The GARDENER'S YEARBOOK
1995

The GARDENER'S YEARBOOK
1995

EDITORS
Charles Quest-Ritson
&
Christopher Blair

MACMILLAN

First published 1994 by Pan Macmillan Ltd
This Edition published 1995 by Macmillan Reference Books
a division of Macmillan Publishers Ltd London
and Basingstoke

Associated companies throughout the world

ISBN 0-333-606450

Copyright © Charles Quest-Ritson & Christopher Blair 1994, 1995

The right of Charles Quest-Ritson & Christopher Blair to be identified
as the authors of this work has been asserted by them in accordance
with the Copyright, Designs and Patents Act of 1988.

All rights reserved. No reproduction, copy or transmission of
this publication may be made without written permission. No paragraph
of this publication may be reproduced, copied or transmitted
save with written permission or in accordance with the provisions of
the Copyright Act 1956 (as amended). Any person who does
any unauthorized act in relation to this publication may be
liable to criminal prosecution and civil claims for damages.

1 3 5 7 9 8 6 4 2

Note: Whilst every care has been taken to ensure that the information
contained in this directory is both accurate and up-to-date, neither the
editor nor the publisher accept any liability to any party for loss or
damage occurred by reliance placed on the information contained in this
book or through omissions or errors, howsoever caused.

A CIP catalogue record for this book is available from
the British Library.

Data management and typesetting by Hodgson Associates, Tunbridge Wells, Kent
Printed and bound in Great Britain by
BPC Hazell Books Ltd
A Member of The British Printing Company Ltd

Contents

		Page
	Introduction	vii
1	Calendar	1
2	Shows	56
3	A Digest of 1994 Gardening News	65
4	New Plants	72
5	Latest Scientific Research	82
6	Garden Restorations	87
7	Weather Records	90
8	Societies	106
9	Gardening Clubs	127
10	Nurseries & Garden Centres	128
11	Nursery Specialities	233
12	Importing & Exporting Plants	242
13	Seedsmen	246
14	Overgrown & Undergrown	251
15	Gardens	252
16	Garden Features	374
17	English Heritage Garden Grades	380
18	Garden Supplies	391
19	Organic Gardening	413
20	Buying in Bulk	416
21	Professional Services	419
22	Organisations	449
23	Colleges and Horticultural Education	457
24	Grant-making Trusts	471
25	Horticultural Libraries	477
26	Specialist Bookshops	481
27	Books, Periodicals & Videos	484
28	Holidays	496
29	Germany: Gärten und Pflanzen für Engländer	502
30	France	506

31	Health & Safety	507
32	Britain in Bloom	510
33	Charities	511
34	Nomenclature Changes	514
35	Royal Warrants	518
36	Garden Theft	520
	Index	523

Introduction

Welcome to the second edition of *The Gardener's Yearbook*. For this year the contents have been completely updated and expanded. New readers will find dates of gardening events for the whole of 1995, as well as descriptions of nurseries and gardens in the British Isles; lists of garden designers and specialist societies; reviews of books and shows; information on safety in the garden and tips on bulk buying; and a great deal besides. Between the contents list at the front and the comprehensive index at the back is a compendium of up-to-date information on every aspect of gardening for anyone who is interested in the subject. Regular readers will notice especially new sections on garden security and on some of the excellent German nurseries. In this National Trust Centenary year, we would also direct your attention to the many Trust gardens which are described in the Gardens section, and their celebration events which are listed in the Calendar. Note also that we have incorporated the new UK phone codes throughout, and that the opening times of many garden centres now reflect the changed Sunday Trading laws in England and Wales. Gardeners are always in need of help and advice. Names and addresses, facts and figures: there are thousands here. If the book does not contain the answer to a particular question, then it should at least point you to where the answer can be found. We hope it will supply a need for a single source of reliable and up to date knowledge for all those who want or need to find out more. There is a balance to be struck between comprehensiveness and selection. Individual sections of the book lean more to one or other of these aims, but we hope that there are few serious omissions. Given the scope, we have had to rely to a great extent on information which has been submitted to us by third parties. Not everyone who was approached has replied – or replied in time – and this explains some gaps. Inclusion or exclusion should not be construed as a recommendation or condemnation. Several sections of the book are arranged by county or region. We have tried to give the actual county in every case, regardless of postal addresses or postcodes. Please use the index or look under adjacent counties in cases of difficulty. You will also find a number of common abbreviations used freely throughout the text, including AGS – the Alpine Garden Society; EC – the European Community; MAFF – Ministry of Agriculture, Fisheries and Food; NAFAS – the National Association of Flower Arrangement Societies; NCCPG – the National Council for the Conservation of Plants and Gardens; NGS – National Gardens Scheme; RHS – Royal Horticultural Society; RNRS – the Royal National Rose Society; SGS – Scotland's Garden Scheme; SRGC – Scottish Rock Garden Club. The editors are very grateful to the many people who have helped in the compilation of this work. First and foremost we want to thank all the garden owners, nurseries, horticulturists, colleges, societies, tour operators, products suppliers and every one else who has responded to our requests for information. We are greatly indebted to them for their assistance, and regret that it is not always possible to give each the personal attention which they are due. Particular thanks go the staff of the Alpine Garden Society; William Christie and Beryl Hunter at the Edinburgh Climate Station; English Heritage; MAFF; the National Trust; the NCCPG; the Northern Horticultural Society; and Emma Kropf, Anne Louise Limm and others at the Royal Horticultural Society. We must also acknowledge the considerable input of others who have worked with us on this project: Julian Ashby; Mark Griffiths; Lin Hawthorne; John Hodgson and his team; Barbara Levy; Jenny Page; Dominic Taylor; Anna Thatcher and Robert Updegraff. Finally thanks are due for their help and forbearance, to Camilla Blair, to Madeline Quest-Ritson; and above all to Brigid Quest-Ritson, whose labours are represented throughout these pages.

Calendar

The calendar, with a week to a page, lists events up and down the country which may be of interest to gardeners. Typically they include lectures and talks, shows, gardening workshops and demonstrations, garden walks, and plant sales. In order to cram in as many as possible, the details are deliberately concise. Many entries give a contact number or an address. Further information may also be found in entries in other sections of the book – say for a society or a garden. Turn to the index first. A number of organisations, most notably the Royal Horticultural Society, have such extensive programmes that to save space, and avoid repetition, their details appear in shortened form. Full titles and booking details, where applicable, are given below. Although we have tried to be as accurate as possible, much of the information has been obtained well in advance. Arrangements can change at short notice, so do check with the organisers or in the press nearer the time, especially if you intend to travel any distance. The RHS journal, *The Garden*, publishes monthly up to date information on events at its gardens and those at Harlow Carr, Ness Gardens and the Hillier Arboretum, among others.

Garden Events

Write to Garden Events, Honeysuckle Cottage, Maulden MK45 2DL for details and advance booking for their garden shows. There are discounts for pre-booked groups.

Harlow Carr

Harlow Carr Botanical Gardens, Crag Lane, Harrogate, North Yorkshire HG3 1QB. The home of the Northern Horticultural Society. Walks and demonstrations are free, and there is no need to book. Contact the Education Officer for details of the courses (01423 565418).

Hillier Arboretum

Sir Harold Hillier Gardens and Arboretum, Jermyns Lane, Ampfield, Romsey, Hampshire SO51 0QA. The gardens and grounds are now managed by Hampshire County Council. Meet in the car park for walks: no need to book. You must book in advance for the workshops (01794 368787).

National Trust

A leaflet containing booking details and other information about events at National Trust gardens in its centenary year can be obtained by sending a sae (29p) to The Events Co-ordinator, The National Trust, 36 Queen Anne's Gate, London SW1H 9AS. Almost all events require prior booking: contact the venue.

Ness

Ness Botanic Gardens, Ness, Neston, Cheshire L64 4AY. The gardens belong to the University of Liverpool. Book in advance for courses and other events. Lectures are free, but you will have to pay the normal garden admission charge (0151 336 7769).

RHS Hyde Hall

The RHS Garden, Hyde Hall, Rettendon, Chelmsford, Essex CM3 8ET. Walks are held at the garden, but other events take place at nearby Writtle College, Writtle, Chelmsford. Apply to the Administrator for tickets for both venues; for further information call 01245 400256.

RHS Pershore

RHS Regional Centre at Pershore, Pershore College of Horticulture, Avonbank, Pershore, Hereford & Worcester WR10 3JP. Write to the Administrative Secretary for tickets for the many events here: details from 01386 554609.

RHS Lectures

For tickets to both regional and London lectures, apply in writing to The Secretary (RHS Lectures), P O Box 313, Vincent Square, London SW1P 2PE. Tickets are normally free for RHS members.

2 Calendar

RHS Rosemoor:
The RHS Garden, Rosemoor, Great Torrington, Devon EX38 8PH. For tickets to the regular demonstrations and walks you should write to the Administrator. Some demonstrations are also staged at Cannington College, Bridgwater. The booking procedure is the same. More details are available on 01805 624067.

RHS Wisley
Walks, demonstrations and other events are held throughout the year at the RHS Garden, Wisley, Woking, Surrey GU23 6QB. Events, which are open to members and non-members, must be booked in advance. Write to the Director at Wisley. For more information ring 01483 224234.

Ryton Organic Gardens
Ryton on Dunsmore, Coventry, West Midlands CV8 3LG. Home of the Henry Doubleday Research Association and the National Centre for Organic Gardening (01203 303517).

Westminster Flower Shows
The RHS Westminster Flower Shows take place in the RHS Halls, Vincent Square and Greycoat Street, London. The nearest underground stations are St James's Park and Victoria. Recorded information is available on 0171 828 1744. RHS members are admitted free.

The attitude of societies towards admitting non-members to their lectures and events varies. More details appear in the Societies section. In general, though, clubs and societies exist for their members, so if you are interested in their events you probably ought to become a member. National societies who have local groups should be able to put you in touch with one near you. Most societies also hold open shows and plant sales (the AGS and NCCPG among them): the public is more than welcome at these events.

EVENTS	DIARY	
		MON 26
		TUE 27
		WED 28
		THU 29
		FRI 30
		SAT 31
Walk; New Year's Day tour, Hillier Arboretum: 2 pm. • European Nature Conservation Year	G. J. Graham, d. 1878; plant collector in Mexico (*Salvia grahami*)	**SUN** 1

4 January

Diary		Events
Mon 2	Sir Harold Hillier, b. 1905; nurseryman and arboriculturist (Hillier Arboretum, Hampshire)	
Tue 3		
Wed 4	Rev. Stephen Hales, d. 1761; (*Halesia*)	
Thu 5	Thomas Nuttall, b. 1786; botanist and rhododendron collector	
Fri 6		
Sat 7		
Sun 8	Sir Herbert Maxwell, b. 1845; plantsman	Lecture; In the footsteps of Forrest, Ness: 2 pm.

JANUARY

EVENTS

EVENTS	DIARY	
Lecture; Crocuses, David P. Stephens. North London AGS, Oakwood Methodist Church Hall (opposite tube station): 7.30 pm.		MON 9
Demonstration; Garden in January, RHS at Pershore.	Nicolas Culpeper, d. 1654; herbalist; Arthur Bulley, b. 1861; founder of Bees Ltd	TUE 10
Demonstration; RHS Wisley. Propagation of glasshouse plants. • Demonstration; Grafting, RHS Hyde Hall at Writtle.	William Curtis, b. 1746; founder of *The Botanical Magazine*	WED 11
Demonstration; Fruit garden tasks, RHS at Pershore.	Hon. Rev. William Herbert, b. 1778; *Herbertia*; George Loudon, d. 1714; designer at Chatsworth and Castle Howard	THU 12
Course; Winter interest, Harlow Carr.	Hon. Vicary Gibbs, d. 1932; creator of garden at Aldenham	FRI 13
Demonstration; Propagation 1, RHS at Pershore. • Walk; Witch hazels, Hillier Arboretum: 11 am & 2 pm.	Walter Hood Fitch, d. 1892; illustrated Hooker's *Rhododendrons of Sikkim-Himalaya*	SAT 14
Demonstration; RHS Wisley. Propagation of glasshouse plants. • Walk; Winter colour, RHS Wisley. • Walk; Witch hazels, Hillier Arboretum: 11 am & 2 pm. • Lecture; An alpine gardener in New Zealand, Ness: 2 pm.		SUN 15

6 JANUARY

DIARY		EVENTS
MON 16	Sir Jeremiah Colman, d. 1942; orchid breeder and mustard manufacturer	
TUE 17	Rev. John Ray, d. 1705; early naturalist	Demonstration; Garden design 1, RHS at Pershore. • RHS Lecture; Decorative vegetable gardens, Joy Larkcom: Ayr.
WED 18	Sir Andrew Balfour, b. 1630; co-founder of Edinburgh Botanic Garden	Workshop; Grafting, Hillier Arboretum. • RHS Lecture; Salads the year round, Joy Larkcom: Aberdeen. • Lecture; Plants and weather, Prof. Last. Friends of RBG, Edinburgh: 7.30 pm.
THU 19		Lecture; Vegetable forum, RHS at Pershore. • Walk; Harlow Carr: 2pm.
FRI 20	Ferdinand Bauer, b. 1760; botanical artist	
SAT 21		Workshop; Painting: watercolours, RHS at Pershore. • Walk; Witch hazels, Hillier Arboretum: 11 am & 2 pm.
SUN 22	George Bunyard, d. 1919; pomologist and rosarian	Walk; Changing face of Wisley, RHS Wisley. • Walk; Witch hazels, Hillier Arboretum: 11 am & 2 pm. • Lecture; The white man in Borneo, Ness: 2 pm.

January 7

Events

Walk; Changing face of Wisley, RHS Wisley.

24 - 25 January; RHS Flower Show, Westminster: 11 am - 7 pm. With botanical paintings and ornamental plant competitions.
• Lecture; International historic gardens, RHS Hyde Hall at Writtle. • Workshop; Conservatories, RHS at Pershore.
• RHS/Welsh Historic Gardens Trust Lecture; A green thought in a green shade, Lord Morris of Castle Morris. Westminster: 2.15 pm.

Walk; Winter structure, RHS Rosemoor. • Also: RHS Flower Show: 10 am - 5 pm

Lecture; Repton in the West Midlands, RHS at Pershore.

Workshop; Painting: oils, RHS at Pershore.

Lecture; Britain's garden heritage, Ness: 2 pm.

Diary

	Mon 23
Henry Merryweather, b. 1839; nurseryman ('Bramley's Seedling')	**Tue** 24
Lionel de Rothschild, b. 1882; creator of Exbury Gardens, Hampshire	**Wed** 25
Hugh, 5th Earl Annesley, b. 1831; creator of garden at Castlewellan, Co. Down	**Thu** 26
Lord Grenfell, d. 1925; president of the RHS	**Fri** 27
Mark Fenwick, d. 1945; creator of garden at Abbotswood, Gloucestershire	**Sat** 28
Lord Digby, d. 1964; creator of garden at Minterne, Dorset	**Sun** 29

JANUARY • FEBRUARY

DIARY		EVENTS
MON 30	George Ehret, b. 1708; botanical artist	
TUE 31	Hugh Falconer, d. 1865; botanist in India (*Rhododendron falconeri*)	Demonstration; Conifer identification, RHS at Pershore.
WED 1		
THU 2	Aylmer Bourke Lambert, b. 1761; botanist	Exhibition; The Revival of the Palladian Style, at the Royal Academy until 2 April (0171 439 4996). • Demonstration; Sweet peas, RHS at Pershore.
FRI 3	Col. Frederick Bailey, b. 1882; soldier and botanist (*Meconopsis baileyi* syn. *betonicifolia*)	Course; The late 18th century house and garden, Harlow Carr.
SAT 4	Jacob Bobart, d. 1680; first gardener at Oxford Botanic Garden	Lecture; *Galanthus*, RHS at Pershore.
SUN 5	John Lindley, b. 1799; botanist and bibliophile	Walk; Winter interest under glass, RHS Wisley. • Walk; Winter scents, Hillier Arboretum: 2 pm. • Garden open; Snowdrops and plant sale, Chelsea Physic Garden: 10 am - 3 pm. • Lecture; Lessons from garden plants in the wild, Ness: 2 pm.

FEBRUARY 9

EVENTS | DIARY

EVENTS	DIARY	
Lecture; AGM, and talk by Les Pettit. North London AGS, Oakwood Methodist Church Hall (opposite tube station): 7.30 pm.	Sir Lancelot 'Capability' Brown, d. 1783; landscaper	MON 6
Demonstration; Garden in February, RHS at Pershore. • Course; Garden construction, Harlow Carr.	Canon Henry Ellacombe, d. 1916; plantsman and writer (*In a Gloucestershire Garden*); George Maw, d. 1912; (*Monograph of Genus Crocus*)	TUE 7
Demonstration; RHS Wisley. Plants under glass. • Walk; Winter, RHS Hyde Hall at Writtle. • AGM and lecture; Friends of RBG, Edinburgh: 7.30 pm. • Lecture; Creating a labour saving garden, Peter Blake. Cornwall Garden Society, Lord Eliot Hotel, Liskeard.	John Sipthorp, d. 1796; botanist	WED 8
Workshop; Painting: botanical, RHS at Pershore.	William Bartram, b. 1739; American botanist	THU 9
Lecture; With the AGS in the Andes, Capt. Peter Erskine, East Kent AGS, Furley Hall, Ashford: 7.45 pm.	Rev. William Colenso, d. 1899; botanist in New Zealand	FRI 10
11 - 12 February; Orchid weekend. Plant Centre, RHS Wisley. Free of charge. • Demonstration; Propagation 2: grafting, RHS at Pershore. • Lecture; Androsaces, George Smith. Bristol AGS, Westbury on Trym.	Robert Gathorne-Hardy, d. 1973; garden writer	SAT 11
Demonstration; RHS Wisley. Plants under glass. • Demonstrations; Stone walls; raised beds, RHS Rosemoor. • Garden open; Snowdrops and plant sale, Chelsea Physic Garden: 10 am - 3 pm. • Snowdrop Sunday; Belton House, Lincolnshire (NT): 11 am - 3 pm. • Lecture; Plants of the Moroccan serpentine, Ness: 2 pm. • Also: Orchid weekend, RHS Wisley.	Charles Darwin, b. 1809; naturalist	SUN 12

FEBRUARY

DIARY		EVENTS
MON 13	Sir Joseph Banks, b. 1743; botanist (*Banksia*)	
TUE 14		Demonstration; Garden design 2, RHS at Pershore. • Workshop; Children and gardens (for adults), Hillier Arboretum. • Course; Rose pruning, Harlow Carr. • RHS Lecture; Gertrude Jekyll, Sally Festing: Chelmsford.
WED 15	E. H. Wilson, b. 1876; collector (*Magnolia wilsonii*); Archibald Menzies, d. 1842; introduced *Araucaria araucana*	Flower Arrangers' Day; Susan Philips, RHS Wisley. • Workshop; Children and gardens (for adults), Hillier Arboretum. • RHS Lecture; Clematis in the garden, Raymond Evison: Shrewsbury.
THU 16		Lecture; Futuristic indoor gardening techniques, RHS at Pershore.
FRI 17	Reginald Farrer, b. 1880; plant collector	17 - 18 February; Conference on The Georgian Villa, at New Burlington Place (Georgian Group). • Course; Creative gardening: foliage, Harlow Carr.
SAT 18	Clarence Elliott, d. 1969; nurseryman and plantsman	Workshop; Winter fruit pruning, RHS at Pershore. • Course; Bedding plants from seed, Harlow Carr.
SUN 19	William Nesfield, b. 1793; garden designer at Arley Hall, Cheshire and RBG, Kew	Lecture; Plants for moist shade, Ness: 2 pm.

FEBRUARY 11

EVENTS

DIARY

Events	Diary	Day
20 - 24 February; International Rose Symposium, Antibes, France. INRA and ISHS.		MON 20
21 - 22 February; RHS Flower Show, Westminster: 11 am - 7 pm. With botanical paintings and ornamental plant competitions. • RHS Annual General Meeting: 2 pm. RHS Hall, Vincent Square. • Lecture; Conservatory plants, RHS Hyde Hall at Writtle. • Workshop; Soil testing, RHS at Pershore. • Course; Pruning, Harlow Carr.	John Lewis, d. 1963; retailer and creator of Longstock Water Gardens, Hampshire	TUE 21
Demonstration; RHS Wisley. Propagating rock garden plants. • Demonstration; Winter colour, RHS Rosemoor at Cannington. • Workshop; Conifer identification, Hillier Arboretum. • RHS Lecture; Flower arrangement demonstration, George Smith. Westminster: 2.15 pm. • Also: RHS Flower Show: 10 am - 5 pm.		WED 22
Lecture; Garden history, RHS at Pershore. • Walk; Trials officer, Harlow Carr: 2 pm.	Sir William Chambers, b. 1723; architect at Kew	THU 23
24 - 26 February; Winter Study weekend, American Rock Garden Society, Seattle WA (00 1 914 762 2948).	Lord Mitford, b. 1837; bamboo expert	FRI 24
AGS Early Spring Show. • Cyclamen Society show, RHS Wisley. • Course; Constructing rock gardens, Harlow Carr. • RHS Lecture; AGS expedition to Japan, Timothy Walker: Bournemouth.	George Don, d. 1856; plant collector	SAT 25
Demonstration; RHS Wisley. Propagating rock garden plants. • Tour; endangered species, RBG, Kew: 2 pm. • Lecture; Plant inspiration in embroidery, Ness: 2 pm.		SUN 26

FEBRUARY • MARCH

DIARY		EVENTS
MON 27	Mrs C. W. Earle, d. 1925; popular gardening writer	
TUE 28		Demonstration; Grafting fruit, RHS at Pershore. • Course; Propagation: introduction, Harlow Carr. • Course; Garden design, Coton Manor Garden (01234 826077).• RHS Lecture; Plant diseases and disorders, Audrey Brooks: Derby.
WED 1	Lady Clara Vyvyan, d. 1976; Cornish gardener and writer	Tour; Green physician, RBG, Kew: 11 am. • Demonstration; RHS Wisley. Rose pruning. • Demonstration; Pruning shrubs and trees, RHS Hyde Hall at Writtle. • AGM and RHS Lecture; My favourite plants, Anne Swithinbank: Pershore: 6.45 pm.
THU 2	Rev. William Wilks, d. 1923; breeder of Shirley poppies	Lecture; Hellebores, RHS at Pershore: 2 pm. • RHS Lecture; Alternative tour of Wisley, Pippa Greenwood: Brecon.
FRI 3	Batty Langley, d. 1751; landscaper	Course; High Victorian house and garden, Harlow Carr.
SAT 4		4 - 5 March; Growing from seed weekend. Plant Centre, RHS Wisley. Free of charge. • Tour; Temperate House, RBG, Kew: 2 pm. • Pruning demonstration, Gardens of the Rose, Hertfordshire. • Demonstration; Propagation 3, RHS at Pershore. • Grafting while you wait; Brogdale, Kent (01795 535286). • Lecture; Plants of China, Christopher Brickell. East Kent NCCPG at HRI, East Malling: 2 pm.
SUN 5		Tour; Trees in winter, RBG, Kew: 2 pm • Demonstration; RHS Wisley. Rose pruning. • Pruning demonstration; Gardens of the Rose, Hertfordshire. • Walk; Touch of spring, Hillier Arboretum: 2 pm. • Lecture; Weather or not at Ness, Ness: 2 pm. • Also: Seed weekend, RHS Wisley.

MARCH 13

EVENTS

National Trust centenary events throughout the season at Studley Royal, North Yorkshire. Phone for details (01765 608888). • Lecture; Cultivation of primulas, John Lonsdale. North London AGS, Oakwood Methodist Church Hall (opposite tube station): 7.30 pm. •6 - 7 March; Garden design course, Coton Manor Garden (01234 826077).

Lecture; RHS Hyde Hall at Writtle. • Demonstration; Garden in March, RHS at Pershore. • Course; Pruning, Harlow Carr.

8 - 11 March; 50th anniversary celebrations, American Camellia Society. • Plant auction; Friends of RBG, Edinburgh: 7.30 pm. • Walk; Glendurgan Garden, Cornwall (NT): 4.30 pm. • Demonstration; RHS Wisley. Planting fruit trees. • Demonstration; Roses, RHS Rosemoor. • Lecture: Roses for the West Country, RHS Rosemoor: 11 am. • Lecture; Covering walls with plants, Peter Rose. Cornwall Garden Society, St Michael's Hotel, Falmouth.

Demonstration; Alpines, RHS at Pershore. • Course; Propagation: further techniques, Harlow Carr. • Lecture; Andrew Lawson, plant photographer, Chelsea Physic: 6.45 pm. • Lecture; *Digitalis,* John Williams: Warwickshire NCCPG.

RHS Lecture; Older roses, Hazel le Rougetel: Cambridge. • Lecture; Hardy orchids, Sandra Bell. East Kent AGS, Furley Hall, Ashford: 7.45 pm. • Lecture; Late colour in the rock garden, Dilys Davies. Bristol AGS, Westbury on Trym: 7 pm.

11 - 12 March; RHS Orchid Show, Westminster: 10 am - 5 pm. • 11 - 12 March; Glasgow Evergreen Show, People's Palace, Glasgow. • AGS Loughborough Show. • AGM; RNRS at the Linnaean Society, London. • Demonstration; Window boxes - for Malvern Spring Show, RHS at Pershore. • Course; Getting the best out of your roses, RHS Wisley. • Course; Garden pests and diseases, Harlow Carr.

Demonstration; RHS Wisley. Planting fruit trees. • Lecture; Everest: mountain, people and plants, Ness: 2 pm. • Walk; Crocuses, with Head Gardener, Myddleton House Gardens, London (01992 713838). • Also: RHS Orchid Show: 10 am - 4 pm; Glasgow Evergreen show.

DIARY

General Sir Henry Collett, b. 1836; botanist and introducer of *Rosa gigantea*

MON 6

TUE 7

William Roscoe, b. 1753; (*Roscoea*)

WED 8

John Fothergill, b. 1712; physician and gardener (*Fothergilla*)

THU 9

FRI 10

Frederick Balfour, b. 1873; creator of arboretum at Dawyck, Borders

SAT 11

John Aubrey, b. 1626; naturalist and antiquarian; André le Nôtre, b. 1613; French royal gardener

SUN 12

14 March

DIARY		EVENTS
MON 13	George Forrest, b. 1873; plant collector (*Rhododendron forrestii*)	13 - 14 March; Garden design course, Coton Manor Garden (01234 826077).
TUE 14		14 - 15 March; RHS Early Spring Show, Westminster: 11 am - 7 pm. Ornamental plant, early camellia, early rhododendron, and early daffodil competitions. • Demonstration; Garden design 3, RHS at Pershore. • Demonstration; Flower arranging, Harlow Carr. • Course; Low maintenance gardening, Harlow Carr. • RHS Lecture; Horticulture of the Commonwealth War Graves Commission, Derek Parker. Westminster: 2.15 pm.
WED 15	Rev. George Engleheart, d. 1936; daffodil breeder	Flower Arrangers' Day; Fred Wilkinson, RHS Wisley. • Demonstration; RHS Wisley. Container gardening. • Demonstration; Heathers, RHS Hyde Hall at Writtle. • RHS Lecture; Blooming containers, Tim Miles: Kidderminster. • Also: RHS Early Spring Show: 10 am - 5 pm.
THU 16		Lecture; Early flowering herbaceous plants, RHS at Pershore: 2 pm. • RHS Lecture; Bulbs, Brian Mathew: Bristol. •Seminar; Alpines, Paul Ingwersen, Gardeners' Academy, Coton Manaor Garden (01234 826077).
FRI 17	Ferdinand Bauer, d. 1826; botanical artist	Course; Climbers and wall shrubs, Harlow Carr.
SAT 18		AGS Kent Show. • AGS Morecambe Show. • Lecture; Bulbs and corms, RHS at Pershore: 10 am. • Course; Bonsai, Harlow Carr. • Course; Analysis of garden soils, Ness.
SUN 19		Demonstration; RHS Wisley. Container gardening. • Demonstration; Bulbs, RHS Rosemoor. • Lecture; Biology of the compost heap, Ness: 2 pm.

MARCH 15

EVENTS

- 20 - 21 March; Garden design course, Coton Manor Garden (01234 826077).

Demonstration; Weed control, RHS at Pershore. • Course; Spring baskets, Harlow Carr.

Walk; Glendurgan Garden, Cornwall (NT): 4.30 pm. • Demonstration; RHS Wisley. Vegetables. • Demonstration; Growing from seed, RHS Rosemoor at Cannington. • Workshop; Flower arranging, Hillier Arboretum. • Course; Soil management, Harlow Carr. • RHS Lecture; Garden design, Elizabeth Banks: Ponteland.

Lecture; Heather gardens, RHS at Pershore. • Walk; Head gardener, Harlow Carr: 2 pm. • RHS Lecture; Trekking in the East Himalaya, Mark Watson: Beverley. • Seminar; Special Plants, James Compton, Roger Grounds and Michael Jefferson-Brown, Coton Manor Garden (01234 826077).

RHS Lecture; Successful water gardening, Bill Heritage: Newport, Isle of Wight.

25 March - 2 April; Spring Gardens Week, Leeds Castle, Kent. • 25 - 26 March; Alpines weekend. Plant Centre, RHS Wisley. Free of charge. • 25 -26 March; Garden design weekend, RHS at Pershore. • AGS East Lancashire Show; Hopwood Hall, Middleton: 11.30 am - 4.30 pm (01706 356385). • Rare Plants Fair: Bingham Hall, Cirencester (01249 782042): 11 am - 4 pm. • Course; Plants from cuttings, Harlow Carr. • Lecture; Kitchen Gardens, Susan Campbell. Gloucestershire Gardens & Landscape Trust.

Walk; Early flowering trees and shrubs, RHS Wisley. • Demonstration; Vegetables, RHS Wisley. • Lecture; What will you see in the woods?, Ness: 2 pm. • Plant sale and garden open; For the Cornwall Garden Society. Porthpean House, Cornwall. • Also: Alpines weekend, RHS Wisley.

DIARY

Sir Isacc Newton, d. 1727; scientist and apple grower — **MON 20**

Wilfrid Fox, b. 1876; creator of Winkworth Arboretum, Surrey — **TUE 21**

Sir James Horlick, b. 1886; creator of Achamore Gardens, Strathclyde — **WED 22**

Augustine Henry, d. 1930; plant collector (*Lilium henryi*) — **THU 23**

Mark Catesby, b. 1682; botanist and artist — **FRI 24**

John Standish, b. 1814; nurseryman — **SAT 25**

Robert Bolton, d. 1949; sweet pea breeder — **SUN 26**

16 MARCH • APRIL

DIARY		EVENTS
MON 27	Charles Raffill, d. 1951; plantsman	Walk; Early flowering trees and shrubs, RHS Wisley. • Lecture; HRH Prince Charles's garden, Rosemary Verey (NT). Purcell Room, London (0171 928 8800). • Course; The Essential Gardener (6 days), at Gardeners' Academy, Coton Manor Garden (01234 826077).
TUE 28		Demonstration; Tomatoes, RHS at Pershore. • Course; Spring hanging baskets, Harlow Carr. • RHS Lecture; The living collections at Kew, John Simmons: Southampton.
WED 29	Sir Edwin Lutyens, b. 1869; architect	Demonstration; Woodland garden, RHS Hyde Hall at Writtle. • Workshop; How does your garden grow?, Hillier Arboretum.
THU 30		Lecture; Vegetable forum, RHS at Pershore. • RHS Lecture; Garden planning for different climates, Tom Wright: Whitland. • Workshop; Roses in Garden Design, Hazel le Rougetel and Philip Harkness at Gardeners' Academy (01234 826077).
FRI 31	William Dallimore, b. 1871; supervised Bedgebury National Pinetum, Kent	RHS Lecture; Plants of the Drakensberg, James Compton: Penventon Hotel, Redruth.
SAT 1		AGS Northumberland Show. • Spring show, Napier Hall, Hide Place, London. Orchid Society of Great Britain. • Bulb display (until Easter): teaching greenhouse, Harlow Carr. • Garden walk; Antony House, Cornwall (NT) (01752 812191). • Workshop; Propagation 4: division, RHS at Pershore. • Plant sale and show; North London AGS, Oakwood Methodist Church Hall (opposite tube station): 2 - 4 pm.
SUN 2	J. J. Dillenius, d. 1747; German botanist	Rare Plants Fair: Battersea Town Hall (01249 782042): 2 - 5 pm. • Walk; Buds and bulbs, Hillier Arboretum: 2 pm. • Walk; Pottering in the park: for children. Beningbrough Hall, North Yorkshire (NT): 2 pm.

APRIL 17

EVENTS

EVENTS	DIARY	
Garden tour; Nunnington Hall, North Yorkshire (NT): 3 pm. • Lecture; Alpines in the open garden, W. Barron. North London AGS, Oakwood Methodist Church Hall (opposite tube station): 7.30 pm.		MON 3
Demonstration; Garden in April, RHS at Pershore. • Course; Principles of Gardening: Spring, Caroline Holmes. Museum of Garden History. • Walk; Mottisfont Abbey, Hampshire (NT): 2 pm. • Walk; The Vyne, Hampshire (NT): 2 pm.	William Gumbleton, d. 1911; Irish botanist; Ronald Gunn, b. 1808; collector (*Eucalyptus gunnii*)	TUE 4
Flower Arrangers' Day; Mary Gwyther, RHS Wisley. • Demonstration; Early vegetables, RHS Rosemoor. • Course; Botanical illustration, Harlow Carr. • Walk; Spring, RHS Rosemoor. • Walkabout; Birmingham Botanical Gardens & Glasshouses. • RHS Lecture; Origins of the Romantic garden, Allen Paterson: Dublin.		WED 5
6 - 7 April; Conserving Europe's Bees. Symposium organised by International Bee Research Association and the Linnaean Society of London (0171 434 4479). • Demonstration; Easter flower arranging, RHS at Pershore. • Spring Flowers garden tour, Anglesey Abbey, Cambridgeshire (NT).	Henry Broughton, Lord Fairhaven, d. 1973; art collector and garden maker	THU 6
Course; Late 19th century and Edwardian house and garden, Harlow Carr. • Garden walk; with Michael Marshall, Dunster Castle, Somerset (NT): 11 am. • RHS Lecture; Courageous gardening, Stephen Anderton: Nottingham. • Lecture; Ernest Wilson Memorial Lecture, Archie Skinner, Town Hall, Chipping Campden, Gloucestershire (01386 840164).		FRI 7
8 - 9 April; Gateshead Spring Flower Show (including Rosecarpe show) (0191 490 1616). • 8 - 9 April; Rainbow Craft fair, Capesthorne Hall, Cheshire. • 8 - 9 April; Alpines in sinks and troughs, RHS Rosemoor. Free of charge. • AGS Nottingham Show. • Primula Show; Village Hall, Datchet, Berkshire: 2 - 4 pm. National Auricula and Primula Society (Southern). • Lecture; Climbers and wall shrubs, RHS at Pershore: 10 am.	John Claudius Loudon, b. 1783; (*Encyclopedia of Gardening*)	SAT 8
Orchid show; Birmingham Botanical Gardens & Glasshouses: 11 am - 4 pm. • AGS Dublin Show. • Rare Plants Fair: Pavilion, Bath (01249 782042): 2 - 5 pm. • Walk; Alpines and rock garden, RHS Wisley. • Walk; Spring, Norton Priory, Cheshire: 2.30 pm. • Walk; Gibside, Tyne & Wear (NT): 2 pm. • Also: Alpine weekend, RHS Rosemoor; Gateshead Spring Flower Show; Craft fair, Capesthorne Hall.	Francis Bacon, Viscount St Albans, d. 1626; Lord Chancellor and writer	SUN 9

18 April

Diary		Events
Mon 10	William Purdom, b. 1880; plant collector	Walk; Alpines and rock garden, RHS Wisley. • RHS Lecture; RHS garden at Wisley, Jim Gardiner: St Andrews.
Tue 11	Benjamin Maund, d. 1864; publisher (*Botanic Garden*)	11 - 12 April; RHS Flower Show, Westminster: 11 am - 7 pm. Ornamental plant, camellia and daffodil competitions. • Demonstrations; RHS Wisley. Plant diseases; Plant pests. • Demonstration; Garden design 4, RHS at Pershore. • RHS Masters Memorial Lecture; Plant responses to stressful environments, Prof. Geoffrey Dixon. Westminster: 2 pm. • Lecture; Propagation, Birmingham Botanical Gardens & Glasshouses. • Kitchen garden exhibition; Tatton Park, Cheshire (NT).
Wed 12	William Kent, d. 1748; landscaper	Walk; Glendurgan Garden, Cornwall (NT): 4.30 pm. • Walk; With David Masters, Nymans Garden, West Sussex (NT): 2.30 pm. • Also: RHS Flower Show: 10 am - 5 pm.
Thu 13	Robert Fortune, d. 1880; plant hunter	Demonstrations; RHS Wisley. Plant diseases; Plant pests. • Walk; Education officer, Harlow Carr: 2 pm. • Lecture; Pelargoniums, Hazel Key: Warwickshire NCCPG.
Fri 14	Walter Bentley, d. 1953; creator of garden at Quarry Wood, Berkshire	14 - 17 April; Childrens Easter Quiz, Harlow Carr.
Sat 15	Rev. Adam Buddle, d. 1715; (*Buddleja*)	15 - 17 April; Spring Gardening Show, Capel Manor (Garden Events). • AGS Cleveland Show. • AGS South West Show.
Sun 16	Henry, 2nd Lord Aberconway, b. 1879; president of the RHS (1931 - 1955)	Daffodil Day and plant sale; High Beeches, West Sussex: 10 am - 5 pm. Also: Spring Gardening Show, Capel Manor.

APRIL 19

EVENTS

DIARY

Garden tour; Ormesby Hall, Cleveland (NT): 2.30 pm. • Also: Spring Gardening Show, Capel Manor.	Col. Frederick Bailey, d. 1967; soldier and botanist	MON 17
Demonstration; RHS Wisley. Biological pest control.	Erasmus Darwin, d. 1802; scientist and poet (Botanic Garden)	TUE 18
19 - 23 April; Sydney Garden Festival, Darling Harbour. • 19 - 21 April; Evolution of Plant Architecture: International Symposium at the Linnaean Society, London and RBG, Kew (0171 434 4479). • 19 - 21 April; International conference on valuing of natural science collections, Manchester University • Demonstration; RHS Wisley. Propagating hardy plants. • Demonstrations; Growing and using waterside plants, RHS Rosemoor. • Walk; Hinton Ampner, Hampshire (NT): 2.15 pm. • Walks; Claremont Landscape Garden, Surrey. Every Wednesday (2.30 pm) until 28 September. • 19 - 21 April; Botanical painting workshop, Harlow Carr. • Walk; Spring, RHS Hyde Hall at Writtle. • Lecture; Colour in the garden, Philip Knox. RIC Museum, Truro.	Adrian Haworth, b.1768; (Haworthia)	WED 19
20 - 23 April; Harrogate Spring Flower Show, Valley Gardens, Harrogate: 9.30 am - 6 pm. More details in Shows section. • Demonstration; Fruit garden tasks, RHS at Pershore. • Demonstration; Sinks and troughs, Harlow Carr. • Course; Flower photography, Harlow Carr.	Peter Barr, b. 1820; botanist and daffodil breeder	THU 20
Lecture; Ranunculaceae, Michael Myers. East Kent AGS, Furley Hall, Ashford: 7.45 pm. • Lecture; Eastern Mediterranean plants, Drs P. and P. Watts, Bristol AGS, Westbury on Trym: 7 pm. • Also: Harrogate Spring Flower Show: 9.30 am - 6 pm.		FRI 21
22 - 23 April; Cornwall Garden Society Spring Flower Show, Lanhydrock (NT) (01208 73320): 10 am - 5.30 pm. 22 - 23 April; Festival of Gardening, Borde Hill (Garden Events). • Garden tour; Baddesley Clinton, Warwickshire (NT): 10.30 am. • Demonstration; RHS Wisley. Propagating hardy plants. • Course; Rock garden plants, RHS Wisley. • Also: Harrogate Spring Flower Show: 9.30 am - 6 pm.	James Anderson, d. 1842; botanist and plant collector (Carex andersonii)	SAT 22
Calke Abbey Plant Sale, Ticknall, Derbyshire: 10 am - 5 pm. • Walk; Bluebells and daffodils, Hatchlands Park, Surrey (NT): 10 am. • Open Day; Pulmonaria National Collection at Stillingfleet Lodge Nurseries, North Yorkshire: 1.30 - 5 pm (01904 728506). • Plant sale; East Kent NCCPG, Squerryes Court, Westerham: 2 - 5 pm. • Course; Traditional orchards workshop, Brogdale, Kent (01795 535346). • Walk; Ness. • Also: Harrogate Spring Flower Show: 9.30 am - 4.30 pm; Flower Show, Lanydrock: 10 am - 4.30 pm.	Harold Comber, d. 1969; plant collector and lily breeder	SUN 23

20 APRIL • MAY

DIARY		EVENTS
MON 24	Sir Jeremiah Colman, b. 1859; mustard maker and orchid breeder	
TUE 25		Lecture; Woodland and shade planting, RHS at Pershore: 2 pm. • Course; Flower arranging course begins, Harlow Carr. • Course; Salad garden, Harlow Carr. • Lecture; Five centuries of gardening: 1, Christopher Thacker. Museum of Garden History. • Walk; Mount Stewart, Co. Down (NT): 7.30 pm. • RHS Lecture; Coastal gardens, Simon Goodenough: Aberystwyth.
WED 26	Sam McGredy II, d. 1926; rose breeder	Walk; Glendurgan Garden, Cornwall (NT): 4.30 pm. • Walkabout; Birmingham Botanical Gardens & Glasshouses. • Demonstration; Vegetables, RHS Wisley. • Workshop; Hanging baskets, Hillier Arboretum. • Course; Making a kitchen and herb garden, Harlow Carr. • Lecture; With RNRS, Friends of RBG, Edinburgh: 7.30 pm. • RHS Lecture: Jade Dragon Snow Mountain of Yunnan, RHS Rosemoor: 3 pm. • Lecture; North American Introductions, Andrew Sawyer: Cragside, Northumberland (NT/ NCCPG): 7 pm. • Grafting mature fruit trees, RHS Hyde Hall at Writtle.
THU 27	Lawrence Johnston, d. 1958; creator of Hidcote Manor, Gloucestershire	27 - 30 April; Botanical drawing course, RHS Wisley. • National *Malus* Collection, RHS Hyde Hall. • Walk; Curator, Harlow Carr: 2 pm. • Courses; Garden design; Garden history (City & Guilds) begin, Harlow Carr. • Lecture; Herb gardens, RHS at Pershore. • Lecture; The work of RBG, Edinburgh, Ness: 2 pm. • Lecture; Medieval and Tudor gardens, Sylvia Landsberg. Gloucestershire Gardens & Landscape Trust.
FRI 28	Charles Sturt, b. 1795; botanist in Australia	Course; Using bulbs, Harlow Carr. • Seminar; Herb Society and Northern Horticultural Society, Harlow Carr.
SAT 29	Rev. Samuel Goodenough, b. 1743; founder and first treasurer of the Linnaean Society	29 - 30 April; Gardening for wildlife weekend. Plant Centre, RHS Wisley. Free of charge. • Auricula Show; Church House, Holy Trinity Church, SW7: 2 - 4 pm. • AGS Ulster Show. • Workshop; Hanging baskets, Hillier Arboretum. • Demonstration; Gardening techniques, Rowallane, Co. Down (NT) (01238 510131): 3 pm. • Course; Early morning bird watch, Ness.
SUN 30	Sir Gerald Loder, Lord Wakehurst; creator of Wakehurst Place, West Sussex	30 April - 2 May; Woodland gardens management workshop, West Dean College, West Sussex. • Bluebell Day and plant sale; High Beeches, West Sussex: 10 am - 5 pm. • Garden open; Plants for sale, Glenarn, Strathclyde: 2 - 5.30 pm. • Walk; Wisley's birds, RHS Wisley. • Demonstration; Vegetables, RHS Wisley. • Demonstration; Pruning stone fruits, Brogdale, Kent (01795 535286). • Also: Gardening for wildlife weekend, RHS Wisley.

MAY 21

EVENTS

DIARY

Joseph Addison, b. 1672; writer and theorist	**MON** 1
2 - 3 May; RHS Flower Show, Westminster: 11 am - 7 pm. Ornamental plant and camellia competitions; daffodil show. • Demonstration; Garden in May, RHS at Pershore. • RHS Queen Elizabeth The Queen Mother Bursary Lecture; Chilean plants in British gardens: Sabina Knees and Martin Gardner. Westminster: 2.15 pm. • RHS/RNRS Courtney Page Lecture; Climbers and ramblers, Charles Quest-Ritson. Westminster: 6 pm. • Lecture; Five centuries of gardening: 2, Christopher Thacker. Museum of Garden History. • Walk; Emmetts Garden, Kent (NT): 7 pm.	Sir John Heathcoat Amory, b. 1894; creator of garden at Knightshayes, Devon — **TUE** 2
3 - 4 May; Craft Fair; Gardens of the Rose, Hertfordshire. • Demonstration; Small trees and shrubs, RHS Hyde Hall at Writtle. • Course; Botanical illustration course begins, Harlow Carr. • Walk; Hillier Arboretum: 2 pm. • Walkabout; Birmingham Botanical Gardens & Glasshouses. • Garden tour; Belton House, Lincolnshire (NT): 7 pm. • Also: RHS Flower Show: 10 am - 5 pm.	George Sherriff, b. 1898; plant hunter — **WED** 3
Garden tours; Kedleston Hall, Derbyshire (NT). Thursdays in May and June: 6 pm. • Garden tour; North American plants, Upton House, Oxfordshire (NT): 2.30 pm. • Also: Craft Fair, Gardens of the Rose.	**THU** 4
5 - 7 May; Malvern Spring Gardening Show, Three Counties Showground, Malvern: 9 am - 6 pm. More details in Shows section (01684 892751).	Hugh Dickson, d. 1904; rose breeder; Alexander Maule, d. 1884; Maule's quince — **FRI** 5
6 - 8 May; Flower Parade, Spalding, Lincolnshire (01775 724843). • 6 - 7 May; Climbers weekend. Plant Centre, RHS Rosemoor. • 6 - 7 May; Bonsai weekend, Leonardslee Gardens, West Sussex • 6 - 7 May; British Orchid Congress, Worthing. • 6 - 7 May; Spring Flower Festival and blossom weekend, Brogdale, Kent (01795 535286). • AGS East Anglia Show. • AGS East Cheshire Show. • Tulip Show; Wakefield & North of England Tulip Society Dutch Show, Wrenthorpe. • Scottish Rhododendron Society show, Pathfoot Building, Stirling University. • Garden tour; Nunnington Hall, North Yorkshire (NT): 3 pm. • Seedling exchange; Harlow Carr: 11 am. • Garden tour; Speke Hall, Merseyside (NT). • Also: Malvern Show: 9 am - 6 pm.	**SAT** 6
Walk; RHS Wisley. • Walk; Winkworth Arboretum, Surrey (NT): 10.30 am. • Walk; Hillier Arboretum: 2 pm. • Walk; Blossom and bluebells, Beningbrough Hall, North Yorkshire (NT): 9 am. • Plantsman's Day; Dunham Massey, Cheshire (NT): 11 am-5 pm.	E. A. Bowles, d. 1954; plantsman and writer — **SUN** 7

22 MAY

DIARY		EVENTS
MON 8	Thomas Baines, d. 1875; artist, explorer and botanist (*Aloe bainesii*)	Rare Plants Fair: Dyffryn, Cardiff (01249 782042): 12 - 4 pm. • Plant sale; Friends of Ness Gardens. • Course; The small greenhouse, Harlow Carr. • Course; Practical beekeeping course begins, Harlow Carr. • Walk; Trees, shrubs and perennials, RHS Wisley. • Also: Flower parade, Spalding.
TUE 9	Charles Turner, d. 1885; nurseryman	Course; SLR flower photography, Harlow Carr. • Lecture; Ferns for the alpine garden, RHS at Pershore. • Lecture; Container gardening, Birmingham Botanical Gardens & Glasshouses.
WED 10	Rev. H. H. d'Ombrain, b. 1818; rosarian	10 - 12 May; Royal Ulster Show (01232 665225). • 10 - 14 May; American Rhododendron Society Fiftieth Anniversary Convention, Portland, Oregon, USA. • 10 - 30 May; Exhibition. My favourite garden. Museum of Garden History. • Flower Arrangers' Day; Keith Smithers, RHS Wisley. • Rhododendron event, Plant Centre, RHS Wisley. Free of charge. • Garden walk; Antony House, Cornwall (NT) (01752 812191). • Walk; Glendurgan Garden, Cornwall (NT): 4.30 pm. • Walk; Woodland plants and early perennials, RHS Rosemoor. • Walk; Friends of RBG, Edinburgh. • Walk; With David Masters, Nymans Garden, West Sussex (NT): 2.30 pm. • Walk; Spring, RHS Hyde Hall. • Walk; Hillier Arboretum: 2 pm. • Demonstration; Hanging baskets and window boxes, RHS Rosemoor.
THU 11	Margaret, Duchess of Portland, b. 1715; (The Portland Rose)	11 - 16 May; Tulip festival, Pashley Manor, East Sussex. • Demonstration; Lawn weed control, RHS at Pershore. • Walk; Trials officer, Harlow Carr: 2 pm. • Also: Royal Ulster Show.
FRI 12	Reginald Cory, d. 1934; plant collector and garden maker (Dyffryn Botanic Garden)	AGM; East Kent AGS, Furley Hall, Ashford: 7.45 pm. • Course; Summer hanging baskets, Harlow Carr. • Lecture; Plant hunting on the Sino-Tibetan frontier, Christopher Grey-Wilson. Bristol AGS, Westbury on Trym. • Also: Royal Ulster Show.
SAT 13		13 - 14 May; Orchid festival, Shugborough Estate, Staffordshire (NT). With Central Orchid Society. • 13 - 14 May; Garden open and plant sale, Houghall College, Co. Durham: 11 am - 5 pm. • 13 - 14 May; Herbs, hives and history, Sulgrave Manor, Northants. • 13 - 14 May; Hertfordshire Garden Show (01795 428242). • Savill Garden Plant Fair, Berkshire (01825 712670). • AGS Midland Show. • Garden road show; Kingston Lacy, Dorset (NT). • Course; Bonsai, Harlow Carr. • NGS Open Day and Plant sales, Acorn Bank Garden, Cumbria (NT). • Course; Morning bird watch on the Dee, Ness.
SUN 14	Mary Delany, b. 1700; paper flower artist; E. A. Bowles, b. 1865; (Myddleton House)	Plant Sale; Primrose Fairs, Ryton Organic Gardens, West Midlands: 10 am - 4 pm. • Walk; May-time medley, RHS Wisley. • Walk; Hillier Arboretum: 2 pm. • Exhibition; Tulip display by North of England Tulip Society, Dudmaston, Shropshire (NT).

MAY 23

EVENTS

DIARY

Walk; May-time medley, RHS Wisley. • Garden tour; Hanbury Hall, Hereford & Worcester (NT): 2.15 and 4 pm. • Walk; With Nigel Davis, Sheffield Park, East Sussex (NT): 2 pm.

MON 15

• Course; Summer hanging baskets, Harlow Carr. • Course; Creating a scented and kitchen herb garden, Caroline Holmes. Museum of Garden History. • Walk; Hinton Ampner, Hampshire (NT): 2.15 pm. • Lecture: 3, Christopher Thacker. Museum of Garden History.

Henry Elwes, b. 1846; dendrologist and collector (*Galanthus elwesii*)

TUE 16

Demonstration; Alpine propagation, RHS Hyde Hall at Writtle. • Walk; Hillier Arboretum: 2 pm. • Garden tour; Meet the gardener, Westbury Court Garden, Gloucestershire (NT): 7 pm.

George Glenny, d. 1874; popular gardening writer

WED 17

18 - 20 May; Devon County Show, Westpoint, Clyst St Mary (01392 444777). • Demonstration; Planting containers, RHS Hyde Hall. • Workshop: Container gardening, Coton Manor Garden (01234 826077). • Walk; Curator, Harlow Carr: 2 pm. • Lecture; Garden design 5, RHS at Pershore.

THU 18

19 May - 25 June; Wicklow County Garden Festival. Details from Tourist Office, St Manntans House, Wicklow Town. • 19 - 20 May; Shropshire & West Midlands Show, Agricultural Showground, Shrewsbury (01743 362824). 19 - 21 Journées des Plantes de Courson (00 331 64 58 90 12). • Courses; Hanging baskets; the wild garden, Harlow Carr. • Course; Herbal medicine course starts, West Dean College, West Sussex. • Also: Devon County Show.

FRI 19

20 - 29 May; Clematis Week, Pennells Nurseries, Lincolnshire. • Show; Wakefield & North of England Tulip Society Annual Show, Normanton. • AGS Southport Show. • Lecture; Clematis, RHS at Pershore: 10 am. • Open Day and Gardeners' day; Cliveden, Buckinghamshire(NT). • Garden visit; Broadlands, Hampshire Gardens Trust. • Also: Courson; Devon County Show; Shropshire & West Mid Show.

Richard Cox, d. 1845; brewer ('Cox's Orange Pippin')

SAT 20

Plant sale; Biddulph Grange Garden, Staffordshire (NT). • Plant sale; For NCCPG, The Manor House, Bledlow, Buckinghamshire. • Plant sale; Sizergh Castle, Cumbria (NT) (015396 60070). • Container gardening event, RHS Rosemoor. • Walk; Hillier Arboretum: 2 pm. • Course; Know your garden weeds, Ness. • Also: Courson.

William Cavendish, 6th Duke of Devonshire, b. 1790; garden maker at Chatsworth, Derbyshire

SUN 21

24 May

DIARY		EVENTS
MON 22	Thomas Bridge, b. 1807; introducer of *Victoria amazonica;* Margaret Mee, b. 1909; botanical artist	Garden open; During Chelsea week, Chelsea Physic Garden: 12 - 5 pm. • Chelsea Flower Show; Press Day and Gala Preview.
TUE 23		23 - 26 May; Chelsea Flower Show, Royal Hospital grounds, Chelsea: 8 am - 8 pm. RHS members day (0171 828 1744). See Shows section for more details. • Walk; Mottisfont Abbey, Hampshire (NT): 2 pm. • Walk; Scotney Castle, Kent (NT): 2 pm. • Lecture; Five centuries of gardening: 4, Christopher Thacker. Museum of Garden History.
WED 24		Chelsea Flower Show: 8 am - 8 pm. RHS members day. • 24 - 25 May; Staffordshire County Show, County Showground, Stafford (01785 58060). • Walk; Hillier Arboretum: 2 pm. • Walk; Glendurgan Garden, Cornwall (NT): 4.30 pm.
THU 25	John, 3rd Earl Bute, b. 1713; prime minister and botanist	Chelsea Flower Show: 8 am - 8 pm. • Walk; Wild flowers, Harlow Carr: 2 pm. • Walk; With Fred Hunt (Head Gardener), Stourhead Garden, Wiltshire (NT): 6.30 pm. • Also: Staffordshire County Show.
FRI 26	W. J. Bean, b. 1863; *Trees & Shrubs Hardy in the British Isles*	Chelsea Flower Show: 8 am - 5 pm. • Course; Hanging baskets, Harlow Carr. • Garden walk; Coleton Fishacre Garden, Devon (NT): 6.30 pm.
SAT 27	Countess Amherst, d. 1863; plant collector and patron (*Amherstia*)	27 - 28 May; Scottish Beer Festival, Traquair House, Borders. • 27 - 29 May; Great East Kent Garden Show (01304 201644). • 27 - 29 May; Art fair, Valley Gardens, Harrogate, North Yorkshire. • 27 - 28 May; Herts County Show; County Showground (M1, J9) (01582 792626). • Workshop; Planting patio containers, RHS at Pershore. • Demonstration; Gardening techniques, Rowallane, Co. Down (NT) (01238 510131): 3 pm. • Garden trail; Blue Peter family quiz trail, Ickworth, Suffolk (NT): 11 am - 4 pm.
SUN 28		28 - 31 May; Flower festival. Athelhampton House and Gardens, Dorset. • 28 - 29 May; Kent Garden Show, County Showground, Detling (01795 428242). • Rare Plants Fair: Ashley Manor, Gloucestershire (01249 782042): 11 am - 4 pm. • Azalea Day and plant sale; High Beeches, West Sussex: 10 am - 5 pm. • Walk; Hillier Arboretum: 2 pm. • Garden open; for RNLI, Mellerstain House, Borders. • Band concerts; Sundays until 27 August, at Valley Gardens, Harrogate, North Yorkshire. • Flower festival; St Michael's Mount, Cornwall (NT). • Pipe bands and Highland dances, Floors Castle, Borders. • Also: Herts County Show; East Kent Garden Show.

MAY • JUNE

EVENTS	DIARY	
Surrey County Show, Stoke Park, Guildford (01483 414651). • Also: Flower festival, Athelhampton; East Kent Garden Show; Kent Garden Show; end of Clematis Week, Pennells Nurseries.	Leopold de Rothschild, d. 1917; creator of Ascott, Buckinghamshire	MON 29
30 May - 2 June; Botanical painting workshops, Harlow Carr. • Lecture; RHS Hyde Hall at Writtle. • Lecture; Five centuries of gardening: 5, Christopher Thacker. Museum of Garden History. • Also: Flower festival, Athelhampton.	Alexander Pope, d. 1744; poet and gardener	TUE 30
31 May - 3 June; Royal Bath & West Show, Showground, Shepton Mallet, Somerset (01749 823211). • 31 May - 1 June; Suffolk Show, Bucklesham Road, Ipswich (01473 726847). • Water plants event, Plant Centre, RHS Wisley. Free of charge. • Workshop; Budding, Hillier Arboretum. • Walk; Hillier Arboretum: 2 pm. • Walkabout; Birmingham Botanical Gardens & Glasshouses. • Also: Flower festival, Athelhampton.		WED 31
Demonstration; Small water features, RHS at Pershore. • Walk; Curator, Harlow Carr: 2 pm. • NGS Open day and Garden tour; Kedleston Hall, Derbyshire (NT). • Also: Suffolk Show; Royal Bath & West Show.	William Bull, d. 1902; orchid hybridiser	THU 1
2 - 4 June; Great Garden & Countryside Festival, Holker Hall, Cumbria. • 2 - 3 June; Scottish Area NAFAS show, Town Hall, Falkirk. • Also: Bath & West Show.	Vita Sackville West, d. 1962; creator of Sissinghurst Castle, Kent	FRI 2
3 - 4 June; British Iris Society show, RHS Wisley. • AGS Summer South Show. • 3 - 4 June; Annual Tractor and Engine Weekend, Bressingham Gardens, Norfolk. • 3 - 4 June; Craft fair, Burnby Hall Gardens, Humberside. • Plant sale and open day; Suntrap Garden, Lothian: 10 am - 5 pm. • Herb tour; With the Herb Society, Little Moreton Hall, Cheshire (NT). • Plant sale; For flower arrangers, Treasurer's House, York (NT). • Garden tour; North American plants, with David Lock, Chirk Castle, Clwyd (NT/ NCCPG): 2 pm. • Also: Scottish NAFAS show; Garden & Countryside Festival, Holker Hall; Bath & West Show.	Robert, 8th Baron Petre, b. 1713; introduced *Camellia japonica*	SAT 3
Rare Plants Fair: Battersea Town Hall (01249 782042): 2 - 5 pm. • Vintage car rally; Mellerstain House, Borders. • Plant fair; For NCCPG, Felley Priory, Nottinghamshire: 12 - 4 pm. • Gardening and Country Show, Beaulieu, Hampshire (01590 612345). • Walk; North American plants, Hillier Arboretum: 2 pm. • Walk; Woodland walk, Norton Priory, Cheshire: 2.30 pm • Also: Iris show; Tractor & Engine weekend, Bressingham; Garden & Countryside Festival, Holker Hall; Craft fair, Burnby Hall.	Nathaniel Ward, d. 1868; inventor of Wardian case	SUN 4

26 JUNE

DIARY		EVENTS
MON 5	George Loddiges, d. 1846; nurseryman and artist (*Botanical Cabinet*)	Course; Kitchen gardens, Harlow Carr. • Garden open; Daily during Chelsea Festival week, Chelsea Physic Garden: 12 - 5 pm. • Plant sale; Inverleith Nursery, Friends of RBG, Edinburgh: 2 pm.
TUE 6	Robert Brown, d. 1858; botanist and president of Linnaean Society (*Rosa brunonii*)	6 - 8 June; Annual Meeting, American Rock Garden Society, Pittsfield MA. • 6 - 7 May; British Iris Society show, RHS Wisley. • Demonstration; Garden in June, RHS at Pershore. • Course; Organic gardening, Harlow Carr. • Walk; Emmetts Garden, Kent (NT): 7 pm.
WED 7		7 - 9 June; AGM and conference, National Association of Allotment & Leisure Gardeners. • 7 - 8 June; Landscape Industries '95, National Agricultural Centre, Stoneleigh, Warwickshire (01203 696969). • Demonstration; Propagating hardy plants, RHS Hyde Hall at Writtle. • Walkabout; Birmingham Botanical Gardens & Glasshouses. • Also: Iris show.
THU 8	Mrs C. W. Earle, b. 1836; popular gardening writer; Brenda Colvin, b. 1897; landscape architect; Jospeh Paxton, d. 1865; designer of Crystal Palace	8 - 10 June; South of England Show, Ardingly, West Sussex (01444 892700). • 8 - 10 June; Royal Cornwall Show, Cornwall Showground, Wadebridge (01208 812183). • 8 - 13 June; Rose festival, Pashley Manor, East Sussex. To be confirmed (01580 200692). • 8 - 11 June; Botanical drawing course, RHS Wisley. • 8 - 9 June; Victorian weekend, Dunster Castle, Somerset (NT). • Walk; Harlow Carr. • Garden walk; Kingston Lacy, Dorset (NT): 7 pm. • Demonstration; Lawns, Anglesey Abbey, Cambridgeshire (NT). • Lecture; *Iris sibirica*, RHS at Pershore. • Also: Landscape Industries '95.
FRI 9	E. F. Warburg, d. 1966; botanist (*Quercus warburgii*)	Garden open; Wimpole Hall, Cambridgeshire (NT). • Also: South of England Show; Royal Cornwall Show.
SAT 10	Sir Cecil Hanbury MP, d. 1936; owner and improver of La Mortola gardens	10 - 18 June; Wildlife week, over 300 wildlife trust events. • 10 - 25 June; West Cork Garden Trail, with several new gardens this year (00 353 23 39159). • 10 - 11 June; Gardeners Fair, Burton Agnes Hall, West Yorkshire (01262 490324). • 10 - 11 June; Rainbow Craft Fair, Newby Hall, North Yorkshire. 10 - 11 June; Woburn Flower Show, Garden Events. • Garden open; Gardens of the Rose, Hertfordshire (until 15 October). • Workshop; Propagation 5: softwood cuttings, RHS at Pershore. • Also: South of England Show; Royal Cornwall Show.
SUN 11		Plant Sale; Primrose Fairs, Royal Assembly Rooms, Harrogate: 10 am - 4 pm. • NGS Open Day and plant sales, Acorn Bank Garden, Cumbria (NT). • Walk; Model gardens and seasonal walk, RHS Wisley. • Walk; Roses, Norton Priory, Cheshire: 2.30 pm. • Also: Gardeners Fair, Burton Agnes Hall; Woburn Flower Show.

June 27

Events

Diary

Walk; Model gardens and seasonal walk, RHS Wisley. • Garden tour; Hanbury Hall, Hereford & Worcester (NT): 2.15 and 4 pm. • Course; Growing for showing, Harlow Carr.	**Mon** 12
Course; Wildlife gardening, Harlow Carr. • Rose clinic; Mottisfont Abbey, Hampshire (NT): 7 pm. • Lecture; Pools and water, Birmingham Botanical Gardens & Glasshouses.	**Tue** 13
14 - 18 June; BBC Gardeners' World Live, NEC, Birmingham (0121 767 4333). Includes an RHS Flower Show. More details in Shows section. • 14 - 16 June; Early Summer Flower Show, St Helier, Jersey (01534 37227). • Wildlife breakfasts planned; more details from county wildlife trusts. • Demonstration; Grapes in summer, RHS Wisley. • Walk; Plants for difficult places, RHS Rosemoor. • Walk; Gibside, Tyne & Wear (NT): 2 pm. • Walk; Friends of RBG, Edinburgh. • Course: Summer propagation, RHS Rosemoor.	Cecil Andrews, d. 1951; botanist **Wed** 14
Demonstration; Grapes in summer, RHS Wisley. • Demonstration; Planting containers, Harlow Carr. • Walk; Late season azaleas, Dunham Massey, Greater Manchester (NT): 7 pm. • Walk; Great Chalfield Manor Garden, Wiltshire (NT): 7 pm. • Also: BBC Gardeners' World Live, Birmingham; Early Summer Flower Show, Jersey.	**Thu** 15
16 - 18 June; Essex County Show, Chelmsford (01733 234451). • Demonstration; Grapes in summer, RHS Wisley. • Course; Water gardening, Harlow Carr. • Course; Roses in garden design, West Dean College, West Sussex. • Also: BBC Gardeners' World Live, Birmingham; Early Summer Flower Show, Jersey.	William Paul, b. 1822; rose nurseryman and breeder **Fri** 16
17 - 18 June; Terracotta and herbs weekend. Plant Centre, RHS Wisley. Free of charge. • AGS Summer North Show. • Plant Fair; Saltram, Devon (NT): 11 am - 5 pm. • National Show, British & European Geranium Society, Hinckley, Leicestershire. • Garden tour; Speke Hall, Merseyside (NT). • Also: BBC Gardeners' World Live, Birmingham; Essex County Show.	**Sat** 17
Northern Country Fair, Newby Hall, North Yorkshire. • Garden tours; Displays, and demonstrations, Ormesby Hall, Cleveland (NT). • Also: BBC Gardeners' World Live, Birmingham; Terracotta weekend, RHS Wisley; Essex County Show.	William Cobbett, d. 1835; journalist, writer and horticultural economist **Sun** 18

28 JUNE

DIARY		EVENTS
MON 19	Sir Joseph Banks, d. 1820; botanist	Course; Drawing plants, Harlow Carr.
TUE 20	S. C. Atchley, d. 1936; diplomat and author (*Wild Flowers of Attica*)	20 - 21 June; RHS Flower Show, Westminster: 11 am - 7 pm. • Flower Arrangers' Day School; Carol Firmstone, RHS Wisley. • Demonstration; Biological pest control, RHS at Pershore. • Course; Pests and diseases, Harlow Carr. • Rose clinic; Mottisfont Abbey, Hampshire (NT): 7 pm. • Garden walk; Dunster Castle, Somerset (NT): 7 pm. • RHS Lecture; Wild plants in garden design, Julie Toll. Westminster: 2.15 pm.
WED 21	Sir Thomas Hanbury, b. 1832; creator of gardens at La Mortola and benefactor of Wisley to RHS	21 - 22 June; Lincolnshire County Show, Lincolnshire Showground, Grange de Lings (01522 522900). • Course; Watercolour painting, Harlow Carr. • Walk; Summer, RHS Hyde Hall at Writtle. • Walk; Hinton Ampner, Hampshire (NT): 2.15 pm. • Also: RHS Flower Show: 10 am - 5 pm.
THU 22		22 - 25 June; Royal Highland Show, Ingliston, Edinburgh (0131 333 2444). • 22 - 25 June; Garden design course, Robin Williams, RHS Wisley. • Garden tour; Baddesley Clinton, Warwickshire (NT): 7 pm. •Walk; Sweet peas, RHS Wisley. • Course; Painting course, Cliveden, Buckinghamshire (NT). • Walk; Roses, RHS Hyde Hall. •Demonstration; Garden design 5, RHS at Pershore. • Also: Lincolnshire County Show.
FRI 23	Eleanor Sinclair Rohde, d. 1950; writer	23 - 25 June; Flower festival, Hever Castle, Kent. • Course; Watercolour painting, Harlow Carr. • Also: Royal Highland Show.
SAT 24		24 - 25 June; Organic Gardening Weekend, organised by Henry Doubleday Research Association. • 24 - 25 June; Festival of Gardening, Hatfield House, Hertfordshire: 10 am - 6 pm. • 24 - 25 June; Middlesex County Show (0181 866 1367). • 24 - 25 June; Newbury Garden & Leisure Show, (01635 247111). • Open Day, J Bradshaw & Sons, Busheyfields Nursery: 10 am - 4 pm (01227 375415). • Demonstration; Gardening techniques, Rowallane, Co. Down (NT) (01238 510131): 3 pm. • Course; Garden design, Harlow Carr. • Also: Flower festival, Hever Castle; Royal Highland Show.
SUN 25	David Douglas, b. 1799; plant collector (Douglas Fir); T. W. Girdlestone, d. 1899; rosarian and dahlia breeder	Rare Plants Fair (01249 782042). • Plant Sale; Primrose Fairs, Bressingham Plant Centre, Elton Hall, Cambridgeshire: 10 am - 4 pm. • Garden open; NCCPG opening, Myddleton House Gardens, London. • Walk; Plant diseases, RHS Wisley. • Demonstration; Pests and diseases, RHS Rosemoor. • Course; Summer herb garden, Caroline Holmes. Museum of Garden History. • Exhibition; Old-fashioned roses, Dudmaston, Shropshire (NT).

EVENTS

Garden walk; Daylilies: Antony House, Cornwall (NT) (01752 812191). • Walk; Plant diseases, RHS Wisley.

Courses; Flower arranging; close-up photography, Harlow Carr. • Rose clinic; Mottisfont Abbey, Hampshire (NT): 7 pm. • Lecture and visit; Hidcote, RHS at Pershore. • Garden tour; Lyme Park, Cheshire (NT). • Garden walk; Followed by supper, Barrington Court, Somerset (NT): 7 pm.

28 - 29 June; Royal Norfolk Show, Showground, New Costessey (01603 748931). • Demonstration; Pruning shrubs, RHS Wisley. • Demonstration; Gardening in shade, RHS Rosemoor at Cannington. • Workshop; Drying and preserving, Hillier Arboretum. • Walk; Growing and trialling delphiniums, RHS Wisley. • Walkabout; Birmingham Botanical Gardens & Glasshouses. • Garden tour; North American plants, Upton House, Oxfordshire (NT): 7 pm. • Walk; with Andrew Humphris (Head Gardener), The Courts, Wiltshire (NT): 7 pm.

Malton Show, Malton (01653 693382). • Demonstration; Companion planting, RHS at Pershore. • Walk; Harlow Carr: 2 pm. • Garden walk; With Graham Kendall, Montacute House, Somerset (NT): 7 pm. • Garden visit; Tughill House. Gloucestershire Gardens & Landscape Trust. • Also: Royal Norfolk Show.

30 June - 2 July; Royal Windsor Rose Show (01753 852352).

1 - 2 July; Southampton Balloon and Flower Festival, Southampton Common. Includes National Sweet Pea Society's Provincial Exhibition. • 1 - 2 July; Sandringham Country Weekend, Norfolk. • 1 - 2 July; Bonsai display, Harlow Carr. • 1 - 3 July; Flower festival, Castle Drogo, Devon (NT). • AGS Cheltenham Show. • Garden tour; Nunnington Hall, North Yorkshire (NT): 3 pm. • Also: Royal Windsor Rose Show (includes RNRS Early Summer Show).

Plant Sale; Primrose Fairs, Fulbeck Hall, Grantham: 10 am - 4 pm. • Demonstration; Pruning shrubs, RHS Wisley. • Walk; Summer sensations, Hillier Arboretum: 2 pm. • Walk; Organic gardening, Norton Priory, Cheshire: 2.30 pm. • Lawn mower rally; Trerice, Cornwall (NT). • Also: Flower festival, Castle Drogo; Royal Windsor Rose Show (with RNRS show); Southampton Balloon & Flower festival; Sandringham Country Weekend.

DIARY

Rev. Gilbert White, d. 1793; naturalist — **MON 26**

Allan Cunningham, d. 1839; botanist and collector — **TUE 27**

Robert Stephenson Clarke, b. 1862; creator of Borde Hill, West Sussex — **WED 28**

Henry Doubleday, d. 1875; Quaker scientist — **THU 29**

Sir Joseph Hooker, b. 1817; botanist — **FRI 30**

Henry Doubleday, b. 1875; Quaker scientist — **SAT 1**

Augustine Henry, b. 1857; collector — **SUN 2**

July

Diary		Events
Mon 3		3 - 6 July; Royal Show, Stoneleigh, Warwickshire (01203 696969). • Exhibition of Botanical illustration, Chelsea Physic Garden, until September (0171 352 5646). • Also: Flower festival, Castle Drogo.
Tue 4	Sir Thomas Raffles, d. 1826; (*Rafflesia*)	Preview Day; Hampton Court Palace Flower Show: 11 am - 5 pm. RHS members only. • 4 - 8 July; *She Stoops to Conquer*, Open air theatre, Hidcote Manor Garden. Gloucestershire (NT). • Demonstration; Garden in July, RHS at Pershore. • Garden walk; Lytes Cary Manor Garden, Somerset (NT): 7 pm. • Spanish evening; Includes talk on Spanish plants, Ness. • Also: Royal Show.
Wed 5	Bishop Henry Compton, d. 1713; botanist and creator of Fulham Palace, London	5 - 9 July; Hampton Court Palace Flower Show, Hampton Court Palace grounds: 10 am - 7.30 pm. Includes the British Rose Festival. More details in Shows section. • 5 - 7 July; County Fair, Colby Woodland Garden, Dyfed (NT) (01834 811885). • Demonstration; Budding fruit trees, RHS Wisley. • Demonstration; Grey and silver foliage, RHS Hyde Hall at Writtle. • Workshop; Medicine from the garden, Hillier Arboretum. • Walkabout; Birmingham Botanical Gardens & Glasshouses. • Also: Royal Show.
Thu 6	Sir Harry Veitch, d. 1924; nurseryman and orchidist	6 - 9 July; Garden design course, Robin Williams, RHS Wisley. • Walk; Calke Abbey, Derbyshire (NT): 7 pm. • Garden walk; With Floyd Summerhayes (Head Gardener), Tintinhull House Garden, Somerset (NT): 7 pm. • Demonstration; Fruit garden tasks, RHS at Pershore. • Walk; Education officer, Harlow Carr. • Garden Tour; Herbaceous Borders, Anglesey Abbey, Cambridgeshire (NT). • Also: Hampton Court Palace Flower Show: 10 am - 7.30 pm; County Fair, Colby Woodland Garden; Royal Show.
Fri 7	Henry Hoare, b. 1705; created Stourhead, Wiltshire	Course; Aromatic plants, Harlow Carr. • Also: Hampton Court Palace Flower Show: 10 am - 7.30 pm; County Fair, Colby Woodland Garden.
Sat 8	Rev. James Backhouse, b. 1794; nurseryman and botanist	8 - 9 July; Dagenham Town Show, Central Park (0181 592 4500 Ext. 2632). • 8 - 9 July; South Beds County Show, Toddington Manor (01525 875170). • 8 - 9 June; National Organic Food and Wine Fair, Ryton Organic Gardens, West Midlands. • Also: Hampton Court Palace Flower Show (with RNRS Southern Summer Show): 10 am - 7.30 pm.
Sun 9	Rev. Keble Martin, b. 1877; botanist of Britain	Strawberry Fayre; Brogdale, Kent (01795 535286). • Demonstration; Budding fruit trees, RHS Wisley. • Also: Hampton Court Palace Flower Show (with RNRS Southern Summer Show): 10 am - 5.30 pm; National Organic Food and Wine Fair; Dagenham Town Show; South Beds County Show.

JULY 31

EVENTS

Garden tour; Hanbury Hall, Hereford & Worcester (NT): 2.15 and 4 pm.

11 - 13 July; Great Yorkshire Show, Hookstone Oval, Harrogate (01423 561536). • Lecture; Cut flower garden, RHS at Pershore. • Lecture; Small trees, Birmingham Botanical Gardens & Glasshouses.

Demonstration; Sinks and troughs, RHS Wisley. • Demonstration; Perennials, RHS Rosemoor. • Walk; Friends of RBG, Edinburgh. • Also: Great Yorkshire Show.

13 - 16 July, Waterperry Gardens, Oxfordshire. Art in Action: arts festival in the grounds (01844 339226). • 13 - 15 July; Kent County Show, County Showground, Detling (01622 630975). • Demonstration; Garden design 6, RHS at Pershore. • Walk; Head gardener, Harlow Carr: 2pm. • Also: Great Yorkshire Show.

14 - 16 July; Flower festival, Gibside, Tyne & Wear (NT). • 14 - 16 July; North American Lily Society Show, Alberta, Canada (00 1 403 387 4382) • Course; Propagation, West Dean College. • Walk; Chartwell, Kent (NT): 2 pm. • Also: Kent County Show.

15 - 16 July; Parham House Garden Weekend, West Sussex. (01243 552121). • 15 - 16 July; Durham County Agricultural Show, Lambton Park, Chester le Street (0191 388 5459). • 15 - 16 July; Rose Show, Jersey (01534 856278). • 15 - 16 July; Clematis Weekend, Tropical Bird Gardens, Rode (01373 830326). • National Exhibition; National Sweet Pea Society, at Agricultural Society Show, Newport, Shropshire. • 15 - 16 July; Herbaceous weekend. Plant Centre, RHS Wisley. Free of charge. • 15 - 16 July; Rose weekend, RHS Rosemoor. • 15 - 16 July; Garden events, Shugborough Estate, Staffordshire (NT). • Teesside Rose Society Show, Ormesby Hall, Cleveland (NT): 1 - 5.30 pm. • Centenary event, Stowe Landscape Gardens, Buckinghamshire (NT). • Walk; The Vyne, Hampshire (NT): 2 pm. • Workshop; Plants in close up, RHS at Pershore. • Course; Garden insects, Ness. • Also: Flower festival, Gibside; Kent County Show.

Alton Agricultural Show, Froyle Park (01420 563492). • Historic Vehicle rally, Newby Hall, North Yorkshire. • Walk; Annuals and herbaceous plants, RHS Wisley. • Band concert; Westbury Court, Gloucestershire (NT). • Demonstration; Sinks and troughs, RHS Wisley. • Garden party; Ormesby Hall, Cleveland (NT).

DIARY

Sir F. Stern, d. 1967; creator of Highdown, West Sussex

MON 10

E. C. Buxton, d. 1925; plantsman (*Geranium* 'Buxton's Blue')

TUE 11

David Douglas d. 1834; plant collector

WED 12

John Clare, b. 1793; nature poet

THU 13

FRI 14

William Robinson, b. 1838; writer (*The English Flower Garden*)

SAT 15

SUN 16

32 JULY

Diary		Events
Mon 17	Rev A. T. Boscawen, d. 1939; creator of garden at Ludgvan, Cornwall	Walk; Annuals and herbaceous plants, RHS Wisley.
Tue 18	James Bateman, b. 1811; botanist and writer (*Orchidaceae of Mexico and Guatemala*)	18 - 19 July; RHS Flower Show, Westminster: 11 am - 7 pm. Ornamental plant competition, and summer fruit and vegetable competition. • Demonstration; Penstemon collection, RHS at Pershore. • RHS Lecture; Flower arrangement demonstration, Rosemary Hughes. Westminster: 2.15 pm. • RHS/National Trust for Scotland Lecture; Gardens of the National Trust for Scotland, Duncan Donald. Westminster: 6 pm. • Walk; Hinton Ampner, Hampshire (NT): 2.15 pm.
Wed 19	Thomas Blaikie, d. 1838; landscaper and writer (*Diary of a Scotch Gardener at the French Court*)	19 - 22 July; NAFAS National Show and Competitions, National Agricultural Centre, Stoneleigh. • Driffield Show, Showground, West Yorkshire (01377 257494). • Flower Arrangers' Day; Anne Tonkin, RHS Wisley. • Demonstration; Pruning fruit trees, RHS Wisley. • Demonstration; Summer colour, RHS Rosemoor at Cannington. • Demonstration; Budding fruit and roses, RHS Hyde Hall at Writtle. • Also: RHS Flower Show: 10 am - 5 pm.
Thu 20		Herbaceous perennials, RHS Hyde Hall. • Demonstration and lecture; Drying herbs, RHS at Pershore. • Herb evening; with the Herb Society, Hardwick Hall, Derbyshire (NT). • Walk; Calke Abbey, Derbyshire (NT): 7 pm. • Walk; Trials officer, Harlow Carr: 2 pm. • Also: NAFAS Show, Stoneleigh.
Fri 21		21 - 23 July; Royal Lancashire Show (01254 813769). 21 - 23 July; Summer Gardening Show, Broadlands, Hampshire (Garden Events). • Garden tour; Hardwick Hall, Derbyshire (NT): 2 pm. • Also: NAFAS Show, Stoneleigh.
Sat 22	Charles Babington, d. 1895; Cambridge botanist (*Allium babingtonii*)	22 - 23 July; Gateshead Summer Flower Show. Includes RNRS National Northern Show, and Rosecarpe) (0191 490 1616). • 22 - 23 July; Dartford Festival (01322 343242). • Course; Wisley's National Collections, RHS Wisley. • Demonstration; Lavenders, RHS at Pershore. • NGS Open Day and plant sales, Acorn Bank Garden, Cumbria (NT). • Also: NAFAS show, Stoneleigh; Royal Lancashire Show; Gardening Show, Broadlands.
Sun 23		• NGS Open Day; Plant sale and machinery demonstrations, The Vyne, Hampshire (NT). • Budding while you wait; Brogdale, Kent (01795 535286). • Demonstration; Summer pruning apples and pears, Brogdale, Kent (01795 535286). • Demonstration; Pruning fruit trees, RHS Wisley. • Also: Gateshead Summer Flower Show; Royal Lancashire Show; Dartford Festival; Gardening Show, Broadlands.

July 33

Events

24 - 27 July; Royal Welsh Show, Llanelwedd, Builth Wells (01982 553683). • 24 - 28 July; Botanical painting summer school, Harlow Carr.

25 - 27 July; New Forest & Hampshire County Show, New Park, Brockenhurst (01590 22400). • Demonstration; Plants for the connoisseur, RHS at Pershore. • Summer evening extravaganza; Harlow Carr: 6 - 9 pm. • Garden tour; Westbury Court Garden, Gloucestershire (NT): 7 pm. • Walk; with nigel Marshall, Mount Stewart, Co. Down (NT): 7.30 pm. • Also: Royal Welsh Show.

Sandringham Flower Show, King's Lynn, Norfolk. • Houseplants event, Plant Centre, RHS Wisley. Free of charge. • Walk; Aromatic garden, RHS Rosemoor. • Walkabout; Birmingham Botanical Gardens & Glasshouses. • Demonstration; Vegetables, RHS Rosemoor. • Also: Royal Welsh Show; New Forest & Hampshire County Show.

Walk; Harlow Carr: 2pm. • Walk; Calke Abbey, Derbyshire (NT): 7 pm. • Also: Royal Welsh Show; New Forest & Hampshire County Show.

28 - 30 July; St Helens Show, Sherdley Park. • 28 - 30 July; South East Garden Festival, Kent (01795 844939).

29 - 30 July; National Miniature Show, Gardens of the Rose, Hertfordshire. • 29 - 30 July; Summer Gardening Show, Arley Hall, Cheshire (Garden Events). • Abergavenny & Borders Show (01873 853152). • Garden road show; Mompesson House, Wiltshire (NT): 2 - 6 pm. • Demonstration; Gardening techniques, Rowallane, Co. Down (NT) (01238 510131): 3 pm. • Also: South East Garden Festival; St Helens Show.

Sheep and wool day, Traquair House, Borders. • Garden open; Gunby Hall, Lincolnshire (NT). • Also: RNRS National Miniature Show; Summer Show, Arley Hall; South East Garden Festival; St Helens Show. National Bog Day; events organised by wildlife trusts to highlight the plight of peat bogs.

Diary

Mon 24 — Montagu Allwood, d. 1958; breeder of carnations and pinks

Tue 25 — William Forsyth, d. 1804; co-founder of the RHS (*Forsythia*)

Wed 26 — Joseph Arnold, d. 1818; botanist (*Rafflesia arnoldii*)

Thu 27

Fri 28 — Abraham Cowley, d. 1667; botanist and poet

Sat 29 — E. B. Anderson, d. 1971; plantsman and writer

Sun 30

34 JULY • AUGUST

DIARY

EVENTS

MON 31	Robert Gathorne-Hardy, b. 1902; writer	31 July - 1 August; Turriff Show (01466 780267).
TUE 1	Lord Digby, b. 1894; creator of garden at Minterne, Dorset	Demonstration; Garden in August, RHS at Pershore. • Also: Turriff Show.
WED 2	Joseph Thomson, d. 1895; botanist of Africa	North Devon Show, Plyms Farm, Landkey, Barnstaple (01769 60205). • 2 - 3 August; Taunton Flower Show, Vivary Park (01823 271597). • 2 - 3 August; Bakewell Show, Showground, Bakewell, Derbyshire (01629 812736). • Walkabout; Birmingham Botanical Gardens & Glasshouses. • Course; The salad garden, Caroline Holmes. Museum of Garden History.
THU 3	Sir Joseph Paxton, b. 1801; garden designer	Black Isle Show, Mannsfield, Muir of Ord, Grampian (01463 233957). • Workshop; Childrens workshop, RHS at Pershore. • Walk; Education officer, Harlow Carr: 2 pm. • Garden tour; Statuary collection, Anglesey Abbey, Cambridgeshire (NT): 6.30 pm. • Garden tour; North American plants, Upton House, Oxfordshire (NT): 7 pm. • Also: Bakewell Show.
FRI 4	John Tradescant, Snr, b. 1608; royal gardener	4 - 5 August; Perth Show, South Inch (01738 23780).
SAT 5	S. T. Edwards, b. 1768; botanical artist	5 - 6 August; Organic Gardening Weekend, organised by the HDRA. • 5 - 6 August; City of Oxford Flower Show; Cutteslowe Park (Garden Events).• 5 - 6 August; Traquair Fair, Traquair House, Borders. • 5 - 6 August; Annual fire engine rally, Bressingham Gardens, Norfolk. • Brecon County Show (01568 708760). • Dumfries & Lockerbie Show (01461 203551). • Oswestry Show, Park Hall, Whittington Road (01691 654875). • Grand Victorian Fete; Centenary celebrations, Knightshayes, Devon (NT).
SUN 6	Thomas Laxton, d. 1893; nurseryman	Walk; Dahlias and chrysanthemums, RHS Wisley. • Walk; Summer shrubs, Hillier Arboretum: 2 pm. • Also: Organic Gardening weekend; Fire engine rally, Bressingham; City of Oxford Flower Show.

AUGUST 35

EVENTS	DIARY	
Walk; Dahlias and chrysanthemums, RHS Wisley.	John Graefer, d. 1802; botanist and garden designer	**MON** 7
8 - 9 August; *A Midsummer Night's Dream*, open air theatre, Mount Edgcumbe Gardens, Cornwall. • Demonstration; Attracting wildlife, RHS at Pershore. • Walk; Prof. Skelding, Birmingham Botanical Gardens & Glasshouses.	Lady Amelia Hume, d. 1809; gardener	**TUE** 8
Flower Arrangers' Day School; Tineke Robertson, RHS Wisley. • Demonstration; Tender perennials, RHS Rosemoor. • Walk; Summer, RHS Rosemoor. • Walk; Friends of RBG, Edinburgh.	Edward Kent Balls, b. 1892; collector	**WED** 9
10 - 11 August; United Counties Show, Camarthen (01267 232141). • Lecture; Vegetable forum, RHS at Pershore. • Lecture; North American plants at Cragside, Andrew Sawyer: Cragside, Northumberland (NT/NCCPG): 7 pm. • Walk; Head gardener, Harlow Carr: 2 pm.	Frank Ludlow, b. 1885; plant collector	**THU** 10
11 - 13 August; Ambleside Summer Flower & Craft Show (015394 32252). • Walk; Chartwell, Kent (NT): 2 pm. • Also: United Counties Show.	James Pulham, d. 1898; ('Pulhamite stone')	**FRI** 11
12 - 13 August; Wisley Flower Show, RHS Garden, Wisley: 10 am - 6 pm (01483 224234). Includes British Gladiolus Society National Show. • 12 - 13 August; Springfields Summer Flower Show, Spalding, Lincolnshire (01775 724843). • 12 - 13 August; Australian Winter Garden Festival, Rouse Hill. With the Society for Growing Australian Plants. • 12 - 13 August; Howden Agricultural & Horticultural Show (01757 630247). • Musical evening; Garden quartets, Greys Court, Oxfordshire (NT): 7 pm.	Rev. Samuel Goodenough, d. 1827; founder of Linnaean Society	**SAT** 12
Summer fruits day; Brogdale, Kent (01795 535286). • Walk; Heathers, RHS Wisley. • Also: Wisley Flower Show, RHS Garden, Wisley: 9 am - 5 pm; Springfields Summer Flower show; Howden Show.		**SUN** 13

AUGUST

DIARY		EVENTS
MON 14	James Dickson, d. 1822; (*Dicksonia*)	Walk; Heathers, RHS Wisley. • Garden tour; Hanbury Hall, Hereford & Worcester (NT): 2.15 and 4 pm.
TUE 15		15 - 16 August; RHS Flower Show, Westminster: 11 am - 7 pm. Ornamental plant and gladiolus competitions. Includes Saintpaulia & Houseplant Society show. • 15 - 16 August; Anglesey Show, Gwalchmai, Anglesey (01407 720072). • 15 - 17 August; Pembrokeshire County Show, Withybush, Haverfordwest (01437 764331). • Tour; Specially for children, Mottisfont Abbey, Hampshire (NT): 2 pm. • RHS Lecture; Naturalised plants and native plants, Richard Mabey. Westminster: 2.15 pm.
WED 16		16 - 17 August; Summer Flower Show, St Helier, Jersey (01534 37227). • Walk; Hinton Ampner, Hampshire (NT): 2.15 pm. • Also: RHS Flower Show: 10 am - 5 pm; Anglesey Show; Pembrokeshire County Show.
THU 17	Lord Lambourne, b. 1847; RHS president (*Malus* 'Lord Lambourne')	17 - 19 August; Southport Flower Show, Victoria Park. • Denbighshire & Flintshire Show, The Green, Denbigh (01352 712131). • Walk; Trials officer, Harlow Carr: 2 pm. • Also: Pembrokeshire County Show; Jersey Summer Flower Show.
FRI 18		Southport Flower Show continues.
SAT 19	Ellen Willmott, b. 1858; plantsman and patron; Jane Wells Loudon, b. 1807; writer	19 - 20 August; Bolton Show, Leverhulme Park, Bolton (01204 22311 Ext. 4070). • Skelton Horticultural & Agricultural Show, Cumbria. • 19 - 20 August; Clematis. Plant Centre, RHS Wisley. Free of charge. • Jazz concert and picnic; Coleton Fishacre Garden, Devon (NT). • Garden road show; With Christine Brain (Head Gardener), Barrington Court, Somerset (NT): 2 - 6 pm. • Also: Southport Flower Show.
SUN 20	Huttleston, Lord Fairhaven, d. 1966; creator of garden at Angelesey Abbey, Cambridgeshire	Pashley Gardens Plant Fair, Ticehurst, West Sussex. 25 specialist nurseries, plus antiquarian books and garden sundries (01580 200692). • Haymaking and craft fair; with shire horses, High Beeches, West Sussex: 10 am - 5 pm. • Walk; Something nasty in the garden, RHS Wisley. • Also: Clematis weekend, RHS Wisley; Bolton Show.

AUGUST

EVENTS

EVENTS	DIARY	
Walk; Something nasty in the garden, RHS Wisley.	James McBean, d. 1910; orchid nurseryman	MON 21
		TUE 22
Demonstration; Paving, RHS Rosemoor at Cannington.	F. C. Puddle, d. 1952; creator of Bodnant Gardens, Clwyd	WED 23
24 - 26 August; Ayr Flower Show, Rozelle Park. • Walk; Hydrangeas, Dunham Massey, Greater Manchester (NT): 7 pm. • Walk; With Andrew Humphris, The Courts, Wiltshire (NT): 7 pm. • Walk; Curator, Harlow Carr: 2 pm. • Exhibition and lecture; David Shepherd, Radnorshire Wildlife Trust: Metropole Hotel, Llandrindod Wells.	A. W. Haworth, d. 1833; cactus botanist (*Haworthia*)	THU 24
25 - 26 August; Guernsey North Show & Battle of Flowers, Saumarez Park, Guernsey (01481 723555). • Course; Flint and stone walling, West Dean College, West Sussex. • Family barbecue; Ness: 6 pm. • Also: Ayr Flower show.		FRI 25
26 - 28 August; Rosecarpe Flower Show, Belsay Hall, Northumberland. • 26 - 28 August; NAFAS Flower festival, Douai Abbey, Buckinghamshire. 26 - 28 August; Festival of Gardening, Audley End, Essex (Garden Events). • 26 - 28 August; Art fair, Valley Gardens, Harrogate, North Yorkshire. • Savill Garden Plant Fair, Berkshire (01825 712670). • Flower and Vegetable Show; Federation of Edinburgh & District Allotments and Gardens (0131 664 1601). • Demonstration; Gardening techniques, Rowallane, Co. Down (NT) (01238 510131): 3 pm. • Poynton Show, Cheshire (01625 872065). • Also: Ayr Flower show; Guernsey North Show & Battle of Flowers.		SAT 26
27 - 28 August; Aintree Show (017408 77324). • 27 - 28 August; Eye Show (01379 870224). • 27 - 28 August; Havering Show. London Borough of Havering (01708 772879). • Pipe bands; Floors Castle, Borders. • Also: Rosecarpe Flower Show; Festival of Gardening, Audley End.	Lionel, 2nd Baron Rothschild, d. 1937; (*Gloriosa rothschildiana*)	SUN 27

38 AUGUST • SEPTEMBER

DIARY

EVENTS

MON 28	Neil McEacharn, b. 1885; creator of Villa Taranto	Aylsham Show, Blickling Hall, Norfolk (01263 732432). • Keswick Show, Crossings Field, High Hill, Keswick, Cumbria (017687 79737). • Madresfield Show, Malvern (01684 576604). • Treasure Hunt; Ness: 10.30 am. • Also: Rosecarpe Flower Show; Aintree Show; Festival of Gardening, Audley End.
TUE 29		
WED 30	Marianne North, d. 1890; botanical artist	Demonstration; Digging, manuring and composting, RHS Wisley. • Walkabout; Birmingham Botanical Gardens & Glasshouses.
THU 31	Huttleston, Lord Fairhaven, b. 1896; creator of garden at Anglesey Abbey, Cambridgeshire	Walk; Education officer, Harlow Carr: 2 pm.
FRI 1		1 - 3 September; National Vegetable Society Show, Dundee.
SAT 2	Marion Cran, d. 1942; garden writer	2 - 3 September; Gardeners' Weekend, Kings Heath Park, Birmingham (0121 235 3008). • 2 - 3 September; Faversham Hop Festival, Brogdale, Kent (01795 535286). • 2 - 3 September; Craft show and garden open weekend, Bressingham Gardens, Norfolk. 2 - 3 September; Late Summer Flower Show, Capel Manor (Garden Events). • Moreton in Marsh Show, Batsford Road, Moreton in Marsh, Gloucestershire (01608 651908). • Walk; Ness. • Also: National Vegetable Society Show.
SUN 3	Sir Frederick Moore, b. 1857; Irish botanist	Demonstration; Digging, manuring and composting, RHS Wisley. • Walk; Hillier Arboretum: 2 pm. • Also: Faversham Hop Festival, Brogdale; National Vegetable Society Show; Craft show, Bressingham; Gardeners' weekend, Birmingham; Capel Manor Show.

Events

Lecture; Wild orchids of Southern Europe and the Mediterranean, G. S. Phillips. North London AGS, Oakwood Methodist Church Hall (opposite tube station): 7.30 pm.

Demonstration; Garden in September, RHS at Pershore.

National Dahlia Society Show, RHS Westminster (01628 473500). • 6 - 7 September; 50th Cheltenham Flower Show (01242 514867). • Garden tour; Belton House, Lincolnshire (NT) 7 pm. • Walkabout; Birmingham Botanical Gardens & Glasshouses.

7 - 9 September; South West NAFAS area Flower festival, Bristol Cathedral, Avon. • Colour in late summer, RHS Hyde Hall. • Workshop; Autumnal hanging baskets, RHS at Pershore. • Garden tour; Dahlias, Anglesey Abbey, Cambridgeshire (NT). • Also: Cheltenham Flower Show.

8 - 11 September; Heather Society conference, Dublin City University. • Course; Managing the large garden, West Dean College, West Sussex. • Walk; Growing and trialling dahlias, RHS Wisley. • Also: NAFAS festival, Bristol Cathedral.

9 - 10 September; National Chrysanthemum Society Great Autumn Show, Bingley Hall, Stafford. • Penistone Show, Penistone Showground (Contact: Huthwaite Bank, Old Mill Lane, Thurgoland, Sheffield S30 7AG). • Romsey Show, Hampshire (01794 517521). • Demonstration; Topiary and training, RHS at Pershore. • Course; Bat watch, Ness. • Garden tour; Nunnington Hall, North Yorkshire (NT): 3 pm. • Also: Heather Society conference; NAFAS festival, Bristol Cathedral.

Town & Country Show, Dereham Road, New Costessey, Norwich (01603 748931). • Gardeners' open day; Wallington, Northumberland (NT). • Plant sale; Beningbrough Hall, North Yorkshire (NT). • Walk; Fruit, RHS Wisley. • Also: Heather Society conference; Chrysanthemum Show, Stafford.

Diary

Mon 4

Tue 5

Wed 6

Thu 7

Fri 8

Captain William Bligh, b. 1754, introducer of bread fruits to the West Indies; George Ehret, d. 1770; botanical artist

Sat 9

George Bentham, d. 1884; taxonomist

Sun 10

40 SEPTEMBER

DIARY		EVENTS
MON 11	Hon. Charles Hamilton, d. 1786; garden at Painshill, Surrey	Walk; Fruit, RHS Wisley. • Garden tour; Hanbury Hall, Hereford & Worcester (NT): 2.15 and 4 pm. • Also: Heather Society conference.
TUE 12		12 - 13 September; RHS Great Autumn Show, Westminster: 10 am - 7 pm. • Demonstration; Autumn conservatory displays, RHS at Pershore. • RHS/National Trust Centenary Celebration Lecture; Plant collections of the National Trust, Christopher Brickell. Westminster: 2.15 pm. • RHS/Worshipful Company of Gardeners Lecture; Gardens of the City of London, David Jones. Westminster: 6 pm. • Garden tour; Westbury Court Garden, Gloucestershire (NT): 2 pm.
WED 13	Hon. Sir David Bowes-Lyon, d. 1964; president of the RHS	Flower Arrangers' Day; Gayle Derrick, RHS Wisley. • Walk; Flower arranger's garden, RHS Rosemoor. • Walk; Friends of RBG, Edinburgh. • Garden open; Meet the gardener, Clumber Park, Nottinghamshire (NT). • Course: Flower arranging, RHS Rosemoor. • RHS/NCCPG/BNCS Lecture; Malmaison carnations, Jim Marshall. Westminster: 2.15 pm. • Also: RHS Great Autumn Show: 10 am - 5 pm.
THU 14	Alicia Amherst, d. 1941; garden historian	14 - 17 September; Botanical drawing course, RHS Wisley. • Demonstration; Cottage garden plants, RHS at Pershore. • RHS Lecture; History of English gardens, Daphne Vince-Prue: Macclesfield.
FRI 15	André le Nôtre, d. 1700; Louis XIV's gardener	15 - 17 September; Harrogate Great Autumn Show, Great Yorkshire Showground, Hookstone Oval. Includes shows by specialist societies. See Shows section for more details. • 15 - 17 September; Autumn Horticultural Show, with Kent Federation of Horticultural Societies, Brogdale, Kent (01795 535286). • 15 - 18 September; Flower festival, Leeds Castle, Kent. • 15 - 17 September; AGS Sussex weekend. • Lecture; European orchids, Tom Norman. Bristol AGS, Westbury on Trym.
SAT 16	Robert Fortune, b. 1812; collector; introduced tea to India from China	Harrogate Great Autumn Show, including the National Kelsae Onion Festival. • 16 - 17 September; Newbury & Royal County of Berkshire Show (01635 247111). • 16 - 17 September; Conservatory weekend. Plant Centre, RHS Wisley. • 16 - 17 September; Rainbow Craft Fair, Newby Hall, North Yorkshire. • 16 - 17 September; Needlework weekend, Traquair House, Borders. • Workshops; Indoor hanging baskets; winter hanging baskets, Hillier Arboretum. • Also: Autumn Horticultural Show, Brogdale; Flower festival, Leeds Castle.
SUN 17	Peter Barr, b. 1820; botanist and daffodil breeder	Show and plant sale; Walled Garden, Norton Priory, Cheshire: 2 pm. • Plant sale; East Kent NCCPG with specialist nurseries, Goodnestone Park, Kent: 11 am - 5 pm. • Choosing and siting plants event. Plant Centre, RHS Rosemoor.

SEPTEMBER

EVENTS

RHS Lecture; The ever-flowering Spring, John Basford: Middlesbrough. • Also: Flower festival, Leeds Castle, Kent.	George Paul, d. 1921; rose nurseryman — **MON 18**
Demonstration; Chrysanthemums, RHS at Pershore. • RHS Lecture; Historic trees and Chinese gardens, Leo Pemberton: Ross-on-Wye. • Walk; Hinton Ampner, Hampshire (NT): 2.15 pm.	George Sherriff, d. 1962; plant hunter — **TUE 19**
Frome Cheese Show, Showfield, Frome, Somerset (01373 463600). • Demonstration; Harvesting and storing vegetables, RHS Wisley. • Demonstration; Apples, RHS Hyde Hall at Writtle. • Workshop; Fungal foray, Hillier Arboretum. • Walk; Ness. • RHS Lecture; Glasshouses, Ray Waite: Dorchester.	Percy Cane, b. 1881; writer and designer (Dartington Hall, Devon) — **WED 20**
Demonstration; Small fruit gardens, RHS at Pershore. • Walk; Head gardener, Harlow Carr: 2 pm. • RHS Lecture; Three influential lady gardeners, Trevor Bath: Birmingham.	**THU 21**
22 - 24 September; Home Counties Area NAFAS, Flower festival, Knebworth House, Hertfordshire. • 22 - 25 September; American Rhododendron Society Western Regional Conference, Vancouver Island, British Columbia, Canada.	John Bartram, d. 1777; botanist ('the greatest natural botanist in the world': Linnaeus) — **FRI 22**
Stokesley Show, Cleveland (01642 713349). • 23 - 24 September; Rainbow Craft fair, Capesthorne Hall, Cheshire. • AGS Wirral Show. • Workshop; Propagation 6: semi-ripe cuttings, RHS at Pershore. • 23 - 24 September; Natural History Book Fair, RBG, Kew. • Also: NAFAS flower festival, Knebworth.	**SAT 23**
Rare Plants Fair: Battersea Town Hall (01249 782042): 2 - 5 pm. • Demonstration; Harvesting and storing vegetables, RHS Wisley. • Also: NAFAS flower festival, Knebworth; Book Fair, RBG, Kew; Craft fair, Capesthorne Hall.	**SUN 24**

SEPTEMBER • OCTOBER

DIARY		EVENTS
MON 25		Nidderdale Show, Bewerley Park, Pateley Bridge, North Yorkshire (01423 770888). • RHS Lecture; Mediterranean plants, John Main: Preston.
TUE 26		Lecture; Spring bulbs, RHS at Pershore. • RHS Lecture; National Trust gardens, Jim Marshall: Edinburgh.
WED 27		Demonstration; Lawns, RHS Wisley. • Demonstration; Garden history, RHS Rosemoor at Cannington. • Demonstration; Outdoor grape growing, RHS Hyde Hall at Writtle. • Walkabout; Birmingham Botanical Gardens & Glasshouses. • RHS Lecture; Soft fruit varieties, Ken Muir: Fishguard.
THU 28	Sir Henry Wickham, d. 1928; plant collector	Demonstration; Saving seed, RHS at Pershore.
FRI 29		29 September - 1 October; Apple Fair, with the Brogdale Horticultural Trust. Apples and produce for sale. Museum of Garden History, London.
SAT 30	James Aitchison, d. 1898; botanist in India (*Rosa ecae*); Decimus Burton, b. 1800; designed Temperate House, Kew	30 September - 1 October; Malvern Autumn Show, Three Counties Showground, Malvern: 9 am - 6 pm. New show (01684 892751). • 30 September - 1 October; Autumn Flower Show, Milton Keynes (Garden Events). • Conference; One day conference, Bristol AGS, Bristol University Students Building, Queen Street. • Demonstration; Gardening techniques, Rowallane, Co. Down (NT) (01238 510131): 3 pm. • Course; Planning and planting a fruit garden, Brogdale, Kent (01795 535286). • Also: Apple Fair, Museum of Garden History.
SUN 1		South of England Autumn Show, Ardingly, West Sussex (01444 892700). • Demonstration; Lawns, RHS Wisley. • Walk; Hillier Arboretum: 2 pm. • Walk; Autumn colour, Hatchlands Park, Surrey (NT): 10 am. • Also: Malvern Autumn Show: 9 am - 5 pm; Apple Fair, Museum of Garden History; Flower Show, Milton Keynes.

OCTOBER

EVENTS	DIARY	
Apple month; Various events and displays during October at Nunnington Hall, North Yorkshire (NT) (01439 748283). • Lecture; Campanulaceae, Peter Lewis. North London AGS, Oakwood Methodist Church Hall (opposite tube station): 7.30 pm.		MON 2
3 - 4 October; RHS Flower Show, Westminster: 11 am - 7 pm. Autumn fruit and vegetable competition and ornamental plant competition. • Demonstration; Garden in October, RHS at Pershore. • RHS/NVS Lecture; Vegetable workshop, Michael Day and Derrick Turner. Westminster: 2.15 pm. • Walk; Scotney Castle, Kent (NT): 2 pm.		TUE 3
4 - 5 October; Autumn Flower Show, St Helier, Jersey (01534 37227). • Demonstration; Glasshouse management, RHS Wisley. • Demonstration; Indoor gardening, RHS Rosemoor. • Walk; Mists and mellow fruitfulness, RHS Rosemoor. • Walkabout; Birmingham Botanical Gardens & Glasshouses. • Walk; Hillier Arboretum: 2 pm. • Demonstration; Hedges and windbreaks, RHS Hyde Hall at Writtle. • Also: RHS Flower Show: 10 am - 5 pm.	Franz Bauer, b. 1758; botanical artist	WED 4
5 - 8 October; Botanical drawing course, RHS Wisley. • Demonstration; Fruit garden tasks, RHS at Pershore. • Garden tour; NCCPG *Aster* collection, Upton House, Oxfordshire (NT): 2.30 pm. • Also: Autumn Flower Show, Jersey.	Sir Moritz Schomburgk, b. 1811; botanist	THU 5
Garden road show; plant sales, at Stourhead Garden, Wiltshire (NT): 2 - 6 pm.		FRI 6
Workshop; Photography, RHS at Pershore. • RHS Lecture; Climbing and wall plants, Ken Burras: Windermere. • Herb evening; Talk and tour, with the Herb Society, Ham House, London (NT): 9.30 am.		SAT 7
Demonstration; Glasshouse management, RHS Wisley. • Walk; Hillier Arboretum: 2 pm.	George Hibbert, d. 1837; (*Hibbertia*)	SUN 8

October

Diary		Events
Mon 9	William Aiton, d. 1849; superintendent of RBG, Kew	9 - 12 October; Flower festival, Compton Castle, Devon (NT). • Apple Day celebrations planned this month at Trerice, Cornwall (NT). Phone for details (01637 875404).
Tue 10	Thomas Fairchild, d. 1729; raised first scientific hybrid (*Dianthus caryophyllus* x *barbatus*)	Lecture; Garden history from paintings, RHS at Pershore: 2 pm. • Walk; Emmetts Garden, Kent (NT): 2 pm. • RHS Lecture; Alpines, Paul Ingwersen: Durham. • Also: Flower festival, Compton Castle.
Wed 11	Alexander Dickson, d. 1890; founder of rose nursery	Demonstration; Paths and patios, RHS Wisley. • Demonstration; Collecting and processing seed, RHS Hyde Hall at Writtle. • Walk; Hillier Arboretum: 2 pm. • Lecture: Making a small formal garden, RHS Rosemoor: 2.30 pm. • RHS Lecture; Victorian walled garden, Peter Thoday: Mold. • Walk; Autumn, RHS Hyde Hall. • Also: Flower festival, Compton Castle.
Thu 12	Thomas Rochford, d. 1901; nursery founder	Lecture; Trees, RHS at Pershore. • Walk; Autumn colour, Harlow Carr: 2 pm. • RHS Lecture; Structural plants, Christopher Bailes: Cheltenham. • Lecture; Historic Hampshire roses, Hazel le Rougetel, Hampshire Gardens Trust. • Also: Flower festival, Compton Castle.
Fri 13	Mary Kingsley, b. 1862; botanist and traveller	Course; The Arts and Crafts Garden, West Dean College, West Sussex.
Sat 14		14 - 22 October; Wildlife Heritage week, Warwickshire Wildlife Trust. • 14 - 15 October; Garden design weekend, RHS at Pershore. • AGS Sussex Show. • AGM; Friends of Ness Gardens. • RHS Lecture; Bulbs in the garden, Michael Jefferson-Brown: Cannington.
Sun 15	George Russell, d. 1951; lupin breeder	Garden open; Last opening of the season, Gardens of the Rose, Hertfordshire. • Covered bazaar and plant sale; High Beeches, West Sussex: 10 am - 5 pm. • Walk; Autumn colour, RHS Wisley. • Walk; Hillier Arboretum: 2 pm. • Walk; The Vyne, Hampshire (NT): 2 pm. • Walk; Including advice, Winkworth Arboretum, Surrey (NT). • Demonstration; Paths and patios, RHS Wisley. • Fruit event. Plant Centre, RHS Rosemoor. • Apple Day celebrations; Attingham Park, Shropshire (NT). • RHS Lecture; Rhododendrons for smaller gardens, Kenneth Cox: Ness.

OCTOBER 45

EVENTS

Walk; Autumn colour, RHS Wisley. • Walk; With Nigel Davis, Sheffield Park, East Sussex (NT): 2 pm. • RHS Lecture; Plant hunting in Central and South America, Martin Gardner: York.

17 - 23 October; Flower festival, Killerton, Devon (NT). • Walk; Mottisfont Abbey, Hampshire (NT): 2 pm. • Lecture; Stylised hedging, RHS at Pershore. • Course; Principles of gardening: Autumn, Caroline Holmes. Museum of Garden History.

18 - 19 October; Devon and Cornwall area NAFAS show, Torquay. • Flower Arrangers' Day; Sheila Macqueen, RHS Wisley. • Demonstration; Autumn colours, RHS Rosemoor at Cannington. • Walk; Hillier Arboretum: 2 pm. • RHS Lecture; Flowers of Greece and Crete, Christopher Grey-Wilson: Oxford.

Lecture; Sandford Park, John Milner. At Cheltenham Art Gallery & Museum. • Demonstration; Dried flowers, RHS at Pershore. • Also: NAFAS show, Torquay.

20 - 22 October; Journées des Plantes de Courson; the Autumn series of this prestigious show, south of Paris (00 33 1 64 58 90 12). • 20 - 22 October; Apple celebrations, Brogdale, Kent (01795 535286). • RHS Lecture; Flowers of Ireland's limestone wilderness, Charles Nelson: Woodbridge. • Lecture; Unusual bulbs for the open garden, Jack Elliott. Bristol AGS, Westbury on Trym: 7 pm.

21 - 22 October; Fruit tasting. Plant Centre, RHS Wisley. Free of charge. • Apple Day celebrations: RHS at Pershore; Brogdale; Norton Priory, Cheshire: 2 pm; Sulgrave Manor, Northamptonshire.

Walk; Hillier Arboretum: 2 pm. • Lecture; Glories of autumn, Ness: 2 pm. • Apple Day celebrations: Killerton, Devon (NT); Fruit tasting weekend, RHS Wisley; Brogdale; Kent; Sulgrave Manor, Northamptonshire.

DIARY

Reginald Farrer, d. 1920; collector (*Viburnum farreri*) — **MON 16**

Thomas Rivers, d. 1877; fruit hybridiser — **TUE 17**

Nicolas Culpeper, b. 1616; herbalist — **WED 18**

Sir Thomas Browne, b. 1605, d. 1682; writer (*The Garden of Cyrus*); E. A. Bunyard, d. 1939; writer (*Old Garden Roses*) — **THU 19**

Friedrich Welwitsch, d. 1872; botanist — **FRI 20**

SAT 21

James Cocker, d. 1880; nurseryman — **SUN 22**

46 OCTOBER

DIARY		EVENTS
MON 23	Rev. H. H. d'Ombrain, d. 1905; rosarian	23 October - 6 November; Exhibition. Flowers and seeds in pencil and watercolour, Valerie Oxley. Museum of Garden History.
TUE 24	Marianne North, b. 1830; botanical artist	Demonstration; Barks, stems and evergreens, RHS at Pershore. • Open Day; Landscape and woodland day, Felbrigg Hall, Norfolk (NT). • Lecture; On a day with Beth Chatto, by Michael Leech, RHS at Pershore.
WED 25	James Sowerby, d. 1822; botanical artist	Demonstration; Propagating hardy plants, RHS Hyde Hall at Writtle. • Walk; Hillier Arboretum: 2 pm. • Walkabout; Birmingham Botanical Gardens & Glasshouses.
THU 26		Demonstration; Pruning shrub, rambling and climbing roses, RHS Hyde Hall. • Demonstration; Edible fungi, RHS at Pershore. • Scandinavian evening; Includes talk on Scandinavian flora, Ness.
FRI 27	Rev. Clarence Bicknell, b. 1842; botanist of the Riviera	
SAT 28	James Aitchison, b. 1836; botanist; Collingwood Ingram, b. 1880; *Prunus* expert	28 - 29 October; Open Weekend, H Woolman (Dorridge), West Midlands: 2 - 5 pm (01564 776283). • 28 - 29 October; Plant sale, Rowallane, Co. Down (NT): 2 pm. • Plant sale; Norton Priory, Cheshire: 1 pm. • Demonstration; Gardening techniques, Rowallane, Co. Down (NT) (01238 510131): 3 pm. • Garden tour; Autumn colour, Anglesey Abbey, Cambridgeshire (NT): 2 pm. • Walk; with Nigel Marshall, Mount Stewart, Co. Down (NT): 2.30 pm.
SUN 29		Open Weekend, H Woolman (Dorridge), West Midlands: 11 am - 5 pm. • Lecture; Tree planting in India, Ness: 2 pm. • Walk; Hillier Arboretum: 2 pm. • Also: Plant sale, Rowallane.

OCTOBER • NOVEMBER

EVENTS	DIARY	
	John Kennedy, b. 1759; nurseryman (*Kennedia*)	MON 30
31 October - 1 November; RHS Flower Show, Westminster: 11 am - 7 pm. Botanical paintings and ornamental plant competition. • Walk; With Fred Hunt, Stourhead Garden, Wiltshire (NT): 11 am. • Demonstration; Dry stone walling, RHS at Pershore. • RHS Lecture; Berried treasure, Dr Hugh McAllister. Westminster: 2.15 pm.	John Evelyn, b. 1620; naturalist and diarist	TUE 31
Lecture; Planning and creating a herb garden, Caroline Holmes. Museum of Garden History. • Also: RHS Flower Show: 10 am - 5 pm.	Fred Streeter, d. 1975; broadcaster; Russell Page, b. 1906; writer and designer	WED 1
Lecture; Restoration of Painswick Rococo Garden, RHS at Pershore.	James Kelway, b. 1815; nurseryman; John Waterer, d. 1868; nurseryman	THU 2
RHS Lecture; Alpines in the garden, Peter Cunnington: Peterborough.	Clarence Elliott, b. 1881; nurseryman and plantsman; Robert Stephenson Clarke, d. 1948; creator of Borde Hill, West Sussex	FRI 3
4 - 5 November; National Chrysanthemum Society Show, RHS Westminster (01788 569039). • Fireworks; Leeds Castle, Kent.	William Dykes, b. 1877; iris breeder	SAT 4
Walk; Autumn, RHS Rosemoor. • Walk; Autumn fruits, Hillier Arboretum: 2 pm. • Walk; Birds in winter, Norton Priory, Cheshire: 1.30 pm. • Lecture; Another side of Ness, Ness: 2 pm. • Also: National Chrysanthemum Society Show.	Richard Bradley, d. 1732; Cambridge botanist and writer	SUN 5

48 NOVEMBER

DIARY		EVENTS
MON 6	Frank Kingdon Ward, b. 1885; plant collector	Walk; Chrysanthemums and other plants under glass, RHS Wisley. • Exhibition; Valerie Oxley exhibition: last day. Museum of Garden History. • Lecture; Wyoming, Chris Norton. North London AGS, Oakwood Methodist Church Hall (opposite tube station): 7.30 pm.
TUE 7	William Dallimore; d. 1959; dendrologist	Demonstration; Garden in November, RHS at Pershore. • Course; Pruning, Ness.
WED 8		Demonstration; Trees, RHS Wisley. • Walk; Autumn, RHS Hyde Hall at Writtle.
THU 9	Thomas Bridges, d. 1865; introducer of *Victoria amazonica*	Lecture; The latest seeds, RHS at Pershore. • RHS Lecture; Plants for busy gardeners, Nigel Colborn: Bath.
FRI 10	Robert Harkness, d. 1920; rose nurseryman	
SAT 11	E. J. Lowe, b. 1825; pteridologist	
SUN 12		Demonstration; Trees, RHS Wisley. • Lecture; Plants, wild and cultivated, Ness: 2 pm.

NOVEMBER 49

EVENTS	DIARY	
		MON 13
Demonstration; Hedges and shrubs for security, RHS at Pershore. • RHS Lecture; Britain's garden heritage, from the sea, Dennis Woodland: Glasgow.	Rev. A. Foster-Melliar, d. 1904; rosarian	TUE 14
Demonstration; Pruning fruit trees, RHS Wisley. • Demonstration; Fruit pruning, RHS Hyde Hall at Writtle. • RHS Lecture; Britain in Bloom, Ashley Stephenson: Norwich.		WED 15
RHS Lecture; Year-round bulb garden, Christine Skelmersdale: Melton Mowbray.		THU 16
Demonstration; Pruning fruit trees, RHS Wisley. • Lecture; Turkish delights, Dr and Mrs Wallis. Bristol AGS, Westbury on Trym: 7 pm.	Rev. William Colenso, b. 1841; botanist (*Myosotis colensoi*)	FRI 17
Demonstration; Herbaceous borders, RHS at Pershore.		SAT 18
Demonstration; Pruning fruit trees, RHS Wisley. • Demonstration; Pruning fruit trees, Brogdale, Kent (01795 535286). • Lecture; ICI, naturally, Ness: 2 pm.	Thomas Meehan, d. 1901; collector (*Meehania*)	SUN 19

50 NOVEMBER

DIARY		EVENTS
MON 20		
TUE 21		21 - 22 November; RHS Flower Show, Westminster: 11 am - 7 pm. Botanical paintings, ornamental plant and late apple and pear competitions. Includes Orchid Society of Great Britain's Autumn Show. • Demonstration; Shade loving perennials, RHS Hyde Hall at Writtle. • Lecture; Fruit tree pruning, RHS at Pershore. • RHS/Glasnevin Botanic Gardens Bicentenary Celebration Lecture; Irish Botany and the plants of the Glasnevin Botanic Gardens, Donal Synott. Westminster: 2.15 pm.
WED 22		Demonstration; Pruning outdoor grapes, RHS Wisley. • Demonstration; Christmas plants, RHS Rosemoor at Cannington. • Also: RHS Flower Show: 10 am - 5 pm.
THU 23	Charles Babington, b. 1808; botanist (*Allium babingtonii*)	Demonstration; Pruning outdoor grapes, RHS Wisley. • Lecture; Vegetable forum, RHS at Pershore.
FRI 24		
SAT 25	John Downie, d. 1892; nurseryman (*Malus* 'John Downie')	Workshop; Winter fruit pruning, RHS at Pershore.
SUN 26	Henry Elwes, d. 1922; dendrologist and collector	Demonstration; Grafting fruit, Brogdale, Kent (01795 535286). • Lecture; Norwegian coastal voyage, Ness: 2 pm.

NOVEMBER • DECEMBER

EVENTS	DIARY	
	James Bateman, d. 1897; orchidist and writer	MON 27
Demonstration; Stems, barks and evergreens, RHS at Pershore. • RHS Lecture; Adapting ideas from Chelsea to your garden, Faith Whiten: Consett.		TUE 28
Flower Arrangers' Day; Barbara Collier, RHS Wisley.	Gertrude Jekyll, b. 1843; garden designer and writer	WED 29
Demonstration; Healing remedies from flowers, RHS at Pershore. • Walk; National Tree Week walk, Harlow Carr: 2 pm.	Sir Isaac Balfour, d. 1922; Edinburgh botanist	THU 30
	William Dykes, d. 1925; iris breeder	FRI 1
	Sir Alfred Parsons, b. 1847; botanical artist (*Genus Rosa*)	SAT 2
Walk; Yuletide tour, Hillier Arboretum: 2 pm. • Lecture; Birches in the wild and garden, Ness: 2 pm.		SUN 3

December

Diary		Events
Mon 4	Hugh Armytage-Moore, d. 1954; creator of Rowallane, Co. Down	Walk; Conifers, including slow growing types, RHS Wisley. • Lecture; Snow melt plants, Jolyon Lea. North London AGS, Oakwood Methodist Church Hall (opposite tube station): 7.30 pm.
Tue 5	Constance Spry, b. 1886; flower arranger and writer	Botany for gardeners; RHS Hyde Hall at Writtle. • Demonstration; Garden in December, RHS at Pershore.
Wed 6		London & Overseas area NAFAS show, Church House, Westminster. • Walk; Winter, RHS Rosemoor. • Course: Christmas decorations from the garden, RHS Rosemoor. Demonstration; Winter fruit pruning, Ryton Organic Gardens, Coventry (01203 303517).
Thu 7	Captain William Bligh, d. 1817; Master of *The Bounty* (*Blighia*, akee fruit)	Demonstration; Christmas decorations, RHS at Pershore. • Walk; Curator, Harlow Carr: 2 pm. • Lecture; Lectures for sixth formers, Ness: 2 pm.
Fri 8	Gertrude Jekyll, d. 1932; garden designer and writer	
Sat 9	Lord Penzance, d. 1899; rose hybridiser (Rose 'Lord Penzance'); Johann Reinhold Forster, d. 1798; Cook's naturalist	9 - 10 December; Christmas weekend. Plant Centre, RHS Wisley. Free of charge. • Workshop; Evergreen swags and table decorations, Hillier Arboretum.
Sun 10	George Maw, b. 1832; collector and *Crocus* expert	Christmas weekend, RHS Wisley continues.

DECEMBER 53

EVENTS	DIARY	
	Franz Bauer, d. 1840; botanical artist	**MON** 11
12 - 13 December; RHS Christmas Show, Westminster: 11 am - 7 pm. • RHS Lecture; Fragrance in the garden, Kay Sanecki: Altrincham. • RHS Lecture; Christmas flower arrangement demonstration, Jose Allen. Westminster: 2.15 pm.	Erasmus Darwin, b. 1731; scientist and poet (*Botanic Garden*)	**TUE** 12
RHS Christmas Show: 10 am - 5 pm. Course; Planning a vegetable garden day, Ryton Organic Gardens, Coventry (01203 303517).		**WED** 13
Workshop; Christmas flower arranging, RHS at Pershore. • Christmas event; Ness: 7 pm.	John Loudon, d. 1843; writer and landscaper	**THU** 14
	Hugh, 5th Earl Annesley, d. 1908; creator of Castlewellan, Co. Down	**FRI** 15
		SAT 16
	Charles Hurst, d. 1947; Cambridge geneticist; hybridiser with roses and orchids	**SUN** 17

DIARY

MON 18 — Philip Miller, d. 1771; writer

TUE 19

WED 20 — James Gordon, d. 1780; nurseryman (*Gordonia*); Sir Reginald Blomfield, b. 1856; garden designer and writer

THU 21 — Charles Lawson, d. 1873; nurseryman (*Cupressus lawsonii*)

FRI 22

SAT 23 — Sir Thomas Neame, b. 1885; founder of East Malling Research Station

SUN 24 — Frances, Viscountess Wolseley, d. 1936; gardener

EVENTS

EVENTS

DIARY

Christmas Day	**MON** 25
John Fothergill, d. 1780; amateur botanist	**TUE** 26
Sir Thomas Gage, d. 1820; plant collector (*Gagea*); Sir Reginald Blomfield, d. 1942; garden designer and writer (*The Formal Garden in England*)	**WED** 27
Joseph Arnold, b. 1782; botanist (*Rafflesia arnoldii*)	**THU** 28
G. P. Baker, d. 1951; textile manufacturer and alpine botanist	**FRI** 29
	SAT 30
Isabella Preston, d. 1965; Canadian hybridiser of *Syringa*	**SUN** 31

2

Shows

NOTES FROM THE RHS SHOWS 1994

The Hampton Court Palace Flower Show at the beginning of July is now the world's largest annual flower show. It has over 800 exhibitors, about 100 more than the Chelsea Flower Show. Hampton Court has 200,000 visitors: Chelsea is restricted to 170,000. The statistics are impressive. Last year, the Show occupied 25 acres of the Home Park at Hampton Court. There were 28 show gardens and 11 water gardens. The 8 marquees boasted more than 1 million blooms between them and put 350,000 square feet under canvas, the equivalent of 80 tennis courts. A total of 31 gold medals were awarded by the RHS in the Floral Marquee. 1995 will be the sixth year of the Show.

Shows are big business. All the most successful shows have some degree of participation by the RHS. The Harrogate Great Autumn Flower Show is now the largest autumn flower event in Europe. This year it will move from the exhibition halls in the centre of Harrogate to the Great Yorkshire Showground on the edge of town. An extra day will be added, making it a three-day show for the first time. Harrogate is organised jointly by the RHS and the North of England Horticultural Society.

The Malvern Spring Gardening Show in May is shared by the RHS and the Three Counties Agricultural Society. Last year it attracted 67,427 visitors, an increase of more than 3,000 on 1993. Such shows are less formal than the London ones: some of the stands look more like market stalls than nurseries. The best stand at Malvern last year was the exhibit of cacti and succulents put on by Southfields Nurseries of Lancashire, that would have done credit to a Westminster show. The RHS medal-winners tend to be those who combine high-quality stock with professional presentation.

At the BBC *Gardeners' World* Live show at the National Exhibition Centre in Birmingham in mid June, the RHS awarded more than 20 gold medals. Visitors are already calling it the 'Chelsea of the Midlands'.

Many of the new shows are profitable: some are not. Profit is what counts: if it does not make money for the organisers, the show will not survive for long. Some are more successful than others. The Southport Show has been going for many years and is an established success. Attendances last year were up by 15 per cent on 1993's figure, and the organisers felt sufficiently secure about the future to take a 60-year lease of the Show's site at Victoria Park. The wonderful show at nearby Holker Hall has been going for three years but has yet to break even.

The Spring Gardening Festival (at Wembley in 1993 and Olympia in 1994) will not be repeated this year. The Show was an unfortunate mixture of the horticultural and the non-horticultural: Stena Sea Link and Allied Dunbar were prominent exhibitors last year with apparently little in common with the other stands.

The Olympia Show also contained both the ugliest and the silliest exhibits of 1994. The hideous central stand, which took up far too much space, was a glass pyramid with bands of scarlet tulips running across its surfaces: it was sponsored by the Netherland's Board of Tourism. The silliest exhibit was the 'Boat Race Blues', designed by Anne Jennings and built by Capel Manor, who should have known better. Commissioned to demonstrate how seasonal bedding could be used effectively with other plants, it depicted an imaginary disaster during the University Boat Race, with one of the crews sinking.

The success of any horticultural show depends on its floral exhibits and these, in turn, depend upon a hard core of stalwart nurserymen. There is a small number of reliable exhibitors, all too often taken for granted, who never fail to mount an interesting exhibit. Among the best are the great modern plantsmen's nurseries. No RHS show would be the same without such exhibitors as Mallet Court Nursery, The Bluebell Nursery, Burncoose & South Down Nurseries, The Botanic Nursery and Green Farm Plants.

Mallet Court Nursery specialises in exotic trees and shrubs: at Hampton Court it showed the purple-leaved form of *Cercis canadensis* called 'Forest Pansy' and *Magnolia grandiflora* 'La Treve'. At the Show on 15 and 16 March, The Bluebell Nursery introduced *Salix caprea* 'Curlilocks' in a stand principally composed of bold foliage forms – *Brachyglottis rotundifolia, Pinus patula* and *Cordyline australis*. The willow will be a useful addition to the list of contorted growers, and is likely to prove more resistant to disease than *Salix matsudana* 'Tortuosa' and *Salix* 'Erythroflexuosa'. At Hampton Court, The Bluebell Nursery showed the seldom seen *Hibiscus syriacus* 'Meehanii', which has a very distinctive variegation. A fortnight later it brought *Maackia chinensis* in flower to a Westminster show. The Bluebell Nursery is particularly good at importing new varieties, and there is a dearth of plantsman's nurseries in the East Midlands.

Burncoose & South Down Nurseries have become identified with the substantial exhibits which they bring up from Cornwall. In 1994 they were rewarded with the prestigious Monument stand at Chelsea. The Botanic Nursery mounted one of the best exhibits at Chelsea, *Digitalis* from its National Collection. Its centre-piece was a magnificent plant of the bronze-flowered shrubby *Isoplexis sceptrum* from Madeira, which the exhibitors believe had never been seen at Chelsea before.

During the course of the year Green Farm Plants established themselves as regular exhibitors. Their exhibit at Hampton Court, though one of the smallest, was one of the best in the Show. Everything was arranged in white and blue, while among the most unusual plants were the variegated *Gaura lindheimeri* 'Corrie's Gold' and a white form of *Dierama pulcherrimum*. There is an art to creating a pretty display. Cheshire Herbs manage to make a simple collection of herbal plants look attractive: the skill lies partly in colour separation and contrasts of form, and partly in drawing the design together with a certain symmetry.

But the shows must also attract new exhibitors of quality. Last year the Ancient Society of York Florists exhibited for the first time at the Harrogate Great Autumn Show. It is the oldest horticultural society in the country. The Great Autumn Show at Westminster saw the first ever exhibit at an RHS show by the Chelsea Physic Garden, the oldest such garden in the country. It was made entirely of seeds of all shapes and sizes.

The RHS is always able to attract interesting new nurseries, such as Barnsdale Plants of Leicestershire who made their début at the unfashionable June Show. A novice exhibitor at the Olympia Show in April was D'Arcy & Everest. Their stand at the Great Autumn Show displayed a number of unusual plants shortly to be introduced into the trade for the first time, including the pink-flowered *Gentiana* 'Ishizuchii' from Japan and *Asplenium septentrionale* which was, until a couple of years ago, believed to be extinct in England.

Some of the best exhibits for the education of visitors to RHS shows were mounted by specialist societies and groups of the Society itself. A fine exhibit by the RHS Rhododendron, 'Camellia' and Magnolia Group at the June Show was an opportunity to see a large number of late-flowering hybrid rhododendrons, including the uncommon 'Margaret Falmouth' and 'Azor', both with huge trusses of flowers. The Fruit Group of the RHS set up a display at the Great Autumn Show called Fruit through the Ages which showed how apples and pears have developed. The 'Black Worcester' and 'Bergamotte d'Automne' pears are thought to date back to the Middle Ages. Such educational displays are one of the greatest rewards of visiting an RHS show.

The Fruit and Vegetable Committee was founded on 5 July 1858 and is the oldest standing committee of the RHS. Its aim has always been to 'examine and report upon all Fruits or Esculents brought under their notice; collecting information concerning the qualities of Fruits grown in different parts of the United Kingdom, and advising the Council generally as to the best modes of increasing the Society's power of promoting the improvement of Fruits and Esculents cultivated in Great Britain and Ireland'.

The NCCPG is a regular exhibitor, and the consistently high standard of its exhibits is all the more remarkable when one remembers that most are mounted by enthusiastic amateurs. Possibly the best stand at any show in 1994 was the NCCPG's exhibit of snowdrops on the 22 and 23 February, which was awarded a gold medal. Indeed, many believe that it was the best exhibit of snowdrops there has ever been. It included such rare forms as *Galanthus* 'Greenish' and *Galanthus nivalis* 'Walrus' and a new form of *Galanthus nivalis* called 'Pagoda', which was awarded a Preliminary Commendation. The organisers were also able to show flowers of *Lathraea clandestina* and the large-flowered imbricated *Hepatica nobilis* 'Coerulea Plena', recently imported from the Czech Republic.

The Hampshire Group of the NCCPG mounted a separate stand of hellebores at the same show to display the current state of hybridisation within the genus. It included some double forms: 'Wolverton Hybrid' was outstanding. Such exhibits are a great credit to the NCCPG.

At Chelsea, the NCCPG's official entry concentrated upon those popular garden plants, the hardy geraniums. It divided them up geographically and topped the exhibit with a large specimen of the monocarpic *Geranium maderense* from Madeira. There was good representation of *Geranium* species from New Zealand and Australia, which are only now beginning to come into wider cultivation, and of South African species.

At Hampton Court the NCCPG tent showed plants from no less than 34 National Collections. Some of the best were the National Collection of *Ceanothus* from Torbay Hospital, the Malmaison carnations, of great historic interest even if the shape of their flowers is not to everyone's taste, and a wide range of cannas from Brocking's Exotics. Botanic Nursery turned up with the National Collection of *Digitalis* again, and included some interesting hybrids between *Digtalis obscura* and *Digitalis parviflora*.

In July, Marwood Hill and the Lakeland Horticultural Society sent up to Westminster a magnificent exhibit of astilbes from their National Collections to occupy a substantial position in the middle of the New Hall. It included a fine selection of the hybrids bred by Georg Arends during the first fifty years of this century, and was graded to show the genus's variability in colour and height.

Sometimes nurserymen put on a first-rate educational exhibit of a single genus. The *Primula allionii* forms and hybrids, from the huge flowers of 'Ken's Seedling' to the dainty albino 'Avalanche', which W E Th. Ingwersen Ltd showed on 15 and 16 March were particularly interesting for visitors. Two stands at Chelsea were also excellent: a magnificent exhibit composed almost entirely of onions, *Allium* species and hybrids from Rupert Bowlby, and a small stand from Butterfields Pleiones which showed the sheer variety of these collectable orchids. Of special interest were hybrids between *formosana* and *limprichtii* and between *formosana* and *confusa* including 'Shantung' and 'Golden Plover', which have pink outer segments and a yellow lip marked with red – a striking combination.

Not all such exhibits are so stimulating. The collection of *Nerine* seedlings from Springbank Nurseries in the Isle of Wight at the Great Autumn Show proved how far UK breeders have to go before they can hope to match the achievements of leading hybridists overseas.

The best of the society exhibits at Chelsea was mounted by the Alpine Garden Society. All its plants, including the cascades of beautiful saxifrages, were supplied by amateur and professional members of the Society. Within a small compass were also a small pool where sarracenias thrived, a gravel garden, peat garden, woodland garden and every imaginable Alpine habitat. The stand even had sempervivums oozing out of the railway sleepers which made up its sides.

Yet more commendable because of the effort it required to mount, was a wonderful display of *Clematis* from Latvia at the August Westminster Show, sponsored by the International Clematis Society. Latvian-bred varieties included a form the *Clematis integrifolia* called 'Aljonushka' (large-flowered, pinky-purple, darker reverses) and two *Clematis* × *jackmannii* types – white 'Valgedamm' with seven broad petals, and dark purple 'Gunda'. Latvian breeders over the last fifty years have raised many good varieties, some of which should find a permanent place in British gardens. It is clear that, since the War, all through Central and Eastern Europe the hybridisation and selection of garden plants have been undertaken on a much larger scale than we realised.

Another novice exhibitor at the Great Autumn Show was the Eric Young Orchid Foundation from Jersey. It showed nothing but forms and hybrids of *Phragmipedium*, in whose breeding it has been actively involved. The colours passed from brilliant scarlet to pink and maroon. Some of the hybrids were over a hundred years old. The sizes and colours of the Foundation's recent seedlings were exceptional and, in addition to a gold medal for the stand as a whole, individual plants received a First Class Certificate and two Awards of Merit. It is greatly to the credit of the RHS that it can attract such exhibitors, for whom there is no obvious benefit in return for the time and labour needed to furnish a stand and attend the Show.

One of the attractions at RHS shows in recent years has been the displays of material from the Lindley Library's collections. The staff of the Library have been able to complement the main exhibits in the show with well-structured and neatly annotated exhibits of their own. At the beginning of May, they chose watercolours of tulips and rhododendrons to match the competitions. In April it offered a small exhibit of books and prints from the Cory bequests. It included books with hand-painted illustrations, some of the most valuable examples of botanical art.

Every RHS show at Westminster has at least one competition. However, garden owners are becoming less competitive – at least in the floral classes, if not where fruit and vegetables are concerned. The rose competition on 3 and 4 May had only two entrants. But for entries from the Clyne Gardens at Swansea, High Beeches in West Sussex and J. A. Fox of Holmwood House in East Sussex, the rhododendron competition at the same show would also have been a wash-out. Quantity is no guide to quality. The camellia competition in April was poorly supported, but the exhibit of twelve different blooms which won the Leonardslee Bowl for Mrs C. Petherick of Porthpean House, Cornwall, included the most perfect specimen of *Camellia* 'Augusto Leal de Gouveia Pinto' probably ever seen at a British show.

Some competitions were nevertheless well supported. Those run by the British National Carnation Society and the Delphinium Society on 21 and 22 June were the best for a long time: the form and freshness of the perpetual flowering carnations were particularly noticeable. Likewise the competitions at the Great Autumn Show were better supported than in recent years. Notable exhibits included *Cornus kousa* var. *chinensis* and *Davidia involucrata* in fruit, and the turquoise-blue grapes of *Ampelopsis brevipedunculata*.

Competition in the fruit and vegetable classes remains intense. The Harrogate Great Autumn Flower Show has become the forum for an annual record-breaking onion competition. Last year 62 onions from dozens of British growers battled it out and the world record was broken not once, but three times during the weigh-in. The winner emerged at 12lb 4oz, an astonishing 1lb 2oz heavier than the world record set in 1992.

During the early part of 1994 the RHS found itself embroiled in a controversy about the awarding of medals to exhibitors who buy in their stock, rather than growing it themselves. The Society would much rather have exhibitors buy flowers to fill a space than mount an empty exhibit, which might happen if all their flowers were, for example, wiped out by frost. The judges look at a stand and pronounce on its merits without regard for the origin of the plant material. That explains why one of the gold medals at Chelsea in 1994 was awarded to a company who bought its lilies in the cut-flower market. One experienced exhibitor, Michael Marriott, the nursery manager of David Austin Roses, said that he had always assumed growers exhibited only their own produce: 'If they can't grow all their own, they should not be there at all.'

The RHS takes the view that there is nothing wrong with an exhibitor buying in his plants, or borrowing them. It is, however, concerned that the public should not be misled. The Show's organiser Stephen Bennett asked trade exhibitors to make it clear, by putting a notice on their stands, if any of their flowers were not home-grown. Many other exhibitors at Chelsea went so far as to hang up a poster announcing that 'The plants on this exhibit have all been grown at our nurseries'. Mr Bennett commented: 'If you say that plants should be grown by the exhibitor, how do you define 'grown by'? Does it mean grown from seed? Clearly that would be ridiculous in the case of a hundred-year-old bonsai.'

Nevertheless the RHS cannot find an easy definition that is going to be fair to everyone, above all to the visiting public.

A fortnight after Chelsea, the RHS was involved in another confrontation at the BBC *Gardeners' World* Live exhibition in Birmingham when it banned Heather Hedgehog, the man-sized pink mascot of the British Heather Growers' Association. 'By no stretch of the imagination can Heather Hedgehog be perceived to be within the spirit of an

RHS Flower Show,' commented the Society. 'It is not appropriate to have a gimmicky creature bouncing about while the public are in. Exhibitors are not permitted to incorporate anything which, in the opinion of the Society, detracts from the presentation of the plants.'

This rule does not apply to model gardens at Chelsea. One highly acclaimed exhibit last year was a reconstruction of a long-forgotten, deserted and ruined garden in the grounds of Donhead Hall near Shaftesbury. The focal feature was a tumbledown greenhouse with only a few panes of glass left, together with a tangle of brambles, a rusted pump, and part of the old boiler-house. The organisers claimed it would 'encourage those who see it to appreciate how many wonderful old gardens exist all over Britain and how tenuous their survival is'. Others argued that the reconstruction of a perfectly ordinary garden, in a state of dereliction, serves no useful or artistic purpose.

Some commentators also observed that nowadays there is too much trying to be different at Chelsea, rather than striving to be better. Everyone has to think of something new. There is always a danger when the professionals lose touch with popular taste: it marks the beginning of the end of any art form.

But Chelsea is different, and Chelsea also has its old traditions. The splendid exhibit of delphiniums and begonias from Blackmore and Langdon, all perfectly grown and of enormous size, was another example of a fashion that is fading from modern shows. So was the display of lupins from Woodfield Brothers of Stratford-on-Avon: solid erect spikes ranging from cream and white to crimson and violet.

Chelsea also boasts wonderful displays of tropical plants, some quite modest, like the exotic orchids from Malaysia against a background of palms and bananas, and others almost gaudy in their opulence: the Belgian flower trade's stand had arches of variegated aechmeas and a false ceiling strung with hanging sarracenias.

Chelsea is a good place for spotting trends. Last year's show illustrated the recent proliferation of such specialist interests as cacti, bonsai and carnivorous plants. Also symptomatic of changes in taste were magnificent displays from fern nurseries. Fibrex Nurseries of Warwickshire showed antipodean *Dicksonia antarctica* alongside such British endemics as *Athyrium filix-femina* 'Frizelliae' and *Osmunda regalis purpurascens*. The tree ferns from Rickards Hardy Ferns Ltd of Tenbury Wells were arranged geographically and included such rarities as *Dryopteris wallichiana* from Central Asia with long, extremely hairy stems.

Chelsea also gives space to minority interests. An exhibit from the rather un-Brazilian Flower Club of São Paulo drew attention to the richness of the plants available in a country where there is a large expatriate English community. Its members design their gardens not with English plants but in the English style, and use plants that grow well in or are native to that part of Brazil. The members of the club who came to Chelsea were as keen to learn from others as they were to show what they can already do.

And that seems to be the difference between Chelsea and Hampton Court. Chelsea is for proper gardeners up from the country. Hampton Court is a jolly day out for Londoners.

Gold Medals Awarded at the Principal Flower Shows in 1994

The Chelsea Flower Show

Gardens: Capel Manor National Gardening Centre (Zeneca Garden); Daily Telegraph; Harpers & Queen (Classical Garden); Sunday Express (Railway Cottage Garden); Peter Tinsley (Rock and Water Garden); Faith and Geoffrey Whiten (Classic FM Garden); Wyevale Garden Centres (A Garden for Children); YOU Magazine with Yardley (Mr Maidment's Garden)

Exhibits of plants: African Violet Centre (saintpaulias); Alpine Garden Society (rock garden plants); Jacques Amand (bulbous plants); David Austin (roses); Avon Bulbs (bulbous plants); Steven Bailey (carnations, pinks, alstroemerias and gypsophila); Peter Beales Roses (roses); Belgium (ONDAH) (ornamentals, azaleas and house plants); Blackmore & Langdon (begonias and delphiniums); S & N Brackley (sweet peas); Bressingham Gardens (hardy plants); British Bedding and Pot Plant Association (bedding and pot plants); Burncoose & South Down Nurseries (trees, shrubs and ornamental plants); Burnham Nurseries (orchids); Butterfields Nursery (pleiones); Carnivorous Plant Society (carnivorous plants); Cedarwood Lily Farm (lilies); Cheshire Herbs (herbs); Devine Nurseries (chrysanthemums); Dibleys (streptocarpus); Fryer's Nurseries (roses); Glebe Cottage Plants (cottage garden plants); Goldbrook Plants (hostas and perennials); Greenacre Nursery (carnations and pinks); Hardy's Cottage Garden Plants (herbaceous perennials, lavateras and flowering shrubs); R Harkness & Co. (roses); Herons Bonsai (bonsai); Heather and Brian Hiley (tender and unusual perennials); Hillier Nurseries (trees, shrubs, roses and ground cover plants); The Hop Shop (dried flowers, herbs and grasses); Ichiyo School of Ikebana (floral arrangements); Interflora (FTDA) British Unit (floral arrangements); Malaysia Tourism Promotion Board (tropical plants and orchids); Mattocks Roses (roses); McBeans Orchids (orchids); Ken Muir (strawberry plants); NAFAS (floral arrangements); Notcutts Nurseries (trees, shrubs, roses, conifers and perennials); Oakleigh Nurseries (fuchsias and pelargoniums); Oxford Botanic Garden (ferns); Potterton & Martin/Peter Orme Landscapes (alpine, rock garden, dwarf shrubs, conifers and aquatic plants); G Reuthe (rhododendrons and azaleas); Rickard's Hardy Ferns (ferns); Diane Sewell (sweet peas); South Africa Blooms Abroad (South African native plants); Southfield Nurseries (cacti and succulents); Swanland Nurseries (pelargoniums); Tropical Rain Forest (bromeliads); Valley Clematis Nursery (clematis); J Walkers Bulbs (daffodils); Woodfield Brothers (lupins)

Courtyard Gardens: Wisborough Green Horticultural Society

Professional Floristry: Berry & Saunders; Richardson Florist

Floral Arrangements: Abingdon Flower Club; Durban Flower Art Club; Helderberg Flower Club, Cape; Lymington Flower Club; National Panel of Floral Art Judges of Zimbabwe

RHS Great Autumn Show

Aylett Nurseries (dahlias); S & N Brackley (sweet peas); Burncoose & South Down Nurseries (trees, shrubs and herbaceous plants); Bushukan Bonsai (bonsai); Heather and Brian Hiley (tender perennials); The Hop Shop (dried flowers, grasses and hops); Toobees Nursery (succulent flora of Madagascar)

Hampton Court Palace Flower Show

Gardens: Age Concern/Timbron (Re-generation); Agriframes (The Wedding Basket)

Floral marquee: African Violet Centre (saintpaulias); Jacques Amand (lilies); Steven Bailey (carnations and pinks); S & N Brackley (sweet peas); Bressingham Gardens (hardy plants); Burncoose & South Down Nurseries (lilies); Burncoose & South Down Nurseries (trees, shrubs and ornamental plants); Bushukan Bonsai (bonsai); Cheshire Herbs (culinary, medicinal and aromatic herbs); Fibrex Nurseries (hardy ferns, hederas and pelargoniums); Goldbrook Plants (hostas and perennials); Green Farm Plants (herbaceous perennials); Heather and Brian Hiley (unusual perennials); Interflora (floral arrangements); Jekka's Herb Farm (herbs); LeGrice Roses (roses); Marks & Spencer (indoor and outdoor plants and cut flowers); Mattocks Roses (roses); Notcutts Nurseries (trees, shrubs, roses, climbers and perennials); Oldbury Nurseries (fuchsias); Potash Nursery (fuchsias); Rickard's Hardy Ferns (ferns); Diane Sewell (sweet peas); Peter J Smith (alstroemerias); Southfield Nurseries (cacti and succulents); Swanland Nurseries (pelargoniums); Three Counties Nurseries (garden pinks); Tropical Rain Forest (bromeliads and air plants); Valley Clematis Nursery (clematis); Vesutor Airplants (tillandsias and other bromeliads)

Aquatics: Dorking Aquatics (The Silent Pool); LWL Landscapes (The Water Lover's Garden); Very Interesting Rock Company (A Show Garden)

Daily Mail International Pavilion: Magnolia Variations (Trinidad and Tobago); Pantiles Plant & Garden Centre (Australasia)

RHS Show at BBC *Gardeners' World Live*

Steven Bailey (carnations, pinks, alstroemerias and gypsophila); Belfast City Council Parks Section (foliage and flowering plants); S & N Brackley (sweet peas); Bressingham Gardens (hardy plants); Burncoose & South Down Nurseries (trees and shrubs); Burncoose & South Down Nurseries (lilies); Cheshire Herbs (herbs); Federation of British Bonsai Societies (bonsai); Fuchsiavale Nurseries (fuchsias); Heather and Brian Hiley (tender perennials); Potash Nursery (fuchsias); Potterton & Martin/Peter Orme Landscapes (alpines, dwarf shrubs and foliage plants); Roualeyn Nursery (fuchsias); Diane Sewell (sweet peas); Peter J Smith (alstroemerias, limoniums and freesias); Southfield Nurseries (cacti and succulents); Three Counties Nurseries (garden pinks);

Philip Tivey & Sons (dahlias and chrysanthemums); Westfield Cacti (cacti and succulents); Woodfield Nurseries (lupins and delphiniums).

Horticultural Shows

Ayr Flower Show
Kyle & Carrick District Council, 30 Miller Road, Ayr KA7 2AY
☎ 01292 282842
CONTACT Mr P. M. Gibbs, Leisure Services
DATES 24 to 26 August
LOCATION Rozelle Park, Ayr
PARKING AND TRAVEL On site

The times and prices for this summer flower show were not confirmed when we went to press. Contact the organisers for more details.

BBC *Gardeners' World* Live
BBC Haymarket Exhibitions, 60 Waldegrave Road, Teddington TW11 8LG
☎ 0181 943 5000
DATES 14 to 18 June
LOCATION National Exhibition Centre, Birmingham
OPEN 10 am – 6 pm, daily
TICKETS Adults £10; RHS members (in advance) £8.50; Children (under 14) free. Ticket hotline: 0121 767 4333
GROUPS Contact organisers
PARKING AND TRAVEL Parking on site

This is proving a useful addition to the show calendar with its mixture of displays and demonstrations. The NEC location, though lacking atmosphere, has easy access and parking. Attractions include a large out of London RHS show, in a big marquee, and feature gardens. The RHS advisory desk will be present.

Chelsea Flower Show
Shows Department, Royal Horticultural Society, 80 Vincent Square SW1P 2PE
☎ 0171 828 1744/ 834 4333
CONTACT See the January edition of *The Garden*
DATES 23 to 26 May
LOCATION Royal Hospital, Chelsea, London
OPEN 23 – 25 May: 8 am – 8 pm; 27 May: 8 am – 5 pm
TICKETS 23, 24 May (members only): £15 (£8 from 3.30 pm); 25 May: members £12; public £23 (£13 after 3.30 pm, £6 after 5.30pm); 26 May: members £10; public £20
GROUPS No discounts for groups
PARKING AND TRAVEL Battersea Park, with free shuttle bus. Public transport recommended (Sloane Square underground or shuttle from Victoria station)

The world-famous annual flower show remains the most prestigious event in the horticultural calendar. Nurseries, societies and charities create display stands and gardens in the huge marquee, and outside in the grounds of The Royal Hospital. An exceptional range of garden furniture, machinery and other products is displayed outside, and items can be bought or ordered. Press attention usually centres on the display gardens: months of work goes into these beautifully staged displays which only last a week. There is a large flower-arranging marquee and a pavilion devoted to garden designers. Numbers are restricted, and even so the Show is often very crowded. RHS members have two days set aside exclusively for them, and can buy tickets at preferential rates. Early morning and late evening are the best times to visit, especially if it is hot.

Gateshead Summer Flower Show
Gateshead Metropolitan Borough Council, Prince Consort Road, Gateshead NE8 4HJ
☎ 0191 490 1616 ext. 272
CONTACT Leisure Services
DATES 22 to 23 July
LOCATION Gateshead Central Nursery, Whickham Highway
OPEN 22 July: 10 am – 7 pm; 23 July: 10 am – 5.30 pm
TICKETS 23 July: £3; 24 July: £2
PARKING AND TRAVEL Free parking

Expanding show which is organised by Gateshead Metropolitan Borough and a local gardening society, Rosecarpe (the North of England Rose, Sweet Pea and Carnation Society). There is also a Spring Show on 8 – 9 April.

The Great Garden and Countryside Festival
Holker Hall, Cark in Cartmel, Grange over Sands LA11 7PL
☎ 015395 58838
CONTACT Show Director
DATES 2 to 4 June
LOCATION Holker Hall, Cumbria: west of Grange over Sands on B5277 and B5278
OPEN 2 June: 10 am – 5.30 pm; 3 June: 10 am – 7.30 pm; 4 June: 10 am – 5.30 pm
TICKETS £6 Adults; £5 OAPs; £3 Children under 12 free
GROUPS Discounts for groups of 20 or more. Booking forms available from show office

The Show covers horticulture, the countryside and the environment. The theme this year is Gardens of the Senses. There will be modern as well as traditional crafts, advice centres, floral art demonstrations and a gardeners' Question Time.

Hampton Court Palace Flower Show
Shows Department, Royal Horticultural Society, 80 Vincent Square SW1P 2PE
☎ 0171 828 1744/ 834 4333
CONTACT Shows Department
DATES 5 to 9 July; Preview day, 4 July
LOCATION Hampton Court Palace, East Molesey, Surrey
OPEN 4 July: 11 am – 6 pm; 5 to 8 July: 10 am – 7.30 pm; 9 July: 10am – 5.30 pm

Shows

TICKETS 4, £20 (members only); 5 – 9, members £11 (after 3 pm £7); public £14 (after 3 pm £8)
GROUPS Affiliated societies £11; others £12.50 (10 or more, booked in advance); OAP groups £11.50
PARKING AND TRAVEL £6; after 3 pm, £3
FACILITIES FOR THE DISABLED Free parking; one escort admitted free

Spread between eight main marquees, with additional stands and tents over a wide area, this is now the biggest gardening show of its kind in the world. Unlike Chelsea the exhibitors can sell direct from their stands on all days. The Show is also recommended for those who now find Chelsea too crowded. The Royal National Rose Society's British Rose Festival is held at the Show. A Gala Evening will be held on Preview Day with music and fireworks.

Harrogate Great Autumn Flower Show
The North of England Horticultural Society, 4a South Park Road, Harrogate HG1 5QU
☎ 01423 561049
CONTACT Show Organiser
DATES 15 to 17 September
LOCATION Great Yorkshire Showground, Hookstone Oval, Harrogate
GROUPS Discounts apply for advance bookings: phone for details

As well as displays from nurseries and other trade stands, this show is particularly recommended for the society competitions (including dahlias and chrysanthemums), and for the National Kelsae Onion Festival (Saturday only). There is a flower arrangement section too.

Harrogate Spring Flower Show
North of England Horticultural Society, 4a South Park Road, Harrogate HG1 5QU
☎ 01423 561049
CONTACT Show Secretary
DATES 20 to 23 April
LOCATION Valley Gardens, Harrogate
OPEN 20 to 22 April: 9.30 am – 6 pm; 23 April: 9.30 am – 4.30 pm.
TICKETS Day tickets: 20, £8.50; 21, £7; 22, £7.50; 23, £6. RHS members, £1.50 less. Reduced afternoon rates
GROUPS Discounts for groups of 20 and over. Apply by 7 April

The Show is jointly run by the North of England Horticultural Society and the Royal Horticultural Society. As well as trade stands from nurseries, there will be shows and competitions run by the Alpine Garden Society, the Daffodil Society, and the National Association of Flower Arrangement Societies. The RHS advisory team will be present to answer horticultural questions.

Journées des Plantes de Courson
Domaine de Courson, 91680 Courson de Monteloup, France
☎ 00 33 64 58 90 12
DATES 19 to 21 May; 20 to 22 October
LOCATION 20 miles south of Paris
PARKING AND TRAVEL On site

Prestigious French show held twice yearly in a country house setting near Paris.

Malvern Autumn Show
Three Counties Agricultural Society, The Showground, Malvern WR13 6NW
☎ 01684 892751
DATES 30 September to 1 October
LOCATION Three Counties Showground
OPEN 30 September: 9 am – 6pm; 1 October: 9 am – 5 pm
TICKETS RHS members £3; public £4
GROUPS £2.40 for affiliated society groups of 10 or more

New horticultural show starting this year. It will include countryside activities and rural crafts.

Malvern Spring Gardening Show
Three Counties Agricultural Society, The Showground, Malvern WR13 6NW
☎ 01684 892751
CONTACT Show Secretary
DATES 5 to 7 May
LOCATION Three Counties Showground, Malvern
OPEN 5 May: 9 am – 6 pm; 6 May: 9 am – 6 pm; 7 May: 9 am – 5 pm
TICKETS £6 (£5 if booked before 28 April); £3.50 for RHS and Three Counties Agricultural Society members
GROUPS £4.50 affiliated society groups of 10 or more
PARKING AND TRAVEL Free car parking

The Malvern Spring Gardening Show is organised by the Three Counties Agricultural Society and the Royal Horticultural Society together. The dramatic setting and rural location give this show its own unique character. The exhibitors include a wide range of nurseries, both national and local, and numerous products and sundries stands. The RHS advisory team is present. There is also a large floral art section.

Shrewsbury Flower Show
Quarry Lodge, Shrewsbury SY1 1RN
☎ 01743 364051
CONTACT Show Secretary
DATES 11 to 12 August
LOCATION The Quarry, Shrewsbury
OPEN 11 August: 11 am – 10 pm; 12 August: 10 am – 10 pm
TICKETS Details from the show office
GROUPS 1 free ticket for groups of 20 or more

Shows

A large, traditional flower show. The Show closes with a firework display on both nights.

Southport Flower Show
42 Hoghton Street, Southport PR9 0PQ
CONTACT Show Administrator
DATES 17 to 19 August
LOCATION Victoria Park, Southport
OPEN 17 August: 9 am – 7.30 pm; 18 August: 9 am – 8.30 pm; 19 August: 9 am – 5.30 pm
TICKETS In advance: £6 Adults; £5 OAPs; £2.50 Children (12-16); On the gate: £7, £6 and £3
GROUPS 15% discount for groups of 20 and over, booked in advance

Prestigious annual flower show which draws over 100,000 visitors. Nice northern flavour with lots of local nurseries who do not attend the numerous southern shows and some southerners who come to be beside the sea. The theme this year is The Future.

Wisley Flower Show
RHS Garden, Wisley, Woking GU23 6QB
☎ 01483 224234
DATES 12 to 13 August
LOCATION RHS Garden, Wisley
OPEN 12 August: 10 am – 6 pm; 13 August: 9 am – 5 pm
TICKETS Normal garden admission rates (£4.50); RHS members free
GROUPS £3.75 for advance bookings of over 20: 12 August only
PARKING AND TRAVEL Free parking

The setting in the garden at Wisley is a major attraction of this smallish show. The nurseries attending will be selling plants. This year the Flower Show hosts the British Gladiolus Society's Show. The RHS Garden is only open to RHS members on Sunday 13 August.

Floral events

NAFAS Devon & Cornwall Area Show and Exhibition
DATES 18 to 19 October
LOCATION Livermead Hotel, Torquay

NAFAS Home Counties Area Festival
DATES 22 to 24 September
LOCATION Knebworth House, Hertfordshire

NAFAS London & Overseas Area Show
DATES 6 December
LOCATION Church House, Westminster

NAFAS National Competitions
DATES 19 to 22 July
LOCATION Stoneleigh, Warwickshire

NAFAS Scottish Area Show
DATES 2 to 3 June
LOCATION Town Hall, Falkirk

NAFAS South West Area Festival
DATES 7 to 9 September
LOCATION Bristol Cathedral

A Digest of 1994 Gardening News

On 5 January the Department of the Environment published the Inspector's report on the proposed development of a clay pigeon range near the Gardens of the Rose in Hertfordshire. The developers' appeal against refusal to grant planning permission was dismissed. The Royal National Rose Society was one of many local protesters who were obliged to spend several thousand pounds to oppose the original application and to be represented at the appeal. But, had either succeeded, the noise of the shooting range would have destroyed the enjoyment of visitors to the Society's gardens.

The English Tourist Board announced in January that garden visiting had increased by 6 per cent in the course of 1993. The top attraction was Hampton Court Palace, with 1.1 million visitors.

Also in January it was announced that the showy red and yellow patio rose 'Duchess of York' had been renamed 'Sunseeker'. The rose was bred by Pat Dickson and introduced at the Chelsea Flower Show in 1992. It became the third most popular patio rose in its first season, according to Cants of Colchester's annual rankings. However, when revealing photographs of the Duchess of York began to appear in British newspapers, sales of the variety slumped. The 1993 rankings were published at the beginning of January 1994 and showed that the rose had lost its place in the top five patio varieties. Pat Dickson spoke to rose growers about a possible change of name. According to a report by Michael Leapman in the *Independent on Sunday*, a majority believed that 'a rose by almost any other name would sell more sweetly'.

A report in the January 1994 newsletter of the International Dendrology Society drew attention to the success of scientists in establishing an arboretum in Greenland. In a small and limited area on the south west coast, natural conditions and an average temperature in July and August of 10–11° C allow a limited amount of experimental tree planting. Indeed, natural species form a shrubby forest on the sheltered slopes, where a birch, *Betula pubescens* ssp. *tortuosa*, grows up to 6 metres high, together with scattered specimens of *Sorbus groenlandica*, a close relation of *Sorbus decora*. The Greenland arboretum covers about 200 hectares and has approximately 45,000 plants of about 70 species culled from over 300 provenances. The principal sources have been collections in the Rockies, Alaska, the Yukon, Scandinavia, Labrador and Archangelesk. The purpose of the arboretum is not only to educate and give pleasure to the people of Greenland but also to facilitate selections for small-scale forestry, Christmas tree production, shelter belts and ornamental horticulture in similar polar regions.

In January, the Department of Transport announced the proposed route of the Channel Tunnel Rail Link from St Pancras to Ashford in Kent. It led immediately to protests from the National Trust, angered that the Link should cross the grounds of Cobham Park near Rochester. The house at Cobham Park is listed Grade I and is currently undergoing restoration at a cost of more than £500,000. The eighteenth-century landscape was not included in English Heritage's listing of the parks and gardens of Kent, but 'the scheme as proposed is environmentally unsustainable', commented the Chairman of the National Trust, Lord Chorley.

In the same month, The Director-General of the RHS, Gordon Rae, announced that the Society intends to build a new national Centre for Horticultural Science at its gardens at Wisley, by the year 2000. Despite its name, the Centre will not concentrate on scientific research. The emphasis will be on providing facilities for conferences, teaching, demonstrations and lectures to develop the Society's educational commitment. Presumably, it will also generate income for the Society.

The RHS also announced that it had acquired *The Plant Finder*, and when the 1994–95 edition was published in April it carried the Society's name. *The Plant Finder* was first compiled in 1987 by Chris Philip, with Dr Tony Lord as the botanical editor. It has been one of the great success stories of modern horticultural publishing and has established itself firmly as one of those books which most keen gardeners buy annually, or at least every other year. It has an annual print run of about 25,000 copies.

In a letter to *The Times* dated 24 January 1994, the headmaster of Dauntsey's School in Wiltshire highlighted the problems caused by the unrestricted breeding of Canada geese. He had visited Stourhead Gardens and noticed that the National Trust was offering, at 15 pence each, small brown paper bags labelled 'Feed the Ducks'. Children who persuaded their parents to accept the Trust's invitation found themselves feeding a host of voracious and aggressive Canada geese. The breed has been multiplying unchecked in recent years: *The Gardener's Yearbook* has already commented on how its presence has spoiled the lawns at Kew Gardens. The headmaster said that he would willingly pay rather more than 15 pence for a suitably filled bag labelled 'Poison the Canada Geese'.

In February, Rosemary Verey was Sue Lawley's guest on Radio 4's *Desert Island Discs*. It was the first time for many years that a garden designer has appeared on the programme. Among the eight records she chose to accompany her on her desert island was one sung by Elton John, the popular singer whom Mrs Verey has for some years now been advising on his garden.

Early in February the entire *Gardeners' Question Time* team defected from BBC Radio 4 to Classic FM, and reassembled as *Classic Gardening Forum*. The news intensified the debate about whether the BBC was wise to farm out such programmes to independent companies. The new chairman of GQT, Eric Robson, promised a livelier style of presentation, aimed at a younger audience. The RHS appeared to have no doubt where its sympathies lay: it invited *Classic Gardening Forum* to broadcast from the Chelsea Flower Show on 25 May. This was the first time that such a programme had ever been recorded at Chelsea, and all visitors to the Show were able to put their questions to the presenter, Dr Stefan Buzacki, and his panellists Daphne Ledward, Fred Downham and Sue Phillips.

Robin Herbert retired in February after ten years as President of the RHS. His presidency was marked by a remarkable growth in the membership, resources and influence of the Society which has now appointed him President Emeritus. In June he was awarded a CBE in the Queen's Birthday Honours for his services to horticulture.

In March the prestigious International Dendrology Society (IDS) announced that its Council proposed to ask members at their annual general meeting in May to approve a reconstitution of the Society. This involved the creation and registration of a new company as a registered charity in England, and the subsequent transfer to it of all the IDS's assets. The old Society would be dissolved, and the ex-members would immediately start a new Society whose council of management would nominate the directors of the new charitable company. This complicated manoeuvre was made necessary by a peculiarity of English law. Apparently, all the Council members of the old Society were deemed to be charitable trustees of the Society and its assets. That, of itself, created no problem, but there was another legal requirement that did: a majority of the trustees must be resident in England or Wales. In fact, only eight of the forty-three members of the Council satisfied this condition and a majority had been resident elsewhere since the Society first became an English charity, twenty years ago. 'We were therefore operating outside the law,' concluded the Chairman, Michael Bonn.

Early in the year a report from the General, Municipal and Boilermakers' Union attacked the local authority economies which had rendered public parks unsafe and affected maintenance standards. The report, *Grounds for Concern*, argues that this is the direct result of compulsory tendering, which has meant that detailed contract conditions are enforced regardless of the vagaries of the weather. Job descriptions dictate that certain tasks should be undertaken at given intervals on a strict rota: if grass has to be cut once a week in April, then it must be cut whether it has actually grown or not. Even councils that have been able to preserve employment for their workforce by awarding contracts to existing staff, have had to accept manning reductions. A typical example is the London Borough of Hammersmith and Fulham. Here, the number of people employed to maintain its 400 acres of public amenity has fallen one quarter from 107 to 80. The condition of the scented garden at Ravenscourt Park reflects this: once a feature that qualified for an enthusiastic description in *The Good Gardens Guide*, the garden is now overrun by nettles and brambles.

At the Royal National Rose Society's annual general meeting in London on 12 March, it was revealed that membership of the Society had dropped to between 16,000 and 16,500. This represents a decline of 14 per cent since 1993. The principal explanation given at the meeting was the age profile of the Society's members: many who joined in vigorous middle age thirty years ago are now dying off. In the 1960s, the Society's membership exceeded 100,000, more than the RHS then enjoyed. Other reasons postulated for the decline of the Society's fortunes are: competition from generalist societies like the RHS; the falling incomes which elderly people have experienced because of the effect of low interest rates; the Society's emphasis upon old-fashioned shows and exhibitions; its failure to treat roses as plants for mixed borders; and its omission to develop a substantial emphasis upon historic roses to reflect current tastes and fashions.

In March *Gardening Which?* surveyed the quality of the plants sold by garden centres throughout the country. They identified three problems: poor stock from the wholesaler, lack of care by the retailer, and old plants on sale when they should have been withdrawn. In one Wiltshire garden centre, more than a quarter of the trees and shrubs were considered 'not fit for sale'. Independent garden centres were generally no better or worse than those which were part of a chain. Nor was there any difference between members and non-members of the Garden Centre Association. Critics replied that old stock that has survived starvation and neglect sometimes grows away all the better in the garden. A greater risk lies in buying plants which have not been hardened off properly.

Statistics released in March by the Forestry Authority of England throw an interesting light upon trends in forestry planting. Tree planting has increased considerably. Woodland owners are planting three times more new trees than ten years ago and two and a half times as much broad-leaf planting is carried out now than coniferous. The figures for 1993–4, released later in the year, indicated a further increase in the amount of grant-aided broad-leaf planting.

New Planting	broad-leaved	5530 hectares
	conifer	558 hectares
Restocking	broad-leaved	2614 hectares
	conifer	1494 hectares

The Forestry Authority believes that the availability of grant aid has been decisive in establishing these trends. It points out that no more than 200–300 hectares per annum are now planted by private owners without Forestry Authority grants.

Biologists at the Cornwall Biological Records Unit attached to Exeter University set up a register in April to monitor the movement of flat 'killer' worms from New Zealand. These attack the larger, more rounded earthworm, reduce its body to pulp and suck up what remains. The Director of the Unit, Adrian Spalding, says that the worms were first seen in Cornwall during the 1980s, although there have been more recent reports in Manchester and in Kingsbridge, Devon. These killer worms are neither a serious nor a long-term threat to soil ecology. 'Luckily they will only pounce on small earthworms,' said Spalding. 'When they have exhausted the supply, they move on to a neighbouring garden, allowing the population to build up again.'

Published in April, a new book *Aspects of Aristocracy* by the social historian Professor David Cannadine, examined the attitudes of Vita Sackville-West and Nigel Nicolson and found them full of 'irrational social prejudices'. Cannadine claimed that any flowers remotely tinted with the middle classes or the suburbs were ruthlessly excluded from Sissinghurst. Azaleas were unsuitable because they were 'Ascot, Sunningdale sort of plants'; rhododendrons were like 'fat stockbrokers, who we do not want to have to dinner'.

A report entitled 'Commercial Horticulture and Garden Centres', published by ICC Communications in May, concluded that garden centre sales had recovered from the recession and would continue to do so. It predicted that spending on garden products would increase by more than 35 per cent, in real terms, over the next five years. The study was based on the financial results of 125 leading companies over three years ending in April 1993. The star performers in 1993-4 were Wyevale Garden Centres, Notcutts Nurseries and Kennedys, all of which reported both higher sales and higher profits. Other indices, including pre-tax margins and returns on capital, indicated that the upturn in the economy has been reflected in garden centre sales. The eight centres which reported 1993-4 figures all showed better results: four of them had turned pre-tax losses in 1992-3 into profits for 1993-4. One particular trend discerned by the analysts is a growth in the sales of conservatories and patios. This has also stimulated demand for indoor and patio plants.

In a letter to the summer edition of *Tree News*, published by the Tree Council, Alan Mitchell criticised the magazine for including articles which perpetuate the myth that our trees are in decline. Mitchell poured scorn on the argument that the crown of a tree becomes thinner in response to pollution: it is a factor of growing old. 'A picture of a dead beech is no evidence of anything beyond the fact that beech are not immortal. There are millions of them dead or dying, and there always have been.'

The theft of moss from natural sites is a growing problem. Moss is widely used in hanging baskets and has a high commercial value. During the summer, Derbyshire police led the way by mounting the first prosecutions for stealing moss under the Wildlife and Countryside Act 1981. Meanwhile Derbyshire Wildlife Trust introduced regular patrols to protect one of its nature reserves from moss thieves.

On 5 July it was announced that Fisons Horticulture had been sold to its senior management for about £50 million and changed its name to Levington Horticulture. The deal included the entire UK operation and its well-known brands, including Levington composts, Evergreen fertilizers and the Murphy range of garden chemicals. The business has a leading position in the market with 26 per cent of the retail sector and annual sales of £47 million, giving rise to a profit of £3.8 million in its last financial year.

Every year, at its main show at the Hampton Court Palace Show, the Royal National Rose Society holds a fragrance competition. In July, over 9,000 votes were cast by visitors who were invited to use their noses to vote for the three varieties which they found the most fragrant of the ten staged. When all the votes at the end of the six-day Show were added together, the final results were as follows:

Variety	Introduced	Votes
Mary-Jean	1991	1550
Margaret Merrill	1977	1516
Rosemary Harkness	1985	1321
Korresia	1974	1130
City of London	1988	1076
Double Delight	1977	1037
Paul Shirville	1983	849
Royal William	1984	490
Samaritan	1991	278
Rosy Future	1991	85

It may be noted that of the first three winners all were raised by the late Jack Harkness of R. Harkness & Co. of Hitchin.

There was an unexpected excitement at the Hampton Court Flower Show. The Home Park, where the Show took place, is normally home to the famous herd of fallow deer. As many gardeners know to their cost, these lovable pests are extremely fond of rosebuds and young rose foliage. The Show took place in a heatwave, and many exhibitors in the Rose Society's marquee left their reserve specimens outside the tent to keep cool: these are used to refresh the rose exhibits over successive days of the Show. Unfortunately, the deer found their way back into the Home Park at night, sniffed out the roses and proceeded to devour the bunches of half-open blooms.

The debate intensified about the use of peat for horticultural purposes. It culminated in a conference entitled Growing Wiser, held at Kew Gardens on 11 August 1994 and sponsored by the Wildlife Trusts. The purpose was to promote the message that garden plants do not need peat and that peat-free alternatives are as good if not better. The conference resolved: to let all local authorities know that specifying peat-free services 'should no longer present a problem'; to spread the message to growers that peat-free products are being used successfully; to discuss with the industry a timetable for phasing out peat use; to encourage retailers to promote peat-free products; and to lobby the government to break 'the industry's dependence on peat'. The conference report, also called *Growing Wiser*, indicated that the protagonists are highly committed to their cause. 'The campaign to protect peatlands is not going to go away: it is gathering momentum,' it declared. The report also quoted, with approval, the Director of the Council for British Archaeology, who said: 'To shred Anglo-Saxon manuscripts for mulching gardens would be considered outrageous. Commercial peat extraction can have the same effect on a human record which is thousands of years older.' Some of the papers were criticised for being unsound, based more upon faith than scientific argument. The Chairman of the Peat Producers Association, Phil Parry, pointed out that the peat industry has voluntarily taken many expensive steps to address the legitimate anxieties of the environmental lobby. 'Peat is vital to the horticultural industry and the amateur gardener,' he said. 'There is no viable alternative for many of its uses.'

In August it was reported that a team of scientists at Leicester University had isolated a gene that stops plants competing with each other for light. The result is that they put more effort into producing seeds, fruit, leaves and roots. The discovery is expected to transform both agriculture and horticulture by allowing farmers, growers and home gardeners to grow crops and ornamental plants more closely together.

At the end of September, the Robert and Lisa Sainsbury Charitable Trust handed over to the Royal Botanic Gardens at Kew a small bus which will make the gardens more accessible to disabled people. The gift will interest readers for two reasons. First, because it was designed by Sir Norman Foster, the international architect whose work has caused its fair share of controversy. Second, because the bus obtains up to one third of its energy from solar cells mounted on the roof. The rest of its fuel comes from rechargeable on-board batteries and the result, according to Sir Norman, is that 'it is so quiet it's as if it's not there. It's like a mobile glass bubble.' Fully loaded, the bus can hold eighteen people, three of them in wheelchairs, and will travel at a maximum speed of 10 miles per hour, the limit on Kew's roads.

In October, Levington Horticulture was a party to the declaration of the South Solway Mosses National Nature Reserve, the first to recognise the international significance of the peatland raised mire habitat that occurs in the southern side of the Solway Firth. Raised mires are peatland which has grown above the surrounding ground level. It may have taken as much as 7,000 years to accumulate and, once lost, can never be completely restored. There are only about 445 hectares of active raised mire vegetation in England. English Nature warmly congratulated Levington Horticulture for its generous donation to the nation

Obituaries 1994

Professor Tom Hewer died on 15 March 1994, aged 90. Hewer was a Bristolian through and through. His father was a corn dealer in the city, he attended Bristol Grammar School, read medicine at Bristol University and returned at the early age of 35 to take the Chair of Pathology at the University where he ended as Pro-Vice Chancellor. Tall, good looking and charming, Hewer combined a languid manner with great conversational skills, personal energy and determination. His career as a plant hunter began when he retired in 1969. Over the next 15 years, he mounted a series of tough expeditions to Turkey, Iran and Afghanistan whose successes included the discovery of 20 new plant species. Three are named after him: *Iris heweri, Acantholimon heweri* and *Bellevalia heweri*. His garden at Vine House, Henbury was a plantsman's paradise and a repository of rare and unusual garden plants. Few of his own collections ended up in the garden: his expeditions were usually undertaken for the benefit of such institutes and gardens as Kew, Edinburgh and Cambridge. Tom Hewer particularly enjoyed the companionship of visitors with whom he could share his enthusiasm for plants. It was an interest which was fortunately inherited by all four of his children for whom the garden at Vine House itself played an important part in their horticultural education.

Alvilde Lees-Milne died on 18 March 1994 aged 84. Behind a manner that was outwardly brusque, perhaps even formidable, lay a curiosity about other people and an acceptance of their eccentricities. Alvilde Lees-Milne was herself unconventional, particularly in her private life: she was great friend of Vita Sackville-West. It was when she was making her first garden in the 1950s at Roquebrune in the South of France, after she married James Lees-Milne, that she found the inspiration which was to dominate all her gardens – the French Classic style based on geometrical formalities. She applied this at Alderley Grange in Gloucester, and later at Essex House, Badminton. Both are small in scale – smallness is a feature of the Gloucestershire School – but her inability to 'think big' did not prevent her from designing gardens for such different persons as Mick Jagger and President Valéry Giscard d'Estaing. She also served on the National Trust's panel of garden advisers, and on the Council of the National Gardens Scheme. But it is as the editor, with Rosemary Verey, of *The Englishwoman's Garden* (1980) and its sequel *The Englishman's Garden* (1982) that she will best be remembered. A series of lady or gentleman gardeners described how they had made their gardens and told the reader what they considered to be their successes. The owners wrote their own chapters, and many supplied photographs: the editors gently edited, and the books were runaway best-sellers.

Jack Harkness was born on 29 June 1919 and died on 18 June 1994 aged 75. His grandfather was one of the founders of the family horticultural firm, but Jack's father was not engaged in horticulture; he was a civil servant instead. Jack left Whitgift School at 16 and spent 2 years apprenticed to the Slieve Donard Nursery in Co Down, but his return to the family firm was interrupted by war service with the Hertfordshire Regiment where he rose to the rank of Major and was mentioned in Dispatches for his service in Burma. Jack will be remembered above all for his achievements as a rose breeder and a writer. His rose breeding activites spanned only 25 years from 1961 but he introduced more good roses than any modern English breeder: more than 200 varieties, which brought him over 500 international awards. Jack re-established his family firm of R. Harkness & Co of Hitchin as one of the great modern rose breeders. His most adventurous work was with *Rosa persica*; no other breeder has ever enjoyed such success in raising hybrids of this difficult and obscure species on the taxonomic fringe of the genus. Several of the crosses were introduced commercially, including 'Euphrates' and 'Tigris'. 'Alexander', 'Amber Queen', 'Compassion', 'Margaret Merrill', 'Mountbatten' and 'Yesterday' are among his most famous roses and, although the bulk of his work was undertaken with conventional hybrid teas and floribundas, his most lasting and successful creations followed the use of unusual breeding material – not only *Rosa persica* but also the early polyantha roses and the pioneering work with European dog rose hybrids of the German Wilhelm Kordes. Jack also developed the new roses which are neither shrubs, nor polyanthas, nor ground cover, but have something in common with all of them. After his retirement to Suffolk, he would return to Hitchin every spring to spend 3 months monitoring his annual crop of thousands of new seedlings and to set about the new season's programme of hybridisation, which was planned in great detail during the winter months. Jack was always willing to discuss his work with anyone who was interested. He was genuinely fond of humankind and bound the rose world together by the affection and respect with which he treated people. Jack Harkness should also be remembered for his extraordinary gift with words: under his editorship, the *Rose Annual* of the RNRS reached a peak of quality which we are unlikely ever to see again. His own books included *Roses* (1980) and *The Makers of Heavenly Roses* (1985) where erudition, charm and the knack of accurate observation are combined in a rare degree. Jack's majestic prose made him the best English writer on roses since Dean Hole in the nineteenth century. His *The Makers of Heavenly Roses* was a work of original research which has never received achieved the commercial success it deserved. The basis of his success as a rose breeder was that he found qualities in seedlings which a lesser man would have overlooked. It was the same with people; he enjoyed an enormous circle of friends, each of whom he liked for qualities that were different and special. A fortnight after he died, the R. Harkness & Co stand at the Hampton Court Show was a tribute to his memory, composed entirely of varieties which Jack raised, from 'Margaret Merrill' and 'Amber Queen' to his latest and last introductions, the pink 'L'Aimant', yellow 'Conquest', and 'Renaissance' which is an improvement on 'Margaret Merrill'. The nursery also showed 'St John', a white floribunda which will be released this year.

John van Geest died on 22 July 1994 aged 88. Born in the Netherlands, he founded the well-known company that imports bananas from the West Indies. His first venture in England, however, was connected with the export of Dutch bulbs to this country. Early in the 1930s he pedalled round eastern England selling bulbs which had been specially treated for forcing. However, by the time he had got his stock through the obstructive Customs & Excise Department, much of the effect of the treatment was lost. Van Geest realised that he would have to grow his bulbs in England and then subject them to forcing treatment in this country. The business flourished. By 1976 the Company was the world's largest grower and distributor of bulbs, growing 200m bulbs yearly on 5,000 acres of prime fenland. Van Geest became a British subject in 1951 and was much liked and respected in the industry for his quiet professionalism and thoughtful management.

Nancy Lancaster died on 19 August 1994 shortly before her 97th birthday. Born in Virginia, but a niece of Lady Astor, her first English house was Ditchley Park in Oxfordshire where the extraordinarily influential garden which she created from scratch has now all but disappeared. Ditchley was elegant: a series of formal terrace gardens, intended to be admired from the windows of the house. In 1954 she bought Haseley Court and, before moving into the Coach House next door, she made another formal garden, richly and colourfully planted. Her influence on garden style and indeed on furnishings and interior decoration was immense, especially after she acquired Colefax and Fowler in partnership with the late John Fowler. Nancy Lancaster had strong views on colours: so long as there was enough green she felt anything went with anything. This argument, though perfectly logical, did gain her the reputation of an experimentalist. She was influenced in her early days by Ogden Codman, one of the earliest American exponents of interior decoration. Nancy Lancaster however saw gardens as an integral part of houses. Gardens were the exterior of a house, and as such, as important as the interior. Among the designers who helped her were Norah Lindsay, Geoffrey Jellicoe and Russell Page, but she was very much a hands on gardener who liked to work at the weeding and pruning herself. She worked very hard, often until nightfall. A BBC documentary shown in autumn 1993 had a memorable sequence of Nancy Lancaster, then aged 95, whizzing round the garden in an electric chair and asking the camera crew to help her with the dead-heading. Even more eloquent of her sense of style were scenes of her head gardener being required, as his first duty every morning, to take a tape recorder into the garden to record the dawn chorus for Nancy Lancaster to listen to later when she ate her breakfast in bed.

Roberto Burle Marx died on 4 June aged 84, widely acclaimed as the greatest designer of gardens and parks of his generation, perhaps of the entire twentieth century. Marx was a Brazilian nationalist, born to a German Jewish father and a French mother. After leaving school he travelled to Berlin at the age of 19 to study painting and drawing. The collection of Brazilian flowers in the Berlin Botanic Garden fascinated him and, on his return to Rio, he sought to combine his artistic talents with a growing passion for plants. He became one of the greatest experts on the Brazilian flora so that over 13 previously unknown species are now described as *burlemarxii*. His first design commission in 1934 was an ecological park at Recife and over the next 60 years Marx designed more than 2,000 parks and gardens. His best known works are the huge bayfront gardens at Rio, linked to the Copacabana Beach, and the creation of the flamingo waterfront in Rio in the 1950s, said to be the largest landscaping project in the world. Marx's skill came from combining the fine and decorative disciplines that he learnt as a student, and especially the design of fabrics and jewellery, with his landscaping of gardens. His own garden near Rio was a flowing design whose strength rested on the sheer scale of the scheme and the accuracy of his line. In particular, he was a passionate advocate of big bold groupings, composed entirely of the same species: nothing could be more different from the traditional Anglo-Saxon herbaceous border, which he disdainfully dismissed as a 'salad'. Marx cultivated over 3,500 species of plants on his estate near Rio, many of them collected and named by him in the jungles of Brazil. His garden extended to 80 hectares and the collection was larger than that in Rio's famous botanic garden, but the plants were always second to the design. He donated the estate to the Brazilian Government, which hopes to keep it open as a permanent monument to Roberto Burle Marx's genius

4
New Plants

New varieties and cultivars of plants don't just arrive in seed catalogues and nurseries. They may be the result of years of top secret work at a horticultural research laboratory or they may have turned up in someone's back garden. Either way, a keen eye and a good deal of patience are at least as important as scientific and horticultural knowledge in the business of breeding new cultivars of garden plants. Genetic engineering may change the picture one day, but raising new plants is as yet an area where in theory the amateur can participate with the professionals.

For thousand of years, mankind has cultivated plants for food, fuel, clothing and ornament. The process of cultivation creates environments which differ from the wild. In order to flourish under their new living conditions, wild species taken into cultivation usually change genetically, that is, they evolve under domestication.

Selection by the new environment, and by man, exerts powerful evolutionary pressures: crops that have been cultivated for millennia may have evolved so far that their wild parents are a matter of speculation.

Plant breeding can be defined as the fixation of a desirable combination of genes in a cultivar.

There are broadly two types of cultivars: those where a good genetic combination is maintained by avoiding the genetic mixing associated with sexual reproduction – these are clonal cultivars, propagated vegetatively; and those where genetic recombination is manipulated to produce the desired genetic mix in seed-propagated cultivars. Both types are of great importance in horticultural crops. With a few exceptions, clonal cultivars are derived from perennial species (trees, shrubs, divisible herbaceous plants, or species with perennating organs such as bulbs, runners, stolons or tubers), while seed-propagated cultivars derive from annual or biennial species.

There are two stages of development. First you have to breed or select a new form which is good enough to be introduced. Then you have the problems of propagating it in sufficient quantities, and marketing and selling your new variety. Trial and error may be enough for the first stage, but you can turn to the specialist societies for advice also. Most will have knowledgeable members who can point you in the right direction and warn you against such problems as genetic incompatibility between certain species or sections within a genus. Some are more active still and make breeding material available to their members.

The Hardy Plant Society has published a useful booklet, *Raising New Plants*, which contains general information about the mechanics of plant breeding and details of how the society can help you take your hobby a stage further. The classic guide is W. J. C. Lawrence's *Practical Plant Breeding*. Many books which are devoted to individual genera include useful material on the genetic history of breeding and on how to raise new varieties.

Propagating and marketing a new plant are probably best left to the professionals, unless the plant is only likely to appeal to a small group of enthusiasts. You can test the water by sending your plant for trial at the RHS, the Royal National Rose Society, or one of the other societies which organise trials for specific genera. RHS members can also enter a plant for an award by taking it to one of the society's shows. The experts on the judging committees will assess its potential and may recommend the plant for an award or advise further trials.

A more high profile approach is to ask a commercial nursery do the work for you. Keep an eye out for the nurseries which regularly bring novelties into commerce, and contact one which handles plants of the right type. The major seed companies, for example, are always looking out for new strains which they can promote in their annual catalogues.

Some have formal schemes to encourage amateur hybridisers. Thompson & Morgan produces an easy to understand leaflet which explains its procedures and gives tips on how to get started, including some plants which are easy for the beginner to experiment with.

Blooms of Bressingham are among the nurseries which are always interested in potential new additions to their list, and have a department whose sole function is to handle such plants. We give the way they deal with new plants here as an illustration. In the first instance Blooms require a photograph and a letter which describes in what way the plant is different from existing varieties. Their experienced staff will quickly recognise an improvement in type. Do not send any plant material until they ask for it. If they think the plant may be of commercial quality, they will propagate and evaluate it for up to two years. During this period Blooms keep meticulous records of its growth and performance, and also inform you of its progress; they are always careful to acknowledge the original raiser. If it still looks good after trialling, they will consider taking out Plant Breeders Rights for the plant, after discussing this with you. A major new introduction could be marketed in Europe, the USA and worldwide, through their agency network: the rights apply overseas too. Financial arrangements would be negotiated, which could be royalty-based or an outright purchase.

Self-satisfaction and local glory aside, there is a chance of making money from your intervention in nature's handiwork. Yet on your own the expense of registering your interest in the plant may prove prohibitive. The legislation in the Plant Varieties and Seeds Act 1964 and the Plant Breeders Rights (Fees) Regulations 1990 lays down stringent procedures including trials and evaluations (see below). At every stage of the process a hefty fee is payable. The result has been that PBR is usually only resorted to – even by the trade – for plants that have the chance of outstanding commercial success and which are expensive to develop. The main categories are roses, chrysanthemums and pelargoniums. Look in *The Plant Finder*, where such plants are marked.

From *The Plant Finder* you will also see that in some genera varieties proliferate for no good reason. Gardeners and nurseryman all suffer from indiscriminate introductions, which detract from the better plants and confuse the public. The following points, which echo the stages of the PBR system, offer some ground rules for hybridisers:

1. Make sure that a 'new' plant really is new. It could be growing somewhere else under a different name. In the past it was common for the same plant to circulate under several different names at once, and the confusion has not yet been eradicated. Don't add to this problem. Check against specimens in botanic gardens or the NCCPG National Collections: a trained eye may be needed.

2. Confirm that the plant is distinct in its ornamental features (as opposed to botanical characteristics). Find a variety that is closest to yours and note every way in which the two plants differ. If there is nothing else like it, you may be onto a winner.

3. Increase your stocks. This is not just a preliminary to distributing it. The form may not be stable or may be difficult to replicate. Bulk up the plants and grow them on to see how they behave. The recent introduction *Lavatera* 'Barnsley' seemed to have no drawbacks until it showed a tendency to revert back to the ordinary form of *Lavatera thuringiaca*.

4. If the plant is raised from seed, then you must make sure that it will come true from seed. You will require several generations of further crosses to develop a pure seed strain.

That said, there is no need to be put off. Hybridising is fun and frequently addictive. All your attempts, even the disastrous ones, will produce unique results. Even if you never seem to be getting anywhere there is nothing to stop you from trying again. And again.

AWARDS AND NEW PLANTS

Many horticultural institutes, private and public, carry out tests and assessments on new and established varieties of plant. These include *Fleuroselect*, which is mainly concerned with annuals grown from seed for summer bedding; the *Royal Horticultural Society*, which runs both temporary and permanent trials of a very wide selection of annuals, perennials, shrubs, bulbs, fruit and vegetables; the *Northern Horticultural Society*, which tests the same range as the RHS, but limits its assessments to fewer varieties; and the *Royal National Rose Society*, which conducts three-year tests on over 200 new rose varieties every year. We report many of these institutions below. *Gardening Which?* also undertakes useful trials of many types of plant, from annuals to trees, and publishes the results month-by-month in *Gardening Which?* There is an emphasis upon established varieties, rather than novelties. The results of all these trials are a good test of what is on the market and what may be expected when the introducers have been able to bulk up their stocks to a commercial volume. One source of information about new varieties of plants and seeds is the *Plant Varieties and Seeds Gazette*, published by MAFF, which operates the whole system of Plant Breeders Rights in the UK. The Gazette is published monthly and lists applications for Plant Breeders Rights, withdrawals of applications, and decisions affecting them.

New Plants of 1994

Dicksons Nurseries of Newtownards consider 'Acapulco' a great breakthrough. Colin Dickson regards it as the best cut-flower rose that Dicksons have ever bred. It is an attractive colour combination of primrose yellow, deep pink and salmon. Dicksons are famous for hybrid teas and their latest deep crimson introduction 'Leslie's Dream' is a worthy modern example, ideal for exhibition. 'Our Molly' was named for Molly Frizzell, until recently President of the Rose Society of Northern Ireland: this is a shrub rose with bright crimson single flowers carried in great profusion on a neat hummocky bush. Dicksons regard 'Shine On' as their best patio rose so far with attractive flowers of pink and orange but they are also introducing a cerise pink low growing floribunda under the name of 'Party Trick' and a deep pink sport of 'The Fairy' from Holland under the name of 'Lovely Fairy'.

Fryers Roses launched their new bedding variety 'Warm Wishes' at Chelsea. It has a very strong scent and a colour described a soft peachy coral. The bush itself is intermediate between a hybrid tea and a floribunda: flowers appear sometimes singly and sometimes in clusters.

Cants of Colchester have named their latest introduction 'Sally's Rose' to celebrate the 21st birthday of Sally Ann Cant-Pawsey. The rose is something between a short floribunda and a patio rose, pink with hints of cream and apricot.

David Austin Roses brought out five new varieties in 1994: 'Eglantine', a strongly scented pale pink rose named after Eglantine Jebb, the founder of Save the Children Fund; 'Radio Times', deep pink with neat rosette blooms and an old-fashioned scent, brought out to celebrate the 70th birthday of the *Radio Times* magazine; 'Molyneux', golden yellow, named in honour of Wolverhampton Wanderers' new stadium; 'Trevor Griffiths', a strongly scented dusky pink which commemorates the great New Zealand rose specialist of that name; and 'John Clare', with cupped cerise pink flowers, to celebrate the 200th anniversary of the birth of the poet.

There has been a dearth of good new climbing roses in recent years but Mattocks introduced two at Chelsea: the vigorous 'White Cloud' and copper orange 'Sunrise', which blooms in profusion. Mattocks also reintroduced a traditional hybrid tea of golden red colour called 'Cleopatra' and introduced Kordes' deep pink shrub rose 'Dornroschenschloß Sababurg' under the name 'Romantic Hedgerose'. The latest in the County series of ground cover roses is 'Cambridgeshire', a mixture of pink and salmon. Mattocks are particularly pleased to be introducing the 1994 Rose of the Year 'Festival', a short healthy floribunda with crimson flowers and a silvery reverse to the petals.

Peter Beales has introduced two new ground cover varieties under the names of 'Summer Sunrise' and 'Summer Sunset'. They have a lot in common but of the two perhaps Summer Sunrise is the better with bright pink semi-double flowers.

Harkness introduced five new roses from which a proportion of the proceeds of sale during the first season will go to charitable causes: 'Compassionate Friends' in aid of the charity of that name; 'Conquest', launched in association with the Imperial Cancer Research Fund; 'Hand in Hand', to raise cash for *Action for Children*; 'St John', to support the work of the Order of St John; and 'City Girl' to provide scholarships at the City of London School for Girls.

Blackmore and Langdon introduced four new varieties of tuberous begonias at Chelsea; 'Fire Dance', a bright orange *pendula*; 'Memories', pale coral, very double; 'Gipsy Maiden', an attractive wavy-edged salmon; and 'Mr Steve', a very handsome white picotee variety with dark crimson edging, named after the late Stephen Langdon who bred many of the best modern varieties.

Unwins Seeds have introduced two unusual radishes to their collection of Chinese vegetables.

'Mantang-hong' is said to have a white and green outer skin, bright magenta flesh and a nutty taste, while 'Cherokee' has pure white flesh but a bright pink skin and hotter flavour. Clearly 'Cherokee' is a conventional radish, but 'Mantong-hong' is said to be capable of reaching the size of a tennis ball. Unwins also offer two forms of Chinese cabbage: 'Mibuna' and 'Tah Tsai Ryokusai'. We wonder whether Unwins will find that these names, phonetically lifted from the Chinese, are a discouragement to making them popular in Britain.

Blooms of Bressingham introduced three new herbaceous plants in May 1994. One is a dark red *Astrantia* named 'Ruby Glow', and another is a form of candytuft with particularly thick white flowers called *Iberis sempervirens* 'Dick Self', but the star of the Chelsea Flower Show was a new variegated form of Jacob's Ladder *Polemonium coeruleum* 'Brise d'Anjou'. Variegated forms of *Polemonium* have been known to occur in the past but they are not always very stable. Blooms of Bressingham claim that the variegation of their new variety is fixed. It certainly looks striking early in the season: later, the colour tends to fade. The flowers are really incidental to the foliage. It occurred in a French nursery, in the Anjou region of France. *Polemonium coeruleum* 'Brise d'Anjou' was awarded an RHS Certificate of Preliminary Commendation after its debut at Chelsea Flower Show. Blooms was inundated with orders: it was thought that the sales potential was more than £100,000 in 1994 alone.

The alpine specialists Potterton & Martin have introduced a variegated form of *Phlox subulata* under the name of 'Nettleton Variation'. It was first noticed as a sport on a plant of 'Alexander Surprise' some years ago but not introduced until last year. *Phlox subulata* 'Nettleton Variation' is in every respect the same as its parent, well known for its pinky red flowers, but the leaves are variegated.

At the BBC *Gardeners' World* Live Show at NEC Birmingham in June 1994, the Belfast Botanical Gardens showed a new conifer called × *Cupressocyparis leylandii* 'Olive's Green'. This is a sport of the famous 'Castlewellan Gold' which occurred recently on the Breagh Orchard Nurseries (137 Gifford Road, Breagh, Portadown (01762 333498)) in Northern Ireland. It is likely to become a popular hedging plant.

Bluebell Nursery of Derbyshire is offering a new maple hybrid introduced from America and patented under the name *Acer* × *freemannii* 'Autumn Fantasy'. It is said to be a medium-sized, very hardy tree with intensely ruby red autumn colour. It prefers a lime free soil. Bluebell Nursery also offers a promising new hybrid magnolia known as *Magnolia* × *Butterflies'*. This makes a large deciduous shrub with deep yellow cup-shaped flowers in spring. It is said to give the best results in a lime-free soil and a warm sunny position.

Thompson & Morgan, the Ipswich-based seed company has always had a high media profile. This year they decided to open their trial grounds for the first time to the public for two days in August. Over 4,000 trial varieties were on show including several new items which will be introduced in 1995. Two for which the company predicts a great demand are *Laurentia* 'Blue Star', with lightly-scented, violet-coloured star-shaped flowers, ideal for hanging baskets and *Wahlenbergia undulata* 'Melton Bluebird' whose dark blue flowers fade gradually almost to pink, with a spreading habit and long flowering season that is also expected to be very popular for containers.

The National Council for the Conservation of Plants and Gardens (NCCPG) will launch a Heritage Plant promotion to publicise a number of old and new 'garden-worthy' plants which need to be protected by making them more widely available. The six plants are *Geranium lindavicum* 'Apple Blossom', *Geranium* 'Gillian Perrin', *Euphorbia* 'Lambrook Gold', *Symphytum* 'Lambrook Sunrise', *Artemisia absynthium* 'Lambrook Mist' and 'The Lambrook Rose' which is grown in European gardens under its correct name of 'Verschuren'. It is regrettable that the NCCPG, which has played such an important part in sorting out the nomenclature of old varieties, should add to confusion by renaming a plant in contravention of the International Convention on Botanic Names. It is also a shame that the plants are only available at nine garden centres, all in the south of England: RHS Wisley, Surrey; RHS Rosemoor, Devon; Whitehall Garden Centre, Wiltshire; Webbs of Wychbold, Worcestershire; Wilton House Garden Centre, Salisbury, Wiltshire; Squires Garden Centres, Middlesex and Surrey; Forest Lodge Garden Centre, Farnham, Surrey; Fulham Palace Garden Centre, London and Hurrans Garden Centre, Churchdown, Gloucestershire.

Plant Breeders Rights

The registered owner of Plant Breeders Rights is entitled, while that registration lasts, to have the exclusive right to sell propagating material or seed of the variety in question or to authorise others to do so. He enjoys, in effect, a plant patent. It is a cardinal rule of the system that the new variety should not have been offered for sale already: new means new. Samples are submitted to MAFF, who must be satisfied that the variety is clearly distinguishable in its characteristics from all other varieties and that it is both stable and uniform or homogeneous.

Most applications relate to agricultural crops, particularly grasses, fodders and brassicas. Among vegetables, the most significant subject for applications for Plant Breeders Rights is the potato. The grant lasts for twenty-five years and the varieties which are still registered (and producing royalties for the owners) include 'Cara', 'Maris Bard', 'Pentland Javelin' and 'Wilja'. Among the horticulturally important genera, chrysanthemums (as MAFF continues to call them, in preference to the more modern *Dendranthema*), pelargoniums and roses are the main plants, but especially roses. You can be certain that almost all the great roses of the last twenty years have been properly registered, including such important roses as 'Silver Jubilee' and 'Royal William'. Unfortunately, however, they are almost invariably registered under code names which continue to be used for legal purposes: the actual cultivar name under which the variety will be marketed will be different, and usually differs from one country to another. For example, the November 1993 edition of the Plant Varieties and Seeds Gazette listed 58 new varieties of rose to which it was proposed to grant Plant Breeders Rights. Most of the famous breeders names were on the list – Austin, Harkness, Cocker, Kordes and Dickson among them – but all the roses had code names and there is no saying, at this stage, what JACPURR, COCJABBY or DICJOON will turn into.

THE ROYAL NATIONAL ROSE SOCIETY

International Rose Trials 1994 – List of Awards made by the Trials Committee of the Royal National Rose Society

The list of roses receiving awards from the Royal National Rose Society is very much less interesting than it used to be when the varieties put to trial were released into commerce with proper names before being sent to trial. It is difficult to get excited about a rose such as this year's winner of the President's International Trophy which is known as 1721-87 and whose real identity may not be revealed for a year or two to come. That said, it was quite an exceptional winner, by the largest margin seen for many years. There are, however, three interesting points emerging from the list that follows. First, there is a strong move away from traditional hybrid teas and floribundas (now known at the RNRS as large flowered roses and clustered flowered roses respectively) towards ground cover, miniature and shrub roses of one sort or another. Second, despite the move away from disclosing the parentage of new roses, it is clear that certain lines are emerging which will have a significant influence on the future, in particular, the polyantha types like 'Eyeopener'. Third, British and Irish rose breeders are falling to competition from abroad and, in particular, from Germany. Kordes, Noack and Tantau between them account for almost half the new roses to win awards. The only British breeder to feature more than twice is the relative newcomer Chris Warner.

The President's International Trophy for the best new seedling rose of the year and a Gold Medal

1721-87. Ground Cover Shrub. Bright pink, semi-double. Light scent. Short, spreading. Foliage small, glossy.
Parentage undisclosed
Raiser: Noack

The Henry Edland Memorial Medal for the best scented variety and a Certificate of Merit

MT 84324. Floribunda. Pink, semi-double. Several flowers in a cluster. Good scent. Medium height, bushy. Foliage dense, glossy.

Parentage undisclosed
Raiser: Tantau

Certificates of Merit

POUlmo. Floribunda. Red, double. Many flowers in a cluster. Little scent. Medium height. Upright growth, small foliage.
Parentage: Seedling × Seedling
Raiser: Poulsen

B4089. Shrub. Deep yellow, semi-double. Many flowers in a cluster. Moderate scent. Short, bushy.
Parentage: Seedling × Seedling
Raiser: Interplant

Trial Ground Certificate and The Torridge Award for the best award winning rose bred by an amateur.

GUEscan. Hybrid Tea. Yellow suffused red, double. Light scent. Medium height, bushy growth.
Parentage: 'Fulton Mackay' × 'Freedom'
Raiser: Guest

Trial Ground Certificates

KORsaku. Shrub. Pink, single. Several flowers in a cluster. Good scent. Short, spreading, bushy. Foliage *rugosa* type.
Parentage: undisclosed
Raiser: Kordes

CHEWpobey. Ground Cover. Light vermillion, yellow eye. Single. Very many flowers in a cluster. Little scent. Very short, bushy. Small foliage.
Parentage: ('Anna Ford' × 'Little Darling') × 'Eyeopener'
Raiser: Warner

CHEWfires. Climbing Miniature. Light vermillion, yellow reverse, semi-double. Several flowers in a cluster. Little scent. Short-growing climber.
Parentage: 'Rosalie Coral' × 'Mary Sumner'
Raiser: Warner

MACbunber. Shrub. Red, white eye, semi-double. Several flowers in a cluster. Little scent. Short, spreading.
Parentage: 'Trumpeter' × 'Eyeopener'
Raiser: McGredy

WAX87A. Shrub. Pink, single. Very many flowers in a cluster. Short, spreading.
Parentage: 'Ballerina' Seedling
Raiser: Watson

B78-87. Shrub. Amber, paler reverse, semi-double. Many flowers in a cluster. Moderate scent. Short, upright.
Parentage: Seedling × Seedling
Raiser: Interplant

B788-88. Shrub. Golden veined red, single. Very many flowers in a cluster. Light scent. Short, spreading.
Parentage: Seedling × Seedling
Raiser: Interplant

CHEWmagwel. Shrub. Apricot, paler reverse, single. Several flowers in a cluster. Little scent. Medium height, upright.
Parentage: 'Sweet Magic' × 'Warm Welcome'
Raiser: Warner

ARB No 919. Shrub. Cream/cerise edge, single. Many blooms in a cluster. Little scent. Medium height, upright.
Parentage: MEIpoque × ('Regens-berg' × 'Fair Play')
Raiser: Meilland

AB 249B. Climber. Deep apricot, double. Few flowers in a cluster; scent good. Short-growing climber.
Parentage: 'High Sheriff' × 'Basildon Bond'
Raiser: Harkness

'Ring of Fire'. Dwarf Floribunda. Amber edged red, double. Several flowers in a cluster. Little scent. Short, bushy.
Parentage: 'Pink Petticoat' × 'Gold Badge'
Raiser: Moore

1314-87. Floribunda. Russet red, semi-double. Few flowers in a cluster. Moderate scent. Medium height, bushy. Foliage good, reddish new growth.
Parentage: 'Champion' × Seedling
Raiser: Noack

'Roussillon'. Floribunda. Dark red/white eye, semi-double. Many flowers in a cluster. Little scent. Medium height, bushy.
Parentage: Seedling × Seedling
Raiser: Dickson

HARimity. Floribunda. Yellow, semi-double. Few flowers in a cluster. Little scent. Medium height, upright.

78 New Plants

Parentage: 'Rosemary Harkness' × 'Golden Years'
Raiser: Harkness

PEAvanguard. Deep pink, double. Many flowers in a cluster. Light scent. Medium height, bushy.
Parentage: Seedling × Seedling
Raiser: Limes New Roses

MT 8899. Shrub. Blush pink, semi-double. Many flowers in a cluster. Light scent. Short, spreading. Foliage small, glossy.
Parentage: undisclosed
Raiser: Tantau

POUlgode. Dwarf Floribunda. Soft yellow, semi-double. Several flowers in a cluster. Light scent. Short, bushy.
Parentage: Seedling × Seedling
Raiser: Poulsen

DICuniform. Floribunda. Red, single. Many flowers in a cluster. Little scent. Medium height, bushy.
Parentage: 'Little Prince' × 'Eyeopener'
Raiser: Dickson

Trial Ground Certificates awarded at the end of the second year

MT 89146. Ground Cover/Shrub. Light yellow, double. Several flowers in a cluster. Moderate scent. Short, spreading.
Parentage: undisclosed
Raiser: Tantau.

CHEWsunford. Shrub. Deep yellow, semi-double. Several flowers in a cluster. Little scent. Short, bushy. Foliage small, glossy.
Parentage: 'Pam Ayres' × 'Laura Ford'
Raiser: Warner

KORarec. Ground Cover. Red/white eye, single. Many flowers in a cluster. Little scent. Very short, trailing. Foliage glossy.
Parentage: undisclosed
Raiser: Kordes

'Gourmet Popcorn'. Dwarf Floribunda. White, semi-double. Many flowers in a cluster. Good scent. Short, bushy. Foliage small.
Parentage: Sport of 'Popcorn'
Raiser: Desamero

THE ROYAL HORTICULTURAL SOCIETY

Permanent trials are conducted at Wisley with border carnations, early-flowering chrysanthemums, daffodils, dahlias, day-lilies, delphiniums, garden pinks, irises and sweet peas. Permanent trials of camellias are situated on nearby Battleston Hill. These trials continue from year to year with periodic replanting, at which time additions and removals are made. Results of trials are published in the horticultural press and in publications of the RHS available to members on request from the trials office at Wisley.

The RHS's main system of awards has, however, been radically overhauled, following the publication last year of its new Award of Garden Merit (AGM). This is the highest award that the Society can give a plant and in the past it was only bestowed irregularly. In practice, the earlier awards were often outclassed by later varieties and, once an award was given, there was no system for taking it away. Four years ago the RHS put the whole problem out to a series of committees whose task was to identify those ornamental plants, fruit and vegetables 'of the highest garden value, whether for cultivation in the open or under glass'. It was important that the plants should be reasonably widely available and carry a hardiness rating. The upshot is a list of 3,300 plants which are now designated carriers of the AGM.

The awards are not however intended as a selection. The criteria remain overall excellence, sound constitution and adaptability in cultivation. Nothing was excluded because there were others of equal quality and, as a result, the list contains nearly 200 roses, 73 camellias and 67 varieties of clematis. Nor did the committees put a premium on rarity: among the names are such common or garden trees as *Betula pendula, Fagus sylvatica* and *Fraxinus excelsior* – birch, beech and ash to you and me, and very good garden plants too. An innovative system of rolling awards has been instituted so that new plants can be added and fading stars deleted once they have reached the decline stage.

The RHS has approved the introduction of a new 'kite-mark' for good garden plants which receive the Award of Garden Merit. The symbol has the shape of a trophy which the society hopes will be widely adopted by gardening publications and on plant tags at nurseries and garden centres. The trophy symbol will simplify the decision-making process for gardeners who want a plant which offers the best all-round garden value.

In order to qualify as an AGM plant, it should be of outstanding excellence for garden decoration or use; be available in the trade; be of good constitution; and require neither highly specialist growing conditions or care. AGMs are only awarded after a period of assessment by the relevant committee of the RHS. That assessment may take the form of a trial at one of the RHS gardens or similar venue; visits to specialist collections; round table discussions which draw on the expertise and experience of committee members.

There follows a selection of the AGM awards made at the Wisley Trials during the course of 1994. Full details are available from the RHS.

Award of Garden Merit (unless otherwise stated)
(Source: Trials Office, RHS Garden, Wisley)

Alstroemeria (open ground)
Alhambra, Apollo, Coronet, Flaming Star, Friendship, Golden Delight, Orange Delight, Orange Gem, Orange Glory, Princess Carmina, Princess Caroline, Princess Elizabeth, Princess Juliana, Princess Mira, Solent Crest, Solent Rose, Yellow Friendship, Yellow Crown

Alstroemeria (under glass)
Amanda, Amor, Bianca, Diamond, Fiona, Helios, Princess Carmina, Princess Elizabeth, Princess Grace, Princess Mira, Rebecca, Rhapsody, Tiara, White Libelle

Begonia (Tuberous, including pendular types; open ground)
Clips Yellow, Cora, Fortune Red, Memory Fiery Red, Memory Mix, Memory Rose, Memory Salmon Pink, Memory White, Musical Rosepink, Musical Scarlet, Panorama Scarlet, Pin Up

Begonia (Pendular types; hanging baskets and pots)
Illumination Orange, Illumination Salmon Pink

Border Carnations (RHS and British National Carnation Society; cultivars for the open border)
Alfriston, Bryony Lisa, Chris Crew, David Saunders, Flanders, Hazel Ruth, Howard Hitchcock, Jean Knight, Maisie Neal, Riccardo, Spinfield Buff, Spinfield Bridesmaid, Tamsin Fifield, Uncle Teddy

Heading Broccoli and Cauliflower (coloured types)
Alverda, Esmeraldo, Limelight, Marmalade, Minaret, Red Lion, Violet Queen, Violetta Italia

Carrot (Early Nantes Types, November sown in frames)
Evora, Nasha, Natan, Sytan; also Panther, Napoli

Celery (Green and self-blanching types, excluding trench celery)
Crystal, Galaxy, Green Cathedral, Loret, Octavius, Starlight, Victoria

Autumn-flowering Crocus
C. cartwrightianus 'Albus', C. goulimyi 'Mani White', C. hadriaticus, C. kotschyanus subsp. cappadocius, C. laevigatus, C. longiflorus, C. ochroleucus, C. serotinus subsp. clusii, C. speciosus 'Albus', C. 'Zephyr'

Dahlias (RHS and National Dahlia Society)
Almand's Climax, Arthur Hills, Autumn Lustre, Barbarry Dominion, Dana Iris, Fascination, Geerlings Queeny, Hamari Accord, Ice Cream Beauty, Jeannette Carter, John Street, Karenglen, Mariner's Light, Nationwide, Orange Mullet, Pink Pastelle, Preston Park, Scottish Relation, Video, Wootton Impact, Yellow Hammer, Yelno Harmony, Young Pippa

Delphinium (Seed raised, for general garden use)
Pink Dream, Southern Maidens, Southern Countess, Southern Countrymen, Zeeland Light Blues

Early-Flowering Chrysanthemums (Wisley and Bradford trials; RHS and National Chrysanthemum Society. Grown as spray cultivars for garden decoration)
Apricot Margaret, Emily, Gold Enbee Wedding, Good Life Sombrero, Nathalie, Pennine Club, Pennine Ginger, Pennine Goal, Pennine Lotus, Pennine Magnet, Salmon Enbee Wedding, Salmon Pennine Rose, Yellow Pennine Oriel

Early-Flowering Chrysanthemums (as above, but disbudded cultivars)
George Griffiths, Linda Welch, Pink Julie Ann

Dodecatheon
D. dentatum, D. hendersonii 'Inverleith', D. meadia 'Splendidum'

Erythronium

80 New Plants

Erythronium californicum, E. 'Eirene', E. 'Margaret Mathew', E. 'Minnehaha', E. 'Susanna'

Irises (RHS and British Iris Society; *Iris spuria*)
Shelford Giant, Belise, Sunny Day

Irises (RHS and British Iris Society; Intermediate Bearded Irises)
Bromyard, Bronzaire, Cannington Skies, Eye Magic, Fierce Fire, Katie-Koo, Maui Moonlight, Pale Shades, Peggy Chambers, Purple Landscape, Raspberry Blush, Saltwood, Sarah Taylor, Sweet Kate, Tarot, Vinho Verde

Irises (RHS and British Iris Society; Pacific Coast Irises)
Big Money, Broadleigh Carolyn, Golden Waves, Lavender Royal, Lincoln Imp, Little Tilgates, Pajaro Dunes, Ring O'Roses, Rio del Mar, Roaring Camp, Short Order

Lettuces (Crisphead types, summer heading)
Beatrice, El Toro, Ice Cube, Kelvin, Leopard, Malika, Minigreen, Roxette, Strada

Pelargoniums (Regal types)
Ann Hoystead, Askham Fringed Aztec, Bodey's Picotee, Bushfire, Carisbrooke, Eileen Postle, Fareham, Fringed Aztec, Gemma Jewel, Georgina Blythe, Joy, Julia, Lavender Grand Slam, Margaret Soley, Royal Princess, Sefton, Splendour, White Glory

Pelargoniums (Angel types)
Catford Belle, Darmsden, Kettlebaston, Spanish Angel, Starlight Magic, The Barle, The Tone, Tip Top Duet, Velvet Duet, Wayward Angel

Pelargoniums (Decorative types)
Lara Maid, Sancho Panza, Variegated Mme Layal

Garden Pinks (RHS and British National Carnation Society; cultivars for the open border)
Bovey Belle, Coronation Ruby, Cranmere Pool, Cyril's Joy, Frances Isabel, Houndspool Cheryl, Laurie Belle, Louise's Choice, Rose Joy, Sheila's Choice, Tamsin

Salvia (Bedding types)
Blue Victory, Cambridge Blue, Cleopatra Mixed, Cleopatra Rose, Cleopatra Salmon, Flare, Phoenix Mixed, Red Arrow, Scarlet King, Scarlet Queen, Sizzler Deep Salmon, Sizzler Lavender, Sizzler Purple, White Victory

Spring Cabbage (Hearted types for August sowing)
Advance, Aladdin, Avoncrest, Jason, King Greens, Prince Greens, Pyramid

Sweet Peas (RHS and National Sweet Pea Society; short cultivar for garden decoration, no support)
Explorer

Sweet Peas (RHS and National Sweet Pea Society; tall cultivars for garden decoration)
Apricot Queen, Bishop Rock, Borderline, Colin Unwin, Jayne Amanda, Jilly, Marmalade Skies, Mrs Bernard Jones, Noel Sutton, Royal Flush, Southbourne, Toby Robinson, White Supreme

Sweet Peas (RHS and National Sweet Pea Society; tall cultivars for exhibition)
Award of Merit: Anne Barron; Preliminary Commendation: Just James, Karen, Miranda Crafer, Moorland Beauty

FLEUROSELECT

Current *Fleuroselect* Gold Medals
Begonia tuberosa 'Pin Up'
Bellis perennis 'Robella'
Callistephus chinensis 'Starlight Rose'
Centaurea cyanus 'Florence Pink'
Centaurea cyanus 'Florence White'
Cosmos bipinnatus 'Sonata'
Dianthus chinensis 'Raspberry Parfait'
Dianthus chinensis 'Strawberry Parfait'
Dianthus hybrida 'Color Magician'
Eschscholtzia californica 'Dalli'
Gazania splendens 'Garden Sun'
Impatiens walleriana 'Mega Orange Star'
Limonium sinuatum 'Forever Gold'
Nierembergia 'Mont Blanc'
Pelargonium × *hortorum* 'Orange Appeal'
Salvia coccinea 'Lady-in-Red'
Tagetes patula 'Safari Tangerine'
Verbena hybrida 'Peaches and Cream'
Verbena speciosa 'Imagination'
Viola 'Velour Blue'
Viola 'Imperial Frosty Rose'
Viola 'Imperial Gold Princess'
Viola 'Jolly Joker'
Viola 'Padparadja'

Four gold medals were awarded for the Fleuroselect 1995 recommendations (*Source* Unwins):

Fuchsia 'Florabelle'. Red and purple semi-double flowers; good branching habit; designed for hanging baskets.

Papaver orientalis 'Pizzicato'. A dwarf-growing strain in a wide selection of colours – scarlet, orange, salmon, mauve, pink, and white.

Lobelia speciosa 'Fan Scarlet'. A compact growing strain with scarlet blooms contrasting with bronzy green foliage. Flowers in one year from seed from an early sowing.

Nicotiana 'Havana Appleblossom'. Pink flowers with a deeper rose reverse to the petals giving an overall effect of a bicolor. This is widely considered the best of this year's Fleuroselect winners.

Latest Scientific Research

A vast corpus of horticultural research is undertaken by universities, institutes, nurserymen and enthusiasts all over the world, and many of the results are published in obscure journals. Several organisations compile abstracts of these publications, so that students and researchers can know what is happening in their particular fields. By far the best is *Horticultural Abstracts*, published by CAB International Information Services, Wallingford, Oxfordshire, OX10 8DE (tel: 01491 832111, fax: 01491 833508), and most of the papers which we summarise here have appeared, or will appear, every year in its pages, alongside more than 10,000 other horticultural abstracts. The amateur has something useful to learn from every one.

Readers with wider interests should consult *Plant Breeding Abstracts*, also published by CAB International Information Services.

Breeding woody ornamentals at East Malling, with particular reference to *Sambucus nigra*. K. R. Tobutt. *Acta Horticulturae* (1992) No 320, pp. 63–68. Horticulture Research International, East Malling, West Malling, Kent ME19 6BJ, UK.

The HRI at East Malling has for the last ten years been principally concerned with developing *Buddleja*, *Pieris*, *Syringa*, *Malus* and *Sambucus*. This will result, in due course, in the introduction to commerce of dwarf buddlejas in various colours, red-leaved crab-apples with columnar habit and good resistance to disease, pieris which are resistant to lime-induced chlorosis, lilacs with large flowers and pinnatifid leaves, and elders with various combinations of leaf colour and laciniation. This account of breeding of new forms of elder is particularly interesting. A programme of crosses with the forms of *Sambucus nigra* known as 'Aurea', 'Guincho Purple' and 'Laciniata' indicated that yellow and purple leaf forms were caused by a single dominant gene, while laciniation was due to a single recessive. Tests are currently being carried out on a number of cut-leaved seedlings with red or yellow leaves, which may be compared to Japanese maples in delicacy but are adaptable to a much wider choice of soils.

***Sorbus domestica* L., New to Wales and the British Isles.** M. Hampton and Q. O. N. Kay. *Watsonia* (1994) 20.

A stand of the true service tree, *Sorbus domestica*, has been discovered growing on inaccessible ledges on a south-facing limestone sea in southern Glamorgan. The discovery was originally made in May 1983 by Marc Hampton, an amateur botanist living near Cardiff, and confirmed by Dr Quentin Kay, a research botanist in the School of Biological Sciences at the University of Wales in Swansea. The discovery gives rise to several interesting problems. First, the site has long been a favourite venue for botanical excursions and it would seem impossible that any long-established but undiscovered species of tree could exist there. This is explained because, when not in fruit, *Sorbus domestica* can easily be confused with the rowan *Sorbus aucuparia*. *Sorbus domestica* is the service tree: the fruit is large, hard and greenish-brown, whereas the ripe fruit of a rowan is small, soft and red. The new colony seldom sets fruit. Second, the colony seems much older than at first supposed. The trees themselves are wind-blown, almost prostrate in some cases and fairly small – no more than 15 ft (5 m) at most, but ring counts of sections from dead branches show that they are extremely slow growing and suggest that some of the larger living trunks are about 400 years old. These trunks often show the stumps of older dead trunks embedded in their bases, which indicates that the individual trees may be much older, conceivably thousands of years old, but periodically produce replacement trunks from basal shoots. Third, comparisons of trees from the new site in South Glamorgan were made with the descendants of the last known supposedly native example of *Sorbus domestica*, a single tree which was said to have grown in the Wyre Forest in Worcestershire until 1862. Those descendants are seedlings grown in such botanic gardens as Oxford. Chromosome examinations showed that the Glamorgan stand of *Sorbus domestica* was closely related to the Wyre Forest specimen while all other cultivated trees, from stands in continental Europe, differed in their genetic make-up more substantially. This suggests that the Glamorgan populations and the Wyre Forest tree were descended from the same original edge-of-range colonising stock.

Promotion of apple tree growth and fruit production by the EBW-4 strain of *Bacillus subtilis* in apple replant disease soil. R. S. Utkhede and E. M. Smith. *Canadian Journal of Microbiology* (1992) 38 (12) pp. 1270-73.

Many members of the Rosaceae are vulnerable to 'specific replant disease', a blanket term for a cocktail of toxins which inhibit growth when such important crops as roses and fruit trees are planted in the same soil as the genus has recently been growing. No uniform explanation for the disease has been given, but sterilising the soil prevents its occurrence and this has hitherto been the commonest means of avoiding the problem. This field trial at Kelowna in British Columbia over a five-year period compared traditional fumigation of the soil with Formalin with the effect of drenching with a bacteria called *Bacillus subtilis*. Growth rate and fruit yield were measured in large plantations of Macintosh apples on an M26 rootstock. A particular strain of *Bacillus subtilis* was found to have a beneficial effect upon growth and fruit yield, better than treatment with Formalin. Since Formalin treatment sterilises the soil, it follows that the bacillus actually has a positive effect. Clearly the potential for selected strains of bacteria not only to avoid such problems as specific replant disease, but actually to increase growth and production, has implications for every type of crop.

Ergebnisse aus Modellversuchen zur Bewurzelung von Ziergeholzen. M. Jacob, A. Plietzsch and K. Schulze. *Gartenbau Magazin* (1991) 38 (3) pp. 44-46.

This short article is another account of the beneficial effect of a form of *Bacillus subtilis* bacteria, in this case upon the rooting and establishment of certain ornamental species. The strain known as race T99 was cultured and suspended in a peat/gravel mixture used for striking cuttings. Compared to a control, which did not contain this bacillus, some species rooted very much more easily than normally. Such difficult taxa such as *Tilia tomentosa*, *Syringa vulgaris* and *Hamamelis virginiana* were noticeably easier to root and subsequently establish. The reason for this is not clear, but it has long been suspected by scientists that there is a symbiotic relationship between plants and certain forms of bacilli and fungi.

Sélection du cassis et de la framboise pour la France. V. Bellenot-Kapusta. *Arboriculture Fruitière* (1993) No 457, pp. 24-30.

This is a summary of research on breeding blackcurrants and raspberries at the French National Research Institute at Angers over the last twenty years. The aim of the blackcurrant breeding programme has been to produce fruit with the right degree of acidity and colour, and a low chilling requirement, on plants that are self-fertile and resistant to pathogens. In the case of raspberries, resistance to phytophthera is an essential requirement, as are the taste and aroma of the fruit, both fresh and frozen. As the breeding programmes proceeded, four blackcurrant varieties and two raspberries were registered for Plant Breeders Rights in France. The blackcurrant varieties were 'Berger' (a sport of 'Noir de Bourgogne'), 'Kifon' ('Ogevin' × 'Tessima'), 'Troll' ('Tessima' × 'Crossdown') and 'Andega' ('Noir de Bourgogne' × 'Tessima'). The two raspberries were 'Warwi' ('Washington' × 'Williamet') and 'Miko' ('Mija' × 'Rose de Côte d'Or'). The point of interest to readers of *The Gardener's Yearbook* is that none of these varieties is available in the UK. Moreover, with the single exception of 'Blackdown' (available from one nursery), none of their parents is available here either. Climatic differences offer only a partial explanation. All fruit varieties, old and new, tend to have a strong local and regional following, and not to be widely grown outside their country of origin. Obviously, there are exceptions: the great grape and apple varieties spring immediately to mind. But breeders have long known that the greatest advances in hybrid vigour are made through crossing the offspring of lines that have become inbred. We therefore suggest that British hybridisers in search of fame and fortune should choose French varieties as the basis of their breeding programmes and cross them with varieties from other countries, including the United Kingdom.

Magnolia × *gotoburgensis*. T. G. Nitzelius. *Magnolia* (1992) 28 (1) pp. 1–5.

Papers which describe a new hybrid in all its botanic detail and give it a scientific name are seldom interesting. This article, however, is an exception. *Magnolia* × *gotoburgensis* is the result of crossing *Magnolia wilsonii* and *Magnolia hypoleuca*. *Magnolia wilsonii* is a useful species because it grows quickly from seed and flowers when young. The flowers, however, are vulnerable to late frost damage. Nor is the plant as a whole among the hardier species: it does not survive in continental Europe or North America. *Magnolia hypoleuca* is less conspicuous in flower, but an extremely hardy tree. The importance of × *gotoburgensis* is that a proportion of the seedlings bearing this name will exhibit both the beauty of *Magnolia wilsonii* and the hardiness of *Magnolia hypoleuca*. Two of the three original clones were planted in Western Sweden and have thrived in a part of the country where no magnolia would normally be considered hardy.

Flower bud hardiness of *Forsythia* cultivars. S. McNamara and H. Pellett. *Journal of Environmental Horticulture* (1993) 11 (1) pp. 35–38.

Minnesota is one of the coldest parts of the North American continent. The University of Minnesota undertook to profile the winter hardiness of six recent cultivars of forsythia and to compare them with three old favourites: *Forsythia* × *intermedia* 'Beatrix Farrand' and *Forsythia ovata* 'Ottawa' and 'Robusta'. The trials concentrated upon the hardiness of the flower buds and compared their resistance to extreme cold at three different times of the year: early in the winter, in the middle of winter and finally in late winter when the plants were beginning to emerge from hibernation. All nine cultivars proved hardy early in the winter and in midwinter: they survived temperatures in excess of −30°C. The six new varieties, 'Meruloc', 'Northern Gold', 'Northern Sun' (all bred from *Forsythia ovata* × *Forsythia europaea*), 'New Hampshire Gold' (*Forsythia ovata* × *intermedia*), 'Sunrise' (*Forsythia ovata* hybrid) and 'Vermont Sun' (*Forsythia mandshurica*) were hardier than the three older cultivars but only to a factor of 4°C at most. Since temperatures in the British Isles seldom, if ever, drop below −25°C, this study may appear to have no direct implications for the horticultural industry here. However, the varieties which 'de-acclimatize' earlier in spring were less hardy than the others by the middle of March. There are therefore two interesting points to note. First, winter hardiness varies at different stages in the season. This explains why plants may be most vulnerable to late spring frosts. Second, forsythias do not de-hibernate until they experience warmth after a period of cold. They are reluctant to flower if they have not suffered at least some cold during the winter. This in turn explains why forsythias flower earlier in Kent than in Cornwall. On the evidence of this experiment, however, forms and hybrids of *Forsythia mandshurica* (which is little grown on this side of the Atlantic) will flower earlier in the west than in the east: a possible subject for further experiment?

High tunnels extend tomato and pepper production. M. P. N. Gent. *Bulletin of the Connecticut Agricultural Experiment Station* (1991) No. 893, 16 pp. Tomato production in heated and unheated greenhouses. G. N. Mavrogianopoulos, P. Choustoulakis and S. Kyritsis. *Agricoltura Mediterranea* (1993) 123 (1) pp. 30–34.

These are reports of two very different trials, carried out in different parts of the world for quite different purposes and yet, when run together, they point to the same very useful conclusion: large unheated polytunnels offer better value than other structures whether heated or unheated. Cost is the significant factor here – cost/value.

Two *Pelargonium* species from Turkey and northern Iraq. M. A. T. Johnson and B. Mathew. *Kew Magazine* (1993) 10 (3) pp. 124–28.

Most *Pelargonium* species come from southern Africa but the genus also includes a number of geographical outliers with interesting genetic potential. *P. endlicherianum* and *P. quercetorum*, from Turkey and Iraq respectively, are interesting because they are frost hardy and semi-shrubby. Their magenta-carmine flowers are not large, but the two upper petals are very much bigger than the three lower ones, as is often the case with cultivated varieties of pelargonium. *P. quercetorum* is confined to a small area where the borders of Turkey, Iran and Iraq meet: it grows on steep limestone slopes in clearings of *Quercus libani* woodland. *P. endlicherianum* is more widely spread throughout Anatolia. Neither is common in cultivation – indeed, *P. quercetorum* is not available from any nursery listed in *The Plant Finder*. However, *P. endlicherianum* is becoming more widely available and its importance lies in the potential for breeding hardy shrubby pelargoniums by judicious crosses with other tender species with large flowers from southern Africa.

Science Vol 260 pp. 214–216 reports the discovery of a new and potentially cheaper source of taxol, the anti-cancer drug hitherto known only from the inner bark of the Pacific yew *Taxus brevifolia*.

As the yew is both rare and slow-growing, and contains only very small quantities of the drug, taxol was considered prohibitively expensive to manufacture artificially: it took six 100-year-old trees to gather enough to treat one patient for one year. However, *Science* reports that a team from Montana State University has discovered an alternative source of taxol – a fungus that lives in the bark of the yew. It has long been known that some fungi produce, from their own processes, the same chemicals as their host plants. Fifty different species of fungi which parasitise yew trees were examined until one was found that produced taxol. Undoubtedly this discovery hastens the possibility of finding a cheaper source of the drug in large quantities, but the Montana State University researchers say that they still do not know why the fungus produces taxol in the first place.

Taxol has been much in the news this year. One story concerned the supply of yew hedge clippings from National Trust gardens to several research laboratories. Another recounted how scientists at the University of Manchester Institute of Science and Technology (UMIST) had turned to the Forestry Commission at Bedgebury Pinetum for assistance in finding alternative sources of Taxol.

Bedgebury has almost seventy different types of yew from all over the world. Not only does each type of yew have its own unique chemical properties, but Bedgebury also holds individual records for each of the specimens detailing its history and origin. If a type proved useful to researchers, fresh sources in acceptable quantities could easily be identified and the chemical mass produced as a result of cloning the most suitable forms.

Hardy nursery stock production in England and Wales. R. Crane, A. J. Errington and P. Woodlock. Department of Agricultural Economics and Management, University of Reading *Special Studies in Agricultural Economics* (1993) No 23, xvi and 35 pp. ISBN 0-7049-05388.

This is the first survey of hardy nursery stock in England and Wales for twenty years. The writers estimate the value of total annual sales in the industry to be between £230m and £250m, of which between £180m and £200m is represented by container stock. Shrubs amount to 60 per cent by value of production. As for open ground stock, roses and trees each account for about 20 per cent of production. The industry is polarised towards larger growers: 10 per cent of producers are responsible for 75 per cent of output. Fifty per cent of production comes from East Anglia and the South East. This survey is invaluable for anyone who is concerned for the future of nurseries in this country. Two of the surprises in the report, which is very comprehensively supported with statistical evidence, are that the wholesale sector is now larger than the retail, and that sales to the amenity market are now greater than sales to individuals.

Nashi: Klima, Markt und Anbau. P. Rusterholz and M. Kellerhals. *Schweizerische Zeitschrift für Obst- und Weinbau* (1991) 127 (18) pp. 476-87.

The Swiss have identified Nashi pears (*Pyrus pyrifolia* cvs.) as a crop with commercial potential for a continental climate. This study discusses the market, the cultivation needs of Nashi pears, and how to harvest and pack them for sale. Nineteen leading varieties are then listed in a table which describes their origin, appearance, quality and vigour. Readers may also be interested to know that a number of research institutes have begun to cross Nashi pears with our own forms of *Pyrus domestica*.

Variation in the shoot production of 'Sonia' cut rose plants, originating from grafting scions of different nodal positions. D. O. de Vries and L. A. Dubois. *Gartenbauwissenschaft* (1992) 57 (2) pp. 64–8.

It has long been supposed, but seldom put to empirical proof, that the performance of vegetatively propagated plants is affected by the choice of propagating material. In this experiment, plants of the cut flower rose 'Sonia' were propagated from different parts of a shoot: in effect it was cut into eleven pieces, each with a leaf and bud, and these were grafted on two very different rootstocks, known in the trade as *Rosa indica* 'Major' and *Rosa canina* 'Inermis'. Rather to the researchers' surprise, the choice of rootstock had little effect on the growth of the grafts. However, their position on the original shoot of 'Sonia' had a considerable bearing upon the performance of the plant. Those taken from the bottom of the shoot were better in two notable ways: they produced many more flowering shoots, and they gave an improved flower yield of up to 30 per cent. Delayed juvenility of the newer wood is one explanation for this phenomenon. It should also be remembered that, generally speaking, new wood is better for propagation than old. Amateur gardeners find that the advantage of propagating from a particular part of the plant is averaged down over the years. This report will therefore be of most interest to the cut flower industry, where quick regeneration is critical to yields.

Towards the somatic hybridisation of shrubby and climbing honeysuckles. D. Georges, L. Decourte and S. J. Ochatt. *Acta Horticulturae* (1993) No. 336, pp. 327–32, ISBN 90-6605-385-2.

Many scientists believe that the future of plant breeding lies not with the wind and the bees, but in laboratory test-tubes. Protoplast fusion is their catch-phrase: it means the creation of hybrids *in vitro* that would not otherwise be viable. The French government station at Angers has begun to experiment with *Lonicera*, with a view to combining the best qualities of those members of the genus which are hardy floriferous shrubs with the large-flowered strongly scented climbers. It has chosen *Lonicera fragrantissima* and *Lonicera periclymenum* 'Serotina' and *Lonicera × brownii* 'Dropmore Scarlet' as subjects for experiment. One of the prerequisites of successful hybridisation under such circumstances is to find out, largely by trial and experiment, how to grow on the artificially created cell so that it becomes established as a plant. This account explains how French researchers have succeeded in excising the protoplasts of the parent forms and grown them through to become viable plantlets by using a number of different growth hormones. The scientists can now concentrate on creating new cells by somatic fusion. It is therefore likely that, in a few years, we shall see hybrids which combine the best qualities of both parts of the genus. Imagine, for example, *Lonicera nitida* with flowers like a honeysuckle, or *Lonicera fragrantissima* with large orange flowers all through winter.

Hardiness

The American Rhododendron Society has adopted a new definition of hardiness for rhododendron hybrids and clones of rhododendron species. We recommend it to our readers as a useful contribution towards an understanding of a problem that exercises everyone who is involved in gardening and horticulture. The ARS definition, which can obviously be applied to plants other than rhododendrons, is as follows: 'Cold hardiness is the temperature range through which damage to flower bud, leaf or plant structure can be expected to occur, in a plant at least five years of age and in good health.' Note that the plant should be in good health and old enough to have an established woody structure. 'Flower bud damage' is quantified as enough to detract from a normal floral display.

Many factors apart from the health and age of a plant can affect its hardiness: unseasonal cold weather or warmth prior to cold, as well as exposure, site, and snow cover. The ARS gives a temperature range of two figures. The lower figure is the lowest temperature after which a plant has been observed to perform normally, and the higher figure is the highest temperature after which cold damage has been observed. If, for example, the range were expressed as $-10\,°C$ to $-5\,°C$, it would mean that the plant in question had been observed to perform normally after a temperature of $-10\,°C$ (for example, when temperatures fell gradually and the cold period was brief), and that under different circumstances the same clone had sustained some damage at a temperature of $-5\,°C$, perhaps because the cold endured for longer or came at a time of the year when the plant was more vulnerable.

Garden Restorations

The restoration of the King's Privy Garden at Hampton Court Palace will be the big story of 1995. Sir Roy Strong considers it 'the single most important site in English garden history' and believes that the present re-creation of the Privy Garden by Historic Royal Palaces is the boldest and most important garden restoration undertaken since the Second World War. In 1701, King William laid out an elaborate broderie design, which incorporated clipped hollies and yews, when he decided to make Hampton Court Palace his main official residence. Henry Wise was the royal gardener and the Privy Garden ran right down to the River Thames. It survived until the mid-eighteenth century, when the garden was replanted in an informal manner, more typical of late eighteenth century romantic taste. Contemporary archives, including perspectives by Knyff, have been used to supplement the work of garden archaeologists, who have played a particularly important part in the restoration. Trial excavations revealed that the 1701 layout was perfectly preserved, just eighteen inches beneath the surface of the existing garden. As part of the restoration, plants of the correct species have been propagated and special eighteenth century turf grown in the Palace nursery. The contract for the hard landscape was awarded to Waterers Landscape Ltd in July last year. The landscaping began with the remodelling of the banks on either side of the Privy Garden. Paths were laid out in the autumn of 1994 and trees planted during the course of the winter, and in early spring 1995. The whole garden will be finished by July.

The National Gardens Scheme paid £250,000 to the National Trust from the proceeds of 1993's *Gardens Open to the Public*. The restoration projects which benefited included a substantial renewal programme for the rhododendrons at Rowallane in Co. Down; rejuvenation of Gertrude Jekyll's rose borders at Lindisfarne Castle in Northumberland; irrigation schemes at Killerton and Overbecks in Devon; and funding the nursery at Dunham Massey in Greater Manchester.

In consultation with the National Trust, Lord Rothschild has restored the gardens at Waddesdon Manor in Buckinghamshire as they were at the beginning of the twentieth century. Waddesdon was renowned for the opulence and colour of its plantings. The big parterre on the south terrace, grassed over after the First World War, has been returned to its original shapes, using the same ribbon planting technique and reproducing the old colour combinations. The bedding plants are raised in the Waddesdon nursery: two complete schemes are planted out each year.

At Greys Court in Oxfordshire the National Trust reopened the reconstructed ice-house. Ice-houses were a common sight on great estates during the eighteenth and nineteenth centuries. The ice-house at Greys is of unmortared brick infilled with rubble and topped with a conical thatched roof. The National Trust announced its intention to create a new ornamental vegetable garden in the old kitchen garden.

At Osterley Park in Greater London, the Trust has begun to replant the pleasure grounds with species used in the late eighteenth and early nineteenth centuries. The newly-restored Adam garden house will soon be filled with orange trees.

Speke Hall in Liverpool, another Trust property, has been awarded the prestigious Europa Nostra Diploma for restoration and conservation work.

A steady increase in visitors to Wisley, estimated at 10 per cent per annum in recent years, has forced the RHS to make good the impact which this rise in numbers has had upon the fabric of the garden. One effect of so many trampling feet is the erosion of the grass, never very resilient on the thin sandy soil. However, the Society's groundsmen have succeeded in incorporating recycled chopped-up car tyres into the lawns to reduce erosion. The presence of the rubber in the top few centimetres of the soil makes for a more open texture and reduces compaction of the soil's structure. It also increases the porosity of the soil and enables water to penetrate further. This in turn allows the grass itself to root deeper. Taken together, these benefits have proved effective in counteracting the constant wear and tear. The principle was later taken up at Killerton in Devon and at other National Trust properties. In some cases small pieces of rubber were simply mixed with the topsoil and the turf relaid over the top, while in others rubber was sprinkled on the grass as a top dressing where it soon bedded in.

During the winter of 1993-4, a substantial alteration was made to the classic eighteenth century grounds of Corsham Court in Wiltshire by the late Lord Methuen, who died later in the year. Corsham Court is one of the few estates in the West Country which was worked on by both Capability Brown and Humphry Repton. Lord Methuen decided to remove the iron fence which separated the park from the garden and replace it with a new ha-ha, the first to be built for many years. One and a half metres high and some 75 metres long, the ha-ha separates the lawns from the park beyond. Planning permission was obtained after consultation with English Heritage, and work began in the autumn of 1993. Some 60 tons of local stone, 12 cubic metres of concrete and 6 tons of cement were needed. When it was finished, in time for the 1994 season, the result was impressive. Seen from the park, the ha-ha was still conspicuous for the bright yellowness of its unweathered stone, but the sweep of the view from the east wing of the house was immeasurably improved.

The Royal Botanic Gardens at Kew have been active in the reintroduction to the wild of endangered species. These have included the Toromiro tree, *Sophora toromiro*, which has been extinct in its natural home, Easter Island, for forty years, and *Hibiscus liliiflorus*, a beautiful flowering shrub, whose natural population has been reduced to just two plants on the island of Rodriguez in the Indian Ocean. Kew scientists have propagated these species and started to reintroduce them to their original homes. 'Islands have a particularly high proportion of the world's endangered plants,' says Mike Maunder of Kew's Conservation Unit, which has launched a £40,000 appeal to help safeguard the future of endangered plant species on remote oceanic islands. The money will go to nursery facilities on the islands to propagate endangered species and to bring local conservation workers to Kew to learn how to save rare plants and manage their habitats.

The Brogdale Horticultural Trust announced plans for a substantial expansion of its gardens, where over 4,000 cultivars of fruit, from apples to nuts and quinces, are already grown. The aim of the development plan is to attract more visitors and create a 'living history' of the development of fruit culture. The main feature is a series of twelve gardens showing the history of fruit cultivation from medieval times to the present day, together with ten or so demonstration gardens for modern fruit culture. A model nursery will show how fruit trees are budded, grafted and trained, while an adjacent area will have the full range of tree shapes and sizes.

In November, the Crarae Gardens Charitable Trust launched an appeal to raise £500,000 to maintain the famous Argyllshire woodland garden. The garden at Crarae was started by Sir George Campbell in 1925, who planted a natural glen with rare conifers and rhododendrons. Graham Rose describes Crarae in the *Good Gardens Guide 1994* as the United Kingdom's most outstanding woodland garden. Others agree: twenty years ago in his classic book *The English Garden*, Edward Hyams devoted an entire chapter to Crarae. The aim of the appeal is to provide sufficient capital to secure its endowment. The funds are needed to generate the income to remake, replant and restore the garden where necessary. Further details are available from John Harman, Ardbeag Cottage, Barremman, Clynder, Strathclyde G84 0QN.

At Prior Park in Avon, the National Trust has completed its master plan based on detailed historical surveys and begun its restoration of the park. The landscape will be restored as originally laid out by Ralph Allen in the mid-eighteenth century. Repairs to the famous Palladian Bridge are a high priority, and archaeological excavations have begun to trace the original position and route of paths around the garden. These digs have unearthed the remains of a pond, a feature that was not previously recorded. Prior Park may be opened to the public later this year. Meanwhile, some guided walks are available: for further information, telephone 01985 847777.

At **Wimpole Hall** in Cambridgeshire, the National Trust has begun to re-create a formal mid-nineteenth century parterre in the north garden, with the help of funds donated to the National Trust by the National Gardens Scheme. The new parterre will contain 1 km of box hedging, and 24,000 bedding plants will be grown every year to fill it. The Trust is also clearing the north park and dredging one of the two eighteenth century lakes created by Capability Brown. The lower lake has been dry for forty years but will be refilled later this year. The Trust will then turn its attention to the restoration of the upper lake.

Work on the early eighteenth century sunken box parterre, fruit orchard and 'wilderness' at **Hanbury Hall** in Hereford & Worcester is now virtually complete. The only outstanding tasks are the completion of two summerhouses and two pavilions, the installation of iron railings and gates, and the replacement of some garden urns.

The Orchard House at **Cragside** in Northumberland, the largest structure of its type to survive today, has reopened following restoration. Work has now begun on the fernery and the Italian carpet bedding garden.

The renovation of the gardens at **Wightwick Manor** in the West Midlands is nearing completion. The 'Mathematical Bridge' has recently been repaired, and will be a means of access to a newly planted garden called the Bridge Garden. The National Trust has also rebuilt the long-neglected Peach House to its original design.

Substantial restoration works have now been completed at **Culross Palace**, which was originally purchased by the National Trust for Scotland in 1932 but, until recently, was managed by Historic Scotland. In November 1991 the National Trust for Scotland took back full responsibility for the Palace and a model seventeenth century garden has been created on the steeply sloping and terraced ground behind the house. The garden has the design and plants that a successful merchant of the late sixteenth century would have kept for his own enjoyment and for the support of his household.

In reply to a parliamentary question last year, it was revealed that the following gardens had been selected for financial assistance under the EC Historic Garden Award Scheme for the conservation of gardens: Painshill Park, Surrey; Harewood Park, North Yorkshire; Brantwood, Cumbria; Hanbury Hall, West Midlands and Prior Park, Avon.

A list of the unsuccessful applicants makes disturbing reading. These are gardens where restoration projects are planned but may not be implemented until funds are available. The sheer numbers hint at the scale of the need. Among them: Haughton Hall and Tushingham Hall in Cheshire; Penjerrick, Heligan and Prideaux Place in Cornwall; Marks Hall and Cressing Temple in Essex; Burton Constable Hall in Humberside; Ickworth Park in Suffolk; Hammerwood Park and West Dean in West Sussex; Hazelbury Manor in Wiltshire; and People's Park and Kirkstall Abbey Monastery Gardens in West Yorkshire.

Weather Records

We are publishing complete weather records for the twelve months of September 1993 to August 1994. The data comes from the Met. Office and was collected at the meteorological stations of five important gardens around the British Isles: the Royal Botanic Garden, Edinburgh; RHS/Wisley, Surrey; the University of Liverpool's Ness Gardens, Cheshire; Trelissick, Cornwall; and Rowallane in Northern Ireland.

The information is given on a day-by-day basis, without averaging, so that readers can see the fluctuations within any period of their choice. Close study reveals patterns that may help to explain plant growth and offer a general guide to seasonal variations.

Review of 1994

The start of 1994 was characterised by heavy rainfall as successive fronts swept in from the Atlantic, affecting the whole British Isles, but most particularly the south of England. The National Rivers Authority issued more than 150 flood alerts in the region. Many nurserymen were affected because their fields were waterlogged, and this prevented them from lifting their stock, whose despatch had already been delayed by the long period of abnormally low temperatures in December 1993. Nevertheless, the absence of cold temperatures encouraged early growth: snowdrops were flowering in most parts of the British Isles by the end of January.

A high-pressure zone over Norway, which coincided with the winter Olympics at Lillehammer, brought cold easterly winds to the whole of the British Isles during the last two weeks of February. At first it was south west Britain which recorded the lowest temperatures, but the coldest daily averages were later experienced in northern England and the Highlands. Snow fell in every region: as much as 6 ins (15 cms) was recorded on two occasions in parts of Yorkshire.

Aberdeen experienced the dullest February since records began: only 37 hours of sunshine. By the beginning of March, the season in most parts of the British Isles was only about one week in advance of the average. Cold weather continued to affect northern Britain throughout March and April, so that gardens in Scotland had little to show at the start of the tourist season.

May was cold and wet for most of the British Isles. The Midlands and the South were particularly badly affected by much heavier and more persistent rainfall than usual, and prolonged periods of cool temperatures. Widespread ground frosts and some air frosts did considerable damage in the south of England at the end of the month: the night of 28-9 May saw temperatures plunge below zero.

At the end of June, a heatwave began in most of England and southern Scotland, and lasted until the first week of August. Temperatures exceeded 30°C in much of the country on more than one occasion, and the daily maxima in the South consistently reached 25°C. August too was warmer than average in most parts of the British Isles, but September was wet and cool, which delayed the onset of the autumn colour. However, October was the second warmest since records began and the exceptionally mild weather continued almost without interruption until the end of November.

Royal Botanic Garden – Edinburgh

Date	Max (°C)	Min (°C)	Rainfall (mm)	Sunshine (hrs)	Date	Max (°C)	Min (°C)	Rainfall (mm)	Sunshine (hrs)
Sept 1	21.9	8.0	0.0	8.3	Nov 1	8.8	6.4	0.0	0.0
2	19.2	10.3	0.2	3.2	2	8.3	6.6	0.0	0.0
3	14.4	10.6	0.0	1.9	3	9.5	7.2	17.2	0.0
4	15.7	8.9	0.0	8.4	4	11.6	7.5	0.1	0.0
5	15.5	7.1	0.0	5.7	5	10.0	6.1	1.7	0.0
6	15.0	7.0	0.0	1.9	6	10.0	7.4	0.1	0.0
7	14.9	11.2	0.0	0.1	7	9.5	8.1	3.2	0.0
8	13.7	10.5	9.1	0.0	8	8.4	7.5	2.3	0.1
9	16.5	11.0	1.1	2.8	9	10.7	4.7	0.6	0.1
10	16.6	12.7	10.7	0.6	10	6.8	-1.1	0.0	3.5
11	16.9	11.5	0.0	4.0	11	8.0	-0.4	0.0	5.3
12	15.2	7.5	0.3	8.7	12	8.9	3.6	2.4	3.0
13	13.2	11.7	2.7	0.0	13	5.3	-2.0	3.4	3.6
14	11.6	8.4	7.2	0.5	14	7.9	-0.9	0.1	4.9
15	11.4	8.3	5.3	0.0	15	9.6	-2.0	0.4	0.3
16	12.4	8.5	1.5	0.8	16	9.5	-0.8	0.0	2.0
17	14.3	4.2	0.3	3.1	17	8.9	0.9	0.0	5.7
18	16.9	5.7	2.1	3.4	18	4.5	-0.9	0.0	0.0
19	16.9	9.8	6.1	0.2	19	7.0	-3.4	0.0	6.1
20	18.5	10.3	0.0	6.5	20	4.7	-5.8	1.5	2.2
21	17.8	8.6	0.0	6.1	21	3.4	-4.7	1.5	3.4
22	16.9	6.2	0.0	8.1	22	2.0	-2.2	0.6	0.6
23	15.9	7.5	0.0	6.8	23	2.0	-0.4	0.0	0.4
24	14.1	7.9	1.6	1.5	24	1.7	-4.5	0.2	2.7
25	14.2	2.7	0.0	10.8	25	6.9	-3.0	0.9	1.1
26	13.9	2.5	0.0	5.0	26	5.4	-2.5	0.1	4.4
27	12.7	1.4	0.0	9.6	27	7.3	-2.5	0.0	2.1
28	12.2	-0.2	0.0	8.0	28	5.0	-0.6	0.0	0.1
29	13.9	2.5	0.2	0.0	29	5.1	0.9	3.1	0.0
30	15.6	8.0	1.7	6.9	30	7.9	1.8	0.0	4.0
Oct 1	12.9	10.1	11.3	0.5	Dec 1	8.9	1.6	8.2	0.8
2	13.9	9.3	0.5	0.3	2	11.5	5.7	5.5	0.6
3	14.0	8.5	7.8	1.5	3	11.0	7.2	4.7	0.0
4	14.1	8.4	0.1	7.9	4	8.8	4.4	0.2	5.5
5	12.5	2.2	24.7	2.5	5	9.6	4.5	0.0	2.3
6	11.4	8.2	11.1	0.0	6	9.5	7.2	2.2	0.5
7	12.5	9.1	12.2	0.1	7	4.7	2.0	0.0	3.2
8	13.9	6.9	1.8	8.2	8	5.5	1.6	26.5	0.0
9	12.0	9.5	26.3	0.0	9	7.0	1.9	2.4	2.9
10	11.9	8.4	2.6	0.2	10	6.1	2.0	2.4	0.8
11	11.2	7.1	3.1	0.9	11	5.2	2.0	0.0	2.0
12	10.5	6.2	0.1	1.4	12	5.6	-2.9	12.1	0.0
13	8.5	-0.1	0.0	3.9	13	6.0	0.9	0.2	0.0
14	8.7	-0.5	0.0	9.3	14	5.8	-2.9	4.3	0.0
15	7.7	-0.6	0.0	8.0	15	4.5	2.4	4.3	1.4
16	6.6	-2.2	0.0	6.0	16	5.0	-0.4	0.0	4.3
17	9.0	-4.6	0.0	8.7	17	11.0	1.0	2.3	0.2
18	11.0	-3.2	0.0	9.5	18	13.1	1.5	4.2	0.0
19	11.6	0.0	2.5	0.7	19	7.7	6.4	0.2	2.3
20	10.9	7.5	0.1	3.9	20	1.5	-2.8	0.0	1.6
21	9.4	4.5	0.0	8.0	21	4.5	-5.9	0.3	3.0
22	9.3	-0.4	0.0	5.0	22	4.2	-0.5	0.0	1.1
23	12.0	1.5	0.0	5.5	23	4.7	1.1	7.1	0.0
24	11.9	6.8	0.0	5.3	24	3.3	0.4	0.0	2.1
25	10.5	1.2	0.0	7.9	25	2.8	-0.2	1.0	0.2
26	6.9	0.9	0.0	0.0	26	0.0	-2.7	0.0	0.7
27	7.6	4.6	0.0	0.3	27	1.7	-3.6	1.9	2.2
28	8.6	0.2	0.0	0.0	28	7.7	-3.2	5.6	0.0
29	8.3	5.5	0.0	0.0	29	7.5	0.1	2.4	3.8
30	9.9	5.4	0.0	5.3	30	3.4	0.8	0.0	0.9
31	9.0	1.6	0.0	0.0	31	2.9	-2.6	0.0	1.8

Date	Max (°C)	Min (°C)	Rainfall (mm)	Sunshine (hrs)	Date	Max (°C)	Min (°C)	Rainfall (mm)	Sunshine (hrs)
Jan 1	4.2	-1.3	2.7	4.4	Mar 1	4.9	1.8	1.1	0.0
2	4.8	0.0	1.2	0.1	2	8.5	2.3	6.0	5.3
3	4.4	0.6	1.5	0.0	3	6.3	3.7	2.5	6.4
4	2.9	-0.9	0.2	1.9	4	10.6	3.8	5.7	0.0
5	4.5	-2.9	9.2	0.0	5	8.9	5.0	1.9	3.8
6	4.9	2.5	2.0	0.0	6	10.5	2.2	0.1	4.4
7	5.0	1.8	0.0	1.6	7	12.2	6.5	1.8	1.7
8	5.0	-2.1	0.5	0.0	8	12.1	9.1	6.8	0.1
9	7.7	0.5	1.9	0.0	9	8.8	3.8	8.1	4.0
10	7.6	2.4	0.0	2.2	10	9.4	1.0	1.0	5.1
11	7.2	0.7	0.8	0.8	11	8.3	4.5	0.2	4.5
12	9.0	1.3	3.4	0.1	12	8.0	2.5	2.3	3.9
13	8.4	3.5	5.0	3.3	13	11.1	2.9	5.7	7.2
14	6.4	4.0	4.3	3.2	14	11.0	3.5	0.3	5.5
15	2.9	-2.0	0.0	0.5	15	7.1	1.9	2.0	7.8
16	3.3	-2.5	0.0	4.3	16	4.5	0.6	1.9	3.5
17	6.5	-2.0	0.0	1.1	17	7.0	0.7	0.0	5.6
18	8.7	-0.5	0.4	0.0	18	4.9	1.7	0.9	0.1
19	8.2	1.9	0.5	4.7	19	8.0	0.1	0.0	9.6
20	10.0	1.6	0.0	0.0	20	8.0	1.0	0.0	4.1
21	10.6	8.1	0.1	1.5	21	11.7	-2.9	2.3	0.1
22	8.0	4.7	3.0	1.5	22	12.8	1.7	12.4	6.6
23	4.1	2.5	0.0	4.9	23	9.6	9.4	5.7	0.6
24	10.0	2.1	3.2	0.0	24	8.5	2.9	2.9	6.3
25	7.5	2.9	7.0	1.1	25	9.7	4.8	0.4	5.8
26	9.1	1.1	9.3	0.6	26	9.9	1.0	0.0	8.3
27	6.1	2.6	0.7	2.0	27	8.6	1.6	0.6	0.0
28	8.0	0.7	0.4	6.0	28	13.1	5.5	3.5	3.0
29	10.3	-0.1	2.8	0.0	29	10.1	5.3	2.0	6.7
30	5.1	3.4	0.1	4.6	30	11.6	2.1	2.9	1.0
31	8.2	3.9	0.4	2.5	31	10.7	3.9	0.3	5.1
Feb 1	8.6	4.4	2.0	0.0	Apr 1	10.8	3.1	0.0	7.1
2	6.6	1.8	0.0	6.7	2	7.1	2.1	0.0	9.1
3	6.8	-0.8	2.7	0.0	3	9.5	1.8	0.2	0.3
4	8.5	1.9	0.0	0.9	4	6.8	2.6	3.2	6.7
5	8.8	3.4	0.0	1.5	5	8.2	1.1	2.9	6.8
6	8.2	2.5	0.0	1.8	6	9.0	2.3	11.7	6.2
7	7.0	0.7	0.0	2.2	7	6.5	2.7	3.6	0.0
8	7.5	0.5	0.7	2.7	8	4.9	0.1	4.2	0.1
9	8.5	2.6	0.0	5.1	9	6.4	1.4	5.0	0.2
10	8.4	-0.9	0.0	4.5	10	9.3	2.6	0.0	4.2
11	7.6	-0.4	0.0	1.5	11	12.1	-1.0	0.0	0.7
12	7.5	3.0	0.0	5.4	12	10.6	5.8	1.0	4.8
13	4.4	-0.9	0.0	3.8	13	12.0	1.1	0.0	10.1
14	2.6	-0.2	0.0	0.0	14	11.3	1.5	0.0	13.1
15	2.3	-0.8	0.0	0.0	15	9.1	4.5	0.0	9.3
16	3.4	-2.4	0.0	3.6	16	9.7	2.1	0.7	0.0
17	3.4	-6.1	0.0	4.3	17	10.7	5.5	0.1	8.4
18	6.5	-3.6	0.0	2.6	18	11.5	3.7	0.0	0.8
19	4.5	-1.5	0.0	0.4	19	12.1	4.9	0.2	11.7
20	3.8	-0.5	0.7	2.5	20	11.8	2.1	0.0	8.9
21	2.5	-4.4	0.9	1.6	21	8.4	0.4	8.5	0.8
22	3.7	-2.7	0.2	4.4	22	10.5	5.2	4.9	0.0
23	3.2	-1.1	1.0	0.4	23	12.7	4.4	1.2	0.6
24	4.0	0.9	0.2	3.1	24	15.4	5.1	1.1	4.5
25	3.8	1.4	8.6	0.0	25	11.1	3.3	2.3	5.5
26	3.9	1.0	14.2	0.0	26	13.6	5.4	0.0	3.4
27	4.5	1.1	26.2	0.0	27	17.2	9.7	0.0	1.7
28	3.0	2.1	8.5	0.0	28	16.6	12.5	0.6	0.6
					29	17.8	11.0	0.4	7.8
					30	15.8	7.0	0.0	9.9

Royal Botanic Garden – Edinburgh

Date	Max (°C)	Min (°C)	Rainfall (mm)	Sunshine (hrs)	Date	Max (°C)	Min (°C)	Rainfall (mm)	Sunshine (hrs)
May 1	12.5	6.1	0.3	9.4	July 1	21.9	10.5	0.0	9.9
2	13.5	8.4	5.1	0.3	2	15.1	10.5	0.0	0.2
3	14.2	7.0	1.4	2.0	3	14.4	11.8	0.6	0.0
4	13.0	6.8	0.1	4.7	4	16.1	12.0	4.7	0.0
5	14.5	6.0	4.5	2.5	5	20.2	12.5	0.0	6.1
6	14.2	6.1	0.0	10.4	6	16.8	10.2	8.4	3.6
7	13.9	7.3	0.3	7.0	7	17.3	11.6	0.0	4.3
8	15.4	1.2	0.8	9.9	8	21.1	12.0	0.0	4.7
9	14.1	1.7	0.0	9.5	9	18.6	10.9	1.4	0.4
10	16.4	7.3	0.0	5.4	10	17.6	14.0	6.4	0.1
11	12.5	8.2	0.0	4.2	11	17.8	13.5	0.7	0.0
12	14.4	7.5	0.0	9.9	12	18.1	12.6	1.3	0.2
13	15.3	8.0	0.0	10.4	13	18.8	10.1	0.0	11.2
14	12.6	8.1	0.0	10.6	14	21.1	10.3	0.4	4.4
15	10.1	7.6	0.0	0.4	15	17.2	12.7	0.0	4.0
16	11.1	5.7	0.0	9.7	16	18.2	9.7	0.0	5.5
17	10.4	5.4	0.0	10.9	17	20.1	9.2	0.0	10.7
18	10.3	4.1	0.4	8.8	18	19.5	7.9	0.0	13.7
19	10.4	4.8	0.1	11.7	19	21.7	8.8	0.0	12.0
20	10.6	5.1	0.0	7.0	20	23.0	13.8	0.1	7.0
21	11.3	6.7	0.0	0.2	21	19.5	14.6	0.4	1.1
22	13.1	7.5	0.0	10.8	22	18.9	12.3	0.0	7.1
23	12.0	6.1	0.0	7.8	23	19.1	8.5	0.0	13.9
24	10.7	6.0	0.0	6.9	24	20.4	13.2	1.7	2.3
25	11.7	6.7	0.0	8.3	25	21.3	13.9	2.2	7.0
26	10.9	3.0	0.0	6.2	26	20.9	16.7	2.1	4.6
27	12.9	5.9	0.0	11.6	27	20.1	11.7	0.0	9.1
28	14.4	6.4	0.0	7.0	28	20.9	12.9	0.0	13.0
29	15.9	7.5	0.0	5.1	29	20.3	11.1	0.0	3.7
30	15.3	6.4	0.0	6.3	30	22.6	9.8	0.2	7.6
31	16.0	10.3	0.0	0.3	31	19.5	14.4	8.5	2.2
June 1	17.2	10.1	0.0	3.8	Aug 1	23.0	15.2	0.1	7.1
2	17.9	9.0	0.4	4.4	2	22.3	14.3	0.0	7.0
3	16.5	11.3	5.7	2.9	3	19.9	13.1	3.2	0.2
4	14.2	7.5	0.5	14.3	4	23.4	15.6	0.0	4.2
5	15.4	6.3	0.1	11.8	5	19.6	14.7	0.0	3.6
6	16.9	10.5	0.0	3.5	6	18.3	10.4	0.0	8.8
7	15.1	9.9	0.1	7.8	7	16.7	11.0	0.0	0.5
8	14.7	5.8	0.6	13.7	8	19.6	11.1	0.0	10.2
9	15.6	8.1	0.1	8.5	9	15.5	7.8	0.0	0.2
10	18.0	7.3	0.0	6.8	10	15.7	11.0	0.0	2.8
11	17.1	8.3	0.0	4.6	11	16.8	11.4	0.0	6.1
12	20.6	10.4	0.0	11.8	12	18.2	10.9	0.0	2.5
13	24.9	8.8	0.0	15.4	13	16.1	5.1	0.0	6.4
14	15.7	10.3	0.0	10.6	14	16.2	6.4	0.0	4.2
15	14.8	9.6	6.6	5.3	15	19.2	9.4	0.0	5.8
16	12.6	7.5	1.3	0.0	16	16.2	10.6	4.7	0.0
17	15.0	8.0	1.1	0.2	17	19.7	8.8	0.2	6.9
18	14.8	9.4	0.2	0.1	18	17.5	8.8	0.9	4.3
19	17.3	11.0	0.0	12.1	19	17.8	11.4	0.0	8.3
20	19.2	12.5	2.2	2.5	20	19.0	11.1	0.0	8.5
21	15.3	10.4	3.8	2.7	21	19.6	11.9	0.0	8.0
22	15.1	8.5	0.1	13.3	22	21.0	7.6	0.0	4.7
23	16.5	6.7	1.7	4.3	23	17.4	13.8	3.7	2.2
24	17.5	10.7	4.1	1.4	24	18.5	10.1	0.3	6.3
25	18.6	11.4	5.8	0.5	25	18.5	9.7	0.3	3.9
26	17.9	7.4	1.2	0.3	26	16.5	12.0	n/a	9.5
27	22.0	12.7	0.0	8.0	27	15.0	9.5	3.7	9.0
28	21.9	14.1	0.0	12.6	28	14.6	7.9	8.7	1.3
29	17.0	12.1	0.0	9.5	29	17.2	10.1	0.5	8.7
30	21.2	9.4	0.0	9.6	30	17.1	8.9	0.0	2.9
					31	15.6	6.5	0.0	0.0

RHS Wisley, Surrey

Date	Max (°C)	Min (°C)	Rainfall (mm)	Sunshine (hrs)	Date	Max (°C)	Min (°C)	Rainfall (mm)	Sunshine (hrs)
Sept 1	24.2	7.8	0.0	7.6	Nov 1	7.5	6.8	0.0	0.0
2	21.0	7.7	0.0	4.6	2	10.8	5.1	0.0	0.0
3	19.4	10.4	0.0	0.5	3	14.6	5.6	0.0	0.7
4	17.1	3.5	0.0	7.8	4	16.0	10.6	0.2	0.6
5	18.0	2.8	0.0	8.4	5	16.4	10.3	0.0	3.3
6	19.1	4.5	0.0	4.6	6	10.5	6.9	0.0	0.0
7	22.0	9.8	21.8	4.9	7	10.8	7.8	0.0	0.0
8	20.7	13.2	2.8	4.7	8	9.9	7.0	0.0	0.0
9	19.7	15.2	2.1	6.2	9	11.4	-0.6	6.2	0.0
10	15.1	13.2	1.2	2.1	10	13.2	8.3	1.3	0.4
11	18.0	6.0	0.0	3.1	11	10.7	2.2	0.0	5.2
12	15.2	5.6	11.7	0.1	12	12.1	2.8	5.4	7.6
13	16.5	11.2	6.3	2.4	13	13.0	5.1	6.9	0.0
14	15.0	11.6	0.1	1.0	14	8.5	5.6	0.0	2.8
15	15.6	6.7	11.0	1.4	15	10.0	-0.1	0.0	5.2
16	14.8	10.1	0.1	0.8	16	6.9	-1.9	0.0	0.3
17	16.8	8.8	0.0	5.3	17	6.8	-0.8	0.0	7.2
18	17.3	2.5	0.0	8.6	18	6.3	-1.9	0.0	5.8
19	21.1	7.0	0.0	10.2	19	6.7	-3.8	0.0	6.8
20	17.2	11.2	5.0	0.0	20	4.6	-5.3	0.3	2.8
21	19.0	11.2	0.6	8.0	21	1.9	-3.5	0.1	0.5
22	18.7	10.2	0.4	1.0	22	0.0	-6.5	0.0	0.0
23	16.3	6.2	0.1	3.3	23	0.5	-5.2	0.0	0.0
24	16.7	5.9	0.0	4.6	24	6.7	-4.3	0.1	0.4
25	12.5	9.3	1.7	0.0	25	11.8	0.4	0.2	4.0
26	14.0	2.8	1.2	0.0	26	4.5	0.0	0.0	0.0
27	9.4	7.3	4.5	0.0	27	8.1	0.6	0.0	5.0
28	11.6	8.3	1.7	0.0	28	2.5	-0.8	0.0	0.0
29	14.9	7.6	6.3	0.5	29	7.7	-1.1	5.9	3.5
30	14.2	5.7	18.6	3.4	30	9.2	0.8	1.1	0.2
Oct 1	13.4	6.8	26.2	0.4	Dec 1	11.3	4.8	0.5	2.9
2	12.5	9.8	11.2	0.0	2	12.4	4.6	0.1	0.0
3	17.2	6.5	2.0	6.9	3	12.3	9.6	0.8	0.1
4	16.5	9.6	3.2	5.3	4	11.8	9.4	0.0	2.2
5	16.6	9.5	4.2	4.0	5	10.6	3.4	0.0	2.1
6	15.2	10.4	6.1	4.5	6	10.3	5.6	6.5	0.8
7	14.8	9.4	4.4	4.7	7	9.4	6.4	5.1	4.7
8	16.4	8.2	5.7	2.2	8	13.8	3.0	2.3	0.1
9	16.2	8.6	1.3	3.5	9	9.9	8.2	1.0	1.6
10	16.1	8.8	7.9	2.1	10	8.6	6.4	0.0	2.2
11	17.1	10.3	6.7	2.7	11	6.9	2.9	0.1	5.8
12	16.2	11.4	17.1	2.2	12	11.6	1.6	6.6	0.0
13	16.1	11.4	0.2	1.8	13	9.7	4.3	1.0	0.7
14	11.4	7.9	0.0	3.3	14	6.6	-0.8	7.4	4.8
15	11.1	-1.0	0.1	7.7	15	7.4	0.3	0.7	2.8
16	9.5	-3.2	0.0	8.0	16	8.7	4.3	2.6	6.0
17	11.4	-4.2	0.0	5.7	17	10.8	3.8	0.7	0.0
18	12.4	-0.3	0.0	10.0	18	13.7	5.6	9.5	0.0
19	11.1	-3.6	0.0	9.5	19	14.4	10.6	10.1	0.0
20	11.3	-2.1	0.0	5.1	20	7.7	3.2	5.0	0.0
21	9.4	1.7	0.0	4.1	21	6.8	2.2	0.2	3.0
22	11.4	5.5	0.0	4.6	22	9.0	2.0	0.4	1.5
23	10.7	5.5	0.0	0.2	23	8.5	2.6	3.2	0.0
24	10.4	7.5	0.0	0.5	24	4.2	1.8	0.0	0.0
25	12.1	4.9	0.1	1.6	25	3.7	-0.2	0.0	0.6
26	11.3	7.7	0.0	0.0	26	2.8	-1.1	0.0	2.0
27	11.3	8.6	1.5	0.2	27	4.2	-1.6	3.9	4.3
28	12.7	8.3	0.0	1.8	28	9.7	-0.9	1.0	0.0
29	12.1	1.5	0.0	4.7	29	11.3	-0.9	3.4	1.0
30	9.8	6.8	0.0	0.0	30	9.7	5.9	11.6	0.0
31	9.3	7.0	0.0	0.0	31	8.2	5.1	0.2	2.2

RHS Wisley, Surrey

Date	Max (°C)	Min (°C)	Rainfall (mm)	Sunshine (hrs)	Date	Max (°C)	Min (°C)	Rainfall (mm)	Sunshine (hrs)
Jan 1	9.2	-0.1	7.3	3.7	Mar 1	9.0	4.8	1.6	0.9
2	10.4	1.0	0.2	2.0	2	12.1	4.2	0.0	7.1
3	8.3	5.3	11.3	0.3	3	11.9	3.9	0.5	3.6
4	8.9	4.6	8.0	0.0	4	11.5	2.8	0.0	3.7
5	8.7	2.1	5.3	0.5	5	13.6	7.0	0.0	1.8
6	4.2	1.8	15.5	0.0	6	10.4	4.0	0.0	0.5
7	5.0	-0.6	0.0	2.5	7	13.2	7.6	2.7	0.0
8	8.6	-4.5	1.2	0.6	8	12.0	10.0	0.0	0.0
9	9.2	-3.5	17.5	0.0	9	11.3	9.4	0.5	0.0
10	9.4	6.3	0.0	0.0	10	12.4	3.5	0.0	10.0
11	10.3	5.0	4.4	2.5	11	9.7	0.6	0.0	4.5
12	12.6	6.9	2.0	0.0	12	10.8	2.3	0.5	3.9
13	11.4	7.4	2.3	5.1	13	13.9	5.2	0.0	5.4
14	9.2	5.7	1.4	6.0	14	14.7	6.2	0.7	6.6
15	7.1	2.8	5.3	0.0	15	13.7	9.6	0.7	2.6
16	5.0	1.2	0.0	4.6	16	10.5	3.6	0.5	5.9
17	4.0	-1.0	0.0	0.8	17	10.2	2.3	1.5	7.4
18	7.0	-2.0	2.6	0.0	18	11.4	4.7	4.4	0.0
19	7.5	2.9	0.0	4.7	19	10.3	4.4	0.0	8.9
20	9.0	0.3	0.0	0.3	20	10.2	-0.8	1.4	7.7
21	10.0	4.2	0.0	0.8	21	10.6	2.5	1.3	7.5
22	11.5	6.9	1.1	0.3	22	11.5	2.7	5.0	0.0
23	11.9	5.5	2.5	1.3	23	13.0	7.8	0.6	0.0
24	11.0	2.6	1.5	0.0	24	13.7	8.3	0.1	6.9
25	12.3	4.0	3.6	3.2	25	14.2	10.1	1.1	0.8
26	10.8	5.0	0.1	4.8	26	11.0	-4.5	0.0	10.1
27	11.5	6.3	7.0	1.1	27	10.5	0.5	0.6	2.4
28	7.6	3.5	0.6	7.9	28	12.2	6.8	0.0	0.1
29	10.0	-0.2	0.2	0.0	29	14.4	10.4	0.0	5.0
30	9.7	7.3	0.0	5.0	30	16.4	8.8	6.8	1.4
31	8.3	0.8	0.0	0.4	31	11.5	5.8	9.8	4.7
Feb 1	9.2	3.5	5.8	0.0	Apr 1	10.3	7.0	0.7	2.6
2	7.6	0.4	6.1	3.5	2	9.9	2.1	1.3	6.5
3	11.2	1.5	6.6	1.1	3	10.7	0.1	6.9	3.2
4	9.4	4.8	0.0	0.6	4	9.8	4.0	0.8	6.8
5	11.0	-0.3	0.0	6.5	5	10.4	2.5	1.8	7.0
6	9.4	1.2	6.4	1.8	6	11.7	2.6	1.8	9.6
7	9.9	3.7	0.1	7.7	7	10.2	3.6	3.3	3.5
8	9.9	-0.7	0.2	5.6	8	10.9	3.2	9.0	4.9
9	8.8	0.9	0.1	3.8	9	8.5	1.0	4.9	4.7
10	8.9	-0.6	6.4	4.7	10	10.3	1.5	3.0	6.1
11	6.6	1.6	0.8	0.1	11	13.9	2.6	0.0	9.4
12	7.6	-1.9	0.0	6.2	12	12.8	-0.2	6.2	0.2
13	3.3	0.4	0.3	0.7	13	10.5	4.2	0.0	5.0
14	0.5	-5.7	2.5	2.4	14	8.2	2.4	1.4	2.3
15	5.8	-5.7	0.2	0.0	15	10.0	2.8	8.6	0.4
16	8.3	0.5	0.0	0.0	16	11.5	5.0	0.0	3.8
17	7.3	3.2	0.0	0.5	17	9.7	2.5	0.0	3.7
18	7.7	3.6	0.0	0.0	18	8.8	3.4	0.0	2.2
19	6.9	-2.0	0.0	3.7	19	12.8	2.0	0.0	0.2
20	2.6	-0.2	0.0	3.0	20	11.0	6.6	0.0	0.0
21	3.9	-3.9	0.2	8.7	21	14.2	2.2	0.7	7.5
22	2.5	-1.4	7.7	0.0	22	15.5	5.2	6.6	10.6
23	4.6	-0.2	2.0	0.0	23	16.1	10.1	2.9	7.9
24	4.2	2.5	0.0	0.0	24	15.5	7.8	0.0	10.5
25	9.9	1.7	1.6	0.0	25	14.0	3.3	0.0	6.2
26	11.6	3.0	0.0	0.0	26	18.8	9.9	1.3	9.9
27	11.9	8.1	0.1	0.3	27	18.3	10.3	0.0	2.2
28	11.3	7.3	0.6	1.0	28	20.0	11.8	0.0	7.2
					29	22.2	6.0	0.0	6.6
					30	19.9	11.4	0.0	11.0

RHS Wisley, Surrey

Date	Max (°C)	Min (°C)	Rainfall (mm)	Sunshine (hrs)	Date	Max (°C)	Min (°C)	Rainfall (mm)	Sunshine (hrs)
May 1	19.8	3.8	0.0	12.1	July 1	26.6	9.9	0.0	10.6
2	18.3	3.8	0.0	11.5	2	26.8	15.5	0.0	3.6
3	19.0	6.0	1.5	11.2	3	28.0	11.7	5.2	9.9
4	13.6	8.1	2.8	4.9	4	22.9	16.3	0.0	8.6
5	12.6	6.3	4.3	0.0	5	20.7	11.2	2.3	7.2
6	14.9	9.6	0.1	0.3	6	19.9	10.6	0.4	3.8
7	13.4	10.5	6.4	0.2	7	21.5	10.9	7.0	8.9
8	16.6	6.0	0.1	11.3	8	17.7	13.5	1.5	0.0
9	16.4	6.6	0.0	5.1	9	23.9	10.0	0.0	9.5
10	18.2	4.1	0.0	8.8	10	24.8	11.2	0.0	14.2
11	18.2	8.3	5.5	8.7	11	28.8	9.7	0.0	14.0
12	17.6	11.0	0.1	6.0	12	31.2	13.0	2.6	11.6
13	19.7	5.1	0.0	6.5	13	21.1	16.4	0.0	0.0
14	19.1	11.0	9.4	1.4	14	26.2	14.5	0.0	8.4
15	20.3	9.5	0.1	8.5	15	23.9	11.0	0.0	3.6
16	13.3	10.6	13.8	0.0	16	25.5	14.9	0.0	8.6
17	8.9	6.7	4.9	0.0	17	24.3	13.0	0.0	12.5
18	13.3	6.1	0.1	2.8	18	23.8	13.5	0.0	9.3
19	13.2	1.8	0.1	4.8	19	25.7	12.6	0.0	11.9
20	15.0	7.8	3.3	1.2	20	27.6	10.3	0.0	12.5
21	14.5	9.9	14.8	0.0	21	28.2	11.8	0.0	10.9
22	16.5	10.9	8.1	3.3	22	27.0	13.4	0.0	10.7
23	16.6	9.5	4.1	1.9	23	27.5	13.5	0.0	11.8
24	13.6	8.0	1.5	0.0	24	31.4	17.0	0.0	8.8
25	16.4	9.7	6.8	0.3	25	28.7	16.2	0.5	11.3
26	12.6	9.8	1.5	0.0	26	22.6	16.3	0.0	1.0
27	12.0	6.0	0.0	3.2	27	27.0	17.6	2.8	7.4
28	13.5	7.1	0.0	0.4	28	20.7	15.3	0.0	4.0
29	16.5	2.1	0.0	9.6	29	25.0	10.3	0.0	10.7
30	17.3	1.5	0.0	12.8	30	30.4	16.3	0.0	7.8
31	21.0	3.5	0.0	13.2	31	25.4	18.7	0.8	5.4
June 1	24.6	3.5	0.0	10.0	Aug 1	23.7	15.0	0.0	6.7
2	18.6	11.0	0.2	3.5	2	24.2	12.2	1.1	1.8
3	16.4	11.2	0.6	7.1	3	30.0	16.8	0.0	9.5
4	13.1	8.5	6.8	0.0	4	24.0	21.0	0.6	0.4
5	17.0	5.1	0.6	11.2	5	27.1	15.9	0.0	8.1
6	20.9	11.0	0.0	6.3	6	25.6	13.4	0.0	1.6
7	20.2	12.3	3.1	3.2	7	22.4	17.4	0.0	0.7
8	16.8	11.3	0.0	6.0	8	24.2	15.0	0.0	7.7
9	16.0	4.8	0.0	1.0	9	23.4	11.6	0.4	6.4
10	16.5	10.5	0.0	4.3	10	19.0	16.5	8.7	0.0
11	18.6	4.8	0.0	7.0	11	17.3	13.7	6.7	0.0
12	20.8	5.8	0.0	9.9	12	19.0	14.1	0.0	1.7
13	23.0	7.2	0.0	13.3	13	21.5	8.5	0.0	9.8
14	24.2	9.8	0.0	13.7	14	20.0	7.0	0.0	12.1
15	22.6	6.5	0.0	14.2	15	23.5	5.2	0.0	10.9
16	23.6	10.3	0.0	14.7	16	24.6	7.1	1.3	7.5
17	24.3	8.5	0.0	10.7	17	19.2	12.2	0.0	7.2
18	22.5	11.0	0.0	10.9	18	21.5	9.1	2.7	8.7
19	20.3	12.1	0.0	5.9	19	21.9	14.4	0.0	7.6
20	17.0	12.3	0.5	0.1	20	21.2	10.8	0.0	6.1
21	18.0	12.6	0.0	0.1	21	22.5	10.3	0.0	7.3
22	21.2	14.8	0.0	13.1	22	25.8	13.4	0.0	5.6
23	23.6	6.5	0.0	14.1	23	22.6	15.1	0.7	2.4
24	28.4	14.2	7.5	11.8	24	21.6	11.9	2.6	7.4
25	21.9	15.2	0.0	3.2	25	19.5	12.2	3.4	3.3
26	19.8	11.3	0.0	6.2	26	23.2	12.8	0.0	7.0
27	23.9	12.9	0.0	9.9	27	21.7	15.0	0.0	9.5
28	26.5	9.0	0.0	14.2	28	20.0	9.5	0.1	12.3
29	21.5	15.0	0.0	14.0	29	20.4	9.8	0.0	5.9
30	23.7	6.7	0.0	13.3	30	19.0	8.7	0.4	2.1
					31	18.2	10.7	18.1	0.0

Ness Gardens, Cheshire 97

Date	Max (°C)	Min (°C)	Rainfall (mm)	Sunshine (hrs)	Date	Max (°C)	Min (°C)	Rainfall (mm)	Sunshine (hrs)
Sept 1	20.7	10.5	0.0	10.5					
2	18.1	14.3	0.0	1.9	Nov 1	10.3	7.1	0.0	0.1
3	18.5	13.7	0.0	1.8	2	6.5	5.0	3.4	0.0
4	13.7	4.7	0.0	1.1	3	10.0	4.5	0.2	0.0
5	14.7	4.3	0.0	1.3	4	13.6	6.5	0.0	2.1
6	17.6	5.6	0.0	6.6	5	13.3	7.0	0.8	0.0
7	18.9	9.6	9.4	3.4	6	11.2	6.9	0.0	0.0
8	19.5	12.7	5.8	2.3	7	9.3	7.8	0.5	0.0
9	18.0	14.0	3.6	0.2	8	9.6	7.2	1.2	0.0
10	15.2	13.1	0.6	0.6	9	9.4	4.5	9.9	0.0
11	17.2	9.5	0.0	5.6	10	9.4	4.6	9.6	3.6
12	14.8	6.6	20.9	1.7	11	9.6	4.4	1.3	3.1
13	16.2	10.9	3.6	0.8	12	11.1	2.8	2.0	4.3
14	12.9	10.7	3.9	0.0	13	7.1	5.8	14.4	0.0
15	12.8	9.8	2.3	0.2	14	8.5	3.9	0.0	5.1
16	11.8	9.4	3.9	0.2	15	6.4	0.6	0.0	1.2
17	15.5	8.7	0.0	2.0	16	7.1	1.0	0.0	1.8
18	16.2	7.1	0.0	4.7	17	5.6	2.0	0.0	5.5
19	17.7	9.0	2.0	0.0	18	5.1	0.7	0.0	1.3
20	15.6	10.8	0.2	0.0	19	3.9	-0.3	0.0	4.8
21	17.9	9.2	0.2	2.9	20	5.5	-3.3	0.0	3.2
22	17.2	8.3	0.0	9.3	21	3.9	-2.0	0.0	3.0
23	13.7	9.1	0.0	2.7	22	3.8	-3.3	0.0	5.3
24	15.1	8.3	1.0	0.4	23	1.7	-5.1	0.0	0.0
25	13.8	7.9	0.5	9.1	24	3.7	-5.3	0.0	0.0
26	14.9	4.8	0.0	6.9	25	7.6	-2.1	0.4	1.4
27	12.4	4.8	0.0	0.7	26	7.4	-1.1	0.2	0.2
28	14.8	6.0	0.0	6.6	27	5.4	-1.1	0.0	0.0
29	14.7	6.7	1.1	0.3	28	2.3	1.2	0.0	0.0
30	13.1	6.1	5.9	2.7	29	4.5	-1.3	1.5	0.0
Oct 1	14.2	6.1	5.4	4.5	30	8.6	-1.8	0.0	5.2
2	15.1	7.6	0.4	1.8	Dec 1	12.1	1.8	0.6	2.8
3	16.8	5.0	3.0	4.6	2	13.8	2.5	0.1	2.2
4	14.5	7.5	0.7	3.7	3	12.3	10.0	4.7	0.4
5	14.1	8.3	3.4	0.4	4	9.0	5.8	0.0	3.7
6	14.0	7.6	2.2	2.8	5	11.1	3.2	0.2	1.7
7	14.6	9.5	1.2	0.0	6	10.9	5.9	12.0	0.6
8	12.4	3.7	10.2	0.0	7	6.9	2.6	7.0	4.7
9	15.7	8.2	0.0	5.2	8	12.2	1.5	8.9	0.8
10	15.9	7.3	0.0	6.6	9	8.6	4.1	1.4	3.3
11	10.9	4.7	5.2	0.0	10	7.8	3.5	3.2	4.4
12	10.1	8.4	11.5	0.0	11	6.3	2.4	2.7	0.2
13	10.0	7.3	0.0	1.1	12	10.1	2.8	10.9	0.0
14	10.5	1.0	2.4	5.7	13	5.9	0.3	2.1	0.0
15	9.0	2.8	0.0	7.4	14	7.2	-0.3	6.4	0.0
16	8.0	0.0	0.0	7.4	15	7.1	0.2	1.3	4.7
17	10.1	-1.5	0.0	6.7	16	7.0	1.2	2.3	2.0
18	11.8	-0.2	0.0	7.2	17	11.4	3.2	1.3	0.0
19	10.6	-0.2	1.3	4.9	18	13.6	4.5	6.0	0.0
20	10.6	2.4	2.9	0.9	19	12.5	1.9	2.3	1.8
21	9.2	4.9	0.0	6.5	20	4.1	2.9	9.1	0.0
22	11.0	1.8	0.0	4.5	21	6.4	-0.9	6.5	2.6
23	11.0	1.4	0.0	5.6	22	7.3	-0.1	4.0	0.8
24	13.0	1.3	0.0	2.4	23	6.1	2.5	5.8	0.2
25	9.6	5.4	0.0	0.0	24	4.7	2.0	1.2	1.2
26	10.1	6.0	0.0	0.0	25	2.3	0.7	2.9	0.0
27	9.0	7.2	0.0	0.0	26	1.6	-2.0	0.2	0.2
28	10.6	6.3	0.0	0.1	27	1.6	-2.3	5.2	0.1
29	10.3	7.6	0.0	0.0	28	10.1	-1.4	1.8	2.5
30	11.1	7.9	0.0	0.2	29	8.9	0.6	3.8	4.3
31	9.4	7.8	0.0	0.0	30	6.4	2.4	0.7	0.6
					31	6.1	1.9	5.5	3.2

Ness Gardens, Cheshire

Date	Max (°C)	Min (°C)	Rainfall (mm)	Sunshine (hrs)	Date	Max (°C)	Min (°C)	Rainfall (mm)	Sunshine (hrs)
Jan 1	8.3	0.5	6.5	2.8	Mar 1	6.5	3.0	1.8	0.6
2	9.3	0.8	0.0	4.8	2	12.3	3.2	2.3	6.1
3	5.8	2.4	7.6	0.0	3	9.6	4.8	0.0	8.2
4	6.6	0.9	1.4	2.5	4	12.6	3.4	0.0	0.0
5	6.3	0.6	0.2	0.0	5	10.7	4.8	1.4	4.3
6	4.7	-1.0	0.0	1.9	6	11.1	3.3	0.2	0.6
7	6.3	-0.7	0.0	0.7	7	13.2	6.2	0.0	0.9
8	5.3	-2.3	1.6	3.4	8	13.6	10.0	0.8	1.3
9	8.7	-0.7	2.8	0.0	9	10.2	7.2	0.5	1.7
10	7.5	3.5	0.0	0.5	10	10.8	4.1	0.0	8.4
11	10.1	3.3	3.8	0.6	11	8.4	4.2	6.8	0.6
12	10.9	3.2	1.9	0.0	12	10.1	-0.2	1.0	3.2
13	9.6	5.2	0.0	5.1	13	10.9	1.7	0.3	3.7
14	8.4	1.0	0.0	3.5	14	13.6	4.6	5.5	3.7
15	4.9	2.3	0.0	0.0	15	8.5	5.0	0.3	4.8
16	4.7	0.6	0.0	6.0	16	8.6	2.9	1.9	6.3
17	6.2	-1.5	0.0	2.2	17	8.5	2.9	1.0	8.2
18	8.8	-1.4	1.5	0.0	18	9.8	3.4	10.1	0.5
19	7.3	0.4	0.1	5.6	19	7.3	2.7	0.0	6.9
20	10.8	0.3	0.1	0.6	20	8.6	0.9	0.0	2.8
21	10.1	6.6	1.1	0.0	21	10.4	2.2	2.7	1.6
22	10.3	4.4	6.9	4.4	22	14.4	2.7	0.7	2.7
23	7.9	3.6	0.0	4.3	23	15.5	6.9	2.2	2.6
24	11.1	4.0	4.5	0.0	24	10.7	5.1	5.3	4.3
25	9.9	3.6	7.2	3.7	25	12.2	7.1	1.8	4.1
26	10.2	1.7	2.7	1.0	26	10.0	2.0	0.0	9.4
27	8.8	5.8	5.7	1.9	27	8.9	2.3	1.3	0.3
28	9.4	1.5	0.8	5.8	28	14.3	4.6	0.0	2.5
29	11.8	1.4	0.8	1.2	29	10.6	7.1	0.0	10.4
30	7.4	5.3	0.0	6.3	30	11.8	3.9	3.4	0.3
31	9.1	2.6	0.5	2.4	31	10.5	4.1	12.6	4.2
Feb 1	10.3	4.0	2.3	1.9	Apr 1	9.7	4.9	0.9	6.3
2	6.2	0.6	1.7	3.7	2	7.4	1.6	0.0	7.8
3	8.2	-1.2	1.4	0.3	3	10.6	1.4	8.4	0.0
4	10.6	1.2	0.0	5.8	4	7.9	0.2	1.7	6.9
5	10.5	2.5	0.5	1.5	5	8.9	1.9	2.0	7.1
6	7.9	0.7	0.4	0.2	6	10.3	0.5	2.7	4.8
7	8.1	0.6	0.0	5.9	7	8.3	4.0	2.4	5.7
8	7.4	-0.4	0.6	1.6	8	8.2	0.9	9.2	1.5
9	7.9	1.2	0.0	5.6	9	7.3	0.1	4.9	5.2
10	8.7	4.6	9.6	3.8	10	9.8	1.6	0.0	10.2
11	5.6	3.6	0.0	0.0	11	14.3	0.5	1.6	8.3
12	7.0	0.7	0.0	7.6	12	9.3	6.0	0.3	6.0
13	2.5	-0.9	0.0	1.4	13	10.4	3.6	0.0	11.1
14	0.5	-2.6	0.1	0.1	14	11.3	3.2	0.0	11.2
15	1.5	-2.6	0.3	1.2	15	11.2	2.7	0.0	6.7
16	1.9	-2.8	2.4	0.0	16	12.8	1.5	0.0	6.0
17	3.7	-2.0	1.5	0.0	17	13.1	4.2	0.0	5.7
18	4.4	1.0	0.2	0.0	18	10.0	0.3	0.0	2.1
19	3.9	1.4	0.0	0.0	19	9.1	5.4	5.1	0.4
20	4.2	0.7	0.0	6.0	20	11.7	5.9	3.7	1.8
21	3.0	-4.4	0.0	7.4	21	13.4	6.8	1.8	2.0
22	2.7	-5.7	7.9	4.0	22	15.7	7.6	2.1	3.8
23	1.0	-4.0	4.3	0.0	23	17.1	7.8	0.2	4.4
24	4.0	-0.3	0.0	0.2	24	14.6	7.7	0.3	6.3
25	6.4	0.6	8.4	0.0	25	11.5	2.8	2.2	2.3
26	9.0	0.1	1.4	0.5	26	17.1	6.6	0.0	7.4
27	10.1	5.9	0.7	0.0	27	19.3	10.1	0.0	5.7
28	6.6	5.6	1.0	0.0	28	17.0	13.9	0.0	2.4
					29	21.7	8.9	0.0	3.7
					30	12.7	7.9	0.0	11.8

Ness Gardens, Cheshire

Date	Max (°C)	Min (°C)	Rainfall (mm)	Sunshine (hrs)	Date	Max (°C)	Min (°C)	Rainfall (mm)	Sunshine (hrs)
May 1	17.4	3.3	0.1	10.2	July 1	23.5	12.8	0.0	4.0
2	17.5	8.7	0.0	6.5	2	20.5	13.0	0.0	0.0
3	15.3	5.9	1.5	7.6	3	21.7	14.5	1.5	0.6
4	14.1	7.4	0.3	6.8	4	18.8	14.4	4.4	0.0
5	14.6	4.8	0.2	0.0	5	20.3	12.3	1.9	6.0
6	14.7	4.9	2.3	6.5	6	16.4	11.8	5.1	1.1
7	14.7	6.7	0.8	5.2	7	20.7	8.9	0.0	9.1
8	15.5	3.0	2.1	10.3	8	22.2	10.9	0.0	2.8
9	15.7	3.4	0.0	10.6	9	22.1	12.4	0.0	3.7
10	16.0	6.2	0.0	0.2	10	20.4	13.9	0.0	1.5
11	18.1	9.7	0.0	3.4	11	23.6	15.3	0.0	9.4
12	20.0	9.2	0.3	5.3	12	22.4	13.3	0.0	5.7
13	20.8	8.0	0.0	11.8	13	17.9	13.3	0.0	13.1
14	20.3	8.4	20.6	9.9	14	23.0	8.1	0.3	10.1
15	16.6	9.6	0.6	0.0	15	19.2	13.6	0.0	5.3
16	11.2	7.8	0.3	0.0	16	18.6	10.4	0.0	8.8
17	14.4	4.9	0.0	9.3	17	22.8	9.4	0.0	11.8
18	11.0	5.0	0.0	0.7	18	23.4	9.2	0.0	11.9
19	11.7	5.3	0.0	2.2	19	23.6	10.2	0.0	11.8
20	12.0	6.4	0.5	0.1	20	26.1	12.9	0.0	12.1
21	13.7	7.3	9.2	0.1	21	19.6	14.9	2.4	0.1
22	12.6	7.9	0.2	0.0	22	19.9	13.0	0.0	10.8
23	11.7	8.9	0.0	0.0	23	26.2	9.4	0.0	11.8
24	12.3	8.4	1.3	0.1	24	21.8	13.9	18.6	0.9
25	13.4	8.6	0.0	0.2	25	24.2	13.6	0.0	9.0
26	13.3	8.2	0.0	1.1	26	24.1	16.7	13.5	6.6
27	12.1	3.7	0.0	4.4	27	19.4	13.8	0.0	8.4
28	13.4	5.1	0.0	10.8	28	20.2	9.2	0.0	9.5
29	14.5	6.4	0.0	8.5	29	22.8	9.3	0.0	11.3
30	15.9	5.1	0.0	13.0	30	25.8	9.8	1.9	7.1
31	15.6	7.0	0.0	13.1	31	23.9	13.6	2.2	1.3
June 1	17.7	6.0	0.9	2.0	Aug 1	21.8	13.2	4.1	3.3
2	17.8	8.3	0.4	2.7	2	21.3	11.0	2.4	6.4
3	16.1	10.8	2.7	4.3	3	25.4	17.1	7.5	4.1
4	12.7	6.0	0.0	5.6	4	24.9	16.9	0.0	8.5
5	16.0	6.8	1.6	8.4	5	21.0	14.1	0.0	7.7
6	20.3	10.9	0.5	6.8	6	18.8	12.8	0.0	4.8
7	15.7	11.4	6.1	2.0	7	20.5	13.3	0.0	3.9
8	13.1	7.3	0.3	11.3	8	19.8	14.1	0.0	1.8
9	12.0	8.1	0.3	0.1	9	19.5	9.9	0.0	2.6
10	14.3	9.5	0.0	8.6	10	18.9	11.1	0.9	0.4
11	15.5	8.9	0.0	5.2	11	17.4	13.4	0.3	1.3
12	15.7	11.0	0.0	5.8	12	15.3	13.2	0.1	0.2
13	17.5	9.6	0.0	10.4	13	17.1	10.2	0.0	9.8
14	14.9	10.3	0.0	11.2	14	17.2	8.4	0.0	9.4
15	18.8	7.1	0.0	11.9	15	19.6	7.9	0.0	3.1
16	18.6	11.4	0.0	8.0	16	19.8	10.3	5.1	2.1
17	21.0	10.3	0.0	5.3	17	16.4	11.1	4.5	6.9
18	17.2	13.3	0.0	3.7	18	19.5	9.7	0.0	3.1
19	17.7	12.8	0.0	0.3	19	19.1	11.9	0.0	6.2
20	19.1	12.5	0.5	2.2	20	17.1	12.0	0.0	0.0
21	16.4	13.8	7.9	0.0	21	20.7	9.2	0.0	9.6
22	18.0	11.1	0.0	13.7	22	24.2	12.0	0.0	5.2
23	21.5	7.4	0.0	4.5	23	20.6	16.0	0.4	6.0
24	26.2	13.3	1.1	6.8	24	16.6	11.3	0.5	1.1
25	19.6	14.3	0.0	2.1	25	18.2	11.8	6.4	4.9
26	17.8	10.7	0.0	0.2	26	17.4	12.6	1.3	6.9
27	20.4	13.7	0.0	2.7	27	18.4	9.9	0.0	9.0
28	26.2	10.8	0.0	12.8	28	18.1	7.3	1.2	8.1
29	19.4	11.8	0.0	7.0	29	17.2	11.0	0.0	6.3
30	20.0	10.1	0.0	4.6	30	19.3	8.5	0.0	4.6
					31	16.4	10.1	12.1	0.0

Trelissick, Cornwall

Date	Max (°C)	Min (°C)	Rainfall (mm)	Sunshine (hrs)	Date	Max (°C)	Min (°C)	Rainfall (mm)	Sunshine (hrs)
Sept 1	20.5	8.2	0.0		Nov 1	9.7	7.2	0.0	
2	22.2	10.3	0.0		2	12.1	7.2	13.6	
3	19.2	10.2	0.0		3	14.9	9.3	0.1	
4	17.1	9.3	0.0		4	12.7	8.8	0.0	
5	17.8	4.7	0.0		5	13.6	9.0	0.0	
6	18.3	13.4	18.2		6	10.8	4.6	0.0	
7	18.5	14.5	12.8		7	10.4	5.6	0.6	
8	17.3	14.8	15.3		8	11.3	7.2	0.1	
9	16.0	14.5	5.7		9	11.6	1.9	12.5	
10	18.2	11.4	3.8		10	11.8	7.4	1.8	
11	16.8	9.3	11.4		11	11.8	5.4	3.5	
12	14.3	6.9	47.4		12	12.8	3.9	10.6	
13	17.9	10.9	0.1		13	13.1	5.5	16.2	
14	17.4	8.4	0.6		14	10.5	7.1	0.0	
15	16.6	8.0	2.3		15	10.5	-0.8	0.0	
16	16.2	6.4	0.1		16	9.9	5.0	0.0	
17	17.0	3.7	0.0		17	9.4	6.9	0.0	
18	17.7	6.1	0.0		18	9.1	5.5	0.0	
19	17.7	13.2	13.5		19	9.2	6.7	0.0	
20	15.7	12.8	1.1		20	7.3	0.9	0.0	
21	17.3	10.7	1.0		21	5.2	-1.6	0.0	
22	16.5	7.8	1.5		22	4.5	-3.5	0.0	
23	17.8	5.4	0.1		23	9.3	-1.8	18.1	
24	16.9	5.3	0.3		24	11.0	3.4	4.6	
25	15.3	10.1	5.7		25	12.5	3.2	0.2	
26	15.3	5.9	0.0		26	10.7	2.8	0.0	
27	15.5	4.0	0.2		27	9.2	3.1	0.0	
28	16.3	5.6	3.3		28	9.5	2.9	9.2	
29	13.0	11.6	25.7		29	11.9	4.8	18.8	
30	15.0	7.4	13.3		30	11.2	5.2	0.8	
Oct 1	14.2	5.2	11.6		Dec 1	12.2	3.0	0.7	
2	14.4	9.3	1.3		2	13.2	8.1	0.1	
3	15.8	10.9	3.8		3	12.3	10.2	7.3	
4	15.5	7.8	6.2		4	9.8	8.4	0.5	
5	16.2	10.4	13.9		5	12.2	4.5	0.2	
6	16.3	7.6	6.2		6	11.1	6.7	17.3	
7	13.7	3.6	6.1		7	11.9	7.5	7.5	
8	14.9	9.8	5.8		8	12.6	6.1	5.5	
9	15.3	9.5	0.2		9	11.1	7.4	2.3	
10	15.5	7.4	26.7		10	9.6	7.5	12.8	
11	14.3	10.2	11.5		11	10.8	3.7	7.8	
12	15.7	9.7	1.0		12	11.7	4.9	18.9	
13	13.7	10.6	0.0		13	8.6	7.9	2.9	
14	11.4	6.2	0.0		14	8.8	-1.7	18.1	
15	10.8	-0.2	0.0		15	8.3	-0.3	3.3	
16	9.8	0.7	0.0		16	10.7	4.4	0.7	
17	9.8	-0.5	0.0		17	11.9	4.4	3.4	
18	12.2	1.9	0.0		18	13.2	10.2	16.3	
19	10.6	-1.7	0.0		19	13.8	11.7	21.4	
20	12.6	1.0	2.8		20	12.7	6.5	7.5	
21	11.5	3.8	0.0		21	9.5	4.5	2.9	
22	12.3	-0.2	0.0		22	10.4	5.4	1.2	
23	11.8	0.5	0.0		23	8.2	5.2	14.7	
24	9.9	1.7	0.0		24	9.9	3.5	6.7	
25	13.2	4.5	0.0		25	8.3	3.9	2.2	
26	10.9	3.5	0.0		26	4.8	1.1	0.1	
27	10.3	7.4	0.0		27	9.9	0.4	14.9	
28	10.7	8.2	0.1		28	11.3	1.3	1.7	
29	11.5	7.2	0.0		29	11.0	8.4	12.8	
30	8.7	2.0	0.0		30	11.2	4.9	36.5	
31	8.9	4.0	0.0		31	8.9	5.0	2.6	

Trelissick, Cornwall 101

Date	Max (°C)	Min (°C)	Rainfall (mm)	Sunshine (hrs)	Date	Max (°C)	Min (°C)	Rainfall (mm)	Sunshine (hrs)
Jan 1	11.6	2.2	24.0		Mar 1	9.9	4.8	4.0	
2	11.0	3.2	1.6		2	12.3	5.5	0.7	
3	9.7	7.5	7.5		3	11.8	7.6	0.1	
4	9.8	5.2	21.1		4	10.8	3.2	1.6	
5	9.0	5.6	4.2		5	10.2	9.0	0.1	
6	6.3	1.2	4.5		6	10.7	4.3	0.3	
7	8.1	-0.7	0.5		7	11.5	8.7	3.2	
8	10.0	-1.5	10.9		8	10.9	9.5	0.2	
9	11.2	5.8	6.7		9	11.2	8.7	0.8	
10	9.1	6.6	3.7		10	11.7	1.5	0.0	
11	11.8	6.0	13.8		11	10.2	4.2	2.1	
12	11.9	8.2	12.1		12	11.0	2.7	5.1	
13	11.0	6.4	2.8		13	11.9	6.5	0.1	
14	9.8	5.6	2.4		14	13.7	9.2	0.8	
15	10.0	3.0	0.4		15	11.5	10.0	1.6	
16	9.8	1.4	0.0		16	10.7	5.3	1.6	
17	6.6	0.6	0.1		17	10.6	5.5	1.8	
18	8.6	-1.4	6.1		18	12.0	7.2	3.2	
19	8.8	2.0	0.7		19	9.5	6.9	0.1	
20	10.0	0.9	0.1		20	9.9	-0.1	3.6	
21	10.4	7.3	0.9		21	12.3	5.2	0.1	
22	11.3	8.7	2.3		22	11.5	4.8	2.2	
23	11.0	9.1	8.4		23	12.0	9.6	1.2	
24	11.5	6.2	3.7		24	12.8	9.4	2.1	
25	11.4	10.4	0.4		25	12.0	9.9	0.2	
26	10.9	7.7	0.0		26	10.5	1.9	0.0	
27	12.0	8.3	2.7		27	10.8	5.4	11.4	
28	9.9	6.0	0.2		28	13.1	8.5	0.6	
29	10.0	5.8	3.2		29	11.4	10.0	0.6	
30	10.0	8.2	0.1		30	11.1	9.4	16.6	
31	10.8	1.7	2.7		31	11.3	5.6	17.5	
Feb 1	11.2	4.9	8.7		Apr 1	9.6	5.5	5.2	
2	10.7	1.0	24.6		2	8.8	3.0	5.3	
3	9.9	2.9	9.7		3	11.2	2.9	15.9	
4	9.8	6.4	7.2		4	8.9	4.7	7.7	
5	10.3	5.3	0.6		5	9.8	2.7	2.2	
6	10.2	4.8	6.0		6	10.8	5.2	1.1	
7	10.1	1.5	1.1		7	10.1	5.4	0.6	
8	9.8	1.5	5.2		8	9.5	4.7	15.7	
9	9.7	4.5	0.3		9	9.6	2.8	0.4	
10	10.3	-2.9	7.7		10	10.9	5.8	0.0	
11	10.4	-0.5	0.2		11	13.3	0.2	0.1	
12	7.9	7.3	0.4		12	11.1	5.5	0.1	
13	6.0	4.7	0.0		13	11.8	4.4	0.0	
14	-0.5	-2.9	6.8		14	11.7	-0.3	0.0	
15	6.8	-3.6	0.1		15	9.5	-0.1	0.0	
16	10.6	-3.7	0.0		16	11.1	3.7	0.0	
17	10.4	2.3	18.6		17	14.4	2.3	0.0	
18	10.7	7.2	0.0		18	11.8	0.5	0.0	
19	10.3	1.3	21.6		19	11.9	2.0	0.0	
20	7.3	6.4	17.3		20	12.5	5.8	0.1	
21	6.9	1.8	10.1		21	13.5	4.2	0.0	
22	10.2	2.6	13.4		22	12.4	9.3	1.7	
23	11.5	4.8	6.0		23	13.5	9.6	13.0	
24	10.1	6.4	6.0		24	11.8	7.9	0.9	
25	10.9	6.4	14.2		25	12.5	4.5	5.7	
26	10.9	9.4	0.3		26	14.2	6.6	5.2	
27	11.2	9.5	0.0		27	13.4	11.0	0.0	
28	9.4	5.2	0.4		28	15.8	10.5	0.0	
					29	17.5	6.7	0.0	
					30	16.4	9.0	0.0	

Trelissick, Cornwall

Date	Max (°C)	Min (°C)	Rainfall (mm)	Sunshine (hrs)	Date	Max (°C)	Min (°C)	Rainfall (mm)	Sunshine (hrs)
May 1	14.2	4.3	0.0		July 1	20.3	12.0	0.0	
2	13.3	9.0	0.0		2	19.1	10.8	1.7	
3	13.7	8.8	0.3		3	17.1	14.4	8.3	
4	12.8	7.6	0.0		4	17.9	14.4	0.0	
5	12.8	6.8	1.4		5	17.8	11.5	6.4	
6	13.2	7.2	4.2		6	18.1	12.6	0.4	
7	13.1	6.5	0.2		7	16.7	10.0	2.6	
8	13.7	2.1	1.8		8	16.8	12.5	0.0	
9	14.1	2.1	0.0		9	18.7	8.4	0.0	
10	13.3	8.6	13.4		10	18.7	13.6	0.0	
11	13.4	10.4	20.3		11	19.5	12.7	0.0	
12	14.7	9.0	0.0		12	22.0	11.4	0.0	
13	16.6	10.3	0.0		13	21.8	11.7	0.0	
14	14.7	12.6	11.4		14	19.6	10.9	0.1	
15	15.5	10.4	1.2		15	20.7	13.7	0.0	
16	15.9	9.6	8.5		16	21.1	11.0	0.0	
17	11.2	8.1	0.2		17	22.4	11.2	0.0	
18	13.9	3.5	0.0		18	20.7	16.5	0.0	
19	12.5	5.6	4.7		19	23.5	13.4	0.0	
20	12.3	8.8	11.7		20	20.7	14.6	0.0	
21	13.2	8.7	3.1		21	22.4	11.8	0.0	
22	15.2	9.8	0.1		22	21.8	12.8	0.0	
23	14.1	9.0	6.0		23	22.5	11.4	0.0	
24	14.7	8.0	1.0		24	21.8	15.6	0.0	
25	13.3	7.4	14.7		25	20.7	15.3	8.1	
26	14.6	10.4	0.4		26	18.6	16.2	8.9	
27	12.5	9.4	0.0		27	18.0	13.6	0.7	
28	14.4	8.6	0.0		28	19.8	8.9	0.0	
29	15.4	5.6	0.0		29	19.5	7.3	0.0	
30	15.9	4.3	0.0		30	22.4	8.8	0.0	
31	16.5	3.5	0.0		31	20.0	12.7	3.4	
June 1	18.9	7.9	0.0		Aug 1	19.2	14.6	16.8	
2	15.8	10.4	3.0		2	18.4	15.1	4.3	
3	14.2	11.2	12.8		3	20.4	17.3	1.6	
4	14.3	9.1	1.2		4	21.2	15.0	0.0	
5	15.7	5.8	0.6		5	21.7	15.7	0.0	
6	17.1	11.7	0.0		6	21.3	11.4	0.0	
7	18.2	12.2	0.1		7	19.9	12.9	0.0	
8	15.7	10.2	0.0		8	20.4	16.0	0.0	
9	18.3	9.8	0.0		9	17.9	15.6	57.6	
10	15.2	9.7	0.0		10	20.5	15.0	0.0	
11	16.4	7.2	0.0		11	19.6	14.4	0.0	
12	17.4	6.8	0.0		12	18.4	11.1	0.0	
13	18.7	7.5	0.0		13	18.4	7.4	0.0	
14	20.2	8.0	0.0		14	19.2	5.8	0.0	
15	17.8	8.1	0.0		15	20.2	10.2	0.0	
16	19.9	9.9	0.0		16	19.4	11.7	4.7	
17	21.3	8.4	0.0		17	17.5	12.5	0.7	
18	19.4	11.7	0.0		18	17.5	9.3	7.9	
19	16.0	11.9	0.0		19	18.4	15.2	0.1	
20	18.8	12.8	1.2		20	18.7	12.5	0.6	
21	16.4	13.9	0.9		21	18.2	13.6	0.0	
22	19.0	13.0	0.0		22	20.4	13.0	5.2	
23	18.0	8.5	1.9		23	21.8	13.9	0.0	
24	17.4	14.2	1.5		24	18.4	12.1	1.5	
25	18.9	8.5	0.0		25	17.3	12.9	2.2	
26	17.5	10.1	0.0		26	19.4	14.2	2.1	
27	19.0	13.3	0.0		27	18.4	12.6	0.1	
28	21.3	11.9	0.0		28	18.0	9.7	0.0	
29	17.8	9.2	0.0		29	17.8	10.7	4.7	
30	18.0	5.6	0.0		30	15.7	11.9	5.0	
					31	17.0	13.5	2.3	

Rowallane, Co. Down

Date	Max (°C)	Min (°C)	Rainfall (mm)	Sunshine (hrs)	Date	Max (°C)	Min (°C)	Rainfall (mm)	Sunshine (hrs)
Sept 1	22.5	8.0	0.0		Nov 1	8.2	6.1	0.0	
2	18.0	11.8	0.0		2	8.2	5.6	0.0	
3	17.4	11.4	0.0		3	10.1	4.8	1.7	
4	15.3	10.4	0.0		4	12.0	6.4	0.1	
5	14.1	4.4	0.0		5	11.0	3.0	0.1	
6	16.8	6.4	0.0		6	10.9	8.5	3.7	
7	16.6	11.2	16.6		7	9.5	8.0	4.3	
8	15.6	11.0	1.1		8	9.0	3.6	11.9	
9	17.1	11.2	25.1		9	11.1	-0.1	0.2	
10	14.1	13.4	1.0		10	7.3	-0.4	0.0	
11	16.1	8.8	0.3		11	7.9	0.1	0.0	
12	13.3	2.5	5.8		12	7.7	0.7	3.8	
13	14.7	10.0	1.0		13	6.0	0.0	6.1	
14	13.1	8.8	3.0		14	7.9	1.0	0.5	
15	12.1	7.6	0.0		15	8.6	-1.8	0.8	
16	14.1	6.1	0.0		16	8.8	6.4	0.1	
17	16.3	3.2	0.0		17	8.8	4.4	0.0	
18	14.4	6.0	13.2		18	8.3	7.2	0.0	
19	15.4	10.5	5.1		19	8.2	6.4	0.0	
20	17.7	9.4	0.2		20	6.8	-2.7	2.1	
21	17.4	6.9	1.6		21	5.2	-1.1	0.1	
22	14.6	7.3	0.2		22	3.7	-3.9	0.7	
23	15.4	3.4	3.2		23	1.9	-5.5	0.6	
24	14.5	6.7	0.2		24	7.3	-4.8	2.1	
25	15.0	4.2	12.9		25	7.7	1.0	1.8	
26	15.1	3.2	0.1		26	8.4	-3.7	0.0	
27	13.0	2.9	0.0		27	8.1	-2.7	0.0	
28	13.3	2.4	8.9		28	6.1	4.0	6.7	
29	13.9	9.5	8.0		29	8.1	3.3	25.8	
30	12.6	8.1	4.6		30	7.4	0.7	0.7	
Oct 1	12.6	4.8	1.5		Dec 1	10.4	-0.9	4.1	
2	11.6	5.1	0.6		2	11.5	4.8	1.8	
3	13.0	4.6	9.7		3	11.4	9.1	6.3	
4	13.3	1.6	0.3		4	7.8	3.2	0.2	
5	10.2	3.8	25.1		5	9.5	3.4	0.0	
6	10.7	7.3	2.6		6	9.0	5.7	9.9	
7	12.3	7.9	3.0		7	6.7	0.2	13.2	
8	12.2	2.1	5.7		8	11.2	0.4	6.8	
9	14.2	8.7	0.5		9	6.6	3.9	6.1	
10	12.3	6.1	0.0		10	4.3	2.8	7.2	
11	13.3	5.5	0.0		11	4.8	0.1	5.4	
12	9.5	5.3	0.0		12	5.9	0.0	26.5	
13	9.4	2.8	0.0		13	5.3	2.9	0.4	
14	9.0	-2.2	0.0		14	6.0	-2.5	4.2	
15	7.5	-0.5	0.0		15	5.6	0.5	3.1	
16	7.0	-1.8	0.0		16	4.7	1.1	0.2	
17	8.3	-1.2	0.0		17	9.8	0.3	2.1	
18	11.2	-2.7	0.0		18	12.8	2.0	5.8	
19	10.2	0.6	0.6		19	7.0	5.0	0.5	
20	11.2	5.2	0.2		20	3.4	-1.2	0.0	
21	9.4	1.5	0.0		21	5.7	-3.5	2.6	
22	10.4	-0.2	0.0		22	5.8	-0.2	2.4	
23	10.9	0.7	0.0		23	2.8	0.9	4.4	
24	11.7	1.9	0.0		24	2.5	0.0	0.8	
25	9.6	2.0	0.0		25	2.4	-1.1	0.5	
26	9.3	5.6	0.0		26	2.5	-4.1	0.8	
27	8.6	5.6	0.0		27	6.0	-1.9	26.2	
28	9.1	4.8	0.0		28	8.2	1.6	3.3	
29	9.7	6.7	0.0		29	5.1	4.6	0.4	
30	7.7	0.9	0.0		30	3.9	1.4	0.0	
31	8.5	5.8	0.0		31	3.0	-1.7	0.0	

104 Rowallane, Co. Down

Date	Max (°C)	Min (°C)	Rainfall (mm)	Sunshine (hrs)	Date	Max (°C)	Min (°C)	Rainfall (mm)	Sunshine (hrs)
Jan 1	5.1	-1.6	16.8		Mar 1	6.6	-0.3	5.8	
2	7.5	-1.0	6.0		2	10.4	0.4	8.5	
3	5.9	1.0	23.2		3	8.2	1.6	0.3	
4	4.6	-1.6	9.0		4	9.7	1.5	6.0	
5	4.7	-0.1	6.0		5	8.2	3.4	1.0	
6	4.0	-0.8	3.0		6	10.7	3.3	0.4	
7	5.7	-0.1	5.1		7	12.2	6.6	2.7	
8	7.6	-1.8	7.3		8	12.3	9.5	1.8	
9	8.1	0.0	14.9		9	9.2	4.0	0.2	
10	7.7	2.5	0.4		10	9.2	2.4	2.0	
11	9.2	2.9	10.6		11	9.2	3.1	1.0	
12	7.7	0.8	0.2		12	8.2	0.2	1.7	
13	7.7	3.4	0.2		13	10.8	1.9	0.2	
14	7.0	3.2	1.4		14	12.6	4.2	2.9	
15	4.5	-0.9	0.4		15	7.8	2.8	1.5	
16	2.7	-2.0	0.0		16	5.8	0.7	1.9	
17	5.9	-1.7	0.3		17	7.9	0.3	2.9	
18	8.2	0.6	1.5		18	6.0	1.2	4.4	
19	7.6	-1.3	0.8		19	6.6	-0.3	0.8	
20	9.2	0.1	0.4		20	7.1	-1.3	0.0	
21	10.7	6.8	0.0		21	11.6	0.6	5.3	
22	9.1	2.4	1.3		22	13.6	5.0	1.2	
23	5.9	2.2	0.0		23	12.6	9.3	4.1	
24	10.1	-0.1	3.6		24	10.4	2.5	8.5	
25	7.8	1.8	10.2		25	9.4	5.4	1.5	
26	9.3	1.6	5.1		26	10.4	-1.2	1.2	
27	4.8	2.7	8.5		27	9.7	2.2	5.7	
28	9.0	-0.6	2.9		28	13.0	4.9	1.3	
29	10.1	-0.2	1.6		29	11.8	3.9	0.1	
30	10.1	2.8	0.0		30	8.3	3.3	5.9	
31	7.8	1.8	9.0		31	10.1	1.3	1.8	
Feb 1	7.2	2.4	1.6		Apr 1	8.9	3.1	2.1	
2	6.8	1.2	2.5		2	5.9	-0.3	3.0	
3	7.2	-2.2	5.5		3	11.6	-1.0	2.8	
4	7.4	0.6	7.4		4	6.0	-0.2	2.3	
5	7.4	4.9	6.5		5	8.5	0.2	3.7	
6	7.5	0.8	6.9		6	8.6	0.2	2.9	
7	4.3	-0.1	0.4		7	8.7	2.1	3.1	
8	8.1	-0.9	6.0		8	6.9	0.6	3.0	
9	6.6	2.0	0.1		9	8.4	-0.1	5.8	
10	7.1	-1.6	12.8		10	10.7	-0.4	0.1	
11	6.0	1.1	3.1		11	11.6	-0.5	2.1	
12	6.4	4.7	0.1		12	9.7	2.3	1.3	
13	3.9	1.7	0.0		13	11.1	0.4	0.1	
14	1.6	-1.7	0.0		14	11.6	-0.6	0.0	
15	0.1	-0.4	3.4		15	11.1	-0.2	0.0	
16	3.8	-8.2	0.1		16	12.0	-1.5	0.0	
17	5.3	-4.7	4.3		17	13.4	3.5	0.0	
18	5.8	1.2	5.8		18	12.1	1.6	0.2	
19	6.6	4.0	0.2		19	12.6	6.3	0.0	
20	2.7	2.0	0.0		20	10.2	2.5	0.0	
21	2.8	-2.6	0.0		21	9.1	0.3	3.9	
22	2.4	-4.2	18.7		22	10.5	3.3	9.0	
23	1.5	-4.0	4.9		23	12.7	5.8	4.3	
24	2.8	-0.3	0.0		24	11.8	5.8	5.0	
25	6.5	0.5	22.5		25	12.6	0.3	2.0	
26	7.5	0.8	30.2		26	14.6	5.6	0.1	
27	7.6	3.1	7.8		27	18.3	7.2	0.0	
28	5.4	3.2	0.1		28	16.0	10.8	0.1	
					29	16.2	7.4	0.0	
					30	14.0	5.0	0.0	

Rowallane, Co. Down

Date	Max (°C)	Min (°C)	Rainfall (mm)	Sunshine (hrs)	Date	Max (°C)	Min (°C)	Rainfall (mm)	Sunshine (hrs)
May 1	13.1	1.9	0.1		July 1	19.7	9.0	0.0	
2	14.2	7.9	0.0		2	19.5	9.5	0.0	
3	11.7	7.6	5.1		3	18.1	11.7	9.0	
4	10.0	5.7	4.0		4	15.6	12.5	3.1	
5	16.6	5.3	0.4		5	19.3	10.1	4.1	
6	13.6	4.3	0.4		6	17.2	11.1	0.2	
7	13.6	1.4	0.2		7	19.0	6.2	0.1	
8	13.1	-0.4	8.5		8	17.5	6.2	2.9	
9	13.5	1.9	0.0		9	14.0	9.6	5.4	
10	11.8	4.6	18.5		10	16.6	12.5	2.0	
11	14.5	8.4	0.1		11	16.9	11.9	7.1	
12	18.4	7.0	0.7		12	17.0	11.8	1.6	
13	18.8	4.0	0.0		13	18.7	6.6	0.0	
14	18.1	7.4	2.0		14	19.1	7.3	6.1	
15	10.1	7.0	7.1		15	16.5	9.8	0.1	
16	11.6	5.2	0.3		16	16.2	10.0	0.0	
17	11.2	4.8	0.0		17	19.5	5.6	0.0	
18	10.9	-1.4	0.0		18	19.7	6.6	0.0	
19	11.2	1.8	0.0		19	20.3	7.7	0.0	
20	12.1	4.8	0.0		20	22.2	10.4	0.0	
21	13.6	5.4	1.7		21	17.7	13.7	0.2	
22	12.9	5.9	0.1		22	18.5	9.2	0.0	
23	10.8	5.9	0.0		23	21.8	6.9	2.6	
24	12.4	6.9	0.5		24	20.4	14.1	0.2	
25	12.7	6.1	0.1		25	17.5	11.0	8.6	
26	12.7	4.8	0.1		26	21.4	13.2	0.3	
27	11.9	4.8	0.0		27	19.5	10.2	0.3	
28	13.7	3.0	0.0		28	19.4	7.5	0.0	
29	14.7	5.6	0.0		29	19.3	9.6	0.6	
30	17.8	1.8	0.0		30	18.8	12.5	0.0	
31	15.4	6.9	0.0		31	22.3	9.5	2.2	
June 1	16.8	4.6	0.0		Aug 1	21.8	10.3	0.1	
2	15.1	8.9	7.6		2	18.5	12.8	24.5	
3	11.9	8.3	9.0		3	21.0	13.0	1.2	
4	13.1	4.8	0.7		4	23.3	12.6	0.4	
5	15.8	4.0	0.9		5	15.5	13.2	0.0	
6	18.7	10.0	0.2		6	16.5	8.3	0.0	
7	15.6	8.8	0.4		7	18.8	11.8	0.0	
8	12.9	4.3	4.4		8	18.1	12.9	0.0	
9	11.1	7.9	0.6		9	18.5	12.5	0.0	
10	13.7	7.6	0.2		10	16.4	10.7	0.0	
11	14.2	5.4	0.0		11	18.1	9.8	0.0	
12	14.5	9.6	0.0		12	16.0	9.3	0.0	
13	22.5	3.5	0.0		13	15.7	7.0	0.0	
14	14.8	7.1	0.0		14	16.4	8.5	0.0	
15	18.0	8.6	0.0		15	19.4	7.3	4.8	
16	18.5	10.3	0.0		16	18.2	11.6	10.0	
17	14.8	10.3	1.6		17	16.3	9.1	0.2	
18	14.9	10.0	0.4		18	19.6	7.9	1.8	
19	15.5	11.4	1.7		19	16.7	10.7	0.2	
20	17.6	12.2	7.8		20	16.8	9.0	0.0	
21	15.2	9.1	1.4		21	18.0	7.3	4.8	
22	16.3	8.5	0.0		22	17.5	6.3	24.8	
23	15.5	4.7	0.0		23	19.1	11.9	1.2	
24	16.9	10.2	2.7		24	17.0	8.8	2.9	
25	13.3	11.4	0.1		25	19.5	9.0	7.9	
26	17.5	4.6	0.0		26	17.7	8.9	1.4	
27	19.8	10.8	0.0		27	14.9	6.0	2.3	
28	17.4	11.0	1.5		28	15.6	7.4	0.3	
29	17.2	9.1	0.0		29	16.4	9.2	0.0	
30	20.0	6.4	0.0		30	17.0	8.5	0.0	
					31	16.1	6.1	0.0	

8
Societies

Specialist Societies

Alpine Garden Society
AGS Centre, Avon Bank, Pershore, Hereford & Worcester WR10 3JP
☎ 01386 554790   FAX 01386 554801
CONTACT   E. M. Upward (Secretary)
AIMS   To further knowledge of Alpine plants
MEMBERSHIP   13,000
SUBSCRIPTIONS   £13 individual, £16 joint
SERVICES   Lectures; associated gardens; seed scheme; library; publications; advice; awards; shows; journal; special interest and regional groups; outings; the new rock garden opens this year

Founded in 1929. The AGS caters for anyone interested in rock gardening or alpine plants. You join the national organisation which entitles you to numerous benefits including free entry to the twenty or so shows, the bulletin, the seed exchange scheme, and the advisory service. If you wish you can also join one of the 60 local groups: there is a small additional subscription which varies from group to group. You have to be a member of the national AGS in order to join. Local groups organise their own busy programmes of events, including lectures, shows and visits. The *Quarterly Bulletin of the Alpine Garden Society* is an authoritative illustrated magazine which covers alpines in cultivation and in the wild. The AGS organises guided expeditions to many countries for its members, and these are both popular and respected. It also publishes monographs and alpine titles (including the mammoth new alpine encyclopedia), and members can use the slide and postal book libraries. At local level, AGS groups are an excellent and informal way to learn and develop an interest in alpines. Some groups are more active than others: it depends on local demand. Many of the lecturers are acknowledged experts, as will be some of the group members. The dates for the national shows, and a number of group events, appear in our calendar. Most local groups allow members to bring guests and will usually admit visitors for a small charge, though if you expect to attend regularly then you should really sign up properly. AGS headquarters can put you in touch with your nearest group. Active groups include the following: Bedfordshire, Berkshire, Birmingham, Bristol, East Cheshire, Cleveland, Cotswold and Malvern, North Cumbria, Derby, East Dorset, North East England, Exeter, Epping Forest, Hertfordshire, South Humberside, Ipswich, East Kent, Kent Medway, East Lancashire, North Lancashire, Leicester, North London, Nottingham, Oxford, East Surrey, North Staffordshire, Southport, West Sussex, Ulster, North Wales, South Wales, Woking, East Yorkshire, West Yorkshire.

Botanical Society of Scotland
c/o Royal Botanic Garden, Edinburgh, Lothian EH3 5LR
CONTACT   Hon. Secretary
AIMS   To promote the study of plants and exchange botanical information
SUBSCRIPTIONS   £9 basic; £16 including scientific publications
SERVICES   Lectures; publications; journal; regional groups; outings

Founded in 1836: formerly the Botanical Society of Edinburgh. Based in Edinburgh, with regional branches in Scotland, the society includes amateur and professional botanists. It holds regular lectures, conferences and field meetings. Its publications include a newsletter and a scientific journal.

Botanical Society of the British Isles
c/o Dept of Botany, The Natural History Museum, Cromwell Road, London SW7 5BD
CONTACT   Hon. Assistant General Secretary
AIMS   The study of British and Irish flowering plants and ferns
MEMBERSHIP   2,500
SUBSCRIPTIONS   £15, reduced rate for junior members
SERVICES   Lectures; publications; advice; journal; outings

This association of amateur and professional botanists traces its history back to 1836. Three regular publications cover the society's activities, articles on the taxonomy and distribution of plants in the British Isles, and an annual bibliography. The society also arranges conferences, exhibitions and study trips, and undertakes research projects and surveys. Members have access to a panel of experts on the British flora and can buy works on British botany at reduced prices.

Societies 107

British & European Geranium Society
Norwood Chine, 26 Crabtree Lane, Sheffield, South Yorkshire S5 7AY
☎ 0114 2426200   FAX 0114 2425379

CONTACT Public Relations Office
AIMS To promote the Geranium (*Pelargonium*)
MEMBERSHIP 1,000
SUBSCRIPTIONS £5
SERVICES Lectures; associated gardens; library; publications; advice; awards; shows; journal; regional groups; outings; plant finding service

The British & European Geranium Society is dedicated to growing, hybridising and exhibiting pelargoniums. The society is divided into regional groups, and they organise programmes of events including lectures and shows. There is an annual national show; every other year a conference is also staged. Members receive four newsletters and a Year Book. The society has other publications too. A new service is a computerised plant finder which has details of sources for any *pelargonium* which is available in Europe.

British Bonsai Association
c/o Inglenook, 36 McCarthy Way, Wokingham, Berkshire RG11 4UA

CONTACT J. White
AIMS To further interest and participation in bonsai
MEMBERSHIP 80
SUBSCRIPTIONS £12 full, £6 corresponding (1994)
SERVICES Lectures; library; advice; awards; journal

The British Bonsai Association is one of the leading bonsai clubs and exhibitors in the country. Those who cannot make the meetings in London (the first Tuesday of each month) can join as corresponding members. The meetings include lectures, demonstrations and competitions. Members can obtain expert advice and trees are sold at some meetings. There is a quarterly newsletter and a library of bonsai books and magazines.

British Clematis Society
The Tropical Bird Gardens, Rode, Bath, Avon BA3 6QW
☎ 01373 830326   FAX 01373 831288

CONTACT Membership Secretary
AIMS To encourage and extend clematis cultivation, and to share knowledge with fellow members
MEMBERSHIP 550
SUBSCRIPTIONS £10 individual, £12 joint, £5 junior, £15 overseas, £17 overseas joint
SERVICES Lectures; seed scheme; advice; shows; journal; outings; plant sales; demonstrations

A fast-growing society which organises meetings throughout the country and publishes a substantial illustrated journal, *The Clematis*, each year as well as supplements and newsletters. The society organises visits to gardens and nurseries. Members can obtain advice on clematis cultivation and join in the seed exchange programme. The society also produces a list of good clematis gardens and a list of clematis nurseries.

British Fuchsia Society
20 Brodawel, Llannon, Llanelli, Dyfed SA14 6BJ

CONTACT Hon. Secretary
AIMS To further interest in the cultivation of fuchsias
MEMBERSHIP 5,500
SUBSCRIPTIONS £5 individual, £7.50 joint
SERVICES Advice; shows; journal; special interest and regional groups; rooted cuttings

The British Fuchsia Society organises nine regional shows and a London show. Members receive the *Fuchsia Annual* and a twice yearly bulletin, as well as three free rooted cuttings. They can also obtain advice from the society's experts either by post or telephone. Special interest groups are devoted to old cultivars and hybridising. Some three hundred societies are affiliated to the national society, many of which organise programmes of events and festivals.

British Gladiolus Society
24 The Terrace, Mayfield, Ashbourne, Derbyshire DE6 2JL

CONTACT Hon. Secretary
AIMS To stimulate interest in and improve gladiolus growing
MEMBERSHIP 375
SUBSCRIPTIONS £8.50 individual
SERVICES Lectures; seed scheme; library; publications; advice; awards; shows; journal; regional groups

Founded in 1926 the British Gladiolus Society stages three major shows each year: the National (at RHS Wisley this year), Southern and Northern. There are regional groups in Sussex and Buckinghamshire. Members keep in touch with society news through three bulletins and the yearbook, *The Gladiolus Annual*, which is published each spring. The society runs trials at three sites, and also has a book, slide and video library available for members and affiliated societies. Council members can advise on gladiolus cultivation, and the society raises money by distributing cormlets. A small range of booklets on showing and growing gladiolus is also available.

British Hosta & Hemerocallis Society
c/o Cleave House, Sticklepath, Okehampton, Devon EX20 2NN
☎ 01837 840481   FAX 01837 840482

CONTACT Hon. Secretary
AIMS To foster interest in the cultivation of Hostas and Hemerocallis
MEMBERSHIP 250
SUBSCRIPTIONS £8 individual, £10 joint
SERVICES Lectures; library; advice; awards; journal; outings; annual plant auction

Founded in 1981, the British Hosta & Hemerocallis Society has members spread throughout the world. It publishes an annual bulletin, and regular newsletters to keep members informed of news and events. Garden visits and lectures are arranged, and members can borrow by post from the society's specialist and comprehensive library. An annual award is presented to a hosta and a hemerocallis. Expert advice is provided via the secretary. There are eight relevant NCCPG National Collections.

The British Iris Society
The Old Mill House, Shurton, Stogursey, Somerset TA5 1QG
CONTACT Hon. Secretary
AIMS To encourage and improve the cultivation of irises
MEMBERSHIP 1,000
SUBSCRIPTIONS £9 individual
SERVICES Lectures; seed scheme; library; publications; advice; awards; shows; journal; special interest and regional groups; plant sales scheme; lectures for clubs and societies

The British Iris Society was founded in 1922 and caters for all levels of interest in this varied genus. The illustrated *Iris Year Book* is supplemented by three newsletters. The society's programme includes three annual shows and occasional lectures. There are regional groups in Mercia and Kent, and special interest groups for species, Japanese, Siberian and Pacific Coast irises. Members can borrow from the reference library, and the slide collection runs to some 5,000 items. As well as a plant sales scheme there is also a seed distribution scheme, and expert advice is available on request. New hybrids are trialled at Wisley, and the Dykes Medal is awarded to the best British bred hybrid in the trial.

British Ivy Society
14 Holly Grove, Huyton, Merseyside L36 4JA
☎ 0151 489 1083
CONTACT Hon. Secretary
MEMBERSHIP 110
SUBSCRIPTIONS £7.50
SERVICES Advice; journal

Members receive three copies of the journal each year, and can obtain advice on *Hedera* cultivation. Further details from the society.

The British National Carnation Society
3 Canberra Close, Hornchurch, Essex RM12 5TR
CONTACT Secretary
AIMS To improve the cultivation of the *Dianthus* family
MEMBERSHIP Under 1,000
SUBSCRIPTIONS £8 individual
SERVICES Lectures; publications; advice; shows; journal; discount coupon scheme

The British National Carnation Society organises several shows annually. Members receive the illustrated *Carnation Year Book* each year as well as two newsletters. New members can also choose one of the society's cultural booklets when they join. Medals and show cards are available for affiliated societies, and together the society and its affiliates hold area shows throughout the country. A coupon in the autumn newsletter gives a discount on plants from selected nurseries. A panel of experts can be called on to answer questions. Other societies can hire lectures: a fee is charged to non-affiliated societies.

The British Pelargonium & Geranium Society
134 Montrose Avenue, Welling, Kent DA16 2QY
CONTACT Carol and Ron Helyar
AIMS To promote interest in *Pelargonium, Geranium* and other Geraniaceae
MEMBERSHIP 1,500
SUBSCRIPTIONS £6.50 individual and affiliated societies
SERVICES Seed scheme; advice; shows; journal; biennial conference; books on pelargoniums available by post

The British Pelargonium & Geranium Society was founded in 1951. It publishes a Year Book and three issues of *Pelargonium News* annually. The society's annual show, held in June, moves around the country, and includes classes for beginners and flower arrangers. Every other year a conference is held. Members can take advantage of a postal advisory service, and free seeds. They stage publicity and information stands at Chelsea, Malvern and the RHS Westminster shows, and encourage other societies to join as affiliated members.

British Pteridological Society
16 Kirby Corner Road, Canley, Coventry, West Midlands CV4 8GD
CONTACT Hon. General Secretary
AIMS To promote the study and cultivation of ferns and fern allies
MEMBERSHIP 800
SUBSCRIPTIONS £15 individual, £12 optional, £9 student, £25 subscriber
SERVICES Lectures; seed scheme; publications; advice; journal; special interest and regional groups; outings; book sales service; plant exchange scheme

Now over 100 years old, this international society includes amateur and professional members. An annual *Bulletin* contains society news, whilst the *Pteridologist* prints articles and book reviews for the amateur enthusiast. The twice yearly *Fern Gazette* includes more scientific papers: members who do not wish to receive this journal pay the lower optional subscription rate. According to the season activities include indoor meetings and field trips and garden visits. A spore exchange distributes fern spores from all over the world, whilst a plant exchange scheme helps members obtain rarely available or surplus plants. There are regional groups in South East England, the Midlands, Wessex and North

East England. Members can obtain advice on fern cultivation through the Hon. General Secretary.

Carnivorous Plant Society
1 Orchard Close, Ringwood, Hampshire BH24 1LP
CONTACT   Steve Cottell
AIMS   To bring together all those interested in carnivorous plants
MEMBERSHIP   650
SUBSCRIPTIONS   £9 individual, £10 Europe, £13 world
SERVICES   Seed scheme; advice; shows; journal; outings; plant search service

The Carnivorous Plant Society publishes an annual colour journal and four newsletters. They organise a number of events including visits to nurseries, field trips and open days. A plant search scheme is run, and members have free access to the seed bank. The information officer can provide advice on all topics.

The Cottage Garden Society
5 Nixon Close, Thornhill, Dewsbury, West Yorkshire WF12 0JA
CONTACT   Membership Secretary
AIMS   To promote and conserve cottage garden plants and to encourage cottage-style gardens
SUBSCRIPTIONS   £5 individual, £8 joint, £6 overseas, $20 USA
SERVICES   Lectures; seed scheme; publications; shows; journal; regional groups; list of members' gardens which can be visited

The Cottage Garden Society promotes and conserves worthwhile old-fashioned garden plants, and encourages owners of small gardens to garden in the cottage style. Members receive a quarterly bulletin and can take part in the annual seed distribution. The society has a growing number of regional and county groups: each organises lectures, meeting, visits and other events. The society hires out slides to members.

The Cyclamen Society
Tile Barn House, Standen Street, Iden Green, Benenden, Kent TN17 4LB
CONTACT   Peter Moore
AIMS   To further interest in and scientific knowledge of cyclamen
MEMBERSHIP   1,300
SUBSCRIPTIONS   £5 individual, £6 family, £7 overseas
SERVICES   Lectures; associated gardens; seed scheme; library; advice; awards; shows; journal; annual week-end conference

The Cyclamen Society has an international membership but is based in Britain. Its work includes research and conservation, whilst members benefit from the twice yearly journal, a seed distribution scheme and access to expert advice through the society's advisory panel. It exhibits and stages shows, organises meetings and lectures, and maintains a specialist library of literature and slides on cyclamen.

The Delphinium Society
Takakkaw, Ice House Wood, Oxted, Surrey RH8 9DW
CONTACT   Membership Secretary
AIMS   To encourage and extend the culture of delphiniums
MEMBERSHIP   1,500
SUBSCRIPTIONS   £5 individual & joint, £6 overseas
SERVICES   Seed scheme; publications: *Simply Delphiniums*, £2.50; advice; awards; shows; journal

The Delphinium Society dates back to 1928. New members receive a mixed packet of seed when they join, and all members can buy the society's hand pollinated seeds of garden hybrids and species. The illustrated Year Book is a unique source of information about the genus. Two shows, at which cups are awarded, are held each year: in June at Westminster, and in July at Wisley. Members gain free entry to the shows, and can also take advantage of advice on cultivation and a number of social events.

Federation of British Bonsai Societies
Rivendale, 14 Somerville Road, Sutton Coldfield, West Midlands B73 6JA
CONTACT   General Secretary
AIMS   To promote the art of Bonsai in the UK
MEMBERSHIP   70 societies
SUBSCRIPTIONS   £40 society, £10 individual, £20 commercial
SERVICES   Library; publications; advice; awards; shows; journal; regional groups; outings; list of lecturers

The Federation of British Bonsai Societies is the national bonsai organisation, and is a member of the European Bonsai Association. It publishes a newsletter six times a year giving members information on national and worldwide bonsai events. Two national exhibitions are held each year, and every other year up to 400 delegates attend a major bonsai convention. This year the International convention will be on 18-21 August at Hull University. FOBBS keeps a library of slides, films and videos and can provide expert advice through the secretary and chairman. The National Bonsai Collection is held at Birmingham Botanic Gardens and Glasshouses.

The Garden History Society
5 The Knoll, Hereford, Hereford & Worcester HR1 1RU
CONTACT   Membership Secretary
AIMS   To study garden history and preserve parks and gardens
MEMBERSHIP   2,000
SUBSCRIPTIONS   £20
SERVICES   Lectures; journal; regional groups; outings

Founded in 1965. Learned society which is concerned with the study of garden and landscape history. It is also actively involved in conservation and regularly advises local authorities on such issues. The twice yearly journal *Garden History* publishes new research, whilst regular newsletters carry details of conservation matters and society events. These events include lectures and garden visits, at home and abroad. There is a regional group in Scotland. All events are limited to society members only.

The Hardy Plant Society
Little Orchard, Great Comberton, Pershore, Hereford & Worcester WR10 3DP
☎ 01386 710317

CONTACT   Mrs Pam Adams (Adminstrator)
AIMS   To stimulate interest in growing hardy herbaceous plants
MEMBERSHIP   10,000
SUBSCRIPTIONS   £8.50 individual, £10 joint
SERVICES   Lectures; associated gardens; seed scheme; publications; advice; shows; journal; special interest and regional groups; outings; slide library

The Hardy Plant Society has its own garden at the Pershore College of Horticulture. Members join the national society and can then choose to join one of the twenty-eight regional groups. In addition there six special interest groups (Grasses; Hardy Geraniums; Half-hardy plants; Pulmonarias; Paeonies; and Variegated plants) and a correspondence group for those who cannot come to meetings. Two journals are sent to members each year, along with regular newsletters. The national society attends Chelsea and the RHS Westminster shows, whilst area groups patronise local shows and arrange their own programmes of events. An annual seed distribution list is circulated to all members. Members benefit from a horticultural advisory panel headed by the society's vice president, and a slide library from which they can borrow. The society is also involved in conserving old cultivars and introducing new ones, and has produced a number of useful publications. It has grown very fast recently, and is currently undergoing some structural changes. The local groups organise their own busy programmes of meetings, trips and garden visits: the additional cost of joining such a group is usually very small. Full details of the local and specialist groups are available from the national society: only HPS members can join a local or specialist group. Because all HPS events are for HPS members only they are not included in our calendar. Regional groups exist for the following areas: Berkshire; Buckinghamshire, Oxfordshire and Northamptonshire; Cambridgeshire and Bedfordshire; Cheshire; Cornwall; Devon; Essex; Hampshire; Hereford & mid Wales; Hertfordshire; Kent; Lincolnshire; Norfolk and Suffolk; North East England; North London; North West England; Nottinghamshire; Rutland; Shropshire; Somerset; Southern Counties; South Wales; Sussex; Western Counties; West Midlands; West Yorkshire; Wiltshire and Avon.

The Heather Society
Denbeigh, All Saints Road, Creeting St Mary, Ipswich, Suffolk IP6 8PJ
☎ 01449 711220   FAX 01449 711220

CONTACT   Administrator
AIMS   To promote interest in heathers and provide a friendly meeting place for enthusiasts
MEMBERSHIP   1,000
SUBSCRIPTIONS   £6 individual, £7 joint
SERVICES   Publications; advice; shows; journal; regional groups; slide library

The Heather Society was founded in 1963. Members receive the society's authoritative *Year Book* and a twice yearly bulletin of news and events. Competitions are held through the RHS at Westminster. A slide library is maintained, and expert advice on cultivation and other technical queries is available. Regional groups arrange a series of local events, and an annual weekend conference, linked to the AGM, is held at a different location each year. The national reference collections are at Wisley, Surrey and Cherrybank, Perth.

Hebe Society
Rosemergy, Hain Walk, St Ives, Cornwall TR26 2AF

CONTACT   Hon. Secretary
AIMS   To encourage, conserve and extend the cultivation of hebe, parahebe and allied New Zealand plants
MEMBERSHIP   280
SUBSCRIPTIONS   £6 individual, £8 joint, £12 professional
SERVICES   Seed scheme: cuttings exchange; publications; advice; shows; journal; regional groups

An international society, based in Britain. It was established in 1985, and has since expanded its brief to include other New Zealand plants. The society is affiliated to the New Zealand Alpine Garden Society. Quarterly issues of *Hebe News* keep members in touch with activities, and include botanical and horticultural articles. Local groups exist or are being formed in the North West of England, Cornwall and the Cotswolds. The society maintains a slide library, operates a cutting exchange service and produces booklets about hebes and parahebes. Society members can also obtain written advice on request. The national collection is at Rosewarne in Cornwall.

Henry Doubleday Research Association (HDRA)
Ryton Organic Gardens, Ryton on Dunsmore, Coventry, West Midlands CV8 3LG
☎ 01203 303517   FAX 01203 639825

AIMS   To promote and advise on organic gardening, growing and food
SUBSCRIPTIONS   £14 individual, £17 joint; £6 additional for Heritage Seed
SERVICES   Associated gardens; seed scheme; library; publications; advice; journal; regional groups; trials; product discounts

Europe's largest organic organisation. At the Ryton headquarters there is a ten-acre garden, and a reference library which members can use. Members are kept up to date with HDRA events through a quarterly magazine. In addition there are over fifty local groups around the country. The society provides free advice on organic gardening to its members, and they receive discounts on HDRA products and books. They can also join the Heritage Seed programme for £6 (£12 for non-members): this scheme propagates and preserves vegetable varieties which have been squeezed out of commerce by current legislation. Since they are not allowed to be sold, the HDRA gives them away to subscribers. Hand in hand with this project is *The Vegetable Finder*. The HDRA also carries out scientific research, consultancy work for industry and public bodies, and worldwide research and agricultural aid projects.

The Herb Society
134 Buckingham Palace Road, London SW1W 9SA
☎ 0171 823 5583
CONTACT   Nicola Hartopp
AIMS   To bring together all who have an interest in herbs
SUBSCRIPTIONS   £14 individual, £10 senior citizens and under 18, £18 overseas
SERVICES   Lectures; associated garden; journal

Founded in 1927 as the Society of Herbalists, the Society aims to bring together all with an interest in herbs. Members receive three copies of the Society's magazine *Herbs*, and four copies of the newsletter *Herbarium* each year. Seminars and workshops are arranged nationwide in appropriate settings. Information on suppliers, literature and all aspects of growing herbs is available to members. The Society's garden is part of the Henry Doubleday Research Association's new garden at Yalding in Kent.

Ichiyo School of Ikebana
4 Providence Way, Waterbeach, Cambridge, Cambridgeshire CB5 9QJ
CONTACT   Mrs Eileen Gibson (President)
AIMS   To introduce the art of Ikebana
MEMBERSHIP   60
SUBSCRIPTIONS   £15
SERVICES   Lectures; shows; journal

The School holds courses, workshops and demonstrations in Ikebana, and exhibits at major shows, including Chelsea and the RHS Westminster shows.

International Camellia Society
41 Galveston Road, East Putney, London SW15 2RZ
CONTACT   UK Membership Representative
AIMS   To foster the love of camellias and maintain and increase their popularity throughout the world
MEMBERSHIP   1,500
SUBSCRIPTIONS   £8 individual; £11 joint
SERVICES   Associated gardens; advice; shows; journal; regional groups; outings

Founded in 1962. There are now members in 34 countries, including 340 in the UK. The society has several trial grounds around the country; the national collection is at Mount Edgcumbe, Cornwall. Members receive the *International Camellia Journal* annually, and a UK newsletter twice a year. The society takes a stand at the main spring shows, and holds weekend meetings in spring and autumn. Informal advice on camellias is available to members, as is a worldwide network of fellow enthusiasts.

International Dendrology Society
School House, Stannington, Morpeth, Northumberland NE61 6HF
☎ 01670 789621
CONTACT   Secretary
AIMS   To promote the study and conservation of trees, woody plants and shrubs
MEMBERSHIP   1,500
SUBSCRIPTIONS   £25 individual, £250 life
SERVICES   Lectures; seed scheme; publications; journal; regional groups; outings; conservation and research; annual bursary

This prestigious society has a worldwide membership. It encourages and helps fund conservation and research projects by registered charities, and has established a bursary to allow a dendrological student from Eastern Europe to study in the UK for a few months each year. The IDS holds a dendrological symposium every two years; members also receive the year book and newsletters, and can take part in the seed exchange scheme and the excellent botanical tours. Membership is restricted, is at the invitation of existing members only, and is subject to the approval of the council.

International Violet Association
The Bungalow, 119 Scalwell Lane, Seaton, Devon EX12 2ST
CONTACT   Membership Secretary
AIMS   To bring together all those interested in the violet and its near relations
MEMBERSHIP   130
SUBSCRIPTIONS   £10 or $15
SERVICES   Advice; journal

A new and growing international society which originated in the USA, though the president is British. The society is still finding its feet in terms of activities, but its aims include bringing the violet back into gardens, assisting in the preservation of its natural habitats, and recording and introducing new cultivars. Membership is not limited to growers and collectors. A newsletter is produced four times a year, and the president offers an advisory service to European members.

International Water Lily Society
92 London Road, Stapeley, Nantwich, Cheshire CW5 7LH
☎ 01270 628628   📠 01270 624188
CONTACT   Treasurer (IWLS Europe)

112 Societies

AIMS To further interest in all aspects of water gardening
MEMBERSHIP 930
SUBSCRIPTIONS £12.50 individual, £15 family
SERVICES Lectures; library; awards; journal; special interest and regional groups; outings

The International Water Lily Society is based in the USA but has members in 23 countries of the world. The membership spans amateurs and professionals, and the society carries out a range of research and educational work, including hybrid registration. Members receive the quarterly journal. There are lectures at the British branch AGM in October. The National Collection of Water Lilies is held at Burnby Hall, Yorkshire.

Japanese Garden Society
Tatton Park, Knutsford, Cheshire WA16 6QN
☎ 01928 718759

CONTACT M. Dickinson, Hon. Secretary
AIMS To record, conserve and encourage Japanese-style gardens
MEMBERSHIP 215
SUBSCRIPTIONS £15
SERVICES Lectures; library; journal; special interest and regional groups; outings

A new society which is devoted to gardens influenced by the Japanese tradition of design. It aims to compile a register of Japanese gardens in the UK, and to work for the conservation of existing gardens and the creation of new ones. The society organised a visit to Kyoto in 1994.

The Mammillaria Society
26 Glenfield Road, Banstead, Surrey SM7 2DG

CONTACT Hon. Chairman
AIMS To promote interest in the genus *Mammillaria*
MEMBERSHIP 500
SUBSCRIPTIONS £6.50
SERVICES Seed scheme; publications; advice; journal

Founded in 1960. Its interests extend to *Coryphantha* and allied genera as well as *Mammillaria*. Members receive a quarterly illustrated bulletin, and have access to specialised publications. There is an annual seed scheme, and advice is available to any member. Lecturers can be provided for other societies.

Mesemb Study Group
Brenfield, Bolney Road, Ansty, West Sussex RH17 5AW

CONTACT Suzanne Mace
AIMS To further the study and knowledge of *Mesembryanthemum* and related genera
MEMBERSHIP 514
SUBSCRIPTIONS £6 individual; £9 overseas, airmail
SERVICES Lectures; seed scheme; journal; research

Successor to the Mesembryanthemum Society. Aims to operate 'informally but not inefficiently'. Members, about a third of whom live overseas, receive a quarterly bulletin and can take part in the annual seed list. Meetings are arranged irregularly, and announced in the bulletin. A larger event, often including a show, takes place every two or three years. Financial assistance is also available for some research projects.

The National Association of Flower Arrangement Societies
21 Denbigh Street, London SW1V 2HF
☎ 0171 828 5145   FAX 0171 821 0587

CONTACT Secretary
AIMS To encourage a love of flowers and demonstrate their decorative value
MEMBERSHIP 106,000
SUBSCRIPTIONS Payable to local clubs
SERVICES Lectures; library; publications; awards; shows; journal; regional groups; outings; book service

Founded in 1959. NAFAS is the umbrella organisation for nearly 1,500 flower arrangement clubs. The Association is very active in training and teaching arrangers of all skill levels. Local clubs organise demonstrations and competitions, and area groups stage exhibits at NAFAS and local shows. Regular flower festivals are organised to raise money for charitable causes, and arrangements in hospitals are another important part of the NAFAS activity. They also co-ordinate the flowers at Westminster Abbey, and do the arrangements for major occasions including royal weddings. *The Flower Arranger* is circulated quarterly; members can use the book service, and there is a book and slide library at the London headquarters. Prospective members should write to headquarters in the first instance: they will put you in touch with a local club. Subscriptions to these clubs vary and are usually modest. All clubs are represented at area level: the twenty areas are as follows: East of England; South West; Scotland; North East; Three Counties and South Wales; London and Overseas; Surrey; Wessex and Jersey; Home Counties; Berks, Bucks and Oxon; Mercia and North Wales; North West; Kent; Sussex; North Midlands; South Midlands; Devon and Cornwall; Northumberland and Durham; Dorset and Guernsey; Cheshire. We have included details of a number of local and area events in our list of floral shows and in the calendar section.

National Auricula and Primula Society (Southern Section)
67 Warnham Court Road, Carshalton Beeches, Surrey SM5 3ND

CONTACT Hon. Secretary
AIMS To improve and encourage the cultivation of auriculas and hardy primroses
MEMBERSHIP 500
SUBSCRIPTIONS £7
SERVICES Lectures; publications; advice; awards; shows; journal; regional groups

Founded in 1876. Members receive a year book and an annual newsletter. Two shows are held: both usually in

April. This year the Primula show is in Datchet on 8 April and the Auricula show is in Brompton Road, London on 29 April. Plants are for sale at the shows. Members can seek advice on all aspects of primula cultivation and exhibition. The society has corresponding sections serving the Midlands and the West (6 Lawson Close, Saltford, Bristol BS18 3LB) and the North (146 Queens Road, Cheadle Hulme, Cheshire SK8 5HY).

National Begonia Society
7 Springwood Close, Thurgoland, Sheffield, South Yorkshire S30 7AB
CONTACT Hon. Secretary
AIMS To promote and encourage the cultivation of all begonias
MEMBERSHIP 900
SUBSCRIPTIONS £3 individual; £4 joint; additional enrolment fee £4 single; £5 joint (1994)
SERVICES Lectures; publications; advice; awards; shows; journal; regional groups

Established in 1948. The society encourages the cultivation of all types of begonia. New members receive a cultural handbook, and the journal appears three times a year. Meetings are arranged through the regional groups, five of which also organise an annual area show. In addition there is a national show with 26 classes. New cultivars can be submitted for awards to the floral committee. An advisory service is available through the secretary.

National Bonsai Society
30 Dunbar Road, Southport PR8 4RD
CONTACT Tom Ball
AIMS To promote, educate and further interest in bonsai throughout the UK
MEMBERSHIP 700
SUBSCRIPTIONS £5 individual; £6.50 joint (1994)
SERVICES Lectures; library; publications; advice; awards; shows; journal

Members receive *The World of Bonsai* quarterly, and can take advantage of the society's library. The annual show takes place in Southport on the first Saturday in June. The National Bonsai Society meets on the third Tuesday of every month (except in December) at 7.45 pm in the Harry Livingstone Hall, Princes Street, Southport. Visitors are welcome at these meetings.

National Chrysanthemum Society
George Gray House, 8 Amber Business Village, Amber Close, Tamworth, Staffordshire B77 4RD
☎ 01827 310331   FAX 01827 310331
CONTACT Mrs Y. Honnor
AIMS To promote the chrysanthemum and offer advice
MEMBERSHIP 4,500
SUBSCRIPTIONS £10 fellow, £9 senior fellow, £14 family, £5 junior

SERVICES Publications; advice; awards; shows; journal; regional groups

The National Chrysanthemum Society holds two national shows each year: in Bingley Hall, Stafford (September) and the RHS Halls, Westminster (November). The advisory bureau helps with queries about chrysanthemums and handles membership enquiries.

National Council for the Conservation of Plants and Gardens
The Pines, Wisley Garden, Woking, Surrey GU23 6QB
AIMS To encourage the conservation of plants and gardens
MEMBERSHIP 6,500
SERVICES Lectures; publications; shows; journal; regional groups; outings

Founded in 1978. The NCCPG is divided into local and county groups who organise their own programmes of events. The national body works to preserve individual plants and endangered gardens. The society's most successful innovation has been the establishment of National Collections of genera (and part genera). These gather together as many representatives of the genus as possible and form a unique resource. Many can be visited: full details appear in the *1995 National Plant Collections Directory*, which is available from the NCCPG.

National Dahlia Society
19 Sunnybank, Marlow, Buckinghamshire SL7 3BL
☎ 01628 473500
CONTACT General Secretary
AIMS To promote the cultivation of dahlias
MEMBERSHIP 3,500
SUBSCRIPTIONS £10 individual, £8 OAPs, £11 affiliated society
SERVICES Lectures; library; publications; advice; awards; shows; journal; regional groups; judging examinations; classification of new varieties

The National Dahlia Society holds two main shows: in London at the RHS and at Harrogate during the Autumn Show. It runs trials at Bradford and Wisley, and gives an annual award for the best new British and new overseas seedlings. Members receive the society journal twice a year, and can take part in its annual conference and lecture programme. There are regional groups in the home counties and Lancashire, and affiliated societies can use the society's medals and certificates for their own shows. A range of books and pamphlets is available for members at reduced prices.

National Pot Leek Society
147 Sea Road, Fulwell, Sunderland SR6 9PW
☎ 0191 5494274
CONTACT Hon. Secretary
AIMS To improve and encourage leek growing
MEMBERSHIP 1,500
SUBSCRIPTIONS £5

SERVICES Lectures; publications; advice; awards; shows; journal; items for sale

The society produces a year book and two newsletters for its members. Advice can be provided by letter or phone, and the society produces a growing guide *Sound All Round*, and a video *Growing Leeks with the Experts*. Items for sale include measuring equipment and charts as well.

National Society of Allotment and Leisure Gardeners
O'Dell House, Hunters Road, Corby, Northamptonshire NN17 1JE

CONTACT Geoff Stokes
AIMS To help all enjoy the recreation of gardening
MEMBERSHIP 104,000
SUBSCRIPTIONS £6.30 individual, £4.20 associate, 42p per member for societies; £30 local authority membership
SERVICES Seed scheme: Commercial seeds available at reduced prices; publications; advice; journal; regional groups; insurance

National society for allotment holders and other gardeners. Members can join individually or as part of a gardening association. In return they receive the journal and are able to take advantage of NSALG's many services. These include substantial discounts on seeds ordered through the society, and special insurance for allotment property. The society provides free advice on horticultural subjects, and in particular on the legal aspects of allotment gardening, including threatened loss of land and other disputes. It can also advise on suitable forms for leases, rents and agreements. A range of leaflets and fact sheets are available, along with show stationery and awards.

The National Sweet Pea Society
3 Chalk Farm Road, Stokenchurch, High Wycombe, Buckinghamshire HP14 3TB

CONTACT Hon. Secretary
AIMS To encourage the cultivation and improvement of the sweet pea
MEMBERSHIP 1,400
SUBSCRIPTIONS £12 individual, £10 affiliated society
SERVICES Lectures; advice; awards; shows; journal; regional groups; joint RHS/ NSPS trials

The National Sweet Pea Society was founded in 1900. The society's *Annual* appears every June, and further Bulletins appear in February and September. Its two major shows are held in July this year: the National in Newport, Shropshire and the Provincial in Southampton. Each county has an area representative who arranges programmes for local members. The society actively promotes new varieties, and members can send their own seedlings to the trials at Wisley each year.

National Vegetable Society
56 Waun-y-Groes Avenue, Rhiwbini, Cardiff, South Glamorgan CF4 4SZ

MEMBERSHIP 3,500
SUBSCRIPTIONS £7 individual, £8.50 joint, £10 & £13 societies
SERVICES Library; publications; advice; awards; shows; journal; regional groups

The National Vegetable Society was founded in 1960 and caters for individual members and societies. The latter can use the NVS medals and award cards. Membership spans the expert and the novice vegetable grower. The new quarterly National Bulletin and the regional Bulletins that members receive contain advice on all aspects of growing and showing vegetables. A National Newsletter gives details of all Society activities. The National Vegetable Championships are held at a different location each year (Dundee in 1995), and major awards are presented at it. There are regional branches.

National Viola and Pansy Society
c/o 28 Carisbrooke Road, Edgbaston, Birmingham, West Midlands B17 8NW

CONTACT Hon. Secretary
AIMS To encourage the cultivation, exhibition and improvement of violas and pansies
SUBSCRIPTIONS £2 (1994)
SERVICES Library; shows; journal

Founded in 1911. The society encourages and popularises the growing of exhibition varieties, and helps its members with advice on propagation and cultivation. A newsletter is circulated irregularly, and there is an annual show in Handsworth, Birmingham at the end of July. Surplus cuttings and plants form the basis for occasional exchanges.

Northern Horticultural Society
Harlow Carr Botanical Gardens, Crag Lane, Harrogate, North Yorkshire HG3 1QB
☎ 01423 565418

CONTACT Barry S. Nuttall
AIMS To promote the science and practice of horticulture
MEMBERSHIP 11,000
SUBSCRIPTIONS £20
SERVICES Lectures; associated gardens; seed scheme; library; publications; advice; awards; journal; special interest groups

Founded in 1947, the Northern Horticultural Society is a particularly active group. Members receive free entrance to the Harlow Carr Botanical Gardens which are the society's headquarters. The annual programme includes a series of day and longer courses throughout the year at the garden. The garden also trials vegetable and flower varieties specifically for their suitability to northerly climates, and visitors can assess the new and unreleased varieties which are undergoing trial. An illustrated journal, *The Northern Gardener*, appears four times a year. Members can also take advantage of the seed scheme, the reference and lending library, and an advisory service (in writing only). There are special interest sections for alpines, bonsai, bulbs, delphiniums, ferns, rhododendrons and roses. A reciprocal arrangement with the Royal Horticultural Society allows free access to some of the RHS gardens. Many of the society's events are listed in our calendar.

Orchid Society of Great Britain

Athelney, 145 Binscombe Village, Godalming, Surrey GU7 3QL

CONTACT Hon. Secretary
AIMS To encourage amateur growers of orchids
MEMBERSHIP 1,200
SUBSCRIPTIONS £10 individual; £12 double; £5 joining fee
SERVICES Lectures; library; publications; advice; awards; shows; journal; regional groups; outings; plant exchanges and sales

The nationwide orchid society. It produces an informative journal four times a year and stages two major shows annually. In addition there is a monthly meeting in the Napier Hall, London which may include a lecture and a show. The library lends books and slides, and members can obtain cultural advice in person or in writing from the Cultural Adviser. There is a plant exchange forum, and a sales table at most meetings. The society publishes a small booklet on orchid cultivation which is a useful introduction to the subject (£2.50).

The Royal Horticultural Society

P O Box 313, 80 Vincent Square, London SW1P 2PE
☎ 0171 834 4333

CONTACT Membership Department
SUBSCRIPTIONS £23 individual, £12 student, £16 associate; £7 enrolment fee
SERVICES Lectures; associated gardens; seed scheme; library; publications; advice; awards; shows; journal; special interest groups; outings

The premier horticultural society in the country and probably the world. Membership has grown steadily in recent years and the society's activities have expanded correspondingly. As well as the extensive gardens at Wisley in Surrey, there are now also regional gardens at Rosemoor, Devon and Hyde Hall, Essex and a regional centre at Pershore in the West Midlands. Reciprocal arrangements also give full and student members admission to the University of Liverpool Botanic Gardens, Merseyside; the Sir Harold Hillier Gardens and Arboretum, Hampshire; Brogdale in Kent; and the Harlow Carr Botanical Gardens, North Yorkshire; as well as the National Trust's gardens at Hidcote Manor, Gloucestershire; Bodnant, Clwyd; Sheffield Park, East Sussex; and Nymans, West Sussex. There is a full range of courses, lectures and demonstrations at the RHS gardens and Pershore, and a wide variety of regional and London lectures each year. Members are admitted to these events at concessionary rates, and free of charge to most lectures: you should apply for tickets in writing. The show programme is formed around the so-called fortnightly shows in the RHS Halls in Westminster (see our calendar for dates). The halls are less full on Tuesday evenings and on Wednesdays. The RHS and specialist societies hold plant competitions at these shows, and members can bring along plants for exhibition or cultural awards. Schedules are available from the RHS. Members no longer receive free entrance to Chelsea, but they can buy tickets at reduced prices and the Tuesday and Wednesday of Chelsea week are reserved for members. Members are entitled to reduced price admission to the increasing number of shows in which the RHS is now involved, including BBC Gardeners' World Live in Birmingham, the Hampton Court Palace Flower Show, and the established shows at Malvern and Harrogate. The illustrated RHS journal *The Garden* is sent free to members every month. Long a journal of record, the magazine is now back on form with a mixture of society news, horticultural and botanical articles. Its sister title is *The New Plantsman*: aimed at the specialist, there is a separate subscription. A number of other publications are produced, and the society promotes a collection of gardening titles in association with commercial publishers. RHS members are entitled to technical advice from the society's experts: this service is accessible by post, at the society's own shows and a number of other major events which it attends, and in person at Wisley. Members may use and borrow from the Lindley Library in Vincent Square: its holdings are of world standing. A distribution of seed from the Wisley garden is made each year for a nominal charge. The new class of associate member coincides with changes which have been made to the membership privileges. Membership cards are no longer transferable, and the benefits now apply to the named holder only. Members can enrol up to three people who live at their address as associate members: they are entitled to all the normal benefits except free entry to those gardens which are not owned by the RHS; only one copy of the journal is sent to each address. There are some specialist groups (an additional subscription is payable) for Fruit, Lilies, and Rhododendrons and Camellias. Behind the scenes the RHS is involved in scientific and technical horticulture, including its regular trial programme. The trials can be viewed at Wisley (Portsmouth field). The society liaises with national and trade organisations in the interests of horticulture, and is increasingly active in the international arena too. Our calendar lists many events that are organised by the RHS. Up to date information along with precise details of how to book, is published monthly in *The Garden* (which non-members can buy from newsagents). A recorded information line (0171 828 1744) gives details of forthcoming flower shows for members and non-members. A new direct line has been established for membership and subscription enquiries: 0171 821 3000.

The Royal National Rose Society
The Gardens of the Rose, Chiswell Green, St Albans, Hertfordshire AL2 3NR
☎ 01727 850461   FAX 01727 850360

CONTACT   Reception
AIMS   To promote the love of roses
SUBSCRIPTIONS   £15 individual; £20 joint; £7 student; £5 extra for Historic Roses Group
SERVICES   Lectures; associated gardens; library; publications; advice; awards; shows; journal; special interest and regional groups; outings

Founded in 1876. The world's largest specialist plant society has its headquarters near St Albans: the Gardens of the Rose display over 1,700 different roses. Members enter free. The society also maintains 12 regional rose gardens. An illustrated quarterly journal *The Rose* gives news of the society and the rose world, and there are regular shows including the British Rose Festival at the Hampton Court Palace Flower Show. The society always has hundreds of new roses on trial for awards at St Albans: the trial fields can be visited. There is a full advisory service for members and regular pruning demonstrations which anyone can attend (4 – 5 March). There are regional groups in Yorkshire and the North West, and special interest sections for exhibitors and rose breeders (The Amateur Rose Breeders Association). For an additional £5 RNRS members can join the Historic Roses Group, which organises its own programme of events and visits. The first part of the RNRS Rose 2000 Development was started last winter.

The Saintpaulia & Houseplant Society
33 Church Road, Newbury Park, Ilford, Essex IG2 7ET

CONTACT   Hon. Secretary
AIMS   To grow better and more beautiful houseplants, and to help the public to do the same
MEMBERSHIP   650
SUBSCRIPTIONS   £4 individual, £5 joint
SERVICES   Lectures; library; publications; advice; shows; journal; regional groups; outings; *Saintpaulia* leaf distribution

The society is affiliated to the Royal Horticultural Society, and holds regular Tuesday evening meetings at the RHS, usually to coincide with the Westminster shows. There are competitions at the meetings, and an annual show in August. Members receive the bulletin four times a year. The society arranges visits and also has three local groups with their own programmes. Members can borrow from the society's specialist library, and take part in the annual leaf distribution.

Scottish National Sweet Pea, Rose & Carnation Society
72 West George Street, Coatbridge, Lanarkshire, Strathclyde ML5 2DD

CONTACT   Secretary
AIMS   To encourage the growing and showing of the named flowers in Scotland
MEMBERSHIP   100
SUBSCRIPTIONS   £3 (1994)
SERVICES   Associated gardens; advice; awards; shows; journal

The Scottish National Sweet Pea, Rose & Carnation Society produces an annual Year Book in November, and holds a show in August. Some 28 trophies are awarded annually. Sweet Peas and roses are trialled in Glasgow, at Bellahouston Park and Tollcross Park respectively. There is an informal advisory service.

Scottish Rhododendron Society
Stron Ailne, Colintraive, Argyll, Strathclyde PA22 3AS

CONTACT   Hon. Secretary
AIMS   To encourage the cultivation of Rhododendrons
MEMBERSHIP   220
SUBSCRIPTIONS   £19.50
SERVICES   Lectures; associated gardens; seed scheme; publications; advice; awards; shows; journal; regional groups; outings; automatic membership of the American Rhododendron Society

The Scottish Rhododendron Society was founded just over ten years ago to provide a forum at which Scottish growers could meet and exhibit. Many of the best Scottish rhododendron gardens belong, but about a third of the members live outside Scotland. A newsletter is produced three times a year, and there are at least two meetings annually. Their national show, at a different venue each year, is probably the top show in Britain for rhododendrons. Members can purchase a range of books at reduced prices, seek specialist advice through the secretary, and gain free admission to Arduaine Gardens in Strathclyde. The society is also a chapter of the excellent American Rhododendron Society, and members automatically belong directly to the American society too. This gives them the scholarly quarterly journal, access to all the other ARS chapters (from Denmark and Holland to India), and the opportunity to raise seeds from the ARS seed bank.

Scottish Rock Garden Club
1 Hillcrest Road, Bearsden, Glasgow G61 2EB

CONTACT   Mrs J. Thomlinson
AIMS   To promote the cultivation of alpine and peat garden plants
MEMBERSHIP   4,500
SUBSCRIPTIONS   £7 single, £1.50 additional family member or junior membership; £9 overseas

Societies

SERVICES Lectures; seed scheme; library; publications; advice; awards; shows: Organised by nine of the local groups; journal: twice yearly; regional groups; slide library; annual conference

Founded in 1933 this is now the largest horticultural society in Scotland, with overseas members in thirty eight countries. There are regional groups in Ayr, Aberdeen, Belford, Dundee, Edinburgh, Glasgow, Inverness, Kircudbright, Newcastle, Oban, Penrith, Perth, Renfrew, Stirling, St Andrews and Thurso. Each local group is responsible for organising a programme of events including lectures, and some members also open their gardens. The society journal, The Rock Garden, appears twice a year: it is a well-produced and authoritative magazine which covers rock garden plants both in cultivation and in the wild. The seed exchange scheme is among the best of its kind.

The Sempervivum Society
11 Wingle Tye Road, Burgess Hill, West Sussex RH15 9HR

CONTACT Peter J. Mitchell
AIMS The promotion and cultivation of sempervivum and allied plants
MEMBERSHIP 300
SUBSCRIPTIONS £2.50 (1994)
SERVICES Library; publications; advice; journal

Members of the Sempervivum Society receive three newsletters or so a year. The society maintains a specialist library and produces a cultivar register for the genus. Specialist advice is available.

Sino-Himalayan Plant Association
81 Parlaunt Road, Slough, Berkshire SL3 8BE

CONTACT Chris Chadwell (Secretary)
AIMS To bring together and spread information on Sino-Himalayan flora
SUBSCRIPTIONS £8 UK, £10 overseas
SERVICES Associated garden; seed scheme; library; journal

Formed in 1990, this is an informal Association. Members receive a twice-yearly newsletter and meetings take place in varying venues around the country. There is a small display garden and a seed exchange.

The Tomato Growers Club
27 Meadowbrook, Old Oxted, Surrey RH8 9LT

CONTACT Colin Simpson
AIMS To collect and maintain a seed library of open-pollinated tomatoes
MEMBERSHIP 186
SUBSCRIPTIONS None; a minimum purchase of £10 seed or plants in first year only
SERVICES Seed scheme; journal

The club exists to preserve worthwhile strains of tomato varieties which are available to members for trialling: currently about 400 are on offer. There is an annual newsletter and seed catalogue in December. Members can get help with disease problems.

The Wild Flower Society
68 Outwoods Road, Loughborough, Leicestershire LE11 3LY

AIMS To encourage field botany
MEMBERSHIP 1,000
SUBSCRIPTIONS £8 individual; £3.50 junior (1994)
SERVICES Publications; advice; journal; regional groups; outings

Founded in 1886. Activity revolves around their Field Botanists Diary (£5), which contains lists of species. Members are encouraged to record their findings, and there are regular field meetings in summer. The Wild Flower Magazine is circulated three times a year. There is a branch structure, and branch secretaries help with and advise on recording and identification. Young people are particularly encouraged.

Regional Societies

Avon Gardens Trust
9 Mansard Close, Bath, Avon BA2 5LW

CONTACT Andrew King (Secretary)
SUBSCRIPTIONS £7.50 individual, £10 family
SERVICES Lectures; publications; journal; outings

The trust works to conserve the county's gardens through monitoring planning applications and advising owners on surveys and restoration plans. Garden visits and other events are staged for their members. Parks and Gardens of Avon by Stuart Harding and David Lambert was published in 1994.

BBONT
3 Church Cowley Road, Rose Hill, Oxford OX4 3JR
☎ 01865 775476

CONTACT Jacky Akam
MEMBERSHIP 8,000
SUBSCRIPTIONS £16 individual, £24 joint
SERVICES Lectures; publications; advice; journal; regional groups; outings

Berkshire, Buckinghamshire and Oxfordshire Naturalists Trust has over ninety reserves across the three counties, including Bowdown Woods, Dancersend and the Warburg Reserve.

Cheshire Wildlife Trust
Grebe House, Reaseheath, Nantwich, Cheshire CW5 6DA
☎ 01270 610180

CONTACT Mr C. Storey
SUBSCRIPTIONS £16 individual, £18 joint
SERVICES Lectures; publications; advice; journal; regional groups; outings; ecological consultancy

Formerly the Cheshire Conservation Trust, the Trust manages 30 reserves including Red Rocks Marsh and Swettenham Meadows.

Cleveland Wildlife Trust
Bellamy House, Unit 2a, Brighouse Business Village, Riverside Park, Middlesborough, Cleveland TS2 1RT
☎ 01642 253716
SUBSCRIPTIONS £12 individual, £15 joint (1994)
SERVICES Lectures; publications; advice; journal; outings

Formed in 1979 to protect wildlife in the county. They have 13 reserves in hand, including the deciduous woodland of Saltburn Gill.

Cornwall Gardens Society
Top Meadow, St Germans Road, Callington, Cornwall PL17 7EN

CONTACT Hon. General Secretary
AIMS To foster a love and knowledge of plants and gardening
MEMBERSHIP 1,400
SUBSCRIPTIONS £10 individual
SERVICES Lectures; publications; advice; shows; journal; outings; garden openings

A scaled down model of the RHS, with an excellent magazine, good bulletins and a famous show at the end of March. They also organise a garden opening scheme.

Cornwall Gardens Trust
Sweet Thymes, Rose, Truro, Cornwall TR4 9PQ

CONTACT Membership Secretary
AIMS To preserve, enhance and recreate the gardens of Cornwall
SUBSCRIPTIONS £8 individual and joint, £10 gardens and schools, £150 patron
SERVICES Lectures; associated gardens; publications; advice; awards; journal; outings

Formed in 1988. Carries out conservation and preservation work, and organises special events and garden visits for its members.

Cornwall Wildlife Trust
Five Acres, Allet, Truro, Cornwall TR4 9DJ
☎ 01872 73939

CONTACT Trevor Edwards
MEMBERSHIP 4,500
SUBSCRIPTIONS £15 individual, £1 each for additional family members
SERVICES Lectures; publications; advice; journal; outings

The trust has 36 nature reserves covering 3,000 acres. Good sites for botanists include Peters Wood and Ventongimps Moor.

Derbyshire Wildlife Trust
Elvaston Castle, Derby DE72 3EP
☎ 01332 756610
SUBSCRIPTIONS £12 individual, £15 family (1994)
SERVICES Lectures; publications; advice; journal; outings

The trust administers 49 reserves, including Cromford Canal and Spring Wood. DWT publishes Fran Hill's *Wildlife Gardening* (£4.50), and has a series of open gardens in the summer.

Devon Gardens Trust
Lucombe House, Devon County Council, County Hall, Exeter, Devon EX2 4QW
☎ 01884 253803

CONTACT Secretary
AIMS To preserve the gardens of Devon
SUBSCRIPTIONS £5 individual, £8 joint (1994)
SERVICES Lectures; advice; journal; outings

The trust surveys Devon gardens, and works to protect their future. Members benefit from special garden visits and seminars, and are kept informed of the trust's research and conservation work.

Dorset Perennial Group
Ivy Cottage, Aller Lane, Ansty, Dorchester, Dorset DT2 7PX

CONTACT Hon. Secretary
MEMBERSHIP 320
SUBSCRIPTIONS £1
SERVICES Lectures; seed scheme; library; journal; outings

Dorset-based society which used to be the local Hardy Plant Society group: they are no longer connected with the HPS. The programme includes garden visits and talks.

Dorset Wildlife Trust
15 North Square, Dorchester DT1 1HY
☎ 01305 264620   FAX 01305 251120

CONTACT Conservation Officer
MEMBERSHIP 6,800
SUBSCRIPTIONS £12.50 individual, £6 each additional person
SERVICES Lectures; publications; advice; journal; special interest and regional groups; outings

The trust looks after 26 nature reserves including Fontmell Down and Kingcombe Meadows. A Wildlife Garden is being established at Preston near Weymouth.

Dyfed Wildlife Trust
7 Market Street, Haverfordwest, Dyfed SA61 1NF
☎ 01437 765462   FAX 01437 767163

CONTACT Margaret Brooks
MEMBERSHIP 3,000
SERVICES Lectures; publications; advice; journal; outings

The trust, the second oldest in the country, manages 65 reserves including the acid heath of Dowrog Common. The Welsh Wildlife Centre has opened at Cilgerran near Cardigan. The 200 acre reserve includes meadows, a reedbed, woodland and fresh and salt-water marsh.

Essex Wildlife Trust
Fingringhoe Wick Nature Reserve, South Green Road, Fingringhoe, Colchester, Essex CO5 7DN
☎ 01206 729678   FAX 01206 729298
MEMBERSHIP 13,300
SUBSCRIPTIONS £15 individual, £18 joint
SERVICES Lectures; associated gardens; publications; advice; journal; regional groups; outings

The trust manages 80 reserves and has 5 conservation centres. Its reserves include the Danbury complex and Fingringhoe Wick. The trust also sells organic compost and woodchips and gives wildlife gardening advice.

Federation of Edinburgh & District Allotments & Gardens
2 South House Avenue, Edinburgh EH17 8EA
☎ 0131 664 1601
CONTACT Secretary
AIMS To promote the interests of allotment and garden associations in Edinburgh
MEMBERSHIP 25 sites
SUBSCRIPTIONS £20 per site
SERVICES Seed scheme; advice; shows; journal; discounts on garden supplies

The Federation of Edinburgh & District Allotments & Gardens Associations represents about 1,300 individuals on 25 sites. Its main efforts recently have been directed at improving the management and facilities on council run sites, and at making allotments part of the city's leisure provisions. A newsletter is circulated about three times a year and members can obtain seed through the federation. The annual flower and vegetable show is held on the last Saturday in August. Informal advice is available through other members, and they are planning to extend the range of membership services offered.

Friends of Brogdale
The Brogdale Horticultural Trust, Brogdale Farm, Faversham, Kent ME13 8XZ
☎ 01795 535286   FAX 01795 531710
AIMS Fruit research and conservation
SUBSCRIPTIONS £15 ordinary, £25 joint
SERVICES Lectures; advice; journal

The Brogdale Experimental Horticultural Station was bought from the government by the Brogdale Trust in 1991 to safeguard its work. It carries out commercial research and trialling, and maintains exceptional reference collections of fruit varieties, including over 2,300 different apples. Friends receive free entry to the site, priority booking for events, and access to a Friday afternoon information line. There is also a quarterly newsletter.

Friends of the Royal Botanic Garden, Edinburgh
The Royal Botanic Garden, Inverleith Row, Edinburgh EH3 5LR
CONTACT Secretary
AIMS To support the garden and raise funds for its activities
SUBSCRIPTIONS £15 individual; £20 family
SERVICES Lectures; associated gardens; journal

The Friends raise funds for and promote the work of the Royal Botanic Garden, Edinburgh. There is no admission charge to this great garden, but friends have free entry to the three regional gardens (Logan, Dawyck and Younger). There is a regular newsletter, and a series of lectures and other social events.

Friends of the Royal Botanic Gardens, Kew
Cambridge Cottage, Kew Green, Kew, Richmond, Surrey TW9 3AB
☎ 0181 332 5922   FAX 0181 332 5901
CONTACT Dianne Owens
AIMS Fund raising for Royal Botanic Gardens, Kew
MEMBERSHIP 24,000
SUBSCRIPTIONS £32 individual, £43 family, concessions for OAPs & students
SERVICES Lectures; associated gardens; shows; journal; discounts in Kew and Wakehurst Place shops; guest passes

The Friends of the Royal Botanic Gardens, Kew is a relatively new organisation: its aim is to raise funds for Kew's work, hence the highish subscription. That said, free entry to Kew and Wakehurst Place is a valuable benefit for regular visitors, and many will enjoy helping the scientific and conservation work which is carried out from Kew. The Friends' journal *Kew*, published three times a year, is colourful and outstandingly good. Lectures are given monthly throughout the year, and there is an annual plant auction in the autumn. Friends receive discounts on shop purchases, and six complimentary day passes to the gardens for their guests.

Glamorgan Wildlife Trust
Fountain Road, Tondu, Bridgend CF32 0EH
☎ 01656 724100
SUBSCRIPTIONS £12 joint (1994)
SERVICES Lectures; publications; advice; journal; regional groups; outings

The Glamorgan Wildlife Trust administers 47 reserves from woodland to coastal sites, including reserves on the Gower peninsula and Melincourt Falls.

Gloucestershire Gardens & Landscape Trust
Sunny Crest, Eden's Hill, Upleadon, Newent, Gloucestershire GL18 1EE
CONTACT Secretary

120 Societies

AIMS To conserve gardens and landscape
SUBSCRIPTIONS £12 individual, £20 joint
SERVICES Lectures; advice; journal; outings

The trust exists to protect valuable gardens and landscapes. As well as conservation work it has a programme of lectures, garden visits and other events for members.

Gwent Wildlife Trust
16 White Swan Court, Monmouth, Gwent NP5 3NY
SUBSCRIPTIONS £12 individual, £16.50 joint
SERVICES Lectures; publications; advice; journal; outings

The trust was started in 1963 and now has over thirty reserves including Magor Marsh, its first purchase, and Cleddon Shoots.

Hampshire Gardens Trust
Jermyns House, Jermyns Lane, Ampfield, Romsey, Hampshire SO51 0QA
☎ 01794 367752 (mornings)   FAX 01794 368520
CONTACT Secretary
AIMS To care for Hampshire's gardens and parks
SUBSCRIPTIONS £10 individual, £15 joint
SERVICES Lectures; library; advice; journal; outings; research into Hampshire's historic gardens and landscapes

The first of the county gardens trusts, formed with help from Hampshire County Council in 1984. The trust is active in conservation and education work, and has a full programme of events for members also.

Herefordshire Nature Trust
25 Castle Street, Hereford HR1 2NW
☎ 01432 356872
SUBSCRIPTIONS £12 individual, £15 joint (1994)
SERVICES Publications; advice; journal; regional groups; outings

The trust manages over 40 reserves in the county, including those at Great Doward and the woods at Lea and Pagets.

Herts & Middlesex Wildlife Trust
Grebe House, St Michaels Street, St Albans, Hertfordshire AL3 4SN
SUBSCRIPTIONS £15 individual, £20 joint
SERVICES Lectures; publications; advice; journal; outings

The trust looks after some 44 reserves including Old Park Wood and the old chalk downland of Therfield Heath.

Isle of Wight Gardens Trust
Cassies, Billingham, Newport, Isle of Wight PO30 3HD
CONTACT Membership Secretary
SUBSCRIPTIONS £5 individual, £7.50 joint (1994)
SERVICES Lectures; journal; outings

The trust helps to record the island's parks and gardens and to assist in their conservation. Talks and garden visits are staged for members, and they can also get involved in conservation work.

Kent Trust for Nature Conservation
Tyland Barn, Sandling, Maidstone, Kent ME14 3BD
☎ 01622 662012   FAX 01622 671390
CONTACT The Public Relations Officer
SUBSCRIPTIONS £19.50 individual, £24.50 family
SERVICES Lectures; publications; advice; journal; regional groups; outings

The Kent Trust looks after more than 40 reserves including Yockletts Bank, Sladden Wood, Park Gate Down and Hothfield Common.

Leicestershire and Rutland Trust for Nature Conservation
1 West Street, Leicester LE1 6UU
☎ 0116 2553904
SUBSCRIPTIONS £15 individual, £5 each additional person (1994)
SERVICES Lectures; publications; advice; journal; regional groups; outings

The trust manages 37 reserves including Cribb's Meadow and the woodland at Prior's Coppice.

The Lincolnshire Trust for Nature Conservation
Banovallum House, Manor House Street, Horncastle, Lincolnshire LN9 5HF
☎ 01507 526667   FAX 01507 525732
CONTACT Mary Edwards, Promotions Officer
MEMBERSHIP 9,000
SUBSCRIPTIONS £15 individual, £20 joint
SERVICES Lectures; publications; advice; journal; regional groups; outings

The trust (one of the RSNC wildlife trusts) manages over 100 sites including Little Scrubbs Meadow in the Wolds and the dunes at Saltfleetby-Theddlethorpe.

Montgomeryshire Wildlife Trust
Collot House, 20 Severn Street, Welshpool, Montgomeryshire SY21 7AD
☎ 01938 555654
SUBSCRIPTIONS £10 individual, £12 joint
SERVICES Lectures; publications; advice; journal; regional groups; outings

The trust has 12 reserves under management including Llyn Mawr, Roundton Hill and Dyfnant Meadows.

Norfolk Naturalists Trust
72 Cathedral Close, Norwich NR1 4DF
☎ 01603 625540
CONTACT C. Patrick
MEMBERSHIP 14,000
SUBSCRIPTIONS £16 individual, £20 joint

Societies 121

SERVICES Lectures; publications; advice; journal; regional groups; outings

The trust looks after 40 reserves across the county including East Wretham Heath in the Breckland and the pingos (glacial craters) of Thompsons Heath.

North of England Horticultural Society
4a South Park Road, Harrogate, North Yorkshire HG1 5QU

CONTACT Mr A. Ravenscroft
AIMS The promotion of horticulture
MEMBERSHIP 65
SUBSCRIPTIONS £18
SERVICES Publications; shows

The North of England Horticultural Society is the organiser of the two annual shows in Harrogate. This year the Spring Flower Show runs from 20 – 23 April, and the Great Autumn Flower Show takes place from 15-17 September. The society publishes a show directory for each show. Many national, regional and amateur societies attend the shows and are able to provide specialist advice on request.

The North of England Rose, Carnation and Sweet Pea Society
94 Hedgehope Road, Westerhope, Newcastle upon Tyne NE5 4LA

CONTACT General Secretary
AIMS To further interest in the three named flowers, and gardening in general
MEMBERSHIP 300
SUBSCRIPTIONS £2.50
SERVICES Lectures; library; publications; advice; awards; shows; journal; outings

The society – Rosecarpe, for short – was founded in 1938. Its interests extend beyond its three main flowers. Members can attend the regular meetings, usually on the first Monday of most months in the Civic Centre, Gateshead, for lectures or demonstrations. The four shows play an important part in the society's life, notably the Gateshead Spring and Summer Flower Shows organised in association with the Metropolitan Borough Council, and two Rosecarpe Flower Shows. Trophies are presented at all shows. An annual year book is produced, and members can also borrow the society's books and videos, and draw on the advice of the society's experts. Rosecarpe attends other shows and horticultural college events, and is affiliated to the national Rose, Carnation, Sweet Pea and Daffodil societies.

North Wales Wildlife Trust
376 High Street, Bangor, Gwynedd LL57 1YE
☎ 01248 351541

SUBSCRIPTIONS £12 individual, £17 joint
SERVICES Lectures; publications; advice; journal; outings

The trust has 33 reserves in North Wales including mixed woodland at Ddol Uchaf and the dunes of Morfa Bychan.

Northamptonshire Wildlife Trust
Lings House, Billing Lings, Northampton NN3 4BE
☎ 01604 405285

SUBSCRIPTIONS £12 individual, £16 joint (1994)
SERVICES Lectures; publications; advice; journal; outings

The trust looks after 1,500 acres spread over 40 sites. Reserves include High Wood and Meadow and Short Wood.

Nottinghamshire Wildlife Trust
310 Sneinton Dale, Nottingham NG3 7DN
☎ 0115 9588242   FAX 0115 9243175

CONTACT J. Ellis
MEMBERSHIP 3,100
SUBSCRIPTIONS £15 individual, £20 joint
SERVICES Lectures; publications; advice; journal; regional groups; outings

Formed in 1963. The trust looks after 50 reserves including Tresswell Wood and Eakring meadows.

Radnorshire Wildlife Trust
Warwick House, High Street, Llandrindod Wells, Powys LD1 6AG
☎ 01597 823298   FAX 01597 823298

CONTACT Gill Lowing
SUBSCRIPTIONS £12 individual, £15 joint, £8 unwaged
SERVICES Lectures; publications; advice; journal; regional groups; outings

In this sparsely populated county the trust manages reserves which include Bailey Einon and the newly acquired Pentrosfa Mire. There is an Information Centre and shop in Llandrindod Wells.

The Royal Caledonian Horticultural Society
28 Silverknowes Southway, Edinburgh EH4 5PX
☎ 0131 336 5488   FAX 0131 336 1847

CONTACT Hon. Secretary
AIMS The improvement of horticulture in all its branches
MEMBERSHIP 750
SUBSCRIPTIONS £10 individual, £12.50 family
SERVICES Lectures; library; publications; advice; awards; shows; journal; special interest or regional groups; outings

The Royal Caledonian Horticultural Society publishes an annual journal, and a newsletter *Preview* three times a year. There is a regular lecture programme, fortnightly from October to April, whilst in the summer months a series of garden visits takes place. The society's president is the custodian of their library. Three annual shows are organised – spring, summer and autumn – and the society presents two prestigious awards: the

Queen Elizabeth, the Queen Mother Medal, and the Scottish Horticultural Medal.

The Scottish Allotments and Gardens Society
14/1 Hoseasons Gardens, Edinburgh, Lothian EH4 7HQ
CONTACT   The Secretary
AIMS   To promote the interests of allotment holders
MEMBERSHIP   780
SUBSCRIPTIONS   Individuals £1; Sites £1 per plot
SERVICES   Seed scheme; advice; awards; journal; grants for gardeners

Long-established organisation which promotes the interests of allotment holders and societies. You can either join as an individual or as an entire site, in which case your subscription depends on the number of plots. There is a bi-monthly newsletter, and a discount seed scheme. SAGS also receives funds to assist needy gardeners with the upkeep of their plots.

Scottish Wildlife Trust
Cramond House, Cramond Glebe Road, Edinburgh EH4 6NS
CONTACT   Development Officer
MEMBERSHIP   10,000
SUBSCRIPTIONS   £15 individual, £25 joint
SERVICES   Lectures; publications; advice; journal; regional groups; outings

Formed in 1964, the national wildlife conservation body in Scotland. They have over 80 reserves under management including Red Moss of Balerno, Rahoy Hills and Seaton Cliffs.

Somerset Gardens Trust
St Peter's Vicarage, 62 Eastwick Road, Taunton, Somerset TA2 7HD
CONTACT   Membership Secretary
SUBSCRIPTIONS   £10 individual, £15 joint (1994)
SERVICES   Lectures; journal; outings

Works to conserve and protect Somerset's parks and gardens. As well as conservation and education work, talks and garden visits are arranged.

Somerset Wildlife Trust
Fyne Court, Broomfield, Bridgwater, Somerset TA5 2EQ
☎ 01823 451587
CONTACT   Stephanie Leland
MEMBERSHIP   8,100
SUBSCRIPTIONS   £12 individual, £2 for additional members
SERVICES   Lectures; associated gardens; library; publications; advice; shows; journal; special interest and regional groups; outings; wildflower gardening group

The trust now has 60 reserves under management, including Greater Westhay in the Somerset Levels. There is a wildflower gardening group.

Staffordshire Gardens & Parks Trust
c/o Planning Department, South Staffordshire District Council, Wolverhampton Road, Codsall, Wolverhampton WV8 1PX
CONTACT   Secretary
AIMS   To record and encourage the conservation of parks and gardens
SUBSCRIPTIONS   £7.50 individual, £10 joint
SERVICES   Lectures; advice; journal; outings; training; exhibitions

The trust aims to record the county's most valuable gardens and work for their conservation. Members can assist in this task, and take part in study visits. Meetings and lectures are held in Stafford.

Staffordshire Wildlife Trust
Coutts House, Sandon ST18 0DN
☎ 01889 503534   FAX 01889 508422
CONTACT   Pauline Robinson
MEMBERSHIP   2,515
SUBSCRIPTIONS   £12 individual, £15 family
SERVICES   Lectures; journal; regional groups; outings

Part of the RSNC partnership. Over 1,100 acres of land in 30 reserves, including the wetland reserves Loynton Moss, Woodseaves and Branston Water Park.

Suffolk Wildlife Trust
Brooke House, The Green, Ashbocking, Ipswich, Suffolk IP6 9JY
☎ 01473 890089
SUBSCRIPTIONS   £16 individual, £17 joint
SERVICES   Publications; advice; journal; outings; education

The largest of the county wildlife trusts, with 75 reserves. A current concern is the effect of ground water levels on many of these reserves.

Surrey Gardens Trust
c/o Planning Department, Surrey County Council, County Hall, Kingston on Thames, Surrey KT1 2DT
☎ 0181 541 9419
CONTACT   Secretary
MEMBERSHIP   200
SUBSCRIPTIONS   £10 individual, £15 joint
SERVICES   Lectures; advice; journal; outings; research; restoration work

Members receive a twice yearly newsletter, and there is a programme of lectures and garden visits. Those wanting more active involvement may train as recorders, carry out archive research and assist on garden improvement projects.

Surrey Wildlife Trust
School Lane, Pirbright, Woking, Surrey GU24 0JN
SUBSCRIPTIONS   £18 individual, £24 family
SERVICES   Lectures; publications; advice; journal; regional groups; outings

The Surrey Wildlife Trust looks after 24 nature reserves including Nower Wood and the Graeme Hendrey Wood.

Sussex Wildlife Trust
Woods Mill, Henfield, West Sussex BN5 9SD
CONTACT   Woods Mill Manager
MEMBERSHIP   7,500
SUBSCRIPTIONS   £12 individual, £8.50 joint (each)
SERVICES   Lectures; publications; advice; journal; regional groups; outings

Formed in 1961, the trust now looks after 37 separate nature reserves including The Mens, over 7,000 acres in total. Among the attractions at the Woods Mill headquarters is managed hazel coppice.

Urban Wildlife Trust, The West Midlands Wildlife Campaign
Unit 310 Jubilee Trades Centre, 130 Pershore Street, Birmingham B5 6ND
☎ 0121 666 7474   FAX 0121 622 6443
CONTACT   Wendy Burnett
MEMBERSHIP   450
SUBSCRIPTIONS   £11.50, £8
SERVICES   Publications; advice; journal; wildflower nursery

Urban group which encourages and advises on the formation of wildlife areas. They have an environmental centre at Winson Green, and a wildflower nursery.

Wakefield & North of England Tulip Society
70 Wrenthorpe Lane, Wrenthorpe, Wakefield, West Yorkshire WF2 0PT
CONTACT   Hon. Secretary
AIMS   The growing, breeding and showing of English florist tulips
MEMBERSHIP   300
SUBSCRIPTIONS   £4 individual; £5 family
SERVICES   Seed scheme; publications; awards; shows; journal; outings

Long-established society, devoted to florist tulips. They publish an annual journal and hold two shows each year: at Wrenthorpe on 6 May and at Normanton on 20 May this year (contact the secretary to check). Other events include formal and informal meetings and garden visits. Surplus bulbs are distributed in October. *The English Tulip and its History* is available from the society, as are slide lectures.

Warwickshire Wildlife Trust
Brandon Marsh Nature Centre, Brandon Lane, Coventry CV3 3GW
☎ 01203 302912   FAX 01203 639556
SUBSCRIPTIONS   £15 individual, £19 joint
SERVICES   Lectures; publications; advice; journal; regional groups; outings; environmental consultancy

Formerly the Warwickshire Nature Conservation Trust. They manage over 40 reserves including Ryton Woods and Ufton Fields.

Welsh Historic Gardens Trust
Coed-y-Ffynnon, Lampeter Valley, Narberth SA67 8UJ
☎ 01834 83396   FAX 01834 83396
CONTACT   The Trust Secretary
AIMS   To assist in and initiate conservation of gardens and designed landscapes in Wales
MEMBERSHIP   500
SUBSCRIPTIONS   £10 individuals, £15 family
SERVICES   Lectures; advice; journal; regional groups; outings

Through the trust office and local branches this organisation assists and initiates the conservation of important gardens, parks and landscapes. Members can become involved in research, surveying and other conservation work which is carried out at branch level.

The Wildlife Trust for Bedfordshire & Cambridgeshire
Enterprise House, Maris Lane, Trumpington, Cambridge CB2 2LE
☎ 01223 846363   FAX 01223 846085
CONTACT   Suzanne Donovan, Publicity Officer
MEMBERSHIP   8,500
SUBSCRIPTIONS   £13 individual, £16 joint
SERVICES   Lectures; publications; advice; journal; regional groups; outings

Nearly ninety reserves under management, including Totternhoe Knolls and Hayley Wood. There are 15 local groups and other offices in Bedford and Luton.

Wildlife Trust for Bristol, Bath and Avon
Bristol Wildlife Centre, Jacob Wells Road, Bristol, Avon BS8 1DR
SUBSCRIPTIONS   £10 individual, £13 joint
SERVICES   Lectures; publications; advice; journal; outings

Formed in 1980, this is the new name for the Avon Wildlife Trust. 28 nature reserves including Brown's Folly above Bathford.

Wiltshire Gardens Trust
Treglisson, Crowe Lane, Freshford, Bath, Avon BA3 6EB
CONTACT   Hon. Secretary
MEMBERSHIP   595
SUBSCRIPTIONS   £10 individual, £15 joint
SERVICES   Lectures; seed scheme; library; publications; journal; special interest groups; outings

This group doubles as the county garden trust and (for an additional subscription) as the Wiltshire branch of the NCCPG. Their programme includes lectures and garden visits.

Wiltshire Wildlife Trust
18 – 19 High Street, Devizes, Wiltshire SN10 1AT
☎ 01380 725670   FAX 01380 729017
CONTACT   The Marketing Officer
MEMBERSHIP   5,000
SUBSCRIPTIONS   £16 individual, £20 joint
SERVICES   Lectures; publications; advice; journal; outings

Formerly the Wiltshire Trust for Nature Conservation. They look after nearly 40 reserves including a fritillary meadow at Upper Waterhay (late April).

Yorkshire Wildlife Trust
10 Toft Green, York, North Yorkshire YO1 1JT
SUBSCRIPTIONS   £17 individual, £25 joint
SERVICES   Lectures; publications; advice; journal; regional groups; outings

Founded in 1946, and now managing 59 nature reserves. Sites of interest to botanists include Grass Wood and Spurn Head.

Overseas

American Camellia Society
One Massee Lane, Fort Valley, Georgia 31030, USA
☎ 00 1 912-967-2358   FAX 00 1 912-967-2083
CONTACT   Helen Bryan
MEMBERSHIP   4,200
SUBSCRIPTIONS   US – $20 individual, $22.50 joint; non US – $21.50 individual, $24 joint
SERVICES   Lectures; associated gardens; library; publications; advice; awards; shows; journal; special interest and regional groups

The American Camellia Society is based in Massee Lane Gardens. Members have free admission to the gardens and greenhouses. They run workshops and courses. There is an extensive library, gift shop and gallery. The Society celebrates its 50th anniversary, 8 – 11 March.

American Hemerocallis Society
1454 Rebel Drive, Jackson, Mississippi 39211, USA
CONTACT   Membership Secretary
MEMBERSHIP   8,000
SERVICES   Associated gardens; seed scheme; publications; awards; shows; journal; special interest and regional groups

The National Convention will be 22 – 26 June, in Knoxville/Chattanooga, Tennessee.

American Hibiscus Society
P O Box 321540, Cocoa Beach, FL 32932-1540, USA
CONTACT   Executive Secretary
MEMBERSHIP   2,000
SERVICES   Lectures; seed scheme; publications; advice; awards; shows

The Annual Convention will be in Clearwater, Florida in June.

American Horticultural Society
7931 E. Blvd. Dr, Alex, VA 22308-130, USA

American Hosta Society
7802 NE 63rd Street, Vancouver, WA 98662, USA
CONTACT   Membership Secretary

American Iris Society
8426 Vinevalley Drive, Sun Valley, CA 91352, USA
CONTACT   Jeanne Clay Plank, Secretary
MEMBERSHIP   7,000
SERVICES   Lectures; associated gardens; seed scheme; library; publications; advice; awards; shows; journal; special interest and regional groups

A Commemorative Bulletin will mark the 75th anniversary celebrations of the society in May.

American Orchid Society
6000 South Olive Avenue, West Palm Beach, Florida 33405, USA
☎ 00 1 407-585-8666   FAX 00 1 407-585-0654
CONTACT   Lee S. Coke, Executive Director
MEMBERSHIP   28,500
SUBSCRIPTIONS $30 US; $36 non US
SERVICES   Lectures; library; publications; advice; awards; shows; journal; special interest and regional groups

American Rhododendron Society
P O Box 1380, Gloucester, VA 23061, USA
CONTACT   Executive Director

The Society is holding a 50th Celebration Convention in Portland, Oregon 10-14 May.

American Rock Garden Society
P O Box 67, Millwood, NY 10546, USA
☎ 00 1 914-762-2948
CONTACT   Executive secretary
MEMBERSHIP   4,500
SERVICES   Lectures; associated gardens; seed scheme; library; publications; awards; journal; special interest and regional groups

The annual meeting will be 6 – 8 June in Pittsfield MA.

American Rose Society
P O Box 30000, 8877 Jefferson-Paige Road, Shreveport, LA 71130-0030, USA
CONTACT   Membership Secretary

Australian Garden History Society
P O Box 972, Bowral, NSW 2576, Australia
CONTACT   Executive Officer

Bonsai Clubs International
2636 W Mission Road, 277, Tallahassee, FL 32304, USA
CONTACT   Virginia Ellerman

Botanical Society of South Africa
Kirstenbosch, Claremont, Cape Town 7735, South Africa
CONTACT Diana Peters

Cactus & Succulent Society of America
P O Box 3010, Santa Barbara, CA 93130, USA
CONTACT Louise Lippold

Cymbidium Society of America Inc
P O Box 2244, Orange, CA 92669, USA
CONTACT Membership Secretary
MEMBERSHIP 1,300
SERVICES Awards; journal; special interest and regional groups

The Cymbidium Congress will be held in March in conjunction with the Santa Barbara Orchid Show.

Gesellschaft der Heidefreunde
Tangstedter Landstraße 276, 2000 Hamburg 62, Germany
CONTACT Herr Fritz Kircher
German Heather society.

Gesellschaft der Staudenfreunde
Meisenweg 1, 65975 Hattersheim, Germany
CONTACT Geschaftsfuhrer (Secretary)
MEMBERSHIP 4,000
SUBSCRIPTIONS DM50 individual, DM75 joint
SERVICES Seed scheme; journal; special interest and regional groups

The German Perennial Society developed from the Iris and Lily Society but now encompasses all kinds of hardy perennials. There are regional and special interest groups which organise lectures and outings. Members receive the quarterly journal 'Der Staudengarten' and can take part in the seed scheme.

Holly Society of America Inc
11318 West Murdock, Wichita, KS 67212-6609, USA
CONTACT Hon. Secretary

International Aroid Society
P O Box 43-1853, Miami, FL 33143, USA
CONTACT Amy Donovan
MEMBERSHIP 400
SERVICES Publications; advice; awards; shows; journal; regional groups

The Society will have its show at the Fairchild Tropical Garden on 4 September.

International Lilac Society
P O Box 315, Rumford, ME 04276, USA
CONTACT Walter W. Oakes

International Palm Society
P O Box 368, Lawrence, KS 66044, USA
CONTACT Mrs Lynn McKamey

The Magnolia Society Inc
6616 81st Street, Cabin John, Maryland 20818, USA
☎ 00 1 301-320-4296
CONTACT Hon. Secretary
MEMBERSHIP 600
SERVICES Lectures; associated gardens; seed scheme; library; publications; advice; awards; journal; outings

Nederlandse Heidervereniging 'Ericultura'
Esdoornstraat 54, 6681 ZM Bemmel, Netherlands
CONTACT Mr J. Dahm
SERVICES
Dutch Heather society.

New Zealand Alpine Gardening Society
17 Courage Road, Amberley, Canterbury, New Zealand

New Zealand Fuchsia Society Inc
P O Box 11-082, Ellerslie, Auckland, New Zealand 5
CONTACT Miss Joan Byres

New Zealand Gladiolus Council
13 Ramanui Avenue, Hawera, Taranaka, New Zealand

North American Heather Society
P O Box 101, Highland View, Alstead, New Hampshire 03602, USA
CONTACT Hon. Secretary

North American Lily Society Inc
P O Box 272, Owatonna, MN 55060, USA
☎ 00 1 507-451-2170
CONTACT Hon. Secretary
MEMBERSHIP 1,500
SERVICES Seed scheme; library; publications; advice; awards; shows; journal; special interest and regional groups

The North American Lily Society Show will be 14-16 July in Edmonton, Alberta, Canada.

The Rock Garden Club Prague
Mimonska 12/639, 19000 Prague 9, Czech Republic

Rose Hybridizers Association
21 S. Wheaton Road, Horseheads, NY 14845, USA
☎ 00 1 607-562-8592
CONTACT Larry D. Peterson
MEMBERSHIP 425
SUBSCRIPTIONS $8 US, $10 non US
SERVICES Associated gardens; library; publications; advice; awards; journal

The Association meets twice yearly during the American Rose Society National Conventions.

La Société Française des Roses
Parc de la Tete d'Or, 69459 Lyon, France

Société Nationale d'Horticulture de France

84 rue de Grenelle, Paris 75007, France
☎ 00 331 45 48 81 00

The French equivalent of the RHS. There are eighteen different special groups. *Jardins de France*, their magazine, has 10 editions a year.

The Society for Growing Australian Plants

3 Currawang Place, Como West 2226, New South Wales, Australia
☎ 00 2 528 2683   FAX 00 2 528 2683
CONTACT   Hon. Secretary (NSW region)
MEMBERSHIP   4,000
SUBSCRIPTIONS $26 ordinary, $20 concessional, $44 overseas

SERVICES   Lectures; associated gardens; seed scheme; publications; advice; shows; journal; special interest and regional groups; outings

Verein Deutscher Rosenfreunde

Waldseestrasse 14, 76530 Baden-Baden, Germany
☎ 00 49 72 21/31202
CONTACT   Hanni Bastetsko
SUBSCRIPTIONS   DM42 individual, DM50 joint

The German Rose Society holds its Congress in Hildesheim, home of 1,000 year old rose from 6-10 July. Tjhere is a quarterly journal *Rosenbogen* and an annual yearbook.

German rose society.

Western Horticultural Society

P O Box 60507, Palo Alto, CA 94306, USA
CONTACT   Robert Young

9

Gardening Clubs

If you have recently moved to a new area, and want to join a local gardening club, it is sometimes difficult to know where to begin the search. Once you have found one, you will discover that the character and interests of clubs differ enormously. One may be run for people who want to know how to grow vegetables that will win prizes at the Village Show, while a neighbouring club is exclusively concerned with how to acquire rare plants and grow them in artistic colour sequences.

The local library or information centre is most people's starting point: clubs usually send details of their programme of forthcoming events to such institutions. The local newspaper will also publish subsequent reports of those meetings. *Garden News* also contains details of clubs events. If you encounter real problems in discovering a club locally, ask your County Horticultural College for help. The Royal Horticultural Society may also be willing to tell you the name of the nearest club among its many affiliates.

Suppose you fail to find a satisfactory gardening club locally. Why not consider starting your own with the help of a few like-minded friends? You will need to organise a regular time and venue for your events and you will have to think about such important matters as the constitution of the club, the costs and benefits of membership, and the need for third party insurance. That said, the greatest difficulty will be in finding good speakers at a reasonable price. Any reader who has been the secretary of a gardening club will know how taxing this task can prove.

One way to find good speakers is to ask among your friends for recommendations. Many people belong to more than one gardening club and will be able to recommend people that they would like to hear again. The specialist plant societies such as the Alpine Garden Society can also find people local to your society who may be able to talk about their specialisation.

However, the whole problem has been enormously simplified in recent years by *The Horticultural Speakers' Register*, published first by Barbara Abbs and now by the Royal Horticultural Society. It lists over 450 speakers who offer a total of more than 1,800 different lectures, a godsend for hard-pressed secretaries. Speakers are arranged alphabetically, rather than by subject, although it is quite easy to pick out the specialist experts. There are Bill Bossom, Ken Grapes and Colin Horner among others from the RNRS, for example, and Bryan Stevens, Edward Stiff and Dick and Lorna Swinbank among the fuchsia experts. Lecture fees range from nil to £500. For less than £50 you can procure a lecturer of the distinction of James Compton, Brian Halliwell or Tony Lowe, but you might have to pay up to £100 for Elizabeth Banks or Kay Sanecki, while Roy Lancaster will set you back at least £200, probably more. The register gives full details of how far each is prepared to travel, when he is available, and the equipment he brings or needs. Every club secretary should have a copy. The last edition was in 1993, though, so some fees and details may have changed.

10
Nurseries & Garden Centres

We have selected a range of nurseries from the smallest and most specialised to the largest of the garden centres. Between these poles there should be several to suit everyone's needs. There are three ways of finding them. In this section they are listed by county. We have used the post-1974 county names for consistency (so no Middlesex or Rutland), and have adopted the regional divisions of Scotland. The English counties are followed by Wales, Scotland, Northern Ireland, the Channel Islands, the Isle of Man and Eire. Where possible the entries are placed in their geographical counties rather than by their postal address to help those planning a visit. Strict alphabetical order has been followed here, so for example, the rose breeders R Harkness & Co are listed under 'R' and not 'H'. Alternatively, all the nurseries and garden centres appear in the index at the end of the book alphabetically. In the index, initials and prefixes are disregarded (so, 'Harkness & Co, R.'). Finally, the next section, Nursery Specialities, lists many of the nurseries by specialisation. The county name appears there to help you locate the entry in the main listing. We have restricted this list to true specialists: those with an excellent but general range are not included. These specialisations also appear in the main entry for each nursery or garden centre, where appropriate. Please note that the order in which the various specialisations are given is not necessarily a guide to their predominance at the nursery: that information will appear in the main body of each entry.

Mail order is an issue which splits the trade. Most garden centres will not offer this service, and nor will many traditional and smaller nurseries. We have indicated those who do. Buying by post, obviously, means you cannot inspect the plants first. You still have a right to expect healthy specimens nonetheless. Remember that posted plants are likely to be smaller than normal to save on space and postage costs. Your order will also probably be sent in the dormant season when the plant will be better able to cope with a journey through the postal system, and when the nurseryman is less busy. Trees are usually sent by road courier; roses travel cheaply in paper sacks; other plants need careful and time-consuming packing for which you will have to pay.

Some nurseries have demonstration and display gardens: these are mentioned. There are cross-references where necessary to the Gardens section. See also the publications of the National Gardens Scheme and Scotland's Garden Scheme: a number of nurseries open regularly for these charities. Where nurseries have indicated that they are holders of a NCCPG National Collection we have included this information: opening times and further details can be found in *The National Plant Collections Directory* which is available from the NCCPG, The Pines, Wisley Garden, Woking, Surrey GU23 6QB. Other useful publications are *The Plant Finder* for picking out stockists of individual genera and sources of a particular species; and a road atlas for tracking down the nursery site. Garden centres usually observe fixed opening times: traditional nurseries tend to open early and close at dusk; opening hours at smaller nurseries may depend on show and other commitments. Watch out for the effects of the new Sunday Trading laws in England and Wales: large nurseries and garden centres may only open for six hours on Sundays. Smaller nurseries face no restrictions. Of course, some nurseries only operate by mail order: they do not open at all. If in doubt, phone first.

Finally, do not forget that all the dialling codes in the UK will change from 15 April 1995. Most are altered by adding a '1' after the first '0'; five codes change completely. Also, the international code, for dialling abroad, becomes 00 (and not 010). You can use the new codes before 15 April, and we have adopted them throughout.

ENGLAND

AVON

A & A Phipps
62 Samuel White Road, Hanham, Bristol, Avon BS15 3LX
☎ 0117 9607591
CONTACT   Alan Phipps
LOCATION   Ask them for directions
OPEN   Phone first
SPECIALITIES   Cacti and succulents
NEW FOR 1995   Range always changing
CATALOGUE   SAE
MAIL ORDER   Yes; smallish plants only
REFRESHMENTS   Tea and biscuits

Cacti and succulent specialist with both a general and a collector's range of species. Telephone first before calling to make sure someone is in. They also sell seed-grown cacti and succulents to retail and wholesale outlets. The mail order list is issued in April, and they will be at the Bristol University Botanic Garden open days in July and September.

Arne Herbs
Limeburn Nurseries, Chew Magna, Bristol, Avon BS18 8QW
☎ 01275 333399
LOCATION   8 miles south of Bristol, just off B3130
OPEN   10 am – 5 pm, usually. Phone first
SPECIALITIES   Herbs; wild flowers
NEW FOR 1995   Salvias: *S. involucrata*, *S. blancoana*, *S. microphylla*, *S. dorisiana*; *Miscanthus sinensis*, *Onopordum nervosum*
CATALOGUE   £1.50
MAIL ORDER   Yes; no minimum order
DESIGN SERVICE   Arne Herbs

Twin ranges of herbs and native species which can be used for conservation schemes. Fresh-cut herbs available in season too. Advice service for customers. Consultancy for physic gardens.

Blackmore & Langdon
Stanton Nurseries, Pensford, Bristol, Avon BS18 4JL
☎ 01275 332300
CONTACT   Mrs Rosemary Langdon
LOCATION   8 miles south of Bristol on B3130, between A37 Wells road and A38
OPEN   9 am – 5 pm, daily
SPECIALITIES   Begonias; delphiniums, *Phlox*
NEW FOR 1995   New begonias
CATALOGUE   SAE
MAIL ORDER   Yes
SHOWS   Malvern Spring; Southport; Chelsea; BBC GW Live; Hampton Court
GIFT TOKENS   Own

This family business, started in 1901, is still run by the founder's grandchildren. Theirs is a long tradition of showy border plants, notably huge begonias and tall delphiniums. All plants are grown on site.

Brackenwood Garden Centre
131 Nore Road, Portishead, Bristol, Avon BS20 8DU
☎ 01275 843484   FAX 01275 843484
CONTACT   Manager
OPEN   9 am – 5.30 pm, Monday – Saturday; 10 am – 5.30 pm, Sundays. Closed over Christmas
MAIL ORDER   No
SHOP   Yes
REFRESHMENTS   Restaurant and tea room
GARDEN   8-acre woodland garden
DESIGN SERVICE   Brackenwood Garden Centre
GIFT TOKENS   HTA

Garden centre with a wide and constantly changing all-round range. Their florist runs regular flower arranging demonstrations. See also Brackenwood Plant Centre.

Brackenwood Plant Centre
Leigh Court Estate, Pill Road, Abbots Leigh, Bristol, Avon
☎ 01275 375292
CONTACT   J. Maycock or P. Gilmour
OPEN   10 am – 5 pm, spring and summer; 10 am – 4.30 pm, winter
SPECIALITIES   Bamboos; herbaceous perennials; shrubs
MAIL ORDER   No
SHOP   Yes
GARDEN   Wildlife lake with native aquatic species planted; display gardens
DESIGN SERVICE   Brackenwood Nurseries
GIFT TOKENS   HTA

All-round stock, grown at the site. There's also a lake, and display gardens are being created. See also Brackenwood Garden Centre.

C S Lockyer
70 Henfield Road, Coalpit Heath, Bristol, Avon BS17 2UZ
☎ 01454 772219
CONTACT   C. S. Lockyer
LOCATION   Near M4, J19: map in catalogue
OPEN   Most days; phone first
SPECIALITIES   Fuchsias
NEW FOR 1995   Fuchsias 'Barbara', 'Bornemann's Best', 'Crosby Serendipity', 'Fire Mountain', 'Lorna Swinbank', 'Machu Picchu', 'Stanley Cash'
CATALOGUE   3 first class stamps
MAIL ORDER   Yes

GARDEN   Demonstration gardens
SHOWS   RHS Westminster; Malvern Spring; Chelsea; BBC GW Live; Hampton Court
GIFT TOKENS   Own

A specialist fuchsia grower, with young plants of both tender and hardy varieties. Regular talks and demonstrations are held at the nursery to pass on the experience of over 35 years in the business.

Graham's Hardy Plants
Southcroft, North Road, Timsbury, Bath, Avon
BA3 1JN
☎ 01761 472187

CONTACT   Mr G. E. Nicholls
LOCATION   On B3115 in Timsbury
OPEN   10 am – 4.30 pm, Tuesday – Thursday, 1 April to 31 October. Telephone first
SPECIALITIES   Alpines
NEW FOR 1995   *Campanula piperi* 'Alba,' *Eritrichium nanum*
CATALOGUE   SAE
MAIL ORDER   Yes

A small alpine nursery specialising in rare species from North America. The selection of *Eriogonum* and *Penstemon* is particularly interesting for collectors. The nursery attends most AGS shows.

Hannays of Bath
Sydney Wharf Nursery, Bathwick, Bath, Avon
BA2 4ES
☎ 01225 462230

CONTACT   Spencer Hannay
OPEN   10 am – 5 pm, daily. Closed Tuesdays
SPECIALITIES   Herbaceous perennials
NEW FOR 1995   *Dierama*
CATALOGUE   £1.45
MAIL ORDER   No
GARDEN   Display borders
GIFT TOKENS   Own

A rich source of herbaceous plants and shrubs, mainly species. Recommended for both gardeners and collectors. Many plants are grown from seed collected by the Hannays, including *Dierama* species from South Africa. Keep an eye open for the results of trips to the Cape, Lesotho, Uganda, Spain and Nepal in 1993.

Jasmine Cottage Gardens
Jasmine Cottage, 26 Channel Road, Walton St Mary, Clevedon, Avon BS21 7BY
☎ 01275 871850

CONTACT   Margaret and Michael Redgrave
OPEN   Thursdays and by appointment
MAIL ORDER   No
GARDEN   Garden opens for NGS

Small quantities of tender perennials available – pretty cottage garden too.

Jekka's Herb Farm
Rose Cottage, Shellards Lane, Alveston, Bristol, Avon BS12 2SY
☎ 01454 418878   FAX 01454 418878

CONTACT   Mrs J. McVicar
OPEN   Mail order only
SPECIALITIES   Herbs; wild flowers
CATALOGUE   SAE plus £1
MAIL ORDER   Yes; no minimum order
SHOWS   RHS Westminster; Chelsea; BBC GW Live; Hampton Court

A comprehensive and interesting range of herbs and some wild flowers. The business is basically wholesale: retail trade is mail order only. *Jekka's Complete Herb Book* was published by Kyle Cathie in 1994.

Little Creek Nursery
39 Moor Road, Banwell, Weston super Mare, Avon BS24 6EF
☎ 01934 823739

CONTACT   Rhys and Julie Adams
LOCATION   3 miles from M5, J21
OPEN   10.30 am – 4.30 pm, Thursday – Friday, March to August. Phone first at other times
SPECIALITIES   Hellebores, cyclamen
CATALOGUE   3 first class stamps
MAIL ORDER   Yes; no minimum order
SHOWS   Malvern Spring

A small nursery which specialises in *Cyclamen* species (raised from seed), and *Helleborus*, with some perennials too. This year they attend the Bristol, Salisbury and Taunton shows. They hold part of the Cyclamen Society's NCCPG collection – mainly the early-flowering varieties.

Monocot Nursery
Jacklands, Jacklands Bridge, Tickenham, Clevedon, Avon BS21 6SG

CONTACT   Mike Salmon
OPEN   10 am – 6 pm, by appointment
SPECIALITIES   Bulbs; seeds
CATALOGUE   SAE
MAIL ORDER   Yes

Specialist nursery with an amazing collection of bulbous plants (including tubers, rhizomes and corms). The stock is mostly of species, and subspecies, grown from seed, frequently from named collectors and sources. The seed list appears in October. Nursery browsers will find items which are not in the catalogue.

Mount Pleasant Trees
Rockhampton, Berkeley, Avon GL13 9DU
☎ 01454 260348

CONTACT   G. Locke
LOCATION   In Avon, near the Gloucestershire border. Map in catalogue
OPEN   By appointment only
SPECIALITIES   Hedging; trees; *Tilia*

BERKSHIRE Nurseries & Garden Centres

CATALOGUE 3 second class stamps
MAIL ORDER No

Mainly native trees and shrubs for hedging and woodland use. In addition there is an eye-catching selection of specimen trees and shrubs for arboreta. The *Tilia* range is outstanding – the biggest in Europe. Good *Sequoiadendron* and *Ginkgo* collections are other highlights on this enticing list.

National Collection of Passiflora
Greenholm Nurseries Ltd, Kingston Seymour, Clevedon, Avon BS21 6XS
☎ 01934 833350 FAX 01934 833320

CONTACT R. J. R. Vanderplank
LOCATION Kingston Seymour
OPEN 9 am – 1 pm, 2 – 5 pm
SPECIALITIES *Passiflora*
CATALOGUE 2 first class stamps
MAIL ORDER Yes
SHOP Gifts
GARDEN Permanent display and exhibition of passion flowers
SHOWS BBC GW Live; Hampton Court
NCCPG NATIONAL COLLECTIONS *Passiflora*

Passion flowers only. A fascinating proposition for anyone in a position to grow them. The catalogue is detailed, and includes precise temperature requirements. Seeds from the collection are also sold.

Park Garden Centre
Over Lane, Almondsbury, Bristol, Avon BS12 4BP
☎ 01454 612247 FAX 01454 617559

CONTACT Mr J. Billings (plants) and Mrs J. Parrish (shop)
LOCATION North of Bristol, off A38
OPEN 9 am – 6 pm, summer; 9 am – 5 pm, winter, Monday – Saturday. 10 am – 4 pm, Sundays
SHOP Garden machinery, conservatory, Park Koi aquatics
REFRESHMENTS Coffee shop
GARDEN Demonstration rose garden and orchard
DESIGN SERVICE Park Garden Centre
GIFT TOKENS HTA; own

Garden centre with garden products, and machinery and aquatic centres on site. Agents for Hillier plants. Local delivery and design and landscaping services.

Wyevale Garden Centre
Hicks Gate, Keynsham, Bristol, Avon BS18 2AD
☎ 01179 778945 FAX 01179 776436

West Country Geraniums
Staunton Lane, Whitchurch, Bristol, Avon BS14 0QL
☎ 01275 832762

CONTACT Alan Pearce
LOCATION Map in catalogue
OPEN 2 – 5 pm, Monday – Saturday, 1 April to 30 June; phone first at other times

SPECIALITIES Pelargoniums
NEW FOR 1995 3 new pelargoniums
CATALOGUE 3 first class stamps
MAIL ORDER Yes
SHOWS Malvern Spring; Southport; Hampton Court

A selection of all types of pelargoniums is available, as young plants, by post; larger sizes at the nursery. They visit most major shows.

BEDFORDSHIRE

Bloms Bulbs Ltd
Primrose Nurseries, Park Lane, Sharnbrook, Bedfordshire MK44 1LW
☎ 01234 782424 FAX 01234 782495

CONTACT Miss N. Wood
OPEN 9 am – 5 pm, Monday – Friday. Also 9 am – 12 pm, Saturdays, September only
SPECIALITIES Bulbs
CATALOGUE On request
MAIL ORDER Yes
GARDEN Display at Chenies Manor, Buckinghamshire, see Gardens section
SHOWS Malvern Spring; Chelsea

Major bulb growers: their range covers hyacinth, daffodil, and tulip cultivars; they also have species and a wide selection of smaller bulbs.

BERKSHIRE

Bressingham Plant Centre
Dorney Court, Dorney, Windsor, Berkshire SL4 6QP
☎ 01628 669999 FAX 01628 669693

CONTACT Peter Freeman
LOCATION Dorney Court
OPEN 10 am – 5.30 pm, daily except Christmas and Boxing Day
SPECIALITIES Conifers; herbaceous perennials
CATALOGUE £2; see Bressingham Gardens Mail Order
MAIL ORDER As above
REFRESHMENTS Tea room
SHOWS Chelsea; BBC GW Live; Hampton Court
GIFT TOKENS Own

Blooms' first plant centre to be opened away from Norfolk: Alan Bloom inaugurated it in March 1993. They carry the huge range of perennials and conifers for which the company is renowned. The quality is also outstanding. Talks are held at the plant centre. Mail order is available directly from Norfolk: see Bressingham Gardens Mail Order.

Foxgrove Plants
Foxgrove, Enborne, Newbury, Berkshire RG14 6RE
☎ 01635 40554

CONTACT Louise Vockins
LOCATION West of Newbury

OPEN 10 am – 5 pm, Wednesday – Sunday, and Bank Holidays. Closed in August
SPECIALITIES Alpines; snowdrops
CATALOGUE 65p cheque
MAIL ORDER Yes
SHOWS RHS Westminster; Malvern Spring; Chelsea; BBC GW Live; Hampton Court

This small nursery carries a pleasing range of hardy and cottage-garden type plants. Their speciality is snowdrops: they have a number of species, forms and hybrids. The nursery will be at the Harlow, Gillingham and Exeter AGS shows. Plantings can be undertaken, and terracotta pans are available to order.

Gatehampton Nursery
Gatehampton Farm, Goring on Thames, Reading, Berkshire RG8 9LU
☎ 01491 872894

CONTACT Robin Cloke
OPEN 9.30 am – 6 pm, daily
SPECIALITIES Fuchsias
CATALOGUE 2 first class stamps
MAIL ORDER Yes

Fuchsia specialists with a range of 800 varieties besides bedding plants, shrubs and perennials. They have a picnic area by the River Thames, and fishing and camping are possible in summer.

Harrisons Delphiniums
Newbury Cottage, Playhatch, Reading, Berkshire RG4 9QN
☎ 01734 470810

CONTACT Len Harrison
OPEN 12.30 – 5 pm, daily, March to June
SPECIALITIES Delphiniums; seeds
NEW FOR 1995 New named delphiniums
CATALOGUE 1 first class stamp
MAIL ORDER Seeds only

A breeder and nurseryman: the source of the Southern series of *Delphinium elatum* strains. Plants can be collected during opening hours; seed is ready from August.

Henry Street
Swallowfield Road Nursery, Arborfield, Reading, Berkshire RG2 9JY
☎ 01734 761223   FAX 01734 761417

CONTACT Mr M. C. Goold
OPEN 9 am – 5.30 pm, Monday – Saturday; 10 am – 4 pm, Sundays
SPECIALITIES Bedding plants; roses
CATALOGUE On request
MAIL ORDER Yes; bare root only
GARDEN Rose fields open

Rose growers whose range covers all types, in mainly modern varieties. They also sell bedding plants, and carry a general stock at the garden centre.

Hollington Nurseries
Woolton Hill, Newbury, Berkshire RG15 9XT
☎ 01635 253908   FAX 01635 254990

CONTACT Judith and Simon Hopkinson
LOCATION 4 miles south of Newbury, off A343
OPEN 10 am – 5.30 pm, Monday – Saturday; 11 am – 5 pm, Sundays and Bank Holidays, March to September. 10 am – dusk, Monday – Saturday, October to December
SPECIALITIES Climbers; herbs
CATALOGUE SAE plus 50p
MAIL ORDER No
SHOP Herb products
REFRESHMENTS Tea room (summer only)
GARDEN Display gardens in walled garden
DESIGN SERVICE Hollington Nurseries
GIFT TOKENS Own

A large range of herbs and scented plants in containers, as well as roses to plant with them. Herb and wild flower seeds too. They run courses, and have a garden planning service. A series of informal lecture days are organised in June, on using herbs in cookery.

M V Fletcher
70 South Street, Reading, Berkshire RG1 4RA
☎ 01734 571814

CONTACT M. V. Fletcher
OPEN Mail order only or by appointment
SPECIALITIES Mosses
CATALOGUE 2 first class stamps
MAIL ORDER Yes

Something well outside the ambit of the horticultural trade. Mr Fletcher is a private collector who only sells mosses and hepatics (liverworts).

BUCKINGHAMSHIRE

A J Palmer & Son
Denham Court Nursery, Denham Court Drive, Denham, Uxbridge, Buckinghamshire UB9 5PG
☎ 01895 832035

CONTACT Sheila or John Palmer
LOCATION Middle of New Buckinghamshire golf course, near Denham country park
OPEN 9 am – 5 pm, Monday – Saturday, 9.30 am – 1 pm, Sundays, during spring; 9 am – dusk, daily, summer; 9 am – 5 pm, Monday – Saturday, 9.30 am – 1 pm, Sundays, autumn. Closed January
SPECIALITIES Roses
NEW FOR 1995 Rose 'Chatsworth' (1995 Rose of the Year)
CATALOGUE On request
MAIL ORDER Yes; collection only for standards
GARDEN Rose fields
GIFT TOKENS HTA

Specialist rose growers with a range of mainly modern varieties. Opening times vary with the seasons and availability. Containerised plants are available in spring,

BUCKINGHAMSHIRE Nurseries & Garden Centres

from about March to June. From July to October the show field is open for viewing (near the Denham roundabout off the A40). Most of the stock is sold bare rooted in November.

Buckingham Nurseries and Garden Centre
14 Tingewick Road, Buckingham, Buckinghamshire MK18 4AE
☎ 01280 813556   FAX 01280 815491

CONTACT Mrs P. L. Brown
LOCATION 1½ miles west of Buckingham, on A421
OPEN Summer: 8.30 am – 6 pm, Monday – Friday, 9.30 am – 6 pm, Sundays; winter: 8.30 am – 5 pm, Monday – Friday, 9.30 am – 5.30 pm, Sundays
SPECIALITIES Hedging; trees
CATALOGUE On request (September)
MAIL ORDER Yes
SHOP Retail garden shop
GIFT TOKENS HTA

The nursery produces bare root hedging and tree plants for ornamental and forestry use. A selection of container plants, including ones not listed in the catalogue, is sold from the garden centre.

Butterfields Nursery
Harvest Hill, Bourne End, Buckinghamshire SL8 5JJ
☎ 01628 525455
LOCATION Off B476
OPEN 9 am – 5 pm, usually
SPECIALITIES Dahlias; orchids, pleiones
CATALOGUE SAE
MAIL ORDER Yes; pleiones only
GARDEN Dahlia display during season
SHOWS RHS Westminster; Malvern Spring; Chelsea
NCCPG NATIONAL COLLECTIONS *Pleione*

Butterfields has two main but very different specialities: pleiones and dahlias. The *Pleione* species are backed up by an impressive list of hybrids. The dahlia range consists of named varieties for showing, flower arranging and garden use. You are advised to phone before visiting, in case they are at a show.

Chenies Garden Centre
Chenies, Rickmansworth, Buckinghamshire WD3 6EN
☎ 01494 764545   FAX 01494 762216
LOCATION Between Rickmansworth and Amersham, on A404
OPEN 8.30 am – 6 pm, Monday – Saturday, summer; 8.30 am – 5 pm, Monday – Saturday, winter; 10.30 am – 4.30 pm, Sundays
SHOP Garden buildings, fencing, paving, sundries
GIFT TOKENS HTA

General garden centre, with a particularly large display of garden buildings. A design service is available through their sister company, Chenies Landscapes (see entry in Professional Services section).

The Conifer Garden
Hare Lane Nursery, Little Kingshill, Great Missenden, Buckinghamshire HP16 0EF
☎ 01494 890624

CONTACT Mr & Mrs M. P. S. Powell
OPEN 11 am – 4.30 pm, Tuesday – Saturday
SPECIALITIES Conifers
CATALOGUE 2 first class stamps
MAIL ORDER By arrangement
GIFT TOKENS Own

Specialists in conifers of all sizes. The stock is container-grown, and the choice is extensive (500). Talks for garden clubs can be arranged.

Great Gardens of England Ltd
Marlow Garden & Leisure Centre, Pump Lane South, Little Marlow, Buckinghamshire SL7 3RB
☎ 01628 482716   FAX 01628 898135

CONTACT Les Brown (Manager)
LOCATION Off A404, between M4 and M40
OPEN 9 am – 5.30 pm, Monday – Saturday; 10 am – 4 pm, Sundays
GIFT TOKENS HTA; own

Garden centre with a general range for indoor and outdoor gardening. Delivery service available.

Morehavens Camomile Nurseries
28 Denham Lane, Gerrards Cross, Buckinghamshire SL9 0EX
☎ 01494 871563

CONTACT Ann Farmer
OPEN Collection by arrangement
SPECIALITIES Camomile for lawns
CATALOGUE SAE
MAIL ORDER Yes; p & p included
GARDEN Gardens

Camomile lawns by post.

Tamarisk Nurseries
Wing Road, Stewkley, Leighton Buzzard, Buckinghamshire LU7 0JB
☎ 01525 240747   FAX 01525 240747

CONTACT Alan Cupit
LOCATION North Buckinghamshire, between Wing and Stewkley
OPEN 12 – 5 pm, Monday – Friday; 10 am – 6 pm, Saturdays and Sundays, and Bank Holidays
SPECIALITIES Air plants; cacti and succulents; carnivorous plants; conservatory plants; orchids
MAIL ORDER Yes

The range here includes cacti and airplants, as well as orchids, carnivorous plants, alpines and perennials. You are advised to phone first during the show season: they visit Capel Manor, Hatfield House, Suffolk Agricultural and the early and late Newbury shows among others.

Nurseries & Garden Centres CAMBRIDGESHIRE

Waddesdon Plant Centre & Nursery
Queen Street, Waddesdon, Aylesbury, Buckinghamshire HP18 0JW
☎ 01296 658586   FAX 01296 658852
CONTACT Mrs P. Wilson
LOCATION Between Aylesbury and Bicester on A41
OPEN 10 am – 5 pm, daily
DESIGN SERVICE Waddesdon Plant Centre & Nursery
GIFT TOKENS HTA

Bedding plants, herbs and herbaceous perennials. No longer connected with the nearby gardens.

Woodstock Orchids and Automations
Woodstock House, 50 Pound Hill, Great Brickhill, Milton Keynes, Buckinghamshire MK17 9AS
☎ 01525 261352   FAX 01525 261724
CONTACT Bill Gaskell
OPEN By appointment only
SPECIALITIES Orchids
CATALOGUE SAE
MAIL ORDER Yes
SHOWS RHS Westminster; Malvern Spring; Harrogate (Spring); Southport; Chelsea; Hampton Court; Harrogate (Autumn)

Specialists for orchids, wholesale and retail. They advise and instruct would-be growers.

CAMBRIDGESHIRE

Arbor Exotica
The Estate Office, Hall Farm, Weston Colville, Cambridgeshire CB1 5PE
☎ 01223 290328   FAX 01223 290650
CONTACT Mrs E. J. Capewell
LOCATION The nursery is at West Wratting Park, West Wratting, Cambridge (01223 290316)
OPEN By appointment only
SPECIALITIES Trees
NEW FOR 1995 New trees
CATALOGUE £1.50 (refundable with order)
MAIL ORDER Yes; handling charge plus 30p per kilo

Wholesale and retail tree and shrub nursery. The emphasis is on species trees, especially unusual species of exotic origin. These are raised from seed (not grafted) and are container-grown. The main address and telephone number above is for the Estate Office.

Ballerina Trees Ltd
Maris Lane, Trumpington, Cambridge CB2 2LQ
☎ 01223 840411   FAX 01223 842934
CONTACT Mr Sean Gardner
OPEN Sold through garden centres
SPECIALITIES Fruit
CATALOGUE On request
MAIL ORDER No

Their only line is the new compact, columnar apple trees, now in six varieties, including a crab and a cooker.

Bressingham Plant Centre
Elton Hall, Elton, Peterborough, Cambridgeshire PE8 6SH
☎ 01832 280058   FAX 01832 280081
CONTACT Peter Goodman
LOCATION A605, near Oundle
OPEN 10 am – 5.30 pm, daily
SPECIALITIES Alpines; conifers; herbaceous perennials
CATALOGUE £2
MAIL ORDER See Bressingham Gardens, Norfolk
GARDEN Elton Hall, Cambridgeshire, see Gardens section
SHOWS Chelsea; Hampton Court
GIFT TOKENS Own

This is Bressingham's newest venture, in the old walled kitchen garden at Elton Hall, with their classic specialities of well-grown alpines, herbaceous perennials and conifers.

Foliage & Unusual Plants
The Dingle Nursery, Pilsgate, Stamford, Cambridgeshire PE9 3HW
☎ 01780 740775   FAX 01780 740838
CONTACT Margaret Handley
LOCATION Less than a mile from Burghley House, on B1443
OPEN 10 am – 6 pm, 1 March to 14 November. Closed Sunday mornings
SPECIALITIES Foliage plants; herbaceous perennials
CATALOGUE 3 first class stamps
MAIL ORDER Yes; minimum order £10
REFRESHMENTS Picnics welcomed
GARDEN Gardens
GIFT TOKENS Own

The range includes hardy shrubs, perennials, alpines, grasses and conifers. Most are chosen for their coloured or variegated foliage. Group and evening visits are welcome by prior arrangement. The nursery is just inside the Cambridgeshire boundary.

The Herbary Prickwillow
Ely, Cambridgeshire CB7 4SJ
☎ 01353 88456   FAX 01353 88451
CONTACT Jacqueline Petts
OPEN Mail order only
SPECIALITIES Herbs
CATALOGUE SAE
MAIL ORDER Yes
GIFT TOKENS Own

Culinary herbs in pots by post, as well as cut herbs and edible flowers.

Honeysome Aquatic Nursery
The Row, Sutton, Ely, Cambridgeshire CB6 2PF
☎ 01353 778889
CONTACT Mr D. Littlefield
OPEN By appointment

CAMBRIDGESHIRE Nurseries & Garden Centres

SPECIALITIES Aquatic plants; bog plants
NEW FOR 1995 *Nymphaea* 'Candida'
CATALOGUE 2 first class stamps
MAIL ORDER Yes

A source of ornamental aquatics and oxygenators as well as bog and marginal plants. Their pool collections are useful for starting a new pond.

Meadowcroft Fuchsias
Church St Nurseries, Woodhurst, Huntingdon, Cambridgeshire PE17 3BN
☎ 01487 823333

CONTACT D. N. Pickard
LOCATION East of Huntingdon, off A141
OPEN 9 am – 6 pm, weekends and Bank Holidays
SPECIALITIES Fuchsias; pelargoniums
NEW FOR 1995 Several new varieties
CATALOGUE 3 second class stamps
MAIL ORDER Yes
DESIGN SERVICE Meadowcroft Fuchsias
SHOWS RHS Westminster; Chelsea; BBC GW Live; Hampton Court

Wholesale and retail fuchsia specialists, with thirty years' experience. Their range includes regal, zonal and ivy leaf pelargoniums.

Monksilver Nursery
Oakington Road, Cottenham, Cambridgeshire
CB4 4TW
☎ 01954 251555

CONTACT Joe Sharman
LOCATION North of Cambridge: between Oakington and Cottenham
OPEN 10 am – 4 pm, Friday – Saturday, March to June and September
SPECIALITIES Herbaceous perennials; shrubs
NEW FOR 1995 *Lathyrus rotundifolius* 'Tillyperowne', *Lonicera pileata* 'Taff's Medley', *Tricyrtis* 'Hototogisu', *Chaenomeles japonica* 'Contorta', *Allium paradoxum* var. *normale* and many others
CATALOGUE 6 first class stamps
MAIL ORDER Yes
GARDEN Display gardens
NCCPG NATIONAL COLLECTIONS *Galeobdolon*, *Lamium*, *Lathyrus*, *Vinca*

That overused word 'rare' applies here: Monksilver specialise in finding and rescuing some really rare plants. Much of the stock is herbaceous, though there are also some desirable shrubs. Three National Collections are held by the nursery, and part of the Cambridgeshire NCCPG's *Lathyrus* collection is also on display.

Padlock Croft
19 Padlock Road, West Wratting, Cambridgeshire
CB1 5LS
☎ 01223 290383

CONTACT Susan and Peter Lewis
OPEN 10 am – 6 pm, Wednesday – Saturday, April to 15 October. Also open Bank Holiday Mondays and by appointment at other times
SPECIALITIES Alpines; herbaceous perennials
CATALOGUE 4 second class stamps
MAIL ORDER No
GARDEN Padlock Croft, Cambridgeshire, see Gardens section
NCCPG NATIONAL COLLECTIONS *Adenophora*, *Campanula*, *Platycodon*, *Symphyandra*

This small nursery holds the National Collection of *Campanula*: a long list of species and cultivars forms the centre of their range. Other plants on offer include different members of the Campanulaceae and border plants.

Scotsdale Nursery & Garden Centre
120 Cambridge Road, Great Shelford, Cambridge, Cambridgeshire CB2 5JT
☎ 01223 842777   FAX 01223 844340

CONTACT Mrs Caroline Owen
LOCATION 4 miles south of Cambridge, on A1301
OPEN 9 am – 5.30 pm, daily; 10.30 am – 4.30 pm, Sundays
SHOP Garden sundries, furniture, fencing, gifts
REFRESHMENTS Tea room
DESIGN SERVICE Scotsdale Nursery & Garden Centre
GIFT TOKENS HTA

Large garden centre with plants and associated products. Garden design and delivery service.

Simply Plants
17 Duloe Brook, Eaton Socon, Cambridgeshire
PE19 3DW
☎ 01480 475312

CONTACT Christine Dakin
LOCATION Near the A1
OPEN By appointment and on open days
SPECIALITIES Bamboos; grasses
CATALOGUE 2 first class stamps
MAIL ORDER No

The nursery specialises in grasses and bamboos, but has an increasing number of perennials also. Wholesale and retail.

Thyme House Nursery
High Street, Manea, March, Cambridgeshire
PE15 0JA
☎ 01354 680412

CONTACT Mary Ludlow
LOCATION Map in catalogue
OPEN 8 am – 8 pm or dusk, daily, March to October
SPECIALITIES Herbaceous perennials
NEW FOR 1995 Many new plants
CATALOGUE 4 first class stamps
MAIL ORDER Yes
GIFT TOKENS Own

Not a herb specialist, but a general nursery where the emphasis is on good garden plants, rare or better known, perennials, climbers and shrubs. Some half-hardy plants too.

CHESHIRE

Arley Hall Nursery
Arley, Northwich, Cheshire CW9 6NB
☎ 01565 777479

CONTACT Jane Foster
LOCATION 5 miles west of Knutsford
OPEN 12 noon – 5.30 pm, Tuesday – Sunday and Bank Holidays, 27 March to 2 October
SPECIALITIES Herbaceous perennials
CATALOGUE 70p
MAIL ORDER No
GARDEN Arley Hall, Cheshire, see Gardens section
GIFT TOKENS Own

Arley Hall is famed for its herbaceous borders: the nursery concentrates on plants which can be seen growing there.

Bellhouse Nursery
Bellhouse Lane, Moore, Warrington, Cheshire WA4 6TR
☎ 01925 740307 ext 13   FAX 01925 740672

CONTACT Doreen Scott or Elaine Soens
LOCATION 2 miles off M56, J11, towards Warrington
OPEN 10 am – 5 pm, Wednesday – Monday, March to October; 10 am – 4 pm, Wednesday – Monday, February and November. Closed Tuesdays, and in December and January
SPECIALITIES Herbaceous perennials; shrubs
CATALOGUE £1.25
MAIL ORDER No
GARDEN Garden open

A young nursery, which is building up a large and useful range of less common shrubs and perennials.

Bridgemere Nurseries
Bridgemere, Nantwich, Cheshire CW5 7QB
☎ 001270 520381   FAX 01270 520215
LOCATION West of M6, J15 and J16
OPEN 9 am – 8 pm, Monday – Saturday; 10 am – 8 pm, Sunday. Close at 5 pm in winter
MAIL ORDER No
SHOP Garden sundries, gifts, foods
REFRESHMENTS Coffee shop
GARDEN Bridgemere Garden World, Cheshire
SHOWS Chelsea; BBC GW Live
GIFT TOKENS HTA

Astonishing 25-acre nursery cum garden theme park: the largest range of plants in the country including a 'Connoisseur's Corner'. The choice of houseplants is especially notable. Other attractions include five acres of gardens (£1 admission) and the Bridgemere Wildlife Park (01270 520223).

C & K Jones
Goldenfield Nursery, Barrow Lane, Tarvin, Cheshire CH3 8JF
☎ 01829 740663   FAX 01829 741877

CONTACT Christine Slatcher
LOCATION Chester
OPEN 8.30 am – 5 pm, daily
SPECIALITIES Roses
NEW FOR 1995 Roses 'Fiesta', 'The Painter'
CATALOGUE £1
MAIL ORDER Yes
SHOWS RHS Westminster; BBC GW Live; Hampton Court; Harrogate (Autumn); Ayr

Specialist rose growers: the rose fields are at Halghton, Clwyd. Their range includes all types, but they are especially good for newer varieties and introductions.

C M Dickinson
Nanney's Bridge Nursery, Church Minshull, Nantwich, Cheshire CW5 6DY
☎ 01270 522239

CONTACT C. M. Dickinson
SPECIALITIES Herbaceous perennials
CATALOGUE SAE
MAIL ORDER No

A wholesale nursery providing a useful source of herbaceous perennials for landscapers and the trade, including *Erysimum* and *Penstemon* cultivars.

Caddick's Clematis Nursery
Lymm Road, Thelwall, Warrington, Cheshire WA13 0UF
☎ 01925 757196

CONTACT Mrs Caddick
LOCATION Near M6, J20 (M56, J9), by Thelwall viaduct
OPEN 10 am – 5 pm, Tuesday – Sunday, and Bank Holidays, February to mid December
SPECIALITIES *Clematis*
NEW FOR 1995 Many new varieties
CATALOGUE £1
MAIL ORDER Yes
GARDEN Display gardens
GIFT TOKENS Own

Obviously a clematis specialist. Their range of species and cultivars is probably the largest in the country, and it's worth asking for ones that are not shown in the list.

Cheshire Herbs
Fourfields, Forest Road, Little Budworth, Tarporley, Cheshire CW6 9ES
☎ 01829 760578   FAX 01829 760354

CONTACT Libby Riddell
LOCATION On A49, just north of A54 intersection
OPEN 10 am – 5 pm. Closed from Christmas to New Year
SPECIALITIES Herbs; seeds
CATALOGUE On request

MAIL ORDER   Seeds only
SHOP   Herbal products
GARDEN   Herb garden
SHOWS   Southport; Chelsea; BBC GW Live; Hampton Court

An extensive range of pot-grown herbs are on sale, retail and wholesale. The small shop sells associated products, and seeds are available mail order. The nursery holds talks and courses.

F Morrey & Son
Forest Nursery, Kelsall, Tarporley, Cheshire CW6 0SW
☎ 01829 751342   FAX 01829 752449
LOCATION   8 miles east of Chester on A54
OPEN   9 am – 5 pm, Monday – Saturday
SPECIALITIES   Rhododendrons; roses; shrubs; trees
CATALOGUE   20p
MAIL ORDER   No
GIFT TOKENS   HTA

A long-established family nursery. Their range includes trees and shrubs of all kinds, as well as conifers, heathers and roses. Notably good for rhododendrons and azaleas.

The Firs Nursery
Chelford Road, Henbury, Macclesfield, Cheshire SK10 3LH
☎ 01625 426422
CONTACT   Mrs F. J. Bowling
LOCATION   2 miles west of Macclesfield on A537
OPEN   9.30 am – 5 pm, March to September. Closed Wednesdays and Sundays
SPECIALITIES   Alpines; herbaceous perennials
CATALOGUE   2 first class stamps
MAIL ORDER   No
GARDEN   Gardens open with nursery

This small nursery specialises in herbaceous perennials. It also stocks a range of hebes and alpines.

Fryer's Roses Ltd
Manchester Road, Knutsford, Cheshire WA16 0SX
☎ 01565 755455   FAX 01565 653755
CONTACT   Mr G. R. Fryer
LOCATION   On A50, north of Knutsford
OPEN   9 am – 5.30 pm, Monday – Saturday, 10.30 am – 4.30 pm, Sundays
SPECIALITIES   Roses
NEW FOR 1995   Roses 'Belle Epoque', 'Warm Wishes'
CATALOGUE   On request
MAIL ORDER   Yes
SHOP   Garden sundries, pots, dried flowers
SHOWS   Southport; Chelsea; Hampton Court; Harrogate (Autumn)
GIFT TOKENS   HTA; own

Rose growers of largely modern roses. They have a garden centre carrying a full general range, with a special rose centre. The rose fields can be visited in summer.

Gordale Nursery & Garden Centre
Chester High Road, Burton, South Wirral, Cheshire L64 8TF
☎ 0151 336 2116   FAX 0151 336 7818
CONTACT   Jill Nicholson
LOCATION   8 miles west of Chester, on A540
OPEN   9 am – 5 pm, winter; 9 am – 6 pm, summer. Open until 8 pm, Thursdays
SHOP   Sundries, gifts, garden furniture
REFRESHMENTS   Coffee shop
GIFT TOKENS   HTA

Garden centre with a general range of plants and garden products. Delivery service.

Grosvenor Garden Centre
Wrexham Road, Belgrave, Chester, Cheshire CH4 9EB
☎ 01244 682856   FAX 01244 679036
CONTACT   Wendy Kettlewell
LOCATION   South of Chester, on B5445
SHOP   Garden sundries, machinery, gifts
REFRESHMENTS   Orangery café
GARDEN   Sensory garden
DESIGN SERVICE   Druid Designs
GIFT TOKENS   HTA

A large garden centre with a full range of plants and products. Monthly lectures, and a design service through Kate Roscoe of Druid Designs.

Okell's Nurseries
Duddon Heath, Tarporley, Cheshire CW6 0EP
☎ 01829 741512   FAX 01829 741587
CONTACT   Donna Okell
OPEN   9 am – 5.30 pm, daily. Close at 7 pm, Saturday – Sunday, May and June)
SPECIALITIES   Heathers
CATALOGUE   On request
MAIL ORDER   No
SHOP   Garden sundries
GIFT TOKENS   HTA

This wholesale nursery produces heathers in variety (150) and quantity (2.6 million). They also have a retail garden centre which stocks heathers and a general range of plants and sundries.

Phedar Nursery
Bunkers Hill, Romiley, Stockport, Cheshire SK6 3DS
☎ 0161 430 3772   FAX 0161 430 3772
CONTACT   Will McLewin
LOCATION   3 miles east of Stockport
OPEN   By appointment only
SPECIALITIES   Paeonies; seeds; hellebores
CATALOGUE   Large SAE (2 first class stamps)
MAIL ORDER   Yes

A highly specialised source of authentic *Helleborus* and *Paeonia* species, which are only grown from collected material. They also offer fresh seed in August. Other plants from this research nursery include *Erythronium* and *Dodecatheon*.

Robinsons of Whaley Bridge
20 Vaughan Road, Whaley Bridge, Stockport, Cheshire SK12 7JT
☎ 01663 732991
CONTACT   Mr J. E. Robinson
OPEN   Mail order only
SPECIALITIES   *Iris*; violas
CATALOGUE   3 first class stamps
MAIL ORDER   Yes

Very small and specialised. Their charming range consists of *Viola odorata* cultivars, dwarf bearded irises and auriculas.

Stapeley Water Gardens Ltd
London Road, Stapeley, Nantwich, Cheshire CW5 7LH
☎ 01270 623868   FAX 01270 624919
CONTACT   Reception desk
LOCATION   Signed from M6, J16; 1 mile south of Nantwich
OPEN   9 am – 6 pm, Monday – Friday; 10 am – 6 pm, Saturdays; 10 am – 7 pm, Sundays and Bank Holidays, summer; closes at 5 pm, daily, winter
SPECIALITIES   Aquatic plants; bog plants
CATALOGUE   £1 cheque
MAIL ORDER   Yes
SHOP   Garden sundries, water equipment, furniture, gifts, books
REFRESHMENTS   Restaurants
GARDEN   Stapeley Water Gardens Ltd, Cheshire, see Gardens section
SHOWS   Southport; Chelsea; BBC GW Live; Hampton Court; Courson
GIFT TOKENS   Own
NCCPG NATIONAL COLLECTIONS *Nymphaea*

A water gardening centre, with aquatic plants, marginals and poolside varieties as well as all the necessary equipment for ponds and pools. They hold the national water lily collection, here and at Burnby Hall, Humberside. Their French subsidiary (Etablissement Botanique Latour-Marliac) exhibits at Courson.

Ward Fuchsias
5 Pollen Close, Sale, Cheshire M33 3LS
☎ 0161 9736467
CONTACT   Mrs M. Ward
LOCATION   Map in catalogue
OPEN   9.30 am – 5 pm, Tuesday – Sunday, February to June. Closed Mondays
SPECIALITIES   Fuchsias
CATALOGUE   On request
MAIL ORDER   Yes

A specialist fuchsia grower: cuttings by post. Plants and hanging baskets at the nursery, with hostas too.

Weaver Vale Garden Centre
Winnington Lane, Winnington, Northwich, Cheshire CW8 4EE
☎ 01606 79965   FAX 01606 784480
CONTACT   Peter Jones
LOCATION   2 miles north west of Northwich on A533
OPEN   9 am – 6 pm, Monday – Saturday; 10.30 am – 4.30 pm, Sundays. Closes at 5 pm in winter
SHOP   Garden sundries, machinery, conservatories, aquatics
REFRESHMENTS   Coffee shop
GARDEN   Demonstration gardens
DESIGN SERVICE   County Gardens
GIFT TOKENS   HTA

Garden centre with indoor and outdoor plants and associated products. Landscaping and garden design service.

Wilmslow Garden Centre
Manchester Road, Wilmslow, Cheshire SK9 2JN
☎ 01625 525700   FAX 01625 539800
CONTACT   Frank, Neil and Denise
LOCATION   A34
OPEN   9 am – 6 pm, summer; 9 am – 5 pm, winter; 10 am – 5 pm, Sundays (all year). Also 8 pm closing, summer Thursdays
SHOP   Garden sundries, furniture, machinery, pets
REFRESHMENTS   Restaurant, coffee shop
DESIGN SERVICE   Wilmslow Garden Centre
SHOWS   Southport
GIFT TOKENS   HTA

Garden centre selling plants and products. They have a design and landscape capability, and a delivery service.

CLEVELAND

Arcadia Nurseries Ltd
Brasscastle Lane, Nunthorpe, Middlesbrough, Cleveland TS8 9EB
☎ 01642 310782   FAX 01642 300817
CONTACT   Michael V. Birch
LOCATION   On B1365, between Middlesbrough and Stokesley
OPEN   9 am – 7 pm, daily, summer; 9 am – 5 pm, winter; 10.30 am – 4.30 pm, Sundays
SPECIALITIES   Fuchsias
NEW FOR 1995   'Richard John' (hardy fuchsia), 'Nancy Scrivener' (exhibition fuchsia)
CATALOGUE   3 first class stamps
MAIL ORDER   Yes
SHOP   Cold water fish and pool supplies
REFRESHMENTS   Refreshments
GARDEN   Demonstration gardens
GIFT TOKENS   HTA; own

Specialist grower with a huge range of fuchsias; some 1,200 different varieties. Visit between June and September to see them in flower. Their new garden centre opens this year.

Peter Barratt's Garden Centres
Yarm Road, Stockton on Tees, Cleveland TS18 3SQ
☎ 01642 613433   FAX 01642 618185
CONTACT   Keith Crackett
OPEN   9 am – 5.30 pm
SHOP   Garden sundries, aquatics
REFRESHMENTS   Refreshments
GARDEN   Demonstration gardens
DESIGN SERVICE   Peter Barratt's Garden Centres
GIFT TOKENS   HTA
General garden centre with garden and leisure products. Delivery and design service.

Town Farm Nursery
Whitton, Stockton on Tees, Cleveland TS21 1LQ
☎ 01740 31079
CONTACT   F. D. Baker
OPEN   10 am – 6 pm, Friday – Monday. Closed in winter
SPECIALITIES   Alpines; herbaceous perennials; shrubs
CATALOGUE   SAE
MAIL ORDER   Yes
GARDEN   1-acre display garden

A good selection of hardy alpines and perennials, as well as some smaller shrubs. The display gardens are open for nursery visitors.

Westwinds Perennial Plants
Filpoke Lane, High Hesleden, Hartlepool, Cleveland TS27 4BT
☎ 0191 5180225
CONTACT   Harry Blackwood
LOCATION   Off A1086, north of Hartlepool
OPEN   12 noon – 6 pm, Saturdays; 8 am – 8 pm, Sundays and Mondays
SPECIALITIES   Herbaceous perennials
NEW FOR 1995   2 new variegated violas
CATALOGUE   SAE
MAIL ORDER   No
GARDEN   Garden open

A herbaceous plant specialist, but with an expanding range of climbers and shrubs. Mailing list customers get a brightly written newsletter.

CORNWALL

Bosvigo Plants
Bosvigo House, Bosvigo Lane, Truro, Cornwall TR1 3NH
☎ 01872 75774   FAX 01872 41565
CONTACT   Mrs Wendy Perry
LOCATION   ¾ mile from Truro centre. Leave A390 at Highertown (near Sainsburys): 500m down Dobbs Lane
OPEN   11 am – 6 pm, Wednesday – Saturday, March to September. Closed Sundays, Mondays and Tuesdays
SPECIALITIES   Herbaceous perennials
CATALOGUE   4 second class stamps
MAIL ORDER   No

GARDEN   Bosvigo House, Cornwall, see Gardens section

This small nursery concentrates on herbaceous perennials, including many geraniums and violas which can also be seen in the main garden. It is worth asking for other plants from the garden which are not in the catalogue.

Boyton Nursery
Bragg's Hill, Boyton, Launceston, Cornwall PL15 9LP
☎ 01566 776474   FAX 01566 776474
CONTACT   Susan Bean
OPEN   8.30 am – 5.30 pm, summer; 9 am – 5 pm, winter
NEW FOR 1995   Old-fashioned pinks and penstemons
CATALOGUE   2 first class stamps
MAIL ORDER   No
REFRESHMENTS   Yes

Fuchsias, roses, and cottage garden perennials are available from this nursery. There is a separate catalogue for fuchsias.

Bregover Plants
Middlewood, Launceston, Cornwall PL15 7NN
☎ 01566 782661
CONTACT   Jennifer Bousfield
LOCATION   Between Launceston and Liskeard on B3254
OPEN   11 am – 5 pm, Wednesday – Friday, mid March to mid October. Weekends and winter months by appointment
SPECIALITIES   Herbaceous perennials; primulas; violas
CATALOGUE   2 first class stamps
MAIL ORDER   Yes; £2 minimum charge
GARDEN   Cottage garden and stock beds open by appointment

Mainly cottage garden, wild and woodland plants, including old varieties. Occasional lists of primulas and *Viola odorata* cultivars are produced: fellow collectors should peruse the offsets and divisions. If you visit on 1 and 2 July, 2 – 6 pm, the village gardens will be open under the NGS.

Brockings Exotics
Brockings Nursery, North Petherwin, Launceston, Cornwall PL15 8LW
☎ 01566 785533
CONTACT   Ian Cooke
LOCATION   Take signs to Otter Park, then continue into village centre
OPEN   2 – 6 pm, Monday – Saturday
SPECIALITIES   Conservatory plants, cannas, coleus, half-hardy plants
CATALOGUE   3 first class stamps
MAIL ORDER   Yes; £15 minimum order
GARDEN   Display garden
DESIGN SERVICE   Brockings Exotics
SHOWS   RHS Westminster; BBC GW Live; Hampton Court

NCCPG NATIONAL COLLECTIONS *Canna;* coleus
Brockings Exotics sell an outstanding collection of half-hardy perennials. Some are new, many are revived. Strengths include cannas, coleus (old named varieties) and argyranthemums (20).

Burncoose & South Down Nurseries
Gwennap, Redruth, Cornwall TR16 6BJ
☎ 01209 861112   FAX 01209 860011

CONTACT   C. H. Williams
LOCATION   Between Redruth and Falmouth, on A393
OPEN   9 am – 5 pm, Monday – Saturday; 11 am – 5 pm, Sundays
SPECIALITIES   Camellias; conservatory plants; rhododendrons; magnolias
NEW FOR 1995   *Delphinium* 'Princess Caroline'
CATALOGUE   £1
MAIL ORDER   Yes
REFRESHMENTS   Tea room
GARDEN   Burncoose Gardens, beside the nursery
DESIGN SERVICE   Burncoose & South Down Nurseries
SHOWS   RHS Westminster; Malvern Spring; Harrogate (Spring); Southport; Chelsea; BBC GW Live; Hampton Court; Harrogate (Autumn)
GIFT TOKENS   HTA

A very large general range, particularly strong on flowering shrubs and trees, including magnolias. Some good tender and conservatory plants too. Look out for their masterly displays at horticultural shows.

Carnon Downs Garden Centre
Quenchwell Road, Carnon Downs, Truro TR3 4LN
☎ 01872 863058   FAX 01872 862162
LOCATION   Carnon Downs
OPEN   8 am – 5 pm, Monday – Friday; 9 am – 5 pm, Saturdays; 10 am – 5 pm, Sundays
SHOP   Garden sundries, furniture and buildings, pets
REFRESHMENTS   Licensed restaurant
GIFT TOKENS   HTA; own

Garden centre with a large range of ancillary products including garden machinery. The plant centre includes a selection of plants suited to coastal conditions. They can deliver; on site there is also a working pottery and an adventure playground. Large Christmas section, from October.

Duchy of Cornwall Nursery
Cott Road, Lostwithiel, Cornwall PL22 0BW
☎ 01208 872668   FAX 01579 345672

CONTACT   Mr Andrew Carthew (Manager)
LOCATION   Lostwithiel, 1½ miles off A390
OPEN   9 am – 5 pm, Monday – Saturday; 10 am – 5 pm, Sundays. Closed Bank Holidays
SPECIALITIES   Herbaceous perennials; shrubs; trees; half-hardy plants
NEW FOR 1995   Many new plants
CATALOGUE   £1 cheque
MAIL ORDER   No

SHOP   Garden sundries
GARDEN   Woodland walk
GIFT TOKENS   HTA; own

The nursery stocks an extensive general range of all types of plants as well as garden sundries. They are especially good on tender perennials. Set in woods, there is a woodland walk centred on the nursery. They will be at the Royal Cornwall and the Devon shows this year.

Elizabeth Smith
Downside, Bowling Green, Constantine, Falmouth, Cornwall TR11 5AP
☎ 01326 40787

CONTACT   Elizabeth Smith
OPEN   Mail order only
SPECIALITIES   Violets
CATALOGUE   SAE; January
MAIL ORDER   Yes

Mail order nursery devoted exclusively to scented violets: single, double and Parma.

Hardy Exotics Nursery
Gilly Lane, Whitecross, Penzance, Cornwall TR20 8BZ
☎ 01736 740660

CONTACT   Clive Shilton or Julie Smith
LOCATION   Off A30, east of Penzance
OPEN   10 am – 5.30 pm daily, summer; 10 am – 5 pm Monday – Friday, winter
CATALOGUE   4 first class stamps
MAIL ORDER   Yes
GARDEN   Demonstration garden
DESIGN SERVICE   Hardy Exotics

There are many eye-catching plants here. Striking foliage and flowers to enliven your garden, patio or conservatory. A design service is offered as well.

Lanhydrock Gardens
The National Trust, Lanhydrock Gardens, Bodmin, Cornwall PL30 5AD
☎ 01208 72220/ 73320

CONTACT   Mr Teagle
OPEN   11 am – 4.30 pm, April to October
SPECIALITIES   Rhododendrons; shrubs
CATALOGUE   On request
MAIL ORDER   No
REFRESHMENTS   11 am – 4.30 pm, April to October
GARDEN   Lanhydrock, Cornwall, see Gardens section
NCCPG NATIONAL COLLECTIONS *Crocosmia*

There are some herbaceous plants here, but the best of the list is shrubs. You would expect rhododendrons and azaleas, but there are also attractive *Ceanothus* and *Deutzia*.

Little Treasures Nursery
Wheal Treasure, Horsedowns, Cornwall TR14 0NL
☎ 01209 831978

CONTACT   Mrs B. Jackson

OPEN   By appointment, for collection
SPECIALITIES   Herbaceous perennials; shrubs
NEW FOR 1995   80 new plants
CATALOGUE   3 first class stamps
MAIL ORDER   Yes

Perennials, shrubs, climbers and herbs, both hardy and tender. Their eclectic selection concentrates on older and scented varieties. Mail order all year except December.

The Old Mill Herbary
Helland Bridge, Bodmin, Cornwall PL30 4QR
☎ 01208 841206   FAX 01208 841206
CONTACT   Mr and Mrs R. D. Whurr
LOCATION   Helland Bridge: Map ref. 065717
OPEN   10 am – 5 pm, April to October
SPECIALITIES   Herbs
CATALOGUE   6 first class stamps
MAIL ORDER   No
GARDEN   Terraced and water garden, arboretum

The nursery sells a range of herbs. The garden, which includes herbs, bog plants, aquatics and a young arboretum is open at the same times, but ring first.

Porthpean House Gardens
Porthpean, St Austell, Cornwall PL26 6AX
☎ 01726 72888
CONTACT   Mrs Petherick
LOCATION   1½ miles south east of St Austell
OPEN   9 am – 5 pm, Monday – Friday
SPECIALITIES   Camellias
CATALOGUE   On request
MAIL ORDER   No
SHOWS   RHS Westminster

Camellia specialists, and regular award-winning camellia exhibitors.

R A Scamp
14 Roscarrack Close, Falmouth, Cornwall TR11 4PJ
☎ 01326 317959
CONTACT   Ron Scamp
OPEN   Mail order only
SPECIALITIES   Daffodils
CATALOGUE   2 first class stamps
GIFT TOKENS   Own

A specialist daffodil grower and breeder. Very wide range of all types of daffodil including miniatures, species and some of Ron Scamp's own varieties.

Roseland House Nursery
Roseland House, Chacewater, Truro TR4 8QB
☎ 01872 560451
CONTACT   Mr C. Pridham
LOCATION   West of Truro
OPEN   12 noon – 4 pm, Tuesdays, March to July
SPECIALITIES   Climbers; herbaceous perennials
CATALOGUE   2 first class stamps
MAIL ORDER   No
GARDEN   Garden opens for NGS

Climbers, including some clematis and a good choice of hardy and half-hardy (outside Cornwall) perennials.

Trebah Nursery
Trebah, Mawnan Smith, Falmouth, Cornwall TR11 5JZ
☎ 01326 250448   FAX 01326 250781
CONTACT   Philip McMillan Browse
LOCATION   6 miles west of Falmouth, signed from Mawnan Smith
OPEN   10 am – 5 pm, daily
SPECIALITIES   Cacti and succulents; ferns
CATALOGUE   A4 SAE
MAIL ORDER   No
GARDEN   Trebah Garden, Cornwall, see Gardens section
GIFT TOKENS   HTA

The plant centre draws on the collections at Trebah to offer plants suitable for the south west. Good *Agave*, *Yucca* and *Lampranthus*.

Trewithen Nurseries
Grampound Road, Truro, Cornwall TR2 4DD
☎ 01726 882764
CONTACT   Mr M. Taylor
LOCATION   Trewithen
OPEN   Garden and nursery: 10 am – 4.30 pm, Monday – Saturday, March to September. Also, Sundays in April and May only; Nursery only: 8 am – 4.30 pm, Monday – Friday, October to February
SPECIALITIES   Camellias; climbers; rhododendrons
CATALOGUE   £1.50
MAIL ORDER   No
REFRESHMENTS   March to September, when gardens open
GARDEN   Trewithen, Cornwall, see Gardens section

Ornamental shrubs and climbers, especially those for acid soils and sheltered spots. A good choice of rhododendrons, camellias and magnolias.

Wall Cottage Nursery
Lockengate, Bugle, St Austell, Cornwall PL26 8RU
☎ 01208 831259
CONTACT   Mrs J. R. Clark
OPEN   8.30 am – 5 pm, Monday – Saturday
SPECIALITIES   Rhododendrons
CATALOGUE   60p
MAIL ORDER   Yes; minimum order £15

Rhododendron and azalea specialist, with an extensive choice of species and hybrids. Visitors welcome, but they would prefer it if you can make an appointment.

CUMBRIA

Beechcroft Nurseries
Bongate, Appleby, Cumbria CA16 6UE
☎ 017683 51201
CONTACT   Roger Brown
LOCATION   Ask in Appleby

Nurseries & Garden Centres CUMBRIA

OPEN   8 am – 6 pm, Monday – Saturday; 11 am – 6 pm, Sundays. Closed Christmas and New Year's Day
SPECIALITIES   Shrubs; trees
CATALOGUE   £2; SAE only for list of field-grown trees
MAIL ORDER   Field-grown trees, November to April
DESIGN SERVICE   Beechcroft Nurseries
GIFT TOKENS   HTA

A small nursery which specialises in trees and shrubs: both container and field-grown. The rest of the selection is splendidly mixed, running from conifers to vegetables. Gardens designed and planted too.

Beetham Nurseries
Pool Darkin Lane, Beetham, Milnthorpe, Cumbria LA7 7QR
☎ 015395 63630   FAX 015395 64487

CONTACT   S. J. Abbit
LOCATION   Off A6, south of Milnthorpe
OPEN   9 am – 6 pm, daily, in summer; 9 am – dusk, daily, in winter
SPECIALITIES   Shrubs; trees
MAIL ORDER   No
GIFT TOKENS   HTA

The nursery has a tree and shrub range.

Brownthwaite Hardy Plants
Fell Yeat, Casterton, Kirkby Lonsdale, Cumbria LA6 2JW
☎ 015242 71340

CONTACT   Chris Benson
LOCATION   Bull Pot Road in Casterton
OPEN   10 am – 5 pm, Tuesday – Sunday, April to October
SPECIALITIES   Grasses; herbaceous perennials
CATALOGUE   3 first class stamps
MAIL ORDER   Yes
GARDEN   Garden opens for NGS
DESIGN SERVICE   Yes

This Pennine nursery grows and stocks a range of hardy perennials and grasses. The plants can be seen in a garden setting.

Halecat Garden Nurseries
Witherslack, Grange over Sands, Cumbria LA11 6RU
☎ 015395 52229

CONTACT   Mrs M. Stanley and Mrs Y. Langhorn
LOCATION   Between Grange and Levens, off A590
OPEN   9 am – 4.30 pm, Monday – Friday, all year; 2 – 4 pm, Sundays, Easter to October only. Closed Saturdays
SPECIALITIES   Herbaceous perennials; *Hydrangea*
NEW FOR 1995   *Hydrangea macrophylla* 'Universal Red Star', 'Miss Hepburn', 'Blue Sky', 'Snow'
CATALOGUE   45p (1994)
MAIL ORDER   No
GARDEN   Display garden

They specialise in species and cultivars of *Hydrangea*, and also stock an attractive range of perennials for herbaceous and mixed borders.

Hartside Nursery Garden
Alston, Cumbria CA9 3BL
☎ 01434 381372

CONTACT   N. Huntley
LOCATION   1¼ miles south west of Alston on A686 Alston to Penrith road
OPEN   9 am – 5pm, Monday – Friday; 10 am – 4 pm, Saturdays; 12.30 – 4 pm, Sundays; March to October. Other months by appointment
SPECIALITIES   Alpines; ferns
CATALOGUE   £1 each; 3 annually
MAIL ORDER   Yes
GARDEN   12-acre wooded valley
SHOWS   Harrogate (Spring); BBC GW Live; Hampton Court; Harrogate (Autumn); Ayr
GIFT TOKENS   Own

The nursery specialises in alpines, dwarf shrubs and conifers, and hardy ferns: all grown in the North Pennines at altitude. The substantial gardens are also open, and there is a self-catering cottage available.

Hayes Gardenworld Ltd
Lake District Nurseries, Ambleside, Cumbria LA22 0DW
☎ 015394 33434   FAX 015394 34153

LOCATION   South of Ambleside on A591
OPEN   9 am – 6 pm, Monday – Saturday; 10.30 am – 4.30 pm, Sundays
SHOP   Garden sundries, greenhouses, conservatories, aquarium
REFRESHMENTS   Coffee lounge
GARDEN   Gardens open, as above
DESIGN SERVICE   Hayes Gardenworld
GIFT TOKENS   HTA

Established over 200 years ago, and now a major tourist attraction. The garden centre also offers a landscaping and construction service, and assorted leisure activities.

Muncaster Plants
Muncaster Castle, Ravenglass, Cumbria CA18 1RJ
☎ 01229 717357   FAX 01229 7171010

CONTACT   A. J. and S. F. Clark
LOCATION   Off A595, 1 mile east of Ravenglass
OPEN   10 am – 4 pm, daily, April to September. By appointment October to March
SPECIALITIES   Rhododendrons
NEW FOR 1995   More plants of wild origin
CATALOGUE   3 first class stamps
MAIL ORDER   Yes
GARDEN   Muncaster Castle, Cumbria, see Gardens section

The nursery at this famous garden has an exceptional collection of azaleas and rhododendrons. It includes rare species, many under famous collectors' numbers, and older and newer hybrids.

DERBYSHIRE Nurseries & Garden Centres 143

T H Barker & Son
Baines Paddock Nursery, Haverthwaite, Ulverston, Cumbria LA12 8PF
☎ 015395 58236
CONTACT Mrs W. E. Thornley
LOCATION On B5278, 2 miles north of Holker Hall
OPEN 9.30 am – 5.30 pm, daily. Closed Tuesday am, Christmas and Boxing Day
SPECIALITIES Clematis
NEW FOR 1995 Clematis 'Arabella', Clematis 'Caroline'
CATALOGUE 3 first class stamps
MAIL ORDER Yes

This nursery specialises in clematis, both large flowered, small flowered and species. There is range of growing cottage garden plants for collection. The nursery is hidden from the road: watch for the green and gold signs.

Weasdale Nurseries
Newbiggin on Lune, Kirkby Stephen CA17 4LX
☎ 015396 23246   FAX 015396 23277
CONTACT Andrew Forsyth
LOCATION 7 miles from M6, J38, off A685
OPEN 9 am – 5 pm. Plant collection by prior arrangement only
SPECIALITIES Hedging; shrubs; trees
NEW FOR 1995 Koelreuteria paniculata, and several new Forsythia
CATALOGUE £2.50 cheque
MAIL ORDER Yes

Trees and shrubs by mail order, including ornamental, hedging and woodland species. Forty years' mail order experience, from a substantial list. The high situation on the Fells promises hardiness too.

Webbs Garden Centre
Burneside Road, Kendal, Cumbria LA9 4RT
☎ 01539 720068   FAX 01539 727328
LOCATION From M6, J36 take A591 Kendal North road. Turn right downhill at roundabout, then left into Burneside Road
OPEN 9 am – 6 pm, Monday – Saturday; 11 am – 5 pm, Sundays
SHOP Garden sundries, floristry
REFRESHMENTS Restaurant
GIFT TOKENS HTA; own

Garden centre with plants and garden products – the home of the 'Webbs wonderful' lettuce. Special events, competitions and demonstrations are held throughout the year. Delivery service.

DERBYSHIRE

Birchwood Farm Nursery
Portway, Coxbench, Derbyshire DE21 5BE
☎ 01332 880685
CONTACT Mr and Mrs H. S. Crooks
LOCATION Off A38, north of Little Eaton
OPEN 9 am – 5.30 pm, Monday – Tuesday, Thursday – Saturday. Closed Wednesdays and Sundays
SPECIALITIES Herbaceous perennials
GARDEN Garden opens by appointment

The nursery stocks herbaceous perennials and shrubs; composts and fertilisers are available too.

Bluebell Nursery
Blackfordby, Swadlincote, Derbyshire DE11 8AJ
☎ 01283 222091   FAX 01283 218282
CONTACT Robert Vernon
LOCATION Off A50, behind Bluebell Inn in Blackfordby
OPEN 9 am – 5 pm, daily. Closed from Christmas Eve to 2 January
SPECIALITIES Trees
CATALOGUE 50p plus 36p stamp
MAIL ORDER Yes
SHOWS RHS Westminster; Malvern Spring; Chelsea; BBC GW Live; Hampton Court

An attractive mix of carefully chosen trees and shrubs, both cultivars and species. Good on Ilex.

Chatsworth Garden Centre
Calton Lees, Beeley, Matlock, Derbyshire DE4 2NX
☎ 01629 734004   FAX 01629 580503
CONTACT John Tarbatt
LOCATION 1 mile from Chatsworth House
OPEN 9 am – 5 pm, October – February; 9 am – 5.30 pm, March to September; 10.30 am – 4.30 pm, Sundays
SHOP Garden sundries, gifts
REFRESHMENTS Coffee shop
GIFT TOKENS HTA

Garden centre with a range of indoor and outdoor plants, set in a former walled garden of the Chatsworth estate. Delivery service within 20-mile radius.

DHE Plants
Rose Leall, Darley House Estate, Darley Dale, Matlock, Derbyshire DE4 2QH
☎ 01629 732512
CONTACT Peter M. Smith
OPEN By appointment
SPECIALITIES Alpines
NEW FOR 1995 Range changes constantly
CATALOGUE 2 first class stamps
MAIL ORDER Yes; no minimum order; October to April

An alpine nursery whose stock includes particularly good choices of helianthemums (50), saxifrages (150) and sisyrinchiums (20). A regular attender at AGS shows.

Greenleaves Garden Centre Ltd
Birkin Lane, Wingerworth, Chesterfield, Derbyshire S42 6RD
☎ 01246 204214   FAX 01629 580503
CONTACT John Tarbatt

144 Nurseries & Garden Centres DEVON

LOCATION 1 mile west of A61 Tupton roundabout
OPEN 9 am – 5 pm, October to February, 9 am – 5.30 pm, March to September, Monday – Saturday; 10.30 am – 4.30 pm, Sundays
SHOP Landscaping supplies
GARDEN Demonstration garden

Garden centre, with local delivery service. They stock landscaping materials as well as plants, and have an advisory service. Closed between Christmas and New Year.

The Herb Garden
Chesterfield Road, Hardstoft, Pilsley, Chesterfield, Derbyshire S45 8AH
☎ 01246 854268

CONTACT Lynne or Steve Raynor
LOCATION Signed off A6175 and B6014
OPEN 10 am – 6 pm, daily, 1 March to 30 September
SPECIALITIES Herbs
CATALOGUE On request
MAIL ORDER No
SHOP Herb products
REFRESHMENTS Tea room
GARDEN Display gardens
GIFT TOKENS HTA; own

There are four themed display gardens here, with around 250 culinary, medicinal and aromatic herbs for sale. Lots of different lavenders.

Highgates Nursery
166a Crich Lane, Belper, Derbyshire DE56 1EP
☎ 01773 822153

CONTACT Mr and Mrs Straughan
LOCATION Along unclassified road, signed to Ambergate and Ridgeway
OPEN 10 am – 4.30 pm, Monday – Saturday, early March to mid October
SPECIALITIES Alpines; rhododendrons
NEW FOR 1995 Many new items
CATALOGUE 2 first class stamps
MAIL ORDER No
GARDEN Display gardens

There are alpines in abundance at this specialist nursery, as well as a selection of dwarf rhododendrons.

Lea Gardens
Lea, Matlock, Derbyshire DE4 5GH
☎ 01629 534380   FAX 01629 534260

CONTACT Jon and Peter Tye
OPEN 10 am – 7 pm, 20 March to 16 July. Also by appointment for the rest of the year
SPECIALITIES Rhododendrons
CATALOGUE SAE plus 30p
MAIL ORDER Yes; minimum order £15
REFRESHMENTS Refreshments
GARDEN Lea Gardens, Derbyshire, see Gardens section

The plants on sale reflect those which grow in the garden, notably *Rhododendron*, azaleas and *Kalmia*, with the tendency towards dwarf or low-growing varieties.

Matlock Garden Centre Ltd
Nottingham Road, Tansley, Matlock, Derbyshire DE4 5FR
☎ 01629 580500   FAX 01629 580503

CONTACT John Tarbatt
LOCATION 7 miles from M1, J28
OPEN 9 am – 5 pm, October to February; 9 am – 5.30 pm, March to September. 10.30 am – 4.30 pm, Sundays. Closed between Christmas and New Year
SHOP Aquatics
REFRESHMENTS Restaurant
GIFT TOKENS HTA

Garden centre with a hardy plant range and aquatics centre. Delivery within 20-mile radius.

Riley's Chrysanthemums
Alfreton Nurseries, Ashover Road, Woolley Moor, Alfreton, Derbyshire DE55 6FF
☎ 01246 590320

CONTACT Martin Riley
LOCATION On B6036, between Clay Cross and Matlock
OPEN Phone for details; nursery fields open 10 am – 4 pm, Sundays, September only
SPECIALITIES Chrysanthemums
NEW FOR 1995 12 new Pennine outdoor sprays, 8 new earlies
CATALOGUE 25p; September
MAIL ORDER Yes
REFRESHMENTS Pubs nearby
GARDEN Chrysanthemum fields
SHOWS RHS Westminster; Harrogate (Autumn)
GIFT TOKENS Own

Trade and retail nursery devoted to chrysanthemums only. They come in all types, old and new, indoor and outdoor. Cut flowers in season. The fields are open for viewing on Sundays in September; the nursery will be at the National Chrysanthemum Society's Early Show in Stafford.

DEVON

Altoona Nurseries
The Windmill, Tigley, Dartington, Totnes, Devon TQ9 6DW
☎ 01803 868147

CONTACT Paul Harber
LOCATION 1½ miles west of Totnes
OPEN By appointment, any time
SPECIALITIES Acers
CATALOGUE SAE
MAIL ORDER No

Specialists in Japanese acers, *Hamamelis* (witch hazels) and *Daphne*.

Ann & Roger Bowden
Hostas, Sticklepath, Okehampton, Devon EX20 2NN
☎ 0183784 0481
CONTACT   Ann and Roger Bowden
OPEN   By appointment only
SPECIALITIES   Hostas
CATALOGUE   3 first class stamps
MAIL ORDER   Yes; no minimum order, low packing charges
GARDEN   National Collection of hybrid hostas
SHOWS   RHS Westminster; Malvern Spring; BBC GW Live; Hampton Court
NCCPG NATIONAL COLLECTIONS Hybrid *Hosta*

Hostas only. They can be bought individually or as collections from a very extensive range which includes some brightly coloured American hybrids.

Burnham Nurseries
Forches Cross, Newton Abbot, Devon TQ12 6PZ
☎ 01626 52233   FAX 01626 62167
CONTACT   Brian and Ann Rittershausen
LOCATION   Forches Cross: signed from A382
OPEN   10 am – 4 pm, daily
SPECIALITIES   Orchids
CATALOGUE   On request
MAIL ORDER   Yes
SHOP   Sundries
REFRESHMENTS   Light snacks
GARDEN   Visitor centre and display house
SHOWS   RHS Westminster; Chelsea

A very extensive range of orchid species and hybrids. Plants can be seen growing in the display house: current admission is £1.50 for adults. They will be at the British Orchid Congress, Brighton.

Decorative Foliage
Higher Badworthy, South Brent, Devon TQ10 9EG
☎ 01364 72768
CONTACT   Amanda Morris
LOCATION   1½ miles from South Brent
OPEN   Phone first
SPECIALITIES   Foliage plants
CATALOGUE   2 first class stamps
MAIL ORDER   Yes; no minimum order
GARDEN   Garden

A small nursery with an accent on perennials and shrubs that would be useful for flower arranging. The nursery will attend the Savill Garden Fairs on 13 May and 26 August, as well as local NCCPG events.

Feebers Hardy Plants
1 Feebers Cottage, Westwood, Broadclyst, Devon EX5 3DQ
☎ 01404 822118
CONTACT   Mrs Edna Squires
LOCATION   3 miles from Broadclyst, directions in catalogue
OPEN   10 am – 5 pm, Thursdays; 2 – 6 pm, Saturdays; March to July, September and October; or by appointment
SPECIALITIES   South American plants
NEW FOR 1995   *Libertia* and *Geum* grown from Chilean seed
CATALOGUE   Large SAE with 38p stamp
MAIL ORDER   Limited

The heavy clay nursery soil influences their choice of hardy perennials. There is a new range of Chilean plants.

Glebe Cottage Plants
Pixie Lane, Warkleigh, Umberleigh, Devon EX37 9DH
☎ 01769 540554
CONTACT   Carol Klein
LOCATION   5 miles south west of South Molton
OPEN   10 am – 5 pm, Wednesday – Friday
SPECIALITIES   Herbaceous perennials
CATALOGUE   £1.50
MAIL ORDER   Yes
GARDEN   Garden, admission £1
SHOWS   RHS Westminster; Malvern Spring; Harrogate (Spring); Southport; Chelsea; BBC GW Live; Hampton Court; Harrogate (Autumn); Courson

An exceptional list of perennials, with newly discovered species and promising cultivars. Carol Klein has a sharp eye for worthwhile new introductions, yet does not forget the reliable old classics, a talent recognised by 3 Gold Medals at Chelsea. Her own garden has been redesigned.

Greenway Gardens
Churston Ferrers, Brixham, Devon TQ5 0ES
☎ 01803 842382
CONTACT   Roger Clark
LOCATION   South west of Galmpton, towards Greenway ferry
OPEN   2 – 5 pm, Monday – Friday; 10 am – 12 pm, Saturdays
SPECIALITIES   Trees
CATALOGUE   3 second class stamps
MAIL ORDER   Yes
GARDEN   2 walled nursery gardens

An interesting list of mainly trees and shrubs, though no sizes and prices. Specialities include South American species, and plants grown from wild collected seed. On this basis, it sounds like a place to visit if you are in the area.

H & S Wills
2 St Brannocks Park Road, Ilfracombe, Devon EX34 8HU
☎ 01271 863949
CONTACT   H. Wills
OPEN   Mail order only

SPECIALITIES Sempervivums
CATALOGUE 3 first class stamps
MAIL ORDER Yes; minimum order £3

Small mail order only nursery with a large choice of houseleeks: *Sempervivum*, *Jovibarba* and *Rosularia*, both species and cultivars.

The High Garden
Courtwood, Newton Ferrers, Devon PL8 1BW
☎ 01752 872528

CONTACT F. Bennett
OPEN By appointment
SPECIALITIES Rhododendrons; *Pieris*
CATALOGUE 60p
MAIL ORDER Yes

Young plants of *Rhododendron* species and hybrids, Japanese azaleas and *Pieris* are sold from a detailed list. Some *Skimmia* and *Camellia* also available.

Jack's Patch
Newton Road, Bishopsteignton, Teignmouth, Devon TQ14 9PN
☎ 01626 776996

LOCATION Between Teignmouth and Newton Abbot on A381
OPEN 9 am – 5.30 pm, Monday – Saturday; 10 am – 5.30 pm, Bank Holidays; 10.30 am – 4.30 pm, Sundays
SHOP Gifts
REFRESHMENTS Jack's Kitchen
DESIGN SERVICE Jack's Patch
GIFT TOKENS HTA; own

Garden centre providing bedding plants and plants for small gardens among a general range. Most of the stock is grown at their own nurseries.

K & C Cacti
Fern Cottage, West Buckland, Barnstaple, Devon EX32 0SF
☎ 01598 760393

CONTACT Keith and Jane Comer
LOCATION Next to post office, opposite churchyard
OPEN Most days, but phone first
SPECIALITIES Cacti and succulents
CATALOGUE SAE
MAIL ORDER Yes

A good selection of cacti and succulents. Particularly strong on the *Mesembryanthemum* group and on *Haworthia*. Basic prices are low, and they can assemble collections for new collectors.

Kenwith Nursery
The Old Rectory, Littleham, Bideford, Devon EX39 5HW
☎ 01237 473752

CONTACT Gordon C. Haddow
LOCATION Next to parish church in Littleham
OPEN 10 am – 12 pm, 2 – 5 pm, Wednesday – Saturday. Other times by appointment
SPECIALITIES Conifers

CATALOGUE 3 first class stamps
MAIL ORDER Yes
GARDEN Garden contains over 1,000 dwarf conifers, many not grown elsewhere in the country

Just conifers – a very interesting and extensive collection of dwarf and slow-growing species and cultivars. They specialise in grafting. Recommended for enthusiasts, who might also be interested in the comprehensive *World Checklist of Conifers* (from Landsman's Bookshop), which Mr Haddow co-wrote with Humphrey Welch.

Knightshayes Garden Trust
The Garden Office, Knightshayes, Tiverton, Devon EX16 7RG

LOCATION Off A396 between Tiverton and Bampton
OPEN 10.30 am – 5.30 pm, daily, April to October
SPECIALITIES Bulbs
CATALOGUE £2.50
MAIL ORDER No
SHOP National Trust shop
REFRESHMENTS Restaurant
GARDEN Knightshayes Court, Devon, see Gardens section

The nursery sells plants which look good in this National Trust garden, including bulbs and shrubs.

Marwood Hill Gardens
Barnstaple, Devon EX31 4EB
☎ 01271 42528

CONTACT Dr J. A. Smart
OPEN 11 am – 5 pm, daily
SPECIALITIES Australian plants; bog plants; camellias; herbaceous perennials; New Zealand plants; trees
CATALOGUE 70p
MAIL ORDER No
REFRESHMENTS Sundays, Bank Holidays (April to October)
GARDEN Marwood Hill Gardens, Devon, see Gardens section

A charmingly varied assortment of interesting trees, shrubs and perennials propagated from the well-known garden.

Nicky's Rock Garden Nursery
Hillcrest, Broadhayes, Stockland, Honiton, Devon EX14 9EH
☎ 01404 881213

CONTACT Bob and Di Dark
LOCATION 6 miles east of Honiton, off midpoint of north/south road between A30 and A35. Map ref. ST 236027
OPEN 9 am – dusk, daily. Phone first
SPECIALITIES Alpines
CATALOGUE 3 first class stamps
MAIL ORDER No
GARDEN Display gardens

This nursery has a wide and changing selection of alpines and perennials for rock garden planting. Visitors

Devon Nurseries & Garden Centres

are asked to phone for directions in advance. They will be at the AGS Exeter show on 15 April.

North Devon Garden Centre
Ashford, Barnstaple, Devon EX31 4BW
☎ 01271 42880   FAX 01271 23972

CONTACT Miss J. Dellow
LOCATION Between Barnstaple and Braunton on A361
OPEN 9 am – 5 pm, Monday – Saturday; 10 am – 6 pm, Sundays
SHOP Garden sundries, conservatories, mowers, pools
REFRESHMENTS Tea room
GARDEN 2-acre show garden, with lake
DESIGN SERVICE North Devon Garden Centre
GIFT TOKENS HTA

General garden centre including all associated products. They have a landscaping department, and during the season a tropical butterfly house.

Otter Nurseries Ltd
Gosford Road, Ottery St Mary, Devon EX11 1LZ
☎ 01404 815815   FAX 01404 815816

CONTACT Mr S. Jones
LOCATION 1 mile from A30 (towards Ottery St Mary): turn at Brick Monument between Fenny Bridges and Fairmile
OPEN 9 am – 5.30 pm, Monday – Saturday; 10.30 am – 4.30 pm, Sundays. Closed Christmas, Boxing Day and Easter Sunday
CATALOGUE On request
MAIL ORDER No
SHOP Garden sundries, conservatories, greenhouses, machinery
REFRESHMENTS Restaurant
DESIGN SERVICE Otter Nurseries Ltd

Large garden centre with a wide general range of plants and garden products. They also have a nursery, so many of the plants are home-produced.

Perrie Hale Forest Nursery
Northcote Hill, Honiton, Devon EX14 8TH
☎ 01404 43344   FAX 01404 47163

CONTACT Mrs Judith Davey
LOCATION 1 mile north east of Honiton
OPEN Mid November to early April
SPECIALITIES Hedging; trees
NEW FOR 1995 *Pinus muricata, Picea omorika, Alnus rubra, Populus nigra, Populus canescens*
CATALOGUE SAE
MAIL ORDER Yes

Forest trees and hedging plants. This wholesale nursery is happy to deal with the public. They prefer you to collect, but small orders (under 200 plants) can be sent by courier.

Plant World Botanic Gardens
St Marychurch Road, Newton Abbot, Devon TQ12 4SE
☎ 01803 872939

CONTACT Ray Brown
OPEN 9 am – 5 pm, daily. Closed over Christmas
SPECIALITIES Seeds
NEW FOR 1995 *Aquilegia flabellata* 'Silver Edge' (dwarf, variegated), *Silene dioicia* 'Variegata', and hardy South African geraniums
CATALOGUE 3 second class stamps
MAIL ORDER Seeds only
REFRESHMENTS Award-winning farm-fresh ice cream
GARDEN Gardens divided into world habitat zones
NCCPG NATIONAL COLLECTIONS *Primula* (capitatae), *Primula* (cortusoides), *Primula* (farinosae)

The nursery sells a selection of alpines, perennials and shrubs. There is an illustrated seed list with fresh material from the gardens and some collected species. This year there are new variegated forms, true from seed. The gardens are planted out as special habitat zones.

Pleasant View Nursery & Garden
Two Mile Oak, Denbury, Newton Abbot, Devon TQ12 6DG
☎ 01803 813388

CONTACT Mrs Christine Yeo
LOCATION Take A381 from Newton Abbot: right opposite Two Mile Oak garage. Nursery is ¾ mile on the left
OPEN 10 am – 5 pm, Wednesday – Saturday, 22 March to 28 October
SPECIALITIES Shrubs; salvias
NEW FOR 1995 Many new plants
CATALOGUE 4 first class stamps
MAIL ORDER Yes; minimum order £20
GARDEN Garden open Wednesday and Friday afternoons, May to September
SHOWS RHS Westminster
NCCPG NATIONAL COLLECTIONS *Abelia, Salvia*

The nursery carries a selection of rare shrubs for gardens and conservatories, and also a number of *Salvia* from the National Collection. There is a special *Salvia* open day on 27 July (2 – 5 pm). They also hold the *Abelia* collection. The garden opens twice a week in season, and for the National Gardens Scheme on certain weekends. Groups and lectures by arrangement.

Pounsley Plants
Pounsley Combe, Spriddlestone, Brixton, Plymouth, Devon PL9 0DW
☎ 01752 402873

CONTACT Mrs Jane Hollow
LOCATION Telephone or write for directions
OPEN 10 am – 5 pm most days, but check first
SPECIALITIES Clematis; herbaceous perennials
NEW FOR 1995 Old roses

148 Nurseries & Garden Centres DEVON

CATALOGUE SAE plus 2 first class stamps
MAIL ORDER Yes; October to February only
GARDEN Garden open

A small nursery with perennials for cottage garden plantings, and some clematis and old roses too. There is an advice centre, 'Plants for Places'.

R D Plants
Homelea Farm, Tytherleigh, Axminster, Devon EX13 7BG
☎ 01460 220206

CONTACT Mrs Lynda Windsor
LOCATION On A358, just inside the county boundary
OPEN 9 am – 1 pm, 2 – 5.30 pm, March to September. Phone first (between 8.30 and 9.30 am)
SPECIALITIES Herbaceous perennials, woodland plants
NEW FOR 1995 *Antirrhinum* 'Powis Pride', *Platycodon grandiflorus* 'Axminster Striped', *Stachys coccinea* 'Yellow form'
CATALOGUE 3 first class stamps
MAIL ORDER No
GARDEN Small display area

A good variety of perennials, pond and moisture-loving plants. There are some ferns, and the new *Tropaeolum* species, which are available in small quantities only, look interesting. Customers are asked to ring between 8.30 and 9.30 am only.

RHS Enterprises Ltd
RHS Garden, Rosemoor, Great Torrington, Devon EX38 8PH
☎ 01805 624067   FAX 01805 624717

CONTACT J. Gingell
OPEN 10 am – 6 pm, April – September; 10 am – 5 pm, March and October; 10 am – 4 pm, November to February
CATALOGUE No
MAIL ORDER No
SHOP Books, gifts
REFRESHMENTS Restaurant (garden)
GARDEN RHS Garden, Rosemoor, Devon, see Gardens section
SHOWS RHS Westminster; Malvern Spring; Harrogate (Spring); Chelsea; BBC GW Live; Hampton Court; Harrogate (Autumn)
GIFT TOKENS HTA

There is an interesting selection of plants from the garden for sale here, as well as the new visitors' centre. Numerous walks and demonstrations are held here (and at Cannington College, Bridgwater) throughout the year. Both are also open to non-RHS members.

Rowden Gardens
Brentor, Tavistock, Devon PL19 0NG
☎ 01822 810275

CONTACT J. R. L. Carter
LOCATION Phone for details
OPEN 10 am – 5 pm, Saturday – Sunday, and Bank Holiday Mondays. Other times by appointment
SPECIALITIES Aquatic plants; bog plants; herbaceous perennials; *Iris*
CATALOGUE £1.50
MAIL ORDER Yes
GARDEN Garden
DESIGN SERVICE Rowden Gardens
SHOWS RHS Westminster; Malvern Spring; BBC GW Live; Hampton Court
NCCPG NATIONAL COLLECTIONS *Fallopia*, *Persicaria*

Mostly aquatic and moisture-loving plants here. The choice of *Iris*, including *I. ensata* cultivars, is especially good. The nursery draws on the 3,000 varieties in the garden. Groups welcome by arrangement – lectures available.

Sampford Shrubs
Sampford Peverell, Tiverton, Devon EX16 7EW
☎ 01884 821164

CONTACT Martin Hughes-Jones and Sue Proud
LOCATION 1 mile from M5, J27 and Tiverton Parkway station
OPEN 9 am – 5 pm (dusk if earlier), Thursday – Saturday; 10 am – 4 pm, Sundays. Closed over Christmas and January
SPECIALITIES Fruit; rhododendrons; shrubs
NEW FOR 1995 *Euphorbia amygdaloides* 'Brithembottom', *Roscoea cautleoides*, Apple 'Lady's Finger of Lancashire', *Crocosmia* 'James Coey', and more
CATALOGUE Long SAE
MAIL ORDER Yes; winter only

A mixed collection of herbaceous plants and trees and shrubs, with a good selection of fruit. The list is crammed with reliable varieties to grow. They will be at the NCCPG's Devon plant sales.

Scotts Clematis
Lee, Ilfracombe, Devon EX34 8LW
☎ 01271 863366   FAX 01271 863366

CONTACT John Scott
LOCATION 3 miles west of Ilfracombe
OPEN 10 am – 5 pm, February to October. Closed Mondays and Saturdays
SPECIALITIES Clematis
CATALOGUE SAE
MAIL ORDER Yes; minimum order 3 plants
SHOWS Malvern Spring; Southport; BBC GW Live; Hampton Court

Clematis specialists, now producing in excess of 250 varieties at the nursery.

Thornhayes Nursery
Dulford, Cullompton, Devon EX15 2DF
☎ 01884 266746   FAX 01884 266739

CONTACT Kevin Croucher
LOCATION 10 minutes from M5, J28

Dorset Nurseries & Garden Centres

OPEN   By appointment only
SPECIALITIES   Fruit; trees
CATALOGUE   4 first class stamps
MAIL ORDER   Yes

A newish nursery, mainly wholesale. The stock is both open ground and container-grown, and covers a broad spectrum of ornamental and fruit trees, including some hard to get West Country apples (for cider, cooking and eating). The *Sorbus* and *Crataegus* are also good: dendrophiles should take a closer look.

Veryans Plants
Glebe, Coryton, Okehampton, Devon EX20 4PB
☎ 01566 783433

CONTACT   Rebecca Miller
LOCATION   3 miles from A30
OPEN   By appointment only
SPECIALITIES   Herbaceous perennials; primulas
NEW FOR 1995   *Geranium harveyi*, *G. sessiliflorum* ssp. *novae-zelandiae*, *G. sessiliflorum* × *traversii elegans*
CATALOGUE   3 first class stamps
MAIL ORDER   Yes
SHOWS   RHS Westminster; Malvern Spring; BBC GW Live; Hampton Court

Young nursery with a selection of cottage garden plants including *Primula* cultivars and a good collection of penstemons, asters and geraniums.

Westfield Cacti
Kennford, Exeter, Devon EX6 7XD
☎ 01392 832921

CONTACT   Ralph and Marina Northcott
LOCATION   Kennford – at the end of the M5
OPEN   10 am – dusk, daily
SPECIALITIES   Cacti and succulents; seeds
NEW FOR 1995   New *Hoya* cultivars
CATALOGUE   4 first class stamps
MAIL ORDER   Yes
REFRESHMENTS   For groups only
GARDEN   Show house open
SHOWS   RHS Westminster; Malvern Spring; Southport; BBC GW Live; Hampton Court

There is a huge choice of cacti and succulents at this retail and wholesale nursery. The stocks are also impressively large. Seeds and some books are also sold.

Withleigh Nurseries
Withleigh, Tiverton, Devon EX16 8JG
☎ 01884 253351

CONTACT   C. S. Britton
LOCATION   3 miles west of Tiverton on B3137
OPEN   9 am – 5.30 pm, Tuesday – Saturday. Also open Mondays, March to June
SPECIALITIES   Herbaceous perennials; shrubs
MAIL ORDER   No
GARDEN   Garden opens for NGS
GIFT TOKENS   Own

A retail nursery with a range of bedding, herbaceous perennials and shrubs. Visitors are usually allowed in the garden too, which also opens for the NGS.

DORSET

Abbey Plants
Chaffeymoor, Bourton, Gillingham, Dorset SP8 5BY
☎ 01747 840841

CONTACT   Mr K. R. Potts
LOCATION   3 miles east of Wincanton, off A303
OPEN   10 am – 1 pm, 2 – 5 pm, Tuesday – Saturday
MAIL ORDER   No
REFRESHMENTS   At garden: last Sunday of each month and Bank Holidays
GARDEN   Chiffchaffs, Dorset, see Gardens section

The nursery sells a range of flowering shrubs including roses, and herbaceous and alpine plants.

Abbotsbury Gardens
Abbotsbury, Weymouth, Dorset DT3 4LA
☎ 01308 871412/871344

CONTACT   Mr D. Sutton
LOCATION   9 miles west of Weymouth, on the Dorset coast
OPEN   10 am – 5 pm, daily, March to October; 10 am – 3 pm, daily, November to March
SPECIALITIES   Half-hardy plants, subtropical plants
CATALOGUE   £1 plus large SAE
MAIL ORDER   Yes; minimum order £10
SHOP   Garden shop and plant centre
REFRESHMENTS   Yes
GARDEN   Abbotsbury Subtropical Gardens, Dorset, see Gardens section

Attached to these famous gardens, the plant centre naturally specialises in tender and subtropical plants, including penstemons and salvias, and in species which give a tropical effect.

Barthelemy & Co Nurseries
262 Wimborne Road West, Stape Hill, Wimborne, Dorset BH21 2DZ
☎ 01202 874283   FAX 01202 897482

CONTACT   John Skinner
LOCATION   Between Wimborne and Ferndown
OPEN   9 am – 5 pm, Monday – Saturday, 1 April to 31 December. Closed 1 – 2 pm.
SPECIALITIES   Acers
CATALOGUE   SAE
MAIL ORDER   Yes

Specialist growers of acers. They have a large number of grafted *A. palmatum* cultivars besides bare root and pot-grown species seedlings.

Beacon Fuchsias
11 Tuckers Lane, Poole, Dorset BH15 4BT
☎ 01202 685053

CONTACT   Alan and Nancy Franklin
OPEN   10 am – 5 pm, daily, February to July

SPECIALITIES Fuchsias
NEW FOR 1995 New varieties of fuchsia
CATALOGUE 1 first class stamp
MAIL ORDER Yes

There are over 400 hundred fuchsias, varieties and species, available in spring and summer. Bedding and patio plants, with a selection of pelargoniums, can be bought as well.

Bennetts Water Lily Farm
Water Gardens, Putton Lane, Chickerell, Weymouth, Dorset DT3 4AF
☎ 01305 785150   FAX 01305 781619

CONTACT J. Bennett
LOCATION 2 miles west of Weymouth, off B3157 Bridport road
OPEN Tuesday – Sunday, April to September
SPECIALITIES Aquatic plants; bog plants; water lilies
CATALOGUE 3 first class stamps
MAIL ORDER Yes
SHOP Gifts, pond supplies
REFRESHMENTS Tea room, cream teas
GARDEN 6-acre site, with 80 varieties of water lilies

Water lilies, pond plants and marginals in abundance, as well as extensive display ponds. The flowering season is from June to late September, here. They also have tropical varieties to tempt conservatory owners.

C W Groves & Son
Nursery & Garden Centre, West Bay Road, Bridport, Dorset DT6 4BA
☎ 01308 22654   FAX 01308 420888

LOCATION On A35 Bridport bypass, opposite Crown roundabout
OPEN 8.30 am – 5 pm, Monday – Saturday; 10.30 am – 4.30 pm, Sundays
SPECIALITIES Violas
CATALOGUE SAE
MAIL ORDER Yes
REFRESHMENTS Café
GARDEN Summer months: rose beds, asparagus beds, and demonstration vineyard
GIFT TOKENS HTA

A traditional and family-run nursery *cum* garden centre, with a good general range. The firm was founded by the present owner's great-great-grandfather in 1866. Appropriately enough they also specialise in Victorian violets. These named violet cultivars are only sold by mail order, though.

Cherry Tree Nursery (SWOP)
Off New Road Roundabout, Northbourne, Bournemouth, Dorset BH10 7DA
☎ 01202 593537   FAX 01202 590626

CONTACT Ms Jessica Davies
LOCATION Off A347, north of Bournemouth
OPEN 8.30 am – 3.30 pm, Monday – Friday; 9 am – 12 pm, Saturdays (most)
SPECIALITIES Shrubs
NEW FOR 1995 Many new plants
CATALOGUE Large SAE
MAIL ORDER No
GIFT TOKENS Own

A wholesale and retail nursery with an expanding range of shrubs, climbers and conifers. It is run by a charity which provides sheltered work opportunities for adults with mental health problems.

Cranborne Manor Garden Centre
Cranborne, Wimborne, Dorset BH21 5PP
☎ 01725 517248   FAX 01725 517248

CONTACT Miss Sandra Hewitt
LOCATION 10 miles north of Wimborne on B3078
OPEN 9 am – 5 pm, Tuesday – Saturday; 10 am – 5 pm, Sundays and Bank Holidays. Closed Mondays
SPECIALITIES Roses
CATALOGUE £1
MAIL ORDER Roses only; November to February
SHOP Pots and ornaments
GARDEN Cranborne Manor, Dorset. 9 am – 5 pm, Wednesdays only, March to September. See Gardens section
GIFT TOKENS HTA

Among the general stock there is a good choice of herbaceous plants. The specialities, though, are old-fashioned roses and topiary specimens. If you go on a Wednesday (March to September) the garden is also open.

Global Orange Groves UK
PO Box 644, Poole, Dorset BH17 9YB
☎ 01202 691699

CONTACT Mrs Oliver
LOCATION Horton Heath, near Wimborne
OPEN Weekends, when not exhibiting
SPECIALITIES Citrus
CATALOGUE SAE
MAIL ORDER Yes
SHOWS Malvern Spring; Hampton Court

Fruiting citrus trees in containers: they have 32 varieties, including lemons, mandarins and kumquats. Groups are offered a free talk and tour of the nursery. Their special summer and winter fertilisers are recommended for anyone with bedraggled and non-fruiting citrus.

Holme Nurseries
West Holme Farm, West Holme, Wareham, Dorset BH20 6AG
☎ 01929 554716

CONTACT Simon Goldsack
LOCATION On B3070, between Wareham and Lulworth
OPEN 10 am – 5 pm, daily, 1 March to 24 December
CATALOGUE £1
MAIL ORDER No
GIFT TOKENS HTA

Dorset Nurseries & Garden Centres

There is a general range, including herbaceous plants, shrubs, climbers and fruit bushes.

Humphries Garden Centre
Littlemoor Road, Preston, Weymouth, Dorset DT3 6AD
☎ 01305 834766   FAX 01305 832708
CONTACT   Simon Lee or Duncan Cunningham
OPEN   9 am – 5.30 pm, Monday – Saturday; 10.30 am – 4.30 pm, Sunday
CATALOGUE   No
MAIL ORDER   No
SHOP   Garden sundries, pets, pond and pool equipment
REFRESHMENTS   Café
GIFT TOKENS   HTA; own

Macpennys Nurseries
154 Burley Road, Bransgore, Christchurch, Dorset BH23 8DB
☎ 01425 672348
CONTACT   Mr T. M. Lowndes
LOCATION   Between Christchurch and Burley
OPEN   9 am – 5 pm, Monday – Saturday; 2 – 5 pm, Sundays. Closed at Christmas and New Year
CATALOGUE   SAE plus 50p
MAIL ORDER   Yes
GARDEN   4-acre woodland garden
GIFT TOKENS   Own

Long-established nursery with a reliable general range across the plant spectrum. The garden is open for the National Gardens Scheme at the same times. Talks and special openings can be arranged for groups.

Milton Garden Plants
Milton on Stour, Gillingham, Dorset SP8 5PX
☎ 01747 822484   FAX 01747 822484
CONTACT   Sue Hardy
LOCATION   3 miles south of A303 at Mere
OPEN   8.30 am – 5.30 pm, Tuesday – Saturday and Bank Holidays; 10 am – 5 pm, Sundays. Closed Mondays
SPECIALITIES   Herbaceous perennials
CATALOGUE   4 first class stamps; perennials only
MAIL ORDER   No
GARDEN   Display gardens
DESIGN SERVICE   Milton Garden Plants
GIFT TOKENS   HTA; own

Family-run plant centre, with a good general range, notably of hardy perennials.

Naked Cross Nurseries
Waterloo Road, Corfe Mullen, Wimborne, Dorset BH21 3SR
☎ 01202 693256
CONTACT   Mr P. J. French and Mrs J. Paddon
OPEN   9 am – 5 pm, daily
SPECIALITIES   Heathers
CATALOGUE   On request

MAIL ORDER   Yes
Family-run nursery with a choice of heathers and herbaceous perennials.

Orchid Sundries Ltd & Hardy Orchids Ltd
New Gate Farm, Scotchey Lane, Stour Provost, Gillingham, Dorset SP8 5LT
☎ 01747 838368   FAX 01747 838308
CONTACT   N. J. Heywood
OPEN   8 am – 1 pm, 2 – 5 pm, Tuesday – Saturday
SPECIALITIES   Orchids (hardy)
CATALOGUE   On request
MAIL ORDER   Yes
SHOP   Orchid books and sundries
GARDEN   Display garden open by appointment

The business is devoted to hardy orchids, old and new books about them, and the materials needed to grow them.

Three Counties Nurseries
Marshwood, Bridport, Dorset DT6 5QJ
☎ 01297 678257
CONTACT   Mr and Mrs D. C. Hitchcock
OPEN   Mail order only
SPECIALITIES   *Dianthus*
CATALOGUE   2 second class stamps
MAIL ORDER   Yes
SHOWS   RHS Westminster; Chelsea; BBC GW Live; Hampton Court; Malvern; Harrogate (Spring); Harrogate (Autumn)

Dianthus specialists, with a wide choice of garden pinks, including laced, old-fashioned and modern hybrids. They also have alpine *Dianthus* and a new selection of named *D. barbatus* (Sweet Williams). Lectures by arrangement.

Trehane Camellia Nursery
Stapehill Road, Hampreston, Wimborne, Dorset BH21 7NE
☎ 01202 873490   FAX 01202 873490
CONTACT   Miss Jennifer Trehane
LOCATION   Between Ferndown and Wimborne, off A31
OPEN   9 am – 4 pm, Monday – Friday, all year; 10 am – 4.30 pm, Saturdays and Sundays, late February to October
SPECIALITIES   Camellias; blueberry plants
CATALOGUE   £1.50 handbook
MAIL ORDER   Yes
GARDEN   Display house and new display garden
SHOWS   RHS Westminster; Harrogate (Spring); Hampton Court
GIFT TOKENS   Own

Wholesale and retail camellia growers. They have a wide choice of *Camellia* hybrids, and *Magnolia*, *Pieris* and azaleas. They also grow and sell blueberries and cranberries. A new display garden opens this year.

White Veil Fuchsias
Verwood Road, Three Legged Cross, Wimborne, Dorset BH21 6RP
☎ 01202 813998

CONTACT   Robin Case
OPEN   9 am – 1 pm, 2 – 5 pm, daily. Closed for lunch
SPECIALITIES   Fuchsias
CATALOGUE   2 first class stamps
MAIL ORDER   Yes
SHOWS   RHS Westminster; Chelsea; Hampton Court; Malvern; Harrogate (Spring); Harrogate (Autumn)

Fuchsia specialists; they attend the major shows.

CO. DURHAM

Eggleston Hall Gardens
The Cottage, Eggleston Hall, Eggleston, Barnard Castle, Co. Durham DL12 0AG
☎ 01833 50378/650403

CONTACT   Mrs R. H. Gray and Mr Gordon Long
LOCATION   Off the B6278: follow local signs
OPEN   10 am – 5 pm, daily
SPECIALITIES   Foliage plants
NEW FOR 1995   *Lavatera arborea* 'Variegata'
CATALOGUE   £1.50
MAIL ORDER   No
GARDEN   Garden open: 50p entrance charge (or £1 season ticket) covers nursery and garden

The gardens grow a varied selection of plants, with the emphasis on providing year-round material for flower arranging. The wide choice in the plant centre reflects this balance.

Elly Hill Herbs
Elly Hill House, Barmpton, Darlington, Co. Durham DL1 3JF
☎ 01325 464682

CONTACT   Mrs Nina Pagan
LOCATION   2 miles north east of Darlington
OPEN   9.30 am – 12.30 pm, 4 – 5.30 pm, daily, March to October. Phone first
SPECIALITIES   Herbs
CATALOGUE   Large SAE
MAIL ORDER   Herb book only (£4.75, inc. p & p)
REFRESHMENTS   By arrangement, for herb parties
GARDEN   Herb garden

A herb nursery selling herb plants and products. They organise herb parties and give conducted tours to groups. Their book, *Herbs and So On*, is available by post.

Elmridge Gardens Ltd
Coniscliffe Road, Darlington, Co. Durham DL3 8DJ
☎ 01325 462710   FAX 01325 363550

CONTACT   Mr J. Blake
OPEN   8.30 am – 5.30 pm, daily (6.30 pm, April to July)
SPECIALITIES   Bedding plants
CATALOGUE   On request
MAIL ORDER   No

GIFT TOKENS   HTA
Bedding and pot plants, shrubs.

Equatorial Plant Co
7 Gray Lane, Barnard Castle, Co. Durham DL12 8PD
☎ 01833 690519   FAX 01833 690519

CONTACT   Dr R. Warren
LOCATION   South Durham
SPECIALITIES   Orchids
CATALOGUE   SAE
MAIL ORDER   Yes
SHOWS   RHS Westminster

They specialise in laboratory-raised tropical orchids, which are sold at the right size for transplanting. They are active in conservation, including Brazil's coastal rain forest, where introductory orchid tours can be arranged.

Rookhope Nurseries
Rookhope, Upper Weardale, Co. Durham DL13 2DD
☎ 01388 517272

LOCATION   5 miles west of Stanhope, off A689
OPEN   9 am – 5 pm, daily, mid March to end September. Phone first in winter
SPECIALITIES   Alpines; herbaceous perennials
CATALOGUE   3 first class stamps
MAIL ORDER   Limited mail order
REFRESHMENTS   Drinks and sweets
GARDEN   Display gardens
GIFT TOKENS   HTA; own

Hardy garden plants, alpines, perennials and shrubs: all in wide variety. The nursery is high up in the Pennines so the plants are selected for the northern climate.

ESSEX

B & H M Baker
Bourne Brook Nurseries, Greenstead Green, Halstead, Essex CO9 1RJ
☎ 01787 476367

CONTACT   B. and H. M. Baker
LOCATION   Halstead, Essex
OPEN   9 am – 4.30 pm, Monday – Friday; 9 am – 12 pm, 2 – 4.30 pm, Saturdays and Sundays
SPECIALITIES   Fuchsias
CATALOGUE   20p plus first class stamp
MAIL ORDER   No

This fuchsia specialist carries a large range of old and new cultivars, and species. There are bedding plants and hanging baskets in season.

The Beth Chatto Gardens Ltd
Elmstead Market, Colchester, Essex CO7 7DB
☎ 01206 822007   FAX 01206 825933

LOCATION   7 miles east of Colchester on A133
OPEN   9 am – 5 pm, Monday – Saturday, March to October; 9 am – 4 pm, Monday – Friday, November to February
SPECIALITIES   Herbaceous perennials

Essex Nurseries & Garden Centres

CATALOGUE £2.50
MAIL ORDER Yes; £20 minimum order
GARDEN Beth Chatto Gardens, Essex, see Gardens section
GIFT TOKENS Own

The nursery is a prime source for out of the ordinary plants. The selection bears the stamp of a plantswoman with a discerning eye for effective plant combinations.

Bullwood Nursery
54 Woodlands Road, Hockley, Essex SS5 4PY
☎ 01702 203761

CONTACT Derek Fox
LOCATION 3 miles north east of Rayleigh
OPEN 9.30 am – 5.30 pm, Wednesdays and Sundays
SPECIALITIES Lilies
CATALOGUE SAE
MAIL ORDER Yes
GARDEN Volpaia, Essex, see Gardens section

Lilies and liliaceous plants from a plantsman's garden.

Bypass Nurseries
72 Ipswich Road, Colchester, Essex CO1 2YF
☎ 01206 865500   FAX 01206 865810

CONTACT Gina Zimmerman
OPEN 9 am – 5.30 pm, March to October; 9 am – 5 pm, winter
SHOP Conservatories, greenhouses, water and flowers
DESIGN SERVICE Bypass Nurseries
GIFT TOKENS HTA

A traditional garden centre supplying plants, and a range of garden products through franchises. Delivery and landscaping services available.

Cants of Colchester
Nayland Road, Mile End, Colchester, Essex CO4 5EB
☎ 01206 844008   FAX 01206 855371

CONTACT Miss Angela Pawsey
LOCATION North of Colchester, on A134
OPEN Times vary: phone first
SPECIALITIES Roses
NEW FOR 1995 Rose 'Silver Anniversary' (Autumn 1995)
CATALOGUE On request
MAIL ORDER Yes; fixed p & p rates
GARDEN Rose fields are open from the end of June to late September. Free entry, and no need to phone
SHOWS Chelsea; Hampton Court
GIFT TOKENS HTA; own

Dynasty of rose breeders and growers, best known for 'Just Joey', one of the most popular roses of the century. The range is mostly of modern varieties. Callers can obtain containerised plants between April and August, and bare root from November to March: they stress the need to phone before visiting. The nursery will be at the Portsmouth, Kent County and New Forest shows this year.

Copford Bulbs
Dorsetts, Birch Road, Copford, Colchester, Essex CO6 1DR
☎ 01206 330008

CONTACT D. J. Pearce
OPEN By appointment
SPECIALITIES Daffodils, *Cyclamen* (hardy)
CATALOGUE 50p
MAIL ORDER Yes
SHOWS RHS Westminster; Harrogate (Spring); Chelsea; Hampton Court

Daffodils for exhibitors and enthusiasts. They also sell young plants of hardy cyclamen.

The Cottage Garden
Langham Road, Boxted, Colchester, Essex CO4 5HU

CONTACT Alison Smith
LOCATION 4 miles north of Colchester
OPEN 8 am – 6 pm, Monday – Saturday; 9.30 – 6 pm, Sundays, March to June; 8 am – 6 pm, Thursday – Monday, July to February; 9.30 am – 6 pm (or dusk), Sundays
MAIL ORDER No
SHOP Garden antiques, garden sundries
GARDEN Display garden
GIFT TOKENS Own

The nursery sells home-grown plants in variety, including perennials and bulbs. Also on sale are garden sundries and garden antiques.

County Park Nursery
384 Wingletye Lane, Hornchurch, Essex RM11 3BU
☎ 01708 445205

CONTACT Graham Hutchins
LOCATION 2½ miles from M25, J29. Off Wingletye Lane, in Essex Gardens, Hornchurch
OPEN 9 am – 6 pm, Monday – Saturday; 10 am – 5 pm, Sundays; from March to October. Closed Wednesdays. Open in winter by appointment only
SPECIALITIES Australian plants; New Zealand plants; *Hebe*
NEW FOR 1995 Several new additions
CATALOGUE 3 first class stamps
MAIL ORDER No
NCCPG NATIONAL COLLECTIONS *Coprosma*

This small nursery specialises in Antipodean plants, many of them grown from native seed. There are lots of hebes, as well as clematis, *Coprosma* and other genera. The main address is for postal inquiries only. The nursery includes many specimen and stock plants.

Crowther Nurseries and Landscapes
Ongar Road, Abridges, Essex RM4 1AA
☎ 01708 688581   FAX 01078 688677

CONTACT K. Crowther
LOCATION On A113 between Chigwell and Ongar, beside Stapleford Airdrome
OPEN 9 am – 5.30 pm, closed over Christmas

MAIL ORDER No
DESIGN SERVICE Crowther Nurseries and Landscapes
GIFT TOKENS HTA

Nursery and garden centre with a general range and a garden design and contruction service.

The Fens
Old Mill Road, Langham, Colchester, Essex CO4 5NU
☎ 01206 272259

CONTACT Ann Lunn
LOCATION 5 miles north of Colchester, off A12
OPEN 10 am – 5 pm, Thursday and Saturday; Also, daily in April
SPECIALITIES Primulas; *Dicentra*
CATALOGUE 3 first class stamps
MAIL ORDER No
GARDEN Garden opens for NGS
NCCPG NATIONAL COLLECTIONS *Dicentra*

Mainly perennial plants for damp and woodland sites: a wide selection of primulas in particular. The Essex NCCPG group's *Dicentra* collection is held at the nursery.

Flora Exotica
Pasadena, South Green, Fingringhoe, Colchester, Essex CO5 7DR
☎ 01206 729414

CONTACT Mr J. Beddoes
OPEN Mail order only
SPECIALITIES Carnivorous plants; lilies; seeds
CATALOGUE £1.50
MAIL ORDER Yes

Insectivorous plants by mail order: *Pinguicula, Utricularia* and *Nepenthe*, as well as a good choice of *Lilium* bulbs (eighty varieties).

Frances Mount Perennial Plants
1 Steps Farm, Polstead, Colchester, Essex CO6 5AE
☎ 01206 262811

CONTACT Frances Mount
LOCATION 8 miles from Colchester and Sudbury
OPEN 10 am – 5 pm, Tuesday, Wednesday, Saturday, Sunday; 2 – 6 pm, Fridays
SPECIALITIES Herbaceous perennials
CATALOGUE 3 first class stamps
MAIL ORDER Yes; minimum order £6
GARDEN Display garden

A small nursery whose stock includes hardy herbaceous perennials and, notably, over 50 varieties of hardy geraniums.

Glen Chantry
Ishams Chase, Wickham Bishops, Essex CM8 3LG
☎ 01621 891342

CONTACT Mrs Sue Staines
LOCATION Map in catalogue
OPEN 10 am – 4 pm, Fridays and Saturdays, 21 April to 31 October; on garden open days
SPECIALITIES Alpines; herbaceous perennials
CATALOGUE 3 first class stamps
MAIL ORDER No
GARDEN Garden opens for NGS

This is a small nursery with a developing collection of perennials and alpines, dwarf rhododendrons and conifers. Particular interests are *Iris* and *Euphorbia*, and plants for white gardens.

Hull Farm Conifer Centre
John Fryer & Sons, Spring Valley Lane, Ardleigh, Colchester, Essex CO7 7SA
☎ 01206 230045

CONTACT J. Fryer & Sons
OPEN 10 am – 4.30 pm, daily
SPECIALITIES Conifers
CATALOGUE SAE plus 70p
MAIL ORDER No

Over 400 varieties of conifer, in a choice of sizes, but also rhododendrons, camellias and fruit trees. Open ground conifers available from November to April.

Ken Evans Orchids
48 Thundersley Park Road, Benfleet, Essex SS7 1ET
☎ 01268 751619

CONTACT Ken Evans
OPEN By appointment
SPECIALITIES Orchids
CATALOGUE Monthly lists on request
MAIL ORDER Yes

A small specialist orchid nursery with a constantly changing stock.

Ken Muir Nurseries
Honeypot Farm, Weeley Heath, Clacton on Sea, Essex CO16 9BJ
☎ 01255 830181   FAX 01255 831534

CONTACT Ken Muir
LOCATION Between Colchester and Clacton, off A133
OPEN 10 am – 4 pm, daily. Closed Christmas and Boxing Day
SPECIALITIES Fruit
CATALOGUE 3 first class stamps
MAIL ORDER Yes
SHOWS RHS Westminster; Chelsea; BBC GW Live; Hampton Court

Fruit specialist with a substantial mail order business. If the lure of Honeypot Farm isn't enough in itself, then consider the wide range of strawberries, raspberries, other soft fruit and fruit trees. Some of the more popular varieties are grown as slender columns, suitable for smaller gardens and tubs.

Langthorns Plantery
Little Canfield, Dunmow, Essex CM6 1TD
☎ 01371 872611   FAX 01371 872611

CONTACT D. N. Cannon

Essex Nurseries & Garden Centres

LOCATION Between Takeley and Great Dunmow, signed off A120
OPEN 10 am – 5 pm, daily. Closed Christmas to New Year
SPECIALITIES Herbaceous perennials
CATALOGUE £1
MAIL ORDER No
GARDEN Gardens
GIFT TOKENS Own

Hardy plants of all kinds in a very varied and extensive range. The herbaceous section is especially good, and there are interesting alpines, shrubs and trees here too. Langthorns Garden is open the last week of each month.

Mill Race Nursery
New Road, Aldham, Colchester, Essex CO6 3QT
☎ 01206 242324   FAX 01206 241616

CONTACT Bill Mathews or Philip Bell
LOCATION Ford Street, Aldham, off A604
OPEN 9 am – 5.30 pm, daily; 11 am – 5 pm, Sundays
SPECIALITIES Herbaceous perennials; trees
NEW FOR 1995 *Eremurus* hybrids (new colours), new dark blue *Lobelia* selection, new *Gaura* selection
CATALOGUE SAE (A4)
MAIL ORDER No
REFRESHMENTS Refreshments
GARDEN Demonstration gardens
DESIGN SERVICE Mill Race Landscapes Ltd
GIFT TOKENS Own

A large nursery with a wide range of container-grown stock, sold both wholesale and retail. Plant types include conifers, climbers, trees, shrubs, perennials and fruit trees and bushes.

Plantworld
Burnam Road, South Woodham Ferrers, Chelmsford, Essex CM3 5QP
☎ 01245 320482   FAX 01245 320482

CONTACT F. Waterworth
OPEN 10 am – 4 pm, Tuesday – Sunday. Closed Mondays
SPECIALITIES *Tropaeolum speciosum*
CATALOGUE £2
MAIL ORDER Yes

A range of hardy perennials, with a speciality in *Tropaeolum speciosum*.

Rhodes & Rockliffe
2 Nursery Road, Nazeing, Essex EN9 2JE
☎ 01992 463693   FAX 01992 440673

CONTACT David Rhodes
LOCATION Phone for directions
OPEN By appointment only
SPECIALITIES Begonias
NEW FOR 1995 Several new American hybrids
CATALOGUE 2 first class stamps
MAIL ORDER Yes; minimum order £2.50
SHOWS RHS Westminster; Chelsea

Begonia specialists, with some out of the way species and hybrids.

Savill's Clematis Ltd
Hanging Gardens Nurseries, Writtle Bypass, Oxney Green, Writtle, Chelmsford, Essex CM1 5YX
☎ 01245 422245   FAX 01245 422293

CONTACT Robin Savill or Sheila Chapman
LOCATION On A414, Writtle bypass
OPEN 9 am – 6 pm, daily, summer; 9 am – 5 pm, daily, winter
SPECIALITIES Clematis
NEW FOR 1995 New species and hybrids
CATALOGUE 4 first class stamps
MAIL ORDER Yes
GIFT TOKENS HTA

A specialist clematis nursery. The large selection encompasses species, newer hybrids and popular cultivars. There is a general plant range at the parent company, Hanging Gardens Nurseries.

Three Suns Nursery
Spital Road, Maldon, Essex CM9 6SH
☎ 01621 853872

CONTACT Mrs A. Thorogood
LOCATION On A414, south of Maldon
OPEN 9 am – 6 pm
SPECIALITIES Pelargoniums
CATALOGUE 30p
MAIL ORDER Yes
SHOWS RHS Westminster; Hampton Court

A regal pelargonium specialist. There is a good collection of standards and a small general plant range.

Trevor Scott Ornamental Grasses
Thorpe Park Cottage, Thorpe le Soken, Essex CO16 0HN
☎ 01255 861308   FAX 01255 861308

CONTACT Trevor Scott
LOCATION Thorpe le Soken, near Colchester
OPEN By appointment only
SPECIALITIES Grasses
NEW FOR 1995 *Arundinaria pumila*, *Panicum virgatum* 'Rotstrahlbusch', *Pennisetum villosum*, *Phaenosperma globosa*, *Phragmites australis* 'Variegatus' and others
CATALOGUE 5 first class stamps
MAIL ORDER Yes; minimum order £20 plus p & p
GARDEN Garden

A very wide range of grasses for all purposes and situations: there are some other interesting perennials too. Visitors by appointment to the nursery and garden.

Whitehouse Ivies
Brookhill, Halstead Road, Fordham, Colchester, Essex CO6 3LW
☎ 01206 240077

CONTACT R. Whitehouse
LOCATION On A604 (not in Fordham village)

OPEN By appointment
SPECIALITIES Ivies
CATALOGUE £1
MAIL ORDER Yes

The largest retail range of *Hedera* species and cultivars. Over 300 are now available, for climbing, trailing, topiary, ground cover and container use. Most of the business is mail order: the catalogue is fully illustrated. Do phone first if you want to visit the nursery.

GLOUCESTERSHIRE

Andrew Norfield Trees & Seeds
Lower Meend, St Briavels, Gloucestershire
GL15 6RW
☎ 01594 530134   FAX 01594 530113
CONTACT Andrew Norfield
OPEN Mail order only
SPECIALITIES Acers; seeds; trees
CATALOGUE 1 first class stamp
MAIL ORDER Yes
SHOWS Malvern Spring

The tree list sells young container-grown species including *Nothofagus* and *Stewartia*: the list is especially strong on *Acer* and *Betula*. The other side of the business supplies pre-germinated seed of trees, shrubs, house plants, bulbs and herbaceous plants. Here you pay a premium on the ordinary seed price, but do not have to wait for lengthy or difficult germination conditions to be fulfilled.

Cowcombe Farm Herbs
Gipsy Lane, Chalford, Stroud, Gloucestershire
GL6 8HP
☎ 01285 760544
CONTACT Caroline Barnett
LOCATION Between Stroud and Cirencester, near A419, at Aston Down
OPEN 2 – 5 pm, Wednesday – Friday; 10 am – 5 pm, Saturdays and Sundays; Easter to end of October
SPECIALITIES Herbs; seeds; wild flowers
CATALOGUE 2 second class stamps
MAIL ORDER No
GARDEN Herb beds

Herbs and wild plants for sale. They are also the home of the Seed Bank and Exchange scheme: members swop seed from their own collections, the aim being to preserve endangered species. Send 2 second class stamps for details.

Four Counties Nursery
Todenham, Moreton in Marsh, Gloucestershire
GL56 9PN
☎ 01608 650522   FAX 01608 650591
CONTACT Sandra Taylor
LOCATION Cotswolds
OPEN 9 am – 6 pm, Monday – Saturday, 25 March to 21 October; 9 am – 5 pm, Monday – Saturday, 22 October to 24 March. Also 11 am – 5 pm, Sundays, all year
SPECIALITIES Conservatory plants; trees; citrus trees
CATALOGUE £1 plus SAE
MAIL ORDER No
SHOP Farm shop, pick your own fruit
REFRESHMENTS Café (summer only)
GARDEN Demonstration gardens
GIFT TOKENS HTA

Four Counties have an extensive range of trees and shrubs. In addition, they also specialise in conservatory plants, including citrus trees.

Highfield Garden Centre
Bristol Road, Whitminster, Gloucester, Gloucestershire GL2 7PB
☎ 01452 741444   FAX 01452 740750
LOCATION On A38, ½ a mile from M5, J13
OPEN 9 am – 6 pm, Monday – Saturday; 10.30 am – 4.30 pm, Sundays
CATALOGUE On request
MAIL ORDER No
SHOP Sundries, tools
REFRESHMENTS Coffee shop
GIFT TOKENS HTA; own

This is Highfield Nurseries' new garden centre.

Highfield Nurseries
School Lane, Whitminster, Gloucester, Gloucestershire GL2 7PL
☎ 01452 740266   FAX 01452 740750
CONTACT Mrs J. E. Greenway
LOCATION Off A38, ½ a mile from M5, J13
OPEN 9 am – 5 pm, Monday – Friday. Closed Saturdays and Sundays
SPECIALITIES Fruit
CATALOGUE On request
MAIL ORDER Yes
GARDEN Demonstration garden
DESIGN SERVICE Julian Dowle Partnership
SHOWS RHS Westminster; Chelsea; Hampton Court
GIFT TOKENS HTA; own

Large nurseries with an extensive all-round range – good choice of fruit trees and bushes. They have a new garden centre nearby (see above).

Hoo House Nursery
Hoo House, Gloucester Road, Tewkesbury, Gloucestershire GL20 7DA
☎ 01684 293389
CONTACT Mrs Julie Ritchie
LOCATION 2 miles south of Tewkesbury on A38
OPEN 2 – 5 pm, Monday – Saturday
SPECIALITIES Alpines; herbaceous perennials
CATALOGUE 3 first class stamps: specify retail or mail order
MAIL ORDER Yes; October to March only
GIFT TOKENS Own

Gloucestershire Nurseries & Garden Centres

NCCPG NATIONAL COLLECTIONS *Gentiana asclepiadea*, *Platycodon*
A mixed range of alpines and herbaceous plants. The nursery also holds two NCCPG National Collections.

Hunts Court Garden & Nursery
Hunts Court, North Nibley, Dursley, Gloucestershire GL11 6DZ
☎ 01453 547440
CONTACT T. K. Marshall
OPEN 9 am – 5 pm, Tuesday – Saturday and Bank Holiday Mondays in spring. Closed August
SPECIALITIES Roses
MAIL ORDER No
GARDEN Hunts Court Garden, Gloucestershire, see Gardens section
The nursery has a large selection of old-fashioned, shrub, climbing and species roses, with shrubby potentillas, perennials and other shrubs too. There is a planting advisory service.

Hurrans Garden Centre Ltd
Cheltenham Road East, Churchdown, Gloucester, Gloucestershire GL3 1AB
☎ 01452 712232 FAX 01452 857369
CONTACT Miss L. Faulds
LOCATION Between Cheltenham and Gloucester on B4063
OPEN 9 am – 6 pm, Monday – Saturday; 10.30 am – 4.30 pm, Sundays
SHOP Garden products
GARDEN Display garden
DESIGN SERVICE Hurrans Garden Centre Ltd
GIFT TOKENS HTA; own
Garden centre selling plants and garden products only. Delivery service and trained staff.

Just Phlomis
Sunningdale, Grange Court, Westbury on Severn, Gloucestershire GL14 1PL
☎ 01452 760268 FAX 01452 760268
CONTACT Mr J. Mann Taylor
OPEN By appointment
SPECIALITIES *Phlomis*
CATALOGUE 2 second class stamps
MAIL ORDER Yes
There are *Phlomis* only from the National Collection holder.

Kiftsgate Court Gardens
Kiftsgate Court, Chipping Campden, Gloucestershire GL55 6LW
☎ 01386 438777
CONTACT Mr and Mrs Chambers
LOCATION Adjacent to Hidcote Manor
OPEN 2 – 6 pm, Wednesdays, Thursdays, Sundays, and Bank Holidays, April to September; and 2 – 6 pm, Saturdays, June and July only
CATALOGUE No

MAIL ORDER No
REFRESHMENTS Home-made teas
GARDEN Kiftsgate Court, Gloucestershire, see Gardens section
The nursery sells a seasonally varied range of plants propagated from this well-known garden.

Marshall's Malmaisons
4 The Damsells, Tetbury, Gloucestershire GL8 8JA
☎ 01666 502589
CONTACT Jim Marshall
OPEN By appointment only
SPECIALITIES Carnations (Malmaison)
NEW FOR 1995 New variety is being launched at Hampton Court Palace show
CATALOGUE List on request
MAIL ORDER Yes
NCCPG NATIONAL COLLECTIONS *Dianthus* (Malmaison)
Not really a nursery: these are Malmaison carnations from the holder of the National Collection. These named varieties can be posted (collection is preferred).

The Old Manor Nursery
Twyning, Gloucestershire GL20 6DB
☎ 01684 293516
CONTACT Mrs J. Wilder
LOCATION Near M50, J1: take Twyning road from A38 (by golf course)
OPEN 2 – 5 pm, Mondays, March to October. By appointment at other times
SPECIALITIES Alpines
CATALOGUE Large SAE plus 30p
MAIL ORDER No
REFRESHMENTS Tea and biscuits on Bank Holidays
GARDEN Garden open (£1.50)
Mainly alpines, but with a changing range of perennials, shrubs and trees. All are propagated from the garden and can be seen in flower at the appropriate seasons. Groups welcome by arrangement at other times.

Priory Garden Nursery
The Priory, Kemerton, Tewkesbury, Gloucestershire GL20 7JN
☎ 01386 725258
CONTACT Mrs Healing
OPEN 2 – 7 pm, Thursdays only
SPECIALITIES Herbaceous perennials
MAIL ORDER No
GARDEN The Priory, Gloucestershire, see Gardens section
Small nursery selling plants from this Gloucestershire garden which is famous for its late-summer borders.

Sherborne Gardens Nursery
Sherborne Gardens, Sherborne, Cheltenham, Gloucestershire GL54 3DZ
☎ 01451 844522 FAX 01451 844695
CONTACT John Hill

158 Nurseries & Garden Centres GREATER MANCHESTER

LOCATION Off A40, in Sherborne village
OPEN 8 am – 4.30 pm, Monday – Friday; 8 am – 4 pm, Saturdays; other times by appointment; also April to June only, 2 – 5 pm, Sundays
SPECIALITIES Hedging; herbaceous perennials; topiary

The nursery is based around the working collection of garden designer John Hill. Specialities include yew hedging and box topiary. See also his entry in the Professional Services section.

St Annes Vineyard
Wain House, Oxenhall, Newent, Gloucestershire
GL18 1RW
☎ 01989 720313
CONTACT J. David Jenkins
LOCATION West Gloucestershire
OPEN 2 – 7 pm, Wednesday – Sunday
SPECIALITIES Vines
CATALOGUE SAE
MAIL ORDER Yes
SHOP Wine
SHOWS Malvern Spring

Specialist grower of vines for dessert and table wines: they claim to have the largest choice in the United Kingdom. Most of the business is mail order: there are some vines but more wine at the premises.

Thuya Alpine Nursery
Glebelands, Hartpury, Gloucestershire GL19 3BW
☎ 01452 700548
CONTACT Mr S. W. Bond
LOCATION On A417, north west of Gloucester
OPEN 10 am – dark, Saturdays and Bank Holidays; 11 am – dark, Sundays; and by appointment
SPECIALITIES Alpines
CATALOGUE 4 second class stamps
MAIL ORDER Yes

A source of alpines in the broadest sense, including bulbs, dwarf conifers and rhododendrons; also small ericaceous shrubs, with rarities among them.

Westonbirt Plant Centre
Westonbirt Arboretum, Tetbury, Gloucestershire
GL8 8QS
☎ 01666 880544   FAX 01666 880559
CONTACT Glyn R. Toplis
LOCATION On A433, 3 miles south of Tetbury
OPEN 10 am – 6 pm, daily; 10 am – 5 pm in winter
SPECIALITIES Shrubs; trees
CATALOGUE On request
MAIL ORDER Yes
GARDEN Westonbirt Arboretum, see Gardens section
SHOWS Malvern Spring
GIFT TOKENS HTA

As you would expect, the Plant Centre attached to the famous arboretum specialises in trees and shrubs, including varieties propagated from their collections. Good for acers.

GREATER MANCHESTER

Daisy Nook Garden Centre
Daisy Nook, Failsworth, Greater Manchester
M35 9WJ
☎ 0161 681 4245   FAX 0161 688 0822
CONTACT Mr P. Tyler
SHOP Landscape materials
REFRESHMENTS Café
GIFT TOKENS HTA

Garden centre including a fish centre.

Fairy Lane Nurseries
Fairy Lane, Sale, Greater Manchester M33 2JT
☎ 0161 905 1137
CONTACT Janice A. Coxon
LOCATION In the Mersey valley, close to M63, J8
OPEN 10 am – 5.30 pm, Monday – Saturday; 10 am – 5.30 pm, Sundays. Closed over New Year from 19 December
SPECIALITIES Herbaceous perennials
NEW FOR 1995 Many new plants
MAIL ORDER No
SHOP Garden sundries
GARDEN Herb garden
DESIGN SERVICE Fairy Lane Nurseries
GIFT TOKENS HTA

A nursery and garden centre which makes an effort to stock more than just the obvious varieties across its general range. Informal design advice is usually available, and courses are sometimes run.

Primrose Cottage Nursery & Garden Centre
Ringway Road, Moss Nook, Wythenshawe
M22 5WF
☎ 0161 437 1557   FAX 0161 499 9932
CONTACT Miss Caroline Dumville
LOCATION On B566, 1 mile from Manchester airport
OPEN 8.30 am – 6.30 pm, summer, 8.30 am – 5.30 pm, winter, Monday – Saturday; 9.30 am – 5.30 pm, Sundays
SPECIALITIES Bedding plants; herbaceous perennials
NEW FOR 1995 More alpines and perennials
CATALOGUE 2 first class stamps
MAIL ORDER No
GIFT TOKENS HTA

There are new introductions each year to the choice of bedding, basket and patio plants, while the range of alpines and herbaceous plants has almost doubled.

The Vicarage Gardens
Carrington, Urmston, Greater Manchester M31 4AG
☎ 0161 775 2750   FAX 0161 775 3679
CONTACT M. Zugor
LOCATION Greater Manchester

HAMPSHIRE Nurseries & Garden Centres 159

OPEN 10 am – 5.30 pm, daily, April to September; 10 am – 5 pm, daily, October to March. Closed Thursdays all year, and 12.30 – 1.30 pm, weekdays for lunch
CATALOGUE 5 first class stamps
MAIL ORDER Yes; minimum order 5 plants
SHOP Gifts
REFRESHMENTS Coffee shop
GARDEN 5-acre garden
SHOWS RHS Westminster; Malvern Spring; Harrogate (Spring); Southport; Chelsea

Large garden in the hands of a charitable trust. The nursery sells old-fashioned herbaceous plants and alpines, plus some water and bog garden plants. Teas and gifts. They will attend the Bakewell Show this year.

Worsley Hall Nurseries & Garden Centre
Leigh Road, Boothstown, Worsley M28 2LJ
☎ 0161 790 8792

CONTACT J. H. R. Cunliffe
LOCATION Near M62, J13: from the south, turn left on A572 (½ a mile)
OPEN 8 am – 5.30 pm, Monday – Saturday, summer (closes at dusk in winter); 11 am – 5 pm, Sundays, summer; 10 am – 4 pm, Sundays, winter
SHOP Garden sundries
REFRESHMENTS Café
GARDEN Fuchsia Society display bed
GIFT TOKENS HTA

Garden centre and nurseries with a general range of plants and products, including fruit trees and hedging. Delivery service. There is a fuchsia show in July.

HAMPSHIRE

Agars Nursery
Agars Lane, Hordle, Lymington, Hampshire SO41 0FL
☎ 01590 683703

CONTACT George and Diane Tombs
OPEN 10 am – 5 pm, March to October; 10 am – 4 pm, February and November. December and January by appointment. Phone first. Closed Thursdays
SPECIALITIES Iris; Penstemon
CATALOGUE 3 first class stamps
MAIL ORDER Yes; minimum order £15
GARDEN Display garden
DESIGN SERVICE Agars Nursery
GIFT TOKENS Own

A family-run nursery which is strong on Penstemon, irises, osteospermums and salvias. They also stock a range of hardy trees and shrubs.

Apple Court
Hordle Lane, Hordle, Lymington, Hampshire SO41 0HU
☎ 01590 642130   FAX 01590 642130

CONTACT Diana Grenfell or Roger Grounds
LOCATION South of New Forest, just off A337 at Downton crossroads
OPEN 9.30 am – 1 pm, 2 – 5 pm, Thursday –Monday, February to November. Closed last week in August
SPECIALITIES Ferns; grasses; hostas; Hemerocallis
NEW FOR 1995 Hemerocallis 'Apple Court Champagne', Hosta 'Crumples', Hosta 'Silvery Slugproof'
CATALOGUE 4 first class stamps
MAIL ORDER Yes
REFRESHMENTS By prior arrangement for parties
GARDEN Display gardens
DESIGN SERVICE Apple Court
SHOWS Southport; Hampton Court
NCCPG NATIONAL COLLECTIONS Camassia, Hosta (small leaved), Rohdea japonica, Woodwardia

Their main specialisations are hostas and hemerocallis: they have over eighty of each. There is also an interesting selection of ferns and grasses, and a collection of plants for white gardens.

Blackthorn Nursery
Kilmeston, Alresford, Hampshire SO24 0NL
☎ 01962 771796

CONTACT Mrs S. B. White
LOCATION 1 mile south of Cheriton, off A272
OPEN 9 am – 5 pm, Friday and Saturday only, March to 15 October
SPECIALITIES Alpines; herbaceous perennials
CATALOGUE 3 first class stamps
MAIL ORDER No
SHOWS RHS Westminster

Their specialities are daphnes and hellebores (see them at Vincent Square in January). Otherwise, there is a good range of alpine and rock plants, and a covetable, changing selection of other plants grown at the nursery.

Chichester Trees and Shrubs
The Mill Studio, Beaulieu, Hampshire SO42 7YG
☎ 01590 612198   FAX 01590 612194

CONTACT James Chichester
LOCATION Map in catalogue
OPEN 8 am – 4 pm, Monday – Friday
SPECIALITIES Shrubs; trees
CATALOGUE On request
MAIL ORDER Carriage available

This mainly wholesale nursery has masses of container-grown trees and shrubs for landscapers and keen private gardeners. The retail side is Pylewell Nursery (01590 626302).

Christopher Fairweather Ltd
The Garden Centre, High Street, Beaulieu, Hampshire SO42 7YR
☎ 01590 612307   FAX 01590 612615

CONTACT Fairweather's Garden Centre
LOCATION Beaulieu village
OPEN 8.45 am – 5.30 pm, daily
MAIL ORDER No
REFRESHMENTS Refreshments

160   Nurseries & Garden Centres   HAMPSHIRE

GIFT TOKENS   HTA
General garden centre in an attractive old building. They specialise in shrubs, and also organise talks and demonstrations on the premises.

Denmead Geranium Nurseries
Hambledon Road, Denmead, Waterlooville, Hampshire PO7 6PS
☎ 01705 240081

CONTACT   Ivan H. Chance or Mrs K. J. Churcher-Brown
LOCATION   2 miles west of A3, on B2150
OPEN   9 am – 5 pm, Monday – Friday; 9 am – 12.30 pm, Saturdays. Open Saturday afternoons and Sundays in April and May also. Closed Saturdays in August
SPECIALITIES   Pelargoniums
CATALOGUE   3 second class stamps
MAIL ORDER   Yes; minimum order 6 plants

Specialist growers of pelargoniums, including the following classes: zonal, coloured leaf, ivy leaf, Swiss balcony, miniatures, stellars, angels and regals. Nursery visitors can sometimes buy cultivars which do not appear in their list.

Drysdale Garden Exotics
Bowerwood Road, Fordingbridge, Hampshire SP6 1BN
☎ 01425 653010

CONTACT   David Crampton
OPEN   9.30 am – 5.30 pm, Wednesday – Friday; 10 am – 5.30 pm, Sundays
SPECIALITIES   Bamboos; foliage plants; Mediterranean plants
CATALOGUE   3 first class stamps
MAIL ORDER   Yes
GARDEN   Bamboo garden
DESIGN SERVICE   Drysdale Garden Exotics
NCCPG NATIONAL COLLECTIONS   Bamboos

The plants here are chosen for their dramatic foliage and for use in Mediterranean plantings. The bamboo collection is reflected in the number of species available from the nursery.

Exbury Enterprises Ltd
Exbury, Southampton, Hampshire SO4 1AZ
☎ 01703 898625   FAX 01703 243380
LOCATION   3 miles south of Beaulieu, off B3054
OPEN   10 am – 5 pm, daily March to Christmas
SPECIALITIES   Camellias; rhododendrons
CATALOGUE   SAE
MAIL ORDER   Yes
REFRESHMENTS   Restaurant
GARDEN   Exbury Gardens, Hampshire, see Gardens section
SHOWS   RHS Westminster; Chelsea

Plant centre attached to this famous garden: unsurprisingly they specialise in rhododendrons and azaleas but have camellias and *Pieris* too.

Family Trees
P O Box 3, Botley, Hampshire SO3 2EA
☎ 01329 834812

CONTACT   Philip House
LOCATION   1 mile from Botley
OPEN   9.30 am – 12.30 pm, Wednesday and Saturday, mid October to mid April
SPECIALITIES   Fruit
CATALOGUE   On request
MAIL ORDER   Yes; minimum order £35

Many varieties of dessert apples, pears, plums and peaches. They are available as bushes or trained. They also have old roses, hedging and woodland trees, and can graft to order.

Hardy's Cottage Garden Plants
The Walled Garden, Laverstoke Park, Laverstoke, Whitchurch, Hampshire RG28 7NT
☎ 01256 896533   FAX 01256 896572

CONTACT   Mr and Mrs R. K. Hardy
LOCATION   Off B3400 Whitchurch to Overton road
OPEN   9 am – 5.30 pm, Monday – Saturday, March to October
SPECIALITIES   Herbaceous perennials
CATALOGUE   3 first class stamps
MAIL ORDER   No
GARDEN   Display garden under development
DESIGN SERVICE   Hardy's Cottage Garden Plants
SHOWS   RHS Westminster; Malvern Spring; Harrogate (Spring); Southport; Chelsea; BBC GW Live; Hampton Court; Harrogate (Autumn); Ayr

A family-run nursery with a large range of pretty cottage garden perennials and flowering shrubs. Watch out for their attractive exhibits at shows. They also offer a design and construction service.

Hayward's Carnations
The Chace Gardens, 141 Stakes Road, Purbrook, Waterlooville, Hampshire PO7 5PL
☎ 01705 263047

CONTACT   Sales Office
OPEN   Mail order only
SPECIALITIES   *Dianthus*
CATALOGUE   On request
MAIL ORDER   Yes

This long-established, specialist mail-order nursery grows garden pinks, border and perpetual flowering carnations. The plants can be seen flowering in June, by appointment.

Highfield Hollies
Highfield Farm, Hatch Lane, Liss, Hampshire GU33 7NH
☎ 01730 892372

CONTACT   Louise Bendall
LOCATION   ½ a mile off old A3, 4 miles north of Petersfield
OPEN   Phone first

HAMPSHIRE Nurseries & Garden Centres

SPECIALITIES *Ilex*
NEW FOR 1995 *Ilex altaclerensis* 'Ripley Gold'
CATALOGUE List on request
MAIL ORDER By carrier

A holly farm, with handsome hollies grown as specimen trees.

Hillier Garden Centre
Farnham Road, Liss, Hampshire GU33 6LJ
☎ 01730 892196   FAX 01730 893676
LOCATION By A3, B3006 Liss exit
OPEN 9 am – 5.30 pm, Monday – Saturday; 10.30 am – 4.30 pm, Sundays
SPECIALITIES Climbers; conifers; shrubs; trees
CATALOGUE On request
MAIL ORDER No
REFRESHMENTS Coffee shop
GIFT TOKENS HTA; own

See Hillier Nurseries Ltd, Hampshire.

Hillier Nurseries Ltd
Ampfield House, Ampfield, Romsey, Hampshire SO51 9PA
☎ 01794 368733   FAX 01794 368813
CONTACT Sheila Pack
SPECIALITIES Climbers; conifers; shrubs; trees
CATALOGUE On request or from stockists
MAIL ORDER No
SHOP Nine garden centres
GARDEN Sir Harold Hillier Gardens and Arboretum, Hampshire. See Gardens section
SHOWS Chelsea
GIFT TOKENS HTA

Celebrated and long-established wholesale and retail nurseries, best known for their wide range of trees and shrubs, available container- or field-grown in large sizes. They have nine garden centres in southern England. The old mail order list has been replaced by the Hillier Premier Plant Service: the choice of plants has been cut back but distribution has been expanded. Nationwide Hillier stockists now give much wider access to the new, restricted list. Hampshire County Council now runs the arboretum built up by Harold Hillier: the Sir Harold Hillier Gardens and Arboretum, Hampshire. There is a free gardening club which produces a magazine with details of events and product discount vouchers (01794 368966).

Langley Boxwood Nursery
Rake, Liss, Hampshire GU33 7JL
☎ 01730 894467   FAX 01730 894703
CONTACT Elizabeth Braimbridge
LOCATION Near Petersfield
OPEN Monday – Friday. Saturdays and Sundays by appointment
SPECIALITIES Topiary; boxwood
NEW FOR 1995 *Buxus sempervirens* 'Blauer Heinz'
CATALOGUE 4 first class stamps
MAIL ORDER Yes

GARDEN Display garden
NCCPG NATIONAL COLLECTIONS *Buxus*

Specialist growers of box with a comprehensive range for hedging, edging, topiary and as specimens. There are over 50 varieties of *Buxus* here, and some *Taxus* also.

Longstock Park Nursery
Longstock, Stockbridge, Hampshire SO20 6EH
☎ 01264 810894   FAX 01264 810439
CONTACT Mr D. Stuart
OPEN 8.30 am – 4.30 pm, Monday – Saturday; 2 – 5 pm, Sundays, when gardens open
SPECIALITIES Aquatic plants; bog plants; herbaceous perennials; primulas
CATALOGUE £1.50
MAIL ORDER No
GARDEN Longstock Water Gardens, Hampshire, see Gardens section
DESIGN SERVICE Longstock Park Nursery

A good range of conifers, ferns, perennials and shrubs. The nursery is recommended for its aquatic, moisture-loving and marginal plants, many of which are propagated from the adjacent water gardens. Excellent selection of primulas. The gardens, also owned by the John Lewis Partnership, open 2 – 4.30 pm on the first and third Sunday of the month, April to September.

Nine Springs Nursery
24 Winchester Street, Whitchurch, Hampshire RG28 7AL
☎ 01256 892837   FAX 01256 892837
CONTACT Gillian Anderson
OPEN By appointment
SPECIALITIES Aquatic plants
CATALOGUE 1 first class stamp
MAIL ORDER Yes

Retail and wholesale aquatic plant nursery: small plants by post, and larger sizes on site. They can supply plants in a fibre roll to minimise erosion and wildfowl damage. See also Artscapes, Professional Services section.

Oakleigh Nurseries
Petersfield Road, Monkwood, Alresford, Hampshire SO24 0HB
☎ 01962 773344   FAX 01962 772622
CONTACT Miss Sally Smith
OPEN 10 am – 1 pm, 2 – 4.30 pm, Monday – Friday, April to July; 10.30 am – 1 pm, 2 – 4 pm, Sundays, April to June
SPECIALITIES Fuchsias; pelargoniums; epiphyllums
CATALOGUE 3 first class stamps
MAIL ORDER Yes
SHOWS Chelsea; Hampton Court

Specialists for fuchsias (specimens, bush and standards) and pelargoniums (zonal, regal and ivy leaf). They also have a range of Christmas cacti hybrids and *Epiphyllum*. They publish a number of books, and Periwinkle Productions have filmed videos at the nursery.

Peter Trenear Nurseries
Chequers Lane, Eversley Cross, Hampshire
RG27 0NX
☎ 01734 732300

CONTACT Peter Trenear
LOCATION Between Reading and Camberley
OPEN 9 am – 4.30 pm. Closed Sundays
SPECIALITIES Bonsai; shrubs; trees
CATALOGUE 1 first class stamp
MAIL ORDER Yes; no minimum order

Here is a list of young trees and shrubs, including conifers. They can either be planted out in the garden or cultivated as bonsai specimens.

Pound Lane Nurseries
Ampfield, Romsey, Hampshire SO51 9BL
☎ 01703 739685   FAX 01703 740300

CONTACT T. A. Holmes
LOCATION Between North Baddesley and Ampfield
OPEN 8.30 am – 5.30 pm, Monday – Friday; 9.30 am – 5 pm, Saturdays and Sundays
MAIL ORDER No
GARDEN Display gardens
DESIGN SERVICE Pound Lane Nurseries

Wholesale and retail working nursery offering hardy container-grown stock, trees, shrubs and heathers.

Southview Nurseries
Chequers Lane, Eversley Cross, Basingstoke
RG27 0NT
☎ 01734 732206

CONTACT Elaine and Mark Trenear
LOCATION Between Camberley and Reading, off B3272
OPEN 9 am – 4.30 pm, Thursday – Saturday. Closed November to January
SPECIALITIES *Dianthus*; herbaceous perennials
NEW FOR 1995 More old varieties of pinks
CATALOGUE On request
MAIL ORDER Yes; September to May
GARDEN Garden open
SHOWS RHS Westminster; Hampton Court

Specialists for older varieties of named pinks and herbaceous perennials: they can help with historical plantings. Their own garden opens for the National Gardens Scheme for the second time this year.

Spinners
Boldre, Lymington, Hampshire SO41 5QE
☎ 01590 673347

CONTACT P. Chappell
LOCATION Off A337, between Brockenhurst and Lymington
OPEN 10 am – 5 pm, daily. Closed Sundays and Mondays
SPECIALITIES Herbaceous perennials; shrubs; trees
NEW FOR 1995 *Halesia monticola* 'Rosea', *Dendromecon rigida*, *Agapetes* species and others

CATALOGUE 4 first class stamps
MAIL ORDER No
GARDEN Spinners, Hampshire, see Gardens section
DESIGN SERVICE Spinners
GIFT TOKENS Own

There is always plenty of interest at this nursery, attached to a plantsman's garden. The hardy plants are particularly strong, and there are good shrubs and small trees. They can advise on establishing wild gardens.

Steven Bailey
Silver Street, Sway, Lymington, Hampshire
SO41 6ZA
☎ 01590 682227   FAX 01590 683765

CONTACT S. E. Bailey and Ian Perry (Manager)
LOCATION Near Hordle: not Sway village
OPEN 8 am – 4.30 pm, Monday – Friday; 9 am – 4.30 pm, Saturdays, March to December. Also 10 am – 4.30 pm, Sundays, March to June only
SPECIALITIES Bedding plants; *Dianthus*
CATALOGUE 2 first class stamps
MAIL ORDER Yes
SHOWS RHS Westminster; Malvern Spring; Harrogate (Spring); Southport; Chelsea; BBC GW Live; Hampton Court; Harrogate (Autumn)

Long-established specialists for carnations, pinks and alstroemerias. Active on the show circuit, so look out for them. The nursery shop also has a selection of bedding and summer pot plants.

Water Meadow Nursery and Herb Farm
Cheriton, Alresford, Hampshire SO24 0JT
☎ 01962 771895

CONTACT Mrs Sandy Worth
LOCATION Near A272, Winchester to Petersfield road, towards Alresford
OPEN 9 am – 5 pm, Friday – Saturday, and Bank Holidays; 2 – 5 pm, Sundays. March to November
SPECIALITIES Aquatic plants; bog plants; herbaceous perennials; herbs
CATALOGUE 3 first class stamps
MAIL ORDER Yes
GARDEN Display garden open at the same times
DESIGN SERVICE Water Meadow Design & Landscape
SHOWS RHS Westminster; Harrogate (Spring); Hampton Court

There is an extensive range of herbs and perennials here, but the main speciality is in plants that grow near water. Strong on *Nymphaea* (70). Other services include design and landscaping, and wholesale. Contact them for information about talks and workshops.

Wychwood Carp Farm
Farnham Road, Odiham, Basingstoke, Hampshire
RG25 1HS
☎ 01256 702800

CONTACT Ann or Clair Henley

Hereford & Worcester   Nurseries & Garden Centres

LOCATION On A284, 3 miles from M3, J5
OPEN 10 am – 6 pm, daily. Closed Thursdays
SPECIALITIES Aquatic plants; bog plants
NEW FOR 1995 *Ludwigia grandiflora*
CATALOGUE 1 first class stamp
MAIL ORDER Yes
GARDEN Odiham Water Lily Collection
NCCPG NATIONAL COLLECTIONS *Nymphaea*

This is a nursery. They grow water lilies and other aquatics, bog and marginal plants including some rare *Iris ensata* cultivars. The Odiham Water Lily Collection can be visited in summer.

HEREFORD & WORCESTER

Abbey Dore Court Garden
Abbey Dore, Hereford, Hereford & Worcester
HR2 0AD
☎ 01981 240419   FAX 01981 240279

CONTACT Charis Ward
LOCATION Between Hereford and Abergavenny, 3 miles west of A465
OPEN 11 am – 6 pm, Thursday – Tuesday, from first Saturday in March to third Sunday in October
SPECIALITIES Clematis; herbaceous perennials; paeonies
MAIL ORDER No
SHOP Country Gift Gallery
REFRESHMENTS Licensed restaurant, home-made food
GARDEN Abbey Dore Court Garden, Hereford & Worcester, see Gardens section

A small nursery attached to the garden: it is particularly good for perennials and clematis. To see the hellebores before the garden season, telephone for an appointment.

Baker Straw Partnership
Perhill Nurseries, Worcester Road, Great Witley, Hereford & Worcester WR6 6JT
☎ 01299 896329   FAX 01299 896990

CONTACT Mr D. Straw and Mrs S. Straw
LOCATION At Great Witley, on A443
OPEN 9 am – 6 pm, daily
SPECIALITIES Alpines; herbaceous perennials; herbs
NEW FOR 1995 Many new varieties
CATALOGUE 6 second class stamps
MAIL ORDER No

The retail nursery stocks some 2,400 different alpines, herbs and perennials. Notable collections include *Dianthus* (100), thymes (40), penstemons (150) and salvias (90). They also operate a wholesale cash and carry business and deliver to local garden centres.

Bouts Cottage Nurseries
Bouts Lane, Inkberrow, Hereford & Worcester
WR7 4HP
☎ 01386 792923

CONTACT Mark Roberts
OPEN Not open to the public

SPECIALITIES Violas
CATALOGUE SAE
MAIL ORDER Yes; no minimum order
SHOWS Malvern Spring; Chelsea; BBC GW Live

Mail order nursery devoted to old-fashioned violas. The plants can be seen at shows, but the nursery is not open for visiting.

Burford House Tropicals
Burford House Gardens, Tenbury Wells, Worcester, Hereford & Worcester WR15 8HQ
☎ 01584 810777

CONTACT Michael Eden
LOCATION A456 between Tenbury Wells and Ludlow
OPEN 10 am – 6 pm, daily; 10 am – 5 pm, in winter
SPECIALITIES Conservatory plants; house plants
CATALOGUE 4 first class stamps
MAIL ORDER Yes; minimum order £15

Tropical and subtropical plants for the house and conservatory, wholesale and retail. The list includes daisies, showy climbers and a show stopper in *Dichorisandra thyrsiflora* (a blue ginger). Many of the plants are available in specimen sizes. The nursery was previously in Torquay (Tropicana).

Cooks Garden Centre
26 Worcester Road, Stourport on Severn, Hereford & Worcester DY13 5PQ
☎ 01299 826169   FAX 01299 824441

CONTACT Paul N. Cook or Millie Barrett
LOCATION ½ a mile from town centre
OPEN 9 am – 6 pm, daily
SPECIALITIES Bedding plants
NEW FOR 1995 More patio plants
MAIL ORDER Young plant plugs in spring only
SHOWS Malvern Spring; Chelsea; Hampton Court
GIFT TOKENS Own

A garden centre and nursery specialising in bedding plants and hanging baskets.

Cotswold Garden Flowers
1 Waterside, Evesham, Hereford & Worcester
WR11 6BS
☎ 01386 47337

CONTACT Bob Brown
LOCATION Sands Lane, Badsey, Evesham. Continue ⅓ mile after tarmac runs out
OPEN 8 am – 4.30 pm, Monday – Friday. Also open 10 am – 6 pm, Saturdays and Sundays, March to September only. Other times by appointment
SPECIALITIES Herbaceous perennials
NEW FOR 1995 Many new varieties
CATALOGUE On request
MAIL ORDER Yes
GARDEN 1-acre herbaceous display gardens
SHOWS Malvern Spring; BBC GW Live

The nursery stocks a wide selection of herbaceous perennials, all of which have been chosen on the basis of their garden worthiness. There is no phone at the nursery, and garden vistors are advised to bring wellingtons when it's wet. They will be at the Shrewsbury Flower Show.

The Cottage Herbery
Mill House, Boraston, Tenbury Wells, Hereford & Worcester WR15 8LZ
☎ 01584 781575   FAX 01299 266216
CONTACT   K. & R. Hurst
LOCATION   Turn off A456 (Worcester to Leominster), at Peacock Inn, 2 miles east of Tenbury Wells
OPEN   10 am – 6 pm, Sundays only; weekdays by appointment
SPECIALITIES   Herbaceous perennials; herbs
NEW FOR 1995   Astro monardas and Red Indian varieties
CATALOGUE   4 first class stamps
MAIL ORDER   Seeds only
SHOP   Herb products
REFRESHMENTS   Teas, Sundays only
GARDEN   Garden opens every Sunday
SHOWS   RHS Westminster; Malvern Spring; BBC GW Live

A small, specialist nursery whose stock includes herbs and aromatic plants, including *Symphytum*, *Pulmonaria* and *Monarda*. The plants are organically grown in peat-free compost. They will open specially for group visits, and they also hold courses.

Country House Hedging
Sunny Bank House, Eaton Bishop, Hereford & Worcester HR2 9QP
☎ 01981 250692
CONTACT   Elaine Wigg
OPEN   Telephone first
SPECIALITIES   Hedging; topiary
NEW FOR 1995   Winter interest shrubs
CATALOGUE   SAE
MAIL ORDER   Yes

The nursery has recently moved. There is box and yew bare root hedging as well as topiary. Winter interest shrubs are a new addition to their range.

Cranesbill Nursery
White Cottage, Earls Common Road, Stock Green, Redditch, Hereford & Worcester B96 6SZ
☎ 01386 792414
CONTACT   Mrs J. Bates
LOCATION   9 miles west of Worcester, 1½ miles north of A422
OPEN   10 am – 5 pm, Friday – Tuesday
SPECIALITIES   Herbaceous perennials; hardy geraniums
NEW FOR 1995   30 new varieties of hardy geraniums
CATALOGUE   4 first class stamps
MAIL ORDER   Yes
SHOP   Coneybury Plant Centre

GARDEN   Customers can visit the 2-acre garden, open for the NGS

Hardy geraniums are the speciality here – hardly surprising given the name. Yet there is a good selection of other perennials, and some interesting shrubs too. They also operate Coneybury Plant Centre, nearby at Dormston.

D & M Everett
Greenacres Nursery, Bringsty, Worcester, Hereford & Worcester WR6 5TA
☎ 01885 482206   FAX 01885 488160
CONTACT   Daphne Everett
LOCATION   Phone for directions
OPEN   By appointment
SPECIALITIES   Heathers
CATALOGUE   On request; separate wholesale and retail lists
MAIL ORDER   No
REFRESHMENTS   On open days
GARDEN   Owners' garden opens for NGS and Red Cross

A heather specialist, with a mainly wholesale business, though a retail list is available. There are upwards of 200 containerised varieties. The garden opens for charity three times a year.

Eastgrove Cottage Garden Nursery
Sankyns Green, Shrawley, Little Witley, Hereford & Worcester WR6 6LQ
☎ 01299 896389
LOCATION   Between Shrawley (B4196) and Great Witley (A443)
OPEN   2 – 5 pm, Thursday – Monday, 1 April to 31 July; 2 – 5 pm, Thursday – Saturday, 1 September to 15 October. Closed August
SPECIALITIES   Herbaceous perennials
CATALOGUE   5 second class stamps
MAIL ORDER   No
GARDEN   Eastgrove Cottage Garden, Hereford & Worcester, see Gardens section

A large and varied range of interesting plants, all of them propagated from this Worcestershire garden. Mainly perennials, but there is a smaller collection of half-hardy plants too.

Fuchsiavale Nurseries
Worcester Road, Torton, Kidderminster, Hereford & Worcester DY11 7SB
☎ 01299 251162
LOCATION   South of Kidderminster
OPEN   9 am – 5 pm, Monday – Saturday; 10.30 am – 4.30 pm, Sundays; December to August. Closed Easter Sunday
SPECIALITIES   Fuchsias
NEW FOR 1995   American varieties
CATALOGUE   SAE for mail order catalogue
MAIL ORDER   Yes
DESIGN SERVICE   Fuchsiavale Nurseries

HEREFORD & WORCESTER — Nurseries & Garden Centres

SHOWS   Malvern Spring; Harrogate (Spring); Chelsea; Hampton Court

Specialists for fuchsias. Their range of around 300 varieties includes new American cultivars. The full catalogue is available only at the nursery.

The Garden at The Elms
The Elms Farm, Frenchlands Lane, Lower Broadheath, Worcester, Hereford & Worcester WR2 6QU
☎ 01905 640841   FAX 01905 640675
CONTACT   Mrs Emma Stewart
LOCATION   Off B4204, 4 miles west of Worcester
OPEN   10 am – 4 pm, Tuesdays and Wednesdays, 1 April to 30 September
SPECIALITIES   Herbaceous perennials
CATALOGUE   3 first class stamps
MAIL ORDER   No
SHOWS   Malvern Spring

An expanding range of cottage garden plants and hardy perennials is available at this young nursery.

Grange Farm Nursery
Guarlford, Malvern, Hereford & Worcester WR13 6NY
☎ 01684 562544
CONTACT   Mrs C. Nicholls
LOCATION   Malvern
OPEN   9 am – 5.30 pm, summer; 9 am – dusk, winter. Closed over Christmas and New Year
SPECIALITIES   Shrubs; trees
MAIL ORDER   No
SHOWS   Malvern Spring
GIFT TOKENS   HTA

An all-round range of plants, with the emphasis on well-grown trees and shrubs, sold from the retail plant centre. Some garden ornaments and equipment too.

Hayloft Plants
The Hayloft, Cooks Hill, Wick, Pershore, Hereford & Worcester WR10 3PA
☎ 01386 561235
CONTACT   Yvonne Walker
OPEN   Mail order only
SPECIALITIES   Half-hardy plants
CATALOGUE   On request
MAIL ORDER   Yes
SHOWS   Malvern Spring; BBC GW Live

A new nursery with mainly half-hardy stock – penstemons, osteospermums and gazanias for example, and plants for hanging baskets.

Hergest Croft Gardens
Kington, Hereford & Worcester HR5 3EG
☎ 01554 230160
CONTACT   Mrs S. Price
LOCATION   Signed off A44
OPEN   1.30 – 6.30 pm, daily, April to October
SPECIALITIES   Shrubs; trees
MAIL ORDER   No
GARDEN   Hergest Croft Gardens, Hereford & Worcester, see Gardens section

Little-known and rare shrubs and trees, propagated from a garden famed for its trees.

How Caple Court Gardens
How Caple Court, How Caple, Hereford, Hereford & Worcester HR1 4SX
☎ 01989 740626   FAX 01989 740611
CONTACT   Mr P. L. Lee
LOCATION   On B4224, 5 miles north east of Ross on Wye
OPEN   9 am – 5 pm, Monday – Saturday; 10 am – 5 pm, Sundays, May to October
SPECIALITIES   Fruit; roses
MAIL ORDER   No
GARDEN   How Caple Court, Hereford and Worcester, see Gardens section

A lovely country-house mixture of plants: old apples, old roses, perennials and shrubs.

International Acers
Acer Place, Coalash Lane, Hanbury, Bromsgrove, Hereford & Worcester B60 4EY
☎ 01527 821774
CONTACT   D. L. Horton
LOCATION   South of Bromsgrove: ask for map
OPEN   9 am – 5.30 pm, weekends and Bank Holidays. Other times by appointment
SPECIALITIES   Acers
CATALOGUE   SAE
MAIL ORDER   No
DESIGN SERVICE   International Acers

They specialise in maples, with excellent lists of species and *Acer palmatum* cultivars. Worth keeping an eye on.

Marston Exotics
Brampton Lane, Madley, Hereford, Hereford & Worcester HR2 9LX
☎ 01981 251140   FAX 01981 251649
CONTACT   Paul Gardner
OPEN   8 am – 4.30 pm, Monday – Friday, all year; 1 – 5 pm, Saturdays and Sundays, March to October
SPECIALITIES   Carnivorous plants
NEW FOR 1995   *Nepenthe* and *Pinguicula* species
CATALOGUE   £1 guide; list is free
MAIL ORDER   Yes; worldwide
REFRESHMENTS   Refreshments
GARDEN   *Sarracenia* collection open
SHOWS   RHS Westminster; Malvern Spring; Southport; Chelsea; BBC GW Live; Hampton Court
GIFT TOKENS   Own

A formidable range of carnivorous plants – the largest public collection in Europe, they claim. Their range includes species for the house, greenhouse and garden, as well as appropriate accessories.

Merebrook Water Plants
Merebrook Farm, Hanley Swan, Worcester, Hereford & Worcester WR8 0DX
☎ 01684 310950   FAX 01684 310034

CONTACT   Roger Kings
LOCATION   On B4209, near Three Counties Showground
OPEN   10 am – 5 pm, daily
SPECIALITIES   Aquatic plants
NEW FOR 1995   *Nymphaea* 'Norma Gedye'
CATALOGUE   SAE
MAIL ORDER   Yes

Water lilies are supplied ready-planted in baskets. There are aquatic and marginal plants and a special conservation pack of British native species.

Mrs S M Cooper
Firlands Cottage, Bishops Frome, Worcester, Hereford & Worcester WR6 5BA
☎ 01885 490358

CONTACT   Mrs Cooper
OPEN   By appointment
SPECIALITIES   Shrubs; trees
CATALOGUE   SAE
MAIL ORDER   Yes

Rare trees and shrubs species, all grown from seed. The provenance is named on request.

Old Court Nurseries
Walwyn Road, Colwall, Malvern, Hereford & Worcester WR13 6QE
☎ 01684 540416

CONTACT   Meriel Picton
LOCATION   B4218 in Colwall village
OPEN   10 am – 1 pm, 2.15 – 5.30 pm, Wednesday – Sunday, April to October
SPECIALITIES   Herbaceous perennials; Michaelmas daisies
CATALOGUE   2 first class stamps
MAIL ORDER   Yes; asters only
GARDEN   Picton Garden
NCCPG   NATIONAL COLLECTIONS *Aster*

Holders of National Collection of Michaelmas daisies. This is their speciality and there is a very extensive collection of them. There are also many other interesting perennials and cottage-garden type plants here. The garden opens for the National Gardens Scheme, Wednesdays to Sundays, from April to October. Guided tours for groups, by arrangement.

Orcon Exotics
16 Woodside Road, Worcester WR5 2EG
☎ 01905 351649

CONTACT   Mr R. Monk
OPEN   By appointment
SPECIALITIES   Orchids
CATALOGUE   SAE
MAIL ORDER   Yes

A range of orchids and other tropical plants for house and greenhouse. Composts and growing sundries are available too.

R F Beeston
294 Ombersley Road, Worcester, Hereford & Worcester WR3 7HD
☎ 01905 453245

CONTACT   R. F. Beeston
LOCATION   Bevere Nurseries, Bevere, Worcester
OPEN   10 am – 1 pm, 2 – 5 pm, Wednesday – Friday, March to October. Other times by appointment
SPECIALITIES   Alpines; primulas
CATALOGUE   SAE
MAIL ORDER   Yes

Alpine specialist with an emphasis on smaller plants for use in alpine houses, alpine beds and troughs. Strengths include European *Primula* species, *Androsace* and *Dionysia*. They attend most of the AGS shows.

Rickard's Hardy Ferns Ltd
Kyre Park, Tenbury Wells, Hereford & Worcester WR15 8RP
☎ 01885 410282   FAX 01885 410398

CONTACT   Hazel and Martin Rickard
LOCATION   Off B4214 Bromyard road, from Tenbury Wells
OPEN   By appointment: phone first
SPECIALITIES   Ferns; tree ferns
CATALOGUE   SAE
MAIL ORDER   UK and EC only
REFRESHMENTS   2 – 6 pm, weekends and Bank Holidays
GARDEN   2 – 6 pm, April to October, or by appointment
SHOWS   RHS Westminster; Malvern Spring; Chelsea; Hampton Court

Specialists in hardy ferns. They have a great number for sale, and over 900 different varieties in their own collection. Half-hardy tree ferns are also sold.

Rosemary Spreckley
Hailey House, Great Comberton, Pershore, Hereford & Worcester WR10 3DS
☎ 01386 710733

CONTACT   Rosemary Spreckley
LOCATION   Church Street – near the church
OPEN   By appointment only
SPECIALITIES   Penstemons
NEW FOR 1995   New *Erysimum* and *Penstemon*
CATALOGUE   SAE
MAIL ORDER   Yes
GARDEN   Garden

Devoted mainly to *Penstemon* species and cultivars, with a number of *Erysimum* too. Mail order is now available.

Rushfields of Ledbury
Ross Road, Ledbury HR8 2LP
☎ 01531 632004

CONTACT   Mr B. Homewood

HEREFORD & WORCESTER   Nurseries & Garden Centres

LOCATION ½ a mile south west of Ledbury on A449
OPEN 11 am – 5 pm, Wednesday – Saturday
SPECIALITIES Herbaceous perennials
CATALOGUE Large SAE (29p) plus £1
MAIL ORDER Yes; their collections only
SHOWS RHS Westminster; Malvern Spring; Harrogate (Spring); Southport; Chelsea; BBC GW Live; Hampton Court; Harrogate (Autumn)

A good choice of perennials, including geraniums, hardy osteospermums and hostas. Mail order is restricted to their collections. They will also be at the Holker Hall and Shrewsbury shows.

S & E Bond
Gardener's Cottage, Letton, Hereford, Hereford & Worcester HR3 6DH
☎ 01544 328422

CONTACT Sarah Bond
LOCATION A438: 12 miles west of Hereford
OPEN 10 am – 6 pm, Wednesday – Saturday and Bank Holidays; 1 – 5 pm, Sundays. Open March to 24 December
SPECIALITIES Herbaceous perennials
CATALOGUE SAE (A5)
MAIL ORDER Yes
GARDEN Walled garden
SHOWS Malvern Spring

Just herbaceous perennials, and an excellent choice of them too. There is a bias towards shade-lovers. Worth a visit to see what did not make it into the catalogue.

Stone House Cottage Nurseries
Stone, Kidderminster, Hereford & Worcester DY10 4BG
☎ 01562 69902

CONTACT J. F. Arbuthnott
LOCATION 2 miles south east of Kidderminster, on A448
OPEN 10 am – 6 pm, Wednesday – Saturday, March to October. Also Sundays, May – June only
SPECIALITIES Climbers; shrubs
CATALOGUE SAE
MAIL ORDER No
GARDEN Stone House Cottage, Hereford & Worcester, see Gardens section
GIFT TOKENS Own

Wall shrubs and climbers are the speciality here, but there are also some interesting shrubs, old roses (on their own roots) and a constantly changing list of herbaceous plants. The nursery and garden are recommended.

Toad Hall Produce
Frogmore, Weston under Penyard, Hereford & Worcester HR9 5TQ
☎ 01989 750214

CONTACT S. V. North
LOCATION 4 miles south east of Ross on Wye
OPEN 10 am – 6 pm, Mondays, April to September
SPECIALITIES Ground cover plants; herbaceous perennials
CATALOGUE SAE
MAIL ORDER Yes
GARDEN 2-acre garden

This small nursery specialises in hardy geraniums, all of which can be seen in the garden. They have other ground cover and herbaceous plants too.

Treasures of Tenbury Ltd
Burford House Gardens, Tenbury Wells, Worcester, Hereford & Worcester WR15 8HQ
☎ 01584 810777   FAX 01584 810673

CONTACT Pat Cox or Chris Haydon
LOCATION Between Tenbury Wells and Ludlow on A456
OPEN 10 am – 6 pm, daily; 10 am – 5 pm, in winter months
SPECIALITIES Clematis
CATALOGUE Yes
MAIL ORDER No
REFRESHMENTS Buttery open 10 am – 6pm, daily
GARDEN Burford House Gardens, Hereford & Worcester, see Gardens section
GIFT TOKENS HTA

The nursery specialises in herbaceous plants and especially the clematis which characterise the garden.

Webbs of Wychbold
Wychbold, Droitwich, Hereford & Worcester WR9 0DG
☎ 01527 861777   FAX 01527 861284

CONTACT John Grunsell
LOCATION 1 mile north of M5, J5 on A38
OPEN 9 am – 5.45 pm, Monday – Saturday; 10 am – 5 pm, Sundays and Bank Holidays. Close at 5 pm in winter and have some late-night openings in summer
NEW FOR 1995 *Nemesia denticulata* 'Confetti'
CATALOGUE £1
MAIL ORDER No
SHOP Garden sundries
REFRESHMENTS Restaurant
GARDEN Demonstration gardens
DESIGN SERVICE Webbs of Wychbold
SHOWS Malvern Spring; BBC GW Live
GIFT TOKENS HTA; own
NCCPG NATIONAL COLLECTIONS *Potentilla fruticosa*

Forward-looking garden centre and nursery, with an extensive range of good plants and all sorts of sundries and equipment. Design and landscaping service.

Wintergreen Nurseries
Bringsty, Worcester, Hereford & Worcester WR6 5UJ
☎ 01886 821858

CONTACT Stephen Dodd
LOCATION 3 miles east of Bromyard, on A44

168 Nurseries & Garden Centres HERTFORDSHIRE

OPEN 10 am – 5.30 pm, Wednesday – Sunday, March to October
SPECIALITIES Alpines; herbaceous perennials
CATALOGUE 2 second class stamps
MAIL ORDER Yes
GARDEN Display garden
SHOWS Malvern Spring; BBC GW Live

A small nursery which specialises in alpines and perennials: there are also some shrubs.

Wyevale Garden Centres plc
Kings Acre Road, Hereford, Hereford & Worcester HR4 0SE
☎ 01432 276568   FAX 01432 263289
CONTACT Mr Stephen Morgan
OPEN 9 am – 6 pm, summer; 9 am – 5.30 pm, winter
CATALOGUE 99p plant guide
MAIL ORDER No
REFRESHMENTS Yes
SHOWS Malvern Spring; Chelsea
GIFT TOKENS HTA

The country's largest garden centre chain, with 43 centres and another 6 shops. Facilities vary, but all sell the company's illustrated *Good Plant Guide* which covers the Wyevale range. They sell over 2,500 trees and shrubs, backed by a substantial wholesale nursery business. In addition the chain operates a plant-finding service for a £5 deposit. Many of the centres also have pet shops and restaurants.

HERTFORDSHIRE

The Abbots House Garden
10 High Street, Abbots Langley, Hertfordshire WD5 0AR
☎ 01923 264946
CONTACT Dr Peter Tomson and Mrs Joan Gentry
LOCATION 4½ miles north of Watford; 4½ miles south west of St Albans
OPEN 9 am – 1 pm, 2 – 4 pm, Saturdays, March to October; 9 am – 1 pm, Saturdays, November to December
SPECIALITIES Conservatory plants
CATALOGUE 3 second class stamps
MAIL ORDER Yes
GARDEN Open for NGS: 14 May, 18, 20 June, 27 August

A small nursery with a pleasantly mixed range, including shrubs, perennials, half-hardy and conservatory plants. Normally only open Saturdays, but visitors welcome on other days by arrangement.

Aylett Nurseries Ltd
North Orbital Road, London Colney, St Albans, Hertfordshire AL2 1DH
☎ 01727 822555   FAX 01727 823024
CONTACT Mr R. S. Aylett
LOCATION On A414 in Hertfordshire

OPEN 8.30 am – 5.30 pm, Monday – Friday; 8.30 am – 5.30 pm, Saturdays; 9.30 am – 5 pm, Bank Holidays; 10 am – 4 pm, Sundays
SPECIALITIES Dahlias
CATALOGUE On request
MAIL ORDER No
SHOP Garden sundries
REFRESHMENTS Coffee shop
GARDEN Trial grounds
DESIGN SERVICE Aylett Nurseries Ltd
GIFT TOKENS HTA

A general garden centre, including a design service and delivery. Their award-winning speciality is dahlias: they have a large selection of all types, and hold special dahlia weekends in late September.

Gannock Growers
Gannock Green, Sandon, Buntingford, Hertfordshire SG9 0RH
☎ 01763 287386
CONTACT Penny Pyle
LOCATION Map in catalogue
OPEN 10 am – 4 pm, Tuesday – Saturday, 1 March to 31 October
SPECIALITIES Herbaceous perennials
CATALOGUE 3 first class stamps
MAIL ORDER Yes
SHOWS RHS Westminster; Malvern Spring; Hampton Court
GIFT TOKENS Own

Herbaceous perennial specialists with a wide selection of the more unusual species and varieties. They visit lots of shows.

Godly's Roses
Redbourn, St Albans, Hertfordshire AL3 7PS
☎ 01582 792255   FAX 01582 794267
CONTACT Colin and Andy Godly
LOCATION A5183, ½ a mile south of M1, J9
OPEN 9 am – 6 pm, daily
SPECIALITIES Roses
NEW FOR 1995 Selected varieties of the thornless roses, 'Smooth Touch'
CATALOGUE On request
MAIL ORDER Yes; local orders only for standards
SHOP Garden sundries
GARDEN Rose fields
GIFT TOKENS Own

Rose growers with a selection of popular modern varieties. A general range of plants is carried in the garden centre.

Great Gardens of England Ltd
Chipperfield Home & Garden Centre, Tower Hill, Chipperfield, Hertfordshire WD4 9LH
☎ 01442 834364   FAX 01442 834259
CONTACT Mrs Jenny Welch
LOCATION 2 miles west of Kings Langley, off A41

HERTFORDSHIRE Nurseries & Garden Centres

OPEN 9 am – 5.30 pm, Monday – Saturday; 11 am – 5 pm, Sunday
REFRESHMENTS Coffee shop
DESIGN SERVICE Yes
GIFT TOKENS HTA; own

General garden centre, with a range of stock for indoor and outdoor gardening. Delivery service available. The chain has other centres nearby at Chandlers Cross, and at Marlow and Syon Park.

Growing Carpets
Christmas Tree House, High Street, Guilden Morden, Royston, Hertfordshire SG8 0JP
☎ 01763 852705
CONTACT Mrs Eileen Moore
OPEN 11 am – 5 pm, Monday – Saturday, March to October. By appointment only from 1 November to 1 March
SPECIALITIES Ground cover plants
NEW FOR 1995 *Lamium* 'Pink Pewter'; *Sedum* 'Purple Carpet'
CATALOGUE £1
MAIL ORDER Yes; from October
GARDEN Garden, including the whole nursery range

This ground cover nursery offers container-grown plants, and especially spreading perennials and prostrate shrubs. They are happy to give advice. The nursery is signed from the road.

Hopleys Plants Ltd
High Street, Much Hadham, Hertfordshire SG10 6BU
☎ 01279 842509   FAX 01279 843784
CONTACT Mr A. D. Barker
OPEN 9 am – 5 pm, daily; 2 – 5 pm, Sundays. Closed Tuesdays, and January
SPECIALITIES Herbaceous perennials; shrubs
NEW FOR 1995 Several new plants
CATALOGUE 5 first class stamps
MAIL ORDER Yes; autumn only
REFRESHMENTS Self-service
GARDEN Garden open at the same times as the nursery
SHOWS RHS Westminster; Malvern Spring; Harrogate (Spring); Chelsea; BBC GW Live; Hampton Court
GIFT TOKENS Own

An extensive choice of hardy shrubs and perennials, with many half-hardy varieties too. Strong on diascias, osteospermums, penstemons and salvias. Over the last quarter of a century the nursery has been responsible for numerous introductions, the most famous being *Lavatera* 'Barnsley' and *Potentilla fruticosa* 'Red Ace'.

LW Plants
23 Wroxham Way, Harpenden, Hertfordshire AL5 4PP
☎ 01582 768467
CONTACT Mrs M. Easter
OPEN 11 am – 5 pm, most days, phone first
SPECIALITIES Herbs
NEW FOR 1995 36 varieties of thyme

CATALOGUE SAE
MAIL ORDER No
GARDEN Garden opens for NGS

A selection of plants from a plantsman's garden with many thyme varieties.

Notcutts Garden Centre
Hatfield Road, Smallford, St Albans, Hertfordshire AL4 0BR
☎ 01727 853224   FAX 01727 847251
LOCATION On A1057
OPEN 8.30 am – 5.30 pm, Monday – Saturday; 11 am – 5 pm, Sundays. Closes at 5 pm in winter
CATALOGUE £2.50
SHOP Garden sundries, furniture
SHOWS Chelsea; BBC GW Live; Hampton Court
GIFT TOKENS HTA; own

See also Notcutts Nurseries, Suffolk.

R Harkness & Co Ltd
The Rose Gardens, Cambridge Road, Hitchin, Hertfordshire SG4 0JT
☎ 01462 420402   FAX 01462 422170
CONTACT Sales Office
OPEN 9 am – 5.30 pm, Monday – Saturday; 10.30 am – 4 pm Sundays
SPECIALITIES Roses
CATALOGUE On request
MAIL ORDER Yes; winter despatch
SHOP Garden centre
REFRESHMENTS Restaurant
SHOWS Chelsea
GIFT TOKENS HTA

Rose breeders and growers with a range dominated by Hybrid Teas, Cluster Flowered and low-growing varieties. There are also climbers and shrub roses on the list. There is a garden centre on the site too, with a wide range of bulbs, herbaceous plants, shrubs and trees.

Roger Harvey Garden World
The Farm House, Bragbury Lane, Bragbury End, Stevenage, Hertfordshire SG2 8JJ
☎ 01438 811777
CONTACT John Morgan
LOCATION On A602, 2 miles east of A1M, J7
OPEN 9 am – 5.30 pm, Monday – Saturday; 10.30 am – 4.30 pm, Sundays
MAIL ORDER No
SHOP Fish, silk flowers, gifts, pools
REFRESHMENTS Coffee shop
GIFT TOKENS HTA; own

This garden centre complex is set in old farm buildings.

Tokonama Bonsai Nursery
14 London Road, Shenley, Radlett, Hertfordshire WD7 9EN
☎ 01923 857587   FAX 01923 852596
CONTACT Charlotte Dalampira

OPEN 9 am – 5 pm, Monday – Friday; 10 am – 5 pm, Saturdays and Sundays
SPECIALITIES Bonsai
NEW FOR 1995 New bonsai and penjing
CATALOGUE SAE
MAIL ORDER Yes
SHOWS Chelsea; Hampton Court

Bonsai and penjing specialist, offering associated sundries. Workshops, lessons and talks can be arranged.

Top Pots
Westmill Farm, Ware, Hertfordshire SG12 0ES
☎ 01920 465026

CONTACT Peter and Cris Vigus
LOCATION On A602, 1 mile north of Ware
OPEN Times vary according to season, phone to check
SPECIALITIES Fuchsias
MAIL ORDER No

There are 600 varieties of fuchsias, besides hanging baskets and bedding plants. They also supply and install automatic watering systems.

The Van Hage Garden Company
Great Amwell, Ware, Hertfordshire SG12 9RP
☎ 01920 870811   FAX 01920 871861

CONTACT Miss Sandra Cronin
LOCATION Off A10
OPEN 9.30 am – 6 pm, Mondays; 9 am – 6 pm, Tuesdays, Wednesdays, Fridays, Saturdays; 9 am – 7.30 pm, Thursdays; 10.30 am – 4.30 pm, Sundays
SPECIALITIES House plants; seeds
CATALOGUE Seeds only
MAIL ORDER Yes
SHOP House plants, furniture, machinery, wholefoods
REFRESHMENTS Coffee house
GARDEN Display gardens
GIFT TOKENS HTA

Long-established and award-winning garden centre and seed merchants. The garden centre is strong on house plants, and has a large choice of plants. The seed catalogue covers flowers and vegetables, and includes the record-breaking Carrot 'Flak' as well as some untreated seed which is suitable for organic gardeners.

HUMBERSIDE

California Gardens
Howden, Goole, Humberside DN14 7TF
☎ 01430 430824   FAX 01430 432023
LOCATION On A614, near M62, J37
OPEN 9 am – 5 pm, daily
MAIL ORDER No
SHOP Greenhouses, garden buildings, sundries
REFRESHMENTS Coffee lounge
GIFT TOKENS HTA; own

This garden centre carries an all-round range of plants and sundries. They stock Blooms' perennials, and organise demonstrations and garden workshop days.

J & D Marston
Culag, Green Lane, Nafferton, Driffield YO25 0LF
☎ 01377 254487

CONTACT J. or D. Marston
LOCATION Off A166, 2 miles from Driffield
OPEN 1.30 – 4.30 pm, Saturdays and Sundays, Easter to mid September
SPECIALITIES Ferns
CATALOGUE £1
MAIL ORDER Yes

Just ferns from this specialist nursery, but there is a large choice of outdoor and greenhouse species.

Mendle Nursery
Holme, Scunthorpe, Humberside DN16 3RF
☎ 01724 850864

CONTACT Mrs A. Earnshaw
LOCATION Holme
OPEN 10 am – 6 pm, daily
SPECIALITIES Alpines; primulas; sempervivums
CATALOGUE 2 first class stamps
MAIL ORDER Yes; no minimum order

A broad range of alpines, including primulas, *Saxifraga* and lots of sempervivums.

Mires Beck Nursery
Low Mill Lane, North Cave, Brough, Humberside HU15 2NR
☎ 01430 421543

CONTACT Martin Rowland
OPEN 10 am – 4 pm, Wednesday – Saturday, 1 April to 30 September; 10 am – 3 pm, Wednesday – Friday, 1 October to 31 March
SPECIALITIES Herbaceous perennials; wild flowers
CATALOGUE 3 first class stamps
MAIL ORDER Yes

This nursery grows herbaceous perennials and wild flowers. It is run to provide training for the disabled.

Pennell & Sons Ltd
Garden Centre, Humberston Road, Grimsby, Humberside DN36 4RW
☎ 01472 694272   FAX 01472 694272

CONTACT Mr J. R. Cousins
LOCATION Outskirts of Grimsby
OPEN 8.30 am – 5.30 pm, Monday – Saturday; 10 am – 5.30 pm, Sundays and Bank Holidays
SHOP Garden sundries
GIFT TOKENS HTA

Garden centre with a full range. Delivery available.

Stephen H Smith's Garden & Leisure
Trent Valley, Doncaster Road, Scunthorpe, Humberside DN15 8TE
☎ 01724 848950   FAX 01724 271912

CONTACT Neil Parker
LOCATION On A18, ½ a mile east of M181 junction

OPEN 9 am – 6 pm, summer; 9 am – 5.30 pm, winter; 11 am – 5 pm, Sundays
SHOP Garden sundries, furniture, gifts, aquatics
REFRESHMENTS Coffee shop
GIFT TOKENS HTA; own

Garden centre with plants and garden products, including a Hillier Premier Plants agency. Delivery service.

White Cottage Alpines
Eastgate, Rudston, Driffield, Humberside YO25 0UX
☎ 01262 420668

CONTACT Mrs S. E. Cummins
LOCATION Just off B1253 (Bridlington to York: the scenic route)
OPEN 10 am – 5 pm, Thursday – Sunday, and Bank Holiday Mondays. Closed December and January
SPECIALITIES Alpines
NEW FOR 1995 Many new plants
CATALOGUE 2 first class stamps
MAIL ORDER Yes
GARDEN Display troughs

There is an interesting range to be found at this alpine nursery. Among the plants for alpine houses and rock gardens are some American species, and species under collectors' numbers. Shows include the Gateshead Spring and Summer Shows, and the Caulke Abbey Plant Sale.

ISLE OF WIGHT

Deacon's Nursery
Moor View, Godshill, Isle of Wight PO38 3HW
☎ 01983 840750/522243

CONTACT G. D. Deacon
LOCATION Moor View is next to school, off School Crescent
OPEN 8 am – 4 pm, Monday – Friday; 8 am – 2 pm, Saturdays, October to April; 8 am – 6 pm, Monday – Friday; 8 am – 4 pm, Saturdays, April to October
SPECIALITIES Fruit
NEW FOR 1995 Apple 'Cox's Orange Pippin' (self-fertile), thornless gooseberries
CATALOGUE SAE (29p stamp)
MAIL ORDER Yes; no minimum order
GARDEN Public welcome at nursery
GIFT TOKENS HTA

Fruit specialist, with tree and soft fruit of every size and variety. The very comprehensive list includes over 250 apple cultivars. All rootstocks are of virus-free origin.

KENT

Alan C Smith
127 Leaves Green Road, Keston, Kent BR2 6DG
☎ 01959 572531

CONTACT Alan C. Smith
OPEN By appointment only
SPECIALITIES Sempervivums
CATALOGUE 50p

MAIL ORDER Yes
SHOWS RHS Westminster

An amazing range of sempervivums and jovibarbas, including species, hybrids and cultivars: there are about one thousand on offer. A small selection is also available at Westerham Heights Garden Centre, Hawley Corner, Westerham Hill, Westerham TN16 2AW.

Ashenden Nursery
Cranbrook Road, Benenden, Cranbrook, Kent TN17 4ET
☎ 01580 241792

CONTACT Kevin McGarry
LOCATION On B2086 between Cranbrook and Benenden
OPEN 10 am – 4.30 pm, Monday – Saturday. Phone first
SPECIALITIES Alpines; herbaceous perennials
NEW FOR 1995 New *Geum*, *Oenothera*, *Cephalaria* and *Dianthus*
CATALOGUE SAE
MAIL ORDER Yes

Stocks a range of plants for rock gardens. They exhibit at specialist and local shows, including the Savill Garden Plant Fairs, Hatfield's Festival of Gardening, and the Parham House Plant Fair.

Bamboo Nursery Ltd
Kingsgate Cottage, Wittersham, Kent TN30 7NS
☎ 01797 270607   FAX 01797 270825

CONTACT Andy or Fran Sutcliffe
OPEN By appointment
SPECIALITIES Bamboos
CATALOGUE SAE
MAIL ORDER Yes

Mainly wholesale bamboo specialists with a selection of *Arundinaria*, *Sasa* and *Phyllostachys*. Some are available in large sizes.

Brenda Hyatt
1 Toddington Crescent, Bluebell Hill, Chatham, Kent ME5 9QT
☎ 01634 863251

CONTACT Brenda Hyatt
OPEN By appointment
SPECIALITIES Auriculas
CATALOGUE SAE plus 75p
MAIL ORDER Yes
SHOWS RHS Westminster; Malvern Spring; Chelsea
NCCPG NATIONAL COLLECTIONS *Primula auricula* (show)

Auricula specialist – and National Collection holder. The superb range includes stripes, doubles, selfs and alpine specimens. Among the show types available are white-edged, green- and grey-flowered plants. Orders are dealt with in rotation, subject to availability.

Bybrook Barn Garden & Produce Centre
Canterbury Road, Kennington, Ashford, Kent
TN24 9JZ
☎ 01233 631959   FAX 01233 635642
OPEN 9 am – 5.30 pm, Monday – Saturday; 10.30 am – 4.30 pm, Sundays
SHOP   Garden sundries, gifts, furniture
REFRESHMENTS   Refreshments
GIFT TOKENS   HTA

Garden centre stocking garden requirements and indoor plants. A gardening club is run from the premises in spring and summer.

Church Hill Cottage Gardens
Charing Heath, Ashford, Kent TN27 0BU
☎ 01233 712522
CONTACT   Mr and Mrs Metianu
LOCATION   Take Charing Heath road from A20 (Maidstone side of Charing). Turn right at Red Lion, right again after 100 yards, towards church. Garden is 300 yards on right
OPEN   10 am – 5 pm, Tuesday – Sunday, and Bank Holidays. Closed Mondays, and 1 November – 31 January
SPECIALITIES   *Dianthus*; herbaceous perennials
NEW FOR 1995   *Acer rubrum* 'October Glory'
CATALOGUE   3 first class stamps
MAIL ORDER   No
REFRESHMENTS   Red Lion nearby
GARDEN   1½-acre garden, admission £1.50 (times as above)
GIFT TOKENS   Own

The nursery specialises in hardy herbaceous perennials, but there are many *Dianthus*, alpines and shrubs to choose from too. The garden opens too: park in the nearby pub.

Coblands Garden Centre
Eridge Road, Tunbridge Wells, Kent TN4 8HP
☎ 01892 515234
LOCATION   A26, Tunbridge Wells
OPEN   daily
GIFT TOKENS   HTA

Coblands Nursery
Trench Road, Tonbridge, Kent TN10 3HQ
☎ 01732 770999   FAX 01732 770271
LOCATION   Tonbridge
SPECIALITIES   Bamboos; climbers; conifers; ferns; grasses; herbaceous perennials; shrubs; trees
CATALOGUE   Wholesale catalogue only
MAIL ORDER   No
GIFT TOKENS   HTA

A large wholesale nursery which carries a comprehensive range of all types of plants for landscapers and garden centres. They also supply their own garden centres at Tunbridge Wells, and a plant centre at Ightham.

Coblands Plant Centre
Hazeldene Nursery, Sevenoaks Road, Ightham,
☎ 01732 780816
LOCATION   A25
OPEN   daily
GIFT TOKENS   HTA

Connoisseurs' Cacti
51 Chelsfield Lane, Orpington, Kent BR5 4HG
☎ 01689 837781
CONTACT   John Pilbeam
LOCATION   Woodlands Farm, Shire Lane, Farnborough, Kent
OPEN   10.30 am – 2 pm, most days, including weekends
SPECIALITIES   Cacti and succulents
NEW FOR 1995   3 new *Rebutia* hybrids
CATALOGUE   SAE
MAIL ORDER   Yes; UK and EC only
SHOP   Books on cacti
SHOWS   RHS Westminster; Harrogate (Spring); Hampton Court

An extensive range of cacti and succulents (over 20,000 specimens in stock), as well as books on cacti. Particularly strong on *Gymnocalycium*, *Mammillaria*, *Rebutia* and *Sulcorebutia*. The main address is for postal inquiries only.

Downderry Nursery
649 London Road, Ditton, Aylesford, Kent
ME20 6DJ
☎ 01732 840710
CONTACT   Dr Simon J. Charlesworth
OPEN   By appointment only
SPECIALITIES   Lavenders
CATALOGUE   SAE
MAIL ORDER   Yes

A lavender and rosemary specialist. Many species and cultivars are available as rooted cuttings and liners by post, wholesale and retail.

Forward Nurseries
Borough Green Road, Ightham, Kent TN15 9JA
☎ 01732 884726   FAX 01732 886626
CONTACT   Paul van Leeuwen
LOCATION   A25 and A227 roundabout at Borough Green
OPEN   8 am – 5 pm, daily
SPECIALITIES   Hedging; ivies
CATALOGUE   Trade catalogue; retail mail order list
MAIL ORDER   Yes

This mainly wholesale nursery carries a general range. Their retail section specialises in hedging plants (which are available by mail order) and containerised ivy plants.

The Fruit Garden
Mulberry Farm, Woodnesborough, Sandwich, Kent
CT13 0PT
☎ 01304 813454   FAX 01304 813454
CONTACT   Patricia and Peter Dodd

OPEN By appointment only, for collection
SPECIALITIES Fruit
CATALOGUE On request
MAIL ORDER Yes
DESIGN SERVICE The Fruit Garden

A tempting list of fruit trees, with the emphasis on older varieties. They can design fruit gardens, and will bud or graft to order. This service can be done with your own scion wood: a way to propagate a favourite or irreplaceable tree.

Hazeldene Nursery
Dean Street, East Farleigh, Maidstone, Kent
ME15 0PS
☎ 01622 726248

CONTACT Mrs J. Adams
LOCATION 2½ miles south west of Maidstone
OPEN 10 am – 3 pm, Tuesday – Saturday, March to September
SPECIALITIES Seeds; violas
NEW FOR 1995 Viola cornuta 'Misty Guy'
CATALOGUE 2 first class stamps
MAIL ORDER Yes
SHOWS RHS Westminster; Malvern Spring; Harrogate (Spring); Southport; Chelsea; BBC GW Live; Hampton Court; Harrogate (Autumn)

Many kinds of pansies, violas, violets and violettas. These are often available as seed as well as plants. The nursery has amassed five gold medals at Chelsea.

High Banks Nurseries
Slip Mill Road, Hawkhurst, Kent TN18 5AD
☎ 01580 753031   FAX 01580 753031

CONTACT Jeremy Homewood
OPEN 8 am – 4.30 pm, winter; 8.30 am – 5 pm, spring and summer
CATALOGUE Large SAE
MAIL ORDER No

The nursery carries a full, general range of plants.

Iden Croft Herbs
Frittenden Road, Staplehurst, Kent TN12 0DH
☎ 01580 891432   FAX 01580 892416

CONTACT Rosemary Titterington and Marion Browne
LOCATION Signed from A229, south of Staplehurst
OPEN 9 am – 5 pm, Monday – Saturday, all year; 11 am – 5 pm, Sundays and Bank Holidays, March to September only
SPECIALITIES Herbaceous perennials; herbs; wild flowers
NEW FOR 1995 Many new plants
CATALOGUE SAE for list; £2.50 full catalogue
MAIL ORDER Yes
SHOP Herb products, seeds, books
REFRESHMENTS Tea room
GARDEN Herb gardens
DESIGN SERVICE Iden Croft Herbs
GIFT TOKENS HTA

NCCPG NATIONAL COLLECTIONS Origanum, Mentha

Calls itself a 'total herb centre' with some justification. The range of herbs and aromatic plants is both impressive and extensive. Other herb products are on sale too. The main catalogue is very helpful and informative. They hold tours, workshops and other events. The gardens are designed for disabled access.

J Bradshaw & Son
Busheyfields Nursery, Herne, Herne Bay, Kent
CT6 7LJ
☎ 01227 375415   FAX 01227 375415

CONTACT Denis Bradshaw
LOCATION On A291, 2 miles south of A299 junction
OPEN 10 am – 5 pm, Tuesday – Saturday
SPECIALITIES Clematis; climbers
CATALOGUE SAE
MAIL ORDER No
GARDEN Stock fields of Clematis and Lonicera open by appointment, £1
NCCPG NATIONAL COLLECTIONS Lonicera (climbing)

Family nursery. The business was mainly wholesale but from this year they will open a new retail centre. They specialise in clematis, Lonicera and other climbers. The stock fields, with over 100 Lonicera species and over 250 Clematis are open by appointment (special terms for NCCPG and British Clematis Society members). The annual open day will be 24 June, from 10 am – 4 pm.

Keepers Nursery
446 Wateringbury Road, East Malling, Kent
ME19 6JJ
☎ 01622 813008

CONTACT Anne and Mike Cook
LOCATION 5 miles west of Maidstone, between M20 and A26
OPEN By appointment at all reasonable times
SPECIALITIES Fruit
CATALOGUE SAE
MAIL ORDER Yes
GARDEN Open by arrangement
DESIGN SERVICE Keepers Nursery

A very lengthy list of fruit trees, including some lovely names, and a good choice of nuts and soft fruit too. An idea of the scope: over 360 apples, 70 plums, 40 cherries, not to mention medlars, pears and quinces. They will design fruit gardens and orchards, and can advise on maintenance within their area. The grafting service offers to propagate known and unknown varieties for customers. They also hold workshops and courses on propagation and fruit maintenance.

Landscape Plants
Cattamount, Grafty Green, Maidstone, Kent
ME17 2AP
☎ 01622 850245

CONTACT Tom La Dell

OPEN   By appointment
CATALOGUE   2 first class stamps
MAIL ORDER   Yes
GARDEN   Demonstration garden
DESIGN SERVICE   Tom La Dell

A mainly wholesale nursery. Plants have been selected for interesting mass planting and low maintenance by a knowledgeable plantsman. Helpful catalogue.

Layham Garden Centre
Lower Road, Staple, Canterbury, Kent CT3 1LH
☎ 01304 813267   FAX 01304 615349
CONTACT   Andrew Marshall (manager)
LOCATION   8 miles south of Canterbury
OPEN   9 am – 5 pm, Monday – Saturday; 10 am – 5 pm, Sundays
SPECIALITIES   Conifers; herbaceous perennials; roses; shrubs
CATALOGUE   Rose list on request
MAIL ORDER   Yes
REFRESHMENTS   Refreshments
GARDEN   Display gardens, open as garden centre
GIFT TOKENS   HTA

The garden centre carries a general range of plants with a particular accent on roses: the business is backed by its own wholesale nursery, Layham Nurseries (01304 611380).

Longacre Nursery
Longacre, Perry Wood, Selling, Faversham, Kent ME13 9SE
☎ 01227 752254
CONTACT   Dr G. Thomas
LOCATION   East of Selling village
OPEN   2 – 5 pm, April to October
SPECIALITIES   Herbaceous perennials
NEW FOR 1995   Many new plants
CATALOGUE   SAE
MAIL ORDER   No
REFRESHMENTS   Teas on open days
GARDEN   Garden opens for NGS and by appointment
DESIGN SERVICE   Longacre Nursery

The nursery sells a wide variety of hardy perennials. The garden can be visited, and the Thomases offer garden design (especially for borders) and lectures. Groups welcome by appointment. NGS open days this year: 16 – 17 April, 30 April, 1 May, 14 May, 28 – 29 May, 11 June, 25 June, 9 July, 23 July, 27 – 28 August, 10 September.

Madrona Nursery
Harden Road, Lydd, Kent TN29 9LT
☎ 01797 320868
CONTACT   Mr Liam MacKenzie
LOCATION   Map in catalogue
OPEN   2 – 8 pm, Tuesday – Thursday, mid March to end October
SPECIALITIES   Shrubs; trees
CATALOGUE   £1

MAIL ORDER   Yes; minimum carriage charge £8
SHOWS   RHS Westminster; Malvern Spring; Hampton Court
GIFT TOKENS   Own

The emphasis is on interesting and attractive trees and shrubs, including new introductions, but there are also perennials, ferns, grasses and bamboos.

Magnolia Gardens
Stodmarsh Road, Canterbury, Kent CT3 4AG
☎ 01227 463951
CONTACT   Mrs L. A. Pickard
LOCATION   Off A257, just after golf club
OPEN   10 am – 5 pm, Tuesday, Thursday – Sunday; 2 – 5 pm, Wednesday and Friday. Closed Mondays, except Bank Holidays, Wednesday and Friday am
SPECIALITIES   *Magnolia*
MAIL ORDER   No

Magnolias, of course, and a selection of other acid-soil loving shrubs – azaleas and rhododendrons, camellias and *Pieris*.

Marle Place Gardens & Nursery
Marle Place Road, Brenchley, Tonbridge, Kent TN12 7HS   FAX 01892 724099
CONTACT   Mrs Williams
LOCATION   Signed from Brenchley
OPEN   10 am – 5.30 pm
SPECIALITIES   Herbs; wild flowers
CATALOGUE   SAE
MAIL ORDER   Yes
REFRESHMENTS   Tea and cake
GARDEN   Marle Place Gardens
DESIGN SERVICE   Marle Place Gardens & Nursery
NCCPG NATIONAL COLLECTIONS   *Calamintha*, *Santolina*

The nursery grows herbs, aromatic and scented plants in containers. This year more plants from the garden are being introduced. Courses, talks and tours can be arranged: there are two garden design courses on 13 and 15 March.

Notcutts Garden Centre
Tonbridge Road, Pembury, Tunbridge Wells, Kent TN2 4QN
☎ 01892 822636   FAX 01892 825251
LOCATION   From A21, take Pembury Hospital turning
OPEN   8.30 am – 5.30 pm, Monday – Friday; 9 am – 5.30 pm, Saturdays; 11 am – 5 pm, Sundays. Closes at 5 pm in winter
CATALOGUE   £2.50
SHOP   Garden sundries, furniture, buildings, landscape materials
REFRESHMENTS   Charity teas: summer weekends only
DESIGN SERVICE   Nottcutts Landscapes
GIFT TOKENS   HTA; own

Events, including trips to major shows, organised throughout the year: ring for details. See also Notcutts Nurseries, Suffolk.

Oldbury Nurseries
Brissenden Green, Bethersden, Ashford, Kent
TN26 3BJ
☎ 01233 820416

CONTACT Wendy and Peter Dresman
LOCATION 7 miles south west of Ashford, off A28
OPEN 9.30 am – 5 pm, daily, February to June
SPECIALITIES Fuchsias; pelargoniums
CATALOGUE 2 first class stamps
MAIL ORDER No
SHOWS Chelsea; BBC GW Live; Hampton Court

Oldbury Nurseries are specialist fuchsia growers with an extensive range. Some pelargoniums too. Groups are catered for by appointment, February to May.

P De Jager & Sons Ltd
Staplehurst Road, Marden, Kent TN12 9BP
☎ 01622 831235   FAX 01622 832416
LOCATION Between Maidstone and Staplehurst on A229
OPEN 9 am – 5 pm, Monday – Friday; 9 am – 12 pm, Saturdays
SPECIALITIES Bulbs; daffodils
CATALOGUE On request; December, May
MAIL ORDER Yes
GIFT TOKENS Own

Bulbs of all kinds, ranging from well-known *Narcissus* and *Tulipa* varieties to some rare specimen bulbs. All bulbs come from cultivated stocks.

P H Kellett
Laurels Nursery, Benenden, Cranbrook, Kent
TN17 4JU
☎ 01580 240463

CONTACT Mr P. H. Kellett
LOCATION ¾ mile off Benenden to Rolvenden road, towards Dingleden
OPEN 8 am – 5 pm, Monday – Thursday; 8 am – 4 pm, Fridays; 8.30 am – 12 pm, Saturdays. Other times by appointment
SPECIALITIES Trees
CATALOGUE On request
MAIL ORDER No
DESIGN SERVICE P. H. Kellett
GIFT TOKENS HTA

A traditional nursery growing a varied range of trees and shrubs, including roses, conifers, fruit trees and climbers. Plants are both open ground and container-grown: browsers can inspect stock for autumn lifting. Border planning and advice available also.

Pete & Ken Cactus Nursery
Saunders Lane, Ash, Canterbury, Kent CT3 2BX
☎ 01304 812170

CONTACT Ken Burke
LOCATION 10 miles east of Canterbury, off A257
OPEN 9 am – 6 pm, daily
SPECIALITIES Cacti and succulents
CATALOGUE Large SAE
MAIL ORDER Yes

Cacti and succulents specialists, with a particularly good choice of *Lithops*. Not all the varieties appear in the catalogue. They also sell some alpines, fuchsias and shrubs.

Plaxtol Nurseries
The Spoute, Plaxtol, Sevenoaks, Kent TN15 0QR
☎ 01732 810550

CONTACT Tessa and Jenny Forbes
LOCATION On the east side of Plaxtol, off A227
OPEN 10 am – 5 pm, daily. Closed for a fortnight at Christmas
SPECIALITIES Foliage plants
CATALOGUE 2 first class stamps
MAIL ORDER Yes; November to March
GARDEN Garden open for customers
DESIGN SERVICE Plaxtol Nurseries
GIFT TOKENS Own

Trees, shrubs, heathers, conifers and herbaceous plants: all chosen with the flower arranger in mind. They attend the NAFAS competitions at Stoneleigh this year also. A wide range of talks and courses are available at the nursery. They design and construct Japanese gardens, and their own garden is open to customers.

Richard G M Cawthorne
Lower Daltons Nursery, Swanley Village, Swanley, Kent BR8 7NU

CONTACT R. G. M. Cawthorne
LOCATION Map sent to customers who have arranged collection
OPEN Mail order only
SPECIALITIES Violas
NEW FOR 1995 On display at Chelsea
CATALOGUE 70p
MAIL ORDER Yes
SHOWS Chelsea
NCCPG NATIONAL COLLECTIONS *Viola* (Melanium section)

The *Viola* and violetta specialist, with a collection of 550 named varieties and species. Many of these have been bred by Mr Cawthorne, whose outdoor displays are a familiar sight at Chelsea each year. Orders are taken from May to October, and invoiced in January or February. Collection from the nursery is possible in April only.

Rosewood Nurseries
70 Deansway Avenue, Sturry, Canterbury, Kent
CT2 0NN
☎ 01227 711071

CONTACT Chris Searle
OPEN By appointment
SPECIALITIES *Hemerocallis*
CATALOGUE 2 first class stamps
MAIL ORDER No

There is a good selection of *Hemerocallis*, especially newer American varieties; other hardy perennials are grown too.

Rumwood Nurseries
Langley, Maidstone, Kent ME17 3ND
☎ 01622 861477   FAX 01622 863123
CONTACT   James Fermor
LOCATION   On A274
OPEN   9 am – 5 pm, Monday – Saturday; 10 am – 4 pm, Sundays
SPECIALITIES   Roses
CATALOGUE   SAE
MAIL ORDER   Yes
GARDEN   Rose fields June to October
GIFT TOKENS   HTA

A family-run retail and wholesale nursery. They specialise in roses, of which they grow an all-round range, and other hardy nursery stock.

Starborough Nursery
Starborough Road, Marsh Green, Edenbridge, Kent TN8 5RB
☎ 01732 865614
CONTACT   Mrs P. Kindley and Colin Tomlin
LOCATION   Between Edenbridge and Lingfield on B2028
OPEN   10 am – 4.30 pm, Thursday – Monday. Closed Tuesdays, Wednesdays and in January and July
SPECIALITIES   Rhododendrons; trees
CATALOGUE   £1.50
MAIL ORDER   Yes
SHOWS   RHS Westminster; Chelsea

Recently joined forces with G. Reuthe Ltd. They now issue a single catalogue, combining Starborough's trees and shrubs with Reuthe's rhododendrons and azaleas.

Tile Barn Nursery
Standen Street, Iden Green, Benenden, Kent TN17 4LB
☎ 01580 240221
CONTACT   Peter Moore
LOCATION   2 miles south of Benenden; turn left at crossroads in Iden Green
OPEN   9 am – 5 pm, Wednesday – Saturday
SPECIALITIES   *Cyclamen*
CATALOGUE   SAE
MAIL ORDER   Yes
GARDEN   Display garden

Mail order is restricted to their speciality – *Cyclamen* species. Nursery visitors will also find some species of *Crocus, Fritillaria, Leucojum* and *Narcissus*.

Westwood Nursery
65 Yorkland Avenue, Welling, Kent DA16 2LE
☎ 0181 301 0886
CONTACT   Mr S. Edwards
OPEN   Mail order only
SPECIALITIES   Pleiones; hardy orchids

CATALOGUE   SAE; summer, winter
MAIL ORDER   Yes

Hardy orchids and pleiones: suitable for the garden and frost-free greenhouse. Some orchid books too.

LANCASHIRE

Auldene Nurseries Ltd
338 Southport Road, Ulnes Walton, Leyland, Lancashire PR5 3LQ
☎ 01772 600271   FAX 01772 601483
CONTACT   Mr Richard Iddon
LOCATION   3 miles south of Leyland, on A581
OPEN   9 am – 8 pm (or dusk if earlier), daily
SHOP   Books, gifts and sundries
REFRESHMENTS   Coffee shop
DESIGN SERVICE   Auldene Landscapes
GIFT TOKENS   HTA

Family-run garden centre which stocks plants and shrubs, aquatics, seeds, sundries and conservatories. They have a design and landscaping capability, and deliver free locally. Monthly gardening seminars are held, and they run their own gardening club.

Barkers Primrose Nurseries
Whalley Road, Clitheroe, Lancashire BB7 1HT
☎ 01200 23521   FAX 01200 28160
CONTACT   Philip Bradley
LOCATION   Ribble Valley: from M6, J31 follow A59 to Clitheroe
OPEN   9 am – 5.30 pm, Monday – Saturday; 10 am – 5 pm, Sundays and Bank Holidays
SPECIALITIES   Acers; aquatic plants
CATALOGUE   SAE; ornamental trees, roses, fruit trees and bushes
MAIL ORDER   No
GIFT TOKENS   HTA

Nursery and garden centre with a large and varied range of plants, including aquatics and marginals, Japanese acers, trees, shrubs and perennials. Named after the area: they are not *Primula* specialists.

Barton Grange Garden Centre (Bolton)
Wigan Road, Bolton, Lancashire BL3 4RD
☎ 01204 660660   FAX 01204 62525
CONTACT   Jane Stead
LOCATION   ½ a mile from M61, J5, on A58 to Bolton
OPEN   9 am – 5.30 pm, Monday – Saturday (until 8 pm Tuesdays); 10 am – 5.30 pm Sundays
NEW FOR 1995   *Skimmia* 'Chameleon'
SHOP   Garden sundries, gifts
REFRESHMENTS   Café
GARDEN   Display beds and water feature
DESIGN SERVICE   Barton Grange Garden Centre (Bolton)
SHOWS   Chelsea
GIFT TOKENS   HTA

LANCASHIRE Nurseries & Garden Centres

Large garden centre with a full range of plants and associated garden products. They are stockists for the Hilliers Premier Plant Collection. Landscaping and garden maintenance service.

Catforth Gardens
Roots Lane, Catforth, Preston, Lancashire PR4 0JB
☎ 01772 690561/690269

CONTACT   Judith Bradshaw and Chris Moore
LOCATION   From M6, J32 towards Garstang; left at first lights. After 2 miles, right at T junction. Then left into School Lane, by Catford sign. At the end of the road, left again, then first right
OPEN   18 March – 17 September
SPECIALITIES   Herbaceous perennials
CATALOGUE   5 first class stamps
MAIL ORDER   No
GARDEN   Three gardens: admission £1.50
NCCPG NATIONAL COLLECTIONS *Geranium*

The nursery is sandwiched between three gardens which open at the same times. The list is strongest on hardy geraniums (both species and cultivars): they hold a National Collection. Many other herbaceous perennials are also on offer.

Craig House Cacti
94 King Street, Southport, Lancashire PR8 1LG
☎ 01704 545077

CONTACT   George A. McCleod
OPEN   Mail order only
SPECIALITIES   Cacti and succulents
CATALOGUE   Yes
MAIL ORDER   Yes
SHOWS   RHS Westminster; Malvern Spring; Harrogate (Spring); Southport; Chelsea; BBC GW Live; Hampton Court; Harrogate (Autumn); Ayr

Mail order specialists selling cacti, succulents and cycads including Madagascan caudiciform succulents (swollen stemmed). They also exhibit widely, so look out for them at shows, including Shrewsbury, Bath, Cardiff and Leicester.

Croston Cactus
43 Southport Road, Eccleston, Chorley, Lancashire PR7 6ET
☎ 01257 452555

CONTACT   John L. Henshaw
LOCATION   On A581, just east of B5253 junction
OPEN   Saturdays and Sundays only
SPECIALITIES   Cacti and succulents
NEW FOR 1995   *Astrophytum asterias* 'Super Kobuto'
CATALOGUE   2 first class stamps; spring and summer
MAIL ORDER   Yes; no minimum order
SHOWS   Southport

Cacti and succulents aimed chiefly at the enthusiast: many mammillarias and some interesting haworthias. Bromeliads and tillandsias are available at the nursery.

Holden Clough Nursery
Holden, Bolton by Bowland, Clitheroe, Lancashire BB7 4PF
☎ 01200 447615

CONTACT   Mr P. Foley
LOCATION   8 miles north east of Clitheroe, off A59
OPEN   1 – 5 pm, Monday – Thursday; 9 am – 5 pm, Saturdays, all year; 2 – 5pm, Sundays (April and May only)
SPECIALITIES   Alpines; conifers; ferns; grasses; herbaceous perennials; shrubs
NEW FOR 1995   New *Crocosmia*, *Monarda* (mildew resistant), *Platycerium*, and *Superbum*
CATALOGUE   £1.20
MAIL ORDER   Yes; October to March
REFRESHMENTS   Available nearby
SHOWS   RHS Westminster; Harrogate (Spring); Southport; BBC GW Live; Hampton Court; Harrogate (Autumn)
GIFT TOKENS   Own

A long-established working nursery, with a large and very hardy range of interesting alpines, perennials, dwarf conifers, shrubs, ferns and grasses. Please note that this Pennine nursery only opens on Sundays in April and May, and that the last admission on all days is at 4.30 pm.

Pinks & Carnations
22 Chetwyn Avenue, Bromley Cross, Bolton, Lancashire BL7 9BN
☎ 01204 306273   FAX 01204 306273

CONTACT   Ruth or Tom Gillies
OPEN   By appointment only
SPECIALITIES   *Dianthus*
NEW FOR 1995   Hostas and dwarf lupins (collection only)
CATALOGUE   1 first class stamp
MAIL ORDER   Yes
GIFT TOKENS   Own

This wholesale and retail nursery supplies garden pinks, and perpetual flowering and border carnations. Some Malmaison carnations will be available in spring. Canes and plant supports supplied too. A sideline is model wooden cars.

Reginald Kaye Ltd
Waithman Nurseries, Silverdale, Carnforth, Lancashire LA5 0TY
☎ 01524 701252

CONTACT   Mrs Kaye
LOCATION   4 miles north west of Carnforth
OPEN   9 am – 5 pm, Monday – Saturday; 2.30 – 5 pm Sundays
SPECIALITIES   Alpines; ferns; herbaceous perennials
CATALOGUE   60p
MAIL ORDER   Ferns only
GARDEN   New rock garden

Alpine and fern specialists: the list of ferns is being increased this year, and there is a newly-built rock garden.

LEICESTERSHIRE

A & A Thorp
Bungalow No. 5, Main Street, Theddingworth, Lutterworth, Leicestershire LE17 6QZ
☎ 01858 880496

CONTACT   Anita Thorp
LOCATION   Between Market Harborough and Lutterworth, on A427
OPEN   9 am – 6 pm (dusk in winter)
SPECIALITIES   Alpines; woodland plants
CATALOGUE   SAE plus 50p
MAIL ORDER   No

A small nursery which stocks alpine and herbaceous plants in small quantities. The range is large, though. Personal service rather than help yourself.

Askew Nurseries
South Croxton Road, Queniborough, Leicester, Leicestershire LE7 3RX
☎ 01664 840557

CONTACT   Mrs J. L. Longland
LOCATION   Off A607, 2 miles east of Queniborough
OPEN   9 am – 7 pm, Wednesday – Monday, February to September. Closed Tuesdays
SPECIALITIES   Fuchsias
CATALOGUE   3 first class stamps
MAIL ORDER   Yes
GARDEN   Display house

A specialist fuchsia nursery with a large range of cultivars; cuttings are available by post, larger plants from the nursery. Stock plants in flower during July and August. There are tours and talks for groups.

Barnsdale Plants
The Avenue, Exton, Oakham, Leicestershire LE15 8AH
☎ 01572 813200   FAX 01572 813346

CONTACT   Nick Hamilton
LOCATION   Off A606, between Oakham and Stamford
OPEN   10 am – 5 pm, daily, 1 March to 31 October; 10 am – 4 pm, daily, 1 November to 28 February. Closed Christmas and New Year
SPECIALITIES   Herbaceous perennials; shrubs
CATALOGUE   3 first class stamps and A4 envelope
MAIL ORDER   Yes
GARDEN   Gardens being planted
SHOWS   RHS Westminster; Hampton Court
GIFT TOKENS   Own

A pleasing selection of perennials, shrubs and trees is grown by the nursery. Many were originally propagated from the BBC TV garden. All are grown in peat-free compost. Since Barnsdale Garden is not open, a series of gardens in similar style is being planted around the nursery.

Fosse Alpines
33 Leicester Road, Countesthorpe, Leicestershire LE8 5QU
☎ 0116 2778237

CONTACT   Mr T. West
LOCATION   Phone for directions
OPEN   By appointment only
SPECIALITIES   Alpines
CATALOGUE   2 first class stamps
MAIL ORDER   Yes; minimum order £8
REFRESHMENTS   Tea and coffee
GARDEN   Display garden

This small nursery is recommended for its range of rare and unusual alpines. They will provide directions when you make an appointment.

Gandy's Roses Ltd
North Kilworth, Lutterworth, Leicestershire LE17 6HZ
☎ 01858 880398

CONTACT   Mr D. Gandy, Mrs E. Gandy, Miss R. Gandy and Mrs M. Spence
OPEN   Office hours: 9 am – 5 pm, Monday – Saturday; 2 – 5 pm, Sundays
SPECIALITIES   Roses
CATALOGUE   On request
MAIL ORDER   Yes
GARDEN   Rose fields open, July – September
GIFT TOKENS   HTA

Rose growers covering the whole spectrum (600), with a particularly interesting choice of climbers. The nursery also sells shrubs, fruit trees and conifers. Items need to be ordered in advance for winter collection and mail order.

Goscote Nurseries Ltd
Syston Road, Cossington, Leicestershire LE7 4UZ
☎ 01509 812121

CONTACT   D. C. and R. C. Cox
LOCATION   5 miles north of Leicester, on B5328
OPEN   8 am – 5 pm (4.30 pm in winter), Monday – Friday; 9 am – 5 pm, Saturdays; 10 am – 5 pm, Sundays
SPECIALITIES   Conifers; heathers; shrubs; trees
NEW FOR 1995   *Berberis thunbergii* 'Red Rodeo', *Hebe* 'Wiri Charm', *H.* 'Wiri Cloud', *H.* 'Wiri Dawn', *H.* 'Wiri Image', *H.* 'Wiri Joy', *Potentilla fruticosa* 'Chino', *Rhodendendron* 'Goldbuckett', *Mahonia aquifolium* 'Cosmo Crawl'
CATALOGUE   5 second class stamps
MAIL ORDER   Yes; minimum order £10
GARDEN   Display gardens
GIFT TOKENS   Own

An extensive collection of trees, shrubs and conifers, acers and azaleas, is available here from the open ground.

LEICESTERSHIRE Nurseries & Garden Centres 179

The nursery centre also stocks container plants. Planting plans can be drawn up.

The Herb Nursery
Thistleton, Oakham, Leicestershire LE15 7RE
☎ 01572 767658
CONTACT Peter Bench
LOCATION Off A1, north west of Stamford
OPEN 9 am – 6 pm (or dusk), daily
SPECIALITIES Herbs; wild flowers
CATALOGUE SAE
MAIL ORDER No

As well as herbs, there are cottage garden plants and wild flowers in a range of sizes.

Hill Farmhouse Plants
Hill Farmhouse, Cottingham, Market Harborough, Leicestershire LE16 8XS
☎ 01536 770994
CONTACT Richard Cain
LOCATION Map in catalogue
OPEN 9.30 am – 5.30 pm, Saturdays only, 1 March to 31 July and 1 – 30 September
SPECIALITIES Hardy geraniums
NEW FOR 1995 More hardy geraniums
CATALOGUE 2 first class stamps
MAIL ORDER No

There is a large and increasing number of hardy geranium species, forms and cultivars – over 100 – with a useful selection of other perennials.

John Smith & Son
Hilltop Nurseries, Thornton, Coalville, Leicestershire LE67 1AN
☎ 01530 230331 FAX 01530 230331
CONTACT N. Smith
LOCATION 3 miles from M1, J22
OPEN 8 am – 5.30 pm; closed Sundays, except in April and May
SPECIALITIES Fuchsias
CATALOGUE SAE
MAIL ORDER Yes

In addition to a general range, the nursery specialises in rooted fuchsia cuttings, including American and other named varieties.

Kayes Garden Nursery
1700 Melton Road, Rearsby, Leicester, Leicestershire LE7 4YR
☎ 01664 424578
CONTACT Hazel Kaye
LOCATION On A607, north east of Leicester
OPEN 10 am – 5.30 pm, Wednesday – Saturday; 10 am – 12 pm, Sundays
SPECIALITIES Climbers; herbaceous perennials
CATALOGUE 2 first class stamps
MAIL ORDER No
GARDEN Garden opens for NGS

SHOWS BBC GW Live
GIFT TOKENS Own

There is a varied selection of herbaceous plants and some useful climbers at the nursery. Half-day courses are run. The garden is open for the NGS.

Laburnum Nurseries
6 Manor House Gardens, Main Street, Humberstone Village, Leicester, Leicestershire LE5 1AF
☎ 0116 2766522
CONTACT Mr W. M. Johnson
OPEN 9.15 am – 12 pm, 2 – 4.30 pm, Monday – Friday; 9 am – 12 pm, Saturdays and Sundays
SPECIALITIES Fuchsias
CATALOGUE On request
MAIL ORDER Yes

Growers and breeders of *Fuchsia* cultivars. Several new introductions are planned for this year

Linda Gascoigne Wild Flowers
17 Imperial Road, Kibworth Beauchamp, Leicester, Leicestershire LE8 0HR
☎ 0116 2793959
CONTACT Linda Gascoigne
LOCATION Between Leicester and Market Harborough, off A6
OPEN By appointment
SPECIALITIES Wild flowers
CATALOGUE 3 first class stamps
MAIL ORDER Yes; minimum order £5
GARDEN Garden open by appointment

A small nursery with a selection of native flowers and plants which attract wildlife. Linda Gascoigne is also a wildlife artist.

Philip Tivey & Son
28 Wanlip Road, Syston, Leicestershire LE7 8PA
☎ 01162 692968
OPEN 9 am – 5 pm, Monday – Friday; 9 am – 3 pm, Saturdays
SPECIALITIES Chrysanthemums; dahlias
CATALOGUE SAE plus 25p
MAIL ORDER Yes; minimum order £8.50
SHOWS RHS Westminster; Southport; Chelsea; Hampton Court; Harrogate (Autumn)

Specialist growers of dahlias, with mixed collections of chrysanthemums, including Korean and hardy border types, available too.

S & S Perennials
24 Main Street, Normanton le Heath, Leicestershire LE67 2TB
☎ 01530 262250
CONTACT S. Pierce
OPEN Afternoons and weekends
SPECIALITIES Bulbs; irises; lilies
CATALOGUE SAE
MAIL ORDER Yes

LINCOLNSHIRE

C E & D M Nurseries
The Walnuts, 36 Main Street, Baston, Peterborough, Lincolnshire PE6 9PB
CONTACT Colin Fletcher
LOCATION South of Bourne, off A15
OPEN 10 am – 5 pm, Friday – Tuesday. Closed Christmas and Boxing Day
SPECIALITIES Herbaceous perennials
CATALOGUE 2 first class stamps
MAIL ORDER Yes; no minimum order
GARDEN Display gardens

This fenland nursery stocks a dependable selection of hardy herbaceous perennials.

Clive Simms
Woodhurst, Essendine, Stamford, Lincolnshire PE9 4LQ
☎ 01780 55615
CONTACT Clive Simms
OPEN Mail order only
SPECIALITIES Fruit
CATALOGUE 2 first class stamps
MAIL ORDER Yes

Nut trees and uncommon edible fruits. There are all sorts of wonderful curiosities on offer here: recommended.

The Fern Nursery
Grimsby Road, Binbrook, Lincoln LN3 6DH
☎ 01472 398092
CONTACT Neil Timm
OPEN Saturdays and Sundays, April to September, or by appointment
SPECIALITIES Ferns
NEW FOR 1995 *Equisetum variegatum*, *Dryopteris dilatata* 'Jimmy Dyce'
CATALOGUE 2 first class stamps
MAIL ORDER Yes
GARDEN Demonstration garden
DESIGN SERVICE Neil Timm

Hardy ferns only are grown at this nursery; small sizes are available by mail order, larger ones at the nursery.

Glenhirst Cactus Nursery
Station Road, Swineshead, Boston, Lincolnshire PE20 3NX
☎ 01205 820314
CONTACT N. C. and S. A. Bell
LOCATION Just off A17, near Boston
OPEN 10 am – 5 pm, Thursdays, Fridays and Sundays, 1 April to 30 September. By appointment at other times
SPECIALITIES Cacti and succulents; seeds
NEW FOR 1995 Hardy and half-hardy cacti and succulents for outside bedding
CATALOGUE 2 first class stamps
MAIL ORDER Yes
SHOP Books, sundries
GARDEN Desert scree gardens

An extensive range of cacti and succulents, including epiphyllums. More succulents and half-hardy cacti are being added this year, including species which can be used in bedding schemes. They also sell books, seeds and sundries, and are happy to advise on cultivation and display.

Hall Farm Nursery
Hall Farm, Harpswell, Gainsborough, Lincolnshire DN21 5UU
☎ 01427 668412
CONTACT Pam and Mark Tatam
LOCATION 7 miles east of Gainsborough on A631
OPEN Open daily. Closed weekends, December to February
SPECIALITIES Herbaceous perennials
CATALOGUE Large SAE
MAIL ORDER No
REFRESHMENTS Charity days only
GARDEN Garden open daily

A small nursery with an interesting and expanding range of hardy roses, shrubs and perennials. The *Nepeta* species and cultivars are worth looking out for.

Hurdletree Nurseries
Hurdletree Bank, Holbeach Fen, Lincolnshire PE12 6SS
☎ 01406 540505
CONTACT Antony or Alison
LOCATION Off B1168, between Holbeach and Holbeach St John
OPEN Dawn – dusk, daily
SPECIALITIES Bedding plants
CATALOGUE On request
MAIL ORDER Yes
DESIGN SERVICE Hurdletree Nurseries

All year round bedding plants, wholesale and retail and a general plant range too. They do design, landscaping, clearing and maintenance and will also install automatic watering systems for hanging baskets.

J Walkers Bulbs
Washway House Farm, Holbeach, Spalding, Lincolnshire PE12 7PP
☎ 01406 426216   FAX 01406 425468
CONTACT J. W. Walkers
OPEN Mail order only
SPECIALITIES Bulbs; daffodils; lilies
CATALOGUE 2 first class stamps
MAIL ORDER Yes
SHOWS Harrogate (Spring); Chelsea

Specialists in daffodil bulbs of all kinds, including exhibition varieties. They also sell fritillaries and lilies.

This small nursery sells *Cyclamen*, *Erythronium*, *Fritillaria* and *Lilium* species, plus a number of *Iris* cultivars.

LINCOLNSHIRE Nurseries & Garden Centres

Judy's Country Garden
The Villa, Louth Road, South Somercotes, Louth, Lincolnshire LN11 7BW
☎ 01507 358487

CONTACT Judy Harry
LOCATION 8 miles east of Louth
OPEN 9 am – 6 pm, most days, mid March to end September. Phone first to check
SPECIALITIES Herbaceous perennials; herbs
CATALOGUE 3 first class stamps
MAIL ORDER No
GARDEN Garden is open for nursery visitors
DESIGN SERVICE Judy's Country Garden
GIFT TOKENS Own

A small, garden nursery with a range of herbs and perennials, especially the older varieties. Shows include Felley Priory Plant Fair (4 June), and the Gardeners Fair, Burton Agnes Hall (10 – 11 June). Courses, talks and group visits are held.

Kathleen Muncaster Fuchsias
18 Field Lane, Morton, Gainsborough, Lincolnshire DN21 3BY
☎ 01427 612329

CONTACT Kathleen Muncaster
LOCATION See catalogue for map
OPEN 10 am – dusk, February to mid July. Phone first at other times
SPECIALITIES Fuchsias
CATALOGUE 2 first class stamps
MAIL ORDER Limited mail order
GARDEN Garden and stock plants on display

Fuchsia specialist with an extensive range of species, hardy fuchsias and other varieties. The hardy fuchsias can be seen in the garden. They also sell other plants for hanging baskets.

Kathy Wright
Frog Hall Cottage, Wildmore Fen, New York, Lincolnshire LN4 4XH
☎ 01205 280709

CONTACT Kathy Wright
LOCATION On B1192, between New York and Boston
OPEN 12 noon – 5 pm, Tuesdays and Wednesdays, mid February to October; 10 am – 5 pm, Sundays, mid February to June, 3rd Sunday July – October
SPECIALITIES Climbers; shrubs
CATALOGUE Large SAE
MAIL ORDER No

A pleasing selection of container-grown shrubs and climbers.

Martin Nest Nurseries
Grange Cottage, Hemswell, Gainsborough, Lincolnshire DN21 5UP
☎ 01427 668369   FAX 01427 668080

CONTACT M. A. Robinson
LOCATION 6 miles east of Gainsborough on A631
OPEN 10 am – 5 pm, daily
SPECIALITIES Alpines; primulas
CATALOGUE 3 second class stamps
MAIL ORDER Yes
GARDEN Demonstration garden

A good businesslike range of tough pot-grown hardy alpine plants (including primulas, auriculas and saxifrages) for garden centres and individuals.

Orchard Nurseries
Tow Lane, Foston, Grantham, Lincolnshire NG32 2LE
☎ 01400 81354   FAX 01400 81354

CONTACT R. and J. Blenkinship
LOCATION Near A1
OPEN 10 am – 6 pm, daily, 1 March to 1 October
SPECIALITIES Clematis; conservatory plants; herbaceous perennials
NEW FOR 1995 *Clematis lisboa*, *Gaura* 'Corries Gold'
CATALOGUE £1
MAIL ORDER No
GARDEN Display areas
DESIGN SERVICE Orchard Nurseries
GIFT TOKENS Own

The nursery has a good range of the smaller-flowered *Clematis* hybrids, and other climbers, as well as many, many herbaceous plants. They offer garden design.

Potterton and Martin
The Cottage Nursery, Moortown Road, Nettleton, Caistor, Lincolnshire LN7 6HX
☎ 01472 851792   FAX 01742 851792

CONTACT Mr and Mrs Potterton
LOCATION On B1205: leave A46 at Nettleton
OPEN 9 am – 5 pm, daily
SPECIALITIES Alpines; bulbs; carnivorous plants; seeds
CATALOGUE £1 (for annual set)
MAIL ORDER Yes
GARDEN Display gardens
SHOWS RHS Westminster; Harrogate (Spring); Chelsea; BBC GW Live
GIFT TOKENS Own

Alpine and rock plant specialist with an interesting and extensive range, running from the easy to the unusual. Bulbs and seeds too. The nursery holds six Chelsea gold medals, and has won the RHS Farrer Trophy (best alpine display) on several occasions.

Southfield Nurseries
Bourne Road, Morton, Bourne, Lincolnshire PE10 0RH
☎ 01778 570168

CONTACT Mr and Mrs B. Goodey
LOCATION On A15, 1 mile north of traffic lights in Bourne
OPEN 10 am – 5 pm, daily
SPECIALITIES Cacti and succulents
CATALOGUE 1 first class stamp

MAIL ORDER Yes
SHOWS RHS Westminster; Malvern Spring; Harrogate (Spring); Southport; Chelsea; BBC GW Live; Hampton Court; Harrogate (Autumn); Ayr

Cacti and succulent specialist with an extensive choice of plants, all raised from seed at the nursery. Various sizes, including some specimens. Seed sometimes available.

The Valley Clematis Nursery
Willingham Road, Hainton, Lincoln LN3 6LN
☎ 01507 313396   FAX 01507 313705
CONTACT Mr Keith or Mrs Carol Fair
LOCATION Off A157, between Louth and Wragby
OPEN 10 am – 5.30 pm (dusk in winter), daily. Closed Christmas Eve to New Year's Day
SPECIALITIES Clematis
NEW FOR 1995 Clematis 'Iola Fair', 'Firefly'
CATALOGUE £1
MAIL ORDER Yes
SHOWS RHS Westminster; Chelsea; Hampton Court
GIFT TOKENS Own

Clematis specialists with a range of over 350 species and cultivars. Look out for their charming displays at major shows, which received high awards in 1994.

LONDON

Clifton Nurseries
Clifton Villas, Little Venice, London W9 2PH
☎ 0171 289 6851   FAX 0171 286 4515
CONTACT Simon Haines
LOCATION 50 yards from Warwick Avenue Underground
OPEN 8.30 am – 5.30 pm, Monday – Saturday; 10 am – 4 pm, Sundays
SPECIALITIES Conservatory plants; house plants; topiary
MAIL ORDER Van delivery in London
DESIGN SERVICE Clifton Landscape and Design
GIFT TOKENS HTA

A smart, stylish source of good plants for Londoners. They concentrate on town gardens, with containers, topiary, statuary, indoor and conservatory plants.

CTDA
174 Cambridge Street, London SW1V 4QE
☎ 0171 821 1801
CONTACT Dr Basil Smith
OPEN Mail order only
SPECIALITIES Seeds; hardy cyclamen
NEW FOR 1995 Cyclamen coum 'Silver Star', Cyclamen trochopteranthum 'Speckles'
CATALOGUE On request
MAIL ORDER Yes

Hardy cyclamen plants by post; hellebore and cyclamen seed too, including very good forms of Cyclamen coum.

Derek Lloyd Dean
8 Lynwood Close, South Harrow, London HA2 9PR
☎ 0181 864 0899
CONTACT Derek Lloyd Dean
OPEN Mail order only
SPECIALITIES Pelargoniums
NEW FOR 1995 New regal and angel Pelargonium
CATALOGUE 2 first class stamps
MAIL ORDER Yes; minimum order 6 plants
SHOWS RHS Westminster; Chelsea

A pelargonium specialist with an extensive range of rooted cuttings available by mail order only. The list is good on new introductions.

The Garden Centre at Hounslow Heath
462 Staines Road, Hounslow, London TW4 5DS
☎ 0181 572 3211   FAX 0181 572 5623
CONTACT Wendy Upson
OPEN 9 am – 6 pm, Monday – Saturday; 9.30 am – 6 pm, Sundays
SHOP Garden sundries, gifts
REFRESHMENTS Coffee shop
GIFT TOKENS HTA

Garden centre, with plants and sundries. They have a delivery service, and there is also a water-life centre..

Great Gardens of England (Syon) Ltd
The Garden Centre, Syon Park, Brentford TW8 8JG
☎ 0181 568 0134/5   FAX 0181 847 3865
CONTACT Alan Chapman (Manager)
LOCATION 8 miles west of London on A4
OPEN 9 am – 5.30 pm, Monday – Saturday (8 pm Wednesdays); 9.30 am – 6 pm, Sundays
CATALOGUE Lists available
MAIL ORDER Yes
DESIGN SERVICE See Syon Courtyard
GIFT TOKENS HTA; own

Garden centre with a general stock for indoor and outdoor gardening. A delivery service is available, and they offer landscaping through Syon Courtyard. There are other branches of Great Gardens of England at Marlow, Chandlers Cross and Chipperfield.

Jacques Amand Ltd
The Nurseries, Clamp Hill, Stanmore HA7 3JS
☎ 0181 954 8138   FAX 0181 954 6784
CONTACT Matthew Downes
OPEN 9 am – 5 pm, Monday – Saturday, all year; Sundays: 10 am – 4 pm, May, June, September, October, 10 am – 2 pm, February, March, April, August, November. Closed Sundays in January, December and July
SPECIALITIES Bulbs
CATALOGUE On request (retail and wholesale)
MAIL ORDER Yes
GARDEN Garden open all year round
SHOWS RHS Westminster; Malvern Spring; Harrogate (Spring); Southport; Chelsea; BBC GW Live; Hampton Court; Harrogate (Autumn)

NORFOLK Nurseries & Garden Centres

GIFT TOKENS   Own

Celebrated bulb specialists, whose range includes flower bulbs of all types. There are wholesale retail lists. The open day is in April. Look out for the displays at shows.

The Palm Centre
563 Upper Richmond Road West, London SW14 7ED
☎ 0181 876 3223   FAX 0181 876 6888
CONTACT   Martin Gibbons
OPEN   10 am – 6 pm, daily
SPECIALITIES   Palms
CATALOGUE   £1.95, palms; £1.85, cycads
MAIL ORDER   Yes

Specialist in ornamental palms, both hardy and indoor varieties. They come in all sizes from seedlings to specimens. There is also a range of cycads.

Sarracenia Nurseries
Link Side, Courtland Avenue, Mill Hill, London N7 3BG
☎ 0181 959 1570
CONTACT   Michele Brady
OPEN   By appointment
SPECIALITIES   Carnivorous plants
CATALOGUE   On request
MAIL ORDER   Yes

Carnivorous plant specialist. There are easy kinds for beginners besides rare and difficult species. Books and appropriate sundries sold too.

Syon Courtyard
Great Gardens of England (Syon) Ltd, Syon Courtyard, Syon Park, Brentford, London TW8 8JG
☎ 0181 568 3114   FAX 0181 847 3865
CONTACT   Karl Lawrence
LOCATION   8 miles west of London on A4
OPEN   9 am – 5.30 pm, Monday – Saturday; 9.30 am – 6 pm, Sundays
MAIL ORDER   Yes
DESIGN SERVICE   Syon Courtyard
GIFT TOKENS   HTA; own

Attached to the Great Gardens of England garden centre at Syon Park. Supplies landscaping materials and offers a design and landscaping service.

Wyevale Garden Centre
Holloway Lane, Harmondsworth, West Drayton, London UB7 0AD
☎ 0181 897 6075   FAX 0181 759 5739

MERSEYSIDE

Landlife Wildflowers Ltd
The Old Police Station, Lark Lane, Liverpool L17 8UU
☎ 0151 728 7011   FAX 0151 728 8413
CONTACT   Gillian Watson
SPECIALITIES   Seeds; wild flowers
CATALOGUE   Large SAE (35p stamp)
MAIL ORDER   Yes
GIFT TOKENS   Own

This small nursery sells a range of native wild flowers as seeds, small plants and bulbs. All profits go to the environmental charity Landlife. Gift tokens are sold in multiples of £5.

Porter's Fuchsias
12 Hazel Grove, Southport, Merseyside PR8 6AX
☎ 01704 533902   FAX 01704 832196
CONTACT   John Porter
OPEN   10.30 am – 4 pm, Thursday – Sunday, January to 2 May
SPECIALITIES   Fuchsias
NEW FOR 1995   Fuchsias: 'Algerine', 'Barbara Hassey', 'Preston Field', 'Purple Patch', 'Stephanie Morris'
CATALOGUE   2 first class stamps
MAIL ORDER   Yes; January to May only
SHOWS   Southport

A fuchsia specialist, concentrating mainly on modern cultivars, and on show varieties in particular. Orders should be placed before 31 March. Mr Porter also lectures nationwide.

NORFOLK

African Violet Centre
Station Road, Terrington St Clement, King's Lynn, Norfolk PE34 4PL
☎ 01553 828374   FAX 01553 827520
CONTACT   Rev. Tony Clements or Mrs Maggie Garford
LOCATION   3 miles west of King's Lynn, by A17
OPEN   10 am – 5 pm, February to 23 December
SPECIALITIES   African violets; house plants
CATALOGUE   On request: phone 01553 827281
MAIL ORDER   Yes
REFRESHMENTS   Tea room, Easter to September
SHOWS   RHS Westminster; Malvern Spring; Harrogate (Spring); Chelsea; BBC GW Live; Hampton Court; Harrogate (Autumn)

The specialists for saintpaulias, with a huge selection on offer. Other house and garden plants are available in season too.

Bawdeswell Garden Centre
Bawdeswell, Dereham, Norfolk NR20 4SJ
☎ 01362 688387   FAX 01362 688504
CONTACT   Peter Underwood
LOCATION   Between Norwich and Fakenham on A1067
OPEN   8 am – 5.30 pm, summer; 8 am – 5 pm, winter
CATALOGUE   Plant guide 50p
SHOP   Garden sundries, gifts, books
REFRESHMENTS   Coffee shop
GIFT TOKENS   HTA

General garden centre, including conservatories and greenhouses. They operate a design and landscaping service.

Bressingham Gardens Mail Order
Bressingham, Diss, Norfolk IP22 2AB
☎ 01379 687464   FAX 01379 688034
CONTACT Sarah O'Hara
OPEN Mail order only
SPECIALITIES Herbaceous perennials
NEW FOR 1995   *Geranium* × *oxonianum* 'Bressingham's Delight'
CATALOGUE Mail order catalogue; also available from plant centres
MAIL ORDER Yes
SHOWS Chelsea; BBC GW Live; Hampton Court
GIFT TOKENS Own

The mail order section of Bressingham's. It is run separately from the retail plant centres at Bressingham, Dorney Court and Elton Hall. The range is similar: an excellent choice of hardy perennials and alpines, and the trademark small conifers and heathers. Border planning service available.

Bressingham Plant Centre
Bressingham, Diss, Norfolk IP22 2AB
☎ 01379 688133/687464 FAX 01379 688034
CONTACT Tony Fry (Manager)
OPEN 10 am – 5.30 pm daily, except Christmas and Boxing Day
SPECIALITIES Alpines; conifers; herbaceous perennials; shrubs
NEW FOR 1995 *Polemonium* 'Brise d'Anjou', *Verbena* 'Homestead Purple', *Picea glauca* 'Alberta Blue'
CATALOGUE £2 for Bressingham Gardens Mail Order catalogue
MAIL ORDER See Bressingham Gardens Mail Order
REFRESHMENTS New Pavilion tea room
GARDEN Bressingham Gardens, Norfolk, see Gardens section
SHOWS Chelsea; BBC GW Live; Hampton Court
GIFT TOKENS Own

The plant centre here at Bressingham is a model of its type. There are others at Dorney Court, Berkshire and Elton Hall, Cambridgeshire. The mail order side is called Bressingham Gardens and is run separately. The retail range is strong on hardy perennials and shrubs, conifers and heathers. Good quality stock. Pick your own fruit also, in season. A border planning service is available.

British Wild Flower Plants
23 Yarmouth Road, Ormesby St Margaret, Great Yarmouth, Norfolk NR29 3QE
☎ 01493 730244   FAX 01493 730244
CONTACT Linda Laxton
LOCATION 4 miles north east of Great Yarmouth
OPEN By appointment
SPECIALITIES Wild flowers
CATALOGUE SAE
MAIL ORDER Yes
GARDEN Wild flower garden

Wild flowers grown as plugs or pots. The original provenance of the stock plants is named, but none of the sale plants was collected in the wild.

Chris Bowers & Son
Whispering Trees Nursery, Wimbotsham, Norfolk PE34 8QB
☎ 01366 388752
CONTACT Chris Bowers
LOCATION North of Downham Market
OPEN 9 am – 4 pm
SPECIALITIES Fruit
NEW FOR 1995 Strawberries 'Eros', 'Tango'
CATALOGUE £2
MAIL ORDER Yes
SHOWS RHS Westminster

Although many types of plants are stocked the attraction here is the fruit. The excellent selection includes purple raspberries, blueberries and cranberries, and rhubarb cultivars from the National Collection, as well as tree fruits and nuts.

Daphne ffiske Herbs
Rosemary Cottage, The Street, Bramerton, Norwich, Norfolk NR13 7DW
☎ 01508 538187
CONTACT Daphne ffiske
LOCATION 4 miles south east of Norwich, off A146
OPEN 10 am – 4 pm, Thursday – Sunday, March to September
SPECIALITIES Herbs
CATALOGUE SAE
MAIL ORDER Yes

The nursery stocks a selection of herbs and medicinal plants, including those which are attractive to bees. Some annual herbs are sold at the nursery in spring, too.

Four Seasons
Forncett St Mary, Norwich, Norfolk NR16 1JT
☎ 01508 488344   FAX 01508 488478
CONTACT J. P. Metcalf and Richard Ball
OPEN Mail order only
SPECIALITIES Herbaceous perennials
CATALOGUE £1
MAIL ORDER Yes; autumn and spring despatch
SHOWS RHS Westminster; BBC GW Live

An outstanding range of herbaceous perennials, both cultivars and species. Highlights include the asters and *Monarda*. The nursery only trades by mail order, but exhibits regularly at the RHS shows in Vincent Square, Westminster.

Hickling Heath Nursery
Sutton Road, Hickling, Norwich, Norfolk NR12 0AS
☎ 01692 598513
CONTACT B. H. Cogan

NORFOLK Nurseries & Garden Centres 185

LOCATION Off A149, on crossroads to Hickling Broad Staithe
OPEN 9.30 am – 5 pm, Tuesday – Sunday. Closed Mondays, except Bank Holidays
CATALOGUE SAE (A4)
MAIL ORDER No

A family nursery with a pleasing mix of interesting shrubs and herbaceous plants, both species and cultivars.

Hoecroft Plants
Severals Grange, Holt Road, Wood Norton, Dereham, Norfolk NR20 5BL
☎ 01362 844206/860179

CONTACT Miss Jane M. Lister
LOCATION 2 miles north of Guist on B1110
OPEN 10 am – 4 pm, Mondays, Wednesdays and Saturdays
SPECIALITIES Foliage plants; grasses
CATALOGUE £1
MAIL ORDER Yes; no minimum order
DESIGN SERVICE Hoecroft Plants
SHOWS RHS Westminster; Chelsea; Hampton Court
GIFT TOKENS Own

Well-known specialist for variegated and coloured foliage plants, and especially for decorative grasses – over 200 varieties.

Jenny Burgess' Alpine Nursery
Alpine Nursery, Sisland, Norwich, Norfolk NR14 6EF
☎ 01508 520724

CONTACT Jenny Burgess
OPEN By appointment only
SPECIALITIES Alpines
CATALOGUE 2 first class stamps
MAIL ORDER Yes; sisyrinchiums only
NCCPG NATIONAL COLLECTIONS *Sisyrinchium*

An alpine grower, with a strong list of sisyrinchiums, and many campanulas too.

Norfolk Lavender Ltd
Caley Mill, Heacham, King's Lynn, Norfolk PE31 7JE
☎ 01485 570384   FAX 01485 571176
CONTACT Henry Head
LOCATION North of King's Lynn on A149
OPEN 9.30 am – 6 pm, summer; 10.30 am – 4 pm, winter. Closed 24 December to 13 January inclusive
SPECIALITIES Lavenders
CATALOGUE 2 first class stamps
MAIL ORDER Yes; minimum order 6 plants
SHOP Lavender products
REFRESHMENTS Refreshments
GARDEN Lavender collection
NCCPG NATIONAL COLLECTIONS *Lavandula*

They grow and sell hardy and tender *Lavandula*, bare root and in containers respectively. Lavender products are for sale, and the National Collection is on display.

Peter Beales Roses
London Road, Attleborough, Norfolk NR17 1AY
☎ 01953 454707   FAX 01953 456845
LOCATION 2 miles south of Attleborough: leave A11 at Breckland Lodge
OPEN 9 am – 5 pm, Monday – Friday; 9 am – 4.30 pm, Saturdays; 10 am – 4 pm, Sundays
SPECIALITIES Roses
CATALOGUE On request
MAIL ORDER Yes; no minimum order
GARDEN Rose garden
DESIGN SERVICE Peter Beales Roses
SHOWS Chelsea; BBC GW Live; Hampton Court
GIFT TOKENS Own

Specialist grower and collector of older and classic roses. The extensive list has over 1,000 species and varieties, many not available elsewhere. Among the popular and rare items, there is also an interesting selection of early Hybrid Teas. They will design rose gardens, and their own fields can be visited.

Raveningham Gardens
Estate Office, Raveningham Hall, Raveningham, Norwich, Norfolk NR14 6NS
☎ 01508 548222   FAX 01508 548958

CONTACT Alison Bowell
LOCATION 15 miles south east of Norwich
OPEN 9 am – 5.30 pm, Monday – Saturday, April to October; 9 am – 4 pm, Monday – Friday, November – March. Also 2 – 5.30 pm, Sundays and Bank Holidays, late March to mid September
SPECIALITIES Herbaceous perennials
CATALOGUE 3 first class stamps
MAIL ORDER Yes
GARDEN Raveningham Hall, Norfolk, see Gardens section

An interesting list of shrubs and herbaceous perennials, with a bias towards those with good foliage, berries or bark. Look out for *Galanthus* and *Pulmonaria* too. The garden opens with the nursery on Sunday afternoons.

Reads Nursery
Hales Hall, Loddon, Norfolk NR14 6QW
☎ 0150846 395   FAX 0150846 395

CONTACT Judy Read
LOCATION Off A146, 1 mile south of Loddon
OPEN 10 am – 1 pm, 2 – 5 pm, Tuesday – Saturday
SPECIALITIES Climbers; conservatory plants; citrus
CATALOGUE 4 first class stamps
MAIL ORDER Yes
NCCPG NATIONAL COLLECTIONS *Citrus, Ficus, Vitis vinifera*

Long-established family nursery which specialises in citrus and conservatory plants. The mouth-watering list includes excellent collections of both of these, with vines, figs and topiary also.

The Romantic Garden Nursery
Swannington, Norwich, Norfolk NR9 5NW
☎ 01603 261488   FAX 01603 871668

CONTACT John Powles
LOCATION 7 miles north west of Norwich
OPEN 10 am – 5 pm, Wednesdays, Fridays, Saturdays
SPECIALITIES Topiary
CATALOGUE 4 first class stamps
MAIL ORDER Yes
SHOP Gifts and presents
REFRESHMENTS Refreshments
GARDEN Display garden
DESIGN SERVICE The Romantic Garden Nursery
SHOWS Chelsea; Hampton Court
GIFT TOKENS Own

Ornamental standards, bobbles and pyramids in *Cupressus* and *Ilex*, as well as box in animal and other shapes. Clematis and half-hardy plants are also available. They can design where necessary, and sell topiary packages which include a layout and the necessary plants.

Simpsons Nursery
The Plant Centre, High Street, Marsham, Norwich, Norfolk NR10 5QA
☎ 01263 733432

CONTACT Gillian and Jonathan Simpson
LOCATION 2 miles south of Aylsham, off A140
OPEN Daily, summer; Wednesday – Sunday and Bank Holidays, winter
CATALOGUE Ask for details
MAIL ORDER No
DESIGN SERVICE Simpsons Nursery

Nursery and plant centre which stocks home-grown plants, notably conifers and shrubs. They also have a landscaping and tree surgery department. They will be at the Royal Norfolk and the Aylsham Agricultural Shows.

Thorncroft Clematis Nursery
The Lings, Reymerston, Norwich, Norfolk NR9 4QG
☎ 01953 850407

CONTACT Mrs Ruth P. Gooch and Mrs Dorothy Tolver
LOCATION Between Dereham and Wymondham on B1135
OPEN 10 am – 5 pm, daily, March to October. Closed Wednesdays. By appointment only in winter
SPECIALITIES *Clematis*
CATALOGUE 2 first class stamps
MAIL ORDER Carriage can be arranged
GARDEN Display garden
GIFT TOKENS Own

There is a good range of species and cultivars at this *Clematis* specialist. Free pruning demonstrations take place in late February and early March: phone for details. The nursery will be at the Royal Norfolk Show (28–29 June) and the Sandringham Flower Show (26 July).

Trevor White Old Fashioned Roses
Bennetts Brier, The Street, Felthorpe, Norwich, Norfolk NR10 4AB
☎ 01603 755135   FAX 01603 755135

CONTACT Trevor and Vanessa White
OPEN Mail order only
SPECIALITIES Roses
CATALOGUE On request
MAIL ORDER Yes

Mainly wholesale. An interesting choice of old and species shrub and climbing roses. Good quality plants.

Unusual Perennials
Green Lane, Mundford, Norfolk IP26 5HS
☎ 01842 878496

CONTACT Patricia Cooper
LOCATION Off A1065
OPEN 9 am – 6 pm, Monday, Tuesday, Thursday, Friday; 12 noon – 6 pm, Saturdays and Sundays. Closed Wednesdays
SPECIALITIES Herbaceous perennials
NEW FOR 1995 Many new plants
CATALOGUE 4 first class stamps
MAIL ORDER No
GARDEN Garden opens for NGS

British native plants, grasses, herbaceous perennials and marginals – a personal selection with a simple pricing policy.

Van Tubergen UK
Thetford Road, Bressingham, Diss, Norfolk IP22 2AB
☎ 01379 688282   FAX 01379 687227

CONTACT Van Tubergen UK
OPEN Mail order only
SPECIALITIES Bulbs
CATALOGUE 50p
MAIL ORDER Yes
GIFT TOKENS Own

Long-established and famous specialists in flowering bulbs. Start at *Allium* and continue to *Tulipa urumiensis*.

West Acre Gardens
8 Pretoria Cottages, West Acre, King's Lynn, Norfolk PE32 1UJ
☎ 01760 755562   FAX 01760 755989

CONTACT John and Sue Tuite
LOCATION Off A47, south east of King's Lynn
OPEN 9 am – 5 pm, daily, 1 March to 31 October; phone first in winter
SPECIALITIES Alpines; primulas
NEW FOR 1995 New golden *Aubretia*
CATALOGUE Large SAE
MAIL ORDER Yes
GARDEN Display gardens
GIFT TOKENS Own

A new nursery with a general range of rarer plants, particularly alpines, but climbers, herbaceous plants and shrubs are grown as well.

The Wild Flower Centre
Church Farm, Sisland, Norwich, Norfolk NR14 6EF
☎ 01508 520235

CONTACT Mrs D. Corne
LOCATION 1½ miles west of Loddon (A146)
OPEN 9 am – 5 pm. Other times by appointment
SPECIALITIES Wild flowers
CATALOGUE 30p
MAIL ORDER Yes
GARDEN Garden open, March to June

This small centre grows a selection of native and naturalised wild flowers.

NORTHAMPTONSHIRE

E L F Plants, Cramden Nursery
Harborough Road North, Northampton NN2 8LU
☎ 01604 846246

LOCATION Kingsthorpe, Northampton: leave A508 at Kingsthorpe cemetery
OPEN 10 am – 5 pm, Thursday – Saturday. Closed December and January
SPECIALITIES Conifers; shrubs
CATALOGUE 50p plus stamp
MAIL ORDER No
GARDEN Garden
SHOWS RHS Westminster; BBC GW Live

This small nursery specialises in dwarf and small shrubs and conifers that are suitable for rock gardens and borders. Some alpines and heathers too. It's advisable to phone first (evenings only). Garden clubs welcome at any time by arrangement. Shows include the Milton Keynes Garden Show.

F Haynes & Partners
56 Gordon Street, Kettering, Northamptonshire NN16 0RX
☎ 01536 519836

CONTACT Mr Nick Maple
LOCATION Woodford Lane, Lowick – directions in catalogue
OPEN 8.30 am – 4 pm, Monday – Friday
SPECIALITIES Roses
NEW FOR 1995 Thornless roses
CATALOGUE On request
MAIL ORDER Yes
SHOWS Hampton Court; Harrogate (Autumn)
GIFT TOKENS Own

Bare root roses. There is a particularly good selection of varieties for exhibition and miniature roses. The nursery is at Woodford Lane, Lowick. Inquiries and correspondence to 56 Gordon Street, Kettering.

Hill Farm Herbs
Park Walk, Brigstock, Kettering NN14 3HH
☎ 01536 373694   FAX 01536 373246

CONTACT Mr and Mrs Simpson
LOCATION Signed off A6116
OPEN 10.30 am – 5.30 pm, daily, summer; 10.30 am – 4.30 pm, daily, winter. Closed Christmas and Boxing Day
SPECIALITIES Herbs
CATALOGUE 2 second class stamps
MAIL ORDER Yes
SHOP Herb products; dried flowers
REFRESHMENTS Tea shop, Easter to September
GARDEN Display gardens
GIFT TOKENS HTA

The nursery and shops are tucked behind the farm. There is a large range of herbs and cottage garden plants, herb products and seeds.

Mears Ashby Nurseries Ltd
Glebe House, Glebe Road, Mears Ashby, Northamptonshire NN6 0DL
☎ 01604 811811   FAX 01604 812353

CONTACT Janette E. Gaggini
LOCATION Map in catalogue
SPECIALITIES Wisteria
CATALOGUE Retail; £1 and A5 SAE
MAIL ORDER Yes
GIFT TOKENS HTA

A mainly wholesale nursery with a large range of container-grown trees and shrubs. Their retail outlet is Gaggini's Plant Centre. Wisterias are a speciality available at both outlets, and by mail order or carrier.

Ravensthorpe Nursery
6 East Haddon Road, Ravensthorpe, Northamptonshire NN6 8ES
☎ 01604 770548

CONTACT Jean and Richard Wiseman
LOCATION Between Rugby and Northampton, near M1, J18
OPEN 10 am – 6 pm, Tuesday – Sunday, and Bank Holiday Mondays
SPECIALITIES Herbaceous perennials
CATALOGUE 4 first class stamps
MAIL ORDER Yes; no minimum order
GARDEN Display garden being made

This nursery has a sound all-round range of plants, much of the material being home-grown.

NORTHUMBERLAND

Bradley Gardens Nursery
Sled Lane, Wylam, Northumberland NE41 8JL
☎ 01661 852176

CONTACT Mrs Susan Hick
LOCATION Off A695, between Wylam and Crawcrook

188 Nurseries & Garden Centres NOTTINGHAMSHIRE

OPEN   9 am – 4.30 pm, Tuesday – Friday; 9 am – 5 pm, Saturdays and Sundays; mid March to mid October. Closed Mondays and mid October to mid March
SPECIALITIES   Herbs
CATALOGUE   SAE
MAIL ORDER   Cut herbs for caterers only
SHOP   Herb products
GARDEN   Demonstration garden

A herb nursery set in a walled garden. They have pot-grown and cut herbs as well as cottage garden plants. Mail order is limited to cut herbs for caterers.

Halls of Heddon
West Heddon Nurseries, Heddon on the Wall, Newcastle upon Tyne, Northumberland NE15 0JS
☎ 01661 852445

CONTACT   Mrs J. A. Lockey
OPEN   9 am – 5 pm, Monday – Saturday; 10 am – 5 pm, Sundays
SPECIALITIES   Chrysanthemums; dahlias
CATALOGUE   2 second class stamps
MAIL ORDER   Dahlias and chrysanthemums only
GARDEN   Herbaceous borders
SHOWS   Harrogate (Autumn)
GIFT TOKENS   HTA

Specialists in dahlias and chrysanthemums of all types for showing, the garden and as cut flowers. The garden centre carries a general range.

Heighley Gate Garden Centre
Morpeth, Northumberland NE61 3DA
☎ 01670 513416   FAX 01670 510013
LOCATION   3 miles north of Morpeth on A697
OPEN   9 am – 5 pm, Monday – Friday; 9.30 am – 5 pm, weekends
SHOP   Garden sundries, gifts, conservatories
REFRESHMENTS   Coffee shop
GARDEN   Display garden
DESIGN SERVICE   Heighley Gate Garden Centre
GIFT TOKENS   HTA

All round range of plants and garden sundries, including home-grown bedding, house plants and pansies.

Herterton House Gardens & Nursery
Hartington, Cambo, Morpeth, Northumberland NE61 4BN
☎ 01670 774278

CONTACT   Frank Lawley
LOCATION   2 miles north of Cambo, off B6342
OPEN   1.30 – 5.30 pm, daily, April to September, and by appointment. Closed Tuesdays and Thursdays
MAIL ORDER   No
GARDEN   Herterton House Gardens & Nursery, Northumberland, see Gardens section

The nursery stocks a range of herbaceous perennials, particularly older varieties, and some herbs. The garden, which is open at the same times, was featured in *The Englishman's Garden*.

Hexham Herbs
Chesters Walled Garden, Chollerford, Hexham, Northumberland NE46 4BQ
☎ 01434 681483

CONTACT   Mrs S. White
LOCATION   6 miles north of Hexham, next to Chesters Roman fort
OPEN   10 am – 5 pm, Easter to October. Shorter hours in winter
SPECIALITIES   Herbs; wild flowers
CATALOGUE   £1.50 cheque
MAIL ORDER   No
SHOP   Pots, gifts
GARDEN   Hexham Herbs, Northumberland, see Gardens section
DESIGN SERVICE   Hexham Herbs
GIFT TOKENS   Own
NCCPG NATIONAL COLLECTIONS   *Thymus, Origanum (marjoram)*

Specialist herb nursery with a wide range of herbs as plants and freshly cut for cooking. They also stock old roses and wild flowers, and dried flowers and gifts.

Northumbria Nurseries
Castle Gardens, Ford, Berwick upon Tweed, Northumberland TD15 2PZ
☎ 01890 820379   FAX 01890 820594

CONTACT   H. M. Huddleston
LOCATION   Follow tourist signs to Ford and Etal
OPEN   9 am – 6 pm, Monday – Friday, all year; 10 am – 6 pm, Saturdays and Sundays from March to October
SPECIALITIES   Herbaceous perennials
CATALOGUE   £2.30 cheque
MAIL ORDER   Yes (£5 minimum)
GARDEN   Display gardens
DESIGN SERVICE   Hazel M. Huddleston

A wide range of container-grown hardy shrubs and perennials. A design and advisory service is also available. The nursery can be visited at other times by appointment: it closes before 6 pm if it's dark.

Ryal Nursery
East Farm Cottage, Ryal, Northumberland NE20 0SA
☎ 01661 886562

CONTACT   R. F. Hadden
OPEN   1 – 5 pm, Tuesdays; 10 am – 5 pm, Sundays, March to July. Other times by appointment
SPECIALITIES   Alpines; primulas
CATALOGUE   SAE
MAIL ORDER   Yes

Woodland and alpine plants, with good primulas and auriculas too.

NOTTINGHAMSHIRE

The Beeches Nursery
Misson Springs, Doncaster DN10 6ET
☎ 01302 772139

NOTTINGHAMSHIRE Nurseries & Garden Centres

CONTACT R. Desmedt
OPEN 10 am – 5 pm daily, 1 March to 30 June; 10 am – 5 pm Saturdays and Sundays, 1 July to 28 February
SPECIALITIES Pelargoniums
CATALOGUE 2 first class stamps
MAIL ORDER Yes

A pelargonium specialist; a selection of most types and varieties, except species, is available. The plants are grown on to 3-inch pot size.

Brinkley Nurseries
Fiskerton Road, Southwell, Nottinghamshire NG24 0TP
☎ 01636 814501

CONTACT Mrs C. Steven
OPEN 10 am – 5 pm, summer; 10 am – 4 pm, winter
SPECIALITIES Trees
CATALOGUE £2.50
MAIL ORDER Yes; £10 minimum order
GARDEN Garden opens under the NGS, or by arrangement. Admission £1

Containerised trees and shrubs, both retail and wholesale. The choice is large and interesting, and they also carry herbaceous plants. The nurseries are celebrating their 20th anniversary this year: watch out for events.

Cottage Nurseries
Cross Lane, Collingham, Newark, Nottinghamshire NG23 7NY
☎ 01636 893161

CONTACT John and Sheila Hipkiss
LOCATION Off A1133, 8 miles north of Newark
OPEN 10 am – dusk, daily
SPECIALITIES Fuchsias
CATALOGUE 2 first class stamps
MAIL ORDER Yes

Fuchsia specialists with over 500 varieties. There are also plants for hanging baskets, pots and patios and a small general range.

Field House Alpines
Leake Road, Gotham, Nottingham, Nottinghamshire NG11 0JN
☎ 0115 9830278

CONTACT Doug Lochhead and Val Woolley
LOCATION Near M1, J24 (10 mins)
OPEN 9 am – 5 pm, Friday – Wednesday
SPECIALITIES Alpines; primulas; seeds
CATALOGUE 4 first class stamps
MAIL ORDER Yes; primulas, auriculas and seeds
GARDEN Auricula theatre at Calke Abbey, Derbyshire, see Gardens section; covered garden at the nursery

A good range of alpines, both as plants and seed. They are particularly strong on primulas and auriculas. As well as maintaining the auricula theatre at Calke Abbey, Derbyshire they are also organising the specialist plant sale there on 23 April.

Greenwood Gardens
Ollerton Road, Arnold, Nottingham, Nottinghamshire NG5 8PR
☎ 01602 205757   FAX 01602 203100

CONTACT Mr H. J. Tomlinson
LOCATION On A614, north of Arnold
OPEN 10 am – 5 pm, Wednesday – Monday. Closed Tuesdays
SPECIALITIES Bonsai
CATALOGUE SAE and 25p stamp
MAIL ORDER Books and tools only
SHOP Pots, crafts and gifts
SHOWS Harrogate (Spring)

Bonsai specialist. Everything you are likely to need for bonsai can be found here – books, containers, tools, trees and tuition.

Hewthorn Herbs & Wild Flowers
Simkins Farm, Adbolton Lane, West Bridgford, Nottinghamshire NG2 5AS
☎ 0115 9812861

CONTACT Julie Scott
LOCATION South of Nottingham, near National Water Sports Centre
OPEN Weekdays during termtime, and some weekends. Phone first
SPECIALITIES Herbs; wild flowers
CATALOGUE 3 first class stamps
MAIL ORDER Yes; no minimum order
SHOP Cards
GARDEN Garden open for groups by arrangement
GIFT TOKENS Own

The nursery sells native and naturalised wild flowers, herbs, medicinal, culinary and dye plants. The garden is open for groups by arrangement: talks are also possible.

Mill Hill Plants
Mill Hill House, Elston Lane, East Stoke, Newark, Nottinghamshire NG23 5QJ
☎ 01636 525460

CONTACT G. M. Gregory
LOCATION 5 miles south west of Newark. Leave A46 at East Stoke, for Elston; ½ mile down, on right
OPEN 10 am – 6 pm, Wednesday – Sunday, and Bank Holiday Mondays, March to October. Closed Mondays and Tuesdays, and from November to February
SPECIALITIES Alpines; herbaceous perennials; *Iris*
CATALOGUE 3 first class stamps
MAIL ORDER Yes; irises only
GARDEN Garden opens for NGS, and when nursery is open
NCCPG NATIONAL COLLECTIONS *Berberis*

The nursery stocks a range of hardy perennials and alpines. The speciality is bearded irises, which are available by mail order also. Groups welcome by appointment. They will be running propagation workshops in July and September: phone for details.

Nurseries & Garden Centres   OXFORDSHIRE

Naturescape
Coach Gap Lane, Langar, Nottinghamshire
NG13 9HP
☎ 01949 851045   📠 01949 850431
CONTACT   Mr Brian Scarborough
LOCATION   Signed off A46 and A52
OPEN   11 am – 5.30 pm, daily, 1 April to 30 September
SPECIALITIES   Seeds; wild flowers
CATALOGUE   £1 in stamps
MAIL ORDER   Yes, seeds all year, plants September to April
REFRESHMENTS   Tea room
GARDEN   Wildlife garden
GIFT TOKENS   Own

Wild flowers, British native shrubs and trees, and cottage garden favourites available as plants and seeds. The growing fields are open. The visitors' centre is set in a wildlife garden showing different habitats.

Norwell Nursery
Woodhouse Road, Norwell, Newark, Nottinghamshire NG23 6JX
☎ 01636 636337
CONTACT   Dr Andrew Ward
LOCATION   Off A1, 4 miles north of Newark
OPEN   10 am – 5 pm, Saturday – Thursday, May to June; 10 am – 5 pm, Sunday – Thursday, July to April
SPECIALITIES   Herbaceous perennials
NEW FOR 1995   *Lathyrus* sp.; *Salvia* sp.; new grasses
CATALOGUE   2 first class stamps
MAIL ORDER   Yes

There is an expanding range of perennials, including hardy geraniums and alpines. Plants are grown with 'Suscon Green' to prevent vine weevil.

Reuben Shaw & Sons
Hollydene Nurseries & Garden Centre, 121 Moorgreen, Newthorpe, Nottinghamshire NG16 2FF
☎ 01773 714326   📠 01773 714326
CONTACT   James or Reuben Shaw
LOCATION   North west of Nottingham
OPEN   9 am – 5.30 pm, Monday – Saturday; 10.30 am – 4.30 pm, Sunday. Closed at 5 pm, Tuesdays
MAIL ORDER   Blooms and Hillier plants only
SHOP   Dried and silk flowers
GIFT TOKENS   HTA; own

Garden centre and nursery. Stockists for Blooms of Bressingham and Hillier plants.

Richard Stockwell – Rare Plants
64 Weardale Road, Sherwood, Nottingham NG5 1DD
☎ 0115 969 1063   📠 0115 969 1063
CONTACT   Richard Stockwell
LOCATION   Map in catalogue
OPEN   By appointment for collection only
SPECIALITIES   Climbers; seeds
NEW FOR 1995   Many rare species

CATALOGUE   4 second class stamps
MAIL ORDER   Yes

Climbers and dwarf species available as small plants by post or as seed. An aptly named nursery for plantsmen and collectors.

Salley Gardens
Flat 3, 3 Millicent Road, West Bridgford, Nottingham, Nottinghamshire NG2 7LD
☎ 0115 9821366
CONTACT   Richard Lewin
OPEN   By appointment only
SPECIALITIES   Seeds; medicinal plants
NEW FOR 1995   Chinese and Indian medicinal plants
CATALOGUE   On request
MAIL ORDER   Yes; no minimum order

The nursery has moved from Cumbria this year. Oriental medicinal, aromatic and dye plants, with some culinary herbs and perennial wild flowers. The business is mainly mail order, and they also sell seeds. Telephone first at all times.

Wheatcroft Ltd
Landmere Lane, Edwalton, Nottingham NG12 4DE
☎ 0115 9216060   📠 0115 9841247
LOCATION   On A606 3 miles south of Trent Bridge
OPEN   9 am – 6 pm
SPECIALITIES   Roses
NEW FOR 1995   Rose 'Summer Lady'
CATALOGUE   Trade only
MAIL ORDER   Yes
REFRESHMENTS   Refreshments
GIFT TOKENS   HTA

Wholesale rose growers with a retail range of roses and hardy shrubs sold from their own garden centre.

OXFORDSHIRE

The Cuckoo Pen Nursery
Preston Crowmarsh, Wallingford, Oxfordshire OX10 4SL
☎ 01491 835971
CONTACT   Ian Burles
OPEN   By appointment only
CATALOGUE   SAE
MAIL ORDER   Limited
SHOWS   RHS Westminster; Malvern Spring; Harrogate (Spring); Southport; Hampton Court; Harrogate (Autumn); Courson; Ayr

A perennial nursery; specialist planting advice is offered. Most sales are at shows.

Mattock Roses
Nuneham Courtenay, Oxford OX44 9PY
☎ 01865 343265   📠 01865 343267
CONTACT   Mark W. Mattock
LOCATION   On B4015, roundabout Golden Ball (A4074)
OPEN   9 am – 5.30 pm, Monday – Saturday; 11 am – 5 pm, Sundays. Close at 5 pm in winter

SPECIALITIES   Roses
NEW FOR 1995   Roses 'Cambridgeshire', 'White Cloud', 'Sunrise', 'Romantic Hedgrose'
CATALOGUE   On request
MAIL ORDER   Yes
SHOP   Garden sundries, furniture
REFRESHMENTS   Restaurant
GARDEN   Rose fields
SHOWS   RHS Westminster; Chelsea; Hampton Court; Harrogate (Autumn)
GIFT TOKENS   HTA; own

A large choice of all kinds of roses. They are particularly good on ground cover varieties and their own 'County' roses. They are part of Notcutts, and are attached to a Notcutts Garden Centre (01285 343454).

Waterperry Gardens Ltd
Waterperry, Wheatley, Oxfordshire OX33 1JZ
☎ 01844 339226   FAX 01884 339883
LOCATION   Near M40, J8
OPEN   10 am – 5.30 pm, Monday – Friday; 10 am – 6 pm, Saturdays and Sundays. Close at 5 pm in winter
SPECIALITIES   Saxifrages
CATALOGUE   Lists
MAIL ORDER   No
SHOP   Garden sundries
REFRESHMENTS   Tea shop
GARDEN   Waterperry Gardens, Oxfordshire, see Gardens section
GIFT TOKENS   HTA

Among a general stock there are good alpines, notably the saxifrages, and a useful choice of fruit trees. Art in Action – an annual arts and crafts festival in the garden – takes place on 13 – 16 July this year.

The Wildlife Gardening Centre
Witney Road, Kingston Bagpuize, Abingdon, Oxfordshire OX13 5AN
☎ 01865 821660
CONTACT   Jennifer Steel
OPEN   Phone for details
SPECIALITIES   Herbs; seeds; wild flowers; native trees and shrubs
NEW FOR 1995   Many new cottage garden and wild plants
CATALOGUE   3 first class stamps
MAIL ORDER   Yes; no minimum order
GARDEN   Wildlife garden

Wild and cottage-style plants, which have been selected for their ability to attract bees and butterflies. There is a grading system to guide novices. Seeds and bulbs too. The trees and shrubs are not available by mail order.

SHROPSHIRE

Applegarth Nursery
The Elms, Maesbrook, Oswestry, Shropshire SY10 8QF
☎ 01691 831577

CONTACT   Cathy Preston
LOCATION   On B4398, between Knockin and Llanymynech
OPEN   2 – 6 pm, Thursday – Saturday, April to October. Phone first
SPECIALITIES   Wild flowers
CATALOGUE   SAE
MAIL ORDER   No
GARDEN   Display beds

Herbs, cottage garden plants and wild flowers chosen for their appeal to wildlife.

Bucknell Nurseries
Bucknell, Shropshire SY7 EL
☎ 015474 606   FAX 015474 699
CONTACT   Andrew Coull
LOCATION   Off A4113, east of Knighton
OPEN   8 am – 5 pm, Monday – Friday, 10 am – 1 pm, Saturdays
SPECIALITIES   Hedging; trees
CATALOGUE   On request
MAIL ORDER   No
GIFT TOKENS   Own

A wholesale and retail bare-root tree specialist. The range includes forest trees, hedging plants, ornamental trees and shrubs. The nursery undertakes contract planting, fencing and landscaping.

David Austin Roses
Bowling Green Lane, Albrighton, Wolverhampton, Shropshire WV7 3HB
☎ 01902 373931   FAX 01902 372142
CONTACT   Sue Webb
LOCATION   South of M54, J3
OPEN   9 am – 6 pm, Monday – Friday; 10 am – 6 pm, Saturdays and Sundays, April to November. 9 am – 5 pm, Monday – Friday, 10 am – dusk, Saturdays, 12 noon – dusk, Sundays, November to March
SPECIALITIES   Roses
CATALOGUE   On request
MAIL ORDER   Yes
REFRESHMENTS   Refreshments
GARDEN   Rose and herbaceous gardens
SHOWS   Chelsea; BBC GW Live; Hampton Court
GIFT TOKENS   Own

Rose grower and breeder, best known for his popular English Roses strain which combines modern performance standards of flowering with an old-fashioned shape.

Fron Nursery
Fron Issa, Rhiwlas, Oswestry, Shropshire SY10 7JH
☎ 01691 76605
CONTACT   Thoby Miller
LOCATION   Clwyd, Shropshire border
OPEN   By appointment only
SPECIALITIES   Conifers; shrubs; trees
NEW FOR 1995   *Acer pseudosieboldianum, Taxodium mucronatum*

CATALOGUE SAE
MAIL ORDER Yes; £20 minimum order
GARDEN 2-acre woodland garden

An interesting selection of seed-grown trees and shrubs, including conifers: the smaller sizes are mostly containerised, the larger, open ground. The more choice offerings include *Abies amabilis* and *Taxodium mucronatum*. The setting, 1,000 feet up, promises good views as well as hardiness. Many specimens can be seen growing in the woodland planting of native broadleaves with exotics.

Hall Farm Nursery
Kinnerley, Oswestry, Shropshire SY10 8DH
☎ 01691 682219

CONTACT Christine Ffoulkes Jones
OPEN 10 am – 5 pm, Tuesday – Sunday, March to October
SPECIALITIES Herbaceous perennials
CATALOGUE 4 first class stamps
MAIL ORDER No
GARDEN Nursery display beds
SHOWS Malvern Spring; BBC GW Live; Hampton Court

The nursery carries a good range of herbaceous perennials, including a great number of geraniums. Alpines and carnivorous plants are the other specialities. Talks, demonstrations and a garden tour are offered by arrangement for groups.

Hillview Hardy Plants
Worfield, Bridgnorth, Shropshire WV15 5NT
☎ 01746 716454

CONTACT Ingrid Millington
LOCATION Between Worfield and Albrighton, off B4176
OPEN 10 am – 5 pm, Monday – Saturday
SPECIALITIES Alpines; herbaceous perennials; primulas
NEW FOR 1995 *Salvia* × *Samensis* 'La Luna', S. 'Raspberry Royale', *Dahlia* 'David Howard'
CATALOGUE 4 second class stamps
MAIL ORDER Yes
GARDEN Display garden
SHOWS RHS Westminster; Malvern Spring; Harrogate (Spring); Southport; Hampton Court; Harrogate (Autumn); Ayr

Twin ranges of alpines and hardy perennials. There are many different primulas and auriculas too. As well as a busy show schedule, occasional courses are held at the nursery, and they run a stall in Bridgnorth on selected Saturdays.

Kim W Davis
Lingen Alpine Nursery, Lingen, Bucknell, Shropshire SY7 0DY
☎ 01544 267720

CONTACT Kim W. Davis
OPEN 10 am – 6 pm, February to October
SPECIALITIES Alpines; herbaceous perennials

NEW FOR 1995 Many new plants
CATALOGUE SAE
MAIL ORDER Yes; p & p from £5
GARDEN Gardens open
SHOWS Malvern Spring

There is a promising herbaceous range developing at this specialist alpine and rock garden nursery. The catalogue changes by as much as a third each year. Its traditional strengths include plants for alpine houses, screes and troughs.

Merton Nurseries
Holyhead Road, Bicton, Shrewsbury, Shropshire SY3 8EF
☎ 01743 850773   FAX 01743 850773

CONTACT Jessica Pannett
LOCATION On B4380, west of Shrewsbury
OPEN 9 am – 5.30 pm, daily
SPECIALITIES Conifers; herbaceous perennials
SHOP Sundries; floral art materials
GARDEN Herbert Lewis Hospice Garden
GIFT TOKENS HTA; own

This family-run nursery carries a wide general range, but specialises in conifers and perennials. Their show garden opens to support the local hospice.

Nordybank Nurseries
Clee St Margaret, Craven Arms, Shropshire SY7 9EF
☎ 0158475 322

CONTACT Polly Bolton
LOCATION Between Bridgnorth and Ludlow, off B4364
OPEN Mondays, Wednesdays, Sundays, Easter to mid October
SPECIALITIES Herbaceous perennials; herbs; wild flowers
CATALOGUE Large SAE plus 50p
MAIL ORDER No
REFRESHMENTS Teas
GARDEN Rose and flower display garden

A choice of hardy herbaceous plants, with herbs and wild flowers also. Design advice available. The cottage garden opens for the NGS.

Oak Cottage Herb Garden
Nesscliffe, Shrewsbury, Shropshire SY4 1DB
☎ 01743 741262   FAX 01743 741262

CONTACT Edward and Jane Bygott
LOCATION Halfway between Shrewsbury and Oswestry on A5
OPEN Usually 11 am – 6 pm, daily
SPECIALITIES Herbs; wild flowers
CATALOGUE 3 first class stamps
MAIL ORDER Yes
SHOP Herb products, books, seeds
GARDEN Herb garden
DESIGN SERVICE Oak Cottage Herb Garden

A small nursery propagating and selling wild flowers, herbs and cottage garden plants. Small quantities only, but larger orders by arrangement, and the range is extensive. There's also a small shop, and they offer a design and planting service: knot gardens a speciality.

Perrybrook Nursery
Brook Cottage, Wykey, Ruyton XI Towns, Shrewsbury, Shropshire SY4 1JA
☎ 01939 261120

CONTACT   Mrs G. Williams
LOCATION North Shropshire
OPEN   Most days, but telephone first
SPECIALITIES Herbaceous perennials
NEW FOR 1995 Many new varieties, including *Tricyrtis*
CATALOGUE 3 first class stamps
MAIL ORDER No
GARDEN Garden and *Tricyrtis* display

Specialist wholesale and retail nursery with a range of hardy perennials, including primulas. Strong on *Tricyrtis*. There is also a display of agricultural machinery, including a working threshing drum.

The Plantation
The Walled Garden, Delbury Hall, Diddlebury, Craven Arms, Shropshire SY9 9DH
☎ 01584 841603

CONTACT   Nicky Fraser
LOCATION Off B4368, north east of Craven Arms
OPEN   11 am – 5.30 pm, Wednesday – Sunday, March to November. Open Bank Holidays
SPECIALITIES Herbaceous perennials
CATALOGUE A4 SAE
MAIL ORDER No

The emphasis here is on plants for mixed borders, including hardy perennials, English roses and shrubs.

Ridgeway Heather Nursery
Park House, Plaish, Church Stretton, Shropshire SY6 7HY
☎ 01694 771574

CONTACT   Mrs N. Cordingley
LOCATION Off B4371, east of Church Stretton
OPEN   10 am – 5 pm, Tuesday – Sunday; February to December. Closed Mondays and in January
SPECIALITIES Heathers
CATALOGUE On request
MAIL ORDER Yes

A range of hardy container-grown heathers, some dwarf rhododendrons, and conifers as well.

Sue Hawthorne Gardens
The Yews, Clunbury, Craven Arms, Shropshire SY7 0HG
☎ 015887 428

CONTACT   Sue Hawthorne
LOCATION Map in leaflet
OPEN   Phone first
SPECIALITIES Herbaceous perennials
CATALOGUE 3 second class stamps

MAIL ORDER Yes
DESIGN SERVICE Sue Hawthorne Gardens

The nursery specialises in cottage garden plants, mainly herbaceous, particularly those introduced before 1837.

Warner's Roses
Greenfields, Brockton, Newport, Shropshire TF10 9EP
☎ 01952 604217   FAX 01952 604217

CONTACT   Chris and Barbara Warner
LOCATION 2 miles south of Newport
OPEN   9 am – 5 pm, Monday – Saturday; 2 – 5 pm, Sundays, mid July to mid April
SPECIALITIES Roses
NEW FOR 1995 Roses 'Good as Gold', 'Little Rambler'
CATALOGUE On request
MAIL ORDER Yes

Chris Warner is a rose breeder and grower specialising in modern shrub, climbing and ground cover varieties. His seedling fields will interest rosarians.

SOMERSET

Avon Bulbs
Burnt House Farm, Mid-Lambrook, South Petherton, Somerset TA13 5HE
☎ 01460 242177

CONTACT   Mr C. Ireland-Jones
LOCATION 3 miles north west of South Petherton, off A303
OPEN   9 am – 4.30 pm, Thursday – Saturday, mid September to end October, and mid February to end March
SPECIALITIES Bulbs
CATALOGUE 4 second class stamps
MAIL ORDER Yes
GARDEN   Growing area, open as above
SHOWS   RHS Westminster; Malvern Spring; Harrogate (Spring); Chelsea
GIFT TOKENS Own

An impressive variety of bulbs (and close relatives) covering all sizes, seasons and shapes. Opening hours are limited because of the seasonal nature of the business and their show commitments. It is a good idea to check with them before visiting. The striking show exhibits are recommended. They hope to organise an open weekend in the spring.

Bradley Batch Cactus Nursery
64 Bath Road, Ashcott, Bridgwater, Somerset TA7 9QJ
☎ 01458 210256

CONTACT   Mr J. E. White
LOCATION 5 miles from Glastonbury, on A39
OPEN   10 am – 6 pm, Tuesday – Saturday. Closed Mondays. Ring first during summer show season
SPECIALITIES Cacti and succulents

194 Nurseries & Garden Centres SOMERSET

MAIL ORDER No

Cacti, of course, and a wide choice of succulents including *Hoya*, *Epiphyllum* and *Crassula*. They sell mixed cacti seed. They welcome group visits, by appointment, and offer B & B all year round. Shows include Bristol, Royal Cornwall, Cornwall Spring and the South of England Flower Show.

Broadleigh Gardens
Bishops Hull, Taunton, Somerset TA4 1AE
☎ 01823 286231   FAX 01823 323646
OPEN 9 am – 4 pm, Monday – Friday. Viewing only, and collection by prior arrangement
SPECIALITIES Bulbs; daffodils; herbaceous perennials; tulip species
CATALOGUE 2 first class stamps; spring, autumn
MAIL ORDER Yes
GARDEN Gardens open
SHOWS RHS Westminster; Chelsea
GIFT TOKENS Own
NCCPG NATIONAL COLLECTIONS *Narcissus* (miniature)

The nursery is best known as a small-bulb specialist. They now grow almost as many foliage and woodland perennials. Look out for the snowdrops, the many miniature narcissus and species tulips, and a double green *Muscari*. Open for viewing only. Prior arrangement is essential if you want to collect from the nursery.

Cannington College
Cannington, Bridgwater, Somerset TA5 2LS
☎ 01278 652226   FAX 01278 652479
CONTACT Mr S. J. Rudhall
LOCATION 3 miles west of Bridgewater off A 39
OPEN 2 – 5 pm, daily, Easter to October
SPECIALITIES Half-hardy perennials
CATALOGUE On request
MAIL ORDER Yes
REFRESHMENTS Refreshments
GARDEN Extensive gardens
SHOWS Malvern Spring; Chelsea; Hampton Court
NCCPG NATIONAL COLLECTIONS *Abutilon*, *Argyranthemum*, *Ceanothus*, *Cordyline*, *Osteospermum*, *Phormium*, *Wisteria*, *Yucca*

The Somerset county agricultural college at Cannington sells a range of plants propagated at the college. They are known particularly for tender perennials including new *Osteospermum* cultivars. The college holds no less than eight National Collections.

Elworthy Cottage Garden Plants
Elworthy Cottage, Elworthy, Lydeard St Lawrence, Taunton, Somerset TA4 3PX
☎ 01984 56427
CONTACT J. M. Spiller
LOCATION 10 miles north west of Taunton, on B3188 in village centre

OPEN 2 – 5 pm, Tuesdays and Thursdays only, mid March to mid October; also Saturday afternoons in April. Closed August, except by appointment
SPECIALITIES Herbaceous perennials
NEW FOR 1995 New hardy geraniums
CATALOGUE 3 second class stamps
MAIL ORDER No
GARDEN Garden opens for NGS (2 April, 14 May, 17 May, 21 June, 2 July)

A pleasant selection of perennials and cottage garden plants. Strong on geraniums, with over 120 varieties. Will be at the Taunton Flower Show, and local NCCPG sales.

Hadspen Garden and Nursery
Hadspen Garden, Castle Cary, Somerset BA7 7NG
☎ 01749 813707   FAX 01749 813707
CONTACT Nori Pope
LOCATION On A371, 2 miles east of Castle Cary
OPEN 9 am – 6 pm, Thursday – Sunday, and Bank Holidays, 2 March to 1 October
SPECIALITIES Herbaceous perennials; roses
CATALOGUE 3 first class stamps
MAIL ORDER No
REFRESHMENTS Coffee, tea and lunches
GARDEN Hadspen Garden, Somerset, see Gardens section
NCCPG NATIONAL COLLECTIONS *Rodgersia*

The nursery, which is attached to this well-known garden, sells the larger garden-worthy herbaceous plants, such as hostas and rodgersias, as well as clematis and old roses (many of which are on their own roots).

Halsway
Crowcombe, Taunton, Somerset TA4 4BB
☎ 01984 218243
CONTACT T. A. and D. J. Bushen
LOCATION ½ a mile off A358, between Taunton and Minehead
OPEN 10.30 am – dusk, Thursday – Sunday; phone first
SPECIALITIES Begonias; *Solenostemon* (*Coleus*)
NEW FOR 1995 Many new varieties
CATALOGUE SAE for *Begonia* and *Solenostemon*
MAIL ORDER Sometimes

A small nursery with a good choice of begonias and foliage *Solenostemon*, besides a wide and varying selection of garden and house plants. Their greenhouses are Victorian.

Kelways Ltd
Barrymore Farm, Langport, Somerset TA10 9EZ
☎ 01458 250521   FAX 01458 253351
CONTACT Sandra Robinson
LOCATION 10 miles east of Taunton
OPEN 9 am – 5 pm, Monday – Friday; 10 am – 4 pm, Saturdays and Sundays
SPECIALITIES Herbaceous perennials; *Iris*; paeonies
NEW FOR 1995 *Nepeta subsessilis*
CATALOGUE On request (retail and wholesale)

SOMERSET Nurseries & Garden Centres

MAIL ORDER Yes
GARDEN Display garden
SHOWS RHS Westminster; Malvern Spring; Chelsea; BBC GW Live; Hampton Court; Harrogate (Autumn)
GIFT TOKENS HTA

Long famous for their herbaceous and tree paeonies, Kelways also has a large range of irises and day lilies, and an expanding perennial section. A selection of their plants is now also available through some 150 garden centres.

Lower Severalls Herb Nursery
Crewkerne, Somerset TA18 7NX
☎ 01460 73234   FAX 01460 76105

CONTACT Mary R. Cooper
LOCATION 1 mile east of Crewkerne
OPEN 10 am – 5 pm, Monday – Saturday; 2 – 5pm, Sundays. Closed Thursdays
SPECIALITIES Herbaceous perennials; herbs
CATALOGUE 3 first class stamps
MAIL ORDER Yes; minimum order £7 plus p & p
REFRESHMENTS Teas on NGS open days (see Yellow Book)
GARDEN 2-acre garden
DESIGN SERVICE Lower Severalls Herb Nursery

Herbs of all kinds, as you would expect, but there are also good selections of the hardy geraniums and salvias. A herbaceous border design service is available.

Mallet Court Nursery
Curry Mallet, Taunton, Somerset TA3 6SY
☎ 01823 480748   FAX 01823 481009

CONTACT David Williamson
OPEN 9 am – 1 pm, 2 – 5 pm, Mondays to Fridays. Other days by appointment
SPECIALITIES Trees
NEW FOR 1995 *Quercus faginea*, *Acer metcalfii*, *Pterostyrax psilophylla*, *Ilex kusanoi*, *Fagus sylvatica* 'Remeleyensis' and many others
CATALOGUE Large SAE (37p stamp)
MAIL ORDER Yes
DESIGN SERVICE Mallet Court Nursery
SHOWS RHS Westminster; Malvern Spring; Harrogate (Spring); Chelsea; BBC GW Live; Hampton Court; Harrogate (Autumn); Courson

Specialist tree nursery with an excellent list of unusual trees. Particularly good for *Quercus* and *Acer*, and also strong on species from China and Korea. They are currently introducing Japanese maples from the late J. D. Vertrees' collection in the States.

Margery Fish Plant Nursery
East Lambrook Manor, East Lambrook, South Petherton, Somerset TA13 5HL
☎ 01460 240328   FAX 01460 242344

CONTACT Mark Stainer
LOCATION Signed from A303 at South Petherton
OPEN 10 am – 5 pm, Monday – Saturday, March to October; 10 am – 5 pm, Monday – Friday, November to February
SPECIALITIES Herbaceous perennials
NEW FOR 1995 Rose 'The Lambrook Rose' (syn. *R. verschuren*), *Geranium* 'Gillian Perrin'
CATALOGUE 4 first class stamps
MAIL ORDER Yes
REFRESHMENTS Coffee and biscuits; pub opposite
GARDEN East Lambrook Manor, Somerset, see Gardens section
GIFT TOKENS Own
NCCPG NATIONAL COLLECTIONS *Geranium*

A wide and attractive range mainly devoted to hardy herbaceous perennials. Good for *Artemisia*, *Euphorbia* and *Lavandula*: the *Geranium* list is exceptional. The late Margery Fish's garden needs no recommendation.

Mill Cottage Plants
The Mill, Henley Lane, Wookey, Somerset BA5 1AP
☎ 01749 676966

CONTACT Mrs Sally Gregson
LOCATION 2 miles from Wells: ring for directions
OPEN 10 am – 6 pm, Wednesdays, March to September
SPECIALITIES Herbaceous perennials
CATALOGUE 2 first class stamps
MAIL ORDER Yes; minimum order £5; October to March
GARDEN Garden open for groups

The nursery grows a selection of cottage garden type plants, including campanulas, ferns and *Geranium*. Talks and workshops can be arranged, as can design and planting advice. They will be at the South of England and the Bristol Flower Shows.

Monkton Elm Garden Centre
Monkton Heathfield, Taunton, Somerset TA2 8QN
☎ 01823 412381   FAX 01823 412745

CONTACT Mr M. Valuks
LOCATION 2½ miles north east of Taunton
OPEN 9.30 am – 5.30 pm, Monday – Saturday; 11 am – 5 pm, Sundays
SHOP Garden sundries, greenhouses, buildings, aquatics
REFRESHMENTS Restaurant
DESIGN SERVICE Monkton Elm Garden Centre
GIFT TOKENS HTA; own

Large garden centre with a complete range of plants and garden products. They have a design service and can deliver. They will be at the Taunton and the West Country Flower Shows.

Otter's Court Heathers
West Camel, Yeovil, Somerset BA22 7QF
☎ 01935 850285

CONTACT Mrs D. H. Jones
OPEN 9 am – 5.30 pm, Wednesday – Sunday. Closed Mondays and Tuesdays
SPECIALITIES Heathers

CATALOGUE   3 first class stamps
MAIL ORDER   Yes
GARDEN   Display gardens
DESIGN SERVICE   Otter's Court Heathers

This nursery stocks a selection of hardy, lime-tolerant heathers. They offer a design service and can draw up planting plans.

P M A Plant Specialities
Lower Mead, West Hatch, Taunton, Somerset
TA3 5RN
☎ 01823 480774   FAX 01823 481046

CONTACT   Karan Junker
LOCATION   Directions given when appointment made
OPEN   Collection only: by appointment
SPECIALITIES   Acers; trees
NEW FOR 1995   More varieties of *Daphne*
CATALOGUE   5 second class stamps
MAIL ORDER   Yes; no minimum order
GARDEN   Demonstration garden
DESIGN SERVICE   PMA Plant Specialities
SHOWS   Courson

Wholesale growers (with retail trade by mail order) of some interesting container-grown trees and shrubs. Strong on Japanese and snakebark acers, daphnes, magnolias and on tree species of *Cornus*. They also offer design and a specialist pruning service.

Rodney Fuller
Coachman's Cottage, Higher Bratton Seymour, Wincanton, Somerset BA9 8DA

CONTACT   Rodney Fuller
OPEN   Mail order only
SPECIALITIES   Violas
CATALOGUE   SAE
MAIL ORDER   Yes

Very small, and charmingly specialised, viola and violetta cultivars only.

Scotts Nurseries Ltd
Merriott, Somerset TA16 5PL
☎ 01460 72306   FAX 01460 77433

CONTACT   Sales Desk
OPEN   9 am – 5 pm, Monday – Saturday; 10.30 am – 4.30 pm, Sundays
SPECIALITIES   Fruit; roses
CATALOGUE   On request: shrubs and perennials; roses and fruit
MAIL ORDER   Yes
SHOP   Garden sundries
DESIGN SERVICE   Scotts Nurseries Ltd
GIFT TOKENS   HTA

Large nurseries with a very extensive range of field and container-grown plants of all kinds. The garden centre carries container stock, and is strong on fruit trees and shrubs.

Shepton Nursery Garden
Old Wells Road, Shepton Mallet, Somerset
BA4 5XN
☎ 01749 343630

CONTACT   P. W. Boughton
LOCATION   Off B3136 Glastonbury road (signed to Shepton Community Hospital)
OPEN   9.30 am – 5.30 pm, Tuesday – Saturday
SPECIALITIES   Alpines; herbaceous perennials; shrubs
CATALOGUE   4 second class stamps
MAIL ORDER   No
GARDEN   Display gardens

A mixed stock which includes alpines, herbaceous perennials and many shrubs. The nursery is strongest on *Chaenomeles*.

West Somerset Garden Centre
Mart Road, Minehead, Somerset TA24 5BJ
☎ 01643 703812   FAX 01643 706470

CONTACT   Mrs J. Shoulders
LOCATION   Just outside Minehead
OPEN   8 am – 5 pm, Monday – Saturday; 10 am – 4 pm, Sundays. Some winter variation
SPECIALITIES   Bedding plants; shrubs
CATALOGUE   On request; roses; fruit; bedding; trees and shrubs
MAIL ORDER   Yes (p & p at cost)
REFRESHMENTS   Café – home-made food
GIFT TOKENS   HTA; own

Bedding plants produced at the nursery, and a good selection of shrubs, stand out in a general range. Monthly availability lists are produced.

YSJ Seeds
Kingsfield Conservation Nursery, Broadenham Lane, Winsham, Chard, Somerset TA20 4JF
☎ 01460 30070   FAX 01460 30070

CONTACT   Mrs Margaret White
LOCATION   Map in catalogue
OPEN   Phone first
SPECIALITIES   Seeds; trees; wild flowers
CATALOGUE   1 second class stamp
MAIL ORDER   Yes
GIFT TOKENS   Own

The nursery specialises in British native trees and shrubs (of British provenance) either open ground or container-grown. Wild flowers are sold as plugs or as seed. Advice or consultations are available, as are tours for groups.

STAFFORDSHIRE

Bretby Nurseries
Bretby Lane, Burton on Trent, Staffordshire
DE15 0QS
☎ 01283 703355   FAX 01283 704035

CONTACT   Mr David Cartwright

OPEN 9 am – 5 pm, Monday – Saturday; 10.30 am – 4.30 pm, Sundays
CATALOGUE None
MAIL ORDER No
SHOP Gift shop
REFRESHMENTS Tea room
GIFT TOKENS HTA

Retail garden centre and wholesale nursery (Barn Farm Nurseries) which specialise in shrubs.

Byrkley Park Centre
Rangemore, Burton on Trent, Staffordshire DE13 9RN
☎ 01283 716467   FAX 01283 716594
CONTACT Information Desk
LOCATION 5 miles west of Burton on Trent; leave A38 at Branston
OPEN 9 am – 5 pm, Monday – Saturday, October to February; 9 am – 6 pm, March to September; 9 am – 9 pm, Fridays; 10.30 am – 4.30 pm, Sundays
CATALOGUE Leaflets
SHOP Garden products
REFRESHMENTS Tea room and carvery
DESIGN SERVICE Byrkley Park Centre
GIFT TOKENS HTA

Garden centre which has been developed inside a Victorian walled garden. Services include delivery, design and landscaping, play area and farm animals. The Annual Flower Show is on 26 – 28 August.

Heldon Nurseries
Asbourne Road, Spath, Uttoxeter ST14 5AD
☎ 01889 563177
CONTACT Mrs J. H. Tate
OPEN 10 am – sunset, daily
SPECIALITIES Cacti and succulents; carnivorous plants
CATALOGUE SAE
MAIL ORDER Yes
REFRESHMENTS Refreshments
SHOWS Malvern Spring; Hampton Court

Cactus and succulent specialists, with carnivorous plants too. Coach parties welcome. Shows include the Bath & West, Royal Welsh and the Bakewell.

Intakes Farm Plants
Intakes Farm, Sandy Lane, Longsden, Stoke on Trent, Staffordshire ST9 9QQ
☎ 01538 398452
CONTACT Mrs K. Inman
OPEN By appointment only
NEW FOR 1995 *Ballota nigra* 'Intakes Alba', *Geum × intermedium variegatum* 'Muriel'
CATALOGUE SAE
MAIL ORDER No

A small nursery which concentrates on unusual forms of British native and cottage garden plants: double flowers, variegated or coloured leaves and so on.

Jackson's Nurseries
Clifton Campville, Tamworth, Staffordshire B79 0AP
☎ 01827 373307
CONTACT Mrs N. Jackson
LOCATION 3 miles from M42, J11
OPEN 9 am – 5.30 pm, Mondays, Wednesday – Saturday; 10 am – 5 pm, Sundays. Closed Tuesdays
SPECIALITIES Fuchsias
NEW FOR 1995 Fuchsia 'Baby Rose', 'Hilda May', 'Justine Ann', 'Mamie's Choice', 'Ron Venables', 'Sutton 21'
CATALOGUE 2 first class stamps
MAIL ORDER No

Fuchsia specialists, with many cultivars available between March and June. They also have pelargoniums and vegetables, bedding and pot plants in season.

Planters Garden Centre
Woodlands Farm, Freasley, Tamworth, Staffordshire B78 2EY
☎ 01827 251511   FAX 01827 251511
CONTACT Gerald & Christine Ingram
LOCATION 1 mile from M42, J10
OPEN 9 am – 6 pm, Monday – Saturday; 11 am – 5 pm, Sundays
SHOP Garden sundries, greenhouses, gifts, pets
REFRESHMENTS Restaurant, coffee shop
GIFT TOKENS HTA

Garden centre with outdoor and indoor plant ranges, bonsai, garden products, fish and a toy shop. Delivery service.

SUFFOLK

Brian Sulman Pelargoniums
54 Kingsway, Mildenhall, Bury St Edmunds, Suffolk IP28 7HR
☎ 01638 712297
CONTACT Brian Sulman
LOCATION Mildenhall
OPEN Open weekend 10 – 11 June
SPECIALITIES Pelargoniums
CATALOGUE 2 first class stamps
MAIL ORDER Yes; 6 plants minimum
SHOWS RHS Westminster; Malvern Spring; Harrogate (Spring)

A newish venture specialising in pelargoniums, especially regals. The nursery is only open at the June open weekend. Trades from the same address as Pearl Sulman (dwarfs and miniatures) though their businesses are distinct.

Crown Vegetables
Marward House, Stock Corner Farm, Beck Row, Bury St Edmunds, Suffolk IP28 8DW
☎ 01638 712779
CONTACT Mr Trevor Sore
OPEN Mail order only

SPECIALITIES Vegetables
MAIL ORDER Yes

Specialist vegetables by post, including asparagus crowns, artichokes and horseradish.

Denbeigh Heathers
All Saints Road, Creeting St Mary, Ipswich, Suffolk IP6 8PJ
☎ 01449 711220   FAX 01449 711220
CONTACT D. J. Small
LOCATION Creeting St Mary
OPEN Phone first
SPECIALITIES Heathers
NEW FOR 1995 *Calluna vulgaris* 'Alexandra'
CATALOGUE On request
MAIL ORDER Yes

Wholesale and retail hardy heathers, sold as rooted cuttings, mini plants and some larger sizes. There are over 1,000 species and cultivars here: they claim to have the largest range in the world, and are the suppliers to the National Collections.

Fisk's Clematis Nursery
Westleton, Saxmundham, Suffolk IP17 3AJ
☎ 01728 648263
LOCATION Map in catalogue
OPEN 9 am – 5 pm, Monday – Friday, March to October; 9 am – 4 pm, Monday – Friday, November to February; 10 am – 1 pm, 2 – 5 pm, Saturdays and Sundays, April to October
SPECIALITIES Clematis
NEW FOR 1995 Clematis 'Joan Gray', 'Mary Claire', 'Norfolk Queen'
CATALOGUE 4 second class stamps
MAIL ORDER Yes
GARDEN Display garden
GIFT TOKENS Own

A well-known clematis specialist nursery with an extensive list. 'Joan Gray', one of their new varieties this year, is a double form of 'Nelly Moser'.

Fulbrooke Nursery
Home Farm, Westley, Waterless, Newmarket, Suffolk CB8 0RG
☎ 01638 507124
CONTACT Paul Lazard
OPEN By appointment
SPECIALITIES Bamboos
CATALOGUE SAE
MAIL ORDER Yes

Container-grown bamboos: the list includes some uncommon and tender species. Grasses and *Fatsia* too.

G Nice
63 Poplar Hill, Stowmarket, Suffolk IP14 2AU
☎ 01449 613398
CONTACT G. Nice
OPEN 10 am – 4 pm, Friday – Wednesday, February to May. Closed Thursdays

SPECIALITIES Fuchsias
CATALOGUE 2 first class stamps
MAIL ORDER Yes

Fuchsias only are grown here. There are around 400 varieties available as rooted cuttings by post.

Goldbrook Plants
Hoxne, Eye, Suffolk IP21 5AN
☎ 01379 668770
CONTACT Sandra Bond
OPEN 10.30 am – 6 pm, Thursday – Sunday. Other days by appointment. Closed January
SPECIALITIES *Hemerocallis*, hostas
NEW FOR 1995 New *Hosta* and *Hemerocallis* varieties
CATALOGUE 4 first class stamps
MAIL ORDER Yes; winter and spring dispatch
SHOWS RHS Westminster; Chelsea; Hampton Court

An exceptional collection of *Hosta* (over 500), with a good choice of *Hemerocallis* and shade-loving plants too. As exhibitors they have an impressive run of Chelsea gold medals for each of the last six years.

Goulding's Fuchsias
Link Lane, Bentley, Ipswich, Suffolk IP9 2DP
☎ 01473 310058
CONTACT Mr E. J. Goulding
LOCATION Just off A12, midway between Colchester and Ipswich
OPEN 10 am – 5 pm, daily, 7 January to 2 July. Closed Fridays
SPECIALITIES Fuchsias
CATALOGUE 3 first class stamps; December
MAIL ORDER Yes
GIFT TOKENS Own

Specialist fuchsia growers. The following types are sold: new, foreign, basket, bedding, encliandras, triphyllas, species and hardies. They welcome coach parties – by arrangement, and can help name unidentified varieties.

Hartshall Nursery Stock
Hartshall Farm, Walsham le Willows, Bury St Edmunds, Suffolk IP31 3BY
☎ 01359 259238   FAX 01359 259238
CONTACT J. D. L. Wight
LOCATION Between Walsham le Willows and Westhorpe
OPEN 10 am – 4.30 pm, Tuesday – Saturday. Closed Bank Holidays and July
SPECIALITIES Shrubs; trees
CATALOGUE 3 first class stamps
MAIL ORDER No
GIFT TOKENS Own

This shrub and tree nursery combines a wide general range with rarer species for plantsmen. It is also worth asking about their surplus plants and seconds.

Home Meadows Nursery Ltd
Top Street, Martlesham, Woodbridge, Suffolk
IP12 4RD
☎ 01394 382419

CONTACT   S. Denis O'Brien Baker
OPEN   8 am – 5 pm, Monday – Saturday. Closed Sundays
SPECIALITIES   Chrysanthemums
CATALOGUE   SAE
MAIL ORDER   Yes
SHOWS   RHS Westminster; Chelsea
NCCPG NATIONAL COLLECTIONS *Chrysanthemum* (Korean)

As well as a general selection of bedding and herbaceous plants, the main specialities here are Korean and spray chrysanthemums, and their own Meadhome strain of Iceland poppies.

Martins Nursery
Smallwood Green, Bradfield St George, Bury St Edmunds, Suffolk IP30 0AJ
☎ 01449 737698

CONTACT   Richard Martin
LOCATION   6 miles south east of Bury St Edmunds
OPEN   8.30 am – 5 pm, Monday – Saturday
SPECIALITIES   Herbaceous perennials
NEW FOR 1995   Many new varieties
CATALOGUE   SAE
MAIL ORDER   Yes

The nursery stocks hardy herbaceous perennials in useful varieties.

Mickfield Fish and Watergarden Centre
Debenham Road, Mickfield, Stowmarket, Suffolk
IP14 5LP
☎ 01449 711336   FAX 01449 711018

CONTACT   Mr M. C. Burch
OPEN   9.30 am – 5 pm, daily. Closed Christmas, Boxing Day and New Year's Day
SPECIALITIES   Aquatic plants; bog plants
CATALOGUE   50p
MAIL ORDER   Yes
SHOP   Pond products, fish
REFRESHMENTS   Tea room (weekends)
GARDEN   2-acre display gardens
DESIGN SERVICE   Mickfield Fish and Watergarden Centre

Plants for in and around water – aquatic, marginal and moisture-loving species. They also sell liners, pumps, rock and fish, and can design and advise on all sorts of water projects. Shows include the Suffolk and Eye Shows.

Mills Farm Plants and Gardens
Norwich Road, Mendlesham, Suffolk IP14 5NQ
☎ 01449 766425

CONTACT   Sue and Peter Russell
LOCATION   On A410, just south of Mendlesham turning
OPEN   9 am – 5.30 pm, daily. Closed Tuesdays, and January
SPECIALITIES   *Dianthus*; roses
CATALOGUE   2 second class stamps
MAIL ORDER   Yes; pinks and roses only

Mills Farm specialise in *Dianthus* (new and old hybrids, species and rock garden types) and roses: there is a list for each genus. The roses are mostly old-fashioned varieties, in a well-chosen selection. Gardening courses are also held at the nursery, spring and summer (SAE for details). Advice is free.

Mrs S Robinson
21 Bederic Close, Bury St Edmunds, Suffolk
IP32 7DR
☎ 01284 764310

CONTACT   Mrs S. Robinson
LOCATION   Off A14 Bury St Edmunds, Sudbury exit
OPEN   By appointment
SPECIALITIES   Foliage plants
MAILORDER   No
GARDEN   Charity garden openings
DESIGN SERVICE   Sue's Garden Designs

Plants on wheels: Sue Robinson lectures to clubs and societies and brings plants to sell with her. A list of lectures is available. Garden design and plant supply also.

Nareys Garden Centre
Bury Road, Stowmarket, Suffolk IP14 3QD
☎ 01449 612559

CONTACT   J. B. Narey, F. Narey and E. Hicks
LOCATION   West of Stowmarket on A14
OPEN   8.30 am – 5.30 pm, summer; 8.30 am – 5 pm, winter
SHOP   Garden sundries, above-ground swimming pools
DESIGN SERVICE   Nareys Garden Centre
GIFT TOKENS   HTA

General garden centre, producing its own bedding and pot plants. Some landscaping and pool and building installation. Delivery service.

North Green Snowdrops
North Green Only, Stoven, Beccles, Suffolk
NR34 8DG

CONTACT   John Morley
OPEN   Mail order only
SPECIALITIES   Snowdrops
CATALOGUE   4 first class stamps
MAIL ORDER   Yes

A connoisseur's collection of rare *Galanthus* species and cultivars. The nursery only sells by mail order – the plants are sold in the green. See also North Green Seeds under Seedsmen.

Notcutts Nurseries
Woodbridge, Suffolk IP12 4AF
☎ 01394 383344   FAX 01394 385460

CONTACT   Woodbridge Plant Advice Centre

LOCATION Woodbridge, and ten other garden centres
SPECIALITIES Roses; trees; shrubs
CATALOGUE £3.25 by post; £2.50 from garden centres
MAIL ORDER Yes
SHOP Garden sundries
GARDEN Demonstration gardens
DESIGN SERVICE Notcutts Landscapes
SHOWS RHS Westminster; Chelsea; BBC GW Live; Hampton Court
GIFT TOKENS HTA; own

Large wholesale nurseries with a garden centre chain. They are strongest on flowering shrubs and trees, including roses, but they have more or less everything else too. Quality is first-class. They have a design capability through Nottcutts Landscapes who are listed in our Professional Services section.

Paradise Centre

Twinstead Road, Lamarsh, Bures, Suffolk CO8 5EX
☎ 01787 269449   FAX 01787 269449

CONTACT Hedy J. Stapel-Valk
LOCATION Near Bures
OPEN 10 am – 5 pm, Saturdays and Sundays, and Bank Holidays. By appointment at other times
SPECIALITIES Bulbs; herbaceous perennials; seeds
NEW FOR 1995 *Asarum hartwegii*
CATALOGUE 4 first class stamps
MAIL ORDER Yes
REFRESHMENTS In fine weather
GARDEN 5-acre gardens
DESIGN SERVICE Garden Scents
SHOWS RHS Westminster; Malvern Spring; Harrogate (Spring); Chelsea; BBC GW Live; Hampton Court
GIFT TOKENS Own

A garden nursery which specialises in bulbs, herbaceous plants and shade lovers, all grown at the nursery – plus a few seeds. They have in-house design and build through Garden Scents, run by Writtle-trained Alan Mitchell (01206 865040).

Park Green Nurseries

Wetheringsett, Stowmarket, Suffolk IP14 5QH
☎ 01728 860139   FAX 01728 860139

CONTACT Richard and Mary Ford
LOCATION 6 miles north east of Stowmarket
OPEN 10 am – 5.30 pm, Thursday – Monday, March to October
SPECIALITIES Grasses; herbaceous perennials
NEW FOR 1995 New hostas, astilbes and grasses
CATALOGUE 3 first class stamps
MAIL ORDER Yes; no minimum order
REFRESHMENTS Refreshments
SHOWS Malvern Spring; Harrogate (Spring); Southport; Chelsea; BBC GW Live; Hampton Court

This nursery specialises in *Hosta* and *Hemerocallis*, with new cultivars each year. Other specialities include astilbes and ornamental grasses.

Pearl Sulman

54 Kingsway, Mildenhall, Bury St Edmunds, Suffolk IP28 7HR
☎ 01638 712297

CONTACT Pearl Sulman
OPEN Mail order only, except for open weekend, 10 – 11 July
SPECIALITIES Pelargoniums
CATALOGUE 3 first class stamps
MAIL ORDER Yes
REFRESHMENTS Light refreshments on open days
SHOWS Southport; Chelsea; BBC GW Live; Hampton Court

A small nursery which specialises in dwarf and miniature pelargoniums (500). Only open on the second weekend in June, otherwise by mail order. Trades from the same address as Brian Sulman.

Potash Nursery

Cow Green, Bacton, Stowmarket, Suffolk IP14 4HJ
☎ 01449 781671

CONTACT Jim Blythe
LOCATION On B1113, between Stowmarket and Finningham
OPEN 10 am – 5 pm, Saturday – Monday, mid February to end June, or by appointment
SPECIALITIES Fuchsias
CATALOGUE 3 first class stamps
SHOWS RHS Westminster; Malvern Spring; Harrogate (Spring); Southport; Chelsea; Hampton Court; Harrogate (Autumn)

Specialists for fuchsias: their range is available as cuttings or larger plants. They have pelargoniums and indoor cyclamen too. No mail order, but they attend lots of shows.

Smallscapes Nursery

3 Hundon Close, Stradishall, Newmarket CB8 9YF
☎ 01440 820336

CONTACT Stephen and Leigh Sage
LOCATION 6 miles north east of Haverhill on A143
OPEN By appointment: phone first
SPECIALITIES Rooted cuttings
CATALOGUE 4 first class stamps
MAIL ORDER Yes; no minimum order
GARDEN Garden

'We really cannot see the point in paying over £1 per plant in postage to send a litre of compost through the post', say the owners of this distinctive nursery. So they list rooted cuttings and small sizes of alpines, perennials, climbers, trees and shrubs, all designed for safe and cheap carriage. Good value too. Larger plants are available at the nursery.

The Walled Garden

Park Road, Benhall, Saxmundham, Suffolk IP17 1JB
☎ 01728 602510   FAX 01728 602510

CONTACT Mr J. R. Mountain

SURREY Nurseries & Garden Centres

OPEN 9.30 am – 5 pm, Tuesday – Sunday, and Bank Holidays. Closed Sundays, December to February
SPECIALITIES Herbaceous perennials
CATALOGUE 2 first class stamps
MAIL ORDER No
GIFT TOKENS HTA

The nursery has a useful range of good garden plants, climbers, shrubs, perennials and annuals in season. The walled garden itself is being restored and replanted.

SURREY

Beechcroft Nursery
127 Reigate Road, Ewell, Surrey KT17 3DE
☎ 0181 393 4265   FAX 0181 393 4265

CONTACT C. Kimber
LOCATION On A240
OPEN 10 am – 5 pm, summer; 10 am – 4 pm, winter, and Sundays and Bank Holidays
SPECIALITIES Alpines; conifers
CATALOGUE On request
MAIL ORDER No
GARDEN Display garden

A mainly wholesale nursery specialising in the supply of alpines and conifers to nurseries and garden centres. Some retail trade also, and they have bedding plants in season.

Brian Hiley
25 Little Woodcote Estate, Wallington, Surrey SM5 4AU
☎ 0181 647 9679

CONTACT Brian and Heather Hiley
OPEN 9 am – 5 pm, Wednesday – Saturday
SPECIALITIES Half-hardy plants
CATALOGUE 3 first class stamps
MAIL ORDER Yes; £10 minimum order
GARDEN Display gardens
SHOWS RHS Westminster; Malvern Spring; Chelsea; BBC GW Live; Hampton Court

An interesting collection of tender perennials and shrubs: the salvias are particularly good. Among the hardy perennials the penstemons stand out, whilst the show displays last year were outstanding (and deservedly rewarded).

Clay Lane Nursery
3 Clay Lane, South Nutfield, Redhill, Surrey RH1 4EG
☎ 01737 823307

CONTACT K. W. Belton
OPEN 9 am – 5 pm, Tuesdays to Saturdays, 28 January – 31 March; daily, 1 April to 31 August. Closed September to end January
SPECIALITIES Fuchsias
NEW FOR 1995 New fuchsia centre
CATALOGUE 2 first class stamps
MAIL ORDER No

GARDEN Fuchsia garden: June to August

This fuchsia specialist sells a wide range of cultivars and species, including hardy varieties and varieties which are suitable for baskets. The new centre will operate in three stages: rooted cuttings (to mid April); containerised plants (from May); and a full garden display (June to August).

D N Bromage & Co Ltd
St Mary's Gardens, Worplesdon, Guildford, Surrey GU3 3RS
☎ 01483 232893

CONTACT D. N. Bromage amd Mrs R. A. Hughes
LOCATION On A322 Guildford to Bagshot road, next to White Lyon
OPEN 10 am – 4 pm, daily
SPECIALITIES Bonsai
CATALOGUE On request
MAIL ORDER Yes
SHOP Bonsai accessories
SHOWS Chelsea
GIFT TOKENS Own

Bonsai trees and all accessories. Other services include offering a holiday home, hospital and repotting.

Foliage Scented & Herb Plants
Walton Poor Cottage, Ranmore Common, Dorking, Surrey RH5 6SX
☎ 01483 282273

CONTACT Mrs Prudence Calvert
LOCATION From A246 take Greendene Shere turning outside East Horsley. Turn first left at Crocknorth Road. Nursery and garden 1 mile on left (near Ranmore Amrs pub)
OPEN Wednesday – Sunday, and Bank Holidays, March to September
SPECIALITIES Aromatic and scented plants; herbs
NEW FOR 1995 New herbaceous plants, including geraniums
CATALOGUE Yes
MAIL ORDER No
REFRESHMENTS Nearby pub and restaurant
GARDEN Herb gardens and new potager
DESIGN SERVICE Foliage Scented & Herb Plants

The nursery stocks a range of aromatic herbs and shrubs. The herb gardens and potager open at the same times as the nursery, and a 2½-acre garden can also be visited Wednesday to Friday, April to September.

Forest Lodge Garden Centre
Holt Pound, Farnham, Surrey GU10 4LD
☎ 01420 23275   FAX 01420 22376
LOCATION On A325, 2 miles south of Farnham
OPEN 8.30 am – 5.30 pm, Monday – Saturday; 10.30 am – 4.30 pm, Sundays
SHOP Gardening products; gifts
REFRESHMENTS Coffee shop
GARDEN Demonstration gardens
GIFT TOKENS HTA; own

Previous winner of the GCA Garden Centre of the Year Award.

Garden Style
68 Wrecclesham Hill, Farnham, Surrey GU10 4JX
☎ 01252 735331   FAX 01252 735269

CONTACT   John Hanson
LOCATION   On A325, 1 mile south of Farnham
OPEN   8.30 am – 5.30 pm, Monday – Friday; 8.30 am – 12.30 pm, Saturdays
SPECIALITIES   Large-size shrubs and trees
CATALOGUE   On request
MAIL ORDER   No

A wholesale and retail nursery that specialises in specimen sizes in containers. They have climbers, conifers, shrubs and trees from 1m–6m high. The largest container is 1,500 litres.

Green Farm Plants
Bentley, Farnham, Surrey GU10 5JX
☎ 01420 23202   FAX 01420 22382

CONTACT   John Coke and Marina Christopher
LOCATION   North east Hampshire
OPEN   10 am – 6 pm, Wednesday – Saturday, mid March to mid October
SPECIALITIES   Herbaceous perennials
CATALOGUE   3 first class stamps
MAIL ORDER   No
SHOWS   RHS Westminster

This nursery is full of interesting plants, including the results of recent collecting trips. The main groups are hardy and half-hardy perennials, with an increasing number of woodland plants and sun-loving shrubs.

Herons Bonsai Ltd
Herons Bonsai Nursery, Wire Mill Lane, Newchapel, Lingfield, Surrey RH7 6HJ
☎ 01342 832657   FAX 01342 832025

CONTACT   Peter and Dawn Chan
LOCATION   Newchapel
OPEN   9 am – 6 pm, daily
SPECIALITIES   Bonsai; Japanese plants
NEW FOR 1995   Japanese irises
CATALOGUE   SAE plus £1
MAIL ORDER   Yes
SHOP   Bonsai accessories, Japanese items
GARDEN   Display garden
DESIGN SERVICE   Herons Bonsai Ltd
SHOWS   Chelsea; Hampton Court
GIFT TOKENS   Own

Bonsai nursery, with a string of Chelsea golds. As well as trees for indoors and outdoors, there are pots, tools and accessories (retail and wholesale). Bonsai classes and design available.

Hydon Nurseries
Clock Barn Lane, Hydon Heath, Godalming, Surrey GU8 4AZ
☎ 01483 860252   FAX 01483 419937

CONTACT   A. F. George
LOCATION   2 miles east of A3, Milford exit. Near Cheshire Home
OPEN   8 am – 5 pm, Monday – Friday, and Saturdays in season. Closed for lunch 12.45 – 2 pm
SPECIALITIES   Rhododendrons
CATALOGUE   £1.50
MAIL ORDER   Yes; p & p at cost
DESIGN SERVICE   Hydon Nurseries
SHOWS   RHS Westminster; Chelsea
GIFT TOKENS   HTA

Rhododendron and azalea specialists. The extensive range covers all types – among them some tender species and their own *Rhododendron yakushimanum* hybrids. They also stock companion trees and shrubs. They can advise on design and planting.

Kaytie Fisher Nursery
South End Farm, Long Reach, Ockham, Surrey GU23 6PF
☎ 01483 282304

CONTACT   Kaytie Fisher
LOCATION   Map in catalogue
OPEN   10 am – 4.30 pm, daily, May – July; Wednesday – Sunday, April, August, September; Wednesday – Friday, March and October; by appointment, November – February
SPECIALITIES   Herbaceous perennials; roses
CATALOGUE   5 second class stamps
MAIL ORDER   Yes
DESIGN SERVICE   Kaytie Fisher

Older varieties for cottage garden planting unite a pleasing mix of perennials, roses and shrubs. The design service specialises in Victorian and cottage gardens.

Knap Hill Nursery Ltd
Barrs Lane, Knaphill, Woking, Surrey GU21 2JW
☎ 01483 481212   FAX 01483 797261

CONTACT   Miss Daphne Buckle
LOCATION   2½ miles west of Woking, off A322
OPEN   9 am – 5 pm, Monday – Saturday; 10.30 am – 4.30 pm, Sundays
SPECIALITIES   Rhododendrons
CATALOGUE   50p
MAIL ORDER   Yes
SHOP   Garden centre
REFRESHMENTS   Coffee shop and carvery
SHOWS   RHS Westminster; Chelsea
GIFT TOKENS   Own

Garden and nursery which specialises in rhododendrons and azaleas. Their extensive list includes hybrids, dwarf, semi-dwarf and *R. yakushimanum* cultivars, as well as deciduous and evergreen azaleas.

Knights Garden Centre
Limpsfield Road, Chelsham, Surrey CR6 9DZ
☎ 01883 622340   FAX 01883 627252
OPEN   8 am – 5.30 pm, Monday – Saturday, 9 am – 5 pm, Sundays

REFRESHMENTS Yes
GIFT TOKENS HTA; own

One of three Knights garden centres: the others are at Woldingham and Godstone.

Knights Garden Centre
Nag's Hall Nursery, Godstone, Surrey RH9 8DB
☎ 01883 742275   FAX 01883 744429
OPEN 8 am – 5.30 pm, Monday – Saturday; 9 am – 5 pm, Sundays
REFRESHMENTS Yes
GIFT TOKENS HTA; own

General garden centre, including garden sundries and house plants: celebrates its Golden Jubilee this year.

Knights Garden Centre
Rosedene Nursery, Woldingham Road, Woldingham, Surrey CR3 7LA
☎ 01883 653142   FAX 01883 652221
LOCATION Near M25, J6
OPEN 8 am – 5.30 pm, Monday – Saturday; 10.30 am – 4.30 pm, Sundays
SHOP Garden sundries, pond equipment, gifts
REFRESHMENTS Yes
GARDEN Woldingham Dene
GIFT TOKENS HTA; own

The head office of the three Surrey garden centres in the Knights chain. This centre celebrates its silver jubilee this year. Events are held in the adjacent Woldingham Dene, including an annual craft fair.

Little Brook Fuchsias
Ash Green Lane West, Ash Green, Aldershot, Surrey GU12 6HL
☎ 01252 29731

CONTACT Carol Gubler
LOCATION 1 mile from A31
OPEN 9 am – 5 pm, Wednesday – Sunday, and Bank Holidays, 1 January to 1 July. Closed Mondays and Tuesdays
SPECIALITIES Fuchsias
CATALOGUE SAE plus 30p
MAIL ORDER No

Old and new *Fuchsia* varieties in abundance, as well as selected bedding and container plants at the nursery in spring.

Merrist Wood College Plant Shop
Merrist Wood College, Worplesdon, Guildford, Surrey GU3 3PE
☎ 01483 232424   FAX 01483 236518

CONTACT Danny O'Shaughnessy
LOCATION On campus, off A322
OPEN 8 am – 5 pm, Monday – Friday. Selected weekends too: phone first
CATALOGUE On request
MAIL ORDER No
REFRESHMENTS Mornings (during term)
SHOWS Chelsea; Hampton Court

Plants of all descriptions, from bedding to semi-mature trees. Most of it is produced by the students as part of their training.

Millais Nurseries
Crosswater Lane, Churt, Farnham, Surrey GU10 2JN
☎ 01252 792698   FAX 01252 792526

CONTACT David Millais
LOCATION From A287 ½ mile north of Churt, take Jumps Road, and follow signs
OPEN 10 am – 1 pm, 2 – 5 pm, Tuesday – Friday. Also Saturdays, March, April, October, November; and daily, May only
SPECIALITIES Rhododendrons
NEW FOR 1995 *Taliense* series *Rhododendron* from Himalayan collected seed
CATALOGUE 5 second class stamps
MAIL ORDER Yes; minimum order £25; October to March
REFRESHMENTS NGS days only
GARDEN 10-acre woodland garden, May only
GIFT TOKENS Own

A rhododendron and azalea specialist. The extensive range of species and hybrids includes some new Himalayan species. The garden is open in May, with a National Gardens Scheme weekend from 27 – 29 May.

Nettletons Nursery
Ivy Mill Lane, Godstone, Surrey RH9 8NF
☎ 01883 742426   FAX 01883 742426

CONTACT Jonathan Nettleton
LOCATION Near M25, J6: beside the green
OPEN 8.30 am – 1 pm, 2 – 5.30 pm, Monday – Saturday. Also 10 am – 1 pm, Sundays from March to early June. Closed Wednesdays
SPECIALITIES Acers; conifers; shrubs
NEW FOR 1995 *Wisteria* 'Showa Beni Fuji'
CATALOGUE 2 first class stamps
MAIL ORDER No

Acers in great variety (100), as well as many wisterias (15), including a new pure pink variety this year. There are other good trees and shrubs here too, all produced at the nursery.

Notcutts Garden Centre
Waterers Nurseries, London Road, Bagshot, Surrey GU19 5DG
☎ 01276 472288
LOCATION On A30
OPEN 9 am – 5.30 pm, Monday – Saturday; 11 am – 5 pm, Sundays. Closes at 5 pm in winter
SPECIALITIES Rhododendrons; shrubs
CATALOGUE £2.50
MAIL ORDER Details in catalogue
SHOP Garden sundries, furniture, pools, aquatics
REFRESHMENTS Restaurant
DESIGN SERVICE Notcutts Garden Centre
SHOWS Chelsea; BBC GW Live; Hampton Court
GIFT TOKENS HTA; own

Famous old nursery (including a wholesale division). Now part of the Notcutts empire.

Notcutts Garden Centre
Guildford Road, Cranleigh, Surrey GU6 8LT
☎ 01483 274222   FAX 01483 267247
LOCATION   On B2128
OPEN   8.30 am – 5.30 pm, Monday – Saturday; 11 am – 5 pm, Sundays. Closes at 5 pm in winter
SPECIALITIES   Clematis; shrubs; trees
CATALOGUE   £2.50
MAIL ORDER   £30 minimum order
SHOP   Garden sundries, furniture, machinery
REFRESHMENTS   Restaurant
DESIGN SERVICE   Nottcutts Garden Centre (Cranleigh)
SHOWS   Chelsea; BBC GW Live; Hampton Court
GIFT TOKENS   HTA; own

Strong on trees and shrubs, especially *Syringa* and *Clematis* (60 varieties). See also Notcutts Nurseries, Suffolk.

Pantiles Plant & Garden Centre
Almners Road, Lyne, Chertsey, Surrey KT16 0BJ
☎ 01932 872195   FAX 01932 874030
CONTACT   Brendan Gallagher
OPEN   8.30 am – 5.30 pm, Monday – Saturday; 9 am – 5 pm, Sundays
SPECIALITIES   Aquatic plants; bedding plants; shrubs; large specimen trees
CATALOGUE   SAE for availability list
MAIL ORDER   No
REFRESHMENTS   Vending machine
DESIGN SERVICE   Pantiles Plant & Garden Centre
SHOWS   Chelsea; Hampton Court
GIFT TOKENS   HTA

The nursery specialises in outsize container-grown specimens (up to 8 metres), including *Dicksonia antarctica* (tree fern). There is also a good bedding range and an aquatic centre. Full landscaping service also available.

RHS Plant Centre, Wisley
RHS Garden, Wisley, Woking, Surrey GU23 6QB
☎ 01483 211113
LOCATION   RHS Garden, Wisley, near M25, A3 intersection
OPEN   10 am – 6.30 pm, summer; 10 am – 5.30 pm, winter, Mondays – Saturdays. Also Sundays, 10 am – 4 pm, November to February; 11.30 am – 5.30 pm, March to October
CATALOGUE   No
MAIL ORDER   No
SHOP   Garden sundries, seeds, books
REFRESHMENTS   Restaurants
GARDEN   RHS Garden, Wisley, Surrey, see Gardens section
GIFT TOKENS   HTA

Wisley's plant centre carries a very wide and interesting selection of most kinds of plants: one of the best in the country. The adjacent garden is an obvious draw, and there are also good choices of books and seeds and bulbs on site.

Rupert Bowlby
Gatton, Reigate, Surrey RH2 0TA
☎ 01737 642221   FAX 01737 642221
CONTACT   Rupert Bowlby
LOCATION   Near M25, J8: see catalogue for map
OPEN   Saturdays and Sunday afternoons, March, September and October. By appointment at other times
SPECIALITIES   Bulbs
NEW FOR 1995   More *Allium*
CATALOGUE   2 first class stamps
MAIL ORDER   Yes
SHOWS   RHS Westminster; Chelsea; Hampton Court

Bulb specialist, including *Narcissus, Tulipa* and *Fritillaria*. He also has some tender South African plants. The *Allium* collection, which has formed such striking displays in recent years, continues to grow.

Surrey Primroses
Merriewood, Sandy Lane, Milford, Godalming, Surrey GU8 5BJ
☎ 01483 416747
CONTACT   G. J. E. Yates
OPEN   Mail order only
SPECIALITIES   Primulas
CATALOGUE   SAE
MAIL ORDER   Yes; no minimum order

Specialist source of old, named single primrose and polyanthus cultivars. Some 42 varieties of delightful and garden-worthy survivors.

Toobees Exotics
20 Inglewood, Woking, Surrey GU21 3HX
☎ 01483 722600   FAX 01483 751995
CONTACT   Bob Potter
OPEN   Phone first
SPECIALITIES   Cacti and succulents
CATALOGUE   SAE
MAIL ORDER   Yes
SHOWS   RHS Westminster; Hampton Court
GIFT TOKENS   Own

Suppliers of succulents from Africa and Madagascar, including rare species of *Euphorbia*.

V H Humphrey
Westlees Farm, Logmore Lane, Westcott, Dorking, Surrey RH4 3JN
☎ 01306 889827
CONTACT   Mrs P. J. Brown
OPEN   By appointment only, and at May open days
SPECIALITIES   *Iris*
NEW FOR 1995   Japanese and Arilbred irises
CATALOGUE   Large SAE

MAIL ORDER   Yes
SHOWS   RHS Westminster; Chelsea

Irises only, and in abundance. Most of this list consists of bearded *Iris*, but there are also species, pacific coast hybrids, *spuria* and *sibirica* cultivars too. The business is mainly mail order, but there are two open days in May, at flowering time.

The Vernon Geranium Nursery
Cuddington Way, Cheam, Sutton, Surrey SM2 7JB
☎ 0181 393 7616   FAX 0181 786 7437

CONTACT   Derek E. James
OPEN   9.30 am – 5.30 pm, Monday – Saturday; 10 am – 4 pm, Sundays, February to August
SPECIALITIES   Fuchsias; pelargoniums
CATALOGUE   £1.50
MAIL ORDER   Yes; no minimum order
SHOWS   Southport; Chelsea; BBC GW Live; Hampton Court

Specialist growers of pelargoniums (1,100) and fuchsias (100). Plants are available as rooted cuttings by post, and pot-grown plants can be had from the nursery or at shows. The number of pelargonium varieties speaks for itself. Some patio plants are available at the nursery. Open days, 14 – 31 July.

EAST SUSSEX

Axletree Nursery
Starvecrow Lane, Peasmarsh, Rye, East Sussex TN31 6XL
☎ 01797 230470

CONTACT   Dr D. J. Hibberd
LOCATION   2 miles south west of Peasmarsh, off A268. Send SAE for map and directions
OPEN   10 am – 5 pm, Wednesday – Saturday, mid March to end September
SPECIALITIES   Herbaceous perennials, hardy geraniums
NEW FOR 1995   New hardy geraniums
CATALOGUE   4 first class stamps; SAE for autumn mail order list
MAIL ORDER   Hardy geraniums only, in autumn
GARDEN   1-acre garden, containing 3,000 varieties: open same time as nursery

Best known for their substantial list of hardy geraniums: more cultivars are being introduced again this year. There is a good range of other herbaceous perennials too.

Coghurst Nursery
Ivy House Lane, Three Oaks, Hastings, East Sussex TN35 4NP
☎ 01424 756228

CONTACT   Mrs J. Farnfield, Mr and Mrs Edgar
LOCATION   Near Hastings – map in catalogue
OPEN   12 noon – 4.30 pm, Monday – Friday; 10 am – 4.30 pm, Sundays. Closed Saturdays

SPECIALITIES   Camellias; rhododendrons
NEW FOR 1995   Hydrangeas
CATALOGUE   2 second class stamps
MAIL ORDER   Yes; no minimum order
SHOWS   RHS Westminster

Camellia and *Rhododendron* specialists. They stock all types of camellias and rhododendrons, and have a good selection of hydrangeas, eucryphias and other shrubs.

Great Dixter Nurseries
Great Dixter, Northiam, Rye, East Sussex TN31 6PH
☎ 01797 253107

CONTACT   Mrs K. Leighton
LOCATION   Off A28, ½ a mile north of Northiam
OPEN   9 am – 12.30 pm, 1.30 – 5.00 pm, Monday – Friday; 9 am – 12 pm, Saturdays
SPECIALITIES   Clematis
CATALOGUE   75p
MAIL ORDER   Yes; minimum order £10; not from May to August
SHOP   Books
GARDEN   Great Dixter, East Sussex, see Gardens section

The nursery is attached to Christopher Lloyd's famous garden, and copies of his books are on sale here. The nursery specialises in clematis, but the rest of the general range includes many other plants which can be seen in the garden.

Harvest Nurseries
Harvest Cottage, Boonshill Farm, Iden, Rye, East Sussex TN31 7QA
☎ 01797 280493

CONTACT   Mr D. A. Smith
OPEN   Mail order only
SPECIALITIES   Cacti and succulents
CATALOGUE   2 first class stamps
MAIL ORDER   Yes; no minimum order

A mail order only cacti and succulent nursery. They specialise in *Epiphyllum* hybrids. All the plants are propagated at the nursery.

Just Roses
Beales Lane, Northiam, Rye, East Sussex TN31 6QY
☎ 01797 252355

CONTACT   Mr J. H. Banham
OPEN   9 am – 5 pm, Tuesday – Friday; 10 am – 4 pm, Saturdays and Sundays. Closed Mondays
SPECIALITIES   Roses
CATALOGUE   On request
MAIL ORDER   Yes; November to February
GARDEN   Display garden

Specialist rose growers, covering the whole spectrum of the genus. Container roses can be bought from April, while stocks last. Most of the business is bare root, from November on.

Kent Street Nurseries
Sedlescombe, Battle, East Sussex TN33 0SF
☎ 01424 751134

CONTACT Mrs D. Downey
LOCATION 5 miles from Hastings, on A21
OPEN 9 am – dusk, daily
SPECIALITIES Bedding plants; fuchsias; pelargoniums
CATALOGUE SAE plus 2 first class stamps per list
MAIL ORDER Fuchsias only

A general plant range is complemented by over 800 *Fuchsia* and *Pelargonium* varieties, including some older ones. They have separate lists for fuchsias and pelargoniums: specify which one you want.

Lime Cross Nursery
Herstmonceux, Hailsham, East Sussex BN27 4RS
☎ 01323 833229

CONTACT Louise Newman or Bob Bryant
LOCATION East of Herstmonceux, on A271
OPEN 8.30 am – 5 pm, Monday – Saturday; 9.30 am – 5 pm, Sundays
SPECIALITIES Conifers; shrubs; trees
CATALOGUE On request
MAIL ORDER No
GIFT TOKENS HTA

Specialist conifer growers with some 300 varieties and more. There is also a good choice of trees and shrubs among a general plant range.

Long Man Gardens
Lewes Road, Wilmington, Polegate, East Sussex BN26 5RS
☎ 01323 870816

CONTACT O. Menzel
LOCATION On A27 between Wilmington and Milton Gate
OPEN 9 am – 5.30 pm, Tuesday – Sunday. Phone first if possible
SPECIALITIES Conservatory plants
CATALOGUE On request
MAIL ORDER Yes

The nursery specialises in plants for conservatory and greenhouse culture, including an attractive choice of *Hoya* and *Bougainvillea*. They will do mail order, but recommend a visit.

Merriments Gardens
Hawkhurst Road, Hurst Green, East Sussex TN19 7RA
☎ 01580 860666   ℻ 01580 860324

CONTACT Mark Buchele
OPEN 10 am – 5.30 pm, daily
SPECIALITIES Herbaceous perennials
NEW FOR 1995 *Fuchsia boliviana* 'Alba', *Amicia zygomeris*, *Pericallis multiflora*, *Sedum* 'Mörchen', *Stipa barbata*
CATALOGUE 75p
MAIL ORDER No
SHOP Garden sundries
REFRESHMENTS Tea room
GARDEN Show garden
DESIGN SERVICE Merriments Gardens
GIFT TOKENS HTA

Retail nursery growing a range of hardy plants. They also sell garden products, offer a design and landscaping service, and have their own garden club.

Norman Bonsai
3 Westdene Drive, Brighton, East Sussex BN1 5HE
☎ 01273 506476

CONTACT Ken Norman
LOCATION Leonardslee Gardens, Lower Beeding, West Sussex
OPEN 10.30 am – 6 pm, 1 April to 31 October, at Leonardslee Gardens
SPECIALITIES Bonsai
MAIL ORDER No
SHOP Bonsai accessories
REFRESHMENTS Restaurant and tea room
GARDEN Leonardslee Gardens, West Sussex, see Gardens section
SHOWS Chelsea

Imported and British grown bonsai trees and accessories. There is a permanent display at Leonardslee Gardens of part of Mr Norman's personal bonsai collection. Demonstrations and tuition can be arranged, and bonsai design and maintenance services are also offered.

Oakhurst Nursery
Oakhurst, Mardens Hill, Crowborough, East Sussex TN6 1XL
☎ 01892 653273

CONTACT Mrs Stephanie Colton
LOCATION Between A26 and B2188, north west of Crowborough
OPEN 11 am – 5.30 pm, Monday – Friday, mid April to mid September. Phone first
CATALOGUE 2 first class stamps
MAIL ORDER No

This is a small garden nursery with a constantly changing selection of useful perennials.

Perryhill Nurseries
Hartfield, East Sussex TN7 4JP
☎ 01892 770377   ℻ 01892 770929

CONTACT Peter Chapman
LOCATION 1 mile north of Hartfield on B2026
OPEN 9 am – 5 pm, March to October; 9 am – 4.30 pm, November to February
SPECIALITIES Herbaceous perennials; roses
CATALOGUE £1.65
MAIL ORDER No; delivery for large orders
DESIGN SERVICE Perryhill Nurseries
GIFT TOKENS HTA; own

No real specialities, except for the width of the range. Trees, shrubs, herbaceous perennials and roses are all available in quantity, and the varieties are well-chosen. A design and landscaping service is available. The Perryhill Sackville Garden Workshop holds learning days here, often with gardening personalities.

Stone Cross Nurseries & Garden Centre
Rattle Road, Pevensey, East Sussex BN24 5EB
☎ 01323 763250   FAX 01323 460406

CONTACT Mr C. Barker
LOCATION On old A27 between Polegate and Pevensey
OPEN 8.30 am – 5.30 pm, Monday – Saturday; 10 am – 4 pm, Sundays
CATALOGUE Trade catalogue only
MAIL ORDER No
SHOP Sundries
GIFT TOKENS HTA

Wholesale and retail nursery and garden centre with an all-round plant range, mainly home-produced. They also have a pick your own farm.

Usual & Unusual Plants
Onslow House, Magham Down, Hailsham, East Sussex BN27 1PL
☎ 01323 840967   FAX 01323 840967

CONTACT Mrs Jennie Maillard
LOCATION On A271
OPEN 9.30 am – 5.30 pm, daily; but Thursday – Sunday only in August
SPECIALITIES Herbaceous perennials
CATALOGUE SAE plus 1 first class stamp
MAIL ORDER No

Small herbaceous nursery: its specialities include hardy geraniums, *Erysimum*, *Penstemon* and *Euphorbia*.

WEST SUSSEX

Allwood Bros
Mill Nursery, Hassocks, West Sussex BN6 9NB
☎ 01273 844229

CONTACT Mr D. James
OPEN 9 am – 4 pm, Monday – Friday
SPECIALITIES *Dianthus*
CATALOGUE 2 first class stamps
MAIL ORDER Yes
SHOWS Malvern Spring; Chelsea

Allwood Bros sell *Dianthus*, carnations and pinks of all kinds, and at all stages of the plants' development – as seed, plants or cut flowers. Their original postal carnation service started in 1910. A booklet, *Allwoods Guide to Perpetual Flowering Carnations*, is available for £2 by post.

Anthony Archer-Wills Ltd
Broadford Bridge Road, West Chiltington, West Sussex RH20 2LF
☎ 01798 813204   FAX 01798 815080

OPEN By appointment
SPECIALITIES Aquatic plants; bog plants
CATALOGUE On request
MAIL ORDER Yes
DESIGN SERVICE Anthony Archer-Wills Ltd
SHOWS Chelsea

Water nursery belonging to a garden designer: see his entry in Professional Services for more details. The nursery stocks aquatic, marginal and waterside plants. They also sell liners and pumps.

Apuldram Roses
Apuldram Lane, Dell Quay, Chichester, West Sussex PO20 7EF
☎ 01243 785769   FAX 01243 536973

CONTACT Mrs D. Sawday
LOCATION 1 mile south west of Chichester
OPEN 9 am – 5 pm, Monday – Saturday; 10.30 am – 4.30 pm, Sundays and Bank Holidays
SPECIALITIES Roses
NEW FOR 1995 Roses 'Chatsworth', 'Blenheim', 'Harewood', 'Toulouse Lautrec'
CATALOGUE On request
MAIL ORDER Yes
GARDEN Rose fields
DESIGN SERVICE Apuldram Roses
GIFT TOKENS HTA; own

Apuldram sell a mixed range of mainly modern roses. The pruning week is 6 – 11 March, and the open evenings in the rose fields are 6.30 – 8.30 pm, 22 and 29 June.

Architectural Plants
Cooks Farm, Nuthurst, Horsham, West Sussex RH13 6LH
☎ 01403 891772   FAX 01403 891056

CONTACT Angus White and Christine Shaw
LOCATION 3 miles south of Horsham, behind the Black Horse pub in Nuthurst
OPEN 9 am – 5 pm, Monday – Saturday
SPECIALITIES Foliage plants; hardy exotics
CATALOGUE On request
MAIL ORDER Yes; minimum carriage £13
GARDEN Display garden
GIFT TOKENS Own

Somewhat out of the ordinary: they specialise in exotic-looking, evergreen foliage plants, often with stylish, architectural shapes. We particularly like their catalogue: breezily written and easy to use. Larger sizes are available for immediate impact, and they deliver anywhere. Terracotta pots and wheelbarrows of their own design also sold.

Cottage Garden Plants
Mytten Twitten, High Street, Cuckfield, West Sussex RH17 5EN
☎ 01444 456067   FAX 01444 456067

CONTACT   David and Pat Clarke
LOCATION   Cuckfield
OPEN   Times under revision: phone first
SPECIALITIES   Herbaceous perennials
CATALOGUE   3 first class stamps
MAIL ORDER   Yes
SHOWS   RHS Westminster; Malvern Spring; Harrogate (Spring); Chelsea; BBC GW Live; Hampton Court; Harrogate (Autumn)

An appropriately named nursery. Their range is mostly herbaceous, but they sell shrubs and climbers too.

Croftway Nursery
Yapton Road, Barnham, Bognor Regis, West Sussex PO22 0BH
☎ 01243 552121

CONTACT   Graham Spencer
LOCATION   Between Yapton and Barnham, on B2233
OPEN   9 am – 5.30 pm, daily. Closed Wednesdays from November to February, and over Christmas
SPECIALITIES   Herbaceous perennials; *Iris*
CATALOGUE   £1
MAIL ORDER   Bearded *Iris* (sent August), beardless *Iris* and *Geranium* (both sent November) only
REFRESHMENTS   Picnic area available
GARDEN   Display garden and *Iris* fields
DESIGN SERVICE   Croftway Nursery
SHOWS   RHS Westminster; Chelsea; Hampton Court
GIFT TOKENS   Own

This family business specialises in bearded irises, of which they have a very large selection. But they also sell other types, and herbaceous perennials. The display fields are best seen in late May, early June.

Denmans Garden Plant Centre
Clock House, Denmans, Fontwell, Arundel, West Sussex BN18 0SU
☎ 01243 542808   FAX 01243 544064

CONTACT   Pamela Wilson
LOCATION   6 miles east of Chichester, just off westbound A27
OPEN   9 am – 5 pm, daily
CATALOGUE   £2.50
REFRESHMENTS   Café
GARDEN   Denmans, West Sussex, see Gardens section
DESIGN SERVICE   Denmans Ltd

Part of this 1940s garden which is now under designer John Brookes's care. The plant centre, which can be visited separately, sells a good choice of shrubs and other plants, many of them propagated from the garden.

Fleur de Lys
The Lodge, Upperton Farm, Petworth, West Sussex GU28 9BE
☎ 017983 43742   FAX 017983 43742

CONTACT   Lisa Rawley
OPEN   By appointment
SPECIALITIES   Conservatory plants
CATALOGUE   50p
MAIL ORDER   No
SHOWS   Chelsea; Hampton Court

Home visits are arranged to advise on and supply conservatory owners with interesting plants. Predators available for biological control as well.

The Geranium Nursery
Chapel Lane, West Wittering, West Sussex PO20 8QG
☎ 01860 586256

CONTACT   Mrs and Mrs F. W. Mepham
LOCATION   6 miles south of Chichester
OPEN   10 am – 5 pm, Good Friday to early June. Closed Mondays, except Bank Holidays
SPECIALITIES   Pelargoniums
CATALOGUE   2 first class stamps
MAIL ORDER   No
SHOWS   BBC GW Live; Hampton Court

The nursery specialises in dwarf, fancy-leaf and scented pelargoniums, but carries many other members of the genus, too.

Hellyer's Garden Plants
Orchards, Rowfant, Crawley, West Sussex RH10 4NJ
☎ 01342 718280

CONTACT   Penelope Hellyer
LOCATION   Map in catalogue
OPEN   10 am – 4 pm, Friday – Sunday, March to September; and by appointment
SPECIALITIES   Herbaceous perennials
CATALOGUE   2 first class stamps and SAE
MAIL ORDER   No
GARDEN   Garden opens for NGS

A selection of hardy and half-hardy perennials propagated from the garden made by the late Arthur and Grace Hellyer. The garden is now being restored. It opens for the NGS and can also be visited privately by appointment.

Hillier Garden Centre
Brighton Road, Horsham, West Sussex RH13 6QA
☎ 01403 210113   FAX 01403 275144

OPEN   9 am – 5.30 pm, Monday – Saturday (6 pm, April and May); 10.30 am – 4.30 pm, Sundays
SPECIALITIES   Climbers; conifers; trees
CATALOGUE   On request
MAIL ORDER   No
REFRESHMENTS   Coffee shop
DESIGN SERVICE   Hillier Garden Centre (Horsham)

GIFT TOKENS   HTA
See Hillier Nurseries Ltd, Hampshire.

Holly Gate Cactus Nursery
Billingshurst Road, Ashington, West Sussex
RH20 3BA
☎ 01903 892930

CONTACT   Mr T. M. Hewitt
OPEN   9 am – 5 pm, daily. Closed 25 and 26 December
SPECIALITIES   Cacti and succulents; seeds
CATALOGUE   4 second class stamps
MAIL ORDER   Yes
SHOP   Garden sundries
REFRESHMENTS   Refreshments
GARDEN   Cactus garden

One of the largest of the cacti and succulent specialists. The extensive retail and wholesale business includes all types of cacti, with over 50,000 specimens in stock. There is a cactus garden, and monthly special events are held in the spring and summer. They also issue an extensive seed list, and supplementary plant lists: £2 covers all mailings.

Houghton Farm Plants
Houghton Farm, Arundel, West Sussex BN18 9LW
☎ 01798 831100   FAX 01798 831183

CONTACT   R. Lock
LOCATION   In Houghton village, on B2139
OPEN   10 am – 5 pm, Monday – Friday; 2 – 5.30 pm, Sundays, March to October. Closed Saturdays
SPECIALITIES   Herbaceous perennials
CATALOGUE   3 first class stamps
MAIL ORDER   Yes
GARDEN   Display garden

An interesting mixed range of good hardy perennials with some shrubs and variegated plants too. They will be among the southern nurseries at the Parham Park Plant Fair.

Mary & Peter Mitchell
11 Wingle Tye Road, Burgess Hill, West Sussex
RH15 9HR
☎ 01444 236848

CONTACT   Peter Mitchell
OPEN   By appointment only
SPECIALITIES   Sempervivums
CATALOGUE   1 first class stamp
MAIL ORDER   Yes

Specialist growers of *Sempervivum*, *Jovibarba* and *Rosularia*.

Peter J Smith
Chanctonbury Nursery, Rectory Lane, Ashington, West Sussex RH20 3AS
OPEN   Mail order only
SPECIALITIES   *Alstroemeria*
NEW FOR 1995   2 miniature alstroemerias, 'Carmina', 'Marieta'
CATALOGUE   1 first class stamp

MAIL ORDER   Yes
SHOWS   RHS Westminster; Malvern Spring; Chelsea; Hampton Court
GIFT TOKENS   Own

Peter J. Smith is a hybridist of *Limonium* and *Alstroemeria*. He calls his hybrids Princess Lilies. They have a long flowering season, and last well as cut flowers.

Roundstone Garden Centre Ltd
Roundstone Bypass, Angmering, West Sussex
BN16 4BD
☎ 01903 776481   FAX 01903 785433

LOCATION   On A259 at Angmering
OPEN   8.30 am – 5.30 pm, summer and weekends; 9 am – 5 pm, winter
CATALOGUE   On request
SHOP   Garden sundries, buildings, machinery, gifts, aquatics
REFRESHMENTS   Coffee shop
GIFT TOKENS   HTA

Garden hypermarket with a large choice of plants, garden and more general products including foods. Delivery service.

Vesutor Airplants
The Bromeliad Nursery, Marringdean Road, Billingshurst, West Sussex RH14 9EH
☎ 01403 784028   FAX 01403 785373

CONTACT   Liam O'Rourke
OPEN   By appointment. 9 am – 3 pm, Monday – Friday
SPECIALITIES   Air plants; bromeliads
CATALOGUE   £1 handbook; SAE for list
MAIL ORDER   Yes

Specialist grower and retailer of bromeliads, with an outstanding range of *Tillandsia*. They also have orchids and some carnivorous plants ('microplants'). Their wholesale business supplies these plants to many garden centres.

W E Th Ingwersen Ltd
Birch Farm Nursery, Gravetye, East Grinstead, West Sussex RH19 4LE
☎ 01342 810236

CONTACT   Mr M. P. Ingwersen
LOCATION   Sussex, Surrey borders
OPEN   9 am – 1 pm, 1.30 – 4 pm, daily, March to September. Closed Saturdays and Sundays from October to February
SPECIALITIES   Alpines; conifers; seeds; bulbs
CATALOGUE   5 first class stamps
MAIL ORDER   Yes; spring and autumn despatch
GARDEN   Display garden
SHOWS   RHS Westminster; Malvern Spring; Harrogate (Spring); Southport; Chelsea; BBC GW Live; Hampton Court; Harrogate (Autumn)
GIFT TOKENS   HTA

Long-established alpine nursery with an excellent range of popular and less common rock garden plants, including dwarf shrubs and conifers. There is an annual plant sale in late September, and the nursery is worth a browse.

TYNE & WEAR

Birkheads Cottage Garden Nursery
Birkheads Lane, Sunniside, Newcastle upon Tyne, Tyne & Wear NE16 5EL
☎ 01207 232262   FAX 01207 232262
CONTACT   Christine Liddle
LOCATION   5 miles from A1(M) Birtley Services, via A692 or A693, and then A6076: ½ a mile south of Tanfield
OPEN   10 am – 5 pm, Saturdays and Sundays and Bank Holidays, March to mid October; other times by appointment
SPECIALITIES   Alpines; herbaceous perennials
NEW FOR 1995   Many new plants
MAIL ORDER   No
GARDEN   Display gardens: including topiary, pond, herbaceous borders and alpine rockeries
DESIGN SERVICE   Birkheads Cottage Garden Nursery

Small nursery with a varied and informed selection of cultivar and species alpines, perennials and shrubs. Worth a browsing visit. A professional design service is available, and plants can also be supplied from stock.

Peter Barratt's Garden Centres
Gosforth Park, Newcastle upon Tyne, Tyne & Wear NE3 5EN
☎ 0191 236 7111   FAX 0191 236 5496
CONTACT   Sheila Caisley
OPEN   9 am – 5.30 pm
SHOP   Garden sundries, aquatics
REFRESHMENTS   Refreshments
GARDEN   Demonstration gardens
GIFT TOKENS   HTA

Garden centre with a range of garden and leisure products. Delivery service.

WARWICKSHIRE

A D & N Wheeler
Pye Court, Willoughby, Rugby, Warwickshire CV23 8BZ
☎ 01788 890341
CONTACT   Tony Wheeler
LOCATION   Map in catalogue
OPEN   10 am – 4.30 pm, daily, January to June. Phone first at other times
SPECIALITIES   Fuchsias; pelargoniums
NEW FOR 1995   New pelargoniums and fuchsias
CATALOGUE   2 first class stamps
MAIL ORDER   Yes
SHOWS   Malvern Spring; Southport; BBC GW Live

Fuchsia and Pelargonium specialists, with a good range of both. They exhibit at many shows in the Midlands.

Diana Hull
Fog Cottages, 178 Lower Street, Hillmorton, Rugby, Warwickshire CV21 4NX
☎ 01788 536574
CONTACT   Diana Hull
OPEN   By appointment only
SPECIALITIES   Pelargonium (species)
CATALOGUE   SAE
MAIL ORDER   Yes

This small and very specialised nursery concentrates on species pelargoniums: the list gets more and more enticing. Some new hybrids may also be available.

Fibrex Nurseries Ltd
Honeybourne Road, Pebworth, Stratford upon Avon, Warwickshire CV37 8XT
☎ 01789 720788   FAX 01789 721162
CONTACT   Mr R. L. Godard-Key
OPEN   12 noon – 5 pm, Monday – Friday, January to March, September to November; 12 noon – 5 pm, Tuesday – Sunday, April to August
SPECIALITIES   Ferns; pelargoniums; ivies
CATALOGUE   2 first class stamps
MAIL ORDER   Yes
GARDEN   Display gardens
SHOWS   RHS Westminster; Harrogate (Spring); Southport; Chelsea; BBC GW Live; Hampton Court; Harrogate (Autumn)
NCCPG NATIONAL COLLECTIONS   Pelargonium

Specialists for pelargoniums. They hold the National Collection, but plants are for sale from April to August only. The Collection is open then too. Hardy ferns and Hedera are available all year round. There is a fern garden, and a new ivy garden is being planted.

The Hiller Garden and Plant Centre
Dunnington Heath Farm, Dunnington, Alcester, Warwickshire B49 5PD
☎ 01789 490991   FAX 01789 490439
CONTACT   David R. Carvill
LOCATION   On A441, 3 miles south of Alcester
OPEN   10 am – 5 pm, daily
SPECIALITIES   Herbaceous perennials; roses
NEW FOR 1995   Roses
CATALOGUE   2 first class stamps
MAIL ORDER   No
GARDEN   Demonstration garden

A range of old and new roses is joining the perennials available at the plant centre, to coincide with the opening of their rose garden.

John Beach (Nursery) Ltd
9 Grange Gardens, Wellesbourne, Warwickshire CV35 9RL
☎ 01789 840529
CONTACT   John Beach
LOCATION   Tanworth Lane, Henley in Arden, Warwickshire

WILTSHIRE Nurseries & Garden Centres

OPEN 10 am – 4 pm
SPECIALITIES Clematis; fruit; trees
CATALOGUE 6 second class stamps
MAIL ORDER Yes; minimum order 2 plants

Species, small and large-flowered *Clematis*, as well as fruit trees and bushes, and ornamental trees and shrubs. Some specimen sizes are available for impatient gardeners.

Kennedys Garden Centre
Kings Newnham Road, Church Lawford, Rugby, Warwickshire CV23 9EP
☎ 01203 542319   FAX 01203 545524
OPEN 9 am – 6 pm, Monday – Saturday; 10 am – 4 pm, Sundays
REFRESHMENTS Café
GIFT TOKENS HTA; own

Woodfield Bros
Wood End, Clifford Chambers, Stratford on Avon, Warwickshire CV37 8HR
☎ 01789 205618
CONTACT Brian Woodfield
OPEN 9.30 am – 4.30 pm, daily. Closed Sunday afternoons
SPECIALITIES Delphiniums; carnations (exhibition); lupins
CATALOGUE SAE
MAIL ORDER Yes: carnations only
SHOWS RHS Westminster; Chelsea; BBC GW Live

They specialise in perpetual flowering carnations, dahlias and lupins. *Phlox*, *Hosta* and *Begonia* cultivars are usually available also. Mail order is restricted to carnations.

WEST MIDLANDS

Ashwood Nurseries
Greensforge, Kingswinford, West Midlands DY6 0AE
☎ 01384 401996   FAX 01384 401108
CONTACT Mr P. D. Baulk
LOCATION 2 miles west of Kingswinford, near A449
OPEN 9 am – 6 pm, Monday – Saturday; 9.30 am – 6 pm, Sundays. Closed 25 and 26 December
SPECIALITIES *Lewisia*; *Cyclamen*; *Helleborus*; Seeds
CATALOGUE 4 first class stamps
MAIL ORDER Seeds only
SHOP Gift shop
REFRESHMENTS Tea room
GARDEN Display gardens
SHOWS RHS Westminster
GIFT TOKENS HTA
NCCPG NATIONAL COLLECTIONS *Lewisia*

This large nursery carries a wide general range as well as a particularly good selection of hardy cyclamen and hellebores. *Lewisia*, *Cyclamen* and *Helleborus* seeds on sale, as well as *Lewisia* from the National Collection.

H Woolman (Dorridge) Ltd
Grange Road, Dorridge, Solihull, West Midlands B93 8QB
☎ 01564 776283   FAX 01564 770830
LOCATION Near M42, J4 (map in catalogue)
OPEN 8 am – 4.15 pm, Monday – Friday
SPECIALITIES Chrysanthemums
NEW FOR 1995 Many new chrysanthemums, including 'Spartan Fire', 'Peter Fraser', 'Margaret Patricia' and 'Harold Lawson'
CATALOGUE On request; September
MAIL ORDER Yes
GARDEN Open weekend, 28 – 29 October
SHOWS Chelsea

Long-established specialist grower of garden and greenhouse chrysanthemum cultivars. Many new varieties this year: don't miss the annual open weekend, 28 – 29 October.

Notcutts Garden Centre
Stratford Road, Shirley, Solihull, West Midlands B90 4EN
☎ 0121 744 4501
LOCATION Near M42, J4, on Stratford Road
OPEN 9 am – 6 pm, Monday – Saturday; 11 am – 5 pm, Sundays. Closes at 8 pm, Thursdays and Fridays in spring and summer; 5.30 pm closing in winter
CATALOGUE £2.50
SHOP Garden sundries, buildings, furniture
REFRESHMENTS Licensed restaurant
GARDEN Arboretum and display areas
DESIGN SERVICE Notcutts Landscapes
GIFT TOKENS HTA; own

Over 2,000 varieties always in stock. Demonstrations, open evenings and talks are arranged. See also Notcutts Nurseries, Suffolk.

Oscroft's Dahlias
Woodside, Warwick Road, Chadwick End, Solihull, West Midlands B93 0BP
☎ 01564 782450
CONTACT Mrs Nash or Mr Oscroft
LOCATION On A4141, between Knowle and Chadwick End
OPEN 9 am – 6 pm, daily
SPECIALITIES Dahlias
CATALOGUE SAE
MAIL ORDER Yes
GIFT TOKENS Own

Specialists for dahlias. Their wide range is available both as tubers and mini plants. Cut flowers are for sale in season. They have made a series of videos on dahlias.

WILTSHIRE

Barters Farm Nurseries Ltd
Chapmanslade, Westbury, Wiltshire BA13 4AL
☎ 01373 832294   FAX 01373 832677

CONTACT   Duncan Travers
LOCATION   At the Westbury end of the village, on A3098
OPEN   9 am – 5 pm, Monday – Saturday; 10 am – 5 pm, Sundays and Bank Holidays
SPECIALITIES   Ferns; ground cover plants; hedging; trees; half-hardy plants
CATALOGUE   On request
MAIL ORDER   No
GARDEN   The Potter's Garden
DESIGN SERVICE   Barters Farm Nurseries Ltd
SHOWS   Malvern Spring; Hampton Court
GIFT TOKENS   HTA

A retail plant centre operates in conjunction with a wholesale nursery. The range runs from trees, conifers and shrubs (mostly container-grown) to half-hardy and ground cover plants. There are many ferns on offer. Open weekends are held in May, for container gardening, in September, when the nurseries are opened, and for National Tree Week at the end of November.

Botanic Nursery
Bath Road, Atworth, Melksham, Wiltshire SN12 8NU
☎ 01225 706597

CONTACT   Terence and Mary Baker
LOCATION   On A365 in Atworth, behind the clock tower
OPEN   10 am – 5 pm, daily. Closed for lunch 1 – 2 pm; also closed Tuesdays and all of January
SPECIALITIES   Herbaceous perennials; shrubs
CATALOGUE   £1
MAIL ORDER   No
GARDEN   Occasional displays
DESIGN SERVICE   The Botanic Nursery
SHOWS   RHS Westminster; Malvern Spring; Southport; Chelsea; BBC GW Live; Hampton Court; Courson
NCCPG NATIONAL COLLECTIONS   *Digitalis*

Specialists for lime-tolerant plants, including foxgloves, of which they have the National Collection. There is much else of interest here. No mail order, but you can arrange to collect from shows. The landscape company offers design and construction services for larger gardens in southern England.

Bowood Garden Centre
Bowood Estate, Calne, Wiltshire SN11 0LZ
☎ 01249 816828   FAX 01249 821757

CONTACT   Charlotte
LOCATION   Between Chippenham and Calne, on A4
OPEN   10 am – 6 pm, April to October; 10 am – 5 pm, November to March. Closed between Christmas and New Year
SPECIALITIES   Clematis; herbaceous perennials; rhododendrons; roses; shrubs
NEW FOR 1995   *Clematis* 'Arabella'
CATALOGUE   A4 SAE

MAIL ORDER   Yes
SHOP   Gifts and garden sundries
REFRESHMENTS   Snack bar, April to October
GARDEN   Bowood House, Wiltshire, see Gardens section
GIFT TOKENS   Own

Attached to the famous landscape gardens, the garden centre stocks a good range of containerised old-fashioned roses, rhododendrons, clematis, shrubs and perennials. Local delivery is available. They will help with design and quote for planting schemes.

Broadleas Gardens Charitable Trust Ltd
Broadleas, Devizes, Wiltshire SN10 5JQ
☎ 01380 722035

CONTACT   Lady Anne Cowdray
LOCATION   1½ miles south west of Devizes, on A360
OPEN   2 – 6 pm, Wednesday – Thursday, Sunday, April to October
SPECIALITIES   Salvias; *Euonymus*
MAIL ORDER   No
REFRESHMENTS   Home-made teas on summer Sundays
GARDEN   Broadleas, Wiltshire, see Gardens section
NCCPG NATIONAL COLLECTIONS   *Euonymus*

The nursery sells a varied selection of plants propagated from this plantswoman's garden. The emphasis is on salvias and shrubby *Euonymus* species and cultivars.

Corsley Mill, Brigid Quest-Ritson
Highfield House, Shrewton, Salisbury, Wiltshire SP3 4BU

LOCATION   4 miles from Stonehenge, 1 mile north of A303
OPEN   By appointment for collection
SPECIALITIES   Roses
NEW FOR 1995   Rose 'Himmelsauge', 'Maria Lisa'
CATALOGUE   2 first class stamps
MAIL ORDER   Yes; no minimum order
NCCPG NATIONAL COLLECTIONS   *Primula* (European species); *Pyrus* (species)

A small nursery which specialises in roses grown on their own roots: species, shrubs, old-fashioned and climbing.

Heather Bank Nursery
Woodlands, 1 High Street, Littleton Pannell, Devizes, Wiltshire SN10 4EL
☎ 01380 812739

CONTACT   D. and B. Mullan
LOCATION   5 miles south of Devizes
OPEN   9 am – dusk, Saturdays and Sundays, and by appointment
NEW FOR 1995   *Campanula* 'Chettle Charm'
CATALOGUE   2 first class stamps
MAIL ORDER   No
SHOWS   Hampton Court

This small nursery on the edge of Salisbury Plain appropriately grows a selection of lime-tolerant alpines, perennials, shrubs and heathers.

Kennedys Garden Centre
Hyde Road, Swindon, Wiltshire SN2 6SP
☎ 01793 822224   FAX 01793 832934
OPEN   9 am – 6 pm, Monday – Friday; 10 am – 4 pm, Sundays
REFRESHMENTS   Restaurant
GIFT TOKENS   HTA; own

Landford Trees
Landford Lodge, Landford, Salisbury, Wiltshire SP5 2EH
☎ 01794 390808   FAX 01794 390037
CONTACT   Mr C. D. Pilkington
LOCATION   10 miles south east of Salisbury
OPEN   8 am – 5 pm, Monday – Friday
SPECIALITIES   Hedging; trees
CATALOGUE   On request
MAIL ORDER   Yes; minimum order £15
GARDEN   Display plantings
SHOWS   Courson

An interesting range of ornamental, deciduous, field-grown trees – some 600 varieties. In addition many species are now available in containers, and they stock hedging and conifers too. On a different tack, they sell stone urns. Group visits by arrangement.

Longhall Nursery
Stockton, Warminster, Wiltshire BA12 0SE
☎ 01985 850914
CONTACT   Helen and James Dooley
LOCATION   7 miles south east of Warminster, off A36. Near Stockton church
OPEN   9.30 am – 6 pm, Wednesday – Sunday, 22 March to 1 October. Other times by appointment
NEW FOR 1995   *Dierama* and *Clematis* species, *Eryngium pandanifolium*, *Plectranthus argentatus*, *Salvia* 'Argentine Skies'
CATALOGUE   Large SAE
MAIL ORDER   Yes
REFRESHMENTS   Teas on open days
GARDEN   Longhall Gardens

Next door to Longhall Gardens. There's a good choice of lime-tolerant plants, many propagated from the garden. The nursery and garden open day is 17 April. The nursery will be at the London Rare Plant Fairs this year.

The Mead Nursery
Brokerswood, Westbury, Wiltshire BA13 4EG
☎ 01373 859990
CONTACT   Emma Lewis-Dale
LOCATION   Near Rudge, off A36 or A361
OPEN   9 am – 5 pm, Wednesday – Saturday, and Bank Holiday Mondays; 12 noon – 6 pm, Sundays, 1 February to 29 October
SPECIALITIES   Alpines; herbaceous perennials
CATALOGUE   4 first class stamps
MAIL ORDER   No
GARDEN   Display gardens
GIFT TOKENS   Own

A mixed range of alpines and herbaceous perennials, including varieties suitable for trough and tufa plantings. Ready-planted troughs and tufa are also on sale.

Natural Selection
1 Station Cottages, Hullavington, Chippenham, Wiltshire SN14 6ET
☎ 01666 837369
CONTACT   Martin Cragg-Barber
LOCATION   Off A429, south of Malmesbury
OPEN   By appointment
NEW FOR 1995   *Lavatera* 'Chedglow'
CATALOGUE   2 first class stamps
MAIL ORDER   Yes

The nursery seeks out rare British native plants and strange forms of commoner ones. Some species and scented-leaf pelargoniums too.

Sherston Parva Nursery
Malmesbury Road, Sherston, Wiltshire SN16 0LL
☎ 01666 840623
CONTACT   Mrs Margaret Morris
LOCATION   On B4040, west of Malmesbury
OPEN   10 am – 1 pm, 2 – 5 pm, Tuesday – Saturday; 12 noon – 5 pm, Sundays; Easter to 31 October
SPECIALITIES   Clematis; climbers
NEW FOR 1995   *Clematis* 'Sunset', 'Masquerade', 'Ruby Glow'
CATALOGUE   3 first class stamps
MAIL ORDER   Yes
SHOWS   RHS Westminster; Malvern Spring; Hampton Court

There are around 100 clematis at the nursery, besides climbers and shrubs suitable for wall and courtyard planting. The mail order list is shorter.

Special Plants
Laurels Farm, Upper Wraxall, Chippenham, Wiltshire SN14 7AG
☎ 01225 891686
CONTACT   Ms Derry Watkins
LOCATION   Near Bath
OPEN   Most days: phone first
SPECIALITIES   Conservatory plants
CATALOGUE   3 second class stamps
MAIL ORDER   Yes; October to February
SHOWS   RHS Westminster; Harrogate (Spring); BBC GW Live; Hampton Court

Special Plants concentrates on tender perennials, including *Felicia*, *Osteospermum* and *Scaevola*, and on conservatory climbers and small shrubs. One-day courses are held at the nursery, and Ms Watkins organises specialist plant sales, including the Rare Plant Fairs in London and the West.

West Kington Nurseries Ltd
West Kington, Chippenham, Wiltshire SN14 7JG
☎ 01249 782822   FAX 01249 782953
CONTACT   Mrs Barbara Ellis

LOCATION Off A420, 8 miles west of Chippenham
OPEN 10 am – 5 pm, Tuesday – Sunday
SPECIALITIES Alpines; herbaceous perennials; roses
CATALOGUE On request (wholesale)
REFRESHMENTS Teas for groups
GARDEN Pound Hill House Garden, Wiltshire, see Gardens section
DESIGN SERVICE West Kington Nurseries Ltd
SHOWS Malvern Spring; Hampton Court
GIFT TOKENS HTA

Wholesale nursery which deals in alpine and herb-aceous plants. The attached retail plant centre also has a selection of old-fashioned and English roses, and topiary plants. They offer garden design and run courses.

Westdale Nurseries

3 Westdale Nurseries, Holt Road, Bradford on Avon, Wiltshire BA15 1TS
☎ 01225 863258   FAX 01225 863258

CONTACT C. W. or P. A. Clarke
OPEN 9 am – 5.30 pm, daily. Closed Christmas Day
SPECIALITIES *Bougainvillea*
NEW FOR 1995 New *Bougainvillea* varieties
CATALOGUE £1; *Bougainvillea* leaflet 20p
MAIL ORDER Conservatory plants
SHOWS Southport; Hampton Court

A West Country source of *Bougainvillea* in numerous varieties. The nursery also stocks pelargoniums, fuch-sias and conservatory plants, and, starting this year, herbs.

Whitehall Garden Centre Ltd

Lacock, Chippenham, Wiltshire SN15 2LZ
☎ 01249 730204   FAX 01249 730755
LOCATION Between Chippenham and Melksham on A350
OPEN 9 am – 6 pm, Monday – Saturday (5.30 pm in winter); 10.30 am – 4.30 pm, Sundays
SHOP Garden sundries, conservatories, pools, gifts
REFRESHMENTS Restaurant
GARDEN 5-acre gardens
DESIGN SERVICE Whitehall Garden Centre
GIFT TOKENS HTA; own

Large family-run garden centre with plants and garden products. Extensive landscaped gardens, and a land-scaping service in association with a local landscaping firm.

Woodborough Garden Centre

Nursery Farm, Woodborough, Pewsey, Wiltshire SN9 5PF
☎ 01672 851249

CONTACT Mrs Els Brewin
LOCATION 3 miles west of Pewsey
OPEN 9 am – 5 pm
SPECIALITIES Clematis
MAIL ORDER No
REFRESHMENTS Coffee shop planned for 1995

GARDEN Demonstration gardens
GIFT TOKENS HTA

A garden centre on a large daffodil farm, and old flower nursery – Daffodil 'Fortune' was bred here. The garden centre specialises in clematis and spring bulbs. Pick your own fruit, vegetables and flowers. A varied programme of demonstrations is planned.

NORTH YORKSHIRE

Battersby Roses

Peartree Cottage, Old Battersby, Great Ayton, Cleveland, North Yorkshire TS9 6LU
☎ 01642 723402

CONTACT Eric Stainthorpe
LOCATION Between Kildale and Ingleby Greenhow, on the edge of the North Yorkshire moors
OPEN During flowering and planting season
SPECIALITIES Roses
CATALOGUE SAE
MAIL ORDER Yes
SHOWS Harrogate (Autumn)

A family-run specialist growing only roses. They are mainly modern types, with a particular emphasis on exhibition roses. Other interests include roses with a northern connection.

Cruck Cottage Cacti

Cruck Cottage, Cliff Road, Wrelton, Pickering, North Yorkshire YO18 8PJ
☎ 01751 472042

CONTACT Ronald and Dorothy Wood
LOCATION On A170, 3 miles west of Pickering
OPEN 9 am – 12 noon, 1 – 6 pm
SPECIALITIES Cacti and succulents
NEW FOR 1995 New stock arrives twice a year
MAIL ORDER No
GARDEN Gardens of ½ an acre surround the nursery

The nursery sells both large and small specimens of cacti and succulents, and has special collections for begin-ners. Advice is on hand from the owners, and the nursery is accessible for disabled visitors.

Daleside Nurseries

Ripon Road, Killinghall, Harrogate, North Yorkshire HG3 2AY
☎ 01423 506450   FAX 01423 527872
LOCATION 4 miles north of Harrogate (A61)
OPEN 9 am – 5 pm, Monday – Saturday; 10 am – 12 noon, 1.30 – 4.30 pm, Sundays
NEW FOR 1995 Several *Clematis* varieties
CATALOGUE Lists available
MAIL ORDER No
GIFT TOKENS HTA

A general plant range, including clematis, conifers and shrubs. They are happy to provide free advice on garden planning.

NORTH YORKSHIRE Nurseries & Garden Centres

Deanswood Plants
Deanswood, Potteries Lane, Littlethorpe, Ripon, North Yorkshire HG4 3LF
☎ 01765 603441

CONTACT Jacky Barber
OPEN 10 am – 5 pm, April to September. Closed Mondays
SPECIALITIES Bog plants; flower arranging plants
CATALOGUE £1.30; list only, 40p
MAIL ORDER No
GARDEN 2-acre garden opens for NGS and Northern Horticultural Society

A nursery in a streamside garden, specialising in moisture-loving plants. Open in the summer only, from April to September. The garden is open for nursery visitors (donation to NGS), and for groups by appointment. Also a flower-arranging service with trained florists.

Gardenscape
Fairview, Smelthouses, Summerbridge, Harrogate, North Yorkshire HG3 4DH
☎ 01423 780291/01142 678405 FAX 01142 678405

CONTACT Michael D. Myers
LOCATION 12 miles north of Harrogate
OPEN By appointment only, and on open days
SPECIALITIES Bulbs; primulas
NEW FOR 1995 New primulas and hepaticas from Germany
CATALOGUE 3 second class stamps
MAIL ORDER Yes
GARDEN Garden opens under NGS and by appointment
NCCPG NATIONAL COLLECTIONS *Anemone nemorosa, Hepatica, Primula marginata*

This specialist nursery is based around the three National Collections held: *Anemone nemorosa, Primula marginata* and *Hepatica*. Other specialities include *Galanthus* and dwarf bulbs. They also sell hand made stone troughs and ornaments. Open days include 26 February, 12 March, 9 April, 7 May, and 14 May: see Yellow Book and National Plant Collections Directory for more details.

Herb and Heather Garden Centre
Main Road, West Haddesley, Selby, North Yorkshire YO8 8QA
☎ 01757 228279

CONTACT Carole Atkinson
LOCATION 6 miles south of Selby, off A19
OPEN 9.30 am – 5.30 pm, daily. In winter, closed at dusk
SPECIALITIES Heathers; herbs
NEW FOR 1995 Sempervivums
CATALOGUE 3 first class stamps
MAIL ORDER Yes
SHOP Gifts, dried flowers
REFRESHMENTS Tea room
GARDEN Display garden
DESIGN SERVICE Herb and Heather Garden Centre
SHOWS Harrogate (Spring); Harrogate (Autumn)
GIFT TOKENS HTA
NCCPG NATIONAL COLLECTIONS *Santolina*

The main specialities are herbs and heathers, with lots to choose from, but conifers, evergreen shrubs and cottage garden plants are stocked too. The display gardens cover several acres; a new water garden opens this year.

Kettlesing Nurseries
The Old Post Office, Kettlesing, Harrogate, North Yorkshire HG3 2LB
☎ 01423 770831

CONTACT Andrew and Angela Durance
LOCATION Off A59, 6 miles west of Harrogate
OPEN 9 am – 5 pm, Thursday – Monday, March to October
SPECIALITIES Alpines
NEW FOR 1995 *Paraquilegia, Primula deorum, Trillium hibbersonii*
CATALOGUE On request
SHOWS Harrogate (Spring); Harrogate (Autumn)

An alpine and rock plant nursery, with lots of gentians, lewisias and primulas. Their most interesting plants are not always included in the list.

Norden Alpine Nursery
Hirst Road, Carlton, Selby, North Yorkshire DN14 9PX
☎ 01405 861348

CONTACT Mrs N. Walton
OPEN Weekends and Bank Holidays, March – September
SPECIALITIES Alpines; primulas
CATALOGUE 4 second class stamps
MAIL ORDER Yes
REFRESHMENTS B & B
GARDEN Garden

A large range of alpines, including *Campanula, Oxalis, Primula* and *Saxifraga*, propagated from a stock of some 2,000 plants. Bed and Breakfast is available at the nursery.

Oak Tree Nursery
Mill Lane, Barlow, Selby, North Yorkshire YO8 8EY
☎ 01757 618409

CONTACT C. G. and G. M. Plowes
LOCATION 14 miles south of York
OPEN 10 am – 4.30 pm, Tuesday – Sunday. Closed Mondays
SPECIALITIES Herbaceous perennials
CATALOGUE 2 first class stamps
MAIL ORDER No
DESIGN SERVICE Oak Tree Nursery

A range of cottage-garden type plants, mainly herbaceous perennials. Full garden design and construction service. The nursery will be at the Great Yorkshire Show.

Orchard House Nursery
Orchard House, Wormald Green, Harrogate, North Yorkshire HG3 3PX

☎ 01765 677541   FAX 01765 677541

CONTACT   Mr Brian Corner
LOCATION   4 miles south of Ripon on A61
OPEN   8.30 am – 5 pm, Monday – Saturday; 2 – 5 pm, Sundays
SPECIALITIES   Herbaceous perennials
CATALOGUE   4 first class stamps
MAIL ORDER   No
DESIGN SERVICE   Orchard House Nursery
SHOWS   Harrogate (Spring); Harrogate (Autumn)

A fairly new nursery with a mixed range of hardy perennials and cottage-garden type plants. A display garden is being planted.

Perry's Plants
River Garden, Sleights, Whitby, North Yorkshire YO21 1RR

☎ 01947 810329

CONTACT   Mrs Patricia Perry or Richard Perry
LOCATION   2 miles south west of Whitby, on B1410 (near A169)
OPEN   10 am – 5 pm, daily, Easter to end of October
SPECIALITIES   Herbaceous perennials
NEW FOR 1995   *Erysimum* 'Perry's Pumpkin', *E.* 'Perry's Peculiar', *Malva* 'Perry's Blue'
CATALOGUE   SAE
MAIL ORDER   No
REFRESHMENTS   Licensed café
GARDEN   Riverside gardens

Herbaceous plants, including their own new cultivars and others which originated here (including *Osteospermum* 'Stardust'). Boats, putting and croquet in the old Victorian gardens.

R V Roger Ltd
The Nurseries, Pickering, North Yorkshire YO18 7HG

☎ 01751 72226   FAX 01751 76749

CONTACT   Ian Roger
LOCATION   1 mile south of Pickering, on A169 (The Roger Plant Centre)
OPEN   9 am – 5 pm, Monday – Saturday; 1 – 5 pm, Sundays
SPECIALITIES   Fruit
CATALOGUE   £1
MAIL ORDER   Yes
SHOWS   Harrogate (Spring); Southport; Chelsea; BBC GW Live; Hampton Court; Harrogate (Autumn); Ayr
GIFT TOKENS   HTA
NCCPG NATIONAL COLLECTIONS   *Erodium*

The nurseries have a good all-round range including alpines, bulbs, conifers, perennials, roses, and trees and shrubs. They are especially good on fruit trees and bushes, including apples and gooseberries. They celebrate Apple Day (21 October), and attend numerous shows, including Holker Hall, Knebworth, Gateshead and Rochester.

Rarer Plants
Ashfield House, Austfield Lane, Monk Fryston, Leeds, North Yorkshire LS25 5EH

☎ 01977 682263

CONTACT   Anne Watson and Mandy Nicholls
LOCATION   2½ miles from A1, A63 intersection
OPEN   11 am – 3.30 pm, Mondays, Fridays; 11 am – 5 pm, Saturdays and Sundays, Easter to 13 September. Also, 10 am – 4 pm, Sundays, 1 February to Easter, for hellebores only
SPECIALITIES   Herbaceous perennials, *Helleborus*
CATALOGUE   SAE
MAIL ORDER   No

A small nursery with an agreeably mixed stock which includes *Penstemon* hybrids and Ballard strain *Helleborus* hybrids. The nursery is specially open on Sundays from February to Easter for hellebores.

Rivendell Nursery
Menagerie Farm, Skipwith Road, Escrick, York, North Yorkshire YO4 6EH

☎ 01904 728690

CONTACT   Dave Fryer and Gareth Hughes
LOCATION   6 miles south of York: phone for directions
OPEN   10 am – 5 pm, Sundays. Other times by appointment
SPECIALITIES   Conifers; shrubs; organic nursery
CATALOGUE   2 second class stamps
MAIL ORDER   No
GARDEN   Organic vegetable plot
DESIGN SERVICE   Rivendell Nursery

A small wholesale nursery which opens for retail customers on Sundays. The range includes alpines, conifers, heathers and shrubs. The nursery is run organically, and takes part in the HDRA garden opening days.

Stillingfleet Lodge Nurseries
Stillingfleet, North Yorkshire YO4 6HW

☎ 01904 728506   FAX 01904 728506

CONTACT   Vanessa Cook
LOCATION   7 miles south of York: turn opposite the church
OPEN   10 am – 4 pm, Tuesday – Wednesday, Friday – Saturday, 1 April to 18 October
SPECIALITIES   Clematis; grasses; herbaceous perennials
CATALOGUE   5 first class stamps
MAIL ORDER   Yes; winter only
GARDEN   Garden opens for NGS, Wenesday afternoons, May and June
NCCPG NATIONAL COLLECTIONS   *Pulmonaria*

Small nursery with an interesting and extensive range of hardy perennials: good on grey foliage and pulmonarias. Also strong on small-flowered clematis. The *Pulmonaria* collection is open 1.30 – 5 pm, 23 April.

Wyevale Garden Centre
Boroughbridge Road, Poppleton, York, North Yorkshire YO2 6QE
☎ 01904 795920   ℻ 01904 794987

Whitestone Gardens Ltd
Sutton under Whitestone Cliffe, Thirsk, North Yorkshire YO7 2PZ
☎ 01845 597467   ℻ 01845 597467

CONTACT   Roy Mottram
LOCATION   4 miles east of Thirsk on A170
OPEN   Dawn – dusk, daily. Closed Fridays
SPECIALITIES   Cacti and succulents
CATALOGUE   4 second class stamps
MAIL ORDER   Yes
SHOP   Books, sundries
NCCPG NATIONAL COLLECTIONS   Cactus (Borzicactinae)

A lengthy list of cacti and succulents is available at this specialist nursery, which holds the Nactional Collection of the Borzicactinae section of the Cactaceae. They also sell relevant books and sundries.

Woodlands Cottage Nursery
Woodlands Cottage, Summerbridge, Harrogate, North Yorkshire HG3 4BT
☎ 01423 780765

CONTACT   Mrs A. Stark
LOCATION   On B6165, between Harrogate and Pateley Bridge
OPEN   10.30 am – 6 pm, Friday – Monday, 1 April to 30 September, or by appointment
SPECIALITIES   Herbaceous perennials; herbs
CATALOGUE   3 first class stamps
MAIL ORDER   No
GARDEN   Garden open on request
DESIGN SERVICE   Ann Stark

This small nursery specialises in herbs and cottage garden perennials, particularly shade lovers. There is a full design service.

SOUTH YORKSHIRE

Brambling House Alpines
119 Sheffield Road, Warmsworth, Doncaster, South Yorkshire DN4 9QX
☎ 01302 850730

CONTACT   Jane McDonagh
LOCATION   West of Doncaster on A630; near A1M Rotherham exit
OPEN   10 am – 6 pm, spring and autumn. Closed Mondays except Bank Holidays. Phone first in summer
SPECIALITIES   Alpines; sempervivums; *Diascia*
NEW FOR 1995   New *Diascia* – as yet unnamed
CATALOGUE   SAE
MAIL ORDER   Yes; spring and autumn

GARDEN   Garden
A small nursery concentrating on alpines. Look out for their saxifrages and a wide range of *Sempervivum* species and cultivars, as well as auriculas, and *Diascia* from the National Collection. They visit a number of local shows, including Gateshead Spring and the Great Yorkshire.

Ferndale Nursery and Garden Centre Ltd
Dyche Lane, Coal Aston, Sheffield, South Yorkshire S18 6AB
☎ 01246 412763

CONTACT   Kevin Daniels
LOCATION   On Sheffield's southern boundary, off the A61
OPEN   9 am – 5.30 pm (6 pm, March to September), daily
SHOP   Florist, conservatories, greenhouses and garden buildings
REFRESHMENTS   Coffee shop
DESIGN SERVICE   Ferndale Nursery and Garden Centre Ltd
GIFT TOKENS   HTA

A garden centre with a wide general range: stockists of both Hillier's and Blooms' plants. They have a garden design service, and can advise on plant ailments too. Talks, demonstrations and classes are also held, especially in spring and autumn.

Oscroft's Dahlias
Sprotbrough Road, Doncaster DN5 8BE
☎ 01302 785026

LOCATION   North of Doncaster town centre
OPEN   9 am – 6 pm, daily
SPECIALITIES   Dahlias
CATALOGUE   SAE
MAIL ORDER   Yes
GIFT TOKENS   Own

See their main entry under West Midlands.

Scott's Nurseries
Denaby Lane, Old Denaby, Doncaster DN12 4LD
☎ 01709 589906

CONTACT   Mr M. Scott
LOCATION   Off A6023, west of Doncaster
OPEN   9 am – 6 pm, daily
SPECIALITIES   Dahlias
NEW FOR 1995   New dahlias
CATALOGUE   SAE
MAIL ORDER   Yes

Dahlia specialist: many new varieties are due this year.

WEST YORKSHIRE

Armitage's Garden Centre
Pennine Garden Centre, Huddersfield Road, Shelley, Huddersfield, West Yorkshire HD8 8LG
☎ 01484 607248   ℻ 01484 608673

CONTACT   A. Harper
LOCATION   Between Shelley and Skelmanthorpe on the B6116
OPEN   9 am – 5.30 pm, daily. Closes at 8 pm in the summer
SHOP   Garden sundries; cut flowers
REFRESHMENTS   Café
GIFT TOKENS   HTA

Long-established garden centre, stocking trees and shrubs, alpines, house plants, aquatics, greenhouses and garden machinery. Their specialist garden machinery outlet, Mower World, is at the garden centre in Birchencliffe (off the A629).

Greenslacks Nurseries
Ocot Lane, Scammonden, Huddersfield, West Yorkshire HD3 3FR
☎ 01484 842584

CONTACT   Mrs V. K. Tuton
LOCATION   Off A640: see catalogue for map
OPEN   10 am – 4 pm, March to October. Closed Mondays and Tuesdays
SPECIALITIES   Alpines; primulas; sempervivums
NEW FOR 1995   New plants from the Andes, Himalaya, Taiwan and South Africa
CATALOGUE   £1
MAIL ORDER   Yes
GARDEN   Display garden
DESIGN SERVICE   Greenslacks Nurseries

An impressive and interesting list of alpines and hardy succulents. Strengths include Kabschia saxifrages (now porophyllum section) and sempervivums. Their ready-made collections are good value.

Hedgerow Nursery
24 Braithwaite Edge Road, Keighley, West Yorkshire BD22 6RA
☎ 01535 606531

CONTACT   Mr Nigel Hutchinson
OPEN   9 am – 5 pm, Wednesday – Sunday, March to October. Closed Mondays and Tuesdays except Bank Holidays
SPECIALITIES   Alpines; conifers; shrubs
CATALOGUE   3 first class stamps
MAIL ORDER   Yes
NCCPG   NATIONAL COLLECTIONS   *Hebe* (dwarf)

An alpine specialist, including dwarf conifers, rhododendrons and especially *Hebe*.

Mansell & Hatcher Ltd
Cragg Wood Nurseries, Woodlands Drive, Rawdon, Leeds, West Yorkshire LS19 6LQ
☎ 0113 2502016

CONTACT   Allan Long
LOCATION   Leave A658 at Apperley Bridge: follow signs to Woodlands Hospital
OPEN   9 am – 5 pm, Monday – Friday. Closed Bank Holidays. Open some weekends: phone for details
SPECIALITIES   Orchids

CATALOGUE   On request
MAIL ORDER   Yes
SHOWS   RHS Westminster; Malvern Spring; Southport

Long-established orchid growers and hybridisers, with a large range of many genera, species and cultivars, including *Odontoglossum* and *Masdevallia*. They will be at the RHS Westminster Orchid Show on 11 – 12 March.

Newton Hill Alpines
335 Leeds Road, Newton Hill, Wakefield, West Yorkshire WF1 2JH
☎ 01924 377056

CONTACT   Mrs Sheena Vigors
LOCATION   3 miles east of M1, J41
OPEN   9 am – 5 pm, daily. Closed Thursdays
SPECIALITIES   Alpines
NEW FOR 1995   Many new items: small quantities only
CATALOGUE   50p by post
MAIL ORDER   No
GARDEN   Garden opens, as nursery

This mainly wholesale alpine nursery welcomes retail customers too. They are good for saxifrages especially, and also have dwarf conifers and heathers. Shows include Honley, Horbury, Otley and Peniston.

Slack Top Alpines
Hebden Bridge, West Yorkshire HX7 7HA
☎ 01422 845348

CONTACT   Michael and Ron Mitchell
LOCATION   ¾ mile from Heptonstall, between Heptonstall and Hebden Bridge
OPEN   10 am – 6 pm, Wednesday – Sunday and Bank Holidays, 1 March to 31 October; closed Mondays and Tuesdays
SPECIALITIES   Alpines; primulas
CATALOGUE   SAE
MAIL ORDER   No
GARDEN   Display garden

This family nursery set high in the Pennines produces alpine and rock garden plants. There are troughs for sale, and a large show garden.

Springwood Pleiones
35 Heathfield, Adel, Leeds, West Yorkshire LS16 7AB
☎ 0113 2611781

CONTACT   Mr K. Redshaw
OPEN   By appointment
SPECIALITIES   *Pleione*
CATALOGUE   SAE
MAIL ORDER   Yes
SHOWS   Harrogate (Spring); Chelsea

There is a selection of *Pleione* species and varieties; smaller-size bargain lots and bulbils also available.

Stephen H Smith's Garden & Leisure
Aire Valley, Wilsden Road, Harden, Bingley, West Yorkshire BD16 1BL
☎ 01535 274653   FAX 01535 271912
CONTACT   Richard Coggill
LOCATION   Take Wilsden road from B6429 in Harden: the nursery is on the right after 1 mile
OPEN   9 am – 6 pm, summer; 9 am – 5.30 pm, winter; 11 am – 5 pm, Sundays
SHOP   Garden sundries, furniture, aquatics, gifts
REFRESHMENTS   Coffee shop
GIFT TOKENS   HTA; own

Garden centre with plants and garden products: Hillier stockists. The range of indoor plants has been extended. Delivery service.

Stephen H Smith's Garden & Leisure
Wharfe Valley, Pool Road, Otley, West Yorkshire LS21 1DY
☎ 01943 462195   FAX 01943 850074
CONTACT   Peter Scott
LOCATION   1 mile east of Otley on A659
OPEN   9 am – 6 pm, summer; 9 am – 5.30 pm, winter; 11 am – 5 pm, Sundays
SHOP   Garden sundries, furniture, aquatics, gifts
REFRESHMENTS   Coffee shop
GIFT TOKENS   HTA; own

Garden centre with indoor and outdoor plants and garden products: agents for both Hillier and Blooms. Delivery service.

Zephyrwude Irises
48 Blacker Lane, Crigglestone, Wakefield, West Yorkshire WF4 3EW
☎ 01924 252101
CONTACT   Richard L. Brook
LOCATION   1 mile south west of M1, J39, off A636
OPEN   Viewing and ordering: 9 am – dusk, daily, May and June; for collection: by appointment in August and September
SPECIALITIES   *Iris*
CATALOGUE   1 first class stamp (between April and September)
MAIL ORDER   Yes
GARDEN   Display garden open 9 am – dusk, daily, May and June

Specialist growers and importers of modern bearded irises. The range concentrates on miniature and standard dwarf, intermediate, and miniature tall types. There is a selection of border and tall bearded irises too. The list appears in April, for collection or despatch in August and September. The trial fields are open in May and June, 9 am till dusk, but check first.

WALES

CLWYD

Aberconwy Nursery
Graig, Glan Conwy, Colwyn Bay, Clwyd LL28 5TL
☎ 01492 580875

CONTACT   K. G. or R. Lever
LOCATION   South of Glan Conwy, 2nd right off A470. Turn right at top of hill: nursery is on the right
OPEN   9 am – 5 pm, Tuesday – Sunday. Closed Mondays, except Bank Holidays
SPECIALITIES   Alpines
NEW FOR 1995   *Gentiana* 'Shot Silk', *G.* 'Amethyst', *G.* 'Indigo', *G.* 'Serenity', *Paraquilegia anemonoides*
CATALOGUE   2 second class stamps
MAIL ORDER   No
GARDEN   Their own garden, Bryn Meifod, opens for the National Gardens Scheme, by appointment

Mainly alpines, including some interesting primroses, but there are also trees, shrubs and herbaceous plants. They exhibit at the following Alpine Garden Society Shows: Morecambe, Summer South (Merrist Wood), Summer North (Pudsey), Wirral.

Bodnant Garden Nursery Ltd
Tal-y-Cafn, Colwyn Bay, Clwyd LL29 6DG
☎ 01492 650460   FAX 01492 650448

CONTACT   Mrs A. Harvey
LOCATION   Next to Bodnant Gardens, near A55
OPEN   9.30 am – 5 pm, daily
SPECIALITIES   Camellias; rhododendrons; magnolias
CATALOGUE   3 first class stamps
MAIL ORDER   Yes; £10 minimum order
REFRESHMENTS   Yes
GARDEN   Bodnant Gardens, Clwyd, see Gardens section
GIFT TOKENS   Own

The nursery specialises in those plants for which the garden is renowned – rhododendrons, azaleas, magnolias and camellias. There is much else of interest in the wide choice of trees and shrubs here.

C & K Jones
Halghton Nursery, Whitchurch Road, Halghton, Bangor on Dee, Clwyd SY14 7LX
☎ 0194874 685

CONTACT   Paula Woolley
LOCATION   Between Whitchurch and Bangor on Dee, on A525
OPEN   8 am – 5 pm, daily, March – September; 9 am – 4 pm, Friday – Monday, October to February
SPECIALITIES   Roses
CATALOGUE   £1
MAIL ORDER   Yes

C & K Jones's new plant centre. The rose crop is produced here. There are shrubs and conifers on sale too. See C & K Jones, Cheshire for more details.

Celyn Vale Nurseries
Allt-y-Celyn, Carrog, Corwen, Clwyd LL21 9LD
☎ 01490 83671   FAX 01490 83671
CONTACT   Andrew McConnell
LOCATION   3 miles east of Corwen, near A5
OPEN   9 am – 5.30 pm, Monday – Friday
SPECIALITIES   Trees; *Eucalyptus*; Acacias
CATALOGUE   1 first class stamp
MAIL ORDER   Yes; minimum order 3 plants; p & p is included
GARDEN   Extensive *Eucalyptus* plantings

Specialist growers of *Eucalyptus* and acacias: they use seed from high-altitude specimens to maximise hardiness. Retail and wholesale.

Dibleys
Efenechtyd Nurseries, Llanelidan, Ruthin, Clwyd LL15 2LG
☎ 01978 790677
LOCATION   Directions in catalogue
OPEN   9 am – 5 pm, daily, April to September
SPECIALITIES   Begonias; house plants; gesneriads; *Streptocarpus*
CATALOGUE   SAE
MAIL ORDER   Yes
SHOWS   RHS Westminster; Malvern Spring; Harrogate (Spring); Southport; Chelsea; BBC GW Live; Hampton Court; Harrogate (Autumn); Ayr

Varieties and species of *Streptocarpus* are the main speciality here, but the choice extends to other gesneriads, *Coleus* and foliage begonias. Active on the show circuit: they attend more than 50 each year, including Holker Hall, the Bath & West and the Royal Welsh.

Paul Christian Rare Plants
P O Box 468, Wrexham, Clwyd LL13 9XR
☎ 01978 366399   FAX 01978 366399
CONTACT   Dr P. J. Christian
OPEN   Mail order only
SPECIALITIES   Bulbs
CATALOGUE   3 first class stamps; May, December
MAIL ORDER   Yes

Bulb, corm and tuber specialist. An exciting range of rare and enticing small, hardy bulbs and greenhouse subjects. The list changes annually according to the availability of new and rediscovered items. An illustrated book going into more detail than the catalogues is newly published.

DYFED

Cilwern Plants
Cilwern, Talley, Llandeilo, Dyfed SA19 7YH
☎ 01558 685526

CONTACT   Anne Knatchbull-Hugessen
LOCATION   6 miles north of Llandeilo on B4302, before Talley village
OPEN   11 am – 6 pm, daily. Closed Fridays
SPECIALITIES   Herbaceous perennials
CATALOGUE   2 first class stamps
MAIL ORDER   Yes; minimum order £10
GARDEN   2-acre garden being created from scrubland

The nursery sells a range of hardy perennials, including geraniums. There are also shrubs and conifers. A demonstration garden is being formed from the surrounding scrub and swamp.

Exotic Fuchsias
Pen-y-Banc Nursery, Crwbin, Pontyberem, Kidwelly, Dyfed SA17 5DP
☎ 01269 870729

CONTACT   Terry or Susie Evans
LOCATION   Map in catalogue
OPEN   10 am – 5 pm, daily, 1 March to 1 September; and by appointment
SPECIALITIES   Fuchsias
CATALOGUE   On request
MAIL ORDER   Yes
SHOWS   Malvern Spring

Specialists for fuchsias, growing around 600 varieties.

John Shipton (Bulbs)
Y Felin, Henllan Amgoed, Whitland, Dyfed SA34 0SL
☎ 01994 240125

CONTACT   John Shipton
OPEN   By appointment
SPECIALITIES   Bulbs
CATALOGUE   SAE
MAIL ORDER   Yes

This wholesale and retail bulb nursery specialises in British native bulbs, which they guarantee are not taken from wild sources. There are also older daffodil cultivars and perennials for naturalising.

Manorbier Garden Centre
Station Road, Manorbier, Tenby, Dyfed SA70 7SN
☎ 01834 871206   FAX 01834 871678
CONTACT   Mr Roger Thompson
OPEN   9.30 am – 5.30 pm, daily. Closed Christmas and Boxing Day
SPECIALITIES   Shrubs
NEW FOR 1995   New perennials
MAIL ORDER   No
REFRESHMENTS   Restaurant
DESIGN SERVICE   Manorbier Garden Centre
GIFT TOKENS   HTA; own

A garden centre and nurseries with a general range. Maritime plants and new shrub varieties are their speciality. There is a local delivery service.

St Ishmaels Nurseries and Garden Centre
St Ishmaels, Haverfordwest, Dyfed SA62 3SX
☎ 01646 636343 FAX 01646 636343

CONTACT Mr and Mrs D. Phippen
LOCATION Between Milford Haven and Dale
OPEN 9 am – 5.30 pm, daily, summer; 9 am – 5 pm, daily, winter. Closed 4 days at Christmas and New Year
SPECIALITIES Shrubs; trees
MAIL ORDER No
SHOP Florist, silk and dried flowers, gifts, pots, tools, sundries, pond and pool equipment
REFRESHMENTS Coffee shop
DESIGN SERVICE St Ishmaels Nurseries
GIFT TOKENS Own

A large garden centre with a general range, especially trees and shrubs.

SOUTH GLAMORGAN

Fisher Fuchsias
Brynawel Garden Centre Ltd, Sully Road, Penarth, South Glamorgan CF64 3UU
☎ 01222 702660 FAX 01222 702660

CONTACT Miss J. Anderson
LOCATION Map in catalogue
OPEN 9 am – 6 pm, daily, spring and summer; 9 am – dusk, winter; 10 am – 4 pm, Sundays
SPECIALITIES Fuchsias
CATALOGUE 2 second class stamps
MAIL ORDER Yes; cuttings
SHOP Garden centre

Fuchsia specialists with a range of over 700 varieties. Part of the Brynawel Garden Centre. There are pelargoniums and a full range of summer and winter bedding.

GWENT

Waterwheel Nursery
Bully Hole Bottom, Usk Road, Shirenewton, Chepstow, Gwent NP6 6SA
☎ 01291 641577

CONTACT Desmond and Charlotte Evans
LOCATION Turn off B4235 (Chepstow to Usk road) 1½ miles north west of Huntsman Hotel
OPEN 9 am – 6 pm, Monday – Saturday
SPECIALITIES Climbers; herbaceous perennials; trees
CATALOGUE 2 first class stamps
MAIL ORDER Yes; winter only
GARDEN Garden around mill buildings

A wide and interesting choice of perennials, trees and shrubs for different situations. Most of the plants can be seen in the garden. You are advised to phone for directions. Waterwheel will be at the Rare Plant Fairs in the South West (see Calendar for details).

Wye Valley Herbs
The Nurtons, Tintern, Gwent NP6 7NX
☎ 01291 689253

CONTACT A. and E. Wood
LOCATION 7 miles north of M4, J22, opposite 'Old Station Tintern' on A466
OPEN 10.30 am – 5 pm, daily
SPECIALITIES Herbaceous perennials; herbs
NEW FOR 1995 More perennials
CATALOGUE 3 first class stamps
MAIL ORDER No
GARDEN Herb garden, herbaceous beds and wildlife pond

A large collection of organically grown herbs, with a growing selection of perennials and shrubs. All carry the Soil Association symbol.

GWYNEDD

Foxbrush Gardens
Portdinorwic, Y Felinheli, Gwynedd LL56 4JZ
☎ 01248 670463

CONTACT Mrs J. Osborne
LOCATION South west of Bangor
OPEN By appointment
CATALOGUE SAE
MAIL ORDER No
GARDEN Garden opens for NGS

There is a selection of plants from the gardens: herbaceous perennials, dwarf conifers and some camellias. The gardens open occasionally for the NGS.

Gwydir Plants
Plas Muriau, Betws-y-coed, Gwynedd LL24 0HD
☎ 01690 710201 FAX 01690 750379

CONTACT Mrs L. Schärer
LOCATION ¼ mile north of Waterloo Bridge, towards Llanrwst on A470
OPEN 11 am – 6 pm, Tuesday – Sunday, and Bank Holidays, March to October
SPECIALITIES Herbs; wild flowers
CATALOGUE 2 first class stamps
MAIL ORDER No
GARDEN Plas Muriau garden is open under the NGS, 11 am – 6 pm, Thursdays, April to September

This small nursery specialises in herbs, wild flowers and cottage garden plants. They can supply collections for school projects.

Henllys Lodge Plants
Henllys Lodge, Beaumaris, Anglesey, Gwynedd LL58 8HU
☎ 01248 810106

CONTACT Mrs E. Lane
LOCATION Turn left, ½ mile after Beaumaris Castle, and then first left again
OPEN 11 am – 5 pm, daily. Closed Tuesdays and Thursdays

SPECIALITIES   Herbaceous perennials
NEW FOR 1995   *Geranium cantabrigiense* 'Saint Ola', *G. oxonianum* 'Wageningen', *G. phaeum* 'Lily Lovell', *G. robertianum* 'Celtic White', *Osteospermum jucundum*
CATALOGUE   2 first class stamps
MAIL ORDER   No
REFRESHMENTS   Cream teas
GARDEN   Cottage-style garden open under NGS (17 – 18 June, 9 July) and by appointment
DESIGN SERVICE   Henllys Lodge Plants

The nursery stocks a selection of cottage-garden type perennials including many hardy geraniums and plants for shade. They run half-day workshops for small groups on planning and planting a garden, and their own garden is also open.

The Herb Garden & Plant Hunters Nursery
Pentre Berw, Gaerwen, Anglesey, Gwynedd LL60 6LF
☎ 01248 421064

CONTACT   Mr and Mrs D. R. Tremaine-Stevenson
LOCATION   Map in catalogue
OPEN   9 am – 6 pm, Wednesday – Sunday and Bank Holidays. Phone first out of season
SPECIALITIES   Herbs; wild flowers
CATALOGUE   £1 and A5 SAE
MAIL ORDER   Yes

Herbs of all kinds and British native species are the specialities; there are perennials and old roses too.

Holland Arms Garden Centre
Gaerwen, Anglesey, Gwynedd LL60 6LA
☎ 01248 421655

CONTACT   Miss Susan Knock
LOCATION   On A5 in central Anglesey
OPEN   9 am – 5.30 pm, Monday – Saturday; 11 am – 5 pm, Sundays; 10 am – 5.30 pm, Bank Holidays
REFRESHMENTS   Restaurant
GARDEN   Demonstration gardens
GIFT TOKENS   HTA

Large, family-run garden centre, with indoor and outdoor plants. Hillier Premier Collection agent. The very large Christmas display includes a bilingual Santa, and there are lectures and events throughout the year.

Ty'n Garreg Nurseries
Ty'n Garreg, Rhyd-y-Clafdy, Pwllheli, Gwynedd LL53 8PL
☎ 01758 720868   FAX 01758 720868

CONTACT   Nigel Pittard
LOCATION   Off B4415, north west of Pwllheli
OPEN   1 – 5 pm, Thursday – Sunday, 1 April to 1 September
CATALOGUE   2 first class stamps
MAIL ORDER   Yes
GARDEN   Demonstration garden

DESIGN SERVICE   Ty'n Garreg Nurseries

The nursery has an expanding range of perennials, particularly *Aquilegia* and *Agapanthus*. They stock unusual annuals in spring and summer. Large dried flower arrangements are produced to order. There are woodland and kitchen gardens.

Ty'r Orsaf Nursery
Maentwrog Road Station, Ty Nant, Gellilydan, Gwynedd LL41 4RB
☎ 0176685 233

CONTACT   Tony and Molly Faulkner
LOCATION   Between Trawsfynydd and Ffestiniog on A470
OPEN   10 am – 7 pm, summer; 10 am – dusk, winter
SPECIALITIES   Alpines; herbaceous perennials
MAIL ORDER   No
GARDEN   Garden open daily

A pleasantly mixed collection of garden-worthy alpines, hardy perennials and shrubs: specialities include *Geum*, *Sidalcea*, *Potentilla*, and *Scabiosa*.

POWYS

Blooming Things
Y Bwthyn, Cymerau, Glandyfi, Machynlleth, Powys SY20 8SS
☎ 01654 781256

CONTACT   Wyn and Dale Garnes
OPEN   Mail order only
SPECIALITIES   Herbs; wild flowers
CATALOGUE   SAE
MAIL ORDER   Yes

Organically grown herbs, wild flowers and plants for hanging baskets are sent as young plant plugs from this Welsh nursery.

SCOTLAND

BORDERS

Lilliesleaf Nursery
Garden Cottage, Linthill, Lilliesleaf, Borders TD6 9HU
☎ 01835 870415   FAX 01835 870415

CONTACT   T. de Bordes
LOCATION   On B6359, between Midlem and Lilliesleaf
OPEN   9 am – 5 pm, Monday – Saturday; 10 am – 4 pm, Sundays. Closed Sunday – Tuesday, December to March
SPECIALITIES   Herbaceous perennials
MAIL ORDER   No
GARDEN   Walled garden
GIFT TOKENS   Own

General plant range, with the emphasis on perennials.

Dumfries & Galloway Nurseries & Garden Centres

Pringle Plants
Groom's Cottage, Kirklands, Ancrum, Jedburgh, Borders TD8 6UJ
☎ 01835 830354
CONTACT   Dr Jan Boyd
LOCATION   Scottish borders
OPEN   By appointment only
SPECIALITIES   Alpines
CATALOGUE   2 second class stamps
MAIL ORDER   Yes; no minimum order
SHOWS   Ayr

A small nursery which concentrates on dwarf forms of shrubs, conifers, bulbs, alpines and herbaceous plants. Orders can be collected from shows (including the Royal Highland) by arrangement.

CENTRAL

Plantings Garden Nursery
Main Street, Thornhill, By Stirling, Central FK8 3PP
☎ 01786 850683
CONTACT   Robin Price
LOCATION   Map in catalogue
OPEN   9.30 am – 5.30 pm, Fridays and Saturdays, March to October
SPECIALITIES   Herbaceous perennials
CATALOGUE   2 first class stamps
MAIL ORDER   Yes
GARDEN   Norrieston House
GIFT TOKENS   Own

A useful range of herbaceous plants available wholesale and retail, as well as container-grown roses. The garden at Norrieston House opens for Scotland's Garden Scheme.

DUMFRIES & GALLOWAY

Bridge End Nurseries
Gretna Green, Dumfries & Galloway DG16 5HN
☎ 01461 800612
CONTACT   Robin Bird
OPEN   9 am – dusk, daily
SPECIALITIES   Herbaceous perennials
NEW FOR 1995   Lavatera 'Blushing Bride'
MAIL ORDER   No
SHOWS   Malvern Spring; Harrogate (Spring); Southport; Ayr
GIFT TOKENS   Own

Lots of cottage garden plants, both well-known and rarer varieties.

British Wild Plants
Stockerton Nursery, Kirkcudbright, Galloway, Dumfries & Galloway DG6 4XS
☎ 01557 31226
CONTACT   Martin Gould
LOCATION   Phone for details
OPEN   By arrangement
SPECIALITIES   Wild flowers
CATALOGUE   3 first class stamps for guide to garden use of plants
MAIL ORDER   Yes
GARDEN   Display garden

A small nursery with a range of native wild plants for a variety of habitats, including aquatic, coastal, meadow and hedgerow, and woodland. Their stock includes bulbs, trees and shrubs.

Cally Gardens
Gatehouse of Fleet, Castle Douglas, Dumfries & Galloway DG7 2DJ
CONTACT   Michael Wickenden
LOCATION   12 miles west of Castle Douglas, on Gatehouse road off A75
OPEN   10 am – 5.30 pm, Saturdays and Sundays only, Easter to early October
SPECIALITIES   Herbaceous perennials
CATALOGUE   3 first class stamps; November
MAIL ORDER   Yes; £15 minimum order; spring despatch
GARDEN   Eighteenth-century walled garden

A nursery for the horticultural avant-garde. It specialises in perennials from collected and botanic garden seed. Culled from a collection of over 3,000 varieties, the catalogue changes by as much as half each year.

Charter House Hardy Plant Nursery
2 Nunwood, Dumfries, Dumfries & Galloway DG2 0HX
☎ 01387 720363
CONTACT   John Ross
LOCATION   Between Terregles and Newbridge
OPEN   10 am – 5 pm, Saturdays and Sundays and by appointment. Closed 24 December to 31 January.
SPECIALITIES   Alpines; herbaceous perennials
CATALOGUE   3 first class stamps
MAIL ORDER   Yes
GARDEN   Demonstration gardens
GIFT TOKENS   Own
NCCPG NATIONAL COLLECTIONS   Erodium

Here are hardy geraniums and erodiums in abundance, plus a selection of other herbaceous and alpine plants. The demonstration gardens are getting larger. Advice on planting and design.

Craig Lodge Nurseries
Craig Lodge, Balmaclellan, Castle Douglas, Dumfries & Galloway DG7 3QR
☎ 01644 420661
CONTACT   Michael or Sheila Northway
LOCATION   Remote – directions in catalogue
OPEN   10 am – 5 pm, Wednesday – Monday, late March to 31 October
SPECIALITIES   Alpines; primulas
NEW FOR 1995   Many new plants, including Primula cuneifolia
CATALOGUE   4 second class stamps and A5 SAE

MAIL ORDER Yes

This young nursery grows all kinds of alpines, including bulbs and dwarf shrubs. They specialise in plants from wild collected seed.

Craigieburn Classic Plants
By Moffat, Dumfriesshire, Dumfries & Galloway DG10 9LF
☎ 01683 21250   FAX 01683 21250
CONTACT Janet Wheatcroft and Bill Chudziak
LOCATION 2½ miles east of Moffat, on A74. On the left, beyond Craiglochan signs
OPEN 12.30 – 8 pm, Wednesday – Sunday, 17 April to 29 October. Open on Bank Holidays
SPECIALITIES Herbaceous perennials; primulas; half-hardy plants
NEW FOR 1995 *Meconopsis* and South East Asian plants (wild collected)
CATALOGUE £1; October
MAIL ORDER Yes; minimum order £10
GARDEN Craigieburn Woodland Garden, admission £1.50
GIFT TOKENS Own

Set in the garden, the nursery carries an attractive range of perennials, with an emphasis on woodlanders. *Meconopsis* and primulas are among the specialities.

Elizabeth MacGregor
Ellenbank, Tongland Road, Kirkcudbright, Dumfries & Galloway DG6 4UU
☎ 01557 330620   FAX 01557 330620
CONTACT Elizabeth or Alasdair MacGregor
LOCATION On A711, 1 mile north of Kirkcudbright
OPEN 10.30 am – 5.30 pm, Fridays and Saturdays, May to October
SPECIALITIES Herbaceous perennials; violas
CATALOGUE £1
MAIL ORDER Yes
GARDEN Walled garden
SHOWS Ayr
GIFT TOKENS Own

Violas – over 100 of them, are the speciality at this nursery, complemented by a lively selection of perennials and shrubs for cottage garden and mixed border planting.

J Tweedie Fruit Trees
Maryfield Road Nursery, Maryfield, Terregles, Dumfries & Galloway DG2 9TH
☎ 01387 720880
CONTACT John Tweedie
LOCATION 3 miles from Dumfries, between Newbridge and Terregles
OPEN 9.30 am – 2.30 pm, Saturdays, October to March. Other times by appointment
SPECIALITIES Fruit
NEW FOR 1995 Blackcurrant 'Ben Connan', Apple 'Cox's Orange Pippin' (self-fertile), wider range of blueberries and gooseberries

CATALOGUE SAE
MAIL ORDER Yes

A good choice of fruit trees and bushes in new varieties, with some old ones also in the list. During the season fresh soft fruits can be bought.

Plantables
Drambuie, Dalry, Castle Douglas, Dumfries & Galloway DG7 3XR
☎ 016443 349
CONTACT Alan Rumble
LOCATION North of New Galloway, at the end of Garroch Glen
OPEN Mail order only: collection by appointment
SPECIALITIES Alpines; herbaceous perennials; rhododendrons
CATALOGUE 2 first class stamps
MAIL ORDER Yes; no minimum value

The nursery has recently moved from the West Midlands to Kircudbrightshire. It still focuses on plants for small features or for use in small gardens, including dwarf rhododendrons and other shrubs, alpines and herbaceous perennials.

FIFE

Roots Garden Centre Ltd
1 Caskieberran Road, Glenrothes, Fife KY6 2NR
☎ 01592 756407   FAX 01592 758973
CONTACT Jim McGregor
LOCATION Opposite Saltire Centre
OPEN 8.30 am – 5.30 pm, Monday – Friday; 9 am – 5.30 pm, Saturdays; 10 am – 5.30 pm, Sundays
SHOP Garden sundries, furniture, buildings, florist's
DESIGN SERVICE Roots Garden Centre Ltd
GIFT TOKENS HTA

Garden centre with a full range of plants and products. They offer design and landscaping (interior and exterior) and daily delivery.

GRAMPIAN

Aultan Nursery
Newton of Cairnhill, Cuminestown, Turriff, Grampian AB53 7TN
☎ 01888 544702
CONTACT Richard King
CATALOGUE 4 first class stamps
MAIL ORDER Yes

Organically grown herbaceous perennials and shrubs.

Ben Reid & Co
Pinewood Park Nurseries, Countesswells Road, Aberdeen, Grampian AB9 2QL
☎ 01224 318744   FAX 01224 310104
CONTACT Mr Shand
LOCATION Aberdeen

OPEN Garden Centre open 9 am – 5 pm, Monday –
Saturday; 10 am – 5 pm, Sundays
SPECIALITIES Hedging; trees
CATALOGUE On request
MAIL ORDER Yes; £10 minimum order
GIFT TOKENS HTA

Large wholesale nursery which specialises in coniferous and deciduous forest trees, hedging, ornamental trees and shrubs. Their retail plant centre carries a good general range.

Christie Elite Nurseries
Forres, Moray, Grampian IV36 0TW
☎ 01309 672633   FAX 01309 676846

CONTACT Dr S. Thompson
LOCATION Bogton Road, Forres
OPEN 8 am – 5.30 pm, Monday – Saturday; 10 am – 5.30 pm, Sundays
SPECIALITIES Hedging; shrubs; trees
CATALOGUE On request
MAIL ORDER Yes
GIFT TOKENS HTA

Large and long-established nursery and garden centre. A wide range of trees and shrubs, from woodland and hedging species to ornamental varieties. Some fruit trees also.

James Cocker & Sons
Whitemyres, Lang Stracht, Aberdeen, Grampian AB9 2XH
☎ 01224 313261   FAX 01224 312531

OPEN 9 am – 5 pm, daily
SPECIALITIES Roses
NEW FOR 1995 Roses 'Aberdeen Celebration', 'Bishop Elphinstone', 'Festival', 'Renaissance', 'Shine On', and 'Warm Wishes'
CATALOGUE On request; May
MAIL ORDER Yes; no minimum order
SHOP Garden centre
REFRESHMENTS Refreshments
SHOWS RHS Westminster
GIFT TOKENS HTA; own

Rose breeders and growers, with a garden centre too. They have an all-round range of roses, but the emphasis is on the modern, shorter varieties. The firm holds a royal warrant.

Tough Alpine Nursery
Westhaybogs, Tough, Alford, Aberdeenshire, Grampian AB33 8DU
☎ 019755 62783   FAX 019755 62783

CONTACT Mr Fred Carrie
OPEN 10 am – 5 pm, February to October
SPECIALITIES Alpines
CATALOGUE 3 second class stamps
MAIL ORDER Yes; minimum order £10

Retail and wholesale alpine nursery producing a wide range of very hardy alpines in this chilly area.

HIGHLAND

Abriachan Gardens & Nursery
Abriachan Nurseries, Loch Ness Side, Inverness-shire, Highland IV3 6LA
☎ 01463 861232

CONTACT Mrs & Mrs Davidson
LOCATION 9 miles south west of Inverness, on A82
OPEN 9 am – 7 pm (or dusk if earlier), daily, February to November
SPECIALITIES Herbaceous perennials; primulas
NEW FOR 1995 Many new primulas and *Meconopsis*
CATALOGUE 4 first class stamps
MAIL ORDER Yes; no minimum order
GARDEN Large garden open under SGS

Mainly perennials, with a large choice of primroses, particularly the Barnhaven strains. Other interesting ranges including helianthemums and hebes. The garden walk is mapped and labelled.

Ardfearn Nursery
Bunchrew, Highland IV3 6RH
☎ 01463 243250/223607 FAX 01463 7117133

CONTACT Alasdair Sutherland
LOCATION Off A862, west of Inverness
OPEN 9 am – 5.30 pm, daily
SPECIALITIES Alpines; primulas
NEW FOR 1995 Many new plants
CATALOGUE 4 second class stamps
MAIL ORDER Yes
GARDEN Demonstration garden
GIFT TOKENS Own

Alpines and small ericaceous shrubs in quantity are produced at this nursery in a lovely Highland setting. Lots of primulas. The sales area has easy wheelchair access.

Arivegaig Nursery
Acharacle, Argyll, Highland PH36 4LE
☎ 01967 431331

CONTACT Mr E. Stewart
LOCATION Ardnamurchan peninsula, Argyll
OPEN 9 am – 5 pm (or dusk if earlier), daily, Easter to October
SPECIALITIES Half-hardy plants
CATALOGUE 4 first class stamps
MAIL ORDER Yes; p & p at cost

The nursery stocks a general range of all plant types, but especially those which flourish in the milder west coast climate.

Black Isle Nurseries
Munlochy, Highland IV8 8PF
☎ 01463 811246   FAX 01463 811525

CONTACT Elizabeth Burnett
LOCATION Map in catalogue
OPEN 2 – 5 pm, Tuesdays, Wednesdays and Fridays, May to October. Phone first

SPECIALITIES Herbaceous perennials
CATALOGUE 2 first class stamps
MAIL ORDER Yes

A small nursery; an attractive selection of hardy perennials is propagated on site.

Evelix Daffodils
Aird Asaig, Evelix, Dornoch, Sutherland, Highland IV25 3NG
☎ 01862 810715

CONTACT D. C. MacArthur
LOCATION Off A9 at Evelix filling station
OPEN By appointment
SPECIALITIES Daffodils
CATALOGUE 3 first class stamps
MAIL ORDER Yes; minimum order £5

Daffodil breeder with an interesting small range of novelty, exhibition and garden varieties. Watch out for new varieties. Sutherland Soil Services operates from the same address.

Island Plants
The Old Manse, Knock, Point, Isle of Lewis, Highland PA86 0BW
☎ 01851 870281

CONTACT Mr D. Ferris
OPEN 2 – 5 pm, Monday – Saturday
SPECIALITIES New Zealand plants
CATALOGUE 1 first class stamp
MAIL ORDER Yes
SHOWS Ayr

New Zealand plants are the speciality here – lots of hebes, as well as those which tolerate wind and sea spray.

Jack Drake
Inshriach Alpine Nursery, Aviemore, Inverness-shire, Highland PH22 1QS
☎ 01540 651287   FAX 01540 651656

CONTACT J. C. Lawson
LOCATION From B9152 take B970 (ski road) to Coylumbridge, outside Aviemore. Turn right, after the Spey
OPEN 9 am – 5 pm Monday – Friday; 9 am – 4 pm, Saturdays. Closed Sundays
SPECIALITIES Alpines; seeds
CATALOGUE £1
MAIL ORDER Yes; no minimum order
GIFT TOKENS HTA

Highland nursery devoted to alpine and rock garden plants, including species for wild and bog gardens. A seed list is also available, containing about 300 items.

Poyntzfield Herb Nursery
Black Isle, By Dingwall, Ross and Cromarty, Highland IV7 8LX
☎ 01381 610352   FAX 01381 610352

CONTACT Duncan Ross
LOCATION 5 miles west of Cromarty, on B9163
OPEN 1 – 5 pm, Monday – Saturday

SPECIALITIES Herbs
NEW FOR 1995 Tibetan medicinal herbs, Japanese ginseng
CATALOGUE SAE plus 3 first class stamps
MAIL ORDER Yes
GARDEN Display garden
DESIGN SERVICE Poyntzfield Herb Nursery

This range of herbs and aromatic plants from the north of Scotland is grown with an eye on hardiness and vigour as well as scent and flavour. They specialise in native species and medicinal plants.

Speyside Heather Centre
Dulnain Bridge, Inverness-shire, Highland PH26 3PA
☎ 01479 851359   FAX 01479 851396

CONTACT David and Betty Lambie
LOCATION Between Aviemore and Grantown on Spey, off A95
OPEN 9 am – 6 pm, Monday – Saturday; 10 am – 5.30 pm, Sundays
SPECIALITIES Heathers
CATALOGUE £2.25 booklet
MAIL ORDER Yes
SHOP Crafts, garden sundries
REFRESHMENTS Tea room
GARDEN Gardens
GIFT TOKENS Own

Garden centre which specialises in heathers and heather gardening. They have other plants, sundries, crafts and a tea room (Clootie Dumpling Tearoom) where 21 dumpling dishes are on offer.

Uzumara Orchids
9 Port Henderson, Gairloch, Ross-shire, Highland IV21 2AS
☎ 01445 741228

CONTACT Mrs I. F. La Croix
LOCATION 8 miles south west of Gairloch
OPEN By appointment
SPECIALITIES Orchids; *Streptocarpus*
CATALOGUE SAE
MAIL ORDER Yes

A highly specialised nursery offering species orchids from Africa and Madagascar, most of them seed-raised. They also have an exceptional choice of *Streptocarpus* species. Still quite new: the range will expand.

LOTHIAN

Belwood Nurseries Ltd
Mauricewood Mains, Penicuik, Midlothian, Lothian EH26 0NJ
☎ 01968 673621   FAX 01968 678354

CONTACT Ron Low (Sales Manager)
LOCATION Dalkeith (Midlothian) and Meigle (Tayside)
OPEN By appointment only: 8 am – 5 pm, Monday – Friday

SPECIALITIES   Conifers; shrubs; trees
CATALOGUE   On request
MAIL ORDER   Carriage arranged anywhere in mainland UK
REFRESHMENTS   Tea or coffee available
GARDEN   Nursery (300 acres) open by arrangement

A large wholesale nursery, with some 300 acres under production. Retail customers must make an appointment before visiting. Trees, shrubs and conifers are available root-balled or container-grown in various sizes. They specialise in semi-mature specimens, and stock for special projects.

Dobbie & Co Ltd, Melville Garden Centre
Melville Nursery, Lasswade, Midlothian, Lothian EH18 1AZ
☎ 0131 663 1941   FAX 0131 654 2548
CONTACT   J. Oliver
LOCATION   Dalkeith
OPEN   9 am – 5 pm, Monday – Friday; 9 am – 5 pm, Saturdays; 10 am – 5 pm, Sundays. Open till 6 pm from April to August
CATALOGUE   No
SHOP   Garden sundries, buildings, machinery, landscape materials
REFRESHMENTS   Tea room
GARDEN   Demonstration gardens
DESIGN SERVICE   Dobbies Landscape Ltd
GIFT TOKENS   HTA; own

Large garden centre, part of the Dobbies chain. As well as hardy nursery stock and associated garden products, the site includes a bird of prey centre and a butterfly and insect exhibition.

Melville Nurseries
Lasswade, Midlothian, Lothian EH18 1AZ
☎ 0131 663 1944   FAX 0131 654 2548
CONTACT   Cathy Stevenson
OPEN   8.30 am – 5 pm, Monday – Friday
SPECIALITIES   Rhododendrons; shrubs
CATALOGUE   Yes
MAIL ORDER   No
REFRESHMENTS   At garden centre
GARDEN   At garden centre

Wholesale only. Large nursery which specialises in deciduous azaleas and rhododendrons. Specimen shrubs and conifers are available in containers from 20 to 130 litres. There is a Dobbies garden centre next door (see previous entry).

STRATHCLYDE

Ballagan Nursery
Gartocharn Road, Alexandria, Dumbartonshire, Strathclyde G83 8NB
☎ 01389 752947   FAX 01389 711288
CONTACT   Mr Wilson

LOCATION   Between Balloch and Gartocharn on A811
OPEN   9 am – 6 pm, daily
SPECIALITIES   Bedding plants
SHOP   Garden centre
GIFT TOKENS   HTA

Garden centre and nursery dealing in bedding plants, unusual hardy shrubs and trees (including feathered specimens).

Barwinnock Herbs
Barrhill, Girvan, Strathclyde KA26 0RB
☎ 0146 582338
CONTACT   Mon and Dave Holtom
LOCATION   Map in catalogue
OPEN   9 am – 7 pm, Friday – Wednesday, April to October. Closed Thursdays
SPECIALITIES   Herbs
CATALOGUE   3 first class stamps
MAIL ORDER   Yes
GARDEN   Display garden
SHOWS   Ayr

Organically grown culinary, medicinal and aromatic herbs. There is a new garden and farm walks to see wild flowers and rare breeds. Wellies advised.

Burnside Nursery
By Turnberry, Strathclyde KA26 9JH
☎ 01465 714290
CONTACT   Mrs C. Walker
LOCATION   On A77, between Girvan and Turnberry
OPEN   10 am – dusk, Saturdays and Sundays, 1 April to 31 October
SPECIALITIES   Herbaceous perennials
CATALOGUE   3 first class stamps
MAIL ORDER   Yes; spring and summer only
SHOWS   Ayr

The nursery is enthusiastic about their range of *Dicentra* – there is a good selection of hardy geraniums and other perennials as well.

Chatelherault Garden Centre
Chatelherault Country Park, Ferniegair, Hamilton, Lanarkshire, Strathclyde ML3 7UE
☎ 01698 457700
CONTACT   Ranald Mackenzie
OPEN   9 am – 5 pm, Monday – Saturday; 10 am – 5 pm, Sundays
REFRESHMENTS   Restaurant
GIFT TOKENS   HTA

A Dobbies garden centre.

Duncans of Milngavie
Flower & Garden Centre, 101 Main Street, Milngavie, Glasgow, Strathclyde G62 6JJ
☎ 0141 956 2377   FAX 0141 956 6649
CONTACT   Andrew N. Duncan
LOCATION   North of Glasgow, on A81

OPEN 8.30 am – 5.30 pm, Monday – Saturday; 10 am – 5 pm, Sundays
SHOP Florist, garden sundries and furniture
REFRESHMENTS Tea room
GIFT TOKENS HTA

Garden centre and florist with a comprehensive choice of indoor and outdoor plants and associated products. Daily delivery. Annual Christmas event in late November includes a Bavarian band.

Hosta Garden
Kittoch Mill, Carmunnock, Glasgow, Strathclyde G76 9BJ
☎ 0141 644 4712
CONTACT P. A. Jordan
LOCATION Off Busby to Carmunnock road
OPEN By appointment only: phone first
SPECIALITIES Herbaceous perennials
MAIL ORDER No
REFRESHMENTS By arrangement
GARDEN Display gardens
NCCPG NATIONAL COLLECTIONS Hosta

They specialise in hostas, including new American cultivars. Some other perennials too. The nursery and gardens are open on 11 June and 25 June, 2 – 5 pm; otherwise recommended viewing times are between late May and late July. Talks can be arranged for clubs and societies, who can also visit the garden by appointment.

Kinlochlaich House Gardens
Appin, Argyll, Strathclyde PA38 4BD
☎ 01631 730342   FAX 01631 730482
CONTACT D. E. Hutchison (MIHort).
OPEN 9.30 am – 5.30 pm, Monday – Saturday, 10.30 am – 5.30 pm, Sundays, summer; 9.30 am – 4.45 pm, Monday – Saturday only, winter
CATALOGUE No
MAIL ORDER No
GARDEN Kinlochlaich House Gardens
DESIGN SERVICE Lorne Landscapers
GIFT TOKENS Own

The largest garden centre in the West Highlands, with a range of hardy garden plants across the whole spectrum from alpines to trees. Design service through Lorne Landscapers.

Tree Shop
Ardkinglas Estate Nurseries, Cairndow, Strathclyde PA26 8BH
☎ 014996 263   FAX 014996 263
CONTACT Mark Sands
OPEN 9.30 am – 7 pm, daily, April to September; 9.30 am – 5 pm, daily, October to March. Closed in January
SPECIALITIES Rhododendrons; trees
CATALOGUE On request
MAIL ORDER Yes
GIFT TOKENS HTA

Specimen trees, azaleas and rhododendrons, including small species and hybrids. There is also a range of woodwork, including toys and garden furniture.

TAYSIDE

Angus Heathers
10 Guthrie Street, Letham, Tayside DD8 2PS
☎ 01307 818504   FAX 01307 818055
CONTACT David Sturrock
LOCATION Forfar, by Dundee
OPEN 9 am – 5 pm, daily
SPECIALITIES Heathers; gentians
CATALOGUE On request
MAIL ORDER No
GARDEN Demonstration garden

As well as over 130 heathers, they stock a range of gentians, and a number of dwarf and slow-growing conifers which make good companions for the heathers.

Christie's Nursery
Downfield, Main Road, West Muir, Kirriemuir, Tayside DD8 5LP
☎ 01575 572977   FAX 01575 572977
CONTACT Ian or Ann Christie, Ian Martin
LOCATION On A926, 1 mile west of Kirriemuir
OPEN 10 am – 6 pm, daily. November to January by appointment only
SPECIALITIES Alpines
NEW FOR 1995 *Gentiana coelestis* CLD 1087, *G. trichotoma* 'KGB', *Corydalis* × 'Highland Mist', *Narcissus watieri*
CATALOGUE SAE
MAIL ORDER Yes
GARDEN Demonstration garden
SHOWS Ayr
GIFT TOKENS HTA; own

This alpine nursery in the Highlands has some interesting gentians and lewisias. Not all their plants can be sent by courier, but they go to Scottish Rock Garden Society and some AGS shows.

Findlay Clark Ltd
Kinross Garden Centre, Turfhills, Kinross, Tayside KY13 7NQ
☎ 01577 863327   FAX 01577 863442
CONTACT Ms Emma Mitchell
LOCATION Off M90, J6
OPEN 9 am – 5.30 pm, daily
SHOP Gifts, floral art
REFRESHMENTS Le Jardin café
GIFT TOKENS HTA

A Findlay Clark garden centre. Delivery is available.

Glendoick Garden Centre
Glendoick, Perth, Tayside PH2 7NS
☎ 01738 860205/01738 860260   FAX 01738 860735
LOCATION 7 miles from Perth, on A90
OPEN 9 am – 5 pm, winter; 9 am – 6 pm, summer

SPECIALITIES Primulas; rhododendrons
CATALOGUE £1.50 in stamps
MAIL ORDER Yes
GARDEN Glendoick Garden Centre, Tayside, see Gardens section
GIFT TOKENS HTA

The garden centre is open daily at the times shown: the nursery is only open by prior arrangement. Glendoick are specialist growers of rhododendrons and other ericaceous shrubs, with a large and impressive collection, including new hybrids. Among the short list of other plants there are a number of interesting Asiatic primulas from collected seed.

Perth Garden Centre
Crieff Road, Perth, Tayside PH1 2NR
☎ 01738 638555   FAX 01738 633005

CONTACT Alistair Brown
LOCATION Beside Tesco superstore
OPEN 9 am – 7 pm, Monday – Friday, 9 am – 6 pm, Saturdays, 10 am – 6 pm, Sundays, March to June; 9 am – 5 pm, Monday – Saturday, 10 am – 5 pm, Sundays, rest of year
MAIL ORDER No
REFRESHMENTS Restaurant
GIFT TOKENS HTA; own

A Dobbies garden centre, with a Hillier Premier Plants agency. They attend the Dundee show this year.

NORTHERN IRELAND

CO. ANTRIM

Carncairn Daffodils
Carncairn Grange, Broughshane, Ballymena, Co. Antrim BT43 7HF
☎ 01266 861216

CONTACT Mrs R. H. Reade
LOCATION 5 miles from Ballymena, just outside Broughshane
OPEN 10 am – 5 pm, by appointment
SPECIALITIES Daffodils
CATALOGUE On request; March
MAIL ORDER Yes
GARDEN Visitors welcome, by appointment
GIFT TOKENS Own

Raisers and growers of daffodils for exhibition use and garden display. Present at the Belfast Show and most other Northern Ireland shows. They prefer it if callers make an appointment first.

CO. ARMAGH

Brownlow Heathers
148 Avenue Road, Lurgan, Craigavon, Co. Armagh BT66 7BJ
☎ 01762 325732

CONTACT William Crawford
OPEN By appointment
SPECIALITIES Heathers
CATALOGUE SAE
MAIL ORDER Yes

Rooted heather cuttings are sent by post, wholesale and retail.

CO. DOWN

Ballydorn Bulb Farm
Ballydorn Hill, Killinchy, Newtownards, Co. Down BT23 6QB
☎ 01238 541250

CONTACT Sir Frank Harrison
SPECIALITIES Daffodils
CATALOGUE £1
MAIL ORDER Yes

Narcissus breeders and hybridisers since 1946. The unique collection consists solely of their own cultivars, bred for either the show bench or the garden. They were awarded a gold medal in 1993 by the American Daffodil Society for hybridising. They will be at the Northern Ireland Spring Shows.

Ballyrogan Nurseries
The Grange, Ballyrogan, Newtownards, Co. Down BT23 4SD
☎ 01247 810451

CONTACT Gary Dunlop
OPEN Collection only, by prior arrangement
SPECIALITIES Herbaceous perennials
CATALOGUE 2 first class stamps
MAIL ORDER Yes; £10 minimum order
NCCPG NATIONAL COLLECTIONS *Celmisia*, *Crcosmia*, *Euphorbia*

A small part-time nursery selling stock derived from their own large collections. The plants are mostly herbaceous: the crocosmias and euphorbias look particularly interesting.

Daisy Hill Nurseries Ltd
Hospital Road, Newry, Co. Down BT35 8PN
☎ 01693 62474

CONTACT Alan Grills
LOCATION On Newry's western boundary
OPEN 9 am – 5 pm, Monday – Friday
SPECIALITIES Heathers; shrubs; trees
NEW FOR 1995 *Calluna vulgaris* 'Celtic Gold', *Pieris japonica* 'Daisy Hill'
CATALOGUE On request
MAIL ORDER Yes; £5 minimum order
DESIGN SERVICE Daisy Hill Nurseries Ltd
GIFT TOKENS Own

The nursery sells alpines and heathers, shrubs and trees. Strengths include small-flowered and dwarf rhododendrons. They offer a landscaping service within a 25-mile radius.

Dickson Nurseries Ltd
Milecross Road, Newtownards, Co. Down BT23 4SS
☎ 01247 812206   FAX 01247 813366

CONTACT Linda Stewart
OPEN 8 am – 12.30 pm, 1.15 – 5 pm, Monday – Thursday; 8 am – 1 pm, Fridays. Closed Saturdays and Sundays
SPECIALITIES Roses
NEW FOR 1995 Rose 'Benita' (amber/gold Grandiflora); Rose 'Pure Bliss' (soft, two-tone pink blend Hybrid Tea)
CATALOGUE On request
MAIL ORDER Yes
GARDEN Rose fields open, as above
GIFT TOKENS Own

Modern rose breeders, with some distinguished introductions to their credit: there are two new introductions this season, 'Benita' and 'Pure Bliss'. They only sell their own roses, and those of Jackson & Perkins and Interplant.

Lisdoonan Herbs
98 Belfast Road, Saintfield, Co. Down BT24 7HF
☎ 01232 813624

CONTACT Barbara Pilcher
LOCATION Between Carryduff and Saintfield, 6 miles south of Belfast on A7
OPEN Wednesday and Saturday mornings, and by appointment
SPECIALITIES Herbs
NEW FOR 1995 *Borago pygmaea*, *Plantago major* 'Rosularis', *Prostanthera cuneata*
CATALOGUE SAE
MAIL ORDER No
GARDEN Demonstration gardens
DESIGN SERVICE Lisdoonan Herbs

The nursery sells culinary herbs and salad plants, as well as cut herbs. One-day workshops are held during the season and visits to the garden can be arranged. Design advice and planting plans available.

Seaforde Gardens
Seaforde, Downpatrick, Co. Down BT30 8PG
☎ 01396 811225   FAX 01396 811370

CONTACT Patrick Forde
LOCATION Between Belfast and Newcastle
OPEN 10 am – 5 pm, Monday – Saturday; 2 – 6 pm, Sundays. Open Monday – Friday only, November to February
SPECIALITIES Rhododendrons; trees
NEW FOR 1995 *Rhododendron sinofalconeri*, *Rh. excellens*
CATALOGUE On request
MAIL ORDER Yes
REFRESHMENTS Refreshments
GARDEN Gardens, maze and butterfly house
NCCPG NATIONAL COLLECTIONS *Eucryphia*

An interesting collection of trees and shrubs, including some for sheltered spots only. Particularly good for *Rhododendron* and *Eucryphia*. There are also gardens and a tropical butterfly house.

Timpany Nurseries
77 Magheratimpany Road, Ballynahinch, Co. Down BT24 8PA
☎ 01238 562812

CONTACT Susan Tindall
LOCATION 2 miles from Ballynahinch, in Drumlin country
OPEN 10 am – 6 pm, Monday – Saturday. Closed Sundays and Mondays during winter. Phone for an appointment at other times
SPECIALITIES Alpines; herbaceous perennials; primulas
NEW FOR 1995 New *Primula allionii* and Kabschia saxifrages
CATALOGUE 50p
MAIL ORDER Yes
GARDEN Garden

A selection of alpine and rock garden plants, including specimens raised from collected seed. Strong on *Primula* and *Helichrysum*. The garden is open to groups by arrangement. Shows include the AGS Dublin show (8 April), Belfast Flower Show (22 – 23 April), and the AGS Ulster show at Greenmount (29 April).

CO. TYRONE

Brian Duncan Daffodils
Knowehead, 15 Ballynahatty Road, Omagh, Co. Tyrone BT78 1PN
☎ 01662 242931   FAX 01662 242931

CONTACT Elizabeth Ann Duncan
OPEN August and September only
SPECIALITIES Daffodils
NEW FOR 1995 New hybrids
MAIL ORDER Yes; cash with order for new customers

Breeder and grower of novelty and exhibition daffodils.

ISLE OF MAN

Ballalheannagh Gardens
Glen Roy, Lonan, Isle of Man IM4 7QO
☎ 01624 861875

CONTACT Cliff and Maureen Dadd
OPEN 10 am – 1 pm, 2 – 5 pm, daily
SPECIALITIES Australian plants; New Zealand plants; rhododendrons; shrubs
CATALOGUE £1.50
MAIL ORDER Yes; limited
GARDEN Ballalheannagh Gardens
DESIGN SERVICE Ballalheannagh Gardens
GIFT TOKENS Own

There is an extensive range of ericaceous shrubs, including rhododendrons, and many plants from the southern hemisphere. The woodland garden covers 23 acres.

P & S Allanson
Rhendoo, Jurby, Isle of Man IM7 3HB
☎ 01624 880766   FAX 01624 880649

CONTACT   Paul Allanson
OPEN   By appointment only
SPECIALITIES   Australian plants; New Zealand plants
NEW FOR 1995   Many new plants
CATALOGUE   £1.50
MAIL ORDER   Yes

This shrub nursery has many interesting Australian and New Zealand plants, *Hebe*, *Correa* and *Olearia*, besides plants for coastal and windy positions.

EIRE

CO. CORK

Deelish Garden Centre
Deelish, Skibbereen, Co. Cork
☎ 00 353 28 21374   FAX 00 353 28 21374

CONTACT   Rain Chase or Bill Chase
LOCATION   1 mile from Skibbereen: signed from Skibbereen to Ballydrob road
OPEN   10 am – 1 pm, 2 – 6 pm, Monday – Saturday; 2 – 6 pm, Sundays
CATALOGUE   Yes: specialist range only
MAIL ORDER   Delivery in Eire
DESIGN SERVICE   Deelish Garden Centre
GIFT TOKENS   Own

The nursery carries a general range of most types of plants, and – among some more unusual varieties – specialises in plants for coastal situations.

Hosford's Geraniums & Garden Centre
Cappa, Enniskeane, Co. Cork
☎ 00 353 23 39159   FAX 00 353 23 39300

CONTACT   John and David Hosford
LOCATION   5 miles west of Bandon; 1 mile off N71
OPEN   9 am – 6 pm, Monday – Saturday, and holidays, all year; 2 – 5.30 pm, Sundays, March to June, mid September to Christmas only
SPECIALITIES   Pelargoniums; roses
NEW FOR 1995   Several new pelargonium cultivars
CATALOGUE   Lists for pelargoniums, roses, perennials, hedging etc.
MAIL ORDER   Yes; credit cards accepted
DESIGN SERVICE   Hosford's Geranium & Garden Centre
GIFT TOKENS   Own

A general garden centre which also makes a speciality of pelargoniums. The rose list is good, and there are regular talks and demonstrations, including rose pruning on 18 February and a lecture at Coachford Community Centre.

CO. DUBLIN

Flower Centre
754 Howth Road, Blackbanks, Dublin 5, Co. Dublin
☎ 00 353 1 832 7047   FAX 00 353 1 832 7251

CONTACT   Eugene Higgins
LOCATION   5 miles east of Dublin
OPEN   10 am – 1 pm, 2.30 – 6 pm (5 pm, winter)
MAIL ORDER   No
SHOP   Garden sundries
GIFT TOKENS   Own

Well-established Dublin garden centre with a full range of plants.

Mackey's Garden Centre
Castlepark Road, Sandycove, Co. Dublin
☎ 00 353 280 7385   FAX 00 353 284 1922

CONTACT   Breda Roseingrave
LOCATION   5 miles south of Dublin
OPEN   9 am – 5.30 pm, Monday – Saturday; 2 – 5.30 pm, Sundays and Holidays
SPECIALITIES   Australian plants; seeds
CATALOGUE   On request: bulbs, seeds, old roses, modern roses
MAIL ORDER   Yes
SHOP   Garden centre and city shop
GARDEN   Demonstration garden
GIFT TOKENS   Own

The garden centre outlet of a famous old seed merchants (founded in 1777). There are many interesting plants in the all-round range, most notably the Australian collection. Mackey's Seed Ltd is at 22 St Mary Street, Dublin.

Malahide Nurseries Ltd
Mabestown, Malahide, Co. Dublin
☎ 00 353 845 0110   FAX 00 353 845 0872

CONTACT   Miss Ann Nutty
LOCATION   7 miles north of Dublin, opposite Malahide Castle
OPEN   9.30 am – 1 pm, 2 – 5.30 pm, Monday – Friday; 9.30 am – 5.30 pm, Saturdays; 2 – 5.30 pm, Sundays
SPECIALITIES   Aquatic plants
NEW FOR 1995   *Bomarea coldasii*
CATALOGUE   Computer list, on request
MAIL ORDER   Yes
SHOP   Garden products, seeds
GARDEN   2 model gardens
GIFT TOKENS   Own

This nursery, trading from a thatched building, carries a general range of plants and sundries. The aquatic plants are home-grown – as is their own *Pittosporum tenuifolium* 'Nutty's Leprechaun'.

CO. GALWAY

Seaside Nursery and Garden Centre
Claddaghduff, Co. Galway
☎ 00 353 95 44687   FAX 00 353 95 44761

CONTACT Charles Dÿck
LOCATION Claddaghduff (near Clifden)
OPEN 9 am – 1 pm, 2 – 6 pm, Monday – Saturday;
2 – 6 pm, Sundays
SPECIALITIES Coastal plants
NEW FOR 1995 Large selection of *Phormium*
CATALOGUE I£1
MAIL ORDER No
SHOP Pots
DESIGN SERVICE Seaside Nursery and Garden Centre
GIFT TOKENS Own

The nursery specialises in plants for seaside locations, including phormiums, and in plants for containers. They import and sell Italian pots also.

CO. KERRY

Liscahane Nursery and Garden Centre
Ardfert, Co. Kerry
☎ 00 353 66 34222 FAX 00 353 66 34600

CONTACT Don Nolan and Bill Cooley
LOCATION 3½ miles north west of Tralee
OPEN 9 am – 6 pm (or dusk), Tuesday – Saturday; 2 – 6 pm (or dusk) Sundays
GIFT TOKENS Own

A general plant range; particularly those suitable for shelter belts and coastal gardening.

Muckross Garden Centre
Muckross, Killarney, Co. Kerry
☎ 00 353 64 34044 FAX 00 353 64 31114

CONTACT Mr John Fuller
LOCATION 3 miles from Killarney, on Kenmare road
OPEN 10 am – 6 pm, Tuesday – Saturday; 2 – 6 pm, Sundays. Closed Mondays. Restricted opening hours in January and February
NEW FOR 1995 *Rubus* 'Golden Vale'
CATALOGUE Available in September
MAIL ORDER No
DESIGN SERVICE Muckross Garden Centre
GIFT TOKENS Own

Garden centre with a general range: a new shrub nursery is being developed. They have a design and maintenance capacity. The garden centre is opposite the Killarney National Park, and you can stay in their B & B, Friar's Glen.

Ryans Nurseries
Lissivigeen, Killarney, Co. Kerry
☎ 00 353 64 33507

CONTACT Tadhe Ryan
LOCATION 1½ miles from Killarney
OPEN 9 am – 6 pm, Monday – Saturday; 12 noon – 6 pm, Sundays and Bank Holidays
MAIL ORDER No
DESIGN SERVICE Ryans Nurseries
GIFT TOKENS Own

A source of shrubs for the mild climate and acid soil of Kerry, including *Arbutus* and *Dicksonia*.

CO. KILDARE

Johnstown Garden Centre
Naas, Co. Kildare
☎ 00 353 4579138 FAX 00 353 4579073

CONTACT Jim Clarke
LOCATION On N7
OPEN 9.30 am – 6 pm, Monday – Saturday; 12 noon – 6 pm, Sundays
MAIL ORDER No
GIFT TOKENS Own

A garden centre with a general range; the emphasis is on colourful foliage plants.

CO. LEITRIM

Eden Plants
Rossinver, Co. Leitrim
☎ 00 353 72 54122

CONTACT Rod Alston
LOCATION 25 miles north east of Sligo
OPEN 2 – 6 pm, daily
SPECIALITIES Herbs
CATALOGUE I£1 plus SAE
MAIL ORDER Yes; SAE for price list
GARDEN Herb garden

An organic herb nursery: all stock is grown at the nursery under organic conditions.

CO. WATERFORD

Orchardstown Nurseries
Cork Road, Waterford, Co. Waterford
☎ 00 353 51 384273 FAX 00 353 51 384422

CONTACT Ron Dool
LOCATION 4 miles from Waterford, towards Cork
OPEN 9 am – 6 pm, Monday – Saturday; 2 – 6 pm, Sundays
SPECIALITIES Rhododendrons; roses; shrubs; trees
CATALOGUE I£1.50
MAIL ORDER Yes
REFRESHMENTS Refreshments
DESIGN SERVICE Orchardstown Nurseries
GIFT TOKENS Own

Irish nursery, with a wide choice of trees and shrubs, including climbers and rhododendrons, and an excellent choice of roses too.

Nursery Specialities

ACERS
Altoona Nurseries, Devon
Andrew Norfield Trees & Seeds, Gloucestershire
Barkers Primrose Nurseries, Lancashire
Barthelemy & Co Nurseries, Dorset
International Acers, Hereford & Worcester
Nettletons Nursery, Surrey
P M A Plant Specialities, Somerset

AFRICAN VIOLETS
African Violet Centre, Norfolk

AIR PLANTS
Tamarisk Nurseries, Buckinghamshire
Vesutor Airplants, West Sussex

ALPINES
A & A Thorp, Leicestershire
Aberconwy Nursery, Clwyd
Ardfearn Nursery, Highland
Ashenden Nursery, Kent
Baker Straw Partnership, Hereford & Worcester
Beechcroft Nursery, Surrey
Birkheads Cottage Garden Nursery, Tyne & Wear
Blackthorn Nursery, Hampshire
Brambling House Alpines, South Yorkshire
Bressingham Plant Centre, Cambridgeshire
Bressingham Plant Centre, Norfolk
Charter House Hardy Plant Nursery, Dumfries & Galloway
Christie's Nursery, Tayside
Craig Lodge Nurseries, Dumfries & Galloway
DHE Plants, Derbyshire
Field House Alpines, Nottinghamshire
The Firs Nursery, Cheshire
Fosse Alpines, Leicestershire
Foxgrove Plants, Berkshire
Glen Chantry, Essex
Graham's Hardy Plants, Avon
Greenslacks Nurseries, West Yorkshire
Hartside Nursery Garden, Cumbria
Hedgerow Nursery, West Yorkshire
Highgates Nursery, Derbyshire
Hillview Hardy Plants, Shropshire
Holden Clough Nursery, Lancashire
Hoo House Nursery, Gloucestershire
Jack Drake, Highland
Jenny Burgess' Alpine Nursery, Norfolk
Kettlesing Nurseries, North Yorkshire
Kim W Davis, Shropshire
Martin Nest Nurseries, Lincolnshire
The Mead Nursery, Wiltshire
Mendle Nursery, Humberside
Mill Hill Plants, Nottinghamshire
Newton Hill Alpines, West Yorkshire
Nicky's Rock Garden Nursery, Devon
Norden Alpine Nursery, North Yorkshire
The Old Manor Nursery, Gloucestershire
Padlock Croft, Cambridgeshire
Plantables, Dumfries & Galloway
Potterton and Martin, Lincolnshire
Pringle Plants, Borders
R F Beeston, Hereford & Worcester
Reginald Kaye Ltd, Lancashire
Rookhope Nurseries, Co. Durham
Ryal Nursery, Northumberland
Shepton Nursery Garden, Somerset
Slack Top Alpines, West Yorkshire
Thuya Alpine Nursery, Gloucestershire
Timpany Nurseries, Co. Down
Tough Alpine Nursery, Grampian
Town Farm Nursery, Cleveland
Ty'r Orsaf Nursery, Gwynedd
W E Th. Ingwersen Ltd, West Sussex
West Acre Gardens, Norfolk
West Kington Nurseries Ltd, Wiltshire
White Cottage Alpines, Humberside
Wintergreen Nurseries, Hereford & Worcester

AQUATIC PLANTS
Anthony Archer-Wills Ltd, West Sussex
Barkers Primrose Nurseries, Lancashire
Bennetts Water Lily Farm, Dorset
Honeysome Aquatic Nursery, Cambridgeshire
Longstock Park Nursery, Hampshire

Malahide Nurseries Ltd, Co. Dublin
Merebrook Water Plants, Hereford & Worcester
Mickfield Fish and Watergarden Centre, Suffolk
Nine Springs Nursery, Hampshire
Pantiles Plant & Garden Centre, Surrey
Rowden Gardens, Devon
Stapeley Water Gardens Ltd, Cheshire
Water Meadow Nursery and Herb Farm, Hampshire
Wychwood Carp Farm, Hampshire

AROMATIC AND SCENTED PLANTS
Foliage Scented & Herb Plants, Surrey

AUSTRALIAN PLANTS
Ballalheannagh Gardens, Isle of Man
County Park Nursery, Essex
Mackey's Garden Centre, Co. Dublin
Marwood Hill Gardens, Devon
P & S Allanson, Isle of Man
The Seed House, Hampshire

BAMBOOS
Bamboo Nursery Ltd, Kent
Brackenwood Plant Centre, Avon
Coblands Nursery, Kent
Drysdale Garden Exotics, Hampshire
Fulbrooke Nursery, Suffolk
Simply Plants, Cambridgeshire

BEDDING PLANTS
Ballagan Nursery, Strathclyde
Cooks Garden Centre, Hereford & Worcester
Elmridge Gardens Ltd, Co. Durham
Henry Street, Berkshire
Hurdletree Nurseries, Lincolnshire
Kent Street Nurseries, East Sussex
Pantiles Plant & Garden Centre, Surrey
Primrose Cottage Nursery & Garden Centre, Greater Manchester
Steven Bailey, Hampshire
West Somerset Garden Centre, Somerset

BEGONIAS
Blackmore & Langdon, Avon
Dibleys, Clwyd
Halsway, Somerset
Rhodes & Rockliffe, Essex

BOG PLANTS
Anthony Archer-Wills Ltd, West Sussex
Bennetts Water Lily Farm, Dorset
Deanswood Plants, North Yorkshire
Honeysome Aquatic Nursery, Cambridgeshire
Longstock Park Nursery, Hampshire
Marwood Hill Gardens, Devon
Mickfield Fish and Watergarden Centre, Suffolk
Rowden Gardens, Devon
Stapeley Water Gardens Ltd, Cheshire
Water Meadow Nursery and Herb Farm, Hampshire
Wychwood Carp Farm, Hampshire

BONSAI
D N Bromage & Co Ltd, Surrey
Greenwood Gardens, Nottinghamshire
Herons Bonsai Ltd, Surrey
Norman Bonsai, East Sussex
Peter Trenear Nurseries, Hampshire
Tokonama Bonsai Nursery, Hertfordshire

BROMELIADS
Vesutor Airplants, West Sussex

BULBS
Avon Bulbs, Somerset
Bloms Bulbs Ltd, Bedfordshire
Broadleigh Gardens, Somerset
Gardenscape, North Yorkshire
J Walkers Bulbs, Lincolnshire
Jacques Amand Ltd, London
John Shipton (Bulbs), Dyfed
Knightshayes Garden Trust, Devon
Monocot Nursery, Avon
P De Jager & Sons Ltd, Kent
Paradise Centre, Suffolk
Paul Christian Rare Plants, Clwyd
Potterton and Martin, Lincolnshire
Rupert Bowlby, Surrey
S & S Perennials, Leicestershire
Van Tubergen UK, Norfolk

CACTI AND SUCCULENTS
A & A Phipps, Avon
Bradley Batch Cactus Nursery, Somerset
Connoisseurs' Cacti, Kent
Craig House Cacti, Lancashire
Croston Cactus, Lancashire
Cruck Cottage Cacti, North Yorkshire
Glenhirst Cactus Nursery, Lincolnshire
Harvest Nurseries, East Sussex
Heldon Nurseries, Staffordshire
Holly Gate Cactus Nursery, West Sussex
K & C Cacti, Devon
Pete & Ken Cactus Nursery, Kent
Southfield Nurseries, Lincolnshire
Tamarisk Nurseries, Buckinghamshire
Toobees Exotics, Surrey
Trebah Nursery, Cornwall
Westfield Cacti, Devon
Whitestone Gardens Ltd, North Yorkshire

CAMELLIAS
Bodnant Garden Nursery Ltd, Clwyd
Burncoose & South Down Nurseries, Cornwall
Coghurst Nursery, East Sussex
Exbury Enterprises Ltd, Hampshire
Marwood Hill Gardens, Devon
Porthpean House Gardens, Cornwall
Trehane Camellia Nursery, Dorset
Trewithen Nurseries, Cornwall

Nursery Specialities

CARNIVOROUS PLANTS
Flora Exotica, Essex
Heldon Nurseries, Staffordshire
Marston Exotics, Hereford & Worcester
Potterton and Martin, Lincolnshire
Sarracenia Nurseries, London
Tamarisk Nurseries, Buckinghamshire

CHRYSANTHEMUMS
H Woolman (Dorridge) Ltd, West Midlands
Halls of Heddon, Northumberland
Home Meadows Nursery Ltd, Suffolk
Philip Tivey & Son, Leicestershire
Rileys Chrysanthemums, Derbyshire

CITRUS
Four Counties Nursery, Gloucestershire
Global Orange Groves UK, Dorset
Reads Nursery, Norfolk

CLEMATIS
Abbey Dore Court Garden, Hereford & Worcester
Caddick's Clematis Nursery, Cheshire
Fisk's Clematis Nursery, Suffolk
Great Dixter Nurseries, East Sussex
J Bradshaw & Son, Kent
John Beach (Nursery) Ltd, Warwickshire
Notcutts Garden Centre, Surrey
Orchard Nurseries, Lincolnshire
Pounsley Plants, Devon
Savill's Clematis Ltd, Essex
Scotts Clematis, Devon
Sherston Parva Nursery, Wiltshire
Stillingfleet Lodge Nurseries, North Yorkshire
T H Barker & Son, Cumbria
Thorncroft Clematis Nursery, Norfolk
Treasures of Tenbury Ltd, Hereford & Worcester
The Valley Clematis Nursery, Lincolnshire
Woodborough Garden Centre, Wiltshire

CLIMBERS
Coblands Nursery, Kent
Hillier Nurseries Ltd, Hampshire
Hollington Nurseries, Berkshire
J Bradshaw & Son, Kent
Kathy Wright, Lincolnshire
Kayes Garden Nursery, Leicestershire
Reads Nursery, Norfolk
Roseland House Nursery, Cornwall
Sherston Parva Nursery, Wiltshire
Stone House Cottage Nurseries, Hereford & Worcester
Trewithen Nurseries, Cornwall
Waterwheel Nursery, Gwent

CONIFERS
Beechcroft Nursery, Surrey
Belwood Nurseries Ltd, Lothian
Bressingham Plant Centre, Cambridgeshire
Bressingham Plant Centre, Norfolk
Bressingham Plant Centre, Berkshire
Coblands Nursery, Kent
The Conifer Garden, Buckinghamshire
E L F Plants, Cramden Nursery, Northamptonshire
Fron Nursery, Shropshire
Goscote Nurseries Ltd, Leicestershire
Hedgerow Nursery, West Yorkshire
Hillier Nurseries Ltd, Hampshire
Holden Clough Nursery, Lancashire
Hull Farm Conifer Centre, Essex
Kenwith Nursery, Devon
Layham Garden Centre, Kent
Lime Cross Nursery, East Sussex
Merton Nurseries, Shropshire
Nettletons Nursery, Surrey
Rivendell Nursery, North Yorkshire
W E Th. Ingwersen Ltd, West Sussex

CONSERVATORY PLANTS
The Abbots House Garden, Hertfordshire
Brockings Exotics, Cornwall
Burncoose & South Down Nurseries, Cornwall
Clifton Nurseries, London
Fleur de Lys, West Sussex
Four Counties Nursery, Gloucestershire
Long Man Gardens, East Sussex
Orchard Nurseries, Lincolnshire
Reads Nursery, Norfolk
Special Plants, Wiltshire
Tamarisk Nurseries, Buckinghamshire
Tropicana Nursery, Devon

DAFFODILS
Ballydorn Bulb Farm, Co. Down
Broadleigh Gardens, Somerset
Carncairn Daffodils, Co. Antrim
Copford Bulbs, Essex
Evelix Daffodils, Highland
J Walkers Bulbs, Lincolnshire
P De Jager & Sons Ltd, Kent
R A Scamp, Cornwall

DAHLIAS
Aylett Nurseries Ltd, Hertfordshire
Butterfields Nursery, Buckinghamshire
Halls of Heddon, Northumberland
Oscroft's Dahlias, West Midlands
Oscroft's Dahlias, South Yorkshire
Philip Tivey & Son, Leicestershire
Scott's Nurseries, South Yorkshire

DELPHINIUMS
Blackmore & Langdon, Avon
Harrisons Delphiniums, Berkshire
Woodfield Bros, Warwickshire

DIANTHUS
Allwood Bros, West Sussex
Church Hill Cottage Gardens, Kent
Hayward's Carnations, Hampshire
Mills Farm Plants and Gardens, Suffolk
Pinks & Carnations, Lancashire

Southview Nurseries, Hampshire
Steven Bailey, Hampshire
Three Counties Nurseries, Dorset

FERNS
Apple Court, Hampshire
Barters Farm Nurseries Ltd, Wiltshire
Coblands Nursery, Kent
The Fern Nursery, Lincolnshire
Fibrex Nurseries Ltd, Warwickshire
Hartside Nursery Garden, Cumbria
Holden Clough Nursery, Lancashire
J & D Marston, Humberside
Reginald Kaye Ltd, Lancashire
Rickard's Hardy Ferns Ltd, Hereford & Worcester
Trebah Nursery, Cornwall

FOLIAGE PLANTS
Architectural Plants, West Sussex
Decorative Foliage, Devon
Drysdale Garden Exotics, Hampshire
Eggleston Hall Gardens, Co. Durham
Foliage & Unusual Plants, Cambridgeshire
Hoecroft Plants, Norfolk
Mrs S Robinson, Suffolk
Plaxtol Nurseries, Kent

FRUIT
Ballerina Trees Ltd, Cambridgeshire
Chris Bowers & Son, Norfolk
Clive Simms, Lincolnshire
Deacon's Nursery, Isle of Wight
Family Trees, Hampshire
The Fruit Garden, Kent
Highfield Nurseries, Gloucestershire
How Caple Court Gardens, Hereford & Worcester
J Tweedie Fruit Trees, Dumfries & Galloway
John Beach (Nursery) Ltd, Warwickshire
Keepers Nursery, Kent
R V Roger Ltd, North Yorkshire
Sampford Shrubs, Devon
Scotts Nurseries Ltd, Somerset
Thornhayes Nursery, Devon

FUCHSIAS
A D & N Wheeler, Warwickshire
Arcadia Nurseries Ltd., Cleveland
Askew Nurseries, Leicestershire
B & H M Baker, Essex
Beacon Fuchsias, Dorset
C S Lockyer, Avon
Clay Lane Nursery, Surrey
Cottage Nurseries, Nottinghamshire
Exotic Fuchsias, Dyfed
Fuchsiavale Nurseries, Hereford & Worcester
G Nice, Suffolk
Gatehampton Nursery, Berkshire
Gouldings Fuchsias, Suffolk
Jackson's Nurseries, Staffordshire
John Smith & Son, Leicestershire

Kathleen Muncaster Fuchsias, Lincolnshire
Kent Street Nurseries, East Sussex
Little Brook Fuchsias, Surrey
Meadowcroft Fuchsias, Cambridgeshire
Oakleigh Nurseries, Hampshire
Oldbury Nurseries, Kent
Porter's Fuchsias, Merseyside
Potash Nursery, Suffolk
Top Pots, Hertfordshire
The Vernon Geranium Nursery, Surrey
Ward Fuchsias, Cheshire
White Veil Fuchsias, Dorset

GRASSES
Apple Court, Hampshire
Brownthwaite Hardy Plants, Cumbria
Coblands Nursery, Kent
Hoecroft Plants, Norfolk
Holden Clough Nursery, Lancashire
Park Green Nurseries, Suffolk
Simply Plants, Cambridgeshire
Stillingfleet Lodge Nurseries, North Yorkshire
Trevor Scott Ornamental Grasses, Essex

GROUND COVER PLANTS
Barters Farm Nurseries Ltd, Wiltshire
Growing Carpets, Hertfordshire
Toad Hall Produce, Hereford & Worcester

HALF-HARDY PLANTS
Abbotsbury Gardens, Dorset
Arivegaig Nursery, Highland
Barters Farm Nurseries Ltd, Wiltshire
Brian Hiley, Surrey
Brockings Exotics, Cornwall
Craigieburn Classic Plants, Dumfries & Galloway
Duchy of Cornwall Nursery, Cornwall
Hayloft Plants, Hereford & Worcester

HEATHERS
Angus Heathers, Tayside
Brownlow Heathers, Co. Armagh
D & M Everett, Hereford & Worcester
Daisy Hill Nurseries Ltd, Co. Down
Denbeigh Heathers, Suffolk
Goscote Nurseries Ltd, Leicestershire
Herb and Heather Garden Centre, North Yorkshire
Naked Cross Nurseries, Dorset
Okell's Nurseries, Cheshire
Otter's Court Heathers, Somerset
Ridgeway Heather Nursery, Shropshire
Speyside Heather Centre, Highland

HEDGING
Barters Farm Nurseries Ltd, Wiltshire
Ben Reid & Co, Grampian
Buckingham Nurseries and Garden Centre, Buckinghamshire
Bucknell Nurseries, Shropshire
Christie Elite Nurseries, Grampian
Country House Hedging, Hereford & Worcester

Nursery Specialities 237

Forward Nurseries, Kent
Landford Trees, Wiltshire
Mount Pleasant Trees, Avon
Perrie Hale Forest Nursery, Devon
Sherborne Gardens Nursery, Gloucestershire
Weasdale Nurseries, Cumbria

HERBACEOUS PERENNIALS
Abbey Dore Court Garden, Hereford & Worcester
Abriachan Gardens & Nursery, Highland
Arley Hall Nursery, Cheshire
Ashenden Nursery, Kent
Axletree Nursery, East Sussex
Baker Straw Partnership, Hereford & Worcester
Ballyrogan Nurseries, Co. Down
Barnsdale Plants, Leicestershire
Bellhouse Nursery, Cheshire
The Beth Chatto Gardens Ltd, Essex
Birchwood Farm Nursery, Derbyshire
Birkheads Cottage Garden Nursery, Tyne & Wear
Black Isle Nurseries, Highland
Blackthorn Nursery, Hampshire
Bosvigo Plants, Cornwall
Botanic Nursery, Wiltshire
Brackenwood Plant Centre, Avon
Bregover Plants, Cornwall
Bressingham Gardens Mail Order, Norfolk
Bressingham Plant Centre, Cambridgeshire
Bressingham Plant Centre, Norfolk
Bressingham Plant Centre, Berkshire
Bridge End Nurseries, Dumfries & Galloway
Broadleigh Gardens, Somerset
Brownthwaite Hardy Plants, Cumbria
Burnside Nursery, Strathclyde
C E & D M Nurseries, Lincolnshire
C M Dickinson, Cheshire
Cally Gardens, Dumfries & Galloway
Catforth Gardens, Lancashire
Charter House Hardy Plant Nursery, Dumfries & Galloway
Church Hill Cottage Gardens, Kent
Cilwern Plants, Dyfed
Coblands Nursery, Kent
Cotswold Garden Flowers, Hereford & Worcester
Cottage Garden Plants, West Sussex
The Cottage Herbery, Hereford & Worcester
Craigieburn Classic Plants, Dumfries & Galloway
Cranesbill Nursery, Hereford & Worcester
Croftway Nursery, West Sussex
Duchy of Cornwall Nursery, Cornwall
Eastgrove Cottage Garden Nursery, Hereford & Worcester
Elizabeth MacGregor, Dumfries & Galloway
Elworthy Cottage Garden Plants, Somerset
Fairy Lane Nurseries, Greater Manchester
The Firs Nursery, Cheshire
Foliage & Unusual Plants, Cambridgeshire
Four Seasons, Norfolk
Frances Mount Perennial Plants, Essex
Gannock Growers, Hertfordshire
The Garden at The Elms, Hereford & Worcester
Glebe Cottage Plants, Devon
Glen Chantry, Essex
Green Farm Plants, Surrey
Hadspen Garden and Nursery, Somerset
Halecat Garden Nurseries, Cumbria
Hall Farm Nursery, Lincolnshire
Hall Farm Nursery, Shropshire
Hannays of Bath, Avon
Hardy's Cottage Garden Plants, Hampshire
Hellyer's Garden Plants, West Sussex
Henllys Lodge Plants, Gwynedd
The Hiller Garden and Plant Centre, Warwickshire
Hillview Hardy Plants, Shropshire
Holden Clough Nursery, Lancashire
Hoo House Nursery, Gloucestershire
Hosta Garden, Strathclyde
Houghton Farm Plants, West Sussex
Iden Croft Herbs, Kent
Judy's Country Garden, Lincolnshire
Kayes Garden Nursery, Leicestershire
Kaytie Fisher Nursery, Surrey
Kelways Ltd, Somerset
Kim W Davis, Shropshire
Langthorns Plantery, Essex
Layham Garden Centre, Kent
Lilliesleaf Nursery, Borders
Little Treasures Nursery, Cornwall
Longacre Nursery, Kent
Longstock Park Nursery, Hampshire
Lower Severalls Herb Nursery, Somerset
Margery Fish Plant Nursery, Somerset
Martins Nursery, Suffolk
Marwood Hill Gardens, Devon
The Mead Nursery, Wiltshire
Merriments Gardens, East Sussex
Merton Nurseries, Shropshire
Mill Cottage Plants, Somerset
Mill Hill Plants, Nottinghamshire
Mill Race Nursery, Essex
Milton Garden Plants, Dorset
Mires Beck Nursery, Humberside
Monksilver Nursery, Cambridgeshire
Nordybank Nurseries, Shropshire
Northumbria Nurseries, Northumberland
Norwell Nursery, Nottinghamshire
Oak Tree Nursery, North Yorkshire
Old Court Nurseries, Hereford & Worcester
Orchard House Nursery, North Yorkshire
Orchard Nurseries, Lincolnshire
Padlock Croft, Cambridgeshire
Paradise Centre, Suffolk
Park Green Nurseries, Suffolk
Perry's Plants, North Yorkshire
Perrybrook Nursery, Shropshire
Perryhill Nurseries, East Sussex
Plantables, Dumfries & Galloway

238 Nursery Specialities

The Plantation, Shropshire
Plantings Garden Nursery, Central
Pounsley Plants, Devon
Primrose Cottage Nursery & Garden Centre, Greater Manchester
Priory Garden Nursery, Gloucestershire
R D Plants, Devon
Rarer Plants, North Yorkshire
Raveningham Gardens, Norfolk
Ravensthorpe Nursery, Northamptonshire
Reginald Kaye Ltd, Lancashire
Rookhope Nurseries, Co. Durham
Roseland House Nursery, Cornwall
Rowden Gardens, Devon
Rushfields of Ledbury, Hereford & Worcester
S & E Bond, Hereford & Worcester
Shepton Nursery Garden, Somerset
Sherborne Gardens Nursery, Gloucestershire
Southview Nurseries, Hampshire
Spinners, Hampshire
Stillingfleet Lodge Nurseries, North Yorkshire
Sue Hawthorne Gardens, Shropshire
Thyme House Nursery, Cambridgeshire
Timpany Nurseries, Co. Down
Toad Hall Produce, Hereford & Worcester
Town Farm Nursery, Cleveland
Ty'r Orsaf Nursery, Gwynedd
Unusual Perennials, Norfolk
Usual & Unusual Plants, East Sussex
Veryans Plants, Devon
The Walled Garden, Suffolk
Water Meadow Nursery and Herb Farm, Hampshire
Waterwheel Nursery, Gwent
West Kington Nurseries Ltd, Wiltshire
Westwinds Perennial Plants, Cleveland
Wintergreen Nurseries, Hereford & Worcester
Withleigh Nurseries, Devon
Woodlands Cottage Nursery, North Yorkshire
Wye Valley Herbs, Gwent

HERBS
Arne Herbs, Avon
Baker Straw Partnership, Hereford & Worcester
Barwinnock Herbs, Strathclyde
Blooming Things, Powys
Bradley Gardens Nursery, Northumberland
Cheshire Herbs, Cheshire
The Cottage Herbery, Hereford & Worcester
Cowcombe Farm Herbs, Gloucestershire
Daphne ffiske Herbs, Norfolk
Eden Plants, Co. Leitrim
Elly Hill Herbs, Co. Durham
Foliage Scented & Herb Plants, Surrey
Gwydir Plants, Gwynedd
Herb and Heather Garden Centre, North Yorkshire
The Herb Garden, Derbyshire
The Herb Garden & Plant Hunters Nursery, Gwynedd
The Herb Nursery, Leicestershire
The Herbary Prickwillow, Cambridgeshire

Hewthorn Herbs & Wild Flowers, Nottinghamshire
Hexham Herbs, Northumberland
Hill Farm Herbs, Northamptonshire
Hollington Nurseries, Berkshire
Iden Croft Herbs, Kent
Jekka's Herb Farm, Avon
Judy's Country Garden, Lincolnshire
Lisdoonan Herbs, Co. Down
Lower Severalls Herb Nursery, Somerset
LW Plants, Hertfordshire
Marle Place Gardens & Nursery, Kent
Nordybank Nurseries, Shropshire
Oak Cottage Herb Garden, Shropshire
The Old Mill Herbary, Cornwall
Poyntzfield Herb Nursery, Highland
Water Meadow Nursery and Herb Farm, Hampshire
The Wildlife Gardening Centre, Oxfordshire
Woodlands Cottage Nursery, North Yorkshire
Wye Valley Herbs, Gwent

HOUSE PLANTS
African Violet Centre, Norfolk
Clifton Nurseries, London
Dibleys, Clwyd
Tropicana Nursery, Devon
The Van Hage Garden Company, Hertfordshire

IRIS
Agars Nursery, Hampshire
Croftway Nursery, West Sussex
Kelways Ltd, Somerset
Mill Hill Plants, Nottinghamshire
Robinsons of Whaley Bridge, Cheshire
Rowden Gardens, Devon
S & S Perennials, Leicestershire
V H Humphrey, Surrey
Zephyrwude Irises, West Yorkshire

IVIES
Fibrex Nurseries Ltd, Warwickshire
Forward Nurseries, Kent
Whitehouse Ivies, Essex

LILIES
Bullwood Nursery, Essex
Flora Exotica, Essex
J Walkers Bulbs, Lincolnshire
S & S Perennials, Leicestershire

NEW ZEALAND PLANTS
Ballaheannagh Gardens, Isle of Man
County Park Nursery, Essex
Island Plants, Highland
Marwood Hill Gardens, Devon
P & S Allanson, Isle of Man

ORCHIDS
Burnham Nurseries, Devon
Butterfields Nursery, Buckinghamshire
Equatorial Plant Co, Co. Durham
Ken Evans Orchids, Essex

Nursery Specialities

Mansell & Hatcher Ltd, West Yorkshire
Orcon Exotics, Hereford & Worcester
Tamarisk Nurseries, Buckinghamshire
Uzumara Orchids, Highland
Woodstock Orchids and Automations, Buckinghamshire

ORGANIC NURSERIES
Aultan Nursery, Grampian
Barwinnock Herbs, Strathclyde
Blooming Things, Powys
The Cottage Herbery, Hereford & Worcester
Eden Plants, Co. Leitrim
Rivendell Nursery, North Yorkshire
Wye Valley Herbs, Gwent

PAEONIES
Abbey Dore Court Garden, Hereford & Worcester
Kelways Ltd, Somerset
Phedar Nursery, Cheshire

PALMS
The Palm Centre, London

PELARGONIUMS
A D & N Wheeler, Warwickshire
The Beeches Nursery, Nottinghamshire
Brian Sulman Pelargoniums, Suffolk
Denmead Geranium Nurseries, Hampshire
Derek Lloyd Dean, London
Fibrex Nurseries Ltd, Warwickshire
The Geranium Nursery, West Sussex
Hosford's Geraniums & Garden Centre, Co. Cork
Kent Street Nurseries, East Sussex
Meadowcroft Fuchsias, Cambridgeshire
Oakleigh Nurseries, Hampshire
Oldbury Nurseries, Kent
Pearl Sulman, Suffolk
Three Suns Nursery, Essex
The Vernon Geranium Nursery, Surrey
West Country Geraniums, Avon

PRIMULAS
Abriachan Gardens & Nursery, Highland
Ardfearn Nursery, Highland
Bregover Plants, Cornwall
Craig Lodge Nurseries, Dumfries & Galloway
Craigieburn Classic Plants, Dumfries & Galloway
The Fens, Essex
Field House Alpines, Nottinghamshire
Gardenscape, North Yorkshire
Glendoick Garden Centre, Tayside
Greenslacks Nurseries, West Yorkshire
Hillview Hardy Plants, Shropshire
Longstock Park Nursery, Hampshire
Martin Nest Nurseries, Lincolnshire
Mendle Nursery, Humberside
Norden Alpine Nursery, North Yorkshire
R F Beeston, Hereford & Worcester
Ryal Nursery, Northumberland
Slack Top Alpines, West Yorkshire

Surrey Primroses, Surrey
Timpany Nurseries, Co. Down
Veryans Plants, Devon
West Acre Gardens, Norfolk

RHODODENDRONS
Ballalheannagh Gardens, Isle of Man
Bodnant Garden Nursery Ltd, Clwyd
Burncoose & South Down Nurseries, Cornwall
Coghurst Nursery, East Sussex
Exbury Enterprises Ltd, Hampshire
F Morrey & Son, Cheshire
Glendoick Garden Centre, Tayside
The High Garden, Devon
Highgates Nursery, Derbyshire
Hydon Nurseries, Surrey
Knap Hill Nursery Ltd, Surrey
Lanhydrock Gardens, Cornwall
Lea Gardens, Derbyshire
Melville Nurseries, Lothian
Millais Nurseries, Surrey
Muncaster Plants, Cumbria
Notcutts Garden Centre, Surrey
Orchardstown Nurseries, Co. Waterford
Plantables, Dumfries & Galloway
Sampford Shrubs, Devon
Seaforde Gardens, Co. Down
Starborough Nursery, Kent
Tree Shop, Strathclyde
Trewithen Nurseries, Cornwall
Wall Cottage Nursery, Cornwall

ROSES
A J Palmer & Son, Buckinghamshire
Apuldram Roses, West Sussex
Battersby Roses, North Yorkshire
C & K Jones, Cheshire
C & K Jones, Clwyd
Cants of Colchester, Essex
Corsley Mill, Brigid Quest-Ritson, Wiltshire
Cranborne Manor Garden Centre, Dorset
David Austin Roses, Shropshire
Dickson Nurseries Ltd, Co. Down
F Haynes & Partners, Northamptonshire
F Morrey & Son, Cheshire
Fryer's Roses Ltd., Cheshire
Gandy's Roses Ltd, Leicestershire
Godly's Roses, Hertfordshire
Hadspen Garden and Nursery, Somerset
Henry Street, Berkshire
The Hiller Garden and Plant Centre, Warwickshire
Hosford's Geraniums & Garden Centre, Co. Cork
How Caple Court Gardens, Hereford & Worcester
Hunts Court Garden & Nursery, Gloucestershire
James Cocker & Sons, Grampian
Just Roses, East Sussex
Kaytie Fisher Nursery, Surrey
Layham Garden Centre, Kent
Mattock Roses, Oxfordshire

240 Nursery Specialities

Mills Farm Plants and Gardens, Suffolk
Notcutts Nurseries, Suffolk
Orchardstown Nurseries, Co. Waterford
Perryhill Nurseries, East Sussex
Peter Beales Roses, Norfolk
R Harkness & Co Ltd, Hertfordshire
Rumwood Nurseries, Kent
Scotts Nurseries Ltd, Somerset
Trevor White Old Fashioned Roses, Norfolk
Warner's Roses, Shropshire
West Kington Nurseries Ltd, Wiltshire
Wheatcroft Ltd, Nottinghamshire

SEMPERVIVUMS
Alan C Smith, Kent
Brambling House Alpines, South Yorkshire
Greenslacks Nurseries, West Yorkshire
H & S Wills, Devon
Mary & Peter Mitchell, West Sussex
Mendle Nursery, Humberside

SHRUBS
Ballalheannagh Gardens, Isle of Man
Barnsdale Plants, Leicestershire
Beechcroft Nurseries, Cumbria
Beetham Nurseries, Cumbria
Bellhouse Nursery, Cheshire
Belwood Nurseries Ltd, Lothian
Botanic Nursery, Wiltshire
Brackenwood Plant Centre, Avon
Bressingham Plant Centre, Norfolk
Chichester Trees and Shrubs, Hampshire
Christie Elite Nurseries, Grampian
Coblands Nursery, Kent
Daisy Hill Nurseries Ltd, Co. Down
Duchy of Cornwall Nursery, Cornwall
E L F Plants, Cramden Nursery, Northamptonshire
F Morrey & Son, Cheshire
Fron Nursery, Shropshire
Goscote Nurseries Ltd, Leicestershire
Grange Farm Nursery, Hereford & Worcester
Hartshall Nursery Stock, Suffolk
Hedgerow Nursery, West Yorkshire
Hergest Croft Gardens, Hereford & Worcester
Holden Clough Nursery, Lancashire
Kathy Wright, Lincolnshire
Lanhydrock Gardens, Cornwall
Layham Garden Centre, Kent
Lime Cross Nursery, East Sussex
Little Treasures Nursery, Cornwall
Madrona Nursery, Kent
Manorbier Garden Centre, Dyfed
Melville Nurseries, Lothian
Monksilver Nursery, Cambridgeshire
Mrs S M Cooper, Hereford & Worcester
Nettletons Nursery, Surrey
Notcutts Nurseries, Suffolk
Orchardstown Nurseries, Co. Waterford
Pantiles Plant & Garden Centre, Surrey
Peter Trenear Nurseries, Hampshire
Pleasant View Nursery & Garden, Devon
Rivendell Nursery, North Yorkshire
Sampford Shrubs, Devon
Shepton Nursery Garden, Somerset
Spinners, Hampshire
St. Ishmaels Nurseries and Garden Centre, Dyfed
Stone House Cottage Nurseries, Hereford & Worcester
Town Farm Nursery, Cleveland
Weasdale Nurseries, Cumbria
West Somerset Garden Centre, Somerset
Westonbirt Plant Centre, Gloucestershire
Withleigh Nurseries, Devon

SOUTH AMERICAN PLANTS
Feebers Hardy Plants, Devon

SWEET PEAS
S & N Brackley, Buckinghamshire

TOPIARY
Clifton Nurseries, London
Country House Hedging, Hereford & Worcester
Langley Boxwood Nursery, Hampshire
The Romantic Garden Nursery, Norfolk
Sherborne Gardens Nursery, Gloucestershire

TREES
Andrew Norfield Trees & Seeds, Gloucestershire
Arbor Exotica, Cambridgeshire
Barters Farm Nurseries Ltd, Wiltshire
Beechcroft Nurseries, Cumbria
Beetham Nurseries, Cumbria
Belwood Nurseries Ltd, Lothian
Ben Reid & Co, Grampian
Bluebell Nursery, Derbyshire
Brinkley Nurseries, Nottinghamshire
Buckingham Nurseries and Garden Centre, Buckinghamshire
Bucknell Nurseries, Shropshire
Celyn Vale Nurseries, Clwyd
Chichester Trees and Shrubs, Hampshire
Christie Elite Nurseries, Grampian
Coblands Nursery, Kent
Daisy Hill Nurseries Ltd, Co. Down
Duchy of Cornwall Nursery, Cornwall
F Morrey & Son, Cheshire
Four Counties Nursery, Gloucestershire
Fron Nursery, Shropshire
Goscote Nurseries Ltd, Leicestershire
Grange Farm Nursery, Hereford & Worcester
Greenway Gardens, Devon
Hartshall Nursery Stock, Suffolk
Hergest Croft Gardens, Hereford & Worcester
Hillier Nurseries Ltd, Hampshire
John Beach (Nursery) Ltd, Warwickshire
Landford Trees, Wiltshire
Lime Cross Nursery, East Sussex
Madrona Nursery, Kent

Nursery Specialities

Mallet Court Nursery, Somerset
Marwood Hill Gardens, Devon
Mill Race Nursery, Essex
Mount Pleasant Trees, Avon
Mrs S M Cooper, Hereford & Worcester
Notcutts Nurseries, Suffolk
Orchardstown Nurseries, Co. Waterford
P H Kellett, Kent
P M A Plant Specialities, Somerset
Perrie Hale Forest Nursery, Devon
Peter Trenear Nurseries, Hampshire
Seaforde Gardens, Co. Down
Spinners, Hampshire
St Ishmaels Nurseries and Garden Centre, Dyfed
Starborough Nursery, Kent
Thornhayes Nursery, Devon
Tree Shop, Strathclyde
Waterwheel Nursery, Gwent
Weasdale Nurseries, Cumbria
Westonbirt Plant Centre, Gloucestershire
YSJ Seeds, Somerset

VIOLAS

Bouts Cottage Nurseries, Hereford & Worcester
Bregover Plants, Cornwall
C W Groves & Son, Dorset
Elizabeth MacGregor, Dumfries & Galloway
Hazeldene Nursery, Kent
Richard G M Cawthorne, Kent
Robinsons of Whaley Bridge, Cheshire
Rodney Fuller, Somerset

WILD FLOWERS

Applegarth Nursery, Shropshire
Arne Herbs, Avon
Blooming Things, Powys
British Wild Plants, Dumfries & Galloway
Cowcombe Farm Herbs, Gloucestershire
Gwydir Plants, Gwynedd
The Herb Garden & Plant Hunters Nursery, Gwynedd
The Herb Nursery, Leicestershire
Hewthorn Herbs & Wild Flowers, Nottinghamshire
Hexham Herbs, Northumberland
Iden Croft Herbs, Kent
Jekka's Herb Farm, Avon
John Chambers Wild Flower Seeds, Northamptonshire
Landlife Wildflowers Ltd, Merseyside
Linda Gascoigne Wild Flowers, Leicestershire
Marle Place Gardens & Nursery, Kent
Mires Beck Nursery, Humberside
Naturescape, Nottinghamshire
Nordybank Nurseries, Shropshire
Oak Cottage Herb Garden, Shropshire
The Wild Flower Centre, Norfolk
The Wildlife Gardening Centre, Oxfordshire
YSJ Seeds, Somerset

Importing & Exporting Plants

CITES

Before considering the import and export of plants, it is necessary to understand the growing importance of the Convention on International Trade in Endangered Species of Wild Fauna and Flora (CITES). It regulates all the trade in wild plants which are listed in its schedules, and the UK is among its 120 signatories. 'Trade' is not limited to commerce: any movement of specimens across international frontiers constitutes trade for CITES purposes. A plant bought by you on holiday abroad falls within CITES if it is of a species included in the appendices to the Convention. Failure to comply with the rules is a criminal offence.

The list of species is regularly revised. It forbids the import or export of those species which are listed as endangered and restricts trade in those which are at risk of becoming endangered. CITES has several appendices. Appendix I is a list of species which are considered to be most at risk and which can only be traded if they are artificially propagated and carry a licence: it includes seriously endangered species like *Mammillaria pectinifera* and *Vanda coerulea*. Appendix II lists those species which are not currently in danger, but will be at risk if present levels of exploitation continue. It permits trade in wild collected material and seed. The principal genera protected by CITES are *Aloe, Cyclamen, Galanthus, Nepenthes, Sternbergia* and all orchids, cycads and cacti, but it is essential that anyone wishing to buy, sell or collect plants should know what is protected and what is not. That said, you can assume that any plant offered by a reputable nurseryman may legitimately be bought.

The Law of Import and Export

The basis of all the rules about importing and exporting plants is *The Plant Health (Great Britain) Order 1993* (SI No. 1993/1320). It is a fiendishly complicated piece of legislation, which consists of old British regulations which have had European Community directives grafted on to them, but it represents a significant loosening up of the old restrictions.

The Order 'seeks to implement a new system of controls on the movement of plants, plant products and other objects arising from the establishment of the single market within the European Community'. It divides the world into three zones. First there is the European Community. Within the EC, the rules are all the same, and comparatively lax. Second, there is the rest of the world from Switzerland to Vanuatu: by and large these countries get second-class treatment. The keen gardener in Munich can bring plants back from the wildest parts of Sicily or Crete but may not pop across the border to buy them from nurseries in Salzburg or Basle. Finally there are the 'protected zones' within parts of the EC. Here the regulations are stricter still.

The EC and the Rest of the World

The background to the EC's relations with the rest of the world is a story of protectionism masquerading as sound phytosanitary practice. Every nation state had regulations to prevent the entry of harmful organisms which were not already in their areas. All had quarantine stations, ostensibly to protect important crops from potential damage or destruction, but in reality to protect home growers from foreign competition. Since other countries, especially the United States, operated the same restrictions against imports from Europe, the argument was advanced that the export of plants also had to be controlled to ensure that pests and diseases were not spread.

The key was the phytosanitary certificate. Government scientists inspected produce to ensure that it was free from contamination. Armed with a certificate, plants could travel anywhere in the world. In practice, however, the plants were kept in quarantine in the receiving country for long enough to kill them.

Phytosanitary certificates are still needed for the export of a large number of types of plants to many countries and for their import into the EC. The schedules to *The Plant Health (Great Britain) Order 1993* list in great detail the plants, and plant products such as forest bark, that cannot be imported into the EC and those that can come in provided they have been inspected in the country of origin or consignor country, and are accompanied by phytosanitary certificates. Anyone who needs to know the exact extent of the legislation should buy a copy and study it carefully.

The rules are most readily relaxed for those countries nearest to us. (1) Austria and Switzerland enjoy one unique concession: they suffer from no restrictions of the export of seed potatoes (varieties of *Solanum tuberosum*) to the EC. (2) The following genera can be imported into the EC from all non-EC European countries: *Abies* (firs), *Castanea* (sweet chestnuts), *Cedrus* (cedars), *Chaenomeles* (Japanese quinces), *Chamaecyparis* (false cypresses), *Cydonia* (true quinces), *Juniperus* (junipers), *Larix* (larches), *Malus* (apples), *Photinia*, *Picea* (spruces), *Pinus* (pines), *Prunus* (plums, cherries, peaches, almonds and apricots), *Pseudotsuga* (Douglas firs), *Pyrus* (pears), *Quercus* (oaks), *Rosa* (roses) and *Tsuga* (hemlock trees). There is still an absolute ban on their import from outside Europe, subject to certain concessions: *Cydonia*, *Malus*, *Prunus* and *Pyrus* can be imported from all Mediterranean countries, Australia, New Zealand, Canada and the continental states of the USA, while strawberry plants (*Fragaria*) can be brought in from those countries but not from the rest of Europe. (3) However, some plants are banned from entering the EC from whatever source. These include two major economic genera: *Vitis* (grape vines) and *Citrus*. (4) Finally, there are some oddities. Palm trees of the genus *Phoenix* are prohibited from entering the EC from Algeria and Morocco; poplars (*Populus*) may not be imported from any part of North America.

Personal Allowances

How does all this affect the holiday-maker who wants to bring a hibiscus back from his holiday in Tenerife? There is no distinction between wild and cultivated plants so far as the international conservation controls are concerned.

The guiding principle for collecting plants is this: do not touch anything unless: (i) you are sure it is not protected and (ii) you have the permission of the owner. Moreover, you should never endanger the plant community from which you collect, nor take material which you will not be able to grow or use.

You should also remember that seed is generally the best way of bringing back plants because it can be cleaned of any pests it might carry. However, some seeds may bring disease with them (a few, like some *Ligustrum* species, carry viruses) and others may have pathological fungi or bacteria on their surfaces. Dormant cuttings are generally less of a hazard than those in full growth. Rooted plants are riskier still because of the very large numbers of micro-organisms which exist in and around their surfaces. Even washing off all the soil cannot guarantee that the roots are free from nematodes or fungal and bacterial spores.

That said, it is important to be positive and make good use of the possibilities to enrich our gardens, instead of dwelling on risks that are unidentified and unquantifiable. Many people would like to know what they can bring back from their holidays abroad. First, you must be sure that there are no legal restrictions in the country you visit. Then you need to know the regulations which apply in Great Britain.

Never smuggle anything home in your spongebag. Find out what the British authorities allow, and keep within the rules. The basic principle – contrary to widespread belief – is that individuals are free to bring back small quantities of plants and propagating material from anywhere in the world. 'Small quantities' means:

(i) up to 2kg of fruit and raw vegetables (although potatoes are not permitted);
(ii) one bouquet of cut flowers, and
(iii) five packets of seed.

These can be imported from any part of the world, provided that they are only for your personal household use, exhibit no sign of pests or diseases, and accompany you home as part of your personal baggage.

More can be imported from the 'non-EC countries of the Euro-Mediterranean area': this means all European countries, plus Algeria, Cyprus, Egypt, Israel, Jordan, Lebanon, Libya, Malta, Morocco, Tunisia and Turkey. The allowance from these countries is increased to permit two additional items:
(i) 2 kg of bulbs, corms, tubers or rhizomes, and
(ii) five plants.

Once again, there is a proviso that they should only be for your personal household use, exhibit no sign of pests or diseases, and accompany you home as part of your personal baggage.

These regulations apply to children as well as adults and make no distinction between wild-collected and cultivated plants. There is no restriction on the import of flower seeds from any part of the world: the 'five packets' rule therefore applies only to non-flower seeds.

These rules and concessions apply only to Great Britain, and not to Northern Ireland or to any other country. Similar regulations apply within each member-state of the EC, but travellers wishing to take plants abroad should check the local requirements before departure. This is important: there may be some nasty surprises for the unwary. For example, many countries ban the import of apples, pears and plums from Great Britain, because of the widespread incidence of fireblight here.

Further advice on personal allowances is available from the Plant Health Division, MAFF, Whitehall Place (East Block), London SW1A 2HH. MAFF also publishes a leaflet entitled 'Traveller's Guide to Bringing Plants Back From Abroad (Including Wild Plants)'.

Moving Plants within the EC

In general there are no restrictions on private individuals buying plants for their personal use from anywhere in the EC. People who live in protected zones have to comply with the higher plant health standards which exist there. Regulations govern the movement of wholesale material through the EC but again the principle is that free movement is permitted provided that the plants have been inspected at the place of production and are accompanied by a plant passport.

Plant passports are effectively phytosanitary certificates for internal EC use only. They are needed even within a single member-state, for any sale or transport of certain economic plants: hops, potatoes, vines, citrus fruits and members of the Rosaceae which are susceptible to fireblight – *Amelanchier, Chaenomeles, Cotoneaster, Crataegus, Cydonia, Eriobotrya, Malus, Mespilu, Prunus, Pyracantha, Pyrus, Sorbus* and *Stransvaesia*. These genera require a plant passport at all stages down to the retailer.

There is also a much wider category of plants which require a plant passport unless, as is usually the case, they are intended and ready for immediate retail sale. Those plants include the following genera: *Argyranthemum, Aster, Brassica, Castanea, Cucumis, Dendranthema, Dianthus, Exacum, Fragaria, Gerbera, Gysophila, Impatiens, Lactuca, Larix, Leucanthemum, Lupinus, Pelargonium, Picea, Pinus, Platanus, Populus, Pseudotsuga, Quercus, Rubus, Spinacia, Tanacetum, Tsuga* and *Verbena*. To these should be added bulbs and corms of: *Camassia, Chionodoxa, Crocus flava, Galanthus, Galtonia candicans, Gladiolus, Hyacinthus, Iris, Ismene, Muscari, Narcissus, Ornithogalum, Puschkinia, Scilla, Tigridia* and *Tulipa*.

But that is not all. The same regulations apply to a ragbag of plants including all members of the *Solanaceae* (apart from potatoes), all *Persea* species (avocado pears) and all members of the *Araceae, Marantaceae, Musaceae* and *Strelitzaceae* unless their roots have been cut off; and bulbs (and seeds too, rather an unusual stipulation) of onions, leeks and chives. All these require a plant passport unless 'they are intended for immediate retail sale'.

Plant passports are issued by the selling nursery, and the procedures are easily accommodated within the routines of a well-run nursery. Any nursery may apply to MAFF for authority to issue plant passports. If it complies with their requirements, MAFF appoints a member of the nursery's staff to implement the correct procedures. This person's responsibility is to inspect plants in the nursery, keep records and liaise with MAFF.

Detailed information and assistance is available from MAFF offices.

Protected Zones

Protected zones are exceptions to the One Nation Europe policy, which have been negotiated by individual member-states. They are areas (usually countries) which are substantially free from a particular harmful pest or disease and where, as a result, a higher level of plant health control is required to keep them free. Be aware of these exceptions.

Conclusion
Despite appearances, *The Plant Health (Great Britain) Order 1993* represents a significant relaxation of restrictions on the movement of plants. It opens up our gardens to the riches of European nurseries: one glance at the catalogues of leading growers and nurserymen in Holland, France, Italy and Germany is enough to show how much we have to gain from this change of the rules.

13 Seedsmen

Andrew Norfield Trees & Seeds
See Gloucestershire, Nurseries section

Ashwood Nurseries
See West Midlands, Nurseries section

Carters Tested Seeds Ltd
Hele Road, Torquay, Devon TQ2 7QJ
☎ 01803 616156   FAX 01803 615747
OPEN   From stockists only
SPECIALITIES   Seeds
MAIL ORDER   From stockists

Long-established seed company in the Suttons group. The flower and vegetable range is sold through garden centres and some supermarkets. Details of stockists from the company.

Cheshire Herbs
See Cheshire, Nurseries section

Chiltern Seeds
Bortree Stile, Ulverston, Cumbria LA12 7PB
☎ 01229 581137   FAX 01229 584549
CONTACT   Mrs P. A. Burns
OPEN   Mail order only
SPECIALITIES   Seeds
CATALOGUE   On request
MAIL ORDER   Yes
GIFT TOKENS   Own

The distinctive long, tall catalogue lists thousands of species and cultivars from around the world, including garden flowers and vegetables. Always something to interest the adventurous or the armchair gardener. The careful descriptions make it useful for reference too. Orders can be phoned through 24 hours a day.

Chris Chadwell – Freelance Botanist
81 Parlaunt Road, Slough, Berkshire SL3 8DE
CONTACT   Chris Chadwell
LOCATION   5 minutes from M4, J5
OPEN   Mail order
SPECIALITIES   Seeds
CATALOGUE   3 second class stamps
MAIL ORDER   Yes
GARDEN   Display garden, open by appointment

Seeds from the Himalaya. You either subscribe for a share in a collecting expedition, or you can buy from his stocks. Other areas are also available. Many Himalayan species can be seen in the P. N. Kohli Memorial Botanic Garden: not large, but full of unusual species. Mr Chadwell is also secretary of the Sino-Himalayan Plant Association.

Cowcombe Farm Herbs
See Gloucestershire, Nurseries section

CTDA
See London, Nurseries section

D T Brown & Co Ltd
Station Road, Poulton le Fylde, Lancashire FY6 7HX
☎ 01253 882371   FAX 01253 890923
CONTACT   David N. Whittam
OPEN   Mail order only
SPECIALITIES   Seeds
CATALOGUE   On request
MAIL ORDER   Yes
GIFT TOKENS   Own

Flower and vegetable seed merchants, with some young plants, grass seed and horticultural sundries. A large range is sold from their clear and concise catalogue. They issue a separate seed catalogue for commercial growers and florists.

Edwin Tucker & Sons
Brewery Meadow, Stonepark, Ashburton, Devon TQ13 7DG
☎ 01364 652403   FAX 01364 654300
CONTACT   Mrs G. Williams
LOCATION   Ashburton and Crediton
OPEN   Ashburton: 8 am – 5 pm, Monday – Friday. Crediton: 8.30 am – 5 pm, Monday – Saturday.
SPECIALITIES   Seeds
CATALOGUE   On request
MAIL ORDER   Yes
SHOP   Seeds; garden sundries; plants
GIFT TOKENS   HTA

Long-established seed merchants, with a retail and agricultural catalogue. They have over 50 seed potatoes as well as vegetables and garden flowers. Some garden products are also available mail order. There is a country store at the above address and at Commercial Road, Crediton (01363 772202). Their working malthouse (near Newton Abbot railway station) can be visited daily, except Saturdays, from Easter to October (01626 334734).

Emorsgate Seeds
Terrington Court, Popes Lane, Terrington St Clement, King's Lynn, Norfolk PE34 4NT
☎ 01553 829028   📠 01553 829028
CONTACT   Donald MacIntyre
OPEN   Mail order only
SPECIALITIES   Seeds
CATALOGUE   On request
MAIL ORDER   Yes

Wild flowers, wild grasses and mixtures for retail and wholesale customers. The seed stocks are based on native collected seed which is then grown at the farm: the source county is given and stocks are regularly replenished. A good choice of wild and amenity grasses. Flower and grass mixtures are available for different soil types, and some are derived (with permission) from specified nature reserves.

Field House Alpines
See Nottinghamshire, Nurseries section

Flora Exotica
See Essex, Nurseries section

Glenhirst Cactus Nursery
See Lincolnshire, Nurseries section

Harrisons Delphiniums
See Berkshire, Nurseries section

Hazeldene Nursery
See Kent, Nurseries section

Holly Gate Cactus Nursery
See West Sussex, Nurseries section

J E Martin
4 Church Street, Market Harborough, LE16 7AA
☎ 01858 462751   📠 01858 434544
LOCATION   Town centre
OPEN   Mail order
SPECIALITIES   Seeds
NEW INTRODUCTIONS FOR 1995   Potatoes 'Accent', 'Kestrel', 'Swift', 'Valor'
CATALOGUE   On request
MAIL ORDER   Yes
GIFT TOKENS   HTA

Seed potatoes in variety, including 'Pink Fir Apple' and 'Stroma' and 'Kestrel'. Mainly wholesale: they operate in the Midlands, with another shop in Lutterworth.

J E Martin
6 High Street, Lutterworth, Leicestershire
☎ 01455 552799
LOCATION   Town centre
SPECIALITIES   Seeds
NEW INTRODUCTIONS FOR 1995   Potatoes 'Accent', 'Kestrel', 'Swift', 'Valor'
MAIL ORDER   Yes (VISA)
GIFT TOKENS   HTA

Seed potatoes: wholesale and mail order as well.

J W Boyce
Bush Pasture, Lower Carter Street, Fordham, Ely, Cambridgeshire CB7 5JU
☎ 01638 721158
CONTACT   Roger Morley
OPEN   10 am – 12.30 pm, Monday – Friday, 9 am – 12 noon, Saturdays. Closed Sundays
SPECIALITIES   Seeds
CATALOGUE   On request
MAIL ORDER   Yes
GIFT TOKENS   Own

Specialists for pansy seed, including their Soham Surprise strain (developed over the last 80 years). Many other fresh flower and vegetable seeds, which are sold packeted and by weight. Free help and advice.

Jack Drake
See Highland, Nurseries section

James Henderson & Sons
Kingholm Quay, Dumfries, DG1 4SU
☎ 01387 52234   📠 01387 62302
CONTACT   Richard J. and James H. Henderson
OPEN   Mail order only
SPECIALITIES   Seeds
CATALOGUE   SAE
MAIL ORDER   Yes

Wholesale and retails seed potato merchants. They supply many garden centres but you can also order direct. This family firm currently lists 36 varieties including 'Pink Fir Apple', and a special potato fertiliser.

Jim & Jenny Archibald
Bryn Collen, Ffostrasol, Llandysul, Dyfed SA44 5SB
CONTACT   Jim and Jenny Archibald
OPEN   Mail order only
SPECIALITIES   Seeds
CATALOGUE   On request
MAIL ORDER   Yes

Serious alpine seed list for serious alpine enthusiasts. The Archibalds are professional collectors, and the list is based on their extensive trips. It includes detailed collection, cultivation and historical notes. Many species will be unavailable elsewhere.

John Chambers Wild Flower Seeds
15 Westleigh Road, Barton Seagrave, Kettering, Northamptonshire NN15 5AJ
☎ 01933 652562   📠 01933 652576
OPEN   Mail order only
SPECIALITIES   Seeds; wild flowers
CATALOGUE   On request
MAIL ORDER   Yes
SHOP   Books
SHOWS   Malvern Spring; Chelsea; BBC GW Live
GIFT TOKENS   Own

Biggest and best-known of the wild flower merchants, with everything from British natives and butterfly plants to mixtures and grass seeds. There's also a good choice of books in the somewhat frenetic catalogue. Keep an eye out for their Chelsea displays: they hit the jackpot with Best in Show in 1993 for their controversial Seaside Garden.

John Drake Aquilegias
Hardwicke House, Fen Ditton, Cambridge, Cambridgeshire CB5 8TF
☎ 01223 292246
CONTACT L. J. Drake
SPECIALITIES Seeds; aquilegias
CATALOGUE 70p
MAIL ORDER Yes; minimum order £10
GARDEN Hardwicke House, Fen Ditton, Cambridge
NCCPG NATIONAL COLLECTIONS *Aquilegia, Semiaquilegia*

Seeds of *Aquilegia* species and forms, some other kinds too, from an enthusiast and collector. Plants available when garden opens for NGS.

Johnsons Seeds
W W Johnson & Son Ltd, London Road, Boston, Lincolnshire PE21 8AD
☎ 01205 365051   FAX 01205 310148
CONTACT Richard Johnson
OPEN Mail order and nationwide stockists
SPECIALITIES Seeds
CATALOGUE On request
MAIL ORDER Yes
GARDEN July to September
GIFT TOKENS HTA

Founded in 1820 and still run by the Johnson family. Large collection of general flower and vegetable seed available by post. Flower packets contain an illustrated plastic label. The company's products, including its grass seed range, are also sold in shops and garden centres. There's also a wholesale division.

Kings Crown of Kelvedon
Monks Farm, Pantlings Lane, Coggeshall Road, Kelvedon, Essex CO5 9PG
☎ 01376 570000   FAX 01376 571189
OPEN Mail order only
SPECIALITIES Seeds
CATALOGUE On request
MAIL ORDER Yes

Good value retail seed list. All the seed is untreated, so suitable for organic gardeners too. Strong on herbs and sweet peas. They also have a large wholesale flower and vegetable seed business aimed at growers.

Landlife Wildflowers Ltd
See Merseyside, Nurseries section

Mackey's Garden Centre
See Co. Dublin, Nurseries section

Marshalls
S E Marshall & Co Ltd, Wisbech, PE13 2RF
☎ 01945 583407   FAX 01945 588235
CONTACT Val Green
OPEN Mail order
SPECIALITIES Seeds; vegetables
NEW INTRODUCTIONS FOR 1995 New varieties include lablab bean, Asparagus 'Dariana', Broccoli 'Rosalind'
CATALOGUE On request
MAIL ORDER Yes
GIFT TOKENS Own

Fenland seed company which specialises in vegetables and seed potatoes: they have a range of popular flowers too, and own Elm House Nursery (which supplies young plants). Like the other major seed firms they place great emphasis on looking after their customers: there are free seeds for larger orders. Regular opportunities to trial (and report) on varieties before they are properly introduced.

Michael Bennett
Long Compton, Shipton on Stour, CV36 5JN
☎ 01608 686676
CONTACT Michael Bennett
OPEN Mail order only
SPECIALITIES Asparagus seed
CATALOGUE SAE
MAIL ORDER Yes

Asparagus breeder. Kits with instructions, seed, pots, fertiliser and weed killer to plant an asparagus bed using modern strains and methods.

Monocot Nursery
See Avon, Nurseries section

Mr Fothergill's Seeds Ltd
Gazeley Road, Kentford, Newmarket, CB8 7QB
☎ 01638 751887   FAX 01638 751624
CONTACT Catalogues: 01638 751887; Orders: 01638 552512
OPEN Mail order only
SPECIALITIES Seeds
NEW INTRODUCTIONS FOR 1995 Petunia 'Celebrity Encore F1', Impatiens 'Circus Mixed F1', *Papaver orientale* 'Pizzicato', Gazania 'Chansonette Pink Shades', Petunia 'Summertime Carpet F1', Impatiens 'Chelsea Girl F1', Nicotiana 'Havana Appleblossom F1', *Convolvulus* 'Red Ensign', Petunia 'Celebrity Ovation F1'
CATALOGUE On request
MAIL ORDER Yes
GIFT TOKENS Own

General seed company selling flowers, vegetables and some sundries from a colourful catalogue. High standard of service and information.

Naturescape
See Nottinghamshire, Nurseries section

North Green Seeds
North Green Only, Stoven, Beccles, Suffolk
NR34 8DG
CONTACT John Morley
OPEN Mail order only
SPECIALITIES Seeds
CATALOGUE 4 first class stamps
MAIL ORDER Yes

A pleasantly eclectic range of good things from around the world. Order in summer for autumn sowing. See also North Green Snowdrops, in Nurseries & Garden Centres section.

Paradise Centre
See Suffolk, Nurseries section

Peter Grayson – Sweet Pea Seedsman
34 Glenthorne Close, Brampton, Chesterfield, Derbyshire S40 3AR
☎ 01246 278503
CONTACT Peter Grayson
OPEN Mail order only
SPECIALITIES Seeds
NEW INTRODUCTIONS FOR 1995 *Lathyrus tingitanus* 'Harmony'
CATALOGUE On request
MAIL ORDER Yes

A short but enticing list which includes unrivalled collections of *Lathyrus* species, and pre-Spencer Grandifloras (or Heirlooms), and some of Mr Grayson's introductions. 'Harmony', his new hybrid, is a breakthrough. Seed is produced on site.

Phedar Nursery
See Cheshire, Nurseries section

Plant World Botanic Gardens
See Devon, Nurseries section

Potterton and Martin
See Lincolnshire, Nurseries section

Roy Young Seeds
23 Westland Chase, West Winch, King's Lynn, Norfolk PE33 0QH
☎ 01553 840867
CONTACT Roy Young
OPEN Mail order only
SPECIALITIES Seeds
CATALOGUE On request (retail and wholesale)
MAIL ORDER International mail order

Cacti and succulent seeds by post, for retail and wholesale customers. Much of the seed is harvested from their own plants. The *Lithops* range is especially notable. Many items are in short supply, no telephone orders.

S & N Brackley
117 Winslow Road, Wingrave, Aylesbury, Buckinghamshire HP22 4QB
☎ 01296 681384

CONTACT Mrs S. Brackley
OPEN For plant collection, April only; seed,s all times
SPECIALITIES Seeds; sweet peas; vegetables
NEW INTRODUCTIONS FOR 1995 Sweet peas 'Kiri Te Kanawa', 'Rosina'
CATALOGUE On request
MAIL ORDER Yes
SHOWS RHS Westminster; Malvern Spring; Harrogate (Spring); Southport; Chelsea; BBC GW Live; Hampton Court; Harrogate (Autumn)

Sweet pea specialists, both as seeds and young plants: garden and exhibition varieties. You can see their displays at the many – mainly southern – shows which they attend. They also produce exhibition vegetable seeds, with leek and onion plants available in April.

S M McArd
39 West Road, Pointon, Sleaford, NG34 0NA
☎ 01529 240765   FAX 01529 240765
CONTACT S. McArd
OPEN Mail order only
SPECIALITIES Seeds; vegetables
CATALOGUE On request
MAIL ORDER Yes

Carefully selected vegetable seeds divided into such headings as unusual and oriental vegetables, and 'economical F1s'. Bulbs and flower seeds too, plus soft fruit and unusual vegetable plants.

Salley Gardens
See Nottinghamshire, Nurseries section

Samuel Dobie & Son Ltd
Broomhill Way, Torquay, Devon TQ2 7QW
☎ 01803 616281
OPEN Mail order only
SPECIALITIES Seeds
NEW INTRODUCTIONS FOR 1995 *Antirrhinum* F1 'Bells Mixture'; *Pelargonium* 'Vista' series, and more
CATALOGUE On request
MAIL ORDER Yes
GIFT TOKENS Own

General seed company with a catalogue of flower and vegetable varieties. They specialise in young annual plants also, and have a range of garden equipment too.

The Seed House
9a Widley Road, Cosham, Portsmouth, PO6 2DS
☎ 01705 325639

CONTACT Richard Spearing
OPEN Mail order only
SPECIALITIES Australian plants; seeds
CATALOGUE 4 first class stamps
MAIL ORDER Yes; £5 minimum order

Interesting list of Australian native plants, including *Callistemon* and *Eucalyptus* as well as less common genera. The species are chosen with regard to suitability for a European climate.

Seeds-by-Size
45 Crouchfield, Boxmoor, Hemel Hempstead, Hertfordshire HP1 1PA
☎ 01442 251458

CONTACT John Robert Size
OPEN Mail order only
CATALOGUE On request
MAIL ORDER Yes

Over 1,290 vegetable strains, and around 3000 flower varieties. Seeds are sold by weight in any quantity from ½ gram up: the pricing system looks more daunting than it really is. Mr Size is a good source for many old and hard-to-obtain varieties. Take your pick from 175 cabbage varieties, 85 lettuces, 221 sweet peas or 211 petunias, for example.

Stewarts (Nottm) Ltd
The Garden Shop, 3 George Street, Nottingham, Nottinghamshire NG1 3BH
☎ 0115 9476338

CONTACT Brenda Lochhead
LOCATION Nottingham city centre
OPEN 9 am – 5.30 pm
CATALOGUE On request
MAIL ORDER Yes
SHOP Seeds and bulbs; chemicals; fertilisers; sundries
GIFT TOKENS HTA

Long-established seed and bulb merchant. Seeds and bulbs, including potatoes and their own grass seed mixtures. Their Economy collections of flowers and vegetables are packaged by them.

Suttons Seeds
Hele Road, Torquay, Devon TQ2 7QJ
☎ 01803 614455   FAX 01803 615747

CONTACT Customer Services
OPEN Mail order only
SPECIALITIES Seeds
NEW INTRODUCTIONS FOR 1995 Strawberry 'Sweet Sensation', *Mesembryanthemum* 'Harlequin' mixture, *Antirrhinum* 'Candyman' mixture, Poppy 'Pizzicato', *Verbena adonis* 'Light Blue', *Nolana* 'Shooting Star', *Lobelia* 'Riviera Lilac', *Antirrhinum* 'Lipstick'
CATALOGUE On request
MAIL ORDER Yes
SHOWS Chelsea; BBC GW Live
GIFT TOKENS Own

Famous old seed house with a strong catalogue of flower and vegetable varieties as well as a useful range of garden sundries, plants and bulbs.

Thompson & Morgan
Poplar Lane, Ipswich, Suffolk IP8 3BU
☎ 01473 688588   FAX 01473 680199
OPEN See below
NEW INTRODUCTIONS FOR 1995 *Phlox* 'Phlox of Sheep', *Salvia* 'Red Arrow', *Armeria* 'Bees Hybrids Mixed', *Mimulus* 'Andean Nymph', *anagalis monellii*, Marigold 'French Vanilla' Fl hybrid, Poppy 'Pizzicato', *Laurentia axillaris* 'Blue Stars', *Wahlenbergia undulata* 'Melton Blue Bird', Evening Primrose 'Lemon Sunset' Melon-Experimental TM/M01, Beetroot 'Chioggia', Brussel Sprout 'Sheriff Fl Hybrid, Lettuce mini iceberg 'Mini Green'
CATALOGUE On request
MAIL ORDER Yes
REFRESHMENTS Yes
GARDEN Trial grounds
GIFT TOKENS Own

Established in 1855. The T&M list is the world's largest illustrated seed catalogue. It combines a tradition of good new introductions with a wide choice of less easily attainable plants. Like all the major seed companies, they pride themselves on their service to customers. Last year the trial grounds and production facilities opened to the public for the first time. Planned open days this year are on 22 – 23 July and 19 – 20 August.

Unwins Seeds Ltd
Histon, Cambridge, Cambridgeshire CB4 4LE
☎ 01223 236236   FAX 01223 237437

CONTACT Order Department
OPEN Mail order and retailers nationwide
NEW INTRODUCTIONS FOR 1995 *Antirrhinum* 'Bells Mixed' and 'Chimes Mixed', *Begonia semperflorens* 'Lotto Pink', *Lindheimera* 'Sunny Boy'
CATALOGUE On request; October
MAIL ORDER Yes

Long-famous as breeders of sweet peas. Unwins also have a full choice of flowers and vegetables, including mixtures, new introductions and established varieties.

The Van Hage Garden Company
See Hertfordshire, Nurseries section

W E Th. Ingwersen Ltd
See West Sussex, Nurseries section

W Robinson & Sons Ltd
Sunny Bank, Forton, Preston, Lancashire PR3 0BN
☎ 01524 791210   FAX 01524 791933
LOCATION 17 miles north of Preston on A6
OPEN Phone first
CATALOGUE On request
MAIL ORDER Yes
SHOWS RHS Westminster; Southport

Home of the 'Mammoth' seed strain: exhibition and garden vegetable seeds, including the 'Mammoth Improved Onion' and their new climbing french bean 'Kingston Gold'. Seedlings and small plants available.

Westfield Cacti
See Devon, Nurseries section

The Wildlife Gardening Centre
See Oxfordshire, Nurseries section

YSJ Seeds
See Somerset, Nurseries section

Overgrown & Undergrown

This is the editors' personal choice of trees and shrubs which deserve to be more or less grown. They are arranged genus by genus from A to Z, with one absence. We challenge any reader to produce a pair from a genus beginning with X. Some we consider overrated, and some underrated. There are no other value judgements attached: this not a list of Ins and Outs, nor a guide to distinguish the PC from the naff, just a list of trees and shrubs which are overgrown and undergrown.

Overgrown

Aesculus × carnea 'Briotii'
Buddleja davidii 'White Profusion'
Cornus alba 'Sibirica'
Daphne × burkwoodii 'Somerset'
Euonymus europaeus
Fagus sylvatica
Griselinia littoralis 'Variegata'
Hedera colchica
Ilex aquifolium 'Golden Queen'
Juglans nigra
Kerria japonica 'Pleniflora'
Lonicera japonica var. repens
Mahonia × media 'Charity'
Nothofagus antarctica
Osmanthus heterophyllus
Pittosporum tenuifolium 'Warnham Gold'
Quercus rubra
Rosa rugosa
Sambucus nigra f. laciniata
Taxus baccata 'Summergold'
Ulmus × hollandica 'Jacqueline Hillier'
Viburnum opulus 'Compactum'
Weigela florida 'Foliis Purpureis'
Yucca filamentosa
Zelkova serrata

Undergrown

Aesculus × carnea 'Plantierensis'
Buddleja davidii 'White Harlequin'
Cornus alba 'Kesselringii'
Daphne × burkwoodii 'Carol Mackie'
Euonymus europaeus 'Red Cascade'
Fagus orientalis
Griselinia littoralis 'Dixon's Cream'
Hedera azorica
Ilex aquifolium 'Golden Milkmaid'
Juglans ailanthifolia
Kerria japonica 'Picta'
Lonicera similis var. delavayi
Mahonia × media 'Buckland'
Nothofagus betuloïdes
Osmanthus yunnanensis
Pittosporum tenuifolium 'Abbotsbury Gold'
Quercus 'Warburgii'
Rosa virginiana
Sambucus nigra 'Linearis'
Taxus baccata 'Fructu Luteo'
Ulmus parvifolia 'Frosty'
Viburnum opulus 'Nanum'
Weigela 'Looymansii Aurea'
Yucca whipplei
Zelkova carpinifolia

15

Gardens

This section recommends gardens in Great Britain and Ireland. Our aim is to supply sufficient detail to enable readers to decide whether and when to plan a visit. The list is not exhaustive. It offers a selection of the different types of garden which are open to the public: ancient and modern, large and small, public and private. The editors welcome suggestions for additions, deletions or alterations to entries.

Gardens are listed by county or region (for Scotland), and then alphabetically by name. The order is England, Wales, Scotland, Northern Ireland and Eire. This section also serves as a reference source for the rest of the book, where gardens are referred to only by their name, followed by their county, as in Marwood Hill Gardens, Devon, and Rowallane, Co. Down. All the counties of Sussex and Yorkshire appear under S and Y respectively.

The number of gardens open to the public continues to grow. We list about 60 new gardens this year, as well as deleting a few whose owners have died or decided to close. Among those who have died in the course of the year are Col. Patullo of Blairhoyle, George Hastings of Rainthorpe Hall, Norfolk, and Major Martin Gibbs of Sheldon Manor, though fortunately his widow Elsie Gibbs will continue to manage this most welcoming of gardens. Jane Stevens of The Mill House, Oxfordshire, is taking a year off garden opening, and Mrs Spencer has decided she can no longer keep open the miraculous small garden at York Gate designed and planted by her late son Robin.

Chilham Castle in Kent has also closed: it was offered for sale in May at an asking price in the region of £3.5 million but remained unsold as we went to press. Simon Loder has sold Clapton Court in Somerset, and the new owners have chosen to close both the garden and the nursery. In a very few instances gardens have been omitted because the owners have not responded to our requests for up-to-date information.

Some gardens are opening more often: Ramster in Surrey and 45 Sandford Road, Dublin are examples. Butterstream in Co. Meath is one of those which are also opening for a greater part of the day. Among stately homes, we are glad to note that Melbourne Hall in Derbyshire will open more frequently this year. It may be joined by Grimsthorpe Castle in Lincolnshire.

Our source of practical information about directions, opening times, admission charges, parking, loos, disabled facilities, shops and refreshments has been the owners or their staff, backed up by our own enquiries where necessary. The accuracy of these details is not guaranteed, but is believed to be correct at the time of going to press. In order to assist readers who are hoping to arrange a group visit by special appointment, we have taken the unusual step of listing the telephone and fax numbers to which enquiries should be directed. In some cases this is the private telephone line of the owners: readers are strongly urged to respect their privacy. If telephone and fax numbers have been omitted, this is because the owners prefer to receive such requests by letter.

Most gardens offer special rates for pre-booked groups. If details are not given, it is often worth asking whether a reduction is available and what minimum number is acceptable. Not all gardens offer reductions for parties: popular gardens which already suffer from wear and tear may not welcome extra visitors.

Special rates for families are sometimes offered, especially by the larger gardens attached to stately homes, where the garden is only one of many entertainments available to the visitor. There are endless permutations on the numbers of adults/children which constitute a 'family'. It goes without saying that special rates are offered on the basis that children are under the control and supervision of a responsible adult. Season tickets are sometimes available, and are good value for people who live near a large garden or stately home.

National Trust members are usually admitted free to Trust properties: readers are strongly recommended to join the National Trust in any event.

Entrance fees vary, and some owners have told us that they may increase fees in the middle of the season. Others have a high season for a month or so – like Leonardslee in May. Still others have a special day of the week or open days for charity, when the entrance fee is higher. A few owners had not yet fixed their 1995 times or admission charges and, with their agreement, we have therefore indicated that the times or prices quoted are for 1994.

We generally give the prices and times for visiting the garden only. If the house is open at the same time, a supplement may be payable.

Remember that many gardens have a last admission time. Typically it will be 30 or 45 minutes before they close, but it can be much longer. The last admission to Stowe is one hour before it closes, while Stratfield Saye actually closes its gates to visitors at 4 pm, two hours before they are expected to leave.

The guide indicates whether parking is available: this may be at the garden itself or on a public road close to it. Parking may be at some distance from the house. At Saltram in Devon, it is 500 yards away, and this is by no means exceptional. You may expect better parking facilities at a popular property which offers a wide range of entertainments than at a small plantsman's garden in a country lane. In the case of refreshments, however, we have referred only to what is offered within the garden itself, and not to facilities nearby.

We have not specified the nature of the special facilities offered to the disabled, but in most cases it includes loos which are suitable for those in wheelchairs. It is best to enquire in advance of a visit if items of special equipment are required. The National Trust is particularly good at adapting its properties to accommodate the needs of disabled visitors.

It is often a condition of admission that no photograph taken within a garden may be sold or used for public reproduction without the consent of the property owner. Visitors should also remember that almost all gardens admit dogs only if they are kept on a lead.

Information about outsize trees is taken from a fascinating small publication *Champion Trees in the British Isles* by A. F. Mitchell, V. E. Hallett and J. E. J. White (third edition 1990, HMSO £3.80). There are two ways of measuring trees: height and girth. Sometimes the tallest specimen will also have the thickest trunk – but not always. Both the tallest and the biggest can claim to be the champion tree, and we have made this distinction when noting record breakers in gardens.

Tree measurements can never be fully up to date: some records have not been verified since the great gales of 1987 and 1990, but *Champion Trees of the British Isles* clearly indicates where to find the best collections of trees – for example, Westonbirt Arboretum in Gloucestershire and Hergest Croft in Hereford & Worcester. The dominance of conifers in western and central Scotland may also be noted. Further information about trees is available from the Tree Register of the British Isles, c/o Mrs V. Schilling, 2 Church Cottages, Westmeston, Hassocks, West Sussex, BN6 8RJ.

We have noted those NCCPG National Collections which are held at the gardens we list. Not all genera are the subject of a National Collection: there are still some horticulturally important groups of plants which have not yet been seriously collected and studied under the auspices of the NCCPG. Other genera have been split into a number of different collections. This is particularly necessary in the case of such a large genus as *Rhododendron* or one that requires a great variety of growing conditions, as *Euphorbia* does. Moreover, the NCCPG has wisely introduced a system of duplicate collections so that plants are grown in two or more gardens.

The need to maintain duplicate collections and split large genera explains why certain names occur several times in our list of National Collections. That list is not comprehensive. We have only included those of which we have received notice. A full list is available from the NCCPG.

A word about the choice of gardens. Our aim is to be comprehensive but realistic. All major gardens which are open regularly are listed as a matter of course. These include many gardens of the National Trust and the National Trust for Scotland, as well as botanic and public gardens and those attached to stately homes. But many gardens do not open regularly to visitors: the National Gardens Scheme lists over 3,000. We have found space for a selection of these gardens which open only once a year or by appointment. Some guides would omit them on the grounds that it is not worth while to give publicity to gardens which so few people can visit. We take the view that, if a good garden is seldom open, it is all the more important to know when the opportunity to see it will arise.

The starting point for garden visiting must be the Yellow Book which the National Gardens Scheme publishes annually in February under the full title *Gardens of England and Wales Open to the Public*. The Yellow Book is a best seller. Its sales immediately after publication invariably exceed 5,000 copies per week, three times the success rate of its nearest rival among best-selling paperback reference books. It is wonderfully comprehensive and totally undiscriminating. The owners write their own garden entries, with the result that a really good garden may come across as self-deprecatingly boring, while an exciting description can often lead to disappointment. Beware of self-publicists: you can usually spot the hype.

The Yellow Book suffers from another irritating shortcoming: the National Gardens Scheme is reluctant to accept some of the boundary changes which took effect in 1974. East Sussex and West Sussex are still treated as one; Merseyside and Greater Manchester are lumped in with Lancashire; and Oxfordshire incorporates the whole of the Vale of the White Horse, at the expense of Berkshire. Nevertheless, the Yellow Book is the single most important guide to visiting gardens in England and Wales, and the least expensive.

Copies of *Gardens of England and Wales Open to the Public in 1995* are available for £3.75 (including UK postage) from the National Gardens Scheme, Hatchlands Park, East Clandon, Guildford, Surrey GU4 7RT.

Scotland has its own Yellow Book called *The Gardens of Scotland*. This is available from Scotland's Gardens Scheme, 31 Castle Terrace, Edinburgh EH1 2EL, and lists over 300 gardens throughout Scotland. Unfortunately, it divides the country into districts and areas which do not correspond with either the old counties or the new regions. However, there is a separate index, so the guide is not difficult to follow.

The *Gardens of Scotland* shares another defect with the Yellow Book: it does not always mention that some gardens are open at other times, not for the benefit of the Scheme. Indeed, some open for the Scheme only one day a year, and for their own funds for the other 364 days. The 1994 edition of *The Gardens of Scotland* was still a great improvement on previous ones, while the 1995 version remains essential reading for anyone who wishes to visit Scottish gardens, and far too seldom seen south of the border.

We strongly recommend Graham Rose's *The Good Gardens Guide*, which comes out every autumn: the 1995 edition is published by Vermilion and costs £12.99. Its quality is inevitably somewhat uneven because the entries are written by many different hands and the standard of its judgements varies. Nevertheless, it describes many good gardens in detail that is not available elsewhere. Above all, it sorts out and evaluates many of the private gardens in the Yellow Book. *The Good Gardens Guide 1995* itself lists over 1,000 gardens, some across the Channel within a day's driving distance of the Tunnel. It saves so much time and money – not to mention good humour – which would otherwise be lost driving many miles to a disappointing garden, that *The Good Gardens Guide 1995* must be worth every penny of its price.

Patrick Taylor's *The 1994 Gardener's Guide to Britain* (Pavilion, £10.99) is beautifully laid out and illustrated – its author is a publisher. It is also elegantly written and sound in its judgements. It describes rather too few gardens and nurseries, and their geographic spread is sometimes too thin to make it really useful. It is, however, recommended as a point of first reference and its judgements cannot be faulted – accurate, observant and intelligent.

The Good Gardens Guide and *The 1994 Gardener's Guide to Britain* are especially valuable because they list a substantial number of public parks where entry is free and unrestricted. These may not be gardens in the popular sense, but they are often of great interest to garden visitors. Both books include good nurseries: Patrick Taylor in particular recognises that visiting new nurseries is just as enjoyable and important to a keen gardener as seeing other people's gardens.

The most scholarly guide currently in print is *The Blue Guide to Gardens of England* (£14.99). Its scope is limited to about 300 gardens, all in England, but they are described in great detail and often illustrated with drawings and plans of layouts.

Reed Information Services publish an A4 format paperback guide, *Historic Houses, Castles and Gar-*

dens in Great Britain and Ireland. The 1994 edition cost £7.80 and listed about 1,500 historic properties in the United Kingdom and Ireland, including many of the grander gardens in this section. This large, well-illustrated handbook is a most useful source of information for planning a trip, although the garden descriptions tend to be short and bland.

The National Trust Gardens Handbook describes fully about 130 gardens. Most are attached to historic houses. Some are little known, and deservedly so. We have included only those which we believe our readers will find worth visiting. As a handbook, however, it is excellent; the detail includes the altitude and terrain of a garden, and how many gardeners are employed there. It also lists such special features as NCCPG Collections and garden architecture, suggests the best time to visit a garden and, most usefully, tells you when to avoid it. Although it is limited to National Trust properties and its scope does not extend to Scotland or Eire, The National Trust Gardens Handbook is a model guide to gardens: a snip at £3.95.

English Heritage publishes a Guide to English Heritage Properties 1995, which is issued to all members. Although many of its properties are ancient monuments, notably castles and abbeys, English Heritage does own a number of good gardens, including Belsay Hall, Northumberland, and Chiswick House, London. In Scotland, historic gardens are maintained by Historic Scotland and include such important examples as Edzell Castle. There are no gardens of importance maintained by Cadw, the Welsh Historic Monuments Commission, although it is actively involved in assessing the conservation needs of historic landscapes within the principality.

The Ulster Gardens Scheme raises funds every year for work in National Trust Gardens which would not otherwise be possible. It is run by the Northern Ireland region of the National Trust at Rowallane House, Saintfield, Ballynahinch, Co. Down, BT24 7LH (tel. 01238 510721, fax. 01238 511242). It usually lists about a dozen gardens, mainly in Down, Armagh and Derry, and each opens only once. All are smallish private gardens made by the present owners: the Ulster Gardens Scheme eschews the big gardens of the stately homes and the National Trust itself.

The National Gardens Scheme is more established in some parts of England and Wales than others. In the north east, the leading organisation is the Northumbria Gardens Scheme which publishes a brochure, Gardens, Grounds and Woodlands Open in 1995 in aid of the Northumbria branch of the British Red Cross, for which it raised over £36,000 in 1993. Copies of the brochure are available from Croft House, Western Avenue, Newcastle-upon-Tyne NE4 8SR.

In the south west, the Cornwall Garden Society holds sway, and visitors should seek out the Gardens of Cornwall Open Guide, published by the Cornwall Garden Society and the Cornish Tourist Board with support from the National Trust. The guide is a model of helpfulness: it offers comprehensive information about 67 gardens, all the dates associated with the Cornwall Festival of Spring Gardens, and a really useful map – no road is too small.

Tourist boards are an invaluable source of local information. The Scottish Tourist Board publishes an excellent Visitors' Guide to Scotland's Gardens, with details of about 150 top Scottish gardens. There are no photographs, but the garden descriptions are substantial. About 20 gardens are illustrated in a slimline brochure called Visit Scotland's Best, printed by the National Trust for Scotland. The Scottish Highlands and Islands Board also issues an attractive coloured booklet Great Gardens of the Scottish Highlands and Islands: it describes 32 gardens, mainly in Inverness, Ross and Argyll, but gives only the minimum of practical information about facilities and opening times.

The Irish Tourist Board (PO Box 273, Dublin 8) publishes a handsomely illustrated 24-page guide to Gardens of Ireland – The Most Distinguished Gardens Open to the Public. In addition to 34 of the best gardens in Eire, it lists 10 Country House Hotels. The guide is invaluable, and whets the armchair visitor's appetite. Readers should also know of the County Wicklow Gardens Festival, the best in Ireland, which runs from 19 May to 25 June. The festival brochure gives details of about 40 gardens which are open either continuously or at some time during those 5 weeks. Copies are available from Wicklow County Tourism (County Buildings, Wicklow, tel. 00 353 404 69117).

Local promotions abound. Two guides whose initiative we particularly commend are The Teesdale Garden: The Connoisseur's Choice in the Durham Dales, available from Teesdale District Council (43

Galgate, Barnard Castle, Co. Durham, DL12 8EL and *Gardens and Nurseries in Lincolnshire and South Humberside*, available from Lincolnshire and South Humberside Tourism (Lincoln Castle, Lincoln LN1 3AA). The latter is a handsome glossy guide to 53 nurseries and garden centres in the area, 24 gardens that open on a regular basis, and 52 'not so stately' gardens which open only occasionally or by appointment.

ENGLAND

AVON

The American Museum
Claverton Manor, Bath, Avon BA2 7BD
☎ 01225 460503   FAX 01225 480726
OWNER   Trustees of the American Museum in Britain
LOCATION   Off A36 south of Bath
OPEN   1 – 6 pm, Tuesday – Friday, 12 noon – 6 pm, Saturdays, Sundays and Bank Holiday Mondays, 25 March to 5 November
ADMISSION   Adults £2; Children £1 (1994)
FACILITIES   Parking; dogs permitted; loos; access for the disabled; plants for sale; book shop, herb shop and country store; light lunches at weekends; tea, coffee and American cookies
FEATURES   Good collection of trees; herbaceous borders; fine conifers; fruit of special interest; herbs; designed by Roper; old roses and climbers; good topiary; woodland garden; Lynne Le Grice Exhibition (all season; 1995)
ENGLISH HERITAGE GRADE   II
FRIENDS   Apply to Membership Secretary (01225 460503)

15 immaculate acres devoted to elements of American gardening, including a Colonial herb garden ('Colonial' = pre-1778), old roses (best in June) and a pastiche of Mount Vernon. But some say it is *all* a pastiche, a chunk of American folksiness slightly incongruous in the Avon Valley.

Badminton
Chipping Sodbury, Avon GL9 1DB
☎ 01454 218346
OWNER   The Duke of Beaufort
LOCATION   5 miles east of Chipping Sodbury
OPEN   2 – 6 pm, 25 June
ADMISSION   Adults £1.50; Senior Citizens £1; Children (under 10) free
FACILITIES   Parking; dogs permitted; loos; access for the disabled; plants for sale; tea, lemonade, cakes and scones
FEATURES   Herbaceous borders; glasshouses and conservatories to visit; old roses and climbers; subtropical plants
ENGLISH HERITAGE GRADE   I

Since moving to Badminton eleven years ago, the Duchess has begun a series of small formal gardens to the side of the house, which do not interfere with the grand 18th-century vistas across three counties. These modern gardens run into each other like the rooms of the house and are each different in character. Work continues.

Bath Botanic Gardens
Royal Victoria Park, Bath, Avon
☎ 01225 448433   FAX 01225 480072
OWNER   Bath City Council
LOCATION   West of city centre by Upper Bristol Road
OPEN   Dawn – dusk, daily, all year
ADMISSION   Free
FACILITIES   Parking; dogs permitted; facilities for the disabled
FEATURES   Good collection of trees; herbaceous borders; fine conifers; lake; rock garden; old roses and climbers; autumn colour; fine bedding displays; interesting new *Scilla* collection (1995); tallest tree of heaven *Ailanthus altissima* in England (and 9 other record trees)
FRIENDS   Newly formed – telephone 01225 448433 for details. Quarterly newsletter; lectures and tours all through the year
NCCPG NATIONAL COLLECTIONS   *Scilla*

9 acres of trees, shrubs, borders, limestone-loving plants and scented walks. Essentially a 'closed' collection and now run by the Parks Department as a public amenity. Standards are high, maintenance is good, and the seasonal highlights of bulbs and bedding are among the best. Some splendid old trees recall the garden's origin as a private garden.

Crowe Hall
Widcombe Hill, Bath, Avon BA2 6AR
☎ 01225 310322
OWNER   John Barratt
LOCATION   Off A36 up Widcombe Hill
OPEN   2 – 6 pm, 23 March, 23 April, 14 and 28 May, 18 June, 16 July
ADMISSION   Adults £1.50; Children 30p
FACILITIES   Parking; dogs permitted; loos; plants for sale; teas
FEATURES   Follies and garden buildings; rock garden; old roses and climbers
ENGLISH HERITAGE GRADE   II

One of the most extraordinary gardens we know. It looks straight out at the Capability Brown landscape at Prior Park, and 'borrows' it. Below the house is an Italianate terrace, which leads to a ferny rock garden (real rocky outcrops here) and down into a modern garden in the woodland.

Dyrham Park
Chippenham, Avon SN14 8ER
☎ 0117 9372501
OWNER   The National Trust

Avon Gardens 257

LOCATION On A46, 8 miles north of Bath
OPEN 12 noon – 5.30 pm, Saturday – Wednesday, 1 April to 29 October
ADMISSION House and garden £5; Park £1.60
FACILITIES Parking; loos; tea room
FEATURES Herbaceous borders; landscape designed by Humphry Repton; deer park; handsome conservatory
ENGLISH HERITAGE GRADE II*

Fascinating for garden historians, who can study the Kip plan and trace the lines of the 17th-century formal garden which Humphry Repton turned into classic English parkland. But pretty boring for the dedicated plantsman.

Essex House
Badminton, Chipping Sodbury, Avon GL9 1DD
☎ 01454 218288

OWNER James Lees-Milne
LOCATION Far end of Badminton village
OPEN By appointment only, preferably groups
ADMISSION £2 for Macmillan Nurses appeal
FACILITIES Parking; dogs permitted
FEATURES Old roses and climbers; good topiary; pretty parterres; unusual plants; weeping pears

A small garden made by the distinguished garden writer Alvilde Lees-Milne. The formal design uses box edging, topiary, silver foliage and soft colours to create a sense of space and quiet enchantment.

Goldney Hall
Lower Clifton Hill, Clifton, Bristol, Avon BS8 1BH
☎ 0117 9265698 FAX 0117 9293414

OWNER The University of Bristol
LOCATION Top of Constitution Hill
OPEN 2 – 6 pm, for NGS (see Yellow Book)
ADMISSION Adults £1.50; Senior Citizens, Students and Children 75p (1994)
FACILITIES Loos; cream teas in the Orangery
FEATURES Herbaceous borders; follies and garden buildings; fruit of special interest; glasshouses and conservatories to visit; herbs; garden sculpture; interesting for children; holm oak hedge; the *Chronicles of Narnia* were filmed in the grotto
ENGLISH HERITAGE GRADE II*

A Bristol merchant's extravagance, nearly 300 years ago. 10 acres in the middle of the City, with an elegant orangery, a gothic folly tower and the gorgeous Goldney Grotto, which sparkles with crystalline rocks among the shells and follies.

The Manor House, Walton-in-Gordano
Walton-in-Gordano, Clevedon, Bristol, Avon BS21 7AN
☎ 01275 872067

OWNER Simon and Philippa Wills
LOCATION North side of B3124 on Clevedon side of Walton-in-Gordano
OPEN 10 am – 4 pm, Wednesdays and Thursdays, 19 April to 14 September, plus some Sundays for the NGS
ADMISSION Adults £1.50; Children free
FACILITIES Parking; loos; access for the disabled; plants for sale; teas on Sundays and Bank Holidays only
FEATURES Alpines; herbaceous borders; fine conifers; fruit of special interest; gravel or scree garden; herbs; lake; plants for plantsmen; pond; rock garden; climbing roses; modern roses; old roses; woodland garden; particularly good in July-August

A really interesting plantsman's garden on a substantial scale, offering something for every taste, from autumn-flowering bulbs to rare conifers. The range of the Wills's interests is breathtaking and there is always much for the visitor to learn and enjoy, whatever the season. Beautifully maintained, too.

Sherborne Garden
Pear Tree House, Litton, Avon BA3 4PP
☎ 01761 241220

OWNER Mr and Mrs John Southwell
LOCATION ½ a mile west of Litton village
OPEN 11 am – 6 pm, Mondays and Sundays, 4 June to 25 September. Plus 2 April, 7 May and 1 October. Other times by appointment. Parties by arrangement
ADMISSION Adults £1.50; Children free
FACILITIES Parking; dogs permitted; loos; plants for sale; tea and coffee at all times; teas 5 June and 2 October
FEATURES Fine conifers; ecological interest; gravel or scree garden; herbs; lake; plants for plantsmen; rock garden; modern roses; old roses and climbers; woodland garden; collection of hollies (180 varieties) and hardy ferns (100 varieties)

Plantsman's garden, started in a modest way in 1964 on ¾ acre but now extending to nearly 4 acres. Thickly planted, and wild at the edges. The owners are particularly interested in trees and plant them closely in groups for comparison: hence the holly wood, the larch wood and the salicetum (*Salix* = willow). But there is much more than trees and it is a garden to dawdle in and learn from.

University of Bristol Botanic Garden
Bracken Hill, North Road, Leigh Woods, Bristol, Avon BS8 3PF
FAX 0117 9733682

OWNER University of Bristol
LOCATION Take M5, J17 towards Clifton, left into North Road before suspension bridge
OPEN 9 am – 5 pm, Monday – Friday, all year
ADMISSION Free (except on NGS days)
FACILITIES Parking; loos
FEATURES Alpines; good collection of trees; herbaceous borders; fine conifers; ecological interest; glasshouses and conservatories to visit; gravel or scree

garden; herbs; plants for plantsmen; rock garden; *Cistus*; hebes; sempervivums; paeonies; *Aeonium*; salvias
FRIENDS Good programme and privileges (e.g. seed list). Details from Membership Secretary, c/o address above

An educational and accessible garden that bridges the gap between botany and horticulture. Because of the climatic conditions in its unusual position above the Avon gorge, it has a particularly fine collection of South African and New Zealand plants. And of course there is the rare endemic *Sorbus bristoliensis*.

Vine House
Henbury, Bristol, Avon BS10 7AD
☎ 0117 9503573

OWNER Mrs T. F. Hewer
LOCATION On Henbury Road, opposite Crow Lane
OPEN For NGS : see Yellow Book. Also by appointment
ADMISSION Adults £1; Senior Citizens and Children 50p (1994)
FACILITIES Dogs permitted; loos
FEATURES Fine conifers; gravel or scree garden; lake; plants for plantsmen; old roses and climbers; woodland garden; rare trees and shrubs; collected plants; shady 'cliff' garden

The garden of a great plant collector – Tom Hewer's trips to Iran and Afghanistan in the 1960s and 1970s introduced endless good novelties to our gardens. Some are here at Vine House, but much of the garden is a flowing plantsman's paradise, with good forms of trees and shrubs the main theme: *Ribes* × *gordonianum* and a huge *Hydrangea sargentiana*, for instance, often underplanted by naturalised bulbs.

BEDFORDSHIRE

Luton Hoo
The Mansion House, Luton, Bedfordshire LU1 3TQ
☎ 01582 22955   FAX 01582 34437

OWNER Trustees of Luton Hoo Foundation
LOCATION Signposted from J10 of M1
OPEN 12 noon – 5 pm, Friday – Sunday and Bank Holiday Mondays; dates not yet known but probably early April to mid October
ADMISSION Adults £2.50; Senior Citizens and Students £2.25 (1994)
FACILITIES Parking; loos; access for the disabled; plants for sale; gift shop; restaurant; picnic area
FEATURES Herbaceous borders; landscape designed by Capability Brown; fine conifers; gravel or scree garden; lake; rhododendrons and azaleas; rock garden; modern roses; garden sculpture; fine cedars
ENGLISH HERITAGE GRADE II*

The grand Italianate formal gardens include a large rose garden stuffed with colour. But there is a classic early rock garden (c.1900) and a Capability Brown park too.

Odell Castle
Odell, Bedfordshire MK43 7BB
☎ 01234 720240

OWNER Lord Luke
LOCATION North west of Bedford
OPEN 2 – 6 pm, 14 May and 16 July
ADMISSION Adults £1; Children free
FACILITIES Parking; dogs permitted; tea and biscuits
FEATURES Herbaceous borders; fine conifers; modern roses; old roses and climbers

A new garden for a new castle, built in 1962, but drawing on an old landscape with grand old trees. The site is magnificent, with views down to the Ouse valley, and the modern gardens around the house are secondary to it. There are splendid herbaceous borders and a pretty rose garden.

The Swiss Garden
Old Warden, Biggleswade, Bedfordshire
☎ 01234 228330   FAX 01234 228921

OWNER Shuttleworth Trust
LOCATION 1½ miles west of Biggleswade
OPEN 1.30 – 6 pm (but 10 am – 6 pm on Saturdays, Sundays and Bank Holidays), daily except Tuesdays (but *including* Tuesdays in August), 1 March to 30 September; 11 am – 4 pm, Sundays and New Year's day, 1 January to 28 February and 1 to 31 October
ADMISSION Adults £2; Concessions £1; Children 75p
FACILITIES Parking; loos; facilities for the disabled; publications and souvenirs shop; restaurant at neighbouring Shuttleworth collection
FEATURES Fine conifers; follies and garden buildings; lake; garden sculpture; woodland garden; interesting for children; daffodils; rhododendrons; azaleas; Pulhamite grotto; fernery; Swiss cottage; much restoration and replanting (1994–5)
ENGLISH HERITAGE GRADE II*
FRIENDS Details available at the entrance

A rustic, gothic landscape garden from c.1830, now maintained as a public amenity. Winding paths, little bridges across streams, picturesque huts and kiosks, vast conifers and cheerful rhododendrons make a unique experience. Great fun to visit.

Toddington Manor
Toddington, Bedfordshire LU5 6HJ
☎ 01525 872576   FAX 01525 874555

OWNER Sir Neville and Lady Bowman-Shaw
LOCATION Signposted from village
OPEN 11 am – 6 pm, Tuesday – Sunday, plus Bank Holiday Mondays, Easter Saturday – 1 October
ADMISSION Adults £3; Senior Citizens £2; Children £1.50
FACILITIES Parking; dogs permitted; loos; facilities for the disabled; plants for sale; gift shop; home-made teas and light refreshments

FEATURES Herbaceous borders; fine conifers; herbs; pond; modern roses; old roses and climbers; woodland garden; interesting for children; vintage tractors

A newish garden, made by the owners, but rapidly maturing and maintained to the highest standard. It opened to the public for the first time last year, and has been much praised.

Woburn Abbey
Woburn, Bedfordshire MK43 0TP
☎ 01525 290666   FAX 01525 290271

OWNER The Marquess of Tavistock
LOCATION 1½ miles from Woburn on A4012
OPEN 10 am – 5 pm, daily, 27 March to 30 October. Private gardens open for NGS: 11 am – 5 pm, 15 April and 25 June. Maze open: 11 am – 5 pm, 4 June and 6 August only
ADMISSION Park: £5 per car; NGS extra
FACILITIES Parking; loos; two shops; coffee shop (teas and light meals)
FEATURES Landscape designed by Capability Brown; fine conifers; lake; woodland garden; interesting for children; deer park
ENGLISH HERITAGE GRADE I

Not a gardener's garden, though the park has many rare trees: the best way to see the famous redwood avenue is from the cable-car. The private gardens are simple and formal, mainly 19th-century and Italianate, but they include the hornbeam maze which has a Chinese pavilion in the centre.

Wrest Park
Silsoe, Bedfordshire MK45 4HS
☎ 01525 860152

OWNER English Heritage
LOCATION ¾ mile east of Silsoe
OPEN 10 am – 6 pm, Saturdays, Sundays and Bank Holiday Mondays, 1 April to 26 September
ADMISSION Adults £1.80; Concessions £1.35; Children 90p (1994)
FACILITIES Parking; dogs permitted; loos; gift shop; light refreshments
FEATURES Landscape designed by Capability Brown; follies and garden buildings; lake; garden sculpture; grand parterres; long vistas
ENGLISH HERITAGE GRADE I

The 'English Versailles', dominated by a graceful long canal which runs down to the classical domed pavilion built by Thomas Archer in 1710. Capability Brown came here later, but worked around the earlier design; the house later still, in the 1830s. A garden of grandeur.

BERKSHIRE

Englefield House
Englefield, Theale, Reading, Berkshire RG7 5EN
☎ 01734 302221   FAX 01734 302326

OWNER Sir William and Lady Benyon

LOCATION On A340, 1 mile from M4, J12
OPEN 10 am – 6 pm, Mondays (plus Tuesdays and Thursdays from 1 April to 30 June), all year. Opens for the NGS
ADMISSION Adults £2; Children free
FACILITIES Parking; loos; plants for sale; refreshments on NGS days
FEATURES Herbaceous borders; fine conifers; daffodils; rhododendrons and azaleas; old roses and climbers; woodland garden; deer park

A splendid woodland garden with underplantings of maples, viburnums, magnolias and many good shrubs. The Elizabethan house has a formal garden in front of it; wonderful colour borders along its walls.

Folly Farm
Sulhamstead, Reading, Berkshire RG7 4DF
LOCATION On right-hand side in Sulhamstead (coming from A4)
OPEN 2 – 6 pm, 23 April, 29 May, 25 June. Private bookings on written application
ADMISSION £1.50 on open days, otherwise £2.50, for charity
FACILITIES Parking; loos; tea; home-made cakes; biscuits
FEATURES Fruit of special interest; planted by Gertrude Jekyll; lake; modern roses; old roses and climbers; good topiary; lavender; lilies; paeonies; irises; lupins; delphiniums
ENGLISH HERITAGE GRADE II*

One of the most enchanting gardens to come from the partnership between Sir Edwin Lutyens and Gertrude Jekyll, the structure of Folly Farm is intact. The most famous incidents are the canal garden, running up to a double-gabled wing of the house, and the sunken rose garden, where a cruciform bed of lavender rises from a tank of water lilies. The plantings have been adapted to modern conditions and to the owners' taste for floribunda roses. Folly Farm is particularly lovely in spring when drifts of anemones flower under cherries and crabs.

Foxgrove Farm
Enborne, Newbury, Berkshire RG14 6RE
☎ 01635 40554

OWNER Miss Audrey Vockins
LOCATION On edge of village
OPEN 2 – 6 pm, 26 February, 26 March, 29 April, 11 June
ADMISSION Adults £1; Children free
FACILITIES Parking; loos; facilities for the disabled; plants for sale; tea and cakes
FEATURES Herbaceous borders; gravel or scree garden; snowdrops; primulas; spring and autumn bulbs

A plantsman's garden, linked to Louise Vockins's nursery next door. Bulbs, alpines and herbaceous plants are Audrey Vockins's great interest. The hellebores, crocuses and snowdrops give a great display in March;

colchicums are the main reason to visit in October. There are good shrubs, roses and handsome small trees too.

The Harris Garden
Plant Sciences Laboratory, University of Reading, Whiteknights, Reading, Berkshire RG6 2AS
☎ 01734 318071   FAX 01734 750630

OWNER University of Reading
LOCATION On A327, 1 mile south east of Reading
OPEN 2 – 6 pm, 14 May; 9 July; 17 September
ADMISSION Adults £1; Children free
FACILITIES Parking; loos; facilities for the disabled; teas
FEATURES Good collection of trees; herbaceous borders; fine conifers; ecological interest; fruit of special interest; glasshouses and conservatories to visit; gravel or scree garden; herbs; lake; plants for plantsmen; rock garden; modern roses; old roses and climbers; subtropical plants; woodland garden; particularly interesting in winter; Mediterranean shrubs; hardy annuals; heathers; *Primula* dell
FRIENDS The Friends of the Harris garden has an active programme of events and gives members free access to the garden. Ring Dr David Collett (01734 318024) in Department of Applied Statistics
NCCPG NATIONAL COLLECTIONS *Iris*

This is the new botanic garden attached to Reading University, which is the leading centre for teaching economic and amenity horticulture. Started in 1988, there is already much to see and to learn. Visit it now, in the early years, and return as it matures.

Hazelby House
North End, Newbury, Berkshire RG15 0AZ
☎ 01635 253544   FAX 01635 254960

OWNER Mr and Mrs Martin Lane Fox
LOCATION 6 miles south west of Newbury, right off A343 to Ball Hill, ¼ mile on left
OPEN By written appointment only (send SAE)
ADMISSION £3
FACILITIES Parking; loos; plants for sale
FEATURES Herbaceous borders; lake; plants for plantsmen; old roses and climbers; young garden

We have not seen this newish garden, made by Robin Lane Fox's brother, but it has received such universal praise for its tight design and luscious planting that we include it in *The Gardener's Yearbook* nevertheless.

Old Rectory Cottage
Tidmarsh, Pangbourne, Berkshire RG8 8ER
☎ 01734 843241

OWNER Mr and Mrs A. W. A. Baker
LOCATION Small lane on right 200 yards north of Tidmarsh village
OPEN 2 – 6 pm, 23 April, 21 May, 18 June, 9 July
ADMISSION £1
FACILITIES Parking; loos; plants for sale

FEATURES Good collection of trees; herbaceous borders; fine conifers; ecological interest; gravel or scree garden; herbs; lake; plants for plantsmen; rock garden; modern roses; old roses and climbers; woodland garden; particularly good in July-August; *Cydamens*; colchicums; hardy geraniums; snowdrops; plants collected in the wild; small lake; collection of birds; wonderful lilies

This is the marvellous garden of a great plantsman who has collected in all four corners of the world – the introducer of such staples as *Geranium palustre* and *Symphytum caucasicum*. The garden is a treasure house of unusual species, forms and home-made hybrids. Lilies are a special interest in early July – Bill Baker breeds them in thousands.

The Old Rectory, Burghfield
Burghfield, Berkshire RG3 3TH
☎ 01734 833200

OWNER Mr and Mrs R. Merton
LOCATION Right at Hatch Gate Inn and first entrance on right
OPEN 11 am – 4 pm, last Wednesday in month; February to October
ADMISSION Adults £1; Children 50p
FACILITIES Parking; loos; facilities for the disabled; plants for sale; teas
FEATURES Herbaceous borders; gravel or scree garden; herbs; lake; plants for plantsmen; rock garden; modern roses; woodland garden; stone troughs; exotic displays in tubs; hellebores; lilies

Highly acclaimed garden, whose main *tour de force* is a double herbaceous border where plants build up their impact through repetition, backed by yew hedges which get taller towards the end, to cheat the perspective. It leads to a pool framed by dense plantings of strong foliage – ferns, hostas, maples. Would that this delicious garden were open more often.

BUCKINGHAMSHIRE

Ascott House & Gardens
Wing, Buckinghamshire LU7 0PS
☎ 01296 688242

OWNER The National Trust
LOCATION ½ a mile east of Wing
OPEN House and garden: 2 – 5 pm, Tuesday – Sunday, 5 April to 7 May and 1 to 30 September. Garden only: Wednesdays and last Sundays in month; 10 May to 30 August
ADMISSION House and gardens: Adults £5; Children £2.50. Gardens only: Adults £3; Children £1.50
FACILITIES Parking; loos
FEATURES Herbaceous borders; fine conifers; lake; garden sculpture; good topiary; woodland garden; spring bulbs; Dutch garden; tallest *Cedrus atlantica* 'Aurea' in the British Isles
ENGLISH HERITAGE GRADE II

BUCKINGHAMSHIRE Gardens 261

NCCPG NATIONAL COLLECTIONS *Canna*
Opulent late-Victorian extravaganza. Tremendous set-piece fountains by Story, grand terraces, magnificent trees and a giant sundial of box and golden yew. Almost too good to be true.

Blossoms
Cobblers Hill, Great Missenden, Buckinghamshire
☎ 01494 863140

OWNER Dr and Mrs Frank Hytten
LOCATION At Cobblers Hill
OPEN By appointment only
ADMISSION £1.50 for NGS
FACILITIES Access for the disabled
FEATURES Bluebells; herbaceous borders; daffodils; lake; plants for plantsmen; rock garden; woodland garden

A large modern plantsman's garden: 5 acres of very varied habitats from beechwoods to lakes and from screes to cutting borders.

Chenies Manor
Chenies, Rickmansworth, Buckinghamshire
WD3 6ER

OWNER Mrs A. MacLeod Matthews
LOCATION Centre of Chenies village
OPEN 2 – 5 pm, Wednesdays, Thursdays and Bank Holidays, 1 April to 30 September
ADMISSION Garden only, £2; House and garden, £4
FACILITIES Parking; loos; access for the disabled; herbs for sale; tea; coffee; home-made cakes
FEATURES Herbaceous borders; fruit of special interest; herbs; good topiary; physic garden; award-winning maze

3 acres of tightly designed gardens full of variety. A Tudor bulb garden, modelled on Hampton Court; a physic garden for herbs; Edwardian skittle alley; grass labyrinth; beautiful old lawns, yew hedges and walls alive with clever modern colour-conscious planting. Ethereally English.

Chicheley Hall
Chicheley, Newport Pagnell, Buckinghamshire
MK16 9JJ
☎ 01234 391252   FAX 01234 391388

OWNER Mrs John Nutting
LOCATION 2 miles from Newport Pagnell towards Bedford on A422
OPEN 2.30 – 5 pm, Sundays, April, May and August
ADMISSION Garden only: £1.50
FACILITIES Parking; loos; tea room
FEATURES Lake; modern roses; old roses and climbers; woodland garden; historic landscape; spring daffodils
ENGLISH HERITAGE GRADE II*

Not a plantsman's garden, but a historic landscape which includes a formal lake in the French style c.1700 and a modern replanting of an old lime avenue.

Cliveden
Taplow, Maidenhead, Buckinghamshire SL6 0JA
☎ 01628 605069   FAX 01628 669461

OWNER The National Trust
LOCATION 2 miles north of Taplow, M4, J7
OPEN 11 am – 6 pm, daily, March to October; 11 am – 4 pm, daily, November to December
ADMISSION Adults (Grounds) £4; (House) £1; Children half-price
FACILITIES Parking; dogs permitted; loos; access for the disabled; National Trust shop, Wednesday – Sunday; light refreshments and meals, Wednesday – Sunday
FEATURES Herbaceous borders; garden sculpture; woodland garden; plantings by Graham Thomas; particularly interesting in winter
ENGLISH HERITAGE GRADE I
NCCPG NATIONAL COLLECTIONS *Catalpa, Anemone nemorosa, Convallaria*

A vast landscape garden, just stuffed with whatever money could buy: balustrading from the Villa Borghese in Rome, the dramatic 'Fountain of Love' and a huge parterre below the house, now dully planted by the National Trust. The best bits are the Arcadian *Ilex* wood, quite magical, and newly restored rose garden, originally made by Geoffrey Jellicoe in 1932.

Great Barfield
Bradenham, High Wycombe, Buckinghamshire
HP14 4HP
☎ 01494 563741

OWNER Richard Nutt
LOCATION Turn right into village from A4010 and immediately right ½ a mile
OPEN 2 – 5 pm, 19 February. 2 – 5.30 pm, 23 April. 2 – 6 pm, 2 July. 2 – 5 pm, 17 September. Also by appointment
ADMISSION Adults £1; Children (under 16) free
FACILITIES Access for the disabled; plants for sale; home-made teas
FEATURES Herbaceous borders; plants for plantsmen; rock garden; old roses and climbers; woodland garden; particularly interesting in winter; wonderful hellebores and snowdrops in February; lilies (notably martagons) naturalising; colchicums; good autumn colour and fruits; plants, plants, plants!
NCCPG NATIONAL COLLECTIONS *Iris unguicularis, Ranunculus ficaria, Leucojum*

One of the best modern plantsman's gardens in southern England, not least because it is beautifully designed, labelled and maintained. Whatever the season, Great Barfield amazes the visitor by the number and variety of plants in flower and their thoughtful placing.

Hughenden Manor
High Wycombe, Buckinghamshire HP14 4LA
☎ 01494 532580

OWNER The National Trust

LOCATION 1½ miles north of High Wycombe
OPEN 2 – 6 pm, Saturdays and Sundays, March 2 – 6 pm, Wednesdays and Saturdays, 1 April to 31 October; Sundays and Bank Holiday Mondays, 12 noon – 6 pm
ADMISSION Adults £3.30; Groups must book
FACILITIES Parking; loos; facilities for the disabled; National Trust shop
FEATURES Herbaceous borders; formal Victorian parterres; rolling parkland
ENGLISH HERITAGE GRADE II

Not a great garden, but interesting for its association with Disraeli. The garden was made by his wife c.1860 and is a classic formal design of its period. Recently restored, using photographs taken in 1881, the parterre is once again planted with Victorian bedding.

The Manor House, Bledlow
Bledlow, Princes Risborough, Buckinghamshire HP27 9PB
☎ 01844 348499   FAX 01844 274556

OWNER Lord and Lady Carrington
LOCATION Off B4009
OPEN 2 – 6 pm, 7 May and 18 June. Also by appointment
ADMISSION £2
FACILITIES Parking; loos; access for the disabled
FEATURES Herbaceous borders; fruit of special interest; lake; modern roses; old roses and climbers; garden sculpture

Designer garden, firmly designed, prettily planted and well maintained. The kitchen garden is particularly well laid out, with a gazebo in the middle. Fun collection of modern sculptures.

Stowe Landscape Gardens
Stowe, Buckingham, Buckinghamshire MK18 5EH
☎ 01280 822850

OWNER The National Trust
LOCATION 1½ miles north of Buckingham
OPEN 10 am – 5 pm or dusk, daily, 1 to 8 January; 25 March to 29 October, but closed on Tuesdays, Thursdays and Saturdays from 17 April to 2 July and from 4 September to 29 October
ADMISSION Adults £3.80; Family ticket £9.50; Groups by prior arrangement
FACILITIES Parking; dogs permitted; loos; light snacks
FEATURES Landscape designed by Capability Brown, Vanburgh and Bridgeman; worked on by Kent
ENGLISH HERITAGE GRADE I

Mega landscape, considered by some the most important in the history of gardens. The National Trust acquired control from the boys' public school 5 years ago, and the restoration will take many years. Go if you have not been already, and go again if you have. Stowe is not obvious: stomp round slowly, and try to appreciate the historic and symbolic significance of each feature. Read the National Trust's excellent guide and then go round again, this year, next year, every year, and commune with the *genius loci*.

Turn End
Townside, Haddenham, Aylesbury, Buckinghamshire HP17 8BG
☎ 01844 291383

OWNER Mr and Mrs Peter Aldington
LOCATION Rising Sun turning, in Haddenham, 300 yards on left. Park in street
OPEN 2 – 5 pm, Wednesdays, April to June. For NGS; 2 – 6 pm, 11 and 18 June, 17 September. Groups by appointment
ADMISSION Adult £1.50; Children 50p
FACILITIES Loos; plants for sale; teas on NGS days
FEATURES Plants for plantsmen; rock garden; old roses and climbers; ferns; grasses; brilliant design

Only 1 acre, but never was space so used to create an illusion of size. A brilliant series of enclosed gardens, sunken or raised, sunny or shady, each different and yet harmonious, contrasts with lawns, borders and glades. Much featured in the glossies, and deservedly.

Waddesdon Manor
Aylesbury, Buckinghamshire HP18 0JH
☎ 01296 651282   FAX 01296 651293

OWNER The National Trust
LOCATION A41 Bicester and Aylesbury
OPEN 11 am – 5 pm, Wednesday – Sunday and public holidays (but only Wednesdays in July and August), 1 March to 24 December
ADMISSION Adults £3; Children (5–17) £1.50
FACILITIES Parking; loos; facilities for the disabled; shop; tea room
FEATURES Herbaceous borders; lake
ENGLISH HERITAGE GRADE II*

A grand park, splendid formal gardens, a rococo aviary and extravagant bedding are the first-fruits of restoring the grounds of this amazing Rothschild palace. An exciting addition to the National Trust's portfolio of historic gardens.

West Wycombe Park
West Wycombe, Buckinghamshire HP14 3AJ
☎ 01494 524411

OWNER The National Trust
LOCATION West end of West Wycombe on Oxford road
OPEN 2 – 6 pm, Sunday – Thursday, 1 June to 31 August. Also Sundays, Wednesdays and Bank Holidays from 2 April to 31 May
ADMISSION Adults £2.50
FACILITIES Parking
FEATURES Follies and garden buildings; lake; garden sculpture
ENGLISH HERITAGE GRADE I

Early landscape park, with a lake in the shape of a swan. Classical temples and follies, plus three modern eye-catchers designed by Quinlan Terry.

CAMBRIDGESHIRE

Abbots Ripton Hall
Abbots Ripton, Cambridgeshire
☎ 014873 555   FAX 014873 545
OWNER   Lord De Ramsey
LOCATION   Off B1090
OPEN   2 – 6 pm, 6 days (details to be announced), May to August
ADMISSION   Adults £2; reduction for Senior Citizens
FACILITIES   Parking; loos; plants for sale; teas
FEATURES   Herbaceous borders; follies and garden buildings; lake; plants for plantsmen; rock garden; irises; grey border; Chinese bridge; trellis-work; new rose garden planted by Peter Beales
ENGLISH HERITAGE GRADE   II

Humphrey Waterfield, Lanning Roper and Jim Russell all worked here, and few garden owners have had as many gardening friends as Lord and Lady De Ramsey, who made and remade this garden over more than 50 years. The result is a garden of stylish individuality – as witness the gothic trellis-work and the bobbles of yellow *Philadelphus* – but also of great unity: pure enchantment.

Anglesey Abbey
Lode, Cambridgeshire CB5 9EJ
☎ 01223 811200
OWNER   The National Trust
LOCATION   Off B1102
OPEN   11 am – 5.30 pm, Wednesday – Sunday, plus Bank Holiday Mondays, 29 March to 29 October. Plus Mondays and Tuesdays from 10 July to 5 September
ADMISSION   Adults: £3.50 on Sundays, £3 other days
FACILITIES   Parking; loos; facilities for the disabled; plants for sale; National Trust shop; licensed restaurant; picnic area
FEATURES   Herbaceous borders; garden sculpture; landscaping on the grandest scale; long avenues of trees
ENGLISH HERITAGE GRADE   II*

60 years old, no more, but the grounds at Anglesey already deserve to be famous, for they are the grandest made in England this century. Majestic avenues are the stuff of it: visit Anglesey when the horse chestnuts are out and tulips glow in the grass. Large formal gardens, carved out of the flat site by yew hedges, house Lord Fairhaven's collection of homoerotic sculpture. Then there are smaller gardens, said to be more intimate, where thousands of dahlias and hyacinths hit the eye: glorious or vainglorious, Anglesey has no match.

Cambridge University Botanic Garden
Cory Lodge, Bateman Street, Cambridge, Cambridgeshire CB2 1JF
☎ 01223 336265   FAX 01223 336278
OWNER   University of Cambridge
LOCATION   Entrance on Bateman Street, 1 mile to the south of the city centre
OPEN   10 am – 4 pm in winter, (5 pm in spring and autumn, 6 pm in summer), daily, except Christmas and Boxing Day
ADMISSION   Adults £1.50; Senior Citizens and Children £1
FACILITIES   Loos; facilities for the disabled; plants for sale; light refreshments
FEATURES   Good collection of trees; herbaceous borders; fine conifers; ecological interest; glasshouses and conservatories to visit; gravel or scree garden; herbs; lake; rock garden; modern roses; old roses and climbers; subtropical plants; woodland garden; particularly good in July-August; particularly interesting in winter; tallest *Maclura pomifera* in the British Isles (and 6 other record trees)
FRIENDS   A very active association – contact the Friends Administrator 01223 336271
NCCPG NATIONAL COLLECTIONS *Alchemilla, Bergenia, Fritillaria, Geranium, Lonicera, Ribes, Ruscus, Saxifraga, Tulipa*

One of the best botanic gardens in the world for the way it matches amenity and public recreation to education, research, conservation, ecology, systematic taxonomy and horticultural excellence. The two rock gardens, one limestone and the other sandstone, are particularly successful and alone worth a long journey. For all-round interest, Cambridge Botanic Garden runs close to Kew, Wisley and Edinburgh.

Crossing House Garden
Meldreth Road, Shepreth, Royston, Cambridgeshire SG8 6PS
☎ 01763 261071
OWNER   Mr and Mrs D. G. Fuller
LOCATION   8 miles south of Cambridge off A10
OPEN   Dawn – dusk, daily, all year
ADMISSION   Donation to NGS
FACILITIES   Dogs permitted; access for the disabled
FEATURES   Plantsman's garden

One of the wonders of modern gardening, the Crossing House celebrates the achievements of its makers over the last 30 years, on an unpropitious site right beside the main railway line to Cambridge. It contains over 5,000 varieties, densely planted in the cottage style. Peat beds, screes, arches, topiary, pools and raised beds are some of the features which add variety to the most intensely and intensively planted small garden in England.

Docwra's Manor
Shepreth, Royston, Cambridgeshire SG8 6PS
☎ 01763 260235/261557
OWNER   Mrs John Raven
LOCATION   Off A10 to Shepreth
OPEN   10 am – 4 pm, Mondays, Wednesdays and Fridays, all year; 2 – 5 pm, first Sunday of April to October; 10 am – 5 pm, Bank Holiday Mondays. And by appointment. See also Yellow Book

ADMISSION £1.50 (£2.50 for special openings)
FACILITIES Facilities for the disabled; plants for sale; teas for NGS openings
FEATURES Herbaceous borders; ecological interest; fruit of special interest; plants for plantsmen; modern roses; old roses and climbers; Mediterranean plants

Very much a plantsman's garden, whose lush profusion defies the dry, cold site. Docwra's Manor is a series of small gardens – walled, wild, paved and so on – each brimming with rarities. Unstructured and informal, and yet the garden works. Do read John Raven's charming and erudite *The Botanist's Garden*, now in print again.

Elton Hall
Peterborough, Cambridgeshire PE8 6SH
☎ 01832 280223/280468 FAX 01832 280584
OWNER Mr and Mrs William Proby
LOCATION A605 near Oundle
OPEN 2 – 5 pm, Wednesdays and Sundays, July and August. Also Thursdays in August, plus Bank Holiday Sundays and Mondays
ADMISSION House and garden: Adults £3.80; Children £1.90. Garden only: Adults £1.90; Children 90p
FACILITIES Parking; loos; tea room; Blooms garden centre
FEATURES Good collection of trees; herbaceous borders; modern roses; old roses and climbers; garden sculpture; good topiary; handsome hedges; good colour plantings
ENGLISH HERITAGE GRADE II*

The house is a castellated monstrosity, but the Victorian gardens have been energetically restored in recent years and make Elton highly visitable. The knot garden and the collection of old roses are the high spots, best in June.

Hardwicke House
High Ditch Road, Fen Ditton, Cambridge, Cambridgeshire CB5 8TF
☎ 01223 292246
OWNER John Drake
LOCATION ¾ mile from village crossroads
OPEN For NGS, and by appointment
ADMISSION £1.50
FACILITIES Parking; plants for sale
FEATURES Herbaceous borders; plants for plantsmen; bulbs
NCCPG NATIONAL COLLECTIONS *Aquilegia, Semiaquilegia*

Essentially a plantsman's garden with an emphasis on herbaceous plants, roses and bulbs. The owner has a particular interest in Asia Minor, as witnesses an area devoted to Turkish bulbs.

North End House
Grantchester, Cambridge, Cambridgeshire CB3 9NQ
☎ 01223 84023 FAX 0171 437 3736
OWNER Lady Nourse
LOCATION 2 miles south west of Cambridge

OPEN For NGS: see Yellow Book
ADMISSION £1.50 (1994)
FACILITIES Parking; facilities for the disabled; plants for sale; home-made teas in village
FEATURES Herbaceous borders; lake; rock garden; old roses and climbers; young garden
NCCPG NATIONAL COLLECTIONS *Geranium*

A good example of what can be done by discriminating plantsmen in a few years. Interesting too for its National Collection of hardy geraniums.

Padlock Croft
West Wratting, Cambridgeshire CB1 5LS
☎ 01223 290383
OWNER Peter and Susan Lewis
LOCATION 2½ miles off A604 between Linton and Horseheath
OPEN 10 am – 6 pm, Wednesday – Saturday, April to 15 October, or by appointment
ADMISSION Donation
FACILITIES Parking; loos; plants for sale; tea and biscuits by prior arrangement
FEATURES Herbaceous borders; plants for plantsmen; rock garden; new shade garden (1994)
NCCPG NATIONAL COLLECTIONS *Adenophora, Campanula, Symphyandra, Platycodon*

1 acre of plantsmanship, 'interesting' rather than 'exquisite', say the owners. But they do themselves an injustice, because this is a fascinating garden. Plants are crammed in, growing where they will do best. Not only are there four National Collections, but a nursery specialising in Campanulaceae.

Peckover House
North Brink, Wisbech, Cambridgeshire PE13 1JR
☎ 01945 65325
OWNER National Trust
LOCATION Signposted from Wisbech
OPEN House and garden: Sundays and Wednesday. Garden: Saturdays, Mondays and Tuesdays, 1 April to 31 October
ADMISSION House and garden: £2.40. Garden only: £1 (1994)
FACILITIES Parking; loos; facilities for the disabled
FEATURES Herbaceous borders; glasshouses and conservatories to visit; Victorian shrubberies; orangery; fernery; Malmaison carnations; tallest *Acer negundo* in the British Isles
ENGLISH HERITAGE GRADE II

Charming example of a not-too-grand Victorian garden, complete with monkey-puzzle, fernery and spotted laurel shrubberies. One of the orange trees in the conservatory is 200 years old.

Wimpole Hall
Arrington, Royston, Cambridgeshire SG8 0BW
☎ 01223 207257 FAX 01223 207838
OWNER The National Trust
LOCATION On A603, south west of Cambridge

OPEN 1 – 5 pm, Tuesday – Thursday, Saturdays and Sundays, 25 March to 5 November. Bank Holiday Sundays and Mondays, 11 am – 5 pm
ADMISSION House and garden: £4.50. Park only: free
FACILITIES Parking; dogs permitted; loos; facilities for the disabled; National Trust shop; restaurant and tea room
FEATURES Landscape designed by Capability Brown; daffodils; landscape designed by Humphry Repton; old roses and climbers; interesting for children; Chinese bridge; parterres; current holder of Sandford Award
ENGLISH HERITAGE GRADE I

A classical 18th-century landscape where Bridgeman, Brown and Repton have all left their mark. The Victorian parterres and pleasure gardens are being restored but remain grand and simple for the present. Not a flower garden, but a joy to lovers of the landscape style.

CHESHIRE

Adlington Hall
Macclesfield, Cheshire SK10 4LF
☎ 01625 829206   FAX 01625 828756
OWNER Mrs A. S. Barnett Legh
LOCATION 5 miles north of Macclesfield off A523
OPEN 2 – 5.30 pm, Sundays and Bank Holidays, 1 April to 2 October (1994 times and dates)
ADMISSION Gardens: £1 (1994)
FACILITIES Parking; dogs permitted; loos; plants for sale; gift shop and home produce; tea room, home-made cakes, scones
FEATURES Follies and garden buildings; woodland garden
ENGLISH HERITAGE GRADE II*

An old avenue of lime trees, planted in 1688 to celebrate the accession of William and Mary, leads to a woodland 'wilderness' with follies. These include a Shell Cottage, a Temple to Diana, a Chinese bridge and a Hermitage. The new owners are restoring these buildings, and have plans for further developments.

Arley Hall & Gardens
Great Budworth, Northwich, Cheshire CW9 6NA
☎ 01565 777353
OWNER The Hon. Michael Flower
LOCATION 5 miles west of Knutsford
OPEN 12 noon – 5 pm, Tuesday – Sunday, 27 March to 2 October
ADMISSION Adults £2.80
FACILITIES Parking; dogs permitted; loos; access for the disabled; plants for sale; shop; lunches and light refreshments
FEATURES Herbaceous borders; lake; plants for plantsmen; old roses and climbers; good topiary; woodland garden; HHA/Christie's Garden of the Year in 1987; shrub-rose plantings redesigned (1994); grove garden expanded (1995)
ENGLISH HERITAGE GRADE II*

FRIENDS New Friends of Arley Hall & Gardens. Talks, events and voluntary projects. Details from The Membership Secretary, 54 High Street, Great Budworth, Cheshire CW9 6HF

Arley has pleached limes, red *Primula florindae*, clipped *Ilex* cylinders (30 feet high) and pretty old roses. But its claim to fame is the double herbaceous border, backed and buttressed by yew hedges, one of the oldest and still one of the best in England.

Bridgemere Garden World
Bridgemere, Nantwich, Cheshire CW5 7QB
OWNER J. Ravenscroft
LOCATION On A51 south of Nantwich
OPEN 10 am – 6 pm (4 pm in winter), daily, all year
ADMISSION £1
FACILITIES Parking; loos; access for the disabled; plants for sale; several shops, as well as the famous garden centre; refreshments
FEATURES Herbaceous borders; fruit of special interest; glasshouses and conservatories to visit; gravel or scree garden; herbs; lake; plants for plantsmen; rock garden; modern roses; old roses and climbers; woodland garden; young garden; particularly good in July-August

Lots of immaculate show gardens in different styles: too numerous to list, but definitely worth a visit, whatever the season.

Capesthorne Hall
Siddington, Macclesfield, Cheshire SK11 9JY
☎ 01625 861221   FAX 01625 861619
OWNER W. Bromley-Davenport
LOCATION 3 miles south of Alderley Edge
OPEN 12 noon – 6 pm, Sundays, April to September. Plus Wednesdays in May, August and September and Tuesdays and Thursdays in June and July
ADMISSION Adults £2.25; Children £1
FACILITIES Parking; loos; facilities for the disabled; small gift shop; tea rooms
FEATURES Good collection of trees; lake; woodland garden; historic park

Classic English landscape, with some pretty modern planting by Vernon Russell-Smith by the lakes, a 19th-century arboretum and formal gardens.

Cholmondeley Castle Gardens
Malpas, Cheshire SY14 8AH
☎ 01829 720383   FAX 01829 720519
OWNER The Marchioness of Cholmondeley
LOCATION Off A49 Tarporley/ Whitchurch road
OPEN 12 noon – 5.30 pm on Sundays and Bank Holiday Mondays, plus 12 noon – 5 pm on Wednesdays and Thursdays, 2 April to 1 October. And by arrangement
ADMISSION Adults £2.60; Senior Citizens £1.80; Children 75p
FACILITIES Parking; dogs permitted; loos; facilities for the disabled; plants for sale; gift shop; tea room, light lunches, home-made teas

266 Gardens CHESHIRE

FEATURES Good collection of trees; herbaceous borders; fine conifers; follies and garden buildings; lake; rock garden; modern roses; old roses and climbers; woodland garden; Japanese cherry walk; rhododendrons; daffodils and bluebells
ENGLISH HERITAGE GRADE II
FRIENDS 'Friends of Cholmondeley' season ticket

Handsome early 19th-century castle in rolling parkland, redeveloped since the 1960s with horticultural advice from Jim Russell. The results include drifts of modern rhododendrons and azaleas, a very pretty rose garden, tender plants along the terraces, a restored rock garden, good waterside plantings and a great variety of shrubs and underplantings. Highly recommended.

Dorfold Hall
Nantwich, Cheshire CW5 8LD
☎ 01270 625245   FAX 01270 628723

OWNER R. C. Roundell
LOCATION 1 mile west of Nantwich on A534
OPEN 2 – 5 pm, Tuesdays and Bank Holiday Mondays, 1 April to 31 October. See also Yellow Book
ADMISSION House and gardens: Adults £3; Children £2
FACILITIES Parking; loos
FEATURES Bluebells; lake; rhododendrons and azaleas; woodland garden
ENGLISH HERITAGE GRADE II

William Nesfield designed the formal approach, but the main reason for visiting the gardens is the new woodland garden of rhododendrons and other shrubs, leading down to a stream where *Primula pulverulenta* has naturalised in its thousands. Do not miss the incredible hulk of an ancient Spanish chestnut in the stable yard.

Granada Arboretum
Jodrell Bank, Macclesfield, Cheshire SK11 9DL
☎ 01477 571339   FAX 01477 571695

OWNER Manchester University
LOCATION On A535 between Holmes Chapel and Chelford
OPEN 10.30 am – 5.30 pm, daily, 18 March to 31 October; 11 am – 4.30 pm, Saturdays and Sundays, 1 November to 17 March
ADMISSION Grounds, Science Centre and Planetarium: Adults £3.50; Senior Citizens £2.50; Children £1.90
FACILITIES Parking; loos; shop; self-service cafeteria
FEATURES Good collection of trees; lake; modern roses; old roses and climbers; Heather Society's *Calluna* collection
NCCPG NATIONAL COLLECTIONS *Malus, Sorbus*

Better known as the Jodrell Bank Arboretum, and founded by Sir Bernard Lovell in 1971, this arboretum specialises in alders, birches, crab apples, pine and *Sorbus*. Long straight drives lead out from the new visitor's centre, known as the Environmental Discovery Centre, by way of large collections of heaths (*Erica*), heathers (*Calluna*) and old-fashioned roses. The huge radio telescope dominates the site: an awesome presence.

Hare Hill Garden
Garden Lodge, Over Alderley, Macclesfield, Cheshire SK10 4QB
☎ 01625 828981

OWNER The National Trust
LOCATION Between Alderley Edge and Prestbury
OPEN 10 am – 5.30 pm, Wednesdays, Thursdays, Saturday, Sundays and Bank Holiday Mondays (but daily from 12 May to 12 June), 29 March to 29 October
ADMISSION Adults: £2.50; Children £1.25
FACILITIES Parking; loos
FEATURES Herbaceous borders; plants for plantsmen; rock garden; old roses and climbers; garden sculpture; woodland garden

Basically, a woodland garden, thickly planted with trees and underplanted with rhododendrons, azaleas and shrubs by Jim Russell in the 1960s. In the middle is a walled garden which has been developed as a flower garden with a pergola, arbour and tender plants against the walls. Best in May but there are still some rhododendrons to flower with the roses in July.

Little Moreton Hall
Congleton, Cheshire CW12 4SD
☎ 01260 272018

OWNER The National Trust
LOCATION 4 miles south of Congleton on A34
OPEN 12 noon – 5.30 pm, Wednesday – Sunday (closed Good Friday), 1 April to 30 September. Plus 11 am – 5.30 pm on Bank Holiday Mondays and 12 noon – 5.30 pm on Saturdays and Sundays in October
ADMISSION Adults: £3.50; Children £1.80
FACILITIES Parking; loos; plants for sale; restaurant – lunches, coffee, teas
FEATURES Herbaceous borders; fruit of special interest; herbs; Graham Thomas knot garden
ENGLISH HERITAGE GRADE I

Little Moreton Hall is the handsomest timber-framed house in England. When the National Trust asked Graham Thomas to design and plant a suitable period garden, he specified box-edged parterres with yew topiary and gravel infilling – and very fine they are too. In the kitchen garden, a speciality has been made of old varieties of fruit and vegetables. Peaceful, charming and orderly.

Lyme Park
Disley, Cheshire SK12 2NX
☎ 01663 762023   FAX 01663 765035

OWNER The National Trust
LOCATION 6½ miles south east of Stockport on A6, just west of Disley
OPEN 11 am – 5 pm, daily, 1 April to 31 October; 12 noon – 4 pm, daily, 1 November to 24 December
ADMISSION Garden only: £1; Car £3

CHESHIRE Gardens 267

FACILITIES Parking; loos; facilities for the disabled; shop; light refreshments from Easter to October
FEATURES Herbaceous borders; follies and garden buildings; lake; old roses and climbers; spring bulbs; bedding out; orangery by Wyatt; 'Dutch' garden
ENGLISH HERITAGE GRADE II*

There is much of horticultural interest at Lyme, as well as the razzmatazz of a country park: traditional bedding out, two enormous camellias in the conservatory, and a Jekyll-type herbaceous border whose colours run from orange to deepest purple. Best of all is the sunken Dutch garden whose looping box and ivy parterres contain the most extravagant bedding displays.

Ness Botanic Gardens
Neston, South Wirral, Cheshire L64 4AY
☎ 0151 336 2135/7769 FAX 0151 353 1004

OWNER University of Liverpool
LOCATION Signed off A540, Chester to Hoylake
OPEN 9.30 am – 4 pm, daily, 1 November to 28 February; 9.30 am – dusk, daily, 1 March – 31 October
ADMISSION Adults £3.50; Senior Citizens and Students £2.50; Children (under 10) free
FACILITIES Parking; loos; facilities for the disabled; plants for sale; two restaurants
FEATURES Good collection of trees; herbaceous borders; fine conifers; glasshouses and conservatories to visit; gravel or scree garden; herbs; lake; rock garden; old roses and climbers; woodland garden
ENGLISH HERITAGE GRADE II
FRIENDS Season ticket for gardens: single adult £15; double adult £25; single concession £12; double concession £20; family £28. Membership of the 7,500-strong Friends of Ness Gardens gives lectures, a newsletter, and a seed list (maximum 10 packets). Contact Dr Joanna Sharples

Ness was started by A. K. Bulley, who sponsored George Forrest the plant collector, and it was here that many Chinese plants were first grown in Europe – notably candelabra primulas. It retains the sense of being a private garden, not a botanic one. The borders and shrubberies teem with interesting plants: rhododendrons, *Sorbus*, lilies, willows, roses, heathers and conifers – including a magnificent *Sequoia sempervirens* 'Adpressa'. The rock garden is particularly well planted, and the mild climate and acid soil allow a wide variety of different plants to flourish. Ness is one of those gardens where you tend to spend much longer than you intended.

Norton Priory Museum & Gardens
Tudor Road, Runcorn, Cheshire WA7 1SX
☎ 01928 569895

OWNER Norton Priory Museum Trust (Cheshire County Council)
LOCATION Well signposted locally
OPEN 12 noon – 5 pm (but 6 pm at weekends and Bank Holidays), weekdays, 1 April to 31 October
ADMISSION Adults £2.40; Senior Citizens £1.20
FACILITIES Parking; loos; facilities for the disabled; plants for sale; garden produce shop; refreshments at museum site
FEATURES Herbaceous borders; fruit of special interest; herbs; rock garden; modern roses; old roses and climbers; collection of *Cydonia* varieties; current holder of Sandford Award; old pear orchard recently restored (1994)

A new layout in the old walled garden, modelled on 18th-century precedents and intended to instruct and please modern visitors. A cottage garden border, medicinal herb garden and orchard rub shoulders with colour borders, children's gardens and a scented garden. Beyond are 16 acres of woodland garden with Georgian summerhouses and glades by the stream.

Penn
Macclesfield Road, Alderley Edge, Cheshire SK9 7BT
☎ 01625 583334

OWNER R. W. Baldwin
LOCATION ¾ mile east of Alderley village on B5087
OPEN 2 – 5 pm, see Yellow Book for dates
ADMISSION Adults £2; Senior Citizens £1.50; Children 50p
FACILITIES Parking; loos; plants for sale; light refreshments
FEATURES Herbaceous borders; camellias; fine conifers; rhododendrons and azaleas; woodland garden; magnolias; *Embothrium*

Penn is famous for its rhododendrons, thickly planted in the woods above the house, and the wide views across the lawns to the valley. But the range of good plants is very wide, and the collections of magnolias and camellias are also comprehensive.

Peover Hall
Over Peover, Knutsford, Cheshire

OWNER R. Brooks Ltd
LOCATION 3 miles south of Knutsford
OPEN 2 – 4.30 pm, Mondays and Thursdays, 1 May to 30 September
ADMISSION Garden only on Mondays: Adults, £1.50; Children, 50p. House and garden on Thursdays: Adults £2.50; Children £1.50
FACILITIES Parking; loos; access for the disabled; refreshments on Mondays only
FEATURES Herbs; old roses and climbers; good topiary; walled garden; landscaped park; rhododendrons
ENGLISH HERITAGE GRADE II

First a classic 18th-century parkland, then an Edwardian overlay of formal gardens – yew hedges and brick paths. Now Peover has modern plantings too – borders in colour combinations, a herb garden, and a rhododendron dell in the woods.

Rease Heath
Cheshire College of Agriculture, Nantwich, Cheshire
☎ 01270 625131   FAX 01270 625665
OWNER   Cheshire College of Agriculture
LOCATION   1 mile north of Nantwich on A51
OPEN   1.30 – 5 pm, Wednesdays, 24 May to 2 August. Plus College open days 12.30 – 5.30 pm on 21 and 22 May
ADMISSION   Donation
FACILITIES   Parking; loos
FEATURES   Good collection of trees; herbaceous borders; lake; rhododendrons and azaleas; rock garden; modern roses; woodland garden; heather garden; candelabra primulas

Formal gardens, island beds, a woodland garden and a lake with water lilies: there is much to enjoy and learn from here.

Rode Hall
Church Lane, Scholar Green, Stoke on Trent, Cheshire ST7 3QP
☎ 01270 882961   FAX 01270 882962
OWNER   Sir Richard Baker Wilbraham
LOCATION   5 miles south west of Congleton between A34 and A50
OPEN   2 – 5 pm, Wednesdays and Bank Holidays, 1 April to 30 September
ADMISSION   Garden only: £2
FACILITIES   Parking; dogs permitted; loos; plants for sale; garden produce
FEATURES   Landscape designed by Humphry Repton; fine conifers; follies and garden buildings; fruit of special interest; old roses and climbers; good topiary; woodland garden; ice house; rhododendrons; grotto
ENGLISH HERITAGE GRADE   II

Landscaped by Repton c.1790 and given a formal garden by Nesfield in 1860, the main horticultural interest comes from the massed banks of azaleas and rhododendrons in the late Victorian 'Wild Garden'.

Stapeley Water Gardens Ltd
92 London Road, Stapeley, Nantwich, Cheshire CW5 7LH
☎ 01270 623868   FAX 01270 624919
OWNER   Stapeley Water Gardens Ltd
LOCATION   A51, 1 mile south of Nantwich
OPEN   10 am – 5.30 pm, daily, all year, except 25 December
ADMISSION   Palms Tropical Oasis: Adults £3.15; Senior Citizens £2.25; Children £1.65
FACILITIES   Parking; facilities for the disabled; plants for sale; cafeteria and terrace restaurant
FEATURES   Glasshouses and conservatories to visit; lake; subtropical plants; interesting for children; particularly interesting in winter; collection of hardy water lilies; *Victoria regia*, the giant water lily
NCCPG NATIONAL COLLECTIONS *Nymphaea*

Part entertainment, part nursery and part display garden, the Palms Tropical Oasis is worth a visit in its own right. A long rectangular pool in the Moorish style is flanked by tall palms, strelitzias and other showy tropical flowers. Visit in winter.

Tatton Park
Knutsford, Cheshire
☎ 01565 750780   FAX 01565 650179
OWNER   The National Trust (managed by Cheshire County Council)
LOCATION   Off M6, J19 and M56, J 7 – well signposted
OPEN   10.30 am – 6 pm, daily except Mondays, 1 April to 23 October; 11 am – 4 pm, daily, except Mondays, 24 October to 31 March
ADMISSION   Adults £2.50; Children £1.50; Family £7.50
FACILITIES   Parking; loos; facilities for the disabled; plants for sale; shop; hot meals and snacks (summer only)
FEATURES   Good collection of trees; herbaceous borders; landscape designed by Capability Brown; follies and garden buildings; glasshouses and conservatories to visit; lake; oriental features; landscape designed by Humphry Repton; modern roses; rhododendrons and azaleas in May; fernery; current holder of Sandford Award; orangery and fernery newly restored (1994)
ENGLISH HERITAGE GRADE   II*
NCCPG NATIONAL COLLECTIONS *Adiantum, Inula*

Humphry Repton laid out the parkland. Joseph Paxton designed both the formal Italian garden and the exquisite fernery; it claims to be the finest in the United Kingdom. Later came a Japanese garden and Shinto temple, such follies as the African hut, and the mass plantings of rhododendrons and azaleas. Tatton Park is wonderfully well-organised for visitors, and gets better every year.

Tirley Garth Trust
Utkinton, Tarporley, Cheshire CW6 0LZ
☎ 01829 732301   FAX 01829 732265
OWNER   The Tirley Garth Trust
LOCATION   2½ miles north of Tarporley, just north of village of Utkinton on road to Kelsall
OPEN   2 – 6 pm, 21, 28, 29 May and 4 June
ADMISSION   Adults £2.50; Children 50p
FACILITIES   Parking; dogs permitted; loos; home baking, home-made ices
FEATURES   Herbaceous borders; rock garden; modern roses; woodland garden
ENGLISH HERITAGE GRADE   II
FRIENDS   Friends of Tirley Garth: details available from the gardens

Famous example of Thomas Mawson's work: wonderful terraces, paths, retaining walks and garden buildings. Good rhododendrons and azaleas in the woodland below.

CORNWALL

Antony House
Torpoint, Cornwall PL11 2QA
☎ 01752 812364

OWNER The National Trust
LOCATION 5 miles west of Plymouth, 2 miles north west of Torpoint
OPEN 1.30 – 5.30 pm, Tuesdays, Thursdays and Bank Holidays, April to October; also Sundays in June and August
ADMISSION Adults £3.60; Children £1.80
FACILITIES Parking; loos; access for the disabled; tea room
FEATURES Herbaceous borders; landscape designed by Capability Brown; fine conifers; lake; good topiary; woodland garden; magnolias; yew hedges; tallest Japanese loquat *Eriobotrya japonica* in the British Isles
ENGLISH HERITAGE GRADE II
NCCPG NATIONAL COLLECTIONS *Hemerocallis*

A classic 18th-century landscape, influenced by Humphry Repton, in a superb position above the Tamar estuary. Yew hedges nearer the house enclose modern plantings while the kitchen garden houses the vast National Collection of *Hemerocallis* or day lilies.

Antony Woodland Garden
Antony House, Torpoint, Cornwall PL11 2QA
☎ 01752 812364

OWNER The Carew Pole Garden Trust
LOCATION 5 miles west of Plymouth, 2 miles north west of Torpoint
OPEN 11 am – 5.30 pm, daily, March to October
ADMISSION Adults £1.50; Children 50p
FACILITIES Parking; loos; tea room
FEATURES Fine conifers; lake; plants for plantsmen; woodland garden; camellias; magnolias; rhododendrons and azaleas

This is the 'Cornish' part of the grounds at Antony, still controlled by the Carew Pole family rather than the National Trust. They have planted it with the best modern forms of rhododendrons, azaleas, magnolias, camellias and other trees.

Bosahan
Manaccan, Helston, Cornwall TR12 6JL
☎ 01326 231330

OWNER Mrs H. R. Graham-Vivian
LOCATION 1 mile north east of Manaccan village
OPEN 19 and 23 April, 14 May
ADMISSION Adults £1.50; Senior Citizens 50p; Children (under 13) free
FACILITIES Parking; dogs permitted; loos; access for the disabled; plants for sale; teas
FEATURES Herbaceous borders; camellias; rhododendrons and azaleas; subtropical plants; magnolias; tree ferns

5 acres of mature Cornish woodland on the banks of the Helford river, underplanted with tree ferns and other southern hemisphere exotica. Daphne du Maurier is said to have had Bosahan in mind when she wrote *Rebecca*.

Bosvigo House
Bosvigo Lane, Truro, Cornwall TR1 3NH
☎ 01872 75774   [FAX] 01872 41565

OWNER Wendy and Michael Perry
LOCATION ¾ mile from Truro centre. Turn off A390 at Highertown then 500 yards down Dobbs Lane
OPEN 11 am – 6 pm, Wednesday – Saturday, 1 March to 30 September
ADMISSION Adults £1.50; Children 50p
FACILITIES Parking; loos; plants for sale
FEATURES Herbaceous borders; plants for plantsmen; woodland garden; young garden; unusual perenials; Victorian conservatory; colour borders

Not a typical Cornish garden, the emphasis at Bosvigo is upon herbaceous plants, chosen for all their qualities and planted in fine colour combinations. Many are rare: some for sale.

Burncoose Gardens
Gwennap, Redruth, Cornwall TR16 6BJ
☎ 01209 861112   [FAX] 01209 860011

OWNER F. J. Williams
LOCATION Between villages of Lanner and Ponsanooth
OPEN 9 am – 5 pm (open 11 am on Sundays), Monday – Saturday, all year
ADMISSION Adults £1; Children free
FACILITIES Parking; dogs permitted; loos; access for the disabled; important nursery adjacent; teas and light refreshments
FEATURES Bluebells; camellias; fine conifers; plants for plantsmen; rhododendrons and azaleas; woodland garden; magnolias; rare trees and shrubs

30 acres of traditional Cornish woodland garden, planted with ancient rhododendrons and handsome trees, but reinvigorated by extensive shrub planting since 1981 – the result of a partnership between the Williams family and Cornwall's leading nurseryman.

Caerhays Castle
Gorran, St Austell, Cornwall PL26 6LY
☎ 01872 501310   [FAX] 01872 501870

OWNER F. J. Williams
LOCATION Between Mevagissey and Portloe
OPEN 11 am – 4 pm, Monday – Friday, 20 March to 5 May. Charity openings: 26 March, 16 April, 8 May
ADMISSION Adults £2.50; Children (under 14) £1.50
FACILITIES Parking; dogs permitted; loos; plants for sale; tea rooms and beach shop/café in car park
FEATURES Good collection of trees; fine conifers; plants for plantsmen; woodland garden; camellias; magnolias; rhododendrons; tallest specimen of *Emmenop-*

terys henryi in the British Isles, and twelve further record-breaking tree species
ENGLISH HERITAGE GRADE   II*

The Williams family subscribed to many of the great plant-collecting expeditions and the fruits of their labours flourish at Caerhays. Wilson and Forrest are represented by thousands of trees and shrubs, and one of the joys of Caerhays is to stumble upon magnificent old specimens deep in its 100 acres of woodland. There are splendid collections of *Nothofagus* and *Lithocarpus* as well as the 3 genera for which Caerhays is famous – magnolias, camellias and rhododendrons. The original × *williamsii* camellias still flourish, including 'J. C. Williams', 'Mary Christian' and 'St Ewe'. There is much to discover at Caerhays: allow plenty of time.

Carclew Gardens

Perran-ar-Worthal, Truro, Cornwall TR3 7PB
☎ 01872 864070
OWNER   Mrs Robert Chope
LOCATION   A39 east at Perran-ar-Worthal, 1 mile to garden
OPEN   For NGS: see Yellow Book
ADMISSION   Adults £1.50; Children 50p (1994)
FACILITIES   Parking; loos; home-made teas
FEATURES   Herbaceous borders; follies and garden buildings; lake; garden sculpture; rhododendrons; tallest *Pseudolarix amabilis* in the British Isles

The gardens first opened to the public in 1927 and have continued to do so for charity every year since then. Vast hummocks of old rhododendrons, some grown from Sir Joseph Hooker's Himalayan collections nearly 150 years ago. Good trees, including a *Quercus* × *hispanica* which is *not* 'Lucombeana'.

Carwinion

Mawnan Smith, Falmouth, Cornwall TR11 5JA
☎ 01326 250258
OWNER   Anthony Rogers
LOCATION   From Mawnan Smith, turn left at Red Lion, 500 yards up hill on right
OPEN   10 am – 5.30 pm, daily or by appointment, all year
ADMISSION   £2
FACILITIES   Parking; dogs permitted; loos; plants for sale
FEATURES   Fine conifers; ecological interest; lake; subtropical plants; woodland garden; 100 species of bamboo; tree ferns; *Gunnera*; bluebells; new quarry garden planted with ferns (1994)

10 acres of Cornish jungle, exotically thick with rhododendrons, camellias, *Drimys* and the largest collection of bamboos in the South West.

Chyverton

Zelah, Truro, Cornwall TR4 9HD
☎ 01872 540324
OWNER   Mr and Mrs Nigel Holman
LOCATION   1 mile south west of Zelah on A30

OPEN   By appointment; March to June
ADMISSION   Adults £3; Children (under 16) free; Groups (20+) £2.50
FACILITIES   Parking; dogs permitted; loos
FEATURES   Fine conifers; lake; plants for plantsmen; woodland garden; magnolias; *Nothofagus*; extensive new planting (1995)
ENGLISH HERITAGE GRADE   II

The garden of a distinguished writer on gardening who is both a keen plantsman and a landscaper with plants. Magnolias are a special interest: several Chyverton seedlings now bear cultivar names. Many other established plants have also been grown from seed: rhododendron hybrids from Brodick, for instance, and *Eucalyptus nicholii* from a wild collection. But there is much more to interest the plantsman. A large *Berberidopsis corallina* and a lanky red-stemmed hedge of *Luma apiculata* below the house are both outstanding. And the planting continues.

Cotehele

St Dominick, Saltash, Cornwall PL12 6TA
☎ 01579 50909
OWNER   The National Trust
LOCATION   14 miles from Plymouth via Saltash
OPEN   11 am – 5.30 pm (dusk if earlier), daily, all year
ADMISSION   1 April – 31 October, £2.50; rest of year, free
FACILITIES   Parking; loos; facilities for the disabled; plants for sale; refreshments 1 April – 31 October
FEATURES   Good collection of trees; fine conifers; lake; modern roses; good topiary; woodland garden; palms; ferns; pretty dovecote; daffodils
ENGLISH HERITAGE GRADE   II

Broad Victorian terraces below the house support many tender climbers such as *Jasminum mesnyi* while the beds beneath have wallflowers and roses. Down the wooded valley are camellias, rhododendrons and shade-loving plants which thrive in an ancient woodland, kept damp by a small stream.

Glendurgan Gardens

Helford River, Mawnan Smith, Falmouth, Cornwall TR11 5JZ
☎ 01326 250906
OWNER   The National Trust
LOCATION   1 mile west of Mawnan Smith, west to Trebah
OPEN   10 am – 5.30 pm, Tuesday – Saturday, plus Bank Holidays except Good Friday, 1 March to 31 October
ADMISSION   £2.60
FACILITIES   Parking; loos; plants for sale; small shop; light refreshments
FEATURES   Fine conifers; lake; subtropical plants; woodland garden; laurel maze; wild flowers; huge tulip tree; new path opened for National Trust Centenary (1995)

ENGLISH HERITAGE GRADE II
A steep, subtropical valley garden on the Helford River with a good collection of old rhododendrons and camellias. Glendurgan also boasts an extraordinary 1830s maze of clipped cherry laurel, which the National Trust has recently restored. A lovely garden, almost best when just viewed from the top – but the temptation to wander down and into it is irresistible!

Heligan Manor Gardens
Pentewan, St Austell, Cornwall PL26 6EW
☎ 01726 844157/843566 FAX 01726 843023

OWNER The Heligan Manor Gardens Project
LOCATION St Austell to Mevagissey Road, following brown tourist signs
OPEN 10 am – 4.30 pm, daily, all year
ADMISSION Adults £2.80; Senior Citizens £2.40; Children £1.60
FACILITIES Parking; dogs permitted; loos; facilities for the disabled; plants for sale; tea room with light refreshments
FEATURES Follies and garden buildings; rhododendrons and azaleas; rock garden; subtropical plants; woodland garden; beautiful fern gully
ENGLISH HERITAGE GRADE II
FRIENDS Friends subscription, £15, includes newsletters

Heligan – the accent is on the i – calls itself 'The Lost Gardens of Heligan' and has been spectacularly rescued from a jungle of neglect. To date the restoration team has uncovered the Italian garden, the Crystal Grotto, the wishing well, the Bee Boles, a melon garden, the Sundial Garden and other authentic features. The enthusiasm of the restorers is infectious and their achievements are already substantial. They are also adept at getting financial support and publicity, even if the reality does not always match the hype.

Ken Caro
Bicton, Pensilva, Liskeard, Cornwall PL14 5RF
☎ 01579 62446

OWNER Mr and Mrs K. R. Willcock
LOCATION Signed from A390, midway between Callington and Liskeard
OPEN 2 – 6 pm, Sunday – Wednesday, 15 April to 28 June; plus Tuesdays and Wednesdays in July and August
ADMISSION £2
FACILITIES Parking; plants for sale
FEATURES Herbaceous borders; fine conifers; oriental features; plants for plantsmen; aviary and waterfowl; lots of new plantings (1994 and 1995)
NCCPG NATIONAL COLLECTIONS *Pittosporum*

Started in 1970 as 2 acres of intensely planted formal gardens in different styles, and extended in 1993 by taking in a further 2 acres. Very much a plantsman's garden with good herbaceous plants and shrubs, not at all a typical Cornish garden. The owners are flower arrangers: look for architectural plants and original combinations.

Lamorran House
Upper Castle Road, St Mawes, Cornwall TR2 5BZ
☎ 01326 270800 FAX 01326 270801

OWNER Mr and Mrs Robert Dudley-Cooke
LOCATION ½ a mile from village centre
OPEN Wednesdays and Fridays, 1 April to 1 October, and some weekends for NGS. Also by appointment
ADMISSION £2
FACILITIES Parking; loos; plants for sale
FEATURES Good collection of trees; herbaceous borders; fine conifers; follies and garden buildings; lake; oriental features; plants for plantsmen; subtropical plants; young garden

Made since 1980 on a steep site above the sea and tightly designed in the Italian style, but also full of unusual plants. An English Mediterranean garden in Cornwall, say the owners, a mainland Tresco.

Lanhydrock
Bodmin, Cornwall PL30 5AD
☎ 01208 73320

OWNER The National Trust
LOCATION 2½ miles south east of Bodmin
OPEN 11 am – 5.30 pm (5 pm in October), daily except Mondays, 30 March to 31 October
ADMISSION House and garden: £5.40. Garden only: £2.50. Children half-price
FACILITIES Parking; loos; plants for sale; National Trust shop; restaurant and bar, cream teas
FEATURES Herbaceous borders; modern roses; good topiary; woodland garden; Victorian parterres; collection of magnolias
ENGLISH HERITAGE GRADE II*
NCCPG NATIONAL COLLECTIONS *Crocosmia*

A grand mansion, mainly 19th-century, with one of the best formal gardens in Cornwall – clipped yews, box parterres and bedding out, as well as large herbaceous borders which contain the National Collection of *Crocosmia*. The woodlands behind are impressive for their size and colourful rhododendrons in spring. But it is the magnolias which impress the visitor most: 140 different species and cultivars.

Mount Edgcumbe Gardens
Cremyll, Torpoint, Cornwall PL10 1HZ
☎ 01752 822236 FAX 01752 822199

OWNER Cornwall County Council & Plymouth City Council
LOCATION At the end of the B3247, or by ferry from Plymouth
OPEN Formal gardens and park: dawn – dusk, all year. House and Earl's Garden: 11 am – 5.30 pm, Wednesday – Sunday, 31 March to 31 October
ADMISSION House and Earl's Garden: Adults £3. Formal gardens and park: free

FACILITIES Parking; dogs permitted; loos; facilities for the disabled; gift and book shops; camellias for sale; orangery restaurant in formal gardens
FEATURES Good collection of trees; herbaceous borders; fine conifers; daffodils; follies and garden buildings; glasshouses and conservatories to visit; lake; subtropical plants; woodland garden; summer bedding; deer park; formal gardens; fern dell; genuine Victorian rose garden; tallest cork oak *Quercus suber* in the British Isles
ENGLISH HERITAGE GRADE I
NCCPG NATIONAL COLLECTIONS *Camellia*
FRIENDS Contact Mrs C. Gaskell Brown (01752 822236)

A long, stately grass drive runs down from the house to Plymouth Sound, through oak woods interplanted with large ornamental trees. Here is the National Collection of camellias, all meticulously labelled, which will eventually include all 32,000 known varieties. The formal gardens are right down on the waterside, protected by a clipped *Ilex* hedge 30 feet high. There are no less than 10 acres of gardens here, including an Italian garden (c.1790), a French garden (early Victorian), an American garden, a modern New Zealand garden complete with geyser, Milton's Temple, an orangery, a conservatory and the fern dell. Allow plenty of time to do justice to these majestic pleasure gardens.

Pencarrow
Washaway, Bodmin, Cornwall PL30 3AG
☎ 01208 841369

OWNER The Trustees of the Molesworth-St Aubyn family
LOCATION 4 miles north west of Bodmin – signed off the A389 at Washaway
OPEN 1.30 – 5 pm, 14 April to 15 October except Fridays and Saturdays, 11 am – 5 pm from 1 June to 10 September and on Bank Holiday Mondays
ADMISSION House and Garden: Adults £3.80; Children £1.80. Garden only: Adults £1.50; Children free
FACILITIES Parking; dogs permitted; loos; facilities for the disabled; plants for sale; craft centre; light lunches, cream teas
FEATURES Fine conifers; fruit of special interest; lake; rock garden; old roses and climbers; woodland garden; Italian garden; rhododendrons; camellias
ENGLISH HERITAGE GRADE II

A long drive through rhododendrons and vast conifers leads to the pretty Anglo-Palladian house. Below is an Italian garden, laid out in the 1830s, and next to it a great granite rock garden where boulders from Bodmin Moor lie strewn among the trees and shrubs. Pencarrow is famous for its conifers: an ancestor planted one of every known variety in the mid-19th century and the survivors are so venerable that the great Alan Mitchell wrote a guide to them. Recent plantings have concentrated upon rhododendrons (many hundreds of the best modern varieties) and adding new conifers to the old.

It is good to see the fortunes of such a distinguished garden revived.

Penjerrick
Budock, Falmouth, Cornwall TR11 5ED
☎ 01326 250074/01872 870105

OWNER Mrs Rachel Morin
LOCATION 3 miles south west of Falmouth, entrance at junction of lanes opposite Penmoruah Manor Hotel
OPEN 1.30 – 4.30 pm, Wednesdays, Fridays and Sundays, 1 March to 30 September
ADMISSION Adults £1; Children 50p
FACILITIES Parking; dogs permitted
FEATURES Good collection of trees; fine conifers; lake; woodland garden; rhododendrons; camellias; tree ferns
ENGLISH HERITAGE GRADE II

Famous for the Barclayi and Penjerrick hybrid rhododendrons and now a mature woodland garden recovering well from a period of neglect. Very Cornish.

Pine Lodge Gardens
Cuddra, St Austell, Cornwall PL25 3RQ
☎ 01726 73500

OWNER Mr and Mrs Raymond Clemo
LOCATION East of St Austell between Holmbush and Tregrehan
OPEN 1 – 5 pm, 28 May and 25 June for charity. Groups (20+) by appointment at any time of year
ADMISSION Adults £2; Groups £3
FACILITIES Parking; loos; access for the disabled; plants for sale; cream teas on charity days
FEATURES Good collection of trees; herbaceous borders; fine conifers; fruit of special interest; plants for plantsmen; garden sculpture; woodland garden; bog gardens; new 1-acre formal garden made from old orchard (1994); new lake and 4-acre pinetum (1994–95)
NCCPG NATIONAL COLLECTIONS *Grevillea*

A modern garden, rather different from the typical Cornish garden, and fast expanding. There are rhododendrons and azaleas, of course, but they are planted and underplanted with other shrubs and herbaceous plants to create lasting colour effects. The latest developments are very exciting.

Probus Demonstration Garden
Probus, Truro, Cornwall TR2 4HQ
☎ 01726 882597

OWNER Cornwall County Council
LOCATION At east end of village
OPEN 10 am – 5 pm, daily, 1 April to 1 October
ADMISSION £2
FACILITIES Parking; loos; access for the disabled; plants for sale; good shop; light refreshments
FEATURES Alpines; good collection of trees; herbaceous borders; camellias; ecological interest; fruit and vegetables of special interest; glasshouses and conservatories to visit; gravel or scree garden; herbs; plants

for plantsmen; climbing roses; modern roses; old roses; garden sculpture; interesting for children

Probus is quite simply the best place in the South West to learn about gardening. Nor is it just about plants: there are innumerable demonstration plots for lawns, methods of cultivation, composting and shelter. One highly original and useful feature is a geological map of Cornwall, made of rock specimens from every part of the county. Standards are high: everyone will learn more from a visit than they ever imagined possible.

St Michael's Mount
Marazion, Cornwall TR17 0HT
☎ 01736 710507 FAX 01736 711544

OWNER Lord St Levan and the National Trust
LOCATION 1 mile south of Marazion
OPEN 10.30 am – 5.30 pm, Monday – Friday, 1 April to 31 May (plus most weekends during summer)
ADMISSION £2
FACILITIES Loos; plants for sale; refreshments
FEATURES Herbaceous borders; ecological interest; rock garden; subtropical plants; woodland garden; wild *Narcissus*; naturalised *Kniphofia* and *Agapanthus*
ENGLISH HERITAGE GRADE II

A triumph of man's ingenuity in the face of Atlantic gales, salt spray and bare rock with sand for a garden soil. Careful experiment over the generations has enabled the owners to plant a remarkable garden of plants which resist the elements: *Luma apiculata*, rugosa roses, *Correa*, nerines, Hottentot figs and naturalised *Agapanthus*. On the north side, a sparse wood of sycamores and pines gives protection to camellias, azaleas and hydrangeas. There is nothing rare about the plants: the wonder is that they grow at all.

Trebah Garden Trust
Mawnan Smith, Falmouth, Cornwall TR11 5JZ
☎ 01326 250448 FAX 01326 250781

OWNER The Trebah Garden Trust
LOCATION 6 miles south west of Falmouth, signposted from Hillhead roundabout on A39 approach to Falmouth
OPEN 10.30 am – 5 pm (last admission), daily, all year
ADMISSION Adults £2.80; Senior Citizens £2.40; Students (5–15 yrs) and disabled visitors £1; Children (under 5) free
FACILITIES Parking; dogs permitted; loos; excellent nursery; light refreshments, hot and cold drinks
FEATURES Good collection of trees; herbaceous borders; fine conifers; lake; plants for plantsmen; subtropical plants; woodland garden; interesting for children; particularly interesting in winter; Tarzan camp and Tarzan trails for children; access to private beach; tallest hornbeam *Carpinus betulus* in the British Isles and 2 other tree records; restored water garden and new Tasmanian tree-fern glade (1994)
ENGLISH HERITAGE GRADE II

FRIENDS The Trebah Trust is a registered charity which aims to preserve the gardens for posterity: details from 01326 250448

Wonderful Trebah! This lost garden has been vigorously restored and succesfully improved since the Hibberts bought it in 1980. The view from the top is magical – a secret valley which runs right down to the Helford estuary. Vast trees, natural and exotic, line the steep sides, while the central point is held by a group of elegant palms: one is the tallest in the British Isles. Trebah is popular with children, whose curiosity is aroused by trails, quizzes and educational games.

Tregrehan
Par, Cornwall PL24 2SJ
☎ 01726 812438

OWNER T. C. Hudson
LOCATION 1 mile west of St Blazey on A390
OPEN 10.30 am – 5 pm, daily except Easter Sunday, mid March to June, plus September
ADMISSION Adults £2; Children 50p
FACILITIES Parking; loos; facilities for the disabled; plants for sale; teas
FEATURES Good collection of trees; fine conifers; glasshouses and conservatories to visit; plants for plantsmen; woodland garden; camellias; pinetum; walled garden; sunken garden
ENGLISH HERITAGE GRADE II*

An old Cornish garden whose 20 acres include a fine range of Victorian conservatories, tall conifers and lanky rhododendrons. But Tregrehan is best known for the camellias bred there by the late Gillian Carlyon, especially 'Jennifer Carlyon', which won her the Reginald Cory Memorial Cup from the Royal Horticultural Society.

Trehane
Probus, Truro, Cornwall TR2 4JG
☎ 0187 252 270

OWNER David and Simon Trehane
LOCATION Signposted from A39
OPEN 2 – 5 pm, 19 March; 2, 16 and 30 April; 7 and 21 May; 4 and 18 June; 2 and 16 July; 20 August
ADMISSION Adults £1.50; Children free
FACILITIES Parking; dogs permitted; loos; access for the disabled; plants for sale; teas
FEATURES Herbaceous borders; fine conifers; plants for plantsmen; good topiary; woodland garden; bluebells

You would expect camellias from anyone called Trehane, and their eponymous garden has a fine collection. There is, however, no limit to their interests and there are many other good things here, especially herbaceous plants.

Trelissick Garden (Feock)
Feock, Truro, Cornwall TR3 6QL
☎ 01872 862090

OWNER The National Trust

274 Gardens CORNWALL

LOCATION   Take B3289 off main Truro – Falmouth Road
OPEN   10.30 am – 5.30 pm, Monday – Saturday, 12.30 – 5.30 pm, Sunday, 1 March to 31 October; March and October closes at 5 pm
ADMISSION   Adult £3.40; Children £1.70
FACILITIES   Parking; loos; facilities for the disabled; gift and plant shop; refreshments
FEATURES   Fine conifers; fruit of special interest; plants for plantsmen; woodland garden; particularly good in July-August; aromatic plant garden; fig garden; hydrangeas
ENGLISH HERITAGE GRADE   II

Once famous for its fig garden, still maintained by the National Trust, Trelissick is particularly colourful in August and September when the hydrangeas are in full flower. There are over 100 varieties, some in a special walk. But venerable conifers and tender plants are also features: *Rosa bracteata* and *Yucca whipplei* are among the many good things to admire in summer, not to mention the rhododendrons and camellias in spring.

Trengwainton Gardens
Madron, Penzance, Cornwall TR20 8RZ
☎ 01736 63148
OWNER   Lt.-Col. E. T. Bolitho and the National Trust
LOCATION   2 miles north west of Penzance, ½ a mile west of Heamoor
OPEN   10.30 am – 5.30 pm (5 pm in March and October), Wednesday – Saturday and Bank Holidays, 1 March to 31 October
ADMISSION   Adults £2.50; Children £1.25 (1994)
FACILITIES   Parking; dogs permitted; loos; facilities for the disabled; plants for sale; new National Trust shop; coffee, snacks, teas
FEATURES   Fruit of special interest; lake; modern roses; old roses and climbers; subtropical plants; woodland garden; lilies; acacias; *Myosotidium hortensia*; tree ferns
ENGLISH HERITAGE GRADE   II

Trengwainton has the best collection of tender plants on the Cornish mainland, all thanks to the Bolitho family who started planting seriously only in 1925. Much came from original seed from such collectors as Kingdon Ward: some rhododendrons flowered here for the first time in the British Isles, among them RR. *macabeanum*, *elliottii* and *taggianum*. The plants in many Cornish gardens are past their best. Not so at Trengwainton, where so many are in their prime. It is a garden to wander through slowly, giving yourself as much time as you need to enjoy its riches.

Trerice
Newquay, Cornwall TR8 4PG
☎ 01637 875404
OWNER   The National Trust
LOCATION   3 miles south east of Newquay – turn right off A3058 at Kestle Mill

OPEN   11 am – 5.30 pm (5 pm in October), daily except Tuesday, 1 April to 31 October
ADMISSION   House: £3.60. Garden: free
FACILITIES   Parking; loos; plants for sale; National Trust shop; restaurant and tea room
FEATURES   Herbaceous borders; oriental features; modern roses; colour borders; good collection of apple trees

A perfect West Country manor house with pretty Dutch gables, Trerice is unusual among Cornish gardens. It is small and comparatively formal: the design and herbaceous plantings are its best points. It is not surrounded by swirling rhododendron woodland. There is a perfect harmony between the Jacobean architecture and the gardens. Somewhat anomalously, it boasts the largest collection of mid-Victorian to current-day lawnmowers in the country. They are both interesting and fun.

Tresco Abbey
Isles of Scilly, Cornwall TR24 0QQ
☎ 01720 22849   FAX 01720 22807
OWNER   Robert Dorrien Smith
LOCATION   Direct helicopter flight from Penzance
OPEN   10 am – 4 pm, daily, all year
ADMISSION   Adults £3.50; Children (under 14) £1
FACILITIES   Dogs permitted; loos; facilities for the disabled; plants for sale; shop; light refreshments
FEATURES   Herbaceous borders; fine conifers; follies and garden buildings; lake; plants for plantsmen; rock garden; subtropical plants; woodland garden; interesting for children; particularly good in July-August; particularly interesting in winter; cacti; succulents; South African, Australian and New Zealand plants; tallest *Luma apiculata* in the British Isles
ENGLISH HERITAGE GRADE   I
NCCPG NATIONAL COLLECTIONS *Acacia*

Tresco has recovered brilliantly from the arctic weather of January 1987 and the hurricane of January 1990. Kew donated hundreds of plants and English Heritage helped to plant new shelter belts. The amazing profusion of exotica is intact. The helicopter service makes access easier than ever, but it does distract you while actually visiting the garden.

Trewithen
Grampound Road, Truro, Cornwall TR2 4DD
☎ 01726 882763   FAX 01726 882301
OWNER   A. M. J. Galsworthy
LOCATION   A390 between Probus and Grampound
OPEN   10 am – 4.30 pm, Monday – Saturday (and Sundays in April), 1 March to 30 September
ADMISSION   Adults £2.50; Children £1.50; Groups (12+) £2.20
FACILITIES   Parking; dogs permitted; loos; facilities for the disabled; plants for sale; garden shop; tea room with light refreshments

FEATURES Good collection of trees; herbaceous borders; camellias; fine conifers; plants for plantsmen; rhododendrons and azaleas; woodland garden; magnolias; trees and shrubs from collected seed; quarry garden; *Cyclamen*; tallest *Eucryphia cordifolia* in the British Isles and four more record-breaking tree species
ENGLISH HERITAGE GRADE II*

Trewithen's setting is magnificent. Instead of the steep terraces of most Cornish gardens, there is a spacious flat lawn that stretches 200 yards into the distance, with gentle banks of rhododendrons, magnolias and rare shrubs on all sides. It sets the tone for the garden's grandeur, which was entirely the work of George Johnstone in the first half of this century. Johnstone was a great plantsman. He subscribed to plant-hunting expeditions, such as those of Frank Kingdon Ward. Note how he used laurel hedges to divide up the woodland and give structure to the garden. He also had an eye for placing plants to advantage. As a breeder, he gave us *Rhododendron* 'Alison Johnstone', *Ceanothus* 'Trewithen Blue' and *Camellia saluenensis* 'Trewithen White'. The Michelin Guide gives Trewithen its top award of three stars – *vaut le voyage!*

CUMBRIA

Acorn Bank Garden
Acorn Bank, Temple Sowerby, Penrith, Cumbria CA10 1SP
☎ 017683 61893/61281
OWNER The National Trust
LOCATION North of Temple Sowerby, 6 miles east of Penrith on A66
OPEN 10 am – 5.30 pm, daily, 1 April to 31 October
ADMISSION Adults £1.60; Children 80p
FACILITIES Parking; loos; facilities for the disabled; plants for sale; National Trust shop; light refreshments
FEATURES Herbaceous borders; ecological interest; fruit of special interest; glasshouses and conservatories to visit; herbs; old roses and climbers; woodland garden; spring bulbs; woodland walk past mill

Acorn Bank boasts the largest collection (250 varieties) of culinary and medicinal plants in the North, but it is almost better visited in spring when thousands and thousands of daffodils fill the woodland slopes, and the fruit trees flower in the old walled garden. Best of all is the huge quince tree, a wondrous sight in flower or fruit.

Brantwood
Coniston, Cumbria LA21 8AD
☎ 015394 41396
OWNER Brantwood Educational Trust
LOCATION East side of Coniston Water, 2½ miles from Coniston, 4 miles from Hawkshead
OPEN 11 am – 5.30 pm, daily, mid March to mid November. 11 am – 4 pm, Wednesday – Sunday, mid November to mid March
ADMISSION House and garden: £3

FACILITIES Parking; dogs permitted; loos; bookshop and craft gallery; meals, light refreshments and drinks all day
FEATURES Lake; woodland garden; daffodils; bluebells
FRIENDS Friends of Brantwood, very active, ring 015394 41396 for details

Most interesting for being the home of John Ruskin, whose garden is undergoing major restoration with a grant from the European Community. Rhododendron woodland and wonderful views across Coniston Water.

Dalemain
Penrith, Cumbria CA11 0HB
OWNER Robert Hasell-McCosh
LOCATION M6 (J40), A66 (west 1 mile), A592
OPEN 11.15 am – 5 pm, Thursday – Sunday
ADMISSION House and garden: £4; reductions for groups
FACILITIES Parking; loos; facilities for the disabled; gift shop; small plant centre; morning coffee, light lunches, afternoon teas
FEATURES Fruit of special interest; herbs; old roses and climbers; woodland garden; interesting for children; *Meconopsis*; old flower and fruit varieties; adventure playground
ENGLISH HERITAGE GRADE II*
FRIENDS Details from Dalemain Estate Office

This historic garden has a 16th-century terrace, 17th-century parterre and a kitchen garden with fruit trees planted 250 years ago. All have been beautifully restored and replanted with period flowers. Charming and not at all self-conscious.

Graythwaite Hall
Ulverston, Hawkshead, Cumbria LA12 8BA
☎ 015395 31248   FAX 015395 30060
OWNER Graythwaite Estate Co.
LOCATION Between Newby Bridge and Hawkshead
OPEN 10 am – 6 pm, daily, 1 April to 30 June (1994 times and dates)
ADMISSION Adults £2; Children free (1994)
FACILITIES Parking; dogs permitted; loos
FEATURES Good collection of trees; herbaceous borders; rock garden; modern roses; old roses and climbers; good topiary

Thomas Mawson on home ground and at his best. Formal gardens by the house drop down to sweeping lawns; beyond the stream is a woodland with rhododendrons and azaleas.

Holehird
Patterdale Road, Windermere, Cumbria LA23 1NP
☎ 01539 446008
OWNER Lakeland Horticultural Society
LOCATION 1 mile north of Windermere town, off A592
OPEN Dawn – dusk, daily, all year

ADMISSION Donation (minimum £1)
FACILITIES Parking; loos; access for the disabled
FEATURES Herbaceous borders; glasshouses and conservatories to visit; herbs; lake; rock garden; modern roses; old roses and climbers; woodland garden; heathers; hostas; ferns; Victorian garden; walled garden
NCCPG NATIONAL COLLECTIONS *Hydrangea, Astilbe, Polystichum*
FRIENDS The Lakeland Horticultural Society is a registered charity: details from the Secretary

A demonstration and trial garden, maintained almost entirely by local volunteers to promote appropriate horticultural practices for the Lake District. Particularly good to see what flourishes in a cool damp climate: alpines, azaleas, heathers, ferns and much more.

Holker Hall
Cark-in-Cartmel, Grange-over-Sands, Cumbria LA11 7PL
☎ 015395 58328   FAX 015395 58776
OWNER Lord Cavendish of Furness
LOCATION J36 off M6, follow brown and white tourist signs
OPEN 10.30 am – 6 pm, Fridays – Sundays, 1 April to 30 October
ADMISSION Adults £3; Children £1.70 (under 6 free), Family ticket £8.90 (1994)
FACILITIES Parking; loos; facilities for the disabled; plants for sale; shop; clock-tower cafeteria (licensed)
FEATURES Lake; modern roses; woodland garden; rhododendrons; formal gardens; HHA/Christie's Garden of the Year in 1991 and current holder of Sandford Award
ENGLISH HERITAGE GRADE II*
NCCPG NATIONAL COLLECTIONS *Styrax, Halesia, Pterostyrax, Sinojackia*

19th-century formal gardens below the house with scrumptious herbaceous borders. The woodland has rhododendrons and splendid trees: Joseph Paxton planted a monkey-puzzle and Lord George Cavendish the cedars grown from the seeds he brought back from the Holy Land.

Hutton-in-the-Forest
Skelton, Penrith, Cumbria CA11 9TH
☎ 017684 84449   FAX 017684 84571
OWNER Lord Inglewood
LOCATION 3 miles from Exit 41 of M6 on B5305
OPEN House: 1 – 4 pm, Easter Sunday and Monday, then Thursdays, Fridays, Sundays and Bank Holiday Mondays from 31 April to 1 October. Gardens: 11 am – 5 pm, all year except Saturdays and Christmas Day
ADMISSION House and gardens: Adults £3.50; Children (7–16) £1.50. Gardens only: Adults £2; Children free
FACILITIES Parking; dogs permitted; loos; refreshments: 1 – 4 pm, Thursday, Friday and Sunday, 1 May – 30 September

FEATURES Herbaceous borders; good topiary; woodland garden; rhododendrons; herbaceous borders in the walled garden
ENGLISH HERITAGE GRADE II

Handsomely sited house with high Victorian terraces and grand views across the valley. Romantic parkland and good modern plantings. A garden to watch.

Levens Hall
Kendal, Cumbria LA8 0PD
☎ 015395 60321
OWNER C. H. Bagot
LOCATION 5 miles south of Kendal on A6
OPEN 11 am – 5 pm, Sunday – Thursday, 1 April to 30 September
ADMISSION House and garden: Adults £4.20; Children £2.50. Garden only: Adults £2.90; Children £1.80
FACILITIES Parking; loos; access for the disabled; gift shop and plant centre; light lunches and teas
FEATURES Good topiary; summer bedding
ENGLISH HERITAGE GRADE I

Levens means topiary, huge overgrown chunks of box and yew left over from a simple formal parterre laid out in 1694 and supplemented by golden yews in the 19th century. The yew hedges are spangled with *Tropaeoleum speciosum* and the modern parterres are planted annually with 15,000 plants, which makes Levens one of the best places to study the expensive art of bedding out.

Lingholm
Keswick, Cumbria CA12 5UA
☎ 01768 772003   FAX 01768 775213
OWNER Viscount Rochdale
LOCATION Follow signs from Portinscale village
OPEN 10 am – 5 pm, daily, 1 April to 31 October
ADMISSION Adults £2.70; Children free; Groups (20+) £2.20
FACILITIES Parking; loos; facilities for the disabled; plants for sale; tea room from 11 am for morning coffee, light lunches, teas
FEATURES Fine conifers; old roses and climbers; rhododendrons; azaleas; daffodils

Set on the hillside above Derwentwater, the main feature of Lingholm is its rhododendron and azalea woodland. The trees include fine conifers, yet the overall impression is of naturalness and peace.

Muncaster Castle
Ravenglass, Cumbria CA18 1RQ
☎ 01229 717614/203 FAX 01229 717010
OWNER Mrs P. R. Gordon-Duff-Pennington
LOCATION A595, 1 mile east of Ravenglass on west coast of Cumbria
OPEN Grounds: 11 am – 5 pm, daily, all year. Castle: 1 – 4 pm, Tuesday – Sunday, 26 March to 29 October
ADMISSION Gardens: Adults £3; Children £1.60; Family (2+2) £8

FACILITIES Parking; dogs permitted; loos; facilities for the disabled; plants for sale; two gift shops; snacks and full meals
FEATURES Fine conifers; plants for plantsmen; woodland garden; rhododendrons; camellias; maples; tallest *Acer palmatum*, *Nothofagus dombeyi* and *Nothofagus obliqua* in the British Isles
ENGLISH HERITAGE GRADE II*

Visit Muncaster in May, when the rhododendrons are at their peak. Many are grown from the original seed introduced by such plant-hunters as Forrest and Kingdon Ward in the 1920s and 1930s. Muncaster also has a developing collection of hardy hybrid rhododendrons. The castle was revamped 150 years ago: its steep slopes and the lakeland hills behind create an intensely romantic landscape.

Rydal Mount
Ambleside, Cumbria LA22 9LU
☎ 015394 33002

OWNER Rydal Mount Trust (Wordsworth family)
LOCATION 1½ miles north of Ambleside on A591, turn up Rydal Hill
OPEN 9.30 am – 5 pm, 1 March to 31 October; 10 am – 4 pm, 1 November to 28 February
ADMISSION Adults £2.50; Children £1; Groups (10+) and Students £2
FACILITIES Parking; dogs permitted; loos
FEATURES Lake; trees; rhododendrons; newly-found terrace undergoing restoration (1995)
ENGLISH HERITAGE GRADE II

Kept very much as it was in the poet's day, the garden at Rydal Mount is a memorial to William Wordsworth. He believed that a garden should be informal in its design, harmonise with the country and keep its views open.

Sizergh Castle
Kendal, Cumbria LA8 8AE
☎ 015396 60070

OWNER The National Trust
LOCATION 3½ miles south of Kendal
OPEN 12.30 – 5.30 pm, Thursday – Sunday, 1 April to 31 October
ADMISSION Castle and garden: £3.30. Garden only: £1.70
FACILITIES Parking; loos; facilities for the disabled; tea room from 1.30 pm
FEATURES Herbaceous borders; fine conifers; lake; rock garden; old roses and climbers; garden sculpture; hardy geraniums; autumn colour; wild-flower meadow
ENGLISH HERITAGE GRADE II*
NCCPG NATIONAL COLLECTIONS *Asplenium scolopendr, Cystopteris, Dryopteris, Osmunda*

One of the best National Trust gardens, with lots of interest from daffodils and alpines in April to hydrangeas and a hot half-hardy border in September. Best of all is the 1920s rock garden made of local stone, whose dwarf maples and conifers have grown to a great size.

DERBYSHIRE

Calke Abbey
Ticknall, Derbyshire DE7 1LE
☎ 01332 863822

OWNER The National Trust
LOCATION 10 miles south of Derby in village of Ticknall
OPEN 11 am – 5 pm, Wednesday – Saturday
ADMISSION £2
FACILITIES Parking; loos; facilities for the disabled; National Trust gift shop; restaurant
FEATURES Herbaceous borders; fruit and vegetables of special interest; dahlias; good Victorian-style bedding; local varieties of apples and soft fruit; newly restored Orchard House (1995)
ENGLISH HERITAGE GRADE II*

The 'sleeping beauty' house is not really matched by its garden, but when funds are available it will be replanted in the early 19th century style, with period ornamental and fruit varieties, a physic garden and an orangery. In the walled garden is the only surviving auricula theatre, originally built to display the perfection of these beautiful 'florists's' plants.

Chatsworth
Bakewell, Derbyshire DE4 1PP
☎ 01246 582204   FAX 01246 583536

OWNER Chatsworth House Trust
LOCATION 8 miles north of Matlock off B6012
OPEN 11 am – 5 pm, daily, 29 March to 29 October
ADMISSION Adults £3; Senior Citizens £2.50; Children £1.50; Family ticket £8
FACILITIES Dogs permitted; loos; facilities for the disabled; plants for sale in Potting Shed Shop, in Orangery; self-service restaurant, licensed
FEATURES Good collection of trees; landscape designed by Capability Brown; fine conifers; lake; rock garden; modern roses; garden sculpture; good topiary; woodland garden; interesting for children; pinetum; rhododendrons; azaleas; maze; tulip tree avenue; adventure playground; tallest *Nyssa sylvatica* and *Pinus strobus* in the British Isles
ENGLISH HERITAGE GRADE I
FRIENDS Season ticket available, ring 01264 582204

Everyone knows of Chatsworth: 105 acres of Capability Brown, a 'conservative wall' to keep the heat and ripen fruit trees, Paxton's rockeries (huge boulders surrounded by conifers), a serpentine hedge with yews of different hues, enormous *Camellia reticulata* 'Captain Rawes' with trunks 80 cms thick, and of course the famous long cascade. But there is so much more: well-run and fun for all the family. New maze and kitchen garden opened in 1994.

Darley House
Darley Dale, Matlock, Derbyshire DE4 3BP
☎ 01629 733341

OWNER   Mr and Mrs G. H. Briscoe
LOCATION   On A6, 2 miles north of Matlock
OPEN   1 May to 30 September, by appointment only
ADMISSION   Adults £1.50; Children free
FACILITIES   Parking; loos; plants for sale; picture gallery; light refreshments
FEATURES   Herbaceous borders; lake; plantsman's garden

Basically a modern, plantsman's garden, just over an acre, but planted with good colour sense and commendable restraint. Interesting too because it belonged to Sir Joseph Paxton in the 1840s and his layout still gives the whole garden its structure.

Elvaston Castle County Park
Borrowash Road, Elvaston, Derbyshire DE72 3EP
☎ 01332 571342

OWNER   Derbyshire County Council
LOCATION   5 miles south east of Derby. Signed from A6 and A52
OPEN   Dawn – dusk (Old English Garden, 9 am – 5 pm), daily, all year
ADMISSION   Gardens free. Car park 60p midweek, £1.20 weekends, coaches £6
FACILITIES   Parking; dogs permitted; loos; facilities for the disabled; gift shop: Easter – 31st October, 11 am – 4.30 pm, light meals: Easter – 31st Oct, 11 am – 4.30 pm
FEATURES   Herbaceous borders; lake; old roses and climbers; good topiary; particularly interesting in winter
ENGLISH HERITAGE GRADE   II*

A historic garden, once famous for its topiary, and saved from oblivion by Derby County Council 25 years ago. The parterres have been replaced and the walled garden replanted with roses and herbaceous plants, and renamed the Old English Garden.

Haddon Hall
Bakewell, Derbyshire DE45 1LA
☎ 01629 812855   FAX 01629 814379

OWNER   The Duke of Rutland
LOCATION   1½ miles south of Bakewell on A6
OPEN   11 am – 5.45 pm, daily except Sundays in July and August; 1 April to 30 September
ADMISSION   Adults £4.50; Senior Citizens £3.50; Children £2.80; Groups (20+) £3.50
FACILITIES   Parking; loos; coffee, lunch, afternoon teas
FEATURES   Herbaceous borders; climbing roses; modern roses; old roses; good topiary; clematis; delphiniums; Christie's/HHA Garden of the Year in 1994
ENGLISH HERITAGE GRADE   I

Terraced neo-Tudor gardens to complement a castellated Elizabethan prodigy house. Fine balustrading and old yews, spring bulbs and herbaceous borders but, above all, roses, roses, roses.

Hardwick Hall
Doe Lea, Chesterfield, Derbyshire S44 5QJ

OWNER   The National Trust
LOCATION   Signposted from J29 of M1
OPEN   12 noon – 5.30 pm, daily, 1 April to 31 October
ADMISSION   Hall and garden: £5.50 Adults; £2 Children. Garden only: £2 (1994)
FACILITIES   Parking; loos; facilities for the disabled; weekend plant sales only; refreshments Wednesdays, Thursdays, Saturdays and Sundays when Hall is open
FEATURES   Herbaceous borders; old roses and climbers; daffodils; fine hedges; mulberry walk; hollies; herb garden newly replanted (1995)
ENGLISH HERITAGE GRADE   I
NCCPG NATIONAL COLLECTIONS   *Scabiosa caucasica*

The formal gardens are extensive: avenues of hornbeam and yew and a new 'Elizabethan' herb garden (lavender and eglantine) in the kitchen garden. Wonderful old fruit trees, mulberries, old roses and borders. In the park, fine cedars and Hungarian oaks.

Kedleston Hall
Derby, Derbyshire DE22 5JH
☎ 01332 842191   FAX 01332 841972

OWNER   The National Trust
LOCATION   5 miles north west of Derby
OPEN   11 am – 6 pm, Saturday – Wednesday, 1 April to 31 October. Park open all year
ADMISSION   Adults £4.20; Children £2.10
FACILITIES   Parking; loos; National Trust shop; lunches and teas (licensed)
FEATURES   Lake; rhododendrons and azaleas; modern roses; handsome Adam orangery
ENGLISH HERITAGE GRADE   I

The landscaped park runs down to a long lake: impressive and important. The pleasure gardens are neither, but quite jolly in a National Trust sort of way.

Lea Gardens
Lea, Matlock, Derbyshire DE4 5GH
☎ 01629 534380   FAX 01629 534260

OWNER   Mr and Mrs J. Tye
LOCATION   3 miles south east of Matlock
OPEN   10 am – 7 pm, daily, 20 March to 16 July
ADMISSION   Adults £2; Children 50p; Season ticket £3.50. Disabled in wheelchairs free
FACILITIES   Parking; dogs permitted; loos; plants for sale; light refreshments
FEATURES   Rhododendrons and azaleas

This is the garden of a rhododendron lover: over 650 varieties as well as *Kalmia*, magnolias, maples and dwarf conifers. Best in May, when it is frankly spectacular.

Devon Gardens

Melbourne Hall
Melbourne, Derbyshire D73 1EN
☎ 01332 862502
OWNER Lord Ralph Kerr
LOCATION 8 miles south of Derby
OPEN 2 – 6 pm, daily, 1 April to 30 September
ADMISSION Adults £2 (may go up early in the year)
FACILITIES Parking; loos; access for the disabled; shop; refreshments
FEATURES Herbaceous borders; lake; garden sculpture; turf terracing; grand avenues
ENGLISH HERITAGE GRADE I

Near-perfect example of an early 18th century garden, influenced by Le Nôtre. Statues, gravel, *bassins* and the famous yew tunnel.

Renishaw Hall
Renishaw, Sheffield, Derbyshire S31 9WB
☎ 01246 432042/01777 860755
OWNER Sir Reresby Sitwell
LOCATION 2½ miles from M1, J30
OPEN 12 noon – 5 pm, Bank Holiday Sundays and Mondays, plus Sundays in June, July and August
ADMISSION Adults £3; Senior Citizens £2; Children £1
FACILITIES Parking; dogs permitted; loos; access for the disabled; plants for sale; small tea rooms open from 12 noon – 5 pm
FEATURES Herbaceous borders; fine conifers; lake; modern roses; old roses and climbers; woodland garden; daffodils; Italian garden
ENGLISH HERITAGE GRADE II*

Lots of horticultural interest, including a good collection of shrub roses, but best for the formal Italian garden laid out by Sir George Sitwell c.1900, and at last appreciated as a meticulous and scholarly creation.

DEVON

Arlington Court
Arlington, Barnstaple, Devon EX31 4LP
☎ 01271 850296
OWNER The National Trust
LOCATION 8 miles north of Barnstaple on A39
OPEN 11 am – 5.30 pm, Sunday – Friday, 1 April to 31 October
ADMISSION Adults £2.40; Children £1.20 (1994)
FACILITIES Parking; dogs permitted; loos; facilities for the disabled; plants for sale; National Trust shop; restaurant and tea rooms
FEATURES Fine conifers; huge old rhododendrons; Victorian walled garden undergoing restoration (1995)
ENGLISH HERITAGE GRADE II
NCCPG NATIONAL COLLECTIONS *Fraxinus*

Mature parkland on a dead flat site in front of a fine Georgian house. Pretty Victorian formal garden and conservatory. Peacocks.

Bicton Park Gardens
East Budleigh, Budleigh Salterton, Devon EX9 7DP
☎ 01395 568465
OWNER Bicton Park Trust Co.
LOCATION On A376 north of Budleigh Salterton
OPEN 10 am – 6 pm, daily, 16 March to 31 October
ADMISSION Adults £4.70 (1994)
FACILITIES Parking; dogs permitted; loos; facilities for the disabled; shop; self-service restaurant; licensed bar
FEATURES Good collection of trees; herbaceous borders; fine conifers; glasshouses and conservatories to visit; lake; oriental features; plants for plantsmen; modern roses; old roses and climbers; woodland garden; interesting for children; play area; miniature railway
ENGLISH HERITAGE GRADE I

60 acres, beautifully maintained by the college nearby. Italian garden; important trees; oriental garden; American garden; collection of dwarf conifers; more than 2,000 heathers; an avenue of monkey-puzzles; a hermitage; and the finest pre-Paxton palm house built 1815-20 from thousands of tiny panes of glass. Allow lots of time.

Castle Drogo
Drewsteignton, Devon EX6 6PB
☎ 01647 433306   FAX 01647 433186
OWNER The National Trust
LOCATION Drewsteignton village: signs from A30 and Exeter – Okehampton road
OPEN 10.30 am – 5.30 pm, daily, 1 April to 31 October
ADMISSION Adults £2; Children £1
FACILITIES Parking; loos; facilities for the disabled; plants for sale; National Trust shop; self-service tea room, waitress-service restaurant
FEATURES Herbaceous borders; planted by Gertrude Jekyll; designed by Lutyens; rock garden; modern roses; old roses and climbers; woodland garden; interesting for children
ENGLISH HERITAGE GRADE II*

Major 1920s garden high on the edge of Dartmoor. Handsome yew hedges; formal design; rich and spacious herbaceous borders, contrasting with the austere castle on its windy bluff. Weather-beaten, lichen-heavy *Prunus* and acers on the slopes below. All on a vast scale.

Coleton Fishacre Garden
Coleton, Kingswear, Dartmouth, Devon TQ6 0EQ
☎ 01803 752466
OWNER The National Trust
LOCATION 2 miles from Kingswear off Lower-Ferry road
OPEN 10.30 am – 5.30 pm, Wednesday – Friday, Sundays and Bank Holidays, 1 April to 31 October (plus Sundays in March, 2 – 5 pm)
ADMISSION Adults £2.80; Children £1.40; Pre-booked groups £2.20

FACILITIES   Parking; loos; plants for sale; tea hut; snacks and ice creams
FEATURES   Herbaceous borders; plants for plantsmen; subtropical plants; woodland garden; rhododendrons; rare trees; interesting new plantings in the 'Holiwell' area
ENGLISH HERITAGE GRADE   II
20 acres of rhododendron and camellia woodland crashing down a secret valley to the sea. Almost frost-free, the range and size of southern hemisphere trees and shrubs is astounding. Rare bulbs in the warm terraces around the Lutyensesque house.

Dartington Hall
Dartington, Totnes, Devon TQ9 6EL
☎ 01803 862367
OWNER   Dartington Hall Trust
LOCATION   2 miles north west of Totnes
OPEN   Dawn – dusk, daily, all year
ADMISSION   Donation (£2 suggested)
FACILITIES   Parking; loos
FEATURES   Herbaceous borders; lake; garden sculpture; good topiary; woodland garden; magnolias; rhododendrons; camellias; tilt-yard
ENGLISH HERITAGE GRADE   II*
Grand mid-20th century garden with some famous associations. Beatrix Farrand designed the terraces, including the so-called tilt-yard, and Percy Cane built the long staircase and spring plantings on either side. Henry Moore deposited a reclining woman. Some consider the garden grandiose and cold: we think it is magnificent, and wholly appropriate to the scale of house and landscape.

Doctyn Mill
Spekes Valley, Hartland, Devon EX39 6EA
☎ 01237 441369   FAX 01237 441681
OWNER   N. S. and I. D. Pugh
LOCATION   Take road from Hartland to Stoke and follow signposts towards Elmscott
OPEN   10 am – 5 pm, daily, 1 March to 30 September
ADMISSION   Adults £2; Children (under 16) 50p
FACILITIES   Parking; loos; plants for sale; light refreshments
FEATURES   Fruit of special interest; lake; woodland garden; apple orchards
The main attraction is a working water mill, but the garden is developing quickly and the new owners have already made further improvements. Worth watching.

Exeter University Gardens
Exeter, Devon EX4 4PX
☎ 01392 263059   FAX 01392 264547
OWNER   The University of Exeter
LOCATION   3 miles north of city centre, all around University
OPEN   Dawn – dusk, daily, all year
ADMISSION   Free
FACILITIES   Parking; dogs permitted

FEATURES   Fine conifers; rhododendrons and azaleas; tender plants; heathers; summer bedding
NCCPG NATIONAL COLLECTIONS   *Azara*

One of the best university campuses, the gardens are educational, attractive and important. Based on the 19th-century Veitch collections of exotic trees, the plantings were supplemented by Chinese species collected 80 years ago by E. H. Wilson.

The Garden House
Buckland Monachorum, Yelverton, Devon PL20 7LQ
☎ 01822 854769
OWNER   Fortescue Garden Trust
LOCATION   Signed off A386 on Plymouth side of Yelverton
OPEN   10.30 am – 5 pm, daily, 1 March to 30 October
ADMISSION   Adults £2.75; Senior Citizens £2.50; Children 50p
FACILITIES   Parking; loos; plants for sale; tea room open in season with light lunches
FEATURES   Herbaceous borders; gravel or scree garden; plants for plantsmen; rock garden; old roses and climbers; woodland garden; alpine bank; flowering cherries; wisterias; substantial new plantings (1994–95) to quadruple the garden's size

A plantsman's garden, made by the late Lionel Fortescue, who insisted on planting only the best forms of plants. The setting is awesome: a ruined abbey on the edge of Dartmoor. Much of the effect is achieved through rigorous cultivation. Plants are well-fed and firmly controlled: they flourish on the treatment. Exciting new developments on a huge scale.

Gidleigh Park Hotel
Chagford, Devon TQ13 8HH
☎ 01647 432367   FAX 01647 432574
OWNER   Paul Henderson
LOCATION   15 miles west of Exeter. Turn off in Chagford: do not go to Gidleigh
OPEN   Guests of the hotel and restaurant only
ADMISSION   50p for NGS
FACILITIES   Parking; dogs permitted; loos; delicious food in Hotel
FEATURES   Lake; woodland garden

45 acres of woodland on the edge of Dartmoor with a 1920s garden round the Tudorised house. Nothing very rare or special, but the position is stupendous and the sense of space, even grandeur, is enhanced by immaculate maintenance. Innumerable awards for the hotel and restaurant over the last 11 years.

The Gnome Reserve & Pixies' Wildflower Garden
The Pixie Kiln, West Putford, Bradworthy, Devon EX22 7XE
☎ 01409 241 435
OWNER   The Atkin family

Devon Gardens

LOCATION Between Bideford and Holsworthy, signed from A39, A386 and A388
OPEN 10 am – 6 pm, daily, 21 March to 31 October
ADMISSION Adults £1.50; Senior Citizens £1.25; Children £1
FACILITIES Parking; loos; large shop selling gnomes
FEATURES Gnomes and more gnomes

There are four reasons to visit this remarkable conservation centre: first, the 2-acre gnome reserve in a beech wood with a stream; second, the 2-acre pixies' wildflower meadow; third, the kiln where pottery gnomes and pixies are born; fourth, the museum of rare early gnomes.

Hill House Garden
Landscove, Ashburton, Newton Abbot, Devon TQ13 7LY
☎ 01803 762273

OWNER R. and V. A. Hubbard
LOCATION Off A384, follow signs for Landscove
OPEN 11 am – 5 pm, daily, all year
ADMISSION Free
FACILITIES Parking; dogs permitted; loos; facilities for the disabled; plants for sale; garden shop; Mother Hubbard's Tea Room (home made cakes)
FEATURES Fine conifers; glasshouses and conservatories to visit; particularly interesting in winter; daffodils; garden temple; *Cyclamen* and snowdrops

Victorian old vicarage made famous by Edward Hyams' *An Englishman's Garden*. Now the centre of an ambitious young nursery.

Killerton
Broadclyst, Exeter, Devon EX5 3LE
☎ 01392 881345

OWNER The National Trust
LOCATION West side of B3181, Exeter to Cullompton Road
OPEN 11 am – 5.30 pm (dusk in winter), daily, all year
ADMISSION £2.80 (£1 from 1 November to 28 February)
FACILITIES Parking; loos; facilities for the disabled; National Trust shop; small well-run plant centre; waitress-service restaurant and self-service tea room
FEATURES Good collection of trees; fine conifers; daffodils; follies and garden buildings; rhododendrons and azaleas; rock garden; woodland garden; particularly interesting in winter; magnolias; herbaceous borders by William Robinson; alpine garden in disused quarry; drifts of *Crocus tommasinianus*; new wild-flower areas (1995)
ENGLISH HERITAGE GRADE II*

A historic giant among gardens, whose long connections with Veitch's Nursery have bequeathed a great tree collection. Innumerable record-breaking specimens, many from collectors' seed, but one's sense of awe is spoilt by droning traffic on the M5 below.

Knightshayes Garden
Tiverton, Devon EX16 7RH
☎ 01884 253264

OWNER The National Trust
LOCATION Off A396 Tiverton to Bampton Road
OPEN 11 am – 5.30 pm, daily, 1 April to 31 October
ADMISSION Adults £2.70
FACILITIES Parking; loos; plants for sale; National Trust shop; licensed restaurant 10.30 am – 5.30 pm daily, coffee, lunches and teas
FEATURES Herbaceous borders; good topiary; woodland garden; plantings by Graham Thomas; hellebores; *Cyclamen*; bulbs; peat beds
ENGLISH HERITAGE GRADE II*
FRIENDS National Trust Culm & Eve Valleys Centre

Brilliant herbaceous plantings and stunning formal gardens, but Knightshayes is above all a garden in a wood, delightful at all seasons and notable for its high standard of maintenance. The shop has particularly interesting plants for sale. Good new plantings by the adventurous head gardener.

Marwood Hill Gardens
Barnstaple, Devon EX31 4EB
☎ 01271 42528

OWNER Dr J. A. Smart
LOCATION Signed from A361 Barnstaple and Braunton Road
OPEN Dawn – dusk, daily, all year except Christmas Day
ADMISSION Adults £2; Senior Citizens £1.50
FACILITIES Parking; dogs permitted; loos; plants for sale; teas, April – September, Sundays and Bank Holidays only
FEATURES Alpines; good collection of trees; bluebells; bog garden; herbaceous borders; camellias; fine conifers; daffodils; glasshouses and conservatories to visit; gravel or scree garden; lake; plants for plantsmen; rhododendrons and azaleas; rock garden; old roses and climbers; particularly good in July-August; particularly interesting in winter; birches; *Eucalyptus*; camellias; hebes; plants, more plants and yet more plants
NCCPG NATIONAL COLLECTIONS *Astilbe*, *Tulbaghia*, *Iris ensata*

An extraordinary plantsman's garden on a grand scale with masses to look at all through the year. Exciting for its scale, variety, and the energy of its owner.

Overbecks
Sharpitor, Salcombe, Devon TQ8 8LW
☎ 01548 843238

OWNER The National Trust
LOCATION 1 mile south of Salcombe
OPEN 10 am – 8 pm (or dusk, if earlier), daily, all year
ADMISSION Garden only: Adults £2; Children £1
FACILITIES Parking; loos; National Trust shop; tea room for light refreshments

FEATURES Bluebells; subtropical plants; palms; mimosas; *Magnolia campbellii*
ENGLISH HERITAGE GRADE II

A small, intensely planted, almost jungly garden, perched above the Salcombe estuary. The formal terraces (rather 1930s) are stuffed with interesting tender plants: wonderful at Easter.

Paignton Zoo & Botanical Gardens
Totnes Road, Paignton, Devon TQ4 7EU
☎ 01803 557479   FAX 01803 523457

OWNER Whitley Wildlife Conservation Trust
LOCATION On A385 Totnes Road, 1 mile from Paignton
OPEN 10 am – 6 pm (5 pm in winter), daily, all year
ADMISSION Adults £5.75; Senior Citizens £4.60; Children £3.50
FACILITIES Parking; loos; plants for sale; shops; large self-service restaurant
FEATURES Good collection of trees; herbaceous borders; fine conifers; rock garden; interesting for children; glasshouses with tropical plants
NCCPG NATIONAL COLLECTIONS *Buddleia, Sorbaria*

Once a private garden devoted to blue-flowered and blue-leaved plants, now an inspiring combination of zoo, botanic collection, public park and holiday entertainment.

Powderham Castle
Exeter, Devon EX6 8JQ
☎ 01626 890243   FAX 01626 890729

OWNER Lord and Lady Courtenay
LOCATION Off A379 Dawlish to Exeter Road at Kenton
OPEN 10 am – 5.30 pm, daily, Easter to October
ADMISSION Adults £3.95; Senior Citizens £3.75; Children £2.95. Charges include guided tour of castle
FACILITIES Parking; loos; plants for sale; light lunches and cream teas
FEATURES Landscape designed by Capability Brown; modern roses; woodland garden
ENGLISH HERITAGE GRADE II

Not a major garden, but the 18th-century landscaped park is serenely English and there is a cheerful modern rose garden all along the front of the house.

RHS Garden, Rosemoor
Great Torrington, Devon EX38 8PH
☎ 01805 624067   FAX 01805 624717

OWNER The Royal Horticultural Society
LOCATION 1 mile south of Torrington on B3220
OPEN 10 am – 6 pm (5 pm, March and October; 4 pm, November to February), daily, all year
ADMISSION Adults £3; Children £1; Groups (20+) £2.50. RHS members free
FACILITIES Parking; loos; facilities for the disabled; plants for sale; good range of books and gifts; licensed restaurant

FEATURES Fine conifers; fruit of special interest; herbs; lake; plants for plantsmen; modern roses; old roses and climbers; woodland garden; young garden; particularly interesting in winter; large collection of dwarf conifers
NCCPG NATIONAL COLLECTIONS *Cornus, Ilex*

A competent, if uninspired, garden by Lady Anne Palmer which the RHS has made its West Country flagship by pouring money into developing and improving it. Although still young, the new Rosemoor is worth a visit at any season, but please note that the sales and food facilities are open from March to October only.

Saltram
Plympton, Plymouth, Devon PL7 3UH
☎ 01752 335546

OWNER The National Trust
LOCATION 2 miles west of Plympton
OPEN 10.30 am – 5.30 pm, Sunday – Thursday, 1 April to 31 October
ADMISSION Adults £2.20; Children £1.10
FACILITIES Parking; dogs permitted; loos; facilities for the disabled; National Trust shop in stable block; licensed restaurant 12 noon – 5.30 pm; light refreshments
FEATURES Camellias; rhododendrons and azaleas; parkland; handsome orangery; lime avenue
ENGLISH HERITAGE GRADE II*

20 acres of beautiful parkland, whose huge and ancient trees are underplanted with camellias and rhododendrons. Best in spring when the daffodils flower in hosts.

Tapeley Park
Instow, Devon EX39 4NT
☎ 01271 42371

OWNER NDCI Ltd
LOCATION Off A39 between Barnstaple and Bideford
OPEN 10 am – 5 pm, daily, except Mondays and Saturdays, Easter to 30 September
ADMISSION Adults £2.50; Senior Citizens £2; Children £1.50; Season ticket £10
FACILITIES Parking; dogs permitted; loos; facilities for the disabled; plants for sale; gift shop; licensed lunches and cream teas
FEATURES Follies and garden buildings; fruit of special interest; glasshouses and conservatories to visit; lake; woodland garden; interesting for children; British Jousting Centre
ENGLISH HERITAGE GRADE II*
FRIENDS Friends of Tapeley set up last year

Fine Italianate formal garden laid out on several levels c.1900 and planted with tender plants (*Sophora tetraptera* and *Myrtus communis* 'Tarentina'). Beyond are palm trees and a rhododendron woodland: worth exploring. All parts are undergoing restoration and replanting with advice from Mary Keen and Carol Klein.

DORSET Gardens

Wylmington Hayes Gardens
Wilmington, Honiton, Devon EX14 9JZ
☎ 01404 831751   FAX 01404 831826
OWNER   Mr and Mrs P. Saunders
LOCATION   Take A35 east of Honiton for 3½ miles, then right before Stockland TV mast
OPEN   2 – 5 pm, Good Friday to Easter Monday, then Sundays and Bank Holidays to 30 June
ADMISSION   Adults £2.50; Children £1; Disabled in wheelchairs £1
FACILITIES   Parking; loos; facilities for the disabled; plants for sale; gift stand; home-made refreshments and cream teas
FEATURES   Good collection of trees; lake; good topiary; woodland garden

An Edwardian house in the Tudor style, with a formal Italian garden and ornamental woodland planted with rhododendrons, azaleas, camellias, acers and magnolias.

DORSET

Abbotsbury Subtropical Gardens
Abbotsbury, Weymouth, Dorset DT3 4LA
☎ 01305 871387

OWNER   Ilchester Estates
LOCATION   On coast, in village
OPEN   10 am – 5 pm, daily, all year, but closed on Mondays from November to February
ADMISSION   Adults £2.80
FACILITIES   Parking; dogs permitted; loos; plants for sale; shop; refreshments
FEATURES   Good collection of trees; bluebells; camellias; plants for plantsmen; rhododendrons and azaleas; subtropical plants; woodland garden; particularly interesting in winter; magnolias; candelabra primulas; rare trees; free-standing loquat *Eriobotrya japonica*; biggest English oak *Quercus robur* in the British Isles; 3 other record trees
ENGLISH HERITAGE GRADE   I

A woodland garden of splendid specimens and trees of great rarity. Palms, *Eucalyptus*, *Pittosporum* and camellias all grow lushly in the sheltered valley and romantic walled garden. A stylish visitors' centre and excellent nursery make for added value.

Athelhampton House & Gardens
Dorchester, Dorset DT2 7LG
☎ 01305 848363   FAX 01305 848135

OWNER   Patrick Cooke
LOCATION   1 mile east of Puddletown on A35
OPEN   12 noon – 5 pm, Tuesday – Thursday, Sundays and Bank Holiday Mondays, 1 April to October. Plus Mondays and Fridays in July and August
ADMISSION   House and garden: £4.20. Garden only: £2.50
FACILITIES   Parking; loos; plants for sale; shop; refreshments

FEATURES   Lake; good topiary; gazebos; beautiful walls and hedges; two *Metasequoia glyptostroboides* from the orginal seed; Queen Victoria Walk restored (1994) with advice from Penelope Hobhouse
ENGLISH HERITAGE GRADE   I

Inigo Thomas designed this about 100 years ago as the perfect garden for the perfect manor house. Sharply cut pyramids of yew, a long canal with water lilies, and rambling roses in early summer.

Broadlands
Hazelbury Bryan, Sturminster Newton, Dorset DT10 2EE
☎ 01258 817374

OWNER   Mr and Mrs Michael Smith
LOCATION   4 miles south of Sturminster Newton
OPEN   2 – 5.30 pm, 2 and 17 April, 7 May, and Wednesdays from May to August
ADMISSION   Adults £1.70; Children free
FACILITIES   Loos; access for the disabled; plants for sale; refreshments on Wednesdays only
FEATURES   Plants for plantsmen; old roses and climbers; young garden; woodland garden now complete (1995); new raised beds (1995); small wild-flower meadow under construction

An excellent and highly instructive modern garden. There is an infinity of character within its 2 acres, and good plants a-plenty. Island bedding and narrow paths are used to slow down your progress and increase your sense of space, yet there are always glimpses of the prospects to come. Ingenious.

Chiffchaffs
Chaffeymoor, Bourton, Gillingham, Dorset SP8 5BY
☎ 01747 840841

OWNER   Mr and Mrs K. R. Potts
LOCATION   At Wincanton end of Bourton
OPEN   2 – 5.30 pm, Sundays, Wednesdays and Thursdays, April to September (but closed on second Sunday every month)
ADMISSION   £1.50
FACILITIES   Parking; plants for sale; teas on last Sunday in month and Bank Holidays
FEATURES   Plants for plantsmen; old roses and climbers; woodland garden; spring bulbs; dwarf rhododendrons

A thatched cottage, with a promising small nursery attached, and just off the A303. Only 15 years old, the garden has a flowing design, exploits a great variety of habitats and burgeons with good plants.

Compton Acres Gardens
Canford Cliffs Road, Poole, Dorset BH13 7ES
☎ 01202 700778   FAX 01202 707537

OWNER   L. Green
LOCATION   Well-signposted locally
OPEN   10.30 am – 6.30 pm, daily, March to October
ADMISSION   Adults £3.50; Senior Citizens £2.50 (1994)

Gardens DORSET

FACILITIES   Parking; loos; access for the disabled; plants for sale; several shops; tea rooms and light lunches
FEATURES   Fine conifers; follies and garden buildings; oriental features; rock garden; modern roses; garden sculpture; subtropical plants; woodland garden
ENGLISH HERITAGE GRADE   II*

Very touristy, very Bournemouth, and very 1920s. Compton Acres offers 10 totally unconnected but highly entertaining gardens, all in different styles but joined by tarmac paths. Best are the Italian garden, the palm court, the white azaleas in the watery glen which runs down to the harbour, and the stupendous Japanese garden. There is opulence, vulgarity, overcrowding and blatant commercialism, but the standards are among the highest in any garden: no visitor could fail to be cheered up by the bravura of it all.

Cranborne Manor
Cranborne, Wimborne, Dorset BH21 5PP
☎ 01725 517248   FAX 01725 517248

OWNER   Viscount Cranborne
LOCATION   10 miles north of Wimborne on B3078
OPEN   9 am – 5 pm, Wednesdays, 1 March to 30 September
ADMISSION   Adults £2.50; Senior Citizens and Students £2; Children (under 16) 50p
FACILITIES   Parking; loos; garden centre
FEATURES   Herbaceous borders; old roses and climbers; good topiary; parterres; Jacobean mount
ENGLISH HERITAGE GRADE   II*

The garden at Cranborne is modern, but employs Elizabethan elements. Most successful are the parterres: long, low and prettily planted. The mixed borders in the charming courtyard are good too. Very 1970s.

Dean's Court
Wimborne, Dorset BH21 1EE

OWNER   Sir Michael and Lady Hanham
LOCATION   2 minutes walk from central Wimborne
OPEN   For NGS: see Yellow Book
ADMISSION   Adults £1.50; Children 70p (1994)
FACILITIES   Parking; loos; plants for sale; organic herb plants and vegetables; wholefood refreshments, June – September
FEATURES   Herbs; lake; plants for plantsmen; rock garden; old roses and climbers; monastery fishpond; good trees; all organic; tallest *Catalpa bignonioides* in the British Isles

A very wholesome garden: everything, including 150 different herb varieties, is grown without artificial fertilisers, pesticides or herbicides.

Edmondsham House
Edmondsham, Wimborne, Dorset BH21 5RE
☎ 01725 517207

OWNER   Mrs Julia E. Smith
LOCATION   Off B3081 between Cranborne and Verwood
OPEN   2 – 5 pm, Wednesdays and Sundays, 1 April to 31 October
ADMISSION   Adults £1; Children 50p
FACILITIES   Parking; dogs permitted; loos; access for the disabled; plants for sale
FEATURES   Herbaceous borders; fruit of special interest; glasshouses and conservatories to visit; herbs; old roses and climbers; organic kitchen garden

The walled garden is maintained organically, with borders round the sides. It is intensively cultivated and brims with interesting vegetables. Fine trees in the park.

Forde Abbey
Chard, Dorset TA20 4LU
☎ 01460 20231   FAX 01460 20296

OWNER   The Trustees of the G. D. Roper settlement
LOCATION   4 miles south of Chard
OPEN   10 am – 4.30 pm, daily, all year
ADMISSION   Adults £3.25; Senior Citizens £2.75
FACILITIES   Parking; dogs permitted; loos; facilities for the disabled; plants for sale; shop; cafeteria
FEATURES   Good collection of trees; bog garden; herbaceous borders; fine conifers; fruit of special interest; gravel or scree garden; lake; rock garden planted by Jack Drake; HHA/Christie's Garden of the Year in 1993; biggest lime *Tilia cordata* in UK
ENGLISH HERITAGE GRADE   II*

A garden of great variety around the rambling house, part Jacobean, part Gothic. The planting is modern, and includes rhododendrons, azaleas, acers, magnolias, irises, *Meconopsis* and candelabra primulas. But there are also mature Victorian conifers (*Sequoia sempervirens*, *Calocedrus decurrens*), lakes, ponds, streams, cascades, bogs and such oddities as the Beech House.

Ivy Cottage
Aller Lane, Ansty, Dorchester, Dorset DT2 7PX
☎ 01258 880053

OWNER   Anne and Alan Stevens
LOCATION   Midway between Blandford and Dorchester
OPEN   10 am – 5 pm, Thursdays, April to October (1994 times and dates)
ADMISSION   Adults £1.50; Children 30p (1994)
FACILITIES   Parking; plants for sale
FEATURES   Herbaceous borders; plantsman's garden
NCCPG NATIONAL COLLECTIONS   *Trolius*, *Lobelia*

1½ acres of cottage garden made by the present owners over the last 30 years and crammed with interesting things, particularly herbaceous plants and bulbs. Springs and streams, combined with greensand soil, multiply the possibilities – drifts of marsh marigolds and candelabra primulas.

Kingston Lacy
Wimborne Minster, Dorset BH21 4EA

OWNER   The National Trust
LOCATION   1½ miles from Wimborne on B3082 to Blandford

Dorset Gardens

OPEN 11.30 am – 6 pm, Saturday – Wednesday, 1 April to 31 October
ADMISSION £2.20 Adults; £1.10 Children
FACILITIES Parking; loos; access for the disabled; lunches and teas
FEATURES Fine conifers; garden sculpture; Victorian fernery; snowdrops; Dutch parterre; huge cedars of Lebanon planted by visiting royalty; current holder of Sandford Award
ENGLISH HERITAGE GRADE II

250 acres of classic 18th-century parkland, still undergoing restoration by the National Trust, with a cedar avenue, Egyptian obelisk and laurel walk dating from Victorian times.

Kingston Maurward Gardens
Dorset College of Agriculture & Horticulture, Dorchester, Dorset DT2 8PY
☎ 01305 264738   FAX 01305 250059
OWNER Kingston Maurward College
LOCATION 1 mile east of Dorchester from A35
OPEN 1 – 5 pm, daily, 14 April to 15 October
ADMISSION Adults £2.50; Children £1.50
FACILITIES Parking; loos; facilities for the disabled; plants for sale; cakes and drinks
FEATURES Herbaceous borders; daffodils; lake; oriental features; modern roses; old roses and climbers; good topiary; Cyclamen; autumn crocuses
ENGLISH HERITAGE GRADE II*
NCCPG NATIONAL COLLECTIONS Salvia, Penstemon

Kingston Maurward belonged to the Hanbury family who owned La Mortola on the Riviera, and laid out the formal garden here in the Italian style (c.1920). It is being restored in country house style with herbaceous borders and old-fashioned roses, but the old kitchen garden is a splendid modern teaching garden with innumerable demonstrations of what can be grown in Dorset. Highly instructive.

Knoll Gardens
Stapehill Road, Wimborne, Dorset
☎ 01202 873931
OWNER K. Martin
LOCATION Signposted from Ferndown
OPEN 10 am – 6 pm, daily, 1 March to 31 October
ADMISSION Adults £3.50
FACILITIES Parking; loos; access for the disabled; plants for sale; good shop; restaurant and refreshments
FEATURES Herbaceous borders; fine conifers; rhododendrons and azaleas; rock garden; Eucalyptus

Around the massive new rock garden of Purbeck stone are the relics of a higgledy-piggledy plantsman's collection. Visit it now, before it becomes altogether too touristy and loses its charm.

Mapperton House Gardens
Beaminster, Dorset DT8 3NR
☎ 01308 863348
OWNER The Hon. John Montagu
LOCATION Signposted from A303
OPEN 2 – 6 pm, daily, 1 March to 31 October
ADMISSION Adults £2.50; Children (5–18) £1.50 (under 5, free); Disabled in wheelchairs free
FACILITIES Parking; loos; plants for sale; small shop selling terracotta pots
FEATURES Good collection of trees; good topiary
ENGLISH HERITAGE GRADE II*

An old/new garden, steeply terraced down a hidden combe, and dominated by tensions between a theatrical orangery at the top and two long lily pools at the bottom. Great fun.

Minterne
Minterne Magna, Dorchester, Dorset DT2 7AU
☎ 01300 341370   FAX 01300 341747
OWNER Lord Digby
LOCATION On A352 Dorchester to Sherborne road
OPEN 10 am – 7 pm, daily, 1 April to 31 October
ADMISSION Adults £2; Children free
FACILITIES Parking; dogs permitted; loos
FEATURES Rhododendrons and azaleas; woodland garden; cherries; Cyclamen, Lathraea clandestina; tallest Chamaecyparis pisifera 'Filifera' in the United Kingdom – 26 metres high
ENGLISH HERITAGE GRADE II

A woodland garden, best in spring, and well-integrated into the park around the hideous Edwardian house. The oldest rhododendrons came from Hooker's collection, but the remarkable late Lord Digby also supported Farrer, Forrest, Rock and Kingdon Ward, which makes Minterne one of the best Himalayan collections. The walk down a greensand valley to the woodland stream is ravishing, but parts are somewhat weedy and run-down.

Parnham House
Beaminster, Dorset DT8 3NA
☎ 01308 862204   FAX 01308 863494
OWNER Mr and Mrs J. Makepeace
LOCATION On A3066 north of Bridport
OPEN 10 am – 5 pm, Sundays, Wednesdays and Bank Holidays, April to 29 October; and groups by appointment
ADMISSION House and garden: Adults £4; Children (over 10) £2
FACILITIES Parking; dogs permitted; loos; facilities for the disabled; woodware and contemporary crafts; tea, coffee, hot and cold lunches
FEATURES Herbaceous borders; lake; old roses and climbers; good topiary
ENGLISH HERITAGE GRADE II*

A handsome Jacobean mansion, approached through a courtyard, with formal terraces running down to lakes and bluebell woods. The gardens have been restored and imaginatively replanted with mixed borders and, above all, roses. But Parnham offers much more beside: Iris borders, a meadow of fritillaries, an Italian garden, topiary, gazebos, rhododendrons and splendid modern sculptures including a larger-than-life Morecambe and Wise.

Sticky Wicket
Buckland Newton, Dorchester, Dorset DT2 7BY
☎ 01300 345476
OWNER   Peter and Pam Lewis
LOCATION   11 miles from Dorchester and Sherborne
OPEN   10.30 am – 8 pm, Thursdays, 15 June to 14 September
ADMISSION   Adults £1.50; Children £1
FACILITIES   Parking; loos; plants for sale; tea, coffee and home-made cakes
FEATURES   Ecological interest; plants for plantsmen; young garden; made since 1987; good colour associations; new white garden (1995)

An original garden, worth watching. The owners are both designers and conservationists, and their devotion to ecology guides their garden-making. A scented garden, a white garden and a colour wheel are secondary to the need to attract birds, insects and other wildlife. The garden is still expanding: worth seeing now in its youth, and returning to in later years.

CO. DURHAM

Barningham Park
Richmond, Co. Durham DL11 7DW
☎ 01833 621202   FAX 01833 621298
OWNER   Sir Anthony Milbank Bt.
LOCATION   10 miles north west of Scotch Corner, off A66
OPEN   2 – 6 pm, 28 May, 4 June, 24 September
ADMISSION   Adults £2, Children free
FACILITIES   Parking; dogs permitted; loos; plants for sale; home-made teas
FEATURES   Herbaceous borders; lake; rock garden; terraced gardens; rhododendrons

Terraced early 18th-century landscape, leading up to the old bowling green and down to the skating pond. Reworked by keen horticultural Milbanks in the 1920s. Unknown and perhaps underrated: if Barningham were in the Home Counties everyone would rave about it.

The Bowes Museum Garden & Park
Barnard Castle, Co. Durham DL12 8NP
☎ 01833 690606   FAX 01833 37163
OWNER   Durham County Council
LOCATION   ½ mile west of Barnard Castle town
OPEN   10 am – 4 pm, Monday – Saturday, 2 – 4 pm, Sundays, November to February; 10 am – 5 pm, Monday – Saturday, 2 – 5 pm, Sundays, March, April and October; 10 am – 5.30 pm, Monday – Saturday, 2 – 5 pm, Sundays, May to September. Closed 25 December and 1 January
ADMISSION   Adults £2.50; Senior Citizens and Children £1.50 (may increase in April). Garden: free
FACILITIES   Parking; dogs permitted; loos; facilities for the disabled; shop; museum café
FEATURES   Good collection of trees; old roses and climbers; woodland garden; parterre; large monkey-puzzle
ENGLISH HERITAGE GRADE   II
FRIENDS   Friends of Museum and Park: ring 01833 690606 for details

Rather run-down and municipal, but the formal gardens are good and fine trees pepper the park, especially conifers.

Houghall College Gardens
Durham, Co. Durham DH1 3SG
☎ 0191 3861351   FAX 0191 3860419
OWNER   Durham College of Agriculture & Horticulture
LOCATION   Follow A177 from A1 to Durham
OPEN   12.30 – 4.30 pm, daily, all year
ADMISSION   Free
FACILITIES   Parking; loos; facilities for the disabled; plants for sale; shop
FEATURES   Alpines; good collection of trees; bog garden; herbaceous borders; fine conifers; daffodils; glasshouses and conservatories to visit; lake; rock garden; modern roses; woodland garden; heathers; hardy fuchsias; seasonal bedding; excellent young pinetum
FRIENDS   Houghall Horticultural Society linked to the college
NCCPG NATIONAL COLLECTIONS *Sorbus*, *Meconopsis*

A well-run teaching garden attached to the county horticultural college. Many trials are conducted here, for example on the hardiness of fuchsias: 'if it grows at Houghall it will grow anywhere'. The arboretum has more than 500 different trees.

University of Durham Botanic Garden
Hollingside Lane, Durham, Co. Durham DH1 3TN
☎ 0191 374 2671   FAX 0191 374 7478
OWNER   University of Durham
LOCATION   In the south of the City of Durham
OPEN   10 am – 5 pm, daily, 1 April to 31 October; 1 – 4 pm, daily, 1 November to 31 March
ADMISSION   Free
FACILITIES   Parking; loos; facilities for the disabled; plants for sale; tea, coffee, cold drinks and snacks
FEATURES   Good collection of trees; old roses and climbers; primulas; *Meconopsis*; autumn colour; new alpine garden and Mediterranean glasshouse (1995)
FRIENDS   300 members and a full programme – details from the curator

Moved to its present site in 1970, this garden impresses with its youthful energy. The new 'American arboretum' was planted to copy natural associations 12 years ago. A woodland garden dates from 1988, a wetland one from 1989, and 1992 saw the opening of the 'Prince Bishop's Garden' with statues transferred from the Gateshead garden festival.

Westholme Hall
Winston, Darlington, Co. Durham DL2 3QL
☎ 01325 730442
OWNER   Mrs J. H. McBain
LOCATION   On B6274 north towards Staindrop
OPEN   2 – 6 pm, 28 May; 2 and 23 July; 27 August
ADMISSION   Adults £1.50; Children 50p
FACILITIES   Parking; dogs permitted; loos; access for the disabled; plants for sale; tea rooms
FEATURES   Lake; old roses and climbers; rhododendrons

5 acres of late Victorian gardens, recently restored and revived, around a smashing Jacobean house. Designed and planted for all seasons: there are parts for spring (bulbs and azaleas), summer (roses and lilacs) and autumn (herbaceous borders). All is maintained by the owners' own hard work and enthusiasm. Worth a long detour to see.

ESSEX

Audley End
Saffron Walden, Essex
☎ 01799 522399
OWNER   English Heritage
LOCATION   On B1383, 1 mile west of Saffron Walden
OPEN   Garden: 12 noon – 6 pm, Wednesday – Sunday, plus Bank Holiday Mondays, 1 April to 30 September (1994 times and dates)
ADMISSION   Gardens: Adults £2.70; Senior Citizens £2; Children £1.30 (1994)
FACILITIES   Parking; dogs permitted; loos; shop; restaurant and picnic site
FEATURES   Landscape designed by Capability Brown; follies and garden buildings; bedding out; parterre
ENGLISH HERITAGE GRADE   I

Capability Brown landscaped the park but the recent excitement at Audley End has been the reinauguration of the gardenesque formal garden after 10 years of restoration. This dates from the 1830s and has 170 geometric flower beds cut out of the turf and planted with simple perennials.

Beth Chatto Gardens
Elmstead Market, Colchester, Essex CO7 7DB
☎ 01206 822007   FAX 01206 825933
OWNER   Beth Chatto
LOCATION   7 miles east of Colchester
OPEN   9 am – 5 pm, Monday – Saturday, March to October; 9 am – 4 pm, Monday – Friday, November to February. Closed on Bank Holidays
ADMISSION   £2

FACILITIES   Parking; loos; big nursery adjacent to the garden
FEATURES   Herbaceous borders; gravel or scree garden; lake; colour contrasts

Superb modern planting, particularly good for herbaceous plants, chosen for foliage as much as flower: all made by Beth Chatto since 1960. There are two types of planting here and it is the contrast between them which makes the garden. First there are the parts on dry gravelly soil, where Mediterranean plants flourish; second, there are the water and bog gardens made on clay. But gardens are only one of Beth Chatto's gifts: her writings and nearby nursery have made her famous.

RHS Garden, Hyde Hall
Royal Horticultural Society Garden, Rettendon, Chelmsford, Essex CM3 8ET
☎ 01245 400256   FAX 01245 401363
OWNER   Royal Horticultural Society
LOCATION   6 miles south east of Rettendon, signposted from A130
OPEN   11 am – 6 pm, Wednesdays, Thursdays, Saturdays, Sundays and Bank Holidays, 26 March to 29 October
ADMISSION   Adults £2.50; Children (6–16) 50p; Groups (20+) £2
FACILITIES   Parking; loos; facilities for the disabled; plants for sale; bookshop; hot and cold lunches; afternoon teas; tea and coffee
FEATURES   Good collection of trees; herbaceous borders; fine conifers; daffodils; fruit of special interest; glasshouses and conservatories to visit; lake; plants for plantsmen; rock garden; climbing roses; modern roses; old roses; woodland garden; particularly interesting in winter; bearded irises; magnolias; South African bulbs; paeonies
NCCPG NATIONAL COLLECTIONS   *Malus*,   *Viburnum*

Recently acquired by the RHS, this outstanding modern garden (less than 40 years old) should be seen before its character changes. Even now the scale of the planting is outstanding for a private garden and the roses are particularly comprehensive.

Olivers
Olivers Lane, Colchester, Essex CO2 0HJ
☎ 01206 330575   FAX 01206 330336
OWNER   Mr and Mrs David Edwards
LOCATION   3 miles south west of Colchester between B1022 and B1026
OPEN   2 – 5 pm, Wednesdays, 1 April to 30 June; also for NGS: see Yellow Book
ADMISSION   Adults £1.50; Children free
FACILITIES   Parking; loos; facilities for the disabled; plants for sale; tea, coffee and biscuits (except Wednesdays)

FEATURES Herbaceous borders; fruit of special interest; lake; modern roses; old roses and climbers; bluebells; rhododendrons

Quite a modern garden, started in 1960 around 2 small lakes, with an eye-catching walk to one side leading down to a statue of Bacchus. Good plants and planting everywhere, from the parterres by the house to the woodland where roses and rhododendrons flourish. This is the garden of enthusiastic and energetic owners: an inspiration.

Park Farm
Chatham Hall Lane, Great Waltham, Chelmsford, Essex CM3 1BZ
☎ 01245 360871
OWNER J. Cowley and D. Bracey
LOCATION On B1008 north from Chelmsford
OPEN 16, 17 and 30 April; 1, 7, 8, 18 and 19 May; 4, 5, 11, 12, 18, 19, 25 and 26 June; 9 and 10 July
ADMISSION Adults £1; Children 50p
FACILITIES Loos; access for the disabled; plants for sale; teas and home-made cakes
FEATURES Herbaceous borders; plants for plantsmen; old roses and climbers

A young garden, still developing, with good colour combinations and a willingness to experiment. Rooms are enclosed by hedges of box and yew for solidity in winter and there is also a winter garden of hellebores, snowdrops and aconites. Add in a Chinese garden, a garden of the Giants (outsize plants), a hot garden, an arid garden and a Russian garden, and Park Farm is clearly a bundle of fun.

Saling Hall
Great Saling, Braintree, Essex CM7 5DT
OWNER Mr and Mrs Hugh Johnson
LOCATION 2 miles north of the Saling Oak on A120
OPEN 2 – 5 pm, Wednesdays, May, June and July. Also 2 – 6 pm, 25 June. Groups by appointment
ADMISSION £2 for NGS
FACILITIES Parking; loos; facilities for the disabled
FEATURES Good collection of trees; herbaceous borders; fine conifers; lake; oriental features; plants for plantsmen; old roses and climbers
ENGLISH HERITAGE GRADE II

A thinking man's garden, Saling also provokes thought in its visitors. The plantsmanship is impressive, particularly the choice and placing of trees. Some find the changes of mood (Japanese, Mediterranean etc.) confusing; others are stimulated.

Volpaia
54 Woodlands Road, Hockley, Essex SS5 4PY
☎ 01702 203761
OWNER Mr and Mrs Derek B. Fox
LOCATION 3 miles north east of Rayleigh
OPEN 2.30 – 6 pm, Thursdays and Sundays, 1 April to 30 June, or by appointment
ADMISSION Adults £1; Children 30p

FACILITIES Parking; plants for sale; Bullwood Nursery attached; tea and biscuits
FEATURES Herbaceous borders; plants for plantsmen; woodland garden; rhododendron species; liliaceous plants; woodlanders

This is the woodland garden of a keen plantsman who has now turned his hobby into a nursery. Rhododendrons, camellias and magnolias are the main shrubs, underplanted with *Erythronium* and woodland herbaceous plants, plus candelabra primulas in the boggy bits.

GLOUCESTERSHIRE

Abbotswood
Stow-on-the-Wold, Cheltenham, Gloucestershire GL54 1LE
☎ 01451 830173
OWNER Robin Scully
LOCATION 1 mile west of Stow-on-the-Wold
OPEN 2 – 6 pm, 16 April; 7 and 21 May; 4 and 18 June
ADMISSION Adults £2; Children free
FACILITIES Parking; loos; teas
FEATURES Good collection of trees; herbaceous borders; fine conifers; planted by Gertrude Jekyll; lake; plants for plantsmen; rock garden; modern roses; old roses and climbers; good topiary; woodland garden; magnolias; heather garden
ENGLISH HERITAGE GRADE II*

One of the most interesting gardens in the Cotswolds. Handsome formal gardens in front of the house: very Lutyens, very photogenic. A magnificent rock garden with a stream (artificially pumped, but you would never know) which meanders through alpine meadows, bogs and moraines, past dwarf azaleas, primulas, *Lysichiton*, heaths and heathers until it disappears again. There is also a small arboretum, rather overgrown, but with some unusual forms, fascinating to browse around.

Barnsley House
Barnsley, Cirencester, Gloucestershire GL7 5EE
☎ 01285 740281   FAX 01285 740628
OWNER Mrs David Verey
LOCATION On A433/B4425 in Barnsley village
OPEN 10 am – 6 pm, Mondays, Wednesdays, Thursdays and Saturdays, all year
ADMISSION Adults £2; Senior Citizens £1; Children free. Season ticket £4. December to February free. Parties by appointment
FACILITIES Parking; loos; plants for sale
FEATURES Herbaceous borders; follies and garden buildings; fruit of special interest; herbs; plants for plantsmen; old roses and climbers; ornamental *potager*; Simon Verity's sculpture

A compact, modern garden, much copying and much copied. Barnsley is interesting at all seasons, but best

GLOUCESTERSHIRE Gardens

when the little laburnum walk and the purple alliums underneath are in flower together.

Batsford Arboretum
The Estate Office, Moreton-in-Marsh, Gloucestershire GL56 9QF
☎ 01608 650722   FAX 01608 650290
OWNER   The Batsford Foundation (registered charity)
LOCATION   Off A44, along Broadway Road
OPEN   10 am – 5 pm, daily, 1 March to mid November
ADMISSION   Adults £2; Senior Citizens and Children (under 16) £1.50 (provisional prices)
FACILITIES   Parking; dogs permitted; loos; facilities for the disabled; plants for sale; shop; light meals and refreshments
FEATURES   Good collection of trees; fine conifers; oriental features; woodland garden; bluebells; maple glade; tallest *Betula platyphylla* (and six other tree records) in the British Isles
ENGLISH HERITAGE GRADE   I

Batsford has an openness which makes its hillside a joy to wander through, passing from one dendrological marvel to the next. Begun in the 1880s, the Arboretum also has several oriental curiosities brought from Japan by Lord Redesdale – a large bronze Buddha and an oriental rest-house, for instance. Lord Dulverton has renewed the plantings over the last 30 years: both the collection and the amenities are improving all the time.

Berkeley Castle
Berkeley, Gloucestershire GL13 9BQ
☎ 01453 810332
OWNER   John Berkeley
LOCATION   Off A38
OPEN   2 – 5 pm, Tuesday – Sunday, April; 11 am – 5 pm, Tuesday – Saturday, also 2 – 4.30 pm, Sundays, May to September. 11 am – 5 pm, Bank Holiday Mondays
ADMISSION   Garden only: Adults £1; Children 50p
FACILITIES   Parking; loos; shop at Castle Farm; light lunches and afternoon teas
FEATURES   Herbaceous borders; fine conifers; plants for plantsmen; old roses and climbers
ENGLISH HERITAGE GRADE   II*

The grim battlements of Berkeley Castle are host to an extensive collection of tender plants. On three terraces are *Cestrum*, *Cistus* and *Rosa banksiae* among hundreds of plant varieties introduced by the owner's grandfather, a nephew of Ellen Willmott. An Elizabethan-style bowling green and a water-lily pond fit well into the overall scheme.

Bourton House
Bourton-on-the-Hill, Moreton-in-Marsh, Gloucestershire GL56 9AE
OWNER   Mr and Mrs Richard Paice
LOCATION   On A44 west of Moreton-in-Marsh

OPEN   12 noon – 5 pm, Thursdays and Fridays, 25 May to 29 September
ADMISSION   £2.50
FACILITIES   Parking; loos; plants for sale; self-service tea and coffee.
FEATURES   Herbaceous borders; follies and garden buildings; gravel or scree garden; modern roses; old roses and climbers; good topiary
ENGLISH HERITAGE GRADE   II

First laid out by Lanning Roper in the 1960s, but consistently improved by the present owners, the garden at Bourton House is both fashionable and a delight. A knot garden, a small *potager*, a raised pond, the topiary walk, white-painted trellis-work, a croquet lawn, exuberant climbing roses and borders bulging with good colour schemes – purple-leaved *Prunus* with yellow roses, for instance.

Cecily Hill House
Cirencester, Gloucestershire GL7 2EF
☎ 012865 653766
OWNER   Mr and Mrs Rupert de Zoete
LOCATION   West of Cirencester near gates into Park
OPEN   Sunday 15 July; also by appointment mid June to 31 July
ADMISSION   £2 for joint ticket
FACILITIES   Parking; dogs permitted
FEATURES   Herbaceous borders; fruit of special interest; modern roses; old roses and climbers; pots; lilies; ferns; flowering cherries

One of a group of small gardens in Cirencester which open once a year for charity. Cecily Hill House has a particularly attractive kitchen garden.

The Ernest Wilson Memorial Garden
High Street, Chipping Campden, Gloucestershire GL55 6AF
☎ 01386 840764
OWNER   Chipping Campden Town Council
LOCATION   North end of Main Street
OPEN   Dawn – dusk, daily, all year
ADMISSION   Donation
FACILITIES   Dogs permitted; access for the disabled
FEATURES   Herbaceous borders; trees and shrubs

A collection of plants all introduced by Ernest H. Wilson, the greatest of European plant-hunters in China: Chipping Campden was his birthplace. *Acer griseum*, *Clematis montana rubens* and the pocket-handkerchief tree *Davidia involucrata* are among his best-known introductions: all are represented here.

Frampton Court
Frampton-on-Severn, Gloucestershire GL2 7EU
☎ 01452 740698
OWNER   Mrs Peter Clifford
LOCATION   Signed from Frampton-on-Severn
OPEN   By appointment all year; also for NGS, NADFAS and Red Cross
ADMISSION   House and Garden: £3.50; Garden: £1

FACILITIES Parking; dogs permitted; loos
FEATURES Follies and garden buildings; lake
ENGLISH HERITAGE GRADE I

Beautiful and mysterious garden, little changed since 1750. The Dutch water garden – a long rectangular pool – reflects the orangery of Strawberry Hill Gothic design. But do also ask to see the collection of botanical watercolours known as the Frampton Flora.

Hidcote Manor Garden
Hidcote Bartrim, Chipping Campden, Gloucestershire GL55 6LR
☎ 01386 438333

OWNER The National Trust
LOCATION Signposted from B4632, Stratford – Broadway Road
OPEN 11 am – 7 pm, daily, except Tuesday and Friday, 1 April to 31 October
ADMISSION Adults £5; Children £2.50; Family £13.75 (2 adults and up to 4 children)
FACILITIES Parking; loos; access for the disabled; plants for sale; National Trust shop; licensed restaurant, coffee and lunches 11 am – 2 pm, teas 2.15 – 5 pm
FEATURES Herbaceous borders; fine conifers; follies and garden buildings; gravel or scree garden; herbs; lake; plants for plantsmen; rock garden; modern roses; old roses and climbers; good topiary; woodland garden; plantings by Graham Thomas; tallest pink acacia *Robinia* × *ambigua* 'Decaisneana' in the British Isles
ENGLISH HERITAGE GRADE I
NCCPG NATIONAL COLLECTIONS *Paeonia*

Probably the most influential 20th-century garden in the world – certainly the most important and most copied. Essential visiting for all garden owners.

Hodges Barn
Shipton Moyne, Tetbury, Gloucestershire GL8 8PR
☎ 01666 880202   FAX 01367 718096

OWNER Charles Hornby
LOCATION 3 miles south of Tetbury on Malmesbury road from Shipton Moyne
OPEN 2 – 5 pm, Mondays, Tuesdays and Fridays, 1 April to 15 August
ADMISSION £2.50
FACILITIES Parking; dogs permitted; loos; access for the disabled; lime tolerant herbaceous plants for sale; teas by arrangement
FEATURES Herbaceous borders; gravel or scree garden; plants for plantsmen; modern roses; old roses and climbers; good topiary; woodland garden; daffodils; bluebells; *Cyclamen*

A big garden – 6 acres – and all intensively planted. Terraces, courtyards and gardens enclosed by stone walls or yew hedges are planted to give year-round colour. One has *rugosa* roses underplanted with hellebores, forget-me-nots and early bulbs for winter. The woodland garden is almost an arboretum of ornamental trees – birches, maples, whitebeams and magnolias – underplanted with daffodils and primroses. Hodges Barn is a garden of great energy and loveliness.

Hunts Court
North Nibley, Dursley, Gloucestershire GL11 6DZ
☎ 01453 547440

OWNER T. K. Marshall
LOCATION Signposted in centre of village
OPEN 2 – 6 pm, Tuesday – Saturday, all year except August. Opens for the NGS
ADMISSION Adults £1; Children free
FACILITIES Parking; loos; access for the disabled; first-rate nursery attached on NGS days
FEATURES Plants for plantsmen; modern roses; old roses

The best collection of old roses in the west of England, and still expanding. Keith and Margaret Marshall say they have 'the collector's touch of madness': the result is charming, peaceful and educational.

Kiftsgate Court
Chipping Campden, Gloucestershire GL55 6LW
☎ 01386 438777

OWNER Mr and Mrs J. Chambers
LOCATION 3 miles from Chipping Campden opposite Hidcote Manor
OPEN 2 – 6 pm, Wednesdays, Thursdays, Sundays and Bank Holiday Mondays, 1 April to 30 September, plus 2 – 6 pm on Saturdays during June and July
ADMISSION Adults £3; Children £1
FACILITIES Parking; loos; plants for sale; tea room in the house
FEATURES Herbaceous borders; plants for plantsmen; modern roses; old roses and climbers; woodland garden; rose hedges; colour plantings; rare plants
ENGLISH HERITAGE GRADE II*

Famous for its roses, especially the eponymous *Rosa filipes*, Kiftsgate is all about plants and the use of colour. The best example is the yellow border, where gold and orange are set off by occasional blues and purples. After some dull years, everything about Kiftsgate has revived again: new thinking, new plantings and new enthusiasm have restored its excellence.

Lydney Park Gardens
Lydney Park, Gloucestershire GL15 6BU
☎ 01594 842844

OWNER Viscount Bledisloe
LOCATION Off A48 between Lydney and Aylburton
OPEN 11 am – 6 pm, Mondays, Bank Holidays and Wednesdays, 2 April to 4 June; daily, 28 May to 4 June. Closed 21 May
ADMISSION £1 (but £2 on Sundays and Bank Holidays)
FACILITIES Parking; dogs permitted; loos; plants for sale; some souvenirs for sale; light teas
FEATURES Fine conifers; lake; garden sculpture; woodland garden; deer park; rhododendrons, azaleas and camellias

GLOUCESTERSHIRE Gardens 291

A remarkable collection of rhododendrons planted over the last 45 years is the backbone to this extensive woodland garden. And not just rhododendrons, but azaleas and camellias too, all carefully planted to create distinct effects from March to June. The numbers are still growing, and include plants grown from collected seed and hybrids from distinguished breeders, many as yet unnamed, while others have yet to flower. Lydney is now recognised as one of the best rhododendron gardens in England.

Miserden Park
Miserden, Stroud, Gloucestershire GL6 7JA
☎ 01285 821303 FAX 01285 821530
OWNER Major M. T. N. H. Wills
LOCATION Turn right off B4070 between Stroud and Birdlip
OPEN 9.30 am – 4.30 pm, Tuesdays, Wednesdays and Thursdays, 1 April to 30 September
ADMISSION Adults £2
FACILITIES Parking; loos; access for the disabled; plants for sale
FEATURES Good collection of trees; herbaceous borders; fine conifers; planted by Gertrude Jekyll; modern roses; old roses and climbers; good topiary; fritillaries; martagon lilies; domed yew hedges; cedar walk replaced by new avenue (1994–95)
ENGLISH HERITAGE GRADE II*

The Jacobean Cotswold house has wide views across the Golden Valley, while the open spacious gardens lie to the side. Most were laid out in the 1920s – a charming rose garden, the long yew walk and expansive herbaceous borders, but there is also an older arboretum and Edwardian shrubbery.

Owlpen Manor
Uley, Dursley, Gloucestershire GL11 5BZ
☎ 01453 860261 FAX 01453 860819
OWNER Nicholas Mander
LOCATION Off B4066 near Uley
OPEN 2 – 5 pm, Tuesdays, Thursdays, Sundays and Bank Holiday Mondays, 1 April to 30 September. Also Wednesdays in July and August
ADMISSION Adults £3.75; Senior Citizens £3; Children £1.50
FACILITIES Parking; loos; guidebooks and postcards for sale; licensed restaurant in 15th-century barn
FEATURES Lake; old roses and climbers; good topiary
ENGLISH HERITAGE GRADE II

Dreamy Cotswold manor house whose loveliness depends as much upon its site as its garden, but there are terraced gardens with box parterres and topiary yews and plantings of roses and herbs.

Painswick Rococo Garden
Painswick, Stroud, Gloucestershire GL6 6TH
☎ 01452 813204
OWNER Painswick Rococo Garden Trust
LOCATION Outside Painswick on B4073
OPEN 11 am – 5 pm, Wednesday – Sunday, 2 February to 30 November
ADMISSION Adults £2.60; Senior Citizens £2.20; Children £1.30
FACILITIES Parking; dogs permitted; loos; plants for sale; gift shop; licensed restaurant, coffee, teas and light snacks
FEATURES Follies and garden buildings; garden sculpture; woodland garden; snowdrop wood
ENGLISH HERITAGE GRADE II*
FRIENDS The Painswick Rococo Gardens Trust was established in 1988 to preserve the gardens in perpetuity. Details from Lord Dickinson

Only 10 years of restoration work lie behind the unique rococo garden at Painswick which is re-emerging from back-to-nature woodland. A white Venetian gothic exedra, a Doric seat, the plunge pool, an octagonal pigeon house, a gothic gazebo called the Eagle House, a bowling green, the fish pond and a gothic alcove have all been reconstructed in their original positions, thanks to the efforts of Lord Dickinson and the Painswick Rococo Gardens Trust. A remarkable garden and a brilliant achievement.

The Priory
Kemerton, Gloucestershire GL20 7JN
☎ 01386 725258
OWNER The Hon. Mrs Healing
LOCATION In Kemerton village
OPEN 2 – 7 pm, Thursdays, 27 May to 28 September. Plus 28 May, 25 June, 16 July, 6 and 27 August, 10 September
ADMISSION £1.50
FACILITIES Parking; dogs permitted; loos; access for the disabled; plants for sale; refreshments on open Sundays
FEATURES Herbaceous borders; gravel or scree garden; plants for plantsmen; old roses and climbers; particularly good in July-August

The Priory is a late-summer comet, dazzling in August and September when the annuals and tender plants supplement the perennial colour planting. The late Peter Healing spent 50 years perfecting his colour gradings. The results are worth a long journey to see: the crimson border is the best there has ever been.

Rodmarton Manor
Rodmarton, Cirencester, Gloucestershire GL7 6PF
☎ 01285 841253
OWNER Simon Biddulph
LOCATION Off A433 between Cirencester and Tetbury
OPEN 2 – 5 pm, Saturdays, 13 May to 26 August, or by appointment
ADMISSION £2, but £1.50 on Saturdays
FACILITIES Parking; loos; access for the disabled; plants for sale

FEATURES Herbaceous borders; fine conifers; plants for plantsmen; rock garden; modern roses; old roses and climbers; good topiary; woodland garden; new rock garden (1993)
ENGLISH HERITAGE GRADE II*

A splendid Arts and Crafts garden, with a strong design and exuberant planting. Simon Biddulph says there are 18 different areas within the garden, from the trough garden for alpine plants to the famous double herbaceous borders, currently undergoing renovation, which lead to a Cotswold summerhouse. Highly original – contemporary, but made without any contact, with Hidcote. Very photogenic.

Sezincote
Moreton-in-Marsh, Gloucestershire GL56 9AW
OWNER Mr and Mrs D. Peake
LOCATION On A44 to Evesham, 1½ miles out of Moreton-in-Marsh
OPEN 2 – 6 pm, Thursdays, Fridays, Bank Holiday Mondays, 1 January to 30 November
ADMISSION Adults £2.50; Children £1
FACILITIES Parking; loos
FEATURES Good collection of trees; herbaceous borders; landscape designed by Humphry Repton; fine conifers; follies and garden buildings; glasshouses and conservatories to visit; lake; oriental features; garden sculpture; subtropical plants; woodland garden; plantings by Graham Thomas; tallest *Fagus sylvatica* 'Zlatia' and maidenhair tree *Ginkgo biloba* in England
ENGLISH HERITAGE GRADE I

The house was the model for Brighton Pavilion, and seems inseparable from the cruciform Moghul garden that sets off its Indian façade so well: yet this brilliant formal garden was designed as recently as 1965. On the other side are sumptuous borders planted by Graham Thomas and a luscious water garden of candelabra primulas and astilbes around the Temple to Surya, the Snake Bridge and Brahmin bulls. Humphry Repton had a hand in the original landscape, but the modern gardens are far more satisfying.

Snowshill Manor
Broadway, Gloucestershire WR12 7JU
☎ 01386 852410
OWNER The National Trust
LOCATION In Snowshill village
OPEN 1 – 6 pm (5 pm in April & October), daily except Tuesday, 1 April to 31 October, except Good Friday
ADMISSION House and grounds (timed ticket system): Adults £5; Children £2.50; Family ticket £13.75. Gardens only: £2
FACILITIES Parking; loos; National Trust shop
FEATURES Herbaceous borders; follies and garden buildings; old roses and climbers
ENGLISH HERITAGE GRADE II

Praised for its changes of levels and collection of curious artefacts – an armillary sphere and a gilt figure of St George and the Dragon, for instance. Snowshill is as curious as its maker, Charles Wade, and the spooky bric-a-brac which fills his house, but many visitors find it 'charming' or 'interesting'. Perhaps its finest ornament is the head gardener, a splendid fellow who persuaded his employers to let him run Snowshill as a completely organic garden, the National Trust's only one.

Stancombe Park
Dursley, Gloucestershire GL11 6AU
☎ 01453 542815

OWNER Mrs Basil Barlow
LOCATION Off the B4060 between Dursley and Wotton-under-Edge
OPEN 2 – 6 pm, 4 June. Also groups by appointment
ADMISSION Adults £2; Children (under 10) 50p
FACILITIES Parking; dogs permitted; loos; access for the disabled
FEATURES Good collection of trees; herbaceous borders; fine conifers; daffodils; follies and garden buildings; herbs; lake; plants for plantsmen; modern roses; old roses and climbers; garden sculpture; good topiary; woodland garden; temple in folly garden restored (1994–95)
ENGLISH HERITAGE GRADE I

Stancombe has everything: a handsome house above a wooded valley, a flower garden of wondrous prettiness, and a gothic horror of an historic Folly Garden at the valley bottom. Start at the top. Peter Coates, Lanning Roper and Nadia Jennett all worked on the rose gardens and mixed borders by the house: there is more to learn about good modern design and planting here than any garden in Gloucestershire. Then wander down the valley where the path narrows and the incline steepens to a ferny tunnel, and start the circuit of the follies, best described as an open-air ghost-train journey without the ghosts.

Stanway House
Stanway, Cheltenham, Gloucestershire GL54 5PQ
☎ 01386 584469   FAX 01386 584469
OWNER Lord Neidpath
LOCATION On B4077
OPEN 2 – 5 pm, Tuesdays and Thursdays, June to September
ADMISSION Adults £3; Senior Citizens £2.50; Children £1
FACILITIES Parking; dogs permitted; loos
FEATURES Good collection of trees; herbaceous borders; fine conifers; follies and garden buildings
ENGLISH HERITAGE GRADE I

Huge terraces behind the house lead up to a pyramid folly. This was the apex of a vast cascade which ran down to a long still tank, now a grassy plateau halfway up the hillside. Little remains, though there are plans for restoration. Rather poignant.

Stowell Park
Northleach, Gloucestershire GL54 3LE
☎ 01285 720308 📠 01285 720360
OWNER   Lord Vestey
LOCATION   A429 between Cirencester and Northleach
OPEN   2 – 5 pm, 14 May and 25 June
ADMISSION   £2
FACILITIES   Parking; loos; teas
FEATURES   Herbaceous borders; glasshouses and conservatories to visit; old roses and climbers
ENGLISH HERITAGE GRADE   II

A historic landscape in a magnificent position, with a pleasure garden and walled garden, stylishly replanted with advice from Rosemary Verey of nearby Barnsley.

Sudeley Castle
Winchcombe, Gloucestershire GL54 5JD
☎ 01242 602308 📠 01242 602959
OWNER   Lady Ashcombe
LOCATION   8 miles north east of Cheltenham B4632
OPEN   11 am – 5.30 pm, daily
ADMISSION   Adults £3.10; Senior Citizens £2.75; Children £1.40 (1994)
FACILITIES   Parking; loos; facilities for the disabled; plants for sale; good shop, rather up-market; restaurant and tea rooms
FEATURES   Herbaceous borders; fine conifers; follies and garden buildings; herbs; lake; modern roses; old roses and climbers; good topiary; interesting for children; ruins of banqueting hall, now a pretty garden; adventure playground
ENGLISH HERITAGE GRADE   II*

Sudeley tries hard and ought to be a good garden: Jane Fearnley-Whittingstall did the roses and Rosemary Verey planted some borders. There are fine old trees, magnificent Victorian topiary (mounds of green and gold yew) and a raised walk around the pleasure gardens that may be Elizabethan in origin. But it lacks intimacy and some find it too obviously commercial.

Westbury Court
Westbury-on-Severn, Gloucestershire GL14 1PD
☎ 01452 760461
OWNER   The National Trust
LOCATION   9 miles south west of Gloucester on A48
OPEN   11 am – 6 pm, Wednesday – Sunday and Bank Holiday Mondays, 1 April to 31 October except Good Friday
ADMISSION   Adults £2.30; Children £1.15
FACILITIES   Parking; loos; facilities for the disabled; picnic area
FEATURES   Herbaceous borders; fruit of special interest; herbs; lake; old roses and climbers; garden sculpture; good topiary; biggest holm oak *Quercus ilex* in the British Isles; restoration of pool and fountain planned (1995)
ENGLISH HERITAGE GRADE   II*

Restored over the last 20 years to become the best example of a 17th-century Dutch garden in England. A pretty pavilion, tall and slender, looks down along a long tank of water. On the walls are old apple and pear varieties. Parterres, fine modern topiary and a T-shaped tank with a statue of Neptune in the middle make up the rest of the garden, with an opulent rose garden (old varieties only) underplanted with pinks, tulips and herbs. Immaculately maintained.

Westonbirt Arboretum
Westonbirt, Tetbury, Gloucestershire GL8 8QS
☎ 01666 880220 📠 01666 880559
OWNER   Forestry Commission
LOCATION   3 miles south of Tetbury on A433
OPEN   10 am – 8 pm (or dusk if earlier), daily, all year. Visitor centre open 10 am – 5 pm, daily, March to December
ADMISSION   Adults £2.60; Senior Citizens £1.70; Children £1
FACILITIES   Parking; dogs permitted; loos; facilities for the disabled; plants for sale; gift shop; cafeteria
FEATURES   Particularly interesting in winter; new plant centre (1994); 61 species of record-breaking trees, including 21 maples (*Acer* spp.)
ENGLISH HERITAGE GRADE   Salix, *Acer*

The finest and largest arboretum in the British Isles: 500 acres, 17 miles of paths, 4,000 species, 18,000 trees. The maple glade is famous, and so are the bluebells in the part known as Silk Wood. Well managed by the Forestry Commission, whose visitor centre is a marvel of helpfulness. Brightest perhaps in spring and autumn, but the best place we know for a long winter walk.

GREATER MANCHESTER

Dunham Massey
Altrincham, Greater Manchester WA14 4SJ
☎ 0161 941 1025
OWNER   The National Trust
LOCATION   3 miles south west of Altrincham off A56, well-signposted (Dunham Massey Hall and Park)
OPEN   11 am – 5 pm, daily, 1 April to 30 October
ADMISSION   Adults £2; Children £1
FACILITIES   Parking; loos; facilities for the disabled; garden shop; large restaurant
FEATURES   Herbaceous borders; follies and garden buildings; glasshouses and conservatories to visit; lake; good topiary; interesting for children; azaleas; hydrangeas; Edwardian parterre
ENGLISH HERITAGE GRADE   II*

Dunham Massey's 250 acres include an ancient deer park, a medieval moat made into a lake in the 18th century, an Elizabethan mount, an 18th-century orangery and some early landscape avenues. All remain as features of the grounds, but the National Trust has decided to major on its even more interesting Victorian relics – evergreen shrubberies, ferns and colourful bedding out schemes. Even that does not preclude the Trust from planting the most modern forms, such as the hybrids of *Rhododendron yakushimanum* and latest *occidentale* hybrid azaleas. The result is a potent cross-section of historical and modern styles with a solid core of Victorian excellence.

Fletcher Moss Botanical Gardens
Mill Gate Lane, Didsbury, Greater Manchester M20 8SD
☎ 0161 434 1877
OWNER   Manchester City Council
OPEN   8 am – dusk, Monday – Friday, 9 am – dusk, weekends and Bank Holidays, all year
ADMISSION   Free
FACILITIES   Parking; loos; facilities for the disabled; cafeteria
FEATURES   Fine conifers; glasshouses and conservatories to visit; gravel or scree garden; lake; rock garden; old roses and climbers; bulbs; heathers; rhododendrons; orchid house

A model municipal botanic garden, beautifully maintained but free to the public. There are good collections of small conifers, maples and aquatics. Excellent autumn colour: almost as good in spring.

HAMPSHIRE

Bramdean House
Bramdean, Alresford, Hampshire SO24 0JU
☎ 01962 771214   FAX 01962 771095
OWNER   Mr and Mrs H. Wakefield
LOCATION   On A272, between Winchester and Petersfield
OPEN   2 – 5 pm, 20 March, 3, 4, 17 April, 15 May, 19 June, 17 July, 21 August, and by appointment
ADMISSION   Adults £1.50; Children free
FACILITIES   Parking; loos; refreshments
FEATURES   Alpines; herbaceous borders; daffodils; fruit of special interest; plants for plantsmen; rock garden; old roses and climbers; good topiary; handsome cedars; paeonies; pinks; irises; winter aconites; flowering cherries
ENGLISH HERITAGE GRADE   II

Beautifully designed by the late Mrs Feilden and immaculately maintained by her daughter, the gardens at Bramdean are much admired, and rightly so. 2 wide herbaceous borders lead up from the terrace behind the house, against a backdrop of mature beeches and cedars. At the end of the central axis, steps lead to a walled kitchen garden whose central bed is planted with roses and annuals. The vista runs yet further, through an orchard to a gazebo some 300 yards from the house. The views in both directions are stunning.

Brandy Mount House
East Street, Alresford, Hampshire SO24 9EG
☎ 01962 732189
OWNER   Mr and Mrs Michael Baron

LOCATION   Left into East Street from Broad Street, 50 yards first right
OPEN   2 – 5 pm, 12 February, 19 March, 23 April, 7 May, 18 June, and by appointment in snowdrop time
ADMISSION   £1
FACILITIES   Dogs permitted; access for the disabled; extensive plant sales area; refreshments for groups by arrangement
FEATURES   Herbaceous borders; gravel or scree garden; plants for plantsmen; rock garden; woodland garden; young garden; paeony species; cardamines; collected plants
NCCPG NATIONAL COLLECTIONS *Daphne, Galanthus*

Essentially a plantsman's garden, but a plantsman who is also a distinguished plant collector and exhibitor of alpine plants. Linked to a thriving small nursery which is always worth a visit.

Broadlands
Romsey, Hampshire
☎ 01794 516878
OWNER   Lord and Lady Romsey
LOCATION   On Romsey bypass, by town centre roundabout
OPEN   12 noon – 4 pm, daily, except Friday, 1 July to 31 August
ADMISSION   Adults £5; Senior Citizens £4.25; Children (12–16) £3.50
FACILITIES   Parking; loos; facilities for the disabled; plants for sale; gift shop; tea rooms and picnic area by river
FEATURES   Herbaceous borders; landscape designed by Capability Brown; lake; woodland garden
ENGLISH HERITAGE GRADE   II

Classic Capability Brown landscape, handsome old trees and an open park which runs slowly down to a lake and the River Test.

Exbury Gardens
Exbury, Southampton, Hampshire SO4 1AZ
☎ 01703 891203   FAX 01703 243380
OWNER   Edmund de Rothschild
LOCATION   3 miles south of Beaulieu
OPEN   10 am – 5.30 pm (or dusk if earlier), daily, 18 February to 29 October
ADMISSION   Too complicated to detail: from £4.50 for Adults in high season, to £1.50 for Children in low season
FACILITIES   Parking; dogs permitted; loos; facilities for the disabled; plants for sale; hot and cold lunches, cream teas
FEATURES   Herbaceous borders; lake; landscape designed by Humphry Repton; rock garden; old roses and climbers; woodland garden; candelabra primulas; rare trees; much new planting (1994–95); tallest shagbark hickory *Carya ovata* in England (and two other tree records)

HAMPSHIRE Gardens 295

ENGLISH HERITAGE GRADE II*

Rhododendrons, rhododendrons, rhododendrons: over 1 million of them in 200 acres of natural woodland. More than 40 have won awards from the Royal Horticultural Society. But there are magnolias, camellias and rare trees too, many grown from the original seed introduced by famous plant collectors. A place of wonder in May.

Fairfield House
Hambledon, Waterlooville, Hampshire PO7 4RY
☎ 01705 632431

OWNER Mrs Peter Wake
LOCATION East Street, Hambledon
OPEN For NGS, and by appointment
ADMISSION Adults £1.50
FACILITIES Access for the disabled; plants for sale; teas on open day
FEATURES Herbaceous borders; fine conifers; plants for plantsmen; beautifully grown roses; new meadow garden for wild flowers and butterflies (1995)

Fairfield is one of the best private rose gardens in England. Old roses and climbers were the late Peter Wake's main interest and he grew them unusually well. The shrubs are trained up a cat's cradle of string drawn between 5 wooden posts. The results make you gasp – 'Charles de Mills' 10 feet high.

Furzey Gardens
Minstead, Lyndhurst, Hampshire SO4 7GL
☎ 01703 812464

OWNER Furzey Gardens Charitable Trust
LOCATION Off A31 or A337 to Minstead
OPEN 10 am – 5 pm (earlier in winter), daily except Christmas and Boxing Day
ADMISSION March – October: Adults £3; Senior Citizens £2.50; Children £1.50. November – February: Adults £1.50; Senior Citizens £1; Children 50p
FACILITIES Parking; loos; plants for sale; small shop
FEATURES Bluebells; bog garden; camellias; fine conifers; plants for plantsmen; pond; rhododendrons and azaleas; woodland garden; interesting for children; naturalised *Dierama*; heathers; spring bulbs
FRIENDS No Friends Organisation but the gardens are owned by a charitable trust.

Furzey demonstrates how woodland garden effects can be created in quite small areas. Parts are a maze of narrow curving paths running between hedges of Kurume azaleas, unforgettable in April and May, but the late summer flowering of *Eucryphia* runs them close and the autumn colour of *Nyssa*, *Parrotia* and *Enkianthus* is worth a visit in October.

Highclere Castle
Highclere, Newbury, Hampshire RG15 9RN
☎ 01635 255317   FAX 01635 254051

OWNER The Earl of Carnarvon
LOCATION South of Newbury off A34
OPEN 2 – 6 pm, Wednesday – Sunday and Bank Holiday Mondays, July to September
ADMISSION Adults £4; Senior Citizens £3.50; Children and disabled £2.50. Gardens only: £2
FACILITIES Parking; loos; facilities for the disabled; plants for sale; shop; good restaurant
FEATURES Herbaceous borders; landscape designed by Capability Brown; camellias; fine conifers; follies and garden buildings; fruit of special interest; glasshouses and conservatories to visit; rhododendrons and azaleas; good topiary; particularly good in July-August; good collection of cedars; long avenues
ENGLISH HERITAGE GRADE I

A major historic garden – when Capability Brown landscaped it in the 1770s he left intact the avenues and follies of the early 18th century, but the park is dominated now by hundreds of huge cedars. Salvin's imposing house has 365 windows. Jim Russell advised on the planting in the walled garden, though the 'Secret Garden' is not among his best.

Hinton Ampner House
Bramdean, Alresford, Hampshire SO24 0LA
☎ 01962 771305

OWNER The National Trust
LOCATION On A272, 1 mile west of Bramdean
OPEN 1.30 – 5 pm, Tuesdays, Wednesdays, Saturdays, Sundays and Bank Holidays except Easter Monday, 1 April to 30 September
ADMISSION Adults £2.40; Children £1.20
FACILITIES Parking; loos; facilities for the disabled; teas and home-made cakes
FEATURES Garden sculpture; good topiary; daffodils; yew trees
ENGLISH HERITAGE GRADE II

The gardens at Hinton Ampner were laid out by the scholarly Ralph Dutton in the middle of this century with great regard to line, landscape and historical propriety. Statues, buildings, axes and views have been restored with exquisite judgement to lead you subtly along the exact route that Dutton intended. Good plantings, too.

Houghton Lodge
Houghton, Stockbridge, Hampshire SO20 6LQ
☎ 01264 810502/810177

OWNER Martin Busk
LOCATION Off A30 at Stockbridge
OPEN 2 – 5 pm, Mondays, Tuesdays and Fridays; 10 am – 5 pm, Saturdays, Sundays and Bank Holidays, 1 March to 30 September
ADMISSION £2.50. Groups at special rates
FACILITIES Parking; dogs permitted; loos; facilities for the disabled; plants for sale
FEATURES Follies and garden buildings; glasshouses and conservatories to visit; lake; good topiary; daffodils; *Cyclamen*
ENGLISH HERITAGE GRADE II*

A lovely gothic *cottage orné* beside the River Test, restored with advice from David Jacques. Houghton also boasts the first hydroponic greenhouse open to the public, where plants are grown in nutrient-rich solutions instead of soil.

Jenkyn Place
Bentley, Farnham, Hampshire GU10 5LU
☎ 01420 23118

OWNER Mrs Gerald Coke
LOCATION Signposted from Farnham bypass
OPEN 2 – 6 pm, Thursday – Sunday, 7 April to 11 September
ADMISSION Adults £2; Children 75p
FACILITIES Parking; loos; plants for sale
FEATURES Good collection of trees; herbaceous borders; fine conifers; herbs; plants for plantsmen; rock garden; modern roses; old roses and climbers; garden sculpture; woodland garden; tallest red horse chestnut *Aesculus × carnea* 'Briotii' in Britain

The best postwar garden in the Hidcote style, a series of rooms and corridors planted with discrimination and art. Good old roses, heroic herbaceous borders, and something for everyone whatever the weather or season.

Longstock Water Gardens
Longstock, Stockbridge, Hampshire SO20 6EH
☎ 01264 810894   FAX 01264 810430

OWNER John Lewis Partnership
LOCATION 1½ miles north east of Longstock village
OPEN 2 – 5 pm, 1st and 3rd Sunday in the month, 1 April to 30 September
ADMISSION £2 for charity
FACILITIES Parking; loos; facilities for the disabled; plants for sale
FEATURES Herbaceous borders; ecological interest; lake; plants for plantsmen; woodland garden; interesting for children

Quite the most extraordinary and beautiful water garden in England, a little Venice where dozens of islands and all-but-islands are linked by small bridges and intensely planted with water-loving plants. Drifts of astilbes, primulas, kingcups, *Hemerocallis*, musks, water irises and lilies. The ground is so soft that the islands seem to float, and a remarkable accumulation of peat has allowed such calcifuge plants as *Meconopsis betonicifolia* and *Cardiocrinum giganteum* to flourish in this chalky valley. Would that it were open more often.

The Loyalty Garden
Basing House Ruins, Redbridge Lane, Basing, Basingstoke, Hampshire RG24 7HB
☎ 01256 467294   FAX 01256 26283

OWNER Hampshire County Council
LOCATION Signposted from M3, J6
OPEN 2 – 6 pm, Wednesday – Sunday, and Bank Holiday Mondays, 1 April to 1 October
ADMISSION Adults £1.50; Senior Citizens and Children 70p
FACILITIES Parking; dogs permitted; loos; facilities for the disabled; plants for sale; tea room open some Sundays
FEATURES Herbs; parterres

A charming modern garden in the ruins of Old Basing Castle: parterres of sage, *Santolina* and box, and the motto of the Paulet family *Aymez Loyautei*, from which it takes its name.

The Manor House, Upton Grey
Upton Grey, Basingstoke, Hampshire RG25 2RD
☎ 01256 862827

OWNER Mrs John Wallinger
LOCATION In Upton Grey village
OPEN 2 – 4.30 pm, Wednesdays, May to July. Groups (20+) by appointment: guided tours available
ADMISSION £2
FACILITIES Parking; loos; plants for sale
FEATURES Herbaceous borders; planted by Gertrude Jekyll; lake; old roses and climbers
ENGLISH HERITAGE GRADE II

Ros Wallinger has restored this Jekyll garden over the last 10 years using the original planting plans. She has gone to great pains to recreate it exactly in all its Edwardian loveliness. Some of the roses were extinct here until reintroduced from private gardens in France and Italy after years of searching. There is no better place to study Gertrude Jekyll's plantings, but what makes it so special is that it is a 'young' garden again.

Mottisfont Abbey
Romsey, Hampshire SO51 0LJ
☎ 01794 41220

OWNER The National Trust
LOCATION 4 miles north west of Romsey
OPEN 12 noon – 6 pm (8.30 pm in June), Saturday – Wednesday (plus Thursday in June), 1 April to 31 October
ADMISSION £2.50 (but £3.50 in rose season)
FACILITIES Parking; loos; facilities for the disabled; plants for sale; good shop selling books and National Trust smellies; light refreshments
FEATURES Herbaceous borders; herbs; plants for plantsmen; old roses and climbers; plantings by Graham Thomas; biggest London plane tree *Platanus × acerifolia* in the British Isles
ENGLISH HERITAGE GRADE II
NCCPG NATIONAL COLLECTIONS *Platanus, Rosa,*

The park and gardens near the house are stately: Russell Page, Geoffrey Jellicoe and Norah Lindsay all worked here. But it is the old rose collection in the walled garden which has made Mottisfont's name. It is Graham Thomas's best-known work, a collection of all the roses he has discovered, assembled, preserved and made popular through his writings. They are surrounded by excellent herbaceous plantings: purple 'Zigeunerknabe' with yellow *Digitalis grandiflora*, for instance. Surely the best rose garden in Britain.

Sir Harold Hillier Gardens & Arboretum

Jermyns Lane, Ampfield, Romsey, Hampshire SO51 0QA
☎ 01794 368787   FAX 01794 368027
OWNER   Hampshire County Council
LOCATION   Signposted from A31 and A3057
OPEN   10.30 am – 5 pm, Monday – Friday, all year, except public holidays at Christmas and New Year. Plus 10.30 am – 6 pm or dusk on Saturdays and Sundays, from March to November
ADMISSION   March to November: Adults £4; Senior Citizens £3.50; Children £1. December to March: Adults £3; Senior Citizens £2.50; Children £1
FACILITIES   Parking; loos; facilities for the disabled; plants for sale; light refreshments from Easter to end of October, and most weekends
FEATURES   Good collection of trees; herbaceous borders; fine conifers; plants for plantsmen; old roses and climbers; interesting for children; particularly good in July-August; particularly interesting in winter; 1993 winner of Sandford Award; six record tree species
FRIENDS   Details of the Friends scheme are available from the Curator: benefits include trips to other gardens, coffee mornings and a quarterly newsletter
NCCPG NATIONAL COLLECTIONS *Quercus*, *Carpinus*, *Cornus*, *Cotoneaster*, *Ligustrum*, *Lithocarpus*, *Corylus*, *Photinia*, *Pinus*

Quite the most important modern arboretum in the UK, for the number of its taxa – over 11,000 in 160 acres and totalling 40,000 plants. Every part of the garden is an education and a pleasure whatever the season or weather. Exemplary labelling and helpful guidebooks available. Hilliers' nursery shares a car park with the arboretum. Guided walks are given on the first Sunday in each month, and on Wednesdays from May to October (see Calendar section).

Spinners

Boldre, Lymington, Hampshire SO4 5QE
☎ 01590 673347
OWNER   Diana and Peter Chappell
LOCATION   Signed off A337 between Brockenhurst and Lymington
OPEN   10 am – 5 pm, Tuesday – Saturday, all year
ADMISSION   £1.50
FACILITIES   Parking; loos; plants for sale
FEATURES   Good collection of trees; herbaceous borders; fine conifers; gravel or scree garden; plants for plantsmen; woodland garden; rhododendrons; woodland plants; rarities and novelties; biggest *Eucalyptus perriniana* in the British Isles

Only 2 acres, but what a garden! Spinners is a plantsman's paradise, where the enthusiast can spend many happy hours browsing at any time of the year.

Everything is well-labelled and Peter Chappell's nursery sells an extraordinary range of good plants: you always come away with a bootful of novelties.

Stratfield Saye House

Stratfield Saye, Reading, Hampshire RG7 2BT
☎ 01256 882882   FAX 01256 882345
OWNER   The Duke of Wellington
LOCATION   1 mile west of A33 between Reading and Basingstoke
OPEN   11.30 am – 6 pm, daily, except Friday, 1 May to 24 September
ADMISSION   House and garden: £4.50
FACILITIES   Parking; dogs permitted; loos; facilities for the disabled; gift shop; light refreshments
FEATURES   Herbaceous borders; fine conifers; lake; modern roses; old roses and climbers; camellia house in walled garden; American garden; tallest Hungarian oak *Quercus frainetto* in the British Isles
ENGLISH HERITAGE GRADE   II

Not a great garden, but there are some fine incidents: a huge kitchen garden, a large and cheerful rose garden, rhododendrons in the park, and magnificent trees, including wellingtonias, named after the Iron Duke.

Tudor House Garden

Tudor House, Bugle Street, Southampton, Hampshire SO1 0A8
☎ 01703 635904   FAX 01703 339601
OWNER   Southampton City Council
LOCATION   Bugle Street is just off the High Street in the old city
OPEN   10 am – 5 pm, Tuesday – Friday, 10 am – 4 pm, Saturdays, 2 – 5 pm, Sundays, all year
ADMISSION   Museum and garden: Adults £1.50; Children 75p
FACILITIES   Loos; facilities for the disabled
FEATURES   Herbaceous borders; herbs; good topiary; interesting for children

Sylvia Landsberg's unique reconstruction of a Tudor garden with a knot garden, fountain, secret garden and contemporary plantings of herbs and flowering plants all crammed into a tiny area. Some call it a pastiche, others a living dictionary of Tudor garden language.

White Windows

Longparish, Andover, Hampshire SP11 6PB
☎ 01264 720222
OWNER   Mr and Mrs B. Sterndale-Bennett
LOCATION   In village centre
OPEN   2 – 6 pm, by appointment from March to September on Wednesdays. Opens for NGS
ADMISSION   £1.50
FACILITIES   Plants for sale
FEATURES   Herbaceous borders; plants for plantsmen; old roses and climbers; young garden; *Euphorbia*; hellebores

One of the best small modern plantsman's gardens on chalk, remarkable for the way Jane Sterndale-Bennett uses her material. Leaves and stems are as important as flowers, especially in the combinations and contrasts of colour – gold and yellow, blue and silver, and crimsons, pinks and purples. Much use is made of evergreens and variegated plants. Perhaps the most luxuriant chalk garden in Hampshire.

HEREFORD & WORCESTER

Abbey Dore Court Garden
Abbey Dore, Hereford, Hereford & Worcester HR2 0AD
☎ 01981 240419   FAX 01981 240279
OWNER   Mrs Charis Ward
LOCATION   On A465 midway between Hereford and Abergavenny
OPEN   11 am – 6 pm, daily except Wednesdays, 4 March to 22 October. Other times by appointment to see hellebores
ADMISSION   Adults £1.75; Children 50p
FACILITIES   Parking; loos; facilities for the disabled; county gift gallery; teddy bears' loft; good nursery; licensed restaurant, coffee, lunches and teas; all food home-made
FEATURES   Herbaceous borders; fine conifers; plants for plantsmen; rock garden; handsome wellingtonias; ferns; hellebores; much new planting in 1994–5
NCCPG NATIONAL COLLECTIONS *Euphorbia, Sedum*

Plantsman's garden on a damp cold site, with fine borders leading down to the ferny river walk. Growing up, changing, expanding and improving every year: very exciting.

Arrow Cottage
Weobley, Hereford & Worcester HR4 8RN
☎ 01544 318468   FAX 01544 318468
OWNER   Jane and Lance Hattatt
LOCATION   1 mile from Weobley: off Wormsley road, signposted Ledgemoor, then second right, first house on left
OPEN   2 – 5 pm, Wednesday – Friday and Sundays, 1 April to 31 July and 1 to 30 September
ADMISSION   Adults £1.50
FACILITIES   Parking; loos; plants for sale
FEATURES   Herbaceous borders; plants for plantsmen; old roses and climbers; stream; new Gothic Garden

A young and expanding garden, or series of gardens, in modern style. Garden rooms create the space for different styles, but all are maintained to the highest standard. Much plantsmanship and artistry.

Burford House Gardens
Treasures of Tenbury, Tenbury Wells, Hereford & Worcester WR15 8HQ
☎ 01584 810777   FAX 01584 810673
OWNER   Treasures of Tenbury Ltd

LOCATION   A456 between Tenbury Wells and Ludlow
OPEN   10 am – 5 pm (dusk in winter), daily, all year
ADMISSION   Adults £1.95; Children 80p; Groups (25+) £1.60 (by prior arrangement)
FACILITIES   Parking; loos; facilities for the disabled; tea rooms (light lunches, afternoon teas), beverages
FEATURES   Herbaceous borders; fine conifers; plants for plantsmen; old roses and climbers; Rose 'Treasure Trove'
NCCPG NATIONAL COLLECTIONS *Clematis*

A glamorous 4-acre modern garden to complement a stylish Georgian house. The fluid design is enhanced by interesting plants, imaginatively used and comprehensively labelled. There are good roses and herbaceous borders, and a magnificent series of water gardens, but Burford means *Clematis* – 200 varieties – cleverly trained, grown and displayed among shrubs.

Eastgrove Cottage Garden & Nursery
Sankyns Green, Little Witley, Worcester, Hereford & Worcester WR6 6LQ
OWNER   Malcolm and Carol Skinner
LOCATION   On road between Great Witley and Shawley
OPEN   2 – 5 pm, Thursday – Monday, 1 April to 31 July. Also Thursday – Saturday, 1 September to 15 October
ADMISSION   Adults £1.50
FACILITIES   Parking; loos; attached to good small nursery
FEATURES   Good collection of trees; herbaceous borders; herbs; plants for plantsmen; old roses and climbers

A tiny cottage garden attached to a cottage garden nursery. The scale itself is small, but crammed in are herbs, dwarf conifers, a bog garden, a 'secret garden' and all the elements of modern plantsmanship.

Eastnor Castle
Eastnor, Ledbury, Hereford & Worcester
OWNER   Mr James and The Hon. Mrs Hervey-Bathurst
LOCATION   2 miles east of Ledbury
OPEN   12 noon – 5 pm, Sundays and Bank Holiday Mondays, 16 April to 30 September. Also daily except Saturdays in August
ADMISSION   Adults £1.75; Children £1
FACILITIES   Parking; dogs permitted; loos; access for the disabled; souvenirs and gift shop
FEATURES   Good collection of trees; fine conifers; lake; woodland garden; spring bulbs; tallest deodar *Cedrus deodara* (38 metres high) in the British Isles, plus 12 more record trees
ENGLISH HERITAGE GRADE   II*

Eastnor is all about trees. The arboretum planted by Lord Somers 150 years ago is now mature, and full of champion specimens. Many are rare. The conifers are particularly fine in early spring and complement the shaggy neo-Norman castle.

Hergest Croft
Kington, Hereford & Worcester HR5 3EG
☎ 01544 230160   FAX 01544 230160
OWNER   W. L. Banks
LOCATION   A44 on west side
OPEN   1.30 – 6.30 pm, daily, 14 April to 29 October
ADMISSION   Adults £2.50; Children (under 15) free; Groups (20+) £2
FACILITIES   Parking; dogs permitted; loos; plants for sale; home-made teas
FEATURES   Good collection of trees; herbaceous borders; fruit of special interest; old roses and climbers; rhododendrons; tallest *Cercidiphyllum japonicum* and *Davidia vilmoriniana* in the British Isles, among 22 record trees
ENGLISH HERITAGE GRADE   II*
NCCPG NATIONAL COLLECTIONS *Acer*, *Betula*, *Zelkova*

Wonderful woodland garden and arboretum around a whopping Edwardian house. There is no end to the garden's marvels: huge conifers, magnificent birches, scores of interesting oaks, many acres of billowing rhododendrons. Plus good herbaceous borders, alpine collections, autumn gentians and kitchen garden, all on a scale that most of us have forgotten.

How Caple Court
How Caple, Hereford, Hereford & Worcester HR1 4SX
☎ 01989 86626   FAX 01989 86611
OWNER   Mr and Mrs Peter Lee
LOCATION   Signposted on B4224 and A449 junction
OPEN   9.30 am – 5 pm, Monday – Saturday, May to October. Plus 10 am – 5 pm, Sundays, all year
ADMISSION   Adults £2.50; Children £1.25
FACILITIES   Parking; dogs permitted; loos; clothes shop; nursery; ice cream; soft drinks
FEATURES   Fine conifers; old roses and climbers; garden sculpture; good topiary; woodland garden; Italian terraces
FRIENDS   New Friends Association: ask for details

Spectacular formal gardens laid out at the turn of the century (some Italianate, others more Arts and Crafts), and now undergoing restoration. Pergolas, loggias, dramatic terraces and *giardini segreti*, with stunning views across a lushly wooded valley. How Caple is a garden of national importance, unjustly ignored by English Heritage and little-known even locally.

Lakeside
Gaines Road, Whitbourne, Worcester, Hereford & Worcester WR6 5RD
OWNER   Chris Philip and Denys Gueroult
LOCATION   9 miles west of Worcester off A44, at county boundary sign
OPEN   2 – 6 pm, 23 April, 14 May, 18 June

ADMISSION   Adults £1.50; Children free
FACILITIES   Parking; loos; plants for sale; teas
FEATURES   Herbaceous borders; lake; plants for plantsmen; old roses and climbers; woodland garden; young garden; ferns; hollies; heathers

6 acres of dramatic planting by the editor of *The Plant Finder*. Good plants, used well: a garden from which to learn.

Overbury Court
Overbury, Tewkesbury, Hereford & Worcester
OWNER   Mr and Mrs Bruce Bossom
LOCATION   5 miles north east of Tewkesbury
OPEN   2 – 6 pm, 26 March
ADMISSION   Adults £1.50
FACILITIES   Parking; dogs permitted; access for the disabled; plants for sale; home-made teas in village hall
FEATURES   Good topiary; landscaped park; daffodils
ENGLISH HERITAGE GRADE   II*

A peaceful and expansive garden laid out around the large, handsome Georgian house, with a view of the parish church worked in. Geoffrey Jellicoe, Aubrey Waterfield and Russell Page all contributed to the design and planting and the result is a garden of exceptional harmony.

Queen's Wood Arboretum & Country Park
Dinmore Hill, Leominster, Hereford & Worcester HR6 0PY
☎ 0156884 7052   FAX 0156884 305
OWNER   Hereford & Worcester County Council
LOCATION   Midway between Leominster and Hereford on A49
OPEN   9 am – dusk, daily, all year
ADMISSION   Free
FACILITIES   Parking; dogs permitted; loos; facilities for the disabled; gift shop; light meals from 9 am – 5 pm
FEATURES   Bluebells; fine conifers; woodland garden; interesting for children; wood anemones

A vigorous young arboretum, planted over the last 40 years with public amenity in mind. Wonderful for walking, whatever the season, and well run in a friendly, efficient manner so that visitors get the most from it.

Spetchley Park
Worcester, Hereford & Worcester WR5 1RS
☎ 01905 345224
OWNER   R. J. Berkeley
LOCATION   2 miles east of Worcester on A422
OPEN   11 am – 5 pm, Tuesday – Friday, plus Sundays and Bank Holiday Mondays, 1 April to 30 September
ADMISSION   Adults £2.20; Children £1.10
FACILITIES   Parking; loos; access for the disabled; teas and refreshments
FEATURES   Good collection of trees; herbaceous borders; daffodils; lake; plants for plantsmen; rhododen-

drons and azaleas; modern roses; old roses and climbers; particularly good in July-August; deer park
ENGLISH HERITAGE GRADE   II*

In a classic English landscaped park, three generations of Berkeleys have created one of the best plantsman's gardens in the Midlands. Ellen Willmott was the owner's great-aunt and many of the most exciting trees and shrubs date from her time. The planting continues: this garden offers something to everyone.

Stone House Cottage Garden
Stone, Kidderminster, Hereford & Worcester DY10 4BG
☎ 01562 69902   FAX 01562 69902
OWNER   Mr and Mrs James Arbuthnott
LOCATION   In Stone village, 2 miles from Kidderminster on A448
OPEN   10 am – 6 pm, Wednesday – Saturday, 1 March to 31 October. Opens for the NGS
ADMISSION   Adults: £1.50 (1994)
FACILITIES   Parking; loos; access for the disabled; excellent nursery attached
FEATURES   Alpines; herbaceous borders; herbs; plants for plantsmen; climbing roses; old roses; young garden; particularly good in July-August; unusual climbing plants

The garden of a famous nursery, which it matches for the range of beautiful and unusual plants it offers. Exquisite plantings, and an eccentric collection of follies built as towers in the garden walls. Bliss.

Whitfield
Allensmore, Hereford & Worcester HR2 9BA
☎ 0198 121202
OWNER   G. M. Clive
LOCATION   8 miles south west of Hereford on A465
OPEN   2 – 6 pm, 4 June or parties by appointment
ADMISSION   Adults £1.50; Children 50p
FACILITIES   Parking; dogs permitted; loos; access for the disabled; teas on 4 June
FEATURES   Good collection of trees; fine conifers; good topiary; huge grove of redwoods; tallest dwarf alder *Alnus nitida* and durmast oak *Quercus petraea* in the British Isles
ENGLISH HERITAGE GRADE   II

Whitfield has magnificent trees, planted by the Clives over the last 200 years. *Zelkova serrata*, a weeping oak, and a ginkgo planted in 1778 are some of the highlights, but there is nothing to beat the grove of 20 or so *Sequoia sempervirens* now pushing 150 feet in height.

HERTFORDSHIRE

The Beale Arboretum
West Lodge Park, Cockfosters Road, Hadley Wood, Barnet, Hertfordshire EN4 0PY
☎ 0181 440 8211   FAX 0181 449 3698
OWNER   Edward Beale CBE

LOCATION   A111 halfway between M25, J24 and Cockfosters station
OPEN   2 – 5 pm, Wednesdays, 1 April to 31 October. Plus 2 – 5.30 pm, 4 June; 12 noon – 4 pm, 22 October
ADMISSION   £1.50
FACILITIES   Parking; dogs permitted; loos; facilities for the disabled; refreshments
FEATURES   Good collection of trees; fine conifers; lake; woodland garden; trees, trees, trees; 300-year-old specimen of *Arbutus unedo*; new head gardener (1995)
NCCPG NATIONAL COLLECTIONS   *Carpinus betulus*

10 acres of young arboretum, begun 25 years ago and shortly to double in size. Among the older specimens – Victorian cedars and redwoods – is a fine collection of trees planted with a view to the overall effect and underplanted with rhododendrons. Little known as yet, but undoubtedly to be reckoned among the great late 20th-century gardens.

Benington Lordship
Benington, Stevenage, Hertfordshire SG2 7BS
☎ 01438 869668
OWNER   C. H. A. Bott
LOCATION   Off A602, Stevenage – Hertford
OPEN   12 noon – 5 pm, Wednesdays, April to September; 2 – 5 pm, Sundays, April to August
ADMISSION   Adults £2.50; Season ticket £7
FACILITIES   Parking; loos; plants for sale; teas
FEATURES   Herbaceous borders; rock garden; modern roses; old roses and climbers; heather garden; cowslip bank; lots of new plantings (1994-95)
ENGLISH HERITAGE GRADE   II

A Georgian house with the ruins of a Norman castle in the grounds. All has been charmingly replanted in recent years without destroying the older features: a Pulhamite folly, an Edwardian rock garden, and a sense of spacious parkland.

The Gardens of the Rose
Chiswell Green, St Albans, Hertfordshire AL2 3NR
☎ 01727 850461   FAX 01727 850360
OWNER   The Royal National Rose Society
LOCATION   1 mile from junction of M1 and M25
OPEN   9 am – 5 pm (10 am – 6 pm on Sundays and Bank Holidays), daily, 10 June to 15 October
ADMISSION   Adults £4; Groups £3.50; Disabled £3; Members and Children free
FACILITIES   Parking; dogs permitted; loos; facilities for the disabled; plants for sale; shop with rose books and souvenirs; licensed cafeteria
FEATURES   Modern roses; old roses and climbers; particularly good in July-August; first new garden planted (1995) as part of *Rose 2000*

The most comprehensive rose garden in Britain, with a 1960s design which emphasises modern roses but also has excellent collections of old roses, shrub roses, climbers, ramblers, miniatures, ground cover and wild species of rose. 30,000 rose bushes and 1,750 varieties, plus a further 600 unnamed novelties in the trial grounds. There are plans to expand into the fields around the garden over the next few years, if funds are available.

Hatfield House
Hatfield, Hertfordshire AL9 5NQ
☎ 01707 262823   FAX 01707 275719
OWNER   The Marquess of Salisbury
LOCATION   Off A1(M), J4
OPEN   West gardens: 11 am – 6 pm, daily except Good Friday; East gardens: 2 – 5 pm, Mondays only
ADMISSION   Park and garden: Adults £2.80; Senior Citizens £2.50; Children £2.10
FACILITIES   Parking; loos; facilities for the disabled; plants for sale; souvenirs and gift shop; licensed restaurant, coffee shop, snacks and hot lunches
FEATURES   Herbaceous borders; herbs; good topiary; knot gardens; physic garden
ENGLISH HERITAGE GRADE   I

Interesting old/new gardens to suit a historic stately home. An 1890s parterre, very pretty, is the main feature. The new knot garden has plants dating from the 17th century (Lady Salisbury is a stalwart of the Tradescant Trust), but there are *allées, rondpoints*, more knots and parterres: the complete design vocabulary for how-to-Tudorise your garden.

Hill House
Stanstead Abbots, Ware, Hertfordshire SG12 8BX
☎ 01920 870013
OWNER   Mr and Mrs Ronald Pilkington
LOCATION   Between Harlow and Ware
OPEN   2 – 5 pm, 7 May, 4 and 11 June, 16 July
ADMISSION   Adults £2; Children 50p
FACILITIES   Parking; dogs permitted; loos; plants for sale; jewellery and art exhibition in June; home-made teas
FEATURES   Herbaceous borders; glasshouses and conservatories to visit; lake; woodland garden

Outstanding plantings in the old kitchen garden include colour borders of purple and gold, weeping pears, and vegetables all as neat as imaginable. Pretty woodland garden and lush growth around the small lake.

Knebworth House
Knebworth, Stevenage, Hertfordshire SG3 6PY
☎ 01438 812661   FAX 01438 811908
OWNER   Lord Cobbold
LOCATION   Off A1(M), J7
OPEN   12 noon – 5 pm, Tuesday – Sunday, 1 and 2 April, 8 to 23 April, 27 May to 29 June, 4 July to 4 September; plus weekends and Bank Holidays, 29 April to 21 May, and weekends only 9 September to 1 October
ADMISSION   Adults £4.50; Children and Senior Citizens £4 (1994)
FACILITIES   Parking; loos; licensed cafeteria
FEATURES   Herbaceous borders; herbs; planted by Gertrude Jekyll; designed by Lutyens; modern roses;

dogs' cemetery; sunken lawn; gold garden; wilderness; newly replanted Victorian maze (1994)
ENGLISH HERITAGE GRADE   II*
FRIENDS   Knebworth House Education and Preservation Trust – details from the Secretary c/o Knebworth House

Most of the garden was laid out by Lutyens, who married a daughter of the house. It has been well restored over the last 15 years with Jekyll plantings where appropriate. Inventive and harmonious, few gardens make such good use of space and perspective.

St Paul's Walden Bury
Whitwell, Hitchin, Hertfordshire SG4 8BP
☎ 01438 871218   FAX 01438 871229
OWNER   St Paul's Walden Bury Estate Co.
LOCATION   B651, 5 miles south of Hitchin
OPEN   For NGS: see Yellow Book
ADMISSION   Adults £2 (1994)
FACILITIES   Parking; dogs permitted; loos; facilities for the disabled; plants for sale; teas and home-made cakes
FEATURES   Follies and garden buildings; garden sculpture; woodland garden; formal French landscape
ENGLISH HERITAGE GRADE   I

Highly important as a unique example of the French 18th-century style – 3 hedged *allées* lead off into the woodland towards temples, statues and pools. The present owner's father (the Queen Mother's brother) was a past President of the RHS, and was able to blend rhododendrons, azaleas, maples and magnolias (plus much more besides) into parts of the woodland. A garden that appeals to historian, plantsman and artist equally.

HUMBERSIDE

Burnby Hall Gardens
Pocklington, Humberside YO4 2QF
☎ 01759 302068
OWNER   Stewarts Trust
LOCATION   On B1247, 13 miles east of York
OPEN   10 am – 6 pm, daily, 8 April to 8 October
ADMISSION   Adults £2; Senior Citizens £1.50; Children 75p
FACILITIES   Parking; loos; facilities for the disabled; plants for sale; snacks and salads, home-made cakes
FEATURES   Herbaceous borders; fine conifers; lake; rock garden; museum; winner of *Age Concern* award; fortnightly band concerts
NCCPG NATIONAL COLLECTIONS *Nymphaea*

Famed for its water lilies, planted by Frances Perry in the 1930s, but there is much more to Burnby Hall. A rock garden, cheerful modern rose garden and good collection of conifers all contribute to its visitor-friendly style.

Burton Constable Hall

Burton Constable Hall, Hull, Humberside HU11 4LN
☎ 01964 562400   FAX 01964 563229
OWNER   Burton Constable Foundation
LOCATION   Via Hull B1238 to Sproatley, follow HH signs
OPEN   12 noon – 5 pm, Sunday – Thursday, Easter Sunday to 30 September. Plus Saturdays in July and August
ADMISSION   Adults £3.50
FACILITIES   Parking; dogs permitted; loos; facilities for the disabled; shop; light snacks
FEATURES   Herbaceous borders; landscape designed by Capability Brown; lake; woodland garden; interesting for children; fine 18th-century orangery
ENGLISH HERITAGE GRADE   II
FRIENDS   Details from The Secretary, Friends of Burton Constable, Burton Constable, Hull HU11 4LN
Essentially a Capability Brown landscape (his original plans are still shown), but the 19th-century pleasure gardens are being restored and the whole estate will undoubtedly develop excitingly in the future.

Sledmere House

Sledmere, Driffield, Humberside YO25 0XG
☎ 01377 236637   FAX 01377 236560
OWNER   Sir Tatton Sykes
LOCATION   Off A166 between York and Bridlington
OPEN   12 noon – 5 pm, daily except Mondays and Fridays, Easter to 30 September (1994 times and dates)
ADMISSION   Adults £1.50; Senior Citizens and Children £1 (1994)
FACILITIES   Parking; dogs permitted; loos; facilities for the disabled; craft and gift shop; tea terrace and cafeteria
FEATURES   Landscape designed by Capability Brown; fine conifers; modern roses; old roses and climbers; deer park
ENGLISH HERITAGE GRADE   I
Sledmere has a classical Capability Brown landscape: his originals plans can be seen in the library. An Italianate formal garden was added in 1911, with Greek and Roman busts swathed in climbing roses. A new knot garden has been added recently and is growing up quickly. Definitely a garden on the up.

ISLE OF WIGHT

Barton Manor Gardens & Vineyards

Whippingham, East Cowes, Isle of Wight PO32 6LB
☎ 01983 292835   FAX 01983 293923
OWNER   R. Stigwood
LOCATION   Next to Osborne House on East Cowes Road (A3021)
OPEN   10.30 am – 5.30 pm, daily, 1 April to 8 October
ADMISSION   Adults £3.50; Senior Citizens and Parties £3; Children free (1 per adult)
FACILITIES   Parking; loos; facilities for the disabled; gift shop with Barton Manor wines; cafeteria
FEATURES   Herbaceous borders; lake; modern roses; woodland garden; rhododendrons; royal connections; new rose maze (1993); new tree-carving of Dionysius (1994)
NCCPG NATIONAL COLLECTIONS   *Kniphofia, Scilla*
Laid out by Prince Albert, Barton was for many years part of the Osborne estate. He planted some of the best trees, including the cork plantation near the house. Now Barton is run as a commercial vineyard and the gardens are being expanded both for private enjoyment and as a commercial resource.

Mottistone Manor

Newport, Isle of Wight
☎ 01983 740552
OWNER   The National Trust
LOCATION   On B3399 west of Brighstone
OPEN   2 – 5 pm, Wednesdays and Bank Holiday Mondays, 5 April to 27 September
ADMISSION   £1.80
FACILITIES   Parking; dogs permitted; plants for sale
FEATURES   Herbaceous borders; fine conifers; fruit of special interest; modern roses; bluebells; irises
A cleverly designed modern garden on a difficult site – steep and narrow. Much has been terraced and enclosed to allow a rose garden and good herbaceous borders. Most of the rest is given to a wide variety of fruit trees, trained to make avenues and underplanted with vegetables or spring bulbs. A model for this type of planting, and made long before the current fashion for ornamental *potagers*.

North Court

Shorwell, Isle of Wight PO30 3JG
☎ 01983 740415   FAX 01983 740415
OWNER   Mr and Mrs John Harrison
LOCATION   4 miles south west of Newport, off B3323
OPEN   2.30 – 5 pm, Wednesdays, May and June; plus certain Sundays (to be announced), or by appointment
ADMISSION   £1.50
FACILITIES   Parking; dogs permitted; access for the disabled; plants for sale
FEATURES   Herbaceous borders; fruit of special interest; planted by Gertrude Jekyll; lake; plants for plantsmen; modern roses; old roses and climbers; subtropical plants; woodland garden; large plane trees
The Harrison family which owns North Court inherited fine grounds with some magnificent trees and a clear stream at the bottom. John Harrison has extensively replanted it with a plantsman's enthusiasm and a special interest in tender exotica. Definitely a garden to watch in future.

Nunwell House

Brading, Ryde, Isle of Wight PO36 OJQ
☎ 01983 407240
OWNER   Colonel and Mrs J. A. Aylmer
LOCATION   Signed off A3055, 1 mile to the west of Brading

OPEN 10 am – 5 pm, Sunday – Wednesday, 2 July to 27 September
ADMISSION House and garden: Adults £2.80; Senior Citizens £2.30; Children (under 12) 60p
FACILITIES Parking; loos; tea, coffee and biscuits
FEATURES Good collection of trees; ecological interest; herbs; plants for plantsmen; modern roses; garden sculpture; obelisks
ENGLISH HERITAGE GRADE II

A pretty garden, largely replanted by Vernon Russell-Smith about 30 years ago: he also planted a small arboretum. The present owners have added some highly attractive garden ornaments and are restoring the fabric and the plantings after some years of neglect. The work continues: last year they dug up 450 yards of old *Lonicera* hedging!

Owl Cottage
Hoxall Lane, Mottistone, Newport, Isle of Wight PO30 4EE
☎ 01983 740433

OWNER Mrs A. L. Hutchinson
LOCATION Down Hoxall Lane, opposite Mottistone Manor
OPEN 2.30 – 5.30 pm, by appointment, groups only
ADMISSION £1.50
FACILITIES Dogs permitted; access for the disabled
FEATURES Herbaceous borders; plants for plantsmen; modern roses; old roses and climbers

A cottage garden, made entirely by the present owner, and remarkable for the range of colour and variety at all seasons, though it is open only in summer. The best plantsman's garden on the Isle of Wight.

Ventnor Botanic Garden
Undercliff Drive, Ventnor, Isle of Wight PO38 1UL
☎ 01983 855397

OWNER South Wight Borough Council
LOCATION 1½ miles west of Ventnor on A3055
OPEN Dawn – dusk, daily, all year
ADMISSION Garden: free; Show house: 50p. Parking charges
FACILITIES Parking; dogs permitted; loos; facilities for the disabled; cafeteria and bar with snacks, tea coffee, lunches
FEATURES Herbaceous borders; fine conifers; glasshouses and conservatories to visit; herbs; plants for plantsmen; subtropical plants; interesting for children; particularly interesting in winter; palms; olives; bananas; medicinal herbs from all over the world; tallest *Peumus boldus* in UK; largest collection of New Zealand plants in UK
NCCPG NATIONAL COLLECTIONS *Pseudopanax, Coprosma*
FRIENDS Friends of Ventnor Botanic Garden (01983 855397), includes seed list

Originally an offshoot of Hillier's Nursery, the Ventnor Botanic Garden is devoted to exotic plants. Many – perhaps most – are from the southern hemisphere but flourish in the unique microclimate of the 'Undercliff': *Widdringtonia* from Zimbabwe and Tasmanian *Olearia*, for instance. Almost destroyed by the gales of 1987 and 1990, the collection is rapidly coming together again. The young head gardener has a wonderful eye for planting.

KENT

Bedgebury National Pinetum
Goudhurst, Cranbrook, Kent TN17 2SL
☎ 01580 211044   FAX 01580 212423

OWNER Forestry Commission
LOCATION 1 mile east of A21 at Flimwell on B2079
OPEN 10 am – dusk, daily, all year
ADMISSION Adults £1.50; Senior Citizens £1; Children 75p
FACILITIES Parking; dogs permitted; loos; plants for sale; drinks and snacks
FEATURES Fine conifers; lake; woodland garden; particularly interesting in winter; rhododendrons; fungi; tallest *Quercus libani* in UK, plus 5 record conifer species
ENGLISH HERITAGE GRADE II*
FRIENDS Details from the Curator
NCCPG NATIONAL COLLECTIONS *Taxus, Juniperus, Chamaecyparis lawsoniana*

Take any of the trails through this magnificent woodland garden, or go to the excellent Visitors' Centre to see the cone collection, and the new exhibit which tells the story of the Great Storm of 1987. It is difficult to realise that all the plantings are less than 70 years old.

Belmont Park
Belmont, Throwley, Faversham, Kent ME13 0HH
☎ 01795 890202

OWNER The Harris (Belmont) Charity
LOCATION Signposted from A251 at Badlesmere
OPEN 2 – 5 pm, Saturdays, Sundays and Bank Holiday Mondays, Easter Sunday to September
ADMISSION Adults £2; Children 75p
FACILITIES Parking; dogs permitted; loos; facilities for the disabled; plants for sale; teas
FEATURES Good collection of trees; fine conifers; follies and garden buildings; rock garden; shell grotto; rhododendrons; pets' cemetery; pinetum
ENGLISH HERITAGE GRADE II

Quiet parkland surrounds this handsome Samuel Wyatt house, while the pleasure gardens are so obviously for the pleasure of the owners, not for display, that they add considerably to the sense of domesticity. There is nothing spectacular or vulgar about Belmont.

Brogdale
Brogdale Road, Faversham, Kent ME13 8XZ
☎ 01795 535286

OWNER Brogdale Horticultural Trust

304 Gardens KENT

LOCATION 1 mile south west of Faversham
OPEN 10 am – 5 pm, Wednesday – Sunday and Bank Holiday Mondays, Easter to Christmas
FACILITIES Parking; loos; access for the disabled; plants for sale
FEATURES Fruit of special interest; interesting for children

Over 2,000 apple varieties (four times as many as the RHS Gardens at Wisley) and the National Collections of pears, plums and bush fruits, make Brogdale a centre of abiding interest. There are demonstrations, exhibitions, workshops and events throughout the year. Fruit from the collections is sold, and scion wood supplied.

Chartwell
Westerham, Kent TN16 1PS
☎ 01732 866368
OWNER The National Trust
LOCATION A25 to Westerham then signposted from B2026
OPEN 11 am – 5.30 pm, Tuesday – Thursday, 11 am – 5.30 pm, Saturdays, Sundays and Bank Holiday Mondays (closed Tuesday after Bank Holiday Monday), April to October
ADMISSION Adults £2; Children £1
FACILITIES Parking; dogs permitted; loos; facilities for the disabled; National Trust shop; restaurant
FEATURES Lake; rock garden; old roses and climbers
ENGLISH HERITAGE GRADE II*

Chartwell trades on its association with Sir Winston Churchill and offers little to the keen plantsman. However, there is a rose garden planted with the variety 'Winston Churchill' and a deep sense of history throughout.

Crittenden House
Crittenden Road, Matfield, Tonbridge, Kent TN12 7EN
☎ 01892 832554
OWNER B. P. Tompsett
LOCATION 2 miles north of Pembury
OPEN 2 – 6 pm, 2, 16, 17 and 30 April, 14 and 28 May
ADMISSION Adults £2; Children 25p
FACILITIES Parking; loos
FEATURES Herbaceous borders; lake; plants for plantsmen; modern roses; old roses and climbers; *Malus* 'Crittenden'

Plantsman's garden built up by the owner over the last 40 years and still intensifying. Island beds surrounded by grass give an informal structure and there are 3 ponds, each planted differently. Fascinating plants everywhere – many given by famous gardeners and collectors, some collected by Ben Tompsett himself.

Emmetts Garden
Ide Hill, Sevenoaks, Kent TN14 6AY
☎ 01732 750367/750429
OWNER The National Trust
LOCATION Between Sundridge and Ide Hill off B2042

OPEN 1 – 6 pm (last ticket 5 pm), Wednesdays, Sundays and Bank Holiday Mondays, 1 April to 31 October
ADMISSION Adults £2.50; Children £1.30; Pre-booked groups £2
FACILITIES Parking; dogs permitted; loos; tea room 2 – 5 pm (may close in bad weather)
FEATURES Rock garden; modern roses; old roses and climbers; Italianate rose garden; rare trees and shrubs
ENGLISH HERITAGE GRADE II

Boasts 'highest tree top in Kent'. 5 acres of Edwardian opulence, whose formal Italianate rose garden is surrounded by an informal woodland garden laid out with trees and shrubs in the William Robinson style. Fabulous views across the Weald of Kent. Picnic area.

Godington Park
Ashford, Kent TN23 3BW
☎ 01233 620773
OWNER The Godington House Preservation Trust
LOCATION Godington Lane, Potters Corner (A20)
OPEN 2 – 5 pm or by appointment; Sundays and Bank Holidays, 1 June to 30 September. Also Easter Saturday to Monday (1994 times and dates)
ADMISSION 70p (1994)
FACILITIES Parking; loos
FEATURES Lake; modern roses; garden sculpture; good topiary; formal Italianate garden; water lilies
ENGLISH HERITAGE GRADE I

Godington is perhaps the prettiest house in Kent. A Jacobean mansion reworked in the early 1900s by Sir Reginald Blomfield, who made the charming Italian garden (statues, loggia, summerhouse). Add in the 18th-century park and late 19th-century plantings, and you have a garden of great charm and authenticity.

Goodnestone Park
Wingham, Canterbury, Kent CT3 1PL
☎ 01304 840107
OWNER Lord and Lady FitzWalter
LOCATION Follow brown tourist signs from B2046
OPEN 11 am – 5 pm, weekdays, 27 March to 27 October. 12 noon – 6 pm, Sundays, 3 April to 15 October
ADMISSION Adults £2; Senior Citizens £1.80; Children (under 12) free; Disabled in wheelchairs £1; Group (20+) £1.80; Guided Group £2.20
FACILITIES Parking; loos; facilities for the disabled; plants for sale; teas 22 May – 28 August, Wednesdays and Sundays only
FEATURES Herbaceous borders; rock garden; old roses and climbers; woodland garden; cedar walk; rhododendrons
ENGLISH HERITAGE GRADE II*

A handsome Palladian house associated with Jane Austen (her brother married a daughter of the house). Fine parkland, a formal garden in front of the house, a 1930s woodland garden (maples, camellias, azaleas) undergoing modern expansion, and good mixed plantings in the old kitchen garden.

Great Comp
St Mary's Platt, Borough Green, Sevenoaks, Kent TN15 8QS
☎ 01732 886154

OWNER Great Comp Charitable Trust
LOCATION 2 miles east of Borough Green, B2016 off A20
OPEN 11 am – 6 pm, daily, 1 March to 31 October
ADMISSION Adults £2.50; Children £1
FACILITIES Parking; loos; facilities for the disabled; plants for sale; gifts and souvenirs; tea room
FEATURES Herbaceous borders; follies and garden buildings; lake; plants for plantsmen; garden sculpture; woodland garden; ground cover; dwarf conifers; new walled garden (1994)
FRIENDS Great Comp Society, mainly to support the annual music festival in July and September

Great Comp is a controversial garden. Everyone admires the energy of its founder Roderick Cameron, and Clay Jones called it the best garden he had ever seen. Others consider the reliance on heathers, dwarf conifers and ground cover to be tedious, the modern follies hideous, and the meandering design plain boring. But go with an open mind and you will find much to admire.

Hever Castle
Edenbridge, Kent TN8 7NG
☎ 01732 865224   FAX 01732 866796

OWNER Broadland Properties Ltd
LOCATION Near Edenbridge, difficult to find – use a good road map
OPEN 11 am – 5 pm, daily, 14 March to 5 November
ADMISSION Adults £4.30; Senior Citizens £3.80; Children (5–16) £2.50; Family £11.10
FACILITIES Parking; dogs permitted; loos; facilities for the disabled; plant centre; shop; two restaurants
FEATURES Bluebells; herbaceous borders; camellias; fine conifers; follies and garden buildings; lake; rhododendrons and azaleas; modern roses; old roses and climbers; garden sculpture; good topiary; woodland garden; particularly good in July-August; new Tudor herb garden (1995)
ENGLISH HERITAGE GRADE I

One of the most important Edwardian gardens in England. The pretty moated castle sits in a park of oaks and firs (underplanted with rhododendrons) with a maze and formal neo-Tudor garden to one side. The best part is a spectacular Italian garden where a long pergola (cool dripping fountains all along) leads past a series of exquisite Italian gardens, stuffed with sculptures, urns, sarcophagi and other loot brought by William Waldorf Astor from Rome; it finally bursts on to a theatrical terrace and a 35-acre lake, hand-dug by 800 workmen.

Ladham House
Goudhurst, Kent TN17 1DB
☎ 01580 211203

OWNER Betty, Lady Jessel
LOCATION Left at Chequers Inn on Cranbrook road, then right to Curtisden Green
OPEN 11 am – 6 pm, 16 April, 28 May and 9 July. Also by appointment
ADMISSION Adults £2 (£2.50 for private visits); Children (under 12) 50p
FACILITIES Parking; dogs permitted; loos; teas
FEATURES Good collection of trees; herbaceous borders; lake; woodland garden; magnolias

Laid out by a botanist Master of the Rolls in the mid-19th century, and enthusiastically restored and updated by the present owner. Many new plantings and some fine specimens, especially a deep red form of *Magnolia campbellii* which has been named 'Betty Jessel'.

Leeds Castle
Maidstone, Kent ME17 1PL
☎ 01622 765400   FAX 01622 735616

OWNER Leeds Castle Foundation
LOCATION Junction 8 off the M20
OPEN 10 am – 5 pm, 1 March to 31 October (closing early on 24 June and 1 July), 10 am – 3 pm, 1 November to 28 February (closing early on 4 November and closed on 25 December)
ADMISSION Park and gardens: Adults £5.50; Students £4.50; Children £3.30; Disabled Adults £3; Disabled Children £2.50
FACILITIES Parking; loos; facilities for the disabled; plants for sale; shop in Castle greenhouse; refreshments in the 17th-century tithe barn
FEATURES Herbaceous borders; herbs; lake; designed by Page; old roses and climbers; woodland garden; interesting for children; new maze disappears into an underground grotto!
ENGLISH HERITAGE GRADE II*
NCCPG NATIONAL COLLECTIONS *Monarda, Nepeta*

More a romantic castle than a garden, best seen across the lake, Leeds is run by a high-profile charitable trust with a big advertising budget. The results are admirable, though the 'Culpeper Garden' is not one of Russell Page's best plantings.

Long Barn
Long Barn Road, Weald, Sevenoaks, Kent TN14 6NH
☎ 01732 463714

OWNER Mr and Mrs Brandon Gough
LOCATION 3 miles south of Sevenoaks; end of village
OPEN 2 – 5 pm, 18 June, 23 July
ADMISSION Adults £2; Senior Citizens £1; Children 50p
FACILITIES Parking; loos

FEATURES Fruit of special interest; herbs; modern roses; old roses and climbers; rhododendron glade; pergola; parterres; secret garden; white garden
ENGLISH HERITAGE GRADE II*

Chiefly of interest for its association with Harold Nicolson and Vita Sackville-West, and well-restored to their period by the present owners. The strong designs and exuberant plantings of Sissinghurst are all here in their infancy.

Northbourne Court
Northbourne, Deal, Kent CT14 OLW
☎ 01304 611281   FAX 01304 614512

OWNER The Hon. Charles James
LOCATION Just beyond the village centre
OPEN 2 – 6 pm, Sundays, 1 June to 31 August
ADMISSION Adults £2.50; Children and Senior Citizens £1.50
FACILITIES Parking; loos; plants for sale; occasional teas
FEATURES Herbaceous borders; glasshouses and conservatories to visit; good topiary
ENGLISH HERITAGE GRADE II*

A series of smallish flower gardens, each intensely planted with cottagey perennials and, for the most part, arranged by the artist Aubrey Waterfield. Wonderful combinations of colours and shades.

Penshurst Place
Penshurst, Tonbridge, Kent TN11 8DG
☎ 01892 870307   FAX 01892 870866

OWNER Viscount De L'Isle
LOCATION Follow brown tourist signs from Tonbridge
OPEN 11 am – 6 pm, Saturdays and Sundays, March and October; all week, 1 April to 30 September
ADMISSION House and gardens: Adults £4.95; Senior Citizens £4.50; Children £2.75; Family £13. Gardens only: Adult £3.50; Senior Citizens £3; Children £2.25; Guided tours for groups (20+) £5.95. Garden season ticket £7
FACILITIES Parking; loos; access for the disabled; dried flowers for sale; self-service restaurant
FEATURES Herbaceous borders; daffodils; lake; pond; designed by Roper; climbing roses; modern roses; formal Italian garden; spring bulbs; new plant centre (1995)
ENGLISH HERITAGE GRADE I

A garden with substantial genuine Tudor remains, but well restored and developed in recent years. A vast Italianate parterre dominates the immediate pleasure garden: it is planted with scarlet polyantha roses – another is planted as a Union Jack. There are borders by Lanning Roper and John Codrington, a 100-yard bed of paeonies, a new lake, and a brand new garden for the blind, straight off the peg at from the Chelsea Flower Show.

Port Lympne Gardens
Lympne, Hythe, Kent CT21 4PD
☎ 01303 264647   FAX 01303 264944

OWNER John Aspinall
LOCATION Junction 11 off M20, follow sign to Lympne
OPEN 10 am – 5 pm, daily, all year
ADMISSION Adults £6.50; Senior Citizens and Children £4.50 (1994)
FACILITIES Parking; loos; facilities for the disabled; plants for sale; souvenirs and some garden sundries; bar, restaurant, café
FEATURES Herbaceous borders; follies and garden buildings; designed by Page; garden sculpture; good topiary; interesting for children; particularly interesting in winter; dahlias; bedding out; clock garden; best known for its zoo
ENGLISH HERITAGE GRADE II*

More than a zoo, Port Lympne is a stylish and luxurious house, and its garden, on the steepest of slopes high above Romney Marshes, is both dramatic and well-designed. The long, long marble staircase, chessboard garden and dahlia terraces are unique.

Riverhill House Gardens
Sevenoaks, Kent TN15 0RR
☎ 01732 458802

OWNER The Rogers family
LOCATION 2 miles south of Sevenoaks on A225
OPEN 12 noon – 6 pm, Sunday and Bank Holiday weekends, 1 April to 30 June
ADMISSION Adults £2; Children 50p
FACILITIES Parking; loos; small gift shop; home-made teas
FEATURES Bluebells; fine conifers; rhododendrons and azaleas; modern roses
ENGLISH HERITAGE GRADE II

Riverhill is a handsome Queen Anne house with grand views on a stately hillside, surrounded by billowing rhododendrons.

Scotney Castle
Lamberhurst, Tunbridge Wells, Kent TN3 8JN
☎ 01892 890651   FAX 01892 890110

OWNER The National Trust
LOCATION On A21
OPEN 11 am – 6 pm (but 2 – 6 pm on Saturdays and Sundays), Wednesday – Friday, 2 April to 31 October. Plus 12 noon – 6 pm on Bank Holiday Sundays and Mondays
ADMISSION Adults £3.20; Children £1.60 (1994)
FACILITIES Parking; loos; facilities for the disabled; shop
FEATURES Herbs; lake; plants for plantsmen; designed by Roper; woodland garden; rhododendrons; azaleas; water lilies; wisteria; ruins of 14th-century castle
ENGLISH HERITAGE GRADE I

Moated and abandoned castle surrounded by rhododendrons and azaleas: very romantic and very photogenic. Among the ruins are a herb garden and cottage garden, surprisingly appropriate and effective. Lanning Roper had a hand in it.

Sissinghurst Castle Garden
Sissinghurst, Cranbrook, Kent TN17 2AB
☎ 01580 715330/712850 [FAX] 01580 713911

OWNER The National Trust
LOCATION 1 mile east of Sissinghurst village, ½ a mile off A262. Cross-country footpath from village
OPEN 1 – 6.30 pm, Tuesday – Friday, 1 April to 15 October. Plus 10 am – 5.30 pm, Saturdays, Sundays and Good Fridays
ADMISSION Adults £5; Children £2.50 (1994)
FACILITIES Parking; loos; facilities for the disabled; plants for sale; National Trust gift shop; self-service restaurant
FEATURES Herbaceous borders; herbs; plants for plantsmen; old roses and climbers; too many visitors have eroded the fabric of this famous and wonderful garden
ENGLISH HERITAGE GRADE I

Too well-known to need description, Sissinghurst is part of every English gardener's education and a source of wonder and inspiration to which to return time and again. There is a 'timed ticket' system to restrict visitors to 400 at a time, which may mean waiting.

LANCASHIRE

Bank House
Borwick, Carnforth, Lancashire LA6 1JR
☎ 01524 732768

OWNER Mr and Mrs R. G. McBurnie
LOCATION 2 miles north east of Carnforth off A6
OPEN 2 – 6 pm, Sunday, 7 May, 4 June, 2 July, 6 August, 3 September, 1 October
ADMISSION Adults £1; Children 25p
FACILITIES Loos; access for the disabled; tea and coffee
FEATURES Good collection of trees; fruit of special interest; gravel or scree garden; plants for plantsmen; old roses and climbers; woodland garden; collection of carnivorous plants

A successful private garden made over the last 30 years by the present owners. It manages to shoehorn such features as a woodland garden, gravel garden, old-fashioned rose collection and a mini-arboretum into 2 acres. But it works.

Hoghton Tower
Hoghton, Preston, Lancashire PR5 0SH
☎ 01254 852986

OWNER Sir Bernard de Highton Bt.
LOCATION A675 midway between Preston and Blackburn

OPEN 1 – 5 pm, Sundays, Easter to 31 October. Also 11 am – 4 pm, Tuesday – Thursday, July and August
ADMISSION Adults £1; Children (under 5) free
FACILITIES Parking; loos; gift shop; tea room
FEATURES Herbaceous borders; old roses and climbers; rhododendrons and azaleas
ENGLISH HERITAGE GRADE II

A series of spacious courtyards and walled gardens surround this fierce castellated house. Not a great garden, but the setting is impressive and there are fine spring walks in the rhododendron woods below.

Leighton Hall
Carnforth, Lancashire LA5 9ST
☎ 01524 734474   [FAX] 01524 702357

OWNER R. G. Reynolds
LOCATION Signed from A6 junction with M6
OPEN 2 – 5 pm, daily except Saturday and Monday, 1 May to 30 September
ADMISSION Adults £3.30; Children £2.10; Senior Citizens and Groups £2.80
FACILITIES Parking; loos; access for the disabled; plants for sale; gift shop; tea rooms
FEATURES Herbaceous borders; fruit of special interest; herbs; old roses and climbers; 'caterpillar' path maze; first prize, Britain in Bloom 1993 (north west region)

The handsome semi-castellated house is set in lush parkland with the moors as a backdrop, but the garden is in the old walled garden, where rose borders, herbs and the gravel maze bring a touch of fancy to the whole.

Rufford Old Hall
Rufford, Ormskirk, Lancashire
☎ 01704 821254

OWNER The National Trust
LOCATION 7 miles north of Ormskirk on A59
OPEN 12 noon – 6 pm, Saturday – Wednesday, 1 April to 31 October
ADMISSION Garden only: Adults £1.60; Children 80p
FACILITIES Parking; dogs permitted; loos; access for the disabled; National Trust shop; lunches and teas (no lunches on Sundays)
FEATURES Herbaceous borders; rhododendrons and azaleas; old roses and climbers

One of the National Trust's most successful re-creations, the gardens are laid out in Regency style around a remarkable 15th-century timber-framed house.

LEICESTERSHIRE

Belvoir Castle
Belvoir, Grantham, Leicestershire
☎ 01476 870262   [FAX] 01476 870443

OWNER The Duke of Rutland
LOCATION 6 miles west of Grantham

308 Gardens LEICESTERSHIRE

OPEN   11 am – 5 pm, Tuesday – Thursday, Saturdays and Sundays, 1 April to 1 October. Open Bank Holiday Mondays, also Sundays in October
ADMISSION   Castle and gardens: Adults £4.25; Senior Citizens £3; Children £2.75
FACILITIES   Parking; loos; gift shop; refreshments: lunches and teas; picnic site
FEATURES   Herbaceous borders; modern roses; old roses and climbers; woodland garden
ENGLISH HERITAGE GRADE   II

Formal gardens on the Victorian terraces beneath the castle. A pretty woodland garden restored to its 18th-century form.

Burrough House
Burrough on the Hill, Melton Mowbray, Leicestershire LE14 2JQ
☎ 01664 454226
OWNER   Mrs Barbara Keene
LOCATION   6 miles west of Oakham
OPEN   11 am – 5 pm, Sundays and Mondays of Bank Holiday weekends; 1 April to 31 August; 2 – 5 pm, Thursdays and Sundays, 1 June to 31 August
ADMISSION   Weekdays £1.50; Weekends £2
FACILITIES   Parking; loos; access for the disabled; plants for sale; light refreshments
FEATURES   Lake; rock garden; modern roses; woodland garden; rhododendrons; new white summer garden (1995)

A 1920s garden revived and improved by the present owner. A parterre, moon gate, Italian garden, rose garden, paeony border, croquet lawn, woodland walk and secret garden are a measure of what pleasure the garden is designed to offer.

Langham Lodge
Langham, Oakham, Leicestershire LE15 7HZ
OWNER   Mr and Mrs H. M. Hemsley
LOCATION   On Burley road out of Langham
OPEN   11 am – 6 pm, 25 June. Other times in June and July by appointment
ADMISSION   £1
FACILITIES   Parking; access for the disabled; plants for sale; light lunches and teas
FEATURES   Herbaceous borders; fruit of special interest; plants for plantsmen; old roses and climbers; colour borders; interesting new vegetable garden (1995)

A modern plantsman's garden, full of interesting plants, often chosen for their foliage effects. Good shrub roses, which show up well against the stone walls.

Long Close
60 Main Street, Woodhouse Eaves, Loughborough, Leicestershire LE12 8RZ
☎ 01509 890376
OWNER   Mrs George Johnson
LOCATION   4 miles south of Loughborough
OPEN   2 – 6 pm, 2 April, 7 and 28 May. Parties by appointment

ADMISSION   Adults £1.50
FACILITIES   Parking; dogs permitted; plants for sale; teas
FEATURES   Fine conifers; old roses and climbers; woodland garden; rhododendrons; azaleas; heathers

A plantsman's garden, begun by the present owner 45 years ago, and now magnificently mature. 5 acres, crammed into a long narrow site that spreads out at the end into woodland, underplanted with massed rhododendrons and azaleas.

The University of Leicester Botanic Garden
Beaumont Hall, Stoughton Drive, Oadby, Leicestershire LE2 2NA
☎ 0116 717725
OWNER   The University of Leicester
LOCATION   3 miles south of Leicester on A6 London road opposite racecourse
OPEN   10 am – 4 pm (3.30 pm Friday), Monday – Friday, all year
ADMISSION   Free
FACILITIES   Parking; loos; plants for sale
FEATURES   Fine conifers; ecological interest; glasshouses and conservatories to visit; herbs; lake; rock garden; modern roses; old roses and climbers; subtropical plants; woodland garden; cacti; succulents; heathers; tallest *Quercus petraea* 'Mespilifolia' and *Pinus aristata* in the British Isles
FRIENDS   Send for membership form: The Curator, Botany Dept, Leicester University, Leicester LE1 7RH. Membership: newsletters, special access, plant exchanges, meetings once a month and guide
NCCPG NATIONAL COLLECTIONS   *Aubrieta*, *Fuchsia* (hardy vars), *Skimmia*, *Hesperis*, *Chamaecyparis lawsoniana*

16 acres – one of the best modern (early 20th century) botanic gardens, with a wide variety of plants from historic trees to an 1980s ecological meadow.

Wartnaby Gardens
Wartnaby, Melton Mowbray, Leicestershire LE14 3HY
☎ 01664 822549   FAX 01664 822296
OWNER   Lady King
LOCATION   3 miles north of Melton Mowbray on A606. Left at A6 Kettley then 1 mile
OPEN   2 – 6 pm, 21 May, 25 June, 23 July. Groups by appointment
ADMISSION   £2
FACILITIES   Parking; dogs permitted; loos; access for the disabled; plants for sale; refreshments available
FEATURES   Good collection of trees; herbaceous borders; fruit of special interest; glasshouses and conservatories to visit; lake; old roses and climbers; colour borders

A model modern garden, where rare plants are displayed in an endless variety of situations and habitats.

Roses feature significantly, with good herbaceous underplanting and satisfying colour schemes.

Whatton House
Long Whatton, Loughborough, Leicestershire
LE12 SBG
☎ 01509 842302   FAX 01509 842268
OWNER Lord Crawshaw
LOCATION Junction 24, Kegworth A6 towards Hathern
OPEN 2 – 6 pm, Wednesdays, Sundays and Bank Holiday Mondays, Easter to 30 August. Also for NGS
ADMISSION Adults £1.50; Senior Citizens and Children 75p
FACILITIES Parking; dogs permitted; loos; facilities for the disabled; plants for sale; refreshments
FEATURES Good collection of trees; herbaceous borders; follies and garden buildings; fruit of special interest; oriental features; rock garden; modern roses; old roses and climbers; climbing plants; bark temple; canyon garden; Chinese garden
ENGLISH HERITAGE GRADE II

15 acres attached to a garden centre. Most of the features date from c.1900 but there has been much replanting in recent years. The Chinese garden sports some extraordinary mythological figures. There is also a mysterious 'bogey hole'. Great fun to visit.

LINCOLNSHIRE

Belton House
Grantham, Lincolnshire NG32 2LS
☎ 01476 61541/66116   FAX 01476 79071
OWNER The National Trust
LOCATION 3 miles north east of Grantham on the A607
OPEN 11 am – 5.30 pm, Wednesday – Sunday, 1 April to 31 October
ADMISSION Adults £4; Children £2 (1994)
FACILITIES Parking; loos; facilities for the disabled; gift shop; lunches, teas, licensed restaurant
FEATURES Herbaceous borders; follies and garden buildings; glasshouses and conservatories to visit; lake; modern roses; garden sculpture; good topiary; woodland garden; interesting for children; daffodils; adventure playground
ENGLISH HERITAGE GRADE I

Grandeur and amenity go hand in hand at Belton. There are 1,000 acres of wooded deer park, a Wyatville orangery, a Dutch garden and an Italian garden with statues and parterres. But the adventure playground and other facilities make it popular with all ages.

Caythorpe Campus, De Montfort University
Caythorpe, Grantham, Lincolnshire NG32 3EP
☎ 01400 72521   FAX 01400 72722
OWNER De Montfort University

LOCATION East of Caythorpe village
OPEN 1.30 – 5 pm, 10 June. Groups by prior arrangement
ADMISSION £20 per group
FACILITIES Parking; dogs permitted; loos; plants for sale; refreshments by arrangement
FEATURES Herbaceous borders; fine conifers; glasshouses and conservatories to visit; plants for plantsmen; modern roses; old roses and climbers; woodland garden; formal terraces
ENGLISH HERITAGE GRADE II

A teaching garden, and well worth a special visit. The Victorian monkey-puzzle and Edwardian terraces pre-date the modern gardens. These are laid out with demonstration borders and plant collections for roses, irises, annuals, vegetables, herbaceous plants, alpines and a lot more too.

Doddington Hall
Doddington, Lincoln, Lincolnshire LN6 4RU
☎ 01522 694308   FAX 01522 682584
OWNER A. Jarvis
LOCATION Signposted off the A46 Lincoln bypass
OPEN Garden only: 2 – 6 pm, Sundays, 12 March to 30 April. House and garden: Wednesdays, Sundays and Bank Holiday Mondays, 1 May to 30 September
ADMISSION Garden only: £1.80; Children 90p
FACILITIES Parking; loos; facilities for the disabled; licensed restaurant
FEATURES Herbaceous borders; lake; old roses and climbers; turf maze; new wild garden and bog garden; new topiary in courtyard (1995)
ENGLISH HERITAGE GRADE II*

A ravishing Elizabethan house around which successive generations have made a successful Tudor-style garden. Simple and open at the front, Edwardian knots and parterres in the walled garden (thickly and richly planted), and then a modern herb garden and pleached hornbeams. Wonderfully harmonious.

Grimsthorpe Castle Trust Ltd
Grimsthorpe Castle, Bourne, Lincolnshire PE10 0NB
☎ 01778 32205   FAX 01778 32259
OWNER Grimsthorpe & Drummond Castle Trust Ltd
LOCATION On A151 Bourne from Colsterworth road
OPEN Details not available at the time of going to press. Telephone for times, dates and prices
ADMISSION See above
FACILITIES Parking; dogs permitted; loos; access for the disabled; tea rooms
FEATURES Good collection of trees; landscape designed by Capability Brown; lake; modern roses; good topiary
ENGLISH HERITAGE GRADE I

First Capability Brown, then a late-Victorian Italian garden, still maintained with summer bedding. The most interesting feature is a formal vegetable garden, made in the 1960s before the craze for *potagers*, right below the

Italian garden. Well-designed and well-maintained, but is it not too close to the house?

Gunby Hall
Gunby, Spilsby, Lincolnshire PE23 5SS
OWNER   The National Trust
LOCATION   2½ miles north west of Burgh-le-Marsh
OPEN   2 – 6 pm, Wednesdays (plus Thursdays for garden only), 1 April to 30 September
ADMISSION   Garden only: £1.50
FACILITIES   Parking; dogs permitted; loos; access for the disabled; plants for sale
FEATURES   Herbaceous borders; fruit of special interest; herbs; old roses and climbers
ENGLISH HERITAGE GRADE   II

Ignore the parkland and make for the two walled gardens. Here is all the action: rich herbaceous borders, an arched apple walk, shrub roses, herbs and vegetables.

Hall Farm & Nursery
Harpswell, Gainsborough, Lincolnshire DN21 5UU
☎ 01427 668412
OWNER   Pam and Mark Tatam
LOCATION   On A361, 7 miles east of Gainsborough
OPEN   10 am – 6 pm (or dusk, if earlier), daily, all year except Christmas week. For NGS: see Yellow Book
ADMISSION   £1 (1994)
FACILITIES   Parking; loos; good nursery next door
FEATURES   Herbaceous borders; plants for plantsmen; pond; old roses and climbers

Small modern garden, intensely planted as an adjunct to the nursery, and for the owners' pleasure.

Riseholme Hall
Lincolnshire College of Agriculture & Horticulture, Riseholme, Lincolnshire LN2 2LG
☎ 01522 522252   📠 01522 545436
OWNER   De Montfort University, Lincoln
LOCATION   2 miles north of Lincoln on A15
OPEN   10.30 am – 4 pm, 14 May. Also groups by prior arrangement
FACILITIES   Parking; dogs permitted; loos; access for the disabled; refreshments by arrangement
FEATURES   Good collection of trees; herbaceous borders; ecological interest; fruit of special interest; glasshouses and conservatories to visit; lake; rock garden; modern roses; old roses and climbers; woodland garden; heather garden; tender plants
ENGLISH HERITAGE GRADE   II

The old house has an 18th-century landscape – park, lake and broad trees. The Bishop's Walk is Edwardian: tender plants flourish between the yew hedge and brick wall. However the main garden is strictly educational, with demonstrations of roses, herbaceous plants, fruit and vegetables, alpine plants and annuals, all beautifully maintained and meticulously labelled.

Springfields Show Gardens
Spalding, Lincolnshire PE12 6ET
☎ 01775 724843   📠 01775 711209
OWNER   Springfields Horticultural Society Ltd
LOCATION   1 mile from Spalding, off new bypass
OPEN   10 am – 6 pm, daily, 24 March to 1 October
ADMISSION   Adults £2.50; Senior Citizens £2.30
FACILITIES   Parking; loos; facilities for the disabled; plants for sale; gift shop; restaurant and café
FEATURES   Lake; modern roses; woodland garden; millions of bulbs
FRIENDS   Associate Membership available: £10

Originally a cor blimey display garden for the Lincolnshire bulb trade, Springfields now offers fun and colour all through the season, with roses providing the midsummer display and bold bedding taking over until the autumn frosts. An eyeful of a garden, splendidly maintained.

LONDON

17 Fulham Park Gardens
London SW6 4JX
☎ 0171 736 4890
OWNER   Anthony Noel
LOCATION   Near Putney Bridge underground station
OPEN   2.30 – 6 pm, 9 July, 17 September
ADMISSION   Adults £2; Senior Citizens £1
FEATURES   Good topiary; young garden; urns, pots, troughs; striking plantings; seven years old

A town garden where meticulous attention to detail pays off: neatly clipped cubes and box bobbles are one speciality. The planting is profuse but plants are rigorously controlled – just greens and whites, with occasional silvers and golds. The contrasts, juxtapositions and harmonies, though on a small scale, are ingenious. Alas, it feels like a garden for one person only at a time, two at the most – a good-humoured crush on open days.

Cannizaro Park
West Side Common, Wimbledon, London SW19
☎ 0181 946 7649
OWNER   London Borough of Merton
LOCATION   West side of Wimbledon Common
OPEN   8 am – sunset, Monday – Friday, 9 am – sunset, Saturday, Sunday and Bank Holidays, all year
ADMISSION   Free
FACILITIES   Parking; loos; some refreshments at summer weekends
FEATURES   Herbaceous borders; fine conifers; modern roses; woodland garden; azaleas; magnolias; summer bedding
ENGLISH HERITAGE GRADE   II*

Famous for its azaleas, planted about 40 years ago and almost too much of a good thing when in full flower. Little known, even to Londoners, Cannizaro deserves recognition as one of the leading Surrey-type of woodland gardens in the country.

Capel Manor
Bullsmoor Lane, Enfield, London EN1 4RQ
☎ 0181 336 4442

OWNER   Capel Manor Corporation
LOCATION   A10 by J25 on M25
OPEN   10 am – 5.30 pm (or dusk if sooner), daily, all year
ADMISSION   Adults: £3; Senior Citizens: £2; Children: £1.50
FACILITIES   Parking; dogs permitted; loos; facilities for the disabled; plants for sale; small shop; refreshments
FEATURES   Alpines; good collection of trees; herbaceous borders; fine conifers; daffodils; ecological interest; follies and garden buildings; fruit and vegetables of special interest; glasshouses and conservatories to visit; gravel or scree garden; herbs; lake; oriental features; plants for plantsmen; rock garden; modern roses; old roses and climbers; subtropical plants; good topiary; woodland garden; interesting for children
NCCPG NATIONAL COLLECTIONS Achillea, Dahlia, Sarcococca

High-profile demonstration garden attached to a horticultural college. Brilliant for new ideas, especially for small gardens: there is a walled garden, herb garden, knot garden, disabled garden, shade garden, pergola, alpine beds and some historical re-creations. Perhaps the best garden attached to a local authority college.

Chelsea Physic Garden
66 Royal Hospital Road, London SW3 4HS
☎ 0171 352 5646

OWNER   Chelsea Physic Garden Company
LOCATION   Please look at your London A to Z
OPEN   2 – 5 pm, Wednesdays, 2 – 6 pm, Sundays, 2 April to 29 October. Plus 12 noon – 5 pm, 22 to 26 May and 5 to 9 June
ADMISSION   Adults £3; Students, Children and Concessions £1.80
FACILITIES   Loos; facilities for the disabled; plants for sale; teas and lunches 22 – 26 May
FEATURES   Herbaceous borders; glasshouses and conservatories to visit; rock garden; 18th-century rock garden; tallest *Koelreuteria paniculata* in England; new 'Garden of World Medicine' (1995)
ENGLISH HERITAGE GRADE   I
FRIENDS   Friends have unrestricted rights of entry in office hours: worth considering if you live nearby
NCCPG NATIONAL COLLECTIONS Cistus

This oasis of peace between Royal Hospital Road and the Chelsea Embankment started life in 1673 as a pharmacological collection, and has kept its original design, but it also has the oldest rock garden in Europe, the largest olive tree in Britain, a vast number of rare and interesting plants, and probably the last known specimen of the 1920s white Hybrid Tea rose 'Marcia Stanhope'.

Chiswick House
Burlington Lane, Chiswick, London W4 2RP
☎ 0181 742 1225

OWNER   English Heritage
LOCATION   South west London on A4 and A316
OPEN   8 am – dusk, daily, all year
ADMISSION   Free
FACILITIES   Parking; loos; refreshments
FEATURES   Camellias; follies and garden buildings; glasshouses and conservatories to visit; worked on by Kent; lake; modern roses; garden sculpture; parterres; summer bedding; luxuriant evergreens
ENGLISH HERITAGE GRADE   I

Laid out by Bridgeman and Kent for Lord Burlington, Chiswick is the best baroque garden in Britain, and the exquisite house is pure Palladian. A Duke of Devonshire added an Italian renaissance garden early in the 19th century, and a camellia house with slate benches and huge bushes, mainly of old *japonica* varieties. But explore the *pattes d'oie*, *allées* and *Ilex* groves of the main garden on a hot July morning and you might be doing a grand tour of Italy 250 years ago.

Fenton House
Hampstead Grove, London NW3 6RT
☎ 0171 435 3471

OWNER   The National Trust
LOCATION   Entrances in Hampstead Grove near Hampstead underground station
OPEN   2 – 5 pm, Saturdays and Sundays, March. 11 am – 5.30 pm, Saturdays, Sundays and Bank Holiday Mondays, and 2 – 5.30 pm, Monday – Wednesday, April to 31 October
ADMISSION   Adults £3.50; Children £1.75
FEATURES   Herbaceous borders; herbs; old roses and climbers; restored Edwardian garden; new autumn border on north terrace (1995)

A country garden in Hampstead. Neat, terraced gardens near the house, rather more formal at the bottom. Not outstandingly flowerful, but the hedges are good and plants are firmly trained: definitely worth knowing.

Ham House
Richmond, Surrey TW10 7RS
☎ 0181 940 1950

OWNER   The National Trust
LOCATION   On the Thames
OPEN   10.30 am – 6 pm, daily except Fridays, Christmas and New Year, all year
ADMISSION   Gardens: free
FACILITIES   Parking; loos; facilities for the disabled; National Trust shop; restaurant open when house open
FEATURES   Fruit of special interest; herbs; climbing roses; modern roses; parterres; *Ilex* avenue
ENGLISH HERITAGE GRADE   II*

A modern re-creation of the 17th-century original. The best bit is a grand series of hornbeam enclosures with white summerhouses and seats. Less successful is a stodgy parterre of lavender, santolina and box. Acres of crunchy gravel: the National Trust at its most sanitised.

Hampton Court Palace
East Molesey, London KT8 9AU
☎ 0181 781 9500
OWNER   Historic Royal Palaces Agency
LOCATION   North side of Kingston bridge over the Thames, on A308 junction with A309
OPEN   Dawn – dusk, daily, all year
ADMISSION   Free
FACILITIES   Parking; dogs permitted; loos; access for the disabled; shop
FEATURES   Herbaceous borders; fruit of special interest; herbs; lake; modern roses; old roses and climbers; good topiary; interesting for children; particularly good in July-August; famous maze; laburnum walk; knot gardens
ENGLISH HERITAGE GRADE   I

66 acres of famous garden and 600 acres of deer park. Here are some highlights: Charles II's Long Canal with radiating lime avenues to imitate the *pattes d'oie* at Versailles; the broad walk, now a herbaceous border 100 yards long; bowling alleys, tilt-yards, the great maze and the Great Vine (actually 'Black Hamburgh'), the 16th-century Privy Garden, William and Mary's Great Fountain Garden, the priory garden, knot garden and all those bulbs in spring.

Isabella Plantation
Richmond Park, Richmond, London
☎ 0181 948 3209
OWNER   The Royal Parks
LOCATION   Richmond Park
OPEN   Dawn – dusk, daily
ADMISSION   Free
FACILITIES   Parking; dogs permitted; access for the disabled; refreshments
FEATURES   Good collection of trees; fine conifers; lake; woodland garden; kurume azaleas; rhododendrons; primulas
FRIENDS   Friends of Richmond Park. Secretary, Howard Stafford, 0181 789 4601
NCCPG NATIONAL COLLECTIONS   *Rhododendron*

42 acres of rhododendrons and azaleas under a deciduous canopy in Richmond Park. Best in May when the candelabra primulas flower and the hostas are in new leaf. Little known.

Kenwood Park
Hampstead Lane, London NW3
OWNER   English Heritage
LOCATION   North side of Hampstead Heath
OPEN   Dawn – dusk, daily, all year
ADMISSION   Free (to Park)
FACILITIES   Dogs permitted; loos; access for the disabled; refreshments during the daytime

FEATURES   Good collection of trees; herbaceous borders; lake; garden sculpture; woodland garden
ENGLISH HERITAGE GRADE   II*

Superb parkland around glittering lakes: a haven of calm from London's busyness.

The Museum of Garden History
Lambeth Palace Road, London SE1 7LB
☎ 0171 261 1891   FAX 0171 401 8869
OWNER   The Tradescant Trust
LOCATION   Between Lambeth Bridge and Lambeth Palace
OPEN   10.30 am – 4 pm (5 pm on Sundays), Sunday-Friday, 5 March to 10 December
ADMISSION   Donation
FACILITIES   Dogs permitted; loos; access for the disabled; plants for sale; books, cards and gifts; light refreshments
FEATURES   Herbs
FRIENDS   Friends of the Tradescant Trust: ask for details

The garden is small, and secondary to the Museum's collections, but designed as a 17th-century knot garden and planted with plants associated with the Tradescants. A garden for contemplation.

Myddelton House Gardens
Bulls Cross, Enfield, London
☎ 01992 713838
OWNER   Lea Valley Regional Park Authority
LOCATION   Off A10 on to Bullsmoor Lane: signposted at Bulls Cross
OPEN   10 am – 3.30 pm, weekdays except Bank Holidays, all year. Also 28 May, 25 June and 24 September
ADMISSION   Adults £1.20; Concessions (weekdays only) 60p
FACILITIES   Parking; loos; access for the disabled; plants for sale
FEATURES   Good collection of trees; herbaceous borders; fine conifers; daffodils; follies and garden buildings; lake; plants for plantsmen; pond; old roses and climbers; snowdrops; woodland garden; particularly interesting in winter
ENGLISH HERITAGE GRADE   II
FRIENDS   E. A. Bowles of Myddelton House Society c/o The Secretary, 102 Myddelton Avenue, Enfield EN1 4AG
NCCPG NATIONAL COLLECTIONS   *Iris*

Holy ground for plantsmen with a sense of history, E. A. Bowles's garden was abandoned for 30 years. Lea Valley Regional Park Authority has slowly started to restore it. The irises, roses and spring bulbs are still impressive.

Osterley Park
Isleworth, London TW7 4RB
☎ 0181 560 3918
OWNER   The National Trust
LOCATION   5 miles west of central London on A4

NORFOLK Gardens 313

OPEN 9 am – 7.30 pm, daily, all year
FACILITIES Parking; loos; facilities for the disabled; tea room
FEATURES Fruit of special interest; herbs; lake; woodland garden; fine rare oaks; autumn colour
ENGLISH HERITAGE GRADE II*
Classical 18th-century landscape. Fine temple and semicircular conservatory by Robert Adam. Good trees – cedars and oaks; elsewhere, restoration in progress.

Royal Botanic Gardens, Kew
Kew, Richmond, Surrey TW9 3AB
☎ 0181 940 1171
OWNER Trustees of the Royal Botanic Gardens
LOCATION Kew Green, south of Kew bridge, or via District line to Kew Gardens station
OPEN 9.30 am – 6 pm (7 pm at weekends), or 30 minutes before dusk, if earlier, daily, all year. Glasshouses close at 5.30 pm. (Details: 0181 940 1171)
ADMISSION Adults £4 (last hour £2); Senior Citizens and Students £2; Children under 5 free; Disabled in wheelchairs free; Family £10 (2+4); Season ticket £17
FACILITIES Parking; loos; facilities for the disabled; gift and book shop; orangery and pavilion restaurants and bakery
FEATURES Alpines; good collection of trees; herbaceous borders; fine conifers; ecological interest; follies and garden buildings; fruit of special interest; glasshouses and conservatories to visit; gravel or scree garden; herbs; lake; oriental features; plants for plantsmen; rock garden; modern roses; old roses and climbers; garden sculpture; snowdrops; subtropical plants; woodland garden; interesting for children; particularly interesting in winter; heather gardens
ENGLISH HERITAGE GRADE I
FRIENDS Friends of Kew: very active and good value – write or telephone for details

Kew has such superstar status that it needs no description. Go in lilac time, if you wish, but go too in winter when there is much to see both in and out of the glasshouses. Visit the newly-restored Palm House, as well as the new Princess of Wales Conservatory (worth a whole afternoon) and do not miss the alpine house. In summer there are very good bedding out schemes, but the garden is plagued by Canada geese, which foul the grass, and aircraft noise.

Syon Park
Brentford, London TW8 8JF
☎ 0181 560 0881
OWNER The Duke of Northumberland
LOCATION Between Brentford and Isleworth, north bank of Thames
OPEN 10 am – 6 pm, or sunset if earlier, daily, all year
ADMISSION Adults £1.75; Children £1.25 (1994)
FACILITIES Parking; loos; plants for sale; garden centre; shops; restaurants; all the fun of the fair

FEATURES Good collection of trees; herbaceous borders; landscape designed by Capability Brown; fine conifers; follies and garden buildings; glasshouses and conservatories to visit; modern roses; old roses and climbers; woodland garden; interesting for children; cacti; ferns; exhibition of gardening for the disabled; tropical butterfly house
ENGLISH HERITAGE GRADE I
Syon is a mixture of 18th-century landscape, 19th-century horticultural seriousness, 20th-century plantsmanship and 21st-century theme park. Splendid conservatories with good collections, worth visiting in winter.

Walpole House
Chiswick Mall, London W4 2PS
OWNER Mr and Mrs Jeremy Benson
LOCATION Parallel to A4 between Hammersmith flyover and Hogarth roundabout
OPEN 2 – 6 pm, 23 April; 2 – 7 pm, 21 May
ADMISSION Adults £1.50; Senior Citizens and Children 50p
FACILITIES Parking; plants for sale
FEATURES Herbaceous borders; plants for plantsmen; woodland garden
ENGLISH HERITAGE GRADE II
A large town garden, designed and planted in the Hidcote style and made to seem much larger than its ⅔rd acre. Big trees, a large lily-pond and densely planted herbaceous borders all contribute to the sense of *rus in urbe*.

MERSEYSIDE

Croxteth Hall & Country Park
Croxteth Hall Lane, Liverpool, Merseyside L12 0HB
☎ 0151 228 5311   FAX 0151 228 5311
OWNER City of Liverpool
LOCATION Muirhead Avenue East
OPEN 11 am – 5 pm, daily, Easter to 30 September
ADMISSION 60p. Walled garden: 30p
FACILITIES Parking; loos; facilities for the disabled; plants for sale; cafeteria
FEATURES Herbaceous borders; fruit of special interest; glasshouses and conservatories to visit; herbs; interesting for children
NCCPG NATIONAL COLLECTIONS Fuchsia
FRIENDS Friends of Croxteth Hall & Country Park: details from Mr E. E. Jackson

Very much a public amenity, Croxteth Hall majors on fruit, vegetables and herbs – showing in its walled garden what visitors can try at home. Good greenhouses. Heart-warming.

NORFOLK

Blickling Hall
Blickling, Norwich, Norfolk NR11 6NF
☎ 01263 733084   FAX 01263 734924
OWNER The National Trust

LOCATION 1 mile west of Aylsham on B1354
OPEN 11 am – 5 pm, daily except Monday and Thursday, but open every day in July and August; 25 March to 5 November
ADMISSION Adults £2.50; Children £1.25
FACILITIES Parking; loos; facilities for the disabled; plants for sale; National Trust shop; light snacks, lunches and teas
FEATURES Herbaceous borders; landscape designed by Capability Brown; lake; old roses and climbers; woodland garden; herbaceous borders at peak in July-August

The garden with everything. Jacobean mansion, handsomely symmetrical; early landscape (Doric Temple, c.1735); smashing conservatory by Samuel Wyatt; then mid 19th-century parterre by Nesfield (topiary pillars); and 1930s herbaceous colour plantings by Nancy Lindsey (her masterpiece). Fabulous bluebells in the woods.

Bressingham Gardens
Bressingham, Diss, Norfolk IP22 2AB
☎ 0137988 386

OWNER Alan Bloom
LOCATION On main road, 3 miles west of Diss
OPEN 10 am – 5.30 pm, daily, 1 April to 31 October
ADMISSION Adults £3.50
FACILITIES Parking; loos; access for the disabled; plants for sale; refreshments in adjacent plant centre
FEATURES Bog garden; herbaceous borders; fine conifers; lake; plants for plantsmen; particularly good in July-August
FRIENDS Monthly lectures April – October

There is no better place to learn about herbaceous plants – what they look like, how they grow and how to place them. The garden's design exemplifies Bloom's commitment to island beds, which he popularised 25 years ago. The curves suit the site, a small valley known as Foggy Bottom, where lightly wooded meadows run down to a stream. Totally absorbing.

Elsing Hall
Elsing, Dereham, Norfolk NR20 3DX
☎ 01362 637224

OWNER Mr and Mrs D. H. Cargill
LOCATION Ask in village
OPEN 2 – 6 pm, Sundays, 5 June to 31 July and Sundays in September
ADMISSION £2
FACILITIES Parking; dogs permitted; loos; access for the disabled
FEATURES Good collection of trees; fruit of special interest; lake; kitchen garden; formal garden now mature; enlarged collection of old roses (1995)

A garden of great charm, whose owners have planted many good trees, roses and a formal garden to enhance the medieval house and its romantic moat. An avenue of ginkgos, a collection of willows and a small arboretum of trees chosen for their coloured bark are some of the most recent additions.

Fairhaven Gardens Trust
South Walsham, Norwich, Norfolk NR13 6EA
☎ 01603 270449

OWNER Fairhaven Gardens Trust
LOCATION 9 miles north east of Norwich on the B1140
OPEN 11 am – 5.30 pm (Saturdays 2 – 5.30 pm), Tuesday – Sunday, plus Bank Holidays, 14 April to 1 October
ADMISSION Adults £3; Senior Citizens £2; Children £1
FACILITIES Parking; dogs permitted; loos; access for the disabled; small shop; new visitors' centre; new plant sales area; tea room
FEATURES Lake; woodland garden; rhododendrons; lilies; candelabra primulas

Basically an enormous plantsman's garden (200 acres) round one of the Norfolk broads. Rhododendrons and azaleas under a canopy of oak and alder, plus extensive plantings of primulas, *Lysichiton*, astilbes, and other bog plants in and around the water. Bluebells.

Felbrigg Hall
Roughton, Norwich, Norfolk NR11 8PR
☎ 01263 837444   FAX 01263 838297

OWNER The National Trust
LOCATION Entrance off B1436, signed from A148 and A140
OPEN 11 am – 5.30 pm, daily except Tuesdays and Fridays, 25 March to 5 November
ADMISSION £1.90
FACILITIES Parking; loos; facilities for the disabled; National Trust shop; restaurant and tea room
FEATURES Herbaceous borders; fruit of special interest; colchicums
ENGLISH HERITAGE GRADE II*
NCCPG NATIONAL COLLECTIONS *Colchicum*

The best bit of Felbrigg is the walled kitchen garden, oriented on a large brick dovecote flanked by Victorian vineries. Fruit trees are trained against the walls (figs, pears, plums) and the garden laid to neatly grown vegetables with herbaceous borders along the box-edged gravel paths.

Holkham Hall
Holkham, Wells-next-the-Sea, Norfolk

OWNER Viscount Coke
LOCATION Off A149, 2 miles west of Wells
OPEN 11.30 am – 5.30 pm, 3 and 4 April; 2, 29 and 30 May. Then 1.30 – 5 pm, Sunday – Thursday, 31 May to 29 September (1994 times and dates)
ADMISSION Adults £3 (1994)
FACILITIES Parking; loos; access for the disabled; plants for sale; gift shop; refreshments
FEATURES Landscape designed by Capability Brown; lake; garden sculpture

ENGLISH HERITAGE GRADE I
A big landscape garden, worked on by Kent, Brown and Repton. Mighty impressive. In the nearby garden centre is a walled garden with several demonstration gardens – herbs, roses and perennials.

Oxburgh Hall
Oxborough, King's Lynn, Norfolk PE33 9PS
☎ 01366 328258
OWNER   The National Trust
LOCATION   7 miles south west of Swaffham on Stoke Ferry road
OPEN   12 noon – 5.30 pm, Saturday – Wednesday, 25 March to 5 November
ADMISSION   Adults £2; Children £1
FACILITIES   Parking; loos; facilities for the disabled; gift shop; light lunches and tea
FEATURES   Herbaceous borders; fruit of special interest; modern roses; French-style parterre; trained fruit trees
ENGLISH HERITAGE GRADE II
The baroque 19th-century parterre has been replanted by the National Trust with such herbs as rue and santolina, making permanent companions for annuals and bedding plants. Good fruit trees in the walled garden: medlars, quinces and mulberries. Not a great garden, but a good one.

Raveningham Hall
Raveningham, Norwich, Norfolk NR14 6NS
☎ 01508 548122   FAX 01508 548958
OWNER   Sir Nicholas Bacon Bt.
LOCATION   Signed off A146 at Hales
OPEN   1 – 4 pm on Wednesdays, 2 – 5 pm on Sundays and Bank Holiday Mondays, 19 March to 17 September
ADMISSION   Adults £2; Children free
FACILITIES   Parking; dogs permitted; loos; access for the disabled; plants for sale; refreshments on Sundays and Bank Holiday Mondays only
FEATURES   Good collection of trees; herbaceous borders; modern roses
ENGLISH HERITAGE GRADE II
Good taste and good plantsmanship characterise Raveningham, both qualities of the owner's mother who collects and plants with enthusiasm. Rather classy.

Sandringham House
Sandringham, King's Lynn, Norfolk PE35 6EN
☎ 01553 772675   FAX 01485 541371
OWNER   H M The Queen
LOCATION   Signed from A148
OPEN   10.30 am (11.30 am on Sundays) – 5 pm, daily, 13 April to 1 October (except 18 July to 4 August)
ADMISSION   Adults £2.50; Senior Citizens £2; Children £1.50 (1994)
FACILITIES   Parking; loos; facilities for the disabled; plants for sale; gift shop; restaurant and tea rooms
FEATURES   Herbaceous borders; lake; rhododendrons; azaleas; maples; hydrangeas

ENGLISH HERITAGE GRADE II*
The best of the royal gardens. The woodland and lakes are rich with ornamental plantings, and the splendid herbaceous borders were designed by Geoffrey Jellicoe, but it is the scale of it all that most impresses, and the grandeur too.

Sheringham Park
Gardener's Cottage, Sheringham Park, Sheringham, Norfolk NR26 8TB
☎ 01263 823778
OWNER   The National Trust
LOCATION   Junction of A148 and B1157
OPEN   Dawn – dusk, daily, all year
ADMISSION   Adults £2.30
FACILITIES   Parking; dogs permitted; loos; facilities for the disabled
FEATURES   Fine conifers; lake; landscape designed by Humphry Repton; woodland garden; rhododendrons
ENGLISH HERITAGE GRADE II*
One of the best Repton landscapes outstanding, but fleshed out with a great early 20th century collection of rhododendrons and glorified by a classical temple, designed by Repton but not eventually built until 1975. Currently undergoing restoration: interesting to study.

NORTHAMPTONSHIRE

Althorp House
Althorp, Northampton, Northamptonshire NN7 4HQ
☎ 01604 770107   FAX 01604 770107
OWNER   Earl Spencer
LOCATION   Signposted from M1
OPEN   1 – 5 pm, 1, 2 and 14 to 17 April; 6 to 8 and 27 May; 1 to 31 August; 7 to 8 October
ADMISSION   Adults £4.50; Senior Citizens £3.50; Children £2.50
FACILITIES   Parking; loos; facilities for the disabled; gift shop; tea room
FEATURES   Fine conifers; formal gardens; biggest *Abies bracteata* in the British Isles
ENGLISH HERITAGE GRADE I
Interesting more for its royal associations than as a great garden, which it is not. But the 19th-century formal gardens are impressive and the traditional parkland deeply pastoral. New gardens are planned.

Boughton House
Kettering, Northamptonshire NN14 1BJ
☎ 01536 515731   FAX 01536 417255
OWNER   The Duke and Duchess of Buccleugh and The Living Landscape Trust
LOCATION   A43, three miles north of Kettering
OPEN   1 – 5 pm, Saturday – Thursday, 1 May to 1 October. Plus Fridays in August
ADMISSION   Adults £1.50; Children 75p
FACILITIES   Parking; dogs permitted; loos; facilities for the disabled; plants for sale; shop

FEATURES   Herbaceous borders; modern roses; interesting for children; current holder of Sandford Award; adventure playground
ENGLISH HERITAGE GRADE   I

A seriously important landscaped park dating from the early 18th century. Rides, avenues, *allées*, pools, canals and prospects.

Canons Ashby House
Daventry, Northamptonshire NN11 3SD
☎ 01327 860690

OWNER   The National Trust
LOCATION   Signposted from A5
OPEN   1 – 5 pm, Saturday – Wednesday, 1 April to 31 October
ADMISSION   Adults £3.20; Children £1.60
FACILITIES   Parking; dogs permitted; loos; facilities for the disabled; light lunches and teas
FEATURES   Herbaceous borders; fruit of special interest; good topiary
ENGLISH HERITAGE GRADE   II*

A rare survivor among gardens. The Drydens, who owned it, never really took to the landscape movement. The early 18th-century layout is intact and has been carefully restored by the National Trust. The terraces below the house (*very* pretty) are planted with clipped Portugal laurel and period fruit trees. A place to contemplate old Tory values.

Castle Ashby Gardens
Castle Ashby, Northampton, Northamptonshire NN7 1LQ
☎ 01604 696696   FAX 01604 696516

OWNER   Marquess of Northampton
LOCATION   Off A428 between Northampton and Bedford
OPEN   10 am – dusk, daily, all year (1994 times and dates)
ADMISSION   Adults £2; Senior Citizens and Children £1 (1994)
FACILITIES   Parking; dogs permitted; facilities for the disabled; gift shops; refreshments
FEATURES   Good collection of trees; landscape designed by Capability Brown; glasshouses and conservatories to visit; lake; good topiary
ENGLISH HERITAGE GRADE   I

Much thought and money has been spent on restoring the gardens recently. The Italian formal gardens were among the first to be renewed, and the arboretum has been restocked. There is a stylish orangery and greenhouses by Sir Matthew Digby Wyatt but perhaps the best thing about Castle Ashby is the park – 200 acres of it, designed by Capability Brown.

Coton Manor
Guilsborough, Northampton, Northamptonshire NN6 8RQ
☎ 01604 740219   FAX 01604 740838

OWNER   Ian Pasley-Tyler
LOCATION   Signposted from A50 and A428
OPEN   12 noon – 6 pm, Wednesday – Sunday and Bank Holiday Mondays, Easter to 30 September
ADMISSION   Adults £2.70; Senior Citizens £2.10; Children £1
FACILITIES   Parking; dogs permitted; loos; access for the disabled; plants for sale; home produce and gifts; tea room
FEATURES   Herbaceous borders; gravel or scree garden; lake; modern roses; woodland garden; bluebells; waterfowl; fifty different hebes; lots of pots; new herb garden (1994); new wild-flower meadow (1995)

A nicely designed and thoughtfully planted garden – rarities and common plants chosen for effect – made by three generations over 70 years. The standard of maintenance is excellent, but there are rather too many birds for some visitors' tastes.

Cottesbrooke Hall
Northampton, Northamptonshire NN6 8PF
☎ 01604 505808   FAX 01604 505619

OWNER   Captain and Mrs John Macdonald-Buchanan
LOCATION   10 miles north of Northampton
OPEN   2 – 5.30 pm, Thursdays and Bank Holiday Mondays, 20 April to 28 September
ADMISSION   House and garden: Adults £2.50; Children £1.25. Groups by appointment
FACILITIES   Parking; loos; plants for sale; tea, coffee and cold drinks
FEATURES   Herbaceous borders; lake; old roses and climbers; garden sculpture
ENGLISH HERITAGE GRADE   II

The garden with everything: a handsome house, an 18th-century park, lakes, waterfalls, bluebell woods, rhododendrons, acres of daffodils, 27 varieties of snowdrop, half a dozen formal gardens, Scheemaker's statues from Stowe, an armillary garden, pergolas, *allées*, 300-year-old cedars, plants a-plenty, and the signatures of Geoffrey Jellicoe and Sylvia Crowe among the designers who have helped to develop it. If only more people knew of it.

Holdenby House Gardens
Holdenby, Northampton, Northamptonshire NN6 8DJ
☎ 01604 770074   FAX 01604 770962

OWNER   Mr and Mrs James Lowther
LOCATION   Off A50 or A428
OPEN   1 – 6 pm weekdays, 2 – 6 pm, Sundays, 1 – 6 pm, Bank Holiday Sundays and Mondays, 1 April to 30 September (except May Day)
ADMISSION   Adults £2.75; Senior Citizens £2.25; Children £1.75
FACILITIES   Parking; dogs permitted; loos; facilities for the disabled; plants for sale; souvenirs and crafts for sale; tea room in original Victorian kitchen
FEATURES   Herbaceous borders; follies and garden buildings; herbs; old roses and climbers; interesting for

NORTHUMBERLAND Gardens

children; Elizabethan garden; fragrant and silver borders; yew knot; current holder of Sandford Award
ENGLISH HERITAGE GRADE II*

Pretty modern gardens designed and planted by the present owners with help from Rosemary Verey. The Elizabethan garden uses only plants available in 1580.

The Old Rectory, Sudborough
Sudborough, Northamptonshire NN14 3BX
☎ 01832 733247   FAX 01832 733832
OWNER   Mr and Mrs A. P. Huntington
LOCATION   In village centre, by church, off A6116
OPEN   By appointment
ADMISSION   Adults £2; Children free
FACILITIES   Parking; loos; plants for sale
FEATURES   Herbaceous borders; fruit of special interest; herbs; lake; modern roses; old roses and climbers; handsome new *potager*

Neat new garden, 3 acres in size, around a handsome Georgian rectory. Good snowdrops and hellebores; unusual vegetables. The garden is thickly and thoughtfully planted so that every season is rich in interest.

Rockingham Castle
Market Harborough, Northamptonshire LE16 8TH
☎ 01586 770240   FAX 01586 771692
OWNER   Cdr L. M. M. Saunders Watson
LOCATION   2 miles north of Corby on A6003
OPEN   1.30 – 5.30 pm, Sundays, Thursdays, Bank Holiday Mondays and following Tuesdays (plus all Tuesdays in August), Easter Sunday to 30 September
ADMISSION   Adults £2.30
FACILITIES   Parking; dogs permitted; loos; access for the disabled; tea room
FEATURES   Good collection of trees; herbaceous borders; old roses and climbers; current holder of Sandford Award
ENGLISH HERITAGE GRADE II*

12 acres around the historic castle. The formal circular rose garden on the site of the old keep is surrounded by a billowing 400-year-old yew hedge. The wild garden in a ravine was replanted 20 years ago as a mini arboretum: very effective.

Sulgrave Manor
Sulgrave, Banbury, Northamptonshire OX17 2SD
☎ 01295 760205
OWNER   Sulgrave Manor Board
LOCATION   7 miles from Banbury
OPEN   10.30 am – 1 pm (but mornings by appointment only on weekdays except in August), and 2 – 5.30 pm (4.30 pm in March, November and December), daily except Wednesdays (but weekends only in March, November and December), 1 March to 24 December, plus 27 to 29 December
ADMISSION   Adults £3; Children £1.50
FACILITIES   Parking; dogs permitted; loos; plants for sale; tea room

FEATURES   Herbaceous borders; fruit of special interest; herbs; modern roses; good topiary
ENGLISH HERITAGE GRADE II

Famous (and highly visitable) for two reasons: first, its association with George Washington; second, its formal design, unchanged since it was laid out by Sir Reginald Blomfield in 1921.

NORTHUMBERLAND

Belsay Hall
Belsay, Newcastle-upon-Tyne, Northumberland NE20 0DX
☎ 01661 881636   FAX 01661 881043
OWNER   English Heritage
LOCATION   At Belsay on A696 Ponteland to Jedburgh road
OPEN   10 am – 6 pm (4 pm from 1 November to 31 March), daily except 1 January and 24 – 26 December
ADMISSION   Adults £2.40; Concessions £1.80; Children £1.20 (1994)
FACILITIES   Parking; dogs permitted; loos; facilities for the disabled; plants for sale; gift shop; refreshments in summer and at weekends
FEATURES   Fine conifers; rhododendrons and azaleas; rock garden; woodland garden; particularly interesting in winter; tallest surviving *Ulmus procera* in the British Isles
ENGLISH HERITAGE GRADE I
NCCPG NATIONAL COLLECTIONS   *Iris spuria*

Wildly romantic Victorian gardens, including several acres of disused quarry with *Trachycarpus* palms, a sequence of gloomy chasms, splendid woodfuls of hardy hybrid rhododendrons, intensive modern herbaceous plantings, brooding conifers and the ruins of Belsay Castle.

Bide-a-Wee Cottage
Stanton, Netherwitton, Morpeth, Northumberland NE65 8PR
☎ 01670 772 262
OWNER   N. M. Robson
LOCATION   7 miles north west of Morpeth
OPEN   1.30 – 5 pm, Saturdays, 1 April to 26 August
ADMISSION   £1.50
FACILITIES   Parking; new small nursery selling plants from garden
FEATURES   Gravel or scree garden; lake; plants for plantsmen; rock garden

Mark Robson's youth has turned this 10-year-old garden, entirely hidden in a small disused quarry, into something of a cult. But deservedly so, for both design and plantings are brilliant.

Chillingham Castle
Chillingham, Northumberland NE66 5NJ
☎ 01668 215359   FAX 01668 215463
OWNER   Sir Humphry Wakefield Bt.

318 Gardens NORTHUMBERLAND

LOCATION Off A1 between Alnwick and Berwick
OPEN 1.30 – 5.30 pm, daily except Tuesday, 1 May to 1 October. Plus Easter and Bank Holidays
ADMISSION Adults £3.30; Senior Citizens and Children £2.75
FACILITIES Parking; loos; museum, antique and curio shop; tea room
FEATURES Herbaceous borders; lake; modern roses; old roses and climbers; good topiary; woodland garden; daffodils; bluebells; vast yew trees and magnificent redwoods
ENGLISH HERITAGE GRADE II

Chillingham has made great efforts to smarten up for visitors. The results are very encouraging: a 19th-century Italian or Italianate garden, a modern herbaceous border in the old walled garden and splendid hardy hybrid rhododendrons in the woodland walks which surround the lake. Chillingham itself is a formidable medieval castle with amazing views down long, 18th-century rides.

Cragside
Rothbury, Morpeth, Northumberland NE65 7PX
☎ 01669 21267

OWNER The National Trust
LOCATION 15 miles north west of Morpeth off A697 and B6341
OPEN 10.30 am – 5.30 pm, Tuesday – Sunday, 1 April to 30 October
ADMISSION Adults £3.40; Children £1.70
FACILITIES Parking; loos; National Trust shop; refreshments
FEATURES Fine conifers; fruit of special interest; lake; rock garden; old roses and climbers; interesting for children; massive rock garden, rather dimly planted with heathers; Armstrong's hydroelectric system fascinates adults and children alike; Italianate terrace replanted (1995); tallest *Abies nordmanniana* in the British Isles
ENGLISH HERITAGE GRADE II*

2 gardens. The newly-acquired Italianate formal garden has splendid carpet bedding, ferneries and a fruit house with rotating pots. Even more impressive are the rhododendron woods – hundreds and hundreds of acres of 19th-century hybrids, plus trusty *RR. ponticum* and *luteum*, breathtaking in late May.

Herterton House Gardens & Nursery
Hartington, Cambo, Northumberland NE61 6BN
☎ 0167 074 278

OWNER Mr and Mrs Frank Lawley
LOCATION 2 miles north of Cambo
OPEN 1.30 – 5.30 pm, daily except Tuesdays and Thursdays, 1 April to 30 September
ADMISSION £1.50
FACILITIES Parking; loos; plants for sale
FEATURES Herbaceous borders; herbs; plants for plantsmen; good topiary; knot garden

A plantsman's garden attached to a small nursery. The knot garden is famous, and much photographed, full of herbs and pharmacological plants. More impressive still are the herbaceous plantings, all weaving through each other in beautiful colour schemes.

Hexham Herbs
Chesters Walled Garden, Humshaugh, Hexham, Northumberland NE46 4BQ
☎ 01434 681483

OWNER Mrs S. White
LOCATION 6 miles north of Hexham, off B6318 near Chollerford
OPEN 10 am – 5 pm, daily, March to October. Telephone for winter opening times
ADMISSION Adults £1; Children (under 10) free
FACILITIES Parking; loos; access for the disabled; nursery attached
FEATURES Herbs; old roses and climbers; woodland garden; 'Roman' garden; new formal pool garden; new *potager* (1995)
NCCPG NATIONAL COLLECTIONS *Thymus, Origanum*

An energetic and successful small modern nursery garden, strategically placed near the fort at Chesters. The herb collection is remarkable (over 900 varieties) and the design within a brick walled garden is charming.

Howick Hall Gardens
Alnwick, Northumberland NE66 3LB
☎ 01665 577285 FAX 01665 577285

OWNER Howick Trustees Ltd
LOCATION Off B1399 between Longhoughton and Howick
OPEN 1 – 6 pm, daily, 1 April to 31 October
ADMISSION Adults £1.50; Senior Citizens and Children 75p (1994)
FACILITIES Parking; loos
FEATURES Fine conifers; daffodils; lake; plants for plantsmen; rhododendrons and azaleas; old roses and climbers; woodland garden; spring bulbs; *Eucryphia*
ENGLISH HERITAGE GRADE II

Rather an un-Northumbrian garden, because its closeness to the sea makes possible the cultivation of such tender plants as *Carpenteria* and *Ceanothus*. Formal terraces below the house, well planted, but the great joy of the garden at Howick is a small woodland which has acid soil. This was planted in the 1930s with a fine collection of rhododendrons and camellias: other plants are still added. The result looks more west coast than east.

Kirkley Hall Gardens
Ponteland, Northumberland NE20 0AQ
☎ 01661 860808

OWNER Kirkley Hall College
LOCATION Signposted in Ponteland
OPEN 10 am – 5 pm, daily, all year

ADMISSION   Adults £1.50; Senior Citizens and Children 70p
FACILITIES   Parking; loos; access for the disabled; new garden centre under development; light refreshments
FEATURES   Herbaceous borders; fine conifers; fruit and vegetables of special interest; glasshouses and conservatories to visit; plants for plantsmen; pond; woodland garden
NCCPG NATIONAL COLLECTIONS *Hedera, Fagus, Salix*
FRIENDS   Friends of Kirkley Hall

One of the best gardens in the north of England to learn how to garden. The emphasis is on plants – their selection, cultivation and enjoyment. A rising star among gardens.

Wallington Hall
Cambo, Morpeth, Northumberland NE61 4AR
☎ 01670 774283

OWNER   The National Trust
LOCATION   6 miles north west of Belsay (A696)
OPEN   10.30 am – 7 pm (6 pm in October, and 4 pm or dusk, if earlier, from 1 November to 31 March), daily, all year
ADMISSION   Adults £2.20; Children £1.10 (prices may go up early in year)
FACILITIES   Parking; dogs permitted; loos; access for the disabled; restaurant
FEATURES   Herbaceous borders; daffodils; glasshouses and conservatories to visit; lake; rhododendrons and azaleas; old roses and climbers; woodland garden; plantings by Graham Thomas
ENGLISH HERITAGE GRADE   II*
NCCPG NATIONAL COLLECTIONS *Sambucus*

There are three reasons to visit Wallington. First, because Capability Brown was born in nearby Kirkharle. Second, to gawp at the ancient tree-like specimen of *Fuchsia* 'Rose of Castille' in the conservatory. Third, to admire the modern mixed borders (*very* Graham Thomas) in the long, irregular, walled garden, in a sheltered valley far from the house. Worth the journey for any of them, but prepare for a longish walk to the walled garden.

NOTTINGHAMSHIRE

Clumber Park
The Estate Office, Worksop, Nottinghamshire
S80 3AZ
☎ 01909 476592   FAX 01909 500721

OWNER   The National Trust
LOCATION   Off A614 Nottingham Road, 4 miles south of Worksop
OPEN   Park: 10.30 am – 5 pm (6 pm in summer), every day, all year. Garden: Saturdays, Sundays and Bank Holidays, Good Friday – September
ADMISSION   Park: free. Garden: Adults 60p, Children 30p. Car parking £2.50

FACILITIES   Parking; dogs permitted; loos; facilities for the disabled; National Trust shop; restaurant
FEATURES   Herbaceous borders; landscape designed by Capability Brown; follies and garden buildings; fruit of special interest; glasshouses and conservatories to visit; herbs; lake; woodland garden; autumn colour; vineries; old rhubarb cultivars; superb trees; tallest *Ilex aquifolium* 'Laurifolia' in the British Isles
ENGLISH HERITAGE GRADE   I

3,800 acres of thickly wooded parkland with a Gothic chapel, classical bridge, temples, an avenue of cedars, a heroic double avenue of limes and masses of rhododendrons. Good conservatories and a garden tools exhibition in the old walled garden. The scale is enormous: very impressive.

Felley Priory
Underwood, Jacksdale, Nottinghamshire NG16 5FL
☎ 01773 810230/812056

OWNER   The Hon. Mrs Chaworth-Musters
LOCATION   ½ a mile west of M1 on A608
OPEN   9 am – 4 pm, 2nd and 4th Wednesday every month; February to October; 11 am – 4 pm, 23 April and 25 June for NGS
ADMISSION   £1, but £1.50 for NGS
FACILITIES   Parking; dogs permitted; loos; facilities for the disabled; nursery attached; tea room
FEATURES   Herbaceous borders; modern roses; knot gardens, two pergolas and new rose garden, orchard of daffodils; new medieval garden of roses and pinks (1994)

Newish plantsman's garden, attached to small but promising nursery. Handsome yew hedges, only 15 years old, with wavy patterns and bobbles on top. Definitely a garden to watch.

Flintham Hall
Flintham, Newark, Nottinghamshire
☎ 01636 525214

OWNER   Myles Thoroton Hildyard
LOCATION   On A46, 6 miles south of Newark
OPEN   For NGS, see Yellow Book
ADMISSION   £1.50
FACILITIES   Parking; dogs permitted; loos; teas
FEATURES   Good collection of trees; herbaceous borders; follies and garden buildings; lake; woodland garden
ENGLISH HERITAGE GRADE   II*

A large garden, well-maintained and remarkable for its extravagant Victorian conservatory, lushly planted.

Hodsock Priory
Blyth, Worksop, Nottinghamshire S81 0TY
☎ 01909 591204   FAX 01909 591578

OWNER   Sir Andrew and Lady Buchanan
LOCATION   Signed off the B6045 Blyth – Worksop
OPEN   2 – 5 pm, Tuesday – Thursday and Sundays, 1 April to 30 July, but not late May Bank Holiday week-

end. Also 10 am – 4 pm (1 – 4 pm weekends), daily, 1 February to 1 March for snowdrops
ADMISSION   Adults £2; Children free
FACILITIES   Parking; loos; facilities for the disabled; plants for sale; tea room
FEATURES   Herbaceous borders; lake; old roses and climbers; lilies; gardening courses

Richly planted modern garden on an ancient moated site. Excellent rose gardens and mixed borders, plus some fine old trees.

Morton Hall
Ranby, Retford, Nottinghamshire DH22 7HW
☎ 01777 701142

OWNER   Lady Mason
LOCATION   Between A620 and A1, drive on left
OPEN   For NGS: see Yellow Book
ADMISSION   £2 a car or £1.25 per head, whichever is the least (1994)
FACILITIES   Parking; dogs permitted; loos; access for the disabled; teas
FEATURES   Fine conifers; rock garden; woodland garden

A Victorian amateur's arboretum is the basis of the garden at Morton and the splendid nursery which adjoins it. Best in spring, when daffodils and rhododendrons make a blaze of colour, before the grass grows up to turn it into a green garden later.

Newstead Abbey
Newstead Abbey Park, Nottinghamshire NG15 8GE
☎ 01623 793557   FAX 01623 797136

OWNER   Nottingham City Council
LOCATION   4 miles south of Mansfield on A60
OPEN   10 am – 8 pm (5 pm in winter), daily, all year
ADMISSION   Adults £1.60; Children £1; Concessions £1
FACILITIES   Parking; dogs permitted; loos; facilities for the disabled; plants for sale; restaurant and refreshments
FEATURES   Herbs; lake; oriental features; rock garden; modern roses; old roses and climbers
ENGLISH HERITAGE GRADE   I

Chiefly of interest for being the debt-ridden estate Lord Byron inherited and had to sell, but Newstead has a good modern garden. Best are the Japanese garden and substantial rockery. The Council has restored and replanted it all extensively as a public amenity: lots of cheerful roses and summer bedding.

OXFORDSHIRE

Blenheim Palace
Woodstock, Oxford, Oxfordshire OX20 1PX
☎ 01993 811091   FAX 01993 813527

OWNER   The Duke of Marlborough
LOCATION   8 miles north of Oxford

OPEN   10.30 am – 4.45 pm, daily, 13 March to 31 October
ADMISSION   Adults £3; Children £1.50 (1994)
FACILITIES   Parking; loos; plants for sale; good shops; light meals and refreshments
FEATURES   Landscape designed by Capability Brown; follies and garden buildings; herbs; lake; garden sculpture; interesting for children; formal gardens; new maze; current holder of Sandford Award
ENGLISH HERITAGE GRADE   I

The grandest of grand gardens. Vanbrugh, Bridgeman, Hawksmoor and Wise worked here. The huge (2,000-acre) park was laid out by Capability Brown and Achille Duchêne restored the formal baroque gardens in the 1920s; most impressive too are the 8 acres of walled kitchen garden.

Brook Cottage
Well Lane, Alkerton, Banbury, Oxfordshire OX15 6NL
☎ 01295 670303/670590

OWNER   Mr and Mrs D. M. Hodges
LOCATION   6 miles west of Banbury, ½ a mile off A422
OPEN   9 am – 6 pm, Monday – Friday, 1 April to 31 October
ADMISSION   Adults £2; Senior Citizens £1.50; Children free
FACILITIES   Parking; dogs permitted; loos; plants for sale; DIY tea and coffee; groups by arrangement
FEATURES   Herbaceous borders; lake; plants for plantsmen; rock garden; modern roses; old roses and climbers; 40 different clematis

First-rate modern garden made by present owners over the last 30 years. Good plants and good plantings but, above all, a good sense of colour and form. 4 acres: allow lots of time, and follow the suggested route.

Broughton Castle
Banbury, Oxfordshire OX15 5EB
☎ 01295 262624

OWNER   Lord Saye
LOCATION   2½ miles west of Banbury on the B4035
OPEN   2 – 5 pm, Wednesdays and Sundays, 18 May to 14 September. Plus Thursdays in July and August, Bank Holiday Sundays and Mondays (including Easter). NGS days 25 June, 6 July, 6 August
ADMISSION   Castle and gardens: Adults £3.50; Senior Citizens and Students £3; Children £1.50
FACILITIES   Parking; dogs permitted; loos; facilities for the disabled; plants for sale; tea room
FEATURES   Herbaceous borders; planted by Gertrude Jekyll; old roses and climbers
ENGLISH HERITAGE GRADE   II*

Mainly designed and planted by Lanning Roper 25 years ago, with a blue-yellow-white border contrasting with a pink-and-silver one. Neat knot garden with roses and lavender.

Buscot Park
Faringdon, Oxfordshire SN7 8BU
OWNER The National Trust
LOCATION On A417 west of Faringdon
OPEN 2 – 6 pm, Wednesday – Friday, plus 2nd and 4th Saturday and Sunday each month, April to September
ADMISSION Adults £3
FACILITIES Parking; loos; plants for sale; light refreshments
FEATURES Herbaceous borders; follies and garden buildings; fruit of special interest; lake; old roses and climbers; garden sculpture; good topiary; woodland garden; tallest *Pinus nigra* var. *cebennensis* in the British Isles
ENGLISH HERITAGE GRADE II*

One of the most original gardens of this century, planned by Harold Peto as a water garden (long canals and bridges), with a *patte d'oie* groundplan. Peter Coats planted lush herbaceous borders in the 1970s and Tim Rees did a good conversion job in the walled garden 10 years later: vegetables as climbing plants and gooseberries grown as standards are among his quirkier features.

Clock House
Coleshill, Swindon, Oxfordshire SN6 7PT
☎ 01793 762476
OWNER Mr and Mrs Michael Wickham
LOCATION On B4019 between Highworth and Faringdon
OPEN 2 – 6 pm, 14 May, 18 June, 10 September and by appointment
ADMISSION £1.50
FACILITIES Parking; loos; access for the disabled; teas and cakes
FEATURES Herbaceous borders; herbs; old roses and climbers

A garden of charm and vigour, whose borders burgeon with good growth, unusual juxtapositions and original colour schemes. An inspiration.

Faringdon House
Faringdon, Oxfordshire SN7 8AE
☎ 01367 240240/240145
OWNER Sofka Zinovieff
LOCATION Entrance by the church
OPEN 2 – 5 pm, 16 April, for NGS
ADMISSION Adults £1; Children free
FACILITIES Parking; dogs permitted; loos; access for the disabled; plants for sale; teas
FEATURES Herbaceous borders; 18th-century orangery

A handsome house and straightforward landscaped park – at first sight. But the garden is full of dottinesses concocted by the late Lord Berners: a bust of General Havelock sinking below the surface of a lily pond, and a gazebo paved with old pennies. Surreal, but fun.

Greenways
40 Osler Road, Headington, Oxford, Oxfordshire OX3 9BJ
☎ 01865 56767 (evenings) FAX 01865 56646
OWNER Mr and Mrs N. H. N. Coote
LOCATION Osler Road is off London Road, within ring road
OPEN 2 – 6 pm, 7 May, 21 May, 16 July, 13 August, and groups by appointment
ADMISSION £1 on 7 May, otherwise £1.80
FACILITIES Loos; plants for sale; teas
FEATURES Herbaceous borders; plants for plantsmen; subtropical plants; particularly good in July-August

Quite new, and totally different. The Cootes have emphasised the Provençal looks of the house by planting a Mediterranean garden – evergreen hedges, terracotta pots, old oil jars, gravel, parterres – with an exuberance of tender plants including olives, daturas, yuccas, oleanders, *Acanthus* and albizias.

Greystone Cottage
Colmore Lane, Kingwood Common, Henley-on-Thames, Oxfordshire RG9 5NA
☎ 01491 628559 FAX 01491 628839
OWNER Mr and Mrs William Roxburgh
LOCATION Between B481 and Stoke Row road
OPEN 2 – 6 pm, 5 March, 7 May, 18 June and by appointment
ADMISSION Adults £1; Children free
FACILITIES Parking; access for the disabled; small nursery; home-made teas
FEATURES Fine conifers; rock garden; old roses and climbers; woodland garden; snowdrops; hellebores; narcissus; fritillaries

2½ acres of perfect plantsmanship, this garden is full of unusual plants in innumerable mini-habitats. It is inspirational at its March opening, and there are drifts of *Fritillaria meleagris* in May and meadow flowers in June, but every part is highly rewarding at all seasons.

Manor House, Stanton Harcourt
Stanton Harcourt, Oxford, Oxfordshire
☎ 01865 881928
OWNER The Hon. Mrs Gascoigne
LOCATION In village
OPEN 2 – 6 pm, 16, 17, 27 and 30 April; 1, 7, 8, 11, 14, 25, 28 and 29 May; 8, 11, 22 and 25 June; 6, 9,20 and 23 July; 10,13, 24, 27 and 28 August; 7, 10, 21 and 24 September
ADMISSION Adults £3; Children £2
FACILITIES Parking; dogs permitted; loos; access for the disabled; plants for sale; teas
FEATURES Herbaceous borders; daffodils; climbing roses; modern roses

Wonderful late medieval manor house, surrounded by Edwardian gardens in the Elizabethan style. Parts are romantically overgrown. Others have been spruced up in contemporary taste with David Austin roses and espaliered fruit trees.

Mount Skippet
Ramsden, Witney, Oxfordshire OX7 3AP
☎ 01993 868253

OWNER Dr M. A. T. Rogers
LOCATION Take B4022 4 miles north of Witney, turn right to Finstock and immediately right again
OPEN By appointment
ADMISSION £1 for NGS
FACILITIES Parking; loos; access for the disabled; plants for sale
FEATURES Herbaceous borders; glasshouses and conservatories to visit; gravel or scree garden; plants for plantsmen; rock garden; alpine troughs

An alpine plantsman's collection, brimful with rarities in pots, troughs, screes, and raised beds. The owner considers that his garden maintenance is not as good as it used to be, but many visitors disagree and find infinite interest in this beautifully sited 2-acre treasure house for good plants. And not just alpines, but trees, shrubs, bulbs and herbaceous plants too.

Nuneham Courtenay Arboretum
Nuneham Courtenay, Oxfordshire
☎ 01865 276920

OWNER University of Oxford
LOCATION 6 miles south of Oxford on the Henley road
OPEN 10 am – 5 pm (4.30 pm from 1 November to 30 April), Monday – Friday, all year, except Good Friday, Easter Monday and 22 December to 4 January
ADMISSION Donation
FACILITIES Parking
FEATURES Good collection of trees; fine conifers; woodland garden
NCCPG NATIONAL COLLECTIONS Bambuseae

50-acre arboretum developed since 1950 around a nucleus of American conifers planted c.1840. Experimental plantations and conservation areas rub along with cushioned rhododendrons, a bluebell wood and an Acer glade to match Westonbirt.

The Old Rectory, Farnborough
Farnborough, Wantage, Oxfordshire OX12 8NX
☎ 01488 638298

OWNER Mr and Mrs Michael Todhunter
LOCATION In village
OPEN 2 – 6 pm, 23 April, 14 May, 25 June and by appointment
ADMISSION Adults £1.50; Private parties £3 each
FACILITIES Parking
FEATURES Herbaceous borders; old roses and climbers

Excellent modern garden, made by the owners on a high, cold, windy site over the last 25 years. Lots of hedges and thick planting were the keys to survival, but the effect now is of shelter and luxuriance. Splendid double herbaceous border and clever colour plantings.

Oxford Botanic Garden
High Street, Oxford, Oxfordshire OX1 4AX
☎ 01865 276920

OWNER University of Oxford
LOCATION East end of High Street next to river
OPEN 9 am – 5 pm (4.30 pm from October to March), daily, all year except Good Friday and Christmas Day
ADMISSION Donation box, but £1 in summer
FACILITIES Facilities for the disabled
FEATURES Fine conifers; glasshouses and conservatories to visit; herbs; rock garden; modern roses; old roses and climbers; garden sculpture; interesting for children; systematic beds; huge service tree; tallest *Diospyros virginiana* in UK
ENGLISH HERITAGE GRADE I
FRIENDS Friends of Oxford Botanic Garden: details from the Secretary, c/o Oxford University Botanic Garden. Seed list, lectures, use of library, plant sales
NCCPG NATIONAL COLLECTIONS *Euphorbia*

A beautifully laid out, well-labelled, progressive yet classical botanic garden, founded in 1621. Everything you would expect, from ferns to carnivorous plants, but also a grace and calm that is far from the bustle outside.

Rousham House
Steeple Aston, Oxford, Oxfordshire OX5 3QX
☎ 01869 347110/01869 360407

OWNER C. Cottrell-Dormer
LOCATION A4260 then off the B4030
OPEN 10 am – 4.30 pm, daily, all year
ADMISSION Adults £2.50. No children under 15
FACILITIES Parking; loos
FEATURES Lake; old roses and climbers; early 18th-century landscape; worked on by Kent
ENGLISH HERITAGE GRADE I

Rousham is the most perfect surviving example of William Kent's landscaping: *Kentissimo*, according to Horace Walpole. The main axis focuses on Scheemakers's statue of a lion and a horse and down to the River Cherwell. Follow the right sequence: the serpentine landscape lies away to the side. Here are Venus' Vale, the Cold Bath and Townsend's Building, from which the lime walk will lead you to the Praeneste. Rousham is an experience.

Stansfield
49 High Street, Stanford-in-the-Vale, Oxfordshire SN7 8NQ
☎ 01367 710340

OWNER Mr and Mrs D. Keeble
LOCATION Off A417 opposite Vale garage
OPEN 10 am – 4 pm, Tuesdays, 5 April to 27 September
ADMISSION Adults £1; Children free
FACILITIES Parking; access for the disabled

SHROPSHIRE Gardens 323

FEATURES Herbaceous borders; gravel or scree garden; plantsman's garden

A modern plantsman's garden, and a model of what enthusiastic collecting can produce in a few years. Over 2,000 different plants in just over 1 acre, with troughs, screes, open borders and endless micro-habitats. Fascinating.

Waterperry Gardens
Wheatley, Oxford, Oxfordshire OX33 1JZ
☎ 01844 339226   FAX 01844 339883
OWNER School of Economic Science
LOCATION Near J8 on M40, well signed locally
OPEN 10.30 am - 5.30 pm (6 pm on Saturdays and Sundays), daily, March to October; 10 am - 5 pm, daily, November to March
ADMISSION March to October: Adults £2.20; Senior Citizens £1.70; Children £1. November to February: all 75p
FACILITIES Parking; dogs permitted; loos; access for the disabled; plants for sale; home produce, stoneware, books; tea shop; wine licence
FEATURES Herbaceous borders; fine conifers; fruit of special interest; glasshouses and conservatories to visit; herbs; rock garden; modern roses
NCCPG NATIONAL COLLECTIONS Saxifraga

Essentially a teaching garden with a commercial nursery grafted on, Waterperry has a slightly uncoordinated feel to it. But the herbaceous borders and alpine collections are worth the journey.

Westwell Manor
Burford, Oxfordshire OX18 4JT
FAX 0171 371 2178
OWNER Mr and Mrs T. H. Gibson
LOCATION 2 miles from A40, west of Burford roundabout
OPEN 2 - 6.30 pm, 21 May and 2 July
ADMISSION £2
FACILITIES Parking; loos; plants for sale; light teas
FEATURES Herbaceous borders; fruit of special interest; old roses and climbers; good topiary; new allée of pleached limes (1994); pergola planted with green and white climbers (1994)

Busy Cotswold garden with several distinct 'rooms' and well-used converted outbuildings. Roses in profusion, bulbs for spring and climbers draping the walls and hedges.

Wilcote House
Wilcote, Finstock, Oxfordshire OX7 3DY
☎ 01993 868606
OWNER The Hon. Charles Cecil
LOCATION ½ a mile from Finstock on the Northleigh road
OPEN For NGS: see Yellow Book. And by appointment
ADMISSION £1 (1994)

FACILITIES Parking; dogs permitted; loos; access for the disabled; plants for sale; refreshments on open days or by arrangement
FEATURES Good collection of trees; old roses and climbers; laburnum walk

Fast-developing garden around a stunning Jacobethan house. Courtyards and terraces with Mediterranean goodies and climbers. Borders with clever colours and wonderful roses. The arboretum is young and small, but promising.

Woodperry House
Stanton St John, Oxford, Oxfordshire OX33 1AJ
OWNER Mrs R. Lush
LOCATION On Horton-cum-Sindey road ⅓ mile after crossing B4027
OPEN 2 - 5 pm, 14 May and 20 August; groups by appointment
ADMISSION Adults £1.50; Children free
FACILITIES Parking; loos; plants for sale; teas
FEATURES Herbaceous borders; fruit of special interest; lake; garden sculpture; parterres

A large new garden expanding with style and planted with enthusiasm, much influenced by pre-landscape ideas. Avenues of cherry and limes. Parterre with chunky statues. Parkland replanted 1994-95. Restoration of vegetable garden continuing. Definitely a garden to revisit as it grows.

SHROPSHIRE

Benthall Hall
Broseley, Shropshire TF12 5RX
☎ 01952 884028
OWNER The National Trust. Tenants: Mr and Mrs James Benthall
LOCATION 1 mile north west of Broseley (B4375)
OPEN 1.30 - 5.30 pm, Sundays, Wednesdays and Bank Holiday Mondays, April to September
ADMISSION Adults £2
FACILITIES Parking; loos; facilities for the disabled
FEATURES Herbaceous borders; fruit of special interest; glasshouses and conservatories to visit; herbs; old roses and climbers; plantings by Graham Thomas

Smallish, but well-restored with a Graham Thomas rose garden. Home of the 19th-century botanist George Maw. His Mediterranean collection is still the backbone of the garden - Crocus naturalised everywhere.

Erway Farm House
Pentre Coed, Ellesmere, Shropshire SY12 9ED
☎ 01691 75479
OWNER A. A. and B. N. Palmer
LOCATION Signposted from B5068 and B5069
OPEN 2 - 6 pm, last Sunday of month, February to September; plus Easter Saturday - Monday
ADMISSION Adults £1; Children free
FACILITIES Parking; loos; plants for sale

FEATURES   Oriental features; plants for plantsmen; old roses and climbers; snowdrops; hellebores; *Lathraea clandestina*; tulips; cyclamen

A cottage garden full of rare plants, inspired by Margery Fish. Layers of different plants from tiny bulbs to tall trees. Visit early for the snowdrops and *Helleborus orientalis* forms.

Hodnet Hall
Hodnet, Market Drayton, Shropshire TF9 3NN
☎ 01630 685202   FAX 01630 685853
OWNER   A. E. H. Heber-Percy
LOCATION   Near junction of A53 and A442
OPEN   2 – 5 pm, Tuesday – Saturday, 12 noon – 5.30 pm, Sundays and Bank Holiday Mondays, April to September
ADMISSION   Adults £2.60; Senior Citizens £2.10; Children £1 (1994)
FACILITIES   Parking; dogs permitted; loos; access for the disabled; plants for sale; gift shop; 17th-century tea rooms
FEATURES   Herbaceous borders; lake; old roses and climbers; woodland garden; camellias; primulas; rhododendrons; HHA/Christie's Garden of the Year in 1985
ENGLISH HERITAGE GRADE II

A large garden, still expanding, and well-maintained. Best known for the lakes and ponds planted with primulas and aquatics, but the rhododendrons alone demand a visit. Good in late summer too, with hydrangeas and astilbes. One of the greatest 20th-century gardens.

Lower Hall
Worfield, Bridgnorth, Shropshire WV15 5LH
☎ 01746 716207   FAX 01746 716607
OWNER   C. F. Dumbell
LOCATION   In centre of village of Worfield
OPEN   By appointment
ADMISSION   £2
FACILITIES   Loos; access for the disabled; plants for sale; tea and coffee
FEATURES   Herbaceous borders; lake; plants for plantsmen; modern roses; old roses and climbers

Lanning Roper helped to get this splendid garden going 30 years ago. It bestrides the River Worfe and every part has a distinct character. Lush streamside plantings, infinite colour schemes, and a woodland area at the bottom. Formal designs, straight brick paths, a pergola and more colour themes in the old walled garden. One of the best modern gardens and neatly kept.

Preen Manor
Church Preen, Church Stretton, Shropshire SY6 7LQ
☎ 01694 771207
OWNER   Philip Trevor-Jones
LOCATION   From B4371 Much Wenlock – Church Stretton
OPEN   For NGS and by appointment
ADMISSION   Adults £2; Children 50p

FACILITIES   Parking; loos; home-made teas
FEATURES   Fruit of special interest; gravel or scree garden; lake; woodland garden; fern garden

A new garden for an old site, with some original ideas. A chess garden, a collection of plants in handsome old pots, a fern garden and that symbol of the 1990s – a gravel garden. And it gets better every year.

Ruthall Manor
Ditton Priors, Bridgnorth, Shropshire WV16 6TN
☎ 0174 634 608
OWNER   Mr and Mrs G. T. Clarke
LOCATION   Take Weston road from church, then 2nd left
OPEN   2 – 6 pm, NGS open day and by appointment
ADMISSION   £1.50
FACILITIES   Parking; dogs permitted; loos; access for the disabled
FEATURES   Lake; plantsman's garden

1-acre plantsman's garden made over 20 years. Good trees, rare shrubs and lots of ground cover. Pretty pool with aquatics and marginals. Very satisfying.

Swallow Hayes
Rectory Road, Albrighton, Wolverhampton, Shropshire WV7 3EP
☎ 01902 372624
OWNER   Mrs P. Edwards
LOCATION   First lane on right on A41 towards Wolverhampton after garden centre
OPEN   11 am – 4 pm, 8 January; 2 – 6 pm, 30 April, 14 and 28 May. And by appointment
ADMISSION   Adults £1.20; Children 10p
FACILITIES   Parking; dogs permitted; loos; access for the disabled; plants for sale; teas on open days
FEATURES   Herbaceous borders; fine conifers; fruit of special interest; gravel or scree garden; herbs; rock garden
NCCPG NATIONAL COLLECTIONS *Hamaelis*, *Lupinus* (Russell)

25 years of plantsmanship and 3,000 plants have made Swallow Hayes a model modern garden, where ground cover helps to minimise labour and maximise enjoyment. The owners have crazes which add enormously to the visitor's pleasure: the current one is geraniums – over 100 different varieties 'on trial'.

Weston Park
Weston-under-Lizard, Shifnal, Shropshire TF11 8LE
☎ 01952850 207   FAX 01952850 430
OWNER   The Weston Park Foundation
LOCATION   Off the A5 to Telford
OPEN   Easter to mid September (full dates and times not yet known)
ADMISSION   Adults £3; Children £2 (1994)
FACILITIES   Parking; dogs permitted; loos; facilities for the disabled; gift shop; tea rooms
FEATURES   Good collection of trees; landscape designed by Capability Brown; old roses and climbers;

woodland garden; landscaped park; rhododendrons; good new shrub plantings around the Church Pool (1994)
ENGLISH HERITAGE GRADE II*

18th-century landscape with 19th-century Italianate parterre, a temple of Diana and an handsome orangery by Paine. But best for its trees, some of them record-breakers, and the collection of *Nothofagus* planted by the late Lord Bradford.

SOMERSET

Ammerdown Park
Kilmersdown, Radstock, Bath, Somerset BA3 5SH
☎ 01761 437382

OWNER   Lord Hylton
LOCATION   West of Terry Hill crossroads: A362/366
OPEN   11 am – 5 pm, Bank Holiday Mondays, Easter Monday to August
ADMISSION   Adults £3; Children free
FACILITIES   Parking; access for the disabled
FEATURES   Planted by Gertrude Jekyll; designed by Lutyens
ENGLISH HERITAGE GRADE II*

Ammerdown's layout is Lutyens at his most ingenious. The lie of the land precludes right angles, but long straight views cover up the irregularities. Some nice plants, particularly trees, but the design is everything.

Barrington Court
Barrington, Ilminster, Somerset TA19 0NQ
☎ 01460 241480

OWNER   The National Trust
LOCATION   In Barrington village
OPEN   11.30 am – 5.30 pm, Saturday – Thursday, 1 April to 30 September
ADMISSION   Adults £3.10
FACILITIES   Parking; loos; access for the disabled; plants for sale; tea room and licensed restaurant
FEATURES   Good collection of trees; fruit of special interest; planted by Gertrude Jekyll; lake; old roses and climbers; particularly in July-August; rose and *Iris* garden restored to original Jekyll plans (1995)
ENGLISH HERITAGE GRADE II*

There is still an Edwardian opulence about Barrington. Massive plantings of irises, lilies and rich dark dahlias. And good design detail too: the patterns of the brick paving are a study in themselves.

Cannington College Heritage Garden
Cannington, Bridgwater, Somerset TA5 2LS
☎ 01278 652226   FAX 01278 652479

OWNER   Cannington College
LOCATION   3 miles west of Bridgwater on A39
OPEN   2 – 5 pm, daily, 1 April to 31 October
ADMISSION   Adults £1.50; Senior Citizens and Children 75p

FACILITIES   Parking; loos; plants for sale; student canteen open to visitors
FEATURES   Alpines; herbaceous borders; fine conifers; fruit of special interest; glasshouses and conservatories to visit; plants for plantsmen; modern roses; old roses and climbers; subtropical plants
NCCPG NATIONAL COLLECTIONS *Abutilon*, *Argyranthemum*, *Ceanothus*, *Cordyline*, *Osteospermum*, *Phormium*, *Wisteria*, *Yucca*

Cannington has long been the leading West Country college for ornamental horticulture. The collections in its teaching gardens are very extensive and beautifully displayed.

Dunster Castle
Minehead, Somerset TA24 6SL
☎ 01643 821314

OWNER   The National Trust
LOCATION   3 miles south east of Minehead on A39
OPEN   11 am – 4 pm (6 pm from April to September), daily, 1 February to 12 December
ADMISSION   Adults £2.70; Children £1.30; Family £6.50
FACILITIES   Parking; loos; facilities for the disabled; National Trust shop; tea rooms at Dunster Mill
FEATURES   Lake; subtropical plants; woodland garden; particularly interesting in winter; *Arbutus* grove
NCCPG NATIONAL COLLECTIONS *Arbutus*

A Victorian woodland on a steep slope, terraced in places and planted with tender exotica – mimosa, *Beschorneria* and a 150-year-old lemon tree in an unheated conservatory.

East Lambrook Manor
East Lambrook, South Petherton, Somerset TA13 5HL
☎ 01460 240328   FAX 01460 242344

OWNER   Mr and Mrs Andrew Norton
LOCATION   Off A303 at South Petherton
OPEN   10 am – 5 pm, Monday – Saturday, 1 March to 31 October
ADMISSION   Adults £2; Children and Students 50p; Groups by arrangement £1.80
FACILITIES   Parking; loos; book, picture gallery and gift shop; coffee and biscuits
FEATURES   Herbaceous borders; plants for plantsmen; cottage garden plants; geraniums; newly restored 'Silver Garden' and 'Lido'
ENGLISH HERITAGE GRADE I
NCCPG NATIONAL COLLECTIONS *Geranium*

The archetypal super-cottage garden, made by Margery Fish, the popular and influential writer, and ambitiously restored by the present owners. Ground cover, narrow paths and, above all, plants, plants, plants.

Gaulden Manor
Tolland, Lydeard St Lawrence, Somerset TA4 3PN
☎ 01984 7213

OWNER   James Starkie

LOCATION 9 miles north west of Taunton off A358
OPEN 2 – 5.30 pm, Sundays and Thursdays, 1st Sunday in May to 1st Sunday in September. Also Easter Sunday and Bank Holidays
ADMISSION £1.50
FACILITIES Parking; loos; access for the disabled; plants for sale; book and gift shop; tea room
FEATURES Herbaceous borders; herbs; lake; modern roses; old roses and climbers; woodland garden; scent gardens; secret garden

A modern garden, and well-planted. Small garden rooms, each devoted to a different theme (roses, herbs and so on), and a good stream garden made beneath the monks' pond, its sides planted with candelabra primulas, ferns and *Gunnera*.

Greencombe Garden Trust
Porlock, Somerset TA24 8NU
☎ 01643 862363

OWNER Greencombe Garden Trust
LOCATION ½ a mile west of Porlock on left of road to Porlock Weir
OPEN 2 – 6 pm, Saturday – Tuesday, 1 April to 31 July
ADMISSION Adults £2.50; Children (under 16) 50p
FACILITIES Parking; loos; access for the disabled; plants for sale; teas for large groups
FEATURES Herbaceous borders; fine conifers; ecological interest; plants for plantsmen; woodland garden
NCCPG NATIONAL COLLECTIONS *Erythronium, Gaultheria, polystichum, Vaccinium*

Rather a cult garden, an organic show-piece, best for its woodland walks where stately gentleness dominates. Interesting plants galore.

Hadspen Garden
Castle Cary, Somerset BA7 7NG
☎ 0149 813707

OWNER N. and S. Pope
LOCATION 2 miles east of Castle Cary on A371
OPEN 9 am – 6 pm, Thursday – Sunday, and Bank Holiday Mondays, 2 March to 1 October
ADMISSION Adults £2; Children 50p
FACILITIES Parking; loos; facilities for the disabled; nursery; light lunches and teas
FEATURES Herbaceous borders; gravel or scree garden; lake; plants for plantsmen; old roses and climbers; Eric Smith's *Hosta* collection
NCCPG NATIONAL COLLECTIONS *Rodgersia*

Penelope Hobhouse's own first garden, full of good plants and unusual colour combinations. Restored and improved by two active young Canadians.

Hestercombe House
Somerset County Council, Cheddon Fitzpaine, Taunton, Somerset TA2 8LQ
☎ 01823 337222   FAX 01823 413030

OWNER Somerset County Council Fire Brigade
LOCATION 4 miles north of Taunton

OPEN 9 am – 5 pm (but 2 – 5 pm on Saturdays and Sundays), daily, 1 May to 30 September
ADMISSION Adults £2; Senior Citizens £1.50; Children free
FACILITIES Parking; dogs permitted; loos
FEATURES Herbaceous borders; planted by Gertrude Jekyll
ENGLISH HERITAGE GRADE I

Famously restored garden with lots of Lutyens hallmarks: iris-choked rills, pergolas, relieved staircases and pools where reflections twinkle on recessed apses. Gertrude Jekyll's planting is bold and simple, which adds to the vigour. Very photogenic.

Lytes Cary Manor
Charlton Mackrell, Somerton, Somerset TA11 7HU
☎ 01458 223297

OWNER The National Trust
LOCATION Near A303 junction with A372 and A37
OPEN 2 – 6 pm, Mondays, Wednesdays and Saturdays, April to October
ADMISSION Adults £3.70
FACILITIES Parking; loos; access for the disabled
FEATURES Herbaceous borders; garden sculpture; good topiary; plantings by Graham Thomas
ENGLISH HERITAGE GRADE II

Neo-Elizabethan garden to go with the prettiest of manor houses. Yew hedges, hornbeam walks, alleys and lawns. Medlars, quinces and a simple Elizabethan flower border.

Milton Lodge
Old Bristol Road, Wells, Somerset BA5 3AQ
☎ 01749 672168

OWNER D. C. Tudway Quilter
LOCATION Old Bristol road off A39
OPEN 2 – 6 pm, Sunday – Friday, Easter to 31 October
ADMISSION Adults £2; Children (under 14) free
FACILITIES Parking; loos; plants for sale; teas on Sundays (May to August)
FEATURES Good collection of trees; herbaceous borders; modern roses; woodland garden; tallest *Populus alba* in British Isles

Terraced Edwardian garden with stone paving and walling against a backdrop of Wells Cathedral. Yew hedges, good modern plantings, and an 8-acre arboretum in a combe, replanted in recent years.

Montacute House
Montacute, Yeovil, Somerset TA15 6XP
☎ 01935 823289

OWNER The National Trust
LOCATION In Montacute village
OPEN 11.30 am – 5.30 pm (dusk if earlier), daily except Tuesday, all year
ADMISSION Adults £2.60; Children £1.30 (1994)

FACILITIES Parking; loos; facilities for the disabled; plants for sale; light lunches and teas; licensed restaurant
FEATURES Herbaceous borders; lake; old roses and climbers; exquisite gazebos
ENGLISH HERITAGE GRADE I

The garden is subsidiary to the amazing Elizabethan mansion, apart from a border started by Vita Sackville-West, worked over by Phyllis Reiss and finished by Graham Thomas. But it cannot be beaten for its sense of English renaissance grandeur.

Ston Easton Park
Ston Easton, Bath, Somerset BA3 4DF
☎ 01761 241631

OWNER Peter L. Smedley
LOCATION Intersection of A37 and A39
OPEN By appointment, unless visiting restaurant
ADMISSION Free
FACILITIES Parking; dogs permitted; loos; plants for sale; Ston Easton Park is a hotel: all meals available to non-residents
FEATURES Landscape designed by Humphry Repton; fine conifers; follies and garden buildings; fruit of special interest; lake; ice-house
ENGLISH HERITAGE GRADE II

A country house hotel, voted Hotel of the Year in 1992, with a Humphry Repton landscape. His 'red book' still exists. A sham castle and ruined grotto are two of the features he built, but there are fine trees, spacious lawns and the highest standards of maintenance to enjoy, too.

Tintinhull House
Tintinhull, Yeovil, Somerset BA22 8PZ
☎ 01985 847777

OWNER The National Trust
LOCATION In Tintinhull village
OPEN 12 noon – 6 pm, Wednesdays – Sunday, April to September
ADMISSION Adults £3.30; Children £1.65
FACILITIES Parking; loos; access for the disabled; refreshments
FEATURES Herbaceous borders; lake; old roses and climbers; good topiary; particularly good in July-August; colour borders
ENGLISH HERITAGE GRADE II

A series of formal garden rooms, beautifully designed to maximise a small site (only 1½ acres) and planted with rarities in exquisite colour combinations. No labels: they would spoil the dream.

Wayford Manor
Crewkerne, Somerset TA18 8QG
☎ 01460 73253

OWNER Mr and Mrs R. L. Goffe
LOCATION 3 miles south west of Crewkerne off A30 or B3165
OPEN 2 – 6 pm, 9 and 30 April, 14 and 28 May, for NGS, or parties by appointment

ADMISSION Adults £1.50; Children 50p
FACILITIES Parking; dogs permitted; loos; plants for sale; teas
FEATURES Herbaceous borders; follies and garden buildings; lake; garden sculpture; rhododendrons; spring bulbs; maples
ENGLISH HERITAGE GRADE II

One of the best gardens designed by Harold Peto: terraces and courtyards, pools and arbours, balustrades and staircases, Tuscan and Byzantine. Parts are now rather dominated by overgrown shrubs, but the whole garden is presently being restored by the enthusiastic and knowledgeable owners.

STAFFORDSHIRE

Alton Towers
Alton, Stoke-on-Trent, Staffordshire ST10 4DB
☎ 01538 702200   FAX 01538 702724

OWNER Tussauds Group
LOCATION Signposted for miles around
OPEN 9 am – 6/7/8 pm depending on season, daily, all year
ADMISSION Adults £14 (£15 from 29 May to 6 November); Children £10.50 (£11 from 29 May to 6 November); Senior Citizens £5.50
FACILITIES Parking; loos; facilities for the disabled; many restaurants
FEATURES Good collection of trees; herbaceous borders; fine conifers; follies and garden buildings; lake; oriental features; rock garden; modern roses; woodland garden; interesting for children; particularly good in July-August
ENGLISH HERITAGE GRADE I

300 acres of dotty and exuberant display, best seen from the cable-car. Ignore the theme park: the gardens are by and large detached from the razzmatazz. Splendid Victorian conifers and gaudy bedding, magnificently done. A Swiss cottage, Roman bridge, Chinese pagoda, flag tower, and corkscrew fountain. Excellent entertainment but not for contemplative souls. Best in term time.

Biddulph Grange
Biddulph, Stoke-on-Trent, Staffordshire ST8 7SD
☎ 01782 517999

OWNER The National Trust
LOCATION ½ a mile north of Biddulph, 3½ miles south east of Congleton
OPEN 12 noon – 6 pm, Wednesday – Friday (closed Good Friday), 11 am – 6 pm, Saturdays, Sundays and Bank Holiday Mondays, 1 April to 29 October. Also 12 noon – 4 pm, Saturdays and Sundays, 4 November to 17 December
ADMISSION Adults £3.90 (£2 in November and December); Children £1.95; Family £9.75
FACILITIES Parking; loos; facilities for the disabled; gift shop; tea room

FEATURES Follies and garden buildings; lake; oriental features; interesting for children
ENGLISH HERITAGE GRADE I

An oddity among gardens: yews cut as an Egyptian temple; a statue of a sacred cow; a 4-acre Chinese garden complete with Great Wall of China and lookout tower; a bowling green, quoits ground and 'stumpery'. All energetically and successfully restored by the National Trust.

The Dorothy Clive Garden
Willoughbridge, Market Drayton, Staffordshire TF9 4EU
☎ 01630 647237

OWNER Willoughbridge Garden Trust
LOCATION A51, midway between Nantwich and Stone
OPEN 10 am – 5.30 pm, daily, 1 April to 31 October
ADMISSION Adults £2.60; Children £1
FACILITIES Parking; dogs permitted; loos; facilities for the disabled; tea room with beverages and home-baked food
FEATURES Alpines; herbaceous borders; camellias; fine conifers; gravel or scree garden; rock garden; modern roses; old roses and climbers; woodland garden; rhododendrons; azaleas; heather; *Cyclamen*

Meticulously maintained and still expanding, this 40-year-old garden seems ageless. Made on an unpromising site, a cold windy hilltop, it is best perhaps in May, when the woodland quarry is brilliant with rhododendrons. But the scree and rock gardens (reflected in the lake) are hard to beat at any season. Highly recommended.

Moseley Old Hall
Moseley Old Hall Lane, Fordhouses, Staffordshire WV10 7HY
☎ 01902 782808

OWNER The National Trust
LOCATION South of M54 between A449 and A460
OPEN 2 – 5.30 pm, Wednesdays, Saturdays and Sundays (and Tuesdays in July and August), 11 am – 5 pm, Bank Holiday Mondays, 1 April to 29 October
ADMISSION Adults £3.30; Children £1.65; Family £8
FACILITIES Parking; loos; access for the disabled; plants for sale; gift shop; tea room
FEATURES Herbs; good topiary; current holder of Sandford Award

Modern reconstruction of a 17th-century town garden. Neat box parterres, a nut walk and an arched pergola hung with clematis. Plantings all of a period. Quietly inspirational.

Oulton House
Oulton, Stone, Staffordshire ST15 8UR
☎ 01785 813556

OWNER Mr and Mrs John Bridger
LOCATION From Stone take Oulton road and turn left after Oulton sign: 3rd driveway on right
OPEN 25 June to 9 July, by appointment
ADMISSION Adults £1.50; Children 50p
FACILITIES Parking; loos; plants for sale; tea and coffee
FEATURES Herbaceous borders; glasshouses and conservatories to visit; rock garden; old roses and climbers; new mixed border, 100 yards long (1994)

Newish 3-acre garden, made for private enjoyment and full of good plants – roses, rhododendrons, geraniums and clematis – arranged in colour groupings.

Shugborough Hall
Great Haywood, Milford, Staffordshire ST17 0XB
☎ 01889 881388   FAX 01889 881323

OWNER The National Trust
LOCATION Signed from J13, M6
OPEN 11 am – 5 pm, daily, 25 March to 27 October. Also parties by appointment
ADMISSION Vehicles £1.50; Coaches free
FACILITIES Parking; dogs permitted; loos; facilities for the disabled; garden centre; lunches, snacks, tea and evening dinners
FEATURES Herbaceous borders; follies and garden buildings; lake; oriental features; old roses and climbers; woodland garden; plantings by Graham Thomas; interesting for children; current holder of Sandford Award; new herbaceous border (1994); much tree-planting in the park (1994–5)
ENGLISH HERITAGE GRADE I

Classical and neo-classical landscape with Chinese additions and a handsome Nesfield terrace dominated by dumplings of clipped golden yew. 50 oaks in the new arboretum. Rose garden restored by Graham Thomas. All very popular with the locals.

Trentham Park Gardens
Trentham, Stoke-on-Trent, Staffordshire

OWNER Trentham Leisure Ltd
LOCATION Signposted from M6
OPEN 10 am – 6 pm, daily, April to September
ADMISSION Adults £1.50 (1994)
FACILITIES Parking; dogs permitted; loos; access for the disabled; plants for sale; shop; refreshments
FEATURES Good collection of trees; lake; modern roses; interesting for children; Capability Brown landscape; good bedding; play area; boats on the lake
ENGLISH HERITAGE GRADE II*

It is the grand Italian garden designed by Charles Barry that most impresses the visitor, as well as the sheer size of the whole park and its lake. Now it is a popular place for family outings, and caters for many tastes: not for quiet contemplative plantsmen.

Wolseley Garden Park
Wolseley Bridge, Stafford, Staffordshire ST17 0YT
☎ 01889 574888

OWNER Sir Charles Wolseley Bt.
LOCATION 2 miles north of Rugeley at junction of A51 and A513

OPEN 10 am – 6 pm (4 pm from November to March), daily, all year except Christmas Day
ADMISSION Adults £2; Senior Citizens £1.50; Children £1
FACILITIES Parking; loos; access for the disabled; plants for sale; cafeteria
FEATURES Fine conifers; herbs; lake; rock garden; old roses and climbers; young garden; started in 1988
NCCPG NATIONAL COLLECTIONS *Salix*

A brand-new garden developed as part of a leisure investment, complete with Cramphorn's Garden Centre at the gate. Lakes, bulbs, roses and planting on a big scale. Some banalities and vulgarities, but the scale is impressive: judge for yourself.

SUFFOLK

Euston Hall
Euston, Thetford, Suffolk IP24 2QP
☎ 01842 766366   FAX 01842 766764
OWNER The Duke of Grafton
LOCATION On A1088, 3 miles south of Thetford
OPEN 2.30 – 5 pm, Thursdays, 1 June to 28 September, plus 25 June and 3 September
ADMISSION Adults £2.50; Senior Citizens £2; Parties (12+) £2; Children 50p
FACILITIES Parking; loos; access for the disabled; craft shop; home-made teas
FEATURES Landscape designed by Capability Brown; lake; old roses and climbers; William Kent temple and summerhouse
ENGLISH HERITAGE GRADE II*

Classic 18th-century parkland on a sweeping site, formal terraces by the house and a pretty modern garden with shrub roses. Not spectacular, but satisfying.

Haughley Park
Stowmarket, Suffolk IP14 3JY
☎ 01359 240205   FAX 01359 240546
OWNER The Williams family
LOCATION Signed from A45
OPEN 3 – 5.30 pm, Tuesdays, May to September, plus first two Sundays in May
ADMISSION Adults £2; Children £1
FACILITIES Parking; dogs permitted; loos; facilities for the disabled
FEATURES Bluebells; herbaceous borders; rhododendrons and azaleas; woodland garden; lily-of-the-valley; 1,000-year-old oak

Parkland round a Jacobean mansion with competent modern flower gardens and fine trees (*Davidia involucrata*). But the acres of lily-of-the-valley in the woodland garden are worth the journey no matter how far.

Helmingham Hall
Stowmarket, Suffolk IP14 6EF
☎ 01473 890363   FAX 01473 890776
OWNER Lord Tollemache

LOCATION 9 miles north of Ipswich on B1077
OPEN 2 – 6 pm, Sundays, 30 April to 10 September; plus groups on Wednesdays by prior arrangement
ADMISSION Adults £2.80; Senior Citizens £2.60; Groups (30+) £2.30; Children £1.50
FACILITIES Parking; dogs permitted; loos; access for the disabled; plants for sale; shop; tea rooms
FEATURES Herbaceous borders; old roses and climbers; deer park; fine walled garden
ENGLISH HERITAGE GRADE I

Most of the garden is modern, but well done with parterres in the Tudor style to suit the Elizabethan house and planted with old flower varieties. Wonderful modern planting in the walled garden.

Shrubland Hall
Coddenham, Ipswich, Suffolk IP6 9QP
☎ 01473 830221   FAX 01473 832202
OWNER Lord de Saumarez
LOCATION Outside village of Coddenham: come by A14 or A140
OPEN 2 – 6 pm, 16 July
ADMISSION Adults £2; Senior Citizens and Children £1
FACILITIES Parking; loos; plants for sale; tea tent
FEATURES Herbaceous borders; follies and garden buildings; lake; modern roses; woodland garden; box maze; Swiss chalet
ENGLISH HERITAGE GRADE I

A grand Victorian garden designed by Charles Barry and famous for its spectacular Italianate staircase which connects the terrace around the house with the formal gardens below. William Robinson later helped with the planting, both around the formal garden and in the park and woodland gardens beyond. Much restoration and recovery has been completed in recent years: Shrubland is getting better and better.

Somerleyton Hall
Lowestoft, Suffolk NR32 5QQ
☎ 01502 730224   FAX 01502 732143
OWNER Lord and Lady Somerleyton
LOCATION 4 miles north west of Lowestoft off B1074
OPEN 12.30 – 5.30 pm, Sundays and Thursdays, plus Tuesdays and Wednesdays in July and August, Easter Sunday to last Sunday in September
ADMISSION Adults £3.50; Senior Citizens £3; Children £1.60 (1994)
FACILITIES Parking; loos; facilities for the disabled; souvenir gift shop; tea room
FEATURES Glasshouses and conservatories to visit; modern roses; maze; miniature railway; some evening openings (ask for details)
ENGLISH HERITAGE GRADE II*

A grand formal garden around the monstrous Victorian house. Nesfield laid out the terraces, and Paxton built the curving greenhouses. Good 19th-century maze (not too difficult) and masses of cheerful bedding and roses.

Wyken Hall

Stanton, Bury St Edmunds, Suffolk IP31 2DW
☎ 01359 50287   FAX 01359 50240

OWNER   Kenneth Carlisle
LOCATION   Stanton, 9 miles north east from Bury St Edmunds; brown signs from A143 to Wyken Vineyards
OPEN   10 am – 6 pm, Thursdays, Sundays and Bank Holiday Mondays, 1 February to 24 December
ADMISSION   Adults £2; Senior Citizens £1.50; Children free
FACILITIES   Parking; dogs permitted; loos; facilities for the disabled; plants for sale; country store shop; lunches and teas
FEATURES   Herbaceous borders; fine conifers; fruit of special interest; herbs; plants for plantsmen; modern roses; old roses and climbers; woodland garden; award-winning 7-acre vineyard

Well-run estate with modern gardens to complement the Elizabethan house. Knot garden, herb garden, traditional English kitchen garden, wild-flower meadows, nuttery and new copper beech maze. Ancient woodland walk (SSSI).

SURREY

Brook Lodge Farm Cottage

Blackbrook, Dorking, Surrey RH5 4DT
☎ 01306 888368

OWNER   Mrs Basil Kingham
LOCATION   Car park signed by Plough Inn in Blackbrook
OPEN   11 am – 3 pm, 31 May, 21 June, 26 July; 2 – 6 pm, 28 May, 18 June, 23 July, 20 August
ADMISSION   Adults £1.50; Children free
FACILITIES   Parking; loos; access for the disabled; plants for sale; home-made lunches and afternoon cakes
FEATURES   Herbaceous borders; fine conifers; glasshouses and conservatories to visit; herbs; lake; plants for plantsmen; rock garden; old roses and climbers; woodland garden

Planted by the present owner 45 years ago, this garden has matured into a fine plantsman's garden with much variety: shrub roses, a rockery, a woodland walk, herbaceous borders and two cottage gardens.

Chilworth Manor

Chilworth, Guildford, Surrey
☎ 01483 61414

OWNER   Lady Heald
LOCATION   In middle of village, up Blacksmiths Lane
OPEN   2 – 6 pm, 8 and 9 April, 6 and 7 May, 4 and 5 June, 8 and 9 July, 5 and 6 August, or by appointment
ADMISSION   £1.50
FACILITIES   Parking; dogs permitted; loos; facilities for the disabled; teas and cakes
FEATURES   Herbaceous borders; lake; woodland garden; rhododendrons; interesting new plantings; flower arrangements in the house

A remarkable garden, tiered up seven distinct levels, the top three being c.1700 and walled around (beautiful brickwork). Good climbers and shrubs against the walls, and a bog garden in the woods at the bottom.

Clandon Park

West Clandon, Guildford, Surrey GU4 7RQ
☎ 01483 222482

OWNER   The National Trust
LOCATION   Off the A247 at West Clandon
OPEN   1.30 – 5 pm, Saturday – Wednesday and Good Friday, 3 April to 31 October
ADMISSION   Adults £4; Children (under 17) £2
FACILITIES   Parking; loos; access for the disabled; garden centre; restaurant
FEATURES   Landscape designed by Capability Brown; daffodils; parterres; grotto; Dutch garden; Maori summerhouse
ENGLISH HERITAGE GRADE   II

Capability Brown's magnificent mature beeches are now underplanted with gloomy Victorian shrubberies and slabs of comfrey, bergenias and *Geranium macrorrhizum* – the apotheosis of National Trust ground cover. There is a modern pastiche of a Dutch garden in front of the house – competent rather than inspired – but the daffodils in spring are breathtaking.

Claremont Gardens

Portsmouth Road, Esher, Surrey KT10 9JG
☎ 01372 469421

OWNER   The National Trust
LOCATION   On southern edge of town
OPEN   10 am – 6 pm, but 5 pm from November to March and 7 pm on Saturdays, Sundays and Bank Holiday Mondays from April to October, all year (1994 times and dates)
ADMISSION   Adults £2.50 (1994)
FACILITIES   Parking; dogs permitted; loos; access for the disabled; shop; restaurant
FEATURES   Landscape designed by Capability Brown; worked on by Kent; follies and garden buildings; lake; plantings by Graham Thomas; tallest false acacia *Robinia pseudoacacia* in the British Isles
ENGLISH HERITAGE GRADE   I

A vast historic landscape worked over by Vanburgh, Bridgeman, Kent and Capability Brown. The stunning turf amphitheatre is best seen flanked by spreading cedars from across the dark lake. Very popular locally, and apt to get crowded at summer weekends.

Hatchlands

East Clandon, Guildford, Surrey GU4 7RT
☎ 01483 222482

OWNER   The National Trust
LOCATION   Off A246 Guildford – Leatherhead

OPEN 2 – 5 pm, Tuesday – Thursday, Sundays and Bank Holiday Mondays, 1 April to 31 October
ADMISSION Adults £4; Children (under 17) £2
FACILITIES Parking; loos; National Trust shop; restaurant
FEATURES Landscape designed by Capability Brown; planted by Gertrude Jekyll; landscape designed by Humphry Repton; woodland garden

Apart from the Jekyll garden (roses, lupins, box and columbines) Hatchlands is an 18th-century landscape with parkland. But the garden buildings are charming and the National Trust has started to restore and replant it.

Munstead Wood
Heath Lane, Busbridge, Godalming, Surrey GU7 1UN
☎ 01483 417867   FAX 01483 425041
OWNER Sir Robert and Lady Clark
LOCATION Take Heath Lane from B2130, turn left after 400 yards, entrance on right
OPEN For NGS: see Yellow Book
ADMISSION Adults £2; Children 50p (1994)
FACILITIES Parking; loos; access for the disabled; plants for sale; cream teas
FEATURES Herbaceous borders; planted by Gertrude Jekyll; rock garden; old roses and climbers; woodland garden
ENGLISH HERITAGE GRADE I

Gertrude Jekyll's own garden was nearly lost before the Clarks bought it. They have acknowledged that parts are beyond restoration while others have been put back to their original state. But the lawns still end where the birches begin, to make Munstead 'a garden in a wood'.

Painshill Park
Portsmouth Road, Cobham, Surrey KT11 1JE
☎ 01932 868113/864674 FAX 01932 868001
OWNER Painshill Park Trust
LOCATION West of Cobham on A245
OPEN 11 am – 5 pm, Sundays and pre-booked groups any other day, 9 April to 15 October
ADMISSION Adults £3.50; Senior Citizens and Students £3; Children (under 14) £2.50; Groups £2.80
FACILITIES Parking; loos; facilities for the disabled; souvenirs, books, cards; light refreshments
FEATURES Follies and garden buildings; lake; American garden; grotto; Turkish tent; tallest *Juniperus virginiana* in the British Isles
ENGLISH HERITAGE GRADE I

Charles Hamilton went bust making this extravagant gothic landscape in the 1770s. It has been industriously restored over the last 10 years and now looks as new and stagey as ever.

Pinewood House
Heath House Road, Worplesdon Hill, Woking, Surrey GU22 0QU
☎ 01483 473141
OWNER Mr and Mrs J. Van Zwanenberg

LOCATION Turn off A322, opposite Brookwood cemetery wall
OPEN Parties by appointment, 1 April to 31 October
ADMISSION Adults £1.50
FACILITIES Parking; loos; access for the disabled; home-made teas if pre-booked
FEATURES Good collection of trees; fine conifers; glasshouses and conservatories to visit; lake; young garden; wild garden; walled garden; rhododendrons

5 acres of old garden, to go with a new house. Lovely woodland, lakes and underplantings with rhododendrons.

Polesden Lacey
Great Bookham, Dorking, Surrey RH5 6BD
☎ 01372 458203
OWNER The National Trust
LOCATION On southern edge of Dorking – signposted
OPEN 11 am – 6 pm, daily, all year
ADMISSION Adults £2.50
FACILITIES Parking; dogs permitted; loos; access for the disabled; shop; tea rooms
FEATURES Herbaceous borders; herbs; old roses and climbers; garden sculpture; plantings by Graham Thomas
ENGLISH HERITAGE GRADE II*

Best for the long terraced walk, laid out by Sheridan, and the return through an Edwardian-style rose garden whose pergolas drip with ramblers.

Ramster
Chiddingfold, Surrey GU8 4SN
☎ 01428 644422
OWNER Mr and Mrs Paul Gunn
LOCATION 1½ miles south of Chiddingfold on A283
OPEN 2 – 6 pm, daily, 15 April to 30 July. Special early-morning opening for photographers: 13 and 14 May at 7 am. Parties by appointment
ADMISSION Adults £2; Children free
FACILITIES Parking; dogs permitted; loos; facilities for the disabled; plants for sale; home-made teas at weekends or by arrangement
FEATURES Good collection of trees; fine conifers; lake; rhododendrons; camellias; azaleas; bluebells; *Embroidery for Gardeners*' Exhibition, 6 to 19 May 1995

20 acres of Surrey woodland underplanted with camellias, rhododendrons and all manner of rare shrubs by Mrs Gunn's grandmother, 70 years ago. She was the second Lord Aberconway's sister and many of her plants came from Bodnant: some of the rhododendrons and azaleas are her hybrids.

RHS Garden, Wisley
Woking, Surrey GU23 6QB
☎ 01483 224234
OWNER The Royal Horticultural Society
LOCATION Near junction of M25 and A3

OPEN 10 am – 7 pm or dusk if earlier (4.30 pm November to January), daily, all year except Christmas Day. Sundays reserved for RHS members only
ADMISSION Adults £4.70; Children £1.75
FACILITIES Parking; loos; facilities for the disabled; plants for sale; marvellous bookshop and souvenir shop; two restaurants
FEATURES Good collection of trees; herbaceous borders; fine conifers; ecological interest; fruit of special interest; glasshouses and conservatories to visit; gravel or scree garden; herbs; lake; plants for plantsmen; rock garden; modern roses; old roses and climbers; subtropical plants; woodland garden; particularly good in July-August; particularly interesting in winter
ENGLISH HERITAGE GRADE II*
NCCPG NATIONAL COLLECTIONS *Calluna vulgaris, Galanthus, Hosta, Rheum, Cochium, Crocus, Daboecia, Daphne, Erica, Epimedium, Pulmonaria*

Too well-known to need description, Wisley is a garden to visit and revisit in search of new knowledge and inspiration. You can spend a a week there and still find corners you never knew existed.

The Savill Garden
Wick Lane, Windsor, Surrey SL4 2HT
☎ 01753 860222   FAX 01753 859617

OWNER Crown Estate Commission
LOCATION 3 miles west of Egham off the A30, 5 miles from Windsor
OPEN 10 am – 6 pm (4 pm, 1 November to 31 March), daily, except Christmas and Boxing Day
ADMISSION Adults £3.30; Senior Citizens £2.80; Children under 16 free; Groups (20+) £2.80
FACILITIES Parking; loos; plants for sale; gift and book shop; licensed restaurant and picnic area
FEATURES Good collection of trees; herbaceous borders; camellias; gravel or scree garden; lake; plants for plantsmen; rock garden; modern roses; woodland garden; particularly good in July-August; particularly interesting in winter; Kurume azaleas; mahonias; magnolias; magnificent late-summer borders; tallest *Betula populifolia* and *Sorbus* 'Joseph Rock' in the British Isles; vast new glasshouse (1995), rather too intrusive in this sylvan setting
ENGLISH HERITAGE GRADE I
FRIENDS Active Friends Organisation: details from John Bond, Keeper of the Gardens
NCCPG NATIONAL COLLECTIONS *Mahonia, Rhododendron*

Quite simply the finest woodland garden in England, crammed with rhododendrons, magnolias, azaleas, maples, mahonias and hydrangeas and underplanted with drifts of *Meconopsis*, primulas and wild *Narcissus*. The primulas come in monospecific masses, from the earliest *P. rosea* and *P. denticulata* through to *P. florindae* in July and August. But the herbaceous borders are also an inspiration and the gravel garden is one of the oldest and largest.

Vale End
Albury, Guildford, Surrey
☎ 01483 202594   FAX 01483 202296

OWNER Mr and Mrs John Foulsham
LOCATION 500 yards west of Albury on A248
OPEN 10 am – 5 pm, 25 June and 23 July
ADMISSION Adults £1.50; Children free
FACILITIES Parking; dogs permitted; loos; plants for sale; refreshments
FEATURES Herbaceous borders; plants for plantsmen; old roses and climbers

A modern plantsman's garden, the best we know on Bagshot sand, where a love of plants has not been allowed to obscure either the design or the landscape beyond.

The Valley Gardens, Windsor
Windsor Great Park, Wick Road, Englefield Green, Surrey
☎ 01753 860222

OWNER Crown Estate Commission
LOCATION 5 miles from Windsor, off A30 following signs for Savill Garden
OPEN 8 am – 7 pm, or sunset if earlier, daily, all year
ADMISSION Car and occupants £2.60 (use 10p, 50p and £1 coins only)
FACILITIES Parking; dogs permitted; refreshments at the Savill Garden
FEATURES Good collection of trees; fine conifers; lake; plants for plantsmen; woodland garden; deciduous azaleas; hollies; magnolias; heathers; rhododendrons; hydrangeas
NCCPG NATIONAL COLLECTIONS *Ilex, Magnolia, Pernettya, Pieris, Rhododendron*

A larger version of the Savill Garden: all is planted on a royal scale in a wilder woodland setting. Best known is the Punch Bowl, where massed ranks of Kurume azaleas fill a natural combe with amazingly garish mixtures. Other parts are underplanted with hostas, ferns, bergenias and candelabra primulas. There is also a fine pinetum and a good collection of hydrangeas. But the gardens extend to 300 acres: not to be undertaken by the frail or faint-hearted.

Vann
Hambledon, Godalming, Surrey GU8 4EF
☎ 01428 68 3413   FAX 017267 9344

OWNER Mr and Mrs Martin Caroe
LOCATION Signs from A283 at Hambledon on NGS days
OPEN 10 am – 6 pm, daily, 18 to 23 April, 1 to 6 May, and 30 May to 4 June. Also 2 – 7 pm on 30 April. By appointment, 1 April to 30 June
ADMISSION Adults £2.50; Children 50p
FACILITIES Parking; loos; plants for sale; teas by arrangement
FEATURES Bluebells; herbaceous borders; fruit of special interest; planted by Gertrude Jekyll; lake; woodland

garden; wood anemones; newly replanted double border (1994)
ENGLISH HERITAGE GRADE   II

High-profile Gertrude Jekyll garden, well-restored and meticulously maintained by the present Caroes, the third generation to live here. Start at the back of the house and move along the Arts and Crafts pergola which leads straight to the lake. This is the heart of the garden, from which 5 or 6 distinct gardens lead from one to the next and melt into the Surrey woods: among them, a yew walk, a water garden, a woodland cherry walk, a hazel coppice and a woodland garden under vast oaks. The plantings are dense and thoughtful.

Winkworth Arboretum
Hascombe Road, Godalming, Surrey GU8 4AD
☎ 01483 208477

OWNER   The National Trust
LOCATION   2 miles south east of Godalming, off B2130
OPEN   All year, dawn – dusk. Groups *must* pre-book in writing
ADMISSION   Adults £2; Children (5–17) £1
FACILITIES   Parking; dogs permitted; loos; shop; tea room
FEATURES   Good collection of trees; lake; woodland garden; plantings by Graham Thomas; bluebells; wood anemones; autumn colour; tallest *Acer davidii* in the British Isles
NCCPG NATIONAL COLLECTIONS *Sorbus*

Beautiful arboretum, planted with particularly decorative species (maples, *Sorbus*, magnolias and *Hamamelis*) in large groups for maximum effect. Good in May when the azaleas are underscored by bluebells: better still for autumn colour in October.

EAST SUSSEX

Bateman's
Burwash, Etchingham, East Sussex TN19 7DS
☎ 01435 882302

OWNER   The National Trust
LOCATION   Signposted at west end of village
OPEN   11 am – 5.30 pm, Saturday – Wednesday, 1 April to 31 October
ADMISSION   Adults £4; Children £2
FACILITIES   Parking; loos; National Trust shop; restaurant and café
FEATURES   Herbaceous borders; fruit of special interest; herbs; old roses and climbers; interesting for children; arcade planted with pears and clematis; water mill
ENGLISH HERITAGE GRADE   II

10 acres on the banks of the River Dudwell, where Rudyard Kipling lived from 1902 until his death in 1936. Fun for children, because there is a working flour mill, but not spectacular for the knowledgeable gardener, except for the *Campsis grandiflora* on the house.

Bates Green Farm
Arlington, Polegate, East Sussex BN26 6SH
☎ 01323 482039

OWNER   Mr and Mrs J. R. McCutchan
LOCATION   3 miles south west of Hailsham
OPEN   10.30 am – 6 pm, Thursdays, 1 March to 31 October. Also for NGS and by appointment
ADMISSION   £1.50
FACILITIES   Parking; loos; access for the disabled; plants for sale; refreshments by arrangement
FEATURES   Herbaceous borders; lake; rock garden; woodland garden; colour borders; bluebells

Made by the present owners over the last 20 years. Several different areas: a large rock garden, a shady garden, and wonderful mixed borders planted for year-round colour associations. The owners seek perfection, but wonder if they will ever achieve it.

Brickwall House
Frewen College, Northiam, East Sussex TN31 6NL
☎ 01797 223329   [FAX] 01797 42567

OWNER   Frewen Educational Trust
LOCATION   Off B2088
OPEN   2 – 5 pm, Saturdays and Bank Holiday Mondays, 1 April to 30 September
ADMISSION   £2
FACILITIES   Parking; dogs permitted; loos; access for the disabled; postcards and guidebooks but no shop
FEATURES   Good collection of trees; herbaceous borders; herbs; good topiary; young garden; extensively redesigned since 1980
ENGLISH HERITAGE GRADE   II*

Designed as a Stuart garden, to match the house, Brickwall has borders planted exclusively with old-fashioned plants and a chess garden where green and yellow yew shapes are grown in squares of black or white chips. Very neatly maintained.

Charleston Farmhouse
Firle, Lewes, East Sussex BN8 6LL
☎ 01323 811265   [FAX] 01323 811628

OWNER   The Charleston Trust
LOCATION   6 miles east of Lewes on the Eastbourne road
OPEN   2 – 6 pm, Wednesday – Sunday, and Bank Holiday Mondays, April to October
ADMISSION   Adults £1.75; Children (5–16) 75p
FACILITIES   Parking; loos; facilities for the disabled; plants for sale; small shop
FEATURES   Herbaceous borders; follies and garden buildings
FRIENDS   Friends of Charleston: details from the Secretary, c/o Charleston Farmhouse

This witness to the Bloomsbury group is not a gardeners' garden, but full of vivacious quirks and follies. The bric-a-brac which decorates every corner is sometimes amusing, always provocative.

Clinton Lodge
Fletching, Uckfield, East Sussex TN22 3ST
☎ 01825 722952

OWNER   Mr and Mrs M. R. Collum
LOCATION   In main village street
OPEN   2 – 6 pm, 11, 12, 19, 21, 26 June
ADMISSION   £2
FACILITIES   Dogs permitted; loos; access for the disabled; plants for sale; home-made teas
FEATURES   Herbaceous borders; herbs; old roses and climbers; yew hedges; lime walks; *potager*; knot gardens

A rising star among new gardens, designed round a handsome 17th-century house. 6 acres of formal gardens of different periods, starting with a 'medieval' *potager* and an Elizabethan herb garden. The most successful parts are the Pre-Raphaelite walk of lilies and pale roses, and the Victorian herbaceous borders in soft pastel shades.

Cobblers
Mount Pleasant, Jarvis Brook, Crowborough, East Sussex TN6 2ND
☎ 01892 655969

OWNER   Mr and Mrs Martin Furniss
LOCATION   Turn off B2100 into Tollwood Road: ¼ mile on right
OPEN   2.30 – 5.30 pm, 14 and 29 May, 11 and 25 June, 9 and 23 July, 6, 20 and 28 August
ADMISSION   Adults £3; Children £1; including teas
FACILITIES   Parking; loos; access for the disabled; plants for sale; home-made teas
FEATURES   Herbaceous borders; gravel or scree garden; herbs; lake; plants for plantsmen; modern roses

Tightly planned and beautifully planted garden made by an architect who is also a plantsman. There is a great variety of habitats and plants (bog, alpine, hot-coloured, shade-loving) within a design which opens out its perspectives slowly. Colour all season.

Great Dixter
Dixter Road, Northiam, East Sussex TN31 6PH
☎ 01797 253160

OWNER   Christopher Lloyd
LOCATION   Off A28 at Northiam post office
OPEN   2 – 5 pm, daily except Monday, 1 April to 15 October, plus Bank Holiday Mondays
ADMISSION   Adults £2.50; Children 25p
FACILITIES   Parking; loos; plants for sale; gift shop
FEATURES   Herbaceous borders; fruit of special interest; herbs; planted by Gertrude Jekyll; plants for plantsmen; modern roses; old roses and climbers; subtropical plants; good topiary; particularly good in July-August; meadow garden; colour schemes; long border
ENGLISH HERITAGE GRADE   I

Several well-defined enclosures surround the Lutyens house but they change constantly as Christopher Lloyd rethinks, reworks and replants. Dixter is a living lesson in the choice and use of plants, a garden to revisit frequently.

Michelham Priory
Upper Dicker, Hailsham, East Sussex BN27 3QS
☎ 01323 844224   FAX 01323 844030

OWNER   The Sussex Archaeological Society
LOCATION   Signposted from A22 and A27
OPEN   11 am – 5.30 pm, daily, 25 March to 31 October
ADMISSION   Adults £3.50; Senior Citizens £2.90; Children £1.90; Family £9.20 (2+2)
FACILITIES   Parking; loos; facilities for the disabled; plants for sale; restaurant and tea room
FEATURES   Herbaceous borders; fine conifers; herbs; lake; modern roses; old roses and climbers

Previously a 13th-century Augustinian priory with Elizabethan barn, blacksmith's shop, rope museum and moat. Physic garden with medieval herb examples. Working water mill with bakery.

Offham House
Offham, Lewes, East Sussex BN7 3QE
☎ 01273 474824

OWNER   Mr and Mrs H. N. A. Goodman
LOCATION   2½ miles north of Lewes on A275
OPEN   2 – 6 pm, 7 May and 4 June
ADMISSION   Adults £2; Children 50p
FACILITIES   Parking; dogs permitted; loos; access for the disabled; plants for sale; home-made cakes and tea
FEATURES   Good collection of trees; herbaceous borders; fruit of special interest; glasshouses and conservatories to visit; herbs; plants for plantsmen; old roses and climbers; cherry orchard; lilacs

Good modern garden, burgeoning with energy and interest. The plantings are thick and show an eye for good new plants. Lilacs, fritillaries and early purple orchids in spring; shrub roses, paeonies and columbines in June. There is much more for high summer and autumn interest if only the owners could be persuaded to open a little more often!

Pashley Manor
Ticehurst, Wadhurst, East Sussex TN5 7NE
☎ 01580 200692

OWNER   James Sellick
LOCATION   On B2099 between A21 and Ticehurst
OPEN   11 am – 5 pm, Tuesday – Thursday, Saturday and Bank Holiday Mondays, 15 April to 30 September
ADMISSION   Adults £3; Senior Citizens £2.50
FACILITIES   Parking; loos; plants for sale; fresh produce for sale; home-made refreshments on fine days
FEATURES   Fine conifers; follies and garden buildings; glasshouses and conservatories to visit; lake; modern roses; old roses and climbers; Victorian shrubberies; hydrangeas; irises; new golden garden (1993) maturing well
FRIENDS   No friends organisation yet, but Pashley Manor is sponsoring a new annual competition for garden paintings. Details from James Sellick

A new/old garden, made or remade in the Victorian style over the last 10 years with advice from Tony

WEST SUSSEX Gardens 335

Pasley. The results are gentle shapes, spacious expanses, harmonious colours and solid plantings. It gets better every year.

Sheffield Park Garden
Uckfield, East Sussex TN22 3QX
☎ 01825 790231

OWNER   The National Trust
LOCATION   Between East Grinstead and Lewes on A275
OPEN   11 am – 4 pm (6 pm from 1 April to 6 November), Tuesday – Sunday and Bank Holiday Mondays (but Saturdays and Sundays only in March, and Wednesday – Saturday only from 9 November to 17 December), 1 March to 6 November and 9 November to 17 December
ADMISSION   Adults £4; Children £2 (1994)
FACILITIES   Parking; loos; facilities for the disabled; National Trust shop; refreshments nearby
FEATURES   Good collection of trees; landscape designed by Capability Brown; fine conifers; lake; plants for plantsmen; landscape designed by Humphry Repton; woodland garden; plantings by Graham Thomas; daffodils; bluebells; kalmias; autumn crocuses; rhododendrons; tallest *Acer maximowiczianum* (syn. *nikoense*) in the British Isles
ENGLISH HERITAGE GRADE   I
NCCPG NATIONAL COLLECTIONS *Rhododendron*

Little remains of Capability Brown and Repton except the lakes which now reflect the plantings of exotic trees – landscaping on the grandest of scales. Wonderful leaf colours whatever the season, plus gentians in autumn.

Standen
East Grinstead, East Sussex RH19 4NE
☎ 01342 323029

OWNER   The National Trust
LOCATION   2 miles south of East Grinstead, signposted from B2110
OPEN   12.30 – 6 pm, Wednesday – Sunday and Bank Holiday Mondays, 1 April to 29 October
ADMISSION   Weekdays £2.50; Other days £3
FACILITIES   Parking; dogs permitted; loos; National Trust shop; light lunches and afternoon teas
FEATURES   Herbaceous borders; fine conifers; rock garden; old roses and climbers; rhododendrons; azaleas; woodland shrubs

Small Edwardian garden with magnificent views across the valley. A series of enclosed gardens around the house give way to woodland slopes and an old quarry furnished with ferns.

WEST SUSSEX

Berri Court
Yapton, Arundel, West Sussex BN18 0ED
☎ 01243 551663

OWNER   Mr and Mrs John M. Turner
LOCATION   Yapton, 5 miles south west of Arundel, centre of village next to Black Dog pub
OPEN   For NGS: see Yellow Book
ADMISSION   Adults £1; Children 30p
FACILITIES   Parking; dogs permitted; loos; facilities for the disabled; plants for sale
FEATURES   Herbaceous borders; modern roses; old roses and climbers; rhododendrons; *Eucalyptus*; hydrangeas; lily ponds

A plantsman's garden with a compact design, some 3 acres in extent.

Borde Hill Garden
Haywards Heath, West Sussex RH16 1XP
☎ 01444 450326   FAX 01444 440427

OWNER   Borde Hill Garden Ltd
LOCATION   1½ miles north of Haywards Heath
OPEN   10 am – 6 pm, daily, 18 March to 1 October
ADMISSION   Adults £3.50; Senior Citizens £3; Children £1.50
FACILITIES   Parking; dogs permitted; loos; facilities for the disabled; plants for sale; small gift shop; tea rooms, restaurant and pub
FEATURES   Good collection of trees; lake; plants for plantsmen; woodland garden; rhododendrons; azaleas; magnolias; plants from original seed; tallest *Magnolia delavayi*, *Juniperus virginiana* in the British Isles, and 19 other record trees
ENGLISH HERITAGE GRADE   II*

This important woodland garden has a significant collection of rhododendron species grown from such introducers as Forrest and Kingdon Ward. It has recently been revamped for the recreation market and is all the better for the new capital. There are good new borders, a lake, and all sorts of facilities like a smart restaurant: very cockle-warming to see Borde Hill on the up again.

Coates Manor
Fittleworth, Pulborough, West Sussex RH20 1ES
☎ 0179 8865356

OWNER   Mrs S. M. Thorp
LOCATION   ½ a mile off B2138, signposted Coates
OPEN   11 am – 6 pm, 11 – 13 June and by appointment
ADMISSION   Adults £1.50; Children free
FACILITIES   Parking; loos; plants for sale; refreshments on open days
FEATURES   Herbaceous borders; colour planting; foliage plants

A small, neatly designed and intensely planted garden which crams a lifetime's learning into its plantings. Long-term colour effects are its outstanding quality: leaves, berries, trunks, stems, form, shadow and texture are all individually exploited to the maximum. A model of its kind and beautifully maintained.

Cooke's House
West Burton, Pulborough, West Sussex RH20 1HD
☎ 0179 831353

OWNER   Miss J. B. Courtauld

336 Gardens WEST SUSSEX

LOCATION Turn off A29 by White Horse at foot of Bury Hill
OPEN 2 – 6 pm, 23 – 25 April, and by appointment
ADMISSION £1
FACILITIES Parking; loos; access for the disabled
FEATURES Herbaceous borders; old roses and climbers; good topiary
ENGLISH HERITAGE GRADE II

A neat and well-maintained garden, pretty in spring when the primulas and bulbs are out. Even better at midsummer when the roses and herbaceous plants crammed into small enclosures create a sense of great richness and harmony.

Cowdray Park
Midhurst, West Sussex GU29 0AQ
☎ 01730 812423   FAX 01730 815608
OWNER Viscount Cowdray
LOCATION South of A272, 1 mile east of Midhurst
OPEN 2 – 7 pm, 14 May
ADMISSION £1
FACILITIES Parking
FEATURES 300-year-old Lebanon cedar; *Wellingtonia* avenue; rhododendrons; tallest *Chamaecyparis pisifera* (and two other conifers) in the United Kingdom
ENGLISH HERITAGE GRADE II*

Seldom open, but worth a long journey to see the extraordinarily overwrought house and its contemporary (100 years old) collection of trees, particularly conifers. Some are now record-breakers, and the sweeps of rhododendrons and azaleas, especially the hardy hybrids down The Dell, are on the grand scale too. Pretty awesome.

Denmans
Fontwell, Arundel, West Sussex BN18 0SU
☎ 01243 542808   FAX 01243 544064
LOCATION Off A29 or A27, near Fontwell racecourse
OPEN 9 am – 5 pm, daily, mid February to December, or by appointment
ADMISSION Adults £2.25; Senior Citizens £1.85; Children (over 5) £1.25; groups (15+) £1.65
FACILITIES Shop; garden centre; full lunches and teas
FEATURES Herbaceous borders; gravel or scree garden; herbs; lake; old roses and climbers; spring bulbs

This small modern garden is a showpiece for John Brookes's ideas: easy care, using foliage, gravel mulches, contrasts of form, coloured stems, winter bark and plants as elements of design. Garden decoration *in excelsis*.

Gravetye Manor
East Grinstead, West Sussex RH19 4LJ
☎ 01342 810567
OWNER Peter Herbert
LOCATION 4 miles south west of East Grinstead
OPEN Hotel guests only
FACILITIES Parking

FEATURES Good collection of trees; herbaceous borders; fine conifers; lake; plants for plantsmen; old roses and climbers; good topiary; woodland garden; alpine meadow
ENGLISH HERITAGE GRADE II*

William Robinson's own garden, very influential 80 years ago, and scrupulously maintained by Peter Herbert as it was in its prime. Gravetye is still a garden to learn from: there is much to admire and copy.

The High Beeches
Handcross, West Sussex RH17 6HQ
☎ 01444 400589
OWNER High Beeches Gardens Conservation Trust
LOCATION South of B2110, 1 mile east of M23 at Handcross
OPEN 1 – 5 pm, daily, except Wednesdays, 1 April to 30 June and 1 September to 31 October
ADMISSION Adults £3
FACILITIES Parking; loos
FEATURES Good collection of trees; fine conifers; ecological interest; plants for plantsmen; woodland garden; rhododendrons
ENGLISH HERITAGE GRADE II
FRIENDS High Beeches Gardens Conservation Trust is an active organisation with many events of interest to gardeners: details from the Curator
NCCPG NATIONAL COLLECTIONS *Stewartia*

One of the best of the famous Sussex gardens, with splendid rhododendrons, azaleas, magnolias and camellias, but also an emphasis on colour planting, wonderful autumn colour and a policy of letting good plants naturalise. A great credit to the Boscawen family who have devoted 25 years to its maintenance and improvement.

Highdown
Littlehampton Road, Goring-by-Sea, West Sussex BN12 6NY
☎ 01903 239999 ext. 2539
OWNER Worthing Borough Council
LOCATION Signposted from A259
OPEN 10 am – 6 pm (4.30 pm October and November, 4 pm December and January, 4.30 pm February and March), daily (but not weekends from October to March), all year. Closes at 8 pm at weekends and on Bank Holiday Mondays from April to September
ADMISSION Free – donations welcome
FACILITIES Parking; loos; facilities for the disabled; refreshments in high season
FEATURES Good collection of trees; herbaceous borders; fine conifers; plants for plantsmen; rock garden; old roses and climbers; woodland garden; tallest specimen of *Carpinus turczaninowii* in the United Kingdom, a handsome tree
ENGLISH HERITAGE GRADE II*

A very important garden. Its maker, Sir Frederic Stern, was determined to try anything that might grow on chalk. 80 years on, the results are some handsome trees, vigorous roses, and long-forgotten paeony hybrids. Best of all are the naturalised hellebores, tulips and anemones. Alas, Stern made a mistake in leaving it to Worthing Borough Council.

Leonardslee Gardens
Lower Beeding, Horsham, West Sussex RH13 6PP
☎ 01403 891212   FAX 01403 891336
OWNER   R. R. Loder
LOCATION   3 miles south west of Handcross at junction of A279 and A281
OPEN   10 am – 6 pm, daily, 1 April to 31 October
ADMISSION   Adults £3 (£4 in May); Children £2
FACILITIES   Parking; loos; plants for sale; gift shop; licensed restaurant and café
FEATURES   Bluebells; fine conifers; glasshouses and conservatories to visit; lake; oriental features; plants for plantsmen; rhododendrons and azaleas; rock garden; woodland garden; new alpine house; wallabies; summer wild-flower walk; tallest fossil tree *Metasequoia glyptostroboides* and *Magnolia campbellii* in the British Isles
ENGLISH HERITAGE GRADE   I

A spectacular collection of rhododendrons and azaleas is the essence of Leonardslee, and the way they are planted in drifts of one colour. But there are magnolias, camellias and innumerable rare plants, as well as a formidable bonsai collection. The original 80 acres open to the public have just been extended to 240 acres, and are laced with lakes, dells and groves. Ravishing in May.

Nymans
Handcross, Haywards Heath, West Sussex RH17 6EB
☎ 01444 400321
OWNER   The National Trust
LOCATION   Handcross, off the main road
OPEN   11 am – 7 pm, daily, 1 March to 31 October
ADMISSION   Adults £3.80
FACILITIES   Parking; loos; facilities for the disabled; plants for sale; shop; teas
FEATURES   Good collection of trees; herbaceous borders; fine conifers; plants for plantsmen; rock garden; modern roses; old roses and climbers; good topiary; woodland garden; tallest *Magnolia campbellii* 'Alba' in the British Isles
ENGLISH HERITAGE GRADE   II*

The sumptuous mansion in the West Country style has been gutted by fire, but the garden is intact, with opulent herbaceous borders in the walled garden, a pioneering collection of old roses, a stupendous wisteria pergola and vast collections of magnolias and camellias. Yet some say Nymans is overrated.

Parham
Parham House, Pulborough, West Sussex RH20 4HS
☎ 01903 742663
OWNER   Trustees of Parham Estate
LOCATION   On A238 midway between Pulborough and Storrington

OPEN   1 – 6 pm, Wednesdays, Thursdays, Sundays and Bank Holiday Mondays, 3 April to 2 October
ADMISSION   Adults £2.50; Children £1 (1994)
FACILITIES   Parking; dogs permitted; loos; facilities for the disabled; plants for sale; shop; self-service teas
FEATURES   Herbaceous borders; fruit of special interest; lake; plants for plantsmen; old roses and climbers; new maze; HHA/Christie's Garden of the Year in 1990
ENGLISH HERITAGE GRADE   I

An ethereal English garden for the loveliest of Elizabethan manor houses. In the park are a landscaped lake and a cricket ground. The fun for garden lovers is in the old walled garden: lush borders, colour plantings, old and new fruit trees, and all maintained to the highest standard.

Petworth House
Petworth, West Sussex GU28 0AE
☎ 01798 342207
OWNER   The National Trust
LOCATION   At Petworth, well signed
OPEN   House: 12.30 – 6 pm, daily except Mondays and Fridays (open Bank Holidays), 1 April to 31 October. Park: 8 am – 9 pm, or dusk if sooner, daily, all year
ADMISSION   House: Adults £4; Children £2. Park: free
FACILITIES   Parking; loos; facilities for the disabled; shop; restaurant; tea rooms
FEATURES   Herbaceous borders; landscape designed by Capability Brown; lake; woodland garden; deer park; one million daffodils; nine record-holding trees all felled by the Great Gale of 1987
ENGLISH HERITAGE GRADE   I

One of the best Capability Brown landscapes in England sweeps up to the windows of the house itself. The National Trust has decided to add modern attractions: herbaceous borders and acres of azaleas in a new woodland garden. Both park and garden have enjoyed a renaissance since the Great Gale.

Stonehurst
Ardingly, West Sussex RH17 6TN
☎ 01444 892052
OWNER   D. R. Strauss
LOCATION   1 mile north of Ardingly on B2028
OPEN   11 am – 5 pm, 17 April, 14 May, 29 May
ADMISSION   Adults £2.50; Children £1
FACILITIES   Parking; dogs permitted; loos; plants for sale; orchids, rhododendrons and camellias for sale; teas
FEATURES   Herbaceous borders; follies and garden buildings; lake; rock garden; camellias; magnolias; azaleas; SSSI
ENGLISH HERITAGE GRADE   II

Stonehurst is in a rock-lined secret valley, where springs issue to form a series of small lakes, and rare liverworts have special scientific interest. The Strausses have made it known as a garden for rhododendrons, camellias and rare trees and shrubs which regularly win prizes at the RHS shows in London. Well-maintained.

Telegraph House
North Marden, Chichester, West Sussex PO18 9JX
☎ 01730 825206

OWNER   Mr and Mrs Gault
LOCATION   Entrance on B2141, 2 miles south of Harting
OPEN   2 – 6 pm, 17 and 18 June, 15 and 16 July, 1 May to 30 August, by appointment
ADMISSION   Adults £1.50; Children 75p
FACILITIES   Parking; dogs permitted; loos; refreshments on open weekends
FEATURES   Herbaceous borders; old roses and climbers; woodland garden; 1-mile avenue of copper beeches

The house is c.1900 and French in style, but the garden has been made by the present owners over the last 20 years. Yew hedges enclose a series of terraces and intimate gardens: roses, shrubs and herbaceous plantings. Nearby are 150 acres of natural woodland, much of it ancient yew.

Wakehurst Place
Ardingly, Haywards Heath, West Sussex RH17 6TN
☎ 0181 332 5066

OWNER   Royal Botanic Gardens, Kew
LOCATION   On B2028 between Turner's Hill and Ardingly
OPEN   10 am – 7 pm (6 pm in March and October, 5 pm in February and 4 pm from November to January), daily except Christmas Day and New Year's day, all year
ADMISSION   Adults £4 (1994)
FACILITIES   Parking; loos; facilities for the disabled; bookshop and gift shop; light refreshments, plus new restaurant in April
FEATURES   Alpines; good collection of trees; bluebells; bog garden; herbaceous borders; camellias; fine conifers; daffodils; ecological interest; gravel or scree garden; lake; plants for plantsmen; rhododendrons and azaleas; rock garden; old roses and climbers; woodland garden; particularly interesting in winter; Asian heath garden; pinetum; *Cardiocrinum*; tallest scarlet oak *Quercus coccinea* in the British Isles, plus 16 further tree records
ENGLISH HERITAGE GRADE   II*
FRIENDS   Part of the Friends of Kew organisation
NCCPG NATIONAL COLLECTIONS *Betula,   Hypericum, Nothofagus, Skimmia*

Allow plenty of time for Wakehurst: it is very big, and there is much to see. Near the house are the winter garden, two ponds, the new Asian heath garden and the southern hemisphere garden. No garden combines so perfectly the function of a major botanic institute with the sense of being a private garden still.

West Dean Gardens
West Dean, Chichester, West Sussex PO18 0Q2
☎ 01243 811303   [FAX] 01243 811342

OWNER   The Edward James Foundation
LOCATION   6 miles north of Chichester on A286
OPEN   11 am – 6 pm, daily, 1 March to 31 October
ADMISSION   Adults £3; Senior Citizens £2.50; Children £1.50; Groups (20+) £2.50
FACILITIES   Parking; dogs permitted; loos; facilities for the disabled; plants for sale; tea, coffee, sandwiches, etc.
FEATURES   Good collection of trees; fine conifers; fruit of special interest; glasshouses and conservatories to visit; old roses and climbers; museum of old lawn-mowers; tallest *Cupressus goveniana* in UK; newly restored kitchen garden (1994); new Visitors' Centre (1995)
ENGLISH HERITAGE GRADE   II*
NCCPG NATIONAL COLLECTIONS   *Liriodendron, Aesculus*

Laid out in the 1890s and 1900s, West Dean has now been extensively restored: Harold Peto's 100-metre pergola has been replanted with roses; much of the damage to the arboretum caused by the 1987 storm has been made good; and the great range of glasshouses in the walled garden has been repaired – the garden itself planted as a working kitchen garden. Everything about West Dean gets better and better.

Yew Tree Cottage
Crawley Down, Turners Hill, West Sussex RH10 4EY
☎ 01342 714633

OWNER   Mrs K. Hudson
LOCATION   Opposite Grange Farm on B2028
OPEN   2 – 6 pm, for NGS and by appointment
ADMISSION   £1
FACILITIES   Parking; plants for sale; refreshments
FEATURES   Herbaceous borders; fruit of special interest; old roses and climbers; cottage garden style; colour borders

This miraculous small garden (⅓rd acre) has been designed, planted and maintained by the 89-year-old owner over many years and won infinite plaudits for its display of plants in the Jekyll manner. There is no better example of the cottage garden style.

TYNE & WEAR

Bede's World Herb Garden
Bede's World, Church Bank, Jarrow, Tyne & Wear NE32 3DY
☎ 0191 489 2196   [FAX] 0191 428 2361

OWNER   Jarrow 700 AD Ltd
LOCATION   Signposted from A85
OPEN   Dawn – dusk, daily, all year
ADMISSION   Garden only: free
FACILITIES   Parking; loos; facilities for the disabled; plants for sale; shop for herbal products; lunches and light refreshments

FEATURES   Herbs; interesting for children
FRIENDS   Friends of Bede's World

A herb garden based on 9th-century descriptions: a small part of an ambitious enterprise which seeks to impart a feeling for the Anglo-Saxon world.

WARWICKSHIRE

Arbury Hall
Nuneaton, Warwickshire CV10 7PT
☎ 01203 382804   FAX 01203 641147

OWNER   Viscount Daventry
LOCATION   3 miles south east of Nuneaton off the B4102
OPEN   2 – 5.30 pm, Sundays and Mondays, Easter Sunday to 24 September
ADMISSION   Adults £2; Children £1
FACILITIES   Parking; dogs permitted; loos; access for the disabled; gift and crafts shop; tea rooms
FEATURES   Follies and garden buildings; lake; modern roses; old roses and climbers; woodland garden; daffodils; rhododendrons; azaleas; bluebells; wisteria
ENGLISH HERITAGE GRADE   II*

Good trees (especially purple beeches), handsome parkland, lakes and ponds – Arbury has good bones for a garden. Then there are bluebell woods, pollarded limes, a large rose garden, a walled garden and a huge wisteria. Nothing is outstanding in itself, but the ensemble is an oasis of peace on the edge of industrial Daventry and worth the journey from far away.

Charlecote Park
Wellesbourne, Warwick, Warwickshire CV35 9ER
☎ 01789 470277

OWNER   The National Trust
LOCATION   Signed from A429
OPEN   11 am – 6 pm, Friday – Tuesday (closed Good Friday), 1 April to 31 October
ADMISSION   £4; Children (5–16) £2
FACILITIES   Parking; loos; facilities for the disabled; National Trust shop; restaurant
FEATURES   Landscape designed by Capability Brown; fine conifers; glasshouses and conservatories to visit; lake; good topiary; deer park; orangery
ENGLISH HERITAGE GRADE   II*

Fine cedars and a Capability Brown park are the main claims to Charlecote's fame, but the young William Shakespeare is reputed to have poached deer from the park, so the National Trust has planted a border with plants mentioned in his works.

Farnborough Hall
Banbury, Warwickshire OX17 1DU
☎ 01295 690202

OWNER   The National Trust
LOCATION   A423, 6 miles north of Banbury
OPEN   2 – 6 pm, Wednesdays – Saturdays, 1 April to 30 September. Also 7 and 8 May

ADMISSION   Grounds: £1.50; Terrace Walk: £1
FACILITIES   Parking; dogs permitted; loos; access for the disabled
FEATURES   Follies and garden buildings; lake; old roses and climbers; good topiary; woodland garden; newly-restored cascade (1994), now functioning

Sanderson Millar's masterpiece – grand vistas, classical temples and a dominating obelisk. Plus a long curving terraced walk to the adjoining estate of Mollington. No flowers, but space and peace.

Ryton Organic Gardens
Henry Doubleday Research Association, Ryton-on-Dunsmore, Coventry, Warwickshire CV8 3LG
☎ 01203 303517

OWNER   The Henry Doubleday Research Association (HDRA)
LOCATION   5 miles south east of Coventry off A45
OPEN   10 am – 5.30 pm, daily, all year
ADMISSION   Adults £2.50; Senior Citizens £1.75; Children £1.25
FACILITIES   Parking; loos; facilities for the disabled; shop with gardening products, books, food, wine and gifts; organic wholefood restaurant
FEATURES   Herbaceous borders; ecological interest; fruit and vegetables of special interest; glasshouses and conservatories to visit; herbs; plants for plantsmen; rock garden; modern roses; old roses and climbers; woodland garden; interesting for children
FRIENDS   Join the HDRA (see Societies section)

Ryton is the UK centre for organic gardening where experiments are made in using only natural fertilisers and trying to operate without pesticides. It is very well laid out, with dozens of different small gardens, all highly instructive. The staff's commitment is also impressive. You may not be convinced by what you see, but it will make you think. The excellent restaurant and substantial shop will add considerably to your enjoyment.

Sherbourne Park
Sherbourne, Warwick, Warwickshire CV35 8AP
☎ 01926 624255

OWNER   The Hon. Lady Smith-Ryland
LOCATION   A429 between M40 and Barford
OPEN   By appointment
ADMISSION   Adults £2.50; Senior Citizens and Children (13–16) £2
FACILITIES   Parking; dogs permitted; loos; access for the disabled; refreshments by arrangement
FEATURES   Herbaceous borders; lake; plants for plantsmen; old roses and climbers; lilies; frescoed garden pavilion (1994)

35 years of good planning and planting by the present owner has produced a series of smallish enclosed gardens around the house, each distinct and beautifully planted. The shelter of walls and hedges allows such

tender genera as *Olearia* and *Carpenteria* to survive, and sometimes to flourish.

Upton House
Banbury, Warwickshire OX15 6HT
☎ 01295 670266

OWNER   The National Trust
LOCATION   A422, 7 miles north west of Banbury
OPEN   2 – 6 pm, Saturday – Wednesday, 1 April to 31 October
ADMISSION   Adults £2.30; Children £1.15 (Garden only)
FACILITIES   Parking; loos; facilities for the disabled; plants for sale; National Trust shop; tea room
FEATURES   Herbaceous borders; fruit of special interest; lake
ENGLISH HERITAGE GRADE   II*
NCCPG NATIONAL COLLECTIONS *Aster amellus*

High on a ridge near the site of the battle of Edgehill, Upton is terraced right down to the pool at the bottom. The centre-piece is a kitchen garden, reached by flights of Italianate stairs. There are also modern formal gardens, one with standard *Hibiscus* 'Bluebird' underplanted with *Eryngium*, another a rose garden. Further down are a bog garden, a cherry garden and grand herbaceous borders to lead you back to the house. Fascinating, and not at all what you expect when you first see the house.

Warwick Castle
Warwick, Warwickshire CV34 4QU
☎ 01926 495421

OWNER   Tussauds Group
LOCATION   In town centre
OPEN   10 am – 6 pm (5 pm in winter), daily, all year except 25 December
ADMISSION   Adults £7.75 (1994)
FACILITIES   Parking; loos; shop; refreshments nearby
FEATURES   Landscape designed by Capability Brown; fine conifers; old roses and climbers; good topiary
ENGLISH HERITAGE GRADE   I

A classic 18th-century landscape, looking good after recent restoration, to which have been added a late 19th-century formal garden and a 1980s Victorian rose garden, pretty but not very profound.

WEST MIDLANDS

Birmingham Botanical Gardens & Glasshouses
Westbourne Road, Edgbaston, Birmingham, West Midlands B15 3TR
☎ 0121 454 1860

OWNER   Birmingham Botanical & Horticultural Society
LOCATION   2 miles west of city centre
OPEN   9 am (Sunday 10 am) – dusk, daily, all year

ADMISSION   Adults £3 (summer Sundays and Bank Holidays £3.30); Concessions £1.70
FACILITIES   Parking; loos; facilities for the disabled; plants for sale; gift shop; restaurant and light refreshments
FEATURES   Herbaceous borders; fine conifers; fruit of special interest; glasshouses and conservatories to visit; lake; plants for plantsmen; rock garden; modern roses; old roses and climbers; children's gardens; adventure playground; three new 'historic' gardens – Roman, Medieval and Tudor
ENGLISH HERITAGE GRADE   II*
FRIENDS   Membership details available from Reception
NCCPG NATIONAL COLLECTIONS Bonsai, *Verbascum*

Part botanic garden, part public park, wholly delightful, the Birmingham Botanical Gardens can boast a historic layout (John Loudon), rare trees and shrubs, gardens for rhododendrons, roses, herbs and alpines, and four glasshouses (tropical, palm house, orangery and cacti house) as well as a good restaurant, brilliant standards of maintenance and a brass band playing on Sunday afternoons in summer. A garden to enjoy.

Castle Bromwich Hall
Chester Road, Castle Bromwich, West Midlands B36 9BT
☎ 0121 749 4100

OWNER   Castle Bromwich Hall Gardens Trust
LOCATION   5 miles from city centre just off A47
OPEN   1.30 – 4.30 pm, Monday – Thursday. 2 – 6 pm, Saturdays, Sundays and Bank Holiday Mondays
ADMISSION   Adults £2; Concessions £1.50; Children 50p
FACILITIES   Parking; dogs permitted; loos; facilities for the disabled; plants for sale; gift shop; refreshments
FEATURES   Interesting for children; green walks; fruit garden; maze; wilderness; historic garden undergoing restoration
ENGLISH HERITAGE GRADE   II*
FRIENDS   Friends of the Gardens organisation

Garden archaeology at work. Castle Bromwich is being restored as it was in 1700 by a privately funded trust. Quietly awe-inspiring, and the tiny orangery, little more than a summerhouse, is very covetable.

Wightwick Manor
Wightwick, Wolverhampton, West Midlands WV6 8EE
☎ 01902 761108   FAX 01902 764663

OWNER   The National Trust
LOCATION   3 miles west of Wolverhampton on A454
OPEN   11 am (1 pm on Saturdays) – 6 pm, Wednesdays, Thursdays and Saturdays, 1 March to 31 December
ADMISSION   Adults £2; Children £1

FACILITIES Parking; dogs permitted; loos; coffee and soft drinks
FEATURES Herbaceous borders; rock garden; old roses and climbers; good topiary; current holder of Sandford Award; newly-restored peach house (1994); new pergola in rose garden (1994); new 'bridge' garden by the Mathematical Bridge (1995)

High Victorian camp, designed by Thomas Mawson and planted by Alfred Parsons. Topiary, a rose arbour, avenues of Irish yews and a Poets' Corner where all the plants were taken as cuttings from the gardens of literary men – Keats, Tennyson and Dickens among them.

WILTSHIRE

Ashtree Cottage
Kilmington Common, Warminster, Wiltshire
BA12 6QY
☎ 01985 844740

OWNER Mr and Mrs L. J. Lauderdale
LOCATION B3092, ½ a mile north of Stourhead garden; 1 mile west towards Alfred's Tower
OPEN For NGS and by appointment
ADMISSION Adults £2; Children 50p
FACILITIES Parking; small garden nursery
FEATURES Plants for plantsmen; old roses and climbers; young garden

Small high-profile new garden, prettily planted for year-round interest but best at high summer with shrub roses, ramblers and perennials. See *The Garden at Ashtree Cottage* by Wendy Lauderdale (Weidenfeld and Nicolson, 1993).

Avebury Manor
Avebury, Marlborough, Wiltshire
☎ 01985 847777

OWNER The National Trust
LOCATION In the village, well signposted
OPEN 11 am – 5.30 pm, daily except Mondays and Thursdays, 1 April to 31 October (provisional dates)
ADMISSION Adults £3 (provisionally)
FACILITIES Parking; access for the disabled; shop just outside the garden; refreshments in village
FEATURES Herbaceous borders; old roses and climbers; good topiary; double lavender walk

A recent owner did much to revive and restore this great Edwardian garden. It is to be hoped that the National Trust will continue the work.

Bolehyde Manor
Allington, Chippenham, Wiltshire
☎ 01249 652105   FAX 01249 659296

OWNER Earl and Countess Cairns
LOCATION 2 miles west of Chippenham
OPEN 2.30 – 6 pm, 18 June, and by appointment
ADMISSION £1.50
FACILITIES Parking

FEATURES Herbaceous borders; fruit of special interest; plants for plantsmen; old roses and climbers; half-hardy plants

Charming series of enclosed gardens around old stone-built house. Brilliantly developed by the owners with help from Melanie Chambers.

Bowood House
Calne, Wiltshire SN11 0LZ
☎ 01249 812102   FAX 01249 821757

OWNER The Earl of Shelburne
LOCATION Off A4 in Derry Hill village between Calne and Chippenham
OPEN 11 am – 6 pm, daily, 1 April to 29 October
ADMISSION Adults £4.50; Senior Citizens £4; Children £2.30 (1994)
FACILITIES Parking; loos; facilities for the disabled; gift shop and garden centre; buffet lunches and afternoon teas in licensed restaurant
FEATURES Good collection of trees; landscape designed by Capability Brown; fine conifers; follies and garden buildings; lake; landscape designed by Humphry Repton; modern roses; garden sculpture; good topiary; woodland garden; interesting for children; bluebells; immodest sculpture; adventure playground; tallest *Populus* × *canadensis* 'Serotina' in the United Kingdom (and two other tree records)
ENGLISH HERITAGE GRADE I

Beautifully maintained and welcoming, Bowood has something from every period of English garden history. Capability Brown made the lake and Charles Hamilton the famous cascade. There are an important 19th-century pinetum laid out on pre-Linnaean principles, handsome Italianate formal gardens, and modern rhododendron drives in a bluebell wood. Be sure to miss the reclining nude above the formal gardens.

Broadleas
Devizes, Wiltshire
☎ 01380 722035

OWNER Broadleas Gardens Charitable Trust
LOCATION 1 mile south of Devizes
OPEN 2 – 6 pm, Wednesdays, Thursdays and Sundays, 1 April to 31 October
ADMISSION Adults £2; Children £1 (1994)
FACILITIES Parking; loos; access for the disabled; plants for sale; teas on summer Sundays
FEATURES Good collection of trees; herbaceous borders; fine conifers; plants for plantsmen; modern roses; old roses and climbers; woodland garden
ENGLISH HERITAGE GRADE II

Broadleas has a rose garden, grey border, a rock garden and a 'secret' garden hidden behind a hedge of *Prunus* × *blireana*, all near the Regency house. But the main attraction is the Dell, a greensand combe that stretches down to the valley below, its sides just stuffed with good things – rare trees, vast magnolias, sheets of *Primula whitei* and shugmen.

Bryher
Yard Lane, Bromham, Chippenham, Wiltshire
SN15 2DT
☎ 01380 850455

OWNER   Richard and Shirley Packham
LOCATION   Turn right, off A342, 4 miles north of Devizes
OPEN   11 am – 5 pm, Wednesdays, 17 May to 21 June
ADMISSION   £1
FACILITIES   Access for the disabled; plants for sale
FEATURES   Alpines; herbaceous borders; plants for plantsmen; foliage effects

Inspirational young garden where discriminating plantsmanship is combined with a fine eye for harmonies and contrasts of colour, form and texture. Few gardens make such effective use of foliage.

Conock Manor
Devizes, Wiltshire SN10 3QP
☎ 01380 840227

OWNER   Mr and Mrs Bonar Sykes
LOCATION   5 miles south east of Devizes off A342
OPEN   2 – 6 pm, 21 May
ADMISSION   Adults £1.20; Children (under 16) free
FACILITIES   Parking; access for the disabled; some shrubs and herbaceous plants for sale; tea and home-made biscuits
FEATURES   *Cottages ornés*; fine trees and mixed borders; good *Sorbus* and *Eucalyptus*
ENGLISH HERITAGE GRADE   II

Beautiful parkland surrounds this covetable Georgian house. Behind the copper-domed stables an elegant shrub walk meanders past *Sorbus*, maples and magnolias.

Corsham Court
Corsham, Wiltshire SN13 0BZ
☎ 01249 712214

OWNER   The Methuen Trustees
LOCATION   Signposted from A4 Bath – Chippenham
OPEN   2 – 6 pm, daily, 1 August to 30 September
ADMISSION   Adults £2; Senior Citizens £1.50; Children £1
FACILITIES   Parking; dogs permitted; loos; access for the disabled
FEATURES   Good collection of trees; oriental features; designed by Capability Brown and Humphry Repton; amazing oriental plane *Platanus orientalis* whose sweeping limbs have rooted over a huge area
ENGLISH HERITAGE GRADE   II*

Major 18th-century landscape garden, with pretty 1820s flower garden and ambitious modern arboretum: strongly recommended.

The Courts
Holt, Trowbridge, Wiltshire BA14 6RR
☎ 01225 782340

OWNER   The National Trust
LOCATION   In the middle of Holt village
OPEN   2 – 5 pm, Sunday – Friday, 2 April to 31 October
ADMISSION   Adults £2.80; Children £1.40
FACILITIES   Parking; loos; access for the disabled
FEATURES   Herbaceous borders; lake; plants for plantsmen; good topiary; lower pond and leat restored (1994) and will be replanted this year
ENGLISH HERITAGE GRADE   II

1920s masterpiece in the Hidcote style. Rich colour plantings in a series of garden rooms. Excellent plants, beautifully used: well-maintained.

Heale House
Middle Woodford, Salisbury, Wiltshire SP4 6NT
☎ 01722 782504

OWNER   Guy Rasch
LOCATION   Signposted off the western Woodford valley road
OPEN   10 am – 5 pm, daily, all year. NGS days: 6 August and 19 November
ADMISSION   Adults £2.50; Groups (20+) £2.25
FACILITIES   Parking; dogs permitted; loos; access for the disabled; large plant centre; garden and gift shop
FEATURES   Herbaceous borders; fruit of special interest; lake; oriental features; old roses and climbers; snowdrops; Christie's/HHA Garden of the Year in 1984
ENGLISH HERITAGE GRADE   II*

A Peto garden round the prettiest house in Wiltshire. Formal walks, ponds, lawns and balustrading. Rich colours and clever planting. Japanese garden around genuine tea house. Pure enchantment.

Hillbarn House
Great Bedwyn, Marlborough, Wiltshire SN8 3NU

OWNER   Alastair J Buchanan
LOCATION   In High Street, opposite garage
OPEN   For NGS: see Yellow Book
FACILITIES   Loos; tea and biscuits

Lanning Roper's masterpiece makes brilliant use of a small steep site by dividing space to create an illusion of size. Well maintained.

Home Covert
Roundway, Devizes, Wiltshire SN10 2JA
☎ 01380 723407

OWNER   Mr and Mrs John Phillips
LOCATION   1 mile north of Devizes in Roundway village
OPEN   2 – 6 pm, 26 April, 17 May, 21 June, 23 July and 16 August for NGS; any time for parties by appointment; NGS open days
ADMISSION   £2
FACILITIES   Parking; dogs permitted; teas on 23 July
FEATURES   Lake; plants for plantsmen; woodland garden; new pastel border (1994); extensive new woodland plantings (1995)

WILTSHIRE Gardens 343

One of the finest plantsman's gardens in southern England; 'a botanical madhouse' say the owners. Rare trees (*Cercis racemosa*) and shrubs (*Heptacodium jasminoides*): *Lathraea clandestina* and swathes of candelabra primulas in the bog garden.

Iford Manor
Iford, Bradford-on-Avon, Wiltshire BA15 2BA
☎ 01225 863146

OWNER Mrs E. Cartwright-Hignett
LOCATION 7 miles south east of Bath, signed from A36 and Bradford-on-Avon
OPEN 2 – 5 pm, Sundays, April and October. Plus Tuesday – Thursday, Saturdays, Sundays and Bank Holiday Mondays from May to September
ADMISSION Adults £2; Senior Citizens and Children (over 10) £1.50
FACILITIES Parking; dogs permitted; loos; teas on Sundays (May to August)
FEATURES Follies and garden buildings; fruit of special interest; garden sculpture; woodland garden; Italian cypresses and *Phillyrea*; martagon lilies; cyclamen
ENGLISH HERITAGE GRADE I
NCCPG NATIONAL COLLECTIONS *Acanthus*

Harold Peto's own Italianate garden on a steep wooded hillside, meticulously restored and maintained. Romanesque cloister, octagonal cloister and much architectural bric-a-brac. Wonderfully photogenic.

Lackham Country Attractions
Lacock, Chippenham, Wiltshire
☎ 01249 443111   FAX 01249 444474

OWNER Lackham College
LOCATION 3 miles south of Chippenham on A350
OPEN 11 am – 5 pm, daily, Easter to 30 September
ADMISSION Details not yet available
FACILITIES Parking; loos; access for the disabled; plants for sale; souvenirs for sale; coffee shop
FEATURES Alpines; good collection of trees; bluebells; herbaceous borders; daffodils; fruit and vegetables of special interest; glasshouses and conservatories to visit; herbs; plants for plantsmen; modern roses; old roses and climbers; interesting for children; particularly good in July-August; adventure playground; farm museum
NCCPG NATIONAL COLLECTIONS *Populus*
FRIENDS Friends of Lackham Charitable Trust; also Lackham Garden Club. Details on 01249 443111

Among the best of county college gardens, Lackham is a living monument to the knowledge and initiative of Oliver & Ann Menhinnick. The trustees have made further efforts to improve and vary the attractions, but the heart of Lackham is the walled garden, beautifully laid out to educate and delight, with a magnificent glasshouse collection of orchids, tropical fruits and bulbs.

Longleat House
Warminster, Wiltshire BA12 7NW
☎ 01985 844400   FAX 01985 844885

OWNER The Marquess of Bath
LOCATION Off A362 Warminster to Frome road
OPEN Daylight hours, daily, all year except 25 December
ADMISSION Grounds and gardens: Adults £2; Senior Citizens £1.50; Children 50p
FACILITIES Parking; dogs permitted; loos; access for the disabled; shops; cafeterias and restaurants
FEATURES Good collection of trees; herbaceous borders; landscape designed by Capability Brown; fine conifers; glasshouses and conservatories to visit; lake; modern roses; old roses and climbers; good topiary; woodland garden; interesting for children; particularly good in July-August; Safari Park; world's largest maze; newly planted rose maze: the Maze of Love (1995)
ENGLISH HERITAGE GRADE I

Forget the lions and the loins, Longleat has a classic 18th-century landscape by Capability Brown, a home park of 600 acres best seen from Heaven's Gate and a grand Victorian garden reworked by Russell Page in the 1930s. The new Lord Bath has conserved the best and is invigorating the rest of Longleat. Worth another visit.

Oare House
Oare, Marlborough, Wiltshire SN8 4JQ
☎ 01672 62428

OWNER Henry Keswick
LOCATION In village, west side of A345
OPEN 2 – 6 pm, 30 April and 30 July
ADMISSION Adults £1; Children 20p
FACILITIES Parking; dogs permitted; loos; light refreshments
FEATURES Good collection of trees; herbaceous borders; fruit of special interest; modern roses; tall hedges of field maple
ENGLISH HERITAGE GRADE II

Oare has an approach along lime avenues and tall hedges whose grandeur is echoed by the main garden behind. A huge apron of walled lawn, with majestic mixed borders at the sides, leads the eye over a half-hidden swimming pool to a grand ride and on to the Marlborough Downs. Intimacy exists only in some small enclosed gardens to the side and in the kitchen garden. Here are a magnificent herbaceous border in reds and yellows, a tunnel of fruit trees and vegetables in neat rows. A delight.

The Old Vicarage
Edington, Westbury, Wiltshire BA13 4QF
☎ 01380 830512

OWNER John d'Arcy
LOCATION On B3098 in Edington village
OPEN NGS open days or by appointment
ADMISSION £2
FACILITIES Plants for sale
FEATURES Alpines; herbaceous borders; gravel or scree garden; plants for plantsmen; young garden; particularly good in July-August

NCCPG NATIONAL COLLECTIONS *Oenothera*
2 acres of intensively cultivated plantsmanship. The owner is a distinguished plant collector: his garden is immaculately maintained and bristles with new species (*Salvia darcyi*) and living holotypes.

Pound Hill House
West Kington, Chippenham, Wiltshire SN14 7JG
☎ 01249 782822   FAX 01249 782953
OWNER Mr and Mrs Philip Stockitt
LOCATION Signposted in village
OPEN 2 – 5 pm, Wednesday – Sunday, and Bank Holidays, all year
ADMISSION Adults £1.50; Senior Citizens £1
FACILITIES Parking; loos; access for the disabled; adjacent to West Kington Nurseries Plant Centre
FEATURES Alpines; fruit and vegetables of special interest; modern roses; old roses and climbers; woodland garden

The private garden of a discriminating nurseryman, Pound Hill has been developed as a year-round showplace. Stylish new plantings make it a garden to watch.

Roche Court
East Winterslow, Salisbury, Wiltshire SP5 1BG
☎ 01980 862204   FAX 01980 862447
OWNER The Earl and Countess of Bessborough
LOCATION Just south of A30 at Lopcombe corner
OPEN 11 am – 5 pm, Saturdays and Sundays, 1 May to 30 October. Also by appointment
ADMISSION Free
FACILITIES Parking; access for the disabled
FEATURES Herbaceous borders; garden sculpture; woodland garden

As a garden, nothing special, but a show-place for Lady Bessborough's exciting contemporary sculpture shop. Everything is for sale, so the garden is ever-changing.

Sheldon Manor
Chippenham, Wiltshire SN14 0RG
☎ 01259 653120
OWNER Anthony Gibbs
LOCATION Signposted from A420 west of Chippenham
OPEN 12.30 – 6 pm, Thursdays, Sundays and Bank Holidays, Easter to the first Sunday in October
ADMISSION Adults £3 (1994)
FACILITIES Parking; dogs permitted; loos; access for the disabled; plants for sale; shop in house; lunch and tea on open days; parties by arrangement
FEATURES Lake; plants for plantsmen; old roses and climbers; flowering cherries and ornamental apples
ENGLISH HERITAGE GRADE II

The best things about these romantic gardens and their Cotswold manor house are the informal roses (climbers and shrubs), the welcome from the owners and the delicious food in the old stables. Highly recommended.

Stourhead
Stourton, Wiltshire BA12 6QD
☎ 01747 841152
OWNER The National Trust
LOCATION Signposted off A303
OPEN 8 am – 7 pm, or dusk if earlier (5 pm, 19 to 23 July), daily, all year
ADMISSION Adults £4.20; Children £2.20
FACILITIES Parking; dogs permitted; loos; facilities for the disabled; National Trust shop near entrance; famous hotel/pub opposite gate
FEATURES Good collection of trees; bluebells; fine conifers; follies and garden buildings; lake; rhododendrons and azaleas; garden sculpture; woodland garden; interesting for children; tallest tulip tree *Liriodendron tulipifera* in the British Isles, and 7 other record tree species
ENGLISH HERITAGE GRADE I

Whatever the weather or season, Stourhead conveys a sense of majesty and harmony. Try it early on a May morning, before it opens officially, when the air is sweet with azaleas. Or scuff the fallen leaves in late November. Think of it 200 years ago, without the rhododendrons, when all the beech trees were interplanted with spruces. Ponder the 18th-century aesthetic, which esteemed tones and shades more highly than colours. Spot the change from classical to gothic, from Pope to Walpole. And wonder at the National Trust's ability to maintain it so well with only 6 gardeners.

Stourton House
Stourton, Warminster, Wiltshire BA12 6QF
☎ 01747 840417
OWNER Mrs Anthony Bullivant
LOCATION Next to Stourhead, 2 miles north of A303 at Mere
OPEN 11 am – 6 pm, Wednesdays, Thursdays, Sundays and Bank Holiday Mondays, April to November
ADMISSION Adults £2; Children 50p; Groups (12+) £1.50
FACILITIES Parking; loos; facilities for the disabled; plants for sale; teas; light lunches; sticky cakes
FEATURES Herbaceous borders; good topiary; woodland garden; particularly good in July-August; Victorian conservatory; elegantly curving hedges; hosts of daffodils in innumerable shapes, sizes and colours; new borders with Kiwi plants (1995)

This 5-acre old vicarage garden is famous for its dried flowers, thanks to the energy and personality of Elizabeth Bullivant. Strongly recommended at any season: over 200 hydrangea varieties in late summer.

Thompson's Hill
Sherston, Malmesbury, Wiltshire SN16 0PZ
☎ 01666 840766
OWNER Mr and Mrs Sean Cooper
LOCATION At Sherston village church turn left down hill, then right, up hill
OPEN 2 – 6.30 pm, 25 June for NGS

ADMISSION £1.50
FACILITIES Parking; plants for sale
FEATURES Herbaceous borders; old roses and climbers; young garden

Half-acre modern garden, growing up quickly and changing all the time. Well-planted and maintained by its owners' own efforts: almost too tidy. Much featured in the glossies.

Wilton House
Wilton, Salisbury, Wiltshire SP2 0BJ
☎ 01722 743115   FAX 01722 744447

OWNER Earl of Pembroke/Wilton House Trust
LOCATION In village, 2 miles west of Salisbury on A30
OPEN 11 am – 6 pm, daily, 11 April to 29 October
ADMISSION Adults £5.75; Senior Citizens £4.95; Children £3.75
FACILITIES Parking; loos; access for the disabled; plants for sale in adjoining Wilton House garden centre; self-service restaurant
FEATURES Fine conifers; oriental features; old roses and climbers; interesting for children; handsome cedars; famous Palladian bridge; magnificent golden-leaved oak; adventure playground
ENGLISH HERITAGE GRADE I

Sublime 18th-century park around classical Inigo Jones pile famous for its paintings. Recently courting popularity: pretty new rose garden and water garden and ugly new visitors' centre.

Wincombe Park
Donhead St Mary, Shaftesbury, Wiltshire SP7 9AB
☎ 01747 852161

OWNER The Hon. Martin Fortescue
LOCATION Off A350 north of Shaftesbury, follow signs for Wincombe
OPEN 2 – 5.30 pm, 17 May and 18 October; plus groups by appointment
ADMISSION Adults £1.50; Children free
FACILITIES Parking; dogs permitted; loos; plants for sale; tea available in house
FEATURES Herbaceous borders; plantsman's garden

Wonderful borders in the walled garden, planted by the owner's late wife, but nothing can beat the spacious view across the lawns, and a lake, to the wooded combe beyond.

NORTH YORKSHIRE

Beningbrough Hall
Shipton-by-Beningbrough, York, North Yorkshire YO6 1DD
☎ 01904 470666

OWNER The National Trust
LOCATION 8 miles north west of York off the A19

OPEN 11 am – 5.30 pm, Saturday – Wednesday, 1 April to 31 October. Guided tours available most weekends
ADMISSION Adults £3; Children £1.50
FACILITIES Parking; loos; facilities for the disabled; plants for sale; National Trust gift shop; morning coffee; hot and cold lunches; afternoon teas
FEATURES Herbaceous borders; fruit of special interest; lake; oriental features; woodland garden; plantings by Graham Thomas; American garden; good conservatory on house; vast Portuguese laurel *Prunus lusitanica*
ENGLISH HERITAGE GRADE II

Pretty modern National Trust plantings: two small formal gardens, one with reds and oranges and the other with pastel shades, on either side of the early Georgian house and a sumptuous mixed border which grades from hot colours to cool.

Castle Howard
York, North Yorkshire YO6 7DA
☎ 01653 648333   FAX 01653 648462

OWNER Castle Howard Estates Ltd
LOCATION 5 miles south west of Malton
OPEN 10 am – 4.30 pm (last entry), daily, 17 March to 29 October
ADMISSION House and grounds: Adults £6; Children £3; Senior Citizens £5. Grounds only: Adults £4; Children £2 (1994)
FACILITIES Parking; dogs permitted; loos; access for the disabled; shop and plant centre; cafeteria
FEATURES Herbaceous borders; follies and garden buildings; modern roses; old roses and climbers; garden sculpture; woodland garden; biggest *Populus alba* in British Isles; major replanting of roses (1994–5)
ENGLISH HERITAGE GRADE I

Heroic megapark (1,200 hectares) laid out with 5 axes by the 3rd Earl of Carlisle, Vanbrugh and Hawksmoor with important buildings (Temple of the Four Winds, Mausoleum). Grand 1980s rose gardens (slightly Surrey) designed by Jim Russell, with every type of rose from ancient to modern. In Ray Wood, a fine and historic collection of rhododendrons and other ericaceous plants, meticulously labelled. A must for botanist and gardener alike – be prepared to spend all day here – and essential visiting for anyone with a sense of history.

Duncombe Park
Helmsley, North Yorkshire YO6 5EB
☎ 01439 70213   FAX 01439 71114

OWNER Lord Feversham
LOCATION Off A170; signed from Helmsley
OPEN 11 am – 5.30pm or dusk if earlier, Sunday – Thursday, but daily in July and August, May to September. Plus Wednesdays and Sundays in April and October
ADMISSION Adults £2.75; Children £1.50
FACILITIES Parking; loos; gift shop; restaurant

FEATURES   Follies and garden buildings; garden sculpture; Rysbrack statue of Old Father Time
ENGLISH HERITAGE GRADE   I

Major early 18th-century landscape, a grass terrace which sweeps between Vanburgh's Ionic rotunda and a Tuscan temple with views across the valley to Helmsley and the moors, matched only by views from its sister terrace at Rievaulx, in the care of the National Trust.

Harlow Carr Botanical Gardens
Beckwithshaw, Harrogate, North Yorkshire HG3 1QB
☎ 01423 565418

OWNER   Northern Horticultural Society
LOCATION   Crag Lane off Otley Road (B6162), 1½ miles from Harrogate centre
OPEN   9.30 am – 6 pm, or dusk if earlier, daily, all year
ADMISSION   Adults £3.20; Senior Citizens £2.50; Children (under 16) free; Parties (20+) £2.50. Special winter rate (November – February)
FACILITIES   Parking; loos; facilities for the disabled; plants for sale; gift shop; licensed restaurant
FEATURES   Good collection of trees; bluebells; camellias; daffodils; fruit and vegetables of special interest; glasshouses and conservatories to visit; gravel or scree garden; herbs; rock garden; modern roses; old roses and climbers; woodland garden; heathers and alpines; good autumn colour
NCCPG NATIONAL COLLECTIONS *Dryopteris, Polypodium, Rheum, Calluna, Hyperium*

Harlow Carr is quite the best place for northern gardeners to learn about gardening: the Wisley of the north.

Newby Hall
Ripon, North Yorkshire HG4 5AE
☎ 01423 322583   FAX 01423 324452

OWNER   Robin Compton
LOCATION   Off B6265, 2 miles from A1
OPEN   11 am – 5.30 pm, Tuesday – Sunday and Bank Holiday Mondays, April to September
ADMISSION   Adults £3.30; Senior Citizens £2.20; Children and Disabled £2.20 (1994)
FACILITIES   Parking; loos; facilities for the disabled; shop and plant stall; licensed restaurant
FEATURES   Alpines; herbaceous borders; daffodils; lake; plants for plantsmen; rock garden; old roses and climbers; garden sculpture; woodland garden; HHA/Christie's Garden of the Year in 1986; biggest *Acer griseum* and *Sorbus intermedia* in UK; adventure playground
ENGLISH HERITAGE GRADE   II*
NCCPG NATIONAL COLLECTIONS *Cornus*

The garden with everything: firm design, an endless variety of features, great plantsmanship, immaculate maintenance. Its axis is a bold, wide double border stretching endlessly down to the River Ure. Second only to Hidcote as an example of 20th-century gardening. Visit Newby at any season and expect to spend all day there.

Parcevall Hall Gardens
Skyreholme, Skipton, North Yorkshire BD23 6DE
☎ 01756 720311

OWNER   Walsingham College (Yorkshire Properties) Ltd
LOCATION   Off B6160 from Burnsall
OPEN   10 am – 6 pm, daily, Good Friday to 31 October; winter visits by appointment
ADMISSION   Adults £2; Children (5–12) 50p
FACILITIES   Parking; dogs permitted; loos; plants for sale; tea shop (summer weekends)
FEATURES   Fine conifers; lake; rhododendrons and azaleas; rock garden; climbing roses; woodland garden; candelabra primulas
FRIENDS   Yes

Breathtaking architectural layout, and views. Planted by Sir William Milner 70 years ago and best now for its wonderful rhododendrons growing alongside limestone outcrops, daffodils (including 'W P Milner') and *Primula florindae* given by Kingdon Ward now naturalised round the lily pond.

Ripley Castle
Ripley, Harrogate, North Yorkshire HG3 3AY
☎ 01423 770152   FAX 01423 771745

OWNER   Sir Thomas Ingilby Bt.
LOCATION   3½ miles north of Harrogate, off A61
OPEN   11 am – 5 pm (4 pm in March, 3.30 pm November and December), daily, 1 March to 23 December, but closed Monday – Wednesday in March
ADMISSION   Adults £2.25; Senior Citizens £1.75; Children £1 (1994)
FACILITIES   Parking; loos; facilities for the disabled; gift shop with plants, fruit and vegetables; castle tea room
FEATURES   Herbaceous borders; landscape designed by Capability Brown; fruit of special interest; glasshouses and conservatories to visit; herbs; subtropical plants; interesting for children; particularly interesting in winter; birds of prey sanctuary
ENGLISH HERITAGE GRADE   II
NCCPG NATIONAL COLLECTIONS *Hyacinthus*

14th-century castle (restored); Capability Brown landscape; temples; smashing Regency conservatory; Victorian formal garden; evergreen shrubberies (handsome yews); hundreds of thousands of bulbs (daffodils in hosts). A garden with something for everyone.

Sleightholmedale Lodge
Fadmoor, Kirkbymoorside, North Yorkshire YO6 6JG

OWNER   Mrs R. James
LOCATION   Signed from Fadmoor
OPEN   For NGS: see Yellow Book. Also by written appointment
ADMISSION   £1.25

FACILITIES Parking; dogs permitted; loos; plants for sale
FEATURES Herbaceous borders; herbs; plants for plantsmen; modern roses; old roses and climbers; woodland garden

Plantsman's paradise on the edge of the moors: not just azaleas and *Meconopsis* but Mexican and Mediterranean plants too – a triumph for good cultivation and manipulation of the microclimate. Roses of every sort – hundreds of them, perhaps thousands.

Studley Royal
Fountains, Ripon, North Yorkshire HG4 3DZ
☎ 01765 608888   FAX 01765 608889

OWNER The National Trust
LOCATION 3 miles west of Ripon off B6265, via the visitor centre
OPEN 10 am – 5 pm (7 pm in summer) or dusk if sooner; daily, all year, except Fridays from November to January, and 24 and 25 December
ADMISSION Adults £4; Children £2; Family £10. Groups (15+): Adults £3.50; Children £1.70
FACILITIES Parking; dogs permitted; loos; facilities for the disabled; National Trust visitor centre shop; tea room
FEATURES Lake; World Heritage site; 400-acre deer park; biggest *Prunus avium* (bird cherry) in British Isles
ENGLISH HERITAGE GRADE I

Inextricably linked to Fountains Abbey, which forms the focus of an unsurpassed surprise view from Anne Boleyn's Seat, Studley is a classical, geometrical landscape of major importance. Best seen high up from the banqueting-house lawn and the Octagon tower – the formal canal, Moon pools, Grotto Springs, rustic bridge and Temple of Filial Piety.

Sutton Park
Sutton-in-the-Forest, York, North Yorkshire YO6 1DP
☎ 01347 810249

OWNER Mrs N. M. D. Sheffield
LOCATION 8 miles north of York on B1363
OPEN 11 am – 5 pm, daily, Easter to October
ADMISSION £1
FACILITIES Parking; loos; plants for sale occasionally; tea room; private parties by arrangement only
FEATURES Herbaceous borders; landscape designed by Capability Brown; plants for plantsmen; old roses and climbers; woodland garden; Yorkshire and Humberside in Bloom winner for last 3 years; new pond garden in walled garden (1994)

Capability Brown was here 200 years ago, but the joy of Sutton is the formal garden laid out on terraces below the house by Percy Cane in the 1960s, and planted by Mrs Sheffield with exquisite taste. Quite the prettiest garden in Yorkshire.

Thorp Perrow Arboretum
Bedale, North Yorkshire DL8 2PR
☎ 01677 425323   FAX 01677 422710

OWNER Sir John Ropner Bt.
LOCATION On the Well – Ripon road, just south of Bedale
OPEN Dawn – dusk, daily, all year
ADMISSION Adults £2.75; Children, Senior Citizens and Students £1.50
FACILITIES Parking; dogs permitted; loos; facilities for the disabled; plants for sale; tea room
FEATURES Good collection of trees; fine conifers; woodland garden; biggest golden beech *Fagus sylvatica* 'Aurea' in UK
ENGLISH HERITAGE GRADE II
FRIENDS Friends of Thorp Perrow (details from Curator)
NCCPG NATIONAL COLLECTIONS *Juglans, Quercus, Tilia, Fraxinus*

Important modern arboretum undergoing restoration after some years of neglect. Wonderful avenues of laburnum, glades of cherries and coniferous groves.

The Valley Gardens, Harrogate
Harrogate Borough Council, Harrogate, North Yorkshire
☎ 01423 500600 ext. 3211

OWNER Harrogate Borough Council
LOCATION Harrogate
OPEN Dawn – dusk, daily, all year
ADMISSION Free
FACILITIES Parking; dogs permitted; loos; access for the disabled; small cafeteria
FEATURES Herbaceous borders; rock garden; sub-tropical plants; interesting for children; wonderful *Meconopsis* and primulas alongside the stream; children's play area
ENGLISH HERITAGE GRADE II

The best example of plantsmanship in a public garden in England, laid out 1880-1910: the Sun Colonnade, which incorporates an elegant pergola, has just been restored. Alpine rarities in spring, a romantic dell, magnificent dahlia display in late summer and the best colour bedding in Yorkshire.

Yorkshire Museum Gardens
Yorkshire Museum, Museum Gardens, York, North Yorkshire YO1 2DR
☎ 01904 629745   FAX 01904 651221

OWNER North Yorkshire County Council
LOCATION Follow signs for Yorkshire Museum
OPEN 7.30 am – dusk, daily, all year except Christmas Day
ADMISSION Free
FACILITIES Dogs permitted; loos; access for the disabled
FEATURES Rock garden
ENGLISH HERITAGE GRADE II

FRIENDS Yorkshire Philosophical Society
Nice example of an up-market amenity garden round a public heritage site. Laid out by Sir John Naysmith 150 years ago and still basically intact. Good trees, including *Alnus glutinosa* 'Laciniata' and *Fraxinus excelsior* f. *diversifolia*.

SOUTH YORKSHIRE

Sheffield Botanical Gardens
Clarkehouse Road, Sheffield, South Yorkshire S10 2LN
☎ 0114 2500500   FAX 0114 2552375
OWNER   Sheffield Town Trust (administered by City Council)
LOCATION   J33 of M1, follow A57 signs to Glossop, left at Royal Hallamshire Hospital, 500m on left
OPEN   8 am – 8 pm (4 pm in winter), daily, all year
ADMISSION   Free
FACILITIES   Dogs permitted; loos; facilities for the disabled
FEATURES   Herbaceous borders; fine conifers; glasshouses and conservatories to visit; rock garden; modern roses; old roses and climbers; woodland garden; particularly interesting in winter; conservatories by Paxton; peat garden; heath garden
NCCPG NATIONAL COLLECTIONS *Weigela*, *Diervilla*
FRIENDS   Friends (ring 0114 2500500); good lecture programme

Founded in 1833 by public subscription and still burgeoning with civic pride. Good camellias and magnolias, *Erica* and *Sorbus*. Splendid summer bedding too, and lots of seats and waste bins: an exemplary combination of botany and amenity.

Wentworth Castle Gardens
Northern College, Wentworth Castle, Stainborough, Barnsley, South Yorkshire S75 3ET
☎ 01226 285426   FAX 01226 284308
OWNER   Barnsley Metropolitan District Council
LOCATION   3 miles south of Barnsley; 2 miles from M1
OPEN   10 am – 5 pm, Spring Bank Holiday (Sunday and Monday). Parties by arrangement. Guided tours in May and June on Tuesdays and Thursdays at 2 pm (assemble in car park)
ADMISSION   Adults £2; Unwaged, Students and Children £1
FACILITIES   Parking; dogs permitted; loos
FEATURES   Woodland garden; interesting for children; educational collection of rhododendrons
ENGLISH HERITAGE GRADE   I
FRIENDS   Friends of the Gardens Society
NCCPG NATIONAL COLLECTIONS *Rhododendron*

Major landscape garden currently undergoing development as an educational and cultural resource. Twinned with the Kun-ming Academy of Sciences. A garden to watch.

WEST YORKSHIRE

Bramham Park
Wetherby, West Yorkshire LS23 6ND
☎ 01937 844265   FAX 01937 845923
OWNER   George Lane Fox
LOCATION   5 miles south of Wetherby on A1
OPEN   1.15 – 5.30 pm, Tuesday – Thursday and Sundays, 18 June to 3 September. Plus Saturday – Monday of Easter, May and Spring Bank Holiday weekends
ADMISSION   Adults £2; Senior Citizens £1.50; Children £1
FACILITIES   Parking; dogs permitted; loos; facilities for the disabled
FEATURES   Herbaceous borders; daffodils; follies and garden buildings; modern roses; garden sculpture
ENGLISH HERITAGE GRADE   I

Very important pre-landscape formal gardens, laid out in the grand manner by a pupil of Le Nôtre in the early 18th century. There are long straight rides cut through dense woodland, ornamental ponds, cascades, loggias, temples and an obelisk.

Canal Gardens
Roundhay Park, Street Lane, Leeds, West Yorkshire
☎ 0113 2661850
OWNER   Leeds City Council
LOCATION   3 miles north-west of city centre, off A6120 ring road
OPEN   All year, but Tropical World closes at dusk
ADMISSION   Free
FACILITIES   Parking; dogs permitted; loos; access for the disabled; souvenirs; cafeteria by lakeside
FEATURES   Glasshouses and conservatories to visit; lake; modern roses; subtropical plants; particularly interesting in winter; good carpet bedding; orchids; new Desert and Nocturnal houses
ENGLISH HERITAGE GRADE   II
NCCPG NATIONAL COLLECTIONS *Viola*, *Dahlia*

Tropical World glasshouses containing South American rain forest plants, bromeliads, hoyas, cacti and Butterfly House. A wonderful retreat from a Yorkshire winter and a triumph of municipal horticultural excellence.

Golden Acre Park
Otley Road, Bramhope, Leeds, West Yorkshire LS16 5NZ
☎ 0113 2782030
OWNER   Leeds City Council
LOCATION   4 miles north on A660 Otley Road
OPEN   Dawn – dusk, daily, all year
ADMISSION   Free
FACILITIES   Parking; dogs permitted; loos; access for the disabled; gifts/souvenirs; restaurant
FEATURES   Lake; rock garden; large heather garden
NCCPG NATIONAL COLLECTIONS *Syringa*, *Primula auricula*

Part park, part botanic collection, part demonstration garden, part test ground for Fleuroselect; perhaps the best of Leeds' five impressive public gardens.

Harewood House
Harewood House Estate, Leeds, West Yorkshire LS17 9LQ
☎ 0113 2886331   FAX 0113 2886467
OWNER   The Earl of Harewood
LOCATION   Between Leeds and Harrogate on A61
OPEN   10 am – 5 pm, daily, 13 March to 31 October
ADMISSION   House and gardens: Adults £5.75; Children £3
FACILITIES   Parking; loos; plants for sale; refreshments
FEATURES   Landscape designed by Capability Brown; oriental features; woodland garden; interesting for children; adventure playground; Japanese garden; rhododendrons; current holder of Sandford Award
ENGLISH HERITAGE GRADE   I
NCCPG NATIONAL COLLECTIONS *Hosta*

Capability Brown landscaped Harewood, and Charles Barry added the grand Italianate terrace, but Repton and Loudon also had a hand in this most grand of Yorkshire gardens. Well-maintained and welcomingly run.

The Hollies Park
Weetwood Lane, Leeds, West Yorkshire LS16 5NZ
☎ 0113 2782030
OWNER   Leeds City Council
LOCATION   3 miles north of city off A660
OPEN   Dawn – dusk, daily, all year
ADMISSION   Free
FACILITIES   Parking; dogs permitted; loos
FEATURES   Woodland garden; rhododendrons; *Eucryphia*
NCCPG NATIONAL COLLECTIONS *Philadelphus, Deutzia, Hemerocallis, Hosta*

Slightly dilapidated plantsman's garden, under-resourced but well-run by a hard-pressed and enthusiastic team.

Land Farm Gardens
Colden, Hebden Bridge, Halifax, West Yorkshire HX7 7PJ
☎ 01422 842260
OWNER   John Williams
LOCATION   On right, 2 miles from Hebden Bridge on Colden road
OPEN   10 am – 5 pm, Saturdays, Sundays and Bank Holiday Mondays, 1 May to 31 August
ADMISSION   Adults £2
FACILITIES   Parking; loos; plants for sale; art gallery; refreshments pre-booked for parties
FEATURES   Alpines; herbaceous borders; fine conifers; heathers

A pioneering plantsman's garden, 1,000 feet up in the Pennines. Only an acre, but the range of plants that will tolerate the conditions is an eye-opener.

Lotherton Hall
Aberford, Leeds, West Yorkshire
☎ 0113 281 3259
OWNER   Leeds City Council
LOCATION   Off A1, ¾ mile east on B1217
OPEN   Dawn – dusk, daily, all year
ADMISSION   Free
FACILITIES   Parking; loos; facilities for the disabled; shop; cafeteria
FEATURES   Oriental features; modern roses
ENGLISH HERITAGE GRADE   II

Edwardian showpiece-garden, now recovering from neglect and on the move again. Formal rose gardens and lily pond, recently replanted with period varieties.

Temple Newsam Park
Manager's Office, Temple Newsam Park, Leeds 15, West Yorkshire
☎ 0113 2645535
OWNER   Leeds City Council
LOCATION   3 miles south east of city, off A63 Selby road
OPEN   Dawn – dusk, daily, all year
ADMISSION   Free. Admission charge to house
FACILITIES   Parking; dogs permitted; loos; access for the disabled; souvenirs; restaurant
FEATURES   Herbaceous borders; landscape designed by Capability Brown; glasshouses and conservatories to visit; modern roses; old roses and climbers; rhododendrons
ENGLISH HERITAGE GRADE   II
NCCPG NATIONAL COLLECTIONS *Aster novi-belgii, Delphinium, Phlox*

1,200 acres of parkland, now a 'green lung' for Leeds. Cheerful borders in the old walled garden. Somewhat neglected in the past, now undergoing extensive restoration and improvement.

WALES

CLWYD

Bodnant Gardens
Tal-y-Cafn, Colwyn Bay, Clwyd LL28 5RE
☎ 01492 650460   FAX 01492 650448
OWNER   The National Trust
LOCATION   8 miles south of Llandudno and Colwyn Bay on A470. Entrance ½ a mile along Eglwysbach Road
OPEN   10 am – 5 pm, daily, mid-March to 31 October
ADMISSION   Adults £3.90; Children £1.95
FACILITIES   Parking; loos; plants for sale; light lunches, teas, refreshments
FEATURES   Good collection of trees; herbaceous borders; fine conifers; follies and garden buildings; glasshouses and conservatories to visit; lake; plants for plantsmen; woodland garden; rhododendrons; azaleas; magnolias; camellias; tallest Californian redwood *Se-*

quoia sempervirens (47 metres) in the British Isles and 19 further record-breaking tree species
NCCPG NATIONAL COLLECTIONS *Embothrium, Eucryia, Magnolia, Rhododendron*

The greatest garden in Wales, some would say in all Britain. The grand Italianate terraces above a woodland 'dell' are only part of its renown: Bodnant is famous for its laburnum tunnel, white wisterias, vast *Arbutus × andrachnoides*, the 1730s gazebo called the Pin Mill, the green theatre, *Viburnum × bodnantense*, hybrid camellias, huge rhododendrons, flaming *Embothrium*, the two Lords Aberconway, father and son, both past-Presidents of the Royal Horticultural Society, and the three generations of the Puddle family who have been head gardeners.

Chirk Castle
Chirk, Clwyd LL4 5AF
☎ 01691 777701   FAX 01691 774706
OWNER The National Trust
LOCATION ½ a mile west of Chirk off A5
OPEN 11.30 am – 6 pm, daily except Monday and Saturday, 1 April to 30 September. Saturdays, Sundays and Bank Holiday Mondays, 1 October to 30 October
ADMISSION Adults £2; Children £1
FACILITIES Parking; dogs permitted; loos; facilities for the disabled; shop; restaurant and tea room
FEATURES Herbaceous borders; follies and garden buildings; rock garden; modern roses; old roses and climbers; garden sculpture; good topiary; woodland garden; rhododendrons; azaleas; *Eucryphia*; hydrangeas; lime avenue

Chirk has handsome 19th-century formal gardens, one planted with roses and another with billowing yew topiary. There is also a good 1930s collection of trees and shrubs, the relics of a garden by Norah Lindsay. But some say the whole garden is 'a little too National Trust' now.

Erddig
Wrexham, Clwyd LL13 0YT
☎ 01978 355314   FAX 01978 313333
OWNER The National Trust
LOCATION Signposted from A483 and A525
OPEN 11 am – 6 pm (5 pm from 2 to 29 October), Saturday – Wednesday, 14 April to 29 October
ADMISSION House and garden: Adults £5; Children £2.50; Groups pre-booked (20+) £4
FACILITIES Parking; loos; plants for sale; restaurant, tea room
FEATURES Fruit of special interest; lake; old roses and climbers; woodland garden; spring bulbs; current holder of Sandford Award
ENGLISH HERITAGE GRADE I
NCCPG NATIONAL COLLECTIONS *Hedera*

More of a re-creation than a restoration, Erddig today majors on domestic life in the early 18th century. There are old-fashioned fruit trees, an avenue of pleached limes, and a long canal to frame the house, but all are slightly awed by the Victorian overlay – avenues of monkey-puzzles and wellingtonias.

DYFED

Cae Hir
Cribyn, Lampeter, Dyfed SA48 7NG
☎ 01570 470839
OWNER W. Akkermans
LOCATION In village
OPEN 1 – 6 pm, daily except Mondays, but open on Bank Holiday Mondays
ADMISSION Adults £1.50; Senior Citizens £1.25; Children 50p
FACILITIES Parking; dogs permitted; loos; plants for sale; small gift shop; light refreshments
FEATURES Bog garden; herbaceous borders; lake; colour gardens; bonsai; new water garden and new white garden (1995)

Young and expanding garden, only 9 years old. 6 acres have been taken from meadows and made into a series of beautiful colour-conscious gardens by the present owner. Trees, shrubs and herbaceous plants, often used in original ways. Immaculately tidy: Mr Akkermans' energy and achievements are an inspiration.

Colby Woodland Garden
Amroth, Narberth, Dyfed SA67 8PP
☎ 01834 811885
OWNER The National Trust
LOCATION Signposted from A477
OPEN 10 am – 5 pm, daily, 1 April to 5 November
ADMISSION Adults £2.60; Groups (15+) £2.10; Children £1.10
FACILITIES Parking; loos; plants for sale; shop; light refreshments
FEATURES Fine conifers; rhododendrons and azaleas; woodland garden; good trees

A grand woodland garden, best in May when the rhododendrons are in full flower.

The Dingle (Crundale)
Crundale, Haverfordwest, Dyfed SA62 4DJ
☎ 01437 764 370
OWNER Mrs A. J. Jones
LOCATION On the A40 to Haverfordwest turn right on first two roundabouts, fork right then 1st right
OPEN 10 am – 6 pm, Wednesday – Monday, 12 March to 15 October
ADMISSION Adults £1; Children 50p
FACILITIES Parking; loos; access for the disabled; nursery; tea room
FEATURES Herbaceous borders; gravel or scree garden; lake; rock garden; old roses and climbers; woodland garden; young garden; bluebells; primroses
NCCPG NATIONAL COLLECTIONS *Gunnera*

This excellent young garden was started in 1982 to display the plants which Mrs Jones grows in the adjoining nursery – roses, clematis, herbaceous plants and alpines – but it has the feel of a private garden. Plants are arranged to show off their form as well as their flowers and leaf-colours. A good garden – it works well.

Picton Castle
The Rhos, Haverfordwest, Pembrokeshire, Dyfed SA62 4AS
☎ 01437 751326
OWNER   Picton Castle Trust
LOCATION   4 miles east of Haverfordwest off A40
OPEN   10.30 am – 5.30 pm, Tuesday – Sunday and Bank Holidays, 1 April to 30 September
ADMISSION   Adults £2; Children and Senior Citizens £1
FACILITIES   Parking; dogs permitted; loos; facilities for the disabled; plants for sale; garden shop selling surplus garden produce; restaurant
FEATURES   Herbs; woodland garden; rhododendrons; azaleas; camellias

Essentially a 50-acre woodland garden with rhododendrons and similar shrubs planted over the last 50 years, but the Trust is replanting the kitchen garden as a flower garden and visitors can expect further improvements.

Post House Gardens
Cwmbach, Whitland, Dyfed SA34 0DR
☎ 01994 484213
OWNER   Mrs Jo Kenaghan
LOCATION   7 miles north of St Clears (A40)
OPEN   9 am – sunset, daily, all year
ADMISSION   Adults £1.50; Senior Citizens £1; Children 50p
FACILITIES   Parking; dogs permitted; loos; plants for sale; tea and coffee
FEATURES   Good collection of trees; bog garden; herbaceous borders; glasshouses and conservatories to visit; lake; plants for plantsmen; rhododendrons and azaleas; rock garden; old roses and climbers; woodland garden; wood anemones; bluebells; lots of recent planting (1994–5), especially bog plants and shrubs

Four acres of plantsmanship on a long, narrow site above the River Sien, so steep that it appears much larger. Hardy trees and shrubs are the main feature, especially rhododendrons which are also available for purchase, but there are also alpines, *Gunnera*, *Meconopsis* and wonderful wild woodland flowers.

SOUTH GLAMORGAN

Dyffryn Botanic Garden
St Nicholas, Cardiff, South Glamorgan CF5 6SU
☎ 01222 593328   FAX 01222 591366
OWNER   Mid and South Glamorgan County Councils
LOCATION   Exit 33 M4 on A48 then follow signs
OPEN   10 am – 5.30 pm, daily, all year
ADMISSION   Adults £2; Senior Citizens and Children £1.50
FACILITIES   Parking; dogs permitted; loos; access for the disabled; plants for sale on Bank Holidays; refreshments
FEATURES   Good collection of trees; herbaceous borders; fruit of special interest; modern roses; spring bulbs; summer bedding; tallest *Kalopanax septemlobus* (syn. *K. pictus*) in the British Isles and 6 other record trees
NCCPG NATIONAL COLLECTIONS   *Salvia, Dahlia*

55 acres of sumptuous gardens designed by Thomas Mawson around an Edwardian prodigy house. Intended partly for display – there is a Roman garden with a temple and fountain – and partly for the owners' own pleasure, Dyffryn has a huge collection of good plants built up by Reginald Cory in the early years of this century. The garden as a status symbol.

WEST GLAMORGAN

Clyne Gardens
Mumbles Road, Blackpill, Swansea, West Glamorgan
☎ 01792 302420   FAX 01792 302408
OWNER   Swansea City Council
LOCATION   3 miles west of Swansea on coast road
OPEN   Dawn – dusk, daily, all year
ADMISSION   Free
FACILITIES   Parking; dogs permitted; loos; access for the disabled; occasional light refreshments
FEATURES   Herbaceous borders; lake; oriental features; woodland garden; Clyne in Bloom Festival all May
FRIENDS   Details of Friends organisation from Ivor Stokes
NCCPG NATIONAL COLLECTIONS   *Pieris, Enkia thus, Rhododendron*

A well-kept woodland garden in the care of an enthusiastic and knowledgeable staff. Several National Collections and a good range of tender plants, including *maddenii* rhododendrons.

Margam Park
Port Talbot, West Glamorgan SA13 2TJ
☎ 01639 881635   FAX 01639 895897
OWNER   West Glamorgan County Council
LOCATION   Follow directions from J38, M4
OPEN   10 am – 7 pm, daily, summer; 9.30 am – 5 pm, daily, winter
ADMISSION   Adults £3.10; Children £2.05; Family £9.30 (1994)
FACILITIES   Parking; dogs permitted; loos; facilities for the disabled; gift shop; restaurant and light refreshments
FEATURES   Good collection of trees; follies and garden buildings; fruit of special interest; oriental features; modern roses; old roses and climbers; garden sculpture;

interesting for children; bedding out; daffodils; rhododendrons; maze; orangery; tallest bay tree *Laurus nobilis* in the British Isles

A popular country park with lots to interest the garden historian and plantsman. A wonderful range of conservatories and glasshouses, including the orangery for which Margam is famous, big trees and rhododendrons (some grown from Kingdon Ward's seed), and cheerful bedding out. The council has added a collection of dwarf conifers, a permanent exhibition of modern sculptures, a maze (one of the largest in Europe) and a new pergola 450 yards long: further work is promised.

Plantasia
Parc Tawe, Swansea, West Glamorgan SA1 2AL
☎ 01792 474555/302420   FAX 01792 652588

OWNER   Swansea City Council
LOCATION   Off main Eastern approach to Swansea
OPEN   10.30 am – 5.30 pm, Tuesdays – Sundays and Bank Holidays, all year
ADMISSION   Adults £1; Concessions 75p (1994)
FACILITIES   Parking; loos; access for the disabled; souvenirs and plant-related materials; soft drinks
FEATURES   Glasshouses and conservatories to visit; interesting for children; particularly interesting in winter; aviary and tropical fish

A major modern amenity commitment by the go-ahead City Council. Plantasia is a large glasshouse (1,600 sq m) with three climatic zones (arid, tropical, and rain forest) and each is stuffed with exotic plants – palms, strelitzias, tree ferns, *Nepenthe*, cacti and such economic plants as coconuts and pineapple. The perfect goal for a winter expedition.

GWENT

Lower House Farm
Nantyderry, Abergavenny, Gwent NP7 9DP
☎ 01873 880257   FAX 01873 880108

OWNER   Mr and Mrs Glynne Clay
LOCATION   500 yards from Chain Bridge
OPEN   For NGS and by appointment
ADMISSION   Adults £1.50; Children 50p
FACILITIES   Parking; loos; plants for sale; plants on NGS days; teas on NGS days
FEATURES   Good collection of trees; herbaceous borders; fine conifers; herbs; plants for plantsmen; old roses and climbers; *Lathraea clandestina*; good autumn colour

A modern garden, substantially made by the present owners. Many good features, notably the bog garden and fern island, and unusual young trees.

Penpergwm Lodge
Abergavenny, Gwent NP7 9AS
☎ 01873 840208

OWNER   Mrs C. Boyle
LOCATION   3 miles from Abergavenny on B4598

OPEN   2 – 5 pm, Thursday – Saturday, 1 April to 31 October
ADMISSION   Adults £1
FACILITIES   Parking; dogs permitted; loos; access for the disabled; nursery for unusual plants; teas on Sundays

The show garden is attached to an up-and-coming garden school. Clever and satisfying.

GWYNEDD

Bodysgallen Hall
Llandudno, Gwynedd LL30 1RS
☎ 01492 584466   FAX 01492 582519

OWNER   Historic House Hotels Ltd
LOCATION   On right of A470 to Llandudno
OPEN   Daily, all year
ADMISSION   Open only to hotel guests
FACILITIES   Parking; refreshments at hotel
FEATURES   Follies and garden buildings; fruit of special interest; herbs; lake; rock garden; old roses and climbers; woodland garden; knot garden; parterres; splendid new 64 foot obelisk (1993) of local stone

Good gardens and good grounds for a good hotel. Partly 1920s and partly modern, the gardens include a knot garden divided into eight segments, an extremely busy kitchen garden, a little sunken garden with a lily pond and a modern parterre with white floribundas in the old walled garden. Handy for Bodnant.

Cefn Bere
Cae Deintur, Dolgellau, Gwynedd LL40 2YS
☎ 01341 422768

OWNER   Mr and Mrs M. Thomas
LOCATION   At Cae Deintur up short steep hill, left at top, 4th house
OPEN   By appointment from spring to early autumn
ADMISSION   Contribution to NGS
FACILITIES   Parking; plants for sale
FEATURES   Glasshouses and conservatories to visit; plants for plantsmen; old roses and climbers; troughs

A plantsman's garden within a disciplined design: the owners say that it encapsulates their own development as gardeners over the last forty years. A great variety of rare plants within a small compass, especially alpines, dwarf conifers, ferns and evergreens. Wonderful views.

Penrhyn Castle
Bangor, Gwynedd LL57 4HN
☎ 01248 353084   FAX 01248 371281

OWNER   The National Trust
LOCATION   3 miles east of Bangor on A5122, signposted from A55 – A5 junction
OPEN   12 noon – 5 pm (11 am – 5 pm in July and August), daily except Tuesday, 1 April to 31 October (1994 times and dates)
ADMISSION   Adults £4.40; Children £2.20 (1994)

FACILITIES Parking; dogs permitted; facilities for the disabled; plants for sale; light lunches in licensed tea room
FEATURES Good collection of trees; fine conifers; fruit of special interest; lake; subtropical plants; woodland garden; Victorian walled garden; rhododendrons; trees planted by royals

A Norman castle (actually a Victorian fake) with a distant walled garden of parterres and terraces merging into the slopes of rhododendrons and camellias. There is much of dendrological interest: ancient conifers, holm oaks and naturalised *Arbutus* trees.

Plas Brondanw Gardens
Llanfrothen, Penrhyndeudraeth, Gwynedd LL48 6SW
☎ 01766 770484
OWNER Trustees of the Second Portmeirion Foundation
LOCATION On Croesor road off A4085
OPEN 9 am – 5 pm, daily, all year
ADMISSION Adults £1.50; Children 25p (1994)
FEATURES Follies and garden buildings; glasshouses and conservatories to visit; good topiary

Highly original and architectural Edwardian garden laid out by Clough Williams-Ellis 17 years before he began Portmeirion, and now assiduously restored by his granddaughter Menna. One of the best-kept secrets in North Wales, full of such original design ideas as the arbour of four red-twigged limes.

Plas Newydd
Llanfairpwll, Anglesey, Gwynedd LL61 6EQ
☎ 01248 714795
OWNER The National Trust
LOCATION 2 miles south west of Llanfairpwll on A4080
OPEN 11 am – 5 pm, Sunday – Friday, 31 March to 29 September; Fridays and Sundays, 1 to 29 October
ADMISSION Adults £3.80; Children £1.90; Groups £3; Family £9.50
FACILITIES Parking; loos; access for the disabled; National Trust shop; tea room
FEATURES Landscape designed by Capability Brown; fine conifers; follies and garden buildings; lake; landscape designed by Humphry Repton; modern roses; woodland garden; azaleas; magnolias; rhododendrons; maples; new plantings in Italianate garden (1994)

A grand collection of rhododendrons (plus azaleas, magnolias and acers) within a Repton landscape on a spectacular site above the Menai Straits. The fine Italianate garden below the house is 1930s, most surprising.

Plas Penhelig Country House Hotel
Aberdovey, Gwynedd LL35 0NA
☎ 01654 767676   FAX 01654 767783
OWNER Mr and Mrs A. C. Richardson
LOCATION On the hillside above Aberdovey Bay
OPEN Dawn – dusk, daily, 15 March to 31 October
ADMISSION Adults £1; Children 50p
FACILITIES Parking; dogs permitted; loos; Country House Hotel; light meals to full restaurant fare
FEATURES Herbaceous borders; fruit of special interest; glasshouses and conservatories to visit; rock garden; old roses and climbers; subtropical plants; woodland garden; rhododendrons; azaleas; bluebells

14 acres of woodland garden around a hotel on the west coast of Wales. The Richardsons have been reclaiming and replanting it after years of neglect: the results are admirable.

Plas-yn-Rhiw
Rhiw, Pwllheli, Gwynedd LL53 8AB
☎ 01758 780219
OWNER The National Trust
LOCATION 12 miles from Pwllheli on south coast road to Aberdarow
OPEN 12 noon – 5 pm, daily except Saturday, 1 April to 30 September
ADMISSION Adults £2.30; Children £1.15; Family £6
FACILITIES Parking; loos
FEATURES Herbaceous borders; formal gardens

Pretty garden, small and formal, with box-edged parterres filled with billowing cottage garden flowers. A few rhododendrons and camellias beyond.

Portmeirion
Gwynedd LL48 6ET
☎ 01766 770228   FAX 01766 771331
OWNER Portmeirion Ltd
LOCATION Between Penrhyndeudraeth and Portmadog
OPEN 9.30 am – 5.30 pm, daily, all year
ADMISSION Adults £3; Children £1.30
FACILITIES Parking; loos; several shops; refreshments and hotel
FEATURES Rhododendrons and azaleas; subtropical plants; woodland garden

Portmeirion is where the architect Clough Williams-Ellis worked out his Italianate fantasies. The gardens are formal, with a mixture of Mediterranean plants and more exotic palms, but full of architectural bric-à-brac of every period. Fun.

POWYS

The Dingle (Welshpool)
Welshpool, Powys
☎ 01938 555145   FAX 01938 554734
OWNER Mr and Mrs Roy Joseph
LOCATION Left turn to Nurseries off A490 to Llantyllin
OPEN 9 am – 5 pm, daily except Tuesdays, all year
ADMISSION £1
FACILITIES Parking; loos; access for the disabled; good nursery attached

FEATURES   Herbaceous borders; fine conifers; lake; rhododendrons and azaleas; rock garden; colour borders; woodland garden expanded (1994–5)

Steep and stony garden attached to a nursery, but essentially a private garden still. Mainly trees and shrubs, mulched with bark, but some herbaceous plants too, and a stream with bridges leading to a pool.

Dolwen
Cefn Coch, Llanrhaedr-ym-Mochnant, Powys
SY10 0BLL
☎ 01691 780411

OWNER   Mrs Frances Denby
LOCATION   Right at Three Tuns Inn, 1 mile up lane
OPEN   2 – 4.30 pm, Fridays, 1 May to 15 September. Plus last Sunday in month from May to August
ADMISSION   £1
FACILITIES   Parking; loos; plants for sale; tea room
FEATURES   Herbaceous borders; gravel or scree garden; lake; plants for plantsmen; old roses and climbers; garden sculpture; woodland garden; garden school

A plantsman's garden on a steep 4-acre site, energetically made by Mrs Denby over the last 20 years. Beautiful plantings around three large ponds, fed by natural springs and connected by waterfalls. One of the best young gardens in Wales, of ever-growing interest.

Powis Castle
Welshpool, Powys SY21 8RF
☎ 01938 554338   FAX 01938 554336

OWNER   The National Trust
LOCATION   1 mile south of Welshpool off the A483
OPEN   Wednesday – Sunday, 1 April to 31 October, plus Tuesdays in July and August
ADMISSION   Adults £3.80; Children (under 17) £1.90; Family £9.50 (1994)
FACILITIES   Parking; loos; facilities for the disabled; plant shop and gift shop; restaurant for light lunches and teas
FEATURES   Herbaceous borders; glasshouses and conservatories to visit; old roses and climbers; good topiary; woodland garden; plantings by Graham Thomas; particularly good in July-August; tender climbers; colour plantings; largest (i.e. thickest trunk) sessile oak *Quercus petraea* in the British Isles

Famous hanging terraces swamped by bulky overgrown yews and wonderfully rich colour planting by Graham Thomas. Smashing in later summer.

Sir Roger Vaughan's Garden
Tretower Court & Castle, Tretower, Crickhowell, Powys NP5 1RF
☎ 0174 730279

OWNER   CADW: Welsh Historic Monuments
LOCATION   3 miles from Crickhowell on A470
OPEN   9.30 am – 6 pm (3.30 pm in winter), daily, all year
ADMISSION   Adults £2; Concessions £1.50

FACILITIES   Parking; loos; facilities for the disabled; shop in summer months
FEATURES   Herbaceous borders; herbs; old roses and climbers

A garden in 15th-century style, designed and planted in 1991 with a careful eye to authenticity. Features include a flowery lawn, turf seats, beds of herbs, two arbours and an orchard. Highly instructive.

SCOTLAND

BORDERS

Dawyck Botanic Garden
Stobo, Borders EH45 9JV
☎ 01721 760254   FAX 01721 760214

OWNER   Royal Botanic Garden, Edinburgh
LOCATION   8 miles south west of Peebles on B71
OPEN   10 am – 6 pm, daily, 15 March to 22 October
ADMISSION   Adults £2; Senior Citizens £1.50p; Children 50p; Family £4.50
FACILITIES   Parking; loos; facilities for the disabled; plants for sale; gift shop; light refreshments
FEATURES   Good collection of trees; herbaceous borders; fine conifers; glasshouses and conservatories to visit; lake; woodland garden; particularly interesting in winter; *Meconopsis*; Chinese conifers; Dawyck beech; Douglas fir from original seed; tallest *Fagus crenata* in the British Isles, and 8 further record trees

A woodland garden, run as an annexe of the Royal Botanic Garden in Edinburgh and long famous for its trees. The Dawyck beech is the upright, fastigiate form, first found in the policies in the mid 19th century. Edinburgh have underplanted with interesting shrubs, and some herbaceous plants. Dawyck is a getting-better garden.

Manderston
Duns, Borders TD11 3PP
☎ 01361 883450   FAX 01361 882010

OWNER   Lord Palmer
LOCATION   On A6105 east of Duns
OPEN   2 – 5.30 pm, Sundays and Thursdays, 11 May to 28 September, plus 29 May and 28 August. Parties welcome by appointment
ADMISSION   Not available at time of going to press
FACILITIES   Parking; dogs permitted; loos; facilities for the disabled; plants for sale; cream teas and ice cream
FEATURES   Herbaceous borders; fine conifers; lake; rhododendrons and azaleas; good topiary; woodland garden; good bedding out

The house is sort-of-Georgian. Below it are four expansive terraces, with rich planting around clipped yews and hollies. Unfortunately it is possible to visit only a small part of this formal garden. Below are a small lake, a Chinese-style bridge (18th-century) and a woodland garden with modern rhododendrons and azaleas. All is planted and maintained in the grand manner.

Mellerstain
Gordon, Borders TD3 6LG
☎ 01573 410225   FAX 01573 410388

OWNER   Mellerstain Trust
LOCATION   1 mile west of A6089 Kelso – Edinburgh road
OPEN   12.30 – 5 pm, 14 – 17 April; Wednesdays, Friday and Sundays in May, June and September; daily except Saturdays in July and August
ADMISSION   £1.50
FACILITIES   Parking; dogs permitted; loos; access for the disabled; tweed and gift shop; tea room
FEATURES   Lake; modern roses; good topiary; Italian terraced garden by Sir Reginald Blomfield (1909)

The house has extensive views south to the Cheviots. Below it lies Blomfield's formal garden planted with floribunda roses and lavender. Beneath runs the landscape laid out by William and Robert Adam, sauntering down to a lake. Uncompromisingly grand.

Mertoun Gardens
St Boswells, Melrose, Borders TD6 0EA
☎ 01835 823236   FAX 01835 822474

OWNER   Mertoun Gardens Trust
LOCATION   In village of Mertoun
OPEN   2 – 6 pm, Saturdays, Sundays and Bank Holiday Mondays, 1 April to 1 October
ADMISSION   Adults £1; Children 50p
FACILITIES   Parking; loos; access for the disabled
FEATURES   Herbaceous borders; daffodils; glasshouses and conservatories to visit; herbs; pond; vegetables of interest

Originally part of the Duke of Sutherland's estates, Mertoun is best known for its traditional kitchen garden. But the trustees have plans for new developments.

Priorwood Garden
Melrose, Borders TD6 9PX
☎ 01896 822493

OWNER   The National Trust for Scotland
LOCATION   Next to Melrose Abbey
OPEN   10 am (1.30 pm on Sundays) – 5.30 pm, daily, 1 April to 24 December
ADMISSION   Adults £1
FACILITIES   Parking; dogs permitted; plants for sale; dried-flower shop and NTS gift shop
FEATURES   Herbaceous borders; fruit of special interest; herbs; woodland garden

Best known for its shop, everything at Priorwood is geared towards dried flowers. Inspirational.

Traquair House
Innerleithen, Borders EH44 6PW
☎ 01896 830323   FAX 01896 830639

OWNER   Mrs Maxwell Stuart
LOCATION   Signposted from Innerleithen
OPEN   12.30 pm (10.30 am in July and August) – 5.30 pm, daily, 15 April to 30 September. Plus Fridays, Saturdays and Sundays in October
ADMISSION   House and grounds: Adults £3.75; Concessions £3.20; Children £1.75. Grounds only: Adults £1.50; Children £1
FACILITIES   Parking; dogs permitted; loos; access for the disabled; plants for sale; gift shop; restaurant serving lunch and tea
FEATURES   Herbaceous borders; modern roses; woodland garden

The main attraction is a large maze, planted in 1980, of beech and Leyland cypress. The house is a Catholic time warp: the Bear Gates in the park, once the main entrance to the estate, have been closed ever since Bonnie Prince Charlie passed through them for the last time in 1746.

DUMFRIES & GALLOWAY

Arbigland
Kirkbean, Dumfries & Galloway DG2 8BG
☎ 01387 880283

OWNER   Arbigland Estate Trust
LOCATION   South of Kirkbean on A710 Solway coast road
OPEN   2 – 6 pm, Tuesday – Sunday, and Bank Holiday Mondays, 1 May to 30 September
ADMISSION   Adults £2; Senior Citizens £1.50; Children 50p
FACILITIES   Parking; loos; home-made teas
FEATURES   Lake; old roses and climbers; woodland garden; interesting for children; rhododendrons; maples

A woodland garden, with many different features. Best is the area called Japan, where ancient Japanese maples surround a water garden. But there are also a hidden rose garden, splendid large-leaved rhododendrons, and paths down to the sandy shore.

Castle Kennedy
Rephad, Stranraer, Dumfries & Galloway DG9 8BX
☎ 01776 702024   FAX 01776 706248

OWNER   Lochinch Heritage Estate
LOCATION   5 miles east of Stranraer on A75
OPEN   10 am – 5 pm, daily, Easter to 30 September
ADMISSION   Adults £2; Senior Citizens £1.50; Children £1
FACILITIES   Parking; dogs permitted; loos; access for the disabled; plant centre; tea rooms
FEATURES   Herbaceous borders; fine conifers; lake; woodland garden; rhododendrons; *Embothrium*; *Eucryphia*; monkey-puzzle avenue; tallest *Pittosporum tenuifolium* (16 metres) in the British Isles

A huge garden, with early 18th-century rides, avenues and *allées*, a complete 19th-century pinetum, rhododendrons from Hooker's Himalayan expedition, a vast collection of trees and shrubs, and handsome herbaceous plantings in the walled garden. Important and impressive.

Galloway House Gardens
Garlieston, Newton Stewart, Dumfries & Galloway
DG8 8HF
☎ 01988 600680

OWNER   Galloway House Gardens Trust
LOCATION   Off B7004 at Garlieston
OPEN   9 am – 5 pm, daily, 1 March to 31 October
ADMISSION   Adults £1.50; Senior Citizens £1; Children 50p
FACILITIES   Parking; dogs permitted; loos
FEATURES   Camellias; daffodils; rhododendrons and azaleas; snowdrops

Galloway House is where Captain Neil McEacharn learnt to garden, before moving to Lake Maggiore to create the great gardens of Villa Taranto. A vast *Davidia involucrata* dates from his ownership.

Glenwhan Garden
Dunragit, by Stranraer, Dumfries & Galloway
DG9 8PH
☎ 01581 400222

OWNER   Mr and Mrs William Knott
LOCATION   1 mile off A75 at Dunragit village
OPEN   10 am – 5 pm, daily, 1 April to 30 September
ADMISSION   Adults £1.80; Senior Citizens £1.50; Children (over 12) £1
FACILITIES   Parking; dogs permitted; loos; facilities for the disabled; plants for sale; shop; garden restaurant
FEATURES   Lake; plants for plantsmen; old roses and climbers; woodland garden; bluebells; trees and shrubs; new woodland walk and bog garden (1994)

A new garden on a large scale (12 acres), started by the owners in 1979 and worked by them and one gardener. Very much a plantsman's garden, but it uses plants to create effects, and capitalises upon the lie of the land to produce different habitats. The achievement to date is commendable: definitely a garden to watch.

Logan Botanic Gardens
Port Logan, Stranraer, Dumfries & Galloway
DG9 9ND
☎ 01776 860231   FAX 01776 860333

OWNER   Royal Botanic Garden, Edinburgh
LOCATION   14 miles south of Stranraer on B7065
OPEN   10 am – 6 pm, daily, 15 March to 31 October; 28 May for SGS
ADMISSION   Adults £2; Concessions £1.50; Children 50p
FACILITIES   Parking; loos; facilities for the disabled; plants for sale; shop selling books, gifts and local crafts; light meals and refreshments
FEATURES   Good collection of trees; herbaceous borders; fine conifers; fruit of special interest; lake; plants for plantsmen; subtropical plants; woodland garden; particularly good in July-August; tree ferns; *Cardiocrinum*; *Gunnera*; cordylines; *Trachycarpus* palms
FRIENDS   Part of the Friends of the Royal Botanic Garden, Edinburgh

The extraordinary effects of Logan are created by palms, cordylines and tree ferns within the semi-formal setting of a walled garden. Huge gunneras and *Cardiocrinum* pile on the message, but the richness extends also to diversity, for here is one of the great botanic collections of tender exotica, worth a long journey on a sunny day in summer.

Threave School of Horticulture
Castle Douglas, Dumfries & Galloway DG7 1RX
☎ 01556 502575   FAX 01556 502575

OWNER   The National Trust for Scotland
LOCATION   1 mile west of Castle Douglas
OPEN   9.30 am – sunset. Visitor centre closes at 5.30 pm
ADMISSION   Adults £3.50; Senior Citizens and Children £1.80. Group rates £2.80 and £1.40
FACILITIES   Parking; loos; facilities for the disabled; plants for sale; shop; restaurant and snacks
FEATURES   Good collection of trees; herbaceous borders; fine conifers; fruit of special interest; glasshouses and conservatories to visit; lake; plants for plantsmen; rock garden; modern roses; old roses and climbers; woodland garden; peat garden; heath garden
NCCPG NATIONAL COLLECTIONS   *Penstemon*

A teaching garden with a very wide range of attractions – something to interest every gardener, in fact. Developed over the last 30 years with the needs of students at the School of Horticulture, garden-owners and tourists all in mind, Threave has quickly acquired the reputation of a Scottish Wisley. You can spend all day here.

FIFE

Balcaskie
Pittenweem, Fife KY10 2RD

OWNER   Major Sir Ralph Anstruther of that Ilk
LOCATION   Off B9171 to Pittenweem
OPEN   2 – 6 pm, Saturday – Wednesday, 1 June to 31 August (1994 times and dates)
ADMISSION   £1.50 (1994)
FACILITIES   Parking; loos; informal tea and biscuits
FEATURES   Long avenues; parterres; old trees; tender plants

The garden was grandly laid out in the 17th century with parterres below the house and a long straight drive to the sea. Nesfield made terraces where tender climbers shelter in the bays of the retaining walls.

Cambo Gardens
Kingsbarns, St Andrews, Fife KY16 8QD
☎ 01333 450313   FAX 01333 450987

OWNER   Mr and Mrs T. P. N. Erskine
LOCATION   On A917 between Kingsbarns and Crail

OPEN 10 am – 4 pm, daily, all year
ADMISSION Adults £2; Children free
FACILITIES Parking; dogs permitted; loos; access for the disabled; plants for sale
FEATURES Daffodils; old roses and climbers; snowdrops; snowflakes; colchicum meadows; autumn colour

A Victorian walled garden built around the Cambo Burn with a waterfall and elegant oriental bridge. Spectacular when the snowdrops and snowflakes flower.

Falkland Palace
Falkland, Fife KY7 7BU
☎ 01337 857397

OWNER The National Trust for Scotland
LOCATION On A912, 11 miles north of Kirkaldy
OPEN 11 am – 5.30 pm, Monday – Saturday, 1.30 – 5.30 pm, Sundays, 1 April to 24 October
ADMISSION Adults £2; Children £1
FACILITIES Parking; loos; facilities for the disabled; gift shop
FEATURES Herbaceous borders; fruit of special interest; glasshouses and conservatories to visit; modern roses; autumn colour; spectacular delphinium border

Percy Cane's reconstruction of a Scottish renaissance garden, with a herb garden, an astrolabe walk and formal parterres prettily planted in pastel colours.

Hill of Tarvit
Cupar, Fife KY15 5PB
☎ 01334 653127

OWNER The National Trust for Scotland
LOCATION Off A916, 2½ miles south of Cupar
OPEN 9.30 am – sunset, daily, all year round
ADMISSION £1
FACILITIES Parking; loos; facilities for the disabled; shop in house (open in summer)
FEATURES Herbaceous borders; plants for plantsmen; old roses and climbers; woodland garden; heathers

Essentially a plantsman's garden, opulently planted and maintained in keeping with the Lorimer house. The Edwardian plantings, now splendidly mature, have been complemented by modern additions. Highly satisfying.

Kellie Castle
Pittenween, Fife KY10 2RF
☎ 013338 337

OWNER The National Trust for Scotland
LOCATION Signposted from main roads
OPEN 10 am – dusk, daily, all year
ADMISSION Adults £1; Concessions 50p
FACILITIES Parking; loos; access for the disabled; gift shop; tea room
FEATURES Herbaceous borders; fruit of special interest; old roses and climbers; particularly good in July-August; strong design; extended collection of historic vegetables

Robert Lorimer's family house: it was he who remade the garden in its present form, though much of the planting is modern. Only 1 acre, but strong lines and thick planting create a sense of both space and enclosure. Kellie has much to teach modern gardeners.

The Murrel Gardens
The Murrel, Aberdour, Fife KY3 0RN FAX
01383 860157

OWNER J. E. Milne
LOCATION On south side of B9157
OPEN 10 am – 5 pm, Wednesdays, 1 April to 30 September, or by written appointment
ADMISSION £1
FACILITIES Parking; loos; tea, coffee and biscuits
FEATURES Herbaceous borders; lake; plants for plantsmen; modern roses; old roses and climbers

The house is Arts & Crafts, and the garden was laid out in 1910, but thickly replanted by the present owner in 1980. Its protected position allows many tender plants to grow in this normally cool and difficult part of Scotland.

St Andrews Botanic Garden
The Canongate, St Andrews, Fife KY16 8RT
☎ 01334 476452

OWNER North East Fife District Council
LOCATION A915, Largo road, then entrance in The Canongate
OPEN 10 am – 7 pm (4 pm in April and October), daily except Saturdays from 1 October to 31 March, all year
ADMISSION Adults £1; Senior Citizens and Children 50p
FACILITIES Parking; loos; plants for sale
FEATURES Good collection of trees; herbaceous borders; fine conifers; glasshouses and conservatories to visit; gravel or scree garden; lake; rhododendrons and azaleas; rock garden; subtropical plants; woodland garden; interesting for children; particularly interesting in winter; peat beds; orchids; ferns; heath garden; order beds; cacti house re-landscaped (1994)
FRIENDS Friends have lectures, workshops, garden visits, a newsletter and seed scheme: details from Honorary Curator, St Andrews Botanic Garden

Financial constraints obliged the University to abandon control of its botanic garden in 1987, and lease it to the Council. It will be interesting to see what effect this change has upon its educational facilities. So far, so good: the garden's main asset, the peat, rock and water complex (crag, scree, moraine, alpine meadow and bog) is looking pretty good.

GRAMPIAN

Brodie Castle
Brodie, Forres, Moray, Grampian IV36 0TE
☎ 01309 641 371   FAX 01309 641 600
OWNER The National Trust for Scotland

LOCATION Signposted from A96
OPEN 11 am – 5.30 pm (opens 1.30 pm on Sundays), daily, but Saturdays and Sundays only in October; 1 April to 22 October
ADMISSION Adults £3.50; Concessions £1.80
FACILITIES Parking; dogs permitted; loos; facilities for the disabled; NTS shop; small tea room in castle
FEATURES Daffodils; pond; rhododendrons and azaleas; woodland garden

Famous for its daffodils, many bred here at the turn of the century: a glorious sight when they bloom in the lawns around the baronial castle.

Crathes Castle
Near Banchory, Grampian AB31 3QJ
☎ 01330 844 525   FAX 01330 844 797

OWNER The National Trust for Scotland
LOCATION 15 miles west of Aberdeen
OPEN 9.30 am to sunset; daily, all year
ADMISSION Adults £4; Senior Citizens and Children £2
FACILITIES Parking; dogs permitted; loos; facilities for the disabled; plants for sale; NTS shop; restaurant/cafeteria open April to October
FEATURES Herbaceous borders; fine conifers; glasshouses and conservatories to visit; plants for plantsmen; modern roses; old roses and climbers; woodland garden; specimen trees; colour borders; current holder of Sandford Award; tallest *Zelkova* × *verschaffeltii* in the British Isles

Viburnum, *Dianthus* (Malmaison)

Famous for its walled garden, with dreamy high summer borders – pastel shades for long Highland evenings. Only 4 acres but intensively planted.

Cruickshank Botanic Garden
University of Aberdeen, Dept of Plant and Soil Science, St Machar Drive, Aberdeen, Grampian AB9 2UD
☎ 01224 272704

OWNER Aberdeen University
LOCATION Follow signs for Aberdeen University and Old Aberdeen
OPEN 9 am – 4.30 pm, Monday – Friday, all year. Plus 2 – 5 pm, Saturdays and Sundays, 1 May to 30 September
ADMISSION Free
FACILITIES Dogs permitted; access for the disabled
FEATURES Good collection of trees; herbaceous borders; fine conifers; lake; rock garden; old roses and climbers; woodland garden; stone troughs; peat beds
FRIENDS Active and well-established Friends group, with plant sales, lectures, excursions and a seed list. Contact 01224 272704

12 acres of classic botanic garden, with every educational element: rock gardens, an arboretum, collections of native plants, beds which illustrate the history of the rose, water plants and systematic beds. Well worth exploration.

Damside Garden Herbs
by Johnshaven, Montrose, Grampian DD10 0HY
☎ 01561 361496

OWNER Ian and Sheena Cruickshank
LOCATION Signposted off A92 at Johnshaven
OPEN 10 am – 5 pm (4.30 pm in winter), daily, Good Friday to 24 December
ADMISSION Adults £1; Senior Citizens and Children 80p
FACILITIES Parking; loos; access for the disabled; plants for sale; excellent herb shop; non-smoking restaurant and light refreshments
FEATURES Herbs; lake; promising young arboretum

A garden *cum* nursery which sets out to educate, interest and please its visitors. A series of gardens illustrates the history, variety and uses of herbs in such designs as the Celtic Knot garden, the Roman garden and the Monastic garden.

Kildrummy Castle
Kildrummy, Alford, Grampian AB33 8RA
☎ 019755 71203/71277

OWNER Kildrummy Castle Garden Trust
LOCATION On A97, off A944
OPEN 10 am – 5 pm, daily, 1 April to 31 October
ADMISSION Adults £1.70; Children (over 5) 50p
FACILITIES Parking; dogs permitted; loos; access for the disabled; plants for sale; tea and coffee
FEATURES Good collection of trees; lake; plants for plantsmen; old roses and climbers; woodland garden; interesting for children; autumn colour; heathers; play area and nature trails

A romantic glen-garden, laid out nearly 100 years ago. Richly planted pools and ponds, a plantsman's collection on the hillside, and a large mature rock garden made from the natural sandstone. One of the most romantic gardens in Scotland.

Leith Hall
Kennethmont, by Huntly, Aberdeen, Grampian AB54 4QQ
☎ 014643 269

OWNER The National Trust for Scotland
LOCATION On B9002 west of Kennethmont
OPEN 9.30 am to sunset, daily, all year
ADMISSION Free
FACILITIES Parking; loos; facilities for the disabled; refreshments from May to September, 2 – 6 pm
FEATURES Herbaceous borders; rock garden; modern roses; particularly good in July-August; bluebells; recent restorations and improvements

Richly planted borders are the pride of Leith Hall: they are full of colour all through the summer. Also impressive is the rock garden, restored and replanted by that most successful of societies, the Scottish Rock Garden Club. Leith gets better and better.

Old Semeil Herb Garden
Strathdon, Grampian AB36 8XJ
☎ 019756 51343

OWNER Mrs Gillian Cook
LOCATION At Strathdon
OPEN 10 am – 5 pm, daily (but not Thursdays in September, and weekends only in April), 1 April to 30 September
ADMISSION Free
FACILITIES Parking; loos; facilities for the disabled; specialist herb nursery attached; light lunches and teas
FEATURES Herbs

A remarkable garden *cum* nursery, 1,000 feet up in the Highlands, where over 200 varieties of herbs are grown using organic methods.

Pitmedden
Ellon, Grampian AB4 0PD
☎ 01651 842352

OWNER The National Trust for Scotland
LOCATION 1 mile west of Pitmedden on A920
OPEN 10 am – 5.30 pm (last admission 5 pm), daily, 1 May to 30 September
ADMISSION Adults £3; Concessions £1.50
FACILITIES Parking; loos; facilities for the disabled; tea room
FEATURES Herbs; good topiary; gazebos; parterres

A 17th-century formal garden meticulously created by the National Trust for Scotland 40 years ago. It has 3 miles of box hedging and uses 40,000 bedding plants every summer. The result is impressive, satisfying and peaceful, but lacks authenticity.

HIGHLAND

Allangrange
Munlochy, Black Isle, Highland IV8 8NZ
☎ 0146 3811249   FAX 0146 3811407

OWNER Major Allan Cameron
LOCATION Off A9, 5 miles north of Inverness
OPEN 2 – 5.30 pm, 7 May, 11 June and 9 July; or by appointment
ADMISSION £1.50
FACILITIES Parking; dogs permitted; loos; facilities for the disabled; plants for sale; teas in house at £1 per head
FEATURES Lake; old roses and climbers; woodland garden; primulas; rhododendrons; colour borders

Colour gardening by the owner's wife, a botanical artist, has made this one of the loveliest summer gardens in the British Isles. Good spring flowers, too.

Cawdor Castle
Cawdor Castle, Nairn, Highland IV12 5RD
☎ 01667 404615   FAX 01667 404674

OWNER Countess Cawdor
LOCATION Between Inverness and Nairn on B9090
OPEN 10 am – 5.30 pm, daily, 1 May to 1 October
ADMISSION Adults £2.50

FACILITIES Parking; loos; facilities for the disabled; gift shop; licensed restaurant in castle
FEATURES Herbaceous borders; fruit of special interest; old roses and climbers; woodland garden; new maze and paradise garden (1994); newly-restored 17th-century walled garden (1994)

A Victorian garden which has been replanted and, in part, redesigned in recent years by the addition of the holly maze and colour plantings. Elsewhere the combination of old shapes and new plants makes for a garden of exceptional accessibility. Not grand, just charming, while the house is as Scottish a castle as ever was seen.

Dochfour Gardens
Inverness, Highland IV3 6JY
☎ 01463 861218   FAX 01463 861336

OWNER Lord and Lady Burton
LOCATION 5 miles south west of Inverness on the A82
OPEN 10 am – 5 pm, Monday – Friday; 2 – 5 pm, Saturdays and Sundays, 1 April to 31 October
ADMISSION £1.50. Reductions for Senior Citizens and Children
FACILITIES Parking; access for the disabled; plants for sale; no shop, but pick your own fruit in season
FEATURES Rhododendrons and azaleas; good topiary; naturalised daffodils; parterres; water gardens; tallest *Thuja occidentalis* 'Lutea' in the British Isles, plus three further tree records

A substantial garden, landscaped and terraced down to the River Ness. Best when the daffodils and rhododendrons colour the hillside.

Dunrobin Castle Gardens
Golspie, Sutherland, Highland KW10 6RR
☎ 01408 633177/633268 FAX 01408 633800

OWNER The Sutherland Trust
LOCATION 50 miles north of Inverness on A9
OPEN Dawn – dusk, daily, all year round. Castle: 10.30 am – 5.30 pm (4.30 pm at Easter and during May and October), Monday – Saturday, 1 – 5.30 pm, Sunday, Easter and 1 May to 15 October
ADMISSION Castle and garden: Adults £3.70; Children £1.90. Reductions for groups. Gardens free when castle closed
FACILITIES Parking; loos; tea room in castle
FEATURES Herbaceous borders; lake; modern roses; good topiary; woodland garden; formal gardens

Grand terrace gardens, designed by Nesfield, striding down to the Dornoch Forth. Recently replanted and partially restored. New features have been added, like rhododendrons: there will be further improvements.

Inverewe
Poolewe, Ross and Cromarty, Highland IV22 2LQ
☎ 0144 586 441   FAX 0144 586 497

OWNER The National Trust for Scotland
LOCATION On A832, 6 miles north of Gairloch

Gardens LOTHIAN

OPEN 9.30 am – dusk, daily, all year. Visitors' centre open from 1 April to 22 October
ADMISSION Adults £3.50; Senior Citizens and Children £1.80; Groups £2.80
FACILITIES Parking; loos; facilities for the disabled; plants for sale; large shop; new restaurant opens on 1 April
FEATURES Good collection of trees; herbaceous borders; fine conifers; fruit of special interest; lake; plants for plantsmen; rock garden; subtropical plants; woodland garden; particularly good in July-August; autumn colour; *Meconopsis*; candelabra primulas; tallest *Eucalyptus cordata* and *E. gunnii* in the British Isles
NCCPG NATIONAL COLLECTIONS *Clearia, Olearia, Brachyglottis, Ourisia, Rhododendron*

One of the wonders of the horticultural world, a subtropical garden in the north west Highlands. Fabulous large-leaved Himalayan rhododendrons, magnolias, eucalyptus, tree ferns, palms and tender rarities underplanted with drifts of blue poppies and candelabra primulas. Best on a sunny dry day in May, before the midges breed.

Lochalsh Woodland Garden
Balmacara, By Kyle of Lochalsh, Ross, Highland IV40 8DN
☎ 0159 986 231

OWNER The National Trust for Scotland
LOCATION On A87 near Kyle
OPEN 9 am – dusk, daily, all year
ADMISSION Adults £1; Children 50p
FACILITIES Parking; dogs permitted; loos; facilities for the disabled
FEATURES Fine conifers; plants for plantsmen; subtropical plants; woodland garden; ferns; primulas; rhododendrons
NCCPG NATIONAL COLLECTIONS *Arundinaria*

A woodland garden and still developing. The structure is about 100 years old – tall trees, both native and exotic, planted as shelter. Ornamental plantings started about 30 years ago, with rhododendrons from Euan Cox at Glendoick. These are now filled out with other shrubs, especially tender species from Tasmania and New Zealand, and herbaceous underplantings.

LOTHIAN

Dalmeny House
Rosebery Estates, South Queensferry, Lothian EH30 9TQ
☎ 0131 331 1888

OWNER The Earl of Rosebery
LOCATION B924 off A90
OPEN 12 noon – 5.30 pm, Mondays and Tuesdays, 1 – 5.30 pm, Sundays, 1 May to 26 September (1994 times and dates)
ADMISSION Grounds only: free
FACILITIES Parking; access for the disabled; refreshments
FEATURES Fine conifers; lake; woodland garden; rhododendrons and azaleas; wellingtonias

The grounds at Dalmeny are extensive, and visitors are encouraged to see the valley walk with rhododendrons, wellingtonias and other conifers.

Inveresk Lodge Garden
24 Inveresk Village, Musselburgh, Lothian EH21 7TE
OWNER The National Trust for Scotland
LOCATION A6124 south of Musselburgh, 6 miles east of Edinburgh
OPEN 10 am – 4.30 pm, Monday – Friday, 2 – 5 pm, Sundays, all year
ADMISSION Donation
FACILITIES Loos
FEATURES Herbaceous borders; old roses and climbers; plantings by Graham Thomas; raised beds; peat beds

A modern garden, tailor-made for a modest NTS estate and maintained to a high standard. Graham Thomas designed the rose borders. Good climbing plants.

Malleny House Garden
Balerno, Lothian EH14 7AF
☎ 0131 449 2283

OWNER The National Trust for Scotland
LOCATION In Balerno, south west of Edinburgh
OPEN 10 am – dusk, daily, all year. For SGS: 2 – 5 pm, 28 June
ADMISSION Adults £1; Senior Citizens and Children 50p
FACILITIES Parking; loos; access for the disabled
FEATURES Herbaceous borders; fruit and vegetables of special interest; glasshouses and conservatories to visit; herbs; modern roses; old roses and climbers; good topiary; particularly good in July-August; Scottish National Bonsai Collection
FRIENDS The Friends of Malleny enjoy garden visits, lectures and other benefits
NCCPG NATIONAL COLLECTIONS *Rosa*

One of the NTS's best gardens, much praised for its 'personal' quality. The 19th-century shrub roses are underplanted with herbaceous plants which take the display into the autumn. The bonsai collection creates quite another dimension, as do the magnificent conservatory and the huge cones of yew topiary. Very peaceful.

Royal Botanic Garden, Edinburgh
Inverleith Row, Edinburgh, Lothian EH3 5LR
☎ 0131 552 7171   FAX 0131 552 0382

OWNER Board of Trustees & Scottish Office
LOCATION 1 mile north of Princes Street
OPEN 10 am – 6 pm, 1 March to 30 April; 10 am – 8 pm, 1 May to 31 August; 10 am – 6 pm, 1 September to 31 October; 10 am – 4 pm, 1 November to 28 February

ADMISSION Free
FACILITIES Parking; loos; facilities for the disabled; plants for sale; shop; licensed terrace café
FEATURES Alpines; good collection of trees; herbaceous borders; fine conifers; ecological interest; glasshouses and conservatories to visit; gravel or scree garden; herbs; lake; oriental features; rhododendrons and azaleas; rock garden; modern roses; old roses and climbers; garden sculpture; subtropical plants; woodland garden; interesting for children; particularly interesting in winter; peat beds; tallest *Pinus coulteri* in the British Isles, and 12 further tree records
FRIENDS Active Friends of the RBG. Lectures, newsletter, seeds: details from the Friends' Office at the garden

Edinburgh outclasses Kew in several ways – better rock gardens, peat beds, rhododendrons and woodland gardens. And entry is free. Wonderful cantilevered glasshouses and good facilities for people with special needs – children, disabled persons and the blind. Edinburgh also has the highest standards of maintenance. No visitor can fail to respond, above all, to the friendly welcome and helpfulness of all the staff.

Suntrap Garden
43 Gogarbank, Edinburgh, Lothian EH12 9BY
☎ 0131 339 7283

OWNER Oatridge Agricultural College
LOCATION 1 mile west of Edinburgh bypass, between A8 and A71
OPEN 10 am – 4.30 pm, daily, all year, but weekdays only from October to March
ADMISSION Adults £1; Children free
FACILITIES Parking; dogs permitted; facilities for the disabled; plants for sale
FEATURES Alpines; herbaceous borders; daffodils; glasshouses to visit; oriental features; pond; modern roses; vegetables of interest; woodland garden; 'Italian' garden; peat walls
FRIENDS Friends of Suntrap. Annual subscription £3, includes events and visits

A 3-acre demonstration garden attached to Oatridge Agricultural College, one of the best places in Lothian to learn how to be a better gardener.

STRATHCLYDE

Achamore Gardens
Isle of Gigha, Strathclyde PA41 7AD
☎ 015835 267/254   FAX 015835 244

OWNER Holt Leisure Parks Ltd (Mr D. N. Holt)
LOCATION Take Gigha ferry from Tainloan (20 minutes) then easy walking for 1½ miles
OPEN Dawn – dusk, daily, all year
ADMISSION Adults £2; Children £1
FACILITIES Parking; loos; access for the disabled; lunches and teas at Gigha Hotel

FEATURES Good collection of trees; fine conifers; plants for plantsmen; old roses and climbers; subtropical plants; woodland garden; rhododendrons; azaleas; biggest *Larix gmelinii* in the British Isles

One of the best rhododendron gardens in the British Isles, and only 50 years old. Mainly planted by Sir James Horlick with advice from Jim Russell. The collection of large-leaved Himalayan rhododendrons is breathtaking.

Angus Garden
Barguillean, Taynuilt, Strathclyde PA35 1HY
☎ 018662 333   FAX 018662 652

OWNER Sam Macdonald
LOCATION Turn off A85 at Taynuilt
OPEN 9 am – dusk, daily, 1 March to 31 October
ADMISSION Adults £1
FACILITIES Parking; dogs permitted; Barguillean Nursery adjoins the garden
FEATURES Daffodils; rhododendrons and azaleas; woodland garden; primulas; heathers

This young woodland garden on the shores of Loch Angus has a particularly fine collection of modern rhododendrons. It doubles up as a test ground for new hybrids introduced from the USA by the adjacent Barguillean Nurseries. There are plans for a substantial expansion of the gardens to create more summer and autumn interest.

Ardanaiseig Hotel Garden
Ardanaiseig, Kilchrenan, by Taynuilt, Strathclyde PA35 1HE
☎ 018663 333   FAX 018663 222

OWNER Mrs Julia Smith
LOCATION On Loch Awe, 4 miles up from Kilchrenan
OPEN 9 am – 9 pm, or dusk if earlier, daily, 31 March to 30 October
ADMISSION Adults £1; Children free
FACILITIES Parking; dogs permitted; loos; hotel open to garden visitors
FEATURES Bluebells; herbaceous borders; daffodils; rhododendrons and azaleas; woodland garden; maples; magnolias

A fine woodland garden with an important collection of rhododendrons and azaleas, in a stunning position on a promontory. The hotel is famous for its good food.

Ardchattan Priory
Connel, Oban, Strathclyde PA37 1RQ
☎ 01631 75244

OWNER Lt.-Col. R. M. T. Campbell-Preston OBE
LOCATION 5 miles east of Connel Bridge, on the north shore of Loch Etive
OPEN 9 am – 9 pm (or dusk, if earlier), daily, 1 April to 31 October
ADMISSION Adults £1; Children free
FACILITIES Parking; dogs permitted; loos; access for the disabled; plants for sale; craft shop; tea room open daily, 11 am – 6 pm

FEATURES Herbaceous borders; daffodils; rhododendrons and azaleas; rock garden; old roses and climbers; good collection of *Sorbus* species

Good in spring, like all west coast gardens, but Ardchattan is planted mainly for high summer, with an emphasis on roses and herbaceous borders.

Ardtornish Garden
Lochaline, Morvern by Oban, Strathclyde PA34 5XA
☎ 01967 421288

OWNER Mrs John Raven
LOCATION 2 miles north of Lochaline
OPEN 10 am – 5 pm, daily, 1 April to 31 October (1994 times)
ADMISSION £1 (1994)
FACILITIES Parking; dogs permitted; loos; plants for sale
FEATURES Good collection of trees; fine conifers; fruit of special interest; lake; plants for plantsmen; woodland garden; kitchen garden; bluebells; *Gunnera*; rhododendrons

This is Faith Raven's other garden – see Docwra's Manor in Cambridgeshire – and a complete contrast: 28 acres of rocky hillside full of Edwardian hybrid rhododendrons like 'Pink Pearl' and 'Cynthia'. Mrs Raven has actively improved it with a great range of interesting plants. Remote, but worth every inch of the journey.

Arduaine Gardens
Arduaine, by Oban, Argyll, Strathclyde PA34 4XQ
☎ 01852 200366

OWNER The National Trust for Scotland
LOCATION On A816 between Oban and Lochgilphead
OPEN 9.30 am – sunset, daily, all year
ADMISSION Adults £2; Senior Citizens £1
FACILITIES Parking; loos; access for the disabled; no refreshments in the garden, but Loch Melfort Hotel is next door
FEATURES Herbaceous borders; fine conifers; lake; rock garden; subtropical plants; rhododendrons; tallest *Nothofagus antarctica* (26 metres) in the British Isles
NCCPG NATIONAL COLLECTIONS *Ampelopsis, Parthenocissus*

A wonderful rhododendron garden, with a flowing design and a profusion of flower in spring. It was replanted in the 1970s by two nurserymen and now has interest at all seasons. Arduaine is in excellent condition, too.

Bargany Gardens
Bargany, Girvan, Strathclyde KA26 9QL
☎ 01465 871249

OWNER John Dalrymple Hamilton
LOCATION 4 miles on left, B734 from Girvan to Dailly
OPEN 10 am – 7 pm, daily, 1 March to 31 October
ADMISSION Donation

FACILITIES Parking; dogs permitted; access for the disabled; plants for sale
FEATURES Daffodils; rhododendrons and azaleas; rock garden; snowdrops; woodland garden; lily pond

A charming woodland garden with banks of rhododendrons and azaleas around a lily pond. Little known, but undeservedly.

Biggar Park
Biggar, Strathclyde ML12 6JS
☎ 01899 21085

OWNER Captain and Mrs David Barnes
LOCATION South end of Biggar on A702
OPEN By appointment only
ADMISSION £1.50
FACILITIES Parking; dogs permitted; loos; plants for sale; home-made teas on open day
FEATURES Good collection of trees; herbaceous borders; lake; oriental features; plants for plantsmen; rock garden; old roses and climbers; woodland garden; daffodils; fritillaries; *Meconopsis*

10 acres of plantsmanship, with drifts of naturalised fritillaries in spring, and deep traditional herbaceous borders in summer when the garden has its open day.

Brodick Castle
Isle of Arran, Strathclyde KA27 8HY
☎ 01770 302202

OWNER The National Trust for Scotland
LOCATION Ferry from Ardrossan to Brodick, follow signs
OPEN 9.30 am – dusk, daily, all year
ADMISSION Adults £2
FACILITIES Parking; dogs permitted; loos; facilities for the disabled; plants for sale; NTS shop; tea rooms open Easter to October
FEATURES Good collection of trees; herbaceous borders; fine conifers; lake; old roses and climbers; subtropical plants; woodland garden; interesting for children; candelabra primulas; *Meconopsis*; tallest *Embothrium coccineum* (20 metres) and *Leptospermum scoparium* (10 metres) in the British Isles (and two further records); several new trails (1995)
NCCPG NATIONAL COLLECTIONS Rhododendron

Ravishing 60-acre rhododendron garden on sloping woodland in a mild wet climate. Good magnolias, camellias, crinodendrons and olearias too, but they are never a match for the rhododendrons, many from collectors' seed (Forrest, Kingdon Ward and others).

Crarae Gardens
Crarae, by Inverary, Strathclyde PA32 8YA
☎ 01546 86614

OWNER The Crarae Garden Charitable Trust
LOCATION South of Inveraray on A83
OPEN 9 am – 6 pm, daily, Easter to 31 October; daylight hours, daily, 1 November to Easter
ADMISSION Adults £2.50; Children £1.50

FACILITIES Parking; dogs permitted; loos; facilities for the disabled; plants for sale; shop selling books, china and local crafts; light refreshments
FEATURES Good collection of trees; lake; woodland garden; camellias; rhododendrons; eucalyptus; autumn colour; tallest *Eucalyptus coccifera* in the British Isles (and 10 further tree records)
FRIENDS Major appeal launched in October 1994
NCCPG NATIONAL COLLECTIONS *Nothofagus*

50 acres of exotic woodland, centred on a steep glen spanned by wooden bridges. The long but gentle climb up the glen is a pilgrim's progress for plantsmen, past all manner of exotic plants displayed for effect. At the top, you pass out of the enchanted garden into wild moorland: no other garden offers such catharsis.

Culzean Castle & Country Park
Maybole, Ayrshire, Strathclyde KA19 8LE
☎ 016556 269   FAX 016556 615

OWNER The National Trust for Scotland
LOCATION Off A719, west of Maybole and South of Ayr
OPEN 9.30 am – dusk, daily, all year
ADMISSION Garden only: Adults, £3; Children £1.50
FACILITIES Parking; dogs permitted; loos; facilities for the disabled; plants for sale; good shop; self-service restaurant; light refreshments in car park
FEATURES Herbaceous borders; follies and garden buildings; glasshouses to visit; herbs; lake; woodland garden; interesting for children; deer park; formal garden; adventure playground; tallest Irish yew *Taxus baccata* 'Fastigiata' (19 metres) in the British Isles (plus 2 further tree records); current holder of the Sandford Award

An important historic landscape, recently restored and seriously open to the public (400,000 visitors a year). Good trees as well as a gothic camellia house, gazebos and a pagoda.

Glasgow Botanic Garden
Great Western Road, Glasgow, Strathclyde G12 OUE
☎ 0141 334 2422

OWNER Glasgow City Council
LOCATION On A82, 2 miles from city centre
OPEN Grounds: 7 am – dusk, daily, all year. Glasshouses and Kibble Palace: 10 am – 4.45 pm (Main Range: 1 – 4.45 pm), daily, all year
ADMISSION Free
FACILITIES Dogs permitted; loos; facilities for the disabled
FEATURES Good collection of trees; herbaceous borders; fine conifers; glasshouses and conservatories to visit; herbs; lake; rock garden; modern roses; old roses and climbers; good topiary; particularly interesting in winter; beautiful glasshouse (the 'Kibble Palace'); systematic beds

FRIENDS Active Friends organisation with lectures, garden visits and a bimonthly newsletter. Details from the Gardens' office
NCCPG NATIONAL COLLECTIONS *Begonia*, *Dendrobium*, Dicksoniaceae

Most of the elements of the botanic garden are here, including systematic beds and chronological beds, but the glory of Glasgow is the two glasshouses – the Kibble Palace and the Main Range. From tree ferns to palms and from cacti to orchids, the Main Range is an essay in plant types. The Kibble Palace, however, is divided between geographical areas – South Africa, Australia, China, South America, the Canaries and so on. There is no better place to enjoy a winter's day in Glasgow.

Glenarn
Rhu, Helensburgh, Dumbartonshire G84 8LL
☎ 01436 820493

OWNER Mr and Mrs Michael Thornley
LOCATION Turn up Pier Road at Rhu Marina, first right is Glenarn Road
OPEN Dawn – dusk, daily, 21 March to 21 June; special open day on 30 April (2 – 5.30 pm) with plant stall and cream teas
ADMISSION Adults £1; Senior Citizens and Children 50p
FACILITIES Dogs permitted; access for the disabled; plants for sale; refreshments may be booked in advance
FEATURES Fine conifers; lake; plants for plantsmen; rock garden; woodland garden; rhododendrons; *Embothrium*

10 acres of woodland garden, with some rhododendrons dating from Sir Joseph Hooker's Himalayan expedition and others from the 1930s trips of Kingdon Ward and Ludlow & Sheriff. Good hybrids too – the original Gibson plants. But plenty of magnolias, camellias, *Pieris*, and other good plants besides.

Greenbank Garden
Flenders Road, Clarkston, Glasgow G76 8RB
☎ 0141 6393281

OWNER The National Trust for Scotland
LOCATION One mile along Mearns Road from Clarkston Toll, take 1st left
OPEN Garden: 9.30 am – sunset, daily, all year
ADMISSION Adults £2; Concessions £1
FACILITIES Parking; loos; facilities for the disabled; plants for sale; NTS gift shop; light refreshments and drinks
FEATURES Herbaceous borders; fruit of special interest; rock garden; modern roses; old roses and climbers; garden sculpture; woodland garden; garden for the disabled
FRIENDS Friends of Greenbank organise events throughout the year. Details from head gardener
NCCPG NATIONAL COLLECTIONS *Verbena*

Greenbank is a demonstration garden: it was left to the Trust in 1976 on condition that it was developed as a teaching resource for people with small gardens. The walled garden has therefore been divided into a great number of sections which represent different interests and skills: a rock garden, fruit garden, dried flower plot, raised beds, winter garden, and so on.

Torosay Castle & Gardens
Craignure, Isle of Mull, Strathclyde PA65 6AY
☎ 01680 812421   FAX 01680 812470
OWNER   Mr and Mrs C. James
LOCATION   1 mile from Craignure on A849 to Iona
OPEN   9 am – 7 pm (dawn – dusk in winter), daily
ADMISSION   House and gardens: Adults £3.50; Concessions £2.75; Children £1.50. Gardens: Adults £1.50; Others £1
FACILITIES   Parking; dogs permitted; loos; facilities for the disabled; shop planned for 1995; tea room with light lunches and home baking
FEATURES   Oriental features; rock garden; garden sculpture; water garden; *Eucalyptus* walk

The best feature of the gardens at Torosay is the Italian Statue Walk, lined with 19 figures by Antonio Bonazza. The Japanese garden and rock garden add to the sheer variety. The woodland garden is stuffed with interesting specimens: *Eucryphia*, *Embothrium* and *Crinodendron* among many.

The Younger Botanic Garden
Benmore, Dunoon, Strathclyde PA23 8QU
☎ 01369 6261   FAX 01369 6369
OWNER   Board of Trustees/Royal Botanic Garden, Edinburgh
LOCATION   7 miles north of Dunoon on A815
OPEN   10 am – 6 pm, daily, 15 March to 31 October
ADMISSION   Adults £2; Senior Citizens £1.50; Children 50p
FACILITIES   Parking; dogs permitted; loos; facilities for the disabled; plants for sale; gift shop; tea room
FEATURES   Good collection of trees; fine conifers; lake; plants for plantsmen; woodland garden; interesting for children; giant redwood avenue planted in 1863; rhododendrons; ferns

Benmore has been an annexe of the Royal Botanic Garden at Edinburgh since 1929. The mild, wet climate makes possible the cultivation of tender plants from lower altitudes of the Sino-Himalaya, Bhutan, Japan and the New World. Benmore is a living textbook of the genus *Rhododendron*. Their background is of conifers planted early in the 19th century, perhaps the best collection in Scotland.

TAYSIDE

Branklyn Garden
Dundee Road, Perth, Tayside PH2 7BB
☎ 01738 633199
OWNER   The National Trust for Scotland
LOCATION   On Dundee Road, east of Perth on edge of city
OPEN   9.30 am – sunset, daily, 1 March to 31 October
ADMISSION   Adults £2; Senior Citizens £1
FACILITIES   Parking; loos; access for the disabled; plants for sale; small NTS gift shop
FEATURES   Gravel or scree garden; plants for plantsmen; rock garden; rhododendrons; alpines; *Meconopsis grandis* 'Branklyn'
NCCPG NATIONAL COLLECTIONS *Cassiope*, *Paeonia*

The apotheosis of Scottish rock gardening, a small suburban garden absolutely stuffed with rare plants in an ideal microclimate.

Cluny House
by Aberfeldy, Perthshire, Tayside PH15 2JT
☎ 01887 820795
OWNER   Mr J. and Mrs W. Mattingley
LOCATION   3½ miles from Aberfeldy, on the Weem to Strathtay Road
OPEN   10 am – 6 pm, daily, March to October
ADMISSION   Adults £2; Children under 16 free
FACILITIES   Parking; plants for sale
FEATURES   Good collection of trees; fine conifers; plants for plantsmen; woodland garden; *Meconopsis*; primulas; *Cardiocrinum*; tallest *Prunus maackii* in the British Isles
NCCPG NATIONAL COLLECTIONS *Primula*

A plantsman's garden, largely made in the 1950s by Mrs Mattingley's father, who subscribed to the Ludlow & Sherriff expeditions. Superb rhododendrons and, above all, candelabra primulas – sheets of them from April to July.

Drummond Castle Gardens
Muthill, Crieff, Tayside PH7 4HZ
☎ 01764 681257   FAX 01764 681550
OWNER   Grimsthorpe & Drummond Castle Trust Ltd
LOCATION   South of Crieff on A822
OPEN   2 – 6 pm, daily, 1 May to 31 October
ADMISSION   Adults £3; Senior Citizens £2; Children £1
FACILITIES   Parking; loos; access for the disabled; teas on first Sunday in August (charity day)
FEATURES   Fruit of special interest; glasshouses and conservatories to visit; important formal garden

Drummond has probably the most important formal garden in Scotland, laid out c.1830 as a St Andrew's cross, with complex parterres filled with roses, statues, clipped cones, herbaceous plants, gravel and lots more beside. The result is order, shape, structure, mass, profusion and colour.

Edzell Castle
Edzell, Angus, Tayside DD9 7TG
☎ 01365 648631
OWNER   Historic Scotland
LOCATION   On B966 to Edzell village

TAYSIDE Gardens

OPEN   9.30 am – 6 pm, Monday – Saturday, 2– 6pm, Sundays, 1 April to 30 September; 9.30 am – 4 pm, Monday – Saturday, 2 – 4 pm, Sundays, 1 October to 31 March
ADMISSION   Adults £2; Senior Citizens £1.25; Children and Students 75p
FACILITIES   Parking; dogs permitted; loos; facilities for the disabled; plants for sale; shop
FEATURES   Formal garden; new herbaceous border (1995)
FRIENDS   Historic Scotland

A 1930s formal garden in the 17th-century style, designed to be seen from the ruined keep. A quincunx, of sorts, with yew bobbles, box edging and roses in the beds. The four main segments have the motto of the Lindsey family *DUM SPIRO SPERO* cut round their edges in box. Fun, though not a garden to linger in.

Glendoick Gardens
Glendoick, Perth, Tayside PH2 7NS
☎ 0173 8860205   FAX 0173 8860630
OWNER   Mr and Mrs Peter A. Cox
LOCATION   A85 between Perth and Dundee
OPEN   2 – 5 pm, Sundays, 7, 14, 21 and 28 May only
ADMISSION   £1.50
FACILITIES   Parking; loos; famous garden centre attached
FEATURES   Plants for plantsmen; woodland garden; rhododendrons; new arboretum in memory of Euan Cox (1995)
NCCPG NATIONAL COLLECTIONS   *Enkianthus*, *Kalmia*, *Phyllodoce*

Everyone knows of the Glendoick nursery, but the garden is even more important. Started by Farrer's friend Euan Cox in the 1920s, it has one of the best collections of plants, especially rhododendron species, forms and hybrids, in the British Isles. More's the pity that it is so seldom open.

Gowranes
Kinnaird, by Inchture, Tayside PH14 9QY
☎ 01828 86752
OWNER   Professor and Mrs W. W. Park
LOCATION   Midway between Perth and Dundee, 1½ miles north of A85
OPEN   By appointment only
ADMISSION   £2
FACILITIES   Parking; loos; access for the disabled; plants for sale; refreshments by arrangement
FEATURES   Fine conifers; lake; plants for plantsmen; rock garden; woodland garden

A newish plantsman's garden on a steeply sloping site above a burn which has been dammed to create pools and waterfalls. Rhododendrons, camellias, *Pieris* and similar shrubs in the woodland parts: *Gunnera* and candelabra primulas down among the boggy bits.

House of Dun
Montrose, Angus, Tayside DD10 9LQ
☎ 01674 810264
OWNER   The National Trust for Scotland
LOCATION   On A395, halfway between Montrose and Brechin
OPEN   10 am – dusk, daily, all year
ADMISSION   Adults £1
FACILITIES   Parking; dogs permitted; loos; facilities for the disabled; plants for sale; National Trust for Scotland shop; tea room, open with house
FEATURES   Fine conifers; daffodils; fruit of special interest; old roses and climbers; woodland garden

The first thing you notice at the House of Dun, particularly in winter, is the magnificent line of mature wellingtonias, but there are sheets of spring bulbs, an old-fashioned rose garden for summer, and a collection of old fruit trees of interest in the autumn.

House of Pitmuies
House of Pitmuies, by Forfar, Angus, Tayside DD8 2SN
☎ 01241 828245
OWNER   Mrs Farquhar Ogilvie
LOCATION   Off A932 Forfar to Arbroath Road
OPEN   10 am – 5 pm, daily, 1 April to 31 October
ADMISSION   £2
FACILITIES   Parking; dogs permitted; loos; access for the disabled; plants for sale; home-raised plants and produce in season
FEATURES   Herbaceous borders; fruit of special interest; glasshouses and conservatories to visit; lake; modern roses; old roses and climbers; alpine meadow; ferns; colour schemes; *Viola* and *Dianthus* collections; tallest *Ilex aquifolium* 'Argenteomarginata' in the British Isles; new *Acer* walk (1994)

One of the most beautiful modern gardens in Scotland. Laid out and planted in the Hidcote style, Pitmuies has wonderful shrub roses in mixed plantings, clever colour schemes, and innumerable different gardens within the garden: a delphinium border, cherry walk, an alpine meadow for wild flowers, rhododendrons glades, vast hollies and splendid monkey-puzzles inherited from Victorian times. Enchanted and enchanting.

University of Dundee Botanic Garden
Riverside Drive, Dundee, Tayside DD2 1QH
☎ 01382 566939
OWNER   University of Dundee
LOCATION   Signposted from Riverside Drive (A85), near its junction with Perth Road
OPEN   10 am – 4.30 pm (3.30 pm from 1 November to 28 February), Monday – Saturday, all year. Plus 11 am – 4 pm (3 pm from 1 November to 28 February), Sundays, all year
ADMISSION   Adults £1; Senior Citizens and Children 50p

FACILITIES Parking; loos; facilities for the disabled; plants for sale; small souvenirs for sale; DIY soft drinks
FEATURES Fine conifers; ecological interest; glasshouses and conservatories to visit; herbs; lake; subtropical plants; drought-resistant plants; carnivorous plants
FRIENDS Friends: Individual £5, Family £8 per annum minimum. Newsletters, botanical excursions and illustrated lectures

A fine botanic garden which caters well for visitors. As well as historic plant collections, systematic and chronological borders, there are areas which illustrate native plant communities, including both montane and coastal habitats.

NORTHERN IRELAND

Co. Down

Castlewellan National Arboretum
Castlewellan Forest Park, Castlewellan, Co. Down BT25 9KG
☎ 013967 78664

OWNER Department of Agriculture, Forest Services
LOCATION 30 miles south of Belfast, 4 miles west of Newcastle
OPEN 10 am – sunset, daily, all year
ADMISSION £2.50 per car
FACILITIES Parking; dogs permitted; access for the disabled; light refreshments at peak times
FEATURES Good collection of trees; herbaceous borders; fine conifers; plants for plantsmen; woodland garden; particularly interesting in winter; autumn colours; *Embothrium*; *Eucryphia*; tallest *Chamaecyparis nootkatensis* 'Lutea' in the British Isles, plus 5 other tree records

Castlewellan means trees: several record-breakers and many rarities. The heart of the collection is in a huge walled garden, interplanted with rhododendrons and other shrubs. The central path has mixed borders at the top: dwarf rhododendrons are prominent even here. Labelling is good, and the standard of maintenance high. There are plans to make the collections of *Taxus* and *Eucryphia* comprehensive, and to create a fragrant garden for the blind.

Mount Stewart
The National Trust, Mount Stewart Estate, Grey Abbey, Newtownards, Co. Down BT22 2AD
☎ 012477 88636

OWNER The National Trust
LOCATION East of Belfast on A20
OPEN 10.30 am – 6 pm, daily, 1 April to 30 September; plus weekends only in October
ADMISSION Adults £2.70; Children £1.35

FACILITIES Parking; dogs permitted; loos; facilities for the disabled; souvenir shop; refreshments from 1.30 pm
FEATURES Good collection of trees; herbaceous borders; fine conifers; follies and garden buildings; lake; plants for plantsmen; old roses and climbers; good topiary; woodland garden; plantings by Graham Thomas; rare and tender shrubs galore; topiary in Shamrock Garden newly restored (1994)
NCCPG NATIONAL COLLECTIONS *Penstemon, Phormium*

One of the best gardens in the British Isles and very little known outside Ireland. The formal gardens by the house are utterly original: a Spanish garden, statues of mythical beasts, and the red hand of Ulster set in a shamrock surround. Good plants too: *Rosa gigantea* grows on the house walls, and the herbaceous and woodland plantings are brilliant with colour and variety. Better still is the walk around the lake, where rhododendrons flood the woodlands. They are underplanted in places with *Meconopsis* and candelabra primulas and, at one point, you catch a glimpse of a white stag in a glade. For design, variety, plants and plantings, Mount Stewart is a place of miracles. Allow lots of time for your visit.

Rowallane Garden
Saintfield, Ballynahinch, Co. Down BT24 7LH
☎ 01238 510131

OWNER The National Trust
LOCATION One mile south of Saintfield on A7
OPEN 10.30 am – 6 pm, Monday – Friday, 2 – 6 pm, Saturdays and Sundays, 1 April to 31 October; 10.30 am – 5 pm, Monday – Friday, 1 November to 31 March
ADMISSION Adults £2.30 (£1.20 from November to March); Children £1.15; Groups £1.60
FACILITIES Parking; facilities for the disabled; National Trust shop; new Information Centre; light refreshments, 2 – 6 pm, May to August and weekends in April and September
FEATURES Good collection of trees; herbaceous borders; fine conifers; plants for plantsmen; rock garden; woodland garden; rhododendrons and azaleas
NCCPG NATIONAL COLLECTIONS *Penstemon*

52 acres of rhododendrons and azaleas, which started near the house and expanded into the fields beyond as the seedlings came and needed to be planted. No garden can match it on a sunny day in April or May, as you amble from a glade of *Rh. augustinii* forms to a line of *Rh. macabeanum* or back through *Rh. yakushimanum* hybrids.

Co. Fermanagh

Florence Court
Enniskillen, Co. Fermanagh BT92 1DB
☎ 01365 348249

OWNER The National Trust
LOCATION 4 miles from Marble Arch Caves on A32

OPEN House: 1 – 6 pm, daily except Tuesday, 1 June to 31 August; plus Saturdays, Sundays and Bank Holidays in April, May and September. Grounds: 10 am – 7 pm, daily, all year except Christmas Day
ADMISSION Adults £2.50; Children £1.25; Groups (12+) £1.90; Garden/Estate £1.50 per car
FACILITIES Parking; dogs permitted; loos; facilities for the disabled; National Trust shop; light lunches and teas; picnics welcome
FEATURES Good collection of trees; woodland garden; interesting for children; ice-house; water-powered sawmill

Classic 18th-century parkland, with some fine trees, notably the original 'Irish Yew' *Taxus baccata* 'Fastigiata' and a beautiful form of weeping beech with a broad curving crown. The sawmill is fun for children.

CO. LONDONDERRY

Guy Wilson Daffodil Garden
University of Ulster, Coleraine, Co. Londonderry BT52 1SA
☎ 01265 44141   FAX 01265 40912
OWNER University of Ulster at Coleraine
LOCATION Signposted from sports centre
OPEN Dawn – dusk, daily, all year
ADMISSION Free
FACILITIES Parking; dogs permitted; loos; facilities for the disabled
FEATURES Exceptional collection of daffodils; best in second half of April
NCCPG NATIONAL COLLECTIONS *Narcissus*

The name says it all – this is both a celebration of Guy Wilson as a daffodil breeder and a museum of his hybrids. His achievements are revered in Northern Ireland, and rightly so.

EIRE

CO. CORK

Annes Grove Gardens
Castletownroche, nr. Mallow, Co. Cork, Eire
☎ 00 353 22 26145
OWNER Patrick Annesley
LOCATION 1 mile north of Castletownroche on N72
OPEN 10 am – 5 pm, Monday – Saturday, 1 – 6 pm, Sundays, 17 March to 30 September
ADMISSION Adults I£2.50; Senior Citizens and Students I£1.50; Children I£1
FACILITIES Parking; dogs permitted; loos; plants for sale; lunches and teas by arrangement for groups
FEATURES Good collection of trees; herbaceous borders; fine conifers; lake; plants for plantsmen; woodland garden; rhododendrons from wild seeds; rare trees

Annes Grove has long been famous for its 30-acre garden: 'Robinsonian' is the word most often used to describe it. The walled garden has a 17th-century mount with a summer house on top. The river garden is lushly wild with *Lysichiton*, *Gunnera* and candelabra primulas. In the glen garden lies a wonderfully dense collection of rhododendrons and azaleas, many from Kingdon Ward's seed.

Fota
Fota Island, Carrigtwohill, Co. Cork, Eire
☎ 00 353 21 812728   FAX 00 353 21 270244
OWNER Fota Trust Company Ltd
LOCATION 9 miles from Cork city, off Cobh road
OPEN 10 am – 6 pm (2 – 6 pm on Sundays), 2 April to 31 October
ADMISSION Cars I£1.50; Pedestrians free of charge
FACILITIES Parking; dogs permitted; loos; facilities for the disabled
FEATURES Good collection of trees; fine conifers; ecological interest; lake; woodland garden; interesting for children; wildlife park; tallest Italian cypress *Cupressus sempervirens* (25 metres) in the British Isles, plus 10 other record trees

Fota has a handsome formal garden and walled garden, now undergoing restoration, but is famous above all for its trees. As well as a fine collection of Victorian conifers (huge redwoods and wellingtonias), there are flowering mimosas, a wonderful *Cornus capitata* and such tender trees as the Canary Islands palm *Phoenix canariensis*.

Kinoith Garden
Ballymaloe Cookery School, Shanagarry, Co. Cork, Eire
☎ 00 353 21 646785   FAX 00 353 21 646909
OWNER Tim and Darina Allen
LOCATION Ballymaloe, signposted from Castlemartyr and Shanagarry
OPEN 2.30 – 5.30 pm, Monday – Saturday, 1 April to 30 September
ADMISSION I£3
FACILITIES Parking; loos; access for the disabled
FEATURES Herbaceous borders; fruit and vegetables of special interest; old roses and climbers; magnificent formal parterres for herbs

Kinoith is attached to the famous Ballymaloe Cookery School and is full of unusual fruit, vegetables and herbs. Seldom is a functional garden so stylishly designed and planted, or so extensive.

CO. DONEGAL

Ardnamona
Lough Eske, Co. Donegal, Eire
☎ 00 353 73 22650   FAX 00 353 73 22819
OWNER Mr and Mrs Kieran Clarke
LOCATION On Lough Eske, 5 miles north east of Donegal
OPEN 2 – 5 pm, daily, 1 April to 30 June (1994 times)
ADMISSION I£2 (1994)

FACILITIES Parking; bed and breakfast
FEATURES Fine conifers; lake; woodland garden; ancient rhododendrons

A wilderness of huge rhododendrons, some as much as 60 feet high, like a Himalayan forest, now taken in hand, cleared and revitalised.

Glenveagh Castle
Churchill, Letterkenny, Co. Donegal, Eire
☎ 00 353 74 37040   FAX 00 353 74 37072

OWNER The Office of Public Works
LOCATION 14 miles north west of Letterkenny on R251
OPEN 10 am – 6 pm (7 pm on Sundays, June – August), Easter to 31 October. Garden tours, 2 pm (arrive 1.15 pm) on Tuesdays and Thursdays in July and August
ADMISSION Adults I£2; Senior Citizens I£1.50; Students I£1
FACILITIES Parking; loos; access for the disabled; restaurant at visitor centre; tea room at castle
FEATURES Good collection of trees; herbaceous borders; fine conifers; fruit of special interest; glasshouses and conservatories to visit; herbs; plants for plantsmen; modern roses; old roses and climbers; garden sculpture; subtropical plants; woodland garden

Glenveagh was built for its view down the rocky slopes of Lough Veagh, and part of the garden is known as the View Garden. Lanning Roper laid out a formal Italianate courtyard garden. Jim Russell advised on planting. There are wonderful borders and conservatories as well as rhododendrons and camellias. The unusual shrubs are magnificent: tree-like *Griselinia* and *Michelia doltsopa*, for instance.

CO. DUBLIN

45 Sandford Road
Ranelagh, Dublin 6, Co. Dublin, Eire
☎ 00 353 1 4971308

OWNER Helen and Val Dillon
LOCATION Junction of Sandford Road and Marlborough Road
OPEN 2 – 6 pm, daily, March, July and August. Plus Sundays, April to June, and September. Groups by appointment
ADMISSION Adults I£3; Senior citizens I£2
FACILITIES Loos; access for the disabled; plants for sale
FEATURES Herbaceous borders; glasshouses and conservatories to visit; plants for plantsmen; raised beds

A plantsman's garden with a fantastic range of rarities, from snowdrops and hellebores in spring, to tropaeoleums in autumn. Unlike some collectors' gardens, this is immaculately maintained and beautifully designed as a series of garden rooms.

Ardgillan Park
Balbriggan, Co. Dublin, Eire
☎ 00 353 1 849 1200

OWNER Fingal County Council
LOCATION Coast road between Skerries and Balbriggan
OPEN 10 am – 5 pm, daily, all year
FACILITIES Parking; loos; facilities for the disabled; refreshments
FEATURES Herbaceous borders; follies and garden buildings; fruit of special interest; herbs; rock garden; modern roses; old roses and climbers; ice-house; 200-year-old yew walk; restored Victorian glasshouse in rose garden, opening spring 1995

Ardgillan was all but lost in the troubles, but restored 10 years ago by the Council as a public amenity. A new rose garden and herbaceous borders have been added. The 4-acre walled garden is being developed too – it has a herb garden now and fruit trees grown against the walls.

Fairfield Lodge
Monkstown Avenue, Monkstown, Co. Dublin, Eire
☎ 00 353 1 2803912

OWNER John Bourke
LOCATION In Monkstown village
OPEN 2 – 6 pm, Sundays and Bank Holidays, 1 May to 30 September. Groups by appointment
ADMISSION Adults: I£2.50; Concessions I£2
FACILITIES Parking; loos; plants for sale
FEATURES Herbaceous borders; old roses and climbers; colour combinations

A small town garden, made to appear much larger by being divided into a series of outdoor rooms. Formal design, informal planting and clever colour combinations – a modern classic.

Fernhill
Sandyford, Co. Dublin, Eire
☎ 00 353 1 295 6000

OWNER Mrs Sally Walker
LOCATION 7 miles south of central Dublin on the Enniskerry Road
OPEN 11 am – 5 pm (2 – 6 pm on Sundays), Tuesday – Sunday (and Bank Holidays), 1 March to 30 November
ADMISSION Adults I£2.50; Senior Citizens I£1.50; Children I£1
FACILITIES Parking; loos; plants for sale
FEATURES Good collection of trees; herbaceous borders; fine conifers; lake; rock garden; garden sculpture; woodland garden; sculpture exhibitions; rhododendrons

A popular garden on the outskirts of Dublin, with a good collection of rhododendrons and other woodland plants and some magnificent trees c.150 years old. Steep woodland walks and an excellent nursery thrown in.

National Botanic Gardens, Dublin
Glasnevin, Dublin 9, Co. Dublin, Eire
☎ 00 353 1 8734388 FAX 00 353 1 8360080

OWNER Office of Public Works
LOCATION 1 mile north of Dublin near Glasnevin cemetery
OPEN 9 am – 6 pm (4.30 pm in winter), daily except 25 December. Opens at 11 am on Sundays
ADMISSION Free
FACILITIES Loos; facilities for the disabled; refreshments by arrangement
FEATURES Good collection of trees; herbaceous borders; fine conifers; ecological interest; fruit of special interest; glasshouses and conservatories to visit; lake; plants for plantsmen; rock garden; modern roses; old roses and climbers; subtropical plants; woodland garden; particularly interesting in winter; carpet bedding; fern house; tallest hardy rubber tree *Eucommia ulmoides* in the British Isles, plus 8 further tree records
NCCPG NATIONAL COLLECTIONS *Garrya*, *Potentilla fruticosa*

Glasnevin garden greets you with beautiful old-fashioned summer bedding and a bed of *Rosa chinensis* 'Parson's Pink', known here as 'The Last Rose of Summer'. Very much a botanic garden in the old tradition: public education and amenity hand in hand. Richard Turner's elegant curvilinear range of glasshouses has just been restored (1995). Interesting plant collections and some good trees, most notably a weeping Atlantic cedar: allow a full day to do it justice.

Primrose Hill
Primrose Lane, Lucan, Co. Dublin, Eire
☎ 00 353 6280373

OWNER Robin and Cicely Hall
LOCATION Lucan village, at top of Primrose Hill
OPEN 2 – 6 pm, by appointment
ADMISSION I£2
FACILITIES Parking; loos; plants for sale
FEATURES Herbaceous borders; plants for plantsmen; snowdrops

4 acres of intensive plantsmanship, particularly interesting for its rare forms of herbaceous plants and its snowdrops. The planting continues, and includes a small arboretum.

Shackleton Garden
Beech Park, Clonsilla, Co. Dublin, Eire
☎ 00 353 1 8212216

OWNER Shackleton family
LOCATION 1 mile from Clonsilla on the road to Lucan, 9 miles west of Dublin
OPEN 2 – 6 pm, Sundays and Bank Holidays, 6 March to 25 October
ADMISSION Adults I£2.50
FACILITIES Parking; loos; access for the disabled; plants for sale; home-made teas

FEATURES Herbaceous borders; fruit of special interest; old roses and climbers; raised beds

A walled garden, attached to a Regency house. The owners claim to have the largest private collection of herbaceous plants in Ireland: *Celmisia* are a speciality. Gardening day-courses throughout the summer.

Talbot Botanic Gardens
Malahide Castle, Malahide, Co. Dublin, Eire
☎ 00 353 1 845 0954

OWNER Dublin County Council
LOCATION 10 miles north of Dublin on Malahide road
OPEN 2 – 5 pm (or by appointment), daily, 1 May to 30 September
ADMISSION I£1 (1994)
FACILITIES Parking; loos; facilities for the disabled; souvenir shop and refreshments in castle
FEATURES Good collection of trees; fine conifers; plants for plantsmen; woodland garden; Tasmanian plants; new scree bed planted (1994); old Victorian glasshouse 'Messenger' in walled garden (1994)
NCCPG NATIONAL COLLECTIONS *Olearia*

The garden at Malahide was the work of Milo Talbot, a passionate amateur botanist with a particular interest in Tasmanian flowers. He built up a collection of 5,000 different taxa and, since the soil is limey, all are calcicole. Best visited on Wednesday afternoons when guided tours are offered of the walled garden (not otherwise open).

Trinity College Botanic Garden
Palmerston Park, Dartry, Dublin 6, Co. Dublin, Eire
☎ 00 353 1 972070 FAX 00 353 1 7021147

OWNER Trinity College
LOCATION Near Ranelagh, opposite Municipal Park
OPEN 9 am – 5 pm, Monday – Friday, by prior arrangement only
ADMISSION Free
FACILITIES Loos; access for the disabled; occasional plant sales
FEATURES Good collection of trees; herbaceous borders; ecological interest; glasshouses and conservatories to visit; gravel or scree garden; rock garden; old roses and climbers; woodland garden

A charming old-fashioned botanic garden, full interesting plants, including a collection of Irish natives.

CO. KERRY

Derreen
Lauragh, Killarney, Co. Kerry, Eire
☎ 00 353 64 83103

OWNER The Hon. David Bigham
LOCATION 15 miles from Kenmare on the Castletown road
OPEN 11 am – 5.30 pm, daily, 1 April to 30 September (1994 times and dates)
ADMISSION Adults I£2; Children I£1 (1994)

FACILITIES Parking; dogs permitted; loos; facilities for the disabled; teas occasionally available
FEATURES Good collection of trees; fine conifers; lake; plants for plantsmen; rock garden; subtropical plants; woodland garden; tree ferns; rhododendrons

Derreen is quite extraordinary. The rocky outcrops come right to the front door, but the fast lush growth of its trees and shrubs is boundless. Tree ferns *Dicksonia antarctica* and myrtles *Myrtus communis* have gone native, and seed themselves everywhere. Moss, lichen and ferns abound. Large-leaved rhododendrons grow to great heights. Wonderful on a sunny day in late April.

Muckross House & Gardens
Muckross, Killarney, Co. Kerry, Eire
☎ 00 353 064 31440 FAX 00 353 64 33926

OWNER Office of Public Works
LOCATION Near Killarney town
OPEN Dawn – dusk, daily, all year except one week at Christmas
ADMISSION Free
FACILITIES Parking; dogs permitted; loos; facilities for the disabled; lunches, hot and cold snacks daily
FEATURES Good collection of trees; fine conifers; lake; rock garden; woodland garden; rhododendrons; azaleas; good new collection of *Daboecia* (1994); splendid new guide book (1995)

Muckross is in the Killarney National Park, which gives it special interest. There are a young arboretum and some enormous old rhododendrons, but the native woodland is of Scots pines and arbutus trees and, even more exciting for a garden visitor, the rock garden is a natural one, of carboniferous limestone.

CO. KILDARE

Coolcarrigan Gardens
Coolcarrigan, Naas, Co. Kildare, Eire
☎ 00 353 45 63512

OWNER John Wilson-Wright
LOCATION 12 miles north of Naas
OPEN By appointment only, from April to August
ADMISSION I£3
FACILITIES Parking; loos; access for the disabled; plants for sale; refreshments by previous arrangement
FEATURES Good collection of trees; bluebells; herbaceous borders; daffodils; glasshouses and conservatories to visit; lake; plants for plantsmen; rhododendrons and azaleas; rock garden; snowdrops

This garden owes everything to a gale which knocked the heart out of the established plantings in 1974. Harold Hillier advised on the replanting, and the result is one of the best modern collections of trees and shrubs in Ireland. The owners, keen plantsmen, have added late-summer borders and a rock garden.

Japanese Gardens, Tully
Tully, Co. Kildare, Eire
☎ 00 353 45 21617 FAX 00 353 45 22129

OWNER Irish National Stud
LOCATION Signposted in Kildare
OPEN 10.30 am – 5 pm, Monday – Friday, 10.30 am – 6 pm, Saturdays and Bank Holidays, 2 – 6pm, Sundays (11 am June – August), Easter Sunday to 31 October
ADMISSION I£4 adults; I£3 Senior Citizens; I£2 Children (1994)
FACILITIES Parking; loos; access for the disabled; plants for sale; souvenir shop; light refreshments
FEATURES Famous Japanese garden

The garden is a sequence which symbolises Man's journey through life. It was made for Lord Wavertree by Japanese gardeners in the early years of this century.

Lodge Park Walled Garden
Straffan, Co. Kildare, Eire
☎ 00 353 1 628 8412 FAX 00 353 1 627 3477

OWNER Mr and Mrs Robert Guinness
LOCATION Signposted from Maynooth and Kill
OPEN Groups (10+) only, by appointment. 1 May to 30 September
ADMISSION I£2
FACILITIES Parking; loos; gift shop at nearby steam museum
FEATURES Herbaceous borders; modern roses; vegetables of interest

An 18th-century walled garden planted for the owners' use and pleasure, with everything from fruit and vegetables to sweet peas and roses.

CO. KILKENNY

Kilfane Glen & Waterfall
Thomastown, Co. Kilkenny, Eire
☎ 00 353 56 24979 FAX 00 353 56 27491

OWNER Nicholas and Susan Mosse
LOCATION Off N9, 2 miles north of Thomastown
OPEN 2 – 6 pm, Tuesday – Sunday, 15 May to 15 September
ADMISSION Adults I£3; Children I£2
FACILITIES Parking; loos; plants for sale; teas on Sundays, but daily in August
FEATURES Bluebells; follies and garden buildings; woodland garden

A romantic landscape garden laid out in the 1790s and vigorously restored by the present owners. Sit in the tiny *cottage orné*, admire the exquisite form of the waterfall across the ravine, and dream of Rousseau.

CO. LAOIS

Heywood Gardens
Ballinakill, Co. Laois, Eire
☎ 00 353 502 33563

OWNER Office of Public Works

LOCATION   In grounds of Ballinakill College
OPEN   Dawn – dusk, daily, all year
ADMISSION   Free
FACILITIES   Parking
FEATURES   Planted by Gertrude Jekyll; lake; designed by Lutyens; woodland garden

A ravishing garden, originally designed by Lutyens and planted by Jekyll, which was taken into State care late in 1993 and will be carefully restored and replanted. Go now, to see what an Edwardian garden looked like when newly made.

CO. LIMERICK

Ballynacourty
Ballysteen, Co. Limerick, Eire
☎ 00 353 61 396409   FAX 00 353 61 396733

OWNER   George and Michelina Stacpoole
LOCATION   3 miles from Askeaton, on River Shannon
OPEN   By appointment
ADMISSION   I£3
FACILITIES   Parking; dogs permitted; loos; access for the disabled; refreshments by arrangement
FEATURES   Herbaceous borders; old roses and climbers

A fine modern family garden: 4 densely planted acres won from open farmland. Interesting, too, for its selection of lime-tolerant trees and shrubs.

Glin Castle
Glin, Co. Limerick, Eire
☎ 00 353 68 34173   FAX 00 353 68 34364

OWNER   Desmond Fitzgerald, Knight of Glin
LOCATION   On N69 west of Limerick
OPEN   10 am – noon and 2 – 4 pm, daily, 1 May to 30 June. Groups by appointment
ADMISSION   Adults I£3; Groups I£2
FACILITIES   Parking; loos; facilities for the disabled; gate shop
FEATURES   Bluebells; camellias; daffodils; rhododendrons and azaleas; subtropical plants; vegetables of interest

These simple formal gardens run down towards the park and merge with the surrounding woodland. Not a great garden but, taken with the gothicised castle and magnificent position on the Shannon estuary, a place of rare enchantment.

CO. MEATH

Butterstream
Kildalkey Road, Trim, Co. Meath, Eire
☎ 00 353 46 36017   FAX 00 353 46 31702

OWNER   Jim Reynolds
LOCATION   Outskirts of Trim on Kildalkey Road
OPEN   11 am – 6 pm, daily, 1 April to 30 September
ADMISSION   I£3

FACILITIES   Parking; loos; access for the disabled; plants for sale; teas on Sundays, and daily in July and August
FEATURES   Herbaceous borders; fruit of special interest; lake; plants for plantsmen; modern roses; old roses and climbers; colour borders

A series of formal compartments in the Hidcote style around an old farmhouse. Each is different in style, but connected to the next. Butterstream boasts a green garden, a white garden, a hot-coloured garden, a Roman garden, a pool garden (with Tuscan portico reflected in it), an obelisk garden, and many others. The plants are determined by the soil – heavy, cold, limey clay.

CO. OFFALY

Birr Castle Demesne
Birr, Co. Offaly, Eire
☎ 00 353 509 20056   FAX 00 353 509 21583

OWNER   Earl of Rosse
LOCATION   Rosse Row in Birr, Co. Offaly
OPEN   9 am – 6 pm or dusk, daily, all year
ADMISSION   April to October: Adults I£3.20; Children I£1.60. Other times: Adults I£2.60; Children I£1.30
FACILITIES   Parking; dogs permitted; loos; plants for sale; craft shop; good guide books; morning coffee, lunch and tea at gates
FEATURES   Good collection of trees; herbaceous borders; fine conifers; herbs; lake; plants for plantsmen; old roses and climbers; good topiary; woodland garden; *Paeonia* 'Anne Rosse'; *Magnolia* 'Anne Rosse'; pretty Victorian conservatory restored in 1994; winner of all-Ireland Property of the Year Award in 1992; tallest *Acer monspessulanum* and boxwood *Buxus sempervirens* (12 metres) in the British Isles, plus 14 other record species
FRIENDS   Friends of the Birr Castle Demesne organisation: I£18 p.a.; Family I£33 p.a.

The best garden in the Irish Midlands. Birr has 50 hectares of grounds, a huge collection of trees and shrubs, and a wonderful walled garden with a tunnel down the middle. Many of the plants are grown from original collectors' material: some were collected in the wild by the owner's parents, Michael and Anne Rosse. Birr also has the tallest box hedges in the world. In the grounds is the famous telescope, once the largest in the world, and witness to the polymath abilities of the family over the generations.

CO. WATERFORD

Lismore Castle
Lismore, Co. Waterford, Eire
☎ 00 353 58 54424   FAX 00 353 58 54896

OWNER   Lismore Estates
LOCATION   Centre of Lismore
OPEN   1.45 – 4.45 pm, daily, 29 April to 10 September

ADMISSION   Adults I£2.50; Children I£1.50
FACILITIES   Parking; dogs permitted
FEATURES   Herbaceous borders; fruit of special interest; old roses and climbers; woodland garden; yew walk; magnolias; camellias; spring bulbs

Best for the castellated house: the gardens are interesting rather than exceptional, but there is a pretty grove of camellias and an ancient double yew walk. Plus some fine traditional kitchen gardening to be seen in the walled garden.

CO. WEST CORK

Creagh Gardens
Skibbereen, Co. West Cork, Eire
☎ 00 353 28 22121   FAX 00 353 28 22084
OWNER   Creagh Gardens Trust
LOCATION   4 miles from Skibbereen on the Baltimore road
OPEN   10 am – 6 pm, daily, 1 March to 31 October
ADMISSION   Adults I£2; Children I£1
FACILITIES   Parking; loos; access for the disabled; refreshments for groups by prior arrangement
FEATURES   Pond; rhododendrons and azaleas; sub-tropical plants; woodland garden

An exotic woodland, lushly planted by the late Peter and Gwendoline Harold-Barry, in the style of a Douanier Rousseau painting. Wildly wonderful.

CO. WESTMEATH

Tullynally Castle Gardens
Castlepollard, Co. Westmeath, Eire
☎ 00 353 44 61159   FAX 00 353 44 61856
OWNER   The Hon. Mr and Mrs Thomas Pakenham
LOCATION   Signposted from Castlepollard
OPEN   2 – 6 pm, daily, 1 May to 30 September
ADMISSION   Adults I£2; Children 50p
FACILITIES   Parking; dogs permitted; loos; plants for sale; tea room open mid June to mid August
FEATURES   Bluebells; herbaceous borders; daffodils; lake; woodland garden; grotto

A grand garden for a grandly turreted house. Formal terraces lead down to the park and into the woodland gardens. A fine avenue of centennial Irish yews is the centrepiece of the walled garden. Shadows of the ascendancy.

CO. WEXFORD

The John F. Kennedy Arboretum
New Ross, Co. Wexford, Eire
☎ 00 353 51 388171   FAX 00 353 51 388172
OWNER   The Office of Public Works
LOCATION   8 miles south of New Ross off R733
OPEN   10 am – 8 pm, 1 May to 31 August; 10 am – 6.30 pm, April and September; 10 am – 5 pm, 1 October to 31 March

ADMISSION   Adults I£2; Senior Citizens I£1.50; Children and Students I£1; Family I£5; Groups (20+) I£1.50
FACILITIES   Parking; dogs permitted; loos; facilities for the disabled; plants for sale; souvenirs; cafeteria for teas/refreshments
FEATURES   Fine conifers; lake; woodland garden; interesting for children

125 hectares planted over the last 25 years. The statistics are impressive: 4,500 types of trees and shrubs arranged with artistry and all meticulously labelled. There are picnic areas, viewpoints, signposted walks, a vigorous visitors' centre and further hectares of experimental forestry.

Johnstown Castle Gardens
Wexford, Co. Wexford, Eire
☎ 00 353 53 42888   FAX 00 353 53 42004
OWNER   TEAGASC (Food and Agriculture Development Authority)
LOCATION   4 miles south west of Wexford
OPEN   9 am – 5.30 pm, daily, all year
ADMISSION   I£2.50 per car and passengers
FACILITIES   Parking; dogs permitted; loos; access for the disabled; coffee shop with snacks, July and August only
FEATURES   Fine conifers; glasshouses and conservatories to visit; lake; woodland garden; walled gardens; agricultural museum; tallest *Cupressus macrocarpa* (40 metres) in the British Isles

50 acres of ornamental grounds with good trees, tall cordylines, three lakes and the Irish Agricultural Museum.

Ram House Garden
Coolgreany, Gorey, Co. Wexford, Eire
☎ 00 353 402 37238   FAX 00 353 402 31205
OWNER   Godfrey and Lolo Stevens
LOCATION   In Coolgreany village
OPEN   2 – 6 pm, Sundays, Easter to 31 August. Plus Saturdays and Mondays on Bank Holiday weekends, and 20 May to 26 June
ADMISSION   I£2.50
FACILITIES   Parking; loos; paintings for sale; tea room
FEATURES   Herbaceous borders; pond; climbing roses; woodland garden

2 acres laid out in modern style as a series of garden rooms, full of good plants and clever plantings. Utterly charming.

CO. WICKLOW

Mount Usher Gardens
Ashford, Co. Wicklow, Eire
☎ 00 353 404 40205
OWNER   Mrs Madelaine Jay
LOCATION   Ashford, 30 miles south of Dublin on the main road
OPEN   10.30 am – 6 pm, daily, 17 March to 31 October

Co. Wicklow Gardens

ADMISSION Adults I£3; Senior Citizens and Children I£2; Groups (20+) I£2.50 and I£1.50 respectively
FACILITIES Parking; loos; access for the disabled; courtyard shops with pottery, books, furniture; tea room with home-baked food
FEATURES Good collection of trees; herbaceous borders; fine conifers; lake; plants for plantsmen; subtropical plants; woodland garden; spring bulbs; tallest *Eucalyptus dalrympleana* in the British Isles, plus 16 other record tree species

20 acres of garden with the River Vartry through the middle, crowded with rare trees and shrubs – 5,000 different species, some very rare. The self-sown *Pinus montezumae* are justly famous. Good herbaceous plants too, and lilies in July. A truly remarkable plantsman's garden.

Powerscourt Gardens
Powerscourt Estate, Enniskerry, Co. Wicklow, Eire
☎ 00 353 1 2867676 FAX 00 353 1 2863561
OWNER Powerscourt Estate
LOCATION 12 miles south of Dublin off N11

OPEN 9.30 am – 5.30 pm, daily, mid March to 31 October
ADMISSION Adults I£2.80; Students and Senior Citizens I£2.30; Children I£1.70
FACILITIES Parking; dogs permitted; loos; plants for sale; garden centre; tea rooms with light lunches
FEATURES Good collection of trees; fine conifers; lake; oriental features; garden sculpture; woodland garden; interesting for children; tallest *Abies spectabilis* in the British Isles, plus 8 other record tree specimens

Powerscourt is a wonderful mixture of awesome grandeur and sheer fun. It is also extremely well-organised for visitors. The main Italian garden, a stately staircase down to a lake, has Great Sugarloaf Mountain as an off-centre backdrop. It is lined with bedding plants, statues and urns (look out for the sulky cherubs). To one side is the Japanese garden – not strongly Japanese – but full of twists and hummocks and scarlet paintwork. In the arboretum, Alan Mitchell has designed a tree trail. Powerscourt is busy in summer, but you can escape into solitude along the avenue of monkey-puzzles.

16
Garden Features

Graham Thomas

Graham Stuart Thomas's contribution to English gardening is seen everywhere – above all, in his books and in his gardens. We have, however, never found a list of the gardens on which he worked as Gardens Adviser to the National Trust. This list is an attempt to put the record straight. They are gardens in which to study his work, whether as a restorer and maintainer of other men's plantings, or as an original garden designer and plantsman himself.

Beningbrough Hall, North Yorkshire
Benthall Hall, Shropshire
Claremont Gardens, Surrey
Cliveden, Buckinghamshire
Hidcote Manor Garden, Gloucestershire
Inveresk Lodge Garden, Lothian
Knightshayes Garden, Devon
Little Moreton Hall, Cheshire
Lytes Cary Manor, Somerset
Mottisfont Abbey, Hampshire
Mount Stewart, Co. Down
Polesden Lacey, Surrey
Powis Castle, Powys
Sezincote, Gloucestershire
Sheffield Park Garden, East Sussex
Shugborough Hall, Staffordshire
Wallington Hall, Northumberland
Winkworth Arboretum, Surrey

Interesting for Children

Garden visiting is seldom such a pleasure for children as it is for adults: children are quickly bored if a garden has nothing to interest or occupy them. Finding gardens where children can be relied upon not to spoil the outing for older members of the party is difficult. All the gardens we list here pass the boredom test easily, but for widely differing reasons. Some such as Bowood and Wilton House have adventure playgrounds. Others have special facil-ities, often educational, which explain everything to children in such a way that their interest is aroused.

Many of the gardens which have won Sandford awards fit in here, as do such brilliant examples of child management as Trebah. Some have such exciting plants and design features that the gardens themselves can be made to interest the young.

Alton Towers, Staffordshire
Arbigland, Dumfries & Galloway
Bateman's, East Sussex
Bede's World Herb Garden, Tyne & Wear
Belton House, Lincolnshire
Bicton Park Gardens, Devon
Biddulph Grange, Staffordshire
Birmingham Botanical Gardens and
    Glasshouses, West Midlands
Blenheim Palace, Oxfordshire
Boughton House, Northamptonshire
Bowood House, Wiltshire
Brodick Castle, Strathclyde
Brogdale, Kent
Burton Constable Hall, Humberside
Capel Manor, London
Castle Bromwich Hall, West Midlands
Castle Drogo, Devon
Chatsworth, Derbyshire
Cragside, Northumberland
Croxteth Hall and Country Park, Merseyside
Culzean Castle and Country Park, Strathclyde
Dalemain, Cumbria
Dunham Massey, Greater Manchester
Florence Court, Co. Fermanagh
Fota, Co. Cork, Eire
Furzey Gardens, Hampshire
Goldney Hall, Avon
Hampton Court Palace, London
Harewood House, West Yorkshire
Holdenby House Gardens, Northamptonshire

The John F. Kennedy Arboretum, Co. Wexford, Eire
Kildrummy Castle, Grampian
Lackham Country Attractions, Wiltshire
Leeds Castle, Kent
Longleat House, Wiltshire
Longstock Water Gardens, Hampshire
Margam Park, West Glamorgan
Oxford Botanic Garden, Oxfordshire
Paignton Zoo and Botanical Gardens, Devon
Plantasia, West Glamorgan
Port Lympne Gardens, Kent
Powerscourt Gardens, Co. Wicklow, Eire
Probus Demonstration Garden, Cornwall
Queen's Wood Arboretum and Country Park, Hereford & Worcester
Ripley Castle, North Yorkshire
Royal Botanic Garden, Edinburgh, Lothian
Royal Botanic Gardens, Kew, London
Ryton Organic Gardens, Warwickshire
Shugborough Hall, Staffordshire
Sir Harold Hillier Gardens and Arboretum, Hampshire
St Andrews Botanic Garden, Fife
Stapeley Water Gardens Ltd, Cheshire
Stourhead, Wiltshire
Sudeley Castle, Gloucestershire
The Swiss Garden, Bedfordshire
Syon Park, London
Tapeley Park, Devon
Toddington Manor, Bedfordshire
Trebah Garden Trust, Cornwall
Trentham Park Gardens, Staffordshire
Tresco Abbey, Cornwall
Tudor House Garden, Hampshire
The Valley Gardens, Harrogate, North Yorkshire
Ventnor Botanic Garden, Isle of Wight
Wentworth Castle Gardens, South Yorkshire
Wilton House, Wiltshire
Wimpole Hall, Cambridgeshire
Woburn Abbey, Bedfordshire
The Younger Botanic Garden, Strathclyde

Late Opening Hours

Many working people like to visit a garden on summer evenings after they have left their workplace. It is difficult to find good gardens, apart from the best of the public parks: Regent's Park in London is open from dawn to dusk, but is even better at 7 am than 7 pm. Few gardens are more magical than Winkworth Arboretum on a mid May evening, or the great rhododendron collections of Brodick Castle and the Valley Gardens in Windsor Great Park at the same time of year.

Some gardens open late for a few special days each year: it is worth finding out about the evening openings in peak rose time at Mottisfont Abbey, not least because you avoid the afternoon crowds. And if you visit Glenveagh Castle or Inverewe late in the day you may have the gardens entirely to yourself.

Achamore Gardens, Strathclyde
Alton Towers, Staffordshire
Angus Garden, Strathclyde
Ardanaiseig Hotel Garden, Strathclyde
Ardchattan Priory, Strathclyde
Arduaine Gardens, Strathclyde
Brodick Castle, Strathclyde
Canal Gardens, West Yorkshire
Cannizaro Park, London
Castle Ashby Gardens, Northamptonshire
Castlewellan National Arboretum, Co. Down
Chiswick House, London
Clyne Gardens, West Glamorgan
Crossing House Garden, Cambridgeshire
Culzean Castle and Country Park, Strathclyde
Dartington Hall, Devon
Dawyck Botanic Garden, Borders
Dyffryn Botanic Garden, South Glamorgan
Elvaston Castle County Park, Derbyshire
The Ernest Wilson Memorial Garden, Gloucestershire
Glasgow Botanic Garden, Strathclyde
Hampton Court Palace, London
Harlow Carr Botanical Gardens, North Yorkshire
Heale House, Wiltshire
Highdown, West Sussex
The Hollies Park, West Yorkshire
Isabella Plantation, London
Killerton, Devon
Lochalsh Woodland Garden, Highland
Lotherton Hall, West Yorkshire
Malleny House Garden, Lothian
Marwood Hill Gardens, Devon
Muckross House and Gardens, Co. Kerry, Eire
Newstead Abbey, Nottinghamshire
RHS Garden, Rosemoor, Devon
Royal Botanic Garden, Edinburgh, Lothian
Royal Botanic Gardens, Kew, London
Sheffield Botanical Gardens, South Yorkshire

Garden Features

Somerleyton Hall, Suffolk
Stourhead, Wiltshire
Syon Park, London
Temple Newsam Park, West Yorkshire
Torosay Castle and Gardens, Strathclyde
The Valley Gardens, Windsor, Surrey
Ventnor Botanic Garden, Isle of Wight
Wakehurst Place, West Sussex
Westonbirt Arboretum, Gloucestershire
Winkworth Arboretum, Surrey
Yorkshire Museum Gardens, North Yorkshire

Young Gardens

Newly made gardens are a great inspiration to visitors who are starting to make gardens for themselves. The examples we list here are all comparatively young – a few are very new indeed. Some show what plants grow quickly: others reveal the latest ideas on design. The best will motivate you to get going in your own garden.

17 Fulham Park Gardens, London
Ashtree Cottage, Wiltshire
Bosvigo House, Cornwall
Brandy Mount House, Hampshire
Brickwall House, East Sussex
Bridgemere Garden World, Cheshire
Broadlands, Dorset
The Dingle (Crundale), Dyfed
Hazelby House, Berkshire
Lakeside, Hereford & Worcester
Lamorran House, Cornwall
North End House, Cambridgeshire
The Old Vicarage, Wiltshire
Pinewood House, Surrey
RHS Garden, Rosemoor, Devon
Sticky Wicket, Dorset
Stone House Cottage Garden, Hereford & Worcester
Thompson's Hill, Wiltshire
White Windows, Hampshire
Wolseley Garden Park, Staffordshire

Seldom Open to the Public

We often find that a garden we wanted to visit has already had its annual visitors' day. This is a checklist for some of the gardens which open seldom. If you have long nurtured the ambition to visit such gardens as Badminton, Cowdray Park or Munstead Wood, you should look up its open days in the main chapter on gardens, and make a note of the dates when it receives visitors. Then plan your other garden visiting round it.

17 Fulham Park Gardens, London
Abbotswood, Gloucestershire
Badminton, Avon
Bank House, Lancashire
Barningham Park, Co. Durham
The Beale Arboretum, Hertfordshire
Bolehyde Manor, Wiltshire
Brandy Mount House, Hampshire
Brook Lodge Farm Cottage, Surrey
Caythorpe Campus, De Monfort University, Lincolnshire
Cecily Hill House, Gloucestershire
Chyverton, Cornwall
Cowdray Park, West Sussex
Darley House, Derbyshire
Elsing Hall, Norfolk
Fairfield House, Hampshire
Faringdon House, Oxfordshire
Flintham Hall, Nottinghamshire
Folly Farm, Berkshire
Glendoick Gardens, Tayside
Great Barfield, Buckinghamshire
Greenways, Oxfordshire
Hardwicke House, Cambridgeshire
The Harris Garden, Berkshire
Hazelby House, Berkshire
Hillbarn House, Wiltshire
Long Barn, Kent
Longstock Water Gardens, Hampshire
The Manor House, Bledlow, Buckinghamshire
Mottistone Manor, Isle of Wight
Munstead Wood, Surrey
North End House, Cambridgeshire
Odell Castle, Bedfordshire
Offham House, East Sussex
Old Rectory Cottage, Berkshire
The Old Vicarage, Wiltshire
Overbury Court, Hereford & Worcester
Riseholme Hall, Lincolnshire
Shrubland Hall, Suffolk
Stancombe Park, Gloucestershire
Stonehurst, West Sussex
Tirley Garth Trust, Cheshire
White Windows, Hampshire
Wincombe Park, Wiltshire
Yew Tree Cottage, West Sussex

Garden Features

Good to Visit in the Summer Gap

It is easy for a garden to look good in May or June, but much more difficult for it to hold the visitor's interest in the dog days of August. Many people take their annual holidays then, and are mildly disappointed to discover that there are no camellias, magnolias or rhododendrons in flower at Trengwainton or Caerhays. Some gardens, however, make a point of building up to a climax of colour in late summer.

- Alton Towers, Staffordshire
- Barrington Court, Somerset
- Blickling Hall, Norfolk
- Bressingham Gardens, Norfolk
- Bridgemere Garden World, Cheshire
- Cambridge University Botanic Garden, Cambridgeshire
- The Gardens of the Rose, Hertfordshire
- Great Dixter, East Sussex
- Greenways, Oxfordshire
- Hampton Court Palace, London
- Hever Castle, Kent
- Highclere Castle, Hampshire
- Inverewe, Highland
- Kellie Castle, Fife
- Lackham Country Attractions, Wiltshire
- Leith Hall, Grampian
- Logan Botanic Gardens, Dumfries & Galloway
- Longleat House, Wiltshire
- Malleny House Garden, Lothian
- The Manor House, Walton-in-Gordano, Avon
- Marwood Hill Gardens, Devon
- Old Rectory Cottage, Berkshire
- The Old Vicarage, Wiltshire
- Powis Castle, Powys
- The Priory, Gloucestershire
- RHS Garden, Wisley, Surrey
- The Savill Garden, Surrey
- Sir Harold Hillier Gardens and Arboretum, Hampshire
- Spetchley Park, Hereford & Worcester
- Stone House Cottage Garden, Hereford & Worcester
- Stourton House, Wiltshire
- Tintinhull House, Somerset
- Trelissick Garden (Feock), Cornwall
- Tresco Abbey, Cornwall

Underrated – A Personal Choice

We have all visited gardens which were a disappointment. Sometimes, however, we are lucky to stumble on a really smashing garden which no one seems to know about. Here are some gardens we particularly want to visit again soon, and encourage others to do so too. Some are well known, but underrated, while others are little known, but undeservedly.

- Athelhampton House and Gardens, Dorset
- The Beale Arboretum, Hertfordshire
- Chenies Manor, Buckinghamshire
- Cottesbrooke Hall, Northamptonshire
- Crowe Hall, Avon
- Fairhaven Gardens Trust, Norfolk
- Galloway House Gardens, Dumfries & Galloway
- Hinton Ampner House, Hampshire
- How Caple Court, Hereford & Worcester
- Isabella Plantation, London
- Kingston Maurward Gardens, Dorset
- Lower Hall, Shropshire
- Mount Stewart, Co. Down
- Parcevall Hall Gardens, North Yorkshire
- Sleightholmedale Lodge, North Yorkshire
- Spetchley Park, Hereford & Worcester
- St Paul's Walden Bury, Hertfordshire
- Stancombe Park, Gloucestershire
- Thorp Perrow Arboretum, North Yorkshire
- Vine House, Avon
- Wrest Park, Bedfordshire

Winter Gardens

Sometimes the urge to go visiting gardens in winter is very strong, especially in late winter when the sun is higher in the sky and the first signs of new life appear. There are three types of garden worth visiting.

First are those with good glasshouse collections: most botanic gardens are therefore rewarding to explore, whatever the season or weather. Second, are those which have good collections of evergreen trees and shrubs, set off perhaps by the colour of bark and twigs: Bedgebury National Pinetum and Westonbirt Arboretum are both perfect for a brisk winter exploration. Third, there are gardens with a strong floral display in winter, particularly towards the end: such gardens as Great Barfield are thick with hellebores, crocus, *Leucojum* and many other genera, while those in milder regions have camellias, rhododendrons and the first primroses early in the year.

Some gardens qualify on all three counts, though they are few. The Royal Horticultural Society's garden at Wisley is perhaps the best example.

Abbotsbury Subtropical Gardens, Dorset
Bedgebury National Pinetum, Kent
Belsay Hall, Northumberland
Cambridge University Botanic Garden, Cambridgeshire
Canal Gardens, West Yorkshire
Castlewellan National Arboretum, Co. Down
Cliveden, Buckinghamshire
Dawyck Botanic Garden, Borders
Dunster Castle, Somerset
Elvaston Castle County Park, Derbyshire
Glasgow Botanic Garden, Strathclyde
Great Barfield, Buckinghamshire
The Harris Garden, Berkshire
Hill House Garden, Devon
Hyde Hall, Essex
Killerton, Devon
Marwood Hill Gardens, Devon
Myddelton House Gardens, London
National Botanic Gardens, Dublin, Co. Dublin, Eire
Plantasia, West Glamorgan
Port Lympne Gardens, Kent
RHS Garden, Rosemoor, Devon
RHS Garden, Wisley, Surrey
Ripley Castle, North Yorkshire
Royal Botanic Garden, Edinburgh, Lothian
Royal Botanic Gardens, Kew, London
The Savill Garden, Surrey
Sheffield Botanical Gardens, South Yorkshire
Sir Harold Hillier Gardens and Arboretum, Hampshire
St Andrews Botanic Garden, Fife
Stapeley Water Gardens Ltd, Cheshire
Trebah Garden Trust, Cornwall
Tresco Abbey, Cornwall
Ventnor Botanic Garden, Isle of Wight
Wakehurst Place, West Sussex
Westonbirt Arboretum, Gloucestershire

Awards to Gardens

In recent years two schemes for awarding recognition to gardens have started up. Both are private initiatives and, though quite different in their aims,

Holker Hall in Cumbria has had the distinction of winning the Garden of the Year Award in 1991 while also being a current holder of the Sandford Award.

The Garden of the Year Award was introduced jointly by the Historic Houses Association (HHA) and Christie's in 1984. It is designed to recognise the importance of gardens, either in their own right or as settings for historic houses. It reflects public enjoyment of those privately owned gardens which are open regularly to the public, rather than their horticultural excellence, although many winners can claim that too.

All HHA members and Friends of the HHA may vote for any garden which is owned by a member of the HHA, and open regularly to the public. Voting takes place during the course of the year and is never completed until November. Marks are awarded for features of special interest, such as recent restoration work or unusual selections of plants, trees and shrubs. The Award carries no cash prize, but the resulting publicity is helpful in raising visitor numbers. The award winners since its institution have been:

1984 Heale House, Wiltshire
1985 Hodnet Hall, Shropshire
1986 Newby Hall, North Yorkshire
1987 Arley Hall, Cheshire
1988 Barnsley House, Gloucestershire
1989 Brympton d'Evercy, Somerset
1990 Parham Park, West Sussex
1991 Holker Hall, Cumbria
1992 Forde Abbey, Dorset
1993 Haddon Hall, Derbyshire

Details of the 1994 winner will be revealed when the award is presented in spring 1995.

The Sandford Awards should be better known. They are given by the Heritage Education Trust to historic properties, in recognition of the educational facilities they offer school parties. The Trust maintains that a welcome is not enough: the trip must present an educational opportunity. The Award reflects a measure of how well adapted a house or garden is to ensure that visitors get maximum educational value. An award lasts for five years and is then reviewed. It is neither financial nor competitive, but always based on properties meeting five educational criteria:

Garden Features

1 Good liaison between the owners and potential school visitors.
2 Imagination applied to developing the educational potential.
3 The design of educational materials and facilities.
4 Encouraging preparation for a visit, managing that visit effectively and offering good follow-up.
5 The use of interpretive facilities to relate the visit to a school curriculum, and to encourage exciting and imaginative work.

The Heritage Education Trust is principally concerned with historic buildings. It follows that a property can get an award even though it does not use its garden for educational purposes. In practice that happens rarely: educational facilities are usually offered both inside and outside the house.

Two or three properties with gardens receive a Sandford Award every year. Current holders include the following:

Blenheim Palace, Oxfordshire
Boughton House, Northamptonshire
Crathes Castle, Grampian
Drumlarig Castle, Dumfries & Galloway
Erdigg Hall, Clwyd
Harewood House, West Yorkshire
Holdenby House, Northamptonshire
Holker Hall, Cumbria
Kingston Lacey, Dorset
Moseley Old Hall, Staffordshire
Norton Priory, Cheshire
Rockingham Castle, Northamptonshire
Shugborough Hall, Staffordshire
Sir Harold Hillier Gardens, Hampshire
Tatton Park, Cheshire
Wightwick Manor, Isle of Wight
Wimpole Hall, Cambridgeshire

The places which have given thought to the educational needs of visiting children are just as interesting for adults. It saves a great amount of disappointment if everyone can be sure that the place will be well equipped. The presence of a Sandford Award is a guarantee that all manner of educational aids will be available for you to learn more from your visit and thus to enjoy it more fully.

Further details are available from: The Heritage Education Trust, The University College of Ripon and York St John, College Road, Ripon HG4 2QX. Secretary: Martyn Dyer.

17

English Heritage Garden Grades

During the 1980s, the *Historic Buildings and Monuments Commission* for England compiled a register of gardens and parks of special historic interest. The aim was to draw attention to the nation's heritage, so that designed landscapes were not overlooked, for example in plans for new development. The register was largely the work of the distinguished garden historian Dr Christopher Thacker. There are three gradings:

Grade I – Parks and gardens which by reason of their historic layout, features and architectural ornaments considered together are of exceptional interest.

Grade II* – Parks and gardens which by reason of their historic layout, features and architectural ornaments considered together are, if not of exceptional interest, nevertheless of great quality.

Grade II – Parks and gardens which by reason of their historic layout, features and architectural ornaments considered together are of special interest.

These gradings reflect the importance of the garden or park concerned in comparison with other gardens or parks in England as a whole. They are not influenced by the presence of a listed building within the limits of a registered garden or park. If there is such a listed building, its grade may not necessarily be the same, since the building and the garden or park are seldom of equal importance. The register introduced no new regulations and had no effect upon existing planning or building controls.

Only gardens and parks with historic features dating from 1939 or earlier were included in the register. Additions since that date were of no account, because the register was only concerned with a garden's historic interest. In practice that rule was sometimes broken in the case of an influential modern garden: Great Dixter and East Lambrook Manor might not have merited Grade I status in 1939. Parks and gardens differ enormously: a public square or a municipal cemetery may be more important than a good Victorian collection of trees. It has also been suggested that gradings were influenced by the park or garden's actual state and condition.

In the 1994 edition of *The Gardener's Yearbook* we listed only the Grade I and II* gardens. This year we have also included the Grade II gardens, so the list is now as complete as it can be. The register is not closed, but updated from time to time to take account of new knowledge that has come to light since the individual parts were completed. There have been additions to the register as well as upgrades of existing entries. Many graded parks and gardens are open to the public and appear in the main Gardens section of this book, but many others are in private ownership. The Commission was at pains to emphasise that including a garden in the register did not mean that there was any public right of access, other than along public rights of way. That remains the position today.

The register is in forty-six parts, one for each English county: we have shown Cleveland as the separate county it was at the time of the survey. Copies are available from English Heritage, Fortress

English Heritage Garden Grades

House, 23 Savile Row, London W1X 2HE at a price of £3.50 or £4 per county. The information they contain about the individual gardens is very comprehensive. It covers the site; area; dates and designers of key surviving elements; surviving features of the garden or park; and other interesting aspects such as historic associations. There is also a list of published references.

Cadw, the Welsh Historic Monuments Commission, has begun a Register of Parks and Gardens of Special Historic Interest in Wales, with aid from ICOMOS. The Register is similar to English Heritage's and the criteria for selection and grading are comparable. The Register for Gwent was published last year and copies are available from Cadw at a price of £15. The Register for Clwyd will probably be available early this year. Cadw aims to complete the whole of Wales by the end of next year.

Avon
Grade I
- Badminton
- Prior Park

Grade II*
- Ashton Court
- Blaise Hamlet
- Clevedon Court
- Dodington House
- Dyrham Park
- Goldney House
- St Catherine's Court
- Tyntesfield

Grade II
- Arno's Vale Cemetery
- Barrow Court
- Beckford's Ride
- Blaise Castle
- Brenby House
- Claverton Manor
- Crowe Hall
- Kelston Place
- King's Weston
- Leigh Court
- Newton Park
- Oldbury Court
- Rayne Thatch
- Royal Victoria Park
- Stoke Park
- Sydney Gardens
- Thornbury Castle
- Tortworth Park
- Warmley House
- Widcombe Manor

Bedfordshire
Grade I
- Woburn Abbey
- Wrest Park

Grade II*
- Luton Hoo
- Swiss Garden
- Southill Park

Grade II
- Ampthil Park
- Battlesden Place
- Bushmead Priory
- Chicksands
- Flitwick Manor
- The Hasells
- Hinwick Hall
- Hinwick House
- Ickwell Bury
- The Lodge, Sandy

Berkshire
Grade I
- Windsor Great Park

Grade II*
- Ascot Place
- Bearwood College
- The Deanery, Sonning
- Folly Farm
- Frogmore Gardens
- Inkpen House
- Park Place
- Purley Hall

Grade II
- Aldermaston Court
- Basildon Park
- Benham Park
- Caversham Court
- Caversham Park
- Donnington Grove
- Englefield House
- Eton College
- Farley Hall
- Forbury Garden, Reading
- Hamstead Marshall
- Newbold College
- Prospect Place, Reading
- Sandleford Priory
- South Hill Park
- Swallowfield
- Wasing Park

Buckinghamshire
Grade I
- Cliveden
- Stowe
- West Wycombe Park

Grade II*
- Ascott
- Bulstrode Park
- Chenies Place
- Chicheley Hall
- Fawley Court
- Hall Barn
- Hartwell House
- Shardeloes
- Tyringham
- Waddesdon Manor
- Wotton Underwood

Grade II
- Berry Hill
- Chequers
- Claydon
- Denhams Place
- Dropmore
- Gayhurst Court
- Halton House
- Harleyford
- Hughenden
- Huntercombe Manor
- Langley Park
- Latimer Park
- Mentmore Towers

Milton's Cottage
Misserden Abbey
Nashdom Abbey
Taplow Court
Wycombe Abbey

Cambridgeshire
Grade I
   The Backs
   Wimpole Hall
Grade II*
   Anglesey Abbey
   Botanic Gardens, Cambridge
   Burghley House
   Childerley Hall
   Christ's College
   Elton Hall
   Emmanuel College
   King's College
   Longstowe Hall
   Milton Hall
   St John's College
   Thorpe Hall
   Trinity College
Grade II
   Abbots Ripton Hall
   Bourn Hall
   Chippenham
   Croxton Park
   Dullingham
   Gamlingay
   Hamerton
   Hatley Park
   Hilton Maze
   Leighton Bromswold
   Hadingley Hall
   Pampisford Hall
   Peckover House
   Queen's College
   Sawston Hall
   Swaffham Hall
   Trinity Hall
   Wilbraham Temple

Cheshire
Grade II*
   Adlington Hall
   Arley Hall
   Eaton Hall
   Gawsworth Hall
   Lyme Park
   Tatton Park
Grade II
   Cholmondeley Castle
   Combermere Abbey
   Crewe Hall
   Doddington Park
   Dorfold Hall
   Ness Botanic Gardens
   Peover Hall
   Rode Hall
   Tabley House

Cleveland
Grade II*
   Wynyard Park
Grade II
   Albert Park

Cornwall
Grade I
   Mount Edgcumbe
   Port Eliot
   Tresco
Grade II*
   Boconnoc
   Caerhays Castle
   Lanhydrock
   Tregothnan
   Tregrehan
   Trewithen
Grade II
   Antony
   Carclew
   Chyverton Park
   Cotehele
   Glendurgan
   Heligan
   Lamellen
   Menabilly
   Pencarrow
   Penheale
   Penjerrick
   Prideaux Place
   St Michael's Mount
   Trebah
   Trelissick
   Trengwainton
   Trewarthenick
   Werrington

Cumbria
Grade I
   Levens Hall
Grade II*
   Appleby Castle
   Belle Isle
   Dalemain
   Holker Hall
   Muncaster Castle
   Sizergh Castle
Grade II
   Askham Hall
   Corby Castle
   Dallam Tower
   Hutton-in-the-Forest
   Lowther Castle
   The Image Garden, Reagill
   Rydal Hall
   Rydal Mount
   Workington Hall

Derbyshire
Grade I
   Chatsworth
   Haddon Hall
   Hardwick Hall
   Kedleston Hall
   Melbourne Hall
Grade II*
   Bolsover Castle
   Buxton Pavilion Gardens
   Calke Abbey
   Derby Arboretum
   Elvaston Castle
   Heights of Abraham
   Renishaw Hall
   Swarkstone Hall
Grade II
   Ednaston Manor
   Locko Park
   Sudbury Hall

Devon
Grade I
   Bicton
   Endsleigh
Grade II*
   Castle Drogo
   Castle Hill
   Dartington Hall
   Killerton

English Heritage Garden Grades

Knighthayes Court
Lindridge
Luscombe Castle
Mamhead
Saltram House
Tapeley Park
Ugbrooke Park
Wood House
Grade II
   A la Ronde
   Arlington Court
   Bridwell
   Cadhay
   Castle Tor
   Coleton Fishacre
   Combe House
   Flete
   Hayne Manor
   Langdon Court Hotel
   Lupton Park
   Overbecks
   Powderham Castle
   Rockbeare House
   Ranston
   Saunton Court
   Shobrooke Park
   Sydenham House
   Watcombe Park
   Youlston Park

Dorset
Grade I
   Abbotsbury Gardens
   Athelhampton
Grade II*
   Chantmarle
   Charborough Park
   Compton Acres
   Cranborne Manor
   Creech Grange
   Eastbury
   Encombe
   Forde Abbey
   Kingston Maurwood
   Mapperton House
   Melbury Park
   Milton Abbey
   Parnham
   St Giles' House
   Sherborne Castle

Pleasure Gardens, Bournemouth
Grade II
   Anderson Manor
   Beaminster Manor
   Boveridge House School
   Bridehead
   Crichell House
   Kingston Lacy
   Lulworth Castle
   Minterne
   Waterston Manor
   Wimborne Road Cemetery, Bournemouth

Co. Durham
Grade II*
   Raby Castle
   Rokeby Park
Grade II
   Auckland Castle Park
   Bowes Museum
   Brancepeth Castle
   Hardwick Park
   Lartington Hall

Essex
Grade I
   Audley End
   Braxted Park
Grade II*
   Bridge End Gardens
   Copped Hall
   Thorndon Park
Grade II
   Belchamp Hall
   Belhus Park
   Blake Hall
   Boreham House
   Colchester Castle Park
   Danbury Park
   Down Hall
   Faulkbourne Hall
   Glazenwood
   Gosfield Hall
   Hatfield Priory
   Hill Hall
   Hylands Park
   Langleys
   Layer Marney Tower
   The Maze, Saffron Walden

New Hall, Boreham
Quendon Park
Riffhams
St Osyth Priory
Saling Grove
Saling Hall
Shortgrove Park
Spains Hall
Terling Place
Thorpe Hall
Warley Place
Weald Park
Water Garden, Harlow
Wivenhoe House

Gloucestershire
Grade I
   Batsford Park
   Cirencester Park
   Frampton Court
   Hidcote Manor
   Sezincote
   Stancombe Park
   Stanway House
   Westonbirt Arboretum
   Westonbirt House
Grade II*
   Abbotswood
   Barnsley Park
   Berkeley Castle
   Cowley Manor
   Daylesford House
   Highnam Court
   Lypiatt Park
   Miserden Park
   Painswick House
   Rodmarton Manor
   Sudeley Castle
   Westbury Court
Grade II
   Adlestrop Hall
   Adlestrop Park
   Alderley Grange
   Alderley Mount
   Barrington Park
   Bourton House
   Bradley Court
   Chavenage House
   Clearwell Castle
   Dixton Manor
   Eyford Park

384 English Heritage Garden Grades

Flaxley Abbey
Gatcombe Park
Great Rissington Manor
Hatherop Castle
Church House, Lechlade
Lodge Park
Nether Lypiatt Manor
Newark Park
Notgrove Manor
Owlpen Manor
St Mary's, Painswick
Pinbury Park
Pittville Park
Sherborne House
Snowshill Manor
Stowell Park
Toddington Manor
Woodchester Park

Greater London
Grade I
  Bushy Park
  Chelsea Physic Garden
  Chiswick House
  Greenwick Place
  Hampton Court
  Hyde Park
  Kensington Gardens
  Kew Gardens
  Regent's Park
  Richmond Park
  St James's Park
  Syon Park
Grade II*
  Battersea Park
  Bedford Square
  Belair
  Buckingham Palace Gardens
  Cannizaro Park
  City of London Cemetery
  Crystal Palace Park
  Dulwich Park
  Fulham Palace
  Gray's Inn
  Grovelands
  Hall Place
  Ham House
  Highgate Cemetery
  The Hill
  Kensal Green Cemetery
  Kenwood

Lambeth Palace
Lincoln's Inn Fields
Marble Hill
Osterley Park
St George's Gardens
Victoria Embankment
  Gardens
Victoria Park
Waterlow Park
Wimbledon Park
Grade II
  Abney Park Cemetery
  Addington Palace
  Belgrave Square
  Berkeley Square
  Bloomsbury Square
  The Boltons
  Brockwell Park
  Brompton Cemetery
  Broomfield House
  Cadogan Place
  100 Cheyne Walk
  Clissold Park
  Coram's Fields
  Danson Park
  Down House
  Eaton Square
  Eccleston Square
  Edwardes Square
  Finsbury Park
  Foots Cray Park
  Garrick's Villa
  Green Park
  Grosvenor Square
  Grove House
  Gunnersbury Park
  Hampton Court House
  Hans Place
  Hogarth's House
  Holland Park
  Holwood Park
  Horniman Gardens
  Island Gardens
  Keats' House
  Kennington Park
  King George's Park
  Ladbroke Square
  Lamorbey Park
  Manchester Square
  Manor House Gardens

Myatt's Fields
Myddelton House
Norwood Grove
Nunhead Cemetery
Peckham Rye Park
Pope's Grotto
Portman Square
Putney Vale Cemetery
The Rookery, Streatham
Royal Hospital, Chelsea
Ruskin Park
Russell Square
St James's Square
St Luke's Gardens, Chelsea
St Marylebone Cemetery
St Michael's Convent
St Pancras Gardens
St Peter's Square
Southwark Park
Springfield Park
Strawberry Hill
Strawberry House
Sundridge Park
The Temple
Trent Park
Valentine Park
Victoria Tower Gardens
Walpole House
Walpole Park
Wandsworth Park
Wanstead Park
Warwick Square
Well Hall
West Norwood Cemetery

Greater Manchester
Grade II*
  Dunham Massey
Grade II
  Haigh Hall
  Heaton Park
  Philips Park
  Stamford Park
  Wythenshaw Park

Hampshire
Grade I
  Hackwood Park
  Highclere Park
Grade II*
  Avington Park

Bramshill Park
Compton End
Cranbury Park
Exbury House
Houghton Lodge
Lainston House
Leigh Park
March Court
Moundsmere Manor
Pylewell Park
Tylney Hall
The Wakes
Warbrook House

Grade II
Amport Park
Basing House
Bramdean House
Breamore
Broadlands
Brockenhurst Park
Cadland House
Chawton House
Dogmersfield Park
Elvetham Hall
Embley Park
The Grange, Northington
Hale Park
Hurstbourne Park
Laverstock Park
Little Boarhunt
Manor House, Upton Grey
Old Alresford House
Rhinefield
Rotherfield Park
Stratfield Saye Park
Stratton Park
Townhill Park
Victoria Park, Portsmouth
The Vyne

Hereford & Worcester
Grade I
Croome Court
Hagley Hall

Grade II*
Berrington Hall
Croft Castle
Downton Castle
Eastnor Castle
Garnons
Hergest Croft

Holme Lacey
Kentchurch Court
Madresfield Court
Moccas Court
Overbury Court
Rous Lench Court
Spetchley Park
Sufton Court
Witley Court

Grade II
Arley House
Brampton Bryan
Brockhampton Park
Broxwood Court
The Manor House,
  Cleeve Prior
Eywood
Foxley
Gatley
Hanbury Hall
Hartlebury Castle
Hewell Grange
Homme House
Hope End
Kyre Park
Shobdon
Springhill House
Stoke Edith
Westwood Park
Whitfield

Hertfordshire
Grade I
Hatfield House
St Paul's Walden Bury

Grade II*
Ashridge
Bayfordbury
The Garden House, Cottered
Knebworth
Moor Park
Panshanger
Putteridge Bury
Scott's Grotto
Youngsbury

Grade II
Aldenham House
Amwell Grange
Ashwell Bury
Ayot House
Balls Park

Benington Lordship
Broadway, Letchworth
Brocket Hall
Cassiobury Park
Cokehatch
Fanhams Hall
Gobions
Gorhambury
Hexton Manor
Homewood, Knebworth
The Hoo, Kimpton
Howard Park, Letchworth
Julians
Markyatecell Park
Pishiobury
Poles Park
Stanstead Bury
Temple Dinsley
Tewin Water
Tring Park
Woodhall Park
Wormleybury
Wrotham Park

Humberside
Grade I
Sledmere House

Grade II*
Londesborough Park

Grade II
Burton Constable
Dalton Hall
Houghton Hall
Thwaite Hall

Isle of Wight
Grade II*
Osborne

Grade II
Appuldurcombe
Norris Castle
Nunwell
Swainston
Westover

Kent
Grade I
Godington Park
Hever Castle
Knole
Penshurst Place
Scotney Castle

386 English Heritage Garden Grades

    Sissinghurst Castle
Grade II*
    Chartwell
    Chevening
    Chilham Castle
    Cobham Hall
    Combe Bank
    Godmersham Park
    Goodnestone Park
    Groombridge Place
    Hall Place
    Japanese Garden,
      Bitchet Wood
    Leeds Castle
    Linton Park
    Long Barn
    Mereworth Castle
    Northbourne Court
    Port Lympne
Grade II
    Bayham Abbey
    Belmont Park
    Benenden
    Boughton Place
    Calverley Park
    Chatham Dockyards
    Chiddingstone Castle
    Chilston Park
    Doddington Place
    Emmets Garden
    Franks Hall
    Great Maytham
    Hush Heath Manor
    Ightham Court
    Lees Court
    Mount Ephraim
    Olantigh Towers
    Redleaf
    Riverhill House
    The Salutation
    Sandling Park
    Sissinghurst Court
    Somerhill
    Squerryes Court
    Stonewall Park
    Waldershare Park
    Walmer Castle

Lancashire
Grade II*
    Stanley Park
    Stonyhurst College
Grade II
    Ashton Memorial Gardens
    Astley Hall
    Avenham Park
    Capernwray Hall
    Cuerden Hall
    Gawthorpe Hall
    Hoghton Tower
    Lever Park
    Lytham Hall
    Rivington Gardens
    Scarisbrick Hall
    Towneley Park
    Worden Park

Leicestershire
Grade II*
    Coleorton Hall
    Staunton Harold Hall
Grade II
    Abbey Park, Leicester
    Baggrave Hall
    Belvoir Castle
    Bradgate Park
    Burley on the Hill
    Exton Park
    Garendon
    Langton Hall
    Lowesby Hall
    New Walk, Leicester
    Prestwold Hall
    Quenby Hall
    Stamford Hall
    Stapleford Hall
    Victoria Park, Leicester
    Whatton House

Lincolnshire
Grade I
    Belton House
    Brocklesby Park
    Grimsthorpe Castle
Grade II*
    Doddington Hall
    Harlaxton Manor
Grade II
    Aynscoughfee Hall
    Boultham Park
    Caythorpe Court
    Coleby Hall
    Culverthorpe Hall
    Easton Park
    Fillingham Castle
    Gunby Hall
    Hackthorn Hall
    Hainton Hall
    Harrington Hall
    Hartholme Park
    Lincoln Arboretum
    Marston Hall
    Rauceby Hall
    Revesby Abbey
    Riseholme Hall
    Scrivelsby Court
    Stoke Rochford Hall
    Well Hall

Merseyside
Grade I
    Birkenhead Park
Grade II*
    Ince Blundell Hall
    Sefton Park, Liverpool
Grade II
    Anfield Cemetery
    Botanic Gardens, Southport
    Hesketh Park, Southport
    Knowsley Hall
    Prince's Park, Liverpool
    Speke Hall
    Stanley Park, Liverpool
    Thornton Manor
    Windle Hall

Norfolk
Grade I
    Holkham Hall
    Houghton Hall
Grade II*
    Felbrigg Hall
    Gunton Park
    Kimberley Hall
    Melton Constable Hall
    The Pleasaunce, Overstrand
    Sandringham House
    Sheringham Hall
Grade II
    Barningham Hall
    Beeston Hall
    Breccles Hall
    Catton Hall

English Heritage Garden Grades

Elmham Hall
Hanworth Hall
Heydon Hall
Honing Hall
Hunstanton Hall
Intwood Hall
Langley Park
Lexham Hall
Lynford Hall
Mannington Hall
Narford Hall
The Old Rectory, Lyng
Oxburgh Hall
Pickenham Hall
Plantation Garden, Norwich
Rainthorpe Hall
Raveningham Hall
Raynham Park
Salle Park
Sennowe Hall
Shadwell Park
Stiffkey Old Hall
Stradsett Hall
Wolterton Hall

Northamptonshire
Grade I
    Althorp
    Boughton House
    Castle Ashby
    Drayton House
Grade II*
    Canons Ashby
    Easton Neston
    Great Harrowden Hall
    Harrington
    Holdenby House
    Kirby Hall
    Lyveden New Bield
    Rockingham Castle
Grade II
    Ashby St Ledgers
    Aynhoe Park
    Barnwell Manor
    Cottesbrooke Hall
    Courteenhall
    Deene Park
    Fawsley
    Lamport Hall
    Stoke Park
    Sulgrave Manor

Northumberland
Grade I
    Alnwick Castle
    Belsay Hall
Grade II*
    Cragside
    Seaton Delaval
    Wallington
Grade II
    Blagdon
    Chillingham
    Hesleyside
    Howick
    Kirkharle Hall
    Lindisfarne Castle
    Nunwick
    Tillmouth Park

Nottinghamshire
Grade I
    Clumber Park
    Newstead Abbey
    Thoresby Park
Grade II*
    Annesley Hall
    Flintham Hall
    Papplewick Hall
    Shireoaks Hall
Grade II
    Babworth Hall
    Holme Pierrepont Hall
    Nottingham Arboretum
    Rufford Abbey
    Welbeck Abbey

Oxfordshire
Grade I
    Blenheim Palace
    Christ Church
    Magdalen College
    New College
    Nuneham Courtney
    Oxford Botanic Garden
    Rousham
    Shotover
    Stonor
Grade II*
    Ashdown House
    Beckley Park
    Broughton Castle
    Buckland House

    Buscot
    Chastleton House
    Cornbury
    Corpus Christi
    Ditchley
    Garsington Manor
    Greys Court
    Heythrop College
    Merton College
    St Hugh's College
    St John's College
    Sarsden House
    Tackley
    Trinity College
    Worcester College
    Wroxton Abbey
Grade II
    Ascott
    Compton Beauchamp
    Cornwell Manor
    Friar Park
    Hinton Manor
    Kiddington Hall
    Pusey House
    Sandford House
    Shirburn Castle
    Sutton Courtenay Manor
    Swerford
    Yarnton Manor

Shropshire
Grade I
    Hawkstone
Grade II*
    Attingham Park
    Davenport House
    Ludstone Hall
    Millicope Hall
Grade II
    Acton Burnell
    Albrighton Hall
    Aldenham Park
    Badger Dingle
    Boscobel House
    Burwarton House
    Chetwynd Park
    Condover Hall
    Court of Hill
    Dudmaston
    Ferney Hall
    Hatton Grange

English Heritage Garden Grades

Henley Hall
Hodnet Hall
Lilleshall Hall
Linley Hall
Longner Hall
Oakly Park
Orleton Hall
Pitchford Hall
Pradoe
Quarry Park
Wenlock Abbey

Somerset
Grade I
Dunster Castle
East Lambrook
Hestercombe
Mells Manor
Montacute House
Grade II*
Ammerdown House
Barrington Court
Barwick Park
Brympton d'Evercy
The Chantry
Cricket House
Nynehead Court
Orchardleigh
Grade II
Babington House
Bishop's Palace, Wells
Burton Pynsent
Cothelstone Manor
Crowcombe Court
The Deanery, Wells
Fairfield
Halswell Park
Hatch Court
Hazelgrove House
Hinton House
Lytes Cary
Marston House
Mells Park
Nettlecombe Park
Newton Surmaville
Pundisford Park
Redlynch Park
St Audries
Ston Easton Park
Tintinhull House
Ven House

Wayford Manor

Staffordshire
Grade I
Alton Towers
Biddulph Grange
Shugborough
Grade II*
Chillington
Enville
Trentham Park
Weston Park
Grade II
Keele Hall
Sandon Park
Patshull Hall

Suffolk
Grade I
Helmingham Hall
Shrubland Park
Grade II*
Campsey Ashe Park
Euston Park
Heveningham Park
Ickworth Park
Kentwell Hall
Melford Hall
Somerleyton Park
Trinity Hospital
Grade II
Chantry Park
Chilton Hall
Christchurch Mansion
Culford Park
Henham
Tendring Hall Park

Surrey
Grade I
Albury Park
Claremont
Munstead Wood
Painshill
Savill Garden
Virginia Water
Grade II*
Busbridge Lakes
Orchards
Polesden Lacey
St Ann's Hill
Wisley Gardens

Wotton
Grade II
Clandon
The Deepdene
Great Fosters
Greathed Manor
Hethersett
Merrow Grange
Moor Park
Norbury Park
Oatlands
Pyrford Court
Reigate Priory
Titsey Place
Vann
Woodburn

East Sussex
Grade I
Great Dixter
Sheffield Park
Grade II*
Brickwall
Charleston Manor
Eridge Park
Glynde Place
Herstmonceux Castle
The Hoo
Penns in the Rocks
Rotherfield Hall
Grade II
Ashburnham Place
Batemans
Battle Abbey
Bayham Abbey
Brightling Park
Buckhurst Park
Buxted Park
Compton Place
Cotchford Farm
Firle Place
Hammerwood Park
Heathfield Park
Kidbrooke Park
Newick Park
Old Buckhurst
Plumpton Place
Preston Manor
Royal Pavilion, Brighton
Wych Cross Place

English Heritage Garden Grades

West Sussex
Grade I
- Goodwood House
- Leonardslee
- Parham
- Petworth House
- Stansted Park

Grade II*
- Arundel Castle
- Borde Hill
- Brockhurst
- Cowdray House
- Gravetye Manor
- Highdown
- Hollycombe House
- Little Thakeham
- Nymans
- Uppark
- Wakehurst Place
- West Dean

Grade II
- Bignor Park
- Blackdown House
- Burton Park
- Cooke's House
- Heaselands
- The High Beeches
- Knepp Castle
- Lavington Park
- Pitshill
- Rymans
- Slaugham Place
- Stonehurst

Tyne & Wear
Grade II
- Gibside

Grade II
- Axwell Park
- Bradley Park
- Jesmond Dene
- Leazes Park
- Newcastle General Cemetery
- Saltwell Park

Warwickshire
Grade I
- Compton Verney
- Farnborough Hall
- Packwood House
- Warwick Castle

Grade II*
- Arbury Hall
- Baddesley Clinton Hall
- Charlecote Park
- Combe Abbey
- Honington Hall
- Radway Grange
- Ragley Hall
- Upton House

Grade II
- Alscot Park
- Anne Hathaway's Cottage
- Clifford Manor
- Jephson Gardens
- Kenilworth Castle
- Merevale Hall
- Newnham Paddox
- Shakespeare Gardens
- Packington Hall
- Stoneleigh Abbey
- Wooton Hall
- Wroxhall Abbey

West Midlands
Grade I
- The Leasowes

Grade II*
- Birmingham Botanical Gardens
- Castle Bromwich Hall

Grade II
- Aston Hall
- Edgbaston Hall
- Great Barr House
- Highbury Hall
- London Road Cemetery, Coventry
- West Park

Wiltshire
Grade I
- Bowood House
- Iford Manor
- Longleat House
- Stourhead
- Wilton House

Grade II*
- Amesbury Abbey
- Belcombe Court
- Corsham Court
- Fonthill
- Heale House
- Larmer Tree Gardens
- Longford Castle
- The Moot, Downton
- Tottenham Park
- Wardour Castle

Grade II
- Biddesden House
- Conock Manor
- The Courts, Holt
- Dinton House
- Great Chalfield Manor
- The Hall, Bradford-n-von
- Hatch House
- Hazelbury Manor
- Lacock Abbey
- Lake House
- Littlecote House
- Lydiard Park
- Marlborough College
- North Canonry
- Oare House
- Ramsbury Manor
- Rushmoor Park
- Sheldon Manor
- Trafalgar House
- Wilbury House

North Yorkshire
Grade I
- Castle Howard
- Duncombe Park
- Forcett Hall
- Hackfall
- Rievaulx Terrace
- Studley Royal

Grade II*
- Aske Hall
- Ebberston Hall
- Mulgrave Castle
- Newby Hall
- Plumpton Rocks
- St Nicholas, Richmond
- Scampston Hall

Grade II
- Aldby Park
- Allerton Park
- Beningbrough Hall
- Broughton Hall
- Constable Burton Hall
- Gilling Castle

English Heritage Garden Grades

Museum Gardens, York
Newburgh Priory
Norton Conyers
Nun Appleton Hall
Nunnington Hall
Ribston Hall
Ripley Castle
Rudding Park
Swinton Castle
Thorpe Perrow
Valley Gardens, Harrogate

South Yorkshire
Grade I
Wentworth Castle

Grade II*
Sandbeck Park
Wentworth Woodhouse
Grade II
Brodsworth Hall
Cusworth Hall
Hickleton Hall
Wortley Hall

West Yorkshire
Grade I
Bramham Park
Harewood House
Grade II*
Nostell Priory

Oulton Hall
People's Park, Halifax
Grade II
Bretton Hall
Heathcote
Ledston Hall & Park
Lister Park
Lotherton Hall
Roundhay Park
Saltaise Park
Temple Newsam

18

Garden Supplies

A E Headen Ltd
218 High Street, Potters Bar, Hertfordshire EN6 5BJ
☎ 01707 652688

CONTACT Sales Department
PRODUCTS Greenhouses
CATALOGUE On request
MAIL ORDER Yes

Makers of aluminium greenhouses and accessories. Delivery is included for most of the UK.

A T Lee & Co Ltd
32 New Broadway, Tarring Road, Worthing, West Sussex BN11 4HP
☎ 01903 210225 FAX 01903 821936

CONTACT Doreen Teale
PRODUCTS Plant hangers; hanging bags
CATALOGUE On request
MAIL ORDER Yes

Suppliers of plant pot hangers, and hanging growing bags.

Access Garden Products
17 Yelvertoft Road, Crick, Northampton, Northamptonshire NN6 7XS
☎ 01788 822301 FAX 01788 824356

CONTACT Sales Department
PRODUCTS Mini greenhouses; frames; watering systems
NEW PRODUCTS 12" deep mini greenhouse
CATALOGUE On request
MAIL ORDER Yes

Established family firm supplying high-quality aluminium frames and mini greenhouses. They also have a complete range of watering and irrigation systems. Access Irrigation Ltd (01788 823811) supplies sprinkler systems to nurseries and garden centres.

Advancalux
Johnson Street, Southall, London UB2 5DA
☎ 0181 571 7788 FAX 0181 574 1186
PRODUCTS Watering cans
NEW PRODUCTS Green Grecian urns
CATALOGUE Yes

Manufacturers of watering and petrol cans, Grecian urns and tile trim.

Allen Power Equipment Ltd
The Broadway, Didcot, Oxfordshire OX11 8ES
☎ 01235 813936 FAX 01235 811491

CONTACT Lance Bassett
PRODUCTS Garden machinery
NEW PRODUCTS Turf Trooper 60-inch triple mower
CATALOGUE On request
MAIL ORDER Yes

Manufacturers of sprayers, brush and hedge cutters, shredders, hovermowers, and rotary and cylinder garden tractors. They also sell the Echo GB range of powered hand tools.

Alton Greenhouses
Station Works, Fenny Compton, Leamington Spa, Warwickshire CV33 0XB
☎ 01295 770795 FAX 01295 770819

CONTACT Grahame Lester
PRODUCTS Greenhouses
CATALOGUE On request (0800 269850)
MAIL ORDER Yes

Long-established firm producing traditional greenhouses in red cedarwood. They claim superior strength and heat retention over aluminium products.

Anderson & Firmin Ltd
43-4 Hirwaun Industrial Estate, Hirwaun, Aberdare, Mid Glamorgan CF44 9UP
☎ 01685 814000 FAX 01685 814057

CONTACT Mandy Davis
PRODUCTS Garden gloves and footwear; garden sundries; irrigation systems
CATALOGUE On request from Sales Office
MAIL ORDER No

Garden gloves, shoes and boots, garden twine and masses of garden sundries. Distributors of Claber hoses and irrigation systems.

392 Garden Supplies

Andreas Stihl Ltd
Stihl House, Stanhope Road, Camberley, Surrey
GU15 3YT
☎ 01276 20202   FAX 01276 670502
PRODUCTS Garden machinery; lawnmowers and tractors; power tools
CATALOGUE Yes

Stihl manufacture a comprehensive range of chainsaws, brush cutters and hedge trimmers. Viking, their garden division, make lawnmowers, ride-on mowers, shredders, sweepers and cultivators.

Andrew Crace Designs
90 Bourne Lane, Much Hadham, Hertfordshire
SG10 6ER
☎ 01279 842685   FAX 01279 843646
PRODUCTS Plant labels; garden furniture; terracotta pots; garden statuary
CATALOGUE On request
MAIL ORDER Yes

The eclectic collection includes 'Alitag' aluminium plant labels, stylish wooden garden furniture and gazebos. Also bronze sculptures, terracotta pots and bamboo cloches.

Aqua-Soil Products Ltd
Blue Waters Estate, Bovey Tracey, Devon TQ13 9YF
☎ 01626 835135
CONTACT B. K. Read
PRODUCTS Aquatic products; fertilisers
NEW PRODUCTS Decorative biological filter and filter medium
CATALOGUE No
MAIL ORDER No

Manufacturers of products for water gardening including special soils, slow-release fertiliser pellets and filters.

Architectural Heritage Ltd
Taddington Manor, Taddington, Cutsdean, Cheltenham, Gloucestershire GL54 5RY
☎ 01386 584414   FAX 01386 584414
CONTACT Nina Ziegler
PRODUCTS Garden statuary
CATALOGUE On request
MAIL ORDER No

Suppliers of antique garden statuary and reproduction statues. They ship worldwide and can also provide insurance valuations (£50 plus VAT). Interior panelling and fire surrounds also stocked.

Arti Flora
Hanover House, Hook Norton, Oxfordshire
OX15 5NF
☎ 01608 737777   FAX 01608 737983
CONTACT Kris C. Doms
PRODUCTS Silk plants and trees
NEW PRODUCTS Silk fruit trees
CATALOGUE Trade only

Importers of silk plants and trees.

B J Crafts
17 Coopers Wood, Crowborough, East Sussex
TN6 1SW
☎ 01892 655899
CONTACT B. R. or I. J. Welbury
PRODUCTS Water-colours
CATALOGUE On request
MAIL ORDER Yes

Original water-colours of flowers from miniatures to larger compositions.

Barralets of Ealing
Pitshanger Lane, Ealing, London W5 1RH
☎ 0181 997 0576
CONTACT Derek Barralet
PRODUCTS Garden sundries
CATALOGUE No
MAIL ORDER Yes

Garden centre and garden shop which also does mail order.

BCS Tracmaster Ltd
Teknol House, Victoria Road, Burgess Hill, West Sussex RH15 9QF
☎ 01444 247689   FAX 01444 871612
CONTACT Chris Trull
PRODUCTS Garden machinery
NEW PRODUCTS Shredder-chippers
CATALOGUE On request
MAIL ORDER Yes

Suppliers of heavy-duty two-wheeled tractors which handle tasks from grass cutting and cultivating, to trailer towing and snow blowing. Shredder-chippers are a new addition.

Bel Mondo Garden Features
11 Tatnell Road, Honor Oak Park, London SE23 1JX
☎ 0181 291 1920
CONTACT Jamie Ripman
PRODUCTS Fountains; decorative taps and water spouts
NEW PRODUCTS New designs
CATALOGUE On request
MAIL ORDER Yes

Attractive cast iron fountains, wall basins and decorative taps and spouts.

Biotal Industrial Products Ltd
Belasis Business Centre, Coxwold Way, Billingham, Cleveland TS23 4EA
☎ 01642 343437   FAX 01642 343438
CONTACT Eileen Dowdie
PRODUCTS Biological products
CATALOGUE Leaflets
MAIL ORDER No

Biological compost makers and general range of biological products.

Garden Supplies

The birdhouse company
Bartra, Harbour Road, Dalkey, Co. Dublin
☎ 00 353 1 280 1936   FAX 00 353 1 280 0743

CONTACT Simone Stephenson
PRODUCTS Bird houses
NEW PRODUCTS Nesting boxes
CATALOGUE On request
MAIL ORDER Yes

Distinctive hand-painted wooden bird houses.

The Birdtable Company
1 Evendine Corner, Colwall, Malvern, Hereford & Worcester WR1 6DY
☎ 01684 540370   FAX 01684 540370

CONTACT Suzanne Wilesmith
PRODUCTS Dovecotes and bird tables
NEW PRODUCTS Stencilled nesting boxes
CATALOGUE On request

Makers of bird tables, nesting boxes and dovecotes: the GLEE 1994 New Product of the Year Award was given to their wall-mounted box.

Blackwall Products
Unit 1-4, Riverside Industrial Estate, 150 River Way, London SE10 0BH
☎ 0181 305 1431   FAX 0181 305 1418

CONTACT Mrs P. Napier
PRODUCTS Compost bins; cloches; garden sundries
CATALOGUE On request
MAIL ORDER Yes

Manufacturers and suppliers of compost-making bins, water butts and propagating aids and other garden supplies.

Blagdon Water Garden Products Ltd
Bristol Road, Bridgwater, Somerset TA6 4AW
☎ 01278 446464   FAX 01278 446155

CONTACT Dean Franklin
PRODUCTS Water garden products
NEW PRODUCTS Economy pond pumps for beginners
CATALOGUE On request (01934 852973)

Manufacturers of everything needed for building and maintaining water gardens – pools, liners, pumps, filters, fountains, lighting, ornaments, plants and fish.

Blount UK Ltd
6 Station Drive, Bredon, Tewkesbury, Gloucestershire GL20 7HQ
☎ 01684 72736   FAX 01684 73154

CONTACT Chris Prevost
PRODUCTS Hand tools,; garden machinery
NEW PRODUCTS Tree stump grinder
CATALOGUE From dealers
MAIL ORDER No

Manufacturers of Oregon chainsaws, chipper-shredders, sprayers and hand tools, and Dixon ride-on grass cutters.

Bob Andrews Ltd
1 Bilton Industrial Estate, Lovelace Road, Bracknell, Berkshire RG12 8YT
☎ 01344 862111   FAX 01344 861345

CONTACT Roy or Joan
PRODUCTS Garden machinery; sprayers
CATALOGUE On request
MAIL ORDER Only if no local dealer

Powered and wheeled garden machinery for domestic gardeners and professionals, including vacuums, leaf sweepers, scarifiers, sprayers, spreaders and trimmers. Mail order if no local dealer.

Bolingbroke
Rectory Lodge, The Fairland, Hingham, Norfolk NR9 4HN
☎ 01953 850197   FAX 01953 850197

CONTACT Christine Boswell
PRODUCTS Garden furniture; summerhouses
CATALOGUE On request
MAIL ORDER Yes

Manufacturers of wooden garden furniture, summerhouses and pavilions in classic styles.

Bonnington Plastics Ltd
Trent Lane, Castle Donington, Derbyshire DE7 2NP
☎ 01332 811811   FAX 01332 811421

CONTACT James Bloomfield
PRODUCTS Hoses
NEW PRODUCTS Tree ties
CATALOGUE On request
MAIL ORDER No

Manufacturers of garden hoses, hose fittings and sprinklers, and tree ties.

Bosmere Products Ltd
189 Victoria Road North, Fratton Bridge, Portsmouth, Hampshire PO5 1AJ
☎ 01705 863541   FAX 01705 293565

CONTACT Sales Office
PRODUCTS Garden bags and covers; garden sundries
NEW PRODUCTS Mammoth tip bag; topiary shapes
CATALOGUE On request
MAIL ORDER Yes

Tip bags, covers for mowers and garden furniture, topiary frames, hanging basket liners and plant supports.

Boughton Loam Ltd
Telford Way, Telford Way Industrial Estate, Kettering, Northamptonshire NN16 8UN
☎ 01536 510515   FAX 01536 510691

CONTACT Mike Franklin or Richard Chinn
PRODUCTS Composts; turf-dressings
CATALOGUE On request
MAIL ORDER No

394 Garden Supplies

Suppliers of specialist turf-dressings, general horticultural composts and landscaping mixes to the trade and the public.

Brettell & Shaw Ltd
West Street, Quarry Bank, Brierly Hill, West Midlands DY5 2DT
☎ 01384 566838   FAX 01384 569123
CONTACT Alan Instan
PRODUCTS Greenhouse heaters; compost bins; incinerators; watering cans
NEW PRODUCTS Eltex 2200 twin-chimney greenhouse heater
CATALOGUE Leaflets on request

Makers of Eltex paraffin and LP-gas greenhouse heaters. The range has recently been redesigned and extended. Watering cans, composters and incinerators are also available.

Brighton Manufacturing Co
PO Box 61, Alton, Hampshire GU4 3YU
☎ 01420 588546   FAX 01420 588546
CONTACT Janet Brighton
PRODUCTS Plant supports
NEW PRODUCTS Tyrite runner bean and sweet pea support packs
CATALOGUE Leaflets
MAIL ORDER Yes

Wires for training and supporting plants. Can be used on walls, posts or fences.

British Museum Connection
46 Bloomsbury Street, London WC1B 3QQ
☎ 0171 323 1234   FAX 0171 636 7186
CONTACT Carey Wells
PRODUCTS Garden statuary
CATALOGUE On request
MAIL ORDER Yes

Replica classical statues, reliefs and busts from the museum's collection: the reconstituted marble items can be placed outside.

Bulldog Tools Ltd
Clarington Forge, Wigan, Lancashire WN1 3DD
☎ 01942 44281   FAX 01942 824316
CONTACT Jacqui Foulkes
PRODUCTS Hand tools
CATALOGUE On request
MAIL ORDER Yes

Manufacturer of hand tools and other horticultural tools.

Burton McCall Group
163 Parker Drive, Leicester, Leicestershire LE4 0JP
☎ 0116 2340800
CONTACT Sue Isaacs
PRODUCTS Tools; gloves
CATALOGUE On request
MAIL ORDER Yes

Suppliers of hand tools and clothing, including pruning saws, horticultural knives and the top-of-the-range secateurs 'Felco'.

Capital Garden Products Ltd
Gibbs Reed Barn, Pashley Road, Ticehurst, East Sussex TN5 7HE
☎ 01580 201092   FAX 01580 201093
PRODUCTS Architectural features and plant containers
NEW PRODUCTS Wall fountains, urns, Ticehurst tub planter
CATALOGUE On request
MAIL ORDER Yes, if no local retailer

Tanks, urns, tubs and planters in glass fibre, wood, cast lead and *faux* lead, also pedestals, urns, fountains, steel furniture and garden edging tiles.

Chase Organics
Addlestone, Surrey KT15 1HY
☎ 01932 820958   FAX 01932 829322
PRODUCTS Organic supplies; seeds
CATALOGUE On request
MAIL ORDER Yes

Produce *The Organic Gardening Catalogue* in association with the HDRA. A full range of organic supplies and untreated seed is sold: many items are stocked at Ryton Organic Gardens too. Discounts for HDRA members.

Chempak Products
Geddings Road, Hoddesdon, Hertfordshire EN11 0LR
☎ 01992 441888   FAX 01992 467908
CONTACT W. Richardson
PRODUCTS Fertilisers; pesticides; garden sundries; water storing granules; peat alternatives
CATALOGUE On request
MAIL ORDER Yes; (£10 minimum)

A very wide range of garden chemicals and fertilisers, as well as general garden products. Mail order is available through the Garden Direct catalogue.

Chillington Manufacturing Ltd
Camden Street, Walsall Wood, West Midlands WS9 9BJ
☎ 01543 376441   FAX 01543 373030
CONTACT Jeanette Brown
PRODUCTS Wheelbarrows
CATALOGUE On request
MAIL ORDER No

Manufacturers of garden and multi-purpose wheelbarrows in galvanised steel and polypropylene.

Claymore Grass Machinery
Waterloo Industrial Estate, Waterloo Road, Bidford on Avon, Warwickshire B50 4JH
☎ 01789 490177   FAX 01789 490170
CONTACT Nicki Cund

Garden Supplies 395

PRODUCTS Lawnmowers and tractors
Distributors of the Bolens range of lawnmowers, lawn and garden tractors, mulching mowers, sickle bar mowers and chippervacs, as well as Sabo Roberine professional mowers.

Cookson Plantpak Ltd
Burnham Road, Mundon, Maldon, Essex CM9 6NT
☎ 01621 740140   FAX 01621 742400
CONTACT Chris Breed
PRODUCTS Plastic plant pots; plastic plant containers
NEW PRODUCTS Countryside range of terracotta-look pots; wall butt; Chelsea hanging basket with assisted watering
MAIL ORDER No

A very wide range of plastic pots, seed trays, hanging baskets and other plastic items. Sold through garden centres.

Cooper Pegler
North Seaton Industrial Estate, Ashington, Northumberland NE63 0YB
☎ 01670 522225   FAX 01670 523992
CONTACT Lorraine Surtees
PRODUCTS Sprayers
CATALOGUE On request
MAIL ORDER No

Leading suppliers of spraying equipment for gardeners and professional users. The range includes hand-held, knapsack and wheeled sprayers with a full choice of nozzles and appropriate safety equipment.

Cotswold Buildings Ltd
Standlake, Oxfordshire OX8 7QG
☎ 01865 300711   FAX 01865 300284
PRODUCTS Garden buildings
CATALOGUE On request
MAIL ORDER Yes, if no local dealer

Large range of garden buildings and garages. They can install bases and construct nationwide.

Courtyard Designs
Suckley, Worcester, Hereford & Worcester WR6 5EH
☎ 01886 884640   FAX 01886 884444
CONTACT Ursula Mason
PRODUCTS Summerhouses; garden buildings
CATALOGUE On request
MAIL ORDER No

Manufacturers and suppliers of traditional wooden summerhouses and pavilions. Complete service, including installation, offered. They can design to order as well.

Cowbridge Compost
Penllyn Estate Farm, Llwynhelig, Cowbridge, South Glamorgan CF7 7RQ
☎ 01446 774030   FAX 01446 774825
CONTACT John Honfray

PRODUCTS Soil conditioner
NEW PRODUCTS C Bag organic plant food
MAIL ORDER Yes

Fertiliser and composts based on farmyard manure and made in the traditional way.

Crowther of Syon Lodge
Busch Corner, London Road, Isleworth, London TW7 5BH
☎ 0181 560 7978   FAX 0181 568 7572
CONTACT Donald Cameron
PRODUCTS Garden statuary; garden ornaments; architectural stonework
CATALOGUE Photographs available of all stock
MAIL ORDER No

This family-owned business is the oldest specialist for architectural antiques in the country. If you have a specific request they can supply a photograph of appropriate items in stock. Armillary spheres are made on site; the display garden itself is worth a visit.

CSM Lighting Ltd
Unit 8, Malmesbury Business Park, Tetbury Hill, Malmesbury, Wiltshire SN16 9JU
☎ 01666 825450   FAX 01666 825436
CONTACT Peter Harding
PRODUCTS Garden lighting
NEW PRODUCTS Heritage lanterns
CATALOGUE Leaflets on request
MAIL ORDER Yes

Garden, pond and patio lighting, and solar lighting.

Danell
PO Box 44, Hemel Hempstead, Hertfordshire HP1 1XE
☎ 01442 248723   FAX 01442 248723
PRODUCTS Vases
CATALOGUE Leaflets
MAIL ORDER Yes

Hand-assembled glass vases for flower arrangers.

Darlac Products
PO Box 996, Slough, Berkshire SL3 9JF
☎ 01753 547790   FAX 01753 580524
CONTACT Peter Darban
PRODUCTS Garden tools
NEW PRODUCTS New products
CATALOGUE On request
MAIL ORDER Yes

Garden tools including secateurs and a fruit picker; some items feature innovative designs.

David Bell Ltd
Eastfield Drive, Penicuik, Midlothian EH26 8BA
☎ 01968 678480   FAX 01968 678878
CONTACT Mark Sinclair
PRODUCTS Fertilisers; grass seed
CATALOGUE Lawngrass brochure
MAIL ORDER Yes

Garden Supplies

Scottish seed wholesalers who supply grass mixtures, specialised lawn fertilisers and bird feed.

David Craig Design and Production
Units 10-11, Langley Moor Industrial Estate, Langley Moor, Co. Durham DH7 8JE
☎ 0191 386 0384   FAX 0191 386 0384
CONTACT David Craig Kuegler
PRODUCTS Garden furniture; parasols
CATALOGUE On request

Designers and manufacturers of top-quality garden furniture. They use sustainable wood sources only and reclaimed timber (up to 300 years old).

The David Sharp Studio
201a Nottingham Road, Somercotes, Derbyshire DE55 4JG
☎ 01773 606066   FAX 01773 540737
CONTACT Mrs Debbie Todkill
PRODUCTS Garden ornaments
NEW PRODUCTS Busts of Apollo and Diana; vases; urns
CATALOGUE £3
MAIL ORDER Yes

Manufacturers of cast stone balustrading, statuary, urns and vases, benches and fountains.

Dax Products Ltd
PO Box 119, Nottingham, Nottinghamshire NG3 5ED
☎ 01602 609996   FAX 01602 604620
CONTACT Amanda Roberts
PRODUCTS Herbicides
NEW PRODUCTS 'Fungo'
MAIL ORDER Yes

Makers of 'Root Out', a herbicide for trees, stumps, brushwood and weeds. Their new product, 'Fungo', kills moss, algae, lichen and slime.

Defenders Ltd
Freepost, PO Box 131, Wye, Ashford, Kent TN25 5BR
☎ 01233 813121   FAX 01233 813383
CONTACT Geoff Siddons
PRODUCTS Biological controls
NEW PRODUCTS 'Nemaslug'
CATALOGUE On request
MAIL ORDER Yes, telephoned or faxed orders only. No postal orders

Biological controls for professional and amateur gardeners for the following organisms: whitefly, red spider mite, slugs and vine weevils. Thursday despatch to ensure they arrive by the weekend. A sister company of Biological Crop Protection.

Dennis
Ashbourne Road, Kirk Langley, Derby DE6 4NJ
☎ 01332 824777   FAX 01332 824525
CONTACT Michael Smout
PRODUCTS Cylinder mowers; grass care equipment
CATALOGUE On request
MAIL ORDER No

Manufacturers of high-quality cylinder grass cutting equipment for amenity use and large gardens.

Diplex Ltd
PO Box 172, Watford, Hertfordshire WD1 1BX
☎ 01923 231784   FAX 01923 243791
CONTACT Ernest Danzig, Barbara Leach, Sheila Rodel
PRODUCTS Thermometers; rain gauges; weather equipment
NEW PRODUCTS Weather-vane
CATALOGUE On request
MAIL ORDER Yes

Manufacturers of an extensive range of thermometers, rain gauges, frost predictors, and other meteorological measuring equipment for amateur and professional use. Models include inexpensive, decorative and scientific devices.

DIY Plastics (UK) Ltd
Regal Way, Faringdon, Oxfordshire SN7 7XD
☎ 01367 242932   FAX 01367 242200
CONTACT C. L. Stone
PRODUCTS Plastic sheeting
CATALOGUE 2 first class stamps
MAIL ORDER Yes

Plastic sheeting for house and garden use including netting, shading, pond liners and horticultural acrylic sheets.

Dowler and Wakefield
146-56 Weston Lane, Tyseley, Birmingham, West Midlands B11 3RY
☎ 0121 706 0638   FAX 0121 707 6482
CONTACT A. J. Homer
PRODUCTS Greenhouse heaters
CATALOGUE On request
MAIL ORDER Yes

Electric and paraffin greenhouse heaters.

Duckbill Anchors Ltd
Perrywood Business Park, Honeycrock Lane, Salfords, Redhill, Surrey RH1 5DZ
☎ 01737 762300   FAX 01737 773395
CONTACT Adam Lacey
PRODUCTS Tree anchoring systems
CATALOGUE On request

'Platypus' systems for securing newly planted standard and semi-mature trees.

Dupre Vermiculite
Tamworth Road, Hertford, Hertfordshire SG13 7DL
☎ 01992 582541   FAX 01992 553436
CONTACT Freya Denton
PRODUCTS Vermiculite
CATALOGUE On request

Garden Supplies

MAIL ORDER No
Suppliers of horticultural vermiculite, through trade wholesalers. High water-retaining and nutrient-absorbing characteristics.

Durston Peat Products
Avalon Farm, Sharpham, Street, Somerset BA16 9SE
☎ 01458 42688   📠 01458 48327
CONTACT Tony Jones
PRODUCTS Peat-based and alternative growing media and mulches
CATALOGUE On request
MAIL ORDER No

Manufacturer of peat-based composts and growing media, with alternative products including bark, vegetable waste and coir.

E H Thorne (Beehives) Ltd
Louth Road, Wragby, Lincoln, Lincolnshire LN3 5LA
☎ 01673 858555   📠 01673 857004
CONTACT Sales Department
PRODUCTS Bee-keeping equipment
NEW PRODUCTS Honey blending apparatus
CATALOGUE On request
MAIL ORDER Yes

A complete range of bee-keeping equipment.

E P Barrus Ltd
Launton Road, Bicester, Oxfordshire OX6 0UR
☎ 01869 253355   📠 01869 321585
CONTACT Tracy Fowler-Green
PRODUCTS Garden machinery
NEW PRODUCTS Lawnflite 930 garden tractor; 881SP6E rotary mower
CATALOGUE On request
MAIL ORDER No

Makers and distributors of the Lawnflite range of lawnmowers and garden tractors, brush cutters, hedge trimmers, cultivators and chipper-shredders.

Edwin Tucker & Sons Ltd
Brewery Meadow, Stonepark, Ashburton, Devon TQ13 7DG
☎ 01364 652403   📠 01364 654300
CONTACT Mrs G. Williams
PRODUCTS Plastic pots; ties; netting; clothing; chemicals and fertilisers
CATALOGUE On request
MAIL ORDER Yes

Commercial and retail seed merchants. They sell garden seeds mail order, as well as products. See Seeds section for more details.

Eliza Tinsley & Co Ltd
Reddal Hill Road, Cradley Heath, West Midlands B64 5JF
☎ 01384 566066   📠 01384 639156
CONTACT Jackie Jinks
PRODUCTS Garden and hand tools
NEW PRODUCTS Traditional wooden-handled, carbon and stainless steel tools
CATALOGUE On request

Makers of garden tools and accessories, hand tools, and agricultural and contractors' tools.

English Woodlands Biocontrol
Hoyle, Graffham, Petworth, West Sussex GU28 0LR
☎ 01798 867574   📠 01798 867574
CONTACT Mrs Sue Cooper
PRODUCTS Biological controls
CATALOGUE On request
MAIL ORDER Yes

Biological controls for whitefly, red spider mite, aphids, mealy bugs, caterpillars, vine weevils and leafhoppers. Larger quantities are available at professional prices, and they produce a useful guide on the compatibility of garden chemicals with biological controls.

Exmouth Garden Products
Units 7-8 Salterton Workshops, Budleigh Salterton, Devon EX9 6RJ
☎ 01395 442796   📠 01395 442851
CONTACT D. J. Redfern
PRODUCTS Greenhouse equipment; netting
CATALOGUE On request
MAIL ORDER Yes

Greenhouse shelving, staging and accessories, insulation film and netting.

F Peart & Co Ltd
Baltic Works, Baltic Street, Hartlepool, Cleveland TS25 1PW
☎ 01429 263331   📠 01429 262179
CONTACT Mr D. Ridden
PRODUCTS Garden furniture
NEW PRODUCTS Additions to table collection
CATALOGUE On request

Garden furniture, benches, chairs and tables made of teak from sustainable sources.

Fiskars UK Ltd
Bridgend Business Centre, Bridgend, Mid Glamorgan CF31 3XJ
☎ 01656 655595   📠 01656 659582
CONTACT Helen Griffiths
PRODUCTS Hand tools
CATALOGUE On request
MAIL ORDER No

Hand and garden tools carrying the Wilkinson Sword brand name. Design ranges include Garden Devils, Classic, Professional, Power and the Ladies Collection. The UK market leader.

The Flower Arrangers Show Shop
PO Box 38, Stratford upon Avon, Warwickshire CV37 6WJ
CONTACT Mr and Mrs S. E. Grant

398 Garden Supplies

PRODUCTS Floral accessories; containers; figurines
CATALOGUE SAE
MAIL ORDER Yes

Flower arranging accessories, verdigris figurines and dried plant material. Only the figurines and containers are available mail order: look out for the stand at shows.

Forsham Cottage Arks
Goreside Farm, Great Chart, Ashford, Kent TN26 1JU
☎ 01233 820229   FAX 01233 820157
CONTACT Cindy Pellett
PRODUCTS Dovecotes
CATALOGUE On request
MAIL ORDER Yes

Decorative and functional dovecotes and small poultry units for the garden.

Franshams Ltd
Holme Court, Biggleswade, Bedfordshire SG18 9ST
☎ 01767 681900   FAX 01767 683481
CONTACT Mrs Rose Clark
PRODUCTS Garden shoes and boots; pruning saw
CATALOGUE On request
MAIL ORDER Yes

Stylish waterproof shoes and boots for gardeners and other outdoor use, and a folding pruning saw.

Frolics of Winchester
82 Canon Street, Winchester, Hampshire SO23 9JQ
☎ 01962 856384   FAX 01962 844896
CONTACT Robert Dick-Read
PRODUCTS Garden furniture; ornamental trellis
CATALOGUE On request
MAIL ORDER Yes

Manufacturers of wooden garden furniture in stylish designs and of painted trellis-work cut to intricate shapes. Individual pieces made to order as well. Trade and garden designer discounts.

The Fyba Pot Company Ltd
Malvern Road, Knottingley, West Yorkshire WF11 8EG
☎ 01977 677676   FAX 01977 607138
CONTACT Carol Moore
PRODUCTS Horticultural sundries and plant pots
NEW PRODUCTS Pot holders; wall troughs; pond and pool netting
CATALOGUE On request
MAIL ORDER Yes

Manufacturers of biodegradable plant pots, hanging baskets and planters as well as a range of horticultural sundries.

Gardena UK Ltd
Dunhams Lane, Letchworth, Hertfordshire SG6 1BD
☎ 01462 686688   FAX 01462 686789
CONTACT Sales/Spares/Service
PRODUCTS Watering systems; garden tools
CATALOGUE On request
MAIL ORDER No

Manufacturers of watering systems. Also a range of interchangeable tool heads.

Gardenglow Cocoa Shell
79 Loudoun Road, St John's Wood, London, NW8 0DQ
☎ 0171 624 5599   FAX 0171 328 9676
CONTACT Carina Glanville
PRODUCTS Mulches
CATALOGUE On request
MAIL ORDER Yes

Fertilising and soil conditioning mulches made from cocoa shell and coir.

Gayways Lawn Mower Centre
215-17 Watford Road, Harrow, London HA1 3UA
☎ 0181 908 4744   FAX 0181 904 6520
CONTACT Michael Fey
PRODUCTS Lawnmowers; garden machinery; hand tools
MAIL ORDER Yes; nationwide distribution

Garden machinery sales and spares. You can order by telephone for nationwide delivery.

GEEBRO Ltd
South Road, Hailsham, East Sussex BN27 3DT
☎ 01323 840771   FAX 01323 440109
CONTACT Ray Scott
PRODUCTS Garden furniture; tree ties; thermometers
NEW PRODUCTS 'Eurovative' garden sundries
CATALOGUE On request
MAIL ORDER No

Founded over 100 years ago, Lister teak garden furniture in a variety of styles is well-known. The iroko range is called Country. Geebro also sells tree ties, labels and guards for growers, and a range of horticultural sundries under the Rainbow brand name.

Geeco Limited
Gore Road Industrial Estate, New Milton, Hampshire BH25 6SE
☎ 01425 614600   FAX 01425 619463
CONTACT Roger Rackstraw
PRODUCTS Containers; propagators; watering cans
NEW PRODUCTS Recycled plastic and galvanised steel watering cans; indoor and outdoor planters
CATALOGUE On written request
MAIL ORDER No

Manufacturers of watering cans and accessories, hanging baskets, plant containers and propagators.

Gerhardt Pharmaceuticals Ltd
PO Box 777, London SW19 5DY
☎ 0181 944 0505
CONTACT Carolyn Archer
PRODUCTS Insecticides

Garden Supplies 399

Makers of Dethlac insecticidal lacquer and Dethtrap whitefly catcher for greenhouses and conservatories.

Glowcroft Ltd
PO Box 137, Gloucester, Gloucestershire GL4 7YB
☎ 01452 372385   FAX 01452 372381
CONTACT Steve Tarrant
PRODUCTS Water storage granules; horticultural sundries
CATALOGUE On request
MAIL ORDER Yes

Their main product is the water-retaining gel 'SwellGel' which stores up to 400 times its own weight. Other items include a trough to hide growbags and caps for Chinese canes.

Good Directions Ltd
15 Talisman Business Centre, Duncan Road, Park Gate, Southampton, Hampshire SO1 7GA
☎ 01489 577828   FAX 01489 577858
CONTACT Heather Langley-Evans
PRODUCTS Architectural features; weather-vanes; sundials; garden taps
NEW PRODUCTS Cast brass vertical sundials; Italian garden taps; ceramic patio clocks
CATALOGUE On request
MAIL ORDER Yes

Cupolas and clock turrets and clocks, weather-vanes, sundials, decorative garden taps and sprinklers.

Green Gardener Products
41 Strumpshaw Road, Brundall, Norfolk NR13 5PG
☎ 01603 715096
CONTACT John Manners
PRODUCTS Biological controls; water-retentive granules
NEW PRODUCTS Flower pouches; slow-release fertiliser
CATALOGUE On request
MAIL ORDER Yes

Suppliers of biological pest controls for whitefly, red spider mite, vine weevil, aphids and mealy bug. There is a daytime helpline (on the number above); they can advise on integrated pest control using a combination of traps, sprays and controls. The range is being extended to include fertilisers and water-retentive granules.

Greenacres Horticultural Supplies
PO Box 1228, Iver, Buckinghamshire SL0 0EH
☎ 01895 835235   FAX 01753 672906
CONTACT I. Ludford
PRODUCTS Grass seed; fertilisers; lawn products; water storage granules
NEW PRODUCTS Sulphur chips; liquid sulphur
CATALOGUE On request
MAIL ORDER Yes

Suppliers of commercial and amenity products to the amateur gardener. Mail order, local delivery and collection from yard.

Greenspan Designs Ltd
8 Mentmore Close, Kenton, Harrow, London HA3 0EA
☎ 0181 907 8695   FAX 0181 904 4101
PRODUCTS Container systems; growing media
NEW PRODUCTS Grow dice; scented floral globes
CATALOGUE On request
MAIL ORDER Yes

Manufacturers and suppliers of container systems for public and private floral displays, including specially developed growing media. They supply over 80 local authorities and city councils.

Greenvale Farm Ltd
Clapham Lodge, Leeming, Northallerton, North Yorkshire DL7 9LY
☎ 01677 422953   FAX 01677 425358
CONTACT Julie McAfee
PRODUCTS Fertilisers; soil conditioners
MAIL ORDER No

Pelleted poultry manure and organic composted manure sold under the Rooster brand.

GWS Ltd
The Walnuts, Pinfold Lane, Harby, Melton Mowbray, Leicestershire LE14 4BU
☎ 01949 61379   FAX 01949 61487
CONTACT Chris Tetley
PRODUCTS Conservatories
NEW PRODUCTS Pyramid roof
CATALOGUE On request
MAIL ORDER No

Family firm selling UPVC Georgian sun rooms direct to the public. Designed for easy installation and maintenance. Their new Pyramid roof goes well with bungalows.

H₂0
The Stables, Winwick Warren, West Haddon, Northampton, Northamptonshire NN6 7NS
☎ 01788 510529   FAX 01788 510728
CONTACT Richard Allen
PRODUCTS Irrigation systems
CATALOGUE On request
MAIL ORDER Yes

Suppliers and installers of automatic watering systems. Individual service; site visits and estimates are free of charge, and service contracts can be arranged.

Haddonstone Ltd
The Forge House, East Haddon, Northampton, Northamptonshire NN6 8DB
☎ 01604 770711   FAX 01604 770027
CONTACT Sales Department

400   Garden Supplies

PRODUCTS   Garden ornaments; architectural stonework
NEW PRODUCTS   Raphael pedestal and pool surround; Adam finial and pedestal
CATALOGUE   Full colour, 108 pages, £5
MAIL ORDER   Delivery

Leading manufacturers and suppliers of garden ornaments, statuary and architectural stonework in the reconstituted stone material 'Haddonstone'. The range is exceptionally large, but they can design to order also. Antique finishes available.

Hardi Ltd
4-5 Watling Close, Sketchley Meadows, Hinckley, Leicestershire LS10 3EX
☎ 01455 233811   FAX 01455 233815
CONTACT   Pat Holt
PRODUCTS   Sprayers

Suppliers of sprayers and aeration equipment.

Haws Watering Cans
120 Beakes Road, Smethwick, Warley, West Midlands B67 5AB
☎ 0121 420 2494   FAX 0121 429 1668
CONTACT   John Massey
PRODUCTS   Watering cans; sprayers
NEW PRODUCTS   Ceramic watering cans
CATALOGUE   On request
MAIL ORDER   Yes

Watering cans that look like watering cans from this well-known company. They also sell other watering equipment, and supply spares – and cans if necessary – by mail order.

Heritage Leisure
Bencroft Gardens, Bremhill, Calne, Wiltshire SN11 9LA
☎ 01249 740498   FAX 01249 740292
CONTACT   David or Stephen
PRODUCTS   Wooden garden features and wheelbarrows
NEW PRODUCTS   Water features made from barrels
CATALOGUE   Trade price list

Wooden tubs and barrels, wheelbarrows, pumps and water features. The range is sold through garden centres.

Heritage Woodcraft
Unit 5, Shelley Farm, Ower, Romsey, Hampshire SO51 6AS
☎ 01703 814145
CONTACT   David Finch
PRODUCTS   Garden furniture; wooden wheelbarrows
CATALOGUE   Free leaflets
MAIL ORDER   Yes

Traditionally crafted wooden garden furniture made from iroko (derived from managed sources) with a new range in English oak.

Hillhout (UK) Ltd
Harfreys Road, Harfreys Industrial Estate, Great Yarmouth, Norfolk NR31 0LS
☎ 01493 440017   FAX 01493 440019
CONTACT   Mrs R. McIlwham
PRODUCTS   Fencing; wooden garden products; garden buildings
NEW PRODUCTS   Profiled trellis panels; glass terrace panels; garden lighting
CATALOGUE   On request
MAIL ORDER   No

Suppliers and manufacturers of wooden fencing, trellis, pergolas, garden furniture, sandpits and garden buildings.

Homer Pressings
Charles Street, Walsall, West Midlands WS2 9NB
☎ 01922 720111   FAX 01922 29781
CONTACT   Pat Jennings
PRODUCTS   Garden and hand tools
CATALOGUE   Leaflets from agents

Manufacturers of a range of traditional garden and hand tools.

The Hop Shop
Castle Farm, Shoreham, Sevenoaks, Kent TN14 7UB
☎ 01959 523219   FAX 01959 524220
CONTACT   Caroline Alexander
PRODUCTS   Dried flowers and grasses
CATALOGUE   4 first class stamps
MAIL ORDER   Yes

Dried flower producers and suppliers: they won a gold medal at Chelsea. Trade and retail. Their range includes grasses, wheatsheaves and autumnal hop-bines. A new farm shop opened in 1994. Group tours by arrangement in season.

Hotbox Heaters Ltd
7 Gordleton Industrial Park, Sway Road, Lymington, Hampshire SO41 8JD
☎ 01590 683788   FAX 01590 683511
CONTACT   R. Spencer
PRODUCTS   Greenhouse heaters; propagators; lighting
NEW PRODUCTS   Lighting
MAIL ORDER   Yes

Electric and gas heaters and air circulation fans for small greenhouses, with larger units for professional users and hobbyists. There is also a range of propagating benches and horticultural lighting.

Hotterotter Group
The Old Rectory, Bryn, Abergavenny, Gwent NP7 9AP
☎ 01873 840328   FAX 01873 840328
CONTACT   Mrs P. A. Roper-Evans
PRODUCTS   Compost bins
NEW PRODUCTS   Mini rotter
MAIL ORDER   Yes

Garden Supplies 401

Unique insulated compost bin which assembles almost instantly. Designed to maintain the high temperatures necessary to kill weed seeds.

Inhome Limited
Sharston Road, Wythenshawe, Manchester, Greater Manchester M22 4TH
☎ 0161 945 2646   FAX 0161 945 1123

CONTACT Veronica Rosers
PRODUCTS Watering equipment
NEW PRODUCTS Fast flow reel
CATALOGUE On request
MAIL ORDER Yes

Hoses, hose end accessories, fittings and storage.

Interpet Ltd
Interpet House, Vincent Lane, Dorking, Surrey RH4 3YX
☎ 01306 881033   FAX 01306 885009

CONTACT Customer Care Department
PRODUCTS Aquatic products
NEW PRODUCTS 'Aquariom' heaters; 'Aqua Air' air pumps; 'Pond Worker' in-pond filters
CATALOGUE On request
MAIL ORDER No

Comprehensive range of aquatic products for ponds and aquariums, including foods, pumps and chemicals. The company also supplies pet products.

Interval Systems Ltd
PO Box 40, Woking, Surrey GU22 7YU
☎ 01483 727888   FAX 01483 727828

CONTACT Sarah Ford
PRODUCTS Wooden garden features; trellis; wheelbarrows
NEW PRODUCTS Front garden fencing; bridges
CATALOGUE On request
MAIL ORDER Yes, see below

Distributors of Ultra wooden arches, trellis, ornamental fences and bridges; FORT wheelbarrows. Mail order: for Ultra products contact the address above; FORT mail order through Boulder Barrows, 99 Westfield Road, Woking, Surrey, GU22 9QR (01482 730658).

J G S Weathervanes
Unit 6, Broomstick Estate, High Street, Edlesborough, Dunstable, Bedfordshire LU6 2HS
☎ 01525 220360   FAX 01525 222786

CONTACT Mr or Mrs J. Sayer
PRODUCTS Weather-vanes
NEW PRODUCTS Cock-a-hoop three-dimensional weather-vane
CATALOGUE On request
MAIL ORDER Yes

Makers of metal weather-vanes in traditional and more modern designs.

Joanna Sheen Ltd
PO Box 52, Newton Abbot, Devon TQ12 4YF
☎ 01626 872405   FAX 01626 872265

CONTACT Nikki Hadley
PRODUCTS Dried flowers; floral accessories
CATALOGUE SAE (19p); courses: SAE (52p)
MAIL ORDER Yes

Dried flowers and pressed pictures, as well as the components for them. They run courses in these crafts too.

John Deere Ltd
Harby Road, Langar, Nottingham, Nottinghamshire NG13 9HT
☎ 01949 60491   FAX 01949 60490

CONTACT Graham Williams
PRODUCTS Lawnmowers; lawn tractors
CATALOGUE Leaflets

Manufacturers of lawn and groundsmanship machinery from garden and commercial lawnmowers, through to lawn tractors and large tractor units.

John McLauchlan Horticulture
50a Market Place, Thirsk, North Yorkshire YO7 1LH
☎ 01845 525585   FAX 01845 523133

CONTACT John McLauchlan
PRODUCTS Fertilisers; growing media
CATALOGUE On request
MAIL ORDER Yes

Specialist suppliers of growing media to trade and retail customers, including vermiculite, perlite, pumice and biosorb. They also sell fertilisers and some sundries. Mail order service.

Joseph Bentley
Beck Lane, Barrow on Humber, Humberside DN19 7AQ
☎ 01469 532000   FAX 01469 532111

CONTACT G. H. Moxon
PRODUCTS Composts; fertilisers; garden sundries
CATALOGUE On request
MAIL ORDER Yes

Suppliers of a wide range of general and specialist composts and fertilisers including straight fertilisers, organic granules and compost mixes for chrysanthemum and fuchsia growers.

King Easton Ltd
The Green, Station Road, Winchmore Hill, London N21 3NB
☎ 0181 886 8783   FAX 0181 882 2685

CONTACT Brian Easton
PRODUCTS Garden furniture; parasols; gazebos
CATALOGUE On request

A stylish collection of traditional French metal outdoor furniture.

Knight Terrace Pots
West Orchard, Shaftesbury, Dorset SP7 0LJ
☎ 01258 472685
PRODUCTS Garden ornaments
CATALOGUE On request
MAIL ORDER Delivery arranged

Reconstituted stone garden ornaments from simple pots and troughs to elaborate vases, finials and balustrades. The works can be visited by appointment, and they can design or copy originals to order.

Knowle Nets
20 East Road, Bridport, Dorset DT6 4NX
☎ 01308 424342   FAX 01308 458186
CONTACT Sales desk
PRODUCTS Netting; plant supports; fruit cages
CATALOGUE On request
MAIL ORDER Yes

Manufacturers of protective netting and woven sheeting for plant supports, fruit cages and wind-breaks. They also produce sports nets.

Konstsmide UK Ltd
Yew Tree Farm, Hardstoft, Pilsley, Chesterfield, Derbyshire S45 8AE
☎ 01246 852140   FAX 01246 854297
CONTACT Lisbeth Orum
PRODUCTS Outdoor lighting
CATALOGUE On request
MAIL ORDER Yes

Wholesalers of a large range of Swedish outdoor lighting equipment.

Kubota (UK) Ltd
Dormer Road, Thame, Oxfordshire OX9 3UN
☎ 01844 214500   FAX 01844 216685
CONTACT Mr Stuart Ellis
PRODUCTS Lawnmowers; lawn tractors; garden machinery

Garden machinery range including lawnmowers, lawn tractors, compact tractors, hedge trimmers, brush cutters and generators. The range extends to professional and amenity machines.

Kut and Dried
PO Box 50, Penrith, Cumbria CA11 8RY
☎ 01768 892275   FAX 01768 892275
CONTACT Steve Smith
PRODUCTS Dried flower arrangements
NEW PRODUCTS Silk arrangements
CATALOGUE £1
MAIL ORDER Yes

Dried and silk flowers in glass boxes and pictures.

L & P Peat Ltd
Tollund House, 8 Abbey Street, Carlisle CA3 8TX
☎ 01228 22181   FAX 01228 41460
CONTACT Alan Armstrong
PRODUCTS Peat; growing media
NEW PRODUCTS 'Humax Growman' ericaceous compost
MAIL ORDER No

Manufacturers and suppliers of peat and peat-based composts under the 'Humax' brand name. They also supply growers with professional composts.

Langdon (London) Ltd
Ickford, Aylesbury, Buckinghamshire HP18 9JJ
☎ 01844 339337   FAX 01844 339666
CONTACT Joan Field
PRODUCTS Garden sundries
NEW PRODUCTS Bean cane supports; greenhouse clips and hooks
CATALOGUE On request
MAIL ORDER Yes

Manufacturers of the Langard range of plant supports and garden accessories.

Larch-Lap Ltd
PO Box 17, Lichfield Street, Stourport on Severn, Hereford & Worcester DY13 9ES
☎ 01299 823232   FAX 01299 871534
CONTACT Mrs Linda Phillips
PRODUCTS Garden buildings; fencing; trellis
NEW PRODUCTS Composter; 'Maxi' wall store; pergola arbour.
CATALOGUE On request
MAIL ORDER No

Manufacturers of timber and metal garden buildings, fencing and trellis.

Leaky Pipe Systems Ltd
Frith Farm, Dean Street, East Farleigh, Maidstone, Kent ME15 0PR
☎ 01622 746495   FAX 01622 745118
CONTACT Chris Fermor
PRODUCTS Irrigation systems
CATALOGUE Leaflets
MAIL ORDER Yes

Porous rubber hose irrigation system which is made from recycled car tyres. Leaky Pipe can be used in horticultural, amenity and agricultural situations.

Lees Mill Products
Lees Lane, Haworth, West Yorkshire BD22 8RA
☎ 01535 643545   FAX 01535 643572
CONTACT Bob Gent
PRODUCTS Soil conditioner
NEW PRODUCTS 'Dalesman' pellets and granules
CATALOGUE Leaflet
MAIL ORDER No

Organic fertiliser and soil conditioner based on wool fibres and sheep manure.

Garden Supplies 403

Levington Horticulture Ltd
Paper Mill Lane, Bramford, Ipswich, Suffolk IP8 4BZ
☎ 01473 830492   FAX 01473 830386
CONTACT   Consumer Relations Department
PRODUCTS   Composts; fertilisers; garden chemicals; growing media
MAIL ORDER   No

Fisons Horticulture was bought out by its managers and now trades as Levington. The range has not changed and includes Levington composts, Evergreen fertilisers and additives for most garden situations, as well as Murphy products. Available from garden centres. Consumer advice line: 01473 830492.

Link-Stakes Ltd
30 Warwick Road, Upper Boddington, Daventry, Northamptonshire NN11 6DH
☎ 01327 260329   FAX 01327 262428
CONTACT   Madeline Knowles
PRODUCTS   Plant supports; stakes
NEW PRODUCTS   Cloches
CATALOGUE   On request
MAIL ORDER   Yes

Suppliers of interlocking wire plant supports and single stakes. The stakes adapt to a variety of shapes and uses. There is a new range of wire cloches.

Lucas Garden Statuary
Units 7-9, Firsland Park Estate, Henfield Road, Woodmancote, Henfield, West Sussex BN6 9JJ
☎ 01273 494931   FAX 01273 495125
CONTACT   Mr M. S. Lucas
PRODUCTS   Garden ornaments
CATALOGUE   Yes, from retailers
MAIL ORDER   No

Garden statuary, fountains, urns, planters and benches, made from reconstituted stone with an aged finish.

Marston & Langinger Ltd
192 Ebury Street, London SW1W 8UP
☎ 0171 823 6829   FAX 0171 824 8757
PRODUCTS   Conservatories; conservatory furniture
CATALOGUE   On request

Individually designed conservatories with an excellent reputation: the showroom, which also displays their range of conservatory fittings, is in London. The factory is in Norfolk.

Matthew Eden
Pickwick End, Corsham, Wiltshire SN13 0JB
☎ 01249 713335   FAX 01249 713644
CONTACT   Matthew Eden
PRODUCTS   Garden furniture
CATALOGUE   £2.50
MAIL ORDER   Yes

Wirework pergolas, obelisks and chairs; wrought iron garden furniture; wooden benches to Lutyens and earlier designs.

Maxicrop International Ltd
Weldon Road, Corby, Northamptonshire NN17 5US
☎ 01536 402182   FAX 01536 204254
CONTACT   Jenny Paxton
PRODUCTS   Fertilisers
CATALOGUE   On request
MAIL ORDER   Yes (10 litres minimum)

Liquid seaweed extract and fertilisers.

Melcourt
Eight Bells House, Tetbury, Gloucestershire GL8 8JG
☎ 01666 503919   FAX 01666 504398
CONTACT   Mrs Rosemary Latter
PRODUCTS   Mulches; soil conditioners
CATALOGUE   Bulk supplies only
MAIL ORDER   No

Bark and wood-based mulches and soil conditioners, compost additives, play and walk surfaces. No direct retail supply, telephone for local small-load stockists.

Mellors Garden Ceramics
Rosemead, Marshwood, Bridport, Dorset DT6 5QB
☎ 01297 678217
CONTACT   Kate Mellors
PRODUCTS   Garden ornaments; fountains; planters
CATALOGUE   Large SAE
MAIL ORDER   Yes

Waterproof ceramic planters, fountains and garden ornaments in stony blue and sandstone stoneware.

Metpost Ltd
Mardy Road, Cardiff, South Glamorgan CF3 8EX
☎ 01222 777877   FAX 01222 779295
CONTACT   R. Kindred
PRODUCTS   Fencing; trellis
CATALOGUE   On request
MAIL ORDER   Yes

Manufacturers of the 'Metpost' fence fixing stake, and a range of maintenance-free trellis made from recycled polystyrene ('Timbron').

Metro Products Ltd
Eastman House, Fleming Way, Crawley, West Sussex RH10 2UY
☎ 01293 533663   FAX 01293 534500
CONTACT   Rosemarie Heron
PRODUCTS   Plastic plant containers; garden sundries
CATALOGUE   Trade, on request

Manufacturers of self-watering hanging baskets and planters, mulch mats, compost bins and lawn edgings.

Mukaluk
Ian Landless Farming Partnership, Hill Farm, Duns Tew, Bicester, Oxfordshire OX6 4JJ
☎ 01869 347532   FAX 01869 347701
CONTACT   Ian Landless
PRODUCTS   Growing media

Garden Supplies

NEW PRODUCTS Multi-purpose compost; container compost
CATALOGUE Leaflet
MAIL ORDER No

Peat-free composts, mulches and soil conditioners based on farmyard manure.

Natural Pest Control Ltd
Yapton Road, Barnham, Bognor Regis, West Sussex PO22 0AY
☎ 01243 553250   FAX 01243 552879
CONTACT Mr I. E. Worrall
PRODUCTS Biological controls
CATALOGUE On request
MAIL ORDER Yes

Wide variety of predators and parasites to control red spider mite, whitefly, mealy bugs, aphids, leaf miners and thrips. They deal with retail and commercial customers and can arrange advisory visits.

Nehra Cookes Chemicals Ltd
16 Chiltern Close, Warren Wood, Arnold, Nottinghamshire NG5 9PX
☎ 01159 203839   FAX 01159 671734
CONTACT David Nehra
PRODUCTS Garden sundries and herbicides; wrought iron garden features
NEW PRODUCTS Soluble feeds; greenhouse space-saver
MAIL ORDER Wrought iron garden products only

Garden products and chemicals.

Netlon Ltd
Kelly Street, Blackburn, Lancashire BB2 4PJ
☎ 01254 262431   FAX 01254 661624
CONTACT Michael Carr
PRODUCTS Netting; trellis; sheeting
CATALOGUE On request

A wide range of netting and sheet products for plant support and protection. They also sell bubble insulation and ties.

Norbark (Northern Bark Ltd)
6 Northern Road, Belfast, Northern Ireland
☎ 01232 754936   FAX 01232 754937
CONTACT Jack Aaron (01420 85090)
PRODUCTS Horticultural bark
NEW PRODUCTS Moss peat
CATALOGUE Leaflets on request
MAIL ORDER No

Producers of horticultural bark in six different grades for propagation and potting as well as amenity use. Technical advice: 01420 85090.

Nortene
Linenhall House, Stanley Street, Chester, Cheshire CH1 2LR
☎ 01244 346193   FAX 01244 320054
PRODUCTS Netting; sheeting; trellis; garden sundries

NEW PRODUCTS Bamboo canes; wooden trellis
CATALOGUE On request
MAIL ORDER No

Originally known for netting, the range now includes protective films and mulches, plant supports, garden furniture covers, canes, trellis and garden sundries.

Nutscene Garden Products Ltd
Old Brechin Road, Forfar, Tayside DD8 3DX
☎ 01307 468589   FAX 01307 467051
CONTACT Murray Anderson
PRODUCTS Garden twine and sundries
NEW PRODUCTS Bulksavers accessories
CATALOGUE SAE
MAIL ORDER No

Manufacturers of garden twine, tree ties, labels and plant support accessories.

O M Scott & Sons Ltd
115 Princess Street, Chase Terrace, Staffordshire WS7 8JH
☎ 01543 450066   FAX 01543 450067
CONTACT Sales Office
PRODUCTS Fertilisers; lawn spreaders
NEW PRODUCTS Evengreen lawn spreader
CATALOGUE On request
MAIL ORDER No

Suppliers of controlled-release lawn and garden fertilisers, spreaders and a lawn repair patch.

Orchid Sundries Ltd
New Gate Farm, Scotchey Lane, Stour Provost, Gillingham, Dorset SP8 5LT
☎ 01747 838368   FAX 01747 838308
CONTACT N. J. Heywood
PRODUCTS Orchid composts
CATALOGUE SAE
MAIL ORDER Yes

Bark composts for orchid growers, as well as a list of hardy orchids raised from seed.

Organic Concentrates Ltd
3 Broadway Court, Chesham, Buckinghamshire HP5 1EN
☎ 01494 792229   FAX 01494 792199
CONTACT C. J. P. Green
PRODUCTS Organic fertilisers; pesticides; sundries
CATALOGUE On request
MAIL ORDER Yes

Suppliers of the concentrated, dried and sterilised poultry manure '6X', a non-toxic slug killer and some garden tools.

Original Organics Ltd
Unit 4-5, Farthings Lodge Business Centre, Plymtree, Cullompton, Devon EX15 2JY
☎ 01884 277681   FAX 01884 277642
CONTACT Clive Roberts
PRODUCTS Compost bins

Garden Supplies 405

CATALOGUE Leaflets on request
MAIL ORDER Yes

Compost bins for kitchen and garden waste, including the 'Wormery' for Tiger Worm compost.

Ornate Products
26-7 Clivemont Road, Cordwallis Industrial Estate, Maidenhead, Berkshire SL6 7BZ
☎ 01628 25414   FAX 01628 23409
CONTACT Sheila
PRODUCTS Garden ornaments
NEW PRODUCTS Antique terracotta finish
CATALOGUE On request
MAIL ORDER Yes

Ornamental stoneware in classical and contemporary styles.

P J Bridgman & Co Ltd
Barnbridge Works, Lockfield Avenue, Brimsdown, Enfield, London EN3 7PX
☎ 0181 804 7474   FAX 0181 805 0873
CONTACT Sales Office
PRODUCTS Garden furniture
CATALOGUE On request and from stockists
MAIL ORDER No

Wide range of solidly built iroko garden furniture in period styles: many include carved details. Wood is derived from sustainable sources.

Pan Britannica Industries Ltd
Britannica House, Waltham Cross, Hertfordshire EN8 7DY
☎ 01992 623691   FAX 01992 626452
PRODUCTS Composts; fertilisers; herbicides; garden sundries
NEW PRODUCTS 'Bio Cat-u-pult'; 'Bio Topshrub'; 'Baby Bio' twins
CATALOGUE Trade only
MAIL ORDER No

Large garden group with a bestselling range of growing media, garden chemicals and general plant care products, including 'Baby Bio'.

Park Forge
Coryton, Okehampton, Devon EX20 4PG
☎ 01566 783454   FAX 01566 783454
CONTACT Sales Office
PRODUCTS Metal pergolas; arches; weather-vanes
CATALOGUE On request
MAIL ORDER Yes

Manufacturers and suppliers of wire arches and pergolas, weather-vanes and hanging basket trees.

Phostrogen
Corwen, Clwyd LL21 0EE
☎ 01490 412662   FAX 01490 412177
CONTACT Stephen Green
PRODUCTS Fertilisers
CATALOGUE On request

MAIL ORDER No

Manufacturers of soluble and slow-release fertilisers.

Plysu Housewares Ltd
Wolseley Road, Kempston, Bedfordshire MK42 7UD
☎ 01234 841771   FAX 01234 841037
CONTACT Peter Fraser/Kate Beal
PRODUCTS Watering cans; plastic plant containers
NEW PRODUCTS Water butt stand; garden brushware
CATALOGUE On request
MAIL ORDER No

Best known for their household products, Plysu also make plastic watering cans, water butts and plant containers.

Porous Pipe Ltd
PO Box 2, Colne, Lancashire BB8 7BY
☎ 01282 871778   FAX 01282 871785
CONTACT Martin Flutton
PRODUCTS Watering systems
CATALOGUE On request
MAIL ORDER Yes

Manufacturers of porous pipe systems of garden watering.

Power Garden Products
3 Daytona Drive, Allesley, Coventry, West Midlands CV5 9QG
☎ 01676 523062
CONTACT Mrs S. Smith
PRODUCTS Plant supports; cloches
CATALOGUE 1 first class stamp
MAIL ORDER Yes

Mail order garden supplies including Power plant supports and Chase Barn cloches, both of which are only available from Power.

Practicality Brown Ltd
Iver Stud, Iver, Buckinghamshire SL0 9LA
☎ 01753 652022
CONTACT David Middleton
PRODUCTS Mulches
CATALOGUE On request
MAIL ORDER No

Mulches and bark products in various grades for horticultural and amenity use. Prices from £20 a cubic metre. Tree-moving and chipping service available.

Precise Irrigation (UK) Ltd
78 Grove Street, Wantage, Oxfordshire OX12 7BG
☎ 01235 763760   FAX 01235 765467
CONTACT Jeremy Browning and Simon Box
PRODUCTS Irrigation systems
CATALOGUE On request
MAIL ORDER Yes

Designers, suppliers and installers of irrigation systems for domestic and commercial customers. No charge for

406 Garden Supplies

evaluations and quotations. Starter and hanging basket kits available.

Prosol
44 Birkdale Court, Fornham St Martin, Bury St Edmunds, Suffolk IP28 6XF
☎ 01284 706124   FAX 01284 706124
CONTACT Order Department
PRODUCTS Fertilisers
NEW PRODUCTS 'Prosol' mini pack; 'Nutrimist' spray plant food
CATALOGUE Leaflets
MAIL ORDER Yes

Plant foods, natural absorbent material and organic fertilisers.

Pumps 'n' Tubs
Unit H1, Holly Farm Business Park, Honiley, Warwickshire CV8 1NP
☎ 01926 484244   FAX 01926 484047
CONTACT Mr I. J. Eborall
PRODUCTS Containers; water features
NEW PRODUCTS New water features
CATALOGUE On request
MAIL ORDER Yes

Wooden tubs, cast iron pumps and water features which combine the two.

Raffles – Thatched Garden Buildings
Laundry Cottage, Prestwold Hall, Prestwold, Loughborough, Leicestershire LE12 5SQ
☎ 01509 881426   FAX 01509 881426
CONTACT Andrew V. Raffle
PRODUCTS Summerhouses
CATALOGUE On request
MAIL ORDER No

Suppliers of thatched summerhouses and garden buildings, built with traditional materials to old designs. They can also restore existing buildings.

Regency Garden Buildings
Barugh Green Road, Barugh Green, Barnsley, South Yorkshire S75 1JU
☎ 01226 390000   FAX 01226 388886
CONTACT Miss K. J. Lodge
PRODUCTS Garden buildings
NEW PRODUCTS 'Store It'; 'Lucerene'
CATALOGUE On telephone request
MAIL ORDER No

Makers of chalets, summerhouses, sheds and playhouses.

Rehau Ltd
Waterside Drive, Langley, Slough, Berkshire SL3 6EZ
☎ 01753 549974   FAX 01753 544461
CONTACT Cliff Wheatley
PRODUCTS Hoses
NEW PRODUCTS 'Proflex-Professional' hose, 'Floro-Design' hose, starter kits ('Greenlawn' and 'Proflex')
CATALOGUE Trade only
MAIL ORDER No

A range of garden hoses and fittings.

Remanoid
Unit 44, Number One Industrial Estate, Medomsley Road, Consett, Co. Durham DH8 6SZ
☎ 01207 591089   FAX 01207 502512
CONTACT Danielle Chilton
PRODUCTS Aquatic products
CATALOGUE On request
MAIL ORDER Yes

Suppliers of a wide range of pumps and accessories for water gardens and ponds.

Renaissance Bronzes
79 Pimlico Road, London SW1W 8PH
☎ 0171 823 5149   FAX 0171 730 4598
CONTACT Simon Jacques
PRODUCTS Garden statuary
CATALOGUE On request
MAIL ORDER No

Classical and classically styled bronzes for indoor and outdoor positions.

Robus Pottery
Hastingleigh, Ashford, Kent TN2 5JH
☎ 01233 750330   FAX 01233 750330
CONTACT Rosemary Robus
PRODUCTS Terracotta pots; tiles; architectural ceramics
NEW PRODUCTS Roman folly
CATALOGUE On telephone request
MAIL ORDER Yes

Makers of terracotta pots and tiles for floor and roof; statues and fountains. There is a terracotta gazebo and a new Roman folly.

Roebuck Eyot Limited
PO Box 321, Welwyn Garden City, Hertfordshire AL7 1LF
☎ 01707 371105   FAX 01707 339221
CONTACT D. McGillycuddy
PRODUCTS Animal repellent
NEW PRODUCTS 'Renardine 72/2'
CATALOGUE Leaflet (SAE)
MAIL ORDER Yes, from QUADTAG Ltd, Corrys, Roestock Lane, Colney Heath, Hertfordshire AL4 0QW

Makers of 'Renardine' animal repellent for cats, dogs and rabbits. 'Renardine 72/2' repels foxes, badgers and moles.

Roffey Bros Ltd
Throop Road, Bournemouth, Hampshire BH8 0DF
☎ 01202 537777   FAX 01202 532765
CONTACT Robert Parsons or Sarah Williams

Garden Supplies 407

PRODUCTS Commercial composts
NEW PRODUCTS Coir compost
CATALOGUE On request
MAIL ORDER No

Composts and materials for commercial growers and garden retailers, including bark, sterilised loam, coir, grit and leca.

Roger Platts
Faircombe, Maresfield, East Sussex TN22 2EH
☎ 01825 764077   FAX 01825 764077
CONTACT Roger Platts
PRODUCTS Garden furniture; pergolas
CATALOGUE On request
MAIL ORDER Yes

Garden furniture including seats and tables made from cast iron and wood; also oak pergolas.

Ryobi Lawn & Garden (UK) Ltd
Cotteswold Road, Tewkesbury, Gloucestershire GL20 5DJ
☎ 01684 294606   FAX 01684 294909
CONTACT Mrs Ruth Wood
PRODUCTS Powered garden tools
NEW PRODUCTS 16" battery lawnmower
CATALOGUE On request
MAIL ORDER No

Manufacturers of powered garden machinery including hedge trimmers, sweeper vacs, cultivators, chainsaws, trimmers and brush cutters.

Samuel Parkes & Co Ltd
New Road, Willenhall, West Midlands WV1 2BU
☎ 01902 366481   FAX 01902 633789
CONTACT Miss M. Robins or Miss S. Gorman
PRODUCTS Garden tools
CATALOGUE On request
MAIL ORDER No

Long-established manufacturers of a wide range of hand and garden tools.

Sarah Burgoyne Revivals
Whyly, East Hoathly, East Sussex BN8 6EL
☎ 01825 840738
CONTACT Sarah Burgoyne
PRODUCTS Garden furniture
CATALOGUE On request
MAIL ORDER Yes

Old-fashioned garden furniture in beech, including a traditional steamer chair with a fringed canopy.

Scarletts Plantcare
Nayland Road, West Bergholt, Colchester, Essex CO6 3DH
☎ 01206 240466   FAX 01206 242530
CONTACT Carrie Creswell
PRODUCTS Biological controls
CATALOGUE On request
MAIL ORDER Yes

Mail order biological controls for whitefly, red spider mite, vine weevil, thrips, mealy bug, aphids and caterpillars. Flat charge per treatment. Ring the number above for advice.

Shamrock Horticulture Ltd
The Crescent Centre, Temple Back, Bristol, Avon BS1 6EZ
☎ 0117 9211666   FAX 0117 9225501
CONTACT Anne Pearse
PRODUCTS Peat; peat-based composts; peat-free composts
NEW PRODUCTS 'Shamrock Grow-tray' – self-watering planter; extended compost range
CATALOGUE On request
MAIL ORDER No

Major peat supplier with an extended range which includes other compost mixes and conditioners. Includes coconut fibre products. Ring for details of your nearest supplier.

Sheen Garden Developments Ltd
11 Earl Road, East Sheen, London SW14 7JH
☎ 0181 878 8842   FAX 0181 878 8842
CONTACT John Hockley
PRODUCTS Labels
CATALOGUE On request
MAIL ORDER Yes

Professionally engraved plant labels and holders.

Shire Garden Buildings
Brigstock Road, Wisbech, Cambridgeshire PE13 3JJ
☎ 01945 65295   FAX 01945 582673
CONTACT Sales Office
PRODUCTS Garden buildings; greenhouses
CATALOGUE Yes

Manufacturers of ranges of wooden garden sheds, workshops, summerhouses and greenhouses.

Sim and Coventry
Eastham House, Copse Road, Fleetwood, Lancashire FT7 7NY
☎ 01253 778888   FAX 01253 878711
CONTACT Pam Nutall
PRODUCTS Bamboo canes and tree stakes
NEW PRODUCTS Bamboo, plastic and wood trellis; lawn edging and chain fencing
CATALOGUE On request
MAIL ORDER No

Suppliers of bamboo canes, trellis and jardinières; timber trellis and tree stakes, plastic trellis and lawn edging.

Simply Garlands
51 Albion Road, Pitstone, Bedfordshire LU7 9AY
☎ 01296 661425
CONTACT Kathy Rollings
PRODUCTS Floral accessories
CATALOGUE On request
MAIL ORDER Yes

408 Garden Supplies

Plastic cages which link together: used for making floral garlands, swags, pew ends and rings.

Somerset Postal Flowers
Carew Cottage, Crowcombe, Taunton, Somerset TA4 4AD
☎ 019848 314   FAX 019848 611
CONTACT Mrs Rosalind Gill
PRODUCTS Fresh flowers
CATALOGUE On request
MAIL ORDER Yes

Fresh flowers sent by post to addresses in the United Kingdom.

Spear & Jackson Garden Products
Neill Tools Ltd, Handsworth Road, Sheffield, South Yorkshire S13 9BR
☎ 0114 244 9911   FAX 0114 256 1545
CONTACT Linda Collins
PRODUCTS Hand tools; garden tools
NEW PRODUCTS Ergonomic spade and fork 'Back-saver'; new hand tools
CATALOGUE On request
MAIL ORDER No

Manufacturers of a wide range of hand and garden tools under this well-known brand name.

Sportsmark Group Ltd
Sportsmark House, Ealing Road, Brentford, London TW8 0LH
☎ 0181 560 2010/2012 FAX 0181 568 2177
CONTACT Sales
PRODUCTS Marking machines; grass seed and artificial grass
NEW PRODUCTS Flower tower; flower ball
CATALOGUE Leaflet and samples on request
MAIL ORDER Yes

Supplies for groundsmen and sports fields, including marking machines, sports grass seed mixtures and artificial grass.

The Standard Manufacturing Co
55 Woods Lane, Derby, Derbyshire DE3 3UD
☎ 01332 343369   FAX 01332 381531
CONTACT Mrs L. Morris
PRODUCTS Garden tools; cloches
NEW PRODUCTS Long-handled bulb planter
CATALOGUE No
MAIL ORDER Yes

Makers of a range of garden tools, including tree pruners, fruit pickers, sweepers and spreaders as well as cloches.

Stangwrach Leisure Products
Stangwrach, Llanfynydd, Camarthen, Dyfed SA32 7TG
☎ 01558 668287
CONTACT Terry or Grace Maidment
PRODUCTS Garden furniture

CATALOGUE £1
MAIL ORDER Yes

Hardwood garden furniture in strong designs. The timber is sourced only from managed forests.

Starkie & Starkie Ltd
39 The Heathers Industrial Park, Freemen's Common, Leicester, Leicestershire LE2 7SQ
☎ 01533 854772   FAX 01533 854884
CONTACT R. A. Starkie
PRODUCTS Tool sharpening systems
CATALOGUE On request
MAIL ORDER Yes

Suppliers of diamond whetstones and tool sharpening systems.

Strand Marketing Ltd
Barton Hall, Dunstall Road, Barton under Needwood, Burton on Trent, Staffordshire DE13 8DY
☎ 01283 716655   FAX 01283 716880
CONTACT Claire Mitchell
PRODUCTS Conservatories; greenhouses
CATALOGUE On request
MAIL ORDER No

Makers of a range of modern and traditional conservatories in uPVC and timber, aluminium greenhouses and cold frames.

Stratford Power Garden Machinery
4 Marsh Road, Wilmcote, Stratford on Avon, Warwickshire CV37 9XR
☎ 01789 294839   FAX 01789 261119
CONTACT Arnold Coffee
PRODUCTS Garden machinery
NEW PRODUCTS New Texas garden cultivators
CATALOGUE On request
MAIL ORDER Yes

Distributors of the Texas range of garden cultivators, Ikra electric hedge cutters, Bertolini sickle mowers and Zenoah chainsaws.

Stuart Garden Architecture
Burrow Hill Farm, Wiveliscombe, Somerset TA4 2RN
☎ 01984 7458   FAX 01984 7455
CONTACT Shari Fleetwood
PRODUCTS Trellis; wooden garden features; garden furniture
NEW PRODUCTS More planters; folding bench; dual height oval table
CATALOGUE £2
MAIL ORDER Yes

Stylish range of trellis-work, gazebos, pergolas, bridges and garden furniture. All constructed from hardwoods from sustainable sources. Custom design and build available.

Garden Supplies 409

Sunlight Systems
Unit 3, St Mary's Works, Burnmoor Street, Leicester, Leicestershire LE2 7JJ
☎ 0116 2470490   FAX 0116 2470485
CONTACT   Sales Office, Leicester
PRODUCTS   Horticultural lighting
CATALOGUE   On request
MAIL ORDER   Yes

Suppliers of artificial lighting products and systems. Other indoor equipment is also sold. There is a counter service at Unit 347, Stratford Workshops, Burford Road, London E15 2SP.

Sunshine of Africa (UK) Ltd
Afton Manor, Freshwater, Isle of Wight PO40 9TW
☎ 01983 754575   FAX 01983 755388
CONTACT   Miss Anne Parsons
PRODUCTS   Mulches
NEW PRODUCTS   Cocoa Lawn

Garden mulch and lawn care products made from cocoa shell.

Super Natural Ltd
Bore Place Farm, Chiddingstone, Edenbridge, Kent TN8 7AR
☎ 01732 463255   FAX 01732 740264
CONTACT   Miss Caroline Dunmall
PRODUCTS   Organic composts; organic fertilisers
CATALOGUE   On request
MAIL ORDER   From Dig & Delve Organics, Diss (01379 898377)

Organic composts, plant foods and soil conditioners. Also available in commercial sizes. Chiddingstone Brickworks, which makes hand-made bricks and pavers, is under the same ownership.

Supersheds Ltd
Coppice Road, Willaston, Nantwich, Cheshire CW5 6QH
☎ 01270 68121   FAX 01270 669280
CONTACT   I. P. Hill
PRODUCTS   Garden buildings; garden furniture
CATALOGUE   Yes

Manufacturers of a range of garden sheds and garden furniture. Metal garden sheds are supplied too.

Sussex Trugs Ltd
Thomas Smith's Trug Shop, Hailsham Road, Herstmonceux, East Sussex BN27 4LH
☎ 01323 832137/833801   FAX 01323 833801
CONTACT   Robin or Sue Tuppen
PRODUCTS   Garden trugs
CATALOGUE   On request
MAIL ORDER   Yes

Makers of the traditional Sussex trug basket.

Taylor Instruments
28 Chase Road, Park Royal, London NW10 6QN
☎ 0181 838 2898   FAX 0181 965 1591
CONTACT   Stephen Zeal
PRODUCTS   Thermometers
NEW PRODUCTS   Simulated terracotta thermometers and clocks
CATALOGUE   On request
MAIL ORDER   Yes

Thermometers, rain gauges, hygrometers, barometers and weather instruments.

Terrace & Garden Ltd
Orchard House, Patmore End, Ugley, Bishops Stortford, Hertfordshire CM22 6JA
☎ 01799 543289   FAX 01799 543586
CONTACT   Lynne Ellis
PRODUCTS   Decorative taps; windchimes; weathervanes; sundials
NEW PRODUCTS   Bird-houses; garden signs
CATALOGUE   On request
MAIL ORDER   Yes

Decorative and amusing sundials, animal-shaped tap heads, bird-houses, trellises, weather-vanes, path signs and windchimes for garden and home.

Thames Valley Wirework Co Ltd
792 Weston Road, Slough Trading Estate, Slough, Berkshire SL1 4HR
☎ 01753 521992   FAX 01753 574160
CONTACT   Sales Office
PRODUCTS   Plant supports
NEW PRODUCTS   'Gro-Thru' fan trellis for indoor plants
CATALOGUE   SAE
MAIL ORDER   Yes

Manufacturers of 'Gro-Thru' plant supports for herbaceous plants and a range of other supports for indoor and outdoor use.

Thermoforce Ltd
Bentalls Complex, Heybridge, Maldon, Essex CM9 7NW
☎ 01621 858797   FAX 01621 858496
CONTACT   K. A. Merriman
PRODUCTS   Greenhouse equipment
CATALOGUE   On request
MAIL ORDER   Yes

Manufacturers of greenhouse equipment including soil cables, mist units, automatic vents and lighting.

Tildenet Ltd
Longbrook House, Ashtonvale Road, Bristol, Avon BS3 2HA
☎ 01272 669684   FAX 01272 231751
CONTACT   Miss Angie Bunce
PRODUCTS   Netting
CATALOGUE   On request

Garden Supplies

MAIL ORDER No
Manufacturers of netting for perimeters, wind-breaks and ground cover.

Town and Country Products
State House, Morledge Street, Leicester LE1 1TA
☎ 0116 2536001   FAX 0116 2513337
CONTACT Nick Page
PRODUCTS Tool holders; gloves
CATALOGUE On request
MAIL ORDER Yes

Manufacturers and suppliers of pouches and tool holders, and suppliers of Wells Lamont garden and work gloves.

Trade and DIY Products Ltd
The Pump House, Hazelwood Road, Duffield, Belper, Derbyshire DE56 4AA
☎ 01332 842685   FAX 01332 842806
CONTACT Mr R. Barlow
PRODUCTS Sheeting; weed suppressants
NEW PRODUCTS Capillary matting; cloche/tunnel system
CATALOGUE On request
MAIL ORDER Yes

Suppliers of insulating horticultural fleece and 'Plantex' weed suppressant fabric (as used by RBG, Kew) to retail and trade customers.

The Traditional Garden Supply Company Ltd
Unit 12, Hewitts Industrial Estate, Elmbridge Road, Cranleigh, Surrey GU6 8LWD
☎ 01483 273366   FAX 01483 273388
CONTACT Paul Brooks or Jo Blair
PRODUCTS Garden supplies
NEW PRODUCTS Mini greenhouses; cold frames; furniture
CATALOGUE On request; 3 a year
MAIL ORDER Yes

Mail order suppliers of carefully selected garden products: some practical, some decorative. They now have a shop, too.

Trailer Barrow Company
Elsan House, Gordon Road, Buxted, Uckfield, East Sussex TN22 4LW
☎ 01825 733291   FAX 01825 733617
CONTACT Karen Isted
PRODUCTS Wheelbarrows
CATALOGUE On request
MAIL ORDER Yes, if no local stockist

2-wheeled barrows for pulling; larger models for towing.

Trees in Miniature
21 Harrowes Meade, Edgware, London HA8 8RR
☎ 0181 958 3574
CONTACT Burt Coleman

PRODUCTS Replica bonsai trees
CATALOGUE No
MAIL ORDER No

Preserved wood and foliage crafted into replica bonsai trees with audio effects. They have recently introduced an indoor water garden.

Trident Water Garden Products
Carlton Road, Foleshill, Coventry CV6 7FL
☎ 01203 638484   FAX 01203 637891
CONTACT Pam Adamson
PRODUCTS Water gardening and aquatic products
CATALOGUE SAE
MAIL ORDER No

Pumps, preformed pools and pond liners, filtration systems, fountains, lighting and water garden accessories.

Two Wests and Elliott Ltd
Unit 4, Carrwood Road, Sheepbridge Industrial Estate, Chesterfield, Derbyshire S41 9RH
☎ 01246 451077   FAX 01246 260115
CONTACT Mrs J. M. West
PRODUCTS Greenhouse equipment; propagators
CATALOGUE On request
MAIL ORDER Yes

Manufacture and sell a wide range of greenhouse and conservatory equipment including staging, heating, watering, propagation equipment and mini greenhouses. For amateur and professional use. Elliott is the dog.

Vale Garden Houses Ltd
Melton Road, Harlaxton, Grantham, Lincolnshire NG32 1HQ
☎ 01476 64433   FAX 01476 78555
CONTACT Lisa Morton
PRODUCTS Conservatories
CATALOGUE On request
MAIL ORDER No

Individually designed conservatories in period styles for domestic houses. Vale Conservatories Ltd handles larger and commercial projects.

Verdigris Ltd
Walkern Hall Farm, Walkern, Stevenage, Hertfordshire SG2 7HZ
☎ 01438 869346   FAX 01438 869370
CONTACT D. N. C. De Boinville
PRODUCTS Plant labels
CATALOGUE On request
MAIL ORDER No

Copper plant labels, tags and markers.

Vitax Ltd
Owen Street, Coalville, Leicestershire LE67 3DE
☎ 01530 510060   FAX 01530 510299
CONTACT Colin Wetherley-Mein
PRODUCTS Composts; fertilisers and soil improvers; herbicides

Garden Supplies 411

NEW PRODUCTS Lawn sand; compost maker; 'Woolmoss'
CATALOGUE On request
MAIL ORDER No

Makers of a range of composts, lawn care products, fertilisers and plant foods, soil improvers and herbicides.

Wartnaby Gardens
Melton Mowbray, Leicestershire LE14 3HY
☎ 01664 822549   FAX 01664 822231
PRODUCTS Plant labels
CATALOGUE On request
MAIL ORDER Yes

Practical zinc plant labels either as tie-ons or with stems; 14-inch stands are available for the tie-on variety and they also sell marking and engraving equipment.

Wells & Winter
Mereworth, Maidstone, Kent ME18 5NB
☎ 01622 813267
CONTACT Sir John Wells
PRODUCTS Labels; tree ties; apron; clamp for aerial layering
CATALOGUE On request
MAIL ORDER Yes

Good quality plastic, aluminium, zinc and copper labels, tags, and marking equipment. Labels can be pre-engraved to your order. Mail order and shows only. Some other products, and books (at shows only).

Wessex Horticultural Products Ltd
South Newton, Salisbury, Wiltshire SP2 0QW
☎ 01722 742500   FAX 01722 742571
CONTACT Rosemary Henderson
PRODUCTS Growing media; organic products
NEW PRODUCTS Ericaceous compost, 'Cocomoss'; decorative grit
CATALOGUE On request
MAIL ORDER Yes

Manufacturers and suppliers of peat-free and traditional growing media. Their sister company Growing Success Organic Ltd sells slug killer, hanging basket liners and insect traps.

Westland Horticulture
97 Moy Road, Dungannon, Co. Tyrone
☎ 018687 84007   FAX 018687 84077
CONTACT Seamus McGrane
PRODUCTS Growing media; mulches
NEW PRODUCTS Specialise composts; mini chipbark
CATALOGUE On request

Manufacturers and suppliers of Westland composts and growing media including mulches and chipped bark.

Whichford Pottery
Whichford, Shipston on Stour, Warwickshire CV36 5PG
☎ 01608 684416   FAX 01608 684833
CONTACT Jane Lancia

PRODUCTS Terracotta pots
NEW PRODUCTS New designs, including ornamental chickens and cockerels
CATALOGUE 6 first class stamps
MAIL ORDER Yes; £13.50 delivery charge

Hand-made, frost-free terracotta pots in plain and decorated designs. The pottery, which can be visited, handles some very large pieces.

William Sinclair Horticulture
Firth Road, Lincoln, Lincolnshire LN6 7AH
☎ 01522 537561   FAX 01522 513609
CONTACT Advisory Service
PRODUCTS Composts; fertilisers; aggregates; lawn care
MAIL ORDER No

Horticultural conglomerate whose range includes composts, fertilisers and soil conditioners from J. Arthur Bowers; Silvaperl aggregates including sand, gravel and perlite; the Garotta brand compost equipment; and peat-free composts and conditioners.

WOLF Tools
Alton Road, Ross on Wye, Hereford & Worcester HR9 5NE
☎ 01989 767600   FAX 01989 765589
CONTACT R. Wolf
PRODUCTS Hand tools; lawnmowers; garden machinery
CATALOGUE From WOLF and their stockists
MAIL ORDER No

An extensive range of tools for the gardener from this well-known company. Products include garden tools with interchangeable heads, cultivating tools, pruning equipment, lawnmowers and powered machinery.

Woodgrow Horticulture Ltd
84 Burton Road, Findern, Derby, Derbyshire DE65 6BE
☎ 01332 516392   FAX 01332 511481
CONTACT Arnold or Martin Woodhouse
PRODUCTS Landscaping materials
MAIL ORDER Some items

Landscape materials for the landscape trade including bark and wood chips, soil and composts, aggregates and plastic tunnels. A new depot has opened at Findern.

Woodside Horticulture Ltd
Woodside Farm, Dearham, Maryport, Cumbria CA15 7LD
☎ 01900 816579   FAX 01900 876019
CONTACT J. Cox
PRODUCTS Composts; fertilisers
NEW PRODUCTS Professional composts
CATALOGUE Yes

Suppliers and manufacturers of peat and peat-free composts, bark and fertilisers.

Garden Supplies

Yardmaster International
Cahore Road, Draperstown, Co. Londonderry
BT45 7AP
☎ 01648 28449/28270 FAX 01648 28670
CONTACT Matt Brady
PRODUCTS Garden buildings
NEW PRODUCTS New metal shed with 10-year anti-rust warranty
CATALOGUE On request
MAIL ORDER Yes

Flat pack self-assembly metal garden sheds.

Zeneca Garden and Professional
Fernhurst, Haslemere, Surrey GU27 3JE
☎ 01428 645454 FAX 01428 657222
CONTACT Consumer Services
PRODUCTS Pesticides; fertilisers; herbicides; growing media; house-plant care products; biological controls
MAIL ORDER No

Manufacturers and suppliers of a wide range of chemicals and gardening sundries, many of them household names.

# 19

Organic Gardening

The organic gardening movement has developed as a branch of organic agriculture during the latter half of this century, in opposition to the increased use of manufactured pesticides and fertilisers. The principles are based on good husbandry as it was practised before farmers were encouraged to grow food as efficiently as possible for a predominantly urban population.

The growing evidence of damage to the environment by the overuse of chemicals has been a significant factor in the growth of organic trends and ideas. One of the most important catalysts was the publication of *Silent Spring* in 1962, in which Rachel Carson recorded the effects of the excessive use of chemicals in the US: the poisoning of the environment, the destruction of beneficial insects and upsetting the balance of nature.

Early ridicule has given way, if to not intellectual respectability, at least to grudging acceptance of the strength of the organic argument. That said, the 'organic movement', as its faithful like to call themselves, is not helped by the theories and practices of some of its battier devotees.

Many of us are daunted by the commitment that organic gardening appears to demand. We are convinced that organic gardening is a religion, but doubt whether it is really for us. Nevertheless, it is worth investigating and understanding. Fortunately, many of the exponents of organic gardening are good at giving help and advice to those who would like to learn more about its precepts and practicalities.

The main rule of organic gardening is 'to feed the soil, not the plant'. This means maintaining and improving soil fertility with organic materials so that there is no need to depend on fast-acting artificial fertilisers to boost plant growth. It is achieved by the regular application of bulky organic materials which are broken down into humus by micro-organisms in the soil. A soil that is humus-rich is better aerated, more likely to have a good structure, and is better able to hold moisture and nutrients. Put simply, a healthy soil grows healthy plants that are more likely to resist both pests and diseases.

The Soil Association, 86 Colston Street, Bristol BS1 5BB has been one of the prime movers in encouraging an organic approach to soil management and plant health. It administers an approval scheme for bona fide organic growers by awarding the Soil Association symbol and, although orientated towards larger-scale production, can offer advice and information to individuals. It also runs a bookshop.

Some organic gardening schools advocate 'no digging'. They call it 'organic surface cultivation', and point out that, in Nature, the soil remains undisturbed and organic materials accumulate on the surface each year to be drawn down by earthworms and micro-organisms. This can be successful on strong soils but, where the structure is initially week, the soil may deteriorate further.

The Good Gardeners Association, Timber Yard, Two Mile Lane, Highnam, Gloucestershire, GL2 8BR; and *The Irish Organic Farmers and Growers Association*, Killegland Farm, Ashbourne, Co. Meath also offer advice and support to growers, and act as contact points for the dissemination of information.

In the UK the centre for organic gardening is the *Henry Doubleday Research Association (HDRA)*, established in 1954. It has become the largest such organisation in the world. Its permanent headquarters, since 1985, have been at Ryton Gardens, Ryton on Dunsmore, Coventry CV8 3LG. Here are demonstration gardens for fruit, vegetables and flowers, as well as wild-flower gardens and conservation areas: the whole is interspersed with displays of equipment, and strategies and tactics for the natural control of pests are an integral part of the gardens. The message of environmental responsibility is also well told and communicated in many ways, from saving seeds of varieties no longer in commerce to growing suitable trees in small greenhouses for seed to be delivered to the Third World.

The maintenance of soil fertility by applying organic matter is widely accepted as good practice, and at Ryton one can see a range of materials and techniques in use from double-digging to no-dig deep-bed systems. It is also one of the best places to study that symbol of political correctness, the art and science of compost production. Regular recycling of plant waste from garden and kitchen is an important habit for most gardeners.

It is a misconception that organic gardeners do not use fertilisers. The truth is that they use them selectively. Compost and humus almost always need to be supplemented by fertilisers to provide the extra nutrients required, certainly by fruit and vegetables. Some organic fertilisers release their nutrients relatively slowly, including bone-meal, hoof and horn; others, such as dried blood and seaweed-meal, are fast-acting.

The control of pests and diseases by totally organic methods presents the most difficulties to the mainstream gardener. There are several reasons for this. Most of us seek horticultural perfection, and this is compromised by infestations of pests and disease. Ryton itself is a sad sight at the end of September, when all the cabbages are reduced to lace by caterpillars and the tomatoes are white with mildew. It is difficult to stick to organic principles when rose varieties chosen for their resistance to disease are much the worse for blackspot, and others whose resistance to pests and diseases is known to be low are not even grown. The answer is to distinguish between cosmetic damage and damage that seriously and permanently affects the health of the plant, which blackspot seldom does.

The instant effect of most modern chemicals makes reaching for the spray-gun an easy and appealing solution to pest control. Organic gardeners may use selected pesticides but will probably regard their use as short-term crisis management: they prefer to control pests, diseases and weeds chiefly by cultural methods, good hygiene and the rotation of crops to prevent a build-up of harmful agents in the soil and avoid depletion of particular nutrients.

Organic gardeners actively encourage natural predators by growing their food plants and by introducing natural parasites to control such difficult pests as whitefly and spider mite. If they use insecticides, they will choose those of natural origin: these may be less efficient, but they are also less harmful to other animal life than inorganic types, and are not persistent. The organic pesticides most frequently recommended include soft soap, derris, pyrethrum and quassia chips.

Organic gardeners make an analogy with the difference between traditional and alternative medicine: the former treats the symptoms, while the latter seeks a more holistic solution. When applied to gardens, this means adopting a range of strategies and tactics for pest and disease control whose common denominators are that they cause minimum disruption to the ecosystem, and that each tactic employed is co-ordinated with every other to form a multi-pronged plan of defence. The tricks, traps, predators and parasitoids that augment sound cultural practices to form a holistic approach can all be seen at Ryton.

HDRA's practical approach is backed up with advice and information; it also runs a bookshop and specialist library, and co-ordinates some thirty local groups. The HDRA operates in conjunction with *Chase Organics*, Coombelands House, Coombelands Lane, Addlestone, Weybridge, Surrey KT15 1HY and supplies almost everything from biocontrols to books from a joint catalogue.

Gardeners with vegan tendencies are stricter in their expectations. They use rock phosphate, rock potash or seaweed-meal instead of fertilisers derived from animals. Most organic suppliers give guidance in their catalogues on the origin and most appropriate use of their fertiliser products. Amongst them are:

Cumulus Organics, Pinetum Lodge, Churcham, Gloucestershire GL2 8AD, Tel: 01452 750402

All-Gain Organics, 8 Netherlands Road, New Barnet, Hertfordshire EN5 1BN, Tel: 0181 449 1605

Other organisations share the ecological principles of organic gardening, but apply them with a broader brush. Perhaps the best known is the *Centre* for *Alternative Technology*, Machynlleth, Powys, SY20 9AZ, Tel: 01654 2400. This well-established centre demonstrates a range of sustainable technologies, including organic food production. It also runs courses, educational visits and an information service; it sells books and environmentally sound products, and produces a wide range of information sheets, resource lists and reports.

The Permaculture Association, 8 Hunters Moon, Totnes, Devon TQ9 6TJ, tel. 01803 867546, was formed to encourage the practice of permaculture – the conscious use of ecological principles for self-sustaining food production. It offers information and advice on garden design and planting to incorporate many different techniques: organic, ecological and bio-dynamic gardening.

The Bio-Dynamic Agriculture Association, Woodman Lane, Clent, Stourbridge, West Midlands, DY9 9PX, Tel: 01562 884933 promotes bio-dynamic agriculture, offers help and support to all bio-dynamic growers and operates a postal advice service. Bio-dynamics are based on the anthroposophical theories of Rudolph Steiner, and combine organic principles with celestial ones: the phase of the moon is believed to influence planting times. Mainstream organic gardeners regard such practices with a degree of scepticism.

• 20 •
Buying in Bulk

There are considerable savings to be made by buying wholesale or in bulk, although there are a number of other considerations to be taken into account. The first problem is that many wholesalers simply do not deal with the general public and, if they do, they often stipulate a minimum order that can range from fifty to several hundred pounds. Unwillingness to deal with the public is not a result of wholesalers' bloody-mindedness. There are building regulations and health and safety constraints that may prevent them from opening their premises to the public. Moreover, unlike well-run garden centres, wholesalers seldom have the time to give horticultural advice. You should have a clear idea of what you need before you order, so always do your homework first.

One approach to bulk buying is to form a 'co-op' – a garden club – and pool financial resources to meet minimum order requirements. There will still be logistical drawbacks to consider. Bulk orders usually need a spacious delivery and distribution centre, and someone willing to organise the process. A good starting-point for the would-be bulk buyer is the Yellow Pages directory; we have given references here for where to look.

Buying Plants and Seeds

(Yellow pages: Nurseries; Horticultural & Wholesale). For orders of large numbers of plants – hedging, for example – it is always worth considering a direct approach to wholesale nurseries, especially if you are buying as a garden society or group. A number of large country estates and local authorities now run forest tree nurseries, with a good selection of native and forestry species. You can only ask, and they can, at worst, refuse to deal with you. If they are willing to do business with you it will probably be on a 'buyer collects' basis, and payment is likely to be required on collection because, as an indivi-dual, you are unknown to them as a credit risk. Give advance notice of your order and fix an appointment for collection, since plants may be field-grown and require lifting. You need to specify exactly what you want: species, variety, size, numbers, and transplant, whip or half-standard. You can find guidelines to stock sizes in the British Standard for Nursery Stock: BS3936 Pt. 1, from your local reference library.

Some suppliers are willing to make up bulk orders of seed and sundries at a discount to allotment and garden groups. Among them are:

D. T. Brown & Co. Ltd, Station Road, Poulton le Fylde, Lancashire FY6 7HX, Tel: 01253 882371

James Henderson & Sons, Kingholm Quay, Dumfries & Galloway DG1 4SU, Tel: 01387 52234

Seeds-by-Size, 45 Crouchmoor, Boxmoor, Hemel Hempstead, Hertfordshire HP1 1PA, Tel: 01442 251458.

Some well known seed merchants also offer discounts or special terms to clubs and allotment societies; it is always worth asking the sales department if they run such schemes.

Many people – and organisations too – are interested in creating wild-flower meadows, or other conservation features. One of the largest suppliers of wild-flower seed, Emorsgate Seeds, Terrington Court, Terrington St Clement, Kings Lynn, Norfolk PE34 4NT, Tel: 01553 829028, can supply seed in quantities from 100 kg down to 1 gm packets, and are experienced in dealing with schools and local authorities.

Should you need to plant up a whole new herbaceous border, it is a good idea to telephone round nurseries for quotes on your planting list.

Composts, Fertilisers and Sundries.

(Yellow Pages: Agricultural Wholesalers; DIY Stores). For the range of composts that most gardeners use, the large chain DIY superstores have massive buying power and can be very competitive.

Buying in Bulk

It is worth phoning round to compare prices: you may find greater reductions at your local agricultural wholesaler's. Owners of large gardens find they can buy fertilisers and chemicals at agricultural prices for a fraction of the price they would spend at a garden centre, but they have to know the agricultural name for Tumbleweed and understand what 20:10:10 means. The following specialise in bulk supplies:

Joseph Bentley Ltd, Back Lane, Barrow-on-Humber DN19 7AQ, Tel: 01469 532000. Composts, fertilisers and sundries. Minimum order £75; special terms for gardening and allotment societies. Nationwide delivery.

Roffey Bros, Throop Road, Throop, Bournemouth, Dorset BH8 0DF, Tel: 01202 537777. Manufacturers and suppliers of a range of composts, fertilisers and chemicals which they will deliver throughout the South and West. They offer special terms to societies, and have no minimum order, but impose a small delivery charge on smaller orders.

T. Dagg & Sons, 16 Bath St, Glasgow G2 1HA, Tel: 0141 322 2487, Fax: 0141 332 5044. Stockists of a wide range of composts, fertilisers and sundries. They give discounts to allotment societies and offer free local delivery on orders over £20; at normal carriage cost they supply Shetland and the Western Isles.

Manure

(Yellow Pages: Riding Stables; Dairy Farmers). Country gardeners need never be short of muck, although farmers are always busy, so you may need charm and persistence to acquire it, especially if you need it delivered. Many farmers will allow you to collect your own. It is, however, always important to offer payment.

The suburban gardener may be lucky enough to live near a riding stables, although it is likely that you will have to make your own arrangements to collect manure. Prospects are fairly bleak for the committed urbanite: finding a source and collecting sufficient quantities to be worth while may be difficult.

Topsoil

(Yellow Pages: Turf Suppliers; Mushroom Growers; Sugar Refiners; Landscapers). Check also Builders in the Classified section of your local paper. Topsoil is sold loose by the tonne, or cubic metre (1.4 tonnes), and you need to check whether the quoted price includes delivery. Before buying, prepare your site, and consider the logistics of how, when and where you will take delivery. Check on quality before delivery and look out for mixtures containing subsoil, which is always a different colour from proper topsoil. Ask the supplier where it comes from: is it from chalky, sandy, gravel, clay or peaty soils? The geology of the country varies considerably.

Avoid stockpiles that have been stacked high for long periods: they will almost certainly have lost their structure through compaction. Delay planting until any pernicious weeds have shown themselves and deal with them before you plant.

Spent mushroom compost is a valuable bulking material for growing media and mulching. It has a good constitution, but do check the pH: it may be very alkaline due to the lime which is used in the casing.

Sugar beet washings are sometimes offered as a substitute for topsoil, but are probably best regarded only as an ameliorant for very heavy soil. Processing destroys the structure; the resulting dirt is nutritionally very poor, light, and liable to be blown about.

Sheet Mulches and Pond-liners

(Yellow Pages: Agricultural and Horticultural Wholesalers; Plastics – Manufacturers; Suppliers of Film and Sheet). Sheet mulches such as woven poly-propylene, black and clear polythene or spun poly-propylene fleece (used as a floating mulch) can be bought by the roll from agricultural and horticultural wholesalers, or from plastics suppliers. In the long term, this will work out much cheaper, though it may take the average gardener several seasons to use a whole roll. Be sure to store black polythene in cool, dark conditions, since it degenerates in heat and sunlight. Plastics manufacturers and suppliers usually carry a range of butyl, reinforced PVC, and heavy-duty plastics that are suitable for pond and bog garden liners. Remember that most wholesalers have a minimum order.

Bark Mulches

(Yellow Pages: Timber Merchants; Sawmills). Brand-name bark mulches can be almost as expensive as best Axminster, though you can usually be sure that you are buying a clean, uniform product. It will also have been composted to drive off terpenes and phenols that would be harmful if applied directly to plant roots. Aside from transport and delivery, this is the major drawback of buying 'raw' bark and wood chips. Unless the chips have been properly composted, stack them and turn them from time to time for about six months before use. Coarse sawdust or shavings also make good mulches, if composted; be sure that they are not derived from wood that has been treated with preservative. With these qualifications, bark chips, loose bark and sawdust can be had at a fraction of the price of branded mulches, from the above sources. The Forestry Commission, and those local authorities that operate an Urban Forestry enterprise, are alternative sources.

Stone, Sand and Gravel

(Yellow Pages: Quarries; Sand and Gravel Merchants; Stone Merchants). There are considerable savings to be made by buying these 'hard' materials direct from source; the price you pay may be as little as one tenth of the retail price. The more you buy, the cheaper the price per tonne, since transport costs are a major portion of the price. Expect delivery by large tipper lorry and make sure you have the place and space to put the load. Plan where it will be unloaded. Can it be stored there? How far is it from the site? Who will help with the back-breaking barrowing?

Hard Landscaping Materials

(Yellow Pages: Builders' Merchants; DIY Stores; Paving Manufacturers). The bricks, paving and other hard materials that form the structure of your garden are likely to be the single most expensive item in its creation. Large paving manufacturers seldom deal with the public (it is rather like asking ICI to sell you a bottle of aspirin). You might have more joy with small local manufacturers, but have to collect the paving slabs from their factory. Builders' merchants may seem the most logical place to buy, but do not overlook the DIY superstores; they are extremely competitive. As with all bulk orders, consider the logistics of delivery – timing, unloading and space for storage. Paving slabs are surprisingly heavy. Many timber merchants will also offer considerable savings over DIY outlets, and may deliver locally.

21

Professional Services

For even the most enthusiastic gardener there comes a time to call on professional help. Others may turn to the experts more often – for large and demanding jobs, for knowledge and expertise, or for their ideas and inspiration. The good news is that there is no shortage of assistance available out there. Choosing the right person for the right task, however, and making sure that what you get is what you actually want are more tricky. The information in this section is designed to help you on your way.

Employing a professional

The most important job is to decide what you want. You don't have to make all the decisions yourself, but the nature and extent of the work which you are prepared to pay for must be laid out at the start. For small and well-defined tasks such as the removal of a tree limb this should be straightforward enough. For anything more extensive it's vital to discuss and agree the brief with the professional concerned. Many professionals produce detailed information on the way they carry out their business and what clients can expect. Then you need to spell out your requirements on such matters as time scale, the budget, and the degree of finish. It has to be absolutely clear that the professional understands your terms and is able to fulfil them. This process can be time-consuming. Avoid the temptation to rush it. This will avoid many costly misunderstandings and potential disappointments. Among the questions to ask, satisfy yourself on the following:

What are your qualifications? Do you belong to an appropriate professional body?

What levels of third party insurance and public liability insurance do you carry? This is very important for heavy or hazardous work such as tree surgery or construction.

Can I see a portfolio, inspect completed work or contact previous clients to see whether I like your work?

Will you use your own staff or employ outside contractors? Can a designer recommend contractors?

Notes on the lists

Suppliers of professional services are listed alphabetically, by name. In each entry you will find details of the services which the firm offers, the geographical area they operate in, and examples of the kind of projects of which they have experience. A number of the nurseries and garden centres we list also offer garden design and landscaping, ranging in degree from informal (but expert) advice to full design, construction or consultancy services. Such nurseries are indicated here by a cross-reference to their main entry in the Nurseries section.

Professional bodies

Many of the entries include details of the main professional bodies and organisations to which they belong. This information is not definitive, and not everyone has supplied full details, yet it is a useful guide to the sort of service you can expect to find. Firms and practitioners are strictly vetted before they can join these bodies, and this vetting may include inspection of their work and a requirement to carry specified levels of insurance. It is up to you to decide on the level of technical competence and

Professional Services

experience you require. For more details about these bodies see the Organisations section.

FHort Fellow of the Institute of Horticulture
MIHort Member of the Institute of Horticulture
AIHort Associate of the Institute of Horticulture
SGD Fellow or Member of the Society of Garden Designers
ALI Associate of the Landscape Institute
AAAC Arboricultural Association Approved Contractor
FAA Fellow of the Arboricultural Association
BALI British Association of Landscape Industries

Further information

The Institute of Horticulture produces a list of horticultural consultants: to receive a free copy write to the institute at P O Box 313, Vincent Square, London SW1P 2PE. The *Society of Garden Designers* also produces a list of its membership with notes about their careers: free of charge from the Hon. Secretary, Society of Garden Designers, 23 Reigate Road, Ewell, Surrey KT17 1PS. If you contact the *British Association of Landscape Industries* (BALI) at Landscape House, Henry Street, Keighley, West Yorkshire BD21 3DR they can provide a list of BALI members in your area. The *Arboricultural Association*, at Ampfield House, Romsey, Hampshire SO51 9PA can send you a copy of their directory of approved contractors and consultants on request. A *Directory of Registered Landscape Practices*, which includes all the *Landscape Institute*'s members, can be obtained from RIBA shops (£10) and by post (£11) from the Royal Institute of British Architects.

Caveat Emptor

Our list is based on information which the firms themselves have supplied. Accordingly, the presence in or absence from this list of a firm should not be taken as a judgement on the firm or any sort of recommendation. It's your decision whom you employ in the end – and, as so often, the motto is *Buyer Beware*.

Absolute Tree Care

27 Harrison Close, Waltham Chase, Twyford, Berkshire RF10 0LL
☎ 01734 320020
CONTACT Philip Warren
WORKING AREA Berkshire, South Buckinghamshire, South Oxfordshire
ASSOCIATIONS AAAC
SERVICES Arboricultural services
STARTED TRADING 1987

Acres Wild (Landscape & Garden Design)

45a High Street, Billingshurst, West Sussex RH14 9PP
☎ 01403 785385

CONTACT Ian Smith or Debbie Roberts
WORKING AREA Hampshire, Kent, London, Surrey and Sussex
ASSOCIATIONS SGD
SERVICES Garden design
STARTED TRADING 1988
PROJECTS Featured on the BBC's *Gardens by Design*; won the Phoenix Award for Memorial Garden Design (Durrington Cemetery) and Commitment to the Environment Award for a wildlife garden for the London & Edinburgh Insurance Group

Both practitioners have degrees in landscape architecture. Acres Wild won the first Hampton Court Trophy for Garden Design.

Agars Nursery, Hampshire

For full details see Nurseries section

Andrea Parsons – The Parsons Garden

15a Rawsthorn Road, Colchester, Essex CO3 3JH
☎ 01206 570440   FAX 01206 763408

CONTACT Andrea Parsons
WORKING AREA Nationwide
SERVICES Garden design
STARTED TRADING 1990
PROJECTS Help the Aged garden, Chelsea 1994; large private gardens in Essex

Gained a distinction at the College of Garden Design. Garden design for private clients.

Annabel Allhusen

Capstitch House, Compton Abbas, Shaftesbury, Dorset SP7 0NB
☎ 01747 811622

CONTACT Annabel Allhusen
WORKING AREA Devon, Dorset, Hampshire, Somerset and Wiltshire
SERVICES Garden design; horticultural consultancy
STARTED TRADING 1989
PROJECTS Private gardens

Trained at the College of Garden Design. Garden design, including drawings and planting schedules. Consultancy advice and individual border planning also available. Has exhibited recently in the Design Pavilion at Chelsea.

Professional Services

Anthony Archer-Wills Ltd
Broadford Bridge Road, West Chiltington, West Sussex RH20 2LF
☎ 01798 803204   FAX 01798 815080
CONTACT   Lynn Archer-Wills
SERVICES   Garden design; contractors; water and riparian services
PROJECTS   Consultant for water gardens, ponds etc.

Garden designer with particular expertise in water gardens: he can supply the plants and associated products too. His book *The Water Gardener* was published in 1993. See also the Nurseries section.

Anthony du Gard Pasley
3 The Homestead, Corseley Road, Groombridge, Kent TN3 9RN
☎ 01892 864548
CONTACT   Anthony du Gard Pasley
WORKING AREA   Home Counties, south west Scotland and Borders, Europe
ASSOCIATIONS   FLI; FSDG; FSA(Scot)
SERVICES   Garden design; horticultural consultancy; landscape architecture
STARTED TRADING   1972
PROJECTS   Wadhurst Park, Sussex; Hedsor Wharf, Bourne End, Buckinghamshire; La Cléchère, Kockelscheuer, Luxembourg; Château Court St Etienne, Belgium

Landscape architect and garden designer with particular expertise in restoring and altering historic gardens for easier maintenance, without loss of character.

Anthony George & Associates
The Old Brick House, Village Road, Dorney, Windsor, Berkshire SL4 6QJ
☎ 01628 604224   FAX 01628 604401
CONTACT   Anthony George
WORKING AREA   London, Midlands and Southern England
ASSOCIATIONS   ALI; FRSA
SERVICES   Garden design; contractors; arboricultural services; landscape architecture; architectural consultants
STARTED TRADING   1982

Architectural consultants, planners and landscape architects.

Anthony Short & Partners
34 Church Street, Ashbourne, Derbyshire DE6 1AE
☎ 01335 342145   FAX 01335 300624
CONTACT   Anthony Short
WORKING AREA   50-mile radius
ASSOCIATIONS   ALI; RIBA
SERVICES   Garden design; landscape architecture; chartered architects
STARTED TRADING   1966

Architectural and landscape architectural practice.

Antony Young
Ridleys Cheer, Mountain Bower, Chippenham, Wiltshire SN14 7AJ
☎ 01225 891204   FAX 01225 891139
CONTACT   Antony Young
WORKING AREA   UK and Europe
SERVICES   Garden design; horticultural consultancy; contractors; landscape architecture
STARTED TRADING   1990
PROJECTS   Extensive new gardens at Ozleworth Park, Gloucestershire, including shrub, rose, herb and parterre and water gardens.

Apple Court, Hampshire
For full details see Nurseries section

Architectural Landscape Design Ltd
3-5 Kelsey Road, Beckenham, Kent BR3 2LH
☎ 0181 658 4455   FAX 0181 658 2785
CONTACT   Mr Chris Coope
WORKING AREA   1 hour's drive from M25
ASSOCIATIONS   BALI; MIHort
SERVICES   Garden design; contractors; water and riparian services; landscape architecture; irrigation systems
STARTED TRADING   1978
PROJECTS   Design and installation of irrigation system at the Tower of London

Complete landscape service from site clearance through to design, planting and construction. Suppliers and installers of Toro sprinkler systems.

Arne Herbs, Avon
For full details see Nurseries section

Arrow Tree Services
102 Quebec Road, St Leonards on Sea, East Sussex TN38 9HT
☎ 01424 714376
CONTACT   David Archer
WORKING AREA   Kent, London, Surrey and Sussex
ASSOCIATIONS   AAAC
SERVICES   Arboricultural services; water and riparian services
STARTED TRADING   1976
PROJECTS   Restoration of treescape in a 17th-century deer park; restoration of Victorian garden and lake

Artscapes & Theseus Maze Designs
Silk Mill House, 24 Winchester Street, Whitchurch, Hampshire RG28 7DD
☎ 01256 892837   FAX 01256 892837
CONTACT   Graham Burgess
WORKING AREA   UK and overseas
ASSOCIATIONS   FHort
SERVICES   Garden design; water and riparian services; landscape architecture; maze and labyrinth design
STARTED TRADING   1981

422 Professional Services

PROJECTS Rose maze parterre at Longleat House, Wiltshire; a country garden in Berkshire; Water feature, Borax, Guildford; mill garden, Gloucestershire; Lake projects throughout UK

Kew-trained garden designer whose work includes symbolic and historic designs, with a special expertise in mazes.

ASH Consulting Group
15 Carlton Court, Glasgow, Strathclyde G5 9JP
☎ 0141 420 3131   FAX 0141 420 3020

CONTACT Ross Anderson
WORKING AREA UK and overseas
ASSOCIATIONS ALI; AI Hort
SERVICES Garden design; landscape architecture; urban forestry
PROJECTS Annandale Water Motorway Service Station; Riverside Walkway, Inverclyde; Cairngorm Tourism Management Programme

Substantial landscape design and planning group formed by the merger of ASH and Cousins Stephens. There are other branches in Scotland and England. The practice includes landscape architects, ecologists, foresters, town planners, environmental scientists and economists.

Auldene Nurseries Ltd, Lancashire
For full details see Nurseries section

Aylett Nurseries Ltd, Hertfordshire
For full details see Nurseries section

Aylmer Addison Associates
Walnut Tree Farm, Kirstead, Brooke, Norwich, Norfolk NR15 1EG
☎ 01508 50202   FAX 01508 50110

CONTACT Mr Aylmer or Mr Addison
WORKING AREA Cambridgeshire, Norfolk, Suffolk
ASSOCIATIONS AAAC
SERVICES Arboricultural services
STARTED TRADING 1979
PROJECTS Re-pollarding fen bank willows in the Norfolk Broads

Arboricultural work including amenity planting, surgery, the conservation and maintenance of small woodlands, and advice on safety for local authorities.

Barbara Hunt
91 Church Street, Staines, Surrey TW18 4XS
☎ 01784 452919   FAX 01784 452919

CONTACT Barbara Hunt
WORKING AREA London, Surrey, Buckinghamshire, Berkshire, Oxfordshire
ASSOCIATIONS SGD; AIHort
SERVICES Garden design
STARTED TRADING 1980
PROJECTS Designer of best show garden, Hampton Court Show, 1992, 1993 and 1994; plantings in VIP areas at Heathrow.

Has a diploma in three-dimensional design. Undertakes landscape design and consultation for private and commercial clients.

Barton Grange Garden Centre (Bolton), Lancashire
For full details see Nurseries section

Berrys Garden Company Ltd
6 Hodford Road, London NW11 8NP
☎ 0181 209 0194   FAX 0181 458 6442

CONTACT Brian Berry
WORKING AREA Buckinghamshire, Hertfordshire, Middlesex and London north of the Thames
ASSOCIATIONS BALI; SDG
SERVICES Garden design; horticultural consultancy; contractors
STARTED TRADING 1980
PROJECTS Royal Free Hospital; St Thomas More Church, Hampstead and varied residential projects

Landscape design and build, including garden electrics, carpentry, and irrigation and drainage.

Birkheads Cottage Garden Nursery, Tyne & Wear
For full details see Nurseries section

Bonita Bulaitis
6 Watton Road, Ware, Hertfordshire SG12 0AA
☎ 01920 466466

CONTACT Bonita Bulaitis
WORKING AREA UK and Europe
ASSOCIATIONS SGD
SERVICES Garden design; landscape architecture
STARTED TRADING 1987
PROJECTS Riverside house and garden

Trained in Garden Design and now studying for a Landscape Architecture degree. Specialities include low-maintenance gardens with bulbs and perennials, and contemporary garden furniture and structures to her own design.

The Botanic Nursery, Wiltshire
For full details see Nurseries section

Branchline Tree Services
23 Charleston Cottages, Glossop, Derbyshire SK13 8LF
☎ 01457 862954

CONTACT Paul Turkentine
WORKING AREA North West England and Greater Manchester
ASSOCIATIONS AAAC
SERVICES Arboricultural services
STARTED TRADING 1988

Approved local and county council contractors.

Bunny Guinness
Sibberton Lodge, Thornhaugh, Peterborough, Cambridgeshire PE8 6NH
☎ 01780 782518

CONTACT Bunny Guinness
WORKING AREA England and France
ASSOCIATIONS ALI
SERVICES Garden design; horticultural consultancy; landscape architecture; planning appeals and public enquiries
STARTED TRADING 1985
PROJECTS Groombridge Place, Kent; Pound Hill House, Wiltshire

Wide experience in public and private practice. Commissions can be phased over several years and an initial free consultation is offered. Gold Medal winner at Chelsea 1994.

Bypass Nurseries, Essex
For full details see Nurseries section

Byrkley Park Centre, Staffordshire
For full details see Nurseries section

Cabbages & Kings
Wilderness Farm, Wilderness Lane, Hadlow Down, East Sussex TN22 4HU
☎ 01825 830552   FAX 01825 830736

CONTACT Andrew or Ryl Nowell
WORKING AREA UK and overseas (design and planting)
ASSOCIATIONS SGD
SERVICES Garden design; horticultural consultancy; contractors
STARTED TRADING 1989
PROJECTS Cottage garden for BBC TV's *Front Gardens*, 1993

Over 30 years experience designing gardens. They will supply and plant too. Demonstration garden open 1 May to 30 September.

Carol Messham
41 Feversham Drive, Kirbymoorside, York, North Yorkshire YO6 6DH
☎ 01751 432071

CONTACT Carol Messham
WORKING AREA Cheshire, Yorkshire and north west England
SERVICES Garden design; horticultural consultancy; landscape architecture
STARTED TRADING 1988
PROJECTS Private gardens including a small courtyard in Malton, and a 3½ acre garden at Horwich

Landscape architect and garden design consultant. Services include postal design and supervision of contractors; maintenance schedules are included with all plans. Before setting up on her own Carol Messham worked with David Stevens.

Channel Island Tree Service
Frenchmans Cottage, Beechvale, St John, Jersey, Channel Islands JE3 4FL
☎ 01534 862343

CONTACT Ian Averty
WORKING AREA Channel Islands
ASSOCIATIONS AAAC
SERVICES Arboricultural services
STARTED TRADING 1987
PROJECTS Woodland management St Peter's valley; Queens valley reservoir project; St George's School woodland management; Jersey Zoo tree care

The only Arboricultural Association-approved contractor in the islands.

Chenies Landscapes Limited
Bramble Lane, London Road East, Amersham, Buckinghamshire HP7 9DH
☎ 01494 728004   FAX 01494 721403

CONTACT Neil Denton or Brian Toms
WORKING AREA London, south east England and south Midlands
ASSOCIATIONS BALI
SERVICES Garden design; contractors; arboricultural services; landscape architecture; interior landscapes
STARTED TRADING 1961
PROJECTS Gold medal, Chelsea Flower Show 1992, for constructing Fisons' garden

A large firm with specialist construction, maintenance and landscape architecture divisions. Chenies Interiorscape designs and maintains interior schemes, and the group also owns a garden centre and a horticultural machinery outlet.

Chris Burnett Associates
Higher Farm, Barton, Malpas, Cheshire SY14 7HU
☎ 01829 782145   FAX 01829 782146

CONTACT Chris Burnett
WORKING AREA Nationwide
ASSOCIATIONS ALI
SERVICES Garden design; landscape architecture
STARTED TRADING 1984
PROJECTS Large private garden in Oxfordshire; new deer park in Cheshire; historic park restoration for the National Trust; small private garden in Cheshire

Landscape architects.

Chris Yarrow & Associates
Wilderness Wood, Hadlow Down, Uckfield, East Sussex TN22 4HJ
☎ 01825 830509   FAX 01825 830977

CONTACT Chris Yarrow
WORKING AREA Nationwide
ASSOCIATIONS FAA
SERVICES Arboricultural services; recreation and tourism advisory service
STARTED TRADING 1972

424 Professional Services

PROJECTS Management of award-winning Wilderness Wood

Comprehensive forestry advisory service specialising in recreational and tourism aspects. Tree surveys, planning appeals and advice on subsidence claims.

Christopher Maguire
15 Harston Road, Cambridge CB2 5PA
☎ 01233 872800
CONTACT Christopher Maguire
WORKING AREA Cambridge, Essex, Hertfordshire, Bedfordshire
ASSOCIATIONS RIBA; SGD
SERVICES Garden design; landscape architecture
STARTED TRADING 1987
PROJECTS Landscaping schemes for Cambridge Housing Society; projects combining domestic buildings with garden design

Qualified architect, landscape and garden designer. Services available combine all disciplines.

Clifton Landscape and Design
59 Clifton Villas, London W9 2PH
☎ 0171 286 6622   FAX 0171 286 5655
CONTACT Andrew Reed
WORKING AREA Within a 100-mile radius of central London
ASSOCIATIONS BALI
SERVICES Garden design; contractors; arboricultural services; water and riparian services; landscape architecture
STARTED TRADING 1940
PROJECTS Rostock, Germany and many private and commercial projects in London

Full service for private and commercial clients, design, construction, supply of plants (from Clifton Nurseries) and maintenance for interior and exterior landscapes, terraces and roof gardens.

Colin White Tree Surgeon and Forestry Contractor
The Manor House, Colwell, Hexham, Northumberland NE46 4TL
☎ 01434 681598   FAX 01434 681598
CONTACT Colin White
WORKING AREA North east England
ASSOCIATIONS AAAC
SERVICES Arboricultural services
STARTED TRADING 1978
PROJECTS Tree maintenance at English Heritage sites; trackside planting for Tyneside Metro; tree surgery and contract work for MoD

Full arboricultural service including planting, maintenance and chipping.

Colson Stone Partnership
2 Calico House, Clove Hitch Quay, Plantation Wharf, Battersea, London SW11 3TN
☎ 0171 924 3257   FAX 0171 978 5220
CONTACT Richard Stone
WORKING AREA Southern England
ASSOCIATIONS ALI
SERVICES Garden design; horticultural consultancy; landscape architecture
STARTED TRADING 1989
PROJECTS Historic landscape surveys and restoration plans for Endsleigh, Devon; Waddesdon Manor, Buckinghamshire; Elvaston Castle, Derbyshire

Landscape architects with experience of work on historic parks and gardens.

Complete Tree Services
Wayside, Kingston Stert, Chinnor, Oxfordshire OX9 4NL
☎ 01844 351488
CONTACT Steven Burkitt
WORKING AREA Thames Valley and Home Counties
ASSOCIATIONS AAAC
SERVICES Arboricultural services
STARTED TRADING 1982
PROJECTS Restoration of various private and institutional treescapes

Full range of services including 24-hour emergency call-out. Recommended by councils and have worked for the National Trust.

Compton & Compton
Coombe Cottage, Hanging Langford, Salisbury, Wiltshire SP3 4NW
☎ 01722 790436
CONTACT Tania or James Compton
WORKING AREA UK and overseas
SERVICES Garden design; horticultural consultancy
STARTED TRADING 1990

James Compton is Kew-trained; was head gardener at the Chelsea Physic; taught at the English Garden School; author of books and many articles; plant collector (e.g. in Mexico, South Africa, Western USA and Korea); advises on suitable plants for gardens. Tania Compton trained at the English Garden School; gained experience with Rosemary Verey; advises on design and garden style. She is a regular contributor to *House and Garden*.

Conservatory Gardens
17 Hartington Road, Chiswick, London W4 3TL
☎ 0181 994 6109   FAX 0181 547 8241
CONTACT Joan Phelan
WORKING AREA Nationwide
SERVICES Garden design; horticultural consultancy; conservatories
STARTED TRADING 1991
PROJECTS Private conservatories

Help on all aspects of conservatory plants and planting design from a botanist and garden designer team. Pre-building advice and schemes for small gardens are also available, as is a postal service.

Courtyard Garden Design
26 Algar Road, Old Isleworth, London TW7 7AG
☎ 0181 568 5263   FAX 0181 568 5263
CONTACT Sally Court
WORKING AREA UK and overseas
ASSOCIATIONS SGD
SERVICES Garden design; contractors
STARTED TRADING 1989
PROJECTS Clearance and creation of 15-acre garden in Sussex; town garden schemes

Diploma from the Inchbald School of Design. Service includes advice on specific problems, design and planting plans, and the supervision of their installation. Sally Court has won awards at Hampton Court, and also writes and lectures on garden design and history.

D J Tree and Landscape Specialists
94 Halegate Road, Halebank, Widnes, Cheshire WA8 8LY
☎ 0151 425 3212   FAX 0151 425 3212
CONTACT John M. Fahey
WORKING AREA North west England and north Wales
ASSOCIATIONS AAAC; AIHort
SERVICES Arboricultural services
STARTED TRADING 1985
PROJECTS Tree clearance for British Rail

Family company with 24-hour emergency service.

D P O'Callaghan & Associates
Valleyfield, 1a Stratford Road, Aigburth, Liverpool, Merseyside L19 3RE
☎ 0151 494 1108/1525 FAX 0151 427 4541
CONTACT D. P. O'Callaghan or M. Lawson
WORKING AREA UK and Republic of Ireland
ASSOCIATIONS FAA
SERVICES Arboricultural services; consultancy
STARTED TRADING 1982
PROJECTS Arboricultural plans and implementation for Fota Island development, Co. Cork; and Manchester Airport Runway 2 project

Arboricultural consultancy practice which encompasses planning, litigation, project management and environmental impact studies. Satellite offices in Shrewsbury, Devon and Co. Wicklow.

D Wells Landscaping
The Cottage, 15 Park Avenue, Eastbourne, East Sussex BN21 2XG
☎ 01323 502063
CONTACT D. Wells
WORKING AREA 50-mile radius
ASSOCIATIONS BALI; SGD
SERVICES Garden design; contractors
STARTED TRADING 1970
PROJECTS St Wilfrid's Hospice, Eastbourne (1994 BALI Award Winner), and work on a BBC TV set

Landscape firm which specialises in water gardens and natural stonework.

Dagenham Landscapes Ltd
Redcrofts Farm, Ockendon Road, Upminster, Essex RM14 2DJ
☎ 01708 222379
CONTACT Colin Byrne
WORKING AREA Essex and north London
ASSOCIATIONS BALI
SERVICES Garden design; contractors; turf suppliers
STARTED TRADING 1968
PROJECTS Designed and built a stream with rock beds through a mature garden, with bridges linking the different sections of the garden

Garden design and landscape construction service. They also undertake garden maintenance for private and commercial customers, install swimming pools and supply grassland turf.

Daisy Hill Nurseries Ltd, Co. Down
For full details see Nurseries section

Dalrymple Ltd
1 Charlwood Place, Charlwood, Surrey RH6 0EB
☎ 01293 862036   FAX 01293 863167
CONTACT Lucy Dalrymple
WORKING AREA 100-mile radius from Gatwick
ASSOCIATIONS AAAC
SERVICES Arboricultural services
STARTED TRADING 1959

As well as arboricultural work, Dalrymple supply professional forestry machines and winches, including chippers to the National Trust.

David Brown Landscape Design
10 College Road, Impington, Cambridge, Cambridgeshire CB4 4PD
☎ 01223 232366
CONTACT David Brown or Alistair Huck
WORKING AREA Nationwide
ASSOCIATIONS ALI; MIHort
SERVICES Garden design; arboricultural services; landscape architecture
STARTED TRADING 1988
PROJECTS Vision Park, Cambridge; Lucy Cavendish College, Cambridge; St Andrews Park, Norwich and Cotton Valley Nature Area (Anglian Water)

Landscape architects whose work ranges from business parks to garden design. Experienced at tree and vegetation surveys, and can undertake historical research and expert witness work.

David Ireland Landscape Architect
Thames Sailing Barge 'Scone', City Harbour, Off East Ferry Road, Isle of Dogs, London E14 9TF
☎ 0171 515 8828   FAX 0171 515 8826
CONTACT David Ireland

WORKING AREA London, Home Counties and nationwide
ASSOCIATIONS ALI
SERVICES Garden design; horticultural consultancy; contractors; arboricultural services; landscape architecture
STARTED TRADING 1991
PROJECTS 17-acre private garden in Hertfordshire; restoration of ancient woodland in Derby; redesigned two London squares

Landscape architect. Has worked on his own since 1991 offering consultancy and design-and-build services for domestic gardens and commercial landscapes. Based in London, his work includes small town gardens.

David R Sisley
Straight Mile Nursery Gardens, Ongar Road, Brentwood, Essex CM15 9SA
☎ 01277 374439

CONTACT David Sisley
WORKING AREA UK
ASSOCIATIONS BALI; SGD
SERVICES Garden design; horticultural consultancy; contractors

Garden designer based at Straight Mile Nurseries. Services include design and construction within a 40-mile radius or design and supervision nationwide.

David Stevens International Ltd
Stowe Castle Business Park, Stowe, Buckinghamshire MK18 5AB
☎ 01280 821097   FAX 01280 821150

CONTACT Verna Stewart
WORKING AREA UK and worldwide
ASSOCIATIONS BALI; SGD; FIHORT
SERVICES Garden design; contractors; shows consultancy; video and film; product franchising
STARTED TRADING 1972
PROJECTS 10 Gold medals at the Chelsea Flower Show

Undertakes domestic and commercial work all over the UK and abroad. David Stevens is one of the country's best-known garden designers, and has recently been appointed Professor of Garden Design at Middlesex University. He is also a broadcaster and writer.

The Design Studio of Julia Fogg and Susan Santer
St Osyth's, Parsons Fee, Aylesbury, Buckinghamshire HP20 2QZ
☎ 01296 87502/01850 381730   FAX 01296 392825

CONTACT Julia Fogg or Susan Santer
WORKING AREA UK and Europe
ASSOCIATIONS SGD
SERVICES Garden design; horticultural consultancy; contractors; landscape architecture
STARTED TRADING 1989

PROJECTS Town and family gardens; restoring neglected estates; private sculpture park

Design diplomas. Complete garden design service from survey and planting plans through to overall project management. Also carry out commercial and consultancy work.

Diana Baskervyle-Glegg
2 High Street, Fletching, East Sussex TN22 3SS
☎ 01825 723128

CONTACT Diana Baskervyle-Glegg
WORKING AREA UK (mainly Kent and Sussex)
SERVICES Garden design; horticultural consultancy
STARTED TRADING 1964
PROJECTS Polebrook, Hever, Kent; Chalvington House, Sussex

Garden designer who also writes, lectures and runs courses on garden design.

Diana Eldon, Garden Designer
27 Parsons Lane, Bierton, Aylesbury, Buckinghamshire HP22 5DF
☎ 01296 24138

CONTACT Diana Eldon
WORKING AREA 30-mile radius
ASSOCIATIONS SGD
SERVICES Garden design
STARTED TRADING 1991
PROJECTS Private gardens

Large- or small-scale garden design, which aims to be innovative and appropriate to the house. Will design trellis, screens and gateways and can produce an artist's impression of the finished garden if required. Gives talks.

Dobbies Landscape Ltd, Lothian
For full details see Nurseries section

Dolwin & Gray
Alpha House, Crowborough Hill, Crowborough, East Sussex TN6 2EG
☎ 01892 664612   FAX 01892 663636

CONTACT F. Noakes or C. Goss
WORKING AREA South east England
ASSOCIATIONS AAAC; BALI
SERVICES Contractors; arboricultural services; woodland management
STARTED TRADING 1969
PROJECTS Work in St James' Park, and at the Dartford river crossing

The firm provides a wide range of arboricultural contracting and consultancy services.

Douglas Lewis Tree Surgeons
11 The Nashes, Clifford Chambers, Stratford upon Avon, Warwickshire CV37 8JB
☎ 01789 295825   FAX 01789 261496

CONTACT Douglas Lewis
WORKING AREA Midlands

ASSOCIATIONS AAAC
SERVICES Arboricultural services
STARTED TRADING 1979

Full tree service including surveys, written reports and stump grinding.

Dream Gardens
Ings Gate, Flaxman Croft, Copmanthorpe, York, North Yorkshire YO2 3TU
☎ 01904 703833   FAX 01904 709815

CONTACT Keith James
WORKING AREA UK and Europe
ASSOCIATIONS ALI; SGD
SERVICES Garden design; horticultural consultancy; contractors; landscape architecture
STARTED TRADING 1992
PROJECTS Mill garden and landscape, North Yorkshire; country house garden, Warwickshire; town garden, London

Trained in garden design. Specialities include period garden restoration and country house gardens. Handles a wide range of other work including interior landscaping.

Duncan Heather
Heathers of Henley, 34 Kings Road, Henley on Thames, Oxfordshire RG9 2DG
☎ 01491 573577   FAX 01491 411161

CONTACT Duncan Heather
WORKING AREA Nationwide
SERVICES Garden design; contractors; landscape architecture; garden design courses
STARTED TRADING 1987
PROJECTS Twice gold medallist at Hampton Court

Duncan Heather is also the director of the Oxford College of Garden Design.

E K David Landscapes
Marlborough Road, Woking, Surrey GU21 5JG
☎ 01483 767277

CONTACT Karl Moyle
WORKING AREA 15-mile radius of Woking
SERVICES Garden design; contractors
STARTED TRADING 1987
PROJECTS Rock gardens, ponds, herbaceous borders

Merrist Wood trained. Services include garden design and contracting.

Earth Connections
9 Crouch Cross Lane, Boxgrove, Chichester, Sussex PO18 0EF
☎ 01243 533545

CONTACT Mark Laurence
WORKING AREA UK and abroad
STARTED TRADING 1988
PROJECTS Natural reed bed filtration systems; turf roof garden buildings; edible landscapes

Ecological and holistic design or design and build service.

Earth Gardening
2 Bridge Road, Mepal, Ely, Cambridgeshire CB6 2AR
☎ 01353 776191

CONTACT Judy Fox
WORKING AREA Cambridgeshire and postal
SERVICES Garden design
STARTED TRADING 1987
PROJECTS Constructed a ½-acre garden from a wheatfield

Garden designer working locally or by post, with practical horticultural experience.

Eastern Tree Surgery
71b High Street, Teversham, Cambridgeshire CB1 5AG
☎ 01223 292110

CONTACT Paul Cole
WORKING AREA East Anglia
ASSOCIATIONS AAAC
SERVICES Arboricultural services
STARTED TRADING 1974

Care and preservation of ornamental trees.

Elaine Horne
Newfield Cottage, Firbank, Sedbergh, Cumbria LA10 5EN
☎ 015396 20621

CONTACT Elaine Horne
WORKING AREA North west England
SERVICES Garden design; horticultural consultancy; design courses
STARTED TRADING 1988
PROJECTS Conversion of concrete yard into flower garden, Kendal; projects for private gardens in Preston

Trained in landscape design, with experience at Kew and Harlow Carr. She specialises in low-maintenance gardens, and also runs design and planting courses.

Elizabeth Banks Associates Ltd
13 Abercorn Place, London NW8 9EA
☎ 0171 624 5740   FAX 0171 372 0964

CONTACT Mrs Elizabeth Banks
WORKING AREA UK and abroad
ASSOCIATIONS ALI; AIHort
SERVICES Garden design; landscape architecture
STARTED TRADING 1987
PROJECTS Work includes Rosemoor Gardens, Devon; Fort Belvedere, Berkshire; Hinxton Hall, Cambridgeshire and British Embassy, Paris

Landscape practice which has made a name for its work on historical restoration projects. Also active in designing new gardens and advising on land use and garden management. Its varied and impressive client list is matched by EBA's well-qualified personnel, including

428 Professional Services

director Tom Stuart-Smith (ALI), and Dr Todd Longstaffe Gowan.

Elizabeth Huntly Francis
86 Beechwood Drive, St Albans, Hertfordshire AL1 4XZ
☎ 01727 810849   FAX 01727 841219
CONTACT   Elizabeth Huntly Francis
WORKING AREA   Home Counties and south east England
SERVICES   Garden design
STARTED TRADING   1994
PROJECTS   Private garden in Chesham

Garden designer with a degree in Horticulture.

Elizabeth Whateley
48 Glossop Road, Sanderstead, South Croydon, Surrey CR2 0PU
☎ 0181 651 0226
CONTACT   Elizabeth Whateley
WORKING AREA   Kent, London, Surrey and Sussex
ASSOCIATIONS   SGD
SERVICES   Garden design
STARTED TRADING   1986
PROJECTS   Large rural garden near Canterbury; suburban gardens in Bromley, Sutton, Thames Ditton and Croydon; town garden in Clapham.

A full garden design service, including surveys, plans, landscaping and planting. Elizabeth Whateley supervises any contractors, and can provide maintenance schedules and a follow-up consultancy visit when required. The Clapham garden is described in *Small Gardens with Style* by Jill Billington.

Eric Lafoy
12 Lauderdale Drive, Petersham, Richmond, Surrey TW10 7BT
☎ 0181 940 2751   FAX 0181 648 5679
CONTACT   Eric Lafoy
WORKING AREA   London and southern England, France
SERVICES   Garden design; horticultural consultancy
STARTED TRADING   1992
PROJECTS   Private gardens

Trained at the College of Garden Design, native French speaker.

Euro Tree Service
Caxton Lodge Farm, Lodge Lane, Cronton, Widnes, Cheshire WA8 9QA
☎ 0151 424 0333   FAX 0151 430 7836
CONTACT   Simon Walton
WORKING AREA   North west England and Wales
ASSOCIATIONS   AAAC
SERVICES   Arboricultural services
STARTED TRADING   1980

Full arboricultural service, including stump grinding and woodland maintenance. Suppliers of timber, logs, mulch and chippings.

Ferndale Nursery and Garden Centre Ltd, South Yorkshire
For full details see Nurseries section

FFC Landscape Architects / The Garden Design Studio
Birch House, 25 Birch Terrace, Hanley, Stoke on Trent, Staffordshire ST1 3JN
☎ 01782 283272   FAX 01782 283272
CONTACT   Francis Colella
WORKING AREA   Midlands and north west England
ASSOCIATIONS   ALI; SGD
SERVICES   Garden design; landscape architecture
STARTED TRADING   1986
PROJECTS   Private gardens of all sizes; housing association and health centre schemes; golf course and landscape planning

Landscape architects and garden designers providing design services, expert witnesses and design consultancy.

Fiona Harrison
23 Course Side, Ascot, Berkshire SL5 7HH
☎ 01344 24543   FAX 01344 873505
CONTACT   Fiona Harrison
WORKING AREA   50-mile radius
ASSOCIATIONS   SGD
SERVICES   Garden design; horticultural consultancy
STARTED TRADING   1992

Degree in Horticulture, and design course at Pershore. Carries out garden and landscape design, mostly for private clients.

Flintshire Woodlands
The Meal House, Iscoyd Park, Redbrook Lane, Shropshire SY13 3AW
☎ 0194873 502   FAX 0194873 412
WORKING AREA   Wales, Midlands and north west England
ASSOCIATIONS   AAAC
SERVICES   Arboricultural services
STARTED TRADING   1953

A large group whose activities include woodland management, tree care and environmental consultancy.

FMG Garden Designs
21 Crescent Gardens, London SW19 8AJ
☎ 0181 879 3168   FAX 0181 944 1977
CONTACT   Nilla Gallanzi
WORKING AREA   London and Home Counties
ASSOCIATIONS   SGD
SERVICES   Garden design; horticultural consultancy; contractors
STARTED TRADING   1987
PROJECTS   Restoration and maintenance of borders at The Old Rectory, Wimbledon; landscape and design for Victorian house in Belsize Park

Professional Services

Trained in garden design. Creates and supervises the construction and maintenance of gardens with a special expertise in perennial borders.

Fountain Forestry Ltd
Mollington House, Mollington, Banbury, Oxfordshire OX17 1AX
☎ 01295 750000   FAX 01295 750001
CONTACT   T. P. Rose
WORKING AREA   Nationwide
ASSOCIATIONS   BALI; AAAC
SERVICES   Arboricultural services
STARTED TRADING   1957
PROJECTS   Tree surgery for Waddesdon Estate; Thenfold Estate; Milton Keynes Borough Council

The largest privately owned independent forestry and land use company in the country. Through 10 district offices (and another in New England) their range includes woodland services, timber harvesting, tree care, vegetation control and fencing.

Frances Traylen Martin
Saint's Hill House, Penshurst, Tonbridge, Kent TN11 8EN
☎ 01892 870331   FAX 01892 870332
CONTACT   Frances Traylen Martin
WORKING AREA   London, south east and central southern England
SERVICES   Garden design
STARTED TRADING   1992
PROJECTS   Garden for listed barn conversion; design for small arboretum

Trained at the Inchbald School of Garden Design. Won a competition to design a parterre for Kentswell Hall in 1992.

Garden Log
4 Stafford Mansions, Albert Bridge Road, London SW11 4QG
☎ 0171 371 0773   FAX 0171 371 8324
CONTACT   Ned Trier
WORKING AREA   South of England
STARTED TRADING   1990
PROJECTS   Private clients

Garden survey service which compiles a photographic record of private gardens with plant identification and advice on problems.

Garden Solutions by Design
43 Park Drive North, Mirfield, West Yorkshire WF14 9NJ
☎ 01924 495584
CONTACT   John Wilson or Elizabeth Wilson
WORKING AREA   Yorkshire, Lancashire and Isle of Man
SERVICES   Garden design; horticultural consultancy; contractors; landscape architecture
STARTED TRADING   1992
PROJECTS   Japanese garden in Doncaster

Trained in landscape and horticultural technology. They provide a full service from design through to implementation.

Gardens by Graham Evans
20 Grandfield Avenue, Radcliffe on Trent, Nottinghamshire NG12 1AL
☎ 0115 9335737
CONTACT   Graham Evans
WORKING AREA   East Midlands
ASSOCIATIONS   BALI
SERVICES   Garden design; contractors
STARTED TRADING   1986

Garden design and construction.

Gardens of Distinction
The Old Canal Building, East Challow, Wantage, Oxfordshire OX12 9SY
☎ 01235 769532   FAX 01235 770040
CONTACT   Michael Branch
WORKING AREA   Central, southern and northern UK
ASSOCIATIONS   ALI
SERVICES   Garden design; horticultural consultancy; landscape architecture
STARTED TRADING   1968
PROJECTS   Garden court at Channel 4's new Pimlico headquarters

Landscape practice with over 25 years of garden design for private and public clients. Service ranges from horticultural advice to full design. There is a sub-office in Warrington (01925 36855).

Gardenscape
Fairview, Smelthouses, Summerbridge, Harrogate, North Yorkshire HG3 4DH
☎ 01423 780291/01142 678405   FAX 01142 678405
CONTACT   Michael D. Myers
WORKING AREA   UK
ASSOCIATIONS   MIHort
SERVICES   Garden design; horticultural consultancy; contractors; landscape architecture
STARTED TRADING   1993

Garden maintenance and design, as well as horticultural consultancy for ornamentals. Mr Myers also holds three NCCPG National Collections, runs a mail order nursery, and opens his garden for the NGS and NCCPG.

Garden Scents, Suffolk
For full details see Paradix Centre, Suffolk in Nurseries section

Geoffrey Coombs
47 Larcombe Road, Petersfield, Hampshire GU32 3LS
☎ 01730 267417
CONTACT   Geoffrey Coombs
WORKING AREA   30-mile radius
ASSOCIATIONS   SGD
SERVICES   Garden design; horticultural consultancy

430 Professional Services

Formerly garden adviser for the RHS at Vincent Square, now retired. Garden design and consultancy: the latter specialises in trees, shrubs and hardy plants.

Gillian Temple Associates
15 Woodside Avenue, Weston Green, Esher, Surrey KT10 8JQ
☎ 0181 339 0323   FAX 0181 339 0335
CONTACT Gillian Temple
WORKING AREA UK and overseas
ASSOCIATIONS SGD; MIHort
SERVICES Garden design; horticultural consultancy; landscape architecture
STARTED TRADING 1991
PROJECTS Residential developments and show gardens; interior landscape and tropical gardens

Landscape and garden design for both private and commercial clients. Expertise in interior design projects.

Glenda Biggs
Berrylands Farm, Pookbourne Lane, Sayers Common, Sussex BN6 9HD
☎ 01444 881437   FAX 01444 881437
CONTACT Glenda Biggs
WORKING AREA London and south east England
SERVICES Garden design; contractors
STARTED TRADING 1990
PROJECTS Cargo terminal at Immingham, Humberside; private gardens in Berkshire, Hampshire and Sussex

Holds a design diploma.

Golden Landscapes
St Anne, Tuckey Grove, Send Marsh, Ripley, Woking, Surrey GU2 6JG
☎ 01483 225412
CONTACT R. F. Golding
WORKING AREA Nationwide
ASSOCIATIONS AIHort
SERVICES Garden design; contractors
STARTED TRADING 1993

Design and construction service.

Goscote Nurseries Ltd, Leicestershire
For full details see Nurseries section

Grace Landscapes Ltd
Knowl Road, Mirfield, West Yorkshire WF19 9UU
☎ 01924 492645   FAX 01924 480518
CONTACT Tim Grace or Hugh Pawsey
WORKING AREA Midlands and northern England
ASSOCIATIONS BALI
SERVICES Garden design; contractors
PROJECTS Design and build at MoD Catterick Garrison; construction and maintenance, Morrison's Supermarket, Darlington

Specialists in design-and-build contracts for both the commercial and the domestic garden sectors.

Graham A Pavey & Associates
11 Princes Road, Bromham, Bedfordshire MK43 8QD
☎ 01234 823860
CONTACT Chris or Graham Pavey
WORKING AREA Nationwide
SERVICES Garden design; horticultural consultancy
STARTED TRADING 1988
PROJECTS Courtyard garden at Bedford Hospital; 1-acre garden in Peterborough; swimming pool garden in Hitchin

Trained at the English Gardening School. Services include garden and landscape design, planting plans and advice. In addition to their comprehensive service, they offer special design packages for smaller gardens.

Graham King Arboricultural Consultant
Lucombe House, Condicote, Stow on the Wold, Cheltenham, Gloucestershire GL54 1ES
☎ 01451 831738
CONTACT Graham King
WORKING AREA Gloucestershire, Oxfordshire, Wiltshire and Worcestershire
ASSOCIATIONS FAA
SERVICES Garden design; arboricultural services
STARTED TRADING 1981
PROJECTS Planting a 10-acre arboretum

Arboricultural services and garden design.

Green Man Landscapes
The Pines, 18 Church Close, Whittlesford, Cambridgeshire CB2 4NY
☎ 01223 832725
CONTACT Michael or Ann Hood
WORKING AREA East Anglia and Hertfordshire
ASSOCIATIONS BALI; AIHort
SERVICES Garden design; contractors
STARTED TRADING 1982

Small firm specialising in soft landscaping and maintenance by knowledgeable plantsmen.

Greenstone Landscapes
18 Woodmancott Close, Forest Park, Bracknell, Berkshire RG12 3XU
☎ 01344 59042   FAX 01344 59042
CONTACT Bob Mattei
SERVICES Garden design; horticultural consultancy; contractors; water and riparian services
STARTED TRADING 1989
PROJECTS A rock and water garden for a private client

Garden design and construction, particularly with water features.

Ground Control Ltd
Ardmore House, London Road, Billericay, Essex CM12 9HS
☎ 01277 650697/0181 534 1466   FAX 01277 630746

Professional Services 431

CONTACT   Mr S. Harrod or Mr. T. Haddow
WORKING AREA   100-mile radius
ASSOCIATIONS   BALI
SERVICES   Garden design; horticultural consultancy; contractors
STARTED TRADING   1976
PROJECTS   BALI award-winners in 1993 and 1994 for work at the Tower of London

Landscape design and contractors: the firm has an annual turnover in excess of £1m.

Hambrook Landscapes Ltd
Wangfield Lane, Curdridge, Southampton, Hampshire S03 2DA
☎ 01489 780505   FAX 01489 785396
CONTACT   Norman Hambrook
WORKING AREA   South Hampshire
ASSOCIATIONS   BALI
SERVICES   Garden design; horticultural consultancy; contractors; arboricultural services; water and riparian services
STARTED TRADING   1969
PROJECTS   Show gardens at their garden centre

Landscaping and maintenance for private and commercial customers, carried out by full-time professionals. Their garden centre is at 135 Southampton Road, Titchfield, Fareham, Hampshire PO14 4PR.

Hardy's Cottage Garden Plants, Hampshire
For full details see Nurseries section

Hazel M. Huddleston, Northumberland
For full details see Northumbria Nurseries, Northumberland in Nurseries section

Hayes Gardenworld, Cumbria
For full details see Nurseries section

Heath Garden
Heath Hill, Sheriffhales, Shifnal, Shropshire TF11 8RR
☎ 01952 691341
CONTACT   Gordon Malt
WORKING AREA   Shropshire, Staffordshire
ASSOCIATIONS   MIHort
SERVICES   Garden design; horticultural consultancy; contractors; arboricultural services
STARTED TRADING   1989

Trained at RBG Edinburgh, with 25 years of varied experience in horticulture. Comprehensive range of services includes garden design, landscaping work and tree and shrub care.

Heritage Tree Services
Redwood Meadow, Stoke Row, Henley on Thames, Oxfordshire RG9 5QR
☎ 01491 681185   FAX 01491 681185
CONTACT   Hugo Loudon

WORKING AREA   Berkshire, Buckinghamshire, Oxfordshire
ASSOCIATIONS   AAAC
SERVICES   Arboricultural services
STARTED TRADING   1985

Designs for parkland tree planting and sales of semi-mature trees.

Hillier Landscapes
Ampfield House, Ampfield, Romsey, Hampshire SO51 9PA
☎ 01794 368733   FAX 01794 368813
CONTACT   Richard Barnard
WORKING AREA   UK and overseas
ASSOCIATIONS   SGD; MIHort; BALI
SERVICES   Garden design; horticultural consultancy; contractors; arboricultural services; landscape architecture
STARTED TRADING   1864
PROJECTS   Work at the Gothick Villa, Regents Park and for the Downland Housing Association; large estate in Guernsey

Landscape architects offering garden design, consultancy, commercial and industrial landscaping and contract management. Plants are supplied by their own nurseries. Construction and maintenance is also available in the Hillier heartland of southern and western England.

Hollington Nurseries, Berkshire
For full details see Nurseries section

Honey Brothers
New Pond Road, Peasmarsh, Guildford, Surrey GU3 1JR
☎ 01483 61362   FAX 01483 35608
CONTACT   Martyn Honey
WORKING AREA   London and south east England
ASSOCIATIONS   FAA; MIHort
SERVICES   Arboricultural services; forestry supplies: see Garden Supplies section
STARTED TRADING   1960

Also sell garden, arboriculture and forestry equipment and organise training courses on tree work and the use of equipment.

Hydon Nurseries, Surrey
For full details see Nurseries section

Iain Tavendale Arboricultural Consultant
High Bank Farm, Stoney Bank Road, Earby, Colne, Lancashire BB8 6LD
☎ 01282 844191   FAX 01282 844191
CONTACT   Iain Tavendale
WORKING AREA   Lancashire, Yorkshire
ASSOCIATIONS   FAA; AAAC
SERVICES   Arboricultural services
STARTED TRADING   1980

Professional Services

Arboricultural consultant and approved contractor.

International Acers, Hereford & Worcester
For full details see Nurseries section

Jacqui Stubbs Associates
24 Duncan Road, Richmond, Surrey TW9 2JD
☎ 0181 948 0744   FAX 0181 948 0744
CONTACT Jacqui Stubbs
WORKING AREA London and south east England
ASSOCIATIONS SGD
SERVICES Garden design; horticultural consultancy
STARTED TRADING 1986
PROJECTS Sheltered accommodation gardens, Wimbledon; small town gardens, London; large gardens in Surrey

Garden designer for mainly private clients. Advises on construction and/or planting schemes.

Jan Martinez
Everden Farmhouse, Alkham, Dover, Kent CT15 7EH
☎ 01303 893462
CONTACT Jan Martinez
WORKING AREA London and south east England mainly
SERVICES Garden design; horticultural consultancy; contractors; landscape architecture
STARTED TRADING 1968
PROJECTS Landscaping at the Eastern Docks, Port of Dover, and work on a large Surrey garden

Garden and commercial designer, now operating as a solo designer. All forms of exterior design undertaken, with additional qualifications and experience as an interior designer. Broadcasts for Radio Kent.

Jean Bishop & Partner
Wood Farm, Dunston, Norwich, Norfolk NR14 8QD
☎ 01508 470649
CONTACT Jean Bishop & Partner
WORKING AREA Home Counties and East Anglia
SERVICES Garden design; horticultural consultancy; contractors
STARTED TRADING 1984
PROJECTS Victorian terrace in BBC TV *Front Gardens* series

Both partners hold diplomas from Merrist Wood, and work either separately or together on design and construction.

Jean Goldberry Garden Design
71 Frog Lane, West Overton, Marlborough, Wiltshire SN8 4ER
☎ 01672 861416
CONTACT Jean Goldberry
WORKING AREA Worldwide by post
SERVICES Garden design
STARTED TRADING 1982

PROJECTS Designs for BBC *Gardeners' World* programmes, including 'The Long Thin Garden' from the *Front Gardens* series

Garden designer. Operates a special postal service: you supply a plan and photographs prepared to her instructions.

Jennifer Gaylor Garden Design
Mallorn, Ladygate Drive, Grayshott, Hindhead, Surrey GU26 6DR
☎ 01428 606885   FAX 01428 607941
CONTACT Jennifer Gaylor
WORKING AREA UK and France
SERVICES Garden design
STARTED TRADING 1989
PROJECTS Private gardens between ⅓ acre and 5 acres

Holds a design diploma. Complete design service from planning to construction for mainly private clients.

Jeremy Barrell Treecare
25 Hightown Gardens, Ringwood, Hampshire BH24 3EG
☎ 01425 479387   FAX 01425 472269
CONTACT Jeremy Barrell
WORKING AREA Southern England
ASSOCIATIONS FAA; AAAC
SERVICES Arboricultural services
STARTED TRADING 1980

Tree consultancy specialising in reports for insurance and mortgage uses.

Jill Billington Garden Design
100 Fox Lane, London N13 4AX
☎ 0181 886 0898
CONTACT Jill Billington
WORKING AREA UK and overseas
ASSOCIATIONS SGD
SERVICES Garden design
STARTED TRADING 1983

Degree in Fine Art (sculpture). Has designed at Chelsea, and also teaches and lectures on gardens. Her book on small gardens was published last year.

Jill Fenwick
Ray Cottage, 14 Tadworth Street, Tadworth, Surrey KT20 5RN
☎ 01737 352621
CONTACT Jill Fenwick
WORKING AREA London and south east England
SERVICES Garden design; horticultural consultancy
PROJECTS Private gardens in London

Best Garden Designer Award, Hampton Court 1994.

Joanna Stay Garden Design & Consultancy
67 Dalton Street, St Albans, Hertfordshire AL3 5QH
☎ 01727 869765
CONTACT Joanna Stay

WORKING AREA Home Counties; nationwide and abroad
ASSOCIATIONS SGD
SERVICES Garden design; horticultural consultancy
STARTED TRADING 1981
PROJECTS Wildlife gardens; lake and landscaping; courtyard gardens

Trained at Pershore and Oaklands College. Joanna Stay won a Hampton Court Tudor Rose award in 1991.

John A Davies Landscape Consultants
Fernhill Lodge, Llechryd, Cardigan, Dyfed SA43 2QL
☎ 01239 87861   FAX 01239 621004
CONTACT John A. Davies
WORKING AREA International
ASSOCIATIONS SGD; MIHort
SERVICES Garden design; horticultural consultancy; landscape architecture
STARTED TRADING 1967
PROJECTS Recent work includes the Saudi Arabian embassy and the Umm Al Nassan Park in Bahrain. Currently working on the Jiddah Island development for the Bahrain Ministry of Housing and private clients in Bahrain

Chelsea gold medallists. Landscape and garden designers with a subsidiary office in Bahrain, working for private and corporate clients. Bahrain address: PO Box 15560, State of Bahrain (00 973 710122).

John Akeroyd
Lawn Cottage, Fonthill Gifford, Tisbury, Wiltshire SP3 6SG
☎ 01747 871507   FAX 01747 871507
CONTACT Dr John Akeroyd
WORKING AREA Nationwide
STARTED TRADING 1989
PROJECTS Non-native wild flower seed in Britain

Highly qualified professional botanist, writer and lecturer. Advises on conservation and plant identification with a special interest in weeds.

John Brookes, Landscape Designer
Clock House, Denmans, Fontwell, Arundel, West Sussex BN18 0SU
☎ 01243 542808   FAX 01243 544064
CONTACT John Brookes or Michael Zinn
WORKING AREA UK and overseas
SERVICES Garden design; landscape architecture

One of the country's best-known garden designers. They aim to work with you rather than for you. The practice covers a full service, including specifications and implementation. John Brookes also teaches landscape and garden design, and writes and lectures on the subject.

John E M Hill
Sherborne Gardens, Sherborne, Cheltenham, Gloucestershire GL54 3DZ
☎ 01451 844522   FAX 01451 844695

CONTACT J. E. M. Hill
WORKING AREA Gloucestershire, Oxfordshire and adjoining counties
ASSOCIATIONS 1981
SERVICES Garden design; contractors
PROJECTS Le Manoir aux Quat' Saisons, Oxford; Manchester College, Oxford

Country house garden design, construction and restoration. Plants can be supplied by the nurseries. See Sherbourne Gardens Nursery, Gloucestershire in Nurseries section.

John H Lucas
Lansdowne House, 320 Chessington Road, West Ewell, Surrey KT19 9XG
☎ 0181 393 9946
CONTACT John Lucas
WORKING AREA Nationwide
ASSOCIATIONS SGD; AIHort; FIDiagE
SERVICES Garden design; horticultural consultancy
STARTED TRADING 1976
PROJECTS Silver medal for Water Conservation Garden at Hampton Court

Provides a landscape and garden design service, and will oversee contractors' work. A postal service is also offered. John Lucas writes and lectures on gardening topics, and his *Low-Water Gardening* was published last year by Dent.

John Moreland
11 Morrab Place, Penzance, Cornwall TR18 4DG
☎ 01736 67525
CONTACT John Moreland
WORKING AREA UK and Europe
ASSOCIATIONS FLI; SGD
SERVICES Garden design; landscape architecture; woodland and estate management
STARTED TRADING 1970
PROJECTS Chelsea gold medal gardens; de Savary's Land's End Project

Landscape architect and garden designer: works in Britain and abroad on large and small gardens in modern or traditional styles.

Josephine Hindle, Garden Designer and Lecturer
11 Beechfield, Newton Tony, Salisbury, Wiltshire SP4 0HQ
☎ 01980 629323
CONTACT Josephine Hindle
WORKING AREA Wiltshire, Hampshire, Dorset, Somerset
SERVICES Garden design
STARTED TRADING 1992
PROJECTS Private gardens

Trained at the English Gardening School. Garden designer with a fine arts degree: also runs study days and garden design workshops.

434 Professional Services

Joy Jardine, Garden Designer
Heath House, Alldens Lane, Munstead, Godalming, Surrey GU8 4AP
☎ 01483 416961   FAX 01483 416961
CONTACT   Joy Jardine
WORKING AREA   Hampshire, Surrey, Sussex
SERVICES   Garden design
STARTED TRADING   1989
PROJECTS   Small town garden on different levels, Godalming; 'modernist' roof garden, London

Garden design, including planting plans, maintenance schedules and project supervision.

Judith Walton
The Corner House, Foxcombe Lane, Boars Hill, Oxford, Oxfordshire OX1 5DH
☎ 01865 735179
CONTACT   Judith Walton
WORKING AREA   Southern England
ASSOCIATIONS   SGD
SERVICES   Garden design; horticultural consultancy
STARTED TRADING   1990
PROJECTS   Small courtyards and rear garden patios

Trained at the College of Garden Design. Part of Seven Counties Garden Design.

Judy's Country Garden, Lincolnshire
For full details see Nurseries section

Julian and Isabel Bannerman
Hanham Court, Hanham Abbots, Bristol, Avon BS15 3NT
☎ 01272 610593   FAX 01272 611202
CONTACT   Julian or Isabel Bannerman
WORKING AREA   Worldwide
SERVICES   Garden design; contractors; water and riparian services
STARTED TRADING   1987
PROJECTS   Daily Telegraph Garden, Chelsea 1994; Waddesden Manor Dairy water garden, Buckinghamshire

Garden designers with a flair for romantic landscapes. Construction service too.

Julian Treyer-Evans
Magnolia House, 26 Cuckfield Road, Hurstpierpoint, West Sussex BN6 9SA
☎ 01273 834233   FAX 01273 834833
CONTACT   Julian Treyer-Evans
WORKING AREA   Southern England and Australia
ASSOCIATIONS   BALI; MIHort
SERVICES   Garden design; landscape architecture
STARTED TRADING   1977
PROJECTS   Gardens for the headquarters of The Body Shop International, and restoration of a large Federation garden in Freemantle, Western Australia

Garden and landscape designer. A Chelsea exhibitor since 1986, whose track record runs from courtyard gardens to golf courses. Carries out overall designs, but has a special taste for herbaceous planting schemes.

Katherine Shock
369 Woodstock Road, Oxford, Oxfordshire OX2 8AA
☎ 01865 515584
CONTACT   Katherine Shock
WORKING AREA   50-mile radius of Oxford
ASSOCIATIONS   SGD
SERVICES   Garden design
STARTED TRADING   1987
PROJECTS   Large gardens in Oxfordshire

Garden designer, a member of the recently established Oxford Design Associates.

Keepers Nursery, Kent
For full details see Nurseries section

Keir Watson Garden Design
35 Magdalen Road, St Leonards on Sea, East Sussex TN37 6ET
☎ 01424 716958   FAX 01424 716958
CONTACT   Keir Watson
WORKING AREA   Nationwide
SERVICES   Garden design
STARTED TRADING   1989
PROJECTS   NCCPG/*Gardeners' World* Marquee, Hampton Court Show 1994

Garden designer. Specialises in natural or habitat planting schemes.

Keith Banyard Tree Surgeons
Nettletree Farm, Horton Heath, Wimborne, Dorset BH21 7JN
☎ 01202 828800   FAX 01202 820128
CONTACT   Keith Banyard
WORKING AREA   Dorset, Hampshire, Wiltshire
ASSOCIATIONS   AAAC; BALI
SERVICES   Garden design; contractors; arboricultural services
STARTED TRADING   1977
PROJECTS   County and local authority contracts; IBM; Wessex Water

Large firm covering an unusually wide range of disciplines including arboricultural services, tree moving, landscape design and maintenance, fencing and soil improving.

Keith Rushforth
32 Park Lane, Fareham, Hampshire PO16 7JX
☎ 01329 284738   FAX 01329 284738
CONTACT   Keith Rushforth
WORKING AREA   Nationwide
ASSOCIATIONS   FAA; MIHort
SERVICES   Arboricultural services
STARTED TRADING   1984

Arboricultural and horticultural consultant.

Professional Services 435

Ken Higginbotham Garden Landscaping
31 Elmfield, Chapel en le Frith, Stockport, Cheshire SK12 6TZ
☎ 01298 813051
CONTACT K. R. Higginbotham
WORKING AREA Cheshire, Peak District and south Manchester.
ASSOCIATIONS BALI
SERVICES Garden design; contractors; arboricultural services
STARTED TRADING 1979
PROJECTS 1993 BALI award for a large private garden in Chinley
Specialise in the design and construction of private gardens, patios and driveways. Experienced in working with difficult sites. Awarded a Silver-Gilt Medal at Hampton Court 1994 for a rock and water garden.

Kexby Design
12 College Lane, Apley Park, Wellington, Telford, Shropshire TF1 3DH
☎ 01952 249935   FAX 01952 641658
CONTACT John B. Rickell
WORKING AREA Nationwide
ASSOCIATIONS MIHort
SERVICES Garden design; horticultural consultancy; landscape architecture
STARTED TRADING 1982
PROJECTS Garden for the blind in Peterborough; new leisure complex, Tamworth
Wisley-trained designer and horticultural consultant. Many years experience; was landscape manager for Telford New Town. His expertise includes wild gardens. Independent professional witness.

Kinlochlaich House Gardens, Strathclyde
For full details see Nurseries section

Land and Tree Ltd
Ballochyle, Sandbank, Dunoon, Strathclyde PA23 8RD
☎ 01369 6428
CONTACT Chris Taylor
WORKING AREA Scotland
ASSOCIATIONS AAAC
SERVICES Arboricultural services
STARTED TRADING 1987
Carry out all tree work from surveys on amenity woods to commercial forestry.

Landcare
28 Station Road, Holmfirth, Huddersfield, West Yorkshire HD7 1AB
☎ 01484 686462   FAX 01484 688346
CONTACT Matthew Corder
WORKING AREA Midlands and northern England
ASSOCIATIONS ALI; ILAM

SERVICES Garden design; landscape architecture
STARTED TRADING 1988
Landscape architects.

Landscape Design Studio
3 Hatton Mains Cottages, Dalmahoy, Kirknewton, Lothian EH27 8EB
☎ 0131 333 1262
CONTACT Lucy Eyers
WORKING AREA Scotland and northern England
SERVICES Garden design; landscape architecture
STARTED TRADING 1991
Qualified landscape architect: the practice offers landscape architecture and garden design. Postal service available throughout the UK.

Landskip and Prospect
Talley, Llandeilo, Dyfed SA19 7YH
☎ 01558 685567   FAX 01558 685745
CONTACT Dr Andrew Sclater
WORKING AREA UK and Europe
ASSOCIATIONS MIHort
SERVICES Garden design; horticultural consultancy; landscape architecture; historical landscape survey and management plans
STARTED TRADING 1987
PROJECTS Survey and management plan for Culzean Country Park, National Trust for Scotland; many surveys for English Heritage; landscape restoration and/or improvement, parks and private gardens, UK, Belgium and France
Specialists in garden and parkland improvement. They have an associated office in Belgium and have an international practice which includes aesthetic assessment, historical research and landscape management.

LDC Ltd
The Courtyard Offices, Hatchlands, East Clandon, Surrey GU4 7RT
☎ 01483 211616   FAX 01483 211548
CONTACT Bridget Purser
WORKING AREA Southern England
ASSOCIATIONS ALI; BALI
SERVICES Garden design; contractors; landscape architecture
STARTED TRADING 1983
PROJECTS Hurlingham Club, Fulham; The Deanery, Sonning; and for the National Trust at Hatchlands, Clandon
Specialist design-and-build service which is led, unusually, by landscape architects.

Linda Fair - Garden Designer
29 Canons Close, Radlett, Hertfordshire WD7 7ER
☎ 01923 853391   FAX 01923 853391
CONTACT Linda Fair
WORKING AREA Buckinghamshire, north and west London, Hertfordshire
ASSOCIATIONS SGD

436 Professional Services

SERVICES Garden design
STARTED TRADING 1986
Garden designer for mainly private clients.

Lingard + Styles Landscape
Walpole House, 35 Walpole Street, London
SW3 4QS
☎ 0171 930 9233 FAX 0171 930 9152
CONTACT Peter Styles
WORKING AREA UK, Ireland and northern Europe
ASSOCIATIONS FLI; MIHort
SERVICES Garden design; horticultural consultancy; water and riparian services; landscape architecture; architects; architectural historians; interior landscapes
STARTED TRADING 1976
PROJECTS Hotel gardens for Voyager Hotel Group; private gardens

Landscape architects, planning and horticulture consultants. With a Kew-trained senior partner, this award-winning practice has a particular expertise in garden design. Other offices in Cardiff (01222 373140), Llandudno (01492 79892) and Newtown, Powys (01686 27600).

Longacre Nursery, Kent
For full details see Nurseries section

Lotus Landscapes
9 Beresford Close, Frimley Green, Camberley, Surrey
GU16 6LB
☎ 01252 838665 FAX 01252 838665
CONTACT Christine Young
WORKING AREA Berkshire, Hampshire, London and Surrey
ASSOCIATIONS BALI
SERVICES Garden design; contractors
STARTED TRADING 1974

Specialise in the design and construction of private gardens.

Louis Vincent Architectural Garden Designer
2 Ford Cottage, Mamhead Road, Kenton, Exeter, Devon EX6 8LY
☎ 01626 890226
CONTACT Louis Vincent or Anita de Visser
WORKING AREA South west England, Netherlands
ASSOCIATIONS SGD
SERVICES Garden design; horticultural consultancy; landscape architecture
STARTED TRADING 1991

Can provide a full range of design and consultancy services, including fully illustrated plans and architecturally designed garden structures.

Marianne Ford Garden Designs
Manor Farm House, Hulcott, Aylesbury, Buckinghamshire HP22 5AX
☎ 01296 394264 FAX 01296 399007

CONTACT Marianne Ford
WORKING AREA Bedfordshire, Buckinghamshire, Hertfordshire, London and Oxfordshire
ASSOCIATIONS SGD
SERVICES Garden design; horticultural consultancy
STARTED TRADING 1987

Marina Adams Landscape Architects
3 Pembroke Studios, Pembroke Gardens, London
W8 6HX
☎ 0171 602 5790 FAX 0171 602 5790
CONTACT Marina Adams
WORKING AREA UK and overseas
ASSOCIATIONS ALI
SERVICES Garden design; landscape architecture
STARTED TRADING 1968
PROJECTS Properties in Somerset and Surrey; urban squares in Paris; estates and gardens in Greece

Landscape architect with projects in Britain, Europe, Africa and the USA.

Mark Collis Tree Service
9 Harrow Road East, Dorking, Surrey RH4 2AX
☎ 01306 881692 FAX 01306 881692
CONTACT Mark Collis
WORKING AREA Surrey, Sussex and south London
ASSOCIATIONS AAAC
SERVICES Arboricultural services
STARTED TRADING 1986
PROJECTS Tree planting scheme for Epsom marketplace

Tree services including stump removal and specialist planting projects. Free quotations.

Mark Enright Landscapes
Highgate Garden Centre, Townsend Yard, Highgate Village, London N6 5JF
☎ 0181 342 9877 FAX 0181 341 5032
CONTACT Mark Enright or Andrew Wenham
WORKING AREA London, Home Counties and Europe
STARTED TRADING 1969
PROJECTS Kings Park, Stevenage; town and country gardens

Design and construction services.

Mark Lutyens
4 Brief Street, London SE5 9RD
☎ 0171 274 4366 FAX 0171 274 4366
CONTACT Mark Lutyens
WORKING AREA Worldwide
ASSOCIATIONS MLI
SERVICES Garden design; horticultural consultancy; landscape architecture
STARTED TRADING 1983
PROJECTS Private gardens in UK, France and Saudi Arabia

Professional Services 437

Landscape architect and garden consultant. Services include management and horticultural advice, selection and supervision of contractors.

Mark Ross Landscape Architects
Royal Arcade, Broad Street, Pershore, Hereford & Worcester WR10 1AG
☎ 01386 561321   FAX 01386 561961
CONTACT   Mark Ross or Sally Winter
WORKING AREA   England and Wales
ASSOCIATIONS   ALI; MIHort
SERVICES   Garden design; contractors; water and riparian services; landscape architecture; environmental assessment
STARTED TRADING   1990
PROJECTS   Landscaping at the Three Counties Showground, Malvern; retained consultants, National Rivers Authority; private gardens

Landscape architects and environmental assessors.

Mark Westcott Landscape Architects
14 Dufferin Street, London EC1Y 8PD
☎ 0171 251 8787   FAX 0171 490 0102
CONTACT   Mark Westcott or Angelos Wideson
WORKING AREA   Nationwide
ASSOCIATIONS   ALI; RIBA
SERVICES   Garden design; arboricultural services; landscape architecture; architecture
STARTED TRADING   1988
PROJECTS   Wildlife and wetlands garden at Powergen headquarters, Coventry; woodland management and storm-water balancing pond for Equity and Law, Kent; canalside walkway, East London

Architects and landscape architects with additional experience of historic gardens work.

Martin Berkley Landscape Architects
40 Berkeley Street, Glasgow, Strathclyde G3 7DW
☎ 0141 204 1855   FAX 0141 204 1813
CONTACT   Martin Berkley
WORKING AREA   Scotland
ASSOCIATIONS   ALI; ARICS
SERVICES   Garden design; contractors; arboricultural services; landscape architecture
STARTED TRADING   1980
PROJECTS   Laigh Kirk restoration project, Kilmarnock; Blairgowrie Shopping Centre, Coatbridge

Landscape architects.

Mary-Jane Hopes, Garden Designer
218 West Malvern Road, West Malvern, Hereford & Worcester WR14 4BA
☎ 01684 892153   FAX 01684 892155
CONTACT   Mary-Jane Hopes
WORKING AREA   Nationwide
ASSOCIATIONS   SGD; MIHort
SERVICES   Garden design; horticultural consultancy
STARTED TRADING   1984
PROJECTS   Many private gardens

Trained at Pershore and Merrist Wood. Full design service including survey, drawings and planting plans. Can supervise contractors' work and also provides consultancy advice. Specialities include organic and wildlife gardens. Mary-Jane Hopes also writes and lectures.

Merriments Gardens, East Sussex
For full details see Nurseries section

Michael Alwyn Jackson
Ashfield House, Grange Lane, Ingham, Lincolnshire LN1 2YD
☎ 01522 730784   FAX 01522 730784
CONTACT   Michael Alwyn Jackson
WORKING AREA   East Midlands and Yorkshire
ASSOCIATIONS   SGD
SERVICES   Garden design; horticultural consultancy
STARTED TRADING   1975
PROJECTS   President's Enclosures at Lincolnshire Showground; 20-acre parkland and formal garden, Grantham

Trained at Pershore. Emphasizes interesting plant associations.

Michael Littlewood Landscape Designer
Troutwells, Higher Hayne, Roadwater, Watchet, Somerset TA23 0RN
☎ 01984 41330   FAX 01984 41330
CONTACT   Michael Littlewood
WORKING AREA   UK and overseas
ASSOCIATIONS   SGD; FLI
SERVICES   Garden design; horticultural consultancy; water and riparian services; landscape architecture
PROJECTS   Ecological forest gardens and landscapes

Landscape architect since 1960 in UK and New Zealand. Specialises in sustainable developments and permaculture design, including urban forestry. Author of landscaping reference books.

Mickfield Fish and Watergarden Centre, Suffolk
For full details see Nurseries section

Mill Race Landscapes Ltd, Essex
For full details see Mill Race Nurseries, Essex in Nurseries section

Monkton Elm Garden Centre, Somerset
For full details see Nurseries section

Muckross Garden Centre, Co. Kerry
For full details see Nurseries section

Nareys Garden Centre, Suffolk
For full details see Nurseries section

438 Professional Services

Nicholas Roeber Landscapes
19 Vernon Yard, London W11 2DX
☎ 0171 727 0176   FAX 0171 221 1284

CONTACT Nicholas Roeber
WORKING AREA London and Home Counties
SERVICES Garden design; horticultural consultancy; contractors
STARTED TRADING 1987
PROJECTS Formal pool garden in London; walled garden in Dorset; woodland garden in Wiltshire

Provide a comprehensive design and construction service. The team has experience in all aspects of hard and soft landscaping.

Nigel Jeffries Landscapes
30 Yaverland Drive, Bagshot, Surrey GU19 5DX
☎ 01276 476365

CONTACT Nigel Jeffries
WORKING AREA South east England
ASSOCIATIONS BALI
SERVICES Garden design; contractors
STARTED TRADING 1974
PROJECTS Local authority projects and private gardens

Nigel L Philips Landscape and Garden Design
18a Cliffe High Street, Lewes, East Sussex BN7 2AH
☎ 01273 474948   FAX 01273 474948

CONTACT Nigel Philips
WORKING AREA Nationwide
ASSOCIATIONS SGD
SERVICES Garden design
STARTED TRADING 1982

Garden design service is offered nationwide. The landscaping service is restricted to the south and south east.

Noël Kingsbury
Sunbeam Nurseries, Frampton Cotterell, Avon BS17 2AU
☎ 0117 9245602   FAX 0117 9245602

CONTACT Noël Kingsbury
WORKING AREA Southern England, south west Midlands
SERVICES Garden design; horticultural consultancy
STARTED TRADING 1988
PROJECTS Experimental ecosystem plantings; 50-acre garden in Gloucestershire

Garden designer. Specialities include wild-flower planting and habitat creation, herbaceous plantings and conservatories.

North Wales Tree Service
Garmon View, School Hill, Trefriw, Gwynedd LL27 0NJ
☎ 01492 641009

CONTACT J. R. Butters or K. R. Webber
WORKING AREA North Wales and border counties
ASSOCIATIONS AAAC
SERVICES Arboricultural services
STARTED TRADING 1984

General tree works and inspections and reports. They sell wood and wood chips and run arboricultural and forestry training courses.

Nottcutts Landscapes
Ipswich Road, Woodbridge, Suffolk IP12 4AF
☎ 01394 383344

WORKING AREA See below
ASSOCIATIONS BALI; SGD; MIHort
SERVICES Garden design; horticultural consultancy; contractors
STARTED TRADING 1910
PROJECTS Private gardens – from tiny town back gardens to country estates

There are four Nottcutts Landscape Centres, including the Woodbridge centre: between them they cover East Anglia, the south east and the West Midlands. All offer a full design and construction service. The other centres are at: Stratford Road, Shirley, Solihull, West Midlands B90 4EN (0121 733 6201); Daniels Road, Norwich, Norfolk NR4 6QP (01603 54665); and Tonbridge Road, Pembury, Tunbridge Wells, Kent TN2 4QN (01892 823843).

Oak Cottage Herb Garden, Shropshire
For full details see Nurseries section

Orchard Nurseries, Lincolnshire
For full details see Nurseries section

Otter Nurseries Ltd, Devon
For full details see Nurseries section

Otter's Court Heathers, Somerset
For full details see Nurseries section

P H Kellett, Kent
For full details see Nurseries section

PMA Plant Specialities, Somerset
For full details see Nurseries section

P A Searle
85 College Ride, Bagshot, Surrey GU18 5EP
☎ 01276 471586   FAX 01276 471586

CONTACT Paul Searle
WORKING AREA South east England
ASSOCIATIONS AAAC
SERVICES Arboricultural services
STARTED TRADING 1980
PROJECTS Rushmoor Council

P G Biddle
Willowmead, Ickleton Road, Wantage, Oxfordshire OX12 9JA
☎ 01235 762478   FAX 01235 768034

CONTACT Dr P. G. Biddle
WORKING AREA Nationwide

Professional Services 439

ASSOCIATIONS FAA
SERVICES Arboricultural services; consultancy
STARTED TRADING 1972

Arboricultural consultant specialising in root damage to buildings, and building near trees. Other insurance and legal work, including expert witness in accident cases. Dr Biddle is a past Chairman of the Arboricultural Association.

P J Chaffin Tree Surgery
16 The Paddock, Eastbourne, East Sussex BN22 9LJ
☎ 01323 504620   FAX 01323 504620
CONTACT Pete Chaffin
WORKING AREA South east England
ASSOCIATIONS AAAC
SERVICES Arboricultural services
STARTED TRADING 1984

As well as tree services, Pete Chaffin acts as an instructor and assessor for chainsaw courses.

Pantiles Plant & Garden Centre, Surrey
For full details see Nurseries section

Park Garden Centre, Avon
For full details see Nurseries section

Pathfinder Gardening
The Island, Wraysbury, Berkshire TW19 5AS
☎ 01784 482677   FAX 01784 482511
CONTACT Mike Taylor
WORKING AREA London and south of England
SERVICES Contractors
STARTED TRADING 1933
PROJECTS Planting contract for Opel in Germany; extensive works for private client in Hampstead

Landscaping contractors who have built Gold Medal gardens at Chelsea. Their mini excavators can be hired.

Paul Cooper
Ty Bryn, Old Radnor, Presteigne, Powys LL8 2RN
☎ 01544 280374
CONTACT Paul Cooper
WORKING AREA Nationwide
SERVICES Garden design
STARTED TRADING 1990
PROJECTS Best Garden, Chelsea 1992; most controversial garden, Chelsea 1994

Garden designer with a modern approach and style. Lectures on garden design at Hereford College.

Paul Miles
23 Seckford Street, Woodbridge, Suffolk IP12 4LY
☎ 01394 383771   FAX 01394 380340
CONTACT Paul Miles
WORKING AREA International
ASSOCIATIONS MIHort
SERVICES Garden design; horticultural consultancy
STARTED TRADING 1979

PROJECTS Gardens in Majorca and Britain

Wisley trained, but also worked for Ingwersen, Nottcutts Landscape and the National Trust before going freelance. As well as design and consultancy, Paul Miles is an experienced photographer, writer and lecturer.

Paul Norton
6 Bayard Road, Weymouth, Dorset DT3 6AJ
☎ 01305 832511   FAX 01305 832511
CONTACT Paul Norton
WORKING AREA Southern England
ASSOCIATIONS ALI
SERVICES Garden design; landscape architecture
STARTED TRADING 1990

Landscape architects offering design and management services, including historic landscape restoration.

Pelham Landscapes
27 Sun Street, Lewes, East Sussex BN7 2QB
☎ 01273 472408
CONTACT Sue Richards
WORKING AREA Europe
ASSOCIATIONS SGD
SERVICES Garden design
STARTED TRADING 1990
PROJECTS Redesigned garden at Trinity Hospital, Greenwich for the Mercers' Company; private gardens in Oxford, Lewes and Croydon

Trained at Merrist Wood and the Inchbald School. Services range from verbal consultancy to full design service and supervision of contractors. Sue Richards is a corresponding member of the Society of Garden Designers.

Perryhill Nurseries, East Sussex
For full details see Nurseries section

Petal Designs Ltd
76 Addison Road, London W14 8EB
☎ 0171 602 2599   FAX 0171 602 7078
CONTACT Spindrift Al Swaidi
WORKING AREA England, France, Italy, Jordan and USA
SERVICES Garden design; landscape architecture
STARTED TRADING 1989
PROJECTS Private estates

Peter Beales Roses, Norfolk
For full details see Nurseries section

Peter Hemsley
14 Stonethwaite, Woodthorpe, York, North Yorkshire YO2 2SY
☎ 01904 705296
CONTACT Peter Hemsley
WORKING AREA Northern England
ASSOCIATIONS MIHort; FAA
SERVICES Horticultural consultancy; lecturing
STARTED TRADING 1992

440 Professional Services

PROJECTS Restoration of historic parterre at Harewood House; restoration of High Close Arboretum

Tree consultant and lecturer.

Peter Rogers Associates
Northdowns, Titsey Road, Limpsfield, Surrey
RH8 0DF
☎ 01883 715818
CONTACT Peter Rogers
WORKING AREA Nationwide
ASSOCIATIONS SGD; MIHort
SERVICES Garden design; horticultural consultancy; landscape architecture
STARTED TRADING 1973
PROJECTS Extensive sports facility for the London Borough of Merton

Landscape design services for private, commercial and public clients, including the refurbishment of private gardens.

Peter Wynn Arboricultural Consultant
Barclays Bank Chambers, Town Hall Street,
Sowerby Bridge, West Yorkshire HX6 2DY
☎ 01422 834587   FAX 01422 831141
CONTACT Peter Wynn
WORKING AREA Lancashire, Lincolnshire, Midlands, North Wales and Yorkshire
ASSOCIATIONS AAAC
SERVICES Arboricultural services
STARTED TRADING 1976

Arboricultural consultant and expert witness. Vice-President of the International Society of Arboriculture, 1993, and President Elect, 1995.

Planscapes
PO Box 37, Stourport on Severn, Hereford & Worcester DY13 9YT
☎ 01299 250805
CONTACT Fiona Browne
WORKING AREA Nationwide, but especially Midlands
ASSOCIATIONS SGD
SERVICES Garden design; contractors
STARTED TRADING 1991
PROJECTS Projects for private clients

Plantsmanship
20 Wellington Road, Hampton Hill, London
TW12 1JT
☎ 0181 943 4471   FAX 0181 943 1236
CONTACT David Wright or Paula Perowne
WORKING AREA London and Home counties
ASSOCIATIONS BALI; SGD
SERVICES Garden design; contractors
STARTED TRADING 1987
PROJECTS Design and construction of complete gardens for private clients

A full design and construction service is available, or they will work with other designers and specialists.

Their gardens are planned for organic maintenance. Advice on irrigation and lighting can be given.

Plaxtol Nurseries, Kent
For full details see Nurseries section

Private Landscapes
33 Beechcroft Road, London SW17 7BX
☎ 0181 767 0179   FAX 0181 672 7080
CONTACT Janet Nott
WORKING AREA London and south east England
SERVICES Garden design; contractors
STARTED TRADING 1992
PROJECTS Private clients in London and the country

Formal training at the Inchbald School of Garden Design, after gardening and designing privately.

Professional Tree Services
12a Bell Street, Romsey, Hampshire SO51 8GW
☎ 01794 513405   FAX 01794 513405
CONTACT Bill Kowalczyk
WORKING AREA Hampshire and East Wiltshire
ASSOCIATIONS FAA; AAAC
SERVICES Contractors; arboricultural services
STARTED TRADING 1985
PROJECTS Landscaping of a Biblical garden at Romsey Baptist Church

Full arboricultural service for trees and shrubs, including planting and design, surveys and consultancy work.

Provincial Tree Services Ltd
31 Bridge Street, Heywood, Lancashire OL10 1JF
☎ 01706 369355
CONTACT Mervyn C. Simpson
WORKING AREA Greater Manchester
ASSOCIATIONS AAAC
SERVICES Arboricultural services
STARTED TRADING 1979
PROJECTS Tree work on Moss Side development for Manchester City Direct Services

Also at Elizabeth Street Farm, Heywood, Lancashire.

Quartet Design
The Village School, Lillingstone Dayrell,
Buckingham, Buckinghamshire MK18 5AP
☎ 01280 860500   FAX 01280 860468
CONTACT David Newman
WORKING AREA UK and western Europe
ASSOCIATIONS Dip. L Arch; MIHort
SERVICES Garden design; horticultural consultancy; landscape architecture
STARTED TRADING 1986

Landscape architects offering full design and construction services.

Raven Tree Services
Florida Close, Hot Lane Industrial Estate, Burslem, Stoke on Trent, Staffordshire ST6 2DJ
☎ 01782 837755

CONTACT   S. A. Coombes
WORKING AREA   Midlands (contracting); nationwide (consultancy and stump removal)
ASSOCIATIONS   AAAC
SERVICES   Arboricultural services
STARTED TRADING   1980

As well as contracting services, they offer nationwide stump removal and arboricultural consultancy. Chainsaw courses and assessment.

Ray Pitt Landscape Design
The Rest, Bradden Road, Greens Norton, Towcester, Northamptonshire NN12 8BS
☎ 01327 350520
CONTACT   Ray Pitt
WORKING AREA   London, Midlands and most of southern England
ASSOCIATIONS   ALI
SERVICES   Garden design; horticultural consultancy; landscape architecture
STARTED TRADING   1990
PROJECTS   Landscape and design for new primary school in Tower Hamlets, London; housing developments in Bedfordshire, Buckinghamshire, Hertfordshire and Northamptonshire; private gardens.

Landscape architect. Services include tree and hedgerow surveys, and site appraisal and assessment. Lectures on landscape design and amenity horticulture.

Richard Key and Associates
40 Glenham Road, Thame, Oxfordshire OX9 3WD
☎ 01844 213051   FAX 01844 213051
CONTACT   Richard Key
WORKING AREA   South of England
ASSOCIATIONS   SGD
SERVICES   Garden design; contractors; landscape architecture
STARTED TRADING   1994
PROJECTS   Chelsea Flower Show gardens

Landscape and garden design. Richard Key writes on design and construction.

Richard Loader Tree Care Specialists
32 Moors Close, Hurn, Christchurch, Dorset BH23 6AL
☎ 01202 470596   FAX 01202 475880
CONTACT   Simon Jones
WORKING AREA   Dorset, Hampshire, Isle of Wight, East Sussex and Wiltshire
ASSOCIATIONS   FAA; AAAC
SERVICES   Arboricultural services
STARTED TRADING   1977

Tree services and fencing.

Robin Digby
Flint Cottage, 21 St John's Road, Boxmoor, Hemel Hempstead, Hertfordshire HP1 1QF
☎ 01442 232699
CONTACT   Robin Digby

WORKING AREA   Nationwide
SERVICES   Garden design; water and riparian services
STARTED TRADING   1993
PROJECTS   Granite Garden at Hampton Court Show

Design and construction: specialises in Chinese and Japanese gardens and water features.

Robin Williams & Associates
Kennet House, 19 High Street, Hungerford, Berkshire RG17 0NL
☎ 01488 686150   FAX 01488 686124
CONTACT   Robin Williams
WORKING AREA   UK, Europe and USA
ASSOCIATIONS   SGD; FIHort; MCSD; M.APLD (USA)
SERVICES   Garden design; horticultural consultancy
STARTED TRADING   1977

Robin Williams is also co-director of the College of Garden Design Ltd, and is an author and illustrator. His new book *The Garden Designer* is published this year by Frances Lincoln.

The Robinson Penn Partnership
4th Floor, Cathedral Buildings, Dean Street, Newcastle upon Tyne, Tyne & Wear NE1 1PG
☎ 0191 230 4339   FAX 0191 230 5509
CONTACT   Dr Rachel Penn
WORKING AREA   UK and overseas
ASSOCIATIONS   ALI
SERVICES   Garden design; horticultural consultancy; arboricultural services; landscape architecture; ecological assessment and wildlife design
STARTED TRADING   1992
PROJECTS   Courtyard design, Howdon Laboratory, Northumberland Water; landscape design, Wynyard Hall, Cleveland

A partnership of a landscape architect and an environmental scientist. Their work has included large-scale habitat creation, formal landscaping and a mannerist garden for a private client.

Romilt Landscape Design & Construction Ltd
North Wyke Farm, Guildford Road, Normandy, Surrey GU3 2AN
☎ 01483 811933
CONTACT   R. J. Milton
WORKING AREA   Southern England
ASSOCIATIONS   BALI
SERVICES   Garden design; contractors; water and riparian services
STARTED TRADING   1975
PROJECTS   Relined lake for Lewisham Borough Council; private gardens and ponds

Complete design and construction service for gardens and landscapes, including interior landscapes. See also associated companies Abbey Waters Ltd, Water and

442   Professional Services

Riparian Services, and R. J. Milton (01252 710325), Horticultural Consultancy.

Rosemary Barry
25 Colne Park Road, White Colne, Colchester, Essex CO6 2PL
☎ 01787 223214

CONTACT   Rosemary Barry
WORKING AREA   East Anglia
SERVICES   Garden design; horticultural consultancy
STARTED TRADING   1993
PROJECTS   Landscaping of commercial barn conversion; wildlife pond; private gardens

Trained at Otley in Garden Design and Construction with a degree in Conservation. Designs and supervises construction for private and commercial clients. Also gives talks.

Ross Tree Services
The Old Pound, Llangarrow, Ross on Wye, Hereford & Worcester HR9 6PG
☎ 01989 770383

CONTACT   J. P. Ross
WORKING AREA   30-mile radius
ASSOCIATIONS   AAAC
SERVICES   Arboricultural services
STARTED TRADING   1980
PROJECTS   Work for English Heritage and Woodland Trust

Full range of tree surgery and consultancy work, including stump removal.

Roy Finch Tree Care Specialists
Welland Way, Gloucester Road, Welland, Malvern, Hereford & Worcester WR13 6LD
☎ 01684 310700   FAX 01684 310867

CONTACT   Roy Finch or Adrian Hope
WORKING AREA   65-mile radius (contracting); nationwide (consultancy)
ASSOCIATIONS   AAAC; FAA
SERVICES   Contractors; arboricultural services
STARTED TRADING   1967

Full range of arboricultural services and also consultancy work including safety, litigation and conservation matters.

Rupert Golby
South View, Cross Hill Road, Adderbury West, Banbury, Oxfordshire OX17 3EG
☎ 01295 810320

CONTACT   Rupert Golby
WORKING AREA   Central England
SERVICES   Garden design; horticultural consultancy
STARTED TRADING   1986
PROJECTS   Many Cotswold manor gardens; British Embassy Gardens, Rome; mountain garden, Salzburg

Trained at Kew and Wisley. Working from the South Midlands he specialises in recreating the classic English country garden in less maintenance-intensive forms.

Ruskins Arboricultural Group
St Mary's Lane, Upminster, Essex RA14 3HP
☎ 01768 641144   FAX 01768 641155

CONTACT   Robert Wilkins (Operations Manager)
WORKING AREA   UK and overseas
ASSOCIATIONS   BALI
SERVICES   Arboricultural services; tree-moving; boxed specimen trees
STARTED TRADING   1986
PROJECTS   Large construction projects

Large arboricultural group including tree surgery, consultancy and management services. They supply specimen trees and have the biggest tree moving machinery in the UK.

S Warren-Brown
Steet Point, Steerpoint Road, Brixham, Devon PL8 2OQ
☎ 01752 880792/788424   FAX 01752 880792

CONTACT   Mr S. Warren-Brown
WORKING AREA   South Devon
ASSOCIATIONS   SGD
SERVICES   Garden design; horticultural consultancy; contractors
STARTED TRADING   1987

Sally Healey Garden Design
The Studio, Brook Lane, Send, Woking, Surrey GU23 7EY
☎ 01483 222716

CONTACT   Sally Healey
STARTED TRADING   1990
PROJECTS   Gardens for private clients

Garden designer, trained at Merrist Wood and Wisley. Work shown in Berg timber frame house brochure.

Sarah Massey
12 Park Drive, London NW11 7SH
☎ 0181 458 1510   FAX 0181 458 1510

CONTACT   Sarah Massey
WORKING AREA   UK and overseas
SERVICES   Garden design
STARTED TRADING   1991
PROJECTS   Garden in Oxfordshire incorporating ruined mill and mill stream

Sarah Rutherford
4 Wolviston Avenue, York, North Yorkshire YO1 3DD
☎ 01904 430558   FAX 01904 430558

CONTACT   Sarah Rutherford
WORKING AREA   Between London and Edinburgh
ASSOCIATIONS   MIHort
SERVICES   Horticultural consultancy
STARTED TRADING   1993
PROJECTS   Research for Countryside Commission

Professional Services 443

Kew-trained, with a degree in Conservation Studies. Horticultural consultant specialising in conservation, restoration and research of historic gardens.

Sarah Rycroft Landscape Architects
634 Wilmslow Road, Didsbury M20 3QX
☎ 0161 445 6375   FAX 0161 445 6375
CONTACT   Sarah Rycroft
WORKING AREA   Nationwide
ASSOCIATIONS   ALI
SERVICES   Garden design; horticultural consultancy; arboricultural services; landscape architecture
STARTED TRADING   1987
PROJECTS   Public open spaces at Trafford Park; parkland and gardens at Maryland Bank of North America Euro HQ, Chester

Landscape architects and garden designers.

Scotsdale Nursery & Garden Centre, Cambridgeshire
For full details see Nurseries section

Scottlandscape
78 Bousley Rise, Ottershaw, Surrey KT16 0LB
☎ 01932 872667   FAX 01932 872667
CONTACT   Robert Scott
WORKING AREA   South east England
ASSOCIATIONS   BALI
SERVICES   Garden design; horticultural consultancy; contractors; water and riparian services; irrigation systems
STARTED TRADING   1965
PROJECTS   Tudor Rose Award for best garden in show, Hampton Court 1992, 1993 and 1994; planting and maintenance at Heathrow airport

Expanding family firm covering garden design, construction and maintenance. As well as award-winning collaborations with designer Barbara Hunt, they are also involved with Hare Hatch Nursery.

Secret Garden Designs by Christina Oates
Fovant Hut, Fovant, Salisbury, Wiltshire SP3 5LN
☎ 01722 714756
CONTACT   Christina Oates
WORKING AREA   Dorset, Hampshire, Somerset, Wiltshire
SERVICES   Garden design; horticultural consultancy
STARTED TRADING   1990
PROJECTS   Private gardens

Trained at the English Gardening School, and now teaches there. Garden design, including preparation of plans for DIY gardeners and consultancy visits.

Seven Counties Garden Design
143 Manor Green Road, Epsom, Surrey KT19 8LL
☎ 01372 724660/0181 940 2402
CONTACT   Sue De Bock Rowles or Karen Saynor
WORKING AREA   Southern England

SERVICES   Garden design
STARTED TRADING   1990

A chain of affiliated garden designers, all trained at the College of Garden Design. They tackle all sizes and styles of gardens, and can produce surveys, plans and costings. They also run short courses in Garden Design. The eight designers are spread out between Kent and Somerset, and between them cover the south of England. See also under the individual designers: Helen Cahill, Sue de Bock Rowles, Mary Ann Lovegrove, Jeanne Paisley, Karen Saynor, Anthea Sokell and Judith Walton.

Seymours Garden & Leisure Group
Pit House, By-Pass, Ewell, Surrey KT17 1PS
☎ 0181 393 0111   FAX 0181 393 0237
CONTACT   James Seymour
WORKING AREA   London, Surrey and adjoining areas
ASSOCIATIONS   SGD; BALI
SERVICES   Garden design; contractors
STARTED TRADING   1918

James Seymour is a Wisley-trained horticulturist and garden designer, with gold medals at Chelsea and Hampton Court. The firm also acts as contractors, and there is a garden centre on the site.

Silk Morus
2 Heifer Mill Cottages, Mosterton, Beaminster, Dorset DT8 3HG
☎ 01308 868103
CONTACT   Patrick Silk
WORKING AREA   Southern England
SERVICES   Garden design

Designs for private gardens. The services include site visits and consultations, plants and planting.

Simon Richards + Associates
17 St Peter's Road, Cirencester, Gloucestershire GL7 1RE
☎ 01285 650828   FAX 01285 650828
CONTACT   Simon Richards
WORKING AREA   Southern Britain
ASSOCIATIONS   ALI; MIHort
SERVICES   Garden design; landscape architecture
STARTED TRADING   1984
PROJECTS   Retail Outlet Centre, Bicester; Parish Wharf Leisure Centre, Portishead, Bristol

Award-winning landscape architecture practice which aims to combine imaginative hard detailing with low-maintenance planting schemes. Designs are structured to allow development in phases.

Smeeden Foreman Partnership
67 Westbourne Road, Huddersfield HD1 4LG
☎ 01484 456494   FAX 01484 456495
CONTACT   Mark Smeeden or Trevor Foreman
WORKING AREA   Nationwide
ASSOCIATIONS   ALI; MIHort

444 Professional Services

SERVICES Garden design; horticultural consultancy; landscape architecture
STARTED TRADING 1992
PROJECTS Design and refurbishment of 17th-century gardens at Whixley Hall, North Yorkshire; interior planting for public buildings

Landscape architects and environmental planners with horticultural qualifications. Retained consultants to the North East division of the National Rivers Authority.

Sol Jordens
Stocksbridge House, Coombe Bissett, Salisbury, Wiltshire SP5 4LZ
☎ 01722 77573

CONTACT Solbjorg Jordens
WORKING AREA Nationwide
SERVICES Garden design; horticultural consultancy
STARTED TRADING 1987
PROJECTS Gardens for period and conemporary houses

Trained at the College of Garden Design, and with John Brookes. Full range of garden design and consultancy services. Aims to relate the garden to the house and its landscape setting.

Sonya Millman Garden Design
53 Maidenhead Road, Stratford upon Avon, Warwickshire CV37 6XU
☎ 01789 414237   FAX 01789 414237

CONTACT Sonya Millman
WORKING AREA Warwickshire and neighbouring counties
SERVICES Garden design
STARTED TRADING 1992
PROJECTS Private gardens; planting scheme for a health centre

Trained at the English Gardening School. Aims to create spacious contemporary gardens.

Southern Tree Surgeons Ltd
Crawley Down, West Sussex RH10 4HL
☎ 01342 712215/712771 FAX 01342 717662

CONTACT Mr M. Coomber, Area Manager
WORKING AREA Nationwide
ASSOCIATIONS FAA: AAAC; BALI
SERVICES Garden design; arboricultural services
STARTED TRADING 1956

Head office of a large firm of tree surgeons and consultants who work nationwide and in Europe. The firm has a royal warrant, and is the largest of its kind in Europe.

Southern Tree Surgeons Ltd
65a Haywood Street, Leek, Staffordshire ST13 5JH
☎ 01538 384877/372682

CONTACT Mr A. Mellor
WORKING AREA Midlands and northern England
SERVICES Arboricultural services

Southern Tree Surgeons Ltd
52a Cowick Street, Exeter, Devon EX4 1AP
☎ 01392 214690

CONTACT Mr C. Groves
WORKING AREA South and south west England
SERVICES Arboricultural services

Southern Tree Surgeons Ltd
Hartleys Place, Church Lane, Wexham, Slough, Berkshire SL3 6LD
☎ 01753 551100   FAX 01753 553166

CONTACT Mrs L. Bell
WORKING AREA London and Home Counties
SERVICES Arboricultural services

Southern Tree Surgeons Ltd
Tring House, 77 High Street, Tring, Hertfordshire HP23 4AB
☎ 01442 828410

WORKING AREA Bedfordshire, Buckinghamshire and Hertfordshire
SERVICES Arboricultural services

Southern Tree Surgeons Ltd
The Old Kennels, Cirencester Park, Tetbury Road, Cirencester, Gloucestershire GL7 1UR
☎ 01285 652421/654370 FAX 01285 885800

CONTACT Mr B. Robinson
WORKING AREA Gloucestershire, Oxfordshire and Wales
SERVICES Arboricultural services

Southern Tree Surgeons Ltd
Gaywood, Mulhuddart, Co. Dublin
☎ 00 353 1 821 3150

CONTACT Mr A. Worsnop
WORKING AREA Ireland
SERVICES Arboricultural services

Stella Caws Associates
Stratheden, 4 Hardwich Hill, Chepstow, Gwent NP6 5PN
☎ 01291 626645   FAX 01291 626645

CONTACT Stella Caws
WORKING AREA Wales, south Midlands and southern England
ASSOCIATIONS SGD; ALI
SERVICES Garden design; landscape architecture
STARTED TRADING 1990
PROJECTS National Centre for Organic Gardening 3-acre display garden in Kent

Undertakes public and private commissions, with a complete service available for projects of all sizes. Lectures at the Garden Academy.

Stephen J White
8 Torwood Gardens, Bishopstoke, Hampshire SO50 8PD
☎ 01703 692773

Professional Services 445

CONTACT   Stephen J. White
SERVICES   Garden design; horticultural consultancy
STARTED TRADING   1976
PROJECTS   4-acre gardens for Cotswold manor house

Kew-trained garden designer and consultant. He also gives lectures to horticultural societies.

Sue De Bock Rowles Garden Design
143 Manor Green Road, Epsom, Surrey KT19 8LL
☎ 01372 724660   FAX 0171 400 8050
CONTACT   Sue De Bock Rowles
WORKING AREA   London, Kent, Surrey and Sussex
SERVICES   Garden design
STARTED TRADING   1991
PROJECTS   Children's gardens; long narrow town gardens; informal country gardens

Trained at the College of Garden Design. Won the Bradstone Design Award in 1991, and is a member of Seven Counties Garden Design. Offers a comprehensive garden design service. Chelsea medallist.

Sue Pack Garden Design
9 Rudchesters, Bancroft, Milton Keynes, Buckinghamshire MK13 0PH
☎ 01908 317029
CONTACT   Sue Pack
WORKING AREA   Bedfordshire, Buckinghamshire and Oxfordshire, mainly
SERVICES   Garden design
STARTED TRADING   1990
PROJECTS   Italian style courtyard garden; low maintenance garden on a very sloping site

Garden design and consultancy. Has exhibited in the Chelsea Flower Show Design Pavilion in recent years and gives talks on garden design.

Sue's Garden Designs, Suffolk
For full details see Mrs S. Robinson, Suffolk in Nurseries section

Susan Buckley
124 Ashton Lane, Sale, Cheshire M33 5QJ
☎ 0161 905 2327   FAX 0161 905 2327
CONTACT   Susan Buckley
WORKING AREA   North west England
ASSOCIATIONS   ALI
SERVICES   Garden design; landscape architecture
STARTED TRADING   1989
PROJECTS   Commercial and residential development landscape design and improvement work

Landscape architects with 15 years' experience for private and public sector clients. Experienced in conservation of historic gardens, and establishing woodlands and semi-natural habitats.

Susanne John Landscape Design & Consultancy
21 Chester Row, London SW1W 9JF
☎ 0171 730 7409   FAX 0171 730 7409

CONTACT   Susanne John
WORKING AREA   UK and Europe
ASSOCIATIONS   SGD
STARTED TRADING   1993
PROJECTS   22-acre parkland, Gut Gross-Kelle, Germany; London gardens for private clients

Garden and landscape designer. A construction service is available.

Sutton, Griffin & Morgan
Albion House, Oxford Street, Newbury, Berkshire RG13 1JE
☎ 01635 521100   FAX 01635 44188
CONTACT   Roderick Griffin
WORKING AREA   UK and overseas
ASSOCIATIONS   SGD; MIHort
SERVICES   Garden design; horticultural consultancy; water and riparian services; landscape architecture; chartered architects
STARTED TRADING   1910

Part of an architectural practice which also accepts garden design commissions. Recently designed for BBC TV's *Front Gardens*.

Syon Courtyard, London
For full details see Nurseries section

Tom La Dell, Kent
For full details see Nurseries section

Teamwork Landscaping
Myrtle Cottage, Knellers Lane, Totton, Southampton, Hampshire SO40 7EB
☎ 01703 871919
CONTACT   John or Linden Kuyser
WORKING AREA   30-mile radius
ASSOCIATIONS   BALI; SGD
SERVICES   Garden design; contractors
STARTED TRADING   1988

Specialise in the design and construction of domestic gardens.

Tim Brayford Landscapes
The Cliff, Spindlers Road, St Lawrence, Ventnor, Isle of Wight PO38 1XD
☎ 01983 852952   FAX 01983 852952
CONTACT   Tim Brayford
WORKING AREA   Isle of Wight, mainly
ASSOCIATIONS   BALI
SERVICES   Garden design; horticultural consultancy; contractors; water and riparian services
STARTED TRADING   1980
PROJECTS   Work at Velta House Nursing Home, Newport and Isle of Wight Crown Court, Newport

Design and construction, redesign and maintenance undertaken. Gardens are tailored exactly to clients' requirements, including future levels of maintenance.

Tony Benger Landscaping
Burrow Farm Gardens, Dalwood, Axminster, Devon EX13 7ET
☎ 01404 831844   FAX 01404 831844
CONTACT Tony Benger
WORKING AREA Devon, Dorset, Somerset and Avon
ASSOCIATIONS BALI
SERVICES Garden design; contractors
STARTED TRADING 1985
PROJECTS Dorchester Hospice; Weston Super Mare Hospital; Southampton Airport

Design, construction amd maintenance service. The 5-acre garden is open to the public.

Town and Country Landscapes
46 Sanderstead Court Avenue, Sanderstead, South Croydon, Surrey CR2 9AJ
☎ 0181 651 0341
CONTACT Nigel Oates
WORKING AREA South London
SERVICES Garden design; horticultural consultancy; contractors
STARTED TRADING 1988
PROJECTS Courtyard garden, Walton on the Hill; low-maintenance planting on steep bank, Caterham

RHS certificate. Specialises in design and construction of low-maintenance gardens. Arboricultural work with small ornamental and fruit trees only.

Tree Maintenance
Unit 12, Hope Mills, Brinscombe, Stroud, Gloucestershire GL5 2SA
☎ 01453 731212
CONTACT Geoffrey March
WORKING AREA Avon, Gloucestershire, Herefordshire, Oxfordshire, Wiltshire, Worcestershire and South Wales
ASSOCIATIONS AAAC
SERVICES Arboricultural services
STARTED TRADING 1981
PROJECTS Regular maintenance for the National Trust and Woodland Trust, and of the 99 yews in Painswick churchyard.

Reports and surveys, tree surgery and maintenance, including hedge trimming, stump removal and chipping.

Treecare (Arboricultural Specialists)
Oak Tree House, Rosebank Works, Rosebank Way, London W3 6TT
☎ 0181 993 1443   FAX 0181 993 2828
CONTACT Edward Radziwillowicz or Darryl Parkin
WORKING AREA London and south east England
ASSOCIATIONS AAAC
SERVICES Arboricultural services
STARTED TRADING 1982
PROJECTS Contracting work at the Tower of London and Westminster Abbey; property maintenance companies; housing associations

Arboricultural contracting and consultancy work for Local Authorities and private clients.

Treecare
132 Knowsley Road, Norwich, Norfolk NR3 4PU
☎ 01603 612485
CONTACT Nick Coleman or Colin McDonald
WORKING AREA Norfolk
ASSOCIATIONS AAAC
SERVICES Arboricultural services
STARTED TRADING 1989
PROJECTS Tree surgery for Norwich City Football Club, Colmans factory and local authorities

Full arboricultural contracting and consultancy service.

Treemasters
53 Tadworth Street, Tadworth, Surrey KT20 5RG
☎ 01737 812389   FAX 0181 781 0536
CONTACT John Darter
WORKING AREA London and south east England
ASSOCIATIONS AAAC
SERVICES Arboricultural services
STARTED TRADING 1986
PROJECTS Appeared on Channel 4's *Fragile Earth* programme in 1993

Arboricultural contractors.

Trees
Copse Cottage, Hurst Lane, Sedlescombe, East Sussex TN33 0PE
☎ 01424 870479   FAX 01424 870479
CONTACT Mr P. W. Martin
WORKING AREA London and south east England
ASSOCIATIONS AAAC
SERVICES Arboricultural services
STARTED TRADING 1971
PROJECTS Continuing contracting work at Hyde Park, Kensington Gardens and Windsor Castle, St James's Park, Eltham Palace and London boroughs

All tree work including contracting, consultancy and planting. 24-hour call-out, and free advice and estimates.

Treework Services Ltd
Cheston Combe, Church Town, Backwell, Bristol, Avon BS19 3JQ
☎ 01275 464466   FAX 01275 463078
CONTACT Neville Fay
WORKING AREA Bristol and south west England
ASSOCIATIONS AAAC; BALI
SERVICES Garden design; horticultural consultancy
PROJECTS Tree maintenance at Bath Royal Victoria Park and Botanical Gardens; lake construction integrated with ornamental and natural landscape

Tree surgeons, arboricultural consultants, tree planting and landscape and garden designers for private and commercial clients. They combine a wide range of professions with a strong ecological awareness.

Professional Services 447

Treeworld Services
14 Portland Gardens, Tilehurst, Reading, Berkshire
RG3 4QH
☎ 01734 419755 FAX 01734 419755
CONTACT Steven M. Kelleher
WORKING AREA Southern England
ASSOCIATIONS AAAC
SERVICES Arboricultural services
STARTED TRADING 1986
PROJECTS Tree work at Legoland, Windsor

Arboricultural services, including fencing and ground maintenance.

Veronica Adams Garden Design
Lower Hopton Farm, Stoke Lacy, Bromyard,
Hereford & Worcester HR7 4HX
☎ 01885 490294
CONTACT Veronica Adams
WORKING AREA Nationwide
ASSOCIATIONS BALI
SERVICES Garden design; horticultural consultancy
STARTED TRADING 1986
PROJECTS Birtsmorton Court, Worcestershire; courtyard garden Beddingend Farm, Hereford

Trained at the Inchbald School of Design, and in painting at Ruskin School, Oxford. Specialises in gardens for English country houses. Also paints botanical ceramics, porcelain and tiles.

Veronica Ross – Landscape Design
Burnroot Farmhouse, Dinnet, Aboyne, Grampian
AB34 5PN
☎ 013398 86690 FAX 013398 86690
CONTACT Veronica Ross
WORKING AREA North east Scotland
ASSOCIATIONS ALI
SERVICES Garden design; landscape architecture
STARTED TRADING 1989
PROJECTS Visitor access and improvements at RSPB reserve Fowls Heugh; village green and car park at Dinnet

Landscape designer with additional expertise in forest landscape design.

W K W Tree Services
The Grange, Old Teversal, Nottinghamshire
NG17 3JW
☎ 01623 512795 FAX 01623 442329
CONTACT William Kew-Winder
WORKING AREA Derbyshire, Nottinghamshire, South Yorkshire, and adjoining parts of Leicestershire and Lincolnshire
ASSOCIATIONS AAAC
SERVICES Arboricultural services
STARTED TRADING 1980
PROJECTS Woodland management for the Woodland Trust; cable-bracing at Rufford Country Park

Tree contracting and consultancy, including emergency service. Supplies wood chips, bark and logs.

Water Meadow Nursery & Herb Farm, Hampshire
For full details see Nurseries section

Weaver Vale Garden Centre (County Gardens), Cheshire
For full details see Nurseries section

Webbs of Wychbold, Hereford and Worcester
For full details see Nurseries section

West Kington Nurseries Ltd, Wiltshire
For full details see Nurseries section

Westside Forestry
Lower Madeley Farm, Harbours Hill, Belbroughton,
Stourbridge, West Midlands DY9 9XE
☎ 0121 457 9457 FAX 0121 457 9457
CONTACT Mr B. Kenward
WORKING AREA West Midlands
ASSOCIATIONS AAAC
SERVICES Arboricultural services
STARTED TRADING 1976

Tree services and fencing.

Whitehall Garden Centre, Wiltshire
For full details see Nurseries section

Willerby Tree Surgeons Ltd
Albion Lane, Willerby, Humberside HU10 6DT
☎ 01482 651185
CONTACT Mr C. P. Scaife
WORKING AREA North Humberside, North Lincolnshire and North Yorkshire
ASSOCIATIONS AAAC
SERVICES Arboricultural services
STARTED TRADING 1981

Tree surgery and tree consultancy, including surveys and planting.

Wilmslow Garden Centre, Cheshire
For full details see Nurseries section

Wolverhampton Tree Service
150 Lamb Crescent, Wombourn, Wolverhampton,
Staffordshire WV5 0ED
☎ 01902 892652/01831 367508 FAX 01902 892652
CONTACT Bob Smith
WORKING AREA Shropshire, Staffordshire and West Midlands
ASSOCIATIONS AAAC
SERVICES Arboricultural services
STARTED TRADING 1985

Approved contractor for 8 local authorities and British Rail.

448 Professional Services

Woodhams
60 Ledbury Road, London W11 2AJ
☎ 0171 243 3141   FAX 0171 243 3151
CONTACT Pippa Bacon
WORKING AREA UK and overseas
SERVICES Garden design; contractors
STARTED TRADING 1988
PROJECTS Gold Medal winner, Chelsea 1994, 'Mr Maidment's Garden'; country house garden; London gardens and roof terraces

Complete garden design and construction service, including planting and lighting.

Wreford Landscapes
Poulner Hill Nurseries, Forest Corner, Ringwood, Hampshire BH24 3HP
☎ 01425 478600   FAX 01425 480882
CONTACT Jon Burrows and Russell Lugg
WORKING AREA Berkshire, Dorset, Hampshire and Wiltshire
ASSOCIATIONS BALI; AAAC; ALI
SERVICES Garden design; contractors; arboricultural services; water and riparian services; landscape architecture
PROJECTS Maintenance work at Poole Park and Christchurch Borough; water gardens at Haskins Garden Centre, Longham

Zengarden
26 Falkland Road, Barnet, Hertfordshire EN5 4LG
☎ 0181 441 3415
CONTACT Andrew Moffat
WORKING AREA UK and Europe
STARTED TRADING 1994
PROJECTS Garden at Tokonoma Bonsai Nursery, Shenley; rain garden at Carmarthen

Garden designer who specialises in Japanese designs. A full service is available including construction and maintenance.

Organisations

ADAS
ADAS Headquarters, Oxford Spires Business Park, The Boulevard, Kidlington, Oxfordshire OX5 1NZ
☎ 01865 842742

Agricultural & Food Research Council
Polaris House, North Star Avenue, Swindon, Wiltshire SN2 1UH
☎ 01793 413200

All Year Round Chrysanthemum Growers Association
30 Pern Drive, Botley, Hampshire SO3 2GW
☎ 01489 786638
CONTACT   The Secretary

Formed to represent the industry and distribute information to growers. Acts as a liaison between the growers, the government and other bodies. In the past their work has included pest control and the new plant passport scheme. They recently became involved in publicity, and are promoting British Chrysanthemums.

Arboricultural Association
Ampfield House, Romsey, Hampshire SO51 9PA
☎ 01794 368717
CONTACT   The Secretariat

A registered charity and the professional body for arboriculturists. The AA publishes a useful directory of consultants and contractors who have met the organisation's stringent standards for training, work and insurance: contact the Secretariat for details. A range of other publications is also available. There is a local group structure, and keen amateurs can join as part of the Tree Club.

Association of National Park Officers
c/o The Old Vicarage, Bondgate, Helmsley, North Yorkshire YO6 3BP
☎ 01439 70657
CONTACT   S. Copeland

Association of Playing Field Officers & Landscape Managers
1 Cowley Road, Tuffley, Gloucester GL4 0HT
☎ 01452 417693
CONTACT   K. Hill

Botanic Gardens Conservation International
Descanso House, 199 Kew Road, Richmond, Surrey TW9 3BW
☎ 0181 940 0047

British Agricultural & Garden Machinery Association
14 - 16 Church Street, Rickmansworth WD3 1RQ
☎ 01923 720241

British Agrochemicals Association
4 Lincoln Court, Lincoln Road, Peterborough
☎ 01733 349225

Trade association for manufacturers, distributors and retailers of pesticides. Among many useful publications on using chemicals is a guide to the products available for amateur gardeners.

British Association of Landscape Industries (BALI)
Landscape House, Henry Street, Keighley, West Yorkshire BD21 3DR
☎ 01535 606139

The national body representing Landscape Contractors. BALI promotes the interests of its members at national and regional level, and works to maintain high standards in the industry. Member firms are required to carry adequate insurance, to abide by the code of conduct, and to maintain a certain standard in their work (which is subject to inspection). Probationary membership is available for companies which have been trading for less than two years.

British Association of Leisure Parks, Piers & Attractions
25 Kings Terrace, London NW1 0JP
☎ 0171 383 7942
CONTACT   Gerald Oliver (General Secretary)

British Association of Seed Analysts
Whitehall Court, London SW1A 2EQ
☎ 0171 930 3611
CONTACT   Mrs J. Moore

British Association Representing Breeders (BARB)
9 Portland Street, King's Lynn, Norfolk PE30 1PB

Formerly the British Association of Rose Breeders. Collects payments due under Plant Breeders Rights, and promotes protected varieties.

British Bedding & Pot Plant Association
Agriculture House, 25 Knightsbridge, London SW1X 7NJ
☎ 0171 235 5077
CONTACT   Jane Connor

Formerly the Bedding Plant Growers Association, it co-ordinates marketing and publicity for the industry.

British Bee-Keepers' Association
National Agricultural Association, Stoneleigh, Kenilworth, Warwickshire CV8 2LZ
☎ 01203 696679

British Christmas Tree Growers Association
12 Lauriston Road, London SW19 4TQ
☎ 0181 946 2695
CONTACT   Tony Richardson

Mainly to represent the growers and wholesalers.

British Dragonfly Society
1 Haydn Avenue, Purley, Croydon, Surrey CR8 4AG
☎ 0181 668 5859
CONTACT   Jill Silsby

The Society aims to promote and encourage the study and conservation of dragonflies and their natural habitats, especially in the UK.

British Ecological Society
26 Blades Court, Deodar Road, Putney, London SW15 8HU
☎ 0181 871 9797
CONTACT   Dr Rachel J. Hammond

British Herbal Medicine Association
Field House, Lye Hole Lane, Redhill, Bristol, Avon BS18 7TB
☎ 01934 862994
CONTACT   R. A. Hill

The British Landscape Industry Training Organisation
11a North Queen Street, Keighley, West Yorkshire BD21 3DL
☎ 01535 691179

Established in 1993 to co-ordinate training for the landscape sector.

British Mycological Society
Department of Biology, University of Newcastle upon Tyne, Newcastle upon Tyne, Tyne & Wear NE1 7RU
☎ 0191 222 6001
CONTACT   Dr G. Beakes

British Naturalists' Association
48 Russell Way, Higham Ferrers, Wellingborough, Northamptonshire NN9 8EJ
☎ 01933 314672
CONTACT   J. F. Pearton

The Association exists to encourage education, study and research in all branches of natural history and wildlife conservation.

British Orchid Growers Association
2 Golvers Hill Road, Kingsteignton, Newton Abbot, Devon TQ12 3BP
☎ 01626 52065
CONTACT   Mrs A. Rittershausen

British Pest Control Association
3 St James' Court, Friar Gate, Derby, Derbyshire DE1 1ZU
☎ 01322 294288
CONTACT   R. J. Straud

British Pharmacological Society
Royal Free Hospital, School of Medicine, Rowland Hill Street, London NW3 2PF
☎ 0171 794 0500
CONTACT   Dr T. Maclagan

British Retail & Professional Florists Association
49 Meadway, Enfield, London EN3 6NX
☎ 01992 767645
CONTACT   W. Hart

British Seeds Council
Agriculture House, 25 Knightsbridge, London SW1X 7NJ
☎ 0171 235 5077

British Society of Plant Breeders
Woolpack Chambers, Market Street, Ely, Cambridgeshire CB7 4ND
☎ 01353 664211

British Tourist Authority
Thames Tower, Black's Road, Hammersmith, London W6 9EL
☎ 0181 846 9000

A list of British tourist information centres is available. Local centres can often provide information on gardens and events in their area.

British Trust for Conservation Volunteers (BTCV)
36 St Mary's Street, Wallingford, Oxfordshire OX10 0EU
☎ 01491 839766

Carries out practical conservation projects, including tree planting. They run training courses and offer working conservation holidays.

Bulb Distributors Association
Springfield Gardens, Camelgate, Spalding,
Lincolnshire PE12 6ET
☎ 01775 724843
CONTACT P. Atkinson

A trade organisation, founded in 1945, which now has 30 corporate members.

Butterfly Conservation
Box 222, Dedham, Colchester, Essex CO7 6EH
☎ 01206 322342

A thriving society with 7,000 members.

Cadw: Welsh Historic Monuments
Brunel House, 2 Fitzalan Road, Cardiff CF2 1UY
☎ 01222 465511

Commercial Horticultural Association
Links View House, 8 Fulwith Avenue, Harrogate,
North Yorkshire HG2 8HR
☎ 01423 879208
CONTACT Mr Brian Dunsby

A trade organisation for manufacturers and suppliers of goods and services to the commercial horticultural industry. The CHA Suppliers Guide is available to professional horticulturists and the trade.

Common Ground
41 Shelton Street, London WC2H 9HJ
☎ 0171 379 3109

Motivating force for projects which preserve and promote links between the environment and social culture. They publicise National Apple Day (21 October), and have worked on the *Flora Britannica* project. Pomologists should investigate their publications list.

The Conservation Foundation
1 Kensington Gore, London SW7 2AR
☎ 0171 823 8842

Manages and creates environmental programmes with business sponsorship, and assists conservation groups with publicity and funding.

Conservatory Association
2nd Floor, Goodwin House, George Street,
Huntingdon, Cambridgeshire PE18 6BU
☎ 01480 458271

Council for Environmental Education
University of Reading, London Road, Reading,
Berkshire RG1 5AQ
☎ 01734 756061

The national body for the co-ordination and promotion of environmental education in England, Wales & Northern Ireland.

Council for National Parks
London Ecology Centre, 45 Shelton Street, London
WC2H 9HJ
☎ 0171 240 3603

Council for the Protection of Rural England
Warwick House, 25 Buckingham Palace Road,
London SW1W 0PP
☎ 0171 976 6433

Country Houses Association Ltd
41 Kingsway, London WC2B 6UB
☎ 0171 836 1624
CONTACT R. D. Bratby

Founded in 1955 to save buildings (including their grounds and gardens) of historic and architectural merit for the public benefit, the association now has about 2,400 members.

Country Landowners Association
16 Belgrave Square, London SW1X 8PQ
☎ 0171 235 0511

Countryside Commission
John Dower House, Crescent Place, Cheltenham,
Gloucestershire GL50 3RA
☎ 01242 521381

Countryside Council for Wales
Plas Penrhos, Ffordd Penrhos, Bangor, Gwynedd
LL57 2LQ
☎ 01248 370444

English Heritage
Fortress House, 23 Savile Row, London W1X 1AB
☎ 0171 973 3000

English Nature
Northminster House, Peterborough, Cambridgeshire
PE1 1UA
☎ 01733 340345

English Tourist Board
Thames Tower, Black's Road, London W6 9EL
☎ 0181 846 9000

The English Vineyards Association
38 West Park, London SE9 4RH
☎ 0181 857 0452

Fauna & Flora Preservation Society
1 Kensington Gore, London SW7 2AR
☎ 0171 823 8899
CONTACT Amanda Hillier

The society was founded in 1903 and now has over 5,000 individual members.

Federation to Promote Horticulture for the Disabled
252 The Ridgeway, Enfield, London EN2 8AP

Fertiliser Manufacturers Association
Greenhill House, Thorpe Wood, Peterborough
PE3 6GF
☎ 01733 331303

452 Organisations

Flower Council of Holland
Catherine Chambers, 6 - 8 Catherine Street, Salisbury, Wiltshire SP1 2DA
☎ 01722 337505

Flowers & Plants Association
Covent House, New Covent Garden Market, London SW8 5NX
☎ 0171 738 8044

The Forestry Authority
Forest Research Station, Alice Holt Lodge, Wrecclesham, Farnham, Surrey GU10 4LH
☎ 01420 23000

Research advisory service operates from the above address, and from: Northern Research Station, Roslin, Lothian EH25 9SY (0131 445 2176).

Forestry Commission (Scotland)
231 Corstorphine Road, Edinburgh, Lothian EH12 7AT
☎ 0131 334 0303

The Forestry Trust
The Old Estate Office, Englefield Road, Theale, Reading, Berkshire RG7 5DZ
☎ 01734 323523

Education and conservation trust dedicated to sustainable forestry. They have a network of 'Link Woods' and produce an annual guide, *Woodlands to Visit in England and Wales*.

The Garden Centre Association
38 Carey Street, Reading, Berkshire RG1 7JS
☎ 01734 393900

Industry body: 200 of the best garden centres belong. Members are independently inspected.

Garden Industry Manufacturers Association
225 Bristol Road, Birmingham, West Midlands B5 7VB
☎ 0121 446 6688
CONTACT Mrs M. E. Slater

Gardenex – Federation of Garden & Leisure Manufacturers
60 Claremont Road, Surbiton, Surrey KT6 4RH
☎ 0181 339 9259
CONTACT Amanda Sizer

The Federation's function is to promote and expand exports of British garden and leisure products to the EC and overseas markets. It has about 120 corporate members.

Gardening for the Disabled Trust
c/o Hayes Farmhouse, Hayes Lane, Peasmarsh, East Sussex TN31 6XR
CONTACT The Hon. Secretary

Advice, grants and information on every aspect of gardening for disabled people.

Good Gardeners Association
Pinetum Lodge, Churcham, Gloucestershire GL2 8AD
☎ 01452 750402
CONTACT J. D. Wilkin

Guernsey Growers Association
Grange House, The Grange, St Peter Port, Channel Islands
☎ 01481 724227

Health & Safety Executive (HSE)
Information Centre, Broad Lane, Sheffield S3 7HQ
☎ 0114 2892345

Historic Houses Association (HHA)
2 Chester Street, London SW1X 7BB
☎ 0171 259 5688

A representative association of private owners which campaigns on their behalf. Of the 1,300 members nearly 300 houses are open to the public. Membership of the Friends of the HHA gives free admission to these properties. The association's brief includes gardens and designed landscapes.

Historic Scotland
20 Brandon Street, Edinburgh, Lothian EH3 5RA
☎ 0131 244 3101

Responsible for the maintenance of historic houses and gardens in the care of the Secretary of State for Scotland.

Horticultural Association of Retail Traders (HART)
Hallams Court, Littleford Lane, Chilworth, Guildford, Surrey GU4 8QZ
☎ 01483 894808

The trade organisation for independent non-multiple garden centres. Aims to increase its members' profitability and market share by consolidated negotiations and marketing initiatives.

Horticultural Development Council
18 Lavant Street, Petersfield, Hampshire GU32 3EW
☎ 01730 263736

Carries out horticultural research which is funded by an industry levy.

Horticultural Research International
Wellesbourne, Warwickshire CV35 9EF

The main English organisation for research into all aspects of horticulture, with further stations at East Malling and Wye in Kent, and Littlehampton in West Sussex.

Organisations

Horticultural Therapy
Goulds Ground, Vallis Way, Frome, Somerset
BA11 3DW
☎ 01373 464782

Horticultural Trades Association (HTA)
Horticulture House, 19 High Street, Theale, Reading, Berkshire RG7 5AH
☎ 01734 303132

The trade association for amenity and leisure horticulture, with around 1,800 members. They publish a magazine, *Nurseryman and Garden Centre*, and a useful reference *Yearbook*: both are also available to non-members. Business advice and negotiated discounts are provided to members. They promote horticulture generally, including the HTA National Garden Gift Tokens.

Institute of Grassland and Environmental Research (IGER)
Aberystwyth, Dyfed SY23 3EB
☎ 01970 828255

IGER incorporates the Welsh Plant Breeding Station, founded in 1919, and best known for breeding new grasses.

Institute of Groundsmanship
19 - 20 Church Street, The Agora, Wolverton, Milton Keynes MK12 5LG
☎ 01908 312511

The Institute of Horticulture (IoH)
P O Box 313, 80 Vincent Square, London SW1P 2PE
☎ 0171 976 5951
CONTACT   The Secretary

The professional body for horticulturists of all descriptions. The strict membership requirements demand a combination of education and experience. Membership confers recognised professional status. Student membership and career advice are available. The IoH acts as a forum for the collection and dissemination of horticultural information to its members and the public. It also promotes and represents the horticultural industry.

Institute of Leisure and Amenity Management (ILAM)
Lower Basildon, Reading, Berkshire RG8 9NE
☎ 01491 874222

International Association of Horticultural Producers
Postbus 93099, 2509 AB 's-Gravenhage, Netherlands
☎ 00 31 70 381 4631

International Federation of Park & Recreation Administration
The Grotto, Lower Basildon, Reading RG8 9NE
☎ 01491 874222

International Plant Propagators Society
Longfield Nursery, Cleobury Mortimer, Shropshire DY14 0TJ
☎ 0174632 562
CONTACT   Thelma Swash (Secretary)

The Great Britain and Ireland region of an international society. The IPPS is aimed at practical and academic horticulturists. Its motto 'Seek and Share' reflects its aim of bringing together and distributing information about propagation and production techniques.

International Tree Foundation
Sandy Lane, Crawley Down, Crawley, West Sussex RH10 4HS
☎ 01342 712536

Formerly Men of the Trees. International tree planting and conservation organisation (£10 individual).

John Innes Manufacturers Association
Links View House, 8 Fulwith Avenue, Harrogate, North Yorkshire HG2 8HR
☎ 01423 879208
CONTACT   Brian L. Dunsby

The trade organisation for manufacturers of John Innes seed and potting composts. Members have to meet the quality standards: they can then display the seal of approval. JIMA actively promotes the use of loam-based composts by amateur gardeners.

The Landscape Institute
6 - 7 Barnard Mews, London, London SW11 1QU
☎ 0171 738 9166

The professional body for the landscape profession: landscape architects, landscape managers and landscape scientists. The LI sets and maintains standards and accredits educational courses. It represents the profession's interests and disseminates information to its members. Members hold the qualification ALI: a directory of firms where at least one of the principals is a registered member is available from RIBA Publications (0171 251 0791). The Landscape Institute can advise potential clients free of charge about suitable firms for large or specialised projects.

Landscape Research Group
Leuric, North Road, South Kilworth, Lutterworth, Leicestershire LE17 6DU
☎ 01858 575530

A multi-disciplinary body to encourage education, interest and research in landscape.

Leisure and Outdoor Furniture Association Ltd (LOFA)
60 Claremont Road, Surbiton, Surrey KT6 4RH
☎ 0181 390 2022

Housed in the same office as Gardenex, LOFA is a trade association to represent and promote some 56 companies in the garden furniture and barbecue market.

454 Organisations

The Linnaean Society of London
Burlington House, Piccadilly, London W1V 0LQ
☎ 0171 434 4479
CONTACT Dr J. C. Marsden, Executive Secretary

Metropolitan Public Gardens Association
3 Mayfield Road, Croydon, Surrey CR4 6DN
☎ 0181 689 4197

Ministry of Agriculture, Fisheries and Food (MAFF)
3 Whitehall Place, London SW1A 2HH
☎ 0171 270 8080

General enquiries on the above number. See your local telephone directory (under 'Agriculture') for the addresses of MAFF's regional centres.

National Farmers Union
22 Long Acre, London WC2E 9LY
☎ 0171 235 5077

The farmers' trade association has a horticulture section which represents growers. Associated organisations include BGLA Ltd (organisers of two trade exhibitions), British Bedding & Pot Plant Association, and Farm Shop and PYO Associations. Specialist advisers can help members with law, taxation, employment and plant health.

National Gardens Scheme
Hatchlands Park, East Clandon, Guildford, Surrey GU4 7RT
☎ 01483 211535

The National Institute of Medical Herbalists
9 Palace Gate, Exeter EX1 1JA
☎ 01392 426022

National Playing Fields Association
25 Ovington Square, London SW3 1LQ
☎ 0171 584 6445

National Small Woods Association
Red House, Hill Lane, Birmingham, West Midlands B43 6LZ
☎ 0121 358 0461

National Trust
36 Queen Anne's Gate, London SW1H 9AS
☎ 0171 222 9251

Conservation body with many outstanding gardens and landscapes under its care. Membership gives admission to all the Trust's properties, and numerous events will be organised throughout this, its centenary year.

National Trust for Scotland
5 Charlotte Square, Edinburgh EH2 4DU
☎ 0131 226 5922

This Scottish conservation body has a number of excellent gardens in its care; members also receive free entry to National Trust properties under a reciprocal arrangement. Self-catering and working holidays are available.

NIAB
Huntingdon Road, Cambridge CB3 0LE
☎ 01223 276381

The National Institute of Agricultural Botany carries out testing of seeds and other laboratory and environmental research on behalf of the government and commercial customers. The Wisley Handbook, *Vegetable Varieties for the Gardener*, by J. Chowings and M. J. Day passes on the results of NIAB tests.

Northern Ireland Tourist Board
St Anne's Court, 59 North Street, Belfast BT1 1NB
☎ 01232 231221

The Organic Food & Farming Centre
86 Colston Street, Bristol BS1 5BB
☎ 0117 9290661

The Soil Association, British Organic Farmers and the Organic Growers Association are based here.

Plant Breeding International
Maris Lane, Trumpington, Cambridge CB2 2LQ
☎ 01223 840411

Plant Publicity Holland
Goudse Rijweg 1, Postbus 81, 2770 AB Boskoop, Netherlands

Plant Variety Rights Office and Seeds Division
White House Lane, Huntingdon Road, Cambridge CB3 0LF
☎ 01223 277151

Part of the Ministry of Agriculture.

Plantlife
The Natural History Museum, Cromwell Road, London SW7 5BD
☎ 0171 938 9111

Wild plant conservation charity (£15 individual). Projects include rescuing individual species, protecting peat bogs, and the Great Hedge Project.

The Professional Gardeners Guild
Gardeners Cottage, Bramdean House, Alresford, Hampshire SO24 0JU
CONTACT Membership Secretary

Ramblers Association
1 – 5 Wandsworth Road, London SW8 2XX
☎ 0171 582 6878

Rose Growers Association
303 Mile End Road, Colchester, Essex CO4 5EA

Royal Entomological Society
41 Queens Gate, London SW7 5HU
☎ 0171 584 8361

Royal Forestry Society of England, Wales & Northern Ireland
102 High Street, Tring, Hertfordshire HP23 4AF
☎ 0144 282 2028

An active society which seeks to encourage the conservation, improvement and expansion of Britain's woodlands by positive management.

Royal Institute of British Architects (RIBA)
66 Portland Place, London W1N 4AD
☎ 0171 580 5533

Royal Scottish Forestry Society
Camsie House, Charlestown, Dunfermline, Fife KY11 3EZ
☎ 01383 873014
CONTACT Michael Osborne

Royal Society for Nature Conservation
The Green, Witham Park, Waterside South, Lincoln LN5 7JR
☎ 01522 544400

The RSNC Wildlife Trusts Partnership is made up of 47 local wildlife trusts, many of whom are listed in our societies section, and 50 urban groups. They manage nature reserves, campaign on conservation issues, and encourage people to become involved in conservation.

Royal Society for the Protection of Birds (RSPB)
The Lodge, Sandy, Bedfordshire SG19 2DL
☎ 01767 680551

Rural Development Commission
141 Castle Street, Salisbury, Wiltshire SP1 3TP
☎ 01722 336255

A government agency concerned with the economic and social well-being of England's rural communities.

Scotland's Garden Scheme
3 Castle Terrace, Edinburgh EH1 2EL
☎ 0131 229 1870

Scotland's Natural Heritage
12 Hope Terrace, Edinburgh EH9 2AS
☎ 0131 447 4784

Scottish Seed & Nursery Trade Association
12 Bruntisfield Crescent, Edinburgh, Lothian EH10 4HA
☎ 0131 447 1035

Scottish Tourist Board
23 Ravelston Terrace, Edinburgh EH4 3EU
☎ 0131 332 2433

The Scottish Wildlife Trust
25 Johnston Terrace, Edinburgh, Lothian EH1 2NH
☎ 0131 226 4602

Society of Botanical Artists
Burwood House, 15 Union Street, Wells, Somerset BA5 2PU
CONTACT Executive Secretary

The society holds regular open exhibitions and can act as a channel for commissions.

Society of Garden Designers (SGD)
6 Borough Road, Kingston upon Thames, Surrey KT2 6BD
☎ 0181 974 9483
CONTACT Assistant Secretary

A professional body for full-time garden designers. Membership depends upon a combination of training and experience, and work is inspected. The society distributes information about its members to enquirers, and publishes *Vitis*. Members use the initials MSGD and FSGD.

The Society of Floristry
70a Reigate Road, Epsom, Surrey
CONTACT The Secretary

The society, which was started in 1951, works to maintain standards in professional floristry. Part of this work includes professional awards at intermediate level and above. Preliminary qualifications are handled by the NEBAHAI and the City and Guilds of London. The National Diploma of the Society of Floristry is the highest floristry qualification. Members are drawn from all sectors of the industry. The society stages displays and demonstrations, including a stand at the Chelsea Flower Show.

The Tree Council
35 Belgrave Square, London SW1X 8QN
☎ 0171 235 8854

Wales Tourist Board
Brunel House, 2 Fitzalan Road, Cardiff CF2 1UY
☎ 01222 499909

Wildfowl & Wetlands Trust
Slimbridge, Gloucester, Gloucestershire GL2 7BT
☎ 01453 890333

Women's Farm & Garden Association
175 Gloucester Street, Cirencester, Gloucestershire GL7 2DP
☎ 01285 658339

Voluntary organisation for women whose livelihood is connected with the land. Among its activities is the Women's Returners to Amenity Gardening Scheme which arranges placements in private gardens for women wishing to return to work.

456 Organisations

Woodland Trust
Autumn Park, Dysart Road, Grantham, Lincolnshire NG31 6LL
☎ 01476 74297

World Conifer Data Pool
Treetops, Buzzacott Lane, Combe Martin, Devon EX34 0NL
☎ 01271 883761
CONTACT Humphrey Welch and Gordon Haddow

Acts as a collecting agency for data on new conifer introductions from around the world. They have recently published *The World Checklist of Conifers* through Landsman's Bookshop.

Worshipful Company of Gardeners
25 Luke Street, London EC2A 4AR
☎ 0171 739 8200

23
Colleges & Horticultural Education

BERKSHIRE

Berkshire College of Agriculture
Hall Place, Burchetts Green, Maidenhead, Berkshire SL6 6QR
☎ 01628 824444   FAX 01628 824695
CONTACT   Steve Gingell
RANGE OF COURSES   Full and Part Time: Amenity Horticulture; Floristry (NVQ); Garden Centre Retailing; Landscape Design; Parks and Gardens; Countryside Recreation; Environmental Resources (BTEC); Conservation and Recreation; Parks and Gardens; Garden Design; Interior Landscaping; (NCH); RHS General Certificate and Diploma. Extensive programme of short courses
LEVELS   RHS; C&G; NCH; ND; NVQ; BTEC

Big county agricultural college, well-run and serious. Excellent modern brochure, very inspirational.

University of Reading
Department of Horticulture, Plant Science Laboratories, Whiteknights, Reading, Berkshire RG6 2AS
☎ 01734 318071   FAX 01734 750630
CONTACT   Tony Kendle (degree courses), tel. 01734 318374; Sue Simonds (short and amateur courses), Tel. 01734 318294
RANGE OF COURSES   Full and Part Time: Horticulture (BSc); Landscape Management (BSc); Crop Protection (BSc); Certificate in Garden Design (2-year part-time); short courses; amateur courses
LEVELS   Postgraduate; degree

The leading university for Horticulture – Amenity, Commercial, Landscape and Garden Design. The gardens and learning resources are also among the best.

BUCKINGHAMSHIRE

Aylesbury College
Hampden Hall, Stoke Mandeville, Nr. Aylesbury, Buckinghamshire HP22 5TB
☎ 01296 434111   FAX 01296 614175
CONTACT   Mrs Pat Hunt
RANGE OF COURSES   Full and Part Time: Amenity Horticulture (NVQ); Groundsmanship; General Horticulture (RHS); Landscape; Floristry; Countryside Management Amateur: Gardening; Creative Flower Arranging; Bee Keeping
LEVELS   NVQ I and II; RHS

CAMBRIDGESHIRE

Cambridgeshire College of Agriculture & Horticulture
Landbeach Road, Milton, Cambridge, Cambridgeshire CB4 6DB
☎ 01223 860701   FAX 01223 860262
CONTACT   Richard Walpole
RANGE OF COURSES   Horticulture; Landscape; Countryside Management; Groundsmanship
LEVELS   NCH; BTEC First Diploma

There is an emphasis on fruit and vegetable production at the Milton centre. Floristry courses are based at the College's second centre at Wisbech (Tel: 01945 581024).

Nene Valley Adult Education
Prince William School, Herne Road, Oundle, Cambridgeshire PE8 4BS
☎ 01832 273550   FAX (PWS) 274942
CONTACT   Ian Russell

458 Colleges & Horticultural Education

RANGE OF COURSES Part Time: Horticulture; Floristry; Countryside Management; Leisure
LEVELS C&G; RHS

CHESHIRE

Manchester Metropolitan University
Division of Environmental Science, Crewe and Alsager Faculty, Crewe Green Road, Cheshire CW1 1DU
☎ 0161 247 5249   FAX 0161 247 6372
CONTACT Dr Ian W. Eastwood (Head of Division)
RANGE OF COURSES Full Time: Environmental Studies (BSc); Environmental Analysis and Monitoring (HND); Business Leisure and Recreation (BA)
LEVELS Degree; HND

Reaseheath College (Cheshire College of Agriculture)
Reaseheath, Nantwich, Cheshire CW5 6DF
☎ 01270 625131   FAX 01270 625665
CONTACT Stephen M. Davies
RANGE OF COURSES Full and Part Time: Horticulture (NVQ I, II and III; RHS); Arboriculture; Greenkeeping and Turf Management (NVQ II and III); Landscape Design and Construction
LEVELS NVQ Levels I, II and III; RHS; RFS

The Cheshire college for Horticulture. In addition to full-time courses, there is a comprehensive range of day- and block-release courses for the industry.

CUMBRIA

Newton Rigg College
Cumbria College of Agriculture & Forestry, Newton Rigg, Penrith, Cumbria CA11 0AH
☎ 01768 63791   FAX 01768 67249
CONTACT The Information Unit
RANGE OF COURSES Full and Part Time: Amenity Horticulture and Landscaping; Forestry and Woodland Management; Floristry; Environmental and Countryside Management Amateur: Garden Design; Garden Planning and Planting; RHS Courses
LEVELS C&G; ND; HND; RHS; BSc

The college primarily serves the land-based industries and rural economy of Cumbria.

DERBYSHIRE

Broomfield College
Morley, Derby, Derbyshire DE7 6DN
☎ 01332 831345   FAX 01332 830298
CONTACT The Principal
RANGE OF COURSES Full and Part Time: Amenity and Commercial Horticulture; Landscape Design and Construction; Greenkeeping and Sports Turf Management; Floristry; Creative Studies – Flower Arranging; Countryside Management; Organic Agriculture; Smallholders; Chainsaw Use; Pesticide Application; RHS Certificate and Diploma.
LEVELS BTEC First Diploma; HND; HNC; ND; C&G; RHS and MHort RHS; CGLI

The Derbyshire College of Agriculture and Horticulture, with a full range of residential and sandwich courses at all levels. Wide range of adult, day and evening tuition.

DEVON

Bicton School of Horticulture
East Budleigh, Budleigh Salterton, Devon EX9 7BY
☎ 01395 68353   FAX 01395 67502
CONTACT Susan Carter
RANGE OF COURSES Full and Part Time: Horticulture (including RHS; C&G); Landscape; Greenkeeping and Sports Turf Management; Nursery Practice; Floristry and Floral Art; Garden Design
LEVELS BTEC First Diploma; NVQ; RHS; C&G

Courses to suit all levels, gardens open to the public daily.

DORSET

Kingston Maurward College
Kingston Maurwood, Dorchester, Dorset DT2 8PY
☎ 01305 264738   FAX 01305 250059
CONTACT Patt Shean
RANGE OF COURSES Full and Part Time: Amenity Horticulture; Agriculture; Countryside Skills and Management; Arboriculture; Landscape Design; Sports Turf Management Amateur: (RHS) Ornamental Horticulture; Fruit; Vegetables; Glasshouse; Hard Landscaping; Design; Sprayers; Bee Keeping; Chainsaw Use; Flower Arranging; Fun with Flowers; Gardening Demonstrations; Garden Woodwork; Gardening under Glass; Outdoor Recreation and Leisure; Botanical Illustration
LEVELS C&G; BTEC First Diploma; HNC; ND; GNVQ; RHS

A residential county-based horticultural college, 'Dorset's centre of excellence', with a wide range of courses.

DURHAM

Finchale Training College
Durham DH1 5RX
☎ 0191 3862634   FAX 0191 3864962
CONTACT Maureen Skelton
RANGE OF COURSES Horticulture; Forestry Horticulture course covers: Landscape Design; Propagation; Internal Decoration (NVQ I and II, 52 weeks)
LEVELS NVQ I and II

Finchale is a residential centre offering vocational training to adults who have become or are born disabled.

Colleges & Horticultural Education 459

Houghall College
Houghall, Durham, Durham DH1 3SG
☎ 0191 386 1351   FAX 0191 386 0419
CONTACT   Ian Webster
RANGE OF COURSES   Full and Part Time: Horticulture; Landscape; Forestry; Floristry; Arboriculture (NVQ). Amateur: General Horticulture (RHS); The Labour Saving Garden (C&G); Flower Arranging; many short courses
LEVELS   NVQ; C&G; HNC; ND; HND; RHS

ESSEX

Southend Adult Community College
Ambleside Drive, Southend on Sea, Essex SS1 2UP
☎ 01702 610196   FAX 01702 601529
CONTACT   Centre Secretary
RANGE OF COURSES   Amateur: Flower Arranging and Floristry; General Horticulture (RHS)
LEVELS   RHS

Writtle College
Writtle, Chelmsford, Essex CM1 3RR
☎ 01243 420705   FAX 01243 420456
CONTACT   Martin Stimson, Ann Notman (short courses, tel. 01245 420705 ext. 25506)
RANGE OF COURSES   Full time: European Horticulture (MSc); Landscape and Amenity Management (MSc); Horticulture (Landscape and Amenity Management; Crop Technology and Management) (BSc); Landscape and Garden Design (BSc); Commercial Horticulture (HND; ND); Landscape Construction (HND) Amenity Horticulture (ND); Horticulture (FD). Part Time: Master of Horticulture; Diploma in Horticultural Practice; Diploma in Garden Design; Nursery/Interior Landscaping (NVQ II); Greenkeeping/Sports Turf Management (NVQ II); Hard Landscaping (NVQ II); Amenity Horticulture (NVQ III); Floristry (NVQ II). Amateur: RHS General Horticulture; Introduction to Flower Arranging; Introduction to Floristry
LEVELS   MSc; BSc Hons; HND; ND; NVQ;

One of the top horticultural colleges, with a national reputation and a commitment to both amenity and commercial horticulture, as well as floristry and rural studies. Full programme of short courses in conjunction with the RHS.

GLOUCESTERSHIRE

Cheltenham & Gloucester College of Higher Education
Francis Close Hall Campus, Swindon Road, Cheltenham, Gloucestershire GL50 4AZ
☎ 01242 532922   FAX 01242 532997
CONTACT   Richard Sneesby (Landscape Architecture); James Derounian (Countryside Planning)
RANGE OF COURSES   Landscape Architecture; Countryside Planning
LEVELS   Postgraduate; degree

The Garden Academy
Kylemore, Netherend, Gloucestershire GL15 6NL
☎ 01594 529619
CONTACT   Ruth Chivers
RANGE OF COURSES   Amateur Short Courses: Garden Design; Garden Workshops on Design Aspects

HAMPSHIRE

Isle of Wight College of Arts and Technology
Medina Way, Newport, Isle of Wight, Hampshire PO30 5TA
☎ 01983 526631   FAX 01983 521707
CONTACT   Gardening: D. Trevan, J. Fradgly; Cultivation; R. Mew. Floristry: P. Gardiner, M. Alexander, C. Lee.
RANGE OF COURSES   Horticulture; Landscape; Administration and Retailing; Forestry; Countryside Management Botany; Amenity and Commercial Horticulture (NVQ I and II); Countryside Studies (BTEC First Diploma ND). Amateur courses include: Certificate in Gardening (C&G); Seeds/Cuttings; Garden Pond; Tree and Shrub Cultivation; Garden Design; Christmas Flower Arranging; Gardening with Nature
LEVELS   Degree; BTEC First and National Diplomas; RHS; C&G

Sparsholt College Hampshire
Sparsholt, Winchester, Hampshire SO21 2NF
☎ 01962 776210   FAX 01962 776587
CONTACT   Ray Broughton
RANGE OF COURSES   Full and Part Time: Countryside Management; Forestry; Floristry; Domestic/Advanced Garden Design; Gardening (C&G); Greenkeeping; Groundsmanship; Horticulture (RHS Diploma/General); Landscape; Plant Identification
LEVELS   C&G; RHS

Sparsholt is fast developing as one of the leading county colleges in England, highly professional and with an expanding range of part-time and amateur courses, too. Excellent brochures. Demonstrations on Wednesday afternoons. Adults £5; Senior Citizens £4. Topics include: Pests and Diseases; Autumn Lawn Care; Alpines; Borders; Plant Nutrition; Summer Bedding; Ericaceous Plants.

HEREFORD & WORCESTER

Hereford College of Art & Design
Folly Lane, Hereford, Hereford & Worcester HR1 1LT
☎ 01432 273359   FAX 01432 341099
RANGE OF COURSES   Full Time: Garden Design Postgraduate Diploma. Part Time: Garden Design Certificate

HERTFORDSHIRE

Oaklands College
Hatfield Road, St Albans, Hertfordshire AL4 0JA
☎ 01727 850651   FAX 01727 847987

CONTACT Admissions (0727 850651)
RANGE OF COURSES Full and Part Time: Amenity Horticulture (HND; ND); Greenkeeping and Sports Turf Management (NC; HND); Commercial Horticulture (NC); Landscape Construction (NC; ND); Mechanics and Machinery Repair; Amenity Horticulture and Greenkeeping Business Management; Pesticides; Chainsaw Use; Tractor Operation and Maintenance Floristry NC; ND; HND; NVQ I, II and III). Amateur: Garden Design; Flower Arranging Horticultural Mechanics; Greenkeeping (NC); Agriculture and Commercial Horticulture Business Management. Amateur: Flower Arranging; Pesticides; Gardening; Tractors; Chainsaw Use
LEVELS ND; NC; HND; NVQ

One of the leading national providers of commercial horticultural teaching, strongly geared to commercial horticulture. Its graduates have long enjoyed a good reputation for professionalism.

KENT

Hadlow College of Agriculture & Horticulture
Hadlow, Tonbridge, Kent TN11 0AL
☎ 01732 850551   FAX 01732 851957

CONTACT Admissions Secretary
RANGE OF COURSES Full and Part Time: Horticulture (NVQ I and II; NCH; NDH; HND; BA; BSc); Commercial Horticulture (NDH); Landscape and Amenity (NDH); Garden Design (BA); Garden Centre Operations; Retailing; Fruit Production; Conservation and Environmental studies; Groundmanship. Amateur: General Horticulture (RHS)
LEVELS Degree; C&G; HNC; ND; HND; RHS

One of the few colleges offering specialist block-release courses. There is a wide range of courses at Hadlow, also Maidstone and Canterbury. The Horticulture Department covers 60 hectares and houses National Collections of hellebores and anemones.

University of Greenwich
School of Architecture and Landscape, Dartford Campus, Oakfield Lane,, Dartford, Kent DA1 2SZ
☎ 0181 316 8000

CONTACT Tom Turner
RANGE OF COURSES Full Time: Horticulture; Landscape Management; Botany; Commercial Horticulture; Garden Design; Landscape Architecture (all BA); Garden Design (HND)
LEVELS BA; HND

The two Garden Design courses (BA and HND) started in 1993.

Wye College, University of London
Wye, Ashford, Kent TN25 5AH
☎ 01233 812401   FAX 01233 813320

CONTACT The Academic Registrar
RANGE OF COURSES Full Time: Horticulture; Countryside Management; Horticultural Business Management; Rural Environment Studies; Landscape Ecology, Design and Management; Tropical Horticulture and Crop Science
LEVELS All courses lead to a BSc; there are postgraduate courses in Fruit Production and Tropical Horticulture leading to a MSc

The Horticultural Department of London University, and very highly regarded both academically and in business.

LANCASHIRE

Myerscough College
Myerscough Hall, Bilsborrow, Preston, Lancashire PR3 0RY
☎ 01995 640611   FAX 01995 640842

CONTACT The College Registry
RANGE OF COURSES Full and Part Time: Horticultural Technology and Management (BSc Hons); Horticulture (HND; ND; NC; RHS; NVQ II and III); Arboriculture (HND; ND; NC); Turf Science and Golf Course Management (HND); Leisure Studies–Sports Development, Golf and Leisure Club Management (HND); Landscape Practice (ND); Turf Science and Sportsground Management (ND); Groundsmanship and Greenkeeping (NC); Landscape Practice (NC); Commercial Floral Design (HND); Floristry (NC; NVQ II); Leisure Management (CEC) Amateur: Gardening; Flower Arrangement; Flower Painting.
LEVELS BSc; NC; HND; ND; NVQ; CEC

An interesting range of courses from a college with a good reputation.

LEICESTERSHIRE

Kayes Garden Nursery
1700 Melton Road, Rearsby, Leicestershire LE7 8YR
☎ 01664 424578

CONTACT Hazel Kaye
RANGE OF COURSES Amateur half-day courses: Aspects of Border Design; Seasonal Plants

University of Nottingham
Department of Agriculture and Horticulture, Sutton Nonington Campus, Loughborough, Leicestershire LE1 5RD

CONTACT Dr Charles Wright
RANGE OF COURSES Full Time: Horticulture; Agriculture; Environmental Science in Agriculture; Horticul-

Colleges & Horticultural Education 461

ture with Technology; Plant Sciences; Environmental Horticulture
LEVELS Postgraduate; degree
The undergraduate course in Horticulture can be combined with European Studies.

LINCOLNSHIRE

Lincolnshire College of Agriculture DEL
Caythorpe Court, Grantham, Lincolnshire NG32 3EP
☎ 01400 72521   FAX 01400 72722
CONTACT Student Services or Dr N Cheffins
RANGE OF COURSES Horticulture; Landscape; Administration and Retailing; Forestry; Floristry; Countryside Management Master of Horticulture; Agriculture; Agricultural and Horticultural Business Management (12 weeks); Rural Leisure Studies; Garden Design (ANC); Environmental Landscape Management (BTEC); Horticultural Mechanics; Flower Arranging and RHS short courses for amateurs
LEVELS BSc; BA; HND; BTEC First Diploma; NEB; HND
A good range of amateur courses as well as professional tuition leading to the highest levels. There is a General Course in Horticulture for the Visually Impaired available (C&G).

LONDON

Ealing Tertiary College
Norwood Hall Centre, Norwood Green, Southall, London UB2 4LA
☎ 0181 574 2161   FAX 0181 571 9479
CONTACT Len Stocks or Margaret Pamment
RANGE OF COURSES Horticulture; Floristry; Countryside Management; Groundsmanship (Institute of Groundsmanship Cert and Diploma)
LEVELS All courses NVQ

The English Gardening School
Chelsea Physic Garden, 66 Royal Hospital Road, London SW3 4HS
☎ 0171 352 4347   FAX 0171 376 3936
CONTACT The School Manager
RANGE OF COURSES Part Time:1-year diploma course in Garden Design; 2 days a week; 1-year certificate courses in Practical Horticulture and Advanced Practical Horticulture – Plants and Plantsmanship, both 1 day a week; short courses (1–5 days) on such subjects as: Garden History; The Cottage Garden; Planning and Planting; Surveying a Garden; Drawing for Garden Designers. Correspondence: Garden Design 1-year course
LEVELS The School issues its own diploma which is recognised by the Institute of Horticulture
Inspirational course for (mainly) female and mature students. The venue cannot be bettered and the Principal, Rosemary Alexander, is a brilliant communicator. The English Garden School produces confident, stylish garden designers.

Inchbald School of Design
32 Eccleston Square, London SW1V 1PB
☎ 0171 630 9011   FAX 0171 976 5979
CONTACT Andrew Wilson
RANGE OF COURSES Full Time and Short courses: Garden Design; Garden Design History; Garden Design Drawing
LEVELS School examinations, recognised by the Society of Garden Designers
Inchbald runs ten-week courses, plus three-week courses in Garden-Design-Drawing. There are plans to introduce correspondence or distance learning courses.

The Institute – Hampstead Garden Suburb
Central Square, London NW11 7BN
☎ 0181 455 9951
CONTACT Faculty Administrator
RANGE OF COURSES Part Time: Horticulture (RHS General). Amateur: The Flower Garden (5 weeks); Garden Design – The Basics (4 weeks)
LEVELS RHS 1st Year

Lambeth College
Clapham Centre, 45 Clapham Common Southside, London SW4 9ESX
☎ 0171 501 5048
CONTACT Terry Fulham
RANGE OF COURSES Full and Part Time: Amenity Horticulture (NVQ I, II and III); Decorative Horticulture (NEBAHAI); Creation and Management of Urban Wildlife Areas; General Horticulture (RHS)
LEVELS BTEC First Diploma; Training Credits Programme (Horticulture); NEBAHAI; NVQ;

Merton Adult College
Whatley Avenue, Wimbledon, London SW20 9NS
☎ 0181 543 9292   FAX 0181 544 1421
CONTACT Mrs Brenda Gunter
RANGE OF COURSES Amateur: General Horticulture (RHS); Gardening – Garden Design; Flower Decor (C&G); Flower Arranging; Floristry
LEVELS C&G; RHS
A well-run and adventurous adult education college. In addition to the courses there is a Friday evening lecture programme.

University College London
Department of Biology (Darwin), Gower Street, London WC1E 6BT
☎ 0171 387 7050
CONTACT Dr F. B. Goldsmith
RANGE OF COURSES Full Time: Ecology (BSc); Conservation (MSc). Short Courses: some 4-day individual units/modules available to a wider audience

LEVELS Postgraduate degree
The MSc in Conservation is considered an academic trail-blazer.

MANCHESTER
University of Manchester
School of Landscape, Department of Planning and Landscape, Oxford Road, Manchester M13 9PL
CONTACT Director of Landscape Studies
RANGE OF COURSES Full Time: Landscape Planning and Management
LEVELS BSc

MERSEYSIDE
Hugh Baird College
Balliol Road, Bootle, Merseyside PR8 3JX
☎ 0151 922 6704   FAX 0151 934 4469
CONTACT Student Advice Centre (0151 934 4444)
RANGE OF COURSES Floristry; Flower arranging
LEVELS NVQ Levels I, II and III

Knowsley Community College, Landbased Industries
The Kennels, Knowsley Park, Prescot, Merseyside L34 4AQ
☎ 0151 549 1500
CONTACT Ruth Brown
RANGE OF COURSES Full and Part Time: Amenity Horticulture (NVQ I); Amenity Horticulture: Core and Nursery Practice; Interior Soft Landscape Maintenance; Greenkeeping/Sports Turf/Sportsground Maintenance; Arboriculture; Hard Landscaping (all NVQ II)); RHS General Examination; Environmental Conservation (NVQ II and III); Floristry (NVQ I and II; C&G III, IV and V; NC). Amateur: Gardening; Flower Arranging
LEVELS C&G; RHS; NVQ I, II and III; College certificate

Southport College of Art & Technology
Mornington Road, Southport, Merseyside PR9 0TT
☎ 01704 424111/500606 ext.2629
CONTACT Vera Hainsworth
RANGE OF COURSES Amateur: General Horticulture (RHS); Gardening (C&G); Gardening for All
LEVELS C&G; RHS

St Helens College
Newton Campus, Crow Lane East, Newton le Willows, Merseyside WA12 9TT
☎ 0192524656   FAX 01925 220437
CONTACT Dr. Bob Ashcroft
RANGE OF COURSES Horticulture; Landscape; Administration and Retailing; Floristry; Countryside management; Leisure Botany; Floristry (NVQ/NEBAHAI); Environmental Conservation (C&G); Amenity Horticulture and Commercial Horticulture/Garden Centre Operation (NVQ/NEBAHAI); Society of Floristry (evening); Flower Arranging (CGLI); Amateur Gardening (C&G); Decorative Horticulture (NEBABHAI); Chemical Handling; Groundsmanship; ATB Training
LEVELS NEBAHAI (National Examinations Board for Agriculture, Horticulture and Allied Industries); C&G; NVQ
The Floristry section has been designated a 'Centre of Excellence' by the Flower Trades Council

NORFOLK
Easton College
Easton, Norwich, Norfolk NR9 5DX
☎ 01603 742105   FAX 01603 741438
CONTACT Paul Metcalf, tel. 01603 742105 Alan Barson, tel. 01603 712519
RANGE OF COURSES Full and Part Time: Horticulture (BTEC 1st Diploma; NVQ II; RHS); Amenity Horticulture (NDH; NCH); Arboriculture (NDH; NCH; C&G); Landscape (NDH; NCH); Turf (NDH); Garden Design; Advanced Garden Design
LEVELS Degree; RHS; C&G; NCH; ND; HND
Norfolk's college of the countryside, with a wide range of courses geared to commercial and business opportunities. Short courses: Gardening; Bee Keeping; Floristry and Flower Arranging; Horticulture; Landscape and Estate Management. There is also a Chainsaw Use course.

NORTHAMPTONSHIRE
The Gardeners' Academy
PO Box 262, Northampton, Northamptonshire NN6 8RQ
☎ 01234 826077
RANGE OF COURSES Amateur courses: Garden Design; The Essential Gardener; Roses in Garden Design; Plannning a Border
The Gardeners' Academy runs a wide range of courses, seminars and workshops with visiting experts at Coton Manor.

Moulton College
West Street, Moulton, Northamptonshire NN3 1RR
☎ 01604 491131   FAX 01604 491127
CONTACT Stuart Phillips
RANGE OF COURSES Horticulture; Landscape; Administration and Retailing; Floristry; Countryside Management Groundsmanship; Horticultural Therapy (with Coventry University); Business Management (options Horticulture /Floristry); Countryside Management
LEVELS BTEC First Diploma; Preliminary Certificate; C&G; HNC; ND; RHS; NC;
Moulton College used to be the county agricultural college for Northamptonshire and offers both commer-

Colleges & Horticultural Education 463

cial and amenity courses to a high level, including a MHort by correspondence

NOTTINGHAMSHIRE

Brackenhurst College
Southwell, Nottinghamshire NG25 0QF
☎ 01636 812252   FAX 01636 815404
CONTACT   Brian Osborne
RANGE OF COURSES Horticulture; Landscape; Administration and Retailing; Floristry; Countryside Management; Leisure Groundsmanship; Arboriculture; Wide range of day/evening courses; Gardening Certificate (C&G); Chainsaw Operation; Spraying (Pesticides)
LEVELS BTEC First Diploma; ND; HND; NC; HNC; NVQ; Degree (BSc); NEBAHAI; ANC
A county residential college with a wide range of well-run courses, full-time and part-time. Note amateur courses in: Plant Photography; Culinary Horticulture; Victorian Garden; Gardening skills workshop

Greenwood Gardens
Ollerton Road, Arnold, Nottinghamshire NG5 8PR
☎ 0115 9205757
RANGE OF COURSES Amateur half-day courses: Introductory, Intermediate and Advanced Bonsai

Hodsock Priory Garden Courses
Blyth, Worksop, Nottinghamshire S81 0TY
☎ 01909 591204
CONTACT   Lady Buchanan or Kate Garton
RANGE OF COURSES Amateur Day Courses: Elementary Design; Planting for Colour All Year Round; The Mixed Border; Foliage Plants; Container Gardening; Pruning and Propagation

OXFORDSHIRE

Judith Walton
The Corner House, Foxcombe Lane, Boars Hill, Oxford, Oxfordshire OX1 5DH
☎ 01865 735179
CONTACT   Judith Walton
RANGE OF COURSES Amateur short courses: Garden Design

West Oxford College
Warren Farm Centre, Horton-cum-Studley, Oxfordshire OX33 1BY
☎ 01865 351794   FAX 01865 358931
CONTACT   Horticulture: Jeremy Dickson. Short courses: Mary Spiller (Waterperry Horticultural Centre)
RANGE OF COURSES Full and Part Time: Horticulture; Legislative courses e.g. Pesticides; Amenity Horticulture (BTEC; Dip. 2 years; NVQ I and II); Landscape Design (NVQ III). Amateur: Weekend Gardening; Garden Design; Flower Garden; Garden Skills; Down to Earth; Garden Calendar; Pruning Fruit; Growing under Glass.
LEVELS BTEC; diploma; NVQ I and II; RHS General Certificate
This incorporates the Waterperry Horticultural Centre with a strong emphasis on amenity horticulture, reflected in the amateur courses.

SHROPSHIRE

Walford College of Agriculture
Baschurch, Shrewsbury, Shropshire SY11 2HL
☎ 01939 260461   FAX 01939 261112
CONTACT   M Ford, Horticultural Unit, (0743 360266)
RANGE OF COURSES Horticulture; Landscape; Floristry Agriculture; Land Use and Recreation; Land Use and Countryside Skills; Amenity Horticulture (NVQ I and II); Decorative Horticulture; Groundsmanship; Amateur: Flower Arranging (day release); Garden and Landscape Design; Gardening for Leisure and Pleasure; General Exam Horticulture (RHS); Pressed Flower Craft
LEVELS IOG; C&G; NVQ I and II; RHS
Walford started as a local authority college and has a wide range of horticultural and floristry courses

SOMERSET

Cannington College
Cannington, Nr. Bridgwater, Somerset TA5 2LS
☎ 01278 652226
CONTACT   Head of Horticulture or Admissions Department
RANGE OF COURSES Full and Part Time: Amenity Horticulture (NVQ I, II and III); Commercial Horticulture (NVQ II); Landscape; Groundsmanship; Floristry; Countryside Amateur: Landscape and Plantsmanship (RHS; College Diplomas; NVQ)
LEVELS C&G; NVQ I, II and III; Advanced National Certificate; RHS; ND; HND
Perhaps the leading centre for Amenity Horticulture.

College of Garden Design
Cothelstone, Taunton, Somerset TA4 3DP
☎ 01823 433215   FAX 01823 433812
CONTACT   Francis Huntington, Course Administrator
RANGE OF COURSES Garden Design; Summer School in USA
LEVELS Diploma

Horticultural Therapy
Goulds Ground, Vallis Way, Frome, Somerset BA11 3DW
☎ 01373 464782   FAX 01373 464782
CONTACT   Jill McChesney
RANGE OF COURSES Part Time: Therapeutic Horticulture (Diploma). Short courses: Horticultural Therapy

464 Colleges & Horticultural Education

LEVELS Post-Professional Diploma
One of the first colleges to develop a range of horticultural activities for therapeutic use, especially for the handicapped, ill, aged or disadvantaged.

Norton Radstock Technical College
South Hill Park, Radstock, Bath, Somerset
BA3 3RW
☎ 01761 433161

CONTACT Peter Skinner
RANGE OF COURSES Forestry; Countryside Management. Full and Part Time: Horticulture; Landscape; Nursery Stock Production; Interior Landscapes; Pesticides; Arboriculture; The Garden School; Amenity Horticulture (NVQ); Amateur Gardening (option C&G); Chainsaw Techniques
LEVELS NVQ; GNVQ; C&G; BTEC
A higher education college concentrating on NVQs. Many short courses e.g., Safe Use of Pesticides. The Garden School has free introductory evenings.

STAFFORDSHIRE

Staffordshire College of Agriculture
Rodbaston, Penkridge, Staffordshire ST19 5PH
☎ 01785 712209   FAX 01785 715701
CONTACT W D D Fowler
RANGE OF COURSES Horticulture; Landscape; Administration and retailing; Floristry; Countryside management Groundsmanship; Garden Design (Diploma)
LEVELS C&G; NCH; ND and Diploma
Wide range of short courses, including RHS, either at College or on industrial premises. Day and evening courses.

Stoke-on-Trent College
Burslem Campus, Moorland Road, Burslem, Staffordshire ST6 1JJ
☎ 01782 208208   FAX 01782 828106
CONTACT Trevor McKeown
RANGE OF COURSES Full and Part Time: Horticulture (BTEC 1st Diploma; RHS); Groundsmanship; Amenity Horticulture (NVQ I and II); Environmental Conservation (NVQ II); Floristry (NVQ I and II); Flower Arranging (C&G)
LEVELS NVQ I and II; BTEC First Diploma; C&G
Range of full-, part-time and evening courses

SUFFOLK

Otley College of Agriculture & Horticulture
Otley, Ipswich, Suffolk IP6 9EY
☎ 01473 785543   FAX 01473 785353
CONTACT John Blyth
RANGE OF COURSES Horticulture; Landscape; Administration and Retailing; Forestry; Floristry; Countryside Management; Leisure Arboriculture; Garden Design and Construction; Organic Production; Interior Landscaping
LEVELS Postgraduate; Degree; C&G; HNC; ND; BTEC First Diploma; HND; RHS; ANC; NVQ
'Suffolk's Countryside Centre' which offers a MHort in partnership with Writtle College. There is a wide range of courses for young and mature students

SURREY

Constance Spry Ltd
Moor Park House, Moor Park Lane, Farnham, Surrey GU10 1QP
☎ 01252 734477   FAX 01252 712011
CONTACT Mrs Cleary
RANGE OF COURSES Amateur Day and Short Courses: Introduction to Flower Arranging/Floristry; Bridal Flowers; Bouquet Designs; Pedestals; Dried Arrangements; Church Decorations; Decorating a Marquee

Kew School of Horticulture
Royal Botanic Gardens, Kew, Richmond, Surrey TW9 3AB
☎ 0181 332 5545
CONTACT Ian Leese
RANGE OF COURSES Full Time: Horticulture; Botanic Garden Management (2 months)
LEVELS The Kew Diploma is a three-year course at first degree level in Amenity Horticulture and Horticultural Administration. It is recognised as the premier qualification of its kind and vacancies are limited to 16 a year. The list of 'Old Kewites' reads as a *Who's Who* of horticulture.

Merrist Wood College
Worplesdon, Guildford, Surrey GU3 3PE
☎ 01483 232424   FAX 01483 236518
CONTACT The Academic Registrar
RANGE OF COURSES Full and Part Time: Arboriculture (ND; NC; NVQ I–IV); Countryside Studies; Amenity Horticulture (ND; NC; NVQ I, II and III); Plant Production and Garden Centre Management (ND); Nursery Stock Production and Garden Centre Operation (NC); Landscape Studies (HND); Landscape Construction (NC; ND); Garden Design; Floristry (NC; NVQ I and II); Greenkeeping and Sports Turf Management (ND; NC; NVQ) Amateur: Gardening (C&G); Gardening for Pleasure; 2-hour practical courses on various subjects
LEVELS NCH and 3-year NDH (sandwich course) in Arboriculture, Landscape and Nursery Practice. HND in Landscape Contract Management; NVQ in Floristry, Arboriculture, Landscape and Commercial Horticulture.

Colleges & Horticultural Education   465

Merrist Wood is the Surrey college, and one of the leading centres for Amenity Horticulture. Both the staff and the pupils are among the most able nationally.

Royal Botanic Gardens, Kew
Education and Marketing Department, Royal Botanic Gardens, Kew, Richmond, Surrey TW9 3AB
☎ 0181 332 5623

CONTACT Andrew Jamieson or Sarah Oldridge
RANGE OF COURSES Short Courses: Garden Design; Drawing for Garden Designers, Botanical Illustration; Plants in Focus; Plant Conservation Techniques. Amateur: Study days
LEVELS RHS; C&G

Short courses and study days are run by the Education and Marketing Department. There is also a programme for schools.

EAST SUSSEX

Cabbages and Kings
Wilderness Farm, Hadlow Down, East Sussex TN22 4HU
☎ 01825 830552

CONTACT Ryl Nowell
RANGE OF COURSES Amateur Day Course: Garden Design

WEST SUSSEX

Brinsbury College
Brinsbury, North Heath, Pulborough, West Sussex RH20 1DL
☎ 01798 873832   FAX 01798 873832

CONTACT The Administrator
RANGE OF COURSES Full and Part Time: Landscape Studies (BTEC) Landscape Services(NC); Amenity Horticulture (NVQ I and II); Commercial Horticulture (NVQ I and II - Glasshouse and Mushroom Production); Groundsmanship; General Horticulture (RHS) Amateur: Short courses on various topics
LEVELS NVQ; RHS; C&G; NC; HNC; ND; HND

The county agricultural college for West Sussex, offering a wide range of qualifications at most levels. Well-organised.

The Edward James Foundation
West Dean College, Chichester, West Sussex PO18 0QZ
☎ 01243 811301   FAX 01243 811343

CONTACT The College Office
RANGE OF COURSES Short courses for professionals in Garden Management. Short courses and study days in Gardening and Garden History

TYNE & WEAR

University of Newcastle
Faculty of Agriculture, Dept of Town and Country Planning, Newcastle upon Tyne, Tyne & Wear NE1 7RU
☎ 0191 222 7802   FAX 0191 222 8811

CONTACT M. F. Downing (Course Director)
RANGE OF COURSES Landscape Master, Diploma, MA, in Landscape Design; Research options to MPhil/PhD; Agriculture; Tropical Agricultural and Environmental Science (MSc); Agricultural Engineering (MSc); International Agricultural Marketing (MSc)
LEVELS Master; Diploma; MA; MSc; PhD

The landscape design course is geared to Town & Country Planning and Urban Landscape design

WEST MIDLANDS

Bournville College of Further Education
Bristol Road South, Northfield, Birmingham, West Midlands B31 2AJ
☎ 0121 411 1414

CONTACT Mike Hill
RANGE OF COURSES Horticulture Amenity Horticulture (NVQ I and II); RHS Certificate in Horticulture
LEVELS NVQ I and II; RHS

Solihull College
Blossomfield Road, Solihull, West Midlands B91 1SB
☎ 0121 711 2111   FAX 0121 711 2316

CONTACT Ms Dorothy Connolly
RANGE OF COURSES Full and Part Time: Environmental Studies (Warwick BA; BSc); Horticulture (NPTC; RHS); Amenity Horticulture (NVQ I and II); Floristry (NVQ I and II) Amateur: Soils; Garden Machinery; Gardening for the Retired; Redesigning Your Garden; Improve Your House Plants
LEVELS BA; BSc; NVQ I and II

Stourbridge College
Horticulture and Conservation Unit, Leasowes Park Nursery, Leasowes Lane, West Midlands B62 8QF
☎ 0121 550 0007

CONTACT Richard Maw
RANGE OF COURSES Full and Part Time: Horticulture; Floristry; Countryside Management; Amenity Horticulture (NVQ); Groundsmanship (NVQ); Urban and Countryside Conservation (ND; FD); Environmental Conservation – Landscapes and Ecosystems (NVQ) Amateur: General Horticulture (RHS); Chainsaw Use; Pesticides
LEVELS ND; NVQ; RHS; Society of Florists exams

466 Colleges & Horticultural Education

Wulfrun College
Paget Road, Wolverhampton, West Midlands
WV6 0DU
☎ 01902 312062   📠 01902 23070
CONTACT   John Newton or Philip Healey, tel. 01902 312064
RANGE OF COURSES Full and Part Time: Amenity Horticulture (NVQ I and II), General Horticulture (RHS); Spraying Courses for NPTC certificates; Amateur Gardening (C&G)
LEVELS   RHS; C&G

WILTSHIRE

Gardeners' Breaks
Special Plants Nursery, Upper Wraxall, Chippenham, Wiltshire SN14 7AG
☎ 01225 891868
CONTACT   Derry Watkins
RANGE OF COURSES Amateur Day Courses: Taking Cuttings; Taking Seed; Using Your Greenhouse; Pruning

Horticultural Correspondence College
Little Notton Farmhouse, 16 Notton, Lacock, Chippenham, Wiltshire SN15 2NF
☎ Freephone 01800 378918   📠 01249 730326
CONTACT   Janet Elms (freephone 01800 378918)
RANGE OF COURSES Correspondence: Horticulture (RHS, NVQ I and II, MIHort); Garden Landscape and Design Drawing; Garden Planting and Layout Course; Interior Landscaping; Horticulture Principles; Turf Culture (IOG); Arboriculture Theory; Garden Centres; Leisure Gardening; Organic Gardening; Conservation
LEVELS   RHS (MHort); IOG; RFS Certificate; NVQ I and II
This college is one of the great success stories of recent years, largely due to the energy and skills of Oliver Menhinick and his staff. Full (and growing) range of correspondence courses.

Josephine Hindle
11 Beechfield, Newton Tony, Salisbury, Wiltshire SP4 0HQ
☎ 01980 629323
CONTACT   Josephine Hindle
RANGE OF COURSES Amateur Short Courses: Garden Design workshops (at Great Gransden, Cambridge); Art of Gardening study days (at Heale House, Salisbury)

Lackham College
Lacock, Chippenham, Wiltshire SN15 2NY
☎ 01249 443111   📠 01249 444474
CONTACT   Mrs P. J. Dickerson
RANGE OF COURSES Full and Part Time: Countryside Management and Conservation (BTEC/HND); Floristry (BTEC; NVQ I, II, III and IV); Professional Gardening (BTEC; NC; ANC); Organic Horticulture (NC); Amenity Horticulture (NVQ I, II, III and IV); General Horticulture (RHS); Garden Design
LEVELS   NVQ; HNC; ND; RHS; CGLI
One of the most go-ahead county colleges, with a substantial commitment to horticulture and floristry, and excellent demonstration gardens.

WORCESTERSHIRE

Pershore College of Horticulture
Avonbank, Pershore, Worcestershire WR10 3JP
☎ 01386 552443   📠 01386 556528
CONTACT   Garden Design: F. S. Hardy; RHS Exams: D. J. Coombs.
RANGE OF COURSES Full and Part Time: Amenity Horticulture; Landscaping (Design, Construction, Maintenance); Arboriculture; Crop Production; Nursery Stock Production; Retail Horticulture; Horticulture and the Environment; Horticultural Technology; Field Tree Production; Sports Surfaces; Countryside Recreation; Container Plants; Garden Maintenance; RHS: Greenhouse, Vegetables, Fruit, Garden Design, general exam
LEVELS   Degree; C&G; HNC; ND; HND; NVQ; RHS
The only specialist college of horticulture (no other subjects are taught), and a clear market leader. It has been developed to provide education and training for everyone building a career in this industry. Pershore's contribution to every aspect of commercial and amenity horticulture over the last 35 years has been incalculable.

NORTH YORKSHIRE

Askham Bryan College
Askham Bryan, York, North Yorkshire YO2 3PR
☎ 01904 702121   📠 01904 702629
CONTACT   Dr Bruce Rigby (Director of Education)
RANGE OF COURSES Full and Part Time: Horticulture; Landscape; Arboriculture; Urban Forestry; Countryside Management; Amenity Horticulture; Landscape and Garden Design; Environment and Conservation; Land Reclamation; Amenity Horticulture with Aboriculture option; Greenkeeping
LEVELS   BSc Hons; BSc; HND; NDH; NCH; BTEC First Diploma; Diploma Garden Design; C&G; NVQ
The BTEC National Diploma in Urban Forestry is unique in the country.

Craven College of Adult Education
High Street, Skipton, North Yorkshire BD23 1JY
☎ 01756 791411
CONTACT   G Hirst
RANGE OF COURSES Horticulture; Landscape; Forestry; Floristry; Countryside management Groundmasnhip; Amateur Gardening (RHS)
LEVELS   BTEC First Diploma; NVA I and II; C&G; RHS

Colleges & Horticultural Education 467

Harlow Carr Botanical Gardens
Crag Lane, Harrogate, North Yorkshire HG3 1QB
☎ 01423 565418
CONTACT   Dr S. Midgley
RANGE OF COURSES   Full and Part Time: Horticulture (C&G, RHS); Garden Design Amateur: Garden Design; Creative Gardening; Flower Arranging
LEVELS   C&G; RHS

Harlow Carr is the centre of the Northern Horticultural Society and has a varied programme of day and short courses.

SOUTH YORKSHIRE

Barnsley College of Technology
Church Street, Barnsley, South Yorkshire S70 2AX
☎ 01226 730191   FAX 01226 298514
CONTACT   John Sheard
RANGE OF COURSES   Horticulture; Gardening (C&G)
LEVELS   NVQ I and II, C&G; RHS

Well planned courses which appeal to amateurs and professionals.

University of Sheffield
Departmentt of Landscape, Sheffield, South Yorkshire S10 2TN
☎ 0114 282 6205
CONTACT   Helen Woolley
RANGE OF COURSES   Full Time: Landscape Design; Landscape Management (also part time); Research programmes
LEVELS   Postgraduate; degree

A large Landscape teaching unit with over 70 postgraduates: research scholarships available.

WEST YORKSHIRE

Leeds Metropolitan University
Landscape Architecture, Brunswick Building, West Yorkshire LS2 8BU
☎ 0113 2832600   FAX 0113 2833190
CONTACT   Landscape Architecture: Alan Simson. Garden Design: Fleur Gethin
RANGE OF COURSES   Landscape Landscape Architecture (BA Hons, MA and Graduate Diploma); Landscape Conversion Course. Amateurs: The Art of Garden Design (Certificate, no exam, 10 weeks, twice yearly, basic and advanced)
LEVELS   BA Hons; MA; Graduate Diploma; Certificate

Shipley College
Exhibition Road, Saltaire, Shipley, West Yorkshire BD18 3JW
☎ 01274 757222   FAX 01274 757201
CONTACT   John Baker (0274 757222)
RANGE OF COURSES   Full Time: Amenity Horticulture – Garden Design; Interior Landscaping; Urban Landscapes; Creating Landscapes; Environmental Studies; Plant Production; Leisure and Sports (BTEC). Part Time: Amenity Horticulture – Hard Landscaping; Nursery Practice; Interior Soft Landscaping; Greenkeeping; Sports Turf; Sportsground Maintenance (NVQ I and II); Constructing and Restoring Landscapes; Designing and Specifying Landscape Designs; Maintaining Sports Turf (NVQ III); Floristry (NVQ I, II and III). Amateur: General Horticulture (RHS); Amenity Horticulture, Floristry; Flower Arranging RHS General Certificate; Horticulture NVQ I and II; day and evening courses
LEVELS   NVQ levels I, II, III and IV; RHS; ND

Wakefield College
Margaret Street, Wakefield, West Yorkshire WS1 2DH
☎ 01924 370501   FAX 01924 810610
CONTACT   Roger Bennett
RANGE OF COURSES   Horticulture; Landscape; Floristry. Various courses for amateurs
LEVELS   C&G; NVQ I, II and III; RHS

WALES

CLWYD

Welsh College of Horticulture
Northop, Mold, Clwyd CH7 6AA
☎ 01352 840861
CONTACT   Floristry: Marae Kinread
RANGE OF COURSES   Full and Part Time: Horticultural Science – Landscape, Conservation, Amenity Horticulture (HND); Environmental Studies (HE Access and degree with Chester College); Machinery and Mechanisation (C&G; BTEC; ND); Glasshouse Crop Production and Management (BTEC; ND); Garden Centre Studies (BTEC; ND); Greenkeeping (BTEC; ND); Floristry (HNC); Landscape Design (NVQ III); Landscape Construction (NVQ III)
LEVELS   Degrees; C&G; NCH; ND; HND; HE Access; NVQ I, II and III

The leading horticultural college in the Principality – very thorough, professional and go-ahead. The range of courses is impressive, geared to commercial needs. The degree course is based for the first year only at WCH; a further 3 years are taught at Chester College. Short courses: Chainsaw Use; Pesticides

SOUTH GLAMORGAN

Cardiff Institute of Higher Education
Llandaff Centre, Western Avenue, Cardiff, South Glamorgan CF5 2YB
☎ 01222 551111
CONTACT   David Thornton

RANGE OF COURSES Full and Part Time: Horticulture; Groundsmanship (NVQ); Amenity Horticulture (NVQ II; BTEC 1st); Gardening (C&G)
LEVELS BTEC First Diploma; NVQ; C&G
The courses are soundly planned and well taught.

WEST GLAMORGAN

Afan College
Margam, Port Talbot, West Glamorgan SA13 2AL
☎ 01639 883712   FAX 01639 891288
CONTACT Richard Coleman, Margam Country Park, Port Talbot
RANGE OF COURSES Full and Part Time: Amenity Horticulture (NVQ I and II). Amateur: Hanging Baskets (winter/summer); Propagation; Patio Containers; Wooden Containers; Fuchsias; Climbing Plants; Arboriculture
LEVELS NVQ I and II

GWYNEDD

University College of North Wales
School of Agricultural and Forest Sciences, Bangor, Gwynedd LL57 2UW
☎ 01248 382439   FAX 01248 354997
CONTACT Mrs A. Louth
RANGE OF COURSES Forestry; Countryside Management; Agriculture; Wood Sciences; Rural Resource Economics; Soil Sciences; Environmental Science; Agroforestry (all degree courses)
LEVELS Postgraduate; degree

SCOTLAND

DUMFRIES & GALLOWAY

The Barony College
Parkgate, Dumfries & Galloway DG1 3NE
☎ 01387 86251   FAX 01387 86395
CONTACT T. Jones
RANGE OF COURSES Full and Part Time: Amenity Horticulture (SVQ I and II); Greenkeeping (SVQ). Amateur: Amateur Gardening (C&G); one-day courses
LEVELS SVQ; C&G

FIFE

Elmwood College
Carslogie Road, Cupar, Fife KY15 4JB
☎ 01334 52781   FAX 01334 56795
CONTACT Lin Edgcumbe
RANGE OF COURSES Full and Part Time: Horticulture; Interior and Exterior Landscaping; Floristry; Golf Greenkeeping; Computer Aided Landscape Technology; Bee Keeping; Plant Production; Plant Protection; Arboriculture
LEVELS HNC; NC; Scotvec

GRAMPIAN

Aberdeen College
Clinterty Centre, Kinellar, Aberdeen, Grampian AB2 0TN
☎ 01224 640366   FAX 01224 790326
CONTACT Robert Bellfield
RANGE OF COURSES Full and Part Time: Horticulture; Landscape; Nursery Practice; Agricultural Engineering (NC); Arboriculture (Scotvec, 1 year); Chainsaw Operation; Forest Tree Harvesting; Countryside Leisure Recreation and Tourism; Horticultural Engineering (HNC); Pesticide Application (Scotvec); Flower Arranging and Floristry. Amateur: Home and Allotment Gardening; Organic Gardening; Vegetative Propagation
LEVELS HNC; NC; Scotvec modules; ND
Aberdeen College incorporates the former Clinterty Agricultural College.

University of Aberdeen
Department of Agriculture, 581 King Street, Aberdeen, Grampian AB9 1UD
☎ 01224 480291   FAX 01224 273731
CONTACT Professor Robert Naylor
RANGE OF COURSES Full Time: Forestry; Botany; Crop and Soil Science; Tropical Biology; Tropical Environmental Science; Agriculture (BSc); Agricultural Business Management; Arboriculture; Agroforestry; Rural Resources
LEVELS Postgraduate; degree
The Faculty of Science has a good record.

LOTHIAN

Edinburgh College of Art, Heriot-Watt University
School of Landscape Architecture, Lauriston Place, Lothian EH3 9DF
☎ 0131 229 9311   FAX 0131 228 8825
CONTACT Anne Watson
RANGE OF COURSES Full Time: Landscape Architecture
LEVELS Postgraduate degree
Noted for stylish and original design; some bursaries available.

University of Edinburgh
Institute of Ecology and Resource Management, Darwin Building, Mayfield Road, Edinburgh, Lothian EH9 3JU
☎ 0131 650 5421   FAX 0131 662 0478
CONTACT School of Forestry: Dr J. F. Blyth, address as above; Department of Landscape Architecture: Dr J. B. Byrom, 20 Chambers Street, Edinburgh, EH1 1JZ
RANGE OF COURSES Full Time: Forestry; Ecology; Resource Management; Wildlife and Fisheries Management; Forestry and Rural Economy; Environmental

Science; Landscape Architecture. Short Courses: Training for the Tropics (TROPAG); Sustainable Development of the Environment; Tropical Forest Management; Tropical Agroforestry
LEVELS   Postgraduate; degree

A major scientific research institute with a distinguished commitment to tropical botany and husbandry and the highest reputation both among academics and in government.

WEST LOTHIAN

Oatridge Agricultural College
Ecclesmachan, Broxburn, West Lothian EH52 6NH
☎ 01506 854387   FAX 01506 853373

CONTACT   The Principal
RANGE OF COURSES   Full and Part Time: Horticulture; Landscape; Countryside Management; Leisure; Groundsmanship; Greenkeeping and Golf Courses. Amateur: Floristry; Floral Art; Plants for Foliage Effect; House Plants; Hanging Baskets; The Patio; Summer Colour; Pests and Diseases
LEVELS   HNC; SVQ

STRATHCLYDE

Country Courses
Ardfern, By Lochgilphead, Strathclyde PA31 8QN
☎ 018525 609/221   FAX 018525 627

CONTACT   Barbara Service
RANGE OF COURSES   Amateur Short Courses: Landscape Garden Design (2 day); Pruning and Propagation (1 day)

International Correspondence Schools
Clydeway Centre, 8 Elliot Place, Glasgow, Strathclyde G3 8EF
☎ 0141 221 7373   FAX 0141 221 8151 (Glasgow)

CONTACT   Course/Career Advisors
RANGE OF COURSES   Horticulture Intensive Market Gardening (Diploma); Complete Gardening (Diploma); General Exam in Horticulture (RHS)
LEVELS   ICS Diploma; RHS

Offices in Sutton, Surrey, Glasgow and Dublin

Langside College
Department of Horticulture, Woodburn House, 27 Buchanan Drive, Rutherglen, Strathclyde G73 3PF
☎ 0141 647 6300

CONTACT   E. Proudfoot
RANGE OF COURSES   Full and Part Time: Horticulture; Landscape; Hard Landscaping; Forestry; Countryside Management; Greenkeeping/Groundsmanship; Golf Course Management; Leisure Gardening; Flower Arranging
LEVELS   C&G; HNC; RHS

Scottish Agricultural College
Auchincruive, Ayr, Strathclyde KA6 5HW
☎ 01292 520331   FAX 01292 521287

CONTACT   Mrs E. A. Jaffray (Education Liaison Officer)
RANGE OF COURSES   Full and Part Time: Horticulture; Landscape; Countryside Management; Biotechnology; Applied Plant and Animal Science; Rural Resources; Rural Tourism; Rural Business Management; Aquaculture; Environmental Protection; Bee Keeping
LEVELS   Postgraduate; Degree; NCH; ND; HND; College Diploma (Horticulture)

The major centre for Horticulture in Scotland: the degree courses are taught in conjunction with the University of Strathclyde. The emphasis is on commercial horticulture and horticultural management.

TAYSIDE

Angus College
Keptie Road, Arbroath, Tayside DD11 3EA
☎ 01241 72056   FAX 01241 76169

CONTACT   Jim Menzies
RANGE OF COURSES   Full and Part Time: Horticulture (HNC); Horticultural Biology; Landscape; Lawns; Garden Machinery; Propagation (Scotvec National Certificate); Plant Protection; Plant Identification; Conservation Amateur: Patios; Garden Planning; Hanging Baskets

Go-ahead local authority college, 'small and friendly'. Courses can be full time or day release. Amateurs can sometimes join day courses on a part-time basis.

EIRE

CO. CORK

Scoil Stiofáin
Naofa, Traore Road, Cork, Co. Cork, Eire
☎ 00 353 21 961029   FAX 00 353 21 961320

CONTACT   Bernard Brennan
RANGE OF COURSES   Horticulture; Landscape; Greenkeeping
LEVELS   C&G; National Certificate

CO. DUBLIN

Teagasc College of Amenity Horticulture
National Botanic Gardens, Glasnevin, Co. Dublin, Eire
☎ 00 353 1 374388   FAX 00 353 1 377329

CONTACT   The Principal
RANGE OF COURSES   Full Time; Horticulture; Amenity Horticulture (Diploma); Greenkeeping (Certificate)
LEVELS   Diploma; certificate

470 Colleges & Horticultural Education

The courses have the premier setting in the National Botanic Gardens at Glasnevin. Diploma students demonstrate a high level of excellence.

University College Dublin
Department of Crop Science, Horticulture and Forestry, Belfield, Dublin, Co. Dublin, Eire
☎ 00 353 1 2693244 FAX 00 353 1 2837328
CONTACT Course Administrator
RANGE OF COURSES Full Time: Horticulture; Forestry; Botany; Groundsmanship; Commercial/Landscape Horticulture; Plant Protection; Environmental Resource Management; Landscape Architecture; Agricultural Science; Agribusiness and Rural Development
LEVELS BAgrSc degrees
Commercial and Landscape Horticulture are the leading degrees, both geared to getting employment on graduation.

CO. KILKENNY
Kildalton Agricultural & Horticultural College
Piltown, Co. Kilkenny, Eire
☎ 00 353 51 43105 FAX 00 353 51 43446
CONTACT Michael Cowhow
RANGE OF COURSES Commercial Horticulture – Production and Retailing
LEVELS Diploma
One of the leading horticultural schools in the Republic of Ireland.

CO. LOUTH
An Grianan College of Horticulture
Termonfechin, Drogheda, Co. Louth, Eire
☎ 00 353 41 22158
CONTACT Course Administrator
RANGE OF COURSES Full Time: Horticulture; Greenkeeping
LEVELS HNC; ND

CO. MEATH
Salesian College of Horticulture
Warrenstown, Drumree, Co. Meath, Eire
☎ 00 353 1 8259342 FAX 00 353 1 8259632
CONTACT Br J. O'Hare
RANGE OF COURSES Horticulture; Administration and retailing Commercial Horticulture (Diploma, 2-3 years)

Educational Grants & Grant-Making Trusts

Students or would-be students in search of funding for university courses or research projects should look at *The Grants Register* (1995–7 edition) edited by Lisa Williams and published by Macmillan in 1994. It is wonderfully comprehensive: we cannot recommend it too highly. The following is a selection of opportunities which may be of interest to our readers, but it is no substitute for consulting *The Grants Register* directly.

Bedding Plants Foundation, Inc (US)

Harold Bettinger Memorial Scholarship
SUBJECTS Business and/or Marketing of Horticulture
NUMBER OFFERED 1 scholarship
FREQUENCY Annually
VALUE US$1,000
COUNTRY OF STUDY US or Canada
ELIGIBILITY Graduate or undergraduate, horticulture major with a business and/or marketing emphasis (or vice-versa), at an accredited college or university in US or Canada. Any nationality
CLOSING DATE 1 April
Application forms available on request.

John Carew Memorial Scholarship
SUBJECTS Horticulture: bedding or flowering pot plants
NUMBER OFFERED 1 scholarship
FREQUENCY Annually
VALUE US$1,500
COUNTRY OF STUDY US or Canada
ELIGIBILITY Graduates majoring in horticulture at an accredited college or university in US or Canada. Any nationality
CLOSING DATE 1 April
Application forms available on request.

Dumbarton Oaks: Trustees for Harvard University

c/o The Assistant Director, Dumbarton Oaks, 1703 32nd Street NW, Washington DC 20007, US

Dumbarton Oaks Fellowships & Junior Fellowships
PURPOSE Support for study, research or doctoral theses
SUBJECTS Landscape architecture
NUMBER OFFERED 3–4
FREQUENCY Annually
VALUE US$11,000 pa (Junior Fellowships). US$18,000 pa (Fellowships). Plus housing, expenses and travel allowances
TENABLE For full time resident work at Dumbarton Oaks for up to 1 year. Not renewable
COUNTRY OF STUDY US
ELIGIBILITY Higher degree examinations for Junior Fellowship; PhD for Fellowship
CLOSING DATE 1 November
Some Summer Fellowships are available to scholars at any level to cover basic expenses for 6–9 weeks at Dumbarton Oaks

Friends of Israel Educational Trust
c/o John Levy, 25 Lyndale Avenue, London NW2 2QB

Jerusalem Botanical Gardens Scholarship
PURPOSE   To provide the opportunity for botanists and horticulturists to work at the Jerusalem Botanical Gardens
SUBJECTS   Botany and Horticulture
NUMBER OFFERED   Several
FREQUENCY   Annually
VALUE   Cost of return flight and accommodation
TENABLE   At the Jerusalem Botanical Gardens
COUNTRY OF STUDY   Israel
ELIGIBILITY   UK graduates in a relevant subject from recognised colleges and universities
CLOSING DATE   31 March

The Herb Society of America
9019 Kirtland Chardon Road, Mentor, OH 44060

Research & Education Grant
PURPOSE   To further the knowledge and use of herbs

SUBJECTS   Research on herbal projects
NUMBER OFFERED   The grant may be split between two or more candidates
FREQUENCY   Annually
VALUE   Up to US$5,000
TENABLE   For up to 1year
COUNTRY OF STUDY   Unrestricted
ELIGIBILITY   Persons with a programme of scientific, academic or artistic research into herbal plants
CLOSING DATE   31 January

Horticultural Research Institute (US)
c/o Ashby Ruden, Administrator, Suite 500, 1250 I Street NW, Washington, DC 20005

Various grants
PURPOSE   The advancement of the nursery, greenhouse and landscape industry
SUBJECTS   Nursery industry, especially the production and use of woody landscape plants
NUMBER OFFERED   Variable
FREQUENCY   Annually
VALUE   Variable: total budget around US$150,000
TENABLE   Federal or state universities, laboratories, institutes, arboreta or gardens. Sometimes renewable
COUNTRY OF STUDY   US
ELIGIBILITY   Any research project which the Institute considers appropriate
CLOSING DATE   1 May

Horticultural Research International (UK)
c/o Personnel Officer, East Malling, Kent ME19 6BJ

Agricultural & Food Research Council Scholarships
PURPOSE   To assist a student with further studies and training
SUBJECTS   A wide range of horticultural sciences
NUMBER OFFERED   Variable
FREQUENCY   Variable
VALUE   £7,200 pa, plus fees
TENABLE   For 3 years at East Malling, Wye, Littlehampton or Wellesbourne
COUNTRY OF STUDY   UK
ELIGIBILITY   UK honours graduates
CLOSING DATE   28 February

British Society for Horticultural Research Blackman Studentship
PURPOSE   To assist postgraduate study
SUBJECTS   Fields relating to horticulture
NUMBER OFFERED   1 studentship
FREQUENCY   Periodically
VALUE   Maintenance allowance on government scale
TENABLE   3 years
COUNTRY OF STUDY   UK
ELIGIBILITY   British subjects with a first or upper second in a relevant subject from a British Commonwealth university

International Society of Arboriculture
c/o Dr Bruce Roberts, Research Committee Chairman, Department of Botany & Microbiology, Ohio Wesleyan University, Delaware, OH 43015

Grants
PURPOSE   To encourage scientific or educational research on shade and landscape trees
SUBJECTS   Arboriculture
NUMBER OFFERED   Currently 10 grants
FREQUENCY   Annually
VALUE   US$2,500 towards supplies, equipment or technical assistance
TENABLE   1 year
COUNTRY OF STUDY   Any country
ELIGIBILITY   Very wide: any nationality, relevant academic disciplines
CLOSING DATE   1 November
The most favoured proposals are those which will 'help arborists earn their living by daily tree-care work'.

Ministry of Agriculture, Fisheries & Food
c/o Mrs Barbara Keller, Nobel House, 17 Smith Square, London SW1P 3JR

Postgraduate agricultural and food studentships
PURPOSE   To further the education of agricultural and food scientists
SUBJECTS   Many, including horticulture
NUMBER OFFERED   Up to 78 studentships awarded to universities for research leading to a PhD or MSc courses
FREQUENCY   Annually
VALUE   Fees, plus £5,638– £7,072 pa allowance
TENABLE   2–3 years at universities and approved colleges only
COUNTRY OF STUDY   UK

Educational Grants & Grant-Making Trusts

ELIGIBILITY UK resident citizens of UK and Commonwealth, and some EC nationals
CLOSING DATE 31 July
Preference is given to applied research.

The Royal Horticultural Society
c/o W. J. Simpson, 80 Vincent Square, London SW1P 2PE

Blaxall/Valentine Bursary
PURPOSE To fund plant collections
SUBJECTS Horticulture
NUMBER OFFERED 1-3 bursaries a year
FREQUENCY Twice yearly
VALUE Variable: the Society may require contributions from personal resources and/or others
ELIGIBILITY Preference is given to UK and Commonwealth citizens aged 20-35
CLOSING DATE 30 June and 31 December
Report and accounts required on completion.

The Expo '90 Osaka Travel Bursary
PURPOSE To enable young people from UK and Japan to study in each other's country
SUBJECTS Horticulture: mainly short courses and travel projects
NUMBER OFFERED 1 bursary
FREQUENCY Twice yearly
VALUE Variable: the Society may require contributions from personal resources and/or others
COUNTRY OF STUDY UK or Japan
ELIGIBILITY British and Japanese citizens aged 20-35
CLOSING DATE 30 June, 31 December
Report and accounts required on completion.

The Queen Elizabeth The Queen Mother Bursary
PURPOSE To help young horticulturists finance specific projects
SUBJECTS Horticulture: mainly short courses and travel projects
NUMBER OFFERED 1-3 bursaries a year
FREQUENCY Twice yearly
VALUE Variable: the Society may require contributions from personal resources and/or others
COUNTRY OF STUDY No limitations
ELIGIBILITY Preference is given to UK and Commonwealth citizens aged 20-35
CLOSING DATE 30 June, 31 December
Report and accounts required on completion.

The Scottish Agricultural College
c/o The Secretary, Auchincruive, Ayr KA6 5HW

William John Thomson Scholarship
PURPOSE To fund research training
SUBJECTS Agriculture and Horticulture
NUMBER OFFERED 1 scholarship
FREQUENCY Triennially
VALUE Variable

TENABLE At Auchincruive or its outstations, for 3 years
COUNTRY OF STUDY UK
ELIGIBILITY Any graduate in agricultural science working for a higher degree from Glasgow or Strathclyde universities

Woman's National Farm & Garden Association, Inc (US)
c/o Mrs Elmer Braun (Chairwoman), 13 Davis Drive, Saginaw, MI 48602

Sarah Bradley Tyson Memorial Fellowship
PURPOSE To assist with advanced study
SUBJECTS Agriculture or horticulture
NUMBER OFFERED 1 fellowship
FREQUENCY Annually
VALUE US$500
TENABLE An educational institution of accepted standing
COUNTRY OF STUDY US
ELIGIBILITY Men and women, properly qualified, who have proved their ability by several years' experience
CLOSING DATE 15 April
Reports required at end of first semester and on completion.

There are hundreds of private charitable trusts which award funds for horticultural projects. Most of the trusts mentioned in this chapter are listed in the 1993-94 edition of *The Directory of Grant-making Trusts*, an invaluable reference book which readers are urged to consult in full.

All these trusts are known to have supported endeavours which can be classed as 'horticultural'. They may have done so only once, and have no plan to do so again: we cannot tell. If the principal concern of a trust is the welfare of people with disabilities, you can assume that its 'horticultural' interests are limited to projects which help such people.

Most trusts accept applications only from other registered charities, but some are prepared to make an exception to this general rule if an individual puts forward a particularly deserving or imaginative proposal. This list will be of particular interest to gardening clubs and conservation groups.

Blunt Trust, The
C.C. No. 250721
CORRESPONDENT Mrs J. E. Mustoe, 58 Grafton Terrace, London NW5 4HY
TRUSTEES Mrs J. E. Mustoe, Mrs. J. M. Blunt
OBJECTS General charitable purposes. The principal areas of interest include historic buildings, conservation

and ecology, mainly in Wiltshire. Registered charities only: no applications from individuals or students.
FINANCES Year 1991; Income: £9,400
Awards do not normally exceed £100. Only direct applications will be considered.

Cantor Trust, The H. & L.
C.C. No. 220300
CORRESPONDENT H. Cantor, Massada, 478 Ecclesall Road South, Sheffield, South Yorkshire S11 9PZ
TRUSTEES L. Cantor, H. Cantor
OBJECTS General charitable purposes with a preference for those charities which are known to the trustees: registered charities only.
FINANCES Year 1991; Income £36,649; Assets £192,312

Colman Charitable Trust, The Timothy
C.C. No 206129
CORRESPONDENT The Administrator, The Timothy Colman Charitable Trust, Coutts & Co., Trustee Department, 440 Strand, London WC2R 0QS
TRUSTEES Coutts & Co., T. J. A. Colman
OBJECTS General charitable purposes for community life, especially in Norfolk. No grants to individuals.
FINANCES Year 1991; Income £9,404; Grants: £10,560; Assets £201,111
Small one-off cash grants, primarily for projects within the Norfolk area. Conservation and nautical projects favoured. Applications in writing to Coutts & Co.

D'Avigdor Goldsmid Charitable Trust, The Sarah
C.C. No. 233083
CORRESPONDENT Mrs R. C. Teacher, Hadlow Place, Golden Green, Tonbridge, Kent TN11 0BW
TRUSTEES Lady d'Avigdor Goldsmid, Mrs R. C. Teacher, A. J. M. Teacher.
OBJECTS General charitable purposes. Registered charities only: no applications by individuals. Unsuccessful applications not acknowledged.
FINANCES Year 1992; Income £12,078; Grants £12,475; Assets £110,732
Usually one-off grants.

Dixon Charitable Trust, The C. H.
C.C. No. 282936
CORRESPONDENT R. M. Robinson, Messrs. Dixon Ward, 16 The Green, Richmond, Surrey TW9 1QD
TRUSTEES Miss A. Dixon, R. M. Robinson
OBJECTS General charitable purposes
FINANCES Year 1992; Income £19,819; Grants £11,098; Assets £124,223

Glaxo (1972) Charity Trust, The
C.C. No. 265241
CORRESPONDENT The Secretary, The Glaxo (1972) Charity Trust, Glaxo House, Berkeley Avenue, Greenford, Middlesex UB6 0NN
TRUSTEES D. J. Derx, Sir Ralf Dahrendorf, J. M. Hignett

Objects: General charitable purposes, with priority for appeals which advance science and health care. No grants to individuals.
FINANCES Year 1992; Income £396,111; Grants £294,008
Single and recurring donations. Some interest in the preservation of the national heritage. Applications are considered 4 times a year.

Ibbetson Settlement, The Harry
C.C. No. 231131
CORRESPONDENT Dr B. Ibbetson, 39 Cumberland Terrace, Regent's Park, London NW1
TRUSTEES C. Kanter, FCA, Professor W. Fox, CMG
OBJECTS General charitable purposes, especially charities in which the trustees have a special interest or association. Restricted to welfare organisations and certain cultural and educational purposes.
FINANCES Year 1986; Income £5,115; Grants £2,934; Assets £61,193
Recurrent and one-off grants to the handicapped and elderly.

Laing Foundation, The Kirby
C.C. No. 264299
CORRESPONDENT R. M. Harley, Box 1, 133 Page Street, Mill Hill, London NW7 2ER
TRUSTEES Sir Kirby Laing, Lady Laing, S. Webley, D. E. Laing
OBJECTS General charitable purposes but not for education or travel.
FINANCES Year 1991; Income £2,516,199; Grants £1,843,190; Assets £15,112,056
Registered charities only: no gifts to individuals. Meetings approximately quarterly.

Laspen Trust, The, (formerly The Penrhyn Charitable Trust)
C.C. No. 276043
CORRESPONDENT J. C. Douglas Pennant, Penrhyn, Bangor, Gwynedd LL57 4HN
TRUSTEES Lady Janet Douglas Pennant, (Chair); R. C. H. Douglas Pennant, J. C. Douglas Pennant (Secretary)
OBJECTS General charitable purposes, especially the arts, the handicapped, health, welfare and environmental causes. No grants to individuals. Main area of benefit: north Wales, Merseyside, Northern Ireland.
FINANCES Year 1992; Income £8,615; Grants £8,250; Assets £117,807
Usually one-off donations to charities.

Lewis Foundation, The John Spedan
C.C. No. 240473
CORRESPONDENT N. Waldemar Brown, The Secretary, The John Spedan Lewis Foundation, 171 Victoria Street, London SW1E 5NN
TRUSTEES P. T. Lewis, W. H. Melly, Miss D. N. Barrett, H. M. J. King, A. D. Page
OBJECTS General charitable purposes, particularly those that reflect John Lewis's interest in education, the

Educational Grants & Grant-Making Trusts 475

arts, the natural sciences (including horticulture) and the encouragement of disadvantaged talent.
FINANCES Year 1992; Income £28,922; Grants £22,500; Assets £640,734
Mostly straight donations which may be repeated. Preference is given to smaller, more imaginative appeals (but not normally to local branches, individual students or expeditions).

Mackintosh Charitable Trust, The Viscount
C.C. No. 202374
CORRESPONDENT The Rt. Hon. Gwynneth Viscountess Mackintosh of Halifax, The Old Hall, Barford, Norwich, Norfolk NR9 4AY
TRUSTEES The Rt. Hon. Gwynneth Viscountess Mackintosh of Halifax, The Rt. Hon. Viscount Mackintosh of Halifax, The Hon. Diana M. Mackintosh
OBJECTS Relief of poverty, advancement of education, religion, medical science and other charitable purposes. Preference to charities in which the trustees have a special interest. No grants to individuals.
FINANCES Year 1992; Income £15,049; Grants £22,597; Assets £176,286
One-off grants only, except where the trustees spread payment over a number of years. No applications currently sought: income is already committed for the foreseeable future.

Mattock Charitable Trust, The W. T.
C.C. No. 244038
CORRESPONDENT Messrs Blakemores, Pemberton House, 4–6 East Harding Street, London EC4A 3BD
TRUSTEES I. S. Wick FCA, K. G. Coulton, A. C. Salt FCA
OBJECTS General charitable purposes, principally for the blind and disabled. Occasional ecological causes. Registered charities only.
FINANCES Year 1992; Income £5,333; Grants £5,000; Assets £61,202
Usually one-off grants for a specific project.

Nuffield Farming Scholarships Trust, The
C.C. No. 261823
CORRESPONDENT The Director, Nuffield Farming Scholarships Trust, Uckfield, East Sussex TN22 3AY
TRUSTEES Sir Richard Trehane, R. J. Cyster OBE, Captain J. S. Steward OBE FRAgS, C. W. Wharton
OBJECTS The advancement of farming (including horticulture) by the provision of scholarships to study practices and techniques anywhere in the world.
FINANCES Year 1992; Income £143,566; Grants £93,020; Assets £292,934
Travelling scholarships only. No grants for courses or conferences. Applicants must be in agriculture, horticulture, forestry or countryside management.

Rank Prize Funds, The
C.C. No. 263819
CORRESPONDENT Mrs. Judith Delaney (Administrative Secretary), 12 Warwick Square, London SW1V 2AA
Trustees: The Earl of Selbourne KBE DL FRS, Robin Cowen MBE, Dr Jack Edelman CBE DSc, Professor Cyril Hilsum CBE FRS, Sir Alex Jarrett CB, Joseph Rank FRCP Hon., Sir Richard Trehane DSc
OBJECTS Advancement and promotion of knowledge and education in the sciences of crop husbandry, human nutrition and animal nutrition.
FINANCES Year 1991; Income £530,476; Grants £406,586; Assets £7,776,820
The main work of the Funds is organising symposia and awarding prizes. The trustees do not usually consider unsolicited appeals. Grants are not made for general charitable purposes or to individuals for the furtherance of their education or research.

Royal Botanical and Horticultural Society of Manchester and the Northern Counties, The
C.C. No. 226683
Correspondent: A. Pye MA FCA, PO Box 498, 12 Booth Street, Manchester M60 2ED
TRUSTEES Official Custodian for Charities
OBJECTS Promotion of science and art in botany and horticulture by giving financial assistance to local gardens or other projects in the North West.
FINANCES Year 1989; Income £10,207; Grants £7,321; Assets £108,242
Mostly cash payments towards prize money or specific expenditure by horticultural societies, show organisers and gardens of horticultural interest.

Royal Commission for the Exhibition of 1851
C.C. No. 206123
CORRESPONDENT The Secretary, Royal Commission for the Exhibition of 1851, Sherfield Building, Imperial College of Science Technology and Medicine, London SW7 2AZ
TRUSTEES Board of Management
OBJECTS 'To increase the means of industrial education and extend the influence of science and art upon productive industry'.
FINANCES Year 1991; Income £1,000,000; Grants £550,000; Assets £11,914,000
Research fellowships in the pure and applied sciences and in engineering, industrial fellowships and industrial design studentships. Young graduates in engineering or science proposing to make their careers in British industry or wishing to develop their knowledge of industrial design.

Royal Society, The
C.C. No. 207043
CORRESPONDENT The Executive Secretary, The Royal Society, 6 Carlton House Terrace, London SW1Y 5AG

TRUSTEES   Council of The Royal Society
OBJECTS   An independent learned society which promotes national and international activities in the natural sciences. It has over one hundred trust funds.
FINANCES   Year 1992; Income £20,571,000; Grants £17,383,000; Assets £35,000,000
Principally for the advancement of science through research, mainly to post-doctoral scientists. Information is available on request.

Stanley Smith Horticultural Trust
C.C. No. 261925
CORRESPONDENT   Dr James Cullen, Cory Lodge, PO Box 365, Cambridge, CB2 1HR

OBJECTS   The support of amenity horticulture mainly, but not exclusively, in the United Kingdom
FINANCES   Year 1993; Income £110,000
The trustees welcome applications from individuals, organisations and institutions. They try to maintain a balance across the whole area of amenity horticulture and between small (up to £1,500) and larger grants at any time. The Trust has recently supported projects concerned with plant collecting, books on horticultural subjects, garden restoration, research on the production of new hybrids, and the maintenance of garden trainees. Grants are awarded twice a year, in April and October. Applications should be sent to the Director, who can also advise applicants as to how their applications should be presented.

25

Horticultural Libraries

Every keen gardener needs to consult reference books and sometimes to borrow them. Most people start their search for a particular book at their local library. Often the volume is not available at that particular branch, in which case the reader's search application form will be referred to other libraries within the same county, metropolitan area or region. Provided that records are readily accessible, and the software is up-to-date, most books are soon found. Those which are not available within the local area are passed to the Local Libraries Bureau, a federation of libraries which holds catalogues from each of its members. If this fails to locate a copy of the book, then the usual course is to refer the request to the British Library at Boston Spa to search through more and better catalogues until a source is found.

The Document Supply Centre of the British Library will also supply copies of articles free of charge to libraries which request them. It is a rule of this service that the copy must be read on the premises of the requesting library and lent, not given, to the reader. If the reader wishes to purchase it, the local library will sometimes give permission and levy a small charge.

Sometimes a reader needs to discover whether any books exist on a particular subject. The better libraries have extensive bibliographies and union lists of periodical publications. A good starting point is the British Library's catalogue: better still, the catalog of the Library of Congress.

Specialised collections like the Royal Horticultural Society's Lindley Library have extensive archives and large numbers of older books, especially those which were published before the *Copyright Act*, 1911, came into effect. There are six legal deposit libraries which are entitled under the provisions of the Act to receive a free copy of any book published in the United Kingdom. They are: the British Library, The Bodleian Library at Oxford, the Cambridge University Library, the National Library of Scotland, the National Library of Wales and the library of Trinity College, Dublin. Their post-1911 collections of British gardening books are all complete.

Most of the libraries listed here offer such facilities as photocopying services, computer terminals, video viewers, and full microform and microfiche equipment, but not all are available at some of the smaller, more specialised libraries.

Much of the information in this chapter comes from *The Libraries Directory* 1991–93 edited by Richard S. Burnell and published by James Clarke & Co. Ltd of Cambridge, which gives further details of the services offered by each and by hundreds of other libraries throughout Britain and Ireland.

England

The British Library
2 Sheraton Street, London W1V 4BH
☎ 0171 636 1544
OPEN Reading Room, weekdays 9.30 am- 5.30 pm (9 pm on Tuesday-Thursday), Saturday 9.30 am-1 pm.

The British Library is the UK's national library, at the centre of the library and information network. It was established in 1973 to consolidate the library departments of the British Museum, the National Central Library, the National Lending Library for Science and Technology, the British National Bibliography Ltd, and, in 1974, the Office for Scientific and Technical Information. Its services are based on the largest collections in the UK: over 18 million volumes at 18 buildings in London and the Document Supply Centre in West Yorkshire.

478 Horticultural Libraries

Most books and articles relating to horticulture, apart from more recent issues of popular magazines, can be read at the Humanities and Social Sciences reading rooms at the British Museum. A British Library Reader's Pass is needed: information about eligibility is available from the Reader Admissions Office. Some gardening books, especially those which deal with practical or scientific topics, are stored at the Aldwych and Holborn reading rooms of the Science Reference and Information Service which open to the general public without charge or formality, but the great majority of material is at the British Museum.

The British Library is in the process of moving to purpose built accommodation at St Pancras, London NW1 but the planned opening has been delayed several times and will certainly not take place this year, as once envisaged.

Document Supply Centre,
Boston Spa, Wetherby, West Yorkshire LS23 7BQ.
☎ Tel: 01937 546000

The British Library offers two important services from the Document Supply Centre. The first is, in effect, a book-finding service for readers who apply through their local public or college libraries. The other is a rapid loan and photocopy service. The Document Supply Centre subscribes to 55,000 current journals in addition to acquiring monographs, conference proceedings and scientific reports. Some 88 per cent of the 3,750,000 requests received each year are satisfied from stock.

Library and Archives, Royal Botanic Gardens
Kew, Richmond, Surrey TW9 3AE.
☎ Tel: 0181 940 1171   Fax: 0181 332 0920

OPEN Monday-Thursday, 9 am-5.30 pm.

Books are available to bona fide researchers by written appointment only. The library's collection includes: plant taxonomy, distribution and conservation, horticulture, economic botany, plant anatomy, genetics, biochemistry and tropical botany. The library has 164,000 volumes (120,000 monographs), 140,000 pamphlets, 1,800 current periodicals and 3,200 no longer current. The archive collection has 250,000 modern and recent items, including the papers of Sir Joseph Banks, Sir William Hooker, Sir Joseph Hooker and George Bentham.

Ministry of Agriculture, Fisheries and Food Library
3 Whitehall Place, London SW1A 3HH
☎ Tel: 0171 270 8420/21

OPEN Monday-Friday, 9.30 am-5 pm, by prior appointment giving at least 24 hours notice.

The library has 160,000 volumes and subscribes to 2,000 current periodicals. It also publishes a library guide, reading lists and subject bibliographies. We have found it a valuable source, especially for foreign periodicals.

Linnaean Society of London Library
Burlington House, Piccadilly, London W1V 0LQ
☎ Tel: 0171 434 4479   Fax: 0171 287 9364

OPEN Monday-Friday, 10 am-5 pm, by appointment.

The library's collection includes: natural history, taxonomy, botany, the history of science, the history of biology, evolutionary theory and some horticultural studies. Its special collections incorporate the Insch Tea Library, the Balfour Bequest Bird Library and the library of Carolus Linnaeus. It has over 100,000 volumes, nearly 1,000 current periodicals and a good collection of pamphlets, photographs and other illustrations.

Chelsea Physic Garden
66 Royal Hospital Road, London SW3 4HS
☎ Tel: 0171 352 5654

OPEN Monday-Friday, 8 am-3 pm by appointment.

The library concentrates on British and foreign pharmacological, herbal and medicinal studies, and its special collections include historic herbals dating back to 1472, small historic herbaria (e.g. Moore's Clematis), and a general reference collection on medicinal plants.

Consumers' Association Library
2 Marylebone Road, London NW1 4DX
☎ Tel: 0171 486 5544   Fax: 0171 935 1606

OPEN Monday-Friday, 10 am-6 pm.

Admission is at the discretion of the Chief Librarian. Principally concerned with consumer protection, the library has a good collection of gardening sources which are used by the staff of *Gardening Which?*. The library has 3,000 volumes and subscribes to 850 current periodicals.

The Natural History Museum
Library Services, Cromwell Road, London SW7 5BD
☎ Tel: 0171 938 9191   Fax: 0171 938 9290

OPEN Monday-Saturday, 10 am-6 pm. Reader's ticket required.

A large collection of books, focused on life and earth sciences: natural history, botany, entomology, palaeontology, mineralogy, geology, anthropology, zoology and horticulture. Also a good collection of drawings, manuscripts, archives, catalogues and papers. There are 800,000 volumes and 10,000 current periodicals.

Horticultural Libraries 479

The Royal Horticultural Society
Lindley Library, 80 Vincent Square, London SW1P 2PE
☎ Tel: 0171 821 3050

OPEN Monday-Friday, 9.30 am-5.30 pm.

Members of the Society are entitled to use the library at any time during these hours. The library has nearly 50,000 books and the largest collection of nursery catalogues in the UK. It subscribes to a wide range of British and foreign periodicals. It also has an unrivalled collection of horticultural papers and foreign works. Some volumes can be borrowed by post if the members cannot attend the library in person.

Bodleian Library
Broad Street, Oxford OX1 3BG
☎ Tel: 01865 277000 FAX Fax: 01865 277182

OPEN during term time: Monday-Friday, 9 am-8 pm, Saturday, 9 am-1 pm. During vacations: Monday-Friday, 9 am-7 pm, Saturday, 9 am-1 pm.

The library is open to non-University readers on payment for a Reader's Ticket (from £2 for two-day ticket, to £10 for one year). The Bodleian is a copyright library, so the horticultural collection is very comprehensive, although there are comparatively few older works. The Bodleian has a total of 5.5 million volumes and subscribes to 54,800 current periodicals.

Cambridge University Library
West Road, Cambridge CB3 9DR
☎ Tel: 01223 333000 FAX Fax: 01223 333160

OPEN Monday to Friday 9 am-7.15 pm (10 pm during Easter Term), Saturday 9 am-1 pm; closed for some Bank Holidays and for one week in September.

Open to non-members of the University: enquiries in writing to the admissions officer. The library is a copyright library, with a comprehensive collection of 20th-century books on gardening. There are 4 million volumes and nearly 60,000 current periodicals, but these include all subjects.

Writtle Agricultural College Library
Writtle College, Chelmsford, Essex CM1 3RR
☎ Tel: 01245 420705 FAX Fax: 01245 420456

OPEN Term time: Monday-Thursday, 8.45 am-8.30 pm, Friday, 8.45 am-5 pm, Saturday, 9 am-12 pm. During vacations: Monday-Thursday, 8.45 am-5.15 pm, Friday, 8.45 am-4.45 pm.

This is a membership library: apply to the chief librarian for details. The collection includes agriculture, horticulture and other land-based subjects, with related science and management, and there are many historical books relating to agriculture and horticulture. The library has 37,000 volumes and subscribes to 375 current periodicals.

University of Reading Library
P.O. Box 223, Whiteknights, Reading, Berkshire RG6 2AE
☎ Tel: 01734 318770 FAX Fax: 01734 312335

OPEN Term time: Monday-Thursday, 9 am-10.15 pm, Friday, 9 am-7 pm, Saturday, 9 am-12.30 pm, Sunday, 2 pm-6 pm. During vacations: Monday-Friday, 9 am-5 pm.

There is a good natural sciences and agriculture collection as well as horticulture. There are 800,000 volumes and 4,000 current periodicals but these statistics cover all the university's facilities. Nevertheless, Reading has one of the best university collections of horticultural books in the country.

Pershore College of Horticulture Library
Pershore, Worcestershire WR10 3JP
☎ Tel: 01386 552443 FAX Fax: 01386 556528

OPEN Monday-Thursday, 9 am-8 pm, Friday, 9 am-5 pm by appointment.

The horticultural collection covers science, landscaping, management, arboriculture and bee keeping, as well as amenity and commercial horticulture. There are 10,000 volumes, 130 current periodicals and 2,500 pamphlets.

University of Bristol Library
Tyndall Avenue, Bristol BS8 1TJ
☎ Tel: 0117 930 3030 FAX Fax: 0117 925 5334

OPEN in term time: Monday-Thursday, 8.45 am-11 pm, Friday and Saturday, 8.45 am-6 pm, Sunday, 2 pm-8 pm. Christmas vacation: Monday-Thursday, 8.45 am-7 pm, Friday, 8.45 am-4.45 pm. Summer vacation: Monday-Friday, 8.45 am-4.45 pm, Saturday, 8.45 am-1 pm.

Applications to use the library should be made in writing to the University Librarian. The library has some rare botany books but, more importantly, houses the book collection of the Garden History Society. There is a total of 940,000 volumes and 6,500 current periodicals, but these figures include all university faculties.

Horticulture Research International
Wellesbourne Library, Wellesbourne, Warwick CV35 9EF
☎ Tel: 01789 470382 FAX Fax: 01789 470552

Dependent library: Horticulture Research International, East Malling Library, East Malling, Maidstone, Kent ME19 6BJ. Monday-Friday, 8.30 am-5 pm, Friday, 8.30 am-4.30 pm by appointment.

Topics covered include horticulture, plant breeding, entomology, plant pathology, seed technology, genetics, vegetable production, soil science, pesticide science and plant physiology. Wellesbourne has 16,000 volumes and subscribes to 400 current periodicals. There is also a small collection of rare 18th- and 19th-century gardening books and an archive collection of modern books – 'modern' means post 1789.

Wales

Welsh College of Horticulture/ Coleg Garddwriaeth Cymru
Northop, Mold, Clwyd CH7 6AA
☎ Tel: 01352 86861   📠 Fax: 01352 86731

OPEN in term time: Monday-Friday, 9 am-8.30 pm: times variable during the vacation.

Reference only: no borrowing. Subjects include horticulture, floristry, interior landscape, landscape, amenity horticulture, garden centres, retail horticulture, commercial horticulture and greenkeeping. The library has 4,000 volumes and subscribes to 50 current periodicals.

The National Library of Wales/ Llyfrgell Genedlaethol Cymru
Aberystwyth, Dyfed SY23 3BU
☎ Tel: 01970 623816   📠 Fax: 01970 615709

OPEN Monday to Friday 9.30 am-6 pm (5 pm on Saturdays).

Membership open to any person over 18 years of age. A legal deposit ('copyright') library with a large modern collection on horticultural topics. 3 million volumes in all subjects. The library has a good collection of bibliographies on Welsh topics, including aspects of horticulture and garden history.

Scotland

National Library of Scotland
George IV Bridge, Edinburgh EH1 1EW
☎ Tel: 0131 226 4531

OPEN Reading room, weekdays, 9.30 am-8.30 pm (Wednesday 10 am-8.30 pm), Saturday 9.30 am-1 pm. Scottish Science Library, weekdays 9.30 am-5 pm (Wednesday 10 am-8.30 pm).

The Library became the National Library of Scotland by Act of Parliament in 1925. Its collection of printed books and MSS is very large and it has an unrivalled collection of Scottish material. The Reading Room is open to readers for research which cannot conveniently be pursued elsewhere. Admission is by ticket issued to an approved applicant.

The Library, Royal Botanic Garden Edinburgh
Inverleith Row, Edinburgh EH3 5LR
☎ Tel: 0131 552 7171   📠 Fax: 0131 552 0382

OPEN Monday-Thursday, 9 am-5 pm, Friday, 9 am-4.30 pm.

Collection includes: systematic botany, amenity horticulture and landscape architecture: there are 180,000 volumes, 25,000 pamphlets, and the library subscribes to 1,500 current periodicals.

Eire

Trinity College Library
College Street, Dublin 2
☎ Tel: 00 353 1 772941
📠 Fax: 00 353 1 719003

OPEN Monday-Friday 9.30 am-10 pm (5 pm during vacations, 1 pm on Saturdays).

Members of the public may use the library to consult material not available elsewhere. It is a deposit library for both Ireland and Britain. There are 3 million volumes and the library subscribes to 12,000 current periodicals.

26

Specialist Bookshops

New gardening books appear each year in unrelenting numbers. Some are excellent, most more run of the mill. Branches of nationwide chains such as Waterstones and Dillons, Foyles, and the university booksellers, including Heffers and Blackwells, all carry an impressive selection of new books and usually offer mail order or account facilities. Ordinary secondhand bookshops can prove fruitful hunting grounds for reasonably priced gardening books but much of their stock is out of date and best forgotten. The specialists are your most reliable source for older and more recent classics, floras and affordable but worthwhile titles from overlooked authors. They will also have highly illustrated and collectable books: since these appeal also to non-gardeners, you must expect to pay accordingly. The Provincial Booksellers Fairs Association (PBFA) (01763 249212) organises regular sales around the country.

Anna Buxton Books
23 Murrayfield Road, Edinburgh, Lothian EH12 6EP
☎ 0131 337 1747   FAX 0131 337 8174
CONTACT   Mrs Anna Buxton
SPECIALITY   New books; remaindered books; secondhand and antiquarian books; flower arranging; horticulture; illustrated books or prints; Scottish gardening; plant hunters; garden history
CATALOGUE   On request; Christmas supplement
MAIL ORDER   Yes
An attractively produced and readable list, which includes general titles, collectable works and some new books. All books are described alphabetically by author.

Besleys Books
4 Blyburgate, Beccles, Suffolk NR34 9TA
☎ 01502 715762
CONTACT   P. Besley
OPEN   9.30 am – 5 pm. Closed Wednesdays and Sundays and sometimes for lunch. After hours contact 01502 675649
SPECIALITY   Secondhand and antiquarian books; botany; flower arranging; horticulture; illustrated books or prints; natural history; trees and forestry

CATALOGUE   On request; 1 a year
MAIL ORDER   Yes
SHOWS   PBFA
An annotated sectional list: bibliographic details rather than descriptions. A wide selection from general gardening titles to specialist and illustrated books.

BSBI Publications; F & M Perring
Green Acre, Wood Lane, Oundle, Peterborough, Northamptonshire PE8 5TP
☎ 01832 273388   FAX 01832 274568
CONTACT   Mrs Margaret Perring
OPEN   By appointment only
SPECIALITY   New books; botany; natural history
CATALOGUE   On request; regular supplements
MAIL ORDER   Yes
Official agents for the Botanical Society of the British Isles. In addition to the society's publications, they stock local, British and overseas floras and other botanical, conservation and reference titles.

Cassell plc
Stanley House, 3 Fleets Lane, Poole BH15 3AJ
☎ 01202 670581   FAX 01202 666219
CONTACT   Customer Services
OPEN   8.30 am – 5 pm, Monday – Friday
SPECIALITY   New books; botany; flower arranging; general gardening
CATALOGUE   On request
MAIL ORDER   Ring Customer Services
Gardening titles direct from the publisher. This extensive list includes titles from Ward Lock, Blandford and the RHS Wisley Handbooks.

Chantrey Books
24 Cobnar Road, Sheffield, South Yorkshire S8 8QB
☎ 0114 274 8958
CONTACT   Clare Brightman
OPEN   By appointment only
SPECIALITY   Remaindered books; secondhand and antiquarian books; botany; horticulture; illustrated books or prints; natural history; rural life

482 Specialist Bookshops

CATALOGUE   On request: 3 a year
MAIL ORDER   Yes
SHOWS   Malvern Spring; Harrogate (Spring); PBFA

A pleasing general list, divided into subheadings. Some interesting older books too, as well as some natural history and rural titles.

Ivelet Books Ltd
Church Street Bookshop, 26 Church Street, Godalming, Surrey GU7 1EW
☎ 01483 418878   FAX 01483 418656

CONTACT   Mr D. J. and Mrs E. A. Ahern
OPEN   10.30 am – 5.30 pm, Monday – Saturday
SPECIALITY   Secondhand and antiquarian books; botany; horticulture; illustrated books or prints; natural history; architecture and interiors
CATALOGUE   On request: 3 or 4 a year
MAIL ORDER   Yes
SHOWS   Chelsea; PBFA

A good range for gardeners and collectors: the list is strongest on twentieth century classics such as Jekyll and Bowles, and is also a source for standard and historical works. They also specialise in Natural History and Architecture.

John Henly
Brooklands, Walderton, Chichester, West Sussex PO18 9EE
☎ 01705 631426

CONTACT   John Henly
OPEN   By appointment only
SPECIALITY   Secondhand and antiquarian books; botany; horticulture; natural history; trees and forestry; geology
CATALOGUE   On request; 4 a year
MAIL ORDER   Yes
SHOWS   PBFA

The catalogues are helpfully sub-divided into subjects. Individual entries have full bibliographic notes, but descriptions are kept to a minimum. Good for standard works, especially from the mid-twentieth century.

Kew Shop
Mail Order Section, Royal Botanic Gardens, Kew, Richmond, Surrey TW9 3AB
☎ 0181 332 5653

OPEN   9 am – 5 pm for telephone orders; Victoria Gate Shop normally open 9.30 am – 5.30 pm (summer and Christmas period) or until last garden admissions
SPECIALITY   New books; botany; flower arranging; horticulture; natural history; trees and forestry
CATALOGUE   Books and gifts; scientific
MAIL ORDER   Yes

An excellent choice of current horticultural and botanical books, including numerous scientific publications. A large section is devoted to children's books and attractive gift items. Entrance is normally through the garden, but you can get in directly if you give advance notice. The closing time changes with the season (information on 0181 940 1171).

Landsman's Bookshop Ltd
Buckenhill, Bromyard, Hereford & Worcester HR7 4PH
☎ 01885 483420   FAX 01885 483420

CONTACT   K. J. Stewart
OPEN   9 am – 4.30 pm, Monday – Friday, Saturdays by appointment
SPECIALITY   New and secondhand books; remaindered books; botany; flower arranging; general gardening; natural history; trees and forestry
CATALOGUE   £1
MAIL ORDER   Yes
SHOWS   International Spring Gardening Fair; Malvern Spring; Harrogate (Spring); Southport; Chelsea

From their substantial catalogue Landsman's aims to supply all gardening books which are in print. Mainly mail order and through agricultural and horticultural shows. They also have remaindered and secondhand material (of interest to horticultural students). Agriculture is stocked in similar depth, and they publish a few titles of their own.

Lloyds of Kew
9 Mortlake Terrace, Kew, Richmond TW9 3DT
☎ 0181 940 2512

OPEN   10 am – 4 pm, Monday – Friday; 10 am – 5 pm, Saturdays. Closed Wednesdays and Sundays
SPECIALITY   Secondhand and antiquarian books; horticulture; illustrated books or prints
CATALOGUE   On request
SHOWS   Chelsea

Specialists for secondhand and antiquarian gardening books. Tucked away just off Kew Green, the shop also carries a general secondhand stock. They operate a free finding service (without obligation).

Mary Bland
Augop, Evenjobb, Presteigne, Powys LD8 2PA
☎ 01547 560218

CONTACT   Mary Bland
OPEN   By appointment only
SPECIALITY   New books; remaindered books; secondhand and antiquarian books; botany; flower arranging; horticulture; trees and forestry
CATALOGUE   On request; about 3 a year
MAIL ORDER   Yes
SHOWS   RHS Westminster; Chelsea

Good general and collectors stock, with many interesting and reasonably priced titles. The list is divided into sections, with bibliographic details and some descriptions. Prints available at shows. Will search for titles.

Mike Park
351 Sutton Common Road, Sutton, Surrey SM3 9HZ
☎ 0181 641 7796

CONTACT   Mike Park

Specialist Bookshops 483

OPEN Sales mainly mail order and shows; viewing occasionally possible by appointment.
SPECIALITY Horticulture; natural history
MAIL ORDER Yes
SHOWS RHS Westminster

Mike Park is a familiar exhibitor at RHS shows in Vincent Square.

Peter M Daly
Thompson Antiques, 20a Jewry Street, Winchester, Hampshire SO23 8RZ
☎ 01962 867732

CONTACT Peter M. Daly
OPEN 10 am – 4.30 pm, Wednesdays and Fridays; 10am – 1pm, 2 – 5pm, Saturdays. Other times by appointment
SPECIALITY Remaindered books; secondhand and antiquarian books; botany; flower arranging; horticulture; illustrated books or prints; natural history; landscape gardening
CATALOGUE No
MAIL ORDER No
SHOWS PBFA

RHS Enterprises Ltd
RHS Garden, Wisley, Woking, Surrey GU23 6QB
☎ 01483 211113   FAX 01483 211003

CONTACT B. M. C. Ambrose
OPEN 10 am – 5.30 pm, Monday – Saturday, closes at 6.30 pm in summer; 11.30 am – 5.30pm Sundays, March – December, 10 am – 4pm, January, February
SPECIALITY New books; botany; flower arranging; general gardening; illustrated books or prints; natural history; trees and forestry
CATALOGUE On request; 2 a year
MAIL ORDER Yes (01483 211320)
SHOWS RHS Westminster; International Spring Gardening Fair; Malvern Spring; Harrogate (Spring); Southport; Chelsea; BBC GW Live; Hampton Court; Harrogate (Autumn); Ayr

The range of gardening and botanical books on sale at Wisley is among the best in the country. Twice yearly catalogues detail an extensive part of the stock, and allow for mail order purchase. New books only, including many from overseas. The shop also sells gift items.

Search Press Books by Post
Wellwood, North Farm Road, Tunbridge Wells, Kent TN2 3DR
☎ 01892 510850   FAX 01892 515903

CONTACT Barbara Duck and Mary Ellingham
OPEN 8.30 am – 5.30 pm
SPECIALITY Horticulture; organic; crafts
CATALOGUE On request
MAIL ORDER Yes

Mail order service from this craft and organic gardening publisher. Orders are post free over £15.

Summerfield Books
Summerfield House, High Street, Brough, Kirkby Stephen, Cumbria CA17 4BX
☎ 017683 41577   FAX 017683 41577

CONTACT Jon and Sue Atkins
OPEN By appointment
SPECIALITY New books; remaindered books; secondhand and antiquarian books; botany; horticulture; illustrated books or prints; natural history; trees and forestry; country and foreign floras; cryptogams
CATALOGUE On request; 4 a year
MAIL ORDER Yes

Substantial list with an individual style. Very good for floras, cryptogams and forestry titles. Some interesting general titles also. Free finding service.

W C Cousens
The Leat, Lyme Road, Axminster, Devon EX13 5BL
☎ 01297 32921

CONTACT W. C. Cousens
OPEN By appointment only
SPECIALITY Secondhand and antiquarian books; botany; flower arranging; horticulture; illustrated books or prints; trees and forestry
CATALOGUE sae; 4 a year
SHOWS PBFA

Book search facility available.

Wells & Winter
Mere House Barn, Mereworth, Maidstone ME18 5NB
☎ 01622 813627

CONTACT Sir John Wells
OPEN Sell from shows only
SPECIALITY New books; remaindered books; secondhand and antiquarian books; botany; general gardening
MAIL ORDER No
SHOWS RHS Westminster; International Spring Gardening Fair; Malvern Spring; Chelsea; Hampton Court

New and secondhand books: available at shows only. The stand also sells labels and other garden products.

Wyseby House Books
Hazlewood, Broad Layings, Woolton Hill, Newbury, Berkshire RG15 9TS
☎ 01635 253301

CONTACT Dr Tim Oldham
OPEN By appointment
SPECIALITY Remaindered books; secondhand and antiquarian books; botany; horticulture; illustrated books or prints; natural history; trees and forestry
CATALOGUE On request; monthly
MAIL ORDER Yes
SHOWS PBFA

The horticultural titles run from affordable classics of the last 150 years to more recent works. Of interest to both gardeners and specialists. Other areas include biology and zoology.

Books, Periodicals & Videos

New Books 1994

1994 Gardener's Guide to Britain, Patrick Taylor (Pavilion, 1994) £10.99, pbk.
Completely revised: Patrick Taylor has visited all the establishments again this year. An attractively presented and agreeably acute guide.

Alan Toogood's Gardening Under Glass, Alan Toogood (Weidenfeld & Nicolson, 1994) £9.99, pbk.

The Alpine Garden: A Practical Guide to Planning and Planting, Christopher Grey-Wilson (Conran Octopus, 1994) £15.99, RHS Collection.

Annuals & Bedding Plants, Nigel Colborn (Conran Octopus, 1994) £12.99.
This is more about bedding than annuals: 'decorating with colours and textures to create a desired effect'. Nigel Colborn explains the principles: massing, patterns, geometric shapes, and rotating the display. Then he identifies the qualities which go to make a good bedding plant and describes the styles of carpet bedding. He is good on the use of dot plants and the differences between traditional and municipal styles. He gives practical advice on how to raise plants, plan and plant beds, mix colours or separate them, choose combinations, create moods, ring in the seasons, treat yourself to special effects, and tackle difficult sites. The book is not cheap for only 96 pages, but lavishly illustrated and every picture is an integral part of the text. Colborn is an observant writer with a good eye and the gift of lucidity. His apostolic zeal for bedding will convert even a strict and particular plantsman into a born again colourist.

The Art of Botanical Illustration, Wilfrid Blunt and William T Stearn (Antique Collectors' Club, 1994) £25.95, new edition.

The previous editions of this work, in the Collins New Naturalist series, have long been collectors' items themselves. Now revised, and expanded by Blunt's co-writer, Professor Stearn, what will strike those familiar with the earlier editions most is the handsome quality of the illustrations. The murky plates are now replaced by ones which do justice to the text. There is an engaging introduction by Professor Stearn, and though there are now other general surveys of botanical art to choose among, the writing retains its discerning charm, so that no one interested in the subject will want to be without this book.

Best Borders, Tony Lord (Frances Lincoln, 1994).
Expert advice on one of the commonest garden features, yet one which is easily mishandled. This practical guide to planning, planting and maintaining borders comes with twelve planting plans. An appealing combination of successful and famous examples, and the knowledge of a former Gardens Advisor to the National Trust.

Best Climbers, Stefan Buczacki (Hamlyn, 1994) £4.99, pbk.
In association with *Amateur Gardening*.

Best Foliage Shrubs, Stefan Buczacki (Hamlyn, 1994) £4.99, pbk.
In association with *Amateur Gardening*.

Best Shade Plants, Stefan Buczacki (Hamlyn, 1994) £4.99, pbk.
In association with *Amateur Gardening*.

Best Soft Fruit, Stefan Buczacki (Hamlyn, 1994) £4.99, pbk.
In association with *Amateur Gardening*.

The Book of Primroses, Barbara Shaw (David & Charles, 1994) £14.99, pbk.

The Border Book, Anna Pavord (Dorling Kindersley, 1994) £15.99.

Border Pinks and Dianthus, Richard Bird (Batsford, 1994) £25.00.

The Bulb Expert, Dr D. G. Hessayon (Transworld, 1994) £4.99.

Cacti and Succulents in Habitat, Ken Preston-Mafham (Cassell, 1994) £16.99.
150 species photographed in the wild.

Clematis as Companion Plants, Barry Fretwell (Cassell, 1994) £15.99.

Clematis: Queen of Climbers, Jim Fisk (Cassell, 1994) £12.99, pbk, new edn.

Climbers and Wall Plants for Year Round Colour, Jane Taylor (Ward Lock, 1994) £8.99, pbk.

Collins Nature Guide to Wild Flowers, Lippart and Podlech (HarperCollins, 1994) new edn.

Colour in the Winter Garden, Graham Stuart Thomas (Weidenfeld & Nicolson, 1994) £10.99, pbk.

Colour your Garden, Mary Keen (Conran Octopus, 1994) £9.99, pbk.

The Complete Book of Garden Design, David Stevens, Lucy Huntington and Richard Key (Ward Lock, 1994) £12.99, pbk.

The Complete Book of Pruning, Coombs, Blackburne-Maze, Cracknell and Bentley (Ward Lock, 1994) £12.99, pbk.

The Container Garden Month-by-Month, Jackie Bennett (David & Charles, 1994) £14.99.

Cottage Garden, Peter Thurman (Pavilion, 1994) £5.99.

The Cottage Garden: A Practical Guide to Planning and Planting, Sue Phillips (Conran Octopus, 1994) £15.99, Royal Horticultural Society Collection.

Cottage Gardening, (Ward Lock, 1994) £5.99, Ward Lock Master Gardener series, pbk.

Country Gardening, Country Style, Peter Thompson (David & Charles, 1994) £11.99.

Country Houses from the Air, Adrian Tinniswood and Jason Hawkes (Weidenfeld & Nicolson, 1994) £19.99.

Creating Wonderful Window Boxes, Martin Baxendale (Ward Lock, 1994) £4.99, pbk.

Creative Ideas for Small Gardens, Anthony Paul (HarperCollins, 1994) £16.99.

The Creative Water Gardener, Andrew Wilson (Ward Lock, 1994) £14.99.

Cultivation of Hardy Perennials, Richard Bird (Batsford, 1994) £20.00.

Designing the Small Garden, John Patrick (Anaya Publishers, 1994) £14.99, Pleasure of Gardening series.

Dictionary of British and Irish Botanists and Horticulturists, Ray Desmond with Christine Ellwood (Taylor & Francis and The Natural History Museum, London, 1994) new edition.

This substantially revised and updated edition has already replaced its 1977 predecessor on the shelves of libraries: a good sign in itself. It makes it harder, though, to confirm the impression that the new work is not only brought up to date, but much clearer and easier to use too. With brief biographical sketches, and lists of publications and references for a diverse range of celebrated figures and the tantalisingly obscure, anyone researching in the fields of botany and horticulture will owe Ray Desmond a substantial debt. To pick just two of the book's virtues: the individuals are also listed at the back by profession, country and plant expertise; and the locations of manuscript and plant material are given where known.

The Dry Garden, Mark Rumary (Conran Octopus, 1994) £15.99.
This is part of a RHS series, so most of the book is about plants: knowing their uses, choosing and planting them. It has some useful planting plans, with elevations, and good photographs, though rather too many are taken in the Mediterranean. This will never be the definitive work on Dry Gardens, but an agreeable and inspirational bringer of hope to those who wonder how they will ever manage with a dry and difficult site.

The English Cottage Garden, Jane Taylor and Andrew Lawson (Weidenfeld & Nicolson, 1994) £14.99.

Field Guide to the Trees of Britain and North America, Andrew Cleave (Crowood Press, 1994) £10.99.

Field Guide to the Wild Flowers of Britain and North Europe, Bob Gibbons and Paul Davies (Crowood Press, 1994) £9.99

Flora's Gems: Daffodils, Pamela Todd (Little, Brown, 1994) £5.99.

The Flowering Shrub Expert, Dr D. G. Hessayon (Transworld, 1994) £4.99.
Colourful shrubs given the illustrated and factual 'Expert' treatment.

Foliage for Year Round Colour, Jane Taylor (Ward Lock, 1994) £14.99.

Fresh Flower Arranging, Wendy Gardiner (Crowood Press, 1994) £7.99.

Fresh from the Garden, Henrietta Green (Kyle Cathie, 1994) £7.99.
This is the first cookery book from the RHS for fifty years. It concentrates on the use of fresh produce, most of which could be grown in your own garden. The recipes themselves are a combination of the traditional, such as summer pudding, and newer ideas, for example pasta with roast tomatoes. The watercolour illustrations by Sally Maltby are particularly pretty.

Fuchsias: The Complete Handbook, (Cassell, 1994) £16.99.

The Garden Book, David Stevens and Ursula Buchan (Conran Octopus, 1994) £25.00.

The idea behind this book is a strong one: a leading designer and a gardening writer with firm views and lots of practical experierence have collaborated to provide a comprehensive manual and source book for gardeners who aspire to more than a patch of grass and some plink-plonk planting. Garden styles, design principles and the features which contribute to them are discussed in detail with the plants chosen and the reasons for that choice. Gardening techniques are covered in a separate section. Each author is identified throughout, both in the text and in the illustration captions highlighting the balance between design and planting. It is not a book for a quick read on a wet afternoon, but invites and repays study, whether as a source of ideas for a new garden, remaking or enlivening an existing one or just to explore the variety which can be achieved in gardening. The illustrations come from many sources: the careful selection contributes much to the usefulness of this book.

Garden Design, Sylvia Crowe (Garden Art Press, 1994) £30.00, rev 3rd edn.
Long a classic, Dame Sylvia Crowe has updated her study and added new photographs.

The Garden in Flower Month-by-Month, John Kelly (David & Charles, 1994) £14.99.

A Gardener's Guide to Bulbs, Brian Matthew and Philip Swindells (Mitchell Beazley, 1994) £19.99.
Illustrated reference book with over 750 bulbs described.

The Gardener's Guide to Growing Hardy Geraniums, Trevor Bath and Joy Jones (David & Charles, 1994) £16.99.

Gardener's World Book of Water Gardens, Sue Fisher (BBC Books, 1994) £9.99.
Presented in the form of ten practical projects, of varying difficulty and scale. The advice is clear and sensible. I was tempted by several of the designs, and when I lent my copy to a friend, it had spawned two ponds before it was returned.

Gardener's World Perfect Plants for Problem Places, Gay Search (BBC Books, 1994) £9.99.

Gardening in the Shade, Alan Toogood (Ward Lock, 1994) £6.99, pbk.

The Gardens and Villas of Tuscany, Simon Cobley and David Gallant (Weidenfeld & Nicolson, 1994) £7.99, pbk.

Geoff Hamilton's Radio Times Gardening Year, Hamilton, Geoff, and Fisher, Sue (Network Books, 1994) £15.99.
Cheerful but basic guide to month-by-month jobs in the garden.

Geraniums and Pelargoniums, Jan Taylor (Crowood Press, 1994) £9.99, Complete Guide series.

Good Gardens Guide 1995, Graham Rose and Peter King (editors) (Vermilion, 1994) £12.99.

Great Gardens – Great Designers, George Plumptre (Ward Lock, 1994) £20.00.
George Plumptre takes a selection of well known designers of the past hundred years and profiles them by examining some of their more famous work, beginning with Mawson at Graythwaite Hall and ending with Oehms and van Sweden's 1980s design for the Federal Reserve Garden. Although each essay is short, he is most at home describing gardens and their makers and the chronological succession reveals the development of garden design more clearly than the essays on garden history and design which begin and end the book.

The Greenhouse Expert, Dr D. G. Hessayon (Transworld, 1994) £4.99.
The turn of Greenhouses in this record-breaking series of no-nonsense books.

Growing Carnations and Pinks, Fred C. Smith (Ward Lock, 1994) £8.99, pbk.

Growing Clematis, Dr John Howells (Ward Lock, 1994) £8.99, pbk.

Growing Fuchsias, Ron Ewart (Ward Lock, 1994) £8.99, pbk.

A Handbook for Garden Designers, Rosemary Alexander and Karena Batstone (Ward Lock, 1994) £18.99.
Practical guide to producing plans and graphics.

Hanging Baskets, Ray Waite (Cassell and the Royal Horticultural Society, 1994) £3.95, Wisley Handbook, pbk.

Hardy Euphorbias, Roger Turner (Batsford, 1994) £17.99.

Hardy Geraniums, David Hibberd (Cassell and the Royal Horticultural Society, 1994) £3.95, Wisley Handbook, pbk.

The Herb Garden Month-by-Month, Barbara Segall (David & Charles, 1994) £14.99.

Herb Gardens, (Ward Lock, 1994) £5.99, Ward Lock Master Gardener series, pbk.

The Hillier Book of Garden Planning, Keith Rushforth, Roderick Griffin and Dennis Woodland (David & Charles, 1994) £17.99, new edn.

Hillier Guide to Connoisseur's Plants, Alan Toogood (David & Charles, 1994) £14.99, pbk.

The History of Gardens in Britain and Ireland, Christopher Thacker (Weidenfeld & Nicolson, 1994) £19.99.

History of the English Herb Garden, Kay Sanecki (Ward Lock, 1994) £9.99, pbk.
Paperback edition of this stimulating history.

Hostas, Sandra Bond (Ward Lock, 1994) £7.99, Foliage Plants in Garden Design series, pbk.

How to be a Supergardener, Alan Titchmarsh (Ward Lock, 1994) £9.99, pbk.

Books, Periodicals & Videos 487

How to Grow Natural Herbs and Spices for Culinary Uses, Charlotte de la Bédoyère (Search Press, 1994) £4.99.
A practical paperback guide to growing herbs and spices organically.

The Impressionist Garden, Derek Fell (Frances Lincoln, 1994).
By the author of *Renoir's Garden*, this book juxtaposes Impressionist colour theories and their gardens. As well as explaining the relationships between these two arts, the book includes planting plans which allow readers to recreate and reinterpret the Impressionist style for themselves.

In the Japanese Garden, Elizabeth Bibb and Michael Yamashita (Cassell, 1994) £10.99, pbk.

Index of Garden Plants, Mark Griffiths (Macmillan, 1994) £35.00
This magnificent handbook was spun off *The New RHS Dictionary of Gardening* and should be bought by everyone who reads *The Plant Finder*, buys the Yellow Book or is just interested in putting the right name to the right plant. It is not a substitute for the RHS Dictionary, more of a distillation, and will remain the standard work (give or take a few updates and reprints) for 100 years to come. *The Index of Garden Plants* offers an accurate description of some 60,000 plants now in cultivation: invaluable for identifying and distinguishing them. Moreover, it displays the phenomenonal erudition and industry of its young editor in every line of its 1,000 pages. No new book has impressed us more this year. Buy it.

International Book of Trees, Hugh Johnson (Mitchell Beazley, 1994) £19.99.

Ivies, Hazel Key (Cassell and the Royal Horticultural Society, 1994) £3.95, Wisley Handbook, pbk.

Japanese Style Gardens, Maggie Oster (Cassell, 1994) £16.99.

Jekka's Complete Herb Book, Jekka McVicar (Kyle Cathie, 1994) £20.00.
Jekka McVicar knows her herbs, and can communicate her enthusiasm for growing and using them. The book has clear instructions for growing and harvesting herbs, and details of their culinary, medicinal and other uses, including, where necessary, warnings against misuse. She describes the various ways of propagating herbs, how to plan a herb garden and gives designs for several types. It is good to see her emphasize that it is essential for a cook's herb garden to have easy access from the kitchen.

Kew: A World of Plants, Heather Angel (Collins & Brown, 1994) £12.99.
A packager's dream – the story of Kew with photographs by Heather Angel. But it does not really work, because the two do not gel together. Heather Angel's photographs are brilliant: the text is mundane. And there are too many taxonomic errors and botanical mistakes for a respectable outfit like RBG Kew.

Lakeland Gardens, Richard Bird (Ward Lock, 1994) £16.99.
Detailed guide to 30 gardens which can be visited in the Lake District.

Landscape Design for Elderly and Disabled People, Jane Stoneham and Peter Thoday (Packard Publishing, 1994) £25.00.
Distributed by the Antique Collectors' Club.

Magic Muck, Lady Muck (Pavilion, 1994) £9.99.
Lively account of the history, theory and practicalities of compost making.

Magnolias, Dorothy J. Calloway (Batsford, 1994) £35.00.
This excellent study is undoubtedly one of the most important books of its kind to be published last year, and is written by the leading American authority on the genus. Begun as a taxonomic thesis, it is particularly sound on the provenance and introduction of species into cultivation. All known forms, hybrids and varieties are clearly and fully described. This will remain the leading work on the genus for many years – though periodic updates will be needed to take account of new hybridisation in this fast-developing amenity favourite. The bibliography and source references are exceptionally comprehensive, but do not interrupt the text. Written in American English, but strongly recommended.

More Front Gardens, Gay Search (BBC Books, 1994) £14.99.
Six garden designers tackle problem front gardens. The book accompanied the second BBC TV series looking at more front garden difficulties and revisited the earlier gardens. Planting plans and descriptions of the plants used are included to provide a useful source of ideas if you cannot think what to do at the front of the house.

Orchid Growing Basics, Dr Gustav Schoser (Sterling, 1994) £9.99.

Orchids, Peter Arnold (Cassell, 1994) £20.00.

Ornamental Grasses, Bamboos, Rushes and Sedges, Nigel Taylor (Ward Lock, 1994) £7.99, Foliage Plants in Garden Design series, pbk.

The Outdoor Room: Garden Design for Living, David Stevens (Frances Lincoln, 1994).
An attempt to demystify the garden design process by one of the country's most successful garden designers. Planned as 'rooms', or a series of rooms, David Stevens's emphasis is on creating useable spaces. Published in spring.

Palms and Cycads of the World, (Cassell, 1994) £20.00.

The Art of Pebble Mosaics, Maggy Howarth (Search Press, 1994) £10.95.
Enthusiastic and inspirational introduction to the art or craft of making pebble pavements, from the utilitarian

488 Books, Periodicals & Videos

to the most sophisticated modern designs. Photographs from all over the world give a historic overview and there are practical chapters on design, drawing, construction and precasting. The author convinces even the dullest of readers that pebble mosaics are something he will enjoy doing and will do well. Maggy Howarth's own designs are distinctive and show how flexibly the art form can develop in the hands of a gifted modern practitioner.

Penelope Hobhouse on Gardening, Penelope Hobhouse (Frances Lincoln, 1994).
Penelope Hobhouse expounds her gardening philosophy through a charmingly affectionate memoir of her years at Tintinhull. The garden is portrayed in great detail with planting plans and fine photographs by Andrew Lawson, with digressions to discuss favourite plants or gardening techniques. She pays generous tribute to Phyllis Reiss, who laid out the garden over fifty years ago, and plays down her own skills in subtly adapting and continuing the combination of design and planting which make Tintinhull such a satisfying garden to visit.

Planting the Country Way, John Brookes (BBC Books, 1994) £18.99.
John Brookes is attracted by the German trend towards environmental gardening and explores ways of doing this in England. Habitat gardening does not always combine easily with the British tradition of smallish private gardens and this has produced certain inconsistencies in the book.

Practical Bedding Plants, Ian Murray (Crowood Press, 1994) £3.99, Practical Gardening series, pbk.

Practical Pelargonium Growing, Jan Taylor (Crowood Press, 1994) £3.99, Practical Gardening series, pbk.
This compact series provides a good starting point for beginners.

Practical Indoor Gardening, Yvonne Rees (Crowood Press, 1994) £3.99, Practical Gardening series, pbk.

Practical Water Gardening, Yvonne Rees (Crowood Press, 1994) £3.99, Practical Gardening series, pbk.

Practical Wildflower Gardening, Yvonne Rees (Crowood Press, 1994) £3.99, Practical Gardening series, pbk.

Primulas, Mary Robinson (Crowood Press, 1994) £10.99, Complete Guide series.

Pruning and Training Plants, David Joyce (Mitchell Beazley, 1994) £19.99.

Quick & Easy Garden Design Projects, Faith & Geoffrey Whiten (BBC Books, 1994) £14.99.
Middlebrow introduction to garden decoration by two acclaimed modern masters. Rather an unsatisfactory mix of theory and practicalities: much of their success depends on defining their own parameters and telling us how clever they are.

The RHS Gardeners' Encyclopedia of Plants and Flowers, Christopher Brickell Editor in Chief (Dorling Kindersley, 1994) £29.95, Revised edition.
Revised and updated edition with more photographs.

Rock Gardens, (Ward Lock, 1994) £5.99, Ward Lock Master Gardener series, pbk.

Rockeries & Alpine Gardens, Mary Moody (Anaya Publishers, 1994) £14.99, Pleasure of Gardening series.

Sissinghurst, Jane Brown (Weidenfeld & Nicolson, 1994) £9.99, pbk.

Small Gardens with Style, Jill Billington (Ward Lock, 1994) £14.99.
Another designer's guide to garden improvement, with some inspiring before-and-after photographs. Jill Billington has a good eye for geometry and uses space well.

The Stream Garden, David Arscott & Archie Skinner (Ward Lock, 1994) £14.99.

Successful Small Gardens, Roy Strong (Conran Octopus, 1994) £17.99.
Not another book from Roy Strong on Small Gardens? Yes, and thank goodness, because there is no-one so endlessly inventive, or who writes so well and so authoritatively. Roy Strong uses plans and photographs to help his analysis of twenty very different gardens – how they are made, why they are successful, and what commitment they require. It is subtitled 'New Designs for Time-Conscious Gardeners': the message is that good planning, planting and design give best value for time spent on future maintenance. Quite the best of the crop of new books on the subject, and the only one that promises to be a classic.

Succulents: The Illustrated Dictionary, Maurizio Sajeva and Mariangela Constanzo (Cassell, 1994) £30.00.
A substantial companion volume to *Cacti*: 1200 species, all illustrated in colour.

Traditional Gardens, Graham Rose (Dorling Kindersley, 1994) £12.99, pbk.

Using Foliage Plants in the Garden, Jill Billington (Ward Lock, 1994) £8.99, pbk

Variegated Plants, Susan Conder and Andrew Lawson (Cassell, 1994) £25.00.

The Water Garden, Peter Robinson (Conran Octopus, 1994) £15.99.
Fancy a water feature in your garden? Here's how to plan, make, plant and maintain ponds, streams, bogs and lakes. There is nothing about how to integrate it into the rest of your garden: water as a fashion accessory. But the photographs are excellent and, bearing the RHS seal of approval, the book has lots about suitable plants.

Water Garden Plants, David Case (Crowood Press, 1994) £9.99, Complete Guide series.

Water Gardens, (Ward Lock, 1994) £5.99, Ward Lock Master Gardener series, pbk

Waterside Planting, Philip Swindells (Ward Lock, 1994) £8.99, pbk.

Books, Periodicals & Videos

Weed Control in the Garden, Richard Chancellor (Cassell and the Royal Horticultural Society, 1994) £3.95, Wisley Handbook, pbk.

The Well-Planned Garden: A Practical Guide to Planning and Planting, Rupert Golby (Conran Octopus, 1994) £15.99, Royal Horticultural Society Collection.

The Wild Flower Garden: A Practical Guide to Planning and Planting, Noel Kingsbury (Conran Octopus, 1994) £15.99, Royal Horticultural Society Collection. This book outlines the use of wild flowers in conventional and in wild gardens.

Wildlife Garden: Peter Thurman (Pavilion, 1994) £5.99.

New Books 1995

1995 Gardener's Guide to Britain, Patrick Taylor (Pavilion, 1995) £10.99, pbk.

A Landscape Handbook for the Tropics, William Frank Hill (Garden Art Press, 1995) £39.50.

A Medieval Flower Garden, (Pavilion, 1995) £4.99.

A Medieval Herbal Garden, (Pavilion, 1995) £4.99.

The Art of Gardening, Rosemary Verey (Frances Lincoln, 1995) Autumn. A distillation of Rosemary Verey's gardening philosophy and theory combined with practical techniques.

Auriculas, Gwen Baker and Peter Ward (Batsford, 1995) £17.99.

Beds and Borders for Year Round Colour, Jill Cowley (Ward Lock, 1995) £14.99.

Bonsai, Joe Davies (Batsford, 1995).

Bonsai from Native Trees and Shrubs, werner Busch (David & Charles, 1995) £14.99.

The Book of Rhododendrons, Marianne Kneller (David & Charles, 1995) £25.00.

Bulbs and their Garden Uses, Brian Mathew (Batsford, 1995) £25.00.

Bulbs for the Rock Garden, Jack Elliott (Batsford, 1995) £17.99.

Bulbs of the Levant, Ori Fragman (Batsford, 1995) £40.00.

Christopher Brickell's Garden Plants, Christopher Brickell (Pavilion, 1995) £20.00, February. A personal selection of exceptional garden plants discussed in detail.

Chrysanthemums, Baden Locke (Crowood Press, 1995) £9.99, Complete Guide Series.

The Complete Book of Alpine Gardening, Richard Bird & John Kelly (Ward Lock, 1995) £12.99.

The Complete Book of Companion Gardening, Bob Flowerdew (Kyle Cathie, 1995) £9.99, pbk.

The Complete Book of Conservatory Plants, William Davidson & Jane Bland (Ward Lock, 1995) £12.99.

The Complete Book of Hardy Perennials, Richard Bird (Ward Lock, 1995) £12.99.

The Complete Book of Patio and Container Gardening, Robin Williams, Mary-Jane Hopes, Robin Templar Williams (Ward Lock, 1995) £12.99, pbk.

The Complete Book of Roses, John Mattock, Sean McCann, Fred Witchell, Peter Wood (Ward Lock, 1995) £12.99, pbk.

The Confident Gardener, Bryan Davies (Viking, 1995) £9.99.

Container Gardening Through the Year, Malcolm Hillier (Dorling Kindersley, 1995) £12.99.

Cushion Plants for the Rock Garden, Duncan Lowe (Batsford, 1995) £17.99.

Dahlias, Philip Damp (Crowood Press, 1995) £9.99, Complete Guide Series.

Delphiniums, Colin Edwards (Crowood Press, 1995) £9.99, Complete Guide Series.

Easy Gardening Month by Month, Michael Jefferson Brown (David & Charles, 1995) £14.99.

The English Garden Abroad, Charles Quest-Ritson (Viking, 1995) £14.99, pbk.

Euphorbias, Roger Turner (Batsford, 1995) £30.00.

First Time Gardener, Pattie Barron (Conran Octopus, 1995) £14.99.

The Flower Arranger's Garden Month by Month, Leila Aitken (David & Charles, 1995) £14.99.

The Fruit Book, Bob Flowerdew (Kyle Cathie, 1995) £20.00.

Fuchsias and Their Cultivation, Edwin Goulding (Batsford, 1995) £30.00.

Garden Craftsmanship in Yew and Box, Nathaniel Lloyd (Garden Art Press, 1995) £19.95. Reprint of this classic with new colour plates and an introduction by Christopher Lloyd, the author's son.

The Garden Designer, Robin Williams (Frances Lincoln, 1995).

A Garden Designer's Source Book, David Stevens (Conran Octopus, 1995) £20.00.

The Gardener's ABC, John Kelly (Ward Lock, 1995) £7.99. Botanical terms, gardening jargon and Latin terms explained.

The Gardener's Book of Colour, Andrew Lawson (Frances Lincoln, 1995).

The Gardener's Guide to Growing Lilies, Michael Jefferson Brown and Harris Howland (David & Charles, 1995) £16.99.

Gardeners Dictionary of Horticultural Terms, Harold Bagust (Cassell, 1995) £12.99.

Gardening at Sissinghurst, Tony Lord (Frances Lincoln, 1995).

An analysis and examination of the Sissinghurst mystique.

Gardening Made Easy, Jane Fearnley-Whittingstall (Weidenfeld & Nicholson, 1995) £19.99.
Single volume gardening manual written by a well known designer, with informative sections on making or remaking a garden, looking after your garden, and becoming a specialist.

Gardening with Roses, Patrick Taylor (Pavilion, 1995) £9.99, pbk.

Geoffrey Jellicoe: The Studies of a Landscape Designer over 80 Years, Geoffrey Jellicoe (Garden Art Press, 1995) £35.00.
The second volume of this four part series reprints Gardens and Design (1927, with J. C. Shepherd) and three lectures given to the Royal Institute of British Architects in 1936, Gardens of Europe.

Giverny, Behind the Scenes and Through the Seasons, Vivian Russell (Frances Lincoln, 1995).

Great Planting, Lucy Gent (Ward Lock, 1995) £20.00.

Hardy Perennials, Graham Rice (Viking, 1995) £16.00.

Herb Garden Design, Ethne Clarke (Frances Lincoln, 1995).

How to Grow and Use Herbs, Ann Bonar & Daphne MacCarthy (Ward Lock, 1995) £6.99.

Hydrangeas, a Gardener's Guide, Brian Rothera and Toni Lawson-Hall (Batsford, 1995) £25.00.

The Ideal Home Plant Guide, David Joyce (Conran Octopus, 1995) £15.99.

The Illustrated Dictionary of Alpines, Clive Innes (Cassell, 1995) £30.00.

The Kitchen Garden, Andi Clevely (Conran Octopus, 1995) £15.99, RHS Collection.

The National Trust Book of Gardening, Penelope Hobhouse (Pavilion, 1995) £12.99, Pbk revised.
Revised edition in field guide format.

New Cottage Gardener, Geoff Hamilton (BBC Books, 1995) £18.99.

The New Gardener, Pippa Greenwood (Dorling Kindersley, 1995) £14.99.

A Plantsman in Nepal, Roy Lancaster (Antique Collectors' Club, 1995) £35.00, spring.
Revised and updated edition of this account of a modern plant-hunting expedition.

Potted Histories, Paul Simons and John Ruthven (BBC Books, 1995) £9.99.

Practical Bulb Growing, Brian Leverett (Crowood Press, 1995) £3.99, Practical Gardening Series.

Practical Garden Features, Yvonne Rees (Crowood Press, 1995) £3.99, Practical Gardening Series.

Practical Small Gardening, Ian Murray (Crowood Press, 1995) £3.99, Practical Gardening Series.

The RHS Manual of Bulbs, John Bryan (Editor Mark Griffiths) (Macmillan, 1995) £40.00.

The RHS Manual of Orchids, Joyce Stewart (Editor Mark Griffiths) (Macmillan, 1995) £45.00.

The Small Ecological Garden, Sue Stickland (Search Press, 1995).

The Small Garden, Julie Toll (Conran Octopus, 1995) £15.99, RHS Collection.

Truly Tiny Gardens, Thomasina Tarling (Conran Octopus, 1995) £10.99.

The Ultimate Garden Designer, Tim Newbury (Ward Lock, 1995) £20.00.

Vegetables, Roger Phillips and Martyn Rix (Pan Macmillan, 1995) £13.99, pbk.

The Ward Lock Encyclopedia of Gardening, Anita Pereire (Ward Lock, 1995) September.
A practical gardening guide and an illustrated plant directory combined in one volume, written by a well known landscape gardener.

Newspapers, magazines & journals

Amateur Gardening
Westover House, West Quay Road, Poole, Dorset BH15 1JG
☎ 01202 680586   FAX 01202 674335
CONTACT   Janet Salisbury
OWNER   IPC Magazines Ltd
PRICE   77p
FREQUENCY   Weekly
EDITORS/CORRESPONDENTS   Graham Clarke (editor), Stefan Buczacki, Fred Downham, Peter Seabrook, John Kelly
Long running weekly magazine with a distinguished roll call of contributors. Packed with seasonal information and brisk advice for active gardeners.

BBC Gardeners' World
101 Bayham Street, London NW1 0AG
☎ 0171 331 8000
OWNER   Redwood Publishing Ltd
PRICE   £1.70, £20.40 pa
FREQUENCY   Monthly
EDITORS/CORRESPONDENTS   Adam Pascoe (Editor), Kathryn Bradley-Hole (Features)
Good-looking, lavishly illustrated mid-market magazine with a wide readership. The main contributors are the current gardening presenters from BBC radio and television. Subscribers receive a privilege card entitling them to discounts on selected purchases.

Country Garden
Burlton House, Station Road, Newport, Saffron Walden, Essex CB11 3PL
☎ 01799 540927   FAX 01799 541367

Books, Periodicals & Videos   491

OWNER   Broad Leys Publishing Company
PRICE   £1.25; £19.75 pa
FREQUENCY   Monthly
EDITORS/CORRESPONDENTS   Helen Sears (Editor)
Country Garden started as a magazine called Home Farm, for many years the leading publication for small holders and organic gardeners. It was reborn in 1994 as Country Garden and concentrates on environmentally friendly gardening, keeping pets, poultry and animals, practical home interests like crafts and cooking and reports on country shows and fairs.

Country Homes and Interiors
King's Reach Tower, Stamford Street, London SE1 9LS
☎ 0171 261 6433   FAX 0171 261 6895
CONTACT   Editor
OWNER   SouthBank Publishing Ltd/IPC Magazines Ltd
PRICE   £2 (£24 pa)
FREQUENCY   Monthly
There are commissioned articles on gardening topics in this country lifestyle magazine.

Country Life
King's Reach Tower, Stamford Street, London SE1 9LS
☎ 0171 261 7058   FAX 0171 261 5139
OWNER   IPC Magazines Ltd
PRICE   £1.80
FREQUENCY   Weekly
EDITORS/CORRESPONDENTS   Clive Aslet (Editor), Tony Venison (Gardening consultant), Christopher Lloyd, Continues to publish the classic articles on gardens and plants which have made it a journal of record. The photography is excellent. The twin columnists are Christopher Lloyd and Tony Venison: both have a following — Lloyd's column is stylishly written and digressive, Venison's more practical.

Country Living
National Magazine House, 72 Broadwick Street, London W1V 2BP
☎ 0171 439 5000   FAX 0171 439 5093
OWNER   National Magazine Co Ltd
PRICE   £2.00 (£24 pa)
FREQUENCY   Monthly
EDITORS/CORRESPONDENTS   Francine Lawrence (Editor), Miranda Innes (Gardens editor)
Influential magazine for country and would-be country dwellers. Bright tone and a good mix of photographs and writing.

The Daily Telegraph
1 Canada Square, Canary Wharf, London E14 5DT
☎ 0171 538 5000   FAX 0171 538 6242
OWNER   The Telegraph plc
FREQUENCY   Daily
EDITORS/CORRESPONDENTS   Charles Clover (Environment), Fred Whitsey,
A strong gardening team writes for the Telegraph on Saturdays, including Fred Whitsey, Margot Bishop, Adrian Lighter, Kathryn Bradley-Hole and Stephen Lacey. Its varied and topical articles make good reading.

Financial Times
1 Southwark Bridge, London SE1 9HL
☎ 0171 873 3000   FAX 0171 873 3076
OWNER   Pearson plc
FREQUENCY   Daily
EDITORS/CORRESPONDENTS   Robin Lane-Fox (Gardening correspondent),
Robin Lane Fox's stylishly idiosyncratic column appears in the Weekend section of the Saturday FT.

Flora
The Fishing Lodge Studio, 77 Balbridge Road, Wilton, Wiltshire
☎ 01722 743207
CONTACT   Wilton (General Enquiries)
OWNER   Maureen Foster
PRICE   £1.95 (£14.50 pa)
FREQUENCY   6 issues a year
EDITORS/CORRESPONDENTS   R. Bennet (Editor)
Bi-monthly magazine for flower arrangers and florists. The editorial office is in Kent.

The Garden
Apex House, Oundle Road, Peterborough PE2 9NP
☎ 01733 898100   FAX 01733 890657
OWNER   EMAP Apex Publications for the RHS
PRICE   £2.50 (free to RHS members)
FREQUENCY   Monthly
EDITORS/CORRESPONDENTS   Ian Hodgson (Editor), Tradescant (Hugh Johnson), Roy Lancaster, Brent Elliott, Alan Leslie
The Journal of the Royal Horticultural Society. Indispensable journal both for new articles and the repository of information laid up in its back numbers. Currently on the up, with a varied mixture of serious but not solemn articles on plants, gardens and horticultural topics. It also contains extensive up to date news of RHS events.

Garden Answers
Apex House, Oundle Road, Peterborough PE2 9NP
☎ 01733 898100   FAX 01733 898433
CONTACT   Managing editor
OWNER   EMAP Apex Publications
PRICE   £1.65 (£19.80 pa)
FREQUENCY   Monthly
EDITORS/CORRESPONDENTS   Adrienne Wild (Editor)
Illustrated monthly magazine with practical information for keen gardeners.

Garden News
Apex House, Oundle Road, Peterborough, Cambridgeshire PE2 9NP
☎ 01733 898100   FAX 01733 898433
OWNER EMAP Apex Publications Ltd
PRICE 70p (£58.56 pa)
FREQUENCY Weekly
EDITORS/CORRESPONDENTS Andrew Blackford (Editor), Geoff Hodge (Gardening editor),
Weekly colour tabloid to read in the potting shed. Many readers are allotment holders and hobbyists. No-nonsense hands-on approach, with good product and club coverage.

The Gardener
Westover House, West Quay Road, Poole, Dorset BH15 1JG
☎ 01202 687418   FAX 01202 674335
CONTACT Janet Salisbury
OWNER IPC Magzines Ltd
PRICE £1.60
FREQUENCY Monthly
EDITORS/CORRESPONDENTS Graham Clarke (Group editor), David Hurrion (Associate editor)
Monthly magazine which has been revamped since joining the *Amateur Gardening* stable. Well illustrated, good for plants and flowers and aimed at relatively serious gardeners with some experience.

Gardening Which?
2 Castlemead, Gascoyne Way, Hertford X SG14 1LH
☎ 01992 587773
OWNER Consumer's Association
PRICE £47 pa
FREQUENCY 10 issues a year
EDITORS/CORRESPONDENTS Alistair Ayres (Editor)
Consumer led magazine which applies the characteristic *Which?* approach to plants and garden matters. The number above is for subscriptions. Stimulating, opinionated and not as authoritative as you might suppose.

Gardens Illustrated
The Boathouse, Crabtree Lane, London SW6 6LU
☎ 0171 381 6007   FAX 0171 381 3930
CONTACT Editor
OWNER John Brown Publishing Ltd
PRICE £2.95
FREQUENCY 6 issues a year
EDITORS/CORRESPONDENTS Rosie Atkins (Editor), Penelope Hobhouse (Associate editor), Anna Pavord (Associate editor), Patrick Taylor
Bi-monthly magazine with glossy bite-sized articles for smart gardeners. It is set apart by its international coverage, distinguished writing and stylish photography.

The Grower
Warwick House, Swanley, Kent BR8 8HY
☎ 01322 660270   FAX 01322 667633
CONTACT Editor
OWNER Nexus Business Communications Ltd
PRICE £1.05 (£47.50 pa)
FREQUENCY Weekly
EDITORS/CORRESPONDENTS Peter Rogers (Editor)
Trade magazine for those involved in commercial horticulture.

The Guardian
119 Farringdon Road, London EC1R 3ER
☎ 0171 278 2332   FAX 0171 837 2114
OWNER Guardian Newspapers Ltd
FREQUENCY Daily
EDITORS/CORRESPONDENTS Hilary Applegate ('Growbag' column)
Good environmental coverage and regular gardening articles by contributors in the Saturday magazine.

Homes and Gardens
King's Reach Tower, Stamford Street, London SE1 9LS
☎ 0171 261 5000   FAX 0171 261 6247
OWNER IPC Magazines Ltd/ Reed Publishing
PRICE £1.95
FREQUENCY Monthly
EDITORS/CORRESPONDENTS Amanda Evans (Editor), A.M. Cleveley (Gardening correspondent)
Reliable monthly magazine with round-ups of garden news items and features on gardens every month.

Horticulture Week
38 – 42 Hampton Road, Teddington, London TW11 0JE
☎ 0181 943 5000   FAX 0181 943 5673
CONTACT Editor
OWNER Haymarket Magazines Ltd
PRICE £55 pa
FREQUENCY Weekly
EDITORS/CORRESPONDENTS Stovin Hayter (Editor)
Informative weekly business news magazine for anyone who works in commercial and ornamental horticulture.

Hortus
Bryan's Ground, Stapleton, Hereford & Worcester LD8 2LP
☎ 01544 260001   FAX 01544 260015
CONTACT Editor
OWNER David Wheeler
PRICE £30 pa
FREQUENCY Quarterly
EDITORS/CORRESPONDENTS David Wheeler (Editor)
Quarterly journal for thinking gardeners, concentrating on the literary and artistic aspects rather than the practical. The tone is gently scholarly; illustrated with original engravings.

House and Garden
Vogue House, Hanover Square, London WR1 0AD
☎ 0171 499 9080   FAX 0171 493 1345
OWNER Conde Nast Publications Ltd
PRICE £2.30

Books, Periodicals & Videos 493

FREQUENCY Monthly
EDITORS/CORRESPONDENTS Susan Crewe (Editor), Tania Compton (Contributing Editor)
This upmarket glossy magazine has a regular column by Tania Compton, and usually profiles a country house garden among other gardening features.

The Independent
40 City Road, London EC1Y 2DB
☎ 0171 253 1222   FAX 0171 956 1435
OWNER Newspaper Publishing plc
FREQUENCY Daily
EDITORS/CORRESPONDENTS Anna Pavord (Gardening correspondent)
Anna Pavord's well-written Saturday column is frequently the best of the crop. Chosen topics extend beyond the obvious.

The Independent on Sunday
40 City Road, London EC1Y 2DB
☎ 0171 253 1222   FAX 0171 415 1333
OWNER Newspaper Publishing plc
FREQUENCY Weekly
EDITORS/CORRESPONDENTS Mary Keene, Michael Leapman
Interesting though somewhat offbeat gardening articles appear in the Review section.

N & GC
147 – 151 Temple Chambers, Temple Avenue, London EC4 0BP
☎ 0171 583 3030   FAX 0171 583 4068
CONTACT Editorial
OWNER Bouverie Publishing Co Ltd
PRICE £44 pa
FREQUENCY Fortnightly
EDITORS/CORRESPONDENTS Peter Dawson (Editor)
Nurseryman & Garden Centre is the official magazine of the Horticultural Trades Association. Contains industry news and features on plants, people and products for retailers.

The New Plantsman
RHS Subscription Service, P O Box 38, Ashford, Kent TN25 6PR
OWNER Royal Horticultural Society
PRICE £25 pa
FREQUENCY Quarterly
EDITORS/CORRESPONDENTS Christopher Brickell (Editorial consultant), Victoria Matthews (Editor)
The relaunched specialist magazine from the RHS for botanists and keen gardeners. Upmarket articles by expert contributors are set off by colour photographs and botanical illustrations.

The Observer
119 Farringdon Road, London EC1R 3ER
☎ 0171 278 2332
OWNER Guardian Newspapers Ltd
FREQUENCY Weekly

EDITORS/CORRESPONDENTS John Course (Gardening editor),
There is a regular gardening column written by several different writers.

Organic Gardening
P O Box 4, Wiveliscombe, Taunton, Somerset TA4 2QY
☎ 01984 623998   FAX 01984 623998
CONTACT Editor
OWNER Organic Garden (Wardnest Ltd)
PRICE £1.85 (£22.20 pa)
FREQUENCY Monthly
EDITORS/CORRESPONDENTS Basil Kaplan (Editor)
The organic gardening magazine. Covers the whole range of organic approaches, and includes both ornamental and fruit and vegetable gardening.

Pacific Horticulture
P O Box 485, Berkeley, CA 94701, USA
PRICE $20
FREQUENCY Quarterly
The best of the American gardening magazines: well worth subscribing to.

Period House and Its Garden
7 ST John's Road, Harrow, London HA1 2EE
☎ 0181 863 2020
CONTACT Editorial Department
OWNER DMG Home Interest Magazines Ltd
PRICE £2.20 (£24 pa)
FREQUENCY Monthly
EDITORS/CORRESPONDENTS Richard Parker (Editor), Laura Goodhart (Assistant Editor)
Colour monthly for people who live in older houses. Gardening coverage consists of news items and case studies of restorations.

Period Living and Traditional Homes
Victory House, 14 Leicester Place, London WC2H 7BP
☎ 0171 437 9011   FAX 0171 434 0656
CONTACT Editorial department
OWNER EMAP Elan Publications
PRICE £2.30
FREQUENCY Monthly
EDITORS/CORRESPONDENTS Clare Weatherall (Editor), Dominique Coughlin (Features Editor)
Lifestyle monthly magazine with articles for people who want to make appropriate gardens for a period house, or to create a garden in a period style.

Practical Gardening
Apex House, Oundle Road, Peterborough, Cambridgeshire PE2 9NP
☎ 01733 898100   FAX 01733 898433
CONTACT Editor
OWNER EMAP Apex Publications
PRICE £2 (£24 pa)
FREQUENCY Monthly
EDITORS/CORRESPONDENTS Susie Johns (Editor),

Good-looking monthly magazine with strong photography and some informative special supplements.

The Scotsman
20 North Bridge, Edinburgh EH1 1YT
☎ 0131 225 2468 FAX 0131 226 7420
CONTACT David Robinson (Weekend section)
OWNER Scotsman Publications Ltd
FREQUENCY Daily
EDITORS/CORRESPONDENTS David Robinson (Editor, weekend section), Dr David Stuart (Columnist)
Dr David Stuart contributes a weekly column every Saturday.

The Spectator
56 Doughty Street, London WC1N 2LL
☎ 0171 405 1706 FAX 0171 242 0603
OWNER The Spectator (1828) Ltd
PRICE £1.80
FREQUENCY Weekly
EDITORS/CORRESPONDENTS Ursula Buchan (Gardening columnist)
Ursula Buchan writes the more-or-less monthly gardening column in this forthright weekly magazine. Her amusing and intelligent essays should not be missed: an anthology is long overdue.

The Sunday Telegraph
1 Canada Square, Canary Wharf, London E14 5DT
☎ 0171 538 5000 FAX 0171 513 2504
OWNER The Sunday Telegraph plc
FREQUENCY Weekly
EDITORS/CORRESPONDENTS Charles Moore (Editor), Ursula Buchan,
Like its daily sister paper the *Sunday Telegraph* has extensive and interesting coverage. The best of the Sunday papers for gardening interest.

The Sunday Times
1 Pennington Street, London E1 9XW
☎ 0171 782 5000 FAX 0171 782 5658
OWNER News International
FREQUENCY Weekly
EDITORS/CORRESPONDENTS Graham Rose, Dan Pearson
Graham Rose has been joined by Dan Pearson to write the regular columns on gardeners and gardens, but the overall space given to gardens is still disproportionately small.

The Times
1 Pennington Street, London E1 9XN
☎ 0171 782 5000 FAX 0171 488 3242
OWNER News International
FREQUENCY Daily
EDITORS/CORRESPONDENTS George Plumptre, Stephen Anderton

Saturday's articles are practical and informative. There is also a valuable show report on the Wednesday of the regular RHS shows.

The Water Gardener
9 Tufton Street, Ashford, Kent TN23 1QN
☎ 01233 621877 FAX 01233 645669
CONTACT The Editor
OWNER Dog World Publications
PRICE £1.75
FREQUENCY 6 issues a year
EDITORS/CORRESPONDENTS David Papworth (Editor)
New magazine dealing with all aspects of water gardening.

Your Garden
Westover House, West Quay Road, Poole, Dorset BH15 1JG
☎ 01202 680603 FAX 01202 674335
CONTACT Janet Salisbury
OWNER IPC Magazines Ltd
PRICE £1.60
FREQUENCY Monthly
EDITORS/CORRESPONDENTS Graham Clarke (Editor),
New glossy monthly with an enthusiastic approach to medium and small gardens: likely to appeal to new gardeners.

Videos

Brilliant Gardens, £12.95.

A Celebration Of Old Roses, Peter Beales (Vivian Russell Inc Ltd) £12.99 (01787 77307).

Chelsea '94, Alan Titchmarsh (Royal Horticultural Society) £12.99 (01483 211320).

The Complete Guide, (Oscroft's Dahlias) £15.00 (01564 782450) Price includes packing and postage.

Dahlias of Today, (Oscroft's Dahlias) £15.00 (01564 782450) Price includes packing and postage.

The Diary of the Dahlia, (Oscroft's Dahlias) £12.00 (01564 782450) Price includes packing and postage.

Garden Heritage, Roy Lancaster, Geoff Hamilton and John Kelly £13.99.

Gardening under Lights, (GroWell Hydroponics and Plant Lighting Ltd) £15.00 (01675 443950).

Gardens of England and Wales, (Seer TV) £12.99 (01222 751159).

Gardens of England and Wales: Gardeners' Views, (Seer TV) £12.99 (01222 751159).

Gardens of England and Wales: The Tour Continues, (Seer TV) £12.99 (01222 751159).

Growing Leeks with the Experts, (National Pot Leek Society) £21.00 (0191 5494274), price includes packing and postage.

Guide to African Violets, Tony Clements and Anne Swithinbank £14.99.

Books, Periodicals & Videos 495

Guide to Clematis, Steven Bradley £14.99.

Guide to Dried Flowers, Malcolm Hillier £12.99.

Guide to Fuchsias, David Clark, Helen Biddlecombe and Harry Smith (Periwinkle Productions) £14.99 (01489 885645).

Guide to Hanging Baskets, Harry Smith and Helen Biddlecombe (Periwinkle Productions) £14.99 (01489 885645).

Guide to Pelargoniums, Anne Swithinbank, Harry Smith and David Clark (Periwinkle Productions) £14.99 (01489 8856445).

Hydroponic Gardening (GroWell Hydroponics and Plant Lighting Ltd) £12.50 (01675 443950).

The Masters Choice, (Oscroft's Dahlias) £15.00 (01564 782450) Price includes packing and postage.

My World of Dahlias, (Oscroft's Dahlias) £12.00 (01564 782450) Price includes packing and postage.

Secret Gardens, Alan Titchmarsh £12.95.

Training a Standard Fuchsia Vol 1, Pam Hutchinson £19.99.

Treasure Gardens, Alan Titchmarsh £12.95.

Treasure of the Trust, Robert Hardy £13.95.

Wisley through the Seasons: Autumn, (Royal Horticultural Society) £12.99 (01483 211320).

Wisley through the Seasons: Spring, (Royal Horticultural Society) £12.99 (01483 211320).

Wisley through the Seasons: Summer, (Royal Horticultural Society) £12.99 (01483 211320).

Wisley through the Seasons: Winter, (Royal Horticultural Society) £12.99 (01483 211320).

28

Holidays

The following list includes a number of specialised garden and botanical tour operators. In addition to the companies below, some general tour operators will organise holidays which include a significant number of interesting gardens in their itinerary. Several of the horticultural societies arrange their own trips for their members, notably the Alpine Garden Society and also the Royal Horticultural Society (01394 276276). Members of the International Dendrology Society have access to many otherwise closed gardens through the IDS tours: members only, though. The National Trust and the British Trust for Conservation Volunteers both arrange working conservation holidays. Outside the gardening world, Specialtours (0171 730 2297) arranges some very tempting itineraries for the National Art Collections Fund (0171 821 0404).

Accompanied Cape Tours
Hill House, Much Marcle, Ledbury, Hereford & Worcester HR8 2NX
☎ 01531 84210   FAX 01432 351028

CONTACT   Virginia Carlton
1995 TOURS   Western Cape, South Africa
FOUNDED   1991

Small groups of less than ten allow for a flexible programme which can be altered to suit individual interests. A chance to meet and talk with South Africans is an important feature of the trips.

American Horticultural Society
7931 East Boulevard Drive, Alexandria, Virginia 22308, USA
☎ 00 1 703 768 5700   FAX 00 1 703 765 6032

1995 TOURS   Puerto Rico and the Virgin Islands, The Mississippi, Italian Lakes, St Lawrence River, S W USA, Vancouver, Portugal and Madeira, S E Asia and Vietnam
FOUNDED   1922

The tours arm of the American Horticultural Society.

Barfield Travel & Tours
14 Chain Lane, Newark, Nottinghamshire NG24 1AU
☎ 01636 705612   FAX 01636 707600

CONTACT   Mrs G. M. Lewis
1995 TOURS   Portugal, Jersey, British Columbia, Northern Holland, Guernsey
MEMBER   ABTA; IATA; ATOL

Tours for gardeners with additional visits to nearby attractions. Specific destinations are subject to confirmation.

Boxwood Tours: Quality Garden Holidays
56 Spring Road, Abingdon, Oxfordshire OX14 1AN
☎ 01235 532791   FAX 01235 532791

CONTACT   Sue Macdonald
1995 TOURS   Great Britain and Europe
FOUNDED   1990
MEMBER   (Client trust account)

Tours to British and European gardens. Distinguished leaders accompany each tour: both partners are themselves Kew-trained.

Carolanka
Rowden House, Brentnor, Tavistock, Devon PL19 0NG
☎ 01822 810230   FAX 01822 810230

CONTACT   Mrs Carol Cameron
1995 TOURS   Sri Lanka
FOUNDED   1991

Guided tours including visits to botanic gardens. Personalised itineraries can also be arranged to concentrate on gardens.

Cox & Kings Travel
St James Court, 45 Buckingham Gate, London SW1E 6AF
☎ 0171 873 5002

CONTACT   Stephen Bray
1995 TOURS   Greece, Turkey, Cevennes, Carinthia, Western Australia, Wyoming, Canada, Bhutan, Andalusia, Portugal, Switzerland
FOUNDED   1758
MEMBER   ABTA; ATOL; IATA

Specialised botany and natural history tours are accompanied by Roy Cheek, Mary Briggs and others. Garden tours have now been added to their range. Destinations this year include many of the classic botanical areas of Europe.

Holidays 497

David Sayers Travel
54 High Street East, Uppingham, Leicestershire
LE15 9PZ
☎ 01572 821330   📠 01572 821072
CONTACT Andrew Brock Travel
1995 TOURS New Zealand, India, Cyprus, Spain, Azores, Dominica, Normandy, Burma, Czech Republic, Slovakia
FOUNDED 1982
MEMBER ABTA; AITO; ATOL
Specialist garden and botanical tours, operated by Andrew Brock Travel. Kew-trained horticulturist David Sayers accompanies most of the tours.

David Way Associates
Southover, Grove Lane, Hunton, Maidstone, Kent
ME15 0SE
☎ 01622 820876   📠 01622 820645
CONTACT D. W. Way
1995 TOURS Normandy, Aquitaine, Utrecht, Gelderland, Flanders
FOUNDED 1988
Specialise in the low countries and France. Tours are organised for societies and groups, and are often based on private gardens which are not usually open.

Fine Art Travel Ltd
15 Savile Row, London W1X 1AE
☎ 0171 437 8553   📠 0171 437 1733
CONTACT Charles FitzRoy or Jane Rae
1995 TOURS Provence, Bologna, Venice, Burgundy
FOUNDED 1984
There are no tours specifically for gardeners, but this top-end of the market firm has the entrée to many fine gardens. High points of this year's offers include Patrick Bowe as guide to Jas Créma in Provence and Robin Lane-Fox leading a tour to Bologna and Mantua.

Gardeners' Delight
45 Church Road, Saxilby, Lincoln LN1 2HH
☎ 01522 703773
CONTACT John Ramsbotham
1995 TOURS UK and Europe
FOUNDED 1977
Past tours have included a large number of TV gardening personalities as guides or special lecturers: Stephen Anderton, Beth Chatto, Brian Halliday, Daphne Ledward, Peter Seabrook and Geoffrey Smith. This year's destinations include Normandy, Switzerland and the Ghent Floralies, as well as private garden tours in the UK.

Himalayan Kingdoms Ltd
20 The Mall, Clifton, Bristol BS8 4DR
☎ 0117 923 7163   📠 0117 974 4993
CONTACT Steven Berry
1995 TOURS The Himalaya, Central Asia
FOUNDED 1987

MEMBER AITO, ATOL
Not specifically a botanic specialist, but a recent rhododendron hunt found 26 out of 29 available species.

Motts Travel
Station Road, Stoke Mandeville, Aylesbury, Buckinghamshire HP22 5UL
☎ 01296 613831   📠 01296 613175
1995 TOURS Cheshire, Cornwall, Cumbria, Harrogate, Dutch Bulb Fields
MEMBER ABTA
Economic coach holidays to popular gardening areas is one of the specialities of this Midlands-based company.

Naturetrek
Chautara, Bighton, Alresford, Hampshire SO24 9RB
☎ 01962 733051   📠 01962 733368
CONTACT David Mills
1995 TOURS Cyprus, Corsica, Crete, Morocco, Slovakia, Turkey, Greece, Sichuan, Nepal, Bhutan, Sikkim, West Pakistan
FOUNDED 1986
MEMBER AITA; ATOL
Specialist treks to near and far destinations for botanists, ornithologists and naturalists. Treks are graded for difficulty. For the adventurous.

Page & Moy Ltd
136-140 London Road, Leicester LE2 1EN
☎ 0116 252 4444
1995 TOURS Barbados, Paris, Italian Lakes, Somerset and Wiltshire
MEMBER ABTA; ATOL
Offers a wide range of general holidays, as well as these specialist garden tours organised for the National Trust in its Centenary Year.

Southern Africa Travel
1 Pioneer Business Park, Amy Johnson Way, York, North Yorkshire YO3 4TN
☎ 01904 692469   📠 01904 691340
1995 TOURS Cape Province
MEMBER ABTA; ATOL
This company specialises in the entire southern half of the continent, and includes several wildflower and garden-visiting tours in spring.

Swan Hellenic Ltd
77 New Oxford Street, London WC1A 1PP
☎ 0171 831 1515   📠 0171 497 2832
1995 TOURS Mediterranean, Dutch bulbfields
FOUNDED 1954
MEMBER ATOL; ABTA
Among this well-known company's extensive cruises, those to the Mediterranean in spring and river cruises in the Netherlands are accompanied by distinguished botanists.

Trossachs Garden Tours
Orchardlea House, Callander, Perthshire FK17 8BG
☎ 01877 330798   FAX 01877 330543
CONTACT Mrs Hilary Gunkel
1995 TOURS St Andrews, Helensburgh, Newton Stewart, Inverary, Stirling, Melrose, Banchory, Biggar, Drymen
FOUNDED 1989

Attractively packaged weekend and midweek visits for small groups to private and public Scottish gardens, each at its seasonal best.

Voyages Jules Verne
21 Dorset Square, London NW1 6QG
☎ 0171 723 5066   FAX 0171 723 8623
1995 TOURS Ireland, Cornwall, Northern France, Positano, Italian Lakes, Tuscany, Madeira
MEMBER ABTA; ATOL

Most tours are accompanied by a guest lecturer: they include Roy Cheek. Wildlife and sight-seeing trips to further-flung destinations also available.

Hotels with good gardens

Some of the houses attached to historic landscapes have become hotels. In several cases the gardens themselves have been well maintained or even improved by the new owners. Sometimes the gardens remain in good condition but in different ownership: the house is sold separately as a hotel. Many people find the idea of staying in a hotel with a beautiful garden particularly attractive. Here is a selection of hotels with gardens which are good enough to mention in their own right. Their size and services vary considerably, from simple B & B to 5-Star ratings.

Cannizaro House
West Side, Wimbledon Common, London SW19 4UF
☎ 0181 879 14641   FAX 0181 879 7339

An elegant Georgian house right on the edge of Cannizaro Park: see Gardens chapter.

Cliveden House Hotel
Taplow, Maidenhead, Berkshire SL6 0JF
☎ 01628 668561   FAX 01628 661837

One of the greatest gardens in the Thames Valley: see Gardens chapter.

Congham Hall Hotel
Lynn Road, Grimston, King's Lynn, Norfolk PE32 1AH
☎ 01485 600250   FAX 01485 601191

40 acres of parkland and a good kitchen garden: best for its herb garden, with over 300 varieties, many available for purchase.

Five Arrows Hotel
High Street, Waddesdon, Buckinghamshire HP18 0JE
☎ 01296 651727   FAX 01296 658596

On the edge of the Waddesdon estate, with access not only to the gardens (see Gardens chapter), but also to the Rothschild cellars.

Gliffaes Country House Hotel
Crickhowell, Powys NP8 1RH
☎ 01874 730371   FAX 01874 730463

29 acres of grounds; wonderful rhododendrons, maples and conifers.

Gravetye Manor
Vowels Lane, East Grinstead, West Sussex RH19 4LJ

William Robinson's own garden, imaginatively replanted and immaculately maintained: see Gardens chapter.

Greywalls
Muirfield, Gullane, Lothian EH31 2EG
☎ 01620 842144   FAX 01620 842241

Designed by Lutyens, planted by Jekyll: beautifully maintained and restored. Roses everywhere, and innumerable architectural jokes.

Hanbury Manor Hotel
Ware, Hertfordshire SG12 0SD
☎ 01921 487722   FAX 01920 487692

Extensive parkland and immaculately maintained gardens: the walled garden is *extremely* pretty, but there are a secret garden, rose garden, woodland walk and arboretum too.

Hawkstone Park Hotel
Weston-under-Redcastle, Shrewsbury SY4 5UY
☎ 01939 200611   FAX 01939 200311

Historic Grade I park: cliffs; follies; monuments; Swiss bridge; grotto; monkey puzzles; rhododendrons.

Hope End Hotel
Ledbury, Hereford & Worcetser HR8 1JQ
☎ 01531 633613   FAX 01531 636366

Late Georgian landscape garden, laid out by John Loudon for Elizabeth Barrett Browning's father in 1809. Temple, grotto, wooded walks, carp pool and shady seats. Splendid walled garden, all organic.

Lainston House Hotel & Restaurant
Sparsholt, Winchester, Hampshire SO21 2LT
☎ 01962 863588   FAX 01962 776672

63 acres of parkland surround this *very* handsome William & Mary house with a spectacular lime avenue, but the modern flower gardens by the house are a model of mixed planting: small trees, shrubs, roses and herbaceous plants all mixed.

Le Manoir aux Quat' Saisons
Church Road, Great Milton, Oxfordshire OX44 7PD
☎ 01844 278881   FAX 01844 278847

World famous restaurant: 19 rooms. Beautiful flower gardens in the English romantic style and impressive kitchen gardens.

Leeming House Hotel
Watermillock, Ullswater, Penrith, Cumbria CA11 0JJ
☎ 017684 86622   FAX 017684 86443

20 acres above the lake: mature conifers and magnificent rhododendrons.

Little Thakenham Hotel
Merrywood Lane, Storrington, West Sussex RH20 3HE
☎ 01903 744416   FAX 01903 745022

Lutyens house, with a period garden; paved walks and courtyards, a rose pergola and magnificent flowering trees and shrubs.

Long Cross Hotel
Trelights, Port Isaac, Cornwall PL29 3TF
☎ 01208 880243

Dramatic gardens, substantially remade in the Victorian style, with many tender plants.

Meudon Hotel
Mawnan Smith, Falmouth, Cornwall TR11 5HT
☎ 01326 250541   FAX 01326 250543

8 acres of lushly planted valley running down to the Helford estuary: tree ferns, cordylines, drimys, camellias and vast clumps of *Gunnera*.

Middlethorpe Hall
Bishopthorpe Road, York YO2 1QB
☎ 01904 641241   FAX 01904 620176

Handsome modern gardens in the formal style, to complement the William & Mary house: grand old cedar.

Rhinefield House Hotel
Rhinefield, Brockenhurst, Hampshire S042 7QB
☎ 01590 622922   FAX 01590 622800

Grand Italian garden (actually late Victorian), well restored recently: magnificent conifers.

Riber Hall Hotel
Matlock, Derbyshire DE4 5JU
☎ 01629 582795   FAX 01629 580475

Very pretty rock garden, herbaceous borders and mixed plantings near the hotel; splendid bluebell walks in the woods.

South Lodge Hotel
Lower Beeding, Horsham, West Sussex RH13 6PS
☎ 01403 891711   FAX 01403 891766

90 acres of grounds, including a fine collection of mature rhododendrons, conifers, ponds and a rock garden.

Ston Easton Park
Ston Easton, Somerset BA3 4DF
☎ 01761 241631   FAX 01761 241377

Humphry Repton landscape, carefully restored by the hotel owners: see Gardens chapter.

Summer Lodge Hotel
Evershot, Dorchester, Dorset DT2 0JR
☎ 01935 83424   FAX 01935 83005

Many tender plants, and some interesting new plantings by Penelope Hobhouse.

The Beeches Hotel & Plantation Garden
4-6 Earlham Road, Norwich, Norfolk NR2 3DB
☎ 01603 621167   FAX 01603 620151

Famous Victorian garden in the Italian style, lost within the 3 acres of grounds until restored in the 1980s.

The Lygon Arms
Broadway, Hereford & Worcester WR12 7DU
☎ 01386 852255   FAX 01386 858611

Beautiful walled garden of roses and fruit trees: magnificent summer bedding.

Thornbury Castle Hotel
Thornbury, Bristol, Avon BS12 1HH
☎ 01454 281182   FAX 01454 416188

High Victorian formal garden within the castellated *enceinte*.

Tylney Hall Hotel
Rotherwick, Hook, Hampshire RG27 9AZ
☎ 01256 764881   FAX 01256 768141

67 acres of late Victorian exotica: avenues of wellingtonias, Italian garden, lakes and massive rhododendrons. Gertrude Jekyll designed the rock garden.

Willapark Manor Hotel
Bossiney, Tintagel, Cornwall PL34 0BA
☎ 01840 770782

14 acres on a magnificent headland. The owner is a keen gardener: he inherited good rhododendrons and spring flowers, and is extending the display.

Woolley Grange Hotel
Woolley Green, Bradford-on-Avon BA15 1TX
☎ 01225 864705   FAX 01225 864059

Cotswold manorhouse with handsome terraced gardens and lilypool.

Ynyshir Hall
Eglwysfach, Machynlleth, Powys SY20 8TA
☎ 01654 781209   FAX 01654 781366

Splendid old rhododendrons and azaleas in the woods.

In addition, we recommend the following hotels which are listed in the Gardens chapter: Ardnamona, Co. Donegal; Loch Melfort Hotel, Arduaine, Strathclyde; Gidleigh Park, Devon; Kildrummy Castle, Grampian; Owlpen Manor, Gloucestershire; Plas Penhelig, Gwynedd; West Park Lodge, Beale Arboretum, Hertfordshire. If a garden is not separately listed in Chapter 16, you should first ask whether it is ever open to non-patrons. The owners' attitudes to visitors who are not guests of the hotel differ greatly. Cliveden and Waddesdon are examples of hotels whose associated gardens may freely be visited most of the year. Others are open infrequently: the Beale Arboretum, attached to West Park Lodge Hotel, is an instance. And some owners are concerned to emphasize that their gardens are never open to the public, but reserved entirely for the pleasure of visitors to the hotel or restaurant: at Gravetye Manor and Gidleigh Park, for example, the delights of the garden may only be known to guests of the business.

Other accommodation

Several organisations offer bed & breakfast accomodation to keen gardeners. The Hardy Plant Society publishes a list of members who have a B & B business: please send a SAE to Mrs Pam Adams, Little Orchard, Great Comberton, Pershore, Hereford & Worcester, WR10 3DP. We also strongly recommend a pamphlet called Bed and Breakfast for Garden Lovers available from Mrs S. Colquhoun, Handywater Farm, Sibford Gower, Banbury, Oxfordshire OX15 5AE which lists 25 garden owners in the southern half of England who do B & B. The guide also identifies those which are mentioned in the Yellow Book or Good Gardens Guide, so that would-be visitors can do their holiday homework before deciding where to stay. Wolsey Lodge, 17 Chapel Street, Bildeston, Suffolk, IP7 7EP Tel 01449 741297 is a marketing organisation for upmarket B & B in private houses throughout Britain. Several of the properties listed in the Gardens section of The Gardener's Yearbook appear in its pages, including Doctyn Mill in Devon. We are also informed by Alan Bloom that bed & breakfast is offered at Bressingham Hall, adjacent to the famous nursery and gardens near Diss in Norfolk.

If you would like to try a working holiday, the best known organisation is The British Trust for Conservation Volunteers, but the National Trust for Scotland runs some too, and offers holiday lets in a number of its properties.

We recommend The National Trust 1995 Holiday Cottage Brochure, available in return for a donation of £1 from The National Trust in London. The lets may be cottages on the estate, converted lodges, water towers, estate buildings or stables, or even a flat in part of the house itself. Prices vary from about £150 pw to £250 pw. There are two at Cliveden in Buckinghamshire; ten at Cotehele in Cornwall; three at Glendurgan in Cornwall; four at Trelissick in Cornwall; three at Acorn Bank in Cumbria; one at Castle Drogo in Devon; two at Coleton Fishacre in Devon; two at Mottistone Manor in the Isle of Wight; two at Felbrigg Hall in Norfolk; three at Nymans in West Sussex; one at Beningbrough in North Yorkshire; three at Studley Royal in North Yorkshire; one at Bodnant in Clwyd; one at Colby Woodland Garden in Dyfed; one at Powis Castle in Powys; one at Rowallane in Co. Down; one at Florence Court in Co. Fermanagh.

Although it is not a National Trust property, readers may also like to know that the Gothic orangery at Frampton Court in Gloucestershire has been converted into a holiday self-catering home. It is right at the heart of the famous gardens, at the head of the Dutch Canal.

When you go away

Whether you're soaking up sun and sangria in Spain during the winter months or just cruising the Norfolk Broads for a long weekend, how will the garden manage without you? The answer depends on how well it manages when you are there. Work out how much time you spend tending your plot each week and you'll have a pretty good idea what sort of arrangements, if any, will be needed in your absence. After all, if a grudging hour or so at the weekend is par for the course, then it probably won't even notice you're not there. If, on the other hand, hour upon hour, week in, week out, go to grooming the garden to perfection, then either you'll need someone else to keep up the standard till you return, or else you should think about going away at a quieter season horticulturally.

Should you fall somewhere in between, then there is a choice of steps you can take to keep the upper hand. So, given that most people go away in summer, the main problem is protecting your plants from English heat and drought. It helps if you can remove pots and hanging baskets to a place of shade and shelter while you are away. Plants in pots fare even better if you plunge them in the ground and water the earth around them well.

Consider introducing any or all of the following: mulches on the borders, and especially around newly planted trees and shrubs, to reduce the amount of water lost through evaporation; shade netting; capillary matting or plunge beds for pots, inside and out; a time-controlled watering system. This last need not be as expensive as it sounds. Use seepage hoses and/or an electronic clock which switches on after dusk when watering is most effective. And remember that no system is suitable for long periods.

After water, the main problem is growth. Puritanical journalists will advise you to cut the heads of flowers which have not yet faded, or perhaps not even opened, before you leave. Necessary or not, the grass won't cut itself and produce will not pick itself, so you'll have to get a friend or neighbour to fight this battle by proxy. Don't expect them to spare as much time as you would but their little will make all the difference.

For bigger gardens and more intensive cultivation, you will probably need to rely on expert help. Greenhouse gardening is a high-risk activity. Precious specimens are best entrusted to the safe custody of an experienced gardening friend to look after in his or her own greenhouse. If this is impossible, you must find a knowledgeable person to water and ventilate your greenhouse as frequently as you do yourself. Remember that the usual fault of inexperienced caretakers is to overwater everything. Leave long and detailed instructions in writing, run through them point by point, and give a practical demonstration of your requirements. If you don't have a gardener already consider arranging for contract gardeners to fill in for you. You will have to set out their duties precisely, and expect to pay from £10 an hour for their time. Alternatively, you can ask one of the specialist agencies to find you a residential houseminder.

Houseminders carry out the basic domestic and garden duties that you would normally perform yourself. These usually involve caring for pets, answering the telephone, and providing the security of a presence in the house, as well as watering the tomatoes and mowing the lawn. Large gardens or greenhouses which demand hours of commitment may require a higher fee. Most agencies are happy to make special arrangements to accommodate your particular needs. Agencies include:

Animal Aunts
45 Fairview Road, Headley Down, Hampshire GU35 8HQ.
☎ 01428 712611 · FAX 01428 717190

Mainly for people with pets and other animals, particularly those with special requirements.

Holiday Homewatch
Nursery Cottage, Penybont, Llandrindrod Wells, Powys, LD1 5SP.
☎ 01597 851840

Specialise in assignments where there are horses and farm livestock as well as domestic pets to look after.

Housewatch Ltd
Little London, Berden, Bishops Stortford, Hertfordshire CM23 1BE
☎ 01279 777412   FAX 01279 777049

Experienced with both houses and gardens.

Homesitters Ltd
Buckland Wharf, Buckland, Aylesbury, Buckinghamshire HP22 5LQ
☎ 01296 630730

Perhaps the best known agency, Homesitters make a point of emphasising that they recruit mature responsible people as caretakers and investigate their backgrounds for the last twenty years, as well as taking up references. Homesitters are particularly conscious of the problems of garden owners who wish to go on holiday. 'When you are away, can you really expect friends to mow the lawn regularly?' they ask, adding that their terms of reference run 'from watering and mowing to picking and freezing, and potting and pruning'.

29
Germany: Gärten und Pflanzen für Engländer

Germany is the only country in Europe that can and does claim to have gardens and nurseries as good as ours. And with justification, for their great gardens are breathtaking and their nurseries are remarkable for the range and variety of their stock. Gardening in Germany is, however, more often an adjunct to an interest in botany or the romantic spirit than a branch of the decorative arts. That said, the English style of gardening is fashionable nowadays in Germany, as in much of continental Europe, and German lifestyle magazines are full of articles about modern gardens in the post-Jekyll tradition.

German culture is not always admired by the English, nor is Germany the tourist attraction for British visitors that it deserves to be. England and Germany entertain a mutual suspicion. Both are keener to point out the differences between them, in order to assert the superiority of their own gardens, than to see how each can learn from the other and improve upon their knowledge. German garden owners complain that our gardens lack cohesion, that there are too many mood changes, and that we do not integrate our gardens properly with either our houses or the countryside beyond. It is a perennial complaint and one to which there is no answer, except to say that the English aesthetic is different and no less valuable than the German.

In the eighteenth century German landowners were immediately attracted by the English landscape style. Rather than employ the fashionable English designers of the day, they came to England, toured the gardens and went back to Germany to redesign their parkland. The German landscape style is therefore a development of ours: many Germans would argue that the work of such artists as Schell and Lenné was an improvement upon the landscapes of later practitioners of the English school.

Nineteenth-century Germany had its own equivalent of the Arts and Crafts movement in England: *Jugendstil* gardens combined formal design with natural planting. A great tradition of public parks and gardens began at the turn of the century: witness the Lichtenthalerallee at Baden-Baden and the Westfalen Park at Dortmund. Nor can the influence of Karl Foerster in the first fifty years of this century be overemphasised – but how many Britons know of his work, or that of his associate Hermann Mattern, or their rival Ludwig Späth? All were protagonists of a naturalistic style that became the school of habitat gardening, of which the Germans are still the masters and from whom we have much to learn.

Practitioners of habitat gardening dispose their plants, particularly perennials, in a natural manner

Germany: Gärten und Pflanzen für Engländer

and encourage them wherever possible to naturalise. They tolerate plants which we would consider weeds, such as buttercups and thistles, and will often give over a large part of their garden to this sort of wild display, where eventually cultivated plants can at best be said only to enhance what is essentially a natural mix of species.

The Germans are enthusiastic garden visitors but the gardens which open to the public tend to be public parks, botanic collections or princely landscapes, now mainly in state ownership. Germany is a country of truly great gardens. A dozen of the best are: Veitshöchheim at Würzburg; Park Wilhelmshöhe at Kassel; Herrenhausen in Hanover; Rennsteig Garten, Oberhof; Nymphenburg and the Englischer Garten at Munich; Muskau near Wörlitz; Sans Souci at Potsdam; the Tiergarten in Berlin and the Berlin Botanical Gardens; Insel Mainau near Konstanz; and the Rosarium at Sangerhausen. Good, smaller private gardens are seldom open: there is no real equivalent of our National Gardens Scheme. Drive through the suburbs of a German town or city to get a feel for these, impeccably neat and designed for low maintenance.

Anyone who is contemplating garden and nursery visiting in the new Bundesländer, the former East Germany, should allow plenty of time. There is an extensive road improvement programme which can lead to long delays and diversions. Congestion in the towns adds to the problem. It should also be remembered that some nurseries in the East still do not have a telephone.

There is no up-to-date English guide to German gardens, and the most recent book on the subject, *The Private Gardens of Germany* by Ursula Dohna (Weidenfeld, 1986), is not entirely satisfactory. The section of Patrick Bowe's *Gardens of Central Europe* (Antique Collectors' Club, 1992) which deals with eastern Germany has good photographs but a disappointing text. *The Gardens of Europe* by Penelope Hobhouse and Patrick Taylor (George Philip, 1991) is a good introduction to the possibilities.

The leading German publisher of books on gardens and gardening is Verlag Eugen-Ulmer whose current list has over 150 titles. Apart from perhaps half a dozen translated from the English, all the books are written by German experts for German gardeners and give, to English eyes, a totally new perspective on gardens and their design as well as on plants and how to use them.

The most popular garden magazine is *Mein Schöner Garten*, a monthly publication which is roughly comparable to *Practical Gardening*: a more specialised publication is *Gartenpraxis*. There are several specialist plant societies with good publications for members: see chapter 8. The Gesellschaft der Staudenfreunde is a fair match for the Hardy Plant Society, while the Verein Deutscher Rosenfreunde is in most respects better than the RNRS.

German garden centres are almost indistinguishable from ours. They place slightly more emphasis on ground cover, containers and bedding plants than we do, and they tend to sell their plants slightly larger in size than ours. There is also a stronger demand for house plants. Germans are firm believers in compost, manure, fertilisers and muck. Garden centres in Germany are as much to do with lifestyle aspirations as gardening, although credit cards are not as widely used as in England.

German nurseries usually publish a glossy catalogue intended to last several years, with annual updates, pricing or availability lists. These are expensive to produce and you are expected to pay to have one sent to you: if you forget, or decline, you are unlikely to receive the catalogue. Nurserymen will not be pleased by English correspondents who neither pay for the catalogue nor buy from it, so readers are urged to remember that the good name of English gardeners is at stake on this matter of principle.

There follows a selection of some of the better nurseries with a wide range of plants that are not yet known in the UK.

Staudengärtner Klose
Rosenstraße 10, D-34253 Lohfelden bei Kassel
☎ 00 49 561 515555

Catalogue (excellent) DM13. Busy working nursery with a very wide range of herbaceous perennials, grasses, hostas, geraniums and paeonies. The closest equivalent would be Blooms of Bressingham: thoroughly professional. No shrubs or conifers. Mail order in autumn and spring; overseas orders welcome; payment in advance. Although visitors are encouraged to visit the nursery and see the plants at flowering times (best in August–September, they say), there are no plants available for immediate sale. Klose are breeders as well as growers: among a lot of recent introductions are *Calamintha nepeta* ssp. *nepeta* 'Gottfried Kühn' with lilac pink flowers and *Pulmonaria saccharata* 'Morgenlicht' with light blue flowers.

Staudengarten Monika und Wolfgang Urban
Obere Kirschgasse 3, D-96271 Grub am Forst
☎ 00 49 9560 765

Near Coburg. Catalogue DM5. Organically grown herbs and herbaceous perennials. Open 1 April to 1 August, and 15 September to 15 November. Guided tours of the display garden at 11 am the first Saturday of the month April to November. Mail order.

Staudengärtnerei Wolfgang Sprich
Papierweg 20, D-79400 Kandern
☎ 00 49 7626 7443

Between Basel and Freiburg. Nursery specialising in herbaceous perennials for cutting, hardy geraniums and paeonies. Mail order. Open 2–6 pm, Monday–Friday, and 2–5 pm on Saturdays.

Staudengärtnerei Gräfin von Zeppelin
D-79295 Sulzburg-Laufen
☎ 00 49 7634 69716

Between Basel and Freiburg. This extensive and efficiently run nursery is set among the Baden vineyards with its own garden and growing fields. It has a large and interesting list of over 4,000 herbaceous perennials, particularly good for sempervivums, irises, paeonies, delphiniums, geraniums and day lilies. The famous *Iris* collection, some 1,500 varieties, formerly at the nursery, is now at the Basel-Bruglingen Botanic Garden. Mail order. Open 8 am – 12 noon and 1 – 5.30 pm, Monday–Friday and 8 am – 1 pm on Saturdays, but closed on Saturdays from December to February. The nursery is now run by Gräfin von Zeppelin's daughter Frau Aglaia von Rumohr who speaks good English.

Schöppinger Irisgarten
Werner Reinemann, Burgerweg 8, D-48624 Schöppingen

North west Germany, near Ahaus and Gronau. The list is full of the latest and smartest hybrids from all over the world: irises, paeonies, over 250 hostas and more than 600 *Hemerocallis*. It also includes cultivars raised by Herr Reinemann. Prices reflect its appeal: the cheapies are DM10, but there are over 100 cultivars at more than DM100, and prices go up to DM550. There are garden open days in May and July.

Gartenbaubetrieb Schuster
D-19065 Augustenhof
☎ 00 49 3863 2705

Near Schwerin. Water plant specialist with a magnificent list of hardy bog and aquatic plants, including 84 varieties of water lily, 15 forms of *Iris pseudacorus* and 83 forms and hybrids of *Iris sibirica*. Mail order.

Staudenkulturen Stade
Beckenstrang 24, D-46325 Borken-Marbeck
☎ 00 49 2861 2604

North west Germany. Splendid list with exceptionally wide range of herbaceous perennials, grasses, marginal and aquatic plants. Much stock originally came from the USA and the UK, but there is a good quantity of German forms too. Mail order.

Förster Stauden GmbH
Am Raubfang 6, D-14469 Potsdam-Bornim
☎ 00 49 331 20294

Famous wholesale nursery responsible for many good introductions, with a comprehensive list of perennials for landscaping which includes a number of postwar varieties not yet grown in the UK.

Bohlje Pflanzenhandel GmbH
Oldenburger Straße 9, D-26655 Westerstede
☎ 00 49 4488 2203

West of Oldenburg. Large wholesale nursery concentrating on trees, shrubs and conifers, with a particularly handsome list of around 300 rhododendrons and azaleas, chosen for their hardiness and including many German, Danish and Dutch hybrids.

Bayerwald Seerosen (Erhard Oldehoff)
Sieglmühle 2, D-94501 Hauzenberg
☎ 00 49 8586 1693

Near Passau. Aquatics, bog plants and marginals, plus around 60 water lilies, including blue-flowered greenhouse forms and three varieties of the lotus *Nelumbo*. A good display garden. Mail order.

Wolfgang Linnemann
Rheindorfer Straße 49, D-53225 Bonn-Beuel
☎ 00 49 228 471448

Quite the rangiest of tree paeony nurseries, with about 25 American, 50 European, 60 Japanese and 85 Chinese cultivars. Mail order. Not cheap – prices range from DM48 to DM330 – but what a list! Dr Linnemann speaks excellent English.

Alpengarten Pforzheim
Joachim Karl. D-75181 Pforzheim-Wurm
☎ 00 49 7231 70590

Alpine nursery set in a garden. Masses of tufa rockeries, on a deeply wooded south-facing hillside, meticulously labelled and well maintained. A plantsman's paradise, closest perhaps to Ingwersen's in England. Mail order for alpines, rock garden plants, dwarf shrubs and conifers. Reasonable prices. Open daily 8 am – 7 pm, spring to autumn.

Germany: Gärten und Pflanzen für Engländer

Alpine Staudengärtnerei Siegfried Geißler
OT Gorschmitz Nr 14, D-04703 Leisnig/Sachsen

Really rare alpines from a young nursery run by a collector turned professional, who has built it up over twenty years by vigorous correspondence with botanic gardens and collectors all over the world. There is a very pretty, small display garden, arranged geographically, and an ever-changing stock with a constant supply of new items, including fifteen forms and species of dwarf *Salix* not listed in *The Plant Finder*. Mail order.

W. Kordes' Söhne
D-25365 Klein Offenseth-Sparrieshoop
☎ 00 49 4121 48700

Near Hamburg. The German rose-breeding dynasty responsible for many notable modern roses, particularly repeat flowering climbers. Large and efficient mail order service, offering well-grown, healthy plants. They have a rose garden at their offices and will give permission to view the rose fields.

Ingwer J. Jensen GmbH
Am Schloßpark 2b, D-24960 Glucksberg
☎ 00 49 46 31 60100

Near Flensburg. Rose specialist with an extremely long list of interesting old roses and newer varieties, as well as good clematis, climbers, rhododendrons and azaleas. There are four colour catalogues, costing between DM12.50 and DM22.50, plus DM5 p & p. His rose list alone is much longer than any in the UK: Jensen is the kingpin of the old rose movement in Germany. Mail order.

Rosen von Schultheis
Rosenhof, D-6350 Bad Nauheim-Steinfurth
☎ 00 49 6032 81013

The nursery, still run by the family after 125 years, specialises in rare and old roses, though with a representative selection of modern ones. The village is full of rose nurseries, many run by former students and staff. There is a small rose museum. Catalogue DM10.

Rosenschule Martin Weingart,
Hirtengasse 16, D-99947 Bad Langensalza/Ufhoven

Near Gotha. New rose nursery specialising in old, rare and species roses. Mail order. Martin Weingart has had access to the great German national collection of roses at Sangerhausen, and includes a large number of old varieties not available from any other nursery.

Jürgen Krebs
D-27318 Hoyerhagen 130
☎ 00 49 4251 2993

35 km south of Bremen. Mail order. Heath garden specialist, meaning dwarf rhododendrons, azaleas, gaultherias and other small ericaceous shrubs, but especially heathers. Krebs's list of *Calluna vulgaris* cultivars always includes several new forms and some of his own raising, including 'Feuerwerk' and 'Sellingsloh'.

France

Garden Centres

Plants tend to be more expensive at French garden centres than English. The best place to find bargains are ordinary markets, although the quality and range may be indifferent. Terracotta pots, however, are cheap, especially in the south. Generally speaking, everything in France is more expensive for gardeners with the possible exception of small hand tools like trowels.

Large garden centres are spaciously planned but not designed as places to take the family for a day out: there are no cafés or loos. Credit cards are not as widely used as in England, but Visa is accepted more than Access.

Nurseries

France has two 'Plant Finders'. If you wish to know as much as possible about French nurseries, you will need both. The larger of the two is *Où trouver vos plantes* by Anita Pereire & Philippe Bonduels. (Hachette, 1992. Price 98FF). It lists 30,000 plants and 600 nurseries, including a few selected nurseries in Great Britain and Belgium. The second plant finder is *25,000 Plantes – où et comment les acheters*, promoted by La Société Nationale d'Horticulture de France (Maison Rustique, 1993. Price 98FF). Based on 300 nurseries, it lists 500 varieties of *Prunus*, 700 fuchsias, 1400 irises and 1700 roses.

France has some excellent nurseries. Certain plants – irises and paeonies for example – are much more popular than in the UK. Here is a selection of top nurseries:

Pepinières Charentaises, 16310 Montemboeuf, (Charente). Tel: 45 65 02 61. Particularly good for hardy trees and shrubs. Retail and wholesale, mail order and garden centre, bare-root and container-grown stock. Catalogue 40FF.

Eve, Le Bois d'Eve, 77690 La Génévrayes, (Seine-et-Marne). Tel: 64 29 00 98. Excellent all-round nurserymen, selling through mail order and on site. Catalogue 60FF, but cost set against purchases.

Les Jardins de Cotelles, 76370 Derchigny-Graincourt, (Seine-Maritime). Tel: 35 83 61 38. Retail and wholesale specialists in herbaceous plants. Mail order and container grown stock sold at their garden centre. Catalogue 25FF.

Cayeux SA, La Carcaudière, 45500 Poilly-lez-Gien, (Loiret) Tel: 38 67 05 08. Prominent iris specialist.

Iris de Thau, 14 Rue des Logis, 34140 Loupian, (Hérault). Tel: 67 43 82 50. Iris nursery with exceptional list of garden varieties.

Les Roses anciennes de André Eve, Morailles, 45300 Pithivier-le-Vieil, (Loiret). Tel: 38 30 01 30. Old-fashioned rose specialist. Many unavailable in UK. Mail order only. Good display garden.

Ets Rivière, 'La Plaine', 26400 Crest, (Drôme). Tel: 75 25 44 85. Specialists in paeonies. The present owner Michel Rivière published *Le Monde fabuleux des pivoines* in 1992 (205FF, pp.164: 150 varieties photographed in colour).

But there is no substitute for buying *Où trouver vos plantes* or *25,000 Plantes – où et comment les acheter* and finding out about French nurseries for yourself.

31
Health & Safety

In the 1994 edition of *The Gardener's Yearbook* we concentrated upon the new rules relating to Health and Safety which were introduced at the beginning of 1993, for the protection of workers in the horticultural industry. We pointed out that the spirit of the law applies just as much to amateurs, and that every gardening enthusiast should try to work within the regulations' code of practice.

This year we look at two different areas: first, the problem of poisonous plants; and second, the sources of advice about safety in the garden.

Many garden plants are poisonous. Human deaths from eating such plants are few, at least in comparison with the total number of reported plant poisonings and other accidental poisonings. This is partly because only a few plants are really dangerous, and people know which they are and avoid them. Less dangerous plants are toxic only if eaten in large quantities, but, since they are usually highly unpalatable, this is unlikely ever to occur. In fact, in many cases it is not known whether a particular plant is poisonous or not. There are also differences in susceptibility to toxins between individuals and differences in toxicity within some plant species. If it were a legal offence to offer poisonous plants for sale, it would be difficult to agree a definitive list of them.

The really poisonous plants are well known: monkshood (*Aconitum napellus*), laburnum and foxglove, for instance. All parts of these plant are highly poisonous, even when eaten in small quantities. It is said that every year oleanders, so reminiscent of summer holidays in the Mediterranean, cause deaths among people who use the twigs as sticks for barbecues: every part of the plant is fatal. In others, poisons may be restricted to one kind of organ – the rhizome or rootstock as in *Convallaria* and *Iris*, the fruit as in *Daphne*, or the foliage as in *Rheum*: foliage is poisonous in a wide range of plants. The seed coats of the castor oil plant *Ricinus communis* contain ricin, the deadly poison that Bulgarian assassins used to murder Georgy Markov: a tiny quantity of the toxin was injected into his back through the tip of an umbrella.

Young children are most at risk from plant poisoning because they frequently put things into their mouths, and colourful flowers or berries are especially attractive to them. By far the most common age for poisoning incidents is between two and three when a child is curious, highly mobile, but has not yet learnt to avoid danger. The bright red fruits of cuckoo-pint (*Arum maculatum*) are one of the most common causes of poisoning in young children: the shining scarlet berries appear a few inches from the ground and are therefore very accessible to toddlers.

Some plants are so toxic that they cause a serious reaction as soon as they are touched: the American poison ivy. *Toxicodendron radicans* is the best-known example, although people's susceptibility varies considerably. Much more commonly encountered are those whose sap causes skin irritations, such as the giant hogweed *Heracleum mantegazzianum* and common rue *Ruta graveolens*. These make the skin hypersensitive to ultraviolet light. The sap of the plants causes no problems if it is washed off quickly, and has little effect in the dull days of winter. But when the skin comes into contact with the sap and is then exposed to bright sunlight, large blisters can form and, even after the person recovers, leave permanent marks. The entire staff of full-time propagators in a large wholesale nursery in Wiltshire was recently put out of action for six weeks after taking cuttings of rue. The economic consequences were potentially catastrophic.

People's reactions to plants differ enormously. Some of us can handle *Primula obconica* with no trouble: others suffer a violent allergic reaction. Other common allergens are ivy (*Hedera helix*) and chrysanthemums (*Dendranthema*). It is best to wear gloves, just in case.

Hay fever and asthma sufferers need to discover what they are allergic to, then try to avoid the offending plants. It could be anything from tree pollens in February to fungal spores in August. Pollen is the commonest irritant: the solution may be to plant your garden with insect-pollinated plants such as geraniums, irises, delphiniums, hostas and sweet peas. The trouble is that wind-borne irritants travel long distances. Two small booklets are available which sufferers should know about: *Hay Fever in the Garden* by Dr Tim Rich and Dr Tom Smith, which is available free if you send a self-addressed envelope (6" x 8") with two second class stamps to: Hay Fever Booklet, Mary and Merrill Dow Ltd, Lakeside House, Stockley Park, Uxbridge, UB11 1BE; and *Blooming Flowers without the Blooming Pollen* by Geoff Hamilton, which is available from PO Box 6, Hampton TW12 2HE.

It is very difficult to get accurate and coherent statistics for garden injuries. St John Ambulance claims that each year an estimated 300,000 people need hospital treatment for injuries caused by garden accidents. The organisation believes that the most risky places in the garden are paths and terraces, where around 43,000 casualties occur annually. According to a report in *Gardening Which?* in May 1994, over 100,000 people suffer eye injuries every year when gardening. The Royal Society for the Prevention of Accidents (RoSPA) is concerned about the way in which gardeners use electrical tools. 'Garden equipment and tools cause 36,000 serious accidents each year, of which 4,000 are down to hedge trimmers and 6,000 to mowers,' said David Jenkins, RoSPA's Product Safety Advisor, last year. The DTI's Accident and Leisure Research shows that on average twenty-five people die every year from electrical accidents in the home and garden. According to a *Gardening Which?* report in July 1993, electricity in the garden accounts for up to eight deaths a year. Most of us would regard that as statistically insignificant, but the 300,000 injuries mentioned at the top of this paragraph are a sobering figure, if it is correct.

There is, however, no shortage of advice available from well-intentioned charities whose concern it is to prevent accidents from occurring in the first place. The Royal National Institute for the Blind, in association with *Gardening Which?*, has sponsored a helpful pamphlet, *Eye Safety in the Garden*. Copies are available from RNIB, 224 Great Portland Street, London W1N 6AA (Tel: 0171 383 0148). Moreover, The British Safety Council publishes an *Eye Safety Code* for gardeners, which has three rules. First, protect the ends of garden canes with some sort of cover: old rubber gloves, pots, rubber balls and so on. Second, wear safety goggles for all gardening jobs where your eyes could be at risk, for example when pruning, or using hedge trimmers. Third, never spray garden chemicals when it is windy.

RoSPA's advice on electrical tools in the garden is as follows: try out any power tool before using it; clear the garden of children and animals; use a circuit breaker; keep cables slung over your shoulder; wear protective gear, including gloves, goggles and sturdy shoes. General advice is also available from RoSPA, Cannon House, Priory Queensway, Birmingham (Tel: 0121 200 2461), and from such organisations as the National Union of Farm Workers.

St John Ambulance's solution to the problem of accidents in the garden is to suggest that more people take the trouble to learn first aid techniques. It also publishes a sixteen-page pamphlet *First Aid in the Garden*, which is a guide to the major hazards that are likely to be encountered during gardening, and how to treat them. It gives notes on how to deal with such common injuries as blows to the head, burns, stings, strains and sprains. The pamphlet is available from St John Ambulance National HQ, 1 Grosvenor Crescent, London SW1X 7EF: please send a stamped addressed envelope.

Otherwise, safety in the garden is all about taking precautions. It means ensuring that machinery is fit for use and that you know how to operate it correctly; following the manufacturer's instructions; wearing protective clothing, including strong shoes and gloves; donning face masks and earplugs when advisable; choosing the right weather conditions; getting expert training before you use tools such as chainsaws; being wary about borrowing tools and equipment from others, even from your friends; fitting RCDs (residual current devices) to all electrical equipment; keeping up your tetanus jabs; knowing how to respond to an emergency; and having first aid at hand for cuts, bruises, stings and other injuries.

Pesticides legislation is much more clear-cut. Everyone has a legal responsibility to dispose of banned or unwanted garden chemicals in a safe manner. If you have excess stocks of domestic garden chemicals, we advise you to contact the Environmental Health Officer at your local council office for advice. Many councils make periodic collections for disposal. They will take a note of your name and address, the type and quantity of chemical you hold, and keep the information on file until they make their next round of collections. However, a report in *Gardening Which?* in August 1994 discovered that, although councils have a legal duty to assist in the disposal of dangerous chemicals, few local authorities make any provision for it. Neath Council told *Gardening Which?*: 'We just don't have the facilities; it just goes into the refuse waste.' The National Association of Waste Disposal Officers confirmed that, while a few authorities have incinerators, most household chemicals end up in land-filled sites.

Further information on all aspects of safety regulations may be obtained from: The Health and Safety Executive Information Centre, Broad Lane, Sheffield, S3 7HQ (Tel: 0114 289 2345). The Centre also publishes a number of advisory pamphlets and booklets including *Watch Your Back* (avoiding back strain when handling timber and using a chainsaw), *Working with VDUs* and *Poisoning by Pesticides: First Aid*. These titles are available free from its Information Office.

32

Britain in Bloom

This annual competition is probably the largest horticultural event in the country, with well over 1000 entrants each year. Regional competitions take place in seventeen areas each summer and the leading category winners are then entered into the national round. These regional contests often spark off further competitions, so that a town which is entering may award prizes to individuals and businesses within their area as a way of encouraging the community to pull together. The results give pleasure and a sense of pride to the communities themselves, and are a major boost to tourism from home and abroad.

Categories of entrants for the main competition are all based on the size of the population in the villages, towns and cities that take part. Last year, to mark the thirtieth anniversary of the competition, only nominees went through to the final stage, all of them past winners. Judging for the national stage takes place in August and September, with marks for the horticultural display and general tidiness. Potential winners usually combine the collective efforts of the council, local business and private gardeners. Eyesores, areas of neglect and vandalism or graffiti count against the entrants.

Britain in Bloom was started by the late Roy Hay in 1964. Until 1983 it was administered by the British Tourist Authority: the event is now co-ordinated by the Tidy Britain Group at national level. Beautiful Scotland in Bloom and the Wales in Bloom Foundation are responsible for the first stages of the competition in their areas; the regional entrants are completed by twelve English areas and winners from competitions in Northern Ireland (Progressive Ulster), the Isle of Man and Jersey.

Entry forms and advice are available from the regional organisers: contact Britain in Bloom, Tidy Britain Group, The Pier, Wigan WN3 4EX.

1994 Britain in Bloom winners:

Large City (150,000)   Bournemouth
City (75,000 - 150,000)   Bath
Large Town (25,000 - 70,000)   Inverness
Town (10,000 - 25,000)   Stratford upon Avon
Small Town (5,000 - 10,000)   Ryton, Tyne & Wear
Small Country Town (2,000 - 5,000) Moir, Northern Ireland
Large Village (600 - 2,000)   Broughshane, Northern Ireland
Village (under 600)   Thorpe Salvin, South Yorkshire

Regional winners include: *Large City*: Gateshead, Southend on Sea; *City*: Aberdeen, Bedford, Durham, Eastbourne, Oxford, Rushmoor; *Inner City*: Bristol; *Large Town*: Abingdon, Bury St Edmunds, Perth, Salisbury, Washington, Worthing; *Town*: Broadstairs, Barnstaple, Christchurch, Howick, Royston, Spennymore, Whitney; *Small Town*: Battle, Forres, Kidlington, Minehead, Wimborne Minster, Woodbridge; *Small Country Town*: Acle, Arundel, Datchet, Moffat, Ringwood, Sedgefield; *Large Village*: Beaulieu, Broughton, Crowmarsh Gifford, Haughley, Sedlescombe, Warkworth; *Village*: Bray, Catcott, Chawton, Fort Augustus, Halliford, Killingworth, Whissonsett; *Urban Community*: Belton, Eton Highcliffe, Hylton Park Business Centre, (Sunderland), Meads Village; *Best Wee Village*: Brunton (Fife).

33
Charities

Charitable Gifts

Many people wish to support a horticultural charity but do not know how to do so or which to choose. There are two main welfare charities specifically concerned with gardeners and their families: the Royal Gardeners' Orphan Fund and the Gardeners' Royal Benevolent Society (see below for details of their aims and achievements). Many other horticultural organisations enjoy charitable status – most clubs and societies for instance, as well as educational institutes. An ever-increasing number of gardens are registering as charities, from Achamore on the Isle of Gigha to Trebah in Cornwall.

Donations are always welcome and account for a substantial part of the income of every charity, but the benefit can be enhanced if people are willing to structure their giving in a tax-efficient way rather than leave it to impulse. Gifts to charity can be exempted from Income Tax, Capital Gains Tax and Inheritance Tax. Take Income Tax, for example. If you put a ten-pound note in a collecting box, you are giving away money on which you have paid tax, and there is no way in which the charity can have the benefit of that tax. But if you use a covenant, Gift Aid or payroll scheme, the charity can reclaim the basic rate tax which you have already paid so that, with the basic rate at 25 per cent, the £10 is worth £13.33.

A covenant is an undertaking to pay a fixed sum for four or more years. It has to follow the prescribed form and be signed as a deed, in order for the charity to recover the basic rate tax which the giver is deemed to have deducted from the gift. A suitable form would read as follows:

I [Jane Smith] of [13 Acacia Avenue, Newtown, Barsetshire], hereby undertake to pay to [name of charity] for a period of 4 years from the date hereof or during my lifetime, whichever is the shorter, on the [1st] day of [April] in each year such sum as will after the deduction of Income Tax at the basic rate for the time being in force amount to the sum of £[100] such sum to be paid out of my general fund of taxed income.
Dated this [21st] day of [March] [1995]
Signed as a Deed by   [Signed] Jane Smith
the said Jane Smith
in the presence of:
[Signature, name,
address and description
of witness]
[Date]

Gift Aid is the most efficient way for UK residents to make a one-off cash gift to a charity. The donation should be more than £250, and you have to sign a form when making the gift so that the charity can reclaim the tax which you have already paid. There is an advantage to the giver as well as to the charity if you are a higher-rate taxpayer: the charity reclaims tax at the basic rate but the difference (15 per cent) between higher and basic tax rates is reclaimed by the giver. Gift Aid has proved very beneficial to charities.

Payroll giving has been widely introduced and many employees use it to ensure that a small part of their income goes to charity in the form of a regular donation. The charity can claim back the basic tax which has been deducted from your salary by your employer, at no cost to you. The best way to find out more about payroll giving is to speak to your employer.

Legacies in people's wills can make an enormous difference to the fortunes of a charity. The Anthony Pettit bequest funded the acquisition and maintenance of the Alpine Garden Society's new headquarters at Pershore. The gift of Netherbyres has quite transformed the ability of the Gardeners' Royal Benevolent Society to care for elderly retired gardeners and their spouses in Scotland.

We recommend you to seek professional advice when making a legacy. The consequences of getting it wrong can be worse than having no will at all. Equally, it is important not to leave the making of a will until it is too late. By instructing a solicitor to write your will, you can be sure that your wishes are expressed correctly so that your executors can put them into effect. Most charities can put you in touch with a suitable person to undertake the legal drafting.

Finally, it is worth remembering that the best source of advice on every aspect of giving to charity is the Charities Aid Foundation, 48 Pembury Road, Tonbridge, Kent TN9 2JD (Tel: 01732 771333, Fax: 01732 350570). The Charities Aid Foundation is itself a charity. It exists to enable individuals and organisations to improve the quality and value of their donations to charity. 'For more than 130,000 private individuals,' they claim, 'the Charities Aid Foundation is simply the best way to give.'

Many gardening organisations are charities. Most of the national horticultural societies are registered charities – the Hardy Plant Society, for instance – and so are such conservation bodies as the National Council for the Conservation of Plants and Gardens. A growing number of gardens belong to charities, often set up to ensure that they are preserved after the owners who made the gardens are dead: Skibbereen in Co. Cork and Boughton House in Northamptonshire are two new examples this year.

But there are other organisations which are registered charities with a more conventionally 'charitable' purpose. They use their funds to alleviate the needs of people who have been in horticulture for most of their working lives. They are popular with garden owners and are often supported by funds raised by such bodies as the National Gardens Scheme. The main charities working in this field are The Royal Gardeners' Orphan Fund, The Gardeners' Royal Benevolent Society, The National Gardens Scheme Charitable Trust, Scotland's Gardens Scheme and The Worshipful Company of Gardeners.

The Royal Gardeners' Orphan Fund, 48 St Alban's Road, Codicote, Hertfordshire ST4 8UT, Tel: 01428 820783. Secretary: Mrs Kate Wallis. Founded in 1887 to help the orphans of gardeners 'by giving them regular allowances and grants for special purposes'. Since 1985 the Fund has also offered assistance to needy children, not necessarily orphans, whose parents are employed full time in horticulture. The Fund's counselling service advises on such problems as may arise when a family that has been living in tied accommodation has to move elsewhere on the death of the breadwinner, sometimes to a different area and far from friends and familiar surroundings. The Fund is supported by many institutions including The National Gardens Scheme, Scotland's Gardens Scheme, The Worshipful Company of Gardeners, The Royal Horticultural Society and many horticultural and flower clubs around the country. The total value of grants made in 1993 was £40,610.

The Gardeners' Royal Benevolent Society, Bridge House, 139 Kingston Road, Leatherhead, Surrey, KT22 7NT, Tel: 01372 373962, Fax: 01372 362575. Patron: HM Queen Elizabeth The Queen Mother. President: HRH Princess Alice, Duchess of Gloucester. Secretary-Administrator: C. R. C. Bunce. The Society was founded in 1839 by a group of horticultural growers who were appalled by the fate of men, gardeners all their lives, who became too old to work and had to face starvation or the workhouse. The aim of the Society remains, as it always has been, to help gardeners suffering from ill health and to provide pensions in their old age. Income in 1993 included £107,891 from donations and £408,818 from investment income and deposits.

The Gardeners' Royal Benevolent Society has been very active in recent years in expanding its activities. Today there are over 500 pensioners, fifty of whom are resident in the Society's country home, Red Oaks, Henfield, Sussex. Arthur Hellyer spent his last weeks at Red Oaks at the beginning of 1993. The Society also owns a group of seven bungalows at Barton in Cambridgeshire, which are used to accommodate retired gardening couples, some of whom have had to vacate tied cottages on retirement. To meet cases of particular difficulty, the

Society also has a Good Samaritan Fund from which grants are made for such specific purposes as fuel, house repairs and special food in cases of illness.

The Society's Scottish home, Netherbyres at Eyemouth near Berwick-on-Tweed, was given to the Society under the terms of the will of Lt. Col. Simon Furness in 1991 and has grounds of forty acres. In December 1991 the Society opened a small development of sheltered housing bungalows at Kings Stanley in Gloucestershire. The first tenants moved in at the end of September 1992.

The National Gardens Scheme Charitable Trust, Hatchlands Park, East Clandon, Guildford, Surrey GU4 7RT. Administrator and Director: Lt. Col. Dennis Carpenter. Despite its high profile, the National Gardens Scheme was not originally intended as a horticultural charity: when founded in 1927, its purpose was to help elderly district nurses. Best known for the success of its National Gardens Scheme, over 90 per cent of its income comes from the 3,500 or so gardens which are open to the public, and from the sale of its Yellow Book. In 1993 these accounted for an income of £1,442,836, and the scheme paid out a total of £1,216,153 to charities. By far the biggest beneficiary was the Cancer Relief Macmillan Fund (£663,548) and the Gardens Fund of the National Trust (£250,000), but donations were also made to county nursing associations (£36,325), the Queen's Nursing Institute (£68,000), the Nurses' Welfare Service (£45,000), the Gardeners' Royal Benevolent Society (£25,235) and the Royal Gardeners' Orphan Fund (£25,235). The balance was shared among other charities nominated by garden owners who are able to specify that up to 25 per cent of their takings should be directed to such organisations as CAFOD and St John's Ambulance.

Scotland's Gardens Scheme, 31 Castle Terrace, Edinburgh EH1 2EL, Tel: 0131 229 1870. General Organiser: R. S. St Clair-Ford. Over 300 gardens throughout Scotland open for this charity which is closely modelled on the English National Gardens Scheme. Owners are encouraged to open their gardens to the public and the proceeds are then distributed among various charities. In 1992 the total income raised was £212,406, a higher return per garden than the English scheme, and £156,674 was paid out. £43,233 was donated to the Queen's Nursing Institute, Scotland; £47,411 to the Gardens Fund of the National Trust for Scotland; £1,500 to the Gardeners' Royal Benevolent Society and £1,500 to the Royal Gardeners' Orphan Fund. Owners are able to donate up to 40 per cent to a charity of their choice and, as a result, the balance of £63,030 was made available to help and support over 160 different charities.

The Worshipful Company of Gardeners has a Charities Fund which makes grants to deserving projects, such as horticultural therapy schemes and garden designs for special schools. Details are available from the Master.

Nomenclature Changes

In future we are likely to see fewer changes in botanical names. This is one result of the new edition of the International Code of Nomenclature which was published in the summer of 1994.

On average, each species of flowering plant has about five names. This may be unpopular with horticulturalists, but taxonomists have for well over two hundred years adopted the principle of strict priority to determine which name is correct. By far the largest number of name-changes which cause adverse comment are the result of taxonomic study and not of nomenclatural argument. A classic example of this would be the splitting of *Chrysanthemum* into *Argyranthemum* and *Dendranthema*. That said, there have always been irritating changes of name which *are* the result of nomenclatural argument and which annoy botanists as much as they do gardeners.

The Chairman of the Committee on Botanical Nomenclature at the fifteenth International Botanical Congress in Yokohama, Japan, in 1993 concluded that: 'What is now needed is a general awareness that it is no longer necessary to change the name for any reason other than a new taxonomic insight.' If it is true, then this represents the most fundamental alteration to the rules of botanical nomenclature that has been seen for a hundred years, and recognises the great importance of a stable system of scientific naming.

In fact, the Yokohama Congress did not entirely abandon the principles of priority. The relevant part of its resolution reads: 'The Congress urges plant taxonomists to avoid displacing well-established names for purely nomenclatural reasons, whether by changing their application or by the resurrection of long-forgotten names.' The word 'urges' does not amount to an order, although botanists are encouraged to cite the Yokohama resolution rather than make changes which are contrary to its spirit.

To some extent decisions on nomenclature are in the hands of committees. One of the most important resolutions of the Yokohama Conference was that any name can be rejected for any reason, provided that the relevant committee regards its loss as advantageous. If, therefore, a taxonomist finds that an earlier name threatens one in use, he should formally propose the earlier name for rejection. As a result, priority of publication now counts for less than it used to. Similarly, any name can be proposed for conservation if its loss is regarded as disadvantageous by the relevant committee. This power to reject 'good' names (i.e. names that discovered to antedate others far more familiar to gardeners and botanists) and conserve 'bad' ones will lead to much greater stability. These new reolutions recognise the necessity in any language for a concept of common usage – a commonsense position that may free users of plant names from the strictures of historical precedent and formal nitpicking. It remains to be seen how far committees will go to approve or reject suggested changes. Certainly, many horticultural taxonomists hope that nomenclature will be very different in future from that which has bugged them for so much of the twentieth century.

Many gardeners are surprised when they encounter an old plant under a new name: some of us have even bought the same plant twice in the belief that it was two quite different plants. This list of alternative namings is a selection of those which readers are most likely to encounter. We have also given reverse namings, so that readers can work from the familar to the new, whether they are 'right' or 'wrong'. The correct name, according to present

Nomenclature Changes 515

thinking, is in each case highlighted and denoted with a →. We have chosen just changes of genus not new specific changes. Usually only part of the genus is involved. For example, only a few *Antirrhinum* are now known as *Asarina*. If you cannot find a familiar plant under its 'old' name, look under the highlighted genus name.

Acacia → *Albizia*
Acca ← *Feijoa*
Acidanthera → *Gladiolus*
Aconitum → *Eranthis*
Aeonium ← *Sempervivum*
Agapetes ← *Pentapterygium*
Agastache ← *Cedronella*
Agropyron → *Elymus*
Albizia ← *Acacia*
Allium → *Nectaroscordum*
Aloysia ← *Lippia*
Amaryllis → *Hippeastrum*
Ampelopsis ← *Vitis*
Amsonia ← *Rhazya*
Amygdalus → *Prunus*
Anaphalis ← *Gnaphalium*
Anchusa → *Pentaglottis*
Androsace ← *Douglasia*
Anemone → *Hepatica*
Anomatheca ← *Lapeirousia*
Antholyza → *Crocosmia*
Antirrhinum → *Asarina*
Aquilegia → *Semiaquilegia*
Aralia → *Fatsia*
Arctotis ← *Venidium*
Argyranthemum ← *Chrysanthemum*
Arum → *Dracunculus*
Asarina ← *Antirrhinum*
Asarina → *Maurandya*
Asparagus ← *Smilax*
Asperula → *Galium*
Asphodeline ← *Asphodelus*
Asphodelus → *Asphodeline*
Aster → *Boltonia*
Aster → *Felicia*
Aster ← *Microglossa*
Atragene → *Clematis*
Austrocedrus ← *Libocedrus*
Azalea → *Rhododendron*
Azorina ← *Campanula*
Bellevallia ← *Muscari*
Berberis → *Mahonia*
Betonica → *Stachys*
Bidens → *Cosmos*
Blechnum ← *Lomaria*
Bocconia → *Macleaya*
Boltonia ← *Aster*
Boykinia ← *Telesonix*
Brachyglottis ← *Senecio*

Brimeura ← *Hyacinthus*
Brodiaea → *Triteleia*
Brugmansia ← *Datura*
Bupthalmum → *Telekia*
Calla → *Zantedeschia*
Calocedrus ← *Libocedrus*
Camellia ← *Thea*
Campanula → *Azorina*
Cardamine ← *Dentaria*
Carduus → *Cnicus*
Cayratia → *Parthenocissus*
Cedrela → *Toona*
Cedronella → *Agastache*
Celsia → *Verbascum*
Centranthus ← *Valeriana*
Cephalaria ← *Scabiosa*
Cerasus → *Prunus*
Chaenomeles ← *Cydonia*
Chaenomeles → *Pseudocydonia*
Chaenorrhinum ← *Linaria*
Chamaecyparis ← *Cupressus*
Chamaenerion ← *Epilobium*
Chamaepericlymenum → *Cornus*
Chamaerops → *Trachycarpus*
Chamaespartium ← *Genista*
Cheiranthus ← *Erysimum*
Chrysanthemum → *Argyranthemum*
Chrysanthemum → *Dendranthema*
Chrysanthemum → *Leucanthemum*
Chrysanthemopsis → *Rhodanthemum*
Cicerbita ← *Lactuca*
Cineraria → *Senecio*
Cissus ← *Parthenocissus*
Cladothamnus → *Elliottia*
Clarkia ← *Godetia*
Clematis ← *Atragene*
Cleyera ← *Eurya*
Cnicus ← *Carduus*
Coleus → *Plectranthus*
Coleus → *Solenostemon*
Cornus ← *Chamaepericlymenum*
Corynabutilon → *Abutilon*
Cosmos ← *Bidens*
Cotinus ← *Rhus*
Crassula ← *Sedum*
Crinodendron ← *Tricuspidaria*
Crocosmia ← *Antholyza*
Crocosmia ← *Montbretia*
Crocosmia ← *Curtonus*
Crocosmia → *Tritonia*
Cupressus → *Chamaecyparis*
Curtonus → *Crocosmia*
Cydonia → *Chaenomeles*
Cymbalaria ← *Linaria*
Cynara ← *Scolymus*
Cyperus ← *Mariscus*
Cytisus → *Argyrocytisus*
Dactylorhiza ← *Orchis*

Nomenclature Changes

Datura → Brugmansia
Dendranthema ← Chrysanthemum
Dentaria → Cardamine
Desmodium ← Lespedeza
Desmodium → Codariocalyx
Dichelostemma ← Triteleia
Dierama → Dracomontanum
Diervilla → Weigela
Dietes ← Moraea
Dimorphotheca → Osteospermum
Douglasia → Androsace
Dracomontanum ← Dierama
Dracunculus ← Arum
Dregea ← Wattakaka
Drepanostachyum → Himalayacalamus
Drimys → Pseudowintera
Duchesnea ← Fragaria
Echinospartium ← Genista
Edraianthus ← Wahlenbergia
Elliottia ← Cladothamnus
Elymus → Leymus
Endymion → Hyacinthoides
Ensete ← Musa
Epilobium ← Zauschneria
Epilobium ← Chamaenerion
Eranthis ← Aconitum
Erianthus → Saccharum
Erigeron → Haplopappus
Erysimum → Cheiranthus
Eurya → Cleyera
Fatsia ← Aralia
Felicia ← Aster
Ferula → Foeniculum
Filipendula ← Spiraea
Foeniculum ← Ferula
Fragaria → Duchesnea
Galeobdolon → Lamium
Galium ← Asperula
Genista → Chamaespartium
Genista → Echinospartum
Genista → Retama
Gladiolus ← Acidanthera
Gladiolus ← Homoglossum
Glechoma ← Nepeta
Gloxinia → Sinningia
Gnaphalium → Anaphalis
Gnaphalium → Helichrysum
Godetia → Clarkia
Haemaria → Ludisia
Haplopappus ← Erigeron
Hebe → Parahebe
Helianthemum → Tuberaria
Helichrysum ← Gnaphalium
Helichrysum → Ozothamnus
Hepatica ← Anemone
Hermodactylus ← Iris
Hippeastrum ← Amaryllis
Hoheria ← Plagianthus

Homoglossum → Gladiolus
Howea ← Kentia
Hyacinthoides ← Endymion
Hyacinthus → Brimeura
Hymenocallis ← Ismene
Hylotelephium → Sedum
Ipomoea ← Pharbitis
Ismene → Hymenocallis
Iris → Hermodactylus
Jacobinia → Justicia
Jovibarba ← Sempervivum
Justicia ← Jacobinia
Kentia → Howea
Knautia ← Scabiosa
Lactuca → Cicerbita
Lamium ← Galeobdolon
Lapeirousia → Anomatheca
Lavatera ← Malva
Leopoldia → Muscari
Lespedeza → Desmodium
Leucanthemum ← Chrysanthemum
Libocedrus → Austrocedrus
Libocedrus → Calocedrus
Ligularia ← Senecio
Lilium → Nomocharis
Limonium ← Statice
Linaria → Cymbalaria
Linaria ← Chaenorrhinum
Lindera ← Parabenzoin
Lippia → Aloysia
Lippia → Verbena
Lithocarpus ← Quercus
Lithodora ← Lithospermum
Lomaria → Blechnum
Luma ← Myrtus
Lychnis → Silene
Lychnis ← Viscaria
Macleaya ← Bocconia
Mahonia ← Berberis
Malva → Lavatera
Malvastrum ← Anisodontea
Mariscus ← Cyperus
Maurandya → Asarina
Microglossa → Aster
Mimulus ← Diplacus
Montbretia → Crocosmia
Moraea → Dietes
Musa → Ensete
Muscari ← Bellevalia
Muscari ← Leopoldia
Myrtus → Luma
Nepeta → Glechoma
Nectaroscordum ← Allium
Neopanax → Pseudopanax
Nomocharis ← Lilium
Orchis → Dactylorhiza
Osteospermum ← Dimorphotheca
Oxycoccus → Vaccinium

Nomenclature Changes 517

Oxypetalum → *Tweedia*
Ozothamnus ← Helichrysum
Parabenzoin → *Lindera*
Parahebe ← Hebe
Paraquilegia ← Semiaquilegia
Parthenocissus ← Ampelopsis
Parthenocissus → *Cissus*
Pentapterygium → *Agapetes*
Pentaglottis ← Anchusa
Persicaria ← Polygonum
Pharbitis → *Ipomoea*
Photinia ← Stransvaesia
Physoplexis ← Phyteuma
Plagianthus → *Hoheria*
Plectranthus ← Coleus
Polygonum ← Fallopia
Polygonum ← Persicaria
Poterium → *Sanguisorba*
Prunus ← Amygdalus
Prunus ← Cerasus
Pseudocydonia ← Chaenomeles
Pseudopanax ← Neopanax
Pseudowintera ← Drimys
Quercus → *Lithocarpus*
Retama ← Genista
Rhazya → *Amsonia*
Rhodiola ← Sedum
Rhododendron ← Azalea
Rhus → *Cotinus*
Rosularia ← Sedum
Sanguisorba ← Poterium
Scabiosa → *Cephalaria*
Scabiosa → *Knautia*
Schizocodon → *Shortia*
Scolymus → *Cynara*
Sedum → *Crassula*
Sedum → *Rhodiola*
Sedum → *Rosularia*
Semiaquilegia ← Aquilegia
Semiaquilegia ← Paraquilegia
Sempervivum → *Aeonium*
Sempervivum → *Jovibarba*

Senecio → *Brachyglottis*
Senecio ← Cineraria
Senecio → *Ligularia*
Setcreasea → *Tradescantia*
Shortia ← Schizocodon
Silene ← Lychnis
Sinarudinaria → *Fargesia*
Sinningia ← Gloxinia
Smilax → *Asparagus*
Sorbaria ← Spiraea
Spiraea → *Filipendula*
Spiraea → *Sorbaria*
Stachys ← Betonica
Statice → *Limonium*
Stransvaesia → *Photinia*
Telesonix → *Boykinia*
Testudinaria → *Dioscorea*
Thamnocalamus → *Yushania*
Thamnocalamus → *Drepanostachyum*
Thamnocalamus → *Hymalayacalamus*
Thea → *Camellia*
Toona ← Cedrela
Trachycarpus ← Chamaerops
Tradescantia ← Setcreasea
Tricuspidaria → *Crinodendron*
Triteleia → *Brodiaea*
Triteleia → *Dichelostemma*
Tritonia ← Crocosmia
Tuberaria ← Helianthemum
Tweedia ← Oxypetalum
Vaccinium ← Oxycoccus
Valeriana → *Centranthus*
Venidium → *Arctotis*
Verbascum ← Celsia
Verbena ← Lippia
Viscaria → *Lychnis*
Vitis → *Ampelopsis*
Wahlenbergia → *Edraianthus*
Wattakaka → *Dregea*
Weigela ← Diervilla
Zantedeschia ← Calla
Zauschneria → *Epilobium*

35
Royal Warrants

Any tradesman who, for a minimum of five years, has been supplying one or more of the Royal Households who award warrants, may apply for the grant of a Royal Warrant. Further details are available from The Secretary, The Royal Warrant Holders' Association, 7 Buckingham Gate, London SW1E 6JY, Tel: 0171 828 2268, Fax: 0171 834 5912. Here is a list of the warrants currently granted to tradesmen in the horticultural sector.

Royal Warrants Of Appointment To Her Majesty Queen Elizabeth II

Department Of Her Majesty's Privy Purse

List of Tradesmen in the Department of Her Majesty's Privy Purse permitted to style themselves 'By Appointment to Her Majesty The Queen' or 'By Appointment to Her Majesty Queen Elizabeth II' and entitling them to display the Royal Arms:

Abbey Rose Gardens	Rose Growers and Nurserymen,	Burnham
Aberdeen Landscapes & Specialist Tree Service	Tree Surgeon	Inverurie
Atco Ltd	Manufacturers of Motor Mowers	Stowmarket
Bartram Mowers Ltd	Suppliers of Horticultural Equipment	Norwich
Joseph Bentley Ltd	Suppliers of Horticultural Products	Barrow on Humber
Blooms of Bressingham Ltd	Suppliers of Hardy Nursery Stock	Diss
Carters Tested Seeds Ltd	Seedsmen	Torquay
Cocker, James & Sons	Suppliers of Roses	Aberdeen
Darby Nursery Stock Ltd	Suppliers of Ornamental Shrubs and Trees	Thetford
Delamore, R. Ltd	Suppliers of Chrysanthemum Stock	Wisbech
Dobbie & Co. Ltd	Seedsmen and Nurserymen	Lasswade
Paul Double Nurseries Ltd	Tree Nurserymen	Ipswich
Elsoms Seeds Ltd	Seedsmen	Spalding
F. A. Bartlett Tree Expert Co. Ltd (Southern Tree Surgeons)	Tree Surgeons	Crawley
FARGRO Ltd	Horticultural Sundriesmen	Littlehampton
Findlay Clark (Aberdeen)	Seedsmen and Nurserymen	Aberdeen.
Fisons PLC	Manufacturers of Horticultural Products	Ipswich
Hillier Nurseries Ltd	Nurserymen and Seedsmen,	Ampfield
ICI Fertilisers	Manufacturers of Fertilisers	Cleveland
Ken Leech Trees	Fruit Tree Nurserymen	Bulmer Tye, Sudbury

Netlon Ltd — Manufacturers of Plastic Mesh — Blackburn
Ransomes Sims & Jefferies Ltd — Manufacturers of Horticultural Machinery — Ipswich
Ben Reid & Co. Ltd — Nurserymen and Seedsmen — Aberdeen
Frank Rowe — Suppliers of Chrysanthemum Stock — Wellington, Somerset
Peter J. Smith — Suppliers of Horticultural Plants — Ashington
Suttons Seeds Ltd — Seedsmen — Torquay
O. A. Taylor & Sons Bulbs Ltd — Bulb Growers — Holbeach
Vitax Ltd — Manufacturers of Fertilisers and Insecticides — Leicester
Willmot Pertwee Ltd — Suppliers of Horticultural Chemicals — Colchester
William Wood & Sons Ltd — Garden Contractors and Horticultural Builders — Taplow

Royal Warrants Of Appointment To Her Majesty Queen Elizabeth The Queen Mother

List of Tradesmen who hold Warrants of Appointment to Queen Elizabeth The Queen Mother from the Lord Chamberlain to Her Majesty, permitted to style themselves 'By Appointment' to Her Majesty, with authority to display Her Majesty's Arms:

Carters Tested Seeds Ltd — Seedsmen — Torquay
Dettlyn Ltd (Egham Mower Service) — Suppliers of Horticultural Machinery — Winchfield, Hants
Findlay Clark (Aberdeen) — Seedsmen and Nurserymen — Aberdeen
Hillier Nurseries Ltd — Nurserymen and Seedsmen — Winchester
Suttons Seeds Ltd — Seedsmen — Torquay
O. A. Taylor & Sons Bulbs Ltd — Bulb Growers — Holbeach
William Wood & Son Ltd — Garden Contractors and Horticultural Builders — Taplow

Royal Warrants Of Appointment To His Royal Highness The Prince Of Wales

List of Tradesmen who hold Warrants of Appointment to The Prince of Wales, permitted to style themselves 'By Appointment to His Royal Highness', and entitling them to display The Prince of Wales Badge of Three Feathers:

Five Trees Garden Centre & Nursery Ltd — Supplier of Gardening Materials — Tetbury

36
Garden Theft

Theft from gardens open to the public is a growing problem. 'Within the past five years the theft of garden statues and ornaments has risen from almost nothing to nearly fifty per cent of art thefts in this country', according to a report published last year by ICOMOS (The International Council on Monuments and Sites). It is 'ornaments of high quality, which are not so individual as to be easily identified' that are most valuable and vulnerable. Thieves have a particular preference for classical figures and vases in marble, stone or lead. Nineteenth-century gardens in the Italian style contain more statues, urns and other ornaments than those of any other period in the history of English gardens.

ICOMOS is concerned that theft from a historic garden undermines the authenticity of what remains. The damage to our heritage is especially serious for important relict gardens like Powis Castle where, three years ago, five eighteenth-century lead sculptures worth more than £100,000 were stolen. Readers with substantial gardens should consult the Council for the Prevention of Art Theft, c/o Sir Thomas Ingilby Bt., Ripley Castle, Ripley, Harrogate, North Yorkshire HG3 3AY (01423 770152).

Most garden theft is more modest. Garden tractors and mowers are expensive and valuable. Hedgecutters and power saws are highly portable. Seats and tables, sundials and bird-baths, hanging baskets and terracotta pots disappear suddenly.

Nor is it just furniture, machinery and ornaments that are lost: the theft of an entire National Collection some years ago from Ventnor Botanic Garden focused police attention upon the acquisitive side of plantsmanship. Good bonsai specimens are particularly vulnerable to theft. Valuable collections, such as the National Bonsai Collection of Scotland at Malleny, are grown in security compounds protected by alarm systems and guard dogs. In Japan, the best specimens now change hands at up to £150,000 each.

The police take the view that prevention is better than cure. Crime Prevention Officers can advise how to implement simple safety measures without great cost or inconvenience. Inspector Alex Sutherland of Scotland Yard's Crime Prevention Branch declares: 'Whether it is the potential theft of outdoor statues from stately homes, or tools and machinery from garden sheds, we can tell members of the public how to take preventive action.'

The police give the following advice: put away all tools and equipment and ensure that all outside sheds and store cupboards are securely locked; bring your tools inside if you do not have a garden shed or outbuilding; use natural plant protection, such as thorny shrubs; install outside security lighting which is activated automatically by movement or heat; if you have a burglar alarm, extend it to outbuildings and sheds; photograph or video valuable garden plants and ornaments and include close-ups of such distinguishing details as cracks and dents; mark your property with your postcode – this makes stolen property easier to trace and positively identifiable as yours; check that your household insurance policy covers theft from your garden and outbuildings; make sure that your house and garden look occupied and cared for when you are away on holiday; join your local Neighbourhood Watch scheme.

Recent research by the Building Research Establishment confirmed that most burglars are opportunists who decide to commit a crime only if they have a fair chance of success. Much theft is opportunistic: garden owners do not realise how vulnerable they are until after the thief has visited them. Burglars start with no particular target in mind and, if put off for any reason, will abandon it quickly. Their first consideration is cover, meaning easy access for entry and escape. It is often thought that the best property guard is a dog; the barking of a pet may be enough to dissuade an intruder. Guinea-fowl and geese may also be used as alerts.

Allotments are particularly difficult to protect because they are usually far from the holders' homes. Theft from allotments in Nottingham became such a problem last year that Nottingham police set up an Allotment Watch, the first in the country. It was not just flowers and produce that were stolen, but paving slabs and even sheds.

But now the real problem is organised crime: gangs who prospect gardens for their valuable ornaments and ship them overseas. Owners like the National Trust have had to spend huge sums on security. Cable alarms are one way to protect objects in the garden. The base of a statue is fitted with a sensor that reacts to vibration, like a car alarm, and any movement sounds an alarm in the owner's home. One of the most sophisticated systems was developed at Renishaw Hall, Derbyshire, to protect the statuary in the Italian gardens designed by Sir George Sitwell. The Estate Office at Renishaw sells the system to other stately home owners: their trade name is Statue Alarms.

Stolen goods often turn up in auction houses. Keeping a record of auction-house catalogues, and scanning them for specific items which meet the owners' descriptions, is the aim of a company called Thesaurus (Mill Court, Furrlongs, Newport, Isle of Wight PO30 2AA, Tel: 01983 826000) which scans about fifty catalogues every day published throughout Great Britain and is now extending its coverage to Europe and North America.

It has recently taken over *Trace* magazine (address as above, but Tel: 01983 826199) which carries details every month of hundreds of stolen works of art. *Trace*'s aim is to alert dealers to stolen property in circulation. During the week in which we spoke to the editor, Tim Linton, in November last year, the magazine helped to recover thirty items of stolen property worth more than £1 million. The annual subscription is £25 and the magazine is known to circulate in no less than 170 countries. An international readership is crucial to its success: much stolen property ends up in mainland Europe.

Index

17 Fulham Park Gardens, 310
1994 Gardener's Guide to Britain, The, 254
25,000 Plantes – où et comment les trouver, 506
45 Sandford Road, 252, 368
Abbey Dore Court Garden, 163, 298
Abbey Plants, 149
Abbey Rose Gardens, 518
Abbots House Garden, The, 168
Abbots Ripton Hall, 263
Abbotsbury Sub-Tropical Gardens, 149, 283
Abbotswood, 288
Aberconwy Nursery, 219
Aberdeen College, 468
Aberdeen Landscapes & Specialist Tree Service, 518
Abingdon Flower Club, 61
Abriachan Gardens & Nursery, 225
Absolute Tree Care, 420
Access Garden Products, 391
Accompanied Cape Tours, 496
acers, 233
Achamore Gardens, 361, 511
Acorn Bank Garden, 275, 500
Acres Wild (Landscape & Garden Design), 420
Adams Garden Design, Veronica, 447
Adams Landscape Architects, Marina, 436
Adlington Hall, 265
Advancalux, 391
Afan College, 468
African Violet Centre, 60, 61, 183
African violets, 233
Agars Nursery, 159, 420
Agricultural & Food Research Council Scholarships, 473
air plants, 233
Akeroyd, John, 433
All-Gain Organics, 414
Allangrange, 359
Allanson, P & S, 230
Allen Power Equipment Ltd, 391
Allhusen, Annabel, 420
Allotment Watch scheme, 521
Allwood Bros, 207
Alpengarten Pforzheim, 504
Alpine Garden Society, 58, 60, 106, 496
alpines, 233
Alternative Technology, Centre for, 415
Althorp House, 315
Alton Greenhouses, 391
Alton Towers, 327
Altoona Nurseries, 144
Amand Ltd, Jacques, 60, 61, 182
Amateur Gardening, 490
American Camellia Society, 124
American Hemerocallis Society, 124

American Hibiscus Society, 124
American Horticultural Society, 124, 496
American Hosta Society, 124
American Iris Society, 124
American Museum, The, 256
American Orchid Society, 124
American Rhododendron Society, 124
American Rock Garden Society, 124
American Rose Society, 124
Ammerdown Park, 325
An Grianan College of Horticulture, 470
Anderson & Firmin Ltd, 391
Andrews Ltd, Bob, 393
Angel, Heather, 487
Anglesey Abbey, 263
Angus College, 469
Angus Garden, 361
Angus Heathers, 228
Animal Aunts, 501
Antony House, 269
Antony Woodland Garden, 269
Apple Court, 159, 421
Applegarth Nursery, 191
Apuldram Roses, 207
Aqua-Soil Products Ltd, 392
aquatic plants, 233
Arbigland, 355
Arbor Exotica, 134
Arboricultural Association, The, 420
Arbury Hall, 339
Arcadia Nurseries Ltd, 138
Archer-Wills Ltd, Anthony, 207, 421
Archibald, Jim & Jenny, 247
Architectural Heritage Ltd, 392
Architectural Landscape Design Ltd, 421
Architectural Plants, 207
Ardanaiseig Hotel Garden, 361
Ardchattan Priory, 361
Ardfearn Nursery, 225
Ardgillan Park, 368
Ardnamona, 367, 499
Ardtornish Garden, 362
Arduaine Gardens, 362, 499
Arivegaig Nursery, 225
Arley Hall, 265, 378
Arley Hall Nursery, 136
Arlington Court, 280
Armitage's Garden Centre, 217
Arne Herbs, 421
aromatic and scented plants, 234
Arrow Cottage, 298
Arrow Tree Services, 421
Arti Flora, 392
Artscapes & Theseus Maze Designs, 421
Ascott House & Gardens, 260
ASH Consulting Group, 422

Ashenden Nursery, 171
Ashtree Cottage, 341
Ashwood Nurseries, 211, 246
Askew Nurseries, 178
Askham Bryan College, 466
Aspects of Aristocracy, 67
asthma, 508
Atco Ltd, 518
Athelhampton House & Gardens, 283
Audley End, 287
Auldene Nurseries Ltd, 176, 422
Aultan Nursery, 224
Austin Roses, David, 60, 74, 191
Australian Garden History Society, 124
Australian plants, 234
Avebury Manor, 341
Avon, graded gardens in, 381
Avon Bulbs, 193
Avon Gardens Trust, 117
Award of Garden Merit, 79
Axletree Nursery, 205
Aylesbury College, 457
Aylett Nurseries Ltd, 61, 168, 422
Aylmer Addison Associates, 422
Ayr Flower Show, 62
B J Crafts, 392
Bacillus subtilis, 83
Badminton, 256
Bailey, Steven, 60, 61, 162
Baker, B & H M, 152
Baker Straw Partnership, 163
Balcaskie, 356
Ballagan Nursery, 227
Ballaheannagh Gardens, 230
Ballerina Trees Ltd, 134
Ballydorn Bulb Farm, 229
Ballynacourty, 371
Ballyrogan Nurseries, 229
Bamboo Nursery Ltd, 171
bamboos, 234
Bank House, 307
Banks Associates Ltd, Elizabeth, 427
Bannerman, Julian and Isabel, 434
Banyard Tree Surgeons, Keith, 434
Barfield Travel & Tours, 496
Bargany Gardens, 362
bark mulches, buying, 418
Barker & Son, T H, 143
Barkers Primrose Nurseries, 176
Barningham Park, 286
Barnsdale Plants, 57, 178
Barnsley College of Technology, 467
Barnsley House, 288, 378
Barony College, The, 468
Barralets of Ealing, 392
Barratt's Garden Centres, Peter, 139, 210
Barrell Treecare, Jeremy, 432
Barrington Court, 325
Barrus Ltd, E P, 397

524 Index

Barry, Rosemary, 442
Barters Farm Nurseries Ltd, 211
Barthelemy & Co Nurseries, 149
Bartlett Tree Expert Co. Ltd, F. A., 518
Barton Constable Hall, 89
Barton Grange Garden Centre (Bolton), 176, 422
Barton Manor Gardens & Vineyards, 302
Bartram Mowers Ltd, 518
Barwinnock Herbs, 227
Baskervyle-Glegg, Diana, 426
Bateman's, 333
Bates Green Farm, 333
Bath Botanic Gardens, 256
Batsford Arboretum, 289
Battersby Roses, 214
Bawdeswell Garden Centre, 183
Bayerwald Seerosen (Erhard Oldehoff), 504
BBC *Gardeners' World*, 490
BBC *Gardeners' World* Live show, 56, 61, 62
BBONT, 117
BCS Tracmaster Ltd, 392
Beach (Nursery) Ltd, JOHN, 210
Beacon Fuchsias, 149
Beale Arboretum, The, 300, 499
Beales Roses, Peter, 60, 74, 185, 439, 494
bed and breakfast accommodation, 500
bedding plants, 234
Bedding Plants Foundation, Inc, 472
Bede's World Herb Garden, 338
Bedfordshire, graded gardens in, 381
Bedgebury National Pinetum, 303
Beechcroft Nurseries, 141, 201
Beeches Hotel & Plantation Garden, 499
Beeches Nursery, The, 188
Beeston, R F, 166
Beetham Nurseries, 142
begonias, 234
Bel Mondo Garden Features, 392
Belfast City Council Parks Section, 61
Bell Ltd, David, 395
Bellhouse Nursery, 136
Belmont Park, 303
Belsay Hall, 317
Belton House, 309
Belvoir Castle, 307
Belwood Nurseries Ltd, 226
Benger Landscaping, Tony, 446
Beningbrough Hall, 345, 500
Benington Lordship, 300
Bennett, Michael, 248
Bennetts Water Lily Farm, 150
Benthall Hall, 323
Bentley Ltd, Joseph, 401, 417, 518
Berkeley Castle, 289
Berkley Landscape Architects, Martin, 437
Berkshire, graded gardens in, 381
Berkshire College of Agriculture, 457
Berri Court, 335
Berry & Saunders, 61
Berrys Garden Company Ltd, 422
Beth Chatto Gardens Ltd, The, 152, 287
Bettinger Memorial Scholarship, Harold, 472
Bicton Park Gardens, 280
Bicton School of Horticulture, 458
Biddle, P G, 438
Biddlecombe, Helen, 495
Biddulph Grange, 327

Bide-a-Wee Cottage, 317
Biggar Park, 362
Biggs, Glenda, 430
Billington, Jill, 488, 432
Bio-Dynamic Agriculture Association, 415
Biotal Industrial Products Ltd, 392
Birchwood Farm Nursery, 143
birdhouse company, The, 393
Birdtable Company, The, 393
Birkheads Cottage Garden Nursery, 210, 422
Birmingham Botanical Gardens & Glasshouses, 340
Birr Castle Demesne, 371
Bishop & Partner, Jean, 432
Black Isle Nurseries, 225
blackcurrants, new, 83
Blackmore & Langdon, 60, 74, 129
Blackthorn Nursery, 159
Blackwall Products, 393
Blagdon Water Garden Products Ltd, 393
Blairhoyle, 252
Blaxall/Valentine Bursary, 473
Blenheim Palace, 320, 379
Blickling Hall, 313
Bloms Bulbs Ltd, 131
Blooming Things, 222
Blooms of Bressingham Ltd, 73, 75, 518
Blossoms, 261
Blount UK Ltd, 393
Blue Guide to Gardens of Britain, The, 254
Bluebell Nursery, 57, 75, 143
Blunt Trust, The, 473
Bodleian Library, 480
Bodnant Garden Nursery Ltd, 219
Bodnant Gardens, 349, 500
Bodysgallen Hall, 352
bog plants, 234
Bohlje Planzenhandel GmbH, 504
Bolehyde Manor, 341
Bolingbroke, 393
Bond, S & E, 167
Bonnington Plastics Ltd, 393
bonsai, 234
Bonsai Clubs International, 124
Bonsai Societies, Federation of British, 61, 109
books, 484; German, 503; secondhand, 481
bookshops, specialist, 481
Borde Hill Garden, 335
Bosahan, 269
Bosmere Products Ltd, 393
Bosvigo House, 269
Bosvigo Plants, 139
Botanic Nursery, 57, 58, 212, 422
Botanical Society of Scotland, 106
Botanical Society of South Africa, 124
Botanical Society of the British Isles, 106
Boughton House, 315, 379, 512
Boughton Loam Ltd, 393
Bournville College of Further Education, 465
Bourton House, 289
Bouts Cottage Nurseries, 163
Bowden, Ann & Roger, 145
Bowers & Son, Chris, 184
Bowes Museum Garden & Park, The, 286
Bowlby, Rupert, 58, 204
Bowood Garden Centre, 212

Bowood House, 341
Boxwood Tours, 496
Boyce, J W, 247
Boyton Nursery, 139
Brackenhurst College, 463
Brackenwood Garden Centre, 129
Brackenwood Plant Centre, 129
Brackley, S & N, 60, 61, 249
Bradley Batch Cactus Nursery, 193
Bradley Gardens Nursery, 217
Bradley Tyson Memorial Fellowship, Sarah, 473
Bradshaw & Son, J, 173
Brambling House Alpines, 217
Bramdean House, 294
Bramham Park, 348
Branchline Tree Services, 422
Brandy Mount House, 294
Branklyn Garden, 364
Brantwood, 89, 275
Brayford Landscapes, Tim, 445
Bregover Plants, 139
Bressingham Gardens, 60, 314
Bressingham Hall, 500
Bressingham Plant Centre, 131, 134, 184
Bretby Nurseries, 196
Brettell & Shaw Ltd, 394
Brickwall House, 333
Bridge End Nurseries, 223
Bridgemere Garden World, 265
Bridgemere Nurseries, 136
Bridgman & Co Ltd, P J, 405
Brighton Manufacturing Co, 394
Brinkley Nurseries, 189
Brinsbury College, 465
Britain in Bloom, 1994 winners, 510
British & European Geranium Society, 107
British Association of Landscape Industries (BALI), 420
British Bedding and Pot Plant Association, 60
British Bonsai Association, 107
British Clematis Society, 107
British Fuchsia Society, 107
British Gladiolus Society, 107
British Heather Growers' Association, 59
British Hosta & Hemerocallis Society, 107
British Iris Society, The, 108
British Ivy Society, 108
British Library, The, 477
British Museum Connection, 394
British National Carnation Society, 59, 108
British Pelargonium & Geranium Society, 108
British Pteridological Society, 108
British Safety Council, The, 508
British Society for Horticulture Research Blackman Studentship, 472
British Trust for Conservation Volunteers, The, 500
British Wild Flower Plants, 184
British Wild Plants, 223
Broadlands, 283, 294
Broadleas, 341
Broadleas Gardens Charitable Trust Ltd, 212
Broadleigh Gardens, 194
Brockings Exotics, 58, 139
Brodick Castle, 362
Brodie Castle, 357

Index 525

Brogdale Horticultural Trust, 88, 303
Bromage & Co Ltd, D N, 201
bromeliads, 234
Brook Cottage, 320
Brook Lodge Farm Cottage, 330
Brookes, Landscape Designer, John, 433, 488
Broomfield College, 458
Broughton Castle, 320
Brown & Co Ltd, D T, 246, 416
Brown Landscape Design, David, 425
Brownlow Heathers, 229
Brownthwaite Hardy Plants, 142
Bryher, 342
Brympton d'Evercy, 378
Buchan, Ursula, 486
Buckingham Nurseries and Garden Centre, 133
Buckinghamshire, graded gardens in, 381
Buckley, Susan, 445
Bucknell Nurseries, 191
Building Research Establishment, 520
Bulaitis, Bonita, 422
bulbs, 234
Bulldog Tools Ltd, 394
Bullwood Nursery, 153
Burford House Gardens, 298
Burford House Tropicals, 163
Burgess' Alpine Nursery, Jenny, 185
Burgoyne Revivals, Sarah, 407
Burle Marx, Roberto, 71
Burnby Hall Gardens, 301
Burncoose & South Down Nurseries, 57, 60, 61, 140
Burncoose Gardens, 269
Burnett Associates, Chris, 423
Burnham Nurseries, 60, 145
Burnside Nursery, 227
Burrough House, 308
Burton Constable Hall, 302
Burton McCall Group, 394
Buscot Park, 321
Bushukan Bonsai, 61
Butterfields Nursery, 60, 133
Butterfields Pleiones, 58
Butterstream, 252, 371
buying in bulk, 416
buying plants and seeds, 416
Buzacki, Dr Stefan, 66
Bybrook Barn Garden & Produce Centre, 172
Bypass Nurseries, 153, 423
Byrkley Park Centre, 197, 423
C E & D M Nurseries, 180
Cabbages & Kings, 423, 465
cacti, 234
Cactus & Succulent Society of America, 125
Caddick's Clematis Nursery, 136
Cadw, Welsh Historic Monuments Commission, 381
Cae Hir, 350
Caerhays Castle, 269
California Gardens, 170
Calke Abbey, 277
Calloway, Dorothy J., 487
Cally Gardens, 223
Cambo Gardens, 356
Cambridge University Botanic Garden, 263
Cambridge University Library, 480
Cambridgeshire, graded gardens in, 382
Cambridgeshire College of Agriculture and Horticulture, 457

camellias, 234
Canada geese, 66
Canal Gardens, 348
Cannington College, 194, 463
Cannington College Heritage Garden, 325
Cannizaro House, 498
Cannizaro Park, 310
Canons Ashby House, 316
Cantor Trust, The H. & L., 474
Cants of Colchester, 74, 153
Capel Manor, 60, 311
Capesthorne Hall, 265
Capital Garden Products Ltd, 394
Carclew Gardens, 270
Cardiff Institute of Higher Education, 467
Carew Memorial Scholarship, John, 472
Carncairn Daffodils, 229
Carnivorous Plant Society, 60, 109
carnivorous plants, 235
Carnon Downs Garden Centre, 140
Carolanka, 496
Carters Tested Seeds Ltd, 246, 518, 519
Carwinion, 270
Castle Ashby Gardens, 316
Castle Bromwich Hall, 340
Castle Drogo, 280, 500
Castle Howard, 345
Castle Kennedy, 355
Castlewellan National Arboretum, 366
Catforth Gardens, 177
Caves Folly Nurseries, 163
Cawdor Castle, 359
Caws Associates, Stella, 444
Cawthorne, Richard G M, 175
Cayeux SA, 506
Caythorpe Campus, De Montfort University, 309
Cecily Hill House, 289
Cedarwood Lily Farm, 60
Cefn Bere, 352
Celyn Vale Nurseries, 220
Chadwick - Freelance Botanist, Chris, 246
Chaffin Tree Surgery, P J, 439
Chambers Wild Flower Seeds, John, 247
Champion Trees in the British Isles, 253
Channel Island Tree Service, 423
Channel Tunnel Rail Link, 65
Chantry, Glen, 154
charitable gifts, 511
Charities Aid Foundation, 512
Charlecote Park, 339
Charleston Farmhouse, 333
Charter House Hardy Plant Nursery, 223
Chartwell, 304
Chase Organics, 394, 414
Chatelherault Garden Centre, 227
Chatsworth, 277
Chatsworth Garden Centre, 143
Chelsea Flower Show, 60, 62
Chelsea Physic Garden, 57, 311, 478
Cheltenham & Gloucester College of Higher Education, 459
chemicals, disposal of garden, 508
Chempak Products, 394
Chenies Garden Centre, 133
Chenies Landscapes Limited, 423
Chenies Manor, 261
Cherry Tree Nursery (SWOP), 150
Cheshire, graded gardens in, 382
Cheshire Herbs, 57, 60, 61, 136, 246

Cheshire Wildlife Trust, 117
Chicheley Hall, 261
Chichester Trees and Shrubs, 159
Chiffchaffs, 283
Chilham Castle, 252
Chillingham Castle, 317
Chillington Manufacturing Ltd, 394
Chiltern Seeds, 246
Chilworth Manor, 330
Chirk Castle, 350
Chiswick House, 311
Cholmondeley Castle Gardens, 265
Christian Rare Plants, Paul, 220
Christie Elite Nurseries, 225
Christie's Nursery, 228
chrysanthemums, 235
Church Hill Cottage Gardens, 172
Chyverton, 270
Cilwern Plants, 220
CITES, 242
citrus, 235
Clandon Park, 330
Claremont Gardens, 330
Classic Gardening Forum, 66
Clay Lane Nursery, 201
Claymore Grass Machinery, 394
clematis, 235
Clements, Tony, 494
Cleveland, graded gardens in, 382
Cleveland Wildlife Trust, 118
Clifton Landscape and Design, 424
Clifton Nurseries, 182
climbers, 235
Clinton Lodge, 334
Cliveden, 261, 500
Cliveden House Hotel, 498
Clock House, 321
Clumber Park, 319
Cluny House, 364
Clyne Gardens, 59, 351
Coates Manor, 335
Cobblers, 334
Cobham Park, 65
Coblands Garden Centre, 172
Coblands Nursery, 172
Coblands Plant Centre, 172
Cocker & Sons, James, 225, 518
Coghurst Nursery, 205
Colborn, Nigel, 484
Colby Woodland Garden, 350, 500
Coleg Garddwriaeth Cymru, 481
Coleton Fishacre Garden, 280, 500
College of Garden Design, 463
Collis Tree Service, Mark, 436
Colman Charitable Trust, The Timothy, 474
Colson Stone Partnership, 424
Competitions, 59; onion, 59
Complete Tree Services, 424
composts, buying, 417
Compton & Compton, 424
Compton Acres Gardens, 283
Conifer Garden, The, 133
conifers, 235
Connoisseurs' Cacti, 172
Conock Manor, 342
Conservatory Gardens, 424
conservatory plants, 235
Constance Spry Ltd, 464
Consumers' Association Library, 478
Cooke's House, 335
Cooks Garden Centre, 163
Cookson Plantpak Ltd, 395
Coolcarrigan Gardens, 370

Coombs, Geoffrey, 429
Cooper, Mrs S M, 166
Cooper, Paul, 439
Cooper Pegler, 395
Copford Bulbs, 153
Cornwall, graded gardens in, 382
Cornwall Biological Records Unit, 67
Cornwall Gardens Society, 118, 255
Cornwall Gardens Trust, 118
Cornwall Wildlife Trust, 118
Corsham Court, 88, 342
Cotehele, 270, 500
Coton Manor, 316
Cotswold Buildings Ltd, 395
Cotswold Garden Flowers, 163
Cottage Garden, The, 153
Cottage Garden Plants, 208
Cottage Garden Society, The, 109
Cottage Herbery, The, 164
Cottage Nurseries, 189
Cottesbrooke Hall, 316
Council for the Prevention of Art Theft, The, 520
Country Courses, 469
Country Garden, 490
Country Homes and Interiors, 491
Country House Hedging, 164
Country Life, 491
Country Living, 491
County Gardens, Weaver Vale Garden Centre, 424
County Park Nursery, 153
Courts, The, 342
Courtyard Designs, 395
Courtyard Garden Design, 425
Cowbridge Compost, 395
Cowcombe Farm Herbs, 156, 246
Cowdray Park, 336
Cox & Kings Travel, 496
Crace Designs, Andrew, 392
Cragside, 89, 318
Craig Design and Production, David, 396
Craig House Cacti, 177
Craig Lodge Nurseries, 223
Craigieburn Classic Plants, 224
Cranborne Manor, 284
Cranborne Manor Garden Centre, 150
Cranesbill Nursery, 164
Crarae Gardens, 88, 362
Crathes Castle, 358, 379
Craven College of Adult Education, 466
Creagh Gardens, 372
Cressing Temple, 89
crime prevention, 520
Crittenden House, 304
Croftway Nursery, 208
Crossing House Garden, 263
Croston Cactus, 177
Crowe Hall, 256
Crown Vegetables, 197
Crowther Nurseries and Landscapes, 153
Crowther of Syon Lodge, 395
Croxteth Hall & Country Park, 313
Cruck Cottage Cacti, 214
Cruickshank Botanic Garden, 358
CSM Lighting Ltd, 395
CTDA, 182, 246
Cuckoo Pen Nursery, The, 190
Culross Palace, 89
Culzean Castle & Country Park, 363
Cumbria, graded gardens in, 382
Cumulus Organics, 414
Cyclamen Society, The, 109

Cymbidium Society of America Inc, 125
D J Tree and Landscape Specialists, 425
daffodils, 235
Dagenham Landscapes Ltd, 425
Dagg & Sons, T., 417
dahlias, 235
Daily Telegraph, The, 60, 491
Daisy Hill Nurseries Ltd, 229, 425
Daisy Nook Garden Centre, 158
Dalemain, 275
Daleside Nurseries, 214
Dalmeny House, 360
Dalrymple Ltd, 425
Damside Garden Herbs, 358
Danell, 395
Darby Nursery Stock Ltd, 518
D'Arcy & Everest, 57
Darlac Products, 395
Darley House, 278
Dartington Hall, 280
David Landscapes, E K, 427
Davies Landscape Consultants, John A, 433
D'Avigdor Goldschmid Charitable Trust, The Sarah, 474
Davis, Kim W, 192
Dawyck Botanic Garden, 354
Dax Products Ltd, 396
De Bock Rowles Garden Design, Sue, 445
De Jager & Sons Ltd, P, 175
Deacon's Nursery, 171
Dean, Derek Lloyd, 182
Dean's Court, 284
Deanswood Plants, 215
Decorative Foliage, 145
deeds of covenant, 511
Deelish Garden Centre, 231
deer, damage to roses, 68
Deere Ltd, John, 401
Defenders Ltd, 396
Delamore Ltd, R., 518
Delphinium Society, 59, 109
delphiniums, 235
Denbeigh Heathers, 198
Denmans, 336
Denmans Garden Plant Centre, 208
Denmead Geranium Nurseries, 160
Dennis, 396
Derbyshire, graded gardens in, 382
Derbyshire Wildlife Trust, 118
Derreen, 369
Desert Island Discs, 66
Design Studio of Julia Fogg and Susan Santer, The, 426
Desmond, Ray, 485
Dettlyn Ltd, 519
Devine Nurseries, 60
Devon, graded gardens in, 382
Devon Gardens Trust, 118
DHE Plants, 143
Diana Hull, 210
Dianthus, 235
Dibleys, 60, 220
Dickinson, C M, 136
Dickson Nurseries Ltd, 74, 230
Digby, Robin, 441
Dingle, The (Crundale), 350
Dingle, The (Welshpool), 353
Diplex Ltd, 396
Directory of Grant-making Trusts, The, 473
disabled visitors, 253
Dixon Charitable Trust, The C. H., 474
DIY Plastics (UK) Ltd, 396

Dobbie & Co Ltd, 227, 518
Dobbies Landscape Ltd, 426
Dobie & Son Ltd, Samuel, 249
Dochfour Gardens, 359
Doctyn Mill, 280
Document Supply Centre, 477, 478
Docwra's Manor, 263
Doddington Hall, 309
dogs, 253
Dolwen, 354
Dolwin & Gray, 426
Donhead Hall, 60
Dorfold Hall, 266
Dorking Aquatics, 61
Dorothy Clive Garden, The, 328
Dorset, graded gardens in, 383
Dorset Perennial Group, 118
Dorset Wildlife Trust, 118
Double Nurseries Ltd, Paul, 518
Doucment Supply Centre, 477
Dowler and Wakefield, 396
Downderry Nursery, 172
Downham, Fred, 66
Drake, Jack, 226, 247
Drake Aquilegias, John, 248
Dream Gardens, 427
Drumlarig Castle, 379
Drummond Castle Gardens, 364
Drysdale Garden Exotics, 160
du Garl Pasley, Anthony, 421
Duchy of Cornwall Nursery, 140
Duckbill Anchors Ltd, 396
Dumbarton Oaks: Trustees for Harvard University, 471
Duncan Daffodils, Brian, 230
Duncans of Milngavie, 227
Duncombe Park, 345
Dunham Massey, 357
Dunrobin Castle Gardens, 359
Dunster Castle, 325
Dupre Vermiculite, 396
Durban Flower Art Club, 61
Durham, graded gardens in, 383
Durham Massey, 87
Durston Peat Products, 397
Dyfed Wildlife Trust, 118
Dyffryn Botanic Garden, 351
Dyrham Park, 256
E L F Plants, Cramden Nursery, 217
Ealing Tertiary College, 461
Earth Connections, 427
Earth Gardening, 427
East Lambrook Manor, 325
East Sussex, graded gardens in, 388
Eastern Tree Surgery, 427
Eastgrove Cottage Garden & Nursery, 164, 298
Eastnor Castle, 298
Easton College, 462
Eden, Matthew, 403
Eden Plants, 232
Edinburgh College of Art/Heriot-Watt University, 468
Edinburgh & District Allotments & Gardens, Federation of, 119
Edmondsham House, 284
educational grants, 471
Edzell Castle, 364
Eggleston Hall Gardens, 152
Eldon, Garden Designer, Diana, 426
Elly Hill Herbs, 152
Elmridge Gardens Ltd, 152
Elmwood College, 468
Elsing Hall, 314
Elsoms Seeds Ltd, 518

Index 527

Elton Hall, 264
Elvaston Castle County Park, 278
Elworthy Cottage Garden Plants, 194
Emmetts Garden, 304
Emorsgate Seeds, 247, 416
Englefield House, 259
English Gardening School, The, 461
English Heritage Garden Grades, 380
English Nature, 69
English Woodlands Biocontrol, 397
Enright Landscapes, Mark, 436
Equatorial Plant Co, 152
Erddig Hall, 350, 379
Erway Farm House, 323
Essex, graded gardens in, 383
Essex House, 70, 257
Essex Wildlife Trust, 119
Euro Tree Service, 428
Europa Nostra, 87
Euston Hall, 329
Evans Orchids, Ken, 154
Eve, Les roses anciennes de André, 506
Eve, 506
Evelix Daffodils, 226
Everett, D & M, 164
Exbury Enterprises Ltd, 160
Exbury Gardens, 294
Exmouth Garden Products, 397
Exotic Fuchsias, 220
Expo '90 Osaka Travel Bursary, 473
export of plants, 242
Exeter University Gardens, 67, 280
Fair - Garden Designer, Linda, 435
Fairfield House, 295
Fairfield Lodge, 368
Fairhaven Gardens Trust, 314
Fairweather Ltd, Christopher, 159
Fairy Lane Nurseries, 158
Falkland Palace, 357
Family Trees, 160
FARGRO Ltd, 518
Faringdon House, 321
Farnborough Hall, 339
Feebers Hardy Plants, 145
Felbrigg Hall, 314, 500
Fell, Derek, 487
Felley Priory, 319
Fens, The, 154
Fenton House, 311
Fenwick, Jill, 432
Fern Nursery, The, 180
Ferndale Nursery and Garden Centre Ltd, 217, 428
Fernhill, 368
ferns, 236
fertilisers, buying, 417
FFC Landscape Architects/ The Garden Design Studio, 428
ffiske Herbs, Daphne, 184
Fibrex Nurseries Ltd, 60, 61, 210
Field House Alpines, 189, 247
Financial Times, 491
Finch Tree Care Specialists, Roy, 442
Finchale Training College, 458
Findlay Clark Ltd, 228, 518, 519
Fine Art Travel Ltd, 497
Firs Nursery, The, 137
First Aid in the Home, 508
Fish Plant Nursery, Margery, 195
Fisher, Sue, 486
Fisher Fuchsias, 221
Fisher Nursery, Kaytie, 202
Fisk's Clematis Nursery, 198
Fiskars UK Ltd, 397
Fisons Horticulture, 68

Fisons PLC, 518
Five Arrows Hotel, 498
Five Trees Garden Centre & Nursery Ltd, 519
Fletcher, M V, 132
Fletcher Moss Botanical Gardens, 294
Fleur de Lys, 208
Fleuroselect, 80
Flintham Hall, 319
Flintshire Woodlands, 428
Flora, 491
Flora Exotica, 154, 247
floral events, 64
Florence Court, 366, 500
Flower Arrangers Show Shop, The, 397
Flower Centre, 231
FMG Garden Designs, 428
Foliage & Unusual Plants, 134
foliage plants, 236
Foliage Scented & Herb Plants, 201
Folly Farm, 259
Ford Garden Designs, Marianne, 436
Forde Abbey, 284, 378
Forest Lodge Garden Centre, 201
Forestry Authority of England, 67
Forsham Cottage Arks, 398
Förster Stauden GmbH, 504
Forsythia, hardiness, 84
Forward Nurseries, 172
Fosse Alpines, 178
Foster, Sir Norman, 69
Fota, 367
Fountain Forestry Ltd, 429
Four Counties Nursery, 156
Four Seasons, 184
Foxbrush Gardens, 221
Foxgrove Farm, 259
Foxgrove Plants, 131
Frampton Court, 289, 500
France, 506
Franshams Ltd, 398
Friends of Brogdale, 119
Friends of Israel Educational Trust, 472
Friends of the Royal Botanic Garden Edinburgh, 119
Friends of the Royal Botanic Gardens Kew, 119
Frolics of Winchester, 398
Fron Nursery, 191
Frost & Co, 398
fruit, 236
Fruit Garden, The, 172
Fryer's Roses Ltd, 60, 74, 137
fuchsias, 236
Fuchsiavale Nurseries, 61, 164
Fulbrooke Nursery, 198
Fuller, Rodney, 196
Furzey Gardens, 295
Fyba Pot Company Ltd, The, 398
Galloway House Gardens, 356
Gandy's Roses Ltd, 178
Gannock Growers, 168
Garden, The, 491
Garden Academy, The, 459
Garden Answers, 491
Garden at the Elms, The, 165
Garden Centre at Hounslow Heath, The, 182
garden centre sales, 68
garden centres; French, 506
garden chemicals, disposal of, 508
Garden Events, 1
Garden History Society, The, 109
Garden House, The, 280
garden injuries, 508

Garden Log, 429
Garden News, 492
Garden of the Year Award, 378
Garden Scents, 429
Garden Solutions by Design, 429
Garden Style, 202
garden theft, 520
garden visiting, 65
Gardena UK Ltd, 398
Gardener, The, 492
Gardeners' Academy, The, 462
Gardeners' Breaks, 466
Gardeners' Delight, 497
Gardeners' Question Time, 66
Gardeners' Royal Benevolent Society, The, 512
Gardenglow Cocoa Shell, 398
Gardening Which?, 67, 492, 508
gardens; editors' personal choice, 377; for children, 374; German, 503; in the summer gap, 377; late opening hours, 375; seldom open, 376; winter, 377; young, 376
Gardens and Nurseries in Lincolnshire and South Humberside, 255
Gardens by Graham Evans, 429
Gardens Illustrated, 492
Gardens of Distinction, 429
Gardens of England and Wales Open to the Public, 254
Gardens of Scotland, The, 254
Gardens of the Rose, The, 65, 300
Gardenscape, 215, 429
Gascoigne Wild Flowers, Linda, 179
Gatehampton Nursery, 132
Gateshead Summer Flower Show, 62
Gaulden Manor, 325
Gaylor Garden Design, Jennifer, 432
Gayways Lawn Mower Centre, 398
GEEBRO Ltd, 398
Geeco Limited, 398
Geißler, Alpine Staudengärtnerei Siegfried, 505
General Municipal and Boilermakers' Union, 66
George & Associates, Anthony, 421
Geranium Nursery, The, 208
Gerhardt Pharmaceuticals Ltd, 398
Germany, 502
Gesellschaft der Heidefreunde, 125
Gesellschaft der Staudenfreunde, 125
Gidleigh Park Hotel, 280, 499
Gift Aid, 511
Glamorgan Wildlife Trust, 119
Glasgow Botanic Garden, 363
Glaxo (1972) Charity Trust, The, 474
Glebe Cottage Plants, 60, 145
Glenarn, 363
Glendoick Gardens, 365
Glendoick Garden Centre, 228
Glendragon, 500
Glendurgan Gardens, 270
Glenhirst Cactus Nursery, 180, 247
Glenveagh Castle, 368
Glenwhan Garden, 356
Gliffaes Country House Hotel, 498
Glin Castle, 371
Global Orange Groves UK, 150
Gloucestershire, graded gardens in, 383
Gloucestershire Gardens & Landscape Trust, 119
Glowcroft Ltd, 399
Gnome Reserve & Pixies' Wildflower Garden, The, 280
Godington Park, 304

528 Index

Godly's Roses, 168
Golby, Rupert, 442
Goldberry Garden Design, Jean, 432
Goldbrook Plants, 60, 198
Golden Acre Park, 348
Golden Landscapes, 430
Goldney Hall, 257
Good Directions Ltd, 399
Good Gardeners Association, The, 413
Good Gardens Guide, 88, 254
Goodnestone Park, 304
Gordale Nursery & Garden Centre, 137
Goscote Nurseries Ltd, 178, 430
Gouldings Fuchsias, 198
Gowranes, 365
Grace Landscapes Ltd, 430
Graham's Hardy Plants, 130
Granada Arboretum, 266
Grange Farm Nursery, 165
grant-making trusts, 471
grants, educational, 471
Grants Register, The, 471
grasses, 236
gravel, buying, 418
Gravetye Manor, 336, 498
Grayson - Sweet Pea Seedsman, Peter, 249
Graythwaite Hall, 275
Great Barfield, 261
Great Comp, 305
Great Dixter, 334
Great Dixter Nurseries, 205
Great Garden and Countryside Festival, The, 62
Great Gardens of England Ltd, 133, 168, 182
Greater London, graded gardens in, 384
Greater Manchester, graded gardens in, 384
Green, Henrietta, 485
Green Farm Plants, 57, 61, 202
Green Gardener Products, 399
Green Man Landscapes, 430
Greenacre Nursery, 60
Greenacres Horticultural Supplies, 399
Greenbank Garden, 363
Greencombe Garden Trust, 326
Greenland Arboretum, 65
Greenleaves Garden Centre Ltd, 143
Greenslacks Nurseries, 218
Greenspan Designs Ltd, 399
Greenstone Landscapes, 430
Greenvale Farm Ltd, 399
Greenway Gardens, 145
Greenways, 321
Greenwood Gardens, 189, 463
Greys Court, 87
Greystone Cottage, 321
Greywalls, 498
Griffiths, Mark, 487
Grimsthorpe Castle, 252
Grimsthorpe Castle Trust Ltd, 309
Grosvenor Garden Centre, 137
Ground Control Ltd, 430
ground cover plants, 236
Grounds for Concern, 67
Grove Gardens, Annes, 367
Groves & Son, C W, 150
Grower, The, 492
Growing Carpets, 169
Growing Wiser, 68
Guardian, The, 492
Guide to English Heritage Properties 1995, 255
Guinness, Bunny, 423

Gunby Hall, 310
Gwent Wildlife Trust, 120
GWS Ltd, 399
Gwydir Plants, 221
H_2O, 399
Haddon Hall, 278, 378
Haddonstone Ltd, 399
Hadlow College of Agriculture and Horticulture, 460
Hadspen Garden and Nursery, 194, 326
Halecat Garden Nurseries, 142
half-hardy plants, 236
Hall Farm & Nursery, 180, 192, 310
Halls of Heddon, 188
Halsway, 194
Hambrook Landscapes Ltd, 431
Hamilton, Geoff, 494, 508
Hammersmith and Fulham, London Borough of, 67
Hammerwood Park, 89
Hampshire, graded gardens in, 384
Hampshire Gardens Trust, 120
Hampton Court Palace, 65, 87, 312
Hampton Court Palace Flower Show, 56, 61, 62
Hanbury Hall, 89
Hanbury Manor Hotel, 498
Hannays of Bath, 130
Hardi Ltd, 400
Hardwick Hall, 278
Hardwicke House, 264
Hardy Exotics Nursery, 140
hardy nursery stock production, 85
Hardy Plant Society, The, 72, 110, 500
Hardy's Cottage Garden Plants, 61, 160, 431
Hare Hill Garden, 266
Harewood House, 89, 349, 379
Harkness, Jack, 68, 70
Harkness & Co Ltd, R, 61, 74, 169
Harlow Carr Botanical Gardens, 1, 346, 467
Harper's & Queens, 60
Harris Garden, The, 260
Harrison, Fiona, 428
Harrisons Delphiniums, 132, 247
Harrogate Great Autumn Flower Show, 56, 57, 59, 61, 63
Harrogate Spring Flower Show, 63
Hartshall Nursery Stock, 198
Hartside Nursery Garden, 142
Harvest Nurseries, 205
Harvey Garden World, Roger, 169
Hatchlands, 330
Hatfield House, 301
Haughley Park, 329
Haughton Hall, 89
Hawkstone Park Hotel, 498
Haws Watering Cans, 400
Hawthorne Gardens, Sue, 193
hay fever, 508
Hayes Gardenworld Ltd, 142, 431
Hayloft Plants, 165
Haynes & Partners, F, 217
Hayward's Carnations, 160
Hazelbury Manor, 89
Hazelby House, 260
Hazeldene Nursery, 173, 247
Headen Ltd, A E, 391
Heale House, 342, 378
Healey Garden Design, Sally, 442
health and safety, 507
Health and Safety Executive, The, 509
Heath Garden, 431
Heather, Duncan, 427

Heather Bank Nursery, 212
Heather Hedgehog, 59
Heather Society, The, 110
heathers, 236
Hebe Society, 110
Hedgerow Nursery, 218
hedging, 236
Heighley Gate Garden Centre, 188
Heldon Nurseries, 197
Heligan Manor Gardens, 89, 271
Hellyer's Garden Plants, 208
Helmingham Hall, 329
Hemsley, Peter, 439
Henderson & Sons, James, 247, 416
Henllys Lodge Plants, 221
Henry Doubleday Research Association (HDRA), 110, 413
Herb and Heather Garden Centre, 215
Herb Garden, The, 144
Herb Garden & Plant Hunters Nursery, The, 222
Herb Nursery, The, 179
Herb Society, The, 111
Herb Society of America, The, 472
Herbary Prickwillow, The, 134
Herbert CBE, Robin, 66
herbs, 237
Hereford & Worcester, graded gardens in, 385
Hereford College of Art & Design, 459
Herefordshire Nature Trust, 120
Hergest Croft Gardens, 165, 253, 299
Heritage Education Trust, 378, 379
Heritage Leisure, 400
heritage plants, 75
Heritage Tree Services, 431
Heritage Woodcraft, 400
Herons Bonsai Ltd, 61, 202
Herterton House Gardens & Nursery, 188, 318
Hertfordshire, graded gardens in, 385
Herts & Middlesex Wildlife Trust, 120
Hessayon, Dr D. G., 485
Hestercombe House, 326
Hever Castle, 305
Hewer, Professor Tom, 69
Hewthorn Herbs & Wild Flowers, 189
Hexham Herbs, 188, 318
Heywood Gardens, 370
Hickling Heath Nursery, 184
Hidcote Manor Garden, 290
Higginbotham Garden Landscaping, Ken, 435
High Banks Nurseries, 173
High Beeches, 59, 336
High Garden, The, 146
Highclere Castle, 295
Highdown, 336
Highfield Garden Centre, 156
Highfield Hollies, 160
Highfield Nurseries, 156
Highgates Nursery, 144
Hiley, Heather and Brian, 61, 201
Hill, John E M, 433
Hill Farm Herbs, 217
Hill Farmhouse Plants, 179
Hill House, 301
Hill House Garden, 281
Hill of Tarvit, 357
Hillbarn House, 342
Hiller Garden and Plant Centre, The, 210
Hillhout (UK) Ltd, 400
Hillier Garden Centre, 161, 208

Index 529

Hillier Gardens & Arboretum, Sir Harold, 1, 297, 379
Hillier Landscapes, 431
Hillier, Malcolm, 494
Hillier Nurseries Ltd, 61, 161, 518, 519
Hillview Hardy Plants, 192
Himalayan Kingdoms Ltd, 497
Hindle, Garden Designer and Lecturer, Josephine, 433
Hinton Ampner House, 295
Historic Houses, Castles and Gardens of Great Britain and Ireland, 254
Historic Houses Association, 378
Hobhouse, Penelope, 488
Hodges Barn, 290
Hodnet Hall, 324, 378
Hodsock Priory, 319
Hodsock Priory Garden Courses, 463
Hoecroft Plants, 185
Hoghton Tower, 307
Holden Clough Nursery, 177
Holdenby House Gardens, 316, 379
Holehird, 275
holiday cottages, 500
Holiday Homewatch, 501
Holker Hall, 276, 378, 379
Holkham Hall, 314
Holland Arms Garden Centre, 222
Hollies Park, The, 349
Hollington Nurseries, 132, 431
Holly Gate Cactus Nursery, 209, 247
Holly Society of America Inc, 125
Holme Nurseries, 150
Home Covert, 342
Home Meadows Nursery Ltd, 199
Homer Pressings, 400
Homes and Gardens, 492
Homesitters Ltd, 501
Honey Brothers, 431
Honeysome Aquatic Nursery, 134
Hoo House Nursery, 156
Hop Shop, The, 61, 400
Hope End Hotel, 498
Hopes, Garden Designer, Mary-Jane, 437
Hopleys Plants Ltd, 169
Horticultural Abstracts, 82
Horticultural Correspondence College, 466
horticultural libraries, 477
Horticultural Research International, 472, 479
Horticultural Therapy, 463
Horticulture Week, 492
Hortus, 492
Hosford's Geraniums & Garden Centre, 231
Hosta Garden, 228
Hotbox Heaters Ltd, 400
Hotels with good gardens, 498
Hotterotter Group, 400
Houghall College, 459
Houghall College Gardens, 286
Houghton Farm Plants, 209
Houghton Lodge, 295
House and Garden, 492
House of Dun, 365
House of Pitmuies, 365
house plants, 237
Housewatch Ltd, 501
How Caple Court Gardens, 165, 299
Howarth, Maggy, 487
Howick Hall Gardens, 318
Huddleston, Hazel M, 431

Hudson's Historic House and Garden Directory of Great Britain and Ireland, 255
Hugh Baird College, 462
Hughenden Manor, 261
Hull Farm Conifer Centre, 154
Humberside, graded gardens in, 385
Humphrey, V H, 204
Humphries Garden Centre, 151
Hunt, Barbara, 422
Huntly Francis, Elizabeth, 428
Hunts Court Garden & Nursery, 157, 290
Hurdletree Nurseries, 180
Hurrans Garden Centre Ltd, 157
Hutton-in-the-Forest, 276
Hyatt, Brenda, 171
Hyde Hall *see* Royal Horticultural Society
Hydon Nurseries, 202, 431
Ibbetson Settlement, The Harry, 474
Ichiyo School of Ikebana, 61, 111
ICI Fertilisers, 518
Ickworth Park, 89
ICOMOS, 520
Iden Croft Herbs, 173
Iford Manor, 343
import of plants, 242
Inchbald School of Design, 461
Independent, The, 493
Independent on Sunday, The, 493
Ingwersen Ltd, W E Th, 58, 209, 250
Inhome Limited, 401
injuries, garden, 508
The Institute - Hampstead Garden Suburb, 461
Institute of Horticulture, The, 420
Intakes Farm Plants, 197
Interflora, 61
International Acers, 165, 432
International Aroid Society, 125
International Botanical Congress, 514
International Camellia Society, 111
International Clematis Society, 58
International Code of Nomenclature, 514
International Correspondence Schools, 469
International Council on Monuments and Sites, 520
International Dendrology Society, 65, 66, 111
International Lilac Society, 125
International Palm Society, 125
International Rose Trials 1994, 76
International Society of Arboriculture, 472
International Violet Association, 111
International Water Lily Society, 111
Interval Systems Ltd, 401
Inveresk Lodge Garden, 360
Inverewe, 359
Ireland Landscape Architect, David, 425
iris, 278
Iris de Thau, 506
Irish Organic Farmers and Growers Association, The, 413
Irish Tourist Board, 255
Isabella Plantation, 312
Island Plants, 226
Isle of Wight, graded gardens in, 385
Isle of Wight College of Arts and Technology, 459
Isle of Wight Gardens Trust, 120
ivies, 237

Ivy Cottage, 284
J G S Weathervanes, 401
Jack's Patch, 146
Jackson, Michael Alwyn, 437
Jackson's Nurseries, 197
James Foundation, The Edward, 465
Japanese Garden Society, 112
Jardine, Garden Designer, Joy, 434
Jardins de Cotelles, Les, 506
Jasmine Cottage Gardens, 130
Jeffries Landscapes, Nigel, 438
Jekka's Herb Farm, 61, 130
Jenkyn Place, 296
Jensen GmbH, Ingwer J., 505
Jerusalem Botanical Gardens Scholarship, 472
John, Elton, 66
John Landscape Design & Consultancy, Susanne, 445
Johnsons Seeds, 248
Johnstown Castle Gardens, 372
Johnstown Garden Centre, 232
Jones, C & K, 136, 219
Jordens, Sol, 444
Josephine Hindle, 466
Journeés de Plantes de Courson, 63
Judy's Country Garden, 181, 434
Just Phlomis, 157
Just Roses, 205
K & C Cacti, 146
Kaye Ltd, Reginald, 177
Kayes Garden Nursery, 179, 460
Kedleston Hall, 278
Keepers Nursery, 173, 434
Keir Watson Garden Design, 434
Kellett, P H, 175, 438
Kellie Castle, 357
Kelly, John, 494
Kelways Ltd, 194
Ken Caro, 271
Ken Muir Nurseries, 154
Kennedy Arboretum, The John F., 372
Kennedys Garden Centre, 68, 211, 213
Kent, graded gardens in, 385
Kent Street Nurseries, 206
Kent Trust for Nature Conservation, 120
Kenwith Nursery, 146
Kenwood Park, 312
Kettlesing Nurseries, 215
Kew School of Horticulture, 464
Kexby Design, 435
Key and Associates, Richard, 441
Kiftsgate Court Gardens, 157, 290
Kildalton Agricultural and Horticultural College, 470
Kildrummy Castle, 358, 499
Kilfane Glen & Waterfall, 370
killer worms, 67
Killerton, 87, 88, 281
King Arboricultural Consultant, Graham, 430
King Easton Ltd, 401
Kings Crown of Kelvedon, 248
Kingsbury, Noël, 438
Kingston Lacy, 284, 379
Kingston Maurward College, 458
Kingston Maurward Gardens, 285
Kinlochlaich House Gardens, 228, 435
Kinoith Garden, 367
Kirkley Hall Gardens, 318
Kirkstall Abbey Monastery Gardens, 89
Klose, Staudengärtner, 503
Knap Hill Nursery Ltd, 202
Knebworth House, 301

Knight Terrace Pots, 402
Knights Garden Centre, 202, 203, 203
Knightshayes Garden Trust, 146, 281
Knoll Gardens, 285
Knowle Nets, 402
Knowsley Community College, Land-based Industries, 462
Konstsmide UK Ltd, 402
Kordes' Söhne, W., 505
Krebs, Jürgen, 505
Kubota (UK) Ltd, 402
Kut and Dried, 402
L & P Peat Ltd, 402
Laburnum Nurseries, 179
Lackham College, 466
Lackham Country Attractions, 343
Ladham House, 305
Lafoy, Eric, 428
Laing Foundation, The Kirby, 474
Lainston House Hotel & Restraurant, 498
Lakeland Horticultural Society, 58
Lakeside, 299
Lambeth College, 461
Lamorran House, 271
Lancashire, graded gardens in, 386
Lancaster, Nancy, 71
Lancaster, Roy, 494
Land and Tree Ltd, 435
Land Farm Gardens, 349
Landcare, 435
Landford Trees, 213
Landlife Wildflowers Ltd, 183, 248
Landscape Design Studio, 435
Landscape Institute, The, 420
Landscape Plants, 173
landscaping materials, buying, 418
Landskip and Prospect, 435
Langdon (London) Ltd, 402
Langham Lodge, 308
Langley Boxwood Nursery, 161
Langside College, 469
Langthorns Plantery, 154
Lanhydrock Gardens, 140, 271
Larch-Lap Ltd, 402
Laspen Trust, The, 474
Layham Garden Centre, 174
LDC Ltd, 435
Le Manoir aux Quat' Saisons, 498
Lea Gardens, 144, 278
Leach Trees, Ken, 518
Leaky Pipe Systems Ltd, 402
Ledward, Daphne, 66
Lee & Co Ltd, A T, 391
Leeds Castle, 305
Leeds Metropolitan University, 467
Leeming House Hotel, 499
Lees Mill Products, 402
Lees-Milne, Alvilde, 69
legacies, 512
LeGrice Roses, 61
Leicestershire, graded gardens in, 386
Leicestershire and Rutland Trust for Nature Conservation, 120
Leighton Hall, 307
Leith Hall, 358
Leonardslee Gardens, 253, 337
Levens Hall, 276
Levington Horticulture Ltd, 68, 69, 403
Lewis Tree Surgeons, Douglas, 426
libraries, 477
Libraries Directory 1991-93, The, 477
lilies, 237
Lilliesleaf Nursery, 222
Lime Cross Nursery, 206

Lincolnshire, graded gardens in, 386
Lincolnshire College of Agriculture DEL, 461
Lincolnshire Trust for Nature Conservation, The, 120
Lindisfarne Castle, 87
Lindley Library, 59, 477
Lingard + Styles Landscape, 436
Lingholm, 276
Link-Stakes Ltd, 403
Linnaean Society of London Library, 478
Linneman, Wolfgang, 504
Liscahane Nursery and Garden Centre, 232
Lisdoonan Herbs, 230
Lismore Castle, 371
Little Brook Fuchsias, 203
Little Creek Nursery, 130
Little Moreton Hall, 266
Little Thackenham Hotel, 499
Little Treasures Nursery, 140
Littlewood Landscape Designer, Michael, 437
Llyfrgell Genedlaethol Cymru, 481
Loader Tree Care Specialists, Richard, 441
Loch Melfort Hotel, 499
Lochalsh Woodland Garden, 360
Lockyer, C S, 129
Lodge Park Walled Garden, 370
Logan Botanic Gardens, 356
London, graded gardens in, 384
Long Barn, 305
Long Close, 308
Long Cross Hotel, 499
Long Man Gardens, 206
Longacre Nursery, 174, 436
Longhall Nursery, 213
Longleat House, 343
Longstock Park Nursery, 161
Longstock Water Gardens, 296
Lonicera, new hybrids, 86
Lord, Dr Tony, 66
Lotherton Hall, 349
Lotus Landscapes, 436
Lower Hall, 324
Lower House Farm, 352
Lower Severalls Herb Nursery, 195
Loyalty Garden, The, 296
Lucas, John H, 433
Lucas Garden Statuary, 403
Luton Hoo, 258
Lutyens, Mark, 436
LW Plants, 169
LWL Landscapes, 61
Lydney Park Gardens, 290
Lygon Arms, 499
Lyme Park, 266
Lymington Flower Club, 61
Lytes Cary Manor, 326
McArd, S M, 249
McBeans Orchids, 61
MacGregor, Elizabeth, 224
Mackey's Garden Centre, 231, 248
Mackintosh Charitable Trust, The Viscount, 475
McLauchlan Horticulture, John, 401
Macpennys Nurseries, 151
McVicar, Jekka, 487
Madrona Nursery, 174
Magnolia Gardens, 174
Magnolia Society Inc, The, 125
Magnolia × gotoburgensis, 84
Maguire, Christopher, 424

Malahide Nurseries Ltd, 231
Malaysia Tourism Promotion Board, 61
Malleny House Garden, 360, 520
Mallet Court Nursery, 57, 195
Malvern Autumn Show, 63
Malvern Spring Gardening Show, 56, 63
Mammillaria Society, The, 112
Manchester, graded gardens in, 384
Manchester Metropolitan University, 458
Manderston, 354
Manor House, Bledlow, 262
Manor House, Stanton Harcourt, 321
Manor House, Upton Grey, 296
Manor House, Walton-in-Gordano, 257
Manorbier Garden Centre, 220
Mansell & Hatcher Ltd, 218
manure, buying, 417
Mapperton House Gardens, 285
Margam Park, 351
Marks Hall, 89
Marle Place Gardens & Nursery, 174
Marshall's Malmaisons, 157
Marshalls, 248
Marston, J & D, 170
Marston & Langinger Ltd, 403
Marston Exotics, 165
Martin, J E, 247
Martinez, Jan, 432
Martins Nursery, 199
Marwood Hill Gardens, 58, 146, 281
Massey, Sarah, 442
Matlock Garden Centre Ltd, 144
Mattock Charitable Trust, The W. T., 475
Mattocks Roses, 61, 74, 190
Maxicrop International Ltd, 403
Mead Nursery, The, 213
Meadowcroft Fuchsias, 135
Mears Ashby Nurseries Ltd, 217
Melbourne Hall, 252, 279
Melcourt, 403
Mellerstain, 355
Mellors Garden Ceramics, 403
Melville Nurseries, 227
Mendle Nursery, 170
Merebrook Water Plants, 166
Merriments Gardens, 206, 437
Merrist Wood College, 464
Merrist Wood College Plant Shop, 203
Merseyside, graded gardens in, 386
Merton Adult College, 461
Merton Nurseries, 192
Mertoun Gardens, 355
Mesemb Study Group, 112
Messham, Carol, 423
Metpost Ltd, 403
Metro Products Ltd, 403
Meudon Hotel, 499
Michelham Priory, 334
Mickfield Fish and Watergarden Centre, 199, 437
Middlethorpe Hall, 499
Miles, Paul, 439
Mill Cottage Plants, 195
Mill Hill Plants, 189
Mill House, The, 252
Mill Race Nursery, 155
Mill Race Landscapes Ltd, *see* Mill Race Nursery
Millais Nurseries, 203
Millman Garden Design, Sonya, 444
Mills Farm Plants and Gardens, 199
Milton Garden Plants, 151
Milton Lodge, 326

Index 531

Ministry of Agriculture, Fisheries & Food, 472, 478
Minterne, 285
Mires Beck Nursery, 170
Miserden Park, 291
Mitchell, Alan, 68
Mitchell, Mary & Peter, 209
Monksilver Nursery, 135
Monkton Elm Garden Centre, 195, 437
Monocot Nursery, 130, 248
Montacute House, 326
Montgomeryshire Wildlife Trust, 120
Morehavens Camomile Nurseries, 133
Moreland, John, 433
Morrey & Son, F, 137
Morton Hall, 320
Moseley Old Hall, 328, 379
Motts Travel, 497
Mottisfont Abbey, 296
Mottistone Manor, 302, 500
Moulton College, 462
Mount Edgcumbe Gardens, 271
Mount Perennial Plants, Frances, 154
Mount Pleasant Trees, 130
Mount Skippet, 322
Mount Stewart, 366
Mount Usher Gardens, 372
Mr Fothergill's Seeds Ltd, 248
Muckross Garden Centre, 232, 437
Muckross House & Gardens, 370
Muir, Ken, 61
Mukaluk, 403
mulches, buying, 417
Muncaster Castle, 276
Muncaster Fuchsias, Kathleen, 181
Muncaster Plants, 142
Munstead Wood, 331
Murrel Gardens, The, 357
Museum of Garden History, The, 312
Myddelton House Gardens, 312
Myerscough College, 460
N&GC, 493
NAFAS *see* National Association of Flower Arranging Societies
Naked Cross Nurseries, 151
Nareys Garden Centre, 199, 437
Nashi pears, 85
National Association of Flower Arrangement Societies, 61, 112
National Auricula Primula and Society (Southern Section), 112
National Begonia Society, 113
National Bonsai Society, 113
National Botanic Gardens, Dublin, 369
National Chrysanthemum Society, 113
National Collection of Passiflora, 131
National Council for the Conservation of Plants and Gardens (NCCPG), 57, 58, 113; heritage plants, 75; National Collections, 58, 253
National Dahlia Society, 113
National Federation of Flower Arranging Societies; shows and exhibitions, 64
National Gardens Scheme Charitable Trust, The, 87, 254, 513
National Library of Scotland, 480
National Library Wales, 480
National Nature Reserve, 69
National Pot Leek Society, 113
National Society of Allotment and Leisure Gardeners, 114
National Sweet Pea Society, The, 114
National Trust, The, 1, 500
National Trust for Scotland, The, 500

National Trust Gardens Handbook, 255
National Vegetable Society, 114
National Viola and Pansy Society, 114
Natural History Museum, The, 478
Natural Pest Control Ltd, 404
Natural Selection, 213
Naturescape, 190, 248
Naturetrek, 497
Nederlandse Heidervereniging 'Ericultura', 125
Nehra Cookes Chemicals Ltd, 404
Neighbourhood Watch schemes, 520
Nene Valley Adult Education, 457
Ness Botanic Gardens, 1, 267; weather, 97
Nest Nurseries, Martin, 181
Netlon Ltd, 404, 519
Nettletons Nursery, 203
new plants, 72; 1994, 74
New Plantsman, The, 493
New Zealand Alpine Gardening Society, 125
New Zealand Fuchsia Society Inc, 125
New Zealand Gladiolus Council, 125
New Zealand plants, 237
Newby Hall, 346, 378
Newstead Abbey, 320
Newton Hill Alpines, 218
Newton Rigg College, 458
Nice, G, 198
Nicky's Rock Garden Nursery, 146
Nicolson, Nigel, 67
Nine Springs Nursery, 161
nomenclature changes, 514
Norbark (Northern Bark Ltd), 404
Norden Alpine Nursery, 215
Nordybank Nurseries, 192
Norfield Trees & Seeds, Andrew, 156, 246
Norfolk, graded gardens in, 386
Norfolk Lavender Ltd, 185
Norfolk Naturalists Trust, 120
Norman Bonsai, 206
Nortene, 404
North American Heather Society, 125
North American Lily Society Inc, 125
North Court, 302
North Devon Garden Centre, 147
North End House, 264
North Green Seeds, 249
North Green Snowdrops, 199
North of England Horticultural Society, 121
North of England Rose, Carnation and Sweet Pea Society, The, 121
North Wales Tree Service, 438
North Wales Wildlife Trust, 121
North Yorkshire, graded gardens in, 389
Northamptonshire, graded gardens in, 387
Northamptonshire Wildlife Trust, 121
Northbourne Court, 306
Northern Horticultural Society, 114
Northumberland, graded gardens in, 387
Northumbria Gardens Scheme, 255
Northumbria Nurseries, 188
Norton, Paul, 439
Norton Priory Museum & Gardens, 267, 379
Norton Radstock Technical College, 464
Norwell Nursery, 190
Notcutts Garden Centre, 169, 174, 203, 204, 211
Notcutts Landscapes, 438

Notcutts Nurseries, 61, 68, 199
Nottinghamshire, graded gardens in, 387
Nottinghamshire Wildlife Trust, 121
Nuffield Farming Scholarships Trust, The, 475
Nuneham Courtenay Arboretum, 322
Nunwell House, 302
nurseries; French, 506
Nutscene Garden Products Ltd, 404
Nymans, 337, 500
O'Callaghan & Associates, D P, 425
Oak Cottage Herb Garden, 192, 438
Oak Tree Nursery, 215
Oakhurst Nursery, 206
Oaklands College, 460
Oakleigh Nurseries, 61, 161
Oare House, 343
Oatridge Agricultural College, 469
Observer, The, 493
Odell Castle, 258
Offham House, 334
Ohara School of Ikebana, 115
Okell's Nurseries, 137
Old Court Nurseries, 166
Old Manor Nursery, The, 157
Old Mill Herbary, The, 141
Old Rectory, Burghfield, The, 260
Old Rectory, Farnborough, The, 322
Old Rectory, Sudborough, The, 317
Old Rectory Cottage, 260
Old Semeil Herb Garden, 359
Old Vicarage, The, 343
Oldbury Nurseries, 61, 175
Olivers, 287
Orchard House Nursery, 216
Orchard Nurseries, 181, 438
Orchardstown Nurseries, 232
Orchid Society of Great Britain, 115
Orchid Sundries Ltd, 151, 404
Orcon Exotics, 166
Organic Concentrates Ltd, 404
organic gardening, 413
Organic Gardening, 493
organic nurseries, 239
Original Organics Ltd, 404
Ornate Products, 405
Oscroft's Dahlias, 211, 217
Osterley Park, 87, 312
Otley College of Agriculture and Horticulture, 464
Otter Nurseries Ltd, 147, 438
Otter's Court Heathers, 195, 438
Où trouver vos plantes, 506
Oulton House, 328
Overbecks, 87, 281
Overbury Court, 299
overgrown plants, 251
Owl Cottage, 303
Owlpen Manor, 291, 499
Oxburgh Hall, 315
Oxford Botanic Garden, 61, 322
Oxfordshire, graded gardens in, 387
P M A Plant Specialities, 196
Pacific Horticulture, 493
Pack Garden Design, Sue, 445
Padlock Croft, 135, 264
paeonies, 239
Page & Moy Ltd, 497
Paignton Zoo & Botanical Gardens, 282
Painshill Park, 89, 331
Painswick Rococo Garden, 291
Palm Centre, The, 183
Palmer & Son, A J, 132
palms, 239
Pan Britannica Industries Ltd, 405

532 Index

Pantiles Plant & Garden Centre, 61, 204, 439
Paradise Centre, 200, 249
Parcevall Hall Gardens, 346
Parham, 337, 378
Park Farm, 288
Park Forge, 405
Park Garden Centre, 131, 439
Park Green Nurseries, 200
Parkes & Co Ltd, Samuel, 407
Parnham House, 285
Parsons, Andrea - The Parsons Garden, 420
Pashley Manor, 334
Pathfinder Gardening, 439
Pavey & Associates, Graham A, 430
payroll giving, 511
Peart & Co Ltd, F, 397
peat, whole, 68
Peat Producers Association, 69
Peckover House, 264
Pelargonium species, 84
pelargoniums, 239
Pelham Landscapes, 439
Pencarrow, 272
Penjerrick, 89, 272
Penn, 267
Pennell & Sons Ltd, 170
Penpergwm Lodge, 352
Penrhyn Castle, 352
Penrhyn Charitable Trust, The, 475
Penshurst Place, 306
Peover Hall, 267
Pepinières Charentaises, 506
Period House and Its Garden, 493
Period Living and Traditional homes, 493
periodicals, 404
Permaculture Association, The, 415
Perrie Hale Forest Nursery, 147
Perry's Plants, 216
Perrybrook Nursery, 193
Perryhill Nurseries, 206, 439
Pershore College of Horticulture, 466
Pershore College of Horticulture Library, 480
Pershore *see* Royal Horticultural Society
Perth Garden Centre, 229
Petal Designs Ltd, 439
Pete & Ken Cactus Nursery, 175
Petworth House, 337
Phedar Nursery, 137, 249
Philip, Chris, 66
Philips Landscape and Garden Design, Nigel L, 438
Phillips, Sue, 66
Phipps, A & A, 129
Phostrogen, 405
phytosanitary certificates, 243
Picton Castle, 351
Pine Lodge Gardens, 272
Pinewood House, 331
Pinks & Carnations, 177
Pitmedden, 359
Pitt Landscape Design, Ray, 441
Planscapes, 440
plant breeders rights, 73, 76
Plant Breeding Abstracts, 82
Plant Finder, The, 66, 73
Plant Health Order, 242
plant passports, 244
Plant World Botanic Gardens, 147, 249
Plantables, 224
Plantasia, 352
Plantation, The, 193

Planters Garden Centre, 197
Plantings Garden Nursery, 223
Plants, R D, 148
Plantsmanship, 440
Plantworld, 155
Plas Brondanw Gardens, 353
Plas Newydd, 353
Plas Penhelig, 353, 499
Plas-yn-Rhiw, 353
Platts, Roger, 407
Plaxtol Nurseries, 175, 440
Pleasant View Nursery & Garden, 147
Plumptree, George, 486
Plysu Housewares Ltd, 405
poisonous plants, 507
Polesden Lacey, 331
pondliners, buying, 417
Porous Pipe Ltd, 405
Port Lympne Gardens, 306
Porter's Fuchsias, 183
Porthpean House Gardens, 141
Portmeirion, 353
Post House Gardens, 351
Potash Nursery, 61, 200
Potterton & Martin, 61, 75, 181, 249
Pound Hill House, 344
Pound Lane Nurseries, 162
Pounsley Plants, 147
Powderham Castle, 282
Power Garden Products, 405
Powerscourt Gardens, 373
Powis Castle, 354, 520
Poyntzfield Herb Nursery, 226
Practical Gardening, 493
Practicality Brown Ltd, 405
Precise Irrigation (UK) Ltd, 405
Preen Manor, 324
Prideaux Place, 89
Primrose Cottage Nursery & Garden Centre, 158
Primrose Hill, 369
primulas, 239
Pringle Plants, 223
Prior Park, 88, 89
Priorwood Garden, 355
Priory, The, 291
Priory Garden Nursery, 157
Private Landscapes, 440
Probus Demonstration Garden, 272
professional services, 419
Professional Tree Services, 440
Prosol, 406
protected zones, 244
Provincial Booksellers Fairs Association, The, 481
Provincial Tree Services Ltd, 440
Pumps 'n' Tubs, 406
Quartet Design, 440
Queen Elizabeth the Queen Mother Bursary, The, 473
Queen's Wood Arboretum & Country Park, 299
Quest-Ritson - Corsley Mill, Brigid, 212
Radnorshire Wildlife Trust, 121
Rae, Gordon, 66
Raffles - Thatched Garden Buildings, 406
Rainthorpe Hall, 252
Ram House Garden, 372
Ramster, 252, 331
Rank Prize Funds, The, 475
Ransomes Sims & Jefferies Ltd, 519
Rarer Plants, 216
raspberries, new, 83
Raven Tree Services, 440

Raveningham Gardens, 185
Raveningham Hall, 315
Ravenscourt Park, 67
Ravensthorpe Nursery, 217
Reads Nursery, 185
Rease Heath, 268
Reaseheath College (Cheshire College of Agriculture), 458
Regency Garden Buildings, 406
Rehau Ltd, 406
Reid & Co Ltd, Ben, 224, 519
Remanoid, 406
Renaissance Bronzes, 406
Renishaw Hall, 279, 521
Reuthe, G, 61
Rhinefield House Hotel, 499
Rhodes & Rockliffe, 155
rhododendrons, 239
RHS Enterprises Ltd, 148
Riber Hall Hotel, 499
Richards & Associates, Simon, 443
Richardson Florist, 61
Rickard's Hardy Ferns Ltd, 61, 60, 166
Ridgeway Heather Nursery, 193
Rileys Chrysanthemums, 144
Ripley Castle, 346
Riseholme Hall, 310
Rivendell Nursery, 216
Riverhill House Gardens, 306
Rivières, Ets, 506
Robinson, Peter, 488
Robinson & Sons Ltd, W, 250
Robinson, Mrs S, 199
Robinson Penn Partnership, The, 441
Robinsons of Whaley Bridge, 138
Robus Pottery, 406
Roche Court, 344
Rock Garden Club, Prague, The, 125
Rockingham Castle, 317, 379
Rode Hall, 268
Rodmarton Manor, 291
Roeber Landscapes, Nicholas, 438
Roebuck Eyot Limited, 406
Roffey Bros Ltd, 406, 417
Roger Ltd, R V, 216
Rogers Associates, Peter, 440
Romantic Garden Nursery, The, 186
Romilt Landscape Design & Construction Ltd, 441
Rookhope Nurseries, 152
Roots Garden Centre Ltd, 224
Rosaleyn Nursery, 61
Rose Hybridists Association, 125
rose propagation, 86
Roseland House Nursery, 141
Rosemoor *see* Royal Horticultural Society
roses, 239
Rosewood Nurseries, 175
Ross - Landscape Design, Veronica, 447
Ross Landscape Architects, Mark, 437
Ross Tree Services, 442
Rothschild, Lord, 87
Roundstone Garden Centre Ltd, 209
Rousham House, 322
Rowallane Garden, 87, 366; weather, 103
Rowden Gardens, 148
Rowe, Frank, 519
Royal Benevolent Society, The, 511
Royal Botanic Garden, Edinburgh, 360; Library, 480; weather, 91
Royal Botanic Gardens, Kew, 66, 69, 88, 313, 465; library and archives, 478

Index 533

Royal Botanical and Horticultural Society of Manchester and the Northern Counties, The, 475
Royal Caledonian Horticultural Society, The, 121
Royal Commission for the Exhibition of 1851, 475
Royal Gardeners' Orphan Fund, The, 511, 512
Royal Horticultural Society, The, 115, 474, 480; 'bought-in-stock controversy', 59; Centre for Horticultural Science, 66; Fruit Group, 57; Gold Medals, 60; holiday tours, 496; lectures, 1; Plant Centre, Wisley, 204; Rhododendron, Camellia and Magnolia Group, 57; RHS Garden, Hyde Hall, 1, 288; RHS Garden, Pershore, 1; RHS Garden, Rosemoor, 2, 282; RHS Garden, Wisley, 2, 88, 331; Westminster Flower Shows, 2; Wisley Flower Show, 64; Wisley trials, 78; Wisley, weather, 94
Royal National Institute for the Blind, The, 508
Royal National Rose Society, 76, 116; drop in membership, 67; fragrance competition, 68; planning appeal, 65
Royal Society, The, 476
Royal Society for the Prevention of Accidents, The, 508
royal warrants, 518
Rufford Old Hall, 307
Rumary, Mark, 485
Rumwood Nurseries, 176
Rushfields of Ledbury, 166
Rushforth, Keith, 434
Ruskins Arboricultural Group, 442
Ruthall Manor, 324
Rutherford, Sarah, 442
Ryal Nursery, 188
Ryans Nurseries, 232
Rycroft Landscape Architects, Sarah, 443
Rydal Mount, 277
Ryobi Lawn & Garden (UK) Ltd, 407
Ryton Organic Gardens, 2, 339, 413
S & S Perennials, 179
Sackville-West, Vita, 67
safety, 507
Sainsbury Charitable Trust, Robert and Lisa, 69
St Andrews Botanic Garden, 357
St Annes Vineyard, 158
St Helens College, 462
St Ishmaels Nurseries and Garden Centre, 221
St John Ambulance Brigade, 508
St Michael's Mount, 273
St Paul's Walden Bury, 301
Saintpaulia & Houseplant Society, The, 116
Salesian College of Horticulture, 470
Saling Hall, 288
Salley Gardens, 190, 249
Saltram, 253, 282
Sambucus nigra, breeding new, 82
Sampford Shrubs, 148
sand, buying, 418
Sandford Award, 378, 379
Sandringham House, 315
São Paolo, Flower Club of, 60
Sarracenia Nurseries, 183
Savill Garden, The, 332

Savill's Clematis Ltd, 155
Sayers Travel, David, 497
Scamp, R A, 141
Scarletts Plantcare, 407
scented plants, 234
Schöppinger Irisgarten, 504
Schultheis, Rosen von, 505
Schuster, Gartenbaubetrieb, 504
Scoil Stiofáin, 469
Scotland's Gardens Scheme, 513
Scotney Castle, 306
Scotsdale Nursery & Garden Centre, 135, 443
Scotsman, The, 494
Scott & Sons Ltd, O M, 404
Scott's Nurseries, 217
Scottish Agricultural College, 469, 473
Scottish Allotments and Gardens Society, The, 122
Scottish National Sweet Pea, Rose & Carnation Society, 116
Scottish Rhododendron Society, 116
Scottish Rock Garden Club, 117
Scottish Tourist Board, 255
Scottish Wildlife Trust, 122
Scottlandscape, 443
Scotts Clematis, 148
Scotts Nurseries Ltd, 196
Seaforde Gardens, 230
Search, Gay, 488
Searle, P A, 438
Seaside Nursery and Garden Centre, 231
Secret Garden Designs by Christina Oates, 443
Seed House, The, 249
Seeds-by-Size, 250, 416
Sempervivum Society, The, 117
sempervivums, 240
services, professional, 419
Seven Counties Garden Design, 443
Sewell, Diane, 61
Seymours Garden & Leisure Group, 443
Sezincote, 292
Shackleton Garden, 369
Shamrock Horticulture Ltd, 407
Sharp Studio, The David, 396
Shaw & Sons, Reuben, 190
Sheen Garden Developments Ltd, 407
Sheen Ltd, Joanna, 401
Sheffield Botanical Gardens, 348
Sheffield Park Garden, 335
Sheldon Manor, 252, 344
Shepton Nursery Garden, 196
Sherborne Garden, 257
Sherborne Gardens Nursery, 157
Sherbourne Park, 339
Sheringham Park, 315
Sherston Parva Nursery, 213
Shipley College, 467
Shipton (Bulbs), John, 220
Shire Garden Buildings, 407
Shock, Katherine, 434
Short & Partners, Anthony, 421
Shrewsbury Flower Show, 63
Shropshire, graded gardens in, 387
Shrubland Hall, 329
shrubs, 240
Shugborough Hall, 328, 379
Silk Morus, 443
Sim and Coventry, 407
Simms, Clive, 180
Simply Garlands, 407
Simply Plants, 135

Simpsons Nursery, 186
Sinclair Horticulture, William, 411
Sino-Himalayan Plant Association, 117
Sisley, David R, 426
Sissinghurst Castle Garden, 307
Sizergh Castle, 277
Skibbereen, 512
Slack Top Alpines, 218
Sledmere House, 302
Sleightholmedale Lodge, 346
Smallscapes Nursery, 200
Smeeden Foreman Partnership, 443
Smith, Alan C, 171
Smith, Elizabeth, 140
Smith, Harry, 495
Smith, Peter J, 61, 209, 519
Smith & Son, John, 179
Smith Horticultural Trust, The, 476
Smith's Garden & Leisure, Stephen H, 219, 170, 218
Snowshill Manor, 292
Société Française des Roses, La, 125
Société National d'Horticulture de France, 125
Society for Growing Australian Plants, The, 126
Society of Garden Designers, the, 420
Soil Association, The, 413
Solihull College, 465
Somerleyton Hall, 329
Somerset, graded gardens in, 388
Somerset Gardens Trust, 122
Somerset Postal Flowers, 408
Somerset Wildlife Trust, 122
Sorbus domestica, new Colony of, 82
South American plants, 240
South Lodge Hotel, 499
South Solway Mosses, 69
South Yorkshire, graded gardens in, 390
Southend Adult Community College, 459
Southern Africa Travel, 497
Southern Tree Surgeons Ltd, 444
Southfield Nurseries, 56, 61, 181
Southport College of Art and Technology, 462
Southport Flower Show, 56, 64
Southview Nurseries, 162
Spalding, Adrian, 67
Sparsholt College Hampshire, 459
Spear & Jackson Garden Products, 408
Special Plants, 213
Spectator, The, 494
Spedan Lewis Foundation, The John, 474
Speke Hall, 87
Spetchley Park, 299
Speyside Heather Centre, 226
Spinners, 162, 297
Sportsmark Group Ltd, 408
Spreckley, Rosemary, 166
Sprich, Staudengärtnerei Wolfgang, 504
Spring Gardening Festival, 56
Springbank Nurseries, 58
Springfields Show Gardens, 310
Springwood Pleiones, 218
Staffordshire, graded gardens in, 388
Staffordshire College of Agriculture, 464
Staffordshire Gardens & Parks Trust, 122
Staffordshire Wildlife Trust, 122
Stancombe Park, 292
Standard Manufacturing Co, The, 408
Standen, 335

534 Index

Stangwrach Leisure Products, 408
Stansfield, 322
Stanway House, 292
Stapeley Water Gardens Ltd, 138, 268
Starborough Nursery, 176
Starkie & Starkie Ltd, 408
Statue Alarms, 521
Staudenkulturen Stade, 504
Stay Garden Design & Consultancy, Joanna, 432
Stevens, David, 486, 487
Stevens International Ltd, David, 426
Stewarts (Nottm) Ltd, 250
Sticky Wicket, 286
Stihl Ltd, Andreas, 392
Stillingfleet Lodge Nurseries, 216
Stockwell – Rare Plants, Richard, 190
Stoke-on-Trent College, 464
Ston Easton Park, 327, 499
stone, buying, 418
Stone Cross Nurseries & Garden Centre, 207
Stone House Cottage Garden, 300
Stone House Cottage Nurseries, 167
Stonehurst, 337
Stourbridge College, 465
Stourhead, 66, 344
Stourton House, 344
Stowe Landscape Gardens, 253, 262
Stowell Park, 293
Strand Marketing Ltd, 408
Stratfield Saye House, 297
Stratford Power Garden Machinery, 408
Street, Henry, 132
Strong, Sir Roy, 87, 488
Stuart Garden Architecture, 408
Stubbs Associates, Jacqui, 432
Studley Royal, 347, 500
succulents, 234
Sudeley Castle, 293
Sue's Garden Designs, 445
Suffolk, graded gardens in, 388
Suffolk Wildlife Trust, 122
Sulgrave Manor, 317
Sulman, Pearl, 200
Sulman Pelargoniums, Brian, 197
Summer Lodge Hotel, 499
Sunday Express, The, 60
Sunday Telegraph, The, 494
Sunday Times, The, 494
sundries, buying, 417
Sunlight Systems, 409
Sunshine of Africa (UK) Ltd, 409
Suntrap Garden, 361
Super Natural Ltd, 409
Supersheds Ltd, 409
Surrey, graded gardens in, 388
Surrey Gardens Trust, 122
Surrey Primroses, 204
Surrey Wildlife Trust, 122
Sussex Trugs Ltd, 409
Sussex Wildlife Trust, 123
Sutton, Griffin & Morgan, 445
Sutton Park, 347
Suttons Seeds Ltd, 250, 519
Swallow Hayes, 324
Swan Hellenic Ltd, 497
Swanland Nurseries, 61
sweet peas, 240
Swiss Garden, The, 258
Swithinbank, Anne, 494
Syon Courtyard, 183, 445
Syon Park, 313
Talbot Botanic Gardens, 369

Tamarisk Nurseries, 133
Tapeley Park, 282
Tarston Park, 379
Tatton Park, 268
Tavendale Arboricultural Consultant, Iain, 431
taxol, 85
Taylor & Sons Bulbs Ltd, O. A., 519
Taylor Instruments, 409
Teagasc College of Amenity Horticulture, 469
Teamwork Landscaping, 445
Teesdale Garden, The, 255
Telegraph House, 338
Temple Associates, Gillian, 430
Temple Newsam Park, 349
Terrace & Garden Ltd, 409
Thacker, Dr Christopher, 380
Thames Valley Wirework Co Ltd, 409
theft from gardens, 520
Thermoforce Ltd, 409
Thesaurus, 521
Thomas, Graham, 374
Thompson & Morgan, 73, 75, 250
Thompson's Hill, 344
Thomson Scholarship, William John, 473
Thornbury Castle Hotel, 499
Thorncroft Clematis Nursery, 186
Thorne (Beehives) Ltd, E H, 397
Thornhayes Nursery, 148
Thorp, A & A, 178
Thorp Perrow Arboretum, 347
Threave School of Horticulture, 356
Three Counties Nurseries, 61, 151
Three Suns Nursery, 155
Thuya Alpine Nursery, 158
Thyme House Nursery, 135
Tildenet Ltd, 409
Tile Barn Nursery, 176
Times, The, 494
Timpany Nurseries, 230
Tinsley, Peter, 60
Tinsley & Co Ltd, Eliza, 397
Tintinhull House, 327
Tirley Garth Trust, 268
Titchmarsh, Alan, 494, 495
Tivey & Son, Philip, 62, 179
Toad Hall Produce, 167
Toddington Manor, 258
Tokonama Bonsai Nursery, 169
Tomato Growers Club, The, 117
Toobees Exotics, 61, 204
Top Pots, 170
topiary, 240
topsoil, buying, 417
Torosay Castle & Gardens, 364
Tough Alpine Nursery, 225
Town and Country Landscapes, 446
Town and Country Products, 410
Town Farm Nursery, 139
Trace, 521
Trade and DIY Products Ltd, 410
Traditional Garden Supply Company Ltd, The, 410
Trailer Barrow Company, 410
Traquair House, 355
Traylen Martin, Frances, 429
Treasures of Tenbury Ltd, 167
Trebah, 511
Trebah Garden Trust, 273
Trebah Nursery, 141
Tree Maintenance, 446
Tree News, 68
tree planting, 67

Tree Register of the British Isles, 253
Tree Shop, 228
Treecare, 446, 446
Treemasters, 446
Trees, 446
Trees in Miniature, 410
Treework Services Ltd, 446
Treeworld Services, 447
Tregrehan, 273
Trehane, 273
Trehane Camellia Nursery, 151
Trelissick Garden, 273, 500; weather, 100
Trenear Nurseries, Peter, 162
Trengwainton Gardens, 274
Trentham Park Gardens, 328
Trerice, 274
Tresco Abbey, 274
Trevor Scott Ornamental Grasses, 155
Trewithen, 274
Trewithen Nurseries, 141
Treyer-Evans, Julian, 434
trials, Wisley, 78
Trident Water Garden Products, 410
Trinity College Botanic Garden, 369
Trinity College Library, 480
Tropical Rain Forest, 61
Trossachs Garden Tours, 498
trusts, grant-making, 471
Tucker & Sons Ltd, Edwin, 246, 397
Tudor House Garden, 297
Tully Japanese Gardens, 370
Tullynally Castle Gardens, 372
Turn End, 262
Tushingham Hall, 89
Tweedie Fruit Trees, J, 224
Two Wests and Elliott Ltd, 410
Ty'n Garreg Nurseries, 222
Ty'r Orsaf Nursery, 222
Tylney Hall Hotel, 499
Tyne & Wear, graded gardens in, 389
Ulster Gardens Scheme, 255
undergrown plants, 251
University College Dublin, 470
University College London, 461
University College of North Wales, 468
University of Aberdeen, 468
University of Bristol Botanic Garden, 257; Library, 479
University of Dundee Botanic Garden, 365
University of Durham Botanic Garden, 286
University of Edinburgh, 468
University of Greenwich, 460
University of Leicester Botanic Garden, The, 308
University of Manchester, 462
University of Newcastle, 465
University of Nottingham, 460
University of Reading, 457; Library, 479
University of Sheffield, 467
Unusual Perennials, 186
Unwins Seeds Ltd, 74, 250
Upton House, 340
Urban, Staudengarten Monika und Wolfgang, 504
Urban Wildlife Trust, The West Midlands Wildlife Campaign, 123
Usual & Unusual Plants, 207
Uzumara Orchids, 226
Vale End, 332
Vale Garden Houses Ltd, 410
Valley Clematis Nursery, 61, 182
Valley Gardens, Harrogate, The, 347

Index 535

Valley Gardens, Windsor, The, 332
van Geest, John, 70
Van Hage Garden Company, The, 170, 250
Van Tubergen UK, 186
Vann, 332
Vaughan's Garden, Sir Roger, 354
Ventnor Botanic Garden, 303, 520
Verdigris Ltd, 410
Verein Deutscher Rosenfreunde, 126
Verey, Rosemary, 66
Vernon Geranium Nursery, The, 205
Very Interesting Rock Company, 61
Veryans Plants, 149
Vesutor Airplants, 61, 209
Vicarage Gardens, The, 158
videos, 494
Vincent Architectural Garden Designer, Louis, 436
Vine House, 258
violas, 241
Visitors' Guide to Scotland's Gardens, 255
Vitax Ltd, 410, 519
Volpaia, 288
von Zeppelin, Staudengärtnerei Gräfin, 504
Voyage Jules Verne, 498
W K W Tree Services, 447
Waddesdon Manor, 87, 262
Waddesdon Plant Centre & Nursery, 134
Wakefield & North of England Tulip Society, 123
Wakefield College, 467
Wakehurst Place, 338
Walford College of Agriculture, 463
Walkers Bulbs, J, 61, 180
Wall Cottage Nursery, 141
Walled Garden, The, 200
Wallington Hall, 319
Walpole House, 313
Walton, Judith, 434, 463
Ward Fuchsias, 138
Warner's Roses, 193
Warren-Brown, S, 442
Wartnaby Gardens, 308, 411
Warwick Castle, 340
Warwickshire, graded gardens in, 389
Warwickshire Wildlife Trust, 123
Water Gardener, The, 494
Water Meadow Design and Landscape, 447
Water Meadow Nursery and Herb Farm, 162
Waterperry Gardens Ltd, 323, 191
Waterwheel Nursery, 221
Way Associates, David, 497
Wayford Manor, 327
Weasdale Nurseries, 143
weather, 1993-1994, 90
Weaver Vale Garden Centre, 138
Webbs Garden Centre, 143
Webbs of Wychbold, 167, 447
Wells & Winter, 411
Wells Landscaping, D, 425
Welsh College of Horticulture, 466, 480
Welsh Historic Gardens Trust, 123
Welsh Historic Monuments Commission, 381
Weingart, Rosenschule Martin, 505

Wentworth Castle Gardens, 348
Wessex Horticultural Products Ltd, 411
West Acre Gardens, 186
West Country Geraniums, 131
West Dean Gardens, 89, 338
West Kington Nurseries Ltd, 213, 447
West Midlands, graded gardens in, 389
West Oxford College, 463
West Park Lodge, 499
West Somerset Garden Centre, 196
West Sussex, graded gardens in, 388
West Wycombe Park, 262
West Yorkshire, graded gardens in, 390
Westbury Court, 293
Westcott Landscape Architects, Mark, 437
Westdale Nurseries, 214
Western Horticultural Society, 126
Westfield Cacti, 149, 250
Westholme Hall, 287
Westland Horticulture, 411
Westminster Flower Shows, 2
Weston Park, 324
Westonbirt Arboretum, 253, 293
Westonbirt Plant Centre, 158
Westside Forestry, 447
Westwell Manor, 323
Westwinds Perennial Plants, 139
Westwood Nursery, 176
Whateley, Elizabeth, 428
Whatton House, 309
Wheatcroft Ltd, 190
Wheeler, A D & N, 210
Whichford Pottery, 411
White, Stephen J, 444
White Cottage Alpines, 171
White Old Fashioned Roses, Trevor, 186
White Tree Surgeon and Forestry Contractor, Colin, 424
White Veil Fuchsias, 152
White Windows, 297
Whitehall Garden Centre Ltd, 214, 447
Whitehouse Ivies, 155
Whiten, Faith & Geoffrey, 60, 488
Whitestone Gardens Ltd, 217
Whitfield, 300
Wightwick Manor, 89, 340, 379
Wilcote House, 323
Wild Flower Centre, The, 187
Wild Flower Society, The, 117
wild flowers, 241
Wildlife Gardening Centre, The, 191, 250
Wildlife Trust for Bedfordshire & Cambridgeshire, The, 123
Wildlife Trust for Bristol, Bath and Avon, 123
Wildlife Trusts, 68
Willapark Manor Hotel, 499
Willerby Tree Surgeons Ltd, 447
Williams & Associates, Robin, 441
Willmot Pertwee Ltd, 519
Wills, H & S, 145
Wilmslow Garden Centre, 138, 447
Wilson Daffodil Garden, Guy, 367
Wilson Memorial Garden, The Ernest, 289
Wilton House, 345
Wiltshire, graded gardens in, 389
Wiltshire Gardens Trust, 123

Wiltshire Wildlife Trust, 124
Wimpole Hall, 89, 264, 379
Wincombe Park, 345
Winkworth Arboretum, 333
Wintergreen Nurseries, 167
Wisborough Green Horticultural Society, 61
Wisley *see* Royal Horticultural Society
Withleigh Nurseries, 149
Woburn Abbey, 259
Wolden Nurseries & Garden Centre, 183
WOLF Tools, 411
Wolseley Garden Park, 328
Wolsey Lodge, 500
Wolverhampton Tree Service, 447
Woman's National Farm & Garden Association, Inc, 473
Wood & Son Ltd, William, 519
Woodborough Garden Centre, 214
Woodfield Brothers, 60, 61, 211
Woodgrow Horticulture Ltd, 411
Woodhams, 448
Woodlands Cottage Nursery, 217
Woodperry House, 323
Woodside Horticulture Ltd, 411
Woodstock Orchids and Automations, 134
Woolley Grange Hotel, 499
Woolman (Dorridge) Ltd, H, 211
Worshipful Company of Gardeners, The, 513
Worsley Hall Nurseries & Garden Centre, 159
Wreford Landscapes, 448
Wrest Park, 259
Wright, Kathy, 181
Writtle College, 459; Library, 479
Wulfran College, 466
Wychwood Carp Farm, 162
Wye College, University of London, 460
Wye Valley Herbs, 221
Wyevale Garden Centres, 60, 68, 131, 168, 183, 217
Wyken Hall, 330
Wylmington Hayes Gardens, 283
Wynn Arboricultural Consultant, Peter, 440
Yardley, 60
Yardmaster International, 412
Yarrow & Associates, Chris, 423
Yellow Book, 254
Yew Tree Cottage, 338
Ynyshir Hall, 499
York, The Duchess of, 65
York Florists, Ancient Society of, 57
York Gate, 252
Yorkshire Museum Gardens, 347
Yorkshire Wildlife Trust, 124
YOU Magazine, 60
Young, Antony, 421
Young Orchid Foundation, Eric, 58
Young Seeds, Roy, 249
Younger Botanic Garden, The, 364
Your Garden, 494
YSJ Seeds, 196, 250
Zeneca Garden and Professional, 412
Zengarden, 448
Zephyrwude Irises, 219